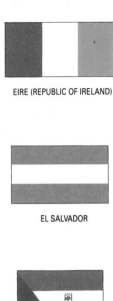

EIRE (REPUBLIC OF IRELAND)

FRANCE
(INCL. FRENCH GUIANA, GUADELOUPE,
FRENCH POLYNESIA, MARTINIQUE, RÉUNION,
ST MARTIN, ST BARTS, WALLIS AND FUTUNA,
NEW CALEDONIA, MAYOTTE,
ST PIERRE & MIQUELON)

GREENLAND

EL SALVADOR

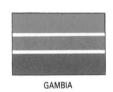

GABON

GRENADA

HONDURAS

ITALY

EQUATORIAL GUINEA

GAMBIA

GUATEMALA

HONG KONG

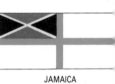

IVORY COAST

ERITREA

GEORGIA

GUINEA

ICELAND

JAMAICA

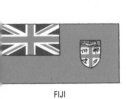

ESTONIA

GERMANY

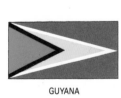

GUINEA-BISSAU

INDIA

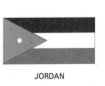

JAPAN

FIJI

GHANA

GUYANA

INDONESIA

JORDAN

FINLAND

GREECE

HAITI

ISRAEL

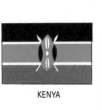

KENYA

WORLD CRUISING
HANDBOOK

Other titles of interest

WORLD CRUISING ROUTES, 4th edition
Jimmy Cornell
ISBN 0-07-013406-5

Here is all the information you need on winds, currents, weather and routes to plan an extended voyage from beginning to end, anywhere in the world. Over 500 cruising routes and 5000 waypoints are given to assist route planning.

ATLANTIC PILOT ATLAS, 2nd edition
James Clarke
ISBN 0-07-011921-X

A complete guide to the weather of the North and South Atlantic, the Mediterranean, and the Caribbean, this is an ideal volume for anyone planning an Atlantic crossing.

THE ATLANTIC CROSSING GUIDE, 4th edition
Ed Gavin McLaren/RCC Pilotage Foundation
ISBN 0-07-026032-X

Totally updated and full of practical advice, this book covers the complete Atlantic circuit. An invaluable aid for those planning a crossing or an extended cruise in these waters.

ADLARD COLES' HEAVY WEATHER SAILING,
30th Anniversary Edition
K Adlard Coles and Peter Bruce
ISBN 0-07-135323-2

The unique classic based on years of experience of sailing in the severest conditions. This new edition contains a wealth of new material with recent accounts of wild weather and ways to survive it.

THE VOYAGER'S HANDBOOK
Beth A Leonard
ISBN 0-07-038143-7

An invaluable handbook for anyone contemplating an extended cruise. It is packed with detailed and up-to-date information on the latest techniques and gear as well as practical advice ranging from motivating the crew to financing your dream.

WORLD CRUISING
HANDBOOK

3rd Edition

Jimmy Cornell

Camden, Maine • New York • Chicago • San Francisco • Lisbon • London
• Madrid • Mexico City • Milan • New Delhi • San Juan • Seoul •
Singapore • Sydney • Toronto

International Marine

A Division of The McGraw-Hill Companies

10 9 8 7 6 5 4 3 2 1

Copyright © Jimmy Cornell 1991, 1996, 2001

Published in Great Britain by Adlard Coles Nautical, an
imprint of A & C Black (Publishers) Ltd, London

All rights reserved. The publisher takes no responsibility
for the use of any of the materials or methods described
in this book, nor for the products thereof. The name
"International Marine" and the International Marine
logo are trademarks of The McGraw-Hill Companies.
Printed in the United States of America.

*The CIP catalog record for this book is available from the
Library of Congress.*
ISBN 0-07-137610-0

Questions regarding the ordering of this book should be
addressed to
The McGraw-Hill Companies
Customer Service Department
P.O. Box 547
Blacklick, OH 43004
Retail customers: 1-800-262-4729
Bookstores: 1-800-722-4726

This book is printed on 60# Finch Opaque by R.R.
Donnelley

For Doina

Whose thorough research work for the first edition of this book ensured its eventual success and who is now applying her many talents to its internet offspring, noonsite.com, the global website for cruising sailors.

NEXT EDITION

The information contained in *World Cruising Handbook* has been compiled from a multitude of sources and, because of its nature, the information needs continual updating. A great effort was made to get all facts right, but as the book covers the entire world it is very difficult to keep up with all the changes. Official sources will be used again for future editions, although no one is in a better position to report on the latest requirements in a particular country than those who are actually cruising there. We therefore need your help to keep this book as up to date as possible by providing the latest information for the sailors who will be following in your wake. So please write to us with any relevant details, new requirements and especially with corrections. Every letter will receive a reply and all substantial contributions will be acknowledged in the next edition. Thank you for your help. Letters should be addressed to:

The Editor
Adlard Coles Nautical
A & C Black (Publishers) Ltd
37 Soho Square
London W1D 3QZ
ENGLAND
www.adlardcoles.co.uk

Contents

Acknowledgements

Updating the information on 185 countries for this edition has been an enormous task, and could not have been accomplished without the generous help of hundreds of people around the world, who wrote, phoned or sent by e-mail updates on the countries they live in or happen to be cruising now. In every instance, I made sure that the help was promptly acknowledged, but my gratitude would not be complete if I did not use this opportunity to mention, albeit briefly, all those who have taken their time to contribute to this book.

First of all, I would like to thank the many government officials for their prompt attention: Amias Moore of the Overseas Territories Department at the Foreign Office in London, who made many valuable comments on the section on Antarctica. Some of my initial contacts were the diplomatic missions of the various countries in London, most of whom dealt with my queries promptly or passed them on to the relevant official in their home country. I therefore wish to thank the following diplomats, all based in London: Ricardas Degutis, Counsellor at the Embassy of Lithuania; Eva Staltmane, Embassy of Latvia; Kouadio Adjumani, Ambassador of the Ivory Coast; Miodrag Maksimovic, Yugoslav Interests Section at the Cyprus High Commission; Fadia Muasher Press Officer at the Jordanian Embassy; Petrina Bachmann, Embassy of Iceland; Yongman Park, First Secretary Embassy of Korea; Andrianarivelo Razafy, Ambassador of Madagascar; M. Bakari, Tanzania High Commission; Guadalupe Romero Silva, Embassy of Honduras; Margarita Aragón, Counsellor, El Salvador Embassy; Zerizer Yousef, Maritime Affairs Attaché, Algerian Embassy; Kyawt Kyawt Khaing, Second Secretary, Embassy of Myanmar.

My grateful thanks also go to the following government officials: Vivienne Kelly, Customs, Noel Synnott, Department of Justice, Equality and Law Reform, Michelle O'Reilly, Central Statistics Office, Colette Edwards, the Heritage Service and Hugh Drumm, Department of Health, all from Ireland; Simon Macphail, Assistant Harbour Master, St Peter Port, Guernsey, José Manuel Velez, former Chairman of the Portuguese Yacht Harbour Association and current Director of European Blue Flag Association for Portugal; Benito Thomas, Chief of Immigration, Republic of Palau; José Guillermo Merlos Guaradado, Port Authority of San Salvador, El Salvador; Tom Nankivell Whangarei Marine Promotion; H.R. Cook, HM Customs & Excise, Dover; Rob Westwood, Norfolk Island Customs; R. Manquant, Customs French Guiana; Marion Herbert, Guyana High Commission, London; Iro Galea, Customs, Malta; Godwin Callus, Malta Maritime Authority; Karianne Nielsen, Customs & Excise Department, Norway; W. Bailey, Comptroller of Customs, Antigua and Barbuda; Kather Smith, Comptroller of Customs, British Virgin Islands; Brian Redfern, New Zealand Customs Service; S. Andrade, Director General Marine Services Division, Seychelles; Jean-Pascal Schaeffer, Marketing Department, Le Port, Réunion; R.J. Aspin, Governor's Office, Montserrat; Geoffrey Fairhurst, Administrator, Ascension Island; Jacques Bajal, Cruise Department Manager, Martinique; Kieth Murray, South Queensland Quarantine Service (AQIS); Roslyn Cameron, Public Relations, Charles Darwin Research Station, Galapagos; Andrés Alcalá, Cartagena Port Authority, Colombia and Nat Aycox, Director of Customs, Honolulu, Hawaii.

I received much valuable information from a number of tourism offices, as increasingly visiting sailors are considered a significant part of the tourism industry, and tourism authorities in many countries are now making visible efforts to provide a suitable infrastructure for cruising yachts. I am grateful to the following for their help: Anthony Dawson, Marketing Manager, Guernsey Tourist Board; Pamela Young, Director, St Helena Tourism Office; Esther Lewis, Montserrat Board of Tourism; Yilmaz Kalfaoglu, North Cyprus Tourism Centre, London; Marc Lubert, Director, and Siti Chanfi of the Mayotte Tourism Board; Aida Duarte Silva and Isabel Duarte of Promex, Cape Verde Islands; Barbara-Jeanne Rudder, Barbados Tourism Authority; Inga Hjallnafoss, Faeroe Islands Tourist Board; Lykke Geisler, Greenland Tourism Office, Copenhagen; Cecile Desnousse, Ministry of Tourism Seychelles; Monique Storra, Tunisian Tourist Office, London; Ida Talagi-Hekesi, Niue Tourism Office; Susie Hill, Jersey Tourism, Channel Islands; Amanda Léonard, Haiti Tourism Office; Patricia Jugan, Tourism Promotion Office, St Pierre & Miquelon; Miljenko Babic, Croatian National Tourist Board; Stanton Carter, Director of Tourism, Dominica.

Many officials at yacht clubs around the world have proven a valuable source of information, especially in countries where yachting is still in its infancy, such as Gintautas Deksnys, Commodore, Achema Yacht Club, Lithuania, Gina Cinskyte, Klaipeda Yacht Club, and Valery Alekseev,

Commodore, Sochi Yacht Club. I am very grateful to Dr Igor Petrov, President of the Black Sea Yachtsmen's Association and founder of KAYRA (Black Sea Cruising Rally), who helped me with the entry on the Ukraine. Also from the Ukraine, I received much useful data from Vladimir and Larissa Tsitsilyuk, Igor Ivanov and Michael Petuhokk, all from the Odessa Marina and Yacht Club. Teoman Arsay and Yalçin Dülger, Assistant General Manager at Ataköy Marina, Istanbul, have all been extremely helpful in clearing up a number of matters regarding their part of the world. They have also been involved with KAYRA, while Hasan Kaçmaz is the initiator of EMYR (Eastern Mediterranean Rally). All these officials have been extremely helpful, as was Brian Hepburn who now runs the successful rallies under the aegis of Island Cruising South Pacific.

The most significant change that has occurred since this book was first published is the outstanding improvement in communications. The internet and electronic mail have made my life much easier, and in the process of trying to find reliable sources for updating my material I have made a new type of contact, my latest cyber-friends. During the six months I was engaged in updating this edition, I received scores of e-mail messages daily from all corners of the world. Outstanding in this help were the following: Luis Oscar Zunino, Director of the Department of Yachting, Prefectura Naval Argentina, who revised the section on Argentina; Jill Outerbridge, of the Bermuda Meetings & Incentives, who updated the entry on Bermuda; Mel and Jackie Norris of the yacht *Drogheda* who contributed to the entries on Venezuela and Bonaire; Dorothy and Richard Walker of *Mariposa*, who sent me valuable material on the Philippines, Sabah, Sarawak, Brunei, where they were cruising at the time; David Stone also sent me additional information on the Philippines; Brian Hull, while cruising Papua New Guinea on *Duck Soup*, revised the entry on that country; George LaMont has kept me up to date on what is happening in the Federated States of Micronesia as well as the Northern Marianas, while Cheryl King revised my entry on Guam; Colin Freshwater, of Cocos Engineering, corrected the material on Cocos Keeling; Håkan Norberg of the Swedish Cruising Association corrected my entry on Sweden, while Sean Stone of Canadian Customs sent me several e-mails that allowed me to thoroughly update the entry on Canada. I am also grateful to Larry Stewart of the yacht *Mischief* for the latest information on Russell Radio and arrival procedures in the Bay of Islands, and to Jürgen and Karin Schulze of *Krios* for the detailed information on the many new marinas in SE Asia.

In several instances, I appealed to earlier contacts who had already helped with the two previous editions. As in the past, their response was prompt and thorough, so I would like to thank Glafkos Cariolou, Manager of Larnaca Marina, who helped me once again with the section on Cyprus; Fathi Soukar, Prince of the Red Sea, who revised the sections on both Egypt and the Suez Canal; Carolyn Wardle, who updated the section on the Bahamas. I was very fortunate in establishing some excellent contacts in St Petersburg where I corresponded with Yuri Yanin of the St Petersburg Central (River) Yacht Club. An older contact in St Petersburg was Dr Grigory Druzhinin, from the radiophysics department at St Petersburg University, who has set up a very useful English-Russian glossary of sailing terms available on his own website: www.phys.spbu.ru/Departments/RadioPhysics/english/Druzhinin.html.

I am greatly indebted to Yusuf Civelekoglu, Director of Bodrum Marina in Turkey, who is very active in simplifying formalities for cruising sailors visiting Turkey, and sent me excellent information on his country. Among the contacts at other marinas around the world I would like to mention: Richard Nadeau, Manager of Plaza Resort Marina, Bonaire; Cees de Jong, Dockmaster, Santa Barbara Marina, Curaçao; Lysanne van Campen, Marketing Assistant, Curaçao Ports Authority; Didier Boulard, Manager, Port Morgan Marina, Haiti; Thomas Herbert, CEO, Port St Charles, Barbados; Dieter Bosch and Brian McKellar, Langkasuka Boat Club, Langkawi; Galo Ortiz, Manager, Puerto Lucia Yacht Club, Salinas. Also involved with cruising boats, and providing a valuable service to visiting sailors, are George and Dorothy Bateman of Opua Radio; Jorge Diena, coxswain of the ADES rescue organisation in Uruguay; Bill Tschan, ABC Trading Company, Rarotonga, Cook Islands; Ricardo Arenas, Servigalapagos; John Racca, John's Service Station Ilocos-Sur, Philippines; Angeli Elliot of Yacht Services Association of Trinidad & Tobago. In the Caribbean, I would like to thank Robbie Ferron of Budget Marine in Sint Maarten, and David Jones, the Caribbean Weather Man, who helped with the sections on the US and British Virgins, while Robert Holbrook, of Admiral Marine Insurance, advised me on insurance during the Caribbean hurricane season.

Work on this edition coincided with the later stages of Millennium Odyssey Canarias, which gave me a unique opportunity to update the information on the forty countries visited by this round the world rally, whether by visiting some of the countries myself, or getting firsthand information from John Ellis and Tom Williams, who ran the rally from beginning to end. John and Tom contributed data on many countries, for which I am very grateful, especially as it was not necessarily in their line of duty. Regine Fauré, who liaised with the sponsor of the rally in the Canaries, contributed to that section. The Millennium Odyssey Canarias was also an excellent opportunity to renew some old friendships, whether from my earlier voyages, or from previous rallies, such as Alan Sitt, now based in Hawaii, who revised the section on Peru; Armen Portugaly of Ashkelon Marina in Israel; Lydia Darham and Adrian Gilson of Marina Bay Marina, Gibraltar; Carlos Ribeiro Ferreira, President of Associaçaõ Naval de Lisboa and Joaquim Pinto Basto; Sandra and Alex Wopper of Alwoplast in Valdivia, Chile; Dominique LeBras and José Zacarias in Salvador da Bahia, who revised the section on Brazil; Michel Alcon, Manager of the Tahiti Yacht Club; Dick Smith of Musket Cove Resort, Fiji; James Pascall of the Moorings base at Secret Harbour, who thoroughly revised the section on Grenada; Andy Stephens, Manager of the Yacht Haven, and Andy Dowden, editor of *Sail Thailand*, both from Phuket, Thailand. The Millennium Odyssey Canarias concluded its circumnavigation at Riva di Traiano Marina in Civitavecchia, near Rome, whose manager Massimo De Notti was a most generous and welcoming host. All these people made valuable contributions to this book, as did my old friend from the Azores, Joao Carlos Fraga, a well-known friend of visiting sailors to those shores. The same can be said of Julie Arias, whose Panama Yacht Services was set up to assist sailors transiting the Panama Canal, and who updated the section on Panama and the Canal.

I have been extremely fortunate in being in contact with several participants in former rallies that I organised, some of whom are still cruising. Outstanding among them is Terence Brownrigg, who sent me detailed reports on several Caribbean countries while cruising there on *Fiskery*. Among former ARC participants I am particularly grateful to Mirek and Lucy Misayat of *Kaprys*, who revised the section on Spain; David Bailey, who recently visited Cuba and Guatemala; Marianne Verdoes, who checked my entry on the Netherlands; Karen Angell-Baustad, who checked that on Norway; while Gulshan Rai, Commissioner Customs and Excise in Goa, sent me excellent updates on the situation in his native India. Previous round the world rally participants helped me on countries where they live or happen to be based now, such as Tadashi Gohda of Kobe and Mr Matsuo of Marine Technical College in Sasebo, who revised the section on Japan, while Roland and Fabienne Schlachter helped with the section on Honduras. Former America 500 participants did the same on their own countries, such as Tihomir Predovic, whose *Runaway* actually won that rally, while Andrzej Arminski of *Mantra* dealt at length with the section on Poland.

Many of the above have become good friends and have remained in contact. It is always a great pleasure to hear from them, especially when their messages are spiced with dry humour as in the case of John Wilson who revised my sections on Fiji and Tuvalu, while Bill Butler of *New Chance* dealt with the entry on Puerto Rico and never missed the opportunity to e-mail me the latest internet jokes.

As with all my previous books, I could appeal to Milt Baker of Bluewater Books and Charts in Fort Lauderdale, who kindly compiled a list of relevant cruising publications. Nearer home, my old friends at Kelvin Hughes in London, Julian van Hasselt, Brian Walker and Ron Haslett, once again proved their unmatched knowledge of maritime publications worldwide.

A number of authors of cruising guides have made valuable contributions to the countries they know best, and I am particularly thankful for the help received from Chris Doyle, the author of several cruising guides to the Caribbean, as well as to Nancy Scott who arranged to send me all his guides in his absence; to Tim Godfrey, whose knowledge of the Maldives is unparalleled, and who is the author of a number of books on the Maldives: *Malvays: Maldives Island Directory*, and *Dive Maldives: A Guide to the Maldives Archipelago*; to Dirk Sieling, who wrote the *Solomon Islands Cruising Guide* and now runs Solomon Charters in Gizo.

Some of the authors continue to cruise on their boats, such as Thomas Müller of *Miz Mae*, who spent several years in Vanuatu, or Gerard van Erp, the author of *ABC-Yachting*. When the authors were not available, their publishers proved to be just as helpful and informative, such as Willie Wilson of Imray, the world's leading cruising guide publisher, who generously supplied copies of all the relevant cruising guides. My German editor and friend, Astrid Breuer-Greiff, thoroughly revised the entry on Germany and I was fortunate in getting many useful tips on China from Oliver Schwarz, also from my German publisher Pietsch Verlage.

Gildas de Gouvello, the managing director of Loisirs Nautiques, has shown great confidence in publishing first my *World Cruising Routes* in a French version, to be followed by a translation of this edition. My sincere thanks to both him and also for Marc Labaume, who translated and edited both books into French and whose valuable comments were greatly appreciated.

Grateful thanks are long overdue to my English editor Carole Edwards who has worked on all previous editions of this book, as well as on its companion *World Cruising Routes*. Janet Murphy, Director of Adlard Coles Nautical, continues to be a faithful friend and supporter, in spite of the problems and difficulties that I occasionally cause her!

As mentioned in these pages, the internet has been in some respects a great help in updating the practical information on many countries, while e-mail has been truly a godsend. I am extremely grateful to my son Ivan for setting up new computers in my offices both in Aups and London, and teaching me several shortcuts, so that I could access the internet quickly and efficiently.

As always, my greatest debt of gratitude is to Gwenda, who, as with some many of my previous projects, stepped in at the right moment and helped me keep my head above water when the sheer volume of new information threatened to drown me in a mass of paperwork. Without her selfless help, this thoroughly revised new edition might never have seen the light of day.

Introduction

The planning stage of a cruise is often just as enjoyable as the voyage itself, letting one's imagination loose on all kinds of possibilities. Yet translating dreams into reality means that a lot of practical questions have to be answered. You might have heard about needing a cruising permit for Indonesia, putting up a bond in French Polynesia or the difficulties of leaving a boat in Thailand, but what about Palau? Tuvalu? Mayotte? The Antarctic? Do yachts go there? *Can* yachts cruise there? Is it worth going at all? Designed as a companion volume to *World Cruising Routes*, the main objective of this book is to serve as a planner for anyone intending to cruise anywhere in the world. While *World Cruising Routes* helps you plan the best way to get to a place, *World Cruising Handbook* aims to let you know what to expect once you have arrived, and the information it contains is what you should know before arriving.

There is no denying the beauty of the cruising life and cruising sailors are rightly envied for the freedom of their lives and the opportunity they have to live unfettered by the constraints of modern urban existence. As with so many things in life, there is a price to pay for this freedom and the beauty of cruising is often spoilt by bureaucracy, unnecessarily complicated formalities and sometimes difficult, unfriendly and even corrupt officials. As many of the countries visited by cruising boats are in the developing world and their population, officials included, are poor in comparison with the owner of a cruising boat, however modest that yacht might be, a yacht is often regarded as a sign of affluence. This might explain the antagonism that is sometimes experienced. The xenophobia and occasionally racism that some officials show towards visiting sailors may well have its roots in the past. Cruising sailors may be paying the price for the injustices suffered by the local population in the colonial past. Whatever the reason for them, these attitudes can mar the pleasure of visiting a country and ways to avoid this are discussed later in the section 'The Right Attitude'.

While on night watch during an Atlantic crossing, I cast my mind back over my first voyage around the world and the many memorable moments spent with my family in some of the most beautiful spots in the world. I tried to recall the few unpleasant incidents and almost without exception they were caused by difficult officials. I then added up the time I must have spent clearing in and out of the 60 countries we visited and I was shocked to come up with a total of some 300 hours. This is equivalent to 40 working days, which means that out of six years sailing I had spent eight weeks sitting in or walking between various offices! It was a terrible thought. While not claiming to give tips on how to reduce this waste of time, this book might nevertheless reduce some of the frustrations by preparing the voyager for what to expect in the countries to be visited, what preparations should be made in advance and what formalities complied with once there. It is the kind of book I wish had existed when I set off on my own voyage.

The background information on each country contained in the following pages should prepare you for your dealings with that country. Similarly, the practical information is meant to give an idea of what is available. Although my original intention was to give full details of existing facilities, including names and addresses, the sheer mass of material precluded this. From personal experience I know it is relatively easy to find out the name and address of a particular workshop or company in most places. Even if one does not speak the language, the ubiquitous Yellow Pages can usually be understood and local sailing enthusiasts or yacht clubs will often help out. This is why the facilities section includes only general notes, as I felt that what is really important to know, for example, is that there is a 75-ton travelift in Darwin, a sailmaker in Tonga, a well-stocked chandlery in Papeete and a lot of frozen lobster trails, if not much else, on Tristan da Cunha. It is equally important to know about the places where little or nothing is available, so that when sailing there one can be prepared to be as self-sufficient as possible. The lack of marine supplies in many popular cruising grounds makes it imperative to carry all essential spares on board.

Originally *World Cruising Handbook* was intended to include only the most important cruising countries on the trade wind route but ended up by embracing virtually the entire world. Research undertaken for one of my previous books, *World Cruising Survey*, has shown that cruising yachts sail to more and more out of the way places, and as there is no cruising information available for those less visited places it was decided to include them in this book, even if information was sometimes scanty. After much debate, the line was drawn at 185 countries and only those that are never or very rarely visited by cruising boats were left out.

Autonomous territories and dependencies have usually been treated as separate entries, because the rules applied to cruising yachts often differ from those of the metropolitan power. Thus, some of the regulations applied in Hawaii differ from those in mainland USA, while French territories in the Caribbean, South Pacific or Indian Ocean often apply different rules even towards French sailors. As some of the major sailing countries, such as the United States, United Kingdom or France, are well covered in other books, only essential information which one should know before arrival has been included. Similarly, major cruising destinations which are well covered in cruising guides and pilots, such as the Bahamas, Virgin Islands, Spain or Greece, have been dealt with succinctly by mentioning only the most relevant facts. Each country has been annotated with details of books where further cruising information can be found.

In the few cases where regulations were unclear or contradictory, I have tried to interpret them and put them in as plain a language as possible. This was not always easy as in some countries the regulations filled a book, while in others the officialese was quite ridiculous. Clarity and conciseness are definitely not attributes of bureaucrats, nor are those who draw up the regulations renowned for their sense of humour, otherwise they might have written differently some of the following gems culled from material sent to us:

'. . . non-human primates may not be imported except for exhibition purposes . . .'

'. . . among articles prohibited are . . . liquor filled candy, lottery tickets, products made by convicts . . . and switchblade knives except for use by a one-armed traveller . . .'

'. . . also enclosed with my letter is The Panama Canal . . .'

Jimmy Cornell

Foreword to the Third Edition

There have been many changes on the world cruising scene since the first edition of this book was published in 1991. Many of those changes have been for the better: better docking and repair facilities, easier financial arrangements thanks to the wider use of credit cards and availability of ATM outlets virtually everywhere, good sources of provisioning even in the most remote places, far better communications everywhere. On the negative side one can list the unnecessarily cumbersome formalities in a few places, the less welcoming attitude towards visiting sailors in some countries, and the higher cost of cruising everywhere. But if all the good things and all the bad things are put in the balance, the scales will tip firmly in favour of the good: it is still a great life for the fortunate few who have the wisdom and courage to be out there cruising.

During the last two years I have had the opportunity to visit many cruising spots around the world, partly as organiser of the Millennium Odyssey Canarias round the world rally, partly as a participant in that exciting event. In 1999 I sailed some 15,000 miles on my *Aventura III*, mostly with only my son Ivan as crew. We started the year sailing from Argentina to the Falklands, then continued to Antarctica – our second visit to the frozen continent. The next six months saw us sail the entire Pacific Ocean from its bottom to the top: Chile, Easter Island, Pitcairn, the Austral, Society and Line Islands, Hawaii, Alaska and British Columbia.

Many of the corrections and additions made to this edition are therefore based on my personal experience, while for the countries that I did not have the opportunity to visit myself, I had to rely on information provided by a variety of sources, which are duly acknowledged in the preceding pages. As we now live in the age of the internet, I had put high hopes in this supposedly inexhaustible source of information. During several busy months I scoured the internet like the most obsessed surfer searching for any bits of information that would be of use in updating this book. The overall result, I must admit, was quite disappointing. Most websites, even when they included some useful information, were hopelessly out of date. Much of the information, when checked against additional sources, was not only obsolete but often inaccurate, so increasingly I had to rely on my personal network of contacts that over the years I have built up around the world. To my great surprise, the best website that I discovered on the internet, from a cruising sailor's point of view, was not that of some great sailing nation, or a major yachting centre, but that of the small island of Niue in the South Pacific. Its website is attractive and well thought out, and includes all the information that anyone planning to visit Niue might need. Quite remarkable is the site of the Panama Canal, where one can follow the transit of vessels through the Miraflores Locks as it happens, thanks to continually updated video images. These two websites, and a few others, were the true gems in a disappointing mass of dross. It only proves the need of a book like this one – at least for the time being.

The absence of a website dedicated to cruising sailors kept returning to me even after I had sent the amended text for the new edition to my publishers. Eventually I realised that the only way to put this right was to create such a website myself. In a similar way, the main reason why I wrote *World Cruising Routes* when I returned from my first circumnavigation was the absence of such a book. That decision, and the book's immediate success, led me to writing *World Cruising Handbook*. The first transatlantic rally in 1986 and the first round the world rally in 1991 followed the same pattern of filling a gap. Now, just when I had decided to retire and go sailing, the same thought process led me to the decision that I should provide something for cruising sailors that is definitely needed. This is how the idea of www.noonsite.com was born.

As in the case of some of my previous projects, I was fortunate in being able to call upon the practical help of my children. Ivan had already designed the highly successful websites for my various rallies, and had written the software for regular position-reporting by individual yachts: a first on the internet. Once again, Ivan generously agreed to support my project by designing the website and writing the necessary software to run it. Doina had done the initial research for the first edition of this book, and her comprehensive knowledge of the countries listed in the following pages made her the ideal person to be the coordinator of the new website. Gwenda, who initially did not approve of me getting involved in yet another time-consuming project, gradually came around to the idea and agreed that it was indeed something that needed to be done.

So I hope that by the time this new edition sees the light of day, www.noonsite.com will be fully developed, and together they will provide you with the necessary information to plan your landfalls, and to complete safely and enjoyably the voyage of your dreams.

Sailing Around the World

The ocean's waves crash on the shore,
That's where the sailboats land,
Any country they come to
Will give them a helping hand.

Every place they visit,
They will have a lot of fun,
They can go many places
Without having to run and run.

Michelle Roberts

(The above poem was one of several submitted by the students at Broken Arrow School, Oklahoma, to the website of the round the world rally which I organised in connection with the Expo '98 world exhibition. It sums up the beauty of cruising to faraway places.)

Jimmy Cornell
Aventura III, St Raphael, Cote d'Azur

SECTION I

1 Formalities

Clearance formalities vary greatly from country to country, being extremely simple in some and ridiculously complicated in others. The complexity of formalities is often a reflection of the nature of the regime in power and it can be safely assumed that the less liberal a country the more complicated its entry formalities. The few exceptions only prove the fact that regardless of the country visited, or the kind of government in power there, formalities should always be taken seriously and even what look like illogical restrictions should always be complied with. Moreover, however lax or strict a country may be known to be, entry formalities must be completed as soon as possible, and the intention to do so must be indicated as soon as one enters that country's territorial waters by flying the Q flag and contacting the relevant authorities by radio.

Documents

The most common documents that are needed when clearing in are the ship's registration papers, radio licence, passports and vaccination certificates. Clearance papers from the last country to be visited may also be requested. Some countries also want to see the original of the third-party insurance for the yacht and a certificate of competence for the captain. If firearms are carried, these should be licensed in the country of origin, as this licence will be requested in many places. Similarly pets must have international health certificates and their anti-rabies and other vaccinations should be kept up to date. Divers who carry scuba diving equipment on board may be asked to show their diving qualification certificates before getting tanks filled. Finally, a prescription or a letter from a doctor specifying the medicine and why it is taken should accompany any medicines containing powerful narcotics or habit-forming drugs, especially those used by a member of the crew on a regular basis, such as heart and blood pressure medication, diuretics, tranquillisers, anti-depressants, stimulants or sleeping tablets.

Several countries require that visiting yachts are properly registered. In the United Kingdom there are two forms of registration. Full British registration is administered by the Registrar of Shipping, who issues a Certificate of British Registry. A simpler alternative is the Small Ship Register, which is administered by the Royal Yachting Association. The International Certificate of Pleasure Navigation is not accepted in some countries, so if planning to cruise further afield, the vessel should have one of the other two types of registration. In the United States yachts can either be registered with the state where the owner lives, or if ownership can be traced to the original owner, the vessel can be documented with the Coast Guard. The latter is generally preferable if cruising abroad.

A certificate of competence, or some document showing the competence of the person in charge of the boat, is now required by officials in many countries. Such a certificate can be obtained in the United Kingdom from the Royal Yachting Association, which issues certificates for different degrees of competence, such as Helmsman, Yachtmaster or Ocean Yachtmaster. In the United States, sailors may obtain a certificate of competence by enrolling for a course on seamanship or pilotage. The US Coast Guard issues licences for captains of boats which carry paying passengers. Such licences are recognised as a mark of competence for operators of commercial craft, including charter yachts carrying six or more persons.

A radio operator's licence, whether for VHF, HF or amateur radio, is required in most countries, although this is rarely checked. Some cruising yachts carry an amateur radio, most of their operators being properly licensed to operate a maritime mobile station. However, in some countries such stations can only be used legally if the operator is in possession of a reciprocal licence issued by the country concerned. In most places this is a simple formality and costs a small fee. In a few countries there are strict restrictions on the use of any radio equipment while in port, while in others, such as Thailand and New Zealand, the use of portable marine VHF radios on land is forbidden.

Although some forms will have to be filled in on the spot, considerable time can be saved by having some papers prepared beforehand. It is always a good idea to have some photocopies of the ship's papers as well as plenty of crew lists, with such details as first name, middle names, surname, date of birth, nationality, passport number and date of expiry of passport as well as details of the boat itself including: name of vessel, flag, type (ie sloop), official registration number, gross and net tonnage, LOA (in feet and metres), call sign, name of registered owner, address of owner. A ship's stamp is greatly appreciated in many countries where, for some strange reason, a rubber stamp has a certain authority.

Visas

One aspect which this book tries to clear up is that of visa requirements. While in some countries these are fairly clear, in others the situation concerning yachts is confusing. Foreign nationals arriving on a yacht can be treated basically in three different ways by the immigration authorities.

1 They are treated the same as ordinary tourists arriving by other means, in which case the usual visa requirements apply.
2 Special visa requirements are applied to those arriving by yacht, which means that in some countries foreign nationals arriving by yacht are treated differently to those visiting the country as ordinary tourists. This may mean that some countries are happy to grant visas on arrival to tourists arriving by air but insist that anyone arriving on a yacht must have obtained their visa in advance. This is often because tourists arriving by air must have an onward ticket to be given a visa, while arriving on a yacht is not always regarded as a guarantee of one's ability to depart by the same means.
3 Sailors are sometimes given special treatment by being allowed to enter a country without a visa, which is required from tourists arriving by other means. Sometimes visas are granted on arrival and occasionally are dispensed with altogether. However, in these cases such special concessions are usually given only for a limited time and may be restricted to the duration of the yacht's stay in port or while cruising certain areas. It may be necessary to obtain an ordinary visa to travel to other parts of the country or to leave the country by other means.

There are several suggestions concerning passports and visas which should be followed to avoid some of the problems that are known to have occurred in the past. If at all possible, passports should have a validity well in excess of the intended period of travel. Some countries insist that passports are valid for at least six months beyond the intended stay in their country.

For countries where a visa is required, this should be obtained well in advance, although one should make sure that the visa will still be valid when one arrives in the respective country as some countries stipulate that the entry must take place within three months of the visa being issued. It is also a good idea to obtain visas for difficult countries, even if it is known that visas can be issued on

arrival. A visa issued by their diplomatic mission abroad sometimes works wonders with local immigration officers. It is mentioned in the text where this is recommended. Wherever possible one should try to obtain a multiple entry visa, particularly for countries with overseas territories or dependencies, such as France (Martinique, Guadeloupe, French Polynesia, New Caledonia, Réunion, St Pierre and Miquelon), Australia (Norfolk Island, Christmas Island and Cocos Keeling) or the USA (Virgin Islands, Puerto Rico, Hawaii and Guam).

Something that must be borne in mind when cruising is that visa regulations do change and often without warning. One should always try to find out the latest situation before sailing to a certain country. As most countries maintain diplomatic missions in neighbouring countries, these are the best places to ask about changes and to apply for any necessary visas. Occasionally regulations change so quickly that even the diplomatic missions do not know about it.

Visa requirements, and the political climate generally, can often change quickly due to the improvement or deterioration of relations between countries. The first edition of this book was written during a period of profound change on the international political scene and at times it was almost impossible to keep up to date with a rapidly changing world. The changes in South Africa have already altered people's attitude to that country, while the process of liberalisation in Eastern Europe has already opened several countries previously barred to foreign cruising boats. Unfortunately not all changes appear to have been for the better and formalities in countries formerly belonging to the Soviet Union continue to be as complicated as before. The situation is further complicated by outbreaks of hostilities in some former Communist countries, so a voyage to any of those countries should be only undertaken with the latest information at hand.

Cruising Permits

In some countries, cruising boats are subjected to special regulations or restrictions concerning their movement. In most places if a cruising permit or transit log is required, it is issued at the first port of entry, so it is not necessary to make any preparations in advance. Any restrictions on the freedom of movement of yachts which do not require a cruising permit to be obtained in advance are discussed in the section on that country. It is most important to know the particular requirements of those permits which must be applied for before one's arrival, so as to make the correct preparations. The regulations pertaining to at least three such countries, Indonesia, Palau and the Galapagos Islands, have been causing great confusion among cruising sailors for years and it is hoped that this book will clear up some of the confusion.

There are various reasons why restrictions on cruising boats are imposed, the main reasons being the protection of remote communities from intrusion, the preservation of natural parks and reserves, or the wish of authorities to keep foreign sailors away from sensitive military areas or detention centres. Restrictions are also increasingly imposed on genuine cruising boats because of the fear by local authorities that a boat chartering illegally might slip through their net. In some places any crew changes are regarded with deep suspicion and boat owners have been asked occasionally to prove that those joining them were not charter guests. In all fairness, it must be said that in many countries charter boats do take advantage of lax laws and operate illegally, pretending to be ordinary cruising boats. The situation has not been helped by some cruising boats doing a bit of chartering on the side without informing the authorities and completing whatever formalities are necessary. After many years of tolerance or ignorance, the authorities in most countries used by charter boats are now aware of what is happening and are trying to get the charter operators to make some contribution to the economy of the country whose beauty they so readily exploit. It is unfortunate that genuine cruising boats have been caught up in this situation, but sailors should try to understand that some of these countries have few resources apart from their picturesque scenery, so their attempts to recoup some of the revenue that others are making out of it should not be condemned too harshly. The same line of thought can be applied to the fees sometimes charged for cruising permits or light dues. These fees, which give access to some of the most beautiful and unspoilt areas of the world, are rarely more than one would pay for two or three nights in a marina anywhere in Europe or North America.

European Union

On 1 January 1993 all countries belonging to the European Union became a single market by enforcing the Single European Act and merging into a common customs and Value Added Tax (VAT) zone. VAT is a special tax which is applied to both goods and services. The rates vary from country to country, and in some countries there are different VAT rates, although the VAT rate charged on boats is invariably the highest. VAT rates vary between 15 per cent in Spain and 25 per cent in Denmark.

Because of the lifting of customs controls within the European Union, the flying of the Q flag is no longer obligatory if one sails from one EU country to another. However, immigration rules still apply and if there are holders of non-EU passports on board, the immigration authorities must be contacted on arrival.

The importation of duty-free goods from one EU country into another is no longer permitted. However, one is allowed to buy duty-free goods outside of the EU, such as the Channel Islands or Gibraltar, and import them into any EU country. In such cases the same allowances apply as those used for air passengers. Where the single market has made a great difference is in lifting all restrictions on the importation of duty-paid goods. In the case of goods bought in normal shops or supermarkets, there are practically no limits provided the goods are bought for your own consumption. There are, however, some limits to the allowance, over which you must prove that the goods are indeed meant for your own consumption. Especially in some of the Nordic countries there are severe restrictions on the importation of alcoholic drinks, even from another EU country. The allowances are quite generous for the UK: 800 cigarettes, 10 litres spirits, 20 litres fortified wines, 90 litres wine and 110 litres beer.

The changes in regulations brought about by the single market, and the way these regulations are applied, have implications both for owners of boats registered in one of the EU countries and to visitors from outside the EU. The 15 countries belonging to the EU are: Italy, France, Germany, Belgium, Luxembourg, the Netherlands, United Kingdom, Ireland, Denmark, Spain, Portugal, Greece, Austria, Finland and Sweden. Island groups belonging to some of those countries, such as the Azores, Madeira, Canaries, Channel Islands or Åland, have a special status and this will be explained in the relevant section. Different regulations also apply in dependent territories, such as Gibraltar or Greenland.

Customs regulations have been largely harmonised and non-EU flagged vessels may now spend a maximum of six months in any one year within the EU, whether in only one or in several of the EU countries. Those who wish to remain longer in any one EU country must deposit the ship's papers with the local customs office, who will put the vessel under bond, or seal. The clock will then be stopped until the owner returns on board. During the period the vessel is in bond, the boat must not move from its berth, and the owner or crew are not allowed to sleep on board, although they may visit the boat and also carry out a certain amount of work.

Non-EU boats remaining inside the EU for over six months, and being used by the owner or the crew during this period, must be imported and VAT paid on the value of the boat. Anyone intending to do this would be well advised to import the boat into one of the EU countries with a lower VAT rate, such as Madeira. The alternative is either to put the boat into temporary bond, so that the clock is stopped, or sail into a non-EU country for the remainder of the year.

The Schengen Agreement

The commitment of European states to free movement of persons led to the creation of the Schengen Agreement, which was signed by Belgium, France, Germany, Luxembourg and the Netherlands in June 1990. Since then, Italy, Spain, Portugal and Austria, as well as Greece and all of the Nordic countries, have joined, although the Nordic countries have not yet ratified the agreement. Schengen abolishes internal border controls between its members, so, for example, a Portuguese person travelling to Spain would not be subject to systematic passport checks.

The removal of internal borders between the participating states obviously means that the criteria for who is allowed across the external border of the Schengen countries is of crucial importance. This is because within the Schengen area, if only one member state had a lax immigration policy or ineffective external controls, the other member states would have reason to fear that they would as a consequence see the entry of large numbers of illegal immigrants. The Schengen countries have therefore committed themselves to abide by a common policy on issuing visas. A uniform visa valid for the entire territory of the Schengen countries is to be introduced. This visa may be issued for visits of up to three months in any one year. Normally, such a visa shall be that of the principal destination. Occasionally a government may decide to temporarily suspend the provisions of the Schengen Agreement, usually in special circum-

stances such as an unexpected influx of refugees following a regional or international crisis (such as Kosovo).

As there are different regulations and requirements for EU or non-EU vessels, they are treated separately.

EU vessels

A boat owned by a resident of the EU has the right to free movement throughout the EU, provided VAT has been paid on that vessel in one of the EU countries. Although there is no legal time limit on the length of time a EU registered boat, VAT paid, can spend in any EU country, it appears that some countries occasionally enforce local regulations once the boat has been in that country for six months.

Although the new regulations came into force in 1993, considerable confusion still reigns. This should improve once the VAT situation is cleared up as there are thousands of boats belonging to EU residents who, for some reason or other, have not paid VAT on their boats. In many cases these boats are based in another EU country than the one where the owner resides and therefore they are liable to VAT. The rules are very clear and a boat belonging to a EU citizen, or flying the flag of a EU country, must be VAT paid. This means that both in home waters and when sailing between any EU countries, such boats should carry evidence of VAT payment. This could be the original boatbuilder's receipt or paid invoice, or some other original document showing clearly that VAT has been paid. Those who are exempt from this rule must have on board a document issued by customs or the relevant authority stating the reasons for such exemption.

Non-EU vessels

Boats owned by non-EU residents and registered outside the EU are entitled to tax free temporary importation into the EU for six months in any 12 month period. The permitted six month period, or temporary importation, applies to the entire EU area and therefore at the end of the six month period the boat must be sailed to a country outside the EU or VAT must be paid. The temporary importation period may be extended, at the discretion of local customs, for various bona fide reasons, such as if the boat is left unattended and unused, if the owner leaves the EU, or if the boat is left in the care of a boatyard for repair.

Those who wish to remain longer in any one EU country must deposit the ship's papers with the local customs office, who will put the vessel under bond. The clock will then be stopped until the owner returns on board. During the period the vessel is in bond, the boat must not move from its berth, and the owner or crew are not allowed to sleep on board.

Non-EU boats remaining inside the EU over six months must be imported and VAT paid on the boat value. Anyone intending to do this would be well advised to import the boat into one of the EU countries with a lower VAT rate, such as Madeira.

There has been a harmonisation of formalities concerning VAT in recent years, but there are still certain inconsistencies so the owners of boats from outside the EU should treat the matter with utmost caution and avoid being caught out. It must be stressed that the above six month VAT relief applies only where the boat is owned and sailed by a person not resident in the customs territory of the EU. The relief is invalidated if the boat is hired, sold or put at the disposal of a EU resident.

It is essential to ascertain on arrival in a new country the exact situation concerning VAT. As non-EU boats are required to contact immigration whenever crossing a border between EU countries, this may be the time to make such enquiries. Generally, however, it may be better to find out the true state of affairs from a fellow sailor before starting to ask questions from the authorities.

Customs procedures in the European Union

Departure from a EU port to another EU port: no formalities required.
Arrival in a EU port directly from another EU port: no formalities for EU vessels and EU citizens. Immigration must be contacted if there are non-EU citizens aboard. Customs must be notified if there is anything to declare, such as firearms.
Departure from a EU port to a non-EU port: customs and immigration must be notified.
Arrival in a EU port from a non-EU port: Q flag must be flown when entering 12 mile limit. Customs and immigration must be contacted on arrival.

European Monetary Union

The European Commission has announced the irrevocably fixed conversion rates between the euro and the currencies of the 11 participating member states. The United Kingdom, Denmark, Sweden have decided not to join the euro at this stage. Greece is joining on 1 January 2002.

Foreign exchange in euros started on 1 January 1999, when the conversion rates were also announced. There will be a gradual changeover period between 1999 and 2001. In all countries that have joined the euro, most prices are already quoted in both the present currency and the euro equivalent during transition. Euro banknotes and coins will start circulating on 1 January 2002, and will be used in parallel with the national currencies. The legal tender of national banknotes will cease on 1 July 2002.

Euro conversion rates

Belgium	1 euro = 40.3399 BEF
Germany	1 euro = 1.95583 DEM
Spain	1 euro = 166.386 ESP
France	1 euro = 6.55957 FRF
Ireland	1 euro = 0.787564 IEP
Italy	1 euro = 1936.27 ITL
Luxembourg	1 euro = 40.3399 LUF
Netherlands	1 euro = 2.20371 NLG
Austria	1 euro = 13.7603 ATS
Portugal	1 euro = 200.482 PTE
Finland	1 euro = 5.94573 FIM
Greece	1 euro = 340.750 GDR

Commonwealth of Independent States (CIS)

The Commonwealth of Independent States was set up in December 1991 after the break-up of the former Soviet Union and consists of 11 republics of the former USSR – the three founder states, Russia, the Ukraine and Belarus; Armenia, Azerbaijan, Georgia, Moldova, and five Central Asian Republics. The CIS headquarters are in Minsk, the capital of Belarus. All the member republics are fully sovereign but the CIS aims towards some sort of economic union and a unified control over strategic nuclear weapons.

Regarding formalities, the CIS has no significance as every member country has its own requirements. The main confusion arises over the fact that within those member states there are autonomous republics or regions, such as the Crimea within Ukraine, or Abhasia and Adjari within Georgia. Russia itself, which has outlets both on the Black Sea and the Baltic, has been included in the section dealing with the Baltic and Northern Europe.

Environment Protection

Few other sports or activities depend so much on the environment as sailing and it is therefore in our best interest to do everything possible to protect it from further destruction.

Anchoring

Anchoring on a coral bottom should be avoided as the anchor and chain will cause irreversible destruction to the live coral. Several countries, such as the Bahamas and Virgin Islands, are now imposing restrictions on anchoring in coral and, to avoid further destruction, are laying mooring buoys in some of the more frequented areas. Cruising sailors should try to set an example by observing these rules.

Garbage

Only biodegradable waste should be disposed of at sea. All other garbage should be collected in plastic bags and disposed of carefully when returning to land.

Holding tanks

Although the use of holding tanks is not yet compulsory throughout the world, in more and more countries the pumping overboard of any waste is prohibited. Holding tanks are now compulsory on many inland waterways and throughout the Baltic. In many ports and marinas pumping out toilets will result in heavy fines. In the USA even boats with holding tanks have been fined for not having the valve handle in the correct position. One other area where the authorities are extremely strict concerning holding tanks is Palau.

Although many cruising boats are not fitted with holding tanks, these should be installed as a matter of priority. As pumping out stations are not yet widely available, in the absence of another alternative the tanks should only be emptied when well away from a port or marina. In some countries tanks may not be pumped out when within six miles of the coast.

Flag Etiquette

Although not all countries insist on it, in theory **the Q flag should be flown as soon as the yacht has entered territorial waters to signal the intention of requesting pratique.** This should be done when entering the 12 mile limit. In this way, one cannot be accused of trying to slip in unnoticed and in fact in some countries yachts have got into trouble for not hoisting the Q flag until they were in port. Also to avoid any misunderstandings, it is advisable to try to contact the authorities on VHF radio, especially in those countries which do not readily welcome yachts.

The courtesy flag should also be flown once the boat enters a nation's territorial waters. The flag should be flown from the starboard spreader in a position above any other flag. The courtesy flag should be in a good state and of reasonable size as some officials

take offence at yachts that fly a torn or tiny flag. In some dependencies or autonomous regions, such as the Canaries, Azores, Tahiti Nui (formerly French Polynesia) or Corsica, it is appreciated if the regional flag is flown together, but below, that of the metropolitan power. Burgees, house flags and courtesy flags as well as ensigns should be lowered at sunset or 2100, whichever is earlier, and hoisted at 0800 in summer and 0900 in winter. It is particularly important to observe this in Scandinavian countries, where people are extremely flag conscious. The courtesy flags of the countries listed in this book are illustrated on the end papers.

The ship should be dressed overall on national days in countries visited. Ships should only be dressed when at anchor or in harbour. Although not essential, and many people are not even aware of it, there is a correct order in which to fly the code signals if the yacht is dressed from bow to stern. This order has been designed to give an interesting variety of both colour and shapes. The correct order, starting from the bow, is: E Q p3 G p8 Z p4 W p6 P p1 1 CODE T Y B X 1st H 3rd D F 2nd U A O M R p2 J p0 N p9 K p7 V p5 L C S. If the vessel is two masted, the line between the two masts starts with Y and ends with O.

The Right Attitude

While the actual completion of formalities is usually a matter about which the captain is at the mercy of local officials, unless he is prepared or able to handle formalities through an agent, many unpleasant experiences can be avoided by a right attitude. The first impressions of a visiting sailor's attitude or behaviour can determine how he or she is treated from the start and one should not be surprised if local officials do not treat someone with respect if that person's attitude shows an obvious disrespect for them, their position, customs, language, religion or colour of skin. Often such an attitude is caused by ignorance, and it is hoped that the information contained in this book will help dispel some of this ignorance. Just as often, such an attitude is caused by a blatant feeling of superiority, which people from developed countries, where most cruising boats come from, sometimes display towards people in developing countries. Such a superior attitude is not always put on deliberately, on the contrary, it is often natural and unnoticed by the person who displays it, but it can and will create an immediate antagonism in the local people that person deals with, who are so well attuned to this condition that they can sense it as soon as people step into their office. It certainly pays to show a little humility. What one would not do at home, one should not do abroad either. Just as one would not behave in a condescending manner towards a US or British customs official, why behave differently towards a Sri Lankan, Tahitian or Sudanese? I have witnessed many incidents when a small dose of politeness and consideration would have resolved matters on the spot without any further aggravation.

An even bigger factor in provoking antagonism is the way some sailors dress, or rather undress, when visiting other countries. It probably does not even occur to them that the way they dress is not only a sign of disrespect for local custom, but can be downright offensive. Particularly when visiting government offices, men should not go barefoot or in rubber thonged sandals, in shorts or singlets. In some countries, such as Brazil, access to government offices is only permitted if properly attired. In many Arab, West Indian, Asian and Latin American countries, shorts are never worn by men in public. Shorts are considered acceptable only for small boys or on a beach. Therefore one should not be offended if officials do not treat someone so dressed with the respect due to the captain of an offshore yacht. Generally a tidy appearance denotes respect for the authorities of the host country and will ensure that one is treated accordingly. The same rules apply when visiting local yacht clubs, where dress rules are often strictly enforced. It is also a good idea to make sure that the boat is tidied up after a long passage, so as to look presentable on arrival, especially in those countries where the yacht is boarded immediately on arrival. Everywhere in the world it is the first impression that counts and it might save one considerable frustration. It might just be the factor that helps the officials decide whether to conduct a search of the yacht or to take your word that you are not carrying anything illegal.

Dress etiquette is a difficult matter as it varies so much from country to country. In some countries, a foreign woman's scanty dress can be interpreted as an indication of her morals, which can lead to sexual harassment and even rape. In most Pacific islands, where bare breasts are considered normal, for a woman to bare her thighs is considered provocative and so very skimpy shorts should be avoided. In Greece women should always cover bare shoulders when entering a church and sometimes their heads too. In Arab countries it is wise for women to wear trousers or long skirts if possible. Footgear should be removed before entering a

Buddhist shrine and although it is permissible to photograph Buddha statues, one should not pose beside them. Footwear should be removed when visiting some Asian homes and also when visiting mosques. In strict Muslim countries, access to mosques is forbidden to nonbelievers. Because the consumption of alcohol is against Muslim belief, one must not be seen consuming alcoholic drinks in public, which may include the cockpit if berthed in a port. Nor should food be consumed in public before sunset during Ramadan. In Muslim countries, dogs are considered unclean and pets are best kept on board. Friday is the day of rest in Muslim countries, when everything is closed. Sunday is observed very religiously in some Pacific countries, particularly Tonga and Fiji, where sporting events are among the activities forbidden on Sundays.

An important rule is not to bribe local officials. Although this might ease matters temporarily for one person, it will certainly make life more difficult for those who follow. There are corrupt officials in many countries and often they attempt to procure a bribe, but if this is firmly resisted, or a detailed official receipt is asked for any money demanded, they may give up. When the boat is inspected, if one feels like offering the boarding officers a drink, there is no reason why one should not do so, although it is preferable to stick to non-alcoholic drinks, particularly in Muslim countries. Generally it is not advisable to make gifts, except perhaps the small token gifts some yachts carry with their logo or name on. It can be difficult to refuse if an official asks for something or for money, but it should be avoided as politely as possible so as not to set a precedent. Occasionally, however, a small gift is virtually impossible to avoid and, in spite of my reluctance to do so, even I had to break my own rules and give a tip to some insistent official.

When clearing in, it is extremely foolish to try and hide anything, because the penalties for possessing undeclared firearms, pets or drugs can be severe. If in doubt it is better to declare more than necessary, especially in those countries where moveable items of value such as cameras and radios have to be written on the declaration. Everything should be declared including prescription drugs, such as strong painkillers, and the relevant prescription or doctor's letter may have to be shown. The official attitude towards illegal drugs is extremely strict everywhere and many countries operate zero tolerance, so if any illegal drugs at all are found, one risks paying a heavy fine, going to prison or possibly losing the boat. One should therefore be very careful about crew picked up casually and what they might have in their possession. This subject should be discussed very seriously with all crew members as the boat could be confiscated if drugs are found on board, and ignorance on the part of the owner or captain is not accepted as an excuse. If a yacht is searched, either the captain or a crew member should accompany the searching officer to prevent anything being planted, which is known to have happened in a few cases. If anything is found, it should not be touched, so as not to leave fingerprints. One should also take a photograph of the official holding the incriminating item where it was found. If arrested, one should alert any other yachts in the vicinity immediately, so they can keep an eye on the yacht and also inform one's embassy or consulate. In a few countries people have been wrongly arrested, kept for 24 hours and then released, only to find on their return that their boat has been ransacked and everything of value taken. Foreign visitors are subject to the laws of the country they are visiting and sailors on cruising boats are not exempt. The powers of one's ambassador or consul are limited and although they may be able to help those that are faced with an emergency situation, they can rarely help someone who has contravened the laws of the country, except to ensure that they receive fair treatment.

2 Health Precautions Worldwide

It is expected that every cruising boat will carry a comprehensive medical kit to deal with a wide range of accidents and possible illnesses, as help at sea in an emergency is not always immediately available. Fortunately infectious or contagious diseases are not a risk while at sea, but these become a hazard when ashore in many parts of the world.

The two greatest health hazards are mosquitos and unsafe drinking water or food. These can be guarded against in several ways. Malaria, yellow fever and dengue fever are among the diseases that are mosquito-borne. If cruising for any length of time in the tropics it is wise to have mosquito screens fitted over hatches or mosquito netting that can be rigged over bunks. One should keep as much of the body covered as possible at sunset and use insect repellants, knockdown sprays or burn coils.

Not all vaccinations give total protection against food and water-borne diseases, so one should be scrupulous about checking water supplies, treating the water or drinking bottled water in dubious areas. Also one should avoid raw vegetables, salads, unpeeled fruit, raw shellfish, ice cream, cream and ice cubes in drinks in risk areas, unless these have been thoroughly washed or prepared by oneself.

It is highly recommended that supplies of sterilised and sealed items such as syringes, needles, sutures, dressings and infusion cannulae are carried. These sterile packs are widely available in kits for travellers and can be given to medical staff if seeking treatment abroad where properly sterilised or disposable equipment is not used or available. This is a precaution to be taken for all countries where there is a risk of Hepatitis B or AIDS from contaminated equipment, blood or blood products. If an accident or emergency needs a blood transfusion in countries where donated blood is not screened or checked properly, it is advisable to contact one's embassy or consulate, as some of them keep a disease-free donor list in certain countries.

Many countries give reciprocal free treatment in an emergency, but this is only on the same terms as that received by nationals of the foreign country concerned. This usually applies to state health-care systems, which leave much to be desired in some countries. For members of the EU, there is a special form (in the UK Form E111 obtainable from post offices), which entitles the person to emergency medical care throughout the EU. The procedure varies from country to country and details are given on the form. For anyone cruising extensively, it is highly recommended that a worldwide medical insurance is taken out to cover any treatment required, especially if sailing to countries where medical care is expensive, such as the USA, Canada or Australia. This insurance will also often provide for an ill person to be flown home for treatment, which is a wise option to take if the emergency occurs in a country with poor medical facilities.

Sufficient time before departure should be allowed for any vaccinations, as some cannot be given at the same time as others. Details on vaccinations required and precautions against specific diseases are summarised below.

AIDS

The Acquired Immune Deficiency Syndrome, commonly called AIDS, is caused by a virus called HIV. Not everyone infected with the HIV virus develops the disease, although they are likely to remain infected and infectious for much of their lives. There is no way to tell if a person is infected without taking an HIV positive test. A few countries have started asking for an HIV test certificate for visitors coming from certain countries where it is prevalent such as East Africa.

The disease is present worldwide, but in certain countries such as Haiti and East Africa the disease is endemic in the general population. The two main ways of catching the AIDS virus is sexual contact or through contaminated blood getting into the body via a transfusion, injection or poorly sterilised medical equipment. The virus cannot be caught by everyday contact, crockery, food, swimming pools or mosquito bites. The obvious precautions are to avoid casual sexual contacts and to use a condom. One should carry sterile medical supplies for emergencies when one may require an injection. One should also avoid medical or dental treatment involving surgery in countries where there is a risk. In many less developed countries blood for transfusion is not properly screened or treated, but there may be ways of obtaining screened blood if the doctor is asked or diplomatic missions are contacted.

Hepatitis B

This is transmitted in a similar way to AIDS, by contact with an infected person or through infected blood or needles. Hepatitis B is found worldwide. There is a vaccination which gives protection, but the course takes up to six months to come to full protection. The best precautions are as those described above for AIDS.

Hepatitis A

This is sometimes called infectious hepatitis and is caught from contaminated food or water and is prevalent in most parts of the world where there is poor sanitation and hygiene. A vaccine, Havrix, is now available, and although expensive, the full course of three injections gives protection for ten years, ideal for long term cruising worldwide. The immunoglobulin injection (HNIG) containing antibodies to Hepatitis A gives protection for six weeks and is an alternative for short visits to vulnerable areas. Otherwise the main precaution is to take scrupulous care over what one eats and drinks as outlined above.

Tetanus

This dangerous disease is found everywhere in the world and results from the tetanus spores entering the body via even a slight scratch or wound. This can easily happen on any dockside, so it is essential that everyone cruising keeps their tetanus vaccination up to date.

Fortunately this vaccination is safe and very effective and if one had a full course as a child, as most people have, a booster is only necessary every ten years. If one has failed to keep this up to date and tetanus – commonly called lockjaw – develops, it can be treated if the patient is got to proper medical facilities immediately. These may not be available in more remote areas.

Tuberculosis

This disease is on the increase again in certain areas of Africa, Asia, Central and South America. If one has been vaccinated against tuberculosis in the past, revaccination is not necessary. Vaccination is only necessary if living or working closely with the indigenous population in these areas. It is unlikely that any cruising sailors would need this vaccination.

Smallpox

This disease has been eradicated worldwide and vaccination against it is no longer necessary.

Measles

Persons born after 1957 should consider a second dose of measles vaccine before travelling abroad.

Typhoid

Typhoid is found almost everywhere except Australia, New Zealand, Europe and North America and it is found especially in conditions of poor hygiene and sanitation. It is caught from contaminated food, water or milk. Sensible precautions are to take care over food and drink, but vaccination against typhoid is recommended for all those sailing outside of the above mentioned areas. There are now two types of typhoid vaccine: Typhoid VI antigen, a single dose vaccine giving protection for three years; and Typhoid TY21A, a live vaccine taken orally as capsules in three doses on alternate days, giving protection for one year.

Poliomyelitis

This disease is found everywhere except Australia, New Zealand, Europe and North America. Anyone cruising outside of these areas should ensure that their vaccination against polio is kept up to date. To commence vaccination, a course of three doses of oral vaccine are given, normally when one is a child. Reinforcing doses should be taken every ten years to continue protection against polio. Polio is transmitted by direct contact with an infected person and sometimes by contaminated water or food.

An extra booster dose of the vaccine should be received by persons over 18 years travelling to Africa, East and SE Asia, the Middle East, the Indian subcontinent and all countries of the former Soviet Union.

Meningococcal Meningitis

This serious disease, which is transmitted by direct contact or droplet infection, has had a rising incidence worldwide. There is a particularly high risk in the meningitis belt, which lies across sub-Saharan Africa and includes Senegal, Gambia and Ivory Coast on the west coast and Sudan, Ethiopia and Kenya on the east coast. There is a season for this disease, from November to May, and pilgrims have taken it to Saudi Arabia during the annual Hadj pilgrimage. Vaccination against meningococcal infection is available for meningitis A and C and this gives protection for three years.

Cholera

Cholera is found in some parts of Africa, Asia, South America and the Middle East and especially in areas of primitive sanitation. The disease is transmitted through contaminated water and food. The cholera vaccine used in the past never worked well and is no longer recommended. For this reason it is not included in the checklist. Scrupulous hygiene is paramount in endemic areas.

Yellow Fever

This disease is only found in some parts of Africa and South America. It is transmitted by the bite of an infected mosquito. Vaccination against yellow fever gives protection for ten years. Vaccination can only be carried out at designated centres, a list of which can be obtained from health authorities, travel agents or one's own doctor. Although yellow fever is found mainly in tropical forest areas and sailors are unlikely to encounter it, the vaccination is compulsory for travel to some countries, even if only visiting the coast or main ports. A vaccination certificate may be required also in subsequent ports if arriving from countries where yellow fever is present. If not possessing a certificate, one may have to be vaccinated on the spot, another reason for carrying those sterile needles and syringes.

Malaria

This is one of the biggest health risks that may be encountered by cruising sailors and some forms of malaria are particularly virulent and can even be fatal. Malaria is prevalent in many parts of Africa, Asia, Central and South America and the western Pacific. The disease is transmitted by mosquitos, so the first precaution is to avoid getting bitten, as outlined earlier.

Prophylactic treatment is available and anti-malarial tablets should be taken two weeks before entering a malarial area, throughout one's stay and for four weeks after departure. The problem has increased because some strains of malaria have become resistant to the drugs in use and therefore different tablets are recommended for particular areas. Although anti-malarial tablets are available over the counter in pharmacies it is wise to check with a doctor or a centre for tropical diseases which are the recommended drugs and doses. The tablets are usually taken once a week and it is essential to take them after food. Children take a dose proportionate to their weight. Advice on malaria prophylaxis changes frequently and no regimen is 100 per cent protective, so it is essential to seek up-to-date advice if cruising in an endemic area. Pregnant women and small children are especially at risk as they have a lower resistance to the disease.

Advice should be sought as some drugs are not suitable for pregnant women, or folic acid supplements should be taken. Those suffering from epilepsy or psoriasis should also seek advice about which prophylactic treatment to take.

Areas particularly important for cruising sailors to take precautions in are Vanuatu, the Solomons and Papua New Guinea in the western Pacific, Guyana, French Guiana in South America, Indonesia, Philippines in South East Asia, and Sri Lanka, Comoros, Mauritius and East Africa in the Indian Ocean.

There is now an immuno-diagnostic kit which can confirm whether or not one has contracted falciparum malaria. The test kit (which needs to be refrigerated) is available from various sources, such as TMVC (Travellers Medical and Vaccination Centre) in Australia. TMVC have a highly informative website dealing with an entire range of tropical and infectious diseases (www.tmvc.com.au).

Rabies

Rabies is endemic virtually worldwide and is usually fatal if not treated immediately, hence the precautions against admitting animals exercised by many island nations which are rabies-free. The disease can be caught if one is bitten, scratched or even licked by an infected animal such as a dog, cat or monkey. Therefore one should not approach or touch any unknown animal. If one is bitten or scratched by an animal one should wash and disinfect the wound thoroughly and get to medical attention fast. There is a rabies vaccination, which is a course of quite unpleasant injections, which should be started immediately. It is not normally recommended to be vaccinated beforehand against rabies unless one is travelling across country in remote parts where treatment is not available. If bitten, one should try and keep the animal under observation or if it is wild or a stray, note the place, description and date of the attack and inform the local police.

Bilharzia

This is also called schistosomiasis and is a deadly disease caught from parasites which have a secondary host in minute snails found in fresh water. Swimming in fresh water lakes or streams should be avoided in much of South America, Africa, Asia and the Caribbean. Bilharzia cannot be caught from swimming in the sea or salt water estuaries.

Diphtheria

Thought to have been eliminated through an extensive immunisation programme, an upsurge in diphtheria in the countries of the former Soviet Union is giving some cause for concern. A low dose children's diphtheria vaccine is recommended for travellers to Romania, Ukraine and Russia (especially St Petersburg and Moscow).

Japanese B Encephalitis

This rare, but often fatal, insect-borne infection is found in Asia from India and Sri Lanka throughout South East Asia as far as Japan and the Philippines, including Indonesia. Vaccination is effective for two years and is available on a named patient basis. It is recommended for stays of more than one month in rural areas during the period June to September.

Ciguatera

This fish poisoning is caught by eating toxic fish from certain reef areas. Local knowledge should be sought whether fish from a certain coral reef area or island are likely to be affected. Fish caught by trolling in the open ocean are not likely to be toxic. One should avoid large fish such as barracuda caught in reef areas and one should avoid repeated meals from such fish as the toxin is cumulative. Fish should always be gutted extremely carefully

and the head, roe or internal organs never eaten.

There is now a test capable of identifying the presence of ciguatoxin in fish flesh. When used properly, Cigua-Check (TM) will test ciguatoxin at levels generally below the level that can cause clinical symptoms in humans. The test kit is available from the Ciguatera Hotline in Hawaii (*Tel.* 808-539-2345) (www.cigua.com).

Reefwalking and Diving Hazards

Many of these hazards can be avoided by wearing footwear when walking on reefs and by looking carefully before touching anything while diving or reefwalking.

The stone fish is an ugly animal looking just like a stone which gives a poisonous sting if stepped on. If stung, one should keep fairly immobile to delay the spread of poison, flush the puncture with vinegar and put the foot in hot water. Wrap a bandage immediately above the wound and seek medical assistance.

Cone shells have a dart which they launch in defence and in a few species this can be deadly. One should avoid picking up live cone shells, but if one is stung, one should treat it like snake venom and seek medical advice.

If stung by the jellyfish called Portuguese Man-of-War, it is important not to rub the sting, but detoxify it with alcohol of some sort – spirits such as rum will do or even perfume. The sting then should be rinsed gently with warm water.

Jellyfish stings should similarly be bathed with vinegar and hot water. If sea urchin spikes are trod on or got into the flesh, one must try to remove all the spikes, sucking them out if necessary. Again soak in hot water and treat with antibiotic cream or powder. For all coral cuts, bites and rashes obtained from marine life, one should wash well with hot water and disinfect to prevent infection.

The Sun

This is one of the most serious dangers encountered by sailors and the power of the sun should never be underestimated. Sunburn should be avoided by using sun screens on exposed skin, covering the head and body until a tan has been acquired. The eyes are particularly vulnerable and should be protected by good sunglasses. When at anchor it is recommended to rig up some kind of cockpit awning.

Not only can the sun burn one's skin painfully, but it can cause the body to overheat. When sailing in very hot climates, particularly in equatorial regions or in the Red Sea, one should drink plenty of non-alcoholic fluids and also slightly increase one's salt intake to counteract salt loss through sweating.

Heat exhaustion

In very hot temperatures, any fatigue, dizziness, headache or muscle cramps should be taken seriously. The person should be cooled by sponging with tepid water or with a fan and given salt and fruit juice or a sugar solution (1 teaspoonful of salt and 4 of sugar to 1 litre of water).

Heat stroke

This is characterised by a sudden dramatic rise in temperature, lack of sweat and odd behaviour. Plenty of water should be given and the skin cooled with water and fans. Medical help will be needed, especially if the person loses consciousness.

Skin cancer

Whilst the above are immediate problems, one of the most serious problems caused by the sun is long term and that is the danger of skin cancer. This is caused by prolonged exposure to the sun and may not show up for many years, but it has afflicted many cruising sailors. The risk of developing skin cancer increases as people grow older, but it is important to prevent over exposure to the sun in children and young people as this is a cumulative risk.

Chronic exposure to the sun is the main cause of skin cancer and the carcinomas usually appear on exposed parts of the body, such as face, scalp, hands, arms and legs. The people at highest risk are those spending long periods outdoors and particularly those with fair skin, light coloured hair and light coloured eyes, such as blue, green or grey. Also more at risk are those who sunburn easily and tan with difficulty. The geographical location is also a factor and the nearer to the equator, the higher the number of cases reported in fair-skinned people.

Ninety per cent of all skin cancers are curable, especially if detected early. Medical advice should be sought for any unusual or persistent change in the skin, whether a growth or a discolouration, or change in size, colour, shape or thickness of any pre-existing moles. Although the incidence of skin cancer has increased and the death rate in the USA has doubled in the last 35 years, in Queensland in Australia, where a public education programme had been established, the death rate has been decreasing despite an increase in the number of cases reported. The increase in incidence is partly due to people living longer and also pursuing a more active outdoor life into their old age. Prevention is the most important factor and so one should avoid prolonged exposure, use sun screens and cover exposed areas.

Health Protection Checklist

Codes

Hep = Hepatitis A, Mal = Malaria, Men = Meningitis, Ty = Typhoid, Pol = Polio, YF = Yellow Fever, r = risk of infection, vaccination recommended, M = mandatory.

Yellow fever

* = vaccination essential if arriving from a country where yellow fever is present. A vaccination certificate will be demanded.

Malaria

* = risk only in certain areas
Area A = Proguanil daily PLUS Chloroquine weekly recommended
Area B = Maloprim weekly PLUS Chloroquine weekly recommended
Area C = Chloroquine weekly OR Proguanil daily recommended
Area D = Mefloquine weekly recommended
Area E = Doxycycline daily recommended

1 Mediterranean and Black Sea

	Hep	Mal	Men	Ty	Pol	YF
Albania	r			r	r	*
Algeria	r			r	r	
Egypt	r	C*		r	r	*
Georgia	r			r	r	
Israel	r			r	r	
Lebanon	r			r	r	*
Libya	r	C*		r	r	*
Morocco	r			r	r	
Montenegro	r			r	r	
Romania	r			r	r	
Syria	r	C*		r	r	*
Tunisia	r			r	r	*
Turkey	r	C*		r	r	

No vaccinations are needed for European countries. Low-dose diphtheria vaccine recommended for travellers to Russia, Romania and Ukraine.

2 Northern Europe

No vaccinations are needed for the Baltic Republics, Belgium, Denmark, Finland, Germany, Netherlands, Norway, Poland or Sweden.

3 Western Europe and North Atlantic Islands

	Hep	Mal	Men	Ty	Pol	YF
Cape Verde Islands	r	A*		r	r	*

No vaccinations are needed for the Azores, Bermuda, Canary Islands, Channel Islands, Faeroes, France, Greenland, Iceland, Ireland, Madeira, Portugal or United Kingdom.

4 West Africa and South Atlantic Islands

	Hep	Mal	Men	Ty	Pol	YF
Ascension				r	r	*
Falkland Islands						
Gambia	r	A/D	r	r	r	r
Ivory Coast	r	D	r	r	r	M
Mauritania	r	D	r	r	r	M
Namibia	r	A*	r	r	r	*
St Helena				r	r	
Senegal	r	D	r	r	r	r
South Africa	r	A*		r	r	*
Tristan da Cunha				r	r	

5 Caribbean

	Hep	Mal	Men	Ty	Pol	YF
Anguilla	r			r	r	*
Antigua/Barbuda	r			r	r	*
Aruba	r			r	r	*
Bahamas	r			r	r	*
Barbados	r			r	r	*
Bonaire	r			r	r	*
British Virgin Islands	r			r	r	
Cayman Islands	r			r	r	
Cuba	r			r	r	
Curaçao	r			r	r	*
Dominica	r			r	r	*
Dominican Rep.	r	C		r	r	
Grenada	r			r	r	*
Guadeloupe	r			r	r	*
Haiti	r	C		r	r	*
Jamaica	r			r	r	*
Martinique	r			r	r	*
Montserrat	r			r	r	*
Puerto Rico	r			r	r	
Saba	r			r	r	*
St Barts	r			r	r	*
St Eustatius	r			r	r	*
St Kitts & Nevis	r			r	r	*
St Lucia	r			r	r	*
St Martin	r			r	r	*
St Vincent & Grenadines	r			r	r	*
Sint Maarten	r			r	r	*
Trinidad	r			r	r	*
Turks & Caicos	r			r	r	*
US Virgin Islands	r			r	r	

6 Central and North America

	Hep	Mal	Men	Ty	Pol	YF
Belize	r	C		r	r	*
Canada						
Costa Rica	r	C*		r	r	
El Salvador	r	C		r	r	*
Guatemala	r	C		r	r	*
Honduras	r	C		r	r	*
Mexico	r	C*		r	r	*
Nicaragua	r	C		r	r	*
Panama	r	A/C*		r	r	r
USA						

7 South America

	Hep	Mal	Men	Ty	Pol	YF
Argentina	r	C*		r	r	
Brazil	r	D*		r	r	r
Chile	r			r	r	
Colombia	r	D		r	r	r
Ecuador	r	A		r	r	r
French Guiana	r	D		r	r	M
Guyana	r	D		r	r	r
Peru	r	A		r	r	r
Suriname	r	D		r	r	r
Uruguay	r			r	r	
Venezuela	r	A/D*		r	r	r

8 North Pacific Islands

	Hep	Mal	Men	Ty	Pol	YF
Federated States of Micronesia	r			r	r	*
Guam	r			r	r	*
Hawaii				r		
Kiribati	r			r	r	*
Marshall Islands	r			r	r	
Northern Marianas	r			r	r	
Palau	r			r	r	

9 South Pacific

	Hep	Mal	Men	Ty	Pol	YF
American Samoa	r			r	r	*
Australia						*
Cook Islands	r			r	r	
Easter Island	r			r	r	*
Galapagos Islands	r			r	r	*
Fiji	r			r	r	*
Juan Fernandez Islands	r			r	r	*
Nauru	r			r	r	*
New Caledonia	r			r	r	*
New Zealand						
Niue	r			r	r	*
Norfolk Island				r	r	*
Papua New Guinea	r	E		r	r	*
Pitcairn	r			r	r	*
Samoa	r			r	r	*
Solomon Islands	r	E		r	r	*
Tahiti Nui (formerly French Polynesia)	r			r	r	*
Tokelau	r			r	r	*
Tonga	r			r	r	*
Tuvalu	r			r	r	*
Vanuatu	r	E		r	r	*
Wallis & Futuna	r			r	r	

10 South East Asia and Far East

	Hep	Mal	Men	Ty	Pol	YF
Brunei	r			r	r	*
China	r	C/D*		r	r	*
Hong Kong	r			r	r	
Indonesia	r	A/D*		r	r	*
Japan					r	
Macao	r			r	r	
Malaysia	r	A		r	r	
Myanmar	r	D		r	r	*
Philippines	r	A*		r	r	*
Singapore	r			r	r	*
South Korea	r			r	r	
Taiwan	r			r	r	*
Thailand	r	E*		r	r	*
Vietnam	r	D*		r	r	

11 North Indian Ocean and Red Sea

	Hep	Mal	Men	Ty	Pol	YF
Bahrain	r			r	r	
Djibouti	r	A	r	r	r	*
Eritrea	r	A	r	r	r	r
Jordan	r			r	r	
Kuwait	r			r	r	
India	r	A	r	r	r	*
Maldives	r			r	r	*
Oman	r	A		r	r	*
Qatar	r			r	r	
Saudi Arabia	r	A*	r	r	r	*
Somalia	r	D	r	r	r	r
Sri Lanka	r	A		r	r	*
Sudan	r	A	r	r	r	r
United Arab Emirates	r			r	r	r
Yemen	r	A*		r	r	*

12 South Indian Ocean

	Hep	Mal	Men	Ty	Pol	YF
Chagos						
Christmas Island				r	r	
Cocos Keeling				r	r	
Comoros	r	C*		r	r	
Kenya	r	D	r	r	r	r
Madagascar	r	D		r	r	*
Mauritius	r	C*		r	r	*
Mayotte	r	C*		r	r	
Mozambique	r	D		r	r	*
Réunion				r	r	*
Seychelles	r			r	r	
Tanzania	r	D	r	r	r	r

Health on the Internet

Health matters are more widely covered on the internet than almost anything else, so I will only mention two sites that are worth visiting as they have a direct relevance to anyone sailing to out-of-the-way places. Highly recommended is the website of Australian-based TMVC (Travellers Medical and Vaccination Centre). TMVC runs a highly informative website dealing with an entire range of tropical and infectious diseases (www.tmvc.com.au). Equally informative and regularly updated is the website of the US-based Center for Disease Control and Prevention (www.cdc.gov/travel).

3 Communications

Radio Communications

Very High Frequency marine radio

VHF radio is the primary means of coastal and short range ship-to-ship communications. VHF Channel 16 (156.8 MHz) is the distress, safety and calling frequency for voice transmissions which, until the complete introduction of the Global Maritime Distress and Safety System (GMDSS), should be monitored by all commercial vessels while at sea. GMDSS has been progressively introduced since 1992. With the advent of GMDSS, commercial vessels have been switching to the semiautomatic alerting system known as Digital Selective Calling (DSC) on Channel 70, as a substitute for Channel 16 voice alerting. Similarly, when GMDSS is fully implemented, those countries which have established a DSC watch on Channel 70 seem likely to dispense with their Channel 16 listening watch. Although DSC equipment is not compulsory on yachts, it seems likely that all yacht owners will have to fit DSC if they want to be heard in an emergency.

In the meantime Channel 16 is supposed to be monitored by all commercial vessels while under way. It is also monitored by coastal radio stations (CRS) as well as coast guards and similar organisations. Most countries maintain a network of coastal radio stations and calls through them can be linked into the national or international telephone system. In order to be able to do this, the VHF marine radio must be licensed in the country of registration and must be operated, or under the control of, a person holding the necessary operator's certificate and call sign (or marine identification number). Where radiotelephone calls are made through a CRS in your own home or abroad, arrangements must be made with the CRS for charging. The alternative is to make accounting arrangements with an accounting authority. Such arrangements should be made before departure so that the calls can be charged to a home account.

Medium and High Frequency marine radio

A large number of cruising yachts are equipped with MF, HF radio transmitters. The main function of these radios is to give the user the possibility to contact coastal radio stations when the vessel is offshore and out of VHF range. Once contacted, a station can place a call in the international telephone system. These radios also have other uses, such as calling coastal stations on medium frequency (MF), receiving weather facsimile broadcasts, monitoring distress frequencies or being used for ship-to-ship communications.

There are certain rules that must be complied with for the operation of HF marine radio. First of all, the operator of such equipment must have an operator's certificate issued by the licensing authority in the country where the vessel is registered. To obtain a licence one usually has to pass an examination, which comprises questions on the operation of the equipment, the procedure for making calls, dealing with emergencies, as well as the regulations governing radio transmissions at sea. There are courses for radio operators run by colleges and various associations, but it is also possible to pass the examination by studying alone. The actual transceiver must also be licensed and the issuing authority will grant the operator an official call sign. In some countries, both the licence and call sign are also valid for a VHF radio. Before leaving home, it is advisable to open an account with an agency recommended by the national telephone company, so that calls made from abroad can be charged to that account.

Most transceivers on cruising yachts are of relatively low power, usually with a maximum output of 150 W. This is not very powerful as far as marine transmitters go, but coupled with a knowledge of propagation, it should be sufficient for the needs of the average sailor wishing to make telephone calls via commercial radio stations. Particularly for those cruising offshore and at great distances from coastal stations, one of the most important factors to master early on is that of propagation. A basic knowledge of this important subject is essential and some of the best books dealing with this matter are those written by and for amateur radio operators.

As part of the new GMDSS infrastructure, Digital Selective Calling (DSC) distress alerting is being introduced on MF and HF, as on VHF. DSC alerting on these bands is likely, ultimately, to replace the listening watch on 2182 kHz and on certain HF frequencies.

Propagation

The distance over which a HF radio signal can travel depends on factors such as transmitter power and antenna gain, but one of the most important aspects is that of radio signal propagation. Radio signals in the ground mode travel along the earth's surface but are rapidly absorbed or masked by other radio frequency emissions. Ground waves are

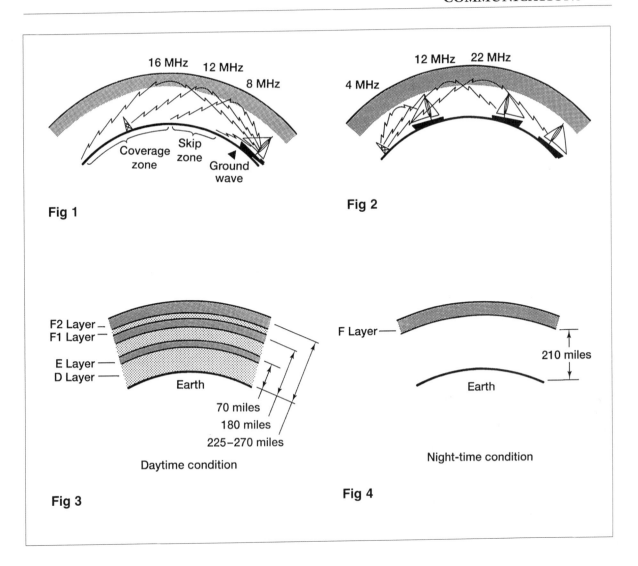

Fig 1

Fig 2

Fig 3 Daytime condition

Fig 4 Night-time condition

most important on medium frequency transmissions in the 2 MHz band. Although some short-range contacts can be made on HF on the ground wave mode, the propagation mode which is paramount to radiotelephone communications over long distances is sky wave propagation. This phenomenon makes worldwide radio communications possible.

In sky wave propagation, radio signals are refracted, or bent, by electricity-conducting layers in the upper atmosphere called the ionosphere. As a result, the signals are bounced back hundreds or thousands of miles from the point of emission. The area between the point of emission and the point at which the signal returns to earth is called the skip zone. The signal in the skip zone itself, in other words the area which has been skipped over,

is either non-existent or negligible (Fig. 1).

The distance that a signal can be skipped depends primarily on a process in the ionosphere called ionisation. Ionisation is caused by several factors, the most important being the ultraviolet light from the sun. It is this ionisation which produces the electricity-conducting layers that refract radio waves. As the earth rotates about its axis gradually turning away from the sun, the density of ions over any given point on the ground changes with increases or decreases in the sun's ionising radiations. This is the explanation for the difference in propagation throughout the day/night cycle. Fortunately, the ionosphere affects each frequency in a different manner. This means that if the point with which one wishes to communicate is skipped over by one frequency, all one has to do is choose a lower or higher frequency in order to reach the desired station. With a little practice, one will soon know which frequencies are best suited for which time of day and also are most likely to travel the required distance.

The lowest, least densely ionised layer of the ionosphere, called the 'D' layer, is located between 30 and 50 miles above the earth's surface. While this layer is not effective in refracting radio waves, it does absorb radio signals and is responsible for most of the weakening radio signal strength in the sky wave mode.

The next layer, called the 'E' layer, is located 70 miles above the earth's surface. This layer is slightly more ionised and is capable of bouncing relatively low frequency waves back to earth. It is particularly useful for short distance propagation, between a few hundred and 1500 miles. The next layer, the 'F1' layer, is located about 180 miles above the earth and is more densely ionised than the 'E' layer. The 'F1' layer is capable of bending higher frequency waves and is most useful for distances around 2000 miles. Finally, the highest layer, 'F2', varies from 225 to 270 miles in altitude and has the greatest density of ions. It is capable of refracting higher frequencies than any other layer and is primarily useful for propagation over distances of 2500 miles or more (Fig. 3).

During the night, when the sun's radiations are absent, the 'D' and 'E' layers disappear, while the 'F1' and 'F2' layers merge to form a single 'F' layer about 210 miles above the earth. This layer is responsible for night sky wave propagation (Fig. 4).

Optimum frequencies

Lower frequencies should be used during periods of low ionisation rather than during periods of high ionisation, in order to communicate over the same distance. It might seem that a frequency which is sufficiently low to be bent back to earth during conditions of low ion density would be suitable for transmission at all times. However, this is not generally the case because absorption of wave energy by the ionosphere increases with increased ionisation and increasing frequency. In other words, during high ionisation periods absorption may so weaken lower frequencies that little or no signal is returned to earth. It is therefore advantageous always to use the highest frequency that will refract down to the area with which one wishes to communicate, since this frequency will be weakened least by absorption.

There are some additional factors which affect radio propagation. Propagation varies not only

with the day/night cycle, but also with the summer/winter cycle as well as the phenomenon known as the 11 year sun-spot cycle. Although all this might sound complicated, in practice one quickly learns how to judge the best conditions to make calls ashore. The most important points to remember are the following:

1   Choose the working frequency of the coastal station you wish to contact. If you hear traffic, it is almost certain that you will be able to communicate with that station on that or any other channel in the same frequency band. It is also likely that the next higher or lower bands may also support communications with that coastal station.

2   In order to become familiar with propagation on various bands, it is useful to listen to traffic lists and other broadcasts from a chosen station and to make a note of the bands which are available at all times.

3   Low frequencies are weakened more than high frequencies during high ionisation periods (day time).

4   High frequencies penetrate the ionosphere at night and are lost in space.

5   Low frequencies are not absorbed at night and can be used for relatively long distance communications during periods of darkness.

The simplest rule to remember is: high ionisation, high frequency – low ionisation, low frequency. In other words, low frequencies should be used at night and high frequencies should be used over long distances during daylight hours.

Because of propagation differences between frequencies, proximity to a station is less important than finding a good clear channel on which to transmit. Communication with more distant stations is primarily a matter of selecting the right frequency band. Since all available maritime mobile channels are shared by countries around the world, it is highly likely that at certain times there will be congestion and interference on some frequencies. It is therefore advisable to equip the transceiver with as many channels as possible for each station. Alternatively, one should ensure that additional frequencies can be quickly dialled if one finds that those preselected do not cover optimum bands. This can occur on radios which have all their frequencies preset by the manufacturer and which do not allow the user to add his own frequencies later on. Transceivers with fixed frequencies are therefore best avoided on cruising yachts. By employing favourable propagation conditions and using the best placed coastal stations, one should be able to maintain contact with land most of the time. Details of coastal radio stations worldwide are given in the British Admiralty List of Radio Signals.

Amateur Short Wave radio

An alternative preferred by many cruising sailors for long-range communications is amateur radio operating on short wave. The frequency bands allocated to amateur radio operators are interspersed with those used by coastal stations broadcasting on the HF marine radio bands. Not only is the mode of transmission similar but the transceivers are almost identical. A licence is needed to operate an amateur set and operators using their sets on yachts must add the suffix MM (maritime mobile) to their call sign. Among the many attractions of amateur radio are the numerous amateur nets that operate all over the world. Some are extremely informative, giving weather forecasts and other data of interest to cruising sailors, while others are just a means of keeping in touch with other yachts cruising in the same part of the world. Many cruising sailors who are not licensed amateur operators listen in regularly to such nets. When installing a short wave transceiver on a cruising boat it is advisable to acquire a unit which will operate on both amateur and marine frequencies.

Autolink

This ship-to-shore service gives vessels with HF, MF or VHF equipment the possibility to dial a telephone number ashore without the need to go through an operator. The onboard signalling unit exchanges channel set-up and telephone number required data with the CRS unit, which then automatically connects the radio channel into the telephone network and completes dialling. The onboard unit also allows messages to be scrambled, which is a clear advantage over the existing system which enables anyone to listen to conversations carried out on standard radio equipment. Scrambled messages are descrambled at the CRS, from where normal speech is fed into the telephone network.

The service is internationally compatible, so that it is possible to dial calls anywhere in the world as long as the nearest country has installed the necessary ground equipment. Autolink is now operational in the following countries, with several more due to come on stream in the future:

VHF: Belgium, Gibraltar, Italy, Malaysia, Portugal, South Africa, Spain and the UK;

MF: Belgium, Portugal, Spain and the UK;

HF: South Africa, Malaysia, Portugal, Spain, the UK and USA.

Cellular telephones

Although originally developed for land use, cellular telephones are found increasingly on yachts.

Land based systems are in wide use on boats, especially when coastal cruising. In the USA there are several operators as well as different systems to choose from. In Europe, the main advance in cellular systems has been the introduction of GSM. This started out as a pan-European cellular system, known initially as Groupe Speciale Mobile (GSM) and, in order to maintain the same initials, is currently known as 'Global System for Mobile communications'. GSM is now operational in most countries in Europe (but not necessarily with comprehensive coastal coverage) as well as countries in the Middle East, Far East, Australia and New Zealand. Because of its wide use throughout the world, the system is also being used by some of the smaller operators in the USA. Operators in each GSM country take out so called roaming agreements with operators in other countries. If you have a GSM telephone and have registered your requirement to operate in other countries, the charges from all networks used will be billed by the home operator. GSM compatible telephones have the advantage of allowing the user to call, or receive calls, in most countries by using the same telephone.

Three main frequencies are used by GSM operators: 900 and 1800 MHz in Europe and most of Asia; 1900 MHz in most of the USA. While these various frequencies continue to be used, it is advisable to acquire a tri-band radio capable of using any of those frequencies. A different frequency is used in the Caribbean, so none of the telephones in use in the USA or Europe are compatible with the local system. Website: www.gsmworld.com.

The first dedicated service for marine users was started in the Eastern Caribbean by Boatphone, a subsidiary of the Cable and Wireless Communications Group. The system is extremely simple to use and calls are dialled as on an ordinary telephone. The Eastern Caribbean is ideal for this kind of operation as most of the time boats are within range of coastal stations. The system in use is the US system, so that anyone from North America can use their own cellular telephones. On arrival in the Caribbean one only needs to contact the Boatphone operator to be issued with a private number. All subsequent calls are charged directly to one of the major credit cards. Yachts which do not possess a cellular phone, or whose system is incompatible with the US system, can either buy or rent a set. A similar system operates in the Bahamas and other systems geared primarily to cruise ships and cruising yachts are being developed in other parts of the world, such as the Mediterranean.

The use of portable telephones will become even more widespread, both on land and on the sea, once some of the satellite networks become established. Such networks, using a system of satellites in low orbit, allow calls to be made to and from anywhere in the world, with very little power, but at a cost that is still higher than the terrestrial-based cellular phones. One of the most reasonably priced systems is Emsat (European Satellite Mobile Telephone) which transmits voice, fax, data, as well as radio-positioning. Emsat uses the Eutelsat satellites positioned in geostationary orbit 36,000 km above the earth. This means that it can only be used in the footprint area of Eutelsat, which is all of Europe and the Mediterranean area as far as the Azores. If the systems are successful, more satellites will be launched to cover at least all of the North Atlantic and the USA. Other satellite telephone systems are described on page 23.

AMVER

The Automated Mutual Assistance Vessel Rescue system (AMVER), operated by the United States Coast Guard, is a maritime mutual assistance organisation which contributes significantly to the coordination of search and rescue operations in many areas of the world. Commercial vessels of all nations making offshore voyages are encouraged to send reports on their movements and periodic position updates to the AMVER centre at Coast Guard New York. This is done either via selected coastal radio stations or Inmarsat. Although not available to pleasure craft, cruising yachts should be aware of this system as it has worked very well in search and rescue operations in the past.

The US Coast Guard monitors continuously certain frequencies, but these frequencies are to be used *only* to transmit details of an emergency and otherwise are meant strictly for listening. The frequencies are also used to transmit information on the location and path of tropical storms.

Ship transmit carrier frequency	*Ship receive carrier frequency*
4134.3 kHz	4428.7 kHz

6200.0 kHz	6506.4 kHz
8241.5 kHz	8765.4 kHz
12342.4 kHz	13113.2 kHz
16534.4 kHz	17307.3 kHz

Maritime Safety Information

This is an international system of radio broadcasts containing information needed for safe navigation. The messages can be received by equipment which automatically monitors MSI frequencies. The information relevant to the individual vessel is then printed out. Messages include navigational and meteorological warnings, forecasts and distress alerts. The main feature of this service is International Navtex, which operates on 518 MHz and which has become the primary means of broadcasting MSI for waters up to 200 miles from the coast of the countries operating a Navtex service. Transmissions are coordinated internationally and mutual interference is avoided by limiting the power of transmitters as well as by time-sharing of the frequency. After a successful debut in the Baltic and North Sea, Navtex has been taken up in many parts of the world and became compulsory on all ships in 1993.

Satellite Communications

Satellite communications systems are used increasingly on cruising yachts.

The inspiration for the maritime satellite communications systems was Intelsat, an organisation which started offering satellite communications in 1965. The system took a big step forward in 1976 with the launch in the USA of the first three maritime satellites in the Marisat programme. In 1979, Inmarsat came into existence to provide satellite communications to civil shipping. By using the existing Marisat system as its core, Inmarsat began commercial services in 1982. Inmarsat is an international organisation comprising about 80 member nations. It is responsible for the operation and maintenance of its satellite system, whereas the ground stations, which provide the connection between the satellites and the world's telecommunications networks, are owned and operated by the countries in which they are located. Maritime satellite communications have seen an explosive development in recent years and although the great majority of users are commercial ships, an increasing number of pleasure yachts use satellite communications. Six Inmarsat satcom systems are in use today, Inmarsat A, B, C, D, E and M.

Inmarsat A

This system is designed primarily for larger vessels or those with sophisticated communications requirements. An Inmarsat A ship earth station (LES) uses Inmarsat satellites to provide high quality connections into the existing international and national telecommunications networks. Each unit is equipped with an automatic push-button telephone and telex machine. Optional equipment includes such facilities as facsimile and data transfer. Making a telephone call via Inmarsat with this equipment is as simple as dialling a call from home.

Another service provided by Inmarsat A terminals is facsimile, from weather charts to letters, newspapers, drawings or plans. Through Inmarsat satellites it is also possible to exchange huge volumes of data between computers ashore and those on board vessels at sea.

The most noticeable feature of an Inmarsat A station on a vessel is its radome, which encloses a parabolic dish antenna. The antenna is motorised so that it tracks the satellite precisely, regardless of ship movement. The size of the radome is the main disadvantage for its installation on yachts smaller than 100 ft (30 m).

Inmarsat B

This is the long term successor of Inmarsat A, but with many new features and more possibilities. Because of the enhanced quality, live television transmissions or video conferencing will be one of its main features, apart from simple voice communications. Because it will require lower satellite power, it will result in lower call charges. The system is being phased in gradually and will eventually replace Inmarsat A. Both systems will run in parallel into the next century. Anyone considering fitting an A or B terminal, which cost about the same, should choose Inmarsat B. The charges for this service are half those charged for 'A'.

Inmarsat M

This is a digital telephone system that can also carry facsimile and low-speed data communications. The equipment is much more compact than both Inmarsat A and B and therefore appeals to owners of small vessels. The radome itself is considerably smaller than the one used on Inmarsat A and weighs only around 44 lb (20 kg). The system is very easy to use and it differs little from an ordinary portable telephone. Voice quality is considered to be better than cellular telephones, though not as good as either 'A' or 'B'. Fax and data transmission is also slower than on 'B'.

Inmarsat Mini-M

This satcom terminal has the same capacities as Inmarsat M by providing voice, data, e-mail and fax communications. Mini-M terminals operate via third generation Inmarsat satellites by using spot-beam technology, which made it possible to considerably reduce the dimensions of the station. As the tariffs are quite reasonable, Mini-M is one of the favourite voice communications systems on sailing boats.

Inmarsat M4

This system allows users to browse the internet at speeds similar to ISDN telephone lines. Initially it is being offered as a mobile land based unit, and coverage is as yet not global.

Inmarsat C

For smaller vessels, criteria such as size, weight, power requirements and cost, make the smaller Inmarsat C system more attractive. The normal installation consists of a small omni-directional antenna plus an electronics package not much bigger than the average VHF radio. This is connected to a personal computer or keyboard and monitor. The power requirements are very modest ranging from 10 W to 50 W.

Inmarsat C is a text-only communications system, which can cope with any kind of language and can interconnect with international telex, electronic mail or data networks. It can also handle computer type graphics. Because transmissions to and from the mobile terminal via the satellite are digital, a message can consist of any type of information that can be reproduced on a computer screen or printer. The system is increasingly simple to use and in 1995 one number dialling was introduced, which simplified matters even more. Electronic mail access for Inmarsat C users is now offered by some of the satcom service providers, and you should contact them first if you wish to receive and transmit e-mail via the onboard satcom system. Inmarsat C terminals can be linked or integrated with a wide variety of navigation systems to provide a continuous global position reporting capability.

Position reporting from the terrestrial Loran, satellite based Transit or GPS systems or onboard dead reckoning equipment can be transmitted automatically either on demand or at fixed intervals. Inmarsat C terminals can be programmed to transmit to a rescue coordination centre a pre-recorded distress message automatically indicating the vessel's latest position.

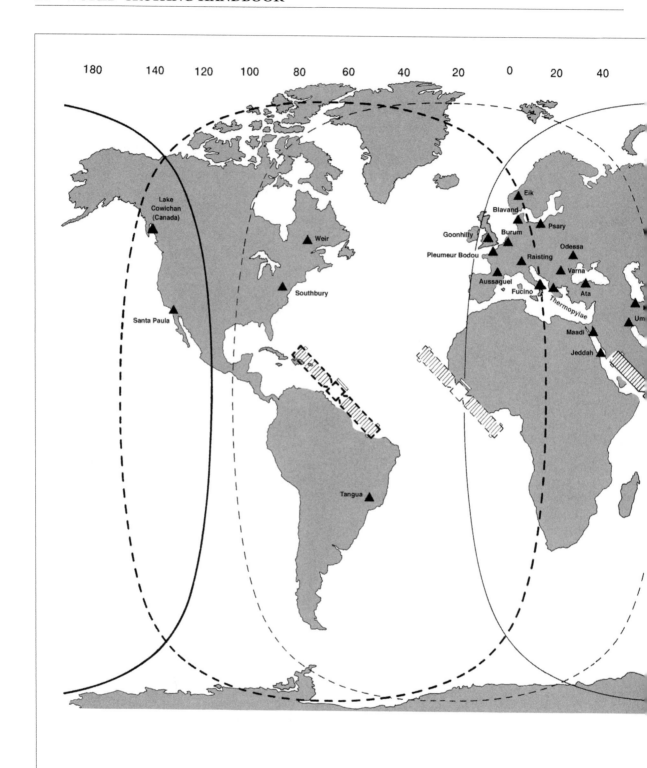

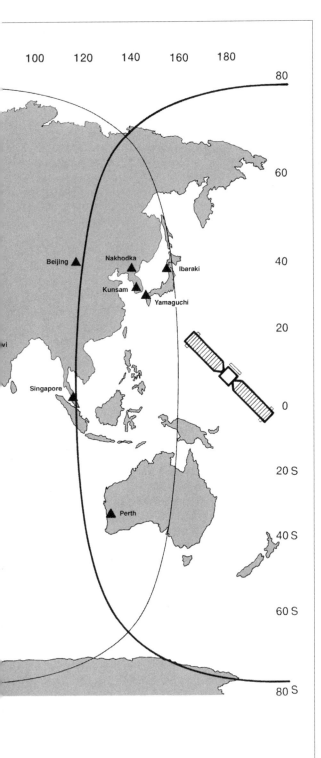

Inmarsat D

This is a global one-way system providing data and report communications to pager-type terminals.

Inmarsat D+

This is a modified version of Inmarsat D by providing two-way communications. Some models have built-in GPS receivers which enable the use of Inmarsat D+ as a mobile tracking system. It was developed mainly for the use of large road haulage operators to enable them to track their trucks, and it is only used marginally by maritime operators.

Inmarsat E

This was developed to transmit distress warnings on the L-band frequencies. Thanks to the geostationary position of Inmarsat satellites warnings of this type of EPIRB may be received by Rescue Coordination Centres (RCC) without delay.

Distress alerting

Every Inmarsat ship station, whether A, B, C or M, is fitted with a special alert mechanism to cope with emergency situations. Usually this is a single 'Distress' button or a special dialling code. Such a distress signal automatically seizes a telephone, telex or data communications channel and connects it automatically via a land earth station (LES) to a rescue coordination centre (RCC). Distress alerts have top priority and because of the reliability of the satellite system, connection is always made automatically regardless of the location of the emergency or the distance to the coast station. Connection for A, B or M may take 15–20 seconds to complete. In the case of 'C', messages are automatically forwarded on a priority basis to the RCC.

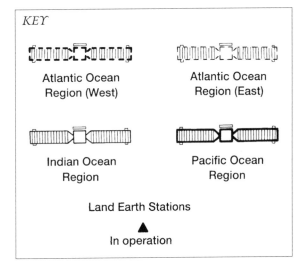

KEY

Atlantic Ocean Region (West)

Atlantic Ocean Region (East)

Indian Ocean Region

Pacific Ocean Region

Land Earth Stations

▲

In operation

All rescue coordination centres are interconnected, often using their own Inmarsat A equipment, so that a distress call is quickly transmitted to the centre dealing with emergencies.

There are more than 30 coast earth stations operating with the Inmarsat system and several more are under construction. Inmarsat operates a number of satellites located in geostationary orbits around the world. Four of these satellites are maintained as operational, but are kept in reserve. The other four are the prime operational satellites and are stationed over the world's three main oceans. Their locations are: AOR-West (54°W), AOR-East (15.5°W), IOR (64.5°E) and POR (178°E). This arrangement gives virtual global coverage.

Global Maritime Distress and Safety System

The International Maritime Organisation has combined all requirements in its specification for GMDSS. The primary aims of GMDSS are to alert search and rescue authorities ashore and to facilitate the coordination of search and rescue operations without delay. Depending on their area of operation, ships will have to carry certain types of communications equipment. Four such areas have been designated:

Area A1: Within range of shore-based VHF DSC coast stations, about 25 miles offshore. Vessels in this area will carry VHF DSC equipment.

Area A2: Within range of shore-based MF DSC coast stations, about 100 miles offshore. Vessels in this area will carry VHF and MF DSC equipment.

Area A3: Within the coverage area of Inmarsat satellites. Vessels in this area will carry VHF and MF DSC equipment, and either HF DSC or satellite equipment.

Area A4: This area is outside of the range of Inmarsat satellites but within the coverage of the polar orbiting COSPAS-SARSAT system. Vessels will need VHF, MF and HF equipment. In all four areas vessels will also have to carry a suitable EPIRB.

A combination of satellite services (Inmarsat and COSPAS-SARSAT), and DSC over terrestrial radio, has provided the means to automate much of the distress alerting process under GMDSS. Initial distress alerts will be transmitted by satellite EPIRB (COSPAS-SARSAT or Inmarsat), or by an Inmarsat terminal, or by DSC on VHF, MF or HF radio. Subsequent communications will be by voice or Narrow Band Direct Printing (NBDP or 'Telex Over Radio') on radio and/or satellite channels. On scene communications will continue to be conducted on VHF Channel 16.

GMDSS implementation commenced in 1992 and is now fully operational. All commercial vessels, which come under GMDSS regulations, are now required to comply by fitting the appropriate equipment and also carrying qualified operators.

GMDSS also has far reaching implications for yacht owners and operators, who are not compelled to fit GMDSS equipment. The fact that many countries intend to cease their listening watch on the international voice distress frequencies (VHF Channel 16, MF 2182 kHz and HF frequencies) means that voluntary equipped craft, such as pleasure vessels, will either have to install GMDSS alerting equipment for VHF, MF/HF or an Inmarsat C unit, which allows an alert to be sent from practically anywhere, or risk their voice distress call going unheard.

COSPAS-SARSAT

This international cooperative search and rescue project was set up in the early 1980s to improve the chances of detecting an emergency and to speed up the response by rescue services. In the United States, the National Oceanic and Atmospheric Administration (NOAA) operates geostationary polar orbiting satellites that monitor weather conditions over the entire globe. In addition to weather and environmental sensors, these polar orbiting satellites also carry search and rescue satellite aided tracking payloads (SARSAT). These payloads are provided by Canada and France. Russia operates a similar system, the payload on the Russian satellites being called COSPAS. The main role of the Russian system is search and rescue, while the NOAA satellites are primarily used for weather purposes and only have a secondary role within the COSPAS-SARSAT system.

The COSPAS spacecraft follow a path inclined 83° to the equator at an altitude of 621 miles (1000 km) and complete a revolution every 106 minutes, compared to the NOAA satellites which are inclined at 99° at an altitude of 528 miles (850 km) and one revolution every 102 minutes. Together the satellites view the whole surface of the earth in less than three hours. The COSPAS-SARSAT satellites handle signals in a similar way. Those on 121.5 MHz are immediately retransmitted on 1544.5 MHz to any LUT (local user terminal) that is in range, whereas 406 MHz signals are processed to establish the identity of the transmitter and stored in an onboard memory to be retransmitted when a LUT comes into view, so that reception by an earth station is assured.

Apart from the spacecraft and their COSPAS-

SARSAT payloads, this system includes the EPIRBs (emergency position indicating radio beacons) on board vessels at sea and ELTs (emergency locator transmitters) on board aircraft, earth receiver stations known as local user terminals (LUT) and mission control centres (MCC). The signal from an EPIRB or ELT triggered by an emergency is received by the satellite, processed and retransmitted to the next LUT to come into view. The LUT uses the data in the signal to calculate the approximate position of the source of the signal. This is transmitted to an MCC, where the most conveniently located rescue coordination centre (RCC) is selected and alerted. Final responsibility for carrying out the search and rescue (SAR) rests with the RCC. There are now around 30 LUTs in operation providing real time coverage over most of the northern hemisphere, Australia and New Zealand, and much of South America.

EPIRB

These lightweight transmitters radiate on one or more of three different frequencies: 121.5 MHz, 243 MHz or 406 MHz. The 243 MHz frequency is monitored only by military aircraft. The 121.5 MHz is used by commercial aircraft and ships and was chosen as the distress frequency before the advent of satellites. The 406 MHz frequency was later chosen to take better advantage of the satellite-based COSPAS-SARSAT system. There is now also a satellite EPIRB, the L-band EPIRB, which operates over the Inmarsat satellites in real time.

The 121.5 MHz frequency will be retained for quite some time as it is carried by ships and aircraft worldwide and it will continue to be monitored by air crews and air traffic control centres. The older frequency has several disadvantages and therefore increasingly offshore cruising yachts are choosing the 406 MHz frequency. Because of the very high incidence of false alarms from EPIRBs operating on 121.5 MHz, it is now unlikely that a search and rescue (SAR) operation will be launched solely because a 121.5 MHz alert has been received. The RCC concerned will want corroborating evidence that there is really a distress situation before sending out SAR aircraft and vessels.

In comparison, the satellite based 406 MHz offers several improvements, such as more accurate location, at an average of 1–3 miles compared to 5–10 miles for the older system. The signals from the new EPIRBs also give the user's identity and they are processed onboard the satellite before being retransmitted. The data is stored in memory for transmission to the next available LUT. This last feature is very important as the 121.5 MHz signals are simply repeated by the satellite and go unheard if there is no earth station within range, whereas the 406 MHz system's storage capability means that COSPAS-SARSAT gives global coverage. The 406 MHz EPIRB, if properly registered ashore with the vessel details and a contact telephone number, which allows the RCC to check that the vessel is at sea in the area indicated and there may be a problem, is much more likely to be taken seriously by the rescue authorities.

Weather Routing

What started off as a service provided to commercial shipping also became available to participants in the major offshore races. Individual boat owners can now subscribe to a number of weather routing services, which will prepare individualised weather forecasts, usually for the next five days, explaining how the various weather systems may evolve during this period. For a boat moving along a certain route, the analysis will also provide such data as wind speed and direction and, depending on the level of service contracted, the forecaster will also advise on the best course to sail so as to make best time towards one's destination. Probably the best known in this field is Bob Rice, whose Weather Window has been used by participants in all major races, from the America's Cup to the Whitbread (now Volvo) Round the World Race. David Jones, a cruising sailor now based in the Virgin Islands, provides a daily service for boats crossing the North Atlantic or cruising in the Caribbean. All these services have their own websites and are easiest contacted by e-mail or via the internet:

www.caribwx.com

www.bobrice weather.com

Some national weather centres now provide a similar service. Although they do not actually offer weather routing as such, they will supply individualised forecasts for given areas at a cost normally lower than that charged by professional weather routing services.

Weather on the internet

This is an unlimited source of information that will undoubtedly revolutionise offshore cruising once the internet becomes more easily accessible when sailing offshore. Although connections tend to be quite costly, boats equipped with Inmarsat A, B and M are now able to connect to the internet and thus have an inexhaustible source of information, as well as access to a host of weather and other essential services. Some of the best sources of information are those provided by US government agencies, such as NOAA, which are also used as raw data by the forecasters providing individualised weather routing. All this information is freely available on the internet, from satellite imagery of the Gulf Stream to the wind speed in any location on the world's oceans. See links below and page 29.

Electronic Mail

Increasingly, cruising sailors rely on this simple and efficient system for communications with home base, friends and business contacts. In the initial stages, e-mail could only be sent and retrieved from telephone lines ashore, but in recent years electronic mail has become a normal feature on many offshore boats. This is due to the improvements made to the two main systems of sending/receiving e-mail at sea: HF based or satcom based. The former uses normal SSB radios and the best known providers of this service are PinOak Digital, SailMail and GlobeEmail. The user needs to buy both the hardware (modem) and software from one of these operators who have a network of coastal radio stations providing virtual worldwide coverage.

www.pinoak.com
www.globewireless.com
www.sailmail.com

The satcom based system is probably easier to use and also more reliable but also more costly to run. E-mail via satcom based systems is offered to Inmarsat C and M users by all service providers. Its disadvantages are that it transmits at very slow speeds and, as one pays by character, it also tends to be rather expensive. A global system of interest to sailors uses the Orbcomm network of satellites and provides worldwide coverage. The hand-held device is marketed by Magellan.

www.inmarsat.org (Details of all Inmarsat systems and service providers)
www.orbcomm.com

Using e-mail on land is much simpler as marinas increasingly provide e-mail access to visiting sailors, so retrieving one's e-mail is no longer a major problem. Even the most remote places now seem to have an internet cafe, which is another source of checking one's e-mail. Those planning to cruise away from home base for long periods would be well advised to choose an internet-based e-mail service (such as Hotmail or Yahoo), and to set this up before leaving home. Cellular telephones are another source for sending or receiving e-mail, although it is limited in range at sea if using one of the terrestrial based systems. This is undoubtedly going to change as satellite telephones become more widely available on cruising boats, as they will enable one to use e-mail as well as to connect to the internet anywhere in the world.

www.yahoo.com
www.hotmail.com

The Internet

The internet is an inexhaustible source of information and useful websites are added to it every day. Using the internet when sailing offshore is, as yet, neither simple nor cheap, but the situation is constantly improving as existing systems are being adapted or new ones being launched. The internet will become widely available in the year 2004 when the Teledesic system comes on stream, a network of 288 satellites providing fast internet access. Below is a list of some of the most useful sites for cruising sailors, whether at sea or in the planning stages of a voyage.

www.noonsite.com (the cruising sailors' website with practical information on all maritime nations of the world and regular updates on the information contained in *World Cruising Handbook*)
www.navcen.uscg.mil (US Coast Guard, useful links safety, weather, GPS, Loran and other navigation systems)
www.nis-mirror.com (alternative site to the above)
www.nemoc.navy.mil (Nemoc (Naval European Meteorology and Oceanography Center) based in Rota, Spain, has the best weather data for the Mediterranean and many useful links to other weather sites.
www.sto-p.com/atol (another useful site for Mediterranean weather)
www.meto.govt.uk (this is the UK Meteorological Office at Bracknell.) It provides a limited service free (such as a shipping forecast in text for the UK and surrounding waters), while some of its services must be paid for. The latter is via the MetWEB service available on: www.meto.govt.uk/MWIntro.html
www.nhc.noaa.gov (US National Hurricane Center)
www.weather.noaa.gov/fax/marine.shtml (marine weather charts)
www.nws.noaa.gov/data.html (forecasts and satellite images)

www.manati.wwb.noaa.gov (ocean surface winds)
www.fermi.jhuapl.edu (Gulf Stream information)
www.mpc.ncep.noaa.gov/graphictextF.html
(Marine Prediction Centers)
www.nws.noaa.gov (US National Weather Center)
www.lumahai.soest.hawaii.edu/Tropical_Weather/
tropical.shtml (tropical storms information)
www.lumahai.soest.hawaii.edu/Tropical_Weather/tropic_atl/tfcst_atl.gif (latest Atlantic
tropical storm track)
http://www.ecmwf.int (European Meteorological Centre)
http://www-imk.physik.uni-karlsruhe.de
(University of Karlsruhe (Germany) Bureau of
Meteorology)
http://www.wetterzentrale.de (another useful
weather site from Germany)
http://www.meteo.fr/temps (Meteo France)
www.bom.gov.au (Australian Bureau of
Meteorology)
www.notmar.com (Canadian Coast Guard)
www.caribwx.com (Caribbean Weather Center)
www.nps.gov (US National Parks including
Glacier Bay and US Virgins Nature Parks)
www2.hawaii.edu/~ogden/piir (Pacific Islands
links)
www.bbc.co.uk/worldservice/index.shtml (BBC
World Service)

Mail

Although more cruising boats are now using faxes, e-mail and satellite communications, the majority continue to communicate by what electronic boffins call, with some justification, snail mail. While sending mail, or even parcels, by the ordinary postal service is simple and quite reliable in most countries of the world, receiving mail is a very different matter. The main problem is the lack of suitable or reliable addresses, and also the flexible schedules of most cruising boats. The obvious solution – of using poste restante or general delivery as a receiving address at the post office in the port of arrival – is not always the most reliable way. One major drawback is that most post offices only keep such mail for a limited period after which it is returned to the sender, but never forwarded. The sorting of incoming mail at the receiving end is rarely systematic and often chaotic, so when expecting mail at poste restante/general delivery one should check not just under one's own surname, but also that of the yacht as well as one's forename. The situation is naturally even worse in countries which use different script.

One should therefore instruct one's correspondents to make sure that the name stands out clearly at the top of the address. It also helps if the envelopes used are of an immediately recognisable colour or appearance, so as to be easily spotted. In larger towns or ports there may be more than one post office, so the letter should be addressed to the Central, Main or General post office. 'To await arrival' should be marked clearly in a box on the envelope. Also, after arriving in a new place, one should check the correct address to be used for post restante or general delivery mail and, if more mail is expected, the correct address should be faxed home. For those without a fax at home, having a reliable fax bureau that will deliver faxes home is a great help if one needs to communicate urgently.

Yacht clubs continue to be a favourite forwarding address. Ideally one should contact the club secretary well in advance to ask permission to use their address and give one's ETA. Yacht clubs usually provide a more reliable address than post offices, and so do marinas. The addresses, telephone and fax numbers of yacht clubs and marinas in the most important ports of the world cruising circuit are listed on the relevant pages for each country included in *World Cruising Handbook*.

Also used by long distance sailors is American Express, which has agencies in most major ports where mail can be received. Advance arrangements for collection are not essential, but the agency should be advised in writing if one is delayed too much as the mail will probably be returned to the sender after about one month. Before leaving a certain port, arrangements should be made to have late arriving mail forwarded to the next port. Naturally, one has to be an American Express card holder to be able to use this service.

Courier services are another, if more expensive, solution to mail collection and forwarding. Unfortunately the service is not as reliable as one is led to believe and even some of the better known companies are known to have failed to live up to expectations. A courier service available from post offices in most countries (called Datapost in the UK) is cheaper and often more reliable than the service offered by private courier companies.

If any of the above systems fail, as most probably they will, one can always revert to the age old system of leaving one's mail in a barrel, as on Floreana Island in the Galapagos. As to waiting for mail to arrive in some remote place, there are many more frustrating things in life than doing this while sitting on the terrace of a friendly yacht club sipping cold beer with the trade wind whispering in the palm trees.

SECTION II

1 Mediterranean and Black Sea

The Mediterranean's reputation as the cradle of western civilisation is undisputed and the beauty of its scenery as well as the wealth of things to see and do ashore more than make up for the less than exhilarating sailing conditions. From the pyramids of Egypt to the Minoan remains on Crete, from the treasures of Asia Minor to the wonders of Ancient Rome, the elegance of the French Riviera or the biblical heritage of Israel, the shores and islands abound in history and many historical sites are close to the sea. The people of the Mediterranean have always looked to the sea for inspiration and so one never has too far to go to get a taste of the fascinating world that has existed for centuries along these shores.

In most parts of the Mediterranean, the sailing season extends from the end of March until November, but is best enjoyed in the spring and autumn when the ports are not crowded and the weather is also more pleasant than at the height of summer. It is possible to sail even in winter but a careful eye has to be kept on the weather as violent storms can occur with little warning. A complete season is the least anyone should plan on spending in the Mediterranean, as distances are deceptive and it is more than 2000 miles from Gibraltar to the Eastern Mediterranean.

If arriving from the Atlantic, it is best to make the long passages first and head straight for the Aegean, if that is one's prime destination. The strong northerly winds that prevail in the Aegean in summer make it advisable to cruise that area from north to south, although it may be difficult to reach the Northern Aegean before the *meltemi* sets in. If an Atlantic crossing is planned at the end of the season, the Eastern Mediterranean should be left by the end of August at the latest so as to be able to cruise leisurely westward. If arriving from the Atlantic later in the year, one can cruise in the Western Mediterranean and, if time permits, plan to spend the following season in the Aegean by heading that way either in the autumn or early the following spring. The choices are easier if arriving in the Mediterranean from the Red Sea, which normally means a spring arrival, in which case the choice is unlimited. Most ports get very crowded in July and August, so during this time one should try to avoid the most popular areas, such as the French Riviera or Greek Cyclades and other known tourist resorts.

The Black Sea has a much shorter season and the winters can be extremely cold, so cruises in that area should be planned for April or early May to September. With the opening up of the area to cruising, yachts are sailing to Russia and the Ukraine, Romania and Bulgaria. Apart from the interest in visiting these formerly closed countries, the cruising attractions are limited, perhaps with the exception of the Georgian coast, where the scenery is more dramatic. A cruise to the Black Sea also has the added reward of a sail through Istanbul, the Bosporus and Dardanelles, an experience which in itself may justify the entire trip.

Yachting facilities are well developed in most parts of the Mediterranean and even countries with no sailing tradition, such as Tunisia or Turkey, have developed excellent facilities in recent years. For major repairs, however, it is still better to go to one of the long established centres such as Palma de Mallorca, Antibes, Malta or Larnaca. There are many other places with good facilities spread all over the Mediterranean, but only those mentioned above offer a comprehensive range of services.

The benign Mediterranean winters attract many cruising yachts who spend the off season in one of the many marinas, the most popular wintering spots being Gibraltar, Spain's Costa del Sol, the Balearics, the Portuguese Algarve, Cyprus, Turkey, Malta and Tunisia. Generally, the southern and eastern shores are warmer and have a better winter climate. As most countries have restrictions on the time a foreign vessel can spend in their waters, it is essential to make sure that the maximum period is not exceeded. The imposition of a maximum six month stay in any 12 months for non-EU boats sailing or merely being based in the European Union has forced the owners of such boats, as well as EU nationals who have not paid tax on their boats, to spend the remaining months in a non-EU area. Although the application of the above regulation has not been particularly strict or thorough, it would be wise not to overstay the stipulated period.

Although the Mediterranean climate makes it possible to live on a boat and even sail for most of the year, for the more adventuresome there is the alternative of heading south at the end of the summer season. From the Western Mediterranean the obvious destinations are the Canaries and Madeira, while the Red Sea beckons to those in the Eastern Mediterranean. Both have become increasingly popular winter destinations in recent years.

ALBANIA

Albania, known as Shqiperia in Albanian, is situated on the Adriatic Sea between Greece and the republic of Montenegro. From the Second World War Albania was ruled by a strict Stalinist regime, which systematically discouraged any contact with the outside world. Relations with western nations were virtually non-existent. From the outside, Albania was seen as a backward enclave within Europe, its separateness enhanced by being the only entirely Muslim country in Europe. The collapse of communism in Eastern Europe has also affected Albania, with moves towards democracy and a normalisation of its relations with the outside world. Foreign yachts can now visit Albania and there are even plans to build a marina in Durres.

The opening up of the country in the early 1990s has brought freedom to the people but has

Map 1: The Mediterranean

— — — Border (unofficial)

ATLANTIC OCEAN
FRANCE
SPAIN
Madrid
Barcelona
Menorca
Mallorca
Ibiza
Balearic Islands
Malaga
Gibraltar
Tangier
Algiers
Oran
Rabat
Casablanca
ALGERIA
MOROCCO

also affected the economy. This has caused high unemployment and has forced many people to emigrate. Greece and Italy are the main targets, which many Albanians try to enter illegally in small boats. Cruising boats sailing the Adriatic should be aware of the possible presence of small unlit boats.

Practical Information

LOCAL TIME: GMT + 1. GMT + 2 end March – end September.

BUOYAGE: IALA A

CURRENCY: Lek

BUSINESS HOURS
Banks: 0700–1400 Monday to Saturday.
Shops: 0700–1200, 1600–1900 Monday to Saturday.

ELECTRICITY: 220 V, 50 Hz

PUBLIC HOLIDAYS
1 January: New Year's Day
8 March: International Women's Day
April: Catholic Easter, Orthodox Easter
28 November: Independence Day
25 December: Christmas
Variable: Small Bayram (end of Ramadan), Great Bayram (Feast of the Sacrifice)

COMMUNICATIONS
International calls can be made from main post offices.
There are flights from Tirana to other European cities.

DIPLOMATIC MISSIONS
In Tirana:
Germany: Rruga Skënderbeu 8.
Tel. (42) 32 050.
Greece: Rruga Frederick Shiroka 3.
Tel. (42) 34 290.
United Kingdom: Vaso Pasha 7/1. Tel. 34 973.
USA: Rruga Labinoti 103. Tel. (42) 33 520.

The situation has been exacerbated by the conflict in neighbouring Kosovo and the intervention of NATO in this province of former Yugoslavia, where the majority of the population is of Albanian origin. The latest situation in this part of the world should be monitored carefully. While approaching Albanian territorial waters, Channel 11 should be monitored as it is the working channel used by the Albanian Coast Guard.

Cruising along the coast offers many possibilities, while one of the main attractions inland is the remarkably well preserved Greek and Roman ruins at Butrint, which is best reached from Saranda. The capital Tirana is 24 miles inland from the port of Durres.

Country Profile

The Ilyrians settled in this region around 2000 BC, ancestors of today's Albanians. Albania was under foreign rule for 2000 years as part of the Roman and Byzantine empires, invaded by Goths, then conquered by the Serbs in the north and

Bulgars in the south, and it has been successively under Greek, Norman, Serbian and Turkish rule. Part of the Ottoman empire until 1912, Albanian independence was declared after several years of uprisings. The First World War saw the state again under occupation by French, Italian and Serbian troops. In 1920 Albania was finally recognised as a sovereign state. From 1922 to 1939 the country was led by Ahmed Zogu, as President and then King Zog I. For much of the Second World War Albania was again occupied by Italy. After the war the communists gained power, and in 1946 proclaimed a peoples' republic. Under Enver Hoxha, a strict Stalinist regime was introduced, although links were broken with the Soviet Union and later China. In 1985 Ramiz Alia replaced Hoxha as leader. In 1990 growing opposition forced the government to end one-party rule. The first free parliamentary elections since 1946 were held in 1992, won by the opposition, under Sali Berisha.

The main elements in the economy are agriculture, mineral extraction (oil and chrome), and livestock raising. Reforms introduced to move towards a market economy have been partly successful but problems of an external debt and institutional weaknesses remain.

The Albanian-speaking population is 3.3 million and is mainly Muslim with some Orthodox Christians and Roman Catholics. Greeks and Macedonians are the largest ethnic minorities as well as Romanians (Vlachs) and gypsies. The capital is Tirana.

The climate is Mediterranean in type, with hot summers and mild winters. The wind in summer is mostly onshore, stronger in the afternoons and dying away at night.

Entry Regulations

Ports of entry

Durres 41°19′N 19°27′E, Vlore (Valona Bay) 40°26′N 19°30′E, Shengjin 41°49′N 19°36′E, Saranda 39°53′N 20°00′E.

Procedure on arrival

The port authority should be contacted on VHF radio before entering any of the official ports. The best facilities are at Durres which is Albania's main port and has regular ferry connections with Italy. Officials will board the boat on arrival.
Durres: This is the main port. Call Port Control on Channel 16, who will direct the boat to an area of the commercial harbour. The port captain occasionally insists that a shipping agent is used to deal with formalities.

Halfway up the coast is the port of Vlore, which has a well-protected fishing harbour called Triport. The entrance into nearby Vlore lagoon has silted up and so access by keeled boats is no longer possible.
Saranda: This is Albania's southernmost port and a convenient place to clear in by boats coming from the south. Proceed to the main quay where officials normally board the boat for clearance.
Shengjin: The port is only 10 miles south of the border from Montenegro. There are shoals off the headland to the north of the harbour so the port should be entered on a bearing of 020 with the leading marks in line.

Immigration

Most nationalities (except Greece, Israel and some Arab nations) do not need to obtain a visa in advance, which is granted, for a fee, on arrival.

Fees

All vessels up to 500 tons pay a $50 clearance fee. Visa fees, plus some port fees.

Restrictions

When sailing along the coast, foreign vessels are required to stay at least three miles offshore.

Boats sailing south to Saranda through the Bay of Porto Palermo will pass through a military zone for which permission must be obtained.

Facilities

Repair facilities are limited in all ports. Fuel and water is available in all ports, even if fuel has to be carried by jerrycans from a fuel station. Best provisioning is in Durres, where one is within reach of the capital Tirana.

Further Reading

Adriatic Pilot
Mediterranean Europe (Lonely Planet)
Mediterranean Almanac

Websites

www.albania.8m.com (Albania Online)
www.artnoir.com/ad (Adriatic Pilot)

ALGERIA

The Democratic and Popular Republic of Algeria lies on the North African coast between Morocco and Tunisia, and has a mixture of African, Oriental and Mediterranean cultures and traditions. Over 700 miles of coastline fronts the Mediterranean, behind which lie mountains and fertile plains, with the vast Sahara desert to the south. Algeria is a huge country, but much of it is uninhabitable desert and mountains, so most of the population live in cities on the northern coastal strip.

Along its entire length, the Algerian coast has no indentations and all the ports are man-made as there are no natural harbours. With very few exceptions, the ports are crowded and polluted, which is the main reason why cruising yachts very seldom go out of their way to stop in Algeria. The one notable exception is Sidi Fredj, west of the capital Algiers, where a tourist development surrounds the harbour, part of which has been converted into a marina.

The conflict between the government forces and the fundamentalist resistance has affected the entire country, which is considered unsafe for travel. Thousands have been killed, increasingly Westerners

Practical Information

LOCAL TIME: GMT. Summer time GMT + 1 May to October.

BUOYAGE: IALA A

CURRENCY: Algerian dinar (AD) of 100 centimes.
AD1000 (about US$200) must be changed on arrival at the official rate. A foreign currency declaration form must be completed on arrival and returned on departure. Also on this form one must declare items such as cameras and other equipment. All exchange receipts must be kept. French franc travellers' cheques are the best type to take. One can only import or export AD50 maximum.

BUSINESS HOURS
Friday is the weekly day of rest.
Banks: hours vary, normally 0900–1500 Sunday to Thursday.
Business: 0800–1200/1400–1730 Saturday to Wednesday, 0800–1200 Thursday.

Shops: 0800–1200/1430–1800 Saturday to Thursday.
Government offices: closed Thursday midday to Saturday morning.

ELECTRICITY: 127/220 V, 50 Hz

PUBLIC HOLIDAYS
1 January: New Year's Day
Prophet's birthday*
1 May
Leilat al Meiraj*
19 June: Revival Day
Start of Ramadan*
5 July: Independence Day
Eid al-Fitr*
Eid al-Adhar*
1 November: Anniversary of the Revolution
Hijara*
Al Ashoura*
*Variable

COMMUNICATIONS
Post office: Algiers, Place Grande Poste for telegrams, 24-hour telephones and telex.
Emergency: dial 14 for police.
There are flights from Algiers to many European and Middle East destinations and some from Oran to European cities.

MEDICAL
Facilities are better in the north.
Emergency treatment is free, for other services doctors and hospitals usually ask for a cash payment.

DIPLOMATIC MISSIONS
In Algiers:
Canada: 27 bis rue des Frères Benhafid, Hydra. Tel. (2) 691 611.
France: 6 rue Larbi Alik, Hydra. Tel. (2) 604 488.
Germany: 165 chemin Findja. Tel. (2) 741 941.
United Kingdom: Résidence Cassiopée, Bâtiment B, 7 chemin des Glycines. Tel. (2) 230 092.
United States: 4 Chemin Cheich Bachir Brahimi. Tel. (2) 691 255/186 854.

---

also, and while the present situation continues, Algeria is best avoided. If forced to make an emergency stop in one of the ports, one should try to do so in one of the larger ports.

Country Profile

Algeria is rare among Mediterranean countries in that the original inhabitants, the Berbers, still make up a sizeable part of the population. The Berbers withdrew to the mountains when invaders came, first the Phoenicians, then the Carthaginians, who controlled the coast around 1100 BC. A thousand years later the area became part of the Roman empire. The Romans were later driven out by the Vandals, followed by the Byzantines and in the seventh century the Arab invasions began. Algeria was ruled by various dynasties as part of the Maghreb together with Morocco and Tunisia. Under Ottoman rule the port of Algiers developed and became a haven for Barbary pirates.

In the nineteenth century France conquered the country and many French settlers immigrated as Algeria was incorporated into France. The Algerians felt alienated, and the 1930s saw the growth of nationalist movements, which became radicalised during the Second World War. In 1954 a rebellion broke out, with Ahmed Ben Bella leading the National Liberation Front (FLN). War with France resulted, and only in 1961 did serious negotiations begin to end this conflict in which over 1 million Algerians lost their lives. A year later Algeria became independent. The first Prime Minister was Ahmed Ben Bella, but although efforts were made to promote economic growth and raise living standards, dissatisfaction continued and in 1965 he was overthrown. A more isolationist foreign policy was followed under Boumediene until his death in 1979. Following severe riots in 1988 the government introduced a programme of political and economic reforms including a move to a pluralist system. The 1991 elections were won by the Islamic fundamentalists, but the ruling government cancelled the results and declared a state of emergency. The fundamentalists' efforts to destabilise the country have become increasingly violent. The 1990s were marked by indiscriminate terrorist attacks and brutal reprisals by the authorities.

The discovery of oil and gas has been important to the economy, and there has been some industrialisation, but the majority of the population work in agriculture. The oil and gas industries were badly hit by the 1980s recession. The economy suffers from a large foreign debt, soaring inflation, and high unemployment especially among the young.

The population is 28 million, being both Arab and Berber, and the majority are Muslim. After independence most settlers of European origin left and many Algerians emigrated to France. Arabic is the official language, but French and Berber are also spoken. Algiers is the capital.

The climate is temperate with hot and dry summers. The winters are mild with some rain along the coast. Prevailing summer winds are easterly, while in winter winds are either from the west or north.

Entry Regulations

Ports of entry
Sidi Fredj 36°46′N 2°51′W, Ghazaouet (Ghazawet) 35°06′N 1°52′W, Oran (Wharan) 35°43′N 0°39′W, Mostaganem (Mestghanem) 35°56′N 0°04′E, Ténes 36°31′N 1°19′E, Algiers (Alger/El Djazair) 36°47′N 3°04′E, Tamenfoust 36°49′N 3°14′E, Dellys 36°55′N 3°55′E, Bejaia 36°45′N 5°06′E, Skikda 36°53′N 6°54′E, Annaba 36°54′N 7°45′E, Beni-Saf 35°18′N 1°23′W, Bouharoun 36°38′N 2°40′W, Collo 37°00′N 6°34′E.

Procedure on arrival
Most ports monitor VHF Channels 12 or 14, but apart from Arabic, only French is usually understood. Yachts must clear in and out of each harbour. Sidi Fredj, which has a marina, is the best port of entry as the officials there are used to yachts. One must clear with customs, police and the military as well.

Customs may search the yacht and will require an inventory. Foreign currency and main dutiable items should be declared. If not the owner of the boat, the captain must have a written authorisation from the owner.

Customs
Firearms need a temporary import licence and detention permit. The firearms are held by police or customs until departure.

Animals must have vaccination certificates.

Immigration
All nationals require visas except Argentina, Bosnia-Hercegovina, Croatia, Guinea, Libya, Macedonia, Mali, Malta, Mauritania, Senegal, Seychelles, Syria, Tunisia, Yemen and Yugoslavia (Serbia and Montenegro). Tourist visas are valid approximately one month. Visas should be obtained in advance from Algerian diplomatic missions and consulates abroad. Visas cannot be issued on arrival. There are Algerian consulates in Morocco and Tunisia. Israeli citizens will be refused entry, and those with Israeli stamps in their passports will have great difficulty obtaining a visa.

Fees
An overtime fee for customs clearance outside office hours is charged.

Port charges are free for under 48 hours, after which there is a charge based on length.

Facilities

Only basic facilities are available in most ports and provisioning in the smaller towns is limited. There are some repair facilities in Sidi Fredj, which has a number of locally owned yachts. There is a 16-ton travelift as well as fuel and water in the marina. In most other ports fuel has to be bought in jerrycans.

Further Reading

Mediterranean Cruising Handbook
Traveller's Guide to North Africa
Morocco, Algeria and Tunisia – a travel survival kit
North Africa

Website

www.algeria-tourism.org (National Tourism Office)

BULGARIA

In the eastern Balkans, Bulgaria has a coastline on the Black Sea. A small boating community thrives around the port of Varna and in spite of the restrictions imposed by the communist regime in the past, Bulgarian sailors have managed to cruise the Mediterranean, take part in the OSTAR transatlantic single-handed race and one intrepid family have even circumnavigated the globe.

Practical Information

LOCAL TIME: GMT + 2. Summer time
GMT + 3. April 1 to September 31.

BUOYAGE: IALA A

CURRENCY: Lev (plural: leva).
Import/export of leva is prohibited.

BUSINESS HOURS
Shops: 0830–1800/1900 Monday to
Saturday; rural areas may close
1200–1500.
Government offices: 0730–1530 Monday to
Friday, also alternate Saturdays.
Banks: 0900–1500 Monday to Friday.

ELECTRICITY: 220 V, 50 Hz

PUBLIC HOLIDAYS
1 January: New Year's Day
3 March: Liberation Day
Orthodox Easter
1–2 May: Labour Days
24 May: Culture Day
24–26 December: Christmas

COMMUNICATIONS
International telephone calls can be made
from post offices open 0830–1730 Monday
to Saturday.
There are international flights from Sofia to
most European capitals and charter flights
from Varna during summer.

MEDICAL
Free emergency treatment is available in
hospitals, although standards are generally
low.

DIPLOMATIC MISSIONS
In Sofia:
United Kingdom: Boulevard Levski
65–67. *Tel.* (2) 885361.
United States: Unit 1335, 1 Saborna
Street. *Tel:* (2) 884801.

In spite of the country's recent liberalisation, visiting boats are still subjected to many restrictions and there are areas closed to foreigners, such as parts of the naval port of Sozopol. Because the authorities do not allow cruising along the coast, one has to clear in and out of every port. The best port to clear in is Varna, where there is a marina-type facility, and where foreign sailors have always been warmly welcomed by the local sailing community. Burgas, the nearest port of entry to the Turkish border, is not recommended as it is a dirty commercial harbour. Other ports, where it may be possible to stop once restrictions are eased, are Kiten, Nessebar, Byala and Balchik.

Country Profile

The Bulgars, of Asiatic origin, crossed the Danube in the seventh century and established the first Bulgarian kingdom, which was later incorporated into the Byzantine Empire. Then the Second Bulgarian Empire was founded by the Asens, until conquered by the Ottoman Turks in 1396. Under Turkish rule some parts of the country were converted to Islam, and Turks settled in the eastern parts.

The Bulgarians rose up against the Turks several times, the most notorious uprising causing the 'Bulgarian atrocities' of 1876 when resistance was brutally crushed. After the Russo-Turkish War of 1877–8, the Congress of Berlin made Bulgaria an autonomous principality under Alexander I, but still dependent on Turkey. Bulgaria was declared an independent kingdom in 1908.

The First Balkan War of 1912 saw Bulgaria join Serbia, Greece and Montenegro against Turkey, but the issue of the partition of Macedonia led to Bulgaria attacking her allies the following year, only to be defeated and losing both Macedonia and Thrace. An ally of Germany in the First World War, Bulgaria invaded Serbia in 1915. As a defeated power, after the war Bulgaria lost her Aegean coast and most of Macedonia. Boris III ruled the country from 1918 to 1943, with an increasingly reactionary regime. In 1944 the Red Army occupied the country and a pro-Soviet government was formed, which declared war on Germany. A republic was proclaimed in 1946, led by the communists, and a socialist state built along Stalinist lines. Bulgaria was one of the last East European countries to respond to the liberalisation occurring in the rest of the communist bloc but in 1990 one party rule ended and free elections were held.

Agriculture remains important, producing mainly wheat and maize, as well as tobacco, fruit and wine which are the main exports. The iron, steel and chemical industries have developed as well as the traditional textile and food industries. Recent moves towards a free market economy have brought problems, especially high inflation.

The population of Bulgaria is 9 million, being mainly Bulgarians, a Slav people, but with Turkish, Macedonian, Armenian, Romanian and gypsy minorities. The Bulgarian language is close to Russian and also uses the Cyrillic alphabet. Turkish and Macedonian are spoken by the respective minorities. Many Bulgarians speak foreign languages, such as French and German but also English. Most Bulgarians are Orthodox Christian and there is also a Muslim minority. The capital is Sofia.

The climate is similar to the Northern Mediterranean, with very hot summers, but colder winters. The prevailing winds of summer are north east, although there is a daily alternation of land and sea breezes.

Entry Regulations

Ports of entry
Burgas 42°30′N 27°29′E, Varna 43°12′N 27°55′E.

Procedure on arrival
One must clear with customs, health and immigration. Officials will visit the yacht on arrival and the crew must remain on board until formalities are completed. The formalities are not complicated, but passports and ship's papers may be retained until departure.
Varna: Port Control maintains 24 hour watch on Channels 16 and 77. Arrivals should be timed for daylight hours. Boats are normally directed to the yacht club marina, located on the starboard side of the entrance to the commercial harbour; if there is no space, an alternative is to moor on the quay south of the ferry terminal.

Customs
Firearms will be impounded until departure. Animals may be confined on board.

Immigration
Passports must be valid at least six months beyond departure.

Visas are required by all nationals except those of Bosnia-Hercegovina, Armenia, Baltic Republics, the CIS, Croatia, Cuba, Czech Republic, Hungary, South Korea, Macedonia, Mongolia, Poland, Romania, Slovak Republic, Slovenia, Tunisia and Yugoslavia. Visas are also not required for US tourists for up to a 30 day stay. Nationals of EU countries may obtain their tourist visas for 30 days on arrival, but it is recommended that nationals of non-EU European countries, Australia, Canada, Israel, Japan, New Zealand, South Africa and most other countries obtain a visa beforehand, although for short stays they can be issued on arrival. The cost of the visa depends on the nationality and whether issued in advance or not.

There is a Bulgarian consulate in Istanbul, where visas are issued in 2 days.

Facilities

Only simple repairs are possible and the best workshops are located in Varna, where there is also a slipway. For any repairs it is best to consult the Varna Yacht Club for advice. The club welcomes visitors, particularly at the beginning of July when it holds its annual regatta from Varna to Kavarna and a yacht can be left there if travelling inland. Provisioning is rather limited, although there is a reasonable selection of fresh produce. Fuel is available in all ports. The best charts for the Black Sea are Turkish and can be bought in Istanbul.

Further Reading

Black Sea Cruising Guide

Website

www.peakview.bg

CROATIA

From Dubrovnik in the south to the Istra peninsula in the north, Croatia has an extensive coastline indented with innumerable bays and there are hundreds of islands that abound in scenic anchorages. Only 66 of some 1000 islands are inhabited. Overshadowed for many years by the Greek islands, which were both better known and more welcoming, the Croatian coast became a popular cruising destination in the 1980s. Large numbers of cruising boats made their permanent base in one of the marinas, the area being also very popular with sailors from neighbouring countries, such as Italy, Austria and Germany. This popularity was accompanied by the rapid development of a considerable number of marinas strategically placed along the coast and on some of the offlying islands.

This idyllic picture was threatened with destruction by the war which followed the breakup of the former Yugoslavia. After a spate of fighting on the coast, which saw the destruction of parts of Dubrovnik, hostilities continued mostly inland.

The Dalmatian islands and most of Northern Croatia were not touched by the war and by the summer of 1999 most damaged buildings as well as the marina in Dubrovnik had been restored. Gradually cruising boats started to return and the situation is now close to what it was before the outbreak of hostilities – with several thousand foreign boats visiting Croatia during the 1999 season. The troubles in Kosovo have only marginally affected Croatia.

Country Profile

The region was populated by Slavs in the sixth century and in the ninth a Croat kingdom was established. Following a dynastic union with Hungary at the end of the eleventh century, most of Croatia remained under Hungarian rule until the First World War. In 1918 Croatia became part of the new Kingdom of Serbs, Croats and Slovenes, renamed Yugoslavia in 1929. After the Second World War Croatia became one of the six Socialist Republics making up the Yugoslav Federation, though Croatian nationalism persisted.

In 1990 a referendum backed full independence for Croatia. This was rejected by the region of Krajina and the other predominantly Serb areas of Croatia, that wished to remain united with Serbia. Conflict broke out in 1991 between Croatian forces on the one hand, and Serb irregulars and the federal army on the other. 1992 marked the arrival of a UN peace-keeping mission, and the international recognition of Croatian independence. After a brief interlude, fighting flared up again after neighbouring Bosnia-Hercegovina followed Croatia's example and also declared independence not recognised by its Serbian minority. In August 1995 the Croatian army took the Krajina region from Serb control, forcing the Serbian population to flee to neighbouring Bosnia and Serbia.

Agriculture dominates in the east, with industry centred around the capital Zagreb. The coast is a popular tourist region. Efforts have been made to stabilise the currency following serious inflation in the early 1990s.

The population numbers around 4.4 million, of which the majority are Croatians, who are Roman Catholics. The Croatian language is a western variant of Serbo-Croat.

On the coast is a Mediterranean climate with mild winters and sunny, dry summers.

Entry Regulations

Ports of entry
Umag 45°26′N 13°31′E, Porec 45°13′N 13°36′E, Rovinj 45°05′N 13°38′E, Pula 44°53′N 13°50′E, Rasa 45°02′N 14°04′E, Rijeka 45°19′N 14°26′E, Mali Losinj 44°32′N 14°28′E, Senj 45°00′N 15°14′E, Maslenica 44°13′N 15°32′E, Zadar 44°07′N 15°14′E, Hvar 43°10′N 16°50′E, Sibenik 43°44′N 15°54′E, Primosten 43°35′N 15°56′E, Split 43°30′N 16°27′E, Ploce 43°02′N 17°25′E, Metkovic 43°06′N 17°33′E, Korcula 42°48′N 17°27′E, Dubrovnik 42°38′N 18°07′E.

All the above ports are open all year. There are also a number of seasonal ports open from 1 April to 30 October: Umag Marina, Novigrad, Kanegra, Sali, Soline, Primosten, Ravni Zakan, Hvar, Vela Luka, Ubli (Lastovo) and Vis.

Procedure on arrival
On arrival from outside Croatia in one of the official ports of entry, one should wait for the officials to come to the yacht for clearance. In marinas, the staff will call the relevant officials. If no one arrives after a reasonable wait the captain should report to the police for passport control, as well as customs and harbour master. The crew must remain on board until formalities are complete. On arrival one must also register with the police and all crew members issued with a registration card.

A cruising permit will be issued for one year and the yacht is free to enter any Croatian port without any further formalities. Restricted areas are usually indicated on the permit. The fee for the cruising permit must be paid in local currency.

Documents needed are the registration certificate, certificate of competence, third party insurance certificate, crew lists, radio licence, and a list of all dutiable items such as alcohol, tobacco and any movable objects not part of the yacht's equipment, such as cameras, portable radios or the outboard engine. A cruising permit will be issued, which must be shown at subsequent stops.

Dubrovnik: Boats are normally directed into Gruz harbour to complete formalities, where there is a dock for yachts, just beyond the ferry terminal.

Customs
Firearms must be declared on arrival and will be sealed and checked again when leaving. All details of the firearms on board must be entered on the cruising permit.

Radio equipment must be declared and an

operator's permit shown. CB and portable VHF radios need a special permit.

Dogs and cats need a veterinary certificate showing that the animal has been vaccinated against rabies between 15 days and six months previously. All animals need a general health certificate.

Yachts left unattended for longer periods, such as for over-wintering, will be bonded by customs. For short periods of absence of up to 20 days the boat can be left in the care of a marina without being bonded.

Immigration

Citizens of all European Union countries with the exception of Greece do not need a visa. Nationals which require a visa: Algeria, Australia, Bosnia-Hercegovina, Bulgaria, Canada, Chile, Czech Republic, Ecuador, Hungary, Japan, Liechtenstein, Macedonia, Malta, Monaco, New Zealand, Norway, Poland, Romania, San Marino, Slovak Republic, Slovenia, South Africa, Sweden, Switzerland, Turkey and the USA. Visas can be obtained on arrival free of charge.

Three months are usually granted on arrival, and this can easily be extended.

Procedure on departure

Boats leaving Croatia must obtain clearance from the harbour master at a port of entry. The vessel must leave Croatian territorial waters immediately after clearance and by the shortest route.

Cruising permit

This is issued on arrival at the port of entry. The permit lasts for the calendar year and covers any number of exits and entries, but must be stamped at each major port by the harbour master and customs.

The permit allows a yacht to cruise along the entire coast including the islands, except for certain prohibited areas.

Restrictions

Areas prohibited to yachts are listed on the cruising permit or will be specified on arrival at the port of entry. It is strictly forbidden to photograph any restricted areas or military installations:

1 Designated parts of the naval ports of Pula, Sibenik, Split (Lora) and Ploce (Bazine).
2 The following are prohibited or protected areas: Navigation is prohibited around Brijuni Island, delimited by the following lines:

Zone I
    1) Rt Barbaren – RT Kadulja
    2) Rt Kadulja – Isle of Supiniæ
    Isle of Supiniæ – Position A (longitude: 44° 52.6'N latitude: 13°42.2'E)
    3) Position A – Position B:

Practical Information

LOCAL TIME: GMT + 1. Summer time GMT + 2, end March to end September.

BUOYAGE: IALA A

CURRENCY: Kuna

BUSINESS HOURS
Banks: 0730–1900 Monday to Friday, 0800–1200 Saturday.
Shops: 0800–2000 Monday to Friday, 0800–1200 Saturday.
Government offices: 0800–1600 Monday to Friday.

ELECTRICITY: 220 V, 50 Hz

PUBLIC HOLIDAYS
1 January: New Year's Day
6 January: Three Kings
Easter Monday
1 May: Labour Day
30 May: Republic Day
22 June: Antifascism Day
5 August: National Holiday
15 August: Assumption
1 November: All Saints' Day
25–26 December: Christmas

COMMUNICATIONS
Public phones take tokens or phone cards. International calls can be made from telephone offices.
The international access code is 00.

There is an international airport at Zagreb with flights to most European capitals. There are some international flights from the airports at Dubrovnik, Pula, Zadar and Split.

DIPLOMATIC MISSIONS
In Zagreb:
Albania: Mother Teresa Charitable Society, Preradoviceva 9.
Australia and Canada: Hotel Esplanade. *Tel.* 435 666.
Germany: Avenija Vukovar 64, 41000 *Tel.* 519 200.
United Kingdom: 12 Ilica, POB 454, 41000 *Tel.* 424 888.
United States: 2 Andrije Hebranga *Tel.* 444 800.

(longitude: 44°52.6'N, latitude: 13°45.1'E)
4) Position B – Position C: (longitude: 44°53.2'N, latitude: 13°46.0'E)
5) Position C – Rt Kamnik

Zone II
The SE part of the Brijuni Island within the line connecting Rt Kavran and Rt Kozlac.
3 Navigation is prohibited in Limski Canal on the western coast of Istria because of a shellfish farm.
4 The protected area in Kornati National Park, which extends from Prolaz Proversa Vela (south of the island Dugi Otok) to the southern point of Kornati Island. All activities that may pollute the sea are strictly prohibited.
5 Navigation is prohibited in several bays because of fish farms located in them. They are listed in pilot books and are marked by buoys or signs onshore.
6 The following sporting activities are prohibited in the interest of safety to swimmers or navigation generally: swimming, windsurfing or waterskiing in ports.
7 Boats must keep at a distance of at least 150 ft (50 m) from marked bathing areas, or sail at least 300 ft (100 m) offshore.

Fees

Overtime is charged after 1500, at weekends and on public holidays. There is a fee for the cruising permit. A navigation security fee, based on LOA, is payable on arrival. The fee is quoted in German marks (may be changed to euros in 2002) and varies from 210 DEM (for a 30 ft/9 m boat) to 350 DEM (for a 40 ft/12 m boat) and 450 DEM for boats over 65 ft/20 m.

Facilities

The reported number of foreign vessels that cleared into Croatia in 1999 was 50,000. Although the actual number of cruising boats was probably much lower, and allowing for the fact that the same boat clearing into the country more than once in the same year may have been counted several times, there is no doubt that Croatia is once again one of the prime cruising destinations in the Mediterranean. To cater for this influx, facilities along the entire Croatian coast are of a very good standard. There are approximately 40 marinas along the coast and as a minimum they have a 10-ton crane and the necessary frame to lift boats up to that weight. There are travelifts with a minimum

capacity of 30 tons at Umag, Cres, Sukosan, Hramina, Murter, Bettina, Mali Losinj, Kremik, Vodice and Dubrovnik. The biggest concentration of boatyards is in the Zadar Sibenik area.

Fuel and provisions are available in most places. Marine equipment is limited and one should carry all essential spares.

Further Reading

Adriatic Pilot
Mediterranean Europe (Lonely Planet)
Mediterranean Almanac

Website

www.htz.hr (National Tourist Board)

CYPRUS

A large island tucked into the eastern corner of the Mediterranean, Cyprus has a strategic position, being within close range of Turkey, Syria, Lebanon and Israel. Ironically it is further from Greece, with which it has the closest ties. Cyprus is an attractive island with a pleasant climate, beautiful mountainous landscape and interesting archaeological sites. According to legend, Aphrodite, the Greek goddess of love, emerged from the sea at Paphos. Recent history has been less romantic and in 1974 the north of the island was invaded by Turkey and now UN troops patrol the ceasefire line between the Republic of Cyprus in the south and Northern Cyprus.

The southern Republic of Cyprus, and Larnaca in particular, has gained great popularity as one of the favourite wintering spots for long-distance cruising yachts. Many of these reach Cyprus after transiting the Suez Canal, while others sail to Cyprus from other parts of the Mediterranean at the end of the cruising season. Lacking natural harbours and anchorages, Cyprus has always been an island to visit from its ports, rather than to cruise around. This has been made even more necessary by the ongoing conflict between Cyprus and Turkey which has reduced the few cruising attractions that the island had in the past. However, the reputation of Cyprus as an excellent base for repairs and reprovisioning has ensured its continuing popularity.

Country Profile

The name Kypros originates from the Greek word for copper. The ancient name of Cyprus was Alasia (meaning 'belonging to the sea'). In ancient times the copper deposits brought considerable wealth to the island and many people came to settle, especially Achaean Ellenes from the mainland. Due to its position Cyprus experienced many invasions and different rulers over the centuries reflecting the history of the region. It was claimed by the Assyrians, Egyptians and Persians, then ruled by Alexander the Great until his death in 323 BC. The Romans were the next to take over and during this time St Paul visited and converted the Roman proconsul in Paphos to Christianity. Later Cyprus became part of the Byzantine Empire until the island was seized by Richard the Lionheart in 1191 during the Crusades. Periods of rule followed by the Franks, Venetians and Ottoman Turks until the late nineteenth century, when the administration was taken over by Britain.

Cyprus was a British colony from 1914 until 1960 when following four years of fighting against the British troops by the Greek Cypriots, the independent Republic of Cyprus was established. Immediately after, intercommunal fighting broke out between the Greek Cypriots and the Turkish Cypriots over the provisions of the London and Zurich 1960 Independence agreement. In 1964 the Turkish Cypriots established a communal administration which was accepted by the Greek Cypriots and the UN. In 1974, as the result of a military coup carried out in mainland Greece by Junta officers, Turkey invaded the north of the island, which has remained under Turkish occupation. In 1983 it became the 'Turkish Republic of Northern Cyprus', but has not been recognised by any other countries except Turkey. The Republic of Cyprus, which controls 60 per cent of the island, is internationally recognised as the government of Cyprus.

Cyprus has an agricultural economy with a small manufacturing industry. Tourism is the main industry of the island and most of the commerce

Practical Information

LOCAL TIME: GMT + 2. Summer time GMT + 3 last weekend in March until last weekend in September.

BUOYAGE: IALA A

CURRENCY: Cyprus pound (C£) of 100 cents.

BUSINESS HOURS
Banks: 0800–1200 Monday to Saturday. Main banks open for exchange in afternoons.
Some exchange facilities open 1530–1730 Monday to Friday.
Business and shops: 0800–1300 Monday to Saturday; afternoons, winter 1430–1730, summer 1600–1900, closed Wednesday and Saturday afternoons all year.
Government offices: 0730/0800–1430/1500 Monday to Friday.
Thursday also 1500–1800.

ELECTRICITY: 220 V, 50 Hz

PUBLIC HOLIDAYS
1 January: New Year's Day
6 January: Epiphany
Kathara Deftera (Orthodox Shrove Tuesday)*
25 March: Greek Revolution (1821) Day
1 April: Greek Cypriot National Day
Orthodox Good Friday, Saturday, Monday* 1 May
15 August: Assumption
1 October: Cyprus Republic Independence Day
28 October: Ohi Day
25, 26 December: Christmas
*Variable

EVENTS
Easter is the biggest event in the Orthodox calendar.
Kataklysmos, which means flood and coincides with Pentecost, is a festival unique to Cyprus.

COMMUNICATIONS
Telephones: CYTA offices. International operator 192.
Post office: 0730–1330 (1300 in summer) Monday to Saturday, some open in the afternoon. Poste restante and afternoon service: King Paul Square, Larnaca; Eleftheria Square, Nicosia; 1 Gladstone Street, Limassol; Themidos and St Paul Streets, Paphos.
Emergency: dial 199.
There are no postal or telephone communications with Northern Cyprus,
except by various banks and some diplomatic missions. There are international flights from Larnaca to many European and Middle East destinations.

MEDICAL
There is a high standard of medical services.
There are decompression chambers at Larnaca General Hospital and at Akrotiri Hospital near Limassol.

DIPLOMATIC MISSIONS
In Nicosia:
Australia: corner L. Stassinou & A. Komninis Street. *Tel.* (2) 473001.
Egypt: 3 Egypt Avenue. Tel. (2) 465144/5.
France: 6 Ploutarchou Street. *Tel.* (2) 465258.
Germany: 10 Nikitara Street. *Tel.* (2) 444362/3/4.
Israel: 4, Gryparis Street. *Tel.* (2) 445195/6.
Lebanon: 1 Vasilissis Olgas Street. *Tel.* (2) 442216.
Syria: corner Androcleous and Thoukidides Street. *Tel.* (2) 474481/2.
United Kingdom: Alexander Pallis Street. *Tel.* (2) 473131.
United States: corner Metochiou & Ploutarchou. *Tel.* (2) 476100.

is in the southern areas of the Greek Republic.

The population of the island is 700,000 and is divided on ethnic grounds. The last census in 1960 found 80 per cent Greek Cypriot and 18 per cent Turkish Cypriot. Since the division of the island, in 1974, over 110,000 Greek Cypriot refugees have left the northern sector for the south. There are small minorities of Armenians, Britons, Maronites and Latins. Greek is the main language of the island and most Greek Cypriots are Orthodox Christians, although there are some other denominations. Turkish is spoken in the northern sector and most Turkish Cypriots are Muslim. English is widely spoken. Nicosia has been the capital since the tenth century and the old walled city can still be seen within the modern metropolis.

Cyprus has an island climate with daily breezes that can get strong in the afternoons. It is usually calm at night. The summers are very hot and humid with temperatures up to 101°F (40°C) in July and August. The winters are generally mild and pleasantly sunny, although gales from the south or east do track across the Mediterranean. September to November are usually the best months for cruising.

Entry Regulations

Ports of entry

Larnaca (marina and port) 34°55'N 33°38'E, Limassol 34°40'N 33°03'E, Paphos 34°45'N 32°25'E.

Procedure on arrival

Information is given for the southern Republic of Cyprus, which lies approximately south of parallel 35°N. Information on Northern Cyprus, which has been occupied by the Turkish army since 1974, is given at the end of this section.

Cyprus Radio maintains continuous watch on VHF Channels 16 and 26. The Cypriot courtesy flag must be flown when entering Cypriot waters. Everyone should remain on board until clearance formalities are completed. Ship's papers will be required by the port authority on arrival. Evidence of insurance may also be requested. A total of five crew lists will be needed.

The captains of boats which have stopped in Northern Cyprus are liable to incur heavy penalties and possibly imprisonment. This is because the authorities in the Republic of Cyprus consider it an illegal act to stop in an area of the island, which is under foreign occupation. This is a very serious matter and mariners are therefore advised to avoid at all cost being caught in the politics of the area.

Customs

Firearms must be declared and surrendered to customs on arrival. Sporting guns require a temporary permit which has to be obtained from the Ministry of the Interior.

For animals, an import permit must be obtained in advance from the Director of the Department of Veterinary Services, Nicosia. Animals must remain on board, which is called home quarantine. Dogs and cats have a six-month quarantine period. Parrots and budgerigars are prohibited.

Antiques may not be exported.

Yachts may stay up to one year without paying taxes, as they are considered to be temporarily imported. For an extension a customs authority is needed. This is normally granted up to a total of five years, any number of visits being cumulative and during this time no taxes are paid. During this period foreign yachts can import spare parts duty-free.

Duty-free stores should be declared on entry and may be removed and retained by customs until departure. Duty-free stores are available 24 hours before departure, spirits being limited to one case per person. Duty-free may be obtained in all ports where there are bonded stores.

Immigration

No visas are required by nationals of most countries in Europe, the Americas, Australia, New Zealand and Japan for stays of up to three months. A permit to stay more than three months may be issued by the Chief Immigration officer, Nicosia. Immigration normally retains passports and each person is issued with a landing permit.

Restrictions

There are military restricted areas along the coasts and yachts should maintain a distance of 1640 ft (500 m) offshore by day and 3280 ft (1000 m) by night unless approaching a port. Spearfishing is prohibited within bathing areas, which are marked by red buoys. A special licence is required for spearfishing with scuba gear. This is issued only to certified divers and is easily obtained from the District Fisheries Departments, on presentation of a certified diving licence. There is no charge. It is forbidden to take antiquities and sponges from the sea.

Facilities

Every autumn, at the end of the cruising season in the Eastern Mediterranean, scores of cruising yachts congregate in Larnaca preparing for hibernation. Their presence has encouraged the setting up of several workshops, which can deal with a complete range of repairs. Woodwork, carpentry and rigging work is undertaken by a boatyard located in the marina, which also operates a 40-ton travelift. Fuel, LPG and nautical charts are all available and there is also a small chandlery with a limited stock of marine supplies. There are several supermarkets and also a fresh produce market nearby. St Raphael Marina (ex-Sheraton Marina) operates in the north part of the bay of Limassol with a full range of services including a boatyard and travelift (60 tons). There is a good selection of marine equipment and the main engine agents are also located in this large commercial harbour.

Further Reading

Mediterranean Cruising Handbook
Mediterranean Almanac
Turkish Waters and Cyprus Pilot

Website

www.cyprustourism.org (Cyprus Tourism Organisation)

NORTHERN CYPRUS

The Turkish Republic of Northern Cyprus is referred to as the 'occupied zone' by the Southern Republic. Visitors may cross into Northern Cyprus with a special pass issued by the Southern authorities, and return the same day, through a frontier checkpoint at Ledra Palace Hotel, Nicosia. Communications by sea from a port in the north to any port in the south is prohibited by the South Cyprus authorities. However, there are no restrictions imposed by North Cyprus authorities for those who wish to visit a port in the north after visiting a port in the south.

Entry Regulations

Ports of entry

Famagusta (Gazimagusa) 35°07'N 33°36'E, Kyrenia (Girne) 35°20'N 33°19'E.

Procedure on arrival

Bearing in mind the warning given earlier concerning visits to Northern Cyprus, those who wish to visit Northern Cyprus can do so, but should request a separate entry form and ask the immigration officer not to stamp their passports, so that they do not face any problems when visiting Southern Cyprus afterwards. North Cyprus immigration officials will be happy to do as requested.

The flag of Northern Cyprus should be flown if approaching Northern Cyprus. The entry formalities are similar to those in Turkey. Visas are issued on arrival. The crew passports may be retained in exchange for landing passes.

Restrictions

There are ill-defined military zones and it is wise to

Practical Information

CURRENCY: Turkish lira are used.

BUSINESS HOURS
Banks: 0800–1200 Monday to Friday, also in winter 1400–1600.
Shops: 0800–1300, 1600–1900 summer, 0900–1300, 1400–1800 winter.
Government offices: summer, Monday to Friday 1530–1800, Mondays only 0730–1400, winter 0800–1300, 1400–1700 Monday to Friday.

PUBLIC HOLIDAYS
1 January: New Year's Day
23 April: Children's Bairam
1 May
19 May: Sports and Youth Bairam
30 August
29 October: Turkish Republic Day
15 November: Northern Cyprus Republic Day
Variable:
Prophet's birthday, Sheker Bairam – Ramadan, 2 days, Qurban Bairam, Feast of Sacrifices, 3 days

COMMUNICATIONS
All mail directed to 'Cyprus' goes automatically to the Southern Republic. The correct postal address for any mail to Northern Cyprus is 'Mersin 10, Turkey' (Cyprus must not appear on the envelope). International calls can be direct dialled with telephone cards, available from Telecommunications Offices. Northern Cyprus can be reached by air via Ercan in Turkey. There are daily sea-bus and ferry services between Kyrenia and Tasucu and ferries three times a week between Famagusta and Mersin. In the summer there are also services from Alanya, Antalya and Anamur.

keep well away from the coast, especially along the north coast and round Cape Andera at the north-eastern end of Karpass Peninsula. In fact because of so many prohibited areas, only the ports of Famagusta and Kyrenia should be approached if sailing to Northern Cyprus.

Facilities

Facilities in Northern Cyprus are limited, with only simple repairs possible in Kyrenia. There is a small slipway capable of hauling out boats of up to 45 ft (14 m). Fuel is available from a station near the port. Provisioning is adequate with prices compa-rable to Turkey but lower than Southern Cyprus.

Further Reading

Turkish Waters and Cyprus Pilot

Website

www.tourism.trnc.net (Tourism Office of Northern Cyprus)

EGYPT

The Pyramids and the Sphinx at Giza, the temples of Luxor and Karnak, the Valleys of the Kings and Queens are some of the places which make Egypt a major tourist destination and most of the visiting sailors also try to see at least some of these ancient sites. Egypt occupies a large area of northern Africa, but most of it is barren, flat desert. It is only the river Nile which makes Egypt cultivable and most of the population lives in the fertile area around this great river. To the west of the Nile lies the Western desert and Libya, while to the east lies the Red Sea, Suez Canal and the Sinai desert.

Most sailors come to know Egypt through tran-siting the Suez Canal and very few yachts sail to Egypt solely to visit the country. For those sailing in the Mediterranean, the only alternative to Port Said is the ancient port of Alexandria. Occasionally yachts manage to obtain a permit to sail up the Nile, which is a fascinating way to see Egypt, although most certainly not the easiest.

Those who approach Egypt from the Red Sea have the opportunity to appreciate the only area of the country which is worth cruising, the reefs and bays that stretch all the way from the Sudanese border to the Gulf of Suez. Day sailing along this coast is the most pleasant way to make progress against the prevailing northerlies. As the Red Sea is increasingly becoming a cruising destination in its own right and yachts sail from the Mediterranean to spend the winter in its more pleasant climate, this coast of Egypt is becoming better known. Whether coming from south or north, the transit-ing of the Suez Canal is an exciting experience, which can be better appreciated now that the for-malities are becoming slightly less complicated.

Terrorist attacks by Islamic fundamentalists against foreign visitors have badly affected tourism, and while this situation continues, the internal sit-uation should be monitored carefully. Probably the best place to visit the ancient monuments at Luxor is from Safaga.

Country Profile

Egypt has 5000 years of recorded history and one of the earliest civilisations in the world. In 3188 BC Menes united the Upper and Lower Kingdoms with Memphis as the capital, and the pyramids were built during this period. After this came the Middle Kingdom, with its centre at Thebes, which is present day Luxor. The New Kingdom, which was the era of Queen Nefertiti and Tutankhamun, established an empire in the sixteenth to the fourteenth cen-turies BC. Invasions from Libya, Nubia, Ethiopia and Assyria brought about the empire's decline. The era of the Pharaohs finally ended with the arrival of Alexander the Great in 332 BC. Alexandria became the new capital, a sophisticated city, which was a centre of Greek culture and civilisation.

Queen Cleopatra's death in 30 BC marked the end of independence. Rome and Byzantium dom-inated until Arab invasions swept across Egypt from the seventh to the tenth centuries and the capital moved to present-day Cairo. In the early sixteenth century the Ottoman Turks gained con-trol and Egypt became an unimportant province of their vast empire.

In 1798 Napoleon's expedition to Egypt opened it up to modern European influence. France's subsequent withdrawal created a power struggle, until the Albanian Muhammed Ali became Sultan. Efforts were made to modernise the country and in 1869 the Suez Canal was opened. Britain occupied Egypt 13 years later, but nationalist feelings grew amongst the Egyptians

Practical Information

LOCAL TIME: GMT + 2

BUOYAGE: IALA A

CURRENCY: Egyptian pound (E£) of 100 piastres. No more than E£100 can be taken out of the country, but unused currency can be changed back before departure. A foreign currency declaration must be made on arrival and exchange receipts should be kept.

BUSINESS HOURS
Friday is the day of rest.
Banks: 0900–1230 Monday to Thursday and Saturday, 1000–1200 Sunday.
Business: summer 0830–1400 Monday to Thursday, winter 0900–1300/1600–1900 except Thursday afternoons and Fridays.
Shops: 0900–1330/1700–2000 Monday to Thursday.
Government offices: summer 0900–1400 Saturday to Thursday except holidays; winter 0900–1300/1600–1900 Monday to Wednesday and Thursday mornings.

ELECTRICITY: 110/220 V, 50 Hz

PUBLIC HOLIDAYS
1 January: New Year's Day
January: Coptic Christmas
1 May: Labour Day
18 June: Republic Day
23 July: Revolution Day
6 October: Armed Forces Day
24 October: Suez Day
23 December: Victory Day
Variable holidays: Islamic New Year, Ashoura, Mouloud, Ramadan, Eid el-Fitr, Eid el-Adha, Hijira, 1st Monday after Coptic Easter, Sham el-Nessim (National Spring Festival). If a holiday falls on a Friday, the following Saturday may also be a holiday.

EVENTS
December Nile festival in Cairo and Luxor.

COMMUNICATIONS
International calls can be dialled direct.
Post offices open daily Saturday to Thursday 0830–1500.

Cairo central post office is open 24 hours. Poste restante is available at main post offices for a small fee.
There are frequent international flights from Cairo to all major cities in Africa, the Middle East and Europe. There are also internal flights to Luxor and Aswan.

MEDICAL
There are good hospitals in Cairo and Alexandria, but poor facilities elsewhere. Treatment for foreigners can be expensive.

DIPLOMATIC MISSIONS
In Cairo:
Canada: 6 Mohammed Fahmi Es Sayed, Garden City. Tel. (2) 3543110.
Sudan: 4 Sharia El Ibrahimi, Garden City. Tel. (2) 3549661.
United Kingdom: Sharia Ahmed Ragheb, Garden City, Tel. (2) 3540852.
United States: Lazouguli Street, Garden City. Tel. (2) 3557371.
In Port Suez: United Kingdom: El Galaa Street. Tel. 334102.
United States: Tel. 229665.

and in 1922 Egypt was recognised as an independent state by Britain, although they occupied the country until 1936 and even after that British troops remained in the Canal area. Amid growing dissatisfaction with Egypt's status and the monarchy, in 1952 a military coup and nationalist revolution led by Gamal Abdel Nasser established a republic. Nasser nationalised the Suez Canal, which provoked the Suez Crisis of 1956, and the military intervention of Israel, France and Britain. Anwar Sadat succeeded Nasser in 1970, establishing better links with the West, and ending the ongoing state of war with Israel in 1979. Sadat was assassinated in 1981, and under President Mubarak relations both with Arab states and Israel have improved considerably.

Egypt is agricultural and half the population work in this domain. There is considerable poverty and high unemployment. However, industry is expanding and tourism, the Suez Canal and oil revenues make important contributions to the economy.

The rapidly rising population now numbers 65 million, comprising Egyptians, Bedouins, Nubians, Arabs and some Italian, Greek and Armenian communities. About 7 million are Copts, who claim to be descendants of the original inhabitants, a Hamitic people who lived along the Nile. Islam is the religion of the majority, although the Copts are Christian, the Coptic church being one of the oldest in existence. There is also a small Jewish community. Arabic is the official language, but some English and French is spoken in the cities. The capital is Cairo, the largest city in Africa.

The summers are very hot with extremely high temperatures both inland and in the Red Sea. Winters are mild with little rain. The prevailing winds are northerly. Occasionally the *khamsin*, a hot dry wind, blows off the land laden with dust and sand reducing visibility. The prevailing winds in the Red Sea are northerly, while along the Mediterranean coast there are daily alternating land and sea breezes.

Entry Regulations

Ports of entry
Alexandria 31°11′N 29°52′E, Port Said 31°15′N 32°18′E, Suez 29°58′N 32°33′E, Hurghada 27°15′N 33°49′E, Safaga 26°44′N 33°56′E, Sharm el Sheik 27°51′N 34°17′E.

Procedure on arrival

The Coast Guard normally maintain a presence in all ports and anchorages, and usually visit the yacht, requesting details of the yacht and its crew. In ports of entry, clearance must be done with customs, health and immigration.

Port Said: Because of the high density of shipping traffic and the difficult approach to Port Said, the harbour should not be entered at night. Yachts are normally met by a pilot boat and directed to the Port Fouad Yacht Club on the eastern side of the harbour. It is usually easier if one is already in contact with a local agent (such as Felix Agency, Fax. + 20 66 333510), who should be contacted first on VHF. He will obtain permission from the port captain for the boat to move directly to the yacht club. If the yacht is transiting the canal and only staying in Port Said as long as it takes to make arrangements for the transit, immigration formalities are simple and no visas will be issued. Those who wish to stay longer and visit other parts of Egypt need to go through the normal entry procedure. See below for further instructions concerning formalities for transiting the Suez Canal.

Suez: Yachts are usually met in the approaches by an agent's boat, who will offer his services, sometimes quite forcefully. It is therefore advisable to have made arrangements in advance with an agent, who can be contacted on Channel 16 and will then meet the yacht on arrival. The agent will obtain permission for the yacht to proceed directly to the Suez Yacht Club. The agent will also arrange for the officials to come to the club for clearance, or will deal himself with all other formalities, including Canal transit. The agent will also bring the Suez Canal pilot to the yacht club on the day of the transit. Otherwise yachts should anchor in the waiting area in Port Ibrahim and contact Port Control on VHF Channel 16 for permission to go to Suez Yacht Club which is located on the left-hand side of the Canal, just beyond the Canal Authority buildings.

Alexandria: Yachts must go to the eastern harbour, and anchor off the Yacht Club of Egypt, who will help with formalities.

Hurghada: Boats are required to go alongside the short jetty next to the police and port launches. Formalities are lengthy if not using an agent. Each arrival must be registered with immigration. Written permission is required to move the boat anywhere within the port, even to get fuel.

Safaga: Call Safaga Port Control on VHF Channel 16 on approach. Calls are usually answered by Safaga Pilot, but not so promptly at night. The port captain insists that boats (especially those arriving from abroad) come alongside the main dock, although this is sometimes unsuitable for small boats. The recommended anchorage (26°47.59'N 33°56.33'E) is in front of the Paradise Hotel. The boat is usually visited first by security police. One should have several crew lists ready. Arms and ammunition should be declared immediately on arrival. The rest of the formalities are completed ashore. The immigration office is at the harbour gates (third floor). Boats are occasionally visited by a quarantine officer who may ask for a fee. The same offices must be visited on departure, even if sailing to another Egyptian port. Non-uniformed police may board the boat before departure.

Outward clearance

If transiting the Canal and not stopping anywhere else after the transit, the outward clearance can be obtained while doing the transit formalities. Yachts may then proceed to sea as soon as they have dropped the pilot. Once outward clearance is obtained, yachts must leave within 24 hours, or obtain another clearance.

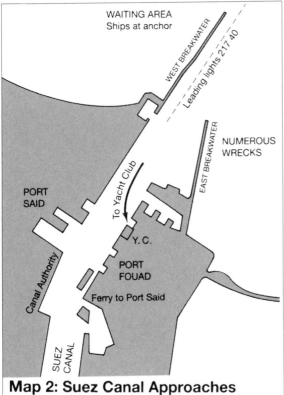

Map 2: Suez Canal Approaches to Port Said

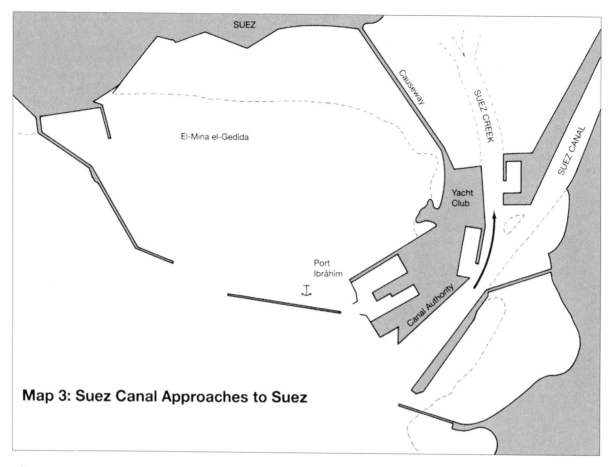

Map 3: Suez Canal Approaches to Suez

Customs
A list of firearms, with their type and details, must be handed to the authorities on arrival.

There are no restrictions on animals.

Yachts may remain in Egypt for a maximum of six months.

Immigration
Visas are not needed by anyone travelling on a yacht transiting the Suez Canal and remaining in the port area. Although most nationalities can obtain a visa on arrival, formalities are much simplified if a visa is obtained in advance. Djibouti is a good place to do this for northbound boats. All nationalities, except those from South Africa, Malta and Arab countries (except Sudan), need a visa. Visa fees vary according to nationality; all fees are lower if obtaining visas in advance.

Tourist visas are issued for any period up to one month and multiple entry visas can be obtained from Egyptian consulates. Visas are valid for three months from the date of issue. An extension to a visa can be obtained from the police. Passports must be valid for six months beyond the visa period. Nationals of Taiwan, Yemen and Libya are not allowed entry. Israeli nationals must have a visa obtained in advance from the Egyptian embassy in Israel. There are Egyptian embassies or consulates in most nearby countries, including Israel (Tel Aviv and Djibouti).

If planning to visit Israel and return to Egypt, it is possible to buy a re-entry permit, which expires one day before the original visa expires.

Cruising permit
This can be obtained on arrival. Outside of the official ports of entry, in other ports and anchorages, one may not go ashore except with special permission from the local authorities. Most anchorages have an army post or military station, who usually ask for the yacht's papers. Yachts coming from Sudan and making overnight stops without going ashore do not normally require a cruising permit. If sheltering from strong winds or making an overnight stop, yachts are normally allowed to stay in Egyptian waters before clearing in at an official

port of entry. If coming from the Red Sea and intending to stop in Egypt before clearing in, it is advisable to have obtained a visa in advance.

Health

Typhoid, tetanus, polio and hepatitis vaccinations are recommended, as is malaria prophylaxis. Quarantine officials will ask for vaccination certificates if coming from a known infected area.

River Nile

A security permit has to be obtained from the Coast Guard as well as permission from the Ministry of Foreign Affairs to navigate the river. The permit is difficult to obtain, although the Yacht Club of Egypt in Alexandria may be able to help. Navigation in the channels is restricted to daytime only. There are several bridges and locks, which open at certain times of the day or on request. Taking photographs of bridges, barrages and dams is strictly forbidden. The maximum draft must not exceed 5 ft (1.5 m). Navigation is only possible during winter, from October to May, when the level of water is higher. The river depth falls considerably during the summer months.

Fees

Overtime is charged after 1400 Saturday to Thursday, all day Friday and public holidays. Departure fees, harbour and light dues. Some fees must be paid every time one clears in or out, even if going to another Egyptian port.

There are various fees for the Suez Canal. In 2000 the following fees were quoted: transit fee and pilotage $122, port authority fee $128, stamp duty, quarantine and immigration $30, plus an additional $10 for each crew member. Agents fees quoted in 2000 were around $350 for southbound boats and $300 for northbound boats.

All agents' and Suez Canal fees must be paid in US dollars, therefore some cash should be carried.

Restrictions

All military zones are prohibited areas.

Spearfishing, the taking of reef fish, collecting of coral, shells and marine animals, are all forbidden in the Red Sea.

Facilities

In both Port Said and Suez, cruising yachts normally berth at the local yacht club, which charges a daily fee. Provisioning is somewhat better in Port Said, which is a duty-free port and stores can be ordered and delivered to the yacht club. There are daily fresh produce markets in both ports. Fuel is sometimes difficult to obtain at the normal pump price, as there is a surcharge for foreign vessels; however, this can be usually avoided. LPG can be found in Suez with the help of the Prince of the Red Sea, a local shipping agent who should be contacted for any kind of help, as he has built up a reputation of being able to fix anything.

The yacht club in Alexandria, located in the eastern harbour, normally allows visitors to use its facilities. There are various workshops known to the yacht club which can undertake engine, electrical and some electronic repairs as well as fibreglass, metal work and carpentry. There are slipways at Alexandria, Port Said and Suez.

Arrangements can be made at any of the clubs to leave the boat while visiting the interior of Egypt. A local watchman should always be employed in such a case. Suez is probably the best place to leave the boat unattended whether to visit Egypt's interior or overland to Israel and Jordan.

Facilities in Hurghada, on the Red Sea, are reasonably good and this is another place where the boat can be left to visit the interior. Provisions are available and also fuel from a pump in the new harbour, north of the naval dockyard. Buying fuel is a complicated matter and can be done via an agent, or by completing all formalities oneself. Larger quantities of water must also be obtained through an agent, or by making the necessary arrangements with one of the hotels. Fuel and water can also be obtained at Safaga, which is a better place from where to visit Luxor.

Neither at Hurghada nor at Safaga should the boat be left unattended.

Procedure for Transiting the Suez Canal

Port Said Captains of yachts intending to transit the Canal will be informed at the yacht club either by their agent or an official of the Canal Authority on the correct procedure to follow. Although time consuming, taking about 2–3 days, the formalities can be carried out by the captain alone and the service of an agent is not essential. The captain first has to visit the Small Craft Department in the main building of the Canal Authority in Port Said. He will be instructed as to the various formalities to be carried out and also the payments to be made. These payments include the transiting fee, insurance policy, ports and lights fee. One can do all necessary formalities oneself, but the relatively small amount of money saved would hardly justify the effort. The following offices must be visited in either Suez (northbound) or Port Said (southbound):

1   Suez Canal small craft office to present ship's documents and request transit.
2   Port immigration to complete arrival forms even by those who do not require a visa.
3   Insurance company to issue insurance certificate.
4   Return to the small craft office to present the insurance certificate.
5   The day before the transit the customs and quarantine offices must be visited to clear the yacht out of country. The officers may visit the yacht too.
6   Port immigration office to present departure form.
7   Red Sea port authority to issue port clearance.
8   Return with the port clearance to the small craft office who will give it to the pilot before the transit.
9   Inspection office for measurement and final inspection before the transit.
10 On the day of the transit, the small craft office will call the skipper to collect the pilot and take him to the yacht club to commence the transit.

    One final piece of advice is that if one has problems in the Canal, such as engine trouble, to contact first the agent, who may be able to find a solution, for the Canal Authority, if contacted, will send a Canal tug and the charges are extremely high.

On the day of the transit the pilot will arrive early in the morning to guide the yacht as far as Ismailia in the NW corner of Lake Timsah, where the yacht must spend the night as yachts are not allowed to transit at night. The crew are not allowed to go ashore. Early the following morning, either the same pilot or another one will continue the transit to Suez. Normally yachts stop at the Suez Yacht Club before continuing into the Red Sea.

Suez After contacting the port authority on VHF Channel 16 and having completed the initial clearance formalities, if permission has been obtained to proceed to Suez Yacht Club, the yacht should make its way to the club. This is located on the left-hand side of the Canal beyond the Canal Administration building. To transit the Canal, the same formalities have to be gone through as those described for Port Said.

Yachts approaching Suez are usually met by one or more agents who offer to complete transit formalities on their behalf. Although not compulsory, it is advisable to employ the services of an agent in Suez, as it is more difficult to complete the formalities alone than in Port Said. If using an agent, all fees should be agreed in advance and the agent should also be asked to specify exactly which fees and services are included. The agent with the best reputation and who handles most cruising yachts in Suez is Fathi Soukar (*Prince of the Red Sea*). He normally monitors VHF Channel 16. *Tel.* + 20 62 222 126, Fax. 330 965, e-mail: princers@gega.net.

The procedure for the transit is identical to the southward passage: the pilot will arrive early in the morning and the night will be spent at Ismailia where the pilot will board the following day and take the vessel to Port Said.

Canal regulations
Yachts must be capable of a consistent speed of 5 knots, which will be checked during the technical inspection. The speed limit in the canal is 9 knots. Yachts normally transit the Canal just after the morning convoy.

Warning
There have been reports of several yachts being run aground, and one severely damaged, due to the incompetence of the Egyptian pilot. It is therefore strongly recommended that at no time should the pilot be allowed to steer the boat, that the latest charts of the Canal are constantly referred to and that if it appears that the pilot is giving wrong instructions, such as advising the person at the helm to leave the main channel to cut a corner, the captain should use his or her commonsense before accepting such advice.

Further Reading

Red Sea Pilot
Mediterranean Cruising Handbook
Africa on a Shoestring

Websites

www.touregypt.net (Official website)
www.suez-canal.com
www.rafimar.com/suez (Canal transit and dues)
www.princeofredsea.com.eg (*Prince of the Red Sea*)

GEORGIA

The most spectacular scenery in the Black Sea and some of the best resorts in the former Soviet Union can now be found in this mountainous country bordering on the eastern shore of the Black Sea. Ethnic strife and economic problems, which have bedevilled other former Soviet republics, have also left their mark on Georgia. There is conflict in the two autonomous republics within Georgia, Abkhazia and Ajaria, as well as the autonomous region of South Ossetia, seeking greater independence from Georgia. Although tension continues in these areas, the situation in much of the country has stabilised and the government is making a determined effort to encourage foreign tourism. The coastal area south of Poti is considered to be safe, which is thought by many to be the most beautiful cruising area in the Black Sea.

Country Profile

The Georgian Republic is part of the Caucasus region. The Caucasian mountains, which stretch from the Black Sea to the Caspian Sea, form a natural frontier so that this whole area was always a refuge of peoples, forming an ethnic mosaic today, and a distinct cultural make-up.

Present-day Georgia was the site of Colchis, from where Jason and the Argonauts stole the Golden Fleece. The ancient Greeks and Romans colonised the area, and in the seventh century it was conquered by the Arabs. From the ninth to the thirteenth century Georgia experienced a considerable renaissance but suffered from the Mongolian invasions, as did the rest of this part of Europe. After losing territories to Iran and the Ottoman Empire in 1783 Georgia put itself under the protection of the Russian Empire. In 1801 it was annexed by Russia.

In 1918 an independent Republic was proclaimed, but the intervention of the Red Army in 1921 saw the establishment of a Soviet regime and in 1922 Georgia became part of the new USSR. Independence was declared in 1991. In 1993, threatened by separatists who controlled the Republic of Abkhazia, Georgia's head of state Edward Shevardnadze called on the help of the Russian army. This led to Georgia's adhesion to the newly founded Commonwealth of Independent States.

The fertile region is a producer of citrus fruit, tea and wine. There are coal, oil, manganese and peat deposits. Industry is dominated by shipbuilding, food processing and fertilisers. The disruption of the Soviet system and ongoing ethnic conflicts have caused economic problems, above all hyper-inflation. The re-election of President Edvard Shevarnadze in 2000 has been accompanied by a return to relative stability, both political and

Practical Information

LOCAL TIME: GMT + 3 (GMT + 4 summer time).

BUOYAGE: IALA A

CURRENCY: Lari. The import and export of local currency is prohibited. Foreign currency can only be exported up to the amount declared on arrival.

BUSINESS HOURS
Banks: 1000–1700 Monday to Friday, closed an hour for lunch.

ELECTRICITY: 220 V, 50 Hz

PUBLIC HOLIDAYS
1 January: New Year
Orthodox Christmas
Orthodox Easter
26 May: Independence Day
28 August: St Marian's Day
14 October: Khetkhob Day (Ancient capital of Georgia)
23 November: St George's Day

COMMUNICATIONS
All outgoing telephone calls go through the operator and long waits are inevitable. The postal system is also very slow. There are air links to Moscow and several West European cities from Tbilisi airport 11 miles (18 km) east of the capital.

MEDICAL
The health service provides free emergency treatment. Medicines must be paid for.

DIPLOMATIC MISSIONS
In Tbilisi:
Germany: Metechi Palace Hotel.
Tel. 744 556/623.
United Kingdom: Metechi Palace Hotel
Tel. 955 497, 998 447.
Turkey: Prospkekt David Agmasenebeli 61.
Tel. 329 52014.
United States: Ulitsa Atoneli 25.
Tel. 933 803/989 968.
In Batumi:
Turkey: Prospekt Memed Abashidze 8.
Tel. 227 4790.

economic, and the long-term prospects of the country are steadily improving.

The population is 5.4 million of which 70 per cent are Georgians and Georgian Orthodox. Other religions are Islam, Eastern Orthodox, Judaism and other Christian denominations. The capital is Tbilissi. The Georgian language is non-Indo European, being part of the Caucasian family, and has its own script. Also spoken are Russian, Ossetian, Abkhazian and Adzharian.

Protected by the Caucasian mountains, the region's climate is very pleasant and mild. On the coast summers are warm and humid.

Entry Regulations

Port of entry
Batumi 41°39′N 41°39′E, Poti 42°09′N 41°39′E.

Procedure on arrival
Formalities must be completed at an official port of entry. Everyone on board should have obtained a visa beforehand. An official invitation may also be required.

Customs
A detailed customs declaration must be completed on arrival, where foreign currency and valuables must be indicated. Firearms on board must also be declared.

Immigration
Russian consulates no longer issue tourist visas valid for Georgia. All nationals require visas except those of Bulgaria and Turkey. Visas can easily be obtained at the Georgian Consulate in Istanbul or on arrival at a port of entry. Otherwise, tour operators can obtain visas, for a fee. The tourist visa fee itself is US$30.

Health
Water should be treated before drinking.

Facilities

An expanding local yachting community and regular visits by the Black Sea Yacht Rally (KAYRA) have been accompanied by a gradual improvement of facilities, and while these are still modest by international standards, most emergency repairs can be done locally. For any help it is best to contact the local yacht clubs in either Batumi or Poti.

Provisioning is good and diesel fuel is available in all ports.

Advance help and practical advice for anyone planning to visit any of the Black Sea countries, not just Georgia, is best obtained from Mr Dülger, Assistant Manager at Ataköy Marina near Istanbul. The marina is located close to the southern end of the Bosphorus. *Tel.* +90 212 560 4270, Fax. 7270, *e-mail*: a_marina@atakoymarina.com.tr.

Further Reading

Black Sea Cruising Guide

Website

www.parliament.ge/tourism (List of useful addresses)

GIBRALTAR

At the crossroads of two seas and two continents, Gibraltar's unique position as the gateway to the Mediterranean has given it an importance far exceeding its small size and population. Only two and a half miles long, barely a mile wide, the peninsula drops sheerly from a height of 1400 ft (427 m) down to the sea. The rock is made of limestone and riddled with caves, a feature used by all its inhabitants throughout the ages.

Very few yachts on their way to or from the Mediterranean fail to stop in this historic port, which has become one of the most frequented yachting centres in the world. Yachts from all parts of the globe call at Gibraltar every year and the facilities at their disposal are some of the best in the area. Although many yachts spend considerable time in Gibraltar, its main function continues to be that of a transit port, a role which the Rock has fulfilled throughout its colourful and often turbulent history. The movement of yachts is virtually continuous, although there are clearly defined peak periods. Spring and early summer sees boats arriving from across the Atlantic or Northern Europe bound for the Mediterranean. The autumn months see a large movement in the opposite direction as many cruising yachts leave the Mediterranean, usually bound for Madeira and the Canaries en route to the Caribbean. Although a convenient place for repairs and reprovisioning,

Gibraltar is also a good place to relax and its cosmopolitan makeup serves this function well.

Country Profile

Prehistoric human remains have been found on the Rock, the early Gibraltarians sheltering in the caves as the Ice Age drew to a close. One of the two Pillars of Hercules, in ancient times Gibraltar marked the limit of the civilised world, beyond which early sailors dared not venture. It was only in the eighth century, with the Moorish expansion into Europe, that people settled. Moorish leader Tarik-ibn-Zeyad conquered most of the Iberian peninsula from this settlement and the Rock was named Tarik's mountain, Gebel Tarik, in his honour, the name evolving eventually into modern day Gibraltar.

The Moors were driven out by the Spanish in

Marina Bay Marina overshadowed by the Rock of Gibraltar.

1462 and under Spanish rule Gibraltar assumed its military importance, with the opening up of the New World and the struggles of Spain, France and Britain to gain maritime supremacy in the region. In 1704 an Anglo-Dutch force seized Gibraltar, which Spain agreed to leave in British hands, as the British had backed the successful contender for the Spanish throne, then in dispute. Later Spanish efforts to recapture the Rock failed repeatedly, the most notable being the Great Siege of 1779–82, the successful defence giving rise to the saying 'safe as the rock of Gibraltar'.

Through all the major wars of the last two centuries, Gibraltar played a crucial part for the British Empire. Used as a base during the Battle of Trafalgar in the Napoleonic Wars, it was here that the body of Admiral Nelson was brought by HMS *Victory*. The Suez Canal further increased the Rock's importance as a provisioning stop. In the two World Wars its position and facilities were greatly appreciated by the Allied navies.

Although still remaining a British colony, since the Second World War Gibraltar has become largely

Practical Information

LOCAL TIME: GMT + 1. Summer time GMT + 2 April to September.

BUOYAGE: IALA A

CURRENCY: The Gibraltar pound is equal to the pound sterling, which can also be used. Spanish pesetas are accepted in many shops.

BUSINESS HOURS
Banks: 0930–1530 Monday to Thursday, Friday 0900–1530, 1630–1800.
Shops: 0930–1300, 1500–1900 Monday to Friday, 0930–1300 Saturday.
Government offices: winter: 0845–1315, 1415–1730; summer: 0800–1430 Monday to Friday.

PUBLIC HOLIDAYS
As for United Kingdom, except:
1 May: May Day
June: Queen's Birthday
4 September: National Day

COMMUNICATIONS
International calls can be dialled direct from public telephones, direct dialling access code 00. Operator connected international calls can be made from Gibraltar Telecom Office, Main St. International telephone calls can also be made from the marinas.
Marina Communications, 2nd floor Neptune House, Marina Bay. Both their telex and fax may be used by clients.
Post office: Main Street, 0900–1300, 1400–1700 Monday to Thursday,

1500–1800 Friday.
Emergency: Police/ambulance 199; fire 190.
There are several daily flights to London and regular flights to Tangiers.

MEDICAL
British subjects can obtain medical treatment at St Bernards Hospital on the same basis as in Britain. EU nationals can obtain similar treatment on presentation of form E111.
International Health Clinic, Neptune House, Marina Bay.

---

self-governing, with an elected House of Assembly. However, under General Franco, Spain renewed her claim, embarking in the 1960s on the fifteenth siege in Gibraltar's history. The frontier was closed and other links cut despite the fact that Gibraltarians had voted overwhelmingly in a referendum to remain with Britain. The death of Franco, subsequent liberalisation of Spain and then the Spanish application to join the European Community made the closed frontier absurd, and finally in April 1985 the border was reopened by Spain.

The Gibraltar Social Democrats, led by Peter Caruana, who favour dialogue with Spain, won the elections in May 1996 and again in March 2000, so the policy of rapprochement with their neighbour is expected to continue.

Tourism is Gibraltar's main industry, one in which yachting plays an important role. The opening of the land border with Spain has had an important effect on Gibraltar's economy. Gibraltar is also expanding in the field of international banking and as a tax haven.

The population of Gibraltar is 30,000. Gibraltarians are a mixture of many nationalities, mainly Spanish and British, but also Genoese, Jewish, Menorcan and Maltese settlers, as well as Portuguese and Moroccan immigrants. Although English is the official language, most of the inhabitants usually speak Spanish amongst themselves. Most Gibraltarians are Christian, although there are also Jewish and Muslim communities living on the Rock.

The tall rock attracts its own weather, often being covered by low cloud. Such mist is often a sign that the *Levanter*, a strong easterly wind, is on its way. Usually caused by an approaching Atlantic low, the latter can reach gale force rapidly, lasting for several days. About 80 per cent of the winds blow either from the east or west. *Poniente* is the name of the westerly wind, which is also preceded by low cloud. With the Atlantic Ocean so near, Gibraltar's weather is not entirely Mediterranean. However, it is generally a pleasant climate with warm summers and mild winters.

Entry Regulations

Port of entry
Gibraltar 36°08′N 05°21′W.

Procedure on arrival
The daytime approach to Gibraltar is straightforward. At night, entry into Gibraltar Bay can be more difficult. The easiest way to find the reporting dock is by heading for the airport runway. The main harbour should not be entered at night, as there are several unlit buoys.

Gibraltar Radio monitors VHF Channel 16 permanently, as do the marinas during office hours. The yellow 'Q' flag must be flown by all yachts, and those that intend to dock at either Marina Bay or Sheppard's Marina must make their way to the reporting dock, reached by rounding the north end of the north mole. Yachts should come alongside this dock in front of the low white official building next to the fuelling station. Customs, immigration and port formalities must be completed immediately on arrival and the offices operate 24 hours a day. After clearance has been completed, one can move to one of the two marinas located nearby. The working channel for all marinas is now 71.

Boats headed for Queensway Marina can complete formalities at the marina office, who will forward the relevant papers to the customs office. If this scheme is successful, it is envisaged that the present customs office will be closed and all clearance formalities will be carried out by the staff of one of the marinas.

Yachts must dock at one of the three marinas, as anchoring or berthing anywhere in the harbour area is only allowed with the permission of the harbour master.

Customs

Firearms must be declared on arrival. Guns are impounded and kept until departure.

Quarantine regulations no longer apply to animals, although they must be declared on arrival.

Any items which yachts wish to import duty free must be reported to customs on arrival.

If sending items out of Gibraltar for repair, customs must inspect them first and be informed of the details. Incoming equipment must be clearly marked 'yacht spares in transit to . . .'.

Yachts can be temporarily imported into Gibraltar without paying duty by a non-resident for a maximum of 18 months within a three-year period. In excess of this time, the yacht becomes eligible for 12 per cent duty. However, yachts can be left unaccompanied in Gibraltar for more than 18 months without paying duty, with the permission of customs, who will place the vessel under bond.

Gibraltar is part of the European Union but outside the VAT area.

Immigration

As a British colony, holders of EU passports do not require visas when visiting Gibraltar. Generally similar immigration rules apply as for Britain, but nationals of countries normally requiring visas for Britain are usually allowed to stop in Gibraltar if they arrive and leave by yacht.

Immigration should be notified of any crew changes, and any passenger or crew member, who is staying ashore while the yacht is in port, must notify Immigration Control at the Waterport Police Station, open 0930–1300 Monday to Friday, also Friday 1530–1700. Immigration must also be informed of the time and date of the yacht's departure.

Warning

Tuna nets are a hazard, especially in the spring and summer, as they are laid along the Spanish coast in the approaches to the Straits of Gibraltar, sometimes several miles offshore. Normally the nets have one or more fishing boats in attendance. The vessel on the seaward end of the net should fly a black flag with 'A' on it by day, and two red lights, or red and white lights on each mast by night. Yachts should pass to seaward of the nets, which often extend 2–3 miles outwards, and float just below the surface. Yachts should not attempt to go between the inner marks and the shore.

Fees

There are no overtime fees.

Facilities

It was the large charter yachts plying between the Mediterranean and Caribbean each season that stimulated Gibraltar into developing its yachting facilities to a high standard. Almost everything can be accomplished here in the way of repair or maintenance, with a wide range of boatyards and workshops providing all essential services. Several companies offer haul-out facilities, either by travel-ift or slipway, some of the latter being able to cope with vessels of several hundred tons. Most major marine product manufacturers are represented by local agents and there is a very well stocked chandlery at Sheppard's Marina. Goods can be air-freighted from Britain in two days. There is also a British Admiralty chart agent in Gibraltar.

Duty-free stores are also available and the price of spirits is probably the lowest in the Mediterranean. Many shops in town sell goods at duty-free prices but even the local taxes are much lower than in the rest of the European Union as VAT (Value Added Tax) is not charged in Gibraltar. Many foreign yachts based in nearby Spanish ports use Gibraltar for both its good repair facilities, duty-free shopping and the easier importation of vital spare parts as compared to Spain.

Provisioning is very good. Most supplies are imported from Britain and prices are reasonable. There is also a good selection of fresh produce, but as virtually all of it is imported either from Spain or Morocco, for a long passage it may be better to shop for fresh produce elsewhere.

Fuel is available from the fuel dock near Marina Bay Marina and also from the CEPSA barge moored on the north side of the inner harbour, close to Queensway Marina.

The best docking facilities are those at Marina Bay, which is now linked to Sheppard's by a walkway. Queensway Marina is reported to be affected by swell in SW winds, but the recent reorientation of the pontoons has improved the situation. All marinas offer reduced winter rates.

Further Reading

Cruising Association Handbook
Straits Sailing Handbook

Websites

www.gibraltar.gi (Gibraltar Tourist Board)
www.gibraltar.gi/port/yachtingmain.html (Yachting information)

GREECE

Spread out in the eastern Mediterranean, Greece consists of the mainland with the capital Athens, the Peloponnese peninsula and a multitude of islands in both the Ionian and Aegean seas, including the large island of Crete to the south.

If one were to grade the top ten cruising destinations in the world according to such criteria as scenic beauty, weather conditions and variety of ports and anchorages, Greece would definitely be among them. If one also takes into account the wealth of things to be seen ashore, as well as that most important ingredient, a pleasant waterfront restaurant or cafe to while away the balmy evening after a hard day's sail, Greece would probably be right at the top of the list.

The Aegean in particular seems to have been tailormade for cruising and after a relatively slow start in the 1970s, yachting in Greece took off at great speed in the 1980s. Although the more popular places are quite crowded, especially during the high season, the situation is not as bad as it may appear from a distance. There are still plenty of less frequented places dotted around the rim of the Aegean and some of the more remote islands rarely see more than a handful of yachts. The crowds are also seasonal and it certainly pays to cruise Greece outside of the peak summer months, ideally around Easter, which is the main holiday in the Greek Orthodox calendar. The autumn months are just as attractive; both winds and weather are more pleasant than in the *meltemi*-swept months of high summer.

More than the pleasant weather and picturesque ports, what makes Greece such a special place is the profusion of historical sites, most of which are within a short distance of the sea. The Greeks have always had an affinity with the sea and nothing they ever built was far from it. Among the sites that should not be missed are those on the mainland, the Acropolis of Athens and the temple at Delphi. On the northern shore of the Peloponnese is ancient Corinth, while not far inland are the ruins of Sparta, the magnificent stadium at Olympia and the impressive fortifications of Mycenae. The islands also abound in sites, such as those at Delos, the birthplace of Apollo and Artemis, or the palace and labyrinth of the legendary King Minos at Knossos on Crete. Closer to modern times are some magnificent churches and monasteries such as those on Patmos, Symi or Chios. Whether afloat or ashore, Greece undoubtedly caters for all tastes.

Country Profile

Greece is considered the birthplace of Western civilisation, and the oldest state in Europe existed on the island of Crete from about 3000 until 1450 BC. Meanwhile on the mainland Indo-European peoples had moved down from the north and settled, developing other states and kingdoms. The events which Homer wrote about later on were probably based on fact. In this legendary time, Greece was divided into many kingdoms, but these came together under Agamemnon, King of Mycenae, to besiege Troy for nine years. Something of a dark age followed this heroic period until a Renaissance occurred in the ninth century BC based on the city-states of Ionia on the Asia Minor coast. In the fifth century BC, Persia, the dominant power of the East, was defeated several times and the city of Athens grew in power and established an empire. After the end of war with Persia and making peace with the bellicose state of Sparta, Athens became the unrivalled cultural centre in the Mediterranean. Alexander of Macedonia established the greatest empire yet seen in Europe

Practical Information

LOCAL TIME: GMT + 2. Summer time GMT + 1 from early April to late September.

BUOYAGE: IALA A

CURRENCY: Drachma (GDR). Euro from 2002. 1 euro = 340.750 GDR. Currency worth more than $1000 must be declared to customs.

BUSINESS HOURS
Banks: 0800–1400 Monday to Friday (some have exchange counters in afternoons and at weekends).
Business: 0800–1330, 1630–1930.
Shops: 0800–1500 Monday, Wednesday, Saturday and 0800–1400/1730–2030 Tuesday, Thursday, Friday.
Government offices: 0730–1430.
Hours may differ in summer.

ELECTRICITY: 220 V, 50 Hz

PUBLIC HOLIDAYS
1 January: New Year's Day
6 January: Epiphany
March: Shrove Monday*
25 March: Independence Day
Good Friday, Easter Monday (Orthodox)*
Whit Tuesday*, 1 May
15 August: Assumption
28 October: Ohi Day
25, 26 December: Christmas
*Variable

EVENTS
The Orthodox Easter is more important than Christmas, and calculated differently to the Catholic and Protestant Easter. Open air festivals of music and drama in summer.

COMMUNICATIONS
International operator 162.
Tourist police *Tel.* 171.
OTE = Telecommunications Organisation, international telephones available in all towns. Metered international calls can also be made from kiosks, tobacconists and shops.
ELTA = Post Office open 0800–1400 Monday to Friday, 0800–1330 Saturday. There are frequent flights from Athens to all parts of the world and also some from Thessalonika. International flights to the islands are mainly charter flights. Frequent ferry services run to all the islands.

DIPLOMATIC MISSIONS
In Athens:
Australia: 37, Odos Dimitriou Soutsou, Ambelokipi. *Tel.* (1) 644-7303.
Canada: 4, Ioannou Gennadiou St. *Tel.* (1) 725-4011.
New Zealand: Semitelou 9, *Tel.* 771-0112.
United Kingdom: 1, Ploutarchou St. *Tel.* (1) 727-2600.
United States: 91, Vasilissis Sophias Blvd. *Tel.* (1) 721-2951.

---

and Asia, stretching as far as Persia. Greece's time of greatness came to an end with the rise of Rome and it became a political backwater. Waves of invasions by Macedonians, Franks and Serbs overran the peninsula.

From the fourteenth century the Ottoman empire dominated the Balkans, and the Turks ruled Greece for four centuries. As the Ottoman empire declined, so Greek nationalism became a growing force. In 1821–2 the Greeks rebelled against the Turks and declared their independence, but this was only recognised after years of war in the 1829 treaty of Adrianopolis. The new state gradually expanded its frontiers to the present day state, incorporating the Ionian islands, Thessaly and Crete, at the expense of Turkey and her Balkan neighbours. Following general dissatisfaction, in 1924 the army proclaimed a republic, although in 1935 the monarchy was restored.

Despite a desire to remain neutral in the Second World War, Greece was invaded by Italy and Germany, and in response a strong resistance movement developed. In 1946 the country became embroiled in a bitter civil war until the communists were defeated in 1949 by General Papagos. His party brought some industrialisation and prosperity, until instability returned in the 1960s. In 1967 a group of army colonels took power and established a dictatorial regime led by Georgios Papadopoulos. The King was deposed and a republic proclaimed in 1973. The crisis which erupted over the invasion of Cyprus by Turkey in 1974 saw the end of the colonels' regime, and a gradual return to democracy and more prosperity. This was also helped by Greece becoming a member of the European Union.

The main industries are shipping and tourism. Agriculture still employs about 20 per cent of the population and fruit, olive oil and tobacco are exported. Fish farming, subsidised by the EU, is a growing industry and may affect yachts as the farms occupy more space in anchorages.

The population of Greece is 10.5 million and the Greek language has its own alphabet of 24 letters still bearing some relationship to Ancient Greek. The majority of Greeks are Orthodox Christian.

Spring and autumn weather is the most pleasant, while the summer is hot and dry. Winters are mild in Crete and Rhodes and cooler as one moves north as well as inland. The prevailing winds of summer are northerly. The seasonal wind of summer, called *etesian* in Greece because of its seasonal character, but better known by its Turkish name *meltemi*, sets in about May and lasts until September. It blows at its strongest in July and August when it can reach force 7 and even 8 on occasions. Violent storms occur only in winter, February being a particularly bad month, but overall the weather is pleasant and extreme conditions are rarely known.

Entry Regulations

Ports of entry
Mainland: Alexandroupolis 40°51′N 25°57′E, Vouliagmeni 37°48′N 23°46′E, Glifada 37°52′N 23°44′E, Itea 38°26′N 22°25′E, Kavala 40°55′N 24°25′E, Lavrion 37°42′N 24°04′E, Piraeus (Zea) 37°56′N 23°38′E, Preveza 38°57′N 20°45′E, Volos 39°21′N 22°56′E, Thessaloniki 40°38′N 22°56′E.
Peloponnese: Kalamata 37°00′N 22°07′E, Katakolon 37°39′N 21°20′E, Nafplion 37°40′N 22°48′E, Patras 38°15′N 21°44′E, Pilos 36°55′N 21°42′E.
Ionian Islands: Argostoli (Cephalonia) 38°12′N 20°29′E, Corfu Port 39°37′N 19°57′E, Zakinthos 37°47′N 20°54′E.
Aegean Islands: Chios 38°23′N 26°09′E, Kos 36°53′N 27°19′E. Lesvos (Mitilini) 39°06′N 26°05′E, Limnos (Mirina) 39°52′N 25°04′E, Rhodos (Mandraki) 36°27′N 28°14′E, Samos (Pithagorion) 37°45′N 27°00′E, Siros 37°26′N 24°57′E.
Crete: Iraklion 35°16′N 25°09′E, Hania 35°31′N 24°01′E, Agios Nikolaos 35°11′N 25°43′E.

Procedure on arrival
The Greek courtesy flag must be flown and also it should be in good condition, as torn or frayed flags are regarded as a sign of disrespect.

As Greece is a member of the European Union, formalities for EU vessels and nationals should be simple, although this does not appear to be always the case. Formalities for non-EU vessels can be just as complicated as before and so the entire procedure is described below, even if in practice this may not be adhered to as strictly by local officials. On arrival in Greece all boats must clear with port authority, customs and health as well as immigration and currency control. The ship's papers will be inspected by the port authority, then customs will issue a transit log, renewable after six months but valid for one year. At subsequent ports this transit log may be inspected by the port authority, mainly in the large ports and occasionally in smaller harbours. The port authorities may also want a passenger and crew list on departure from each port. Where there is no port authority, local police

or customs officials may wish to see the log. Sometimes the log is kept until departure from a port. In principle, the transit log should be issued only to non-EU vessels, or to EU vessels wishing to purchase fuel at duty-free prices. A new document was introduced in 2000 for EU boats; this must be stamped in and out by each port authority.

A fee is charged for the transit log and by customs for each fuel delivery.

Customs
Firearms must be declared.

Cats and dogs require health and rabies inoculation certificates issued in the country of origin, not more than 12 months previously for dogs, six months for cats, and not less than six days before arrival. Birds also need a health certificate.

Immigration
A visa is not required for a visit of up to three months for nationals of the European Union, Andorra, Antigua, Argentina, Australia, Canada, Cyprus, Czech Republic, Ecuador, Hungary, Iceland, Israel, Japan, Liechtenstein, Malta, Mexico, New Zealand, Nicaragua, Norway, St Kitts and Nevis, South Korea, Norway, San Marino, Slovak Republic, Switzerland, Taiwan, the USA and Zimbabwe.

Visas are also not required for nationals of Brazil, Chile, Uruguay for a visit of up to two months, Hong Kong and Peru up to one month and Singapore up to two weeks.

Visas must be issued in advance for all other nationalities and are valid for up to three months, depending on nationality.

Extensions of visas can be obtained from the nearest police station or Aliens Department, Leoforos Alexandros 173, Athens.

Entry may be refused if there are Turkish Cyprus stamps in the passport.

Transit log
This is completed in Greek and English with details of the yacht, crew, fuel and other provisions. The log authorises the yacht to sail in Greek waters for its period of validity. The log must be produced when requested and must also record any crew changes. After six months the log can be renewed for another six months.

Crew and passengers on board a yacht are considered by the authorities to be in transit, and the transit log only authorises day visits inland, the nights being presumed to be spent on board. The harbour master and immigration should be notified if travelling away from the yacht overnight or if an individual leaves Greece by other means such as by air. These changes have to be noted in the transit log and entry and exit stamps put into the passport. Individual passports are not stamped on entry into Greece by yacht, nor is this required for departure with the same yacht. However, if leaving by another means, these stamps are required by immigration at the point of exit.

On departure from Greece, the transit log must be returned to customs at the port of exit. If the yacht is being left in Greece for the winter, the log should be handed in to customs and a new one issued when returning to the yacht. A photocopy of the log should be shown to immigration officials when leaving the country by other means.

Restrictions

Fishing is forbidden with scuba gear and is only permitted with a snorkel in undeveloped areas. Scuba diving is restricted in Greece. Permission should be sought locally before diving.

Chartering by foreign yachts from Greek ports is illegal and is punishable by heavy fines. Because the registered owner of the boat is expected to be on board, if a friend is allowed to use the boat in the owner's absence, a proper document should be prepared, in Greek, stating this.

Canals

Corinth Canal: Opened in 1893, the canal separates mainland Greece from the Peloponnese. It has a length of 4 miles (about 6 km) and a depth of 26 ft (8 m). The canal is state owned, the canal authority being the Corinth Canal SA. The cut is too narrow for ships to pass each other, so one must get permission to proceed. Contact the authorities on VHF Channel 11 for which time to be at the canal entrance. There are waiting areas at both ends. Pilotage is not compulsory.

The pilot service will supply a declaration form, which must be completed and returned to the control tower at the east entrance, where payment is made. Payment is calculated on the net tonnage recorded on the original registration certificate of the vessel. If only gross tonnage is shown, the fees are calculated as 80 per cent of the gross tonnage. If neither tonnage is on the registration certificate, the length of the vessel will be the basis for the calculation.

A vessel can only enter the canal when a permit has been granted by the Canal Service. A blue flag by day and a white light by night indicates entrance is permitted. A red flag by day and two vertical white lights by night show that entry is prohibited.

More details can be obtained from the Corinth Canal Company, 88 Hippocratous Street, Athens.
Evripos Canal: Between Euboea (Evia) Island and the mainland, the bridge only opens at slack tide or when ships can pass with a following tide, as there is a very strong current at other times. There are no tolls for the opening of the Halkis bridge.
Lefkas Canal: This canal separating the island of Lefkas from the mainland has existed since ancient times. It is used mainly by local craft as a short cut to nearby Ionian islands. It has been dredged to a minimum depth of 15 ft (4.5 m). There is no toll. The canal opens on the hour from 0800 to 2200.

Fees

All public harbours now charge a mooring or anchoring fee based on the tonnage and length of the boat. Boats from EU countries pay lower fees than those from non-EU countries, while Greek flagged boats pay even less. There is a basic fee charged at every port for completing the paperwork. The formula used is: G.T. × 100 Dr. The daily mooring fee is LOA (in feet) × 100 Dr. (alongside a quay or pontoon), LOA (in feet) × 33 Dr. (if moored stern or bow to). A lower fee is charged for anchoring. In most ports these fees are charged even if stopping for provisions only, or even to buy fuel.

A controversial fee was introduced in 2000 and it applies to all cruising yachts in Greece. A fee of 2000 Dr. per metre must be paid by each yacht at the first port of entry. However, the rule appears to contradict the principle of free movement within the European Union and may be repelled as it has caused widespread discontent both among sailors and marine-related businesses.

Facilities

The recent expansion in yachting has been accompanied by a parallel development in facilities. Although some of those who know Greece from before may not regard this expansion as a blessing, their alarm is unfounded, as none of the picturesque ports have been ruined by the construction of pontoons in centuries old harbours. Most marinas have been built inside newly built breakwaters or reclaimed land and in most islands yachts still either come stern-to the existing quay, if there is space, or stay at anchor. Most of the new marinas are on the mainland and this is also where the best repair facilities are.

The greatest concentration of facilities is in the

Athens–Piraeus area, where there are several boat-yards with hauling-out facilities and a full range of repair services. Permission is required from the port police to haul out a yacht and also when returning it to the water. Haul-out facilities are available at Alimos, Aretsou, Flisvos, Glifada, Mandraki, Lavrion, Patras, Porto Carras and Zea.

Marine equipment is available at all marinas and also in the ports frequented by cruising or charter boats.

Diesel fuel is widely available, usually on the dock in marinas and most ports. Foreign yachts can buy fuel at duty-free prices, which must be arranged through customs, but formalities are lengthy and complicated. Stations that sell fuel for foreign yachts are marked by blue and yellow diagonal stripes on the quay. Water is available in most ports, but usually one has to pay. In summer in some of the smaller islands it may be difficult to obtain any large quantity of water, so one should try to arrive with full tanks from the mainland. Provisioning is generally good and fresh locally grown produce is available everywhere.

Further Reading

Greek Waters Pilot
Mediterranean Cruising Handbook
Blue Guide Greece
The Greek Islands

Websites

www.gnto.gr (National Tourism Organisation)
www.yachting.gr/links (Useful addresses)

ISRAEL

Israel is a small country on the Eastern Mediterranean shore, but one with a wealth of history and culture. A symbol for three of the world's major religions, settlement of this country has always been hotly disputed.

The coast is low with no natural harbours or anchorages and visiting yachts have the choice of only a few marinas and ports. An unexciting coast-line, stringent security controls and recurring internal problems have kept most cruising yachts away from this interesting country, where yachting facilities have been steadily improving to cater for an expanding resident boating community. The few foreign yachts who make the detour to reach Israel during a cruise of the Eastern Mediterranean are rewarded with the opportunity to visit many of the well-known ancient sites. A sojourn in Israel also provides a unique opportunity to experience and perhaps understand some of the reasons for the continuing tension in the Middle East.

Country Profile

Lying between Africa and Asia on the edge of Europe, this region has had many peoples move back and forth across it throughout its history. Inhabited from earliest times it was known as Canaan and from 1220–1200 BC the Hebrews conquered the country, developing a monarchy with Jerusalem as its capital.

After King Solomon's death his kingdom split into Israel and Judah, was invaded by the Assyrians, and the Israelites scattered. The region was made a province of the Roman empire in 64–63 BC.

In the fourth century the Byzantine Emperor Constantine encouraged the development of Christianity, and many pilgrims travelled to what became known as the Holy Land. The Arabs, adherents of the new religion preached by Mohammed, invaded in the seventh century ending Byzantine rule.

When in the eleventh century the Ottoman Turks captured Jerusalem and refused to cooperate with visiting Christian pilgrims, the Pope called for a liberating crusade. Crusaders came from all over Europe and occupied Jerusalem. The Christian kingdom of Jerusalem lasted until the thirteenth century, after which the Mamelukes of Egypt took over until the Ottoman Turks made it part of their empire in 1517. In the seventeenth and eighteenth centuries Jewish immigration and settlement in Palestine increased, especially from Eastern Europe.

In the First World War the Allies sought Arab and Jewish support to topple the Ottomans, although promises for Jewish aspirations to form a state remained vague. After the war Britain occupied Palestine as a League of Nations mandate. The 1920s and 30s saw many Jews immigrate, and Jewish–Arab relations deteriorate, often into violence. The British tried unsuccessfully to control immigration in an attempt to keep racial tension down, and the Zionist movement carried out terrorist attacks against Britain. The state of Israel was declared unilaterally in 1948, following the withdrawal of British troops. Since then the surrounding Arab countries have been in conflict with the country which they call Palestine. In 1979 some peace came to the area when Israel and Egypt signed a Peace Treaty, but from 1987 the Palestinian revolt (Intifadah) and Jewish settlement in the Occupied Territories kept up tension. In 1993 the mutual recognition of Israel and the Palestinian Liberation Organisation led to an agreement for establishing Palestinian autonomy in the disputed territories.

The peace process continued to be stalled during the Netanyahu government in the late 1990s, but was put back on track with the election of Ehud Barak who worked towards normalising relations with both Syria and the Lebanon.

Industry in Israel is increasingly important for the economy. Agriculture produces enough for domestic needs as well as for export. The tourist industry is developed, and US aid remains considerable. However, the country has had very high inflation, and the economy is not helped by

The Wailing Wall in front of the Mosque of the Rock, two of the major religious sites of the city of Jerusalem.

the costly military budget and lack of mineral resources or water supply.

The population of Israel is 6 million, over half of which are Jews of very mixed cultures and national origins. The rest are mainly Palestinian and concentrated in East Jerusalem, the West Bank and the Gaza area. Hebrew is the national language, but Arabic is spoken by the Palestinians. Also spoken is Yiddish, which is a combination of Hebrew and medieval German, and Ladino, which derives from Hebrew and Spanish. English is widely spoken and many other languages are spoken by recent immigrants. Judaism as practised by Jews in Israel covers many facets from the most orthodox to the most liberal. Some of the Palestinian Arabs are Christian, although the majority are Muslim. Many Christian denominations have a presence in the capital Jerusalem, which has several holy sites for Jews, Christians and Muslims. Israel is also a centre for the Baha'i faith.

The climate is generally temperate, the winters being cool and rainy, the summers hot and dry. In summer, winds along the coast alternate between land and sea breezes.

Practical Information

LOCAL TIME: GMT + 2. Summer time GMT + 3.

BUOYAGE: IALA A

CURRENCY: New shekel (NIS) of 100 agorot. US$ are also used. Payments made in foreign currency are exempt from 15 per cent Value Added Tax (VAT). VAT refunds can be obtained by presenting the receipts of purchases made in foreign currency to a bank before departure.

BUSINESS HOURS
These vary a lot, depending on religion. The Jewish Shabbat from sunset Friday to sunset Saturday means that on Friday afternoon and Saturday, most shops, offices and places of entertainment are closed. Public transport also does not run, Haifa being an exception.
Banks: hours vary, but generally open Sunday to Tuesday, Thursday 0830–1230/1600–1730. Monday, Wednesday 0830–1230. Friday and the eve of holy days 0830–1200.
Business: November to May 0800–1300, 1500–1800, Sunday to Thursday, 0730–1230 Friday.
June to October 0730–1430 Sunday to Thursday, 0730–1230 Friday. Muslim

businesses close Friday, Christian businesses on Sundays.
Shops: 0800–1300, 1600–1900 Monday to Thursday, 0800–1400 Friday.
Government offices: September to May 0700–1300 Sunday to Thursday, 0730–1430 Friday, June to August 0730–1430 Sunday to Thursday, 0730–1300 Friday.

ELECTRICITY: 220 V, 50 Hz

PUBLIC HOLIDAYS
Many of the Jewish holidays are variable.
February/March: Purim – Carnival
February/March: Feast of Passover Holocaust Day
April/May: Independence Day
May/June: Shavuot
September/October: Rosh Ha-Shanah, Day of Judgement
Yom Kippur, Day of Atonement
October: Sukkot
October: Simhat Torah
December/January: 8 days of Hanukkah
Muslim and Christian holidays are kept by those sections of the population.

COMMUNICATIONS
International calls can be made from main post offices. Collect calls can be made

from public phones. International operator: dial 18/03. Public phones need tokens.
International telephone office: 7 Mikve Yisrael St, Tel Aviv. Open Sunday to Thursday 0800–1800, Friday 0800–1400.
Tel Aviv's main post office: 132 Allenby Road on corner of Yehuda Ha Levi St, open Sunday to Thursday 0700–2000, Friday 0700–1400.
Emergency: police 100, ambulance 101, fire service 102.
Most international flights for European and North American destinations leave from Tel Aviv airport.

MEDICAL
Medical care is of a high standard.

DIPLOMATIC MISSIONS
In Tel Aviv:
Egypt: 54 Rehov Babel.
Sunday to Thursday 0900–1100 for visas. Can be collected 1200–1300 the same day. *Tel.* 5464151.
United Kingdom: 192 Hayarkon Street. *Tel.* 5249171/8, Fax. 5243313.
United States: 71 Hayarkon Street. *Tel.* 5197575, Fax. 5102444.
Canada: 3 Nirim, Beit Hasapanut. *Tel.* 6363300.

Entry Regulations

Ports of entry
Haìfa 32°49′N 35°00′E, Ashdod 31°49′N 34°38′E, Eilat 29°33′N 34°57′E, Tel Aviv Marina 32°05′N 34°46′E, Ashkelon 31°41′N 34°33′E, Herzliya 32°10′N 34°48′E.

Procedure on arrival
When 40 miles from the coast, a position report with the yacht details and ETA should be sent via VHF radio to the Israeli Navy. All marinas monitor Channel 16, but use different working channels: 11 at Herzliya, Ashkelon and Eilat, 10 at Tel Aviv, and 9 at Ashdod Marina. Channel 16 must be monitored permanently.

On approaching the coast yachts may be met by an armed patrol boat and asked for details of the yacht and crew. Sometimes the yacht is boarded for inspection while still offshore. On arrival yachts

are met by customs and immigration. The yacht may be searched for arms or explosives.

Customs
Firearms must be declared.

Dogs, cats and birds need a veterinary health certificate issued in the country of origin. Dogs over three months old need a rabies vaccination certificate issued between one year and one month before arrival. If the yacht carries more than two of any of these animals and other species of animal, an import permit issued by the Director of Veterinary Services is required. A written application must be received not less than 10 days before the planned arrival of such animals.

Immigration
Passports must be valid for a minimum of six months from the date of arrival.

Nationals of the following countries do not require visas, or will have them issued free of charge on arrival: the European Union, Argentina, Australia, Bahamas, Barbados, Brazil, Bolivia, Canada, Central African Republic, Chile, Colombia, Costa Rica, Cyprus, Dominican Republic, Ecuador, El Salvador, Fiji, Guatemala, Haiti, Hungary, Hong Kong, Iceland, Jamaica, Japan, Liechtenstein, Malawi, Malta, Mauritius, Mexico, New Zealand, Netherlands Antilles, Norway, Paraguay, Philippines, San Marino, Slovenia, South Africa, St Kitts and Nevis, Surinam, Swaziland, Switzerland, Trinidad, Uruguay, and the USA.

All nationals require an immigration stamp on arrival.

Other nationalities must apply for visas in advance, and pay a fee. Normally a three-month stay is granted on arrival. After three months, one can apply for a visa or extension of a visa at a Ministry of the Interior office. This extension is usually for a further three months. Office hours 0800–1200 Sunday to Thursday. Monday, Wednesday open 1400–1500. Tel Aviv: Shalom Meyer Tower, 9 Ahad Ha'am St. Haifa: Government Building (opposite Municipality), 11 Hassan Shukri St.

Important note If one is planning to visit Arab countries or countries who do not recognise Israel, one may be refused entry to those countries if possessing an Israeli stamp in one's passport. Therefore one should request the Israeli immigration officer not to stamp the passport on arrival and departure. The officials are aware of this problem and usually provide a loose leaf of paper to slip in the passport, which can be stamped. However, if applying for an extension after the initial three months, this will automatically be stamped in the passport.

Cruising permit
This must be applied for within 30 days of arrival.

Restrictions
There are several areas prohibited to yachts. Information on these areas is obtainable from chart suppliers and is drawn on Navy charts, which are available in every marina.

Health
Typhoid and polio vaccinations are recommended.

Fees
Overtime is payable on weekends and public holidays. Harbour fees are calculated on length. There are light fees.

Facilities

Although not a prime cruising destination, Israel's yachting facilities are rapidly expanding as more Israelis discover the pleasures of sailing. The largest sailing community is in Tel Aviv, where the best facilities are concentrated and Tel Aviv Marina offers a good range of services including fuel and water on the dock. There are two chandleries with a good selection close by and marine charts are also available locally. There are various workshops in the area, including haul-out by crane (25 tons). A whole range of repairs can be undertaken, such as engine, electronic, fibreglass or sail repair. There is a small marina at Jaffa, situated close to Tel Aviv. The entrances to both Tel Aviv and Jaffa Marina are difficult and should not be used in strong onshore winds.

Haifa offers a similar range with haul-out facilities, various workshops and docking facilities at the local yacht club. There is also a marina at Akko, north of Haifa. As Haifa tends to be crowded and very dirty, the marina at Akko is to be preferred. Some limited facilities are also available at Eilat, Israel's port on the Red Sea, where the new marina has expanded into the nearby lagoon. New marinas have opened at Ashkelon, Herzliya and Ashdod. Ashekelon Marina has good facilities, including its own 100-ton travelift, and is becoming a favourite among cruising sailors, especially those wishing to spend winter in Israel, afloat or ashore.

Fuel is available in all ports and LPG bottles can also be filled. Provisioning is very good in the larger centres, although imported goods are expensive. Locally produced fruit and vegetables are more reasonable and are among the best to be found in the Mediterranean.

Further Reading

Mediterranean Cruising Handbook
Red Sea Pilot

Websites

www.israel.org (Ministry of External Affairs)
www.index.co.il/tourism (General tourist information)
www.ashkelon.muni.il (Ashkelon Marina)

ITALY

Italy has well over 5000 miles of coastline, surrounded by the Tyrrhenian, Adriatic, Ligurian, Ionian and Mediterranean Seas. Off the west coast there are many small islands and the two large islands of Sardinia and Sicily. The coastline is very varied from the Italian Riviera right down to the south, being mountainous in some areas and low-lying in others. The west coast can be extremely crowded in the summer, especially in the north. July and August are the months to avoid, but in the spring and autumn the coasts are more peaceful and the weather can be very pleasant.

Once the undisputed domain of power boating, many Italians have now discovered the beauty of sailing and to cope with this insatiable demand many marinas have been built, particularly along the Italian Riviera. South of Rome sailing yachts are not so common. The east coast of Italy has been less endowed by nature and is less popular for cruising, even the local sailors often preferring to cruise in neighbouring Croatia. Italy's best cruising spots are spread around the rim of the Tyrrhenian Sea where groups of islands alternate with attractive harbours on the mainland. Some of the most picturesque anchorages are on Sardinia, while close to the Straits of Messina one can either anchor in the shadow of Stromboli or within sight of Mount Etna. Everywhere in Italy there is a lot to see ashore and the proximity of ports or marinas to all tourist attractions makes it easy to visit the main points of interest without leaving the boat for more than a few hours.

Country Profile

The Italian peninsula's earliest inhabitants were Ligurian and Illyrian peoples, and later Etruscans, Greeks and Gauls settled. From the middle of the fourth century BC Rome dominated the peninsula, and expanded to form an empire which at its height stretched around the Mediterranean and north as far as England. The empire declined from the second century AD, and Rome itself fell under waves of barbarian invasions from the east from the fifth century onwards.

The Frankish empire dominated in the eighth century, and was followed by a confused period until the tenth century, when Otto I united the crowns of Germany and Italy into the Holy Roman Empire. Southern Italy was later conquered by the Normans, while semi-independent city-states developed in the north and centre. The power of both the Empire and the Papacy declined, leaving the peninsula divided. By the fifteenth century five main states had emerged, the duchy of Milan, the republics of Florence and Venice, the Papal States, and the kingdom of Naples. Economically prosperous, they fostered the arts as the Renaissance emerged as a new cultural force.

With the Italian Wars (1494–1559) rivalry between small Italian states was intensified by the rivalry of France and Spain, until France abandoned her claims to parts of Italy. Thereafter Spain and later Austria dominated the peninsula.

Italian nationalism and the idea of unification grew rapidly, although there was little success until Piedmont, ruled by Victor Emmanuel II and prime minister Cavour, won victories over Austria in 1859 and gained Lombardy. Central Italy and Naples voted for union with Piedmont and in 1861 the kingdom of Italy was proclaimed. Venice and Rome were acquired, and the latter became the capital of the new state.

In 1915 Italy entered the First World War on the side of the Allies, and in 1919 gained some territory from Austria. A fascist government was formed in 1922 under Benito Mussolini, and a totalitarian state was gradually imposed. In 1936 the Rome–Berlin Axis was formed with Nazi Germany, and Italy entered the Second World War on the side of Germany. Mussolini was overthrown in 1943 following heavy defeats and social unrest. An armistice was signed with the Allies and war declared on Germany. After the war a republic replaced the monarchy, but was weakened by instability until the 1950s, when under the Christian Democrats the economy made a spectacular recovery. A strong left-wing opposition developed and from 1968 political instability returned with a quick succession of governments, until eventually the political parties reached a compromise with Communists and Christian Democrats in power together. Through the 1970s the country suffered from right- and left-wing terrorist activity especially by the Red Brigade. The 1990s have been marked by a rise in the electoral success of right-wing parties, and a nationwide campaign against the Mafia and political corruption.

Italy is traditionally an agricultural country with industry concentrated in the north centred on Milan and Turin. There is still a division between the poorer, more rural south and the industrial north. The economy is diverse, the manufacturing industry being well known for quality production

Practical Information

LOCAL TIME: GMT +1. Summer time GMT + 2 from the last weekend in March to the last weekend in September.

BUOYAGE: IALA A

CURRENCY: Lira (L). Euro from 2002. 1 Euro = 1936.27 ITL.

BUSINESS HOURS
Banks: 0830–1330, 1500–1600 (afternoon opening varies) Monday to Friday.
Business: 0830–1330 Monday to Friday.
Shops: 0830/0900–1300, and 1530/1600–1930/2000 (N. Italy takes a shorter lunch break, but closes earlier).
Government offices: 0830–1345 Monday to Saturday.

ELECTRICITY: 220 V, 50 Hz

PUBLIC HOLIDAYS
1 January: New Year's Day
6 January: Epiphany
Easter Monday
25 April: Liberation Day
1 May: Labour Day
15 August: Assumption
1 November: All Saints
8 December: Immaculate Conception
25, 26 December: Christmas
There are also local feast days on the day of the patron saint.

COMMUNICATIONS
Phone booths need cards. Cards can be bought from post offices, tobacconists and bars. International calls can also be made from ASST or SIP telephone offices. Operator *Tel.* 170. International direct dialling access code is 00. Mail is very unreliable and slow, although private addresses or marinas are better than poste restante. Post Restante: c/o Post Office and adding FERMO POSTA to the name of the locality. Delivery is made at central post office on presentation of passport and payment of a fee.
Emergency: dial 112.
There are regular international flights from most major cities, such as Rome, Milan, Turin, Genoa, Naples, Venice and Palermo.

MEDICAL
EU citizens and nationals of some other countries have access to health care on a reciprocal basis. Private medical treatment is expensive.

DIPLOMATIC MISSIONS
In Rome:
Australia: Via Alessandria 215. *Tel.* 06 852 721.
Albania: 3 v. Asmara. *Tel.* 0686 214 475.
Canada: 27 av. G.B. de Rossi. *Tel.* 06 445 981.
Croatia: 74 v. Bodio. *Tel.* 0636 307 300.
Egypt: 267 v. Salaria. Tel: 068 540 734.
France: 67 p. Farnese. *Tel.* 06 686 011.
Germany: 4 v. D. Mart, Battaglia. *Tel.* 06 492 131.
Greece: vl. G. Rossini. *Tel.* 068 549 630.
Slovenia: 10 v. della Concilliazione. *Tel.* 066 833 009
New Zealand: Via Zara 28. *Tel.* 064 417 171.
United Kingdom: Via XX Settembre 80A. *Tel.* 064 825 441, 064 825 551.
United States: Via Veneto 119/A. *Tel.* 06 46 741.

in cars, domestic appliances and household goods. Italian goods have a reputation for style in fashion, furniture and many other items.

The population is 60 million and the language Italian, although there are some dialects in Sicily, Naples and Sardinia. The majority are Roman Catholic and the capital is Rome, where the Roman Catholic Church has its headquarters in the Vatican City, an autonomous state.

The climate varies from north to south and between the islands. The north can have cold winters, while the south can be extremely hot in summer. Generally the coastal areas have a Mediterranean climate. The summers are hot and dry along the coast. The prevailing winds of summer are NW, although in many areas there is a daily pattern combining land and sea breezes.

Entry Regulations

Ports of entry

There is such a large number of ports and marinas both on the mainland and in the offlying islands that only those where foreign yachts normally clear in have been listed. Most of these are close to cruising routes.

Mainland: Ancona 43°36′N 13°31′E, Anzio 41°27′N 12°38′E, Bari 41°08′N 16°53′E, Brindisi 40°39′N 17°59′E, Chioggia 45°13′N 12°17′E, Civitavecchia (Riva di Traiano) 42°04′N 11°48.6′E, Fiumicino 41°46′N 12°14′E, Genoa 44°25′N 8°55′E, Imperia 43°53′N 8°02′E, La Spezia 44°07′N 9°50′E, Naples 40°51′N 14°16′E, Ravenna 44°25′N 12°27′E, Reggio di Calabria 38°07′N 15°39′E, Salerno 40°41′N 14°46′E, San Remo 43°49′N 7°47′E, Taranto 40°27′N 17°12′E, Trieste 45°39′N 13°48′E, Venice 45°26′N 12°20′E.

Sardinia: Alghero 40°34′N 8°19′E, Arbatax 39°56′N 9°42′E, Cagliari 39°12′N 9°05′E, Carloforte 39°09′N 8°19′E, Olbia 40°55′N 9°34′E, Porto Cervo 41°08′N 9°34′E.

Elba: Porto Azzuro 42°46′N 10°24′E.

Sicily: Catania 37°31′N 15°06′E, Gela 37°04′N 14°15′E, Marsala 37°48′N 12°26′E, Messina 38°12′N 15°34′E, Palermo 38°07′N 13°22′E, Porto Empedocle 37°17′N 13°32′E, Siracusa 37°03′N 15°18′E, Trapani 38°02′N 12°31′E.

Procedure on arrival

Italy is a member of the European Union and therefore vessels arriving from another EU country, with only EU nationals on board, are not required to complete any formalities. Occasionally boats may be subjected to spot checks by customs (Guardia di Finanza), especially in areas known for smuggling. The formalities described below apply primarily to non-EU boats, although EU boats will have to conform to some of them, such as the requirement to have a valid third party insurance certificate on board. It is therefore recommended that any yacht arriving in Italy from abroad should attempt to do so at a port which has customs and immigration offices to which the captain should report on arrival.

Both EU and non-EU boats arriving from a country outside the EU (Malta, Tunisia, Croatia, Albania, etc) must contact customs at the first Italian port. On arrival in a port of entry, boats from non-EU countries must clear with the port captain. One also has to clear with customs and immigration.

Officials are very unlikely to come to a yacht, so the captain must report to their offices. Yachts have got into trouble for failing to report to the authorities.

The captain may be asked to show a certificate of competence; other documents needed are the registration certificate and third-party liability insurance.

Customs

Non-EU boats may only remain in any EU country for a total of six months, so boats arriving in Italy from another EU country will have the time spent there taken into account. At the completion of the six-month period, the boat must leave the EU, or it will have to pay VAT on its estimated value. To avoid this, the boat may be put in bond by informing customs who will seal the boat. The boat can then be left in a boatyard or assigned marina, but cannot be used for the next three months. When the boat is recommissioned, a new period of six months is started.

Firearms must be declared on arrival. The penalty for non-declaration is imprisonment.

Dogs and cats need a health certificate, which must be in Italian as well as the language of the country of origin. This can be obtained from the local veterinary inspector of the Ministry of Agriculture and should state that the animal is free from disease and has been vaccinated against rabies not less than 20 days and not more than 11 months prior to the date of issue of the health certificate. Animals under 12 weeks old do not have to have a rabies vaccination, but must be examined on arrival.

Immigration

No visa is required for a stay of up to three months for nationals of EU countries, other West European countries, Australia, Canada, New Zealand, the USA as well as Argentina, Bermuda, Bolivia, Brazil, Chile, Colombia, Costa Rica, Croatia, Cyprus, Czech Republic, Ecuador, El Salvador, Guatemala, Honduras, Hong Kong, Hungary, Iceland, Jamaica, Japan, Kenya, South Korea, Malaysia, Malta, Mexico, Paraguay, Poland, Singapore, Slovak Republic, Slovenia, Uruguay, Yugoslavia (Serbia and Montenegro), for Venezuela up to two months, and Israel up to one month. Extensions can be obtained from the police.

Insurance

It is illegal for yachts to cruise in Italian waters without valid third-party insurance. Yachts which do not have insurance may not be allowed to leave the harbour until they obtain it. Insurance can be obtained locally from an Italian insurance company.

Diving

Underwater fishing with scuba gear is prohibited. Spearfishing is also prohibited for anyone under 16 years old, within 1640 ft (500 m) of a beach or of a fishing boat at anchor. When underwater, the presence of the diver must be shown by a float with a red flag and yellow diagonal stripe.

Pets

Boats with dogs or cats on board must be able to produce a certificate of health issued by an Italian veterinary inspector stating that the animal is free of disease. To avoid this inspection on arrival, one should have a certificate showing that the animal had been vaccinated against rabies not less than 20 days before the date of the certificate's issue.

Health

Seafood should not be consumed in areas of heavy pollution.

Charter

It is illegal for foreign yachts to charter in Italy. However, if one arrives with a charter party from abroad one can obtain the transit log in the usual way. Neither the charter party nor the crew may be changed while in Italian waters.

Facilities

With a large resident boating population and also

a considerable boat-building industry of its own, yachting facilities in Italy are of a very high standard. Purpose-built marinas or docks for yachts are available almost everywhere and the only deterrent can be the high docking fees charged in some places, some of the highest being those at Porto Cervo in Sardinia.

The best repair facilities are in the north-west of the country where most marinas are concentrated. Conveniently located near Rome, the large marina called Riva di Traiano, two miles south of Civitavecchia, has excellent docking facilities, fuel, chandlery and supermarket. It also offers a complete range of repair facilities as well as a boatyard with two travelifts up to 120 tons. The marina monitors Channel 9 permanently. There are boatyards all around Italy's coasts and for any repair or haul-out one is never too far away from help. Marine supplies and spares, particularly more common makes of diesel engines or outboards, are widely available, although everything is found more easily in the north. Essential spares that are not available locally can be imported free of duty. Fuel and water are available in most ports and LPG containers can also be filled in most places although an adaptor may be necessary. Provisioning is good everywhere and most towns have a fresh produce market with a wide selection of fruit and vegetables. Because of the mild winters in the south of the country, fresh produce is available all year round.

Further Reading

Italian Waters Pilot
Adriatic Pilot
Mediterranean Almanac

Websites

www.enit.it (Italian State Tourism Organisation)
www.etruria.net/reticiviche (Riva di Traiano Marina)

LEBANON

Before being torn apart by civil war, Lebanon was one of the most popular tourist destinations in the Eastern Mediterranean. This beautiful country was also popular with cruising yachts and there used to be a regular movement of small boats between Cyprus and Lebanon. With the return of peace, cruising boats are rediscovering the attractions of this small country ravaged by a senseless war. The best way to see Lebanon's interior, which is now considered safe to travel, perhaps with the exception of the south, is by hired car. The boat can be left in complete safety at the ATCL marina at Jounieh.

Country Profile

The modern state of Lebanon emerged out of the Ottoman Empire at the end of the First World War. In the inter-war period it was under French mandate, and gained full independence during the Second World War. An important commercial centre with a strategic position in the Middle East, its government was quite stable and westernised. However, the Muslims, who make up 50 per cent of the population, felt excluded as it was the right-wing Christians who held the power. Adding to the tension was the immigration of many Palestinian refugees displaced from Israel. In 1958 a Muslim rebellion occurred and the United States intervened to put this down. In the mid-1970s complete civil war broke out, exacerbated by the intervention of Syrian and Israeli forces. With Syrian backing, a Muslim government has established its authority in the state.

A mainly agricultural country, income used to be derived from tourism and trade. Since peace was established, Lebanon is regaining its former role as a centre for banking and financial services.

The population is about 2.8 million, who are Arabic speaking, although both English and French are spoken, especially in Beirut. There are both Muslim and Christian communities and the population is divided along religious lines. The capital Beirut was once a cosmopolitan and prosperous city described as the Paris of the Middle East.

The pleasant climate is Lebanon's main attraction as the weather is mostly sunny. The summers are hot and dry, while the winters are cool and occasionally rainy.

Entry Regulations

Ports of entry
Beirut 33°54′N 35°31′E, Jounieh 33°59′N 35°39′E, Tripoli 34°28′N 35°50′E.

Practical Information

LOCAL TIME: GMT + 2, summer time
GMT + 3.

BUOYAGE: IALA A

CURRENCY: Lebanese pound of 100
piastres.

BUSINESS HOURS
Banks: 0800–1230 Monday to Friday,
0800–1200 Saturdays.
Government offices: 0800–1400.
Business: 0800–1700.

ELECTRICITY
110/220 V 50 Hz

PUBLIC HOLIDAYS
1 January: New Year's Day
9 February: St Maron
22 March: Arab League Anniversary
Easter (Roman Catholic and Orthodox)*
1 May: Labour Day
May: Ascension Day
15 August: Assumption Day
1 November: All Saints' Day
22 November: Independence Day
25 December: Christmas Day
31 December: Evacuation Day

Islamic holidays*:
Leilat al-Meiraj, Mouloud, Al-Fiter, Al-Adha,
Islamic New Year's Day, Achoura.
*variable

COMMUNICATIONS
There are flights from Beirut to various
European and Middle East destinations.

DIPLOMATIC MISSIONS
United Kingdom: Middle East Airlines
Building, Jal el Dib, East Beirut.
Tel. (1) 416-112/410-573.
Also: Shamma Building, Raouche, West
Beirut. *Tel.* (1) 812-849/812-851.
United States: Ali Reza, Avenue de Paris,
Beirut. *Tel.* (1) 361-800.

Procedure on arrival

The Lebanese Navy (call sign Oscar Charlie) should be contacted on VHF Channel 16 when 12 miles offshore and about to enter Lebanese territorial waters. Instructions will be given to proceed to Jounieh, which is the best place to clear into the Lebanon. A clearance number will be allocated to the boat and this number must be given when arriving at the marina. The authorities should be contacted again when 6 miles from the marina entrance. The arrival should be timed to be during daylight hours. The port captain should be contacted on Channel 16 when about to enter the marina to be given directions to a free berth. All formalities are completed in the marina and there are various clearance fees, which can be paid in US dollars.

Boats proceeding along the Lebanese coast between the ports of Beirut, Tripoli, Sidon and Sour must sail within the 12 mile limit and not closer than 3 miles to the coast. Such movement is restricted to daylight hours between 0500 and 2000 local time. When leaving or approaching any of the above ports, a course of 270° or 90° respectively must be steered. The ports of Beirut and Jounieh are open permanently, but Tripoli, Sidon and Sour are only open between 0500 and 2000 local time.

Immigration

All nationalities require visas, issued for stays of two weeks up to three months.

Facilities

The first week at Jounieh Marina is free of charge. Facilities in the marina are of very good standard, but repair facilities are limited. There is a chandlery near the marina and several good supermarkets nearby. Both water and fuel are available in the marina.

Website

www.lebanon.com

LIBYA

Libya has a long stretch of coastline on the southern shore of the Mediterranean between Egypt and Tunisia. The official name of Libya is the Socialist People's Libyan Arab Jamahariya, meaning the state of the masses. The 1969 revolution established a regime based on Arab socialism and tolerating no outside interference, under the rule of Colonel Gaddafi. In 1977 a Jamahariya was declared, which is a combination of democracy and extreme Islam. Since the 1960s massive oil resources have brought the country great wealth.

The economy is dominated by oil production although efforts are being made to diversify into other industries, agriculture, and even tourism, which was always discouraged in the past. Tourists are now slowly beginning to visit Libya, especially such spectacular archaeological remains as the city of Leptis Magna, possibly the best Roman site in the Mediterranean. However, entry formalities remain very difficult.

The same rules apply to cruising yachts as to ordinary tourists and, whatever their means of travel, individual tourists are not welcome. Cruising yachts are therefore advised to avoid Libya and to keep well out of its territorial waters when sailing past its shores. Should there be an emergency which forces a yacht to call at one of the Libyan ports, an attempt should be made to contact the authorities on VHF Channel 16 as soon as one enters Libyan territorial waters. As there is a Libyan law which does not permit foreign ships to retain Israeli flags, stores or literature pertaining to Israel on board, even if these are part of the vessel's navigation equipment, such as Sailing Directions, any such incriminating items should be disposed of before entering a Libyan port.

Every visitor needs a visa in advance, which is difficult to obtain. There are Libyan diplomatic representatives in Malta and Tunis. Travel details could possibly be arranged through one of the newly established private tourism companies based in Libya. Essential information in one's passport must be printed in Arabic. It should be noted that with a Libyan stamp in one's passport, one may have considerable problems going to some other countries, especially the United States. Entry is refused to Israelis, and those with passports containing stamps from Israel.

Diplomatic missions
Australia, Canada, New Zealand, the United Kingdom and the USA do not have official diplomatic relations with Libya.
United Kingdom: British Interests Section c/o Italian Embassy, Shara Uahran 1, Tripoli. *Tel.* (21) 333 1191/2/3.
US Interests Section c/o Belgian Embassy, 1 Sharia Abu Ubaydah ibn al-Jarrah, PO Box 663, Tripoli. *Tel.* (21) 37797.

MALTA

A small archipelago in the middle of the Mediterranean, Malta is a very popular tourist destination. The Republic of Malta consists of three islands, the largest, Malta, being the economic and administrative centre and most heavily populated. Gozo is smaller and picturesque, with the prehis-

toric temple of Ggantija, 5500 years old, while Comino is a very small island between the other two. All three islands are dry, mostly treeless, with rocky coasts. Maltese culture is a mixture of Catholic, Arab and the influence of the Knights of St John who were based there for two hundred years and whose cross became Malta's emblem.

Malta was an important yachting centre before the Balearics, Costa del Sol and Greece became such popular cruising destinations. Malta's convenient location, excellent harbours and good range of repair facilities ensured its leading position for many years until the authorities started imposing various restrictions which cruising sailors resented. Many yachts left never to return and cruising yachts deliberately bypassed Malta. Recently a concerted effort has been made to reverse this trend and yachts are once again discovering the attractions of Malta. Its mild and pleasant winters make it a perfect wintering spot and as the repair facilities are being brought up to their former high standards, Malta is again a good place to refit a yacht between seasons.

Malta's position almost in the centre of the Mediterranean makes it an ideal jumping off point for many other cruising grounds and an increasing number of European yachts make their base on the island. Fortunately there is more to Malta than just its repair and maintenance facilities, as besides the impressive Valletta harbour, there are many delightful anchorages around the islands.

Country Profile

Malta was inhabited from early times, first by the Phoenicians and Greeks, then ruled over by Carthage until the third century BC, when it became part of the Roman Empire. St Paul and St Luke were shipwrecked there in AD 58 when on their way to Rome. After the decline of the Roman Empire, Malta was ruled by Byzantium, the Arabs and then the Normans, who were established in nearby Sicily. The population remained Muslim until the mid-thirteenth century, when non-Christians were expelled and the Arab presence eliminated.

In the sixteenth century Malta became the home of the Knights of the Order of St John of Jerusalem, after they had been driven out of Rhodes by Sultan Suleiman the Magnificent. The Knights resisted all attempts by the Turks to conquer the island, notably in the Great Siege in 1562. The Knights ruled Malta until the end of the eighteenth century, when the islands were fought over by Britain and France until declared British in 1814. Internal self-government was granted in 1821, but political crises led to the constitution being suspended. Malta was badly bombed during the Second World War when the islands were used as a British naval base. Full independence came in 1964 and a republic was declared ten years later. In 1979 the British closed their naval base. In 1990 an application was made to join the European Union.

Until 1979 the main income was millions of pounds that Britain paid to use the facilities on the island. Since then shipbuilding, tourism, agriculture and light industry are the main money earners.

The Maltese population of 360,000 are mainly Catholic and speak Maltese, which is a Semitic language in origin, having 80 per cent Arabic and 20 per cent Romance elements. English and some Italian are also spoken. The capital is Valletta, founded at precisely 2 p.m. 28 March 1566 to prevent any enemies from gaining the strategic Mount Sciberras as they had done in the Great Siege.

The climate is similar to North Africa, with extremely hot, dry summers and mild winters. Prevailing winds throughout the year are north-westerlies. When the hot sirocco wind blows from the south, it comes laden with dust.

Entry Regulations

Ports of entry
Marsamxett harbour (Msida Marina) and Grand Harbour 35°54′N 14°31′E, Gozo (Mgarr Marina) 36°01.5′N 14°18′E.

Procedure on arrival
Yachts must not stop anywhere before a port of entry, or they risk being fined. Valletta Port Control must be contacted on VHF Channels 12 or 16 (24-hour watch) before entering the harbour. During office hours, visitors are normally directed to the reception dock in Msida Marina. Outside office hours clearance is done in the commercial port, Grand Harbour. It is not advisable to enter Marsamxett harbour at night.

Msida: The guest berth is located on the

Round the World Rally start from Valletta.

Breakwater Quay at the opening to Msida Creek. All formalities are carried out at the Yachting Centre located close to Breakwater Quay. Port police (immigration) and customs have officers on duty there. The office hours are 0800–1700 daily, but extended until 2000 from 16 June to 30 September.

Grand Harbour: The Customs House is on Lascaris Wharf. It is possible to come alongside.

Gozo: In summer it is also possible to clear in at Mgarr Marina on Gozo. The customs office there is open 0800–1700 daily, extended until 2000 from 16 June to 30 September.

Procedure on departure

Outward clearance is obtained from the customs and immigration offices at the Yachting Centre in Msida Creek. It is possible to clear out on any day provided the boat is leaving before 0800 the following morning. Outside of office hours, one has to go to the Customs House in Valletta. A receipt for the payment of berthing fees must be obtained first in order to clear out. Customs will require a crew list. It is possible to clear out on a Friday if leaving the following Sunday. Duty-free stores can be obtained before departure – they will be loaded under the supervision of a customs officer, and will be sealed until departure from Maltese waters. After loading duty-free goods, the yacht must leave within 24 hours.

Customs

Firearms will be taken into custody on arrival and returned prior to departure, or sealed on board if there is a suitable locker.

Yachts with animals on board cannot come alongside or moor stern-to and must anchor off. Landing animals is strictly prohibited, even with proper health certificates. As it is illegal to bring animals into Malta, the animal may be destroyed if landed.

Yachts may be kept in Malta tax-free indefinitely, provided that certain conditions and procedures are complied with, such as the owner being a non-resident foreigner and the yacht is not being used for charter. Such yachts are entitled to tax-free spare parts.

Immigration

Visas are not required for nationals of Commonwealth countries (except Bangladesh, Ghana, India, Nigeria and Sri Lanka), West European countries, and nationals of Algeria, Argentina, Bulgaria, Chile, Croatia, Czech Republic, Egypt, Hungary, Indonesia, Israel, Japan, South Korea, Kuwait, Libya, Morocco, Poland, Saudi Arabia, Slovak Republic, Tunisia, Turkey, Uruguay and the United States.

Visas are required by all other nationalities, obtainable from Maltese or British diplomatic missions abroad. Nationals from countries needing a

Practical Information

LOCAL TIME: GMT + 1. Summer time GMT + 2 last Sunday in March to last Sunday in September.

BUOYAGE: IALA A

CURRENCY: Maltese pound (M£). One cannot import more than M£50 and export more than M£25.

BUSINESS HOURS
Banks: 0830–1230 Monday to Friday, also 1430–1600 Tuesday and Friday, 0830–1200 Saturday (to 1130 in summer).
Shops: 0900–1300, 1600–1900 Monday to Saturday.
Business: 0830–1245/1430–1730 Monday to Friday and 0830–1200 Saturday.
Government offices: 0800–1700 winter, 0800–1330 summer Monday to Friday.

ELECTRICITY: 220 V, 50 Hz

PUBLIC HOLIDAYS
1 January: New Year's Day
10 February: Feast of St Paul
19 March: St Joseph's Day
31 March: National Day
Good Friday
1 May: May Day
7 June: Sette Giugno
29 June: Sts Peter and Paul
15 August: Assumption Day
21 September: Independence Day
8 December: Immaculate Conception
13 December: Republic Day
25 December: Christmas Day

EVENTS
Carnival
Good Friday processions

COMMUNICATIONS
International direct dialling is possible from public phones or from one of the Telemalta offices. International operator Tel. 194. There are international flights from Valletta to various European and North African destinations.

MEDICAL
St Luke's Hospital, Gwardamangia. Tel. 241251. Police 191, Ambulance 196.

DIPLOMATIC MISSIONS
Canada: 103 Archbishop St, Valletta. Tel. 233121.
Egypt: 11 Sir Temi Zammut Street, Ta'Xbiex, Tel. 314158.
United Kingdom: 7 St Anne St, Floriana. Tel. 233134.
United States: Development House, St Anne St, Floriana. Tel. 235961.

visa are usually granted one on arrival, especially if staying only a short time.

Immigration officials do not stamp the passports of persons arriving by sea, so if leaving by air, it is necessary to notify the port police, who will stamp passports.

Yachts may remain an indefinite amount of time in Malta, but the length of time people may stay depends on immigration requirements.

Cruising

There are no restrictions on cruising around the archipelago, but Valletta Port Control must be kept informed on VHF Channel 12 of the movement of the yacht while away from the marina.

Diving

It is necessary to obtain a diving permit from the Department of Health if planning to scuba dive in Maltese waters. One needs a medical certificate, two photographs, a logbook and a certificate of qualification as an amateur diver. The permit must be shown if having diving tanks filled in Malta. Spearfishing without a licence is strictly forbidden, and the penalty is a heavy fine. Diving is prohibited in some areas and these are listed on the permit. Any archaeological finds must be reported.

Fees

Clearance is a 24-hour service, but some government offices charge overtime after 1330 in summer and after 1700 in winter.

Facilities

Malta has been blessed by nature with one of the best natural harbours in the Mediterranean and the decline of its traditional role as a Navy base and shipping centre has led to the development of its yachting facilities, which are already among the best in the region. The main marine facilities are in the creeks leading off Marsamxett harbour. A new breakwater at the opening of Msida Creek has increased the protection of the Msida Marina. Lazaretto Creek has stern-to moorings on either side (Lazaretto and Ta'Xbiex quays) and these are used mainly by larger yachts. Most repair facilities and shipyards are situated on Manoel Island. Comprehensive repair facilities are available with several boatyards offering a full range of services, haul-out, maintenance and refits. There is a good selection of marine supplies with all major manufacturers of marine equipment being represented

locally. Several companies specialise in the maintenance of yachts left unattended in Malta for longer periods, as an increasing number of European owners have their yachts permanently based there. Provisioning is good and duty-free stores are also available to yachts in transit.

Further Reading

Mediterranean Cruising Handbook
Italian Waters Pilot (includes section on Malta)

Websites

www.malta.com (Malta Tourism Authority)
www.visitmalta.com (Malta Tourism Authority)
www.digigate.net/maritime (Malta Sailing Federation)

MONACO

Monaco is a small independent principality lying on the southern coast of France, surrounded by the French department of the Alpes Maritimes. Most people know it for its palace, casino and Grand Prix. The Grimaldi family have ruled Monaco since the thirteenth century, the state's independence being recognised by France in 1512. Unlike other small countries in Europe, Monaco was not absorbed by a larger state, although always remaining within the French sphere of influence. A customs union was created between Monaco and France in 1865. Rainier III, prince since 1949, introduced constitutional reforms in 1962. The principality is a prosperous tourist and business centre, with low taxes and no income tax. Of the 28,000 inhabitants, only around 20 per cent are Monégasques.

Immigration

There are no customs controls at the frontiers of France and Monaco. However, all foreigners entering Monaco must have the necessary documents (passport or identity card) and visas, if these are required to enter France. No formalities are needed by nationals of EU countries, nor for those of non-EU countries who have already cleared into France. A stay of up to three months is allowed after which application must be made for a residence permit through the nearest French consulate, who handle all visa applications for Monaco.

Procedure on arrival

Call Port Control on Channel 16 and ask to have a berth assigned. The main port is always crowded and finding a space is so difficult that arriving boats are strongly advised to go directly to Fontvielle, less than half a mile further west. Fontvielle is a fully equipped marina having good services and repair facilities.

Facilities

A full range of services is available in the main port, where several workshops are located on its south side. The fuel dock is in the main port. The latter is geared more to dealing with large yachts, so cruising boats may find Fontvielle less intimidating.

Further Reading

Mediterranean France and Corsica

Website

www.monaco-tourism.com (Government Tourism Office)

MOROCCO

Situated on the north-west shoulder of Africa, Morocco is in some ways the bridge between Africa and Europe. All the main cities lie along the fertile coast, while behind Marrakesh stand the Atlas mountains, which were thought in ancient times to hold up the heavens. The Sahara desert stretches along the south, while to the north are the narrow Straits of Gibraltar.

In spite of its strategic position close to the sailing routes between Europe, the Mediterranean, Madeira and the Canary Islands, Morocco has done very little to develop its yachting facilities. Most of the large ports have a yacht club and there are a certain number of locally owned yachts, but the facilities do not compare with those of the neighbouring countries. Formalities are also complicated and foreign sailors are still regarded with a certain degree of suspicion. Although the coastline and harbours offer limited cruising, the attractions ashore, such as the old quarters and markets of some ports or the country beyond them, may make a visit to Morocco worthwhile.

Country Profile

Morocco was a Berber society from early times, its peoples being the agricultural Masmouda, the nomadic Sanhaja and the Zenata horsemen of the steppes. Over the centuries the country has been invaded by Carthage, Rome, Spain, Portugal and the Arabs, the latter having the most lasting effect. In the eleventh and twelfth centuries AD a Berber dynasty unified the Maghreb and Andalucia into a vast empire and only in 1492 with the fall of Moorish Granada did this link with Spain end. In the sixteenth century a religious revival and reunification came under the Saadi dynasty, driving out the Portuguese traders on the coast and attacking Spain. In the following century the Alaouite dynasty came to power and still rules today. Europeans were kept out and throughout the eighteenth and nineteenth centuries the country remained impervious to change. However, increasing numbers of European traders and explorers eventually forced the sultans to open up to trade. Great power rivalry let Morocco retain its independence until the early twentieth century when the country was divided into Spanish and French protectorates. This provoked a nationalist religious revival, but only after the Second World War did these feelings emerge more strongly.

In 1956 independence was achieved and in 1957 Morocco became a kingdom. In the 1980s King Hassan II played an active role in the Middle East peace process. King Hassan II died in July 1999 and was succeeded by his 36-year-old son, King Mohamed.

A continuing problem has been that of the Western Sahara. Morocco annexed part of it after Spain withdrew, which gave the monarchy popularity at home, but worsened the country's relations with Algeria. The Moroccan occupation was resisted by the Polisario guerillas and, after a long conflict, in 1991 the United Nations negotiated a ceasefire for the area. A referendum on self-determination is planned.

Phosphates are the main export and tourism is increasing rapidly. Wheat and citrus fruit grow in

Practical Information

LOCAL TIME: GMT. Summer time GMT + 1 April to October.

BUOYAGE: IALA A

CURRENCY: Dirham (DH) of 100 centimes. It is illegal to take DH in or out of the country. It is also difficult to change DH back into foreign currency on departure although it is possible if exchange receipts are kept.

BUSINESS HOURS
Sunday is a holiday; some shops also close on Fridays.
Banks: winter 0815–1130/1415–1630 Monday to Friday; summer 0830–1130/1500–1700 Monday to Friday; during Ramadan 0930–1430.
Business and shops: Tangier 0900–1100/1600–2000; rest of the country 0900–1200/1500–1800; during Ramadan 1000–1500.
Government offices: winter 0830–1200/1430–1800 Monday to Friday, 0800–1300 Saturday (summer afternoons open 1600–1900); during Ramadan 1000–1500.

ELECTRICITY: 110/220 V, 50 Hz

PUBLIC HOLIDAYS
1 January: New Year's Day
3 March: Coronation Day
1 May
6 November: Anniversary of the Green March
18 November: Independence Day
Variable Muslim holidays:
Ras el Am (New Year's Day), Ashoura (Memorial Day), Mouloud (Prophet's birthday), Start of Ramadan, Eid-el-Seghir, Eid el-Kebir, Hijra
NB: Mosques cannot be visited by non-Muslims.

COMMUNICATIONS
Most towns have telephone offices, open 24 hours, seven days a week. Phone cards (télécarte) can be bought from kiosks and post offices.
Telephone calls can also be made at the post office.
Post offices (PTT): 0830–1800 in large towns; elsewhere they close 1200–1500. There are international flights to Europe and elsewhere from Casablanca, Tangier, Rabat, Fez, Agadir and Marrakesh. There are flights to the Canary Islands from Agadir and Casablanca. There are ferry services to Southern Spain.

MEDICAL
Casablanca has a good public hospital. Medical facilities are adequate in the larger cities.
Emergency/Police *Tel.* 19, Ambulance *Tel.* 15.

DIPLOMATIC MISSIONS
In Rabat:
Algeria: 46 Avenue Tariq ibn Zayid. *Tel.* (7) 65092.
Canada: 13 bis rue Jaafar As-Sadiq. *Tel.* (7) 72880.
Egypt: 31 Charia Al Jazair, Place Abraham Lincoln.
Mauritania: 11, 266 Souissi. *Tel.* (7) 656678.
Spain: 57 Avenue du Chellah. *Tel.* (7) 704147.
Tunisia: 6 Avenue de Fes. *Tel.* (7) 730576.
United Kingdom: 17 Blvd de la Tour Hassan. *Tel.* (7) 731403.
United States: 2 Avenue de Marrakesh. *Tel.* (7) 62265.
In Casablanca:
United Kingdom: 60 Blvd d'Arifa.
United States: 8 Blvd Moulay Youssef.

---

the fertile coastal areas and much livestock is kept. Economic reforms have had some success in lowering inflation, but there is a large foreign debt and much of the population is poor and illiterate. Many Moroccans have emigrated, especially to France, and remittances sent home by workers overseas are important to the economy.

The population numbers 28 million, being mainly Arab in urban areas and Berber in the more rural regions. The majority are Muslim, but there are also some Christians and Jews. Arabic is the main language, while French is widely spoken, as well as some Berber dialects. The capital Rabat, on the Atlantic coast, replaced the old capital Fez at the start of the twentieth century.

On the coast the climate is one of hot summers and mild winters. Westerly winds predominate on the North African coast in winter, while most of the summer the winds are ENE. On the Atlantic coast summer winds are mostly northerly.

Entry Regulations

Ports of entry
Nador 35°17′N 2°56′W, Al Hoceima 35°15′N 3°54′W, Tangier 35°47′N 5°48′W, Kenitra 34°16′N 6°35′W, Mohammedia 33°43′N 7°22′W, Casablanca 33°37′N 7°36′W, El Jadida 33°16′N 8°31′W, Jorf Lasfar 33°07′N 8°38′W, Safi 32°18′N 9°15′W, Agadir 30°25′N 9°38′W.

Procedure on arrival
All crew members, including the captain, are supposed to remain on board until formalities have been completed, but in practice the captain may have to go ashore to look for the officials in order to report the yacht's arrival and request clearance. He should report first to customs, who will require an inventory and a crew list. Customs often keep the ship's papers until departure. An entry declaration must be filled in at the Capitainerie office (Port Captain's office). Health control is done by Santé Maritime and a complete maritime health

declaration must be made. One must also clear with immigration, who often keep passports until departure. One should be prepared for delays in the return of documents. Yachts must check in with the port captain and police at each port visited. Occasionally photographs may be taken of the boat and crew by officials.

Tangiers: It is possible to come alongside the dock inside the small boat harbour, which is crowded with fishing boats. If the boat is not visited by customs and immigration on arrival, the captain must take the passports and ship's papers to the various offices all located within the harbour area.

Casablanca: Entry formalities can be easily done at the yacht club, as both customs and police have an office there.

El Jadida: The captain should go ashore with the passports and ship's papers and visit customs, immigration and port captain's office, all of which are in the harbour area.

Agadir: One should contact Port Control on VHF Channel 16 and ask permission to come alongside the commercial dock for clearance. The ship's papers must be presented to the port captain who may retain them during the yacht's stay in port. Similarly, the port police will retain passports and issue special passes for access through the harbour gates.

Essaouira: This small port 65 miles south of El Jadida is not an official port of entry, but yachts may call there. All formalities are accomplished at the harbour gate, where the captain must present passports and ship's papers.

Customs

Firearms must be declared on arrival and will be either sealed on board or kept in custody until departure. The penalty for non-declaration of firearms is decided by a military tribunal.

Animals need valid vaccination certificates; if not possessing these, vaccination will be carried out on the spot at the owner's expense and the animal put under observation.

A yacht may remain in Morocco for a temporary importation period of three months. Extensions are possible, but the yacht then may become eligible for duty.

Immigration

Visas are not required by nationals of the following countries: Western European (except the Benelux countries, which require visas), United States, Japan, the Commonwealth, and also Argentina, Bahrain, Brazil, Chile, Congo, Ivory Coast, Guinea, Indonesia, South Korea, Libya, Mali,

Malta, Mexico, Niger, Oman, Peru, Philippines, Qatar, Romania, Saudi Arabia, Senegal, Tunisia, Turkey, UAE and Venezuela. All others require visas, which should be obtained in advance. There are convenient Moroccan representatives in Malaga and Tunis. (Immigration regulations are liable to vary and the latest situation should be checked.)

A three months' stay is normally given. However, for short stays or emergency stops, even nationals of countries that need visas will be allowed to arrive without one.

Visas allow up to 90 days' stay with two entries. Extensions can be obtained from the local police, but one needs a letter of recommendation from one's own embassy.

People may be refused entry if their passport has an Israeli stamp in it. Israeli nationals have been refused entry until now although with the improving situation in Israel and Palestine this may change.

Health

Hepatitis, polio and typhoid inoculations recommended.

Fees

Overtime is charged outside of office hours (0800–1800) on weekdays, all day Sunday and public holidays.

Port charges and pilotage fee if over 50 tons.

Restrictions

There are areas prohibited to yachts and these are mentioned in the Notices to Mariners. If in doubt, one should check with the port captain before leaving for the next port, particularly in the south of the country.

Travel south of Tan Tan into the Western Sahara needs special permission from the military authorities.

Facilities

Provisioning is good in all major ports, although imported goods are expensive. The fresh produce markets are good everywhere, while the one in Tangiers is excellent. In most places fuel must be carried in jerrycans from a fuel station. In some ports men calling themselves 'shipkeepers' offer their services. They will deal with everything and also ensure that nothing is stolen off the yacht.

Repair facilities in the bigger ports are adequate and there are small boatyards in both Tangiers and Casablanca which have dealt with yachts in the past and carried out simple repairs.

Tangiers: Docking facilities for visitors are better than in the past, but two new marinas further east, at Marinasmir and Kabila, both near Tetouan, are a much better alternative to leave the boat if wishing to visit the interior of the country.

Casablanca: There are a number of workshops, which have attained a certain degree of expertise as they have dealt with the French Transat des Alisées every three years during the last decade.

The yacht club lies in the south corner at the base of the mole. It is possible to moor the boat at one of the club buoys. The yacht club welcomes visitors and charges a daily fee for the use of its facilities. Water is available on the club dock, but its quality is questionable. Fuel is available by jerrycan. Repair facilities in town are adequate as there is a large fishing fleet and there is the usual range of workshops and small boatyards. Simple electronic repairs can be done with the help of one of the yacht club members.

El Jadida: Lying approximately 50 miles SW of Casablanca, there is a good anchorage off the harbour entrance, but no protection from the NW swell, which is common in winter.

There is a small harbour, but this is only accessible to shallow drafted vessels. The dinghy can be left at the yacht club, which has no facilities except a restaurant. There is good provisioning in town and an excellent fresh produce market.

Agadir: One can anchor off the yacht club, which welcomes visitors. The dinghy can be left at the yacht club pontoon. Water can be obtained at the same dock, which has sufficient depth at high tide. There is good provisioning in town.

Further Reading

North Africa
Straits Sailing Handbook
North Africa (Lonely Planet)

Website

www.mincom.gov.ma (Ministry of Communications)

ROMANIA

Situated in Eastern Europe with a small outlet to the Black Sea and the river Danube separating it from the Balkans, Romania has always been at the crossroads of East and West. As the only Latin people in Eastern Europe, Romanians have always regarded themselves as different from their neighbours, but nearly half a century of communist rule has almost destroyed traditional life. The profound changes that followed the collapse of the former Soviet empire have allowed Romania to return to the European fold.

The Black Sea coast is flat and lacks natural harbours and anchorages, so from the cruising point of view, Romania has very little to offer with the possible exception of cruising the Danube Delta, one of the largest wildlife sanctuaries in Europe. The Danube itself is navigable along most of its length and yachts have successfully cruised down the Danube from Austria through the Slovak Republic, Hungary, Yugoslavia, Bulgaria and Romania. Sailing the river in the opposite direction is difficult and slow because of the strong current. Boats coming from the Black Sea should enter the Danube at Sulina, from where a dredged branch of the river leads to Tulcea, 40 miles upriver. The trip offers a unique opportunity to see some of the Danube Delta.

Romania can now be reached by a more direct way than through the Mediterranean thanks to the opening of the 107 mile long Main–Danube Canal. This new canal has made it possible to sail across the entire continent of Europe, from the mouth of the Rhine, on the North Sea, to the mouth of the Danube, on the Black Sea. The 2179 mile long waterway can be used by boats drawing not more than 8 ft (2.5 m) and with an air clearance of 19.5 ft (6 m), so as to be able to pass under the many bridges. Some of the bridges in Yugoslavia were destroyed during the NATO bombing of 1999 and until the situation returns to normal river traffic has been severely restricted.

Country Profile

The state of Dacia was fairly developed when conquered by the Romans in AD 106 and it remained a province of the empire until the third century AD, to be followed by invasions by Visigoths, Huns, Lombards and Avars. In the sixth century Slavs settled, and then Bulgarians, while in the eleventh century Hungary conquered Transylvania. From the late thirteenth century the principalities of Wallachia and Moldavia were established, becoming vassals of the Ottoman Empire. After the battle of Mohacs in 1526 Transylvania also fell under Ottoman rule.

Practical Information

LOCAL TIME: GMT + 2. Summer time GMT + 3 from early April until the end of September.

BUOYAGE: IALA A

CURRENCY: Leu (plural lei). The import/export of lei is prohibited. Foreign currency must be declared on arrival and exchange receipts kept to show customs on departure.

BUSINESS HOURS
Banks: 0900–1200, 1300–1500 Monday to Friday.
Shops: 0900–1300, 1500–1800 Monday to Friday, 0900–1300 Saturday.
Government offices: 0700–1500 (0730–1530) Monday to Friday, 0730–1200 on alternate Saturdays.

ELECTRICITY: 220 V, 50 Hz

PUBLIC HOLIDAYS
1, 2 January: New Year's Day
Orthodox Easter
1 May: Labour Day
1 December: National Day
25–26 December: Christmas

COMMUNICATIONS
International telephone calls can be made from the telephone section of the post office (PTTR), as well as from many private businesses offering telephone, fax and telex services.
Post offices open 0730–1900 Monday to Thursday, 0800–1400 Friday and Saturday. There are regular international flights from Bucharest to many European capitals, also some destinations in Asia, Africa and North

America. There are also some international flights from Constanta and Timisoara, as well as a network of internal flights.

MEDICAL
Nationals of certain countries are entitled to free medical care in an emergency. The standards in most hospitals are below the normal European standards.

DIPLOMATIC MISSIONS
In Bucharest:
Canada: Strada Nicolae Iorga 36.
Tel. (01) 506140
Germany: Strada Rabat 21.
Tel. (01) 792 580
United Kingdom: Strada Jules Michelet 24.
Tel. (01) 3120303.
United States: Strada Tudor Arghezi 7–9.
Tel. (01) 3124042.

The three regions were briefly united at the turn of the sixteenth century under Michael the Brave, but in 1691 the Hapsburgs annexed Transylvania, and the Turks hardened their grip over the rest of the region. In the nineteenth century revolutions against Turkish rule failed, and the principalities were for a time jointly occupied by the Turks and Russians. Moldavia and Wallachia were united as Romania in 1861, but only some years later in 1878 was Romania recognised as an independent kingdom.

Joining the First World War on the side of the Allies in 1916, at the peace settlement Romania gained Dobruja, Banat, Bukovina and Transylvania. King Carol II established a dictatorial regime from 1930, until deposed in 1940 by Antonescu who allied with Germany, and entered the war against the Soviet Union in 1941. An armistice was signed with the USSR in 1944 and King Michael ruled until forced to abdicate in 1947. The communists came to power and a people's republic was proclaimed.

In 1965 Nicolae Ceaușescu became General Secretary of the communist party, and thereafter his increasingly repressive rule dominated the country. In 1989 he was overthrown by a revolution and executed, and the Front for National Salvation took power provisionally, then winning free elections in May 1990. The political scene in the 1990s was marked by the generally unsuccessful efforts of a centre-right coalition government to place the country's ailing economy on a sound basis. Continuing inflation and high unemployment have affected most of the population, especially public employees and pensioners.

The economy is dominated by metallurgical, petrochemical and heavy industry. The agricultural sector has been privatised and produces largely wheat, maize and sugar beet. Tourism is developed along the Black Sea coast. Despite Romania's mineral resources and fertile agricultural land, unemployment, inefficiency and high inflation are serious problems.

The population is around 23 million, the majority being Romanian, but with a 2 million minority of Hungarians living mainly in Transylvania. The German minority has dwindled in recent years due to emigration as have the Jewish and Greek communities. Other minorities are Gypsy, Armenian, Turkish and Lippoveni, who are Russians inhabiting the Danube Delta area. Romanian is a Latin language with some Slav and Turkish elements. Minorities speak their own languages and French and English are also widely spoken as foreign languages. The majority are Orthodox Christian, but there are also Catholics and Lutherans. The capital is Bucharest.

The climate is typically temperate with hot summers and cold winters. The winds along the Black Sea coast are very much influenced by the surrounding landmass and in summer there is a daily pattern of land and sea breezes. An onshore breeze comes up around midday and usually dies by dusk to be followed by a land breeze during the night.

Entry Regulations

Ports of entry

Constanta 44°10'N 28°39'E, Sulina 45°09'N 29°39'E Mangalia 43°48'N 28°35'E.

Procedure on arrival

The political changes in Romania have removed most of the restrictions applied to visiting yachts and formalities are generally straightforward. Yachts must clear in and out of each port. Crew should remain on board until formalities have been completed.

Constanta: If wishing to clear in at Constanta one should make for the small boat harbour, Port Tomis, about half a mile north of the main commercial harbour. Call on VHF Channel 67 on approach. The small harbour is under permanent military guard, and it is best to tie up alongside the quay, close to the sentry box. The boat will be visited by customs and immigration, after which the captain may be required to go into the main harbour and clear with the Port Authority. The ship's papers will be kept until departure.

The authorities should be notified at least one hour before departure so they can come to the yacht.

Sulina: It is also possible to clear in at the port of Sulina, at the mouth of the Danube. One can tie up to the main wharf to clear with customs in the Administration Building. Navigating in the river can be very difficult because of the strong current.

Mangalia: Officials will visit the yacht for clearance formalities.

Customs

Firearms must be declared and will be detained.

There are no restrictions on animals, but as there is rabies in Romania, pets should be vaccinated.

A customs declaration must be completed on arrival, where video cameras, personal computers and other valuables should be detailed.

The export of articles of cultural, historical or artistic value is prohibited.

Immigration

According to a decree passed early in 2000, starting on 1 January 2001 nationals of countries who need visas for Romania can no longer obtain these on arrival, but must obtain a visa at one of Romania's diplomatic missions abroad. This regulation has caused much controversy and may be repelled, but anyone travelling to Romania should find out in advance whether this regulation is still in force.

Health

There is a hepatitis risk.

Fees

Visa fee. Harbour fees.

Danube–Black Sea Canal

Cruising yachts may use this Canal, which starts near Constanta and bypasses the Danube Delta. There are certain height restrictions both in the Canal and on the Danube and most yachts will have to lower their masts before entering the Canal.

Facilities

Facilities for yachts outside Tomis are practically non-existent. Facilities at Tomis have been improved, with water and electricity available on the quay. Simple repairs can be undertaken in workshops in either Constanta or Sulina. There are very few local yachts and most of them are kept in Port Tomis. Any of their owners would be the best source of information and advice regarding any repairs that are needed. Provisioning is adequate. Diesel fuel can only be bought in jerrycans from a station in town.

The boat can be left safely at Tomis, if this is arranged with the port captain, by those who wish to visit some of Romania's interior, such as the unique painted churches and monasteries in northern Moldavia.

Further Reading

Black Sea Cruising Guide

Websites

www.turism.ro (Romanian Tourism Promotion Office)
www.embassy.org/romania (General information)

SLOVENIA

Situated between Italy and Croatia, Slovenia has a small stretch of coast on the Istrian peninsula. The area has been hardly affected by the war in the south and boats have continued to cruise here throughout the hostilities in neighbouring Croatia. Although lacking the range of yachting facilities available along the Croatian coast, Slovenia's few ports and marinas are well equipped and most ports are attractive old towns.

Country Profile

During the sixth century AD the Slavic Slovene tribes settled in the region. In 788 it was incorporated into Charlemagne's empire, and in 1278 came under Hapsburg rule. In the nineteenth century a greater cultural and national consciousness developed among the Slovenes. After Austro-Hungary's defeat in 1918 Slovenia became part of the new Kingdom of Serbs, Croats and Slovenes, later renamed Yugoslavia. In 1941–5 the region was partitioned between Germany, Italy and Hungary, and became at the end of the war one of the Socialist Republics of the Yugoslav Federation.

In 1991 Slovenia declared its independence from Yugoslavia; this was recognised by the European Community in 1992.

There are coal and lignite reserves, as well as forestry, fishing and some agriculture. Tourism is also important. A privatisation programme has been undertaken.

The population of 2 million consists mainly of Slovenes, most of whom are Roman Catholic. Slovenian is a Slav language. The capital is Ljubljana.

Entry Regulations

Ports of entry
Koper 45°33′N 13°44′E, Izola 45°33′N 13°40′E, Piran 45°32′N 13°34′E, Portoroz 45°30′N 13°36′E.

Procedure on arrival
On arrival in one of the official ports of entry, one should wait for the officials to come to the yacht for clearance. In marinas, the staff will call the relevant officials. If no official arrives, the captain should report to the police for passport control, as well as customs and harbour master. The crew must remain on board until formalities are completed.

Piran is the most convenient port of entry if coming from either Venice or Croatia. There is a small space next to the fuel dock one can tie to for clearance and all offices are located close to this dock.

Documents needed are the registration certificate, certificate of competence, insurance certificate, crew lists and radio licence. A list must also be prepared of all dutiable items such as alcohol, tobacco and any movable objects not part of the yacht's equipment, such as cameras, portable radios, diving equipment or outboard engine. When clearance is completed, a cruising permit will be issued for a small fee (around US$15 for a 40 ft/12 m boat).

Customs
Firearms must be declared on arrival and will be sealed and checked again when leaving. Radio equipment must be declared and an operator's permit shown.

Practical Information

LOCAL TIME: GMT + 1, Summer time GMT + 2 end March to end October.

BUOYAGE: IALA A

CURRENCY: Tolar (SLT).

BUSINESS HOURS
Banks: 0800–1800 Monday to Friday, 0800–1200 Saturday.
Government offices: 0800–1500 Monday to Friday.

ELECTRICITY: 220 V 50 c

PUBLIC HOLIDAYS
1–2 January: New Year
8 February: Day of Culture
April: Easter Monday
27 April: Resistance Day
1–2 May: Labour Days
25 June: National Statehood Day
15 August: Assumption Day
31 October: Reformation Day
1 November: All Saints' Day
25 December: Christmas Day
26 December: Independence Day

COMMUNICATIONS
Phone cards can be bought at post offices, where public phone booths are located. International access code 00. Koper's main post office and telephone centre is at Muzejski Trg 3, open 0700-1900 Monday to Friday, 0700-1300 Saturday. International airport at Ljubljana.

DIPLOMATIC MISSIONS
In Ljubljana:
Croatia: Gruberjero Nabrezje 6.
United Kingdom: 3 Trg Republike.
Tel. 125 7191.
United States: 4 Ulica Prazakova.
Tel. 301 427.

Dogs and cats need a veterinary certificate showing that the animal has been vaccinated against rabies between 15 days and six months previously. All animals need a general health certificate.

Yachts left unattended for longer periods, such as for wintering, will be bonded by customs.

Immigration

Citizens of all European countries do not need a visa. Citizens of countries that need visas will be issued one on arrival.

Diving

Certain restrictions apply to diving and these should be ascertained when clearing in.

Facilities

There is a fuel quay at Koper Marina and a 30-ton travelift, as well as some repair facilities. There is a full service marina at Portoroz, just south of Piran.

Further Reading

Adriatic Pilot
Mediterranean Europe (Lonely Planet)

Websites

www.uvi.si (Government Public Relations Office)
www.artnoir.com (Adriatic Marinas)

SPAIN

With coasts on both the Atlantic and the Mediterranean, there are four main areas in Spain for cruising, which are all very different. The Atlantic coast is in two sections either side of Portugal, the north-west coast bordering the Bay of Biscay and the smaller south-west coast of Andalucia from the Portuguese border to the Straits of Gibraltar. From Gibraltar the Mediterranean coast stretches the length of the Iberian peninsula to France and the fourth cruising area is the Balearic Islands.

The most attractive natural cruising areas of Spain are situated at its extremes, the north-west Atlantic coast and the Balearics, the islands being one of the Mediterranean's prime yachting centres.

Nature has been generous in these places creating many natural harbours, secluded coves and pretty anchorages. Elsewhere man has had to make his own contribution and as well as old harbours, many attractive new ports have been created, especially along the southern Mediterranean coast, where there are marinas placed at strategic intervals, so that one is never more than a few hours' sail away from the next harbour. There is a lot to see both inland as well as in the ports along the coast in a country of rich culture, where the relaxed Spanish way of life still can be sampled in the many waterfront cafes and restaurants. It is possible to navigate some of the rivers, such as the Guadalquivir where one can sail as far as Seville. Another river that offers even better cruising opportunities is the Guadiana, which forms the border between Spain and Portugal. The river is navigable for some 20 miles as far as Pomarão, and the scenery and wildlife are well worth the detour. The bridge linking the two banks is reported to have a clearance of at least 66 ft (20 m). The southern ports are popular wintering spots, due to the mild winter weather.

In recent years Spain's Mediterranean coast and islands have seen a tremendous development in yachting facilities with new marinas being built everywhere. Initially the development was needed to cope with the demands of foreign sailors, many of whom based their yachts permanently in Spain. With the exception of a few traditional sailing centres such as Mallorca, Barcelona and Cadiz there was little local interest in yachting in Spain, but this is rapidly changing as Spaniards come to enjoy standards of living comparable to those of their partners in the European Union.

Country Profile

The Iberian peninsula was inhabited from Stone Age times, and in the first millennium BC the Celts invaded and mingled with the native Iberians. Phoenician and Greek colonies were established along the coasts. The Carthaginians conquered Spain in the third century BC, but were expelled by the Romans who spread their control over the whole peninsula. After the decline of the Roman Empire, Vandals and Visigoths overran the country and in AD 711 the Moors invaded from North Africa. Spain was gradually reconquered by the Christians from the north, and in 1479 the kingdoms of Castile and Aragon were united under Ferdinand V and Isabella I. In 1492 the Moors were driven from their last stronghold in Granada, and in the same year Christopher Colombus sailed to the New World and claimed it for Spain. The Spaniards explored the Americas over the next century, mainly in search of gold and silver, and established a vast empire.

Spain reached the height of her power in the sixteenth century under Charles V who inherited both the Spanish and Hapsburg thrones. After this, Spanish domination of Europe was slowly eroded, especially by the War of the Spanish Succession (1701–14) after Charles II of Spain died heirless and Louis XIV of France tried to place his own grandson on the throne. Spain lost her European possessions and the succession went to the French Bourbons. In 1808 Napoleon placed his brother Joseph Bonaparte on the Spanish throne, but the Bourbon Ferdinand VII was restored in 1814. His reactionary rule, however, led to the loss of the Latin American colonies.

In the nineteenth century the country was troubled by conflict between the royalists and republicans, and after the war with the United States in 1898 Spain lost Cuba, the Philippines and Puerto Rico. Strong anarchist and nationalist movements developed and in 1923 Primero de Rivera led a coup and established a military dictatorship. The growth of republicanism resulted in the overthrow of the Bourbon monarchy in 1931, but the new republic was faced with strong opposition from the Church and landowners. Civil war broke out in 1936 when the Falangists under General Franco rose against the Popular Front government. In 1939 Franco established a dictatorship, which remained neutral in the Second World War although friendly to the Axis powers. Spain was declared a monarchy in 1947 with Franco the regent for life. Franco died in 1975, succeeded by King Juan Carlos I, and gradually the country returned to democracy. Spain joined the European Community in 1986.

Agriculture still remains of considerable importance to the economy, but industry and services have developed. A traditional trade deficit is helped by tourist revenues but unemployment remains among the highest in the European Union.

The population numbers around 40 million and most Spaniards are Catholic. The various regions of Spain enjoy a high degree of autonomy and although everyone speaks Spanish (Castilian),

Practical Information

LOCAL TIME: GMT + 1. Summer time GMT + 2 April to September.

BUOYAGE: IALA A

CURRENCY: Peseta. Euro from 1 January 2002. 1 euro = 166.386 ESP. No more than 1 million peseta in cash may be imported or exported.

BUSINESS HOURS
Banks: 0900–1400 Monday to Friday, 0900–1200 Saturday.
Business: 0900–1845 winter, 0900–1400/1630–1900 summer, Monday to Friday.
Shops: 0900–1330, 1700–2100 summer, 0900–1300, 1600–2000 winter. Monday to Saturday. Some close Saturday afternoons.
Government offices: 0900–1330. Some are opened to the public on Thursday afternoons.

ELECTRICITY: 220 V, 50 Hz

PUBLIC HOLIDAYS
1 January: New Year's Day
6 January: Epiphany
Maundy Thursday (except Barcelona)
Good Friday
Easter Monday (Barcelona and Palma de Mallorca only)
1 May
Corpus Christi
24 June: St John
25 July: St James' Day (Galicia only)
15 August: Assumption
12 October: Columbus Day
1 November: All Saints' Day
6 December: Constitution Day
8 December: Immaculate Conception (except Barcelona)
25 December: Christmas
26 December (Barcelona and Palma de Mallorca only)

COMMUNICATIONS
International direct dialling is possible from public phones, which have instructions in English. International dialling access code 00. Cheaper rates after 2000. There are also telephone offices (Telefonica) with metered booths in major tourist centres.
All numbers in Spain now have nine digits, so even when dialling local numbers all digits must be dialled.
Post office (correo): telegrams, telex and fax services as well as poste restante (lista de correos).
There are international flights to European destinations from all major centres. Madrid international airport has regular flights to all parts of the world. There is also an excellent network of internal flights, both within peninsular Spain, the Canaries and Balearics.

DIPLOMATIC MISSIONS
In Madrid:
Australia: 2° Edificio Cuzco 1, Paseo de la Castellana 143. Tel. 91 579-0428.
Canada: Edificio Goya, Calle Nuñez de Balboa 35, Apartado 587. Tel. 91 431-4300.
Germany: Fortuny 8. Tel. 91 319-9100.
United Kingdom: Calle de Fernando el Santo 16. Tel. 91 319-0200.
United States: Serrano 75. Tel. 91 577-4000.

other languages and dialects are in wide use. Catalan is the second major language and is spoken in the Catalonia region centred on Barcelona. The Galician and Basque languages are in common use in those regions. The capital of Spain is Madrid.

The climate varies greatly from the Atlantic north coast, which is wet and cool, to the Mediterranean south and east, where summers are very hot and winters mild. The winds are just as varied, the north coast coming under the influence of Atlantic weather systems, with south-westerly to north-westerly winds predominating in winter and northerly winds in summer, although land and sea breezes can be experienced inshore. This is also the case along the south-western coast during summer, while the rest of the year, winds are either easterly or westerly. Alternating sea and land breezes are also characteristic of the Mediterranean coast. The eastern coast and Balearics are occasionally affected by the mistral, a N or NW wind which can rapidly reach gale force.

Entry Regulations

Ports of entry
Because of the large numbers of ports of entry as well as marinas which have customs offices where entry formalities can be completed, only the main ports and marinas are listed which are close to Spain's frontiers and are more commonly used by foreign yachts to clear in.
Atlantic coast: San Sebastian 43°28'N 30°48'W, Santander 43°28'N 3°46'W, Bilbao 43°17'N 2°55'W, Gijon 43°33'N 5°40'W, El Ferrol 43°28'N 8°16'W, La Coruña 43°23'N 8°22'W, Bayona 42°57'N 9°11'W, Vigo 42°14'N 8°40'W, Ayamonte 37°13'N 7°22'W, Huelva 37°07'N 6°49'W, Puerto Sherry 36°36'N 6°13'W, Cadiz 36°30'N 6°20'W, Algeciras 36°07'N 5°26'W.
Mediterranean coast: La Duquesa 36°21'N 15°14'W, Puerto Banus 36°29'N 4°57'W, Málaga 36°41'N 4°26'W, Motril 36°43'N 3°31'W, Almería 36°50'N 2°30'W, Cartagena 37°35'N 0°58'W, Alicante 38°20'N 0°29'W, Denia 38°50'N 0°07'E, Valencia 39°27'N 0°18'W, Tarragona 41°06'N 1°14'E, Barcelona 41°21'N 2°10'E, Palamos 41°50'N 3°08'E.
Balearics: Ibiza 38°54'N 1°28'E, Palma de Mallorca 39°33'N 2°38'E, Andraitx 39°33'N 2°24'E, Alcudia 39°49'N 3°08'E, Mahón 39°52'N 4°19'E.

Procedure on arrival
European Union regulations apply and boats from other EU countries must only clear in when arriving from outside the EU. In practice, however, the authorities expect to be informed of one's arrival even if coming from a neighbouring EU country. As a result of the implementation of the Schengen Agreement, boats having on board nationals of EU countries which are not signatories of the Schengen Agreement must clear immigration at the port of entry into Spain. In the case of non-EU boats, the captain should proceed ashore and clear customs (Aduana) and immigration at a port of entry. Normally officials then come to inspect the boat. In subsequent ports where Guardia Civil and/or customs officials are stationed, the clearance procedure may be repeated, although this varies from place to place. Sometimes the local yacht club or marina inform the authorities about the arrival of foreign yachts and many marinas have their own customs office. After having cleared into Spain, the procedure at subsequent ports seems to depend on the attitude of local officials. However, one should be prepared to show all relevant documents whenever asked. One may be asked for registration papers, crew lists, certificate of competence and proof of marine insurance. Once cleared, yachts are free to stop in ports and anchorages where there are no officials.

For non-EU boats, a temporary importation of up to six months in any one year is possible. If the boat is not in use, one may ask customs to put the boat temporarily in bond or under seal (precinto). This will stop the clock, and the time when the boat had been under seal does not count towards the allowed six-month period.

Procedure on departure
One should clear with immigration and customs on departure from Spain. Customs will record the date of departure on the customs permit if one has one. This permit can be used again if re-entering Spain within the period of its validity. Each arrival and departure must be noted by customs on the permit.

Customs
Firearms and animals must be declared.

Immigration
Visas are not required for nationals of West European countries, Canada and the United States, as well as Argentina, Australia, Bolivia, Brazil, Chile, Colombia, Costa Rica, Croatia, Cyprus, Czech Republic, Ecuador, El Salvador, Guatemala, Honduras, Hungary, Iceland, Israel, Japan, Kenya, South Korea, Malaysia, Malta,

Mexico, New Zealand, Nicaragua, Norway, Panama, Paraguay, Poland, Singapore, Slovak Republic, Slovenia, Uruguay and Venezuela. Children under 14 of any nationality do not require visas if they have their own passports.

Most nationalities are given 90 days' stay on entering Spain. Visas are required for all other nationals or for stays longer than 90 days, to be obtained in advance from a Spanish embassy or consulate abroad.

Often the immigration official does not stamp passports of people entering on yachts, but if planning to leave Spain by another means of transport, an entry stamp (entrada) will be needed.

Charter
Foreign yachts can charter in Spain under certain conditions. Charter vessels must not exceed 72 ft (22 m) LOA nor carry more than 12 passengers. They must comply with the international regulations for the safety of life at sea and have an insurance to cover both crew and passengers. A special permit must be obtained from the local maritime authorities (Comandancia de Marina) and also a licence from customs. Yachts will be granted a five month period (extendable for two further periods of five months) in which to charter. If such vessels are engaged in any kind of fishing, proper licences must be obtained both for the passengers and crew.

Restrictions
The island of Cabrera, in the Balearics, has been declared a national park. Overnight stays are only allowed with a permit obtained from ICONA, in Palma de Mallorca (*Tel.* 971 72 50 10). Boats must not use their own anchors but tie to one of the moorings provided. July and August: one night in every seven nights. June and September: two nights in every seven. There are no restrictions between October and May.

Fees
Overtime is not normally charged, as all formalities are completed during normal working hours and yachts are not expected to clear at other times.

Harbour fees are charged in most ports if there are any facilities provided for yachts.

A special tax or surcharge on docking fees is payable in most ports within the region of Valencia.

Facilities

Although there are marinas all around Spain's coasts, comprehensive repair facilities are only available in the most important yachting centres. The prime yachting centre is Palma de Mallorca, where several companies specialising in marine work have set up base. Facilities in the Balearics generally are probably the best to be found anywhere in Spain. Another centre with good facilities is Barcelona and the surrounding area. There are also good facilities along the Costa del Sol. In recent years, marinas have increased in numbers all along the Mediterranean coast and also in the Balearics. Repair facilities generally have also improved, as has the availability of spare parts and yachting equipment.

Facilities outside the Mediterranean are not so easily available. On the Atlantic coast there are good facilities at the new Puerto Sherry near Cadiz. On the north coast the best range is to be found at La Coruña where the yacht club can be particularly helpful. Most marinas have haul-out facilities, usually by travelift, while in many ports there are slipways dealing with fishing boats.

Marine supplies and spares are not as widely available as one would expect in a country with such a large boating community, both local and foreign. There are chandleries with a good selection of supplies in the main sailing centres, but in smaller ports and marinas the availability of spares is limited.

Yachts in transit can import spares and equipment duty-free but the procedure is not simple. The owner must lodge a cash deposit with the local customs office equal to the value of the imported goods. This is returned when the goods have been placed on the boat under customs supervision. In the absence of a customs officer, the document must be signed by the police before the deposit is returned. In some places it may be necessary to employ the services of a shipping agent.

Spanish charts are available from the Navy office (Comandancia de Marina) in major ports or the Hydrographic Institute in Cadiz. Now that value added tax is charged on diesel fuel bought by yachts, the fuel must be obtained from marinas and not from fishermen's pumps on quays. LPG gas (butane) is widely available and filling stations are located in all major ports. Provisioning is good everywhere and local fresh produce is of very good quality, although its availability may depend on the season.

Most Spanish yacht clubs are exclusive social clubs, where visitors are not particularly welcome. Those which have docking facilities operate on a commercial basis charging visitors marina fees. Dress etiquette is strict and a sloppy appearance is frowned upon.

Spanish North Africa

Ceuta and Melilla are Spanish enclaves on the north coast of Morocco, administered as city provinces of Spain. Also Spanish are the small islands of Alhucemas, Chafarinas and Penon de la Gomera. The cities became Spanish in the fifteenth century, when the Moors were expelled from the Iberian peninsula and remained Spanish when Morocco became independent in 1956. Ceuta and Melilla are important military bases. Visa requirements are the same as for Spain.

Ceuta: There is a small yacht harbour which has pontoons, although it is not very protected from swell. It is a good place for provisioning as the prices are reasonable. Diesel also is cheaper than on the Spanish mainland and Morocco as the town is duty free.

Melilla: Lying 120 miles east along the Moroccan coast from Ceuta, Melilla is not as large. A yacht club is located inside the fishing port, where berthing is provided for visiting yachts.

Canary Islands

As the Canary Islands are an autonomous overseas region of Spain, they are dealt with separately on page 147.

Further Reading

Atlantic Spain and Portugal
East Spain Pilot
Mediterranean Cruising Handbook
Mediterranean Spain
Islas Baleares
Mediterranean Almanac

Websites

www.spaintour.com (National Tourism Office)
www.la-moncloa.es (Official government site)

SYRIA

Syria lies on the coast of the Eastern Mediterranean, which used to be called the Levant as the sun rose there. Its capital Damascus is reputed to be the city which has been continually inhabited for the longest period in the world. In recent years the authorities have adopted a more welcoming attitude towards foreign tourists. As a result, formalities for visiting boats are also somewhat easier and every year a few cruising boats brave the official barriers and call at one of the Syrian ports. The coast lacks natural harbours, and the country is only worth visiting for the ancient sites to be found inland or such medieval landmarks as the Crusader castle Krak des Chevaliers.

Country Profile

In earliest times the Levant coast was a flourishing trading centre, and Damascus has been a thriving city since 5000 BC. Part of the Persian, Greek and

---

Practical Information

LOCAL TIME: GMT + 3

BUOYAGE: IALA A

CURRENCY: Syrian pound (S£) of 100 piastres. S£ are not convertible and export is prohibited.

BUSINESS HOURS
The working week is Saturday to Thursday, Friday being the day of rest. Some businesses run by Christians close on Sundays.
Government offices: 0800–1430.

ELECTRICITY: 110 V, 50 Hz

PUBLIC HOLIDAYS
1 January: New Year's Day
8 March: Revolution Day
21 March: Mothers' Day
Easter*
17 April: Independence Day
1 May: Labour Day
6 May: Martyrs Day
6 October: Tishrin Liberation
16 November: National Day
25 December: Christmas Day
*Variable: end of Ramadan, Al-Adha, Prophet's birthday, Muslim New Year

COMMUNICATIONS
International direct dialling is available.

There are flights from Damascus and Aleppo to Middle East, Asian, North African and European destinations.

DIPLOMATIC MISSIONS
In Damascus:
Australia: 128/A rue Farabi, Mezzeh District. *Tel.* (11) 6664317/6660283.
Canada: near Razi Hospital, Mezzeh Autostrad. *Tel.* (11) 2236892/3330535.
United Kingdom: Immueble Kotob, 11 Rue Kurd Ali, Malki. *Tel.* (11) 3712561/2/3.
United States: Abu Rumaneh, rue Al Mansur, No. 2. *Tel.* (11) 3332315/3332814.

Roman empires and then under the Arabs from the seventh century, the city was sacked by the Mongols, then annexed by the Turks and relegated to the role of a rather unimportant province in the Ottoman Empire. The city of Damascus was liberated from the Turks by the troops of the Arab revolt led by Lawrence of Arabia during the First World War. Syria was placed under French mandate, until independence was achieved at the end of the Second World War. Syria's postwar history has been marked by conflict with Israel. Syria has played an active role in the Lebanese conflict and continues to be involved with the situation in that country. There has been a gradual rapprochement with the West and also talks with Israel aimed at resolving their long standing conflict.

Oil and agriculture are the mainstays of the economy, which has recently experienced a period of rapid growth because of liberal reforms, the private sector being freed of restrictions for the first time.

The Arabic population of 13.5 million are mainly Muslim with sizeable minorities of Christians, Jews, Druzes and others. Some French is spoken as well as Arabic.

The climate is of the Mediterranean type with hot dry summers and mild winters, especially along the coast. The prevailing winds of summer are westerly. A day breeze usually comes up at noon and lasts until sunset.

Entry Regulations

Ports of entry
Lattakia 35°31′N 35°46′E, Banias 35°14′N 35°56′E, Tartous 34°54′N 35°52′E.

Procedure on arrival
Port Control should be contacted prior to arrival on VHF Channel 16. Lattakia is Syria's main port and as its officials are used to dealing with foreign vessels, this is the best port to enter. A new marina is reported to have opened at Tartous, which is a better place to both clear in and use as a base to visit the interior.

Immigration
Visas must be obtained in advance from Syrian consulates or embassies abroad. A letter of recommendation from one's own embassy is required if the visa is not obtained in one's country of residence. Visitors are given a stay of 15 days on arrival. Visas are difficult to obtain, particularly by

nationals of certain countries, such as the United States. Entry is refused to Israeli nationals or to anyone with an Israeli stamp in their passport. Any evidence of a previous visit to Israel is sufficient reason to be forced to leave the country. Visitors must change US$100 on arrival.

Further Reading

Southern Turkey, the Levant and Cyprus

Website

www.syriatourism.org (National Tourism Office)

TUNISIA

Facing the Mediterranean with both its north and east coasts, Tunisia lies between Algeria and Libya. The main towns and good beaches, which are Tunisia's main tourist asset, are situated on the fertile east coast. The country's long association with France has left a noticeable influence in Tunisia's culture and way of life.

Of all the North African countries, Tunisia has approached yachting in the most systematic way. Realising the considerable revenue that can be generated by cruising yachts, the Tunisian government has encouraged the setting up of a chain of marinas and yacht harbours conveniently spaced along Tunisia's entire coast, from Zarzis in the south-east to Tabarka in the west. All ports are within reach of colourful towns and the boat can be left in safety to visit the interior. All this, plus the relatively low prices of the marinas, has recently turned Tunisia into a popular cruising destination, especially for wintering. For those wishing to get a taste of Africa, without actually leaving the Mediterranean, Tunisia is undoubtedly the best choice.

Country Profile

The original inhabitants of North Africa were the Berber, named from the Roman 'barbari'. Therefore the Europeans called the Maghreb, which is present-day Tunisia, Morocco and Algeria, the Barbary coast. In 814 BC Queen Dido

Practical Information

LOCAL TIME: GMT + 1. Summer time GMT + 2, May to October.

BUOYAGE: IALA A

CURRENCY: Tunisian dinar (D) of 1000 millimes (M). The import and export of dinars is illegal. One should only change as much as needed because it is only possible to change back 30% on departure. Exchange receipts should be kept in order to be able to do this.

BUSINESS HOURS
Sunday is normally a holiday, although some keep Friday as a day of rest.
Banks: summer 0800–1100 Monday to Friday; winter 0800–1100/1400–1615 Monday to Thursday, 0800–1100/1330–1515 Friday; during Ramadan 0800–1130/1300–1430 Monday to Friday.
Business: winter 0830–1200/1500–1800 Monday to Friday; summer 0730–1200/1600–1830 Monday to Friday.
Shops: 0830–1300/1500–1800; Saturday 0800–1200.
Food shops: 0700–1300/1530–2100

Monday to Friday all year.
Souks (markets): 0830–1900 all year.
Government offices: winter 0830–1300/1500–1745 Monday to Thursday, 0830–1300 Friday, Saturday; summer 0700–1300 Monday to Saturday.

ELECTRICITY: 110/220 V, 50 Hz

PUBLIC HOLIDAYS
1 January: New Year's Day
18 January: Anniversary of the Revolution
20 March: Independence Day
9 April: Martyr's Day
1 May
1 June: Victory Day
25 July: Anniversary of the Republic
13 August: Women's Day
3 September: Commemoration Day
15 October: Evacuation Day
7 November: Anniversary of Ben Ali's Takeover
Variable holidays: Mouloud, Eid el-Seghir, Eid el-Kebir, Ras El Ham El Hejeri, Achoura

COMMUNICATIONS
Telecommunications Centre (PTT), 29 rue

Gamal Abdel Nasser, Tunis for overseas calls, open 24 hours.
Post office adjacent in rue Charles de Gaulle. Post offices open 0800–1800 (winter), 0730–1330 (summer), 0800–1500 (Ramadan) Monday to Saturday, 0900–1100 Sunday (all year).
There are frequent international flights to many European, Middle East and North African destinations from Tunis and flights from Sfax to Malta and Paris. Internal flights link the main cities of Tunis, Monastir, Sfax, Tozeur and Djerba.

DIPLOMATIC MISSIONS
In Tunis:
Algeria: 136 rue de la Liberté
Tel. (1) 280 055.
Canada: 3 rue de Sénégal, Place Palestine. Tel. (1) 796 577.
Egypt: 16 rue Essayouti, El Menzeh.
Tel. (1) 230004.
Morocco: 39 rue 1 Juin Mutuelleville.
Tel. (1) 782 775.
United Kingdom: 5 place de la Victoire.
Tel. (1) 340 239.
United States: 144 avenue de la Liberté.
Tel. (1) 782 566.

---

fled from Tyre with her followers, establishing the new city of Carthage. Legend says she set fire to herself rather than marry a local prince, while Virgil recounts 700 years later that this was due to the loss of Aeneas sailing back from Troy. It has been said that the island of Jerba was the Land of the Lotus Eaters in Homer's *Odyssey*.

Leaving legends aside, after the fall of Tyre, Carthage prospered and dominated much of the Mediterranean. This great maritime power was eclipsed by the rise of Rome and Carthage was finally destroyed. It was in this struggle with Rome that the Carthaginian general Hannibal took his elephants over the Alps. After the Romans came the Vandals, and then Byzantium ruled over the country. The seventh century brought the Arab invasions and the spread of Islam throughout the region. Following the defeat of the Moors in Spain, many settled in northern Africa, both crafts-men and seafarers. Some took to piracy and attacked Christian ships sailing in the Mediterranean. Tunisia was claimed in the six-teenth century both by the Barbarossa pirates, under Ottoman suzerainty, and Spain, and the

country passed from being a Spanish protectorate to a Turkish military province. Throughout the eighteenth century piracy continued to bring wealth to the coast.

In the nineteenth century Tunisia became a French protectorate, and many French people settled in the country. After the Second World War a guerilla war was waged until independence was granted in 1957 under Habib Bourguiba. Since the 1960s the government has kept close links with Western states.

Tunisia has seen rapid economic growth and is a relatively prosperous country. Income comes mainly from petroleum, olive oil and phosphates. The country has made efforts to industrialise, but agriculture remains important. Tourism is an increasing source of revenue. Unemployment is a problem and many Tunisians work abroad, espe-cially in France and Libya.

The population is around 9 million and is of a mixture which reflects the region's past history, of Arab, Roman, Greek, Spanish, Sicilian, French, Berber and black African origins. In the south the nomadic Bedouin still follow their traditional life.

The main languages are Arabic, Berber and French, the latter being used in education, commerce and administration. Tunis is the bustling modern capital. The majority of the population are Muslim, with Christian and Jewish minorities.

Inland the climate can be very hot in summer, but the winters are mild. Spring and autumn are the best times. Westerly winds prevail along the north coast, but in summer they are usually interrupted by the daily alternating land and sea breezes. Along the east coast the prevailing winds of summer are SE. The occasional sirocco arrives with gale force winds from the south, but is usually short lived.

Entry Regulations

Ports of entry
Tabarka 36°58′N 8°45′E, Bizerte 37°16′N 9°53′E, Sidi Bou Said 36°52′N 10°21′E, La Goulette 36°49′N 10°18′E, Kelibia 36°50′N 11°07′E, El Kantaoui 35°52′N 10°36′E, Sousse 35°50′N 10°39′E, Sfax 34°44′N 10°46′E, Gabes 33°55′N 10°06′E, Djerba (Houmt Souk) 33°53′N 10°52′E, Zarzis 33°30′N 11°07′E. From 2001: Yasmine Hammamet.

Procedure on arrival
On arrival at a port of entry, all persons must remain on board until the formalities are completed. Formalities on arrival are usually simplified by the fact that the various officials will visit the boat, or are often waiting on the quay, when one arrives. Customs require a list of dutiable goods and often wish to see the yacht's insurance papers. They will issue a cruising permit. One must also clear with immigration and the harbour master (marine marchande) to whom harbour dues have to be paid. In subsequent ports officials may retain the permit during one's visit and will request crew lists.

Procedure on departure
When leaving each port, one should pay the harbour fees and check out with the port police, who will want to know the yacht's next destination.

On departure from Tunisia, the cruising permit must be surrendered to customs. It is also necessary to clear with immigration on departure from Tunisia.

Customs
Large quantities of alcoholic drinks may be sealed by customs.

Spare parts can be imported duty-free if clearly marked 'yacht in transit'.

Firearms must be declared to customs on arrival.

Dogs and cats must have health certificates and certificates of vaccination between one and six months old.

Immigration
Visas are not required for many nationals including those of most European countries, Canada, the United States and Japan. Australian citizens can obtain a visa on arrival, while New Zealand citizens require a visa, to be obtained in advance. There is no charge for the visa, which can be renewed after three months.

On arrival, passports are stamped by the police for three months, renewable for another three. One must notify the authorities of any crew changes.

Cruising permit
A cruising permit (triptique) is issued on arrival when clearing in, free of charge. The period of validity will be stated on the permit and is usually three months. It is renewable up to one year. If leaving the yacht in Tunisia, but departing the country by other means, the permit must be returned and customs will put the yacht in containment, during which time one cannot cruise, although crew can remain on board. When wishing to cruise again, one must obtain a new permit. If a yacht is left in Tunisia in the care of a marina or boatyard while the owner is abroad, the validity of the permit can be extended. Unattended boats may remain in Tunisia for any length of time provided customs is informed.

Fees
Harbour dues.

Restrictions
The commercial port of Ghannouch 1.5 miles north of Gabes is prohibited to yachts.

Fishing with scuba gear is forbidden.

Facilities

Yachting facilities are the best in North Africa and as good as in many other parts of the Mediterranean. There are now either new marinas or docks for yachts inside existing harbours along the entire Tunisian coast from Zarzis to Tabarka. There are marinas at Port Kantaoui, Sidi Bou Said, La Goulette and Monastir. La Goulette is nearest to the capital Tunis, while Sidi Bou Said is within walking distance of the ruins of Carthage. There are haul-out facilities at Kantaoui, La Goulette, Monastir and Sfax, where there are also boatyards with a good range of repair facilities. The best facilities are at Sidi Bou Said. Marine supplies are not widely available although there are chandleries attached to most marinas. Provisioning is good everywhere, particularly in Monastir, which has some French-type supermarkets. There are street markets everywhere with a very good selection of fresh produce. In most places fuel is available on the dock, otherwise it can be ordered from a nearby station. LPG bottles can be filled in most ports.

Because of its good facilities, security, attractive prices and simple formalities, Tunisia has become a popular wintering place, especially with owners of boats who wish to avoid spending too long in the EU. Three marinas are most suitable for wintering: Sidi Bou Said, El Kantaoui and Monastir. They have similar amenities and long term fees are negotiable. Equipment or spares from abroad should be addressed to the marina, which will assist in clearing it through customs.

A new full service marina is under construction at Yasmine Hammamet and is scheduled to open in 2001.

Further Reading

North Africa
Mediterranean Cruising Handbook
Africa on a Shoestring
North Africa – a travel survival kit

Websites

www.tourismtunisia.com (National Tourism Office)
www.focusmm.com.au/tunisia (Marina details)

TURKEY

Boasting a long coastline in the Eastern Mediterranean, the Sea of Marmara and the Black Sea, Turkey is almost surrounded by water. Spanning the two shores of the Bosporus and Dardanelles at the meeting point of Europe and Asia, Turkey cannot be labelled as either European or Asian. It is a melting pot of different cultures and civilisations, every one of which has left its indelible mark on the country and many of whose remains can still be seen, from Troy to Ephesus and Byzantium. This latter city became first Constantinople, and then, as Istanbul, the centre of the vast Ottoman Empire.

Most cruising yachts sail in the south-west of the country, although the Sea of Marmara is also worth exploring and a sail through the heart of Istanbul is an exhilarating experience. Negotiating the crowded waters of the Bosporus can be nerve-racking at times, but this is more than made up for by the attractions provided by the Black Sea coast of Turkey. Although lacking in natural harbours, there are several sheltered ports while the spectacular coast can be enjoyed when day sailing from one such port to the next. Some of these ports tend to be crowded with local craft, so it pays to be there during the closed season for fishing, in July and August, when most trawlers are hauled out. One of the most interesting towns to visit is Trabzon.

Although lacking the profusion of islands of its Greek neighbour, along the coast of Asia Minor there are so many bays and coves that one can almost always pick a pretty anchorage within minutes of deciding to drop the anchor. Although the number of yachts cruising Turkey is almost doubling every year, many places are still uncrowded, especially out of the high season and particularly on the southern shore, from Marmaris to Antalya and beyond. In some of the places along that coast, th boat can be anchored in sight of a 2000 year old Lycian tomb and a short walk ashore may lead to a well preserved amphitheatre hidden in the hills. It is memories like these, and not the Byzantine formalities, which make a cruise in Turkey an unforgettable experience.

Country Profile

Turkey was part of the classical world and the Trojan Wars were fought on what is now Turkish soil. During the classical era much of the Asia Minor coast was part of Greece. The Christian Byzantine empire, which succeeded Rome, had its capital at Constantinople, later to become Istanbul under the Ottoman Turks. Towards the end of the thirteenth century the Ottoman state was founded in Asia Minor by Osman I and expanded its territory in the fourteenth century through Asia Minor, into Thrace, capturing Adrianople and Bulgaria. The following century saw further expansion, and in 1453 Mehmed II captured Constantinople. The

Practical Information

LOCAL TIME: GMT + 3. Summer time
GMT + 2.

BUOYAGE: IALA A

CURRENCY: Turkish lira (TL).

BUSINESS HOURS

Although a Muslim country, Saturday and
Sunday are the days of rest for state
offices and most banks. Most businesses
remain open every day, especially during
the tourist season. In summer in Aegean
and Mediterranean regions some places
may be closed in the afternoons.
Banks 0830–1200, 1330–1700 Monday to
Friday.
Shops: 0900–1300/1400–1900 Monday to
Saturday.
Government offices:
0830–1200/1300–1700 Monday to Friday.

ELECTRICITY: 220 V, 50 Hz

PUBLIC HOLIDAYS

1 January: New Year's Day
23 April: Independence Day, Children's Day
1 May: Spring Festival
19 May: Atatürk's Commemoration Day,
Youth and Sports Day
30 August: Victory Day
29 October: Republic Day
Variable religious holidays: Ramadan
(called Ramazan in Turkish) Seker
Bayrami, Kurban Bayrami.

COMMUNICATIONS

International direct dialling phones
(Milletlerarasi) take phone cards.
Post office (PTT): 0830–1200/1300–1700
Monday to Saturday. Main post offices are
open 0800–2100 Monday to Saturday,
0900–1900 Sunday.
PTT services such as telephone are
available in some cities and tourist resorts 24
hours daily.
Poste Restante at main post offices.
Address should be: name (surname first),
Postrestante, Merkez Postanesi, City,
Turkey.
There are international flights from Istanbul
and Ankara to most parts of Europe and
elsewhere. There are several flights from
Izmir and Antalya to European destinations
and many charter flights in the summer. The
international airports at Bodrum and
Dalaman have frequent flights to European
destinations and are most convenient if
cruising in that part of Turkey.

MEDICAL

Treatment in public hospitals is inexpensive,
but better care will be found in one of the
private hospitals. The latter deal with
insurance cases and accept credit cards.
Costs should be agreed in advance and, if
time allows, prices should be compared at
different hospitals.

DIPLOMATIC MISSIONS

In Ankara:
Australia: Nenehatun Cad. 83, Gazi Osman
Pasa. *Tel.* 446 1180.

Bulgaria: Atatürk Bulvari 124. *Tel.* 426 74 55.
Canada: Nenehatun Cad 75 Gazi Osman
Pasa. *Tel.* 436 12 75.
France: Paris Cad 70 Kavaklidere. *Tel.* 426
14 80.
Germany: Atatürk Bulvari 114. *Tel.* 426 54
65.
Greece: Ziya-Ürrahman Cad 9-11 Gazi
Osman Pasa. *Tel.* 436 88 60.
Romania: Bükres Sok 4. *Tel.* 466 37 06.
Russia: Karyagdi Sok 5 Çankaya. *Tel.* 439
21 22.
Ukraine: Cemal Nadir Sok 9 Çankaya. *Tel.*
439 99 73.
United Kingdom: Sehit Ersan Cad. 46/A,
Çankaya. *Tel.* 468 6230.
United States: 110 Atatürk Blvd.
Tel. 468 6110.

In Istanbul:
Bulgaria: Levent Ulus Mah, Zincirliküyü
Caddesi 44. *Tel.* 269 2216.
Canada: Buyukdere Cad. 107/3, Bengun
Hän. *Tel.* 272 5174.
Germany: Inönü Cad, Selim Hatun Camii
Sok 46, Ayazpasha, Taksim. *Tel.* 251 5404.
Greece: Aga Hamam Sok, Beyoglu. *Tel.*
245 0596.
Romania: Siraselviler Caddesi 55.
Russia: Istiklal Caddesi 443, Tünel, Beyoglu.
Tel. 244 2610.
Ukraine: 5th floor, c/o BASCO Shipping
Co., Maliye Caddesi 29
Karaköy. *Tel.* 252 5402.
United Kingdom: Mesrutiyet Cad. 34,
Beyoglu, Tepesbasi. *Tel.* 251 3602.
United States: Mesrutiyet Cad. 104–8,
Tepesbasi, Beyoglu. *Tel.* 251 3602.

empire reached the height of its power under
Suleiman I (1520–66), whose realm stretched
from Hungary and the Balkans to south Russia,
throughout Asia Minor to the Persian Gulf and
across North America as far west as Algeria.
However, after a decisive defeat at Lepanto in
1571, and unsuccessful sieges of Vienna in 1529
and 1683, the empire had reached its limit.

The new powers of Austria and Russia challenged Ottoman dominance in the Balkans,
especially Russia which sought to expand at
Turkish expense. The nineteenth century saw
states in the Balkans and Mediterranean gain independence from an empire weakened by financial
difficulties and lack of reform. The Balkan wars of

1912–13 lost nearly all Turkish territory in
Europe. Dissatisfaction with the regime grew, and
in 1909 the nationalist Young Turks came to
power. In the First World War Ottoman Turkey
fought on Germany's side and on defeat was occupied by the Allies and a harsh treaty imposed. In
1922 Mustafa Kemal led the overthrow of the
Sultanate, renegotiated the peace settlement, and
established a republic. Under the presidency of
Kemal, known as Atatürk, a modern, westernised
Turkey was created as a smaller, more nationally
united state.

Neutral during the Second World War, after the
war Turkey joined NATO. Civil troubles in Turkey
in 1970–72 saw the army intervene to restore

order, and in 1980 there were worse disturbances involving Marxist and Muslim opposition groups as well as Kurdish separatists, leading to the military dissolving parliament and banning political parties. In 1983 civil government was restored. Turkey's application to join the European Union has been postponed due to Turkey's record on human rights. In the meantime Turkey has a special economic relationship with the EU. In the 1990s the Kurdish fight for autonomy has intensified in violence. Turkey's acceptance in 1999 as a candidate member for eventual entry into the EU has somehow relieved the tension but travel in the Kurdish part of Turkey is still best avoided.

Industry is concentrated in the west of the country, while the east is gradually catching up. There are some mineral resources of coal, oil and iron ore.

The population is around 60 million, of which 90 per cent are ethnic Turks. Kurds form the largest minority in the east of the country and there are also Arabs, Georgians, Bulgarians and some Greeks and Armenians.

Turkish is an Ural-Altaic language of the same origins as Finnish and Hungarian. Kurdish and Arabic are also spoken. Many also speak German or English. Most people are Muslim with small minorities of Jews, Greek Orthodox and Syrian Monophysites. The Turks are not quite so fundamentalist as other Muslims and mosques can be visited provided shoes are removed, women cover their heads and arms and men do not wear shorts. Modesty of dress is important outside of tourist areas.

Ankara, which is a new city, has been the capital since 1923. However, Istanbul is still the largest city and a commercial and cultural centre. Istanbul is a spectacular city, spread over two continents, and there is much to see from the Blue Mosque to the Grand Bazaar.

The climate is very varied, but generally can be described as Mediterranean, with hot summers and mild winters. The Black Sea has more extremes and is more humid. The Aegean coast in summer is under the influence of the northerly *meltemi* wind, which blows from about May until the end of August and at its peak can be very strong. Lighter winds prevail along the south coast where nights are usually calm. During the rest of the year, winds are variable.

Entry Regulations

Ports of entry
Canakkale 40°09′N 26°25′E, Bandirma 40°21′N 27°58′E, Tekirdag 40°58′N 27°31′E, Gemlik 40°26′N 29°09′E, Mudanya 40°22.6′N 28°53.5′E, Istanbul 41°00′N 28°58′E, Akcay 39°35′N 26°56′E, Ayvalik 39°19′N 26°41′E, Dikili 39°05′N 26°53′E, Izmir 38°26′N 27°08′E, Cesme 38°19′N 26°20′E, Kuşadasi 37°52′N 27°14′E, Güllük 37°15′N 27°38′E, Bodrum 37°02′N 27°25′E, Datça 36°43′N 27°41′E, Marmaris 36°51′N 28°16′E, Fethiye 36°38′N 29°06′E, Kas 36°11′N 29°38′E, Finike 36°18′N 30°09′E, Kemer 36°35′N 30°34′E, Antalya 36°53′N 30°42′E, Alanya 36°32′N 32°01′E, Anamur 36°01′N 32°48′E, Tasucu 36°19′N 33°53′E, Mersin 36°48′N 34°38′E, Iskenderun 36°36′N 36°10′E.

Black Sea: Sinop 42°01′N 35°09′E, Zonguldak 41°27.6′N 31°46.8′E, Eregli 41°17′N 31°24′E, Bartin 41°41′N 32°13′E, Inebolu 42°00′N 33°46′E, Samsun 41°18′N 36°20′E, Giresun 40°55′N 38°22′E, Trabzon 41°00′N 39°45′E, Rize 41°02′N 40°31′E, Hopa 41°25′N 41°25′E.

Procedure on arrival
Any yacht coming from abroad must fly the Q flag and report to customs and/or customs police at an official port of entry. Either quarantine or customs will be first to inspect the yacht, and then direct the skipper to clear immigration (referred to as 'Polis') and harbour master. If customs is not present, immigration should be visited first. Although officials are represented at some marinas, in most cases it is necessary to visit the various offices to complete clearance formalities and have both transit log and passports stamped. Marians usually act as one's agent and will both provide the transit log and deal with formalities. Each yacht must purchase a transit log (from a marina, chamber of commerce or agency) which is the travel document of the yacht during her stay in Turkey and states the yacht's master, owner, destinations in Turkey and registered inventory. The transit log is valid for three months or until the yacht is laid up. A new log must be purchased and completed on each arrival from abroad.

Customs will stamp the skipper's passport stating that he is accompanied by a yacht. In order to eliminate illicit chartering work, only the owner of a yacht is deemed to be skipper. According to Turkish law, a yacht may have up to four owners. Should an owner not be present, the skipper may be asked to pay a special fee in order to cruise in Turkish waters. Skippers of company-owned boats should have a document showing that he/she is an owner of the company. Ideally, the skipper's name should appear on the registration certificate or on some official proof of ownership. Generally, it is wise to ask for receipts for any payments.

Officials are particular about the Turkish courtesy flag, which must be flown from the correct position between 0800 and sunset when cruising. The courtesy flag may be left up permanently when in port.

In subsequent ports the authorities may wish to see the transit log. There are some regional differences in customs formalities. In the past, some captains have been asked to produce a certificate of competence when clearing and if unable to do so, the yacht was not allowed to leave port.

It is recommended to avoid zigzagging between Turkish and Greek waters. Both countries insist on arrival from abroad to be made only at an official port of entry.

When within 5 miles of the entrance into either the Bosporus or the Dardanelles, boats should contact Traffic Control for further instructions. Although this provision only applies to boats over 20 metres LOA, it is recommended that smaller boats also comply with it. Boats in possession of a transit log are no longer required to stop at Canakkale and may proceed through the Dardanelles without stopping. The regulations are similar for boats going through the Bosporus, who may continue towards ports on the Turkish Black Sea coast without stopping.

Procedure on departure

On departure, Section V of the transit log must be completed and returned to customs. Details of the transit log are also entered on the captain's passport, and this entry must be cancelled by customs on departure from Turkey. One must also clear out with immigration and the harbour master. If Turkey is left in an emergency, without having been able to clear out correctly, the completed Section V should be handed in to a Turkish consulate abroad within one month, otherwise the offending yacht cannot return.

Customs

All types of firearms must be declared, and will be sealed on arrival by customs. Also, diving tanks must be declared.

Animals require a recent health certificate from the country of origin. A rabies vaccination certificate must show that the animal received the vaccination between 15 days and six months before arrival in Turkey.

Antiques cannot be exported. If carpets are

bought, the customs will require to see proof of purchase. Antique objects must be accompanied by a non-objection certificate issued by the Ministry of Culture.

Although the people of Turkey as a whole are extremely hospitable, some of their customs officers leave much to be desired. The formalities are cumbersome and time-consuming and the officials quite unhelpful. Getting the customs duty waived on yacht equipment that has been ordered from abroad is also a lengthy and frustrating procedure, so it might be easier to try and bring any equipment needed into Turkey as personal luggage. In such a case it is advisable to have a copy of the ship's papers as well as some form of proof that the yacht has been left temporarily in Turkey. Items brought in personally with a value over US$300 will be registered into one's passport. This will be cancelled when the entry is transferred to the transit log. Equipment couriered directly should be addressed to the marina. As the yacht has been stamped into the skipper's passport on arrival, those laying up their yacht in Turkey and leaving the country by air should have their passports amended accordingly before going to the airport.

Immigration

In a move to further encourage foreign nationals to base their yachts in Turkey, visa restrictions were considerably eased early in 2000, so that foreign sailors arriving in Turkey on their own yacht are now eligible for a two-year visa at the first application, later a three-year visa, and then a five-year visa. This means that foreign nationals are subject to the same treatment regarding length of stay as their own yachts.

Otherwise, visa regulations stipulate that citizens of the European Union do not need visas for up to three months' stay, except for those of Austria, Ireland, Italy, Portugal, Spain and the United Kingdom, who can obtain a three-month visa on arrival. The latter also applies to citizens of the United States.

Visas are not required for up to a three-month stay for nationals of Australia, Argentina, Bahamas, Bahrain, Barbados, Belize, Canada, Chile, Ecuador, Fiji, Grenada, Iceland, Iran, Israel, Jamaica, Japan, Kenya, South Korea, Kuwait, Liechtenstein, Malaysia, Malta, Mauritius, Monaco, Morocco, New Zealand, Northern Cyprus, Norway, Oman, Qatar, St Lucia, San Marino, Saudi Arabia, Seychelles, Singapore, Switzerland, Trinidad and Tobago, Tunisia, UAE.

For up to two months, visas are not required for

nationals of Bosnia-Hercegovina, Croatia, Indonesia, Macedonia, Romania and Slovenia. For up to one month, for Bolivia, Kazakhstan, Kyrgyzstan and South Africa.

Nationals of the CIS, Czech Republic, Estonia, Hungary, Jordan, Latvia, Lithuania, Poland and the Slovak Republic can obtain one month visas on arrival. Nationals of Guatemala are issued a 15 day visa on arrival.

Visa fees are charged in UK£ for the United Kingdom and Ireland, in US$ for all others, where applicable.

All other nationalities need visas in advance.

Nationals of Taiwan, Greek Cyprus and North Korea may only obtain a visa after providing certain references.

If staying longer than three months one has to apply for a residence permit and must prove adequate financial means. It is easier to leave and return after a reasonable period of time, re-enter Turkey and obtain a further three months, than to apply for an extension.

Anamur on Turkey's south coast.

Transit log

An official transit log is required for all yachts cruising in Turkey. The log is issued at the first port of entry and is valid for a total of five years without paying VAT. Yachts can be left for up to two years in bond at a boatyard or marina.

The transit log has provision for only one crew change. For subsequent changes a new log must be obtained. A new log must be isssued also if there is a change of skipper. Crew changes are amended at the harbour master's office. The owner is expected to be on board and Turkish law does not allow more than four co-owners. If one of the owners is not on board, or proof of ownership is inadequate, a special transit log must be purchased at a cost of US$600.

A great deal of confusion surrounds the regulations concerning restrictions imposed on foreign yachts cruising in Turkey, which are suspected of chartering. A change of crew, even if these are friends of the owner, is sometimes interpreted by some harbour masters as being equivalent to the arrival of a charter party. As a consequence, the yacht in question may be required to buy a new

transit log or pay the charter fee despite the owner's protestations. Regulations have been eased in recent years and the ownership issue is no longer applied with such severity. It is now possible for non-owners, such as delivery skippers, to make one landfall in Turkey, usually to deliver a boat for wintering. Further easing of restrictions are envisaged for the near future.

Wintering
Special formalities must be completed if the yacht is to be left unattended in Turkey and the crew leave the country by other means. The forms are available from marina offices and must be stamped by customs. The passports must be stamped if leaving by other means than by yacht, as the police do not normally stamp passports of people entering by yacht and these stamps are necessary to leave the country overland or by air. The skipper in particular must ensure that customs cancels the yacht endorsement in his/her passport.

Charter
Foreign yachts used for commercial purposes and private foreign yachts without their owners on board may be required to pay the US$600 charter fee. Foreign yachts are now allowed to transport passengers from a foreign port to a Turkish port.

Health
Hepatitis, polio and typhoid vaccinations are recommended.

Fees
A fee is charged for the transit log. This is US$30 for an ordinary log and US$600 if the boat is used for charter work. A navigation aids fee is payable by boats over 30 tons.

Overtime charges seem to vary from place to place, so if at all possible it is advisable to clear in and out during office hours on normal working days.

Restrictions
Prohibited areas for yachts are: no anchoring at the entrance and exit of the Dardanelles (Canakkale Bogazi, especially Gokceada and Bozcaada, region of Kumkale, Mehmetcik, Burnu, Ani, Korfezi); the zone north of the Bosporus, Gulf of Izmir, isles of Uzin and Hekim; the Bay of Karaagac; Oludeniz, Fethiye; parts of the ports of Mersin and Iskenderun; the submarine base in the inner port of Bartin Liman.

Taking archaeological souvenirs can lead to confiscation of the yacht.

Skin diving is permitted everywhere, but diving with tanks is restricted. Divers must have an internationally recognised certificate, have to register with a Turkish diving club and must be accompanied by a Turkish instructor when diving. Fishing is permitted for sport in certain areas, but there is a minimum size for fish caught and also the amount per person is controlled.

Facilities
Yachting facilities are constantly improving and those in the major centres are of a good standard. There are several marinas, the best being at Kuşadasi, Kemer, Bodrum, Marmaris and Atakoy Marina near Istanbul. Apart from the usual services of fuel and water, these marinas also have good repair facilities as well as haul-out facilities. The best repair services are reported to be those at the marinas at Bodrum, Kusadasi and Antalya. For major electronic work, Istanbul and Marmaris are reported to be the best places. Fuel is available in all larger marinas, but in smaller places it may have to be carried in jerrycans. Dirty fuel continues to be a problem, so in certain places the fuel may have to be filtered. Water is available everywhere. LPG (butane) bottles can be filled locally in most places. Turkish charts can be obtained from the Hydrographic Office in Istanbul or some of the chandleries. Marine equipment is available at chandleries in the larger marinas and items that are not in stock can be ordered from the importers and delivered promptly. VAT may be refunded on larger purchases. All major engine manufacturers are represented in Turkey and parts for most common makes are usually manufactured locally and easily available. Provisioning is generally good and there are grocery stores in most marinas or supermarkets in nearby towns. At Trabzon on the Black Sea provisions are adequate and fuel readily available.

Highly recommended as a winter spot are the marinas in SW Turkey at Finike, Kemer and Antalya as the weather is better than in other parts of the Mediterranean and rates are very attractive. Also highly recommended is Bodrum Marina, whose management is known for its determined efforts to welcome foreign sailors and ease formalities for them. Facilities in and around Bodrum have improved greatly in recent years turning it into one of the major yachting centres in the Mediterranean.

Further Reading
Turkish Waters and Cyprus Pilot
Black Sea Cruising Guide

Practical Information

LOCAL TIME: GMT + 2, GMT + 3 summer time end March to end September.

BUOYAGE: IALA A

CURRENCY: Ukraine grynia (UHA), also spelt hryvnia. Exchange kiosks offer the best rates. Hard currency can be changed anywhere, but credit cards are not widely accepted. Paying in hard currency in restaurants and retail shops has been officially banned, but most services aimed at foreign tourists expect to be paid in hard currency.

BUSINESS HOURS
Business: 0900–1300, 1430–1700/1800.
Shops: 0800/0900–1800/1900 weekdays.

ELECTRICITY: 220 V 50 Hz

PUBLIC HOLIDAYS
1–2 January: New Year's Day
7 January: Orthodox Christmas
8 March: International Women's Day
1–2 May: Spring and Labour Days
9 May: Victory Day
24 August: Independence Day

COMMUNICATIONS
International calls can be booked at telephone offices, usually open 24 hours in the main cities, located in post office buildings, but it may be better, though more expensive, to try one of the main hotels. The mail service can be unreliable. Post office and telephone office, Sadovya Street, Odessa.

Odessa airport only has international and internal flights, and there are frequent trains to other CIS cities. The international airport is at Kiev.

Crimea: International calls can be made from the Yalta port authority building. Simferopol, a two hour bus journey from Yalta, has rail and air connections to other cities.

DIPLOMATIC MISSIONS
In Kiev:
Canada:Vul. Yaroslaviv 31.
Tel. (044) 212 21 12.
Germany: Vul. Chkalova 84.
Tel. (044) 216 67 94.
Russia: Vul. R. Luxemburg 5, Hotel Zhovtnevy.
Tel. (044) 291 83 13.
United Kingdom: Vul. Desyatynna 9.
Tel. (044) 228 05 04.
United States: Vul. Yuria Kotsyubinskoho 10.
Tel. (044) 244 73 49.

Websites

www.turkey.org (Official government site)
www.focusmm.com.au/trt (Directory of marinas)
www.access.ch/tuerkei (General information)

Greece and beyond. This interest in yachting should eventually result in better facilities for pleasure craft.

The small country of Moldova, Ukraine's western neighbour, only has a token exit to the Black Sea, on the right bank of the Dniester River.

UKRAINE

Set on the northern shores of the Black Sea, between the Azov Sea and the Danube Delta, the Ukraine has been endowed by nature with many more natural harbours than any of its neighbours. Some of these harbours are on the Azov Sea, an enclosed body of water which until recently was barred to foreign vessels. This almost completely enclosed body of water is reached through a narrow cut, on the shores of which stands the old city of Kerch.

Facilities for yachts are limited but are constantly improving, and the opening of a new marina in Odessa has made a great difference to the comfort of visiting sailors. Several rallies held in the Black Sea in recent years have persuaded the authorities to bring about some considerable improvements to the yachting infrastructure. Independence and the freedom to travel have seen an amazing upsurge in the number of locally built sailing boats, some of which have been enjoying the new found freedom by sailing in large numbers to

Country Profile

Around the fifth century the Slavic peoples established themselves in this region. The Russian State of Kiev was founded in the ninth century and developed by the eleventh century into an advanced civilisation, influenced by Byzantium, only to be ruined in the thirteenth century by Mongolian invasions. By the fourteenth century Lithuania and Poland had annexed all of the Ukraine except for Ruthenia which was under Hungarian domination. During the fifteenth and sixteenth centuries the Cossacks established themselves on the Don and the Dneiper rivers. In the seventeenth century the Ukraine was partitioned between Poland and Russia; in 1709 Tsar Peter the Great crushed a movement to establish an independent Ukraine. Towards the end of the eighteenth century all of the Ukraine came under Russian and Austrian rule.

In 1917 the Ukrainian Soviet Socialist Republic was proclaimed and finally established in 1919, joining together in 1922 with the other Soviet Socialist Republics to form the USSR. From 1941 to 1944 it was occupied by Germany. The Crimea was incorporated into the Ukraine in 1954.

Independence from the USSR was declared in 1991 and the Ukraine was one of the founder members of the Commonwealth of Independent States. In 1994 an accord was signed by the presidents of the Ukraine, Russia and the United States for the dismantling of all nuclear weapons on Ukrainian territory.

The Ukraine has great economic potential, being rich in mineral and chemical deposits and a fertile agricultural region. However, moves towards privatisation have been slower than in Russia and living standards have fallen in the move away from a Soviet economic system. The 1986 Chernobyl nuclear reactor disaster left large land areas contaminated and the process of decontamination takes a substantial part of state expenditure.

The population is around 52 million, of which the majority are Ukrainian, with a large Russian minority of some 12 million. Ukrainian is the official language, and most also speak Russian. Christian Orthodox and Roman Catholic are the main denominations; the Greek Catholic Church, banned in 1946, was relegalised in 1991. The capital is Kiev.

The climate is temperate with hot summers and cold winters. Along the coast, the winds are very much influenced by the surrounding landmass and in summer there is a daily pattern of land and sea breezes. An onshore breeze comes up around midday and usually dies by dusk to be followed by a land breeze during the night.

Entry Regulations

Ports of entry
Odessa 46°28'N 30°45'E, Feodosia 45°02'N 35°24'E, Sevastopol 44°37'N 33°30.8'E (yacht club), Yalta 44°30'N 34°10'E, Kherson 46°37'N 32°36'E, Nikolaev 46°58'N 31°58'E.

Also reported as ports of entry are Kerch 45°13'N 36°28'E and Belograd-Dnestzovski 46°13'N 30°18'E.

Procedure on arrival
Formalities generally are still lengthy and cumbersome and one must be prepared to accept bureaucracy as a fact of life.

All officials will visit the yacht. Captain and crew must remain onboard until all formalities are completed.

Odessa: Arriving vessels must contact Odessa Port Control on Channel 14. It is strongly recommended that all vessels enter Odessa via the Vorontsov gateway on a course due south. Yachts are now directed to the new Odessa Marina (46°29.5'N, 30°45'E), where clearance formalities will be completed. Immigration, customs and quarantine officials will visit the boat. The latter will request a deratting or exemption certificate, in the absence of which a new one will be issued at the cost of $US100. There is also a fee for a health certificate, issued on arrival, at the cost of between $30 and $40.

Procedure on departure
The authorities must be given 24 hours' notice of departure. Entry and exit formalities must be carried out at every port where officials are present, and permission obtained to visit harbours where there are no officials. An ecological certificate must be obtained in the port of departure stating that the vessel had not been guilty of polluting the sea or environment.

Customs
Foreign currency, firearms and narcotics must be declared on arrival.

Caviar and artworks may not be exported without a permit.

Immigration
All citizens need a visa to visit the Ukraine. To obtain a visa in advance one must have an official invitation. The best source is either the Black Sea Yachtsmen's Association (e-mail, bsya@bios.iuf.net, Fax. + 38 692 465 738) or Odessa Marina (e-mail, marina@port.odessa.ua, *Tel.*/Fax. +38 48 729 4335), whose manager will issue such an invitation. Advance help and practical advice for anyone planning to visit any of the Black Sea countries, not just the Ukraine, can be obtained from Mr Dülger, assistant manager at Ataköy Marina near Istanbul. The marina is located close to the southern end of the Bosphorus. *Tel.* +90 212 560 4270, Fax. 7270, e-mail a_marina@atakoymarina.com.tr.

In exceptional situations a visa may be granted on arrival, but only for a very short stay. To simplify matters it is therefore advisable to obtain a visa in advance.

Visas and other arrangements can be made in Istanbul, where the best place to stop is at Ataköy Marina, approximately 5 miles west of the Bosporus. The management of the marina has an arrangement with the authorities in Odessa, as well as with the Odessa Yacht Club, and can also help with the latest information.

The Ukrainian consulate in Istanbul is open Fridays and Saturdays, 0900–1200, near the Bosporus passenger terminal: c/o BASCO Shipping & Trade SA, 5th floor, Maliye Caddesi 29, Karaköy. Intourist, the Russian state tourist agency, offer a visa service for the CIS republics.

Agents
Although formalities can be lengthy, the services of an agent are not compulsory, neither in Odessa nor in other ports. Odessa Marina will act as an agent.

Health
Cholera may be a problem. Water must be treated.

Navigation
Turkish charts are reported as being most up to date.

Some ports may still be closed to foreign vessels; this should be checked on arrival at the first port of entry.

Facilities

Facilities are good at the Odessa Yacht Club, with water and electricity on the quay. Fuel and basic repairs can be arranged through the Bo Arinko Agency at the yacht club. The new marina in Odessa provides docking, fuel, water and electricity and also some repair facilities, including a slipway. Provisioning in Odessa is good, with both fresh produce markets and several supermarkets. There is a new marina (Gold Simvol) at Balaklava, near Sevastopol. Marinas are also planned in Sevastopol itself (Yug), Ochakov, Alushta and Yalta. Yacht clubs at Nikolaev, Kherson and Sevastopol welcome visiting cruising boats. Hard currency shops have sprung up in recent years, selling imported goods at very high prices. At other main ports, fuel and water can be arranged through an agent, for a fee.

CRIMEA

The Crimean peninsula extends south into the Black Sea, with a picturesque coast always popular as a holiday destination, as can be seen by the many resorts, the most famous among them being Yalta. With the opening of this entire region to foreign travel, Crimea is attracting a major share of cruising boats.

In ancient times the region was colonised by the Greeks and Romans, then later suffered invasions by the Goths and Huns, before being settled from the eighth to thirteenth centuries by peoples of Turkish and Mongol origin. It later passed under the rule of the Ottoman Turks, followed by the Russian empire. In 1945 the Tatar population were deported for their alleged collaboration with the Nazi occupiers during the Second World War, and their autonomous republic established in 1921 was suppressed. In 1954 the Crimea was attached to the Ukraine. Following Ukrainian independence, in 1992 Russia contested the status of the Crimea, whose population are mainly Russian. Crimea was subsequently defined as an autonomous republic within the Ukraine. However, Ukraine resisted further moves by the Crimean assembly towards Crimean independence and the autonomy was abolished in 1995.

The population is around 2.6 million, of which some 65 per cent are Russian and 25 per cent Ukrainian. Many of the surviving Tatar population, who are Muslims and Turkish-speakers, have returned since the collapse of the Soviet Union. Simferopol is the capital.

Entry Regulations

Ports of entry
Sevastopol 44°37′N 33°32′E, Yalta 44°30′N 34°10′E.

Procedure on arrival
Yalta: The main commercial harbour is open to the south and with an onshore wind, conditions can become untenable. It may be possible to obtain permission to go to the sheltered commercial harbour, Massandra. Better protection and adequate conditions for visiting yachts will be found at Artek Marina, 7 miles north of Yalta. When contacting the authorities by radio on arrival, one should insist on being allowed to go directly to Artek Marina and complete formalities there.

Sevastopol: While this port remains the site of the ex-USSR Black Sea fleet, the authorities do not welcome foreign yachts. Formalities must be completed at Sevastopol 'Free Port' 3 miles west of Sevastopol.

Facilities

Artek Harbour is a yacht harbour with some basic facilities: fuel is available by jerrycan, and the port captain may be able to help arrange repairs. It is a bus ride into Yalta, where shopping is better; there is a good market for fresh produce. The Yalta Marine Agency may also be able to help with repairs.

Further Reading

Black Sea Cruising Guide

Websites

www.utis.com.ua (National Tourism Office for the Ukraine)
www.ukraine.org (Useful links)

YUGOSLAVIA (Montenegro and Serbia)

The disintegration of the former Socialist Federal Republic of Yugoslavia into its component parts in the early 1990s has led to one of the most senseless wars in European history. Croatia and Slovenia were the first to declare their independence followed by Bosnia-Hercegovina. The Federal Republic of Yugoslavia, declared in 1992, consists of Serbia, its dependencies Kosovo and Vojvodina, and the Republic of Montenegro. Because of its alleged involvement in hostilities in Bosnia-Hercegovina, international sanctions under UN supervision were imposed against Yugoslavia, whose recognition by the international community was made dependent on the finding of a peaceful solution in the areas under its influence. The situation was further aggravated in 1999 by the NATO bombing of Serbia during an aerial campaign of over two months that left the country in ruins. This was in response to Belgrade's refusal to respond to international pressure and put an end to the violence against the Albanian population of Kosovo. A UN force (K-for) was sent into Kosovo, whose continuing status as a province of Yugoslavia is increasingly under threat. Similarly under threat is Montenegro's contin-uing presence in the current federation with Serbia. There is therefore a strong possibility of Montenegro seeking independence at some point in the future.

From the cruising point of view, most of the coastline of former Yugoslavia is now in Croatia, where much of the yachting activity is concentrated. The main attraction of Montenegro's coast is the spectacular Gulf of Kotor which is the longest fjord in southern Europe, and long sandy beaches around the popular resorts of Budva and Ulcinj.

Country Profile

In medieval times Serbia was a prosperous, large state dominating the Balkans until defeated by the Turks in 1389 at the Battle of Kosovo. Independence from Turkey only came in 1878. At the end of the First World War, out of the ruins of the Ottoman and Austro-Hungarian empires, the Kingdom of the Serbs, Croats and Slovenes was formed, renamed Yugoslavia in 1929. In

Practical Information

LOCAL TIME: GMT + 1, summer time GMT + 2 end March to end September.

CURRENCY: Dinar. The dinar is not convertible. Travellers cheques and credit cards cannot be used while the international sanctions last.

ELECTRICITY: 220 V, 50 Hz

BUSINESS HOURS
Banks: 0700–1900 Monday to Friday, 0700–1200 Saturday.
Shops: 0800–1200, 1600–2000 Monday to Friday, close 1500 Saturday.

PUBLIC HOLIDAYS
(not observed in all republics)
1–2 January: New Year
7 January: Orthodox Christmas
1–2 May: Labour Day
9 May: Victory Day
29–30 November: Republic Days
Also: 7 July: Serbian public holiday
13 July: Montenegrin holiday

COMMUNICATIONS
International calls can be booked at main post offices. Many international flights have been cancelled as a result of the sanc-tions, but the situation appears to be gradually returning to normal.

DIPLOMATIC MISSIONS
As a result of the Kosovo crisis, most NATO countries have either withdrawn or scaled down their missions.
United States: Kneza Milosa 50, Belgrade. *Tel.* 645 655. Diplomatic relations are at a low level, but the consular section continues to provide essential services.
United Kingdom: Generala Zdanova 46, Belgrade. *Tel.* 645 055/034. The embassy is temporarily closed.

1945 a republic along Communist lines was set up under the leadership of Josip Broz Tito, who had been prominent in the war-time resistance to German occupation. The new Yugoslavia comprised the six republics of Bosnia-Hercegovina, Croatia, Macedonia, Montenegro, Serbia and Slovenia. After Tito's death in 1980 the Presidency was made collective. From 1988 inter-ethnic tensions worsened and the economic, political and social situation deteriorated.

Serbia opposed the independence of Croatia, Slovenia, Bosnia-Hercegovina and Macedonia in 1991 and 1992, wishing to maintain the Yugoslav Federation. In April 1992 it proclaimed the Federal Republic of Yugoslavia. The numerous Serbs living in Croatia and Bosnia-Hercegovina declared their allegiance to the new state, not recognising the new governments of these two independent republics. International sanctions were imposed on Serbia in June 1992. These were followed by even stronger measures in 1999, when the country was totally isolated by the international community. While this situation continues, cruising boats, especially those flying the flag of one of the NATO countries, are strongly advised to avoid this area. President Milosevic was deposed in 2000 as a first step towards a return to democracy.

The population is around 11 million, the majority being Serb and Orthodox Christians, with a large Hungarian minority (Roman Catholic) in the north of Vojvodina; Albanians, most of them Muslim, constitute the majority of the Kosovo population. There are also other small ethnic minorities. Serbia uses the Cyrillic alphabet, while Montenegro uses both Latin and Cyrillic. The capital of Serbia is Belgrade, where industry is largely centred. The international sanctions have adversely affected the economy, which has remained dependent on agriculture.

Entry Regulations

Ports of entry (Montenegro)

Budva 42°17′N 18°51′E, Bar 42°06′N 19°05′E, Kotor 42°25′N 18°46′E, Ulcinj 41°55′N 19°12′E, Hercegovni 42°27′N 18°32′E.

Procedure on arrival

Yachts approaching the Yugoslav (Montenegro) coast should expect to be intercepted by naval craft patrolling the area. VHF Channel 16 should be monitored permanently and, if contacted by a naval vessel, the radio operator of the yacht will be expected to give the following information: name of yacht, international callsign, flag, port of registration, last port of call, destination. The name of the owner and the general description of the cargo is sometimes also requested.

Bar: Yachts should call harbour control on Channel 16 before proceeding to the customs quay in the commercial harbour for clearance.

Immigration

Most nationalities require visas, which cannot be obtained on arrival. There are consulates in Bucharest, Sofia, Athens and Tirana.

Further Reading

Adriatic Pilot

Websites

www.gov.yu (Federal government)
www.montenegro.com (Montenegro Ministry of Tourism)
www.serbia-info.com (National Tourist Organisation of Serbia)

2 Northern Europe

A relatively short cruising season and inconsistent weather limits Northern Europe to being a cruising destination for yachts sailing from neighbouring countries. However, the Baltic Sea has started attracting more yachts from outside of the area as new cruising grounds open up in Poland, the Baltic republics and Russia.

Yachting is well developed in the Nordic countries who have their own considerable boating community. The traditional links between these countries are strong and yachts flying one of the Nordic flags enjoy many concessions when cruising in other Nordic countries. The rules affecting visiting yachts from other countries are stricter, particularly those concerning onboard stores. For a long-distance cruising yacht this can present serious problems, as the same duty-free allowances apply to foreign nationals arriving by sea as to ordinary tourists coming by land or air.

The situation has changed with Sweden and Finland joining the European Union, so that restrictions applied to non-EU boats do not affect those from other EU countries. There are various concessions and special arrangements which only apply to yachts from Nordic countries (Denmark, Norway, Sweden and Finland).

The major drawback of a cruise in this area is the short sailing season which lasts from June until the end of August. The weather during summer is pleasant and the days are very long with the sun hardly setting in the northern regions. Because the sailing season in the Baltic is so short, this can cause logistical problems for those who come from further away, whether Southern Europe or even across the Atlantic. Generally it is still too cold in April to enjoy cruising, especially if one is used to warm water sailing, so cruises should not be planned to start before May. The best weather can be expected in June and early July, when one has the added bonus of very long days. Midsummer Day has a special significance to all peoples bordering on the Baltic and, especially in Scandinavia, there are popular feasts held on that day. By the end of August, the sailing season is almost over and it is time to either start sailing south or make arrangements for leaving the boat to winter in one of these countries. In this respect Poland and Estonia can be very attractive as there are no restrictions on temporary importation for short periods and the rates are very low by West European or North American standards.

Mooring facilities are good almost everywhere and the yachting associations of Nordic countries have laid down their own moorings which may be used by visitors. Repair facilities are generally good and each country has at least one major yachting centre where more difficult repair jobs can be undertaken. Facilities in the former East Germany are rapidly improving, while those in Poland and the three Baltic republics are slowly getting up to West European standards. Only Russia still has a long way to go, both in regard to its facilities and the complicated formalities to which visiting boats are still subjected.

There are various opportunities for inland cruising, in the lakes and rivers of Sweden or the extensive river and canal systems in Germany, the Netherlands and Belgium. While the inland waterways of Holland or Sweden have great attractions, the busy canals and rivers of continental Europe are generally unsuited for cruising yachts and should be avoided.

Northern Europe is a region of very civilised cruising, but there is a price to pay for this quality of life and even basic provisions can be very expensive. Compensating for this, the Nordic countries have a reputation for extending a very hospitable welcome to visiting sailors and English is widely spoken.

BELGIUM

Situated between France and the Netherlands, Belgium has only a short coastline facing the English Channel and the North Sea. This lack of both coast and natural harbours do not make Belgium an appealing cruising destination. This is not helped by the difficulty of making landfall on the Belgian coast, which is fringed by sandbanks running parallel to the coast. Most foreign cruising yachts visit Belgian ports as a convenient place to stop while sailing north or south through the English Channel or are British yachts on a cross-channel trip. A few visiting yachts use the inland waterway system, which is connected to the extensive European canal network.

Country Profile

This region was originally inhabited by the Celtic Belgae, then was conquered by the Romans and later invaded by the Franks and Vikings. During the Middle Ages small independent principalities developed, while the towns became important commercial centres known especially for their textiles. Under the rule of the House of Burgundy and later the Hapsburgs, the Belgian provinces came under Spanish rule along with the Netherlands.

In 1572 the northern provinces rebelled against

Practical Information

LOCAL TIME: GMT + 1. Summer time GMT + 2 April to October.

BUOYAGE: IALA A

CURRENCY: Belgian franc (BF). Euro from 2002. 1 euro = 40.3399 BEF.

BUSINESS HOURS
Banks: 0900–1630 Monday to Friday.
Business: 0830–1730 Monday to Saturday.
Shops: 0900–1830 Monday to Saturday.
Government offices: 0900–1700 Monday to Friday. Some offices and shops close for lunch.

ELECTRICITY: 220 V, 50 Hz

PUBLIC HOLIDAYS
1 January: New Year's Day
Easter Monday

1 May: Labour Day
Ascension Day
Whit Monday
21 July: National Holiday
15 August: Assumption Day
1 November: All Saints' Day
11 November: Armistice Day
25 December: Christmas Day

COMMUNICATIONS
International dialling access code 00.
Public telephones take 5 or 20 franc coins and phone cards.
Dial 987 for an English-speaking operator for long-distance collect calls. Telegrams can be sent from telegraph offices, open 24 hours. Post offices open 0900–1700 Monday to Friday, Saturday mornings. Brussels is the only large international airport with flights to many destinations worldwide.

MEDICAL
There is no national health service so treatment can be expensive. Most West European countries have reciprocal arrangements for free emergency treatment.
Police *Tel.* 101, Ambulance 100.

DIPLOMATIC MISSIONS
In Brussels:
Australia: Guimard Centre, Rue Guimard 6–8. *Tel.* (2) 2310500.
Canada: Avenue de Tervuren 2. *Tel.* (2) 7356040.
France: Rue Ducale 65. *Tel.* (2) 220 0111.
Germany: Avenue de Tervueren 190. *Tel.* (2) 774 1911.
New Zealand: Blvd du Regent 47–8. *Tel.* (2) 5121040.
United Kingdom: Britannia House, Rue d'Arlon 85. *Tel.* (2) 2876211.
United States: Blvd du Regent 27. *Tel.* (2) 5133830.

King Philip and became independent as the United Provinces, while the southern states remained under Spain. In 1713 they were incorporated into the Austrian Hapsburg Empire. Briefly occupied by France, they proclaimed their independence in 1790 only to be overrun again by their neighbour. Remaining part of France until 1815, Belgium and the Netherlands were then united under the rule of William of Orange. Dissatisfaction with his rule led to the Belgians declaring independence and finally in 1831 the neutral kingdom of Belgium was recognised by the European Great Powers.

In 1948 the Benelux customs union was formed with the Netherlands and Luxembourg and later Belgium joined NATO and the European Community. In 1993 the constitution was revised to make Belgium a federal state, with considerable autonomy given to the three regions of Flanders, Wallonia and Brussels.

Belgium has an export-based economy, with only a small domestic market. Service industries are dominant, although there is a small manufacturing industry and agricultural sector.

The population is 10 million and the country is very densely populated. The Flemish, who are the majority, live mainly in the north, the French-speaking Walloons in the south and there is a small German minority in the east. French, Flemish and German are spoken, being official languages in their respective regions. The population is mainly Roman Catholic, with small Jewish and Protestant minorities. The capital is Brussels, which is one of the main centres of the European Union and NATO, and various other international institutions and companies have their headquarters there.

The climate is mild, humid and wet. The prevailing summer winds are northerly. During the rest of the year winds are mostly W or SW and most winter gales are from the SW. The sea often breaks over the outlying sandbanks especially when the wind blows against the tide.

Entry Regulations

Ports of entry
Antwerp 51°14′N 4°25′E, Nieuwpoort 51°09′N 2°43′E, Ostend 51°14′N 2°55′E, Zeebrugge 51°20′N 3°12′E.

Procedure on arrival
As a member of the European Union, EU regulations apply. As a result of the implementation of the Schengen Agreement, of which Belgium is a signatory, boats having on board nationals of EU countries which are not signatories of the Schengen Agreement, such as the UK, must clear immigration at the point of entry into Belgium.

Yachts are normally boarded on arrival by the maritime police (immigration) and customs. One may be asked to show a VHF radio licence, a copy of the International Regulation for the Prevention of Collisions at Sea, and tide tables. Yachts must be equipped with sufficient safety equipment, and have their name and home port clearly marked on the stern.

Customs

No licence is required for the importation of hunting and sporting firearms, but these should be licensed in one's own country. Two sporting guns, with a maximum of 100 cartridges per gun, can be temporarily imported duty-free. These must be declared to customs on arrival for inspection.

Cats and dogs require a valid rabies vaccination certificate. The vaccination must have been made at least 30 days before the date of arrival in Belgium.

Foreign yachts remaining more than two months in Belgium must obtain a registration plate, as all Belgian yachts have, and pay navigation dues. Further details can be obtained from the Bureau de Perception des Droits de Navigation. The registration plate allows a vessel to stop on navigable waterways or to use their tributaries.

Immigration

Visitors must have a passport valid at least three months beyond their proposed departure date.

Visas are not required for nationals of the following countries provided they do not stay more than three months in any six month period: European Union, Andorra, Argentina, Australia, Brazil, Brunei, Canada, Chile, Costa Rica, Cyprus, Czech Republic, Ecuador, El Salvador, Guatemala, Honduras, Hungary, Iceland, Israel, Jamaica, Japan, South Korea, Liechtenstein, Malawi, Malaysia, Malta, Mexico, Monaco, New Zealand, Nicaragua, Norway, Panama, Paraguay, Poland, San Marino, Singapore, Slovak Republic, Slovenia, Switzerland, Turkey (if EU resident), United States, Uruguay, Vatican City, Venezuela.

All other nationalities require visas, normally issued for three months. For these nationalities, visas for the countries to be visited before and after the visit to Belgium must be obtained prior to application for a visa.

Navigation

When motorsailing, a black cone with its apex down must be hoisted in the rigging. Port entry signals must be obeyed, due to the very heavy shipping traffic in and out of ports.

Inland waterways

Navigation is freely allowed on the Belgian waterways, although there are regulations one should be aware of. There are maximum speed limits on many of the canals and rivers. Vessels must not sail within 60 ft (20 m) of the banks of the River Meuse and the Ghent–Terneuzen canal, and within 25 ft (8 m) on the Lys and the Brussels–Charleroi canal. Full details of the regulations can be obtained in the booklet *Dispositions reglementant la police et la navigation*, available from the offices at the locks. Information is also obtainable from the Ministère des Travaux Publics.

Foreign yachts arriving in Belgium by one of the canals must report to the first navigation tax office, to complete an entry declaration. On departure an exit declaration must also be signed at a navigation tax office. These offices are situated at the locks.

Facilities

The best facilities are concentrated in the ports of Ostend, Zeebrugge and Nieuwport, all of which have yacht clubs and docking facilities. Most repair facilities are available, as well as chandlery, fuel and provisions. There are also good facilities at Antwerp, where there is access to the inland waterways.

Further Reading

Inland Waterways of Belgium
North Sea Harbours and Pilotage
Cruising Association Handbook
North Sea Passage Pilot
The Ministère des Travaux Publics has published a map of the inland waterways.

Website

www.visitbelgium.com (National Tourism Office)

DENMARK

Denmark juts up towards the Scandinavian peninsula from the north-west edge of Europe and is made up of the Jutland peninsula and many islands. Over five hundred make up the Danish archipelago providing excellent cruising opportunities. The islands are scattered over a relatively

Practical Information

LOCAL TIME: GMT + 1, summer time GMT + 2 from late March to October.

BUOYAGE: IALA A

CURRENCY: Danish krone (Dkr) of 100 ore.

BUSINESS HOURS
Banks: 0930–1600 Monday to Friday, to 1800 Thursdays.
Business: 0900–1630 Monday to Friday.
Shops: Monday to Thursday 0900–1700, 0900–1900/2000 Friday, 0900–1300/1400 Saturday.
Government offices: 0900–1630 Monday to Friday.

ELECTRICITY: 220 V, 50 Hz

PUBLIC HOLIDAYS
1 January: New Year's Day
Maundy Thursday, Good Friday and Easter Monday
4th Friday after Easter: Prayer Day
Ascension Day
Whit Monday
5 June p.m.: Constitution Day
24 December p.m.
25 December: Christmas Day

COMMUNICATIONS
International telephone calls can be made from post offices and all coin and card public phones. International operator 113. International dialling access code 00. Reverse charge calls, 0015 to Europe, 0016 outside of Europe.
Emergency: dial 112.
There are flights to all European and many worldwide destinations from Kastrup International airport near Copenhagen.

MEDICAL
There is free emergency treatment for most West European nationals.

DIPLOMATIC MISSIONS
In Copenhagen:
Australia: Kristianagade 21.
Tel. (1) 35 26 22 44.
Canada: Kr. Benikowsgade 1.
Tel. (1) 33 12 22 99.
Estonia: Admiralgade 20. *Tel.* 33 15 18 62.
Lithuania: Bernstorff Svej 214.
Tel. 31 63 62 07.
Russia: Kristianiagade 3. *Tel.* 31 42 55 85.
United Kingdom: Kastelsvej 36–40.
Tel. (1) 35 26 46 00.
United States: Dag Hammarskjolds Alle 24.
Tel. (1) 31 42 31 44.

small area and distances between harbours are never more than a few miles. The most popular cruising area is the archipelago south of the larger islands of Fyn and Sjaelland. In the northern part of Jutland are the perfectly sheltered waters of Limfjord, connecting the North Sea to the Kattegat. A more convenient point of access for yachts coming from the south is the Kiel Canal, which avoids a long detour around the north of Denmark and leads straight into the heart of the Danish archipelago. The Sound between Denmark and Sweden is the main waterway between the North Sea and the Baltic, so there is very heavy shipping in this area.

Country Profile

Denmark has been populated from neolithic times and was one of the most developed areas in the Bronze Age. The Vikings from the region which is now Denmark and Norway became known and feared for their raids and pillaging of the coasts of Western Europe. In the tenth century Denmark was unified and gradually Christianity spread through the country. The marauding lessened, but Danish kings ruled England for some years in the eleventh century. In 1397 the Union of Kalmar brought Denmark, Norway, Sweden, the Faeroes, Iceland and Greenland under the rule of the Danish king. In the sixteenth century this Union broke up and the next two hundred years saw wars with several countries including Sweden, Denmark's main rival in the Baltic.

In the eighteenth century Denmark had a period of economic expansion. It administered Greenland, which became a colony in 1814. From this time Denmark started losing its territories. It had to cede Norway to Sweden at the end of the Napoleonic Wars, as Denmark had been an ally of France. Later war with Austria and Prussia lost Denmark her southern provinces of Schleswig and Holstein. In 1918 Iceland gained independence, although it was still under the Danish crown until 1953. Neutral in the First World War, during the Second World War Denmark was occupied by Germany, although King Christian X remained in the country and encouraged the resistance movement that developed.

The monarchy's powers were limited in 1849, when a liberal constitution was adopted. In the early twentieth century, the growth of the working class brought the socialists into power. During the interwar years the social democrats introduced many social reforms and dominated the political scene until the 1970s. The country has enjoyed prosperity and joined the European Community in 1973.

Farming is the mainstay of the economy. Cereals are grown on the plains and there is much pasture-land for livestock, the main exports being pork,

beef and dairy products. The fishing industry is also important. Industry is developed in the major towns.

The population is 5.1 million and is mainly Lutheran. As well as Danish, Faroese, Greenlandic and German are spoken in some areas. The capital is Copenhagen – in Danish, Kobenhavn.

Denmark has a temperate climate and the winters are cold. The sailing season is limited to the summer which can be fairly wet, although enjoying long days. The prevailing winds in summer are westerly and this is also where most gales come from. Because of the surrounding landmass, the winds can be variable and the weather also changes with little warning.

Entry Regulations

Ports of entry
Jutland: Esbjerg 55°28′N 8°26′E, Frederikshavn 57°26′N 10°33′E, Frederica 55°34′N 9°45′E, Haderslev 55°15′N 9°30′E, Holstebro (Struer) 56°30′N 8°36′E, Horsens 55°51′N 9°52′E, Kolding 55°30′N 9°30′E, Randers 56°28′N

The lively quayside, Copenhagen.

10°03′E, Skive 56°34′N 9°02′E, Sonderborg 54°55′N 9°47′E, Thisted 56°57′N 8°42′E, Vejle 55°43′N 9°33′E, Ålborg 57°03′N 9°55′E, Århus 56°09′N 10°13′E.
Funen (Fyn): Odense 55°25′N 10°23′N, Svendborg 55°03′N 10°37′E.
Sjaelland: Copenhagen 55°42′N 12°37′E, Elsinore 56°02′N 12°37′E, Kalundborg 55°41′N 11°05′E, Korsør 55°20′N 11°08′E, Koge 55°27′N 12°12′E, Naestved 55°14′N 11°45′E.
Lolland: Rodbyhavn 55°39′N 11°21′E.
Falster: Nkobing 54°46′N 11°52′E.
Bornholm: Ronne 55°06′N 14°42′E.

Procedure on arrival
As a member of the European Union, EU regulations apply. Yachts arriving from Greenland, Norway or other EU countries, with nothing to declare, do not have to report to customs on arrival. Others should proceed to a port of entry and report to customs. The captain may be asked for proof of ownership, or a letter authorising the use of the boat. A certificate of competence is

compulsory for the captain of any boat with a displacement of over 20 tons. It should be noted that duty-free allowances are very small and amounts over this are declarable. Customs do check yachts, so if in doubt it is advisable to report to customs. Immigration must be cleared on arrival and departure. A full list of all safety equipment on board may be requested by customs.

Customs

Firearms must be declared.

Animals can be landed, but dogs taken ashore 1 April to 1 September must be kept on a leash.

Yachts may remain without paying duty for three months within a six month period which begins with the yacht's arrival in any Nordic country.

The importation of dairy products is restricted.

If a yacht has a large amount of dutiable goods in excess of the allowed limits, the stores must be placed under customs seal and re-exported aboard the yacht. A deposit must be paid, which will be refunded after departure from Danish waters by returning the certificate supplied by the Danish customs office, after it has been stamped by customs on arrival in the next country confirming that the same amount of goods are on board.

Immigration

Nationals of EU countries do not need a visa and can stay for an unlimited time. However, after six months they must apply for a resident's permit.

US, Canadian, Australian, Japanese and New Zealand nationals are amongst those who do not need a visa for up to a three-month visit, after which a visa must be obtained. An extension can be obtained from the police, but later one will not be allowed back for a further six months.

Navigation

Shipping traffic between the North Sea and the Baltic is heavy and vessels must use the correct lane in traffic separation zones. These are in operation in the northern part of the Sound between Elsinore and Hälsingborg in Sweden, at the Great Belt between Korsør and Sprogoe by Hatter Barn and the Baltic Sea south of Gedser. In Danish waters the Transit Route for very large vessels runs from the Skaw to the Moen SE light vessel northeast of Gedser. In some areas larger ships on the Transit Route are confined by depths to Deep Water Routes; these can be found in the Great Belt east of Samsoe, along the east coast of Langeland, and north-east of Gedser. Yachts should avoid the Transit and Deep Water Routes as the depth con-

ditions do not allow large vessels much room to manoeuvre. Attention should also be paid to port entry regulations and signs.

Restrictions

Prohibited areas are military firing areas, information on which is contained on Danish charts and in the Danish Notices to Mariners. Also marked on Danish charts as restricted are several small uninhabited islands, which are protected areas for seabirds and other wildlife and should not be landed on between 1 April and 1 June. On some of these islands there are signs forbidding landing.

Fishing

Foreign visitors may only use simple hand gear for fishing, for which a permit is required. Permits can be obtained at post offices. Harpoons, traps and nets are forbidden. Permission should be obtained from the owners of the fishing rights before fishing in rivers or estuaries.

Facilities

Fuel is available in most ports and some yacht harbours have their own fuelling dock, although these are more common in fishing harbours. LPG containers can be refilled in the larger centres. Provisioning is excellent throughout Denmark and the quality of food is among the best in the world. Marine supplies are available in all yachting centres, although the prices are very high.

Yachting facilities are good throughout the country and there are either marinas or fishing harbours with mooring facilities for yachts conveniently situated within a short distance of each other. The harbours get very crowded in summer and it is customary to raft up extensively, often several boats deep. The Danish Yachting Association has mooring buoys (marked with 'DS' in black letters) in 23 harbours in Limfjord, the east coast of Jutland, SE coast of Fyn and south coast of Sjaelland. Visiting sailors may not use such buoys.

The best repair facilities are concentrated in and around Copenhagen where there are several marinas, the best known of which is Langelinie close to the centre of the capital. Also close to Copenhagen is the marina at Svanemoellen. There are good facilities at Århus and Ålborg, the latter in Limfjord.

Danish charts are produced by the Royal Danish Administration of Navigation and Hydrography in special editions for yachts. It is essential to have good charts for the smaller channels. The Danish Yachting

Association (Idraettens Hus, 2605 Broendby) publishes an annual handbook with details of rates and facilities for Danish harbours called *Händbog for Tursejlere*. Several local tourist associations also publish leaflets for yachtsmen, which are available from Danish Tourist Association offices.

Further Reading

Cruising Guide to Germany & Denmark
The Baltic Sea
Baltic Southwest Pilot
Cruising Association Handbook

Website

www.dt.dk (Danish Tourist Board)

ESTONIA

Lying on the southern shores of the Baltic Sea between Latvia and Russia, Estonia is a country of low lands and many lakes as well as numerous offshore islands, the largest being Saaremaa and Hiiumaa. Both the Estonian islands in the Gulf of Riga and the offshore islands provide excellent daysailing opportunities.

Although Estonia and the other two Baltic republics, Latvia and Lithuania, have only recently opened their doors to cruising boats, they are rapidly gaining in popularity. With Poland and Russia now also added to the cruising circuit, one can expect the number of visiting boats to increase significantly in coming years, as well as an improvement in facilities.

Country Profile

The Finno-Ugric peoples were the first to settle in this region. They resisted invasions from the Vikings in the ninth century, then the Russians in the eleventh and twelfth centuries; however, despite further resistance, from 1346 Estonia was under the rule of the German Knights, as part of the Livonian Confederation, along with Latvia. From the sixteenth century fierce wars occurred between Russia and Sweden seeking to control Livonia. Swedish rule lasted until 1721, when Estonia became part of the Russian empire.

The indigenous population were little more than serfs all through these centuries of foreign rule; thus, with the emancipation of the serfs in the early nineteenth century, came a growing national revival, with the spread of education and increasingly resistance to Russification. Nationalists took advantage of the Russian Revolution to declare Estonian independence in 1918; they were aided in their resistance to the Red Army by British naval forces and fighters from Scandinavia and Finland. In 1920 the Soviet Union recognised Estonia's independence. Yet the years as a sovereign state were brief: the 1939 Soviet–German pact assigned Estonia to the USSR's sphere of influence, which invaded in 1940 and forced the creation of the Estonian Soviet Socialist Republic. After German occupation in 1941–44, Estonia was reconquered by the Red Army and again became part of the USSR.

With the 1980s policy of glasnost in the USSR, Estonians gave increasingly open support for independence. Yet only after the 19 August 1991 coup in Moscow did their ambitions become reality; on 20 August the Estonian parliament declared independence, which was recognised soon after by the USSR and the international community. The process of democratisation has been very rapid and Estonia is expected to be among the first East European countries to join the European Union.

There are some oil and gas deposits; other important economic activities are forestry, fishing and dairy farming. The government has set about moving from a Soviet-style command economy towards the free market. Estonia has signed a Free Trade Agreement with Latvia and Lithuania.

The population is 1.5 million, mainly Estonians, though Russians make up nearly a third of the population; also small minorities of Ukrainians, Belorussians and Finns. The main religions are Lutheran and Russian Orthodox. Estonian, of the Finno-Ugric family, and Russian are spoken. The capital is Tallinn.

The climate is moderate, with cool summers and mild winters.

Entry Regulations

Ports of entry

Tallinn 59°27'N 24°46'E, Pirita 59°28.2'N 24°29.2'E, Pärnu 58°23'N 24°29'E, Nasva 58°13'N 22°23'E, Lehtma 59°04'N 22°42'E, Narva 59°28'N 28°02'E, Roomassaare, 58°13'N 22°31'E, Veere 58°27'N 22°05'E, Vergi 59°36'N 26°06.5'E.

Practical Information

LOCAL TIME: GMT + 2. Summer time end March to end October GMT + 3

BUOYAGE: IALA A

CURRENCY: Kroon (EKr) of 100 sents.

BUSINESS HOURS
Banks: 0900–1230 Monday to Friday.
Offices: 0900–1300, 1400–1800 Monday to Friday.
Shops: 0800/0900/1000–1800/1900/2000 Monday to Friday, until 1300/1500 Saturday. Some close for lunch.

ELECTRICITY: 220 V, 50 Hz

PUBLIC HOLIDAYS
1 January: New Year's Day
24 February: Independence Day
Good Friday, Easter Monday
1 May: Labour Day
23 June: Victory Day
24 June: Midsummer Day
16 November: Rebirth Day
25, 26 December: Christmas

COMMUNICATIONS
International calls from telephone offices, hotels or via Finnish VHF channels. Private phones may be better. International access code: 08. International operator: 007.
The main post and phone office is at Narva maantee 1, open 0800–2000 Monday–Friday, 0800–1700 Saturday. Also telephone and fax office at Gonsiori 10, open 0800–1900 Monday to Friday.
There is an international airport at Tallinn with flights to all main European countries. There are daily ferries and hydrofoils from Tallinn to Finland and Sweden.

MEDICAL
(Tallinn) 24 hour emergency centre at Sütiste tee 19, Mustamäe. *Tel.* 525 652.
Hospital: Ravi 18.

DIPLOMATIC MISSIONS
In Tallinn:
Finland: Kohtu 4. *Tel.* 610 3200.
Germany: Toom-Kuninga 11. *Tel.* 627 5300.
Latvia: Tõnismägi 10. *Tel.* 646 1313.
Lithuania: Uus tn. 15. *Tel.* 631 4030.
Poland: Pärnu maantee 8. *Tel.* 627 8206.
Russia: Pikk 19. *Tel.* 646 4175.
United Kingdom: Wismari 6. *Tel.* 667 4700.
United States: 2nd floor, Kentmanni 20., *Tel.* 631 2021.

Procedure on arrival

All Estonian harbours are now open to foreign yachts, including the old Russian naval base at Paldiski.

Yachts arriving from abroad must proceed directly to a port with customs and immigration offices. It is recommended to request that the harbour office of the port of departure informs the next port of one's arrival.

Tallinn: The yacht harbour is at Pirita, east of Tallinn port. After passing the outer breakwaters, proceed to the end of the inner breakwater, which is left to starboard, to reach the customs quay situated behind the inner breakwater. Clearance formalities can also be completed at Pirita Marina, which monitors Channel 16.

Customs

Firearms must be declared.

All valuable equipment on board, which can be removed, such as cameras, must be declared.

Duty-free allowances per adult: 10 litres beer, 2 litres alcohol, 200 cigarettes.

Immigration

Visas are not required for citizens of Australia, Bulgaria, Canada, Czech Republic, European Union, Iceland, Hungary, Japan, Latvia, Liechtenstein, Lithuania, Monaco, New Zealand, Poland, Slovakia, Romania, Singapore, Turkey and the USA.

All other countries require a visa, although the citizens of most West European countries may obtain their visa on arrival. Visas are cheaper if obtained in advance. The Baltic states are a one visa zone, so with an Estonian visa you can visit the other two republics, and vice versa.

Because the Baltic Republics have few diplomatic missions abroad, visas for them can also be obtained from a local agent, such as Tiina Coik, ESAIL, Sport Hotel, Pirita Marina, Tallinn, Estonia. *Tel.* (372 2) 238 145, Fax 237 945. The ESTUM agency in Helsinki can also issue visas.

Warning

As in the case of the other Baltic republics, existing British and US charts have many inaccuracies and local charts should be used if at all possible. Attention is drawn to an uncharted rock south of Kihnu, which has already caused the loss of a yacht, in the reported position 58°04.4′N, 24°03.8′E. This danger has been reported to be wrongly depicted also on the latest Russian charts.

Russian charts can be ordered from DML, Olympic Yacht Club, 1 Regati Boulevard, EE 0103 Tallinn, Estonia. The Estonian Offshore Sailing Union publishes a booklet detailing lights and harbours on the Estonian coast.

Facilities

Best facilities are at the Olympic Yacht Marina in Pirita. Buses and trams go into Tallinn centre.

These are the best facilities near Tallinn, with water and electricity on the dock, as well as fuel. Fuel and water is available in all major ports. Adequate facilities are also available at Pärnu, which has a yacht club with pontoon spaces for visitors. There are good repair facilities at the Kalev Yacht Club, in Pirita, and also fuel and LPG. Provisioning is cheaper than in Finland. The Nasva Yacht Club on Saaremaa Island runs a small marina in the old Nasva fishing harbour. There is a slipway and limited repair facilities.

Further Reading

The Baltic Sea
Estonian Lights and Harbours, published by Estonian Offshore Sailing Union
Baltic States & Kaliningrad – a travel survival kit.

Websites

www.tourism.ee (Estonian Tourist Board)
www.tt.ee (Yacht clubs and marinas)
www.estoniaonline.ee

FINLAND

Finland, known as Suomi to its inhabitants, is situated in the far north-east of Europe and is one of the largest countries on the continent. From the rolling agricultural lands of the south the land rises towards the hills and huge forests of the north and the peatlands and treeless fells of Lapland. Finland has, at the last count, some 62,000 lakes, and nearly 3000 miles of coastline, off which lie thousands of islands including the Åland archipelago.

Cruising opportunities in Finland are infinite, either through the many islands or on the lakes, the larger of which are navigable. With a reputed 6500 islands, the offlying Åland archipelago is a world in itself. Unfortunately the sailing season is very short, usually from about the end of May until September, although the summer days do benefit from almost perpetual daylight. With a highly developed and top quality boat building industry, many foreign visitors only sample the cruising delights of Finland when they arrive to take delivery of their new boats and then sail them to warmer waters.

Country Profile

Little is known about the first inhabitants, who arrived in Stone Age times, although the present-day Lapps are probably their descendants. Between two and three thousand years ago the Finno-Ugrian tribes moved west into what is now Hungary, and north-west into Estonia and Finland. The tribes were well established when Christianity spread across the land around the tenth century. Sweden was a continual aggressor in the following centuries and gradually Finland came under the control of the Swedish kings.

The rise of Russia as a great power led to an expansionist policy westwards, and the 1808–9 war led to Finland being incorporated into the Russian empire as a Grand Duchy. Although having some measure of autonomy, a policy of russification was followed and Finnish national resistance to this grew. The Russian Revolution was the chance the Finns had been waiting for and an independent Finland was declared in December 1917, recognised by the Soviet Union three years later.

The interwar years saw a conflict with Sweden over the possession of the Åland Islands, which were eventually awarded to Finland by the League of Nations.

In November 1930 Stalin declared war on Finland after being refused his demands of territory. The Finns fought back fiercely, but despite aid from Sweden they had to cede much of Karelia to the Soviet Union. From 1941 the Finns fought with Germany against Russia, until an armistice with the latter was declared in 1944. After the war Finland had to pay considerable reparations to the Soviet Union, but the country rebuilt itself and embarked on a strong non-aligned policy as an active member of the United Nations, although concluding pacts of mutual assistance with the Soviet Union. Finland joined the European Union in 1995.

Around 65 per cent of Finland is forest, and one of its main resources are forest products, especially paper. Only the south is cultivated, due to the harsher climate further north.

Finland is a sparsely inhabited country with a population of 5.1 million. Finnish and Swedish are the two official languages, and Lappish (or Saame) is a semi-official language. The majority speak Finnish as their mother tongue, although there is a large Swedish speaking minority. English is widely spoken. Lutheran and Orthodox Christian are the two main religions. The capital since 1812 is Helsinki.

Much of the country lies north of the Arctic

Practical Information

LOCAL TIME: GMT + 2. Summer time GMT + 3 from April to October.

BUOYAGE: IALA A

CURRENCY: Markka (Fmk/FIM) of 100 pennies. Euro from 2002. 1 Euro = 5.94573 FIM.

BUSINESS HOURS
Banks: 0915–1615 Monday to Friday.
Shops: 0900–1700 Monday to Friday, 0900–1400 Saturday.
Government offices: 0900–1700 Monday to Friday.

ELECTRICITY: 220 V, 50 Hz

PUBLIC HOLIDAYS
1 January: New Year's Day
Epiphany
Good Friday, Easter Monday
Saturday before Whit Sunday
May Day Eve and Day
Ascension
Midsummer's Eve and Day
1 November: All Saints' Day
6 December: Independence Day
25–26 December: Christmas

COMMUNICATIONS
International dialling code: 00, 990, 999 or 994. Good mobile phone coverage in all Finnish waters.
Post offices 0900–1700 Monday to Friday.
Emergency: dial 112.
VHF Channel 16 should be used to contact the coastal rescue services.
There are many international flights to worldwide destinations from Helsinki and flights to other Nordic countries from Turku.

MEDICAL
State hospitals charge reasonable fees for treatment. Private hospitals are more expensive. Certain West European countries have reciprocal agreements for free treatment.

DIPLOMATIC MISSIONS
In Helsinki:
Canada: Pohjois Esplanadi 25B. *Tel.* (90) 171 141.
Estonia: Kasarmikatu 28. *Tel.* (90) 179 719.
Germany: Krogiuksentie 4b. *Tel.* (90) 458 2355.
Latvia: Bulevardi 5A-18. *Tel.* (90) 605 640.
Russia: Vuorimiehenkatu 6. *Tel.* (90) 661 449.
United Kingdom: Uudenmaankatu 16–20. *Tel.* (90) 661 293.
United States: Itainen Puistotie 14A. *Tel.* (90) 171931.

Circle, however the influence of the Baltic Sea keeps the climate milder than other countries on the same latitude. The sailing season is limited to the summer when the winds are variable. The surrounding landmass affects the winds which can be light in summer.

Entry Regulations

Coastguard stations which perform passport and customs clearance for yachts (from north to south to east):
Röyttä 65°46′N 24°09′E, Virpiniemi 64°20′N 24°25′E, Kalajoki 64°17′N 23°55′E, Kokkola 63°50′N 23°06′E, Vallgrund 63°10′N 21°15′E, Kummelgrund 60°23′N 21°33′E, Susiluoto, Enskär 60°13′N 19°20′E, Maarianhamina (Mariehamn) 60°06′N 19°56′E, Storkubb 59°58′N 20°54′E, Kökar 59°56′N 20°52′E, Nauvo-Pärnäinen (or Üto passport control point) 60°14′N 21°48′E, Hanko 59°49′N 22°55′E, Bågaskär 59°57′N 24°01′E, Porkkala 59°58′N 24°25′E, Suomenlinna 60°09′N 24°59′E, Pirttisaari 60°10′N 25°27′E, Kotka 60°28′N 26°27′E, Haapasaari 60°17′N 27°12′E, Hurppu Frontier guard station, 60°27′N 27°43′E, Nuijamaa border station (on Saimaa Canal).

Ports for passport and customs clearance (where there are no coastguard stations along the channel):
Kemi 65°44′N 24°34′E, Raahe 64°41′N 24°29′E, Pietarsaari 63°41′N 22°24′E, Kaskinen 62°23′N 21°13′E, Pori 61°29′N 21°48′E, Rauma 61°08′N 21°30′E, Uusikaupunki 60°48′N 21°24′E, Mariehamn's West Harbour and Nuijamaa.

Customs clearance is also obtainable from these commercial ports:
Tornio 65°51′N 24°09′E, Haukipudas 65°12′N 25°15′E, Oulu 65°00′N 25°28′E, Vaasa 63°06′N 21°37′E, Kristiinankaupunki (Kristinestad) 62°16′N 21°19′E, Eckerö 60°13′N 19°35′E, Långnäs 60°08′N 20°18′E, Orrengrund 60°23′N 26°17′E, Merikarvia 61°51′N 21°29′E, Naantali 60°28′N 22°01′E, Turku 60°27′N 22°15′E, Tammisaari 59°59′N 23°26′E, Inkoo 60°03′N 24°01′E, Helsinki 60°10′N 24°57′E, Porvoo 60°23′N 25°40′E, Loviisa 60°27′N 26°14′E, Lappeenranta, 61°04′N 28°11′E.

Procedure on arrival

Foreign yachts arriving in Finland must keep to the customs routes, which are channels (marked on the charts) from the open sea to where there are frontier guard stations. Yachts must report to the nearest coastguard station along the channel, or, if there is no station, to the nearest port of entry for customs and immigration formalities. No other routes may be taken, nor should anyone land or come aboard before customs clearance has been completed.

The passport control station should be alerted by radio on VHF Channel 74 (or 16 as standby), or by telephone, approximately one hour before arrival. Although passport control stations work 24 hours, it is recommended that whenever possible boats call there between 0800 and 2000. The vessel may be intercepted by coastguard vessels when arriving in Finnish waters.

If carrying dutiable goods, the yacht will be directed to the nearest customs site after passport inspection.

A yacht registered in one of the Nordic countries, maximum 30 tons net, arriving in Finland from another Nordic country, with no dutiable stores, is only required to notify the nearest coastguard station by VHF or telephone of its passage. The vessel must have only Nordic citizens on board and also that vessel's journey has not and will not extend beyond the Nordic countries.

All vessels entering or leaving Finnish waters must have on board a current crew list signed by the captain.

A clearance declaration is issued on completion of formalities and this must be shown to the authorities at the port of departure. Vessels from other Nordic countries are exempt from this requirement.

Immigration clearance must be done on arrival and departure.

Helsinki: Clearance is done at Suomenlinna Island, southeast of Helsinki, at a special clearance station for yachts. On arrival at the Helsinki traffic control area all vessels over 39 ft (12 m) shall maintain permanent watch on VHF Channel 71. Vessels over 66 ft (20 m) must report to the station the name of the vessel, its route and destination. A similar report must be made before departure.

Customs

For boats built on or after 1 January 1987 and registered in a EU country, evidence has to be produced that VAT has been paid on the boat in one of the EU member states. A boat on which VAT has been paid can be used and docked in Finland without any time limits.

Residents of non-EU countries may leave their boats for the winter at a boatyard providing the boat is to be used the following season. Customs must be notified and it may be necessary to pay a deposit which is refunded when the vessel is in use again. This fee varies (around FIM 5000–10,000). If a vessel is not taken out of the country within one year of arrival, appropriate taxes and fees must be paid. A cheaper alternative is to leave the vessel in a bonded warehouse, for details contact the appropriate port authority.

The following items must be declared to customs and are subject to duties and import restrictions: drugs, firearms and ammunition, alcoholic drinks and tobacco products, endangered species and their products, live animals and plants.

Animals must have rabies vaccination certificates, issued between 30 days and 12 months previously. Animals arriving from rabies-free countries (Sweden, Norway, Iceland, United Kingdom, Ireland) do not need this, as long as they did not visit a country with rabies. All animals should have a valid health certificate.

Excess amounts of alcohol, tobacco and other dutiable goods, must be declared to customs on arrival. Although a member of the EU, Finland still imposes strict limits on the amount of alcoholic drinks or tobacco products that may be imported free of duty into the country. Some age limits also apply, but in general one is only allowed to bring into Finland, if coming from another EU country, 1 litre of spirits, 3 litres of apéritifs, 5 litres of wine and 15 litres of beer, as well as 300 cigarettes. If coming from a non-EU country, the allowances are 1 litre of spirits *or* 2 litres of apéritifs plus 2 litres of wine, 15 litres of beer and 200 cigarettes.

Boats arriving from another EU country have no restrictions on importing foodstuffs for their own use. From non-EU countries only 1 kg of meat or meat products, fish and fishery products, milk, dairy and egg products may be imported. The importation of more than 250 g of caviar must be accompanied by a CITES import or export permit.

Immigration

Nationals of EU or EAA member countries, with the exception of Great Britain and Greece, need only an identity card to enter Finland. All other nationalities require valid passports.

A visa is generally required for nationals of non-European countries and the following: Albania, Bulgaria, Romania, Turkey, former Yugoslavia (excluding Croatia and Slovenia), Russia and CIS countries.

All foreigners wishing to stay in Finland for more than three months or to work must obtain a visa, except nationals of European Union countries, Iceland and Norway.

Compulsory equipment

According to Finnish law, approved lifejackets must be carried for everyone on board. The boat must also be fitted with a fire extinguisher, water emptying equipment, anchor and oars or sweep.

Restrictions

Special permission is needed for voyages through or stops in restricted military areas. The general fairways, marked on charts, which lead through restricted areas may generally be used without permission by foreign vessels for a direct passage without stopping. Yachts must remain within these fairways unless one has special permission to leave them. A foreign vessel may only stop in a restricted area in case of emergency. Yachts may anchor for not more than 48 hours within a restricted area at special designated anchorages and moorings. Permission to stay within a restricted area or to move outside of a fairway must be applied for to the Military Area Headquarters or local coastguard authorities.

There are numerous nature conservation areas where landing and anchoring are forbidden either all year round or during the bird breeding season (1 April–31 July). These restrictions are marked on the nautical charts and on shore. Sailing is permitted in the national parks of the Archipelago Sea, Tammisaari archipelago, eastern part of the Gulf of Finland, Bay of Bothnia, Linnansaari, Koli, Päijänne and Kolovesi. However, national park rules and regulations, including some speed limits and landing restrictions, must be observed.

The Finnish coastguard have the right to stop and search all pleasure boats in Finnish territorial waters. The code flag L is the stopping sign, which may be given visually or by sound.

Navigation

Customs routes and general fairways must be used. The sailing lanes must be followed and these are clearly marked on the charts issued by the Finnish National Board of Navigation, and on reduced size charts. Short or overnight stays and stopovers due to adverse weather are allowed outside of the sailing routes. Yachts may only stop at yacht harbours, anchorages or holiday sites. Yachts leaving the sailing routes must give consideration to other vessels.

The public has the right of free access to outdoor areas, as well as the duty to preserve and not to interfere with nature. One should not anchor close to an inhabited stretch of shore nor land without the owner's permission. Fires should not be lit ashore nor any garbage be thrown overboard.

Fishing

All fishing (except angling with handheld line or rod without a reel for casting and restrictions on the lure) requires an official licence, which may be bought from any post office or bank. Also permission must be obtained from the owner of the fishing rights. Most waters in Finland are under private ownership. Information on local fishing regulations can be obtained from tourist offices, and restrictions on fishing gear and times will be given when applying for the licence.

ÅLAND ISLANDS

These islands are autonomous and some of the regulations applicable in Finland may differ. The flag of the Åland Islands is a red cross with a yellow border on a light blue field. The customs allowances and restrictions on the Åland Islands for boats arriving from EU countries or from Finland itself are the same as those for arrival from non-EU countries. The islands have plenty of visitors' harbours and there are many public jetties where temporary stops can be made. Natural harbours outside of inhabited areas should only be used in emergencies and the landowner's permission asked to anchor. Fishing is only allowed with permission from the owner of the fishing rights, and a fishing licence must be bought, available at shops, service stations and fishing associations. Fishing from the shore is not allowed from 15 April to 15 June.

Saimaa Canal

The Saimaa lake area, reached through the Saimaa Canal leased to Finland by Russia, is now open to foreign yachts. Using this canal requires passing through Russian waters, and for this reason all crew must have valid passports, not identity cards, and the Board of Management of the Canal must be notified of the boat's intentions to use the canal one week in advance. Arriving from along the coast of Finland, the departure inspection is carried out at the coastguard stations of either Santio or Haapasaari island. Alternatively, one may arrive directly from international waters, when the entry inspection is carried out at the customs quay in Nuijamaa.

All vessels are required to have a Russian pilot between the island of Vihrevoi and Brusnitnoe lock. Inspection by the Russian authorities is carried out at these locations. It is possible to visit the Russian city of Vyborg if one has obtained a visa in advance. The Saimaa Canal Board of Management, which publishes a useful 'Instructions for Small Boat Traffic', should be contacted two weeks in advance of arrival. Their address is: Itäinen Kanavatie 2, Fin-53420 Lappeenranta. *Tel.* (358 53) 4585170, Fax. (358 53) 6259210.

Facilities

Provisioning is very good in all ports, as well as on the larger islands where there are villages or holiday resorts. Fuel is available in all ports. Most coastal towns have visitors' harbours and yacht clubs usually have a few berths reserved for visitors. The standard of services varies and repair facilities are available only in the largest ports. With a developed boat-building industry, producing some of the best yachts in the world, repair facilities are of a high standard. The most comprehensive range of repair facilities are to be found in and around the capital Helsinki. Other yachting centres are at Turku, Hanko, Rauma, Loviisa and Pietarsaari, the latter being the home of the famous Swan yachts. Good facilities are also available in Åland with several marinas, the largest in the capital Mariehamn.

Further Reading

The Baltic Sea
With Pleasure Boat to Finland
The National Board of Navigation and the Finnish Travel Association publish a book of harbours, *Käyntisatamat Besökshamnar A Suomen Rannikot* Finnish Cruising Club handbook of anchorages in Åland and the south coast.

Websites

www.finland-tourism.com (Finnish Tourist Board)
www.fma.fi (Finnish Maritime Authority)
www.lappeenranta.fi (Saimaa Canal)

GERMANY

Germany occupies a central position in Europe with coasts on both the North and Baltic Seas. The most important navigable rivers in continental Europe, the Rhine and the Danube, also flow through German territory.

Although one of the most active sailing nations in Europe, Germany is not a cruising destination and most German sailors prefer to do their cruising away from home. One such popular area is the IJselmeer in the Netherlands, which is reputed to have more resident German yachts than locally owned ones. Cruising opportunities on the North Sea coast are rather limited and the restrictions imposed on cruising in some of the German Frisian Islands have reduced the destinations ever further, although the opening up of former East Germany is adding a hitherto unknown corner of the Baltic to the German cruising portfolio. The most attractive part is the island of Rügen and the surrounding area in the Greiswalder Bodden.

The only contact many visiting yachts have with Germany is the Kiel Canal, the convenient shortcut from the North Sea to the Baltic. Those with more time on hand may be tempted to sail up the narrow estuaries to the old Hanseatic ports of Hamburg, Bremen or Lübeck.

Country Profile

The region was settled by Germanic tribes after the collapse of the Roman Empire. Saxony was gradually conquered by the Franks, and the eastern part of Charlemagne's empire divided in 843, and the Kingdom of the East Franks, became the nucleus of the German state. Large feudal duchies developed while the frontiers were attacked by Magyars, Norsemen and Slavs.

In the tenth century the Holy Roman Empire was formed, uniting the crowns of Germany and Italy. In 1273 a Hapsburg was elected Holy Roman Emperor, and the dynasty expanded its territories, although it was unable to establish centralised rule in a region where over 350 small states were endlessly fighting one another.

In the sixteenth century Hapsburg Austria consolidated its power, but the Protestant Reformation split Germany into the Catholic south and the Lutheran north. Religious conflict was followed by the Thirty Years War (1618–48) which completed Germany's devastation, and established a loose confederation of small principalities under the Emperor's nominal rule. The eighteenth century saw the rise of Prussia as a powerful state and German culture flourished. The Holy Roman Empire was finally destroyed during the Napoleonic wars, and in 1815 a German Confederation was formed, dominated by Austrian and Prussian rivalry. Nationalism was a growing force, but the 1848 revolution saw the liberal Frankfurt Parliament fail to unify the country. Austria dominated the Confederation until Otto von Bismarck, in charge of Prussian policy, achieved unification excluding Austria.

In 1871 the German empire was established under the rule of the Prussian Hohenzollern dynasty. Rapid industrialisation followed, and a

Practical Information

LOCAL TIME: GMT + 1. Summer time GMT + 2 April to October.

BUOYAGE: IALA A

CURRENCY: Deutsch mark (DM) of 100 pfennig (pf). Euro from 2002. 1 euro = 1.95583 DM.

BUSINESS HOURS
Banks: 0900–1230, 1330–1600 Monday to Friday, Thursday 0900–1300, 1500–1730. Business: 0830–1700 Monday to Friday. Shops: 0800/0900–1830 Monday to Friday, 0830–1600 Saturday. Government offices: 0900–1230, 1400–1700 Monday to Thursday, to 1500 Friday.

ELECTRICITY: 220 V, 50 Hz

PUBLIC HOLIDAYS
1 January: New Year's Day
6 January: Epiphany*
Good Friday, Easter Monday
1 May: Labour Day
Ascension Day; Whit Monday
15 August: Assumption*
3 October: German Unity Day
31 October: Reformation Day (north only)
1 November: All Saints' Day*
25–26 December: Christmas
* religious holidays in certain Länder
Corpus Christi (south only)

COMMUNICATIONS
International dialling access code 00. International calls from card phones or metered calls from post offices. Post offices open 0800–1800 Monday to Friday, 0800–1200 Saturday. There are regular international flights from Hamburg, Frankfurt, Berlin, Düsseldorf and München.

MEDICAL
Most European countries have a reciprocal agreement with Germany for free emergency treatment; otherwise, treatment is expensive. 24 hour clinic, Eppendorf Hospital, Martinstrasse, Hamburg. *Tel.* 420 8030. Police 110, Ambulance 112.

DIPLOMATIC MISSIONS
In Berlin:
Australia: Friedrichstraße 200. *Tel.* 880 0880.
Canada: Friedrichstr. 95. *Tel.* 261 1161.
New Zealand: Friedrichstr. 60. *Tel.* 206 210.
United Kingdom: Unter den Linden 32/34. *Tel.* 201 840.
United States: Neustädtische Kirchstr. 4-5. *Tel.* 238 5174.
In Hamburg:
United Kingdom: Harvestehuder Weg 8a. *Tel.* 448 0320.
United States: Alsterufer 27. *Tel.* 411 710.

colonial expansionist policy brought Germany into conflict with Britain and France. At the start of the First World War Germany invaded Belgium and France, then Poland, Romania and Serbia. After the German defeat in 1918 a social democratic revolution established the parliamentary Weimar Republic. Some economic recovery was made, but thwarted by the world depression which led to mass unemployment. The 1930s saw the rise of the national socialist party, and its leader Adolf Hitler established a totalitarian regime. Germany's expansionist foreign policy led to the outbreak of the Second World War, when much of Europe was defeated and occupied.

Eventually Germany surrendered in 1945, and the country was occupied by the Soviet Union, United States, France and Britain. The onset of the Cold War led to this division hardening, and in 1949 the Federal Republic (West Germany) and the Democratic Republic (East Germany) were formed. West Germany fostered links with Western Europe, joining NATO and the European Community, and made a rapid economic recovery, while East Germany remained under the Soviet sphere of influence. In 1989 the East German Communist party relinquished power, and the two Germanies were reunited officially on 3 October 1990.

West Germany made a spectacular recovery after the Second World War, becoming one of the leading economic powers in the world. It has a market economy, with a large proportion of its industry geared to export. The agricultural sector is small, but provides much of the domestic need. Service industries are also important. East Germany was the most industrialised of the East European states, having a centralised economy with much of its agriculture collectivised.

The German-speaking population is about 80 million, with a small Danish minority. Catholicism is stronger in the south and Protestantism in the north. Bonn was the capital of the Federal Republic of Germany but all important government departments as well as the parliament are gradually being moved to Berlin, which reverted to its role as national capital at the beginning of this century.

Germany has a temperate climate, with warm summers and cold winters. The coastal areas are generally milder than inland in the winter. In the North Sea the predominating winds are SW or W. The incidence of gales is low in summer but increases in spring and autumn. Gales usually veer from SW to NW producing cross seas. Winds on the Baltic coast are variable.

Entry Regulations

Ports of entry

Bremerhaven 53°33′N 8°35′E, Brunsbüttel 53°54′N 9°08′E, Cuxhaven 53°52′N 8°42′E, Emden 53°21′N 7°11′E, Flensburg 54°48′N 9°26′E, Hamburg 53°33′N 9°58′E, Laboe (Kiel) 54°24′N 10°13′E, Norddeich 53°38′N 7°10′E, Rostock 54°05′N 12°07′E, Stralsund 53°19′N 13°06′E, Travemunde 53°58′N 10°54′E, Wilhelmshaven 53°31′N 8°09′E, Wismar 53°54′N 11°28′E.
Frisian Islands: Borkum 53°35′N 6°40′E, Norderney 53°42′N 7°10′E.

Procedure on arrival

On arrival, the Q flag must be flown, unless arriving from an EU or Scandinavian country. Yachts arriving from a non-EU country must report to customs (Zoll) at one of the ports of entry. Helgoland is not a port of entry and clearance formalities cannot be completed there. Yachts must be registered. The captains of foreign yachts may have to show a certificate of competence, although the rules stipulate that this is not compulsory if such a certificate is not required in the country where the vessel is registered. A radio operator's certificate is compulsory. Duty-free stores must be declared to customs. Immigration must be cleared on arrival and departure.

Laboe, at the entrance of the Kiel fjord, is the customs clearance point for yachts entering or leaving Germany via Kiel.
Kiel Canal: If passing through the Kiel Canal, but not visiting Germany, the 3rd substitute pennant must be flown.

Customs

Firearms must be declared and will be sealed on board.

Animals must have valid health certificates.

Pleasure craft may remain in Germany for up to one year without paying duty.

Immigration

Nationals of all Western European countries, Australia, Canada, Croatia, Czech Republic, Hungary, Israel, Japan, New Zealand, Poland, Slovak Republic, Slovenia and the United States do not need visas for up to three months, after which time a resident's permit must be obtained. As a member of the Schengen Agreement, nationals of countries that need visas for any of the Schengen countries must obtain a visa in advance and clear immigration on arrival.

Restrictions

There are strict anti-pollution regulations in force throughout Germany, but particularly in the Baltic Sea. The disposal of garbage anywhere in the Baltic is forbidden. Degradable foodstuff can only be disposed of overboard more than 12 miles from shore. Special containers are provided in all ports for the disposal of garbage and used oils.

Navigation

When motorsailing, a black cone with its apex pointing downwards must be displayed – failure to do so can result in instant fines. Yachts must carry on board the German collision regulations (Seeschiffahrtsstrasse-nordnung) and the Kiel Canal Rules. The latter can be obtained at the Canal.

Any vessel over 15 tons is considered a merchant ship and must carry a pilot through most state waterways unless one has a Master's Certificate. Harbour authorities will help to make any arrangements for this.

Children under 16 years may not steer a vessel under way in German waters and in certain rivers this minimum age is 21 or 23. Motor boats and sometimes sailing yachts require special permission to use some inland waterways.

KIEL CANAL

The 54 mile long Nord–Ostsee-Kanal (North Sea–Baltic Sea Canal) has strict rules which must be observed by yachts transiting it. A set of the rules, in German (Merkblatt für die Sportschiffahrt auf dem Nord–Ostsee-Kanal), can be obtained at either end of the Canal. The height limit is 129 ft (39.6 m) and there is a speed limit of 15 km/h (8 knots). Yachts are expected to make the transit under power and although sailing is permitted in certain parts, tacking is forbidden and the engine must be on standby.

Boats capable of 6 knots under power can complete the transit in one day. The transit must be accomplished during daylight hours. If this is not possible, a convenient place to stop halfway through is at Rendsburg, which has a yacht club. The transit fee is payable at Holtenau locks.

1 Because of the high amount of radio traffic, the traffic control office or lock-keepers should only be called on VHF radio if absolutely necessary. Transiting vessels must monitor the correct frequencies permanently.

2 Yachts without a pilot may use the canal only

The 54-mile Kiel Canal links the North Sea to the Baltic.

during daylight hours, except in the approaches to the yacht harbours at Brunsbüttel and Holtenau. When waiting at locks, yachts must stay behind commercial vessels.

3   Yachts may moor only in the following places within the limits of the canal:
Brunsbüttel yacht harbour (km 1.8)
Waiting area at N side of Brunsbüttel (km 2.7)
Waiting area at Dückerswisch (km 20.5) – one night only
Waiting area before Gieselau lock (km 40.5).
   Note: foreign yachts which have duty-free stores on board may only stop here if already cleared by customs.
Waiting area at Obereider Lake (Rendsburg harbour) (km 66)
Waiting area at Borgstedter Lake (km 70)
Dock at Flemhuder Lake (km 85.4) – one night only
Holtenau yacht harbour (km 98.5)
In an emergency, yachts may also moor behind the dolphins intended for larger vessels.

4   The light signal for yachts at the end locks are:

Single red light: entry forbidden.
Flashing white light: proceed.
Three vertical red lights: all vessels must stop.

5   Yachts unable to use their engine or without an engine may be towed through at the owner's expense.

6   Yachts without radar must stop in reduced visibility.

Facilities

The best facilities are concentrated around the main sailing centres at Hamburg, Kiel and Bremen. Extensive repair facilities are available in all these places and also a comprehensive range of marine supplies. Marinas and small boatyards are spread around the entire coastline and also in the rivers and estuaries. Fuel, water and LPG are easily available and so are provisions.

Cuxhaven Marina, at the mouth of the Elbe, is an excellent place to prepare for the transit of the Kiel Canal towards the Baltic. Kiel is the place to stop for boats transiting the canal in the opposite direction.

Facilities are rapidly improving in former East

Germany. A marina has opened at Rügen, which now has good repair facilities.

Further Reading

Baltic Southwest Pilot
Cruising Association Handbook
The Baltic Sea
Cruising Guide to Germany and Denmark

Website

www.deutschland-tourismus.de (National Tourism Board)

LATVIA

Latvia lies on the Baltic between Estonia, Russia and Lithuania. Although it offers fewer cruising opportunities than its neighbours, the capital Riga is one of the most attractive cities in Europe. The city lies on the banks of the river Daugava and its old district has a medieval flavour that has miraculously been unaffected by its recent Soviet past.

Country Profile

The first inhabitants on the territory of Latvia appeared in 9000 BC and ancestors of the Baltic Finns lived in the area from about 3000 BC. Baltic tribes, ancestors of today's Latvians, settled the region around 2000 BC, and at the start of the Christian era traded in amber. From the eighth to ninth centuries the Viking trade route to the south passed through present day Lativa. Encroachment by neighbouring Russia was resisted, but in medieval times the crusaders (mainly German) spread Christianity and by 1270 established the state of Livonia. Shortly afterwards Riga was admitted into the Hanseatic League, bringing prosperity to the German knights – although the Baltic peoples remained little more than feudal serfs. After the Livonian War in the sixteenth century, Livonia was divided between Sweden and Poland-Lithuania.

With the new wave of Russian expansion during the eighteenth century, Latvia was included in the Russian Empire. As elsewhere in Europe, the nineteenth century saw a growing national consciousness among the Latvians, culminating in a declaration of independence in 1918. Latvia was recognised by the international community at the beginning of 1921 and admitted to the League of Nations. According to the secret pact between Germany and Russia, Latvia fell under the Soviet sphere of influence and in June 1940 Soviet troops invaded Latvia. In 1941 some 14,000 Latvians were deported to Siberia, Nazi troops invaded in July 1941 and during their occupation 90 per cent of Latvian Jews were killed. In 1944 Latvia again fell under the Soviet Union and some further 43,000 persons were deported.

Soviet occupation lasted until the early 1990s when the restoration of independence was declared

Practical Information

LOCAL TIME: GMT + 2. Summer time end of March to start October GMT + 3

BUOYAGE: IALA A

CURRENCY:
Lats (Lvl) of 100 santims.

BUSINESS HOURS
Banks: 0900–1300, 1400–1530 Monday to Friday.
Shops: 0800/0900/1000–1800/1900/2000 Monday to Friday, until 1300/1500 Saturday. Some close for lunch.

ELECTRICITY: 220 V 50, Hz

PUBLIC HOLIDAYS
1 January: New Year's Day
Good Friday, Easter Monday
1 May: Labour Day
23, 24 June: Midsummer Festival
18 November: National Day
25, 26 December: Christmas
31 December: New Year's Eve

COMMUNICATIONS
Lattelcom. International phone calls can be booked at the main post offices, which also have fax services. International operator: 815. Main post office in Riga, Brivibas bulvaris 21, open 24 hours, also telephone, fax and telegraph services. Telephone office

at Dzirnavu iela, open 0900–2000 daily.
Riga has an international airport with flights to most main European cities.

DIPLOMATIC MISSIONS
In Riga:
Denmark: Pils iela 11. *Tel.* 722 6210.
Finland: Kalpaka bulvaris 1. *Tel.* 733 2005.
Germany: Reina bulvaris 13. *Tel.* 722 9096.
Poland: Elizabetes iela 2. *Tel.* 732 1617.
Russia: Antonijas iela 2. *Tel.* 733 2151.
United Kingdom: Alunana iela 5.
Tel. 733 8126.
United States: 7 Raina Bulevaris.
Tel. 721 0005.

following a referendum. In August 1991 the international community including Russia recognised Latvia as an independent democratic republic.

In 1993 a Free Trade Agreement was signed with Estonia and Lithuania. Latvia is now an associated member of the EU. The economy is largely industrial, with manufacturing industries, as well as some peat deposits, forestry, cattle and dairy farming. Moves from a Soviet-style economy to privatisation and a free market resulted in a decline in living standards, although in recent years there have been signs of improvement.

The population numbers 2.7 million of which just over half are Latvians, a third being Russian, and various smaller minorities: Belorussians, Ukrainians, Poles, Lithuanians, Jews and Gypsies. Latvia is very urbanised and more than a third of the population live in the capital Riga. Lutherans form the traditional majority, though there are other denominations such as Orthodox Christian and Roman Catholic.

The climate is moderate, with cool summers and mild winters.

Entry Regulations

Ports of entry
Riga 56°58′N 24°06′E, Ventspils 57°24′N 21°33′E, Liepaja 56°32′N 21°01′E.

Procedure on arrival
As clearance formalities must be completed at one of the above ports and as only Riga has adequate facilities for yachts, the capital should be the preferred first port of call.

Riga: Situated at the head of the Bay of Riga, arriving yachts should proceed about 8 miles through the large port of Riga as far as the last basin before the bridge. The ferry terminal is located there, where customs and immigration have their offices. Yachts may go directly to the Andrejosta Yacht Centre (the former Latvian Shipping Company Yacht Club). Officials will visit the boat and complete formalities.

Customs
Firearms and ammunition must be declared. A customs declaration must be completed on arrival.

Immigration
Visas are not required by nationals of the USA and most European countries with the exception of Monaco, Bulgaria, Romania, Russia and CIS states. Nationals of Argentina, Australia, Brazil, Bulgaria, Canada, Chile, Cyprus, Israel, Japan, Mexico, Monaco, New Zealand, Paraguay, Republic of Korea, San Marino, Singapore, South Africa, Uruguay and Venezuela require a visa, which in most cases can be obtained on arrival. Nationals of all other countries must have a special invitation from the immigration department in order to obtain a visa.

The Baltic states are a one visa zone, so with a Latvian visa one can visit the other two Republics, and vice versa.

Visa extensions are obtained from the Visa Office, Raina Bulvaris 5, Riga. *Tel.* (2) 2 219 176.

Anchorage
Anchoring is not permitted in the navigation channels and rivers approaching the ports.

Facilities

Riga, and the Andrejosta Yacht Centre in particular, has the best facilities for visiting yachts. The marina is close to the centre of town and has marina type facilities. Repair facilities are limited, but the yacht club will help if necessary and will also arrange deliveries of fuel. The ports of Ventspils and Liepaja are commercial harbours and facilities for yachts are limited. There is a designated dock for visiting yachts at Ventspils, and a yacht harbour at the resort of Jaurmala, a few miles west of Riga.

Further Reading

The Baltic Sea
Baltic States & Kaliningrad – a travel survival kit

Website

www.latviatravel.com (Latvian Tourism Development Agency)

LITHUANIA

Lithuania is the largest and most populous of the three Baltic Republics, lying on the Baltic Sea south of Latvia. Its coast is only some 60 miles long, half of which is on the Courland Spit (Neringa in Lithuanian, Kurshskaya kosa in Russian), a long, narrow sandbar, sheltering the Courland lagoons which can be reached from Klaipeda.

Shallow drafted boats can use the inland waterway that links Klaipeda with Kaliningrad, in the Russian enclave between Poland and Lithuania. Cruising opportunities are few, although shallow drafted boats may explore the northern part of Kurskiy Zaliv, the large inland body of water fronting the Russian enclave of Kaliningrad.

Country Profile

The original inhabitants, known as 'Balts', settled as tribes in this region around 2000 BC. In the early Christian era they resisted invasions from Scandinavia, and in 1240 the Grand Duchy of Lithuania was founded, which successfully resisted the threat of the German Teutonic Knights; by the mid-fifteenth century its rule had extended into the neighbouring Russian lands, almost to the Black Sea. A dynastic union with Poland in 1385 saw the spread of Catholicism (Lithuania was the last European country to become Christian) and a political union came in 1569. Poland came to dominate the union, and the Lithuanian lands were absorbed into the Russian empire in 1795 during the partition of Poland. Many Lithuanians emigrated to America in the nineteenth century, while nationalism grew amongst those who remained.

Occupied by the German army during the First World War, in 1918 Lithuania proclaimed its independence, which was recognised by the Soviet Union in 1920. The Red Army occupied Vilnius in 1919, which was occupied by Poland until 1939. The secret pact of that year, between the Soviet Union and Germany, led to the Soviet invasion of Lithuania in 1940, and after the war Soviet rule was consolidated in what was then the Lithuanian Soviet Socialist Republic.

The 1980s saw Lithuania taking a leading role among the Baltic states in the growing pressure for independence. In March 1990 Lithuania's proclamation of independence was not accepted by the Soviet Union, which sent troops into Vilnius to intimidate the nationalists. The situation changed suddenly with the August 1991 coup in Moscow against Gorbachev; soon afterwards an independent Lithuania was recognised by Russia and the international community. Since 1992 Lithuania has been governed by a democratically elected parliament called the Seimas. The President of the Republic is elected for a term of five years.

In 1993 Lithuania signed a Free Trade Agreement with Estonia and Latvia. An extensive privatisation programme is being undertaken to move away from the Soviet-style command economy, although many have suffered from high inflation and the subsequent decline in living standards. Industry consists mainly of manufacturing, ship building, forestry and fishing; 30 per cent of the population is rural, engaged in dairy and stock farming. There are some oil reserves.

The population numbers 3.8 million, the majority being Lithuanians, most of whom are Roman Catholics, while there is a Russian minority of

Practical Information

LOCAL TIME: GMT +1, summer time end March to end October GMT +2.

BUOYAGE: IALA A

CURRENCY: Litas of 100 centas.

BUSINESS HOURS
Banks 0930–1300 Monday to Friday.

ELECTRICITY: 220 V, 50 Hz

PUBLIC HOLIDAYS
1 January: New Year's Day
16 February: Independence Day
11 March: Restoration of Lithuania's Independence
Good Friday, Easter Monday
2 May: Mother's Day
6 July: Statehood Day
1 November: All Saints' Day
25, 26 December: Christmas

COMMUNICATIONS
International phone calls from a 24-hour telephone centre, Liepu 16 in Klaipeda, or with phone cards. International access code: 8, then after dial tone, 10. For in-country access, also dial 8. Post office at Liepu gatve 16, Klaipeda, open 0900–1900 Monday to Friday, 0900–1600 Saturday. There are international airports at Vilnius and Kaunas with regular flights to other European countries. Palanga airport, 16

miles (25 km) north of Klaipeda, has international flights to Germany and the Scandinavian countries. Buses run from Klaipeda to Vilnius and Riga; there are also ferries to Germany.

DIPLOMATIC MISSIONS
In Vilnius:
Finland: Klaipedos gatve 6. Tel. (22) 221 621.
Germany: Sierakausko gatve 24. Tel. (22) 650 272.
Russia: Latviu 53. Tel. (22) 721 763.
United Kingdom: Antakalnio gatve 2. Tel. (22) 222 070.
United States: Akmenu gatve 6. Tel. (22) 222 737.
In Klaipeda:
Russia: Janonio 24. Tel. 299 674.

under 10 per cent, as well as some Poles, Belorussians and Ukrainians. The official language is Lithuanian although the minorities have the right to the official use of their language where they form a substantial part of the population. The capital is Vilnius.

Summers are generally cool and winters mild.

Entry Regulations

Port of entry
Klaipeda 55°43′N 21°07′E.

Procedure on arrival
Klaipeda: The Sea Canal, which links the port with the Baltic, is well marked. Yachts are directed to the customs pier in the commercial harbour, where customs and immigration formalities are completed. Afterwards yachts are allowed to move to the yacht club, which is located further along the channel on the oppposite bank from Klaipeda town.

Customs
Firearms must be declared. A customs declaration form has to be completed on arrival, on which valuables and foreign currency amounts should be listed. Animals must have health and inoculation certificates.

Duty-free allowances are 1 litre strong spirits, 2 litres wine.

Immigration
Visas are not required by nationals of most European countries, Australia, Canada, Japan, Korea, New Zealand, the United States and Venezuela. Other nationals must obtain a visa, and some of these may be restricted to a maximum of 10 days.

Lithuanian visas are also valid for Latvia and Estonia as the Baltic states are a one-visa zone. Visa fees are lower if obtained in advance. Extensions can be obtained from the Immigration Office, Verkiugatve 3, Vilnius.

Facilities

Klaipeda Yacht Club has good docking and repair facilities. A club launch makes occasional trips to Klaipeda itself, which is situated on the opposite bank of the river. There is also a ferry crossing. There are good train connections to the capital Vilnius.

Visiting yachts may also find a berth at Klub Budys, on the Dange Canal, just south of the immigration office. The club area is reached via an opening bridge and is more convenient for visiting the town.

Repair facilities are limited, although the yacht club might be able to help. Fuel, water and LPG may also have to be arranged via the yacht club.

Further Reading

The Baltic Sea
Baltic States – a travel survival kit

Website

www.tourism.lt (Department of Tourism)

NETHERLANDS

Facing the North Sea between Belgium and Germany, the Netherlands or Low Countries certainly deserve their name. Much of the country is so low that to prevent the encroaching of the sea has always been a battle, and gradually a system of dykes were built to protect the land. It is not correct to call the country 'Holland' as the Netherlands is divided into twelve provinces and this name applies to only two provinces, North Holland and South Holland.

In the Netherlands one is never too far away from water and the centre of the country is occupied by the IJsselmeer, formerly called Zuiderzee, until it was dammed off from the sea. Most cruising is concentrated in the IJsselmeer, Wadden Sea and Frisian Islands, an area of sand dunes, intricate channels and picturesque ports. The western part has deeper water and a keeled yacht has access everywhere, whereas a shallow draft is essential in the eastern part. At IJmuiden one can pass through a lock to reach the IJsselmeer and Amsterdam. Another excellent cruising ground is Zeeland, in the south-west, which can be reached via the Walcheren Canal at Vlissingen or through the locks on the Oosterschelde. Cruising along the North Sea coast is more challenging on account of the strong tides, sand banks and onshore winds. From Vlissingen in the south-west to Delfzijl in the north-east, there are several good yacht harbours in which to shelter in case of bad weather. The Frisian Islands have many sheltered harbours

Practical Information

LOCAL TIME: GMT + 1. Summer time GMT + 2 from the end of March to the end of October.

BUOYAGE: IALA A at sea, and the ISIGNI system in inland waters.

CURRENCY: Gulden (guilder/florin, Fl) of 100 cents. Euro from 2002. 1 euro = 2.20371 NLG.

BUSINESS HOURS
Banks: 0900–1700 Monday to Friday.
Business: 0830–1730 Monday to Friday.
Shops: 0830/0900 to 1730/1800 Monday to Friday, to 1600 Saturday, some until 1900–2100 on Thursdays or Fridays. Small shops may close for lunch and some have a half day closing, often Monday morning. In bigger towns, many shops are open also on Sundays, and in some cases for 24 hours.

Government offices: 0830–1730 Monday to Friday.

ELECTRICITY: 220 V, 50 Hz

PUBLIC HOLIDAYS
1 January: New Year's Day
Good Friday, Easter Monday
30 April: Queen's Day
5 May: Liberation Day
Ascension Day
Whit Monday
24–26 December: Christmas

COMMUNICATIONS
International dialling access code is 00.
Post offices open 0830–1700 Monday to Friday, some also 0830–1200 Saturday.
Amsterdam has a very busy international airport with flights to almost everywhere in the world.
Emergency 112.

MEDICAL
There are reciprocal agreements for free treatment with other European countries.

DIPLOMATIC MISSIONS
In The Hague:
Australia: Carnegielaan 4, 2517 KH.
Tel. (70) 310 8200.
Canada: Sophialaan 7, 2514 JP.
Tel. (70) 311 1600.
New Zealand: Carnegielaaan 10-14, 2517 KH. *Tel.* (70) 346 9324.
United Kingdom: Lange Voorhout 10, 2514 ED. *Tel.* (70) 427 0427.
United States: Lange Voorhout 102, 2514 EJ. *Tel.* (70) 575 5310.

In Amsterdam:
United Kingdom: Koningslaan 44, 1075 AE. *Tel.* (20) 676 4343.
United States: Museumplein 19, 1071 DJ. *Tel.* (20) 575 5310.

on the east side facing the Wadden Sea, which are good starting points to explore the liquid world of the Netherlands.

Country Profile

This region was already peopled by Celtic and Germanic tribes when conquered by the Romans in 57 BC. Overrun by Germanic invasions in the fourth century, later Saxons and Franks settled in different parts. The ninth century brought Norman invasions and the country was divided into feudal duchies, earldoms and bishoprics, then fiefs of the Holy Roman Empire. The twelfth and thirteenth centuries saw the rapid growth of the towns, their prosperity based mainly on the cloth trade. By the fifteenth century, royal marriages, inheritances and purchases led to the area being united under the Duke of Burgundy, and later brought under Spanish rule. During the sixteenth century there was economic expansion, and the ideas of the Protestant Reformation spread. In 1555 Philip II became the new king of Spain and the Netherlands, and his absolutist anti-Protestant policy led to the Calvinist, prosperous northern provinces rebelling. After a long struggle against Spain in 1648 the United Provinces were eventually recognised as an independent country.

The United Provinces later became known as the Netherlands and they made rapid economic progress, becoming a leading maritime power. They established a vast commercial empire in the East Indies, South Africa and Brazil. However, wars with neighbouring powers weakened the state and the eighteenth century led to a decline. France overran the country, forming first the Batavia Republic, then the Kingdom of Holland. In 1814 the Treaty of Paris united the Netherlands and Belgium as an independent entity, but in 1830 Belgium broke away.

A liberal constitution was introduced in 1848. Wilhelmina became Queen in 1890, her reign lasting nearly sixty years. The Netherlands were neutral in the First World War, and occupied by Germany in the Second. After the war the Netherlands enjoyed an economic recovery. Juliana succeeded as Queen in 1948, until her abdication in 1980 in favour of her daughter Beatrice. The Netherlands are a member of Benelux, NATO and the European Community.

Overseas commerce has always been important, and continues to dominate the economy, half the national product being exported. Electrical, food processing, chemical and natural gas industries or service industries such as finance are the main employers of the working population. Agriculture is intensive, often on reclaimed land, mainly raising livestock, and the flowers and market gardening for which the country is renowned.

The population is 15.2 million and is concentrated around the main towns. Amsterdam is the commercial capital, but The Hague is the parliamentary and legal capital. Dutch is the official language, but English is widely spoken. There are both Protestants and Catholics, as well as several other denominations.

The climate is normally temperate, and rainfall is frequent all year round. Temperatures are rarely above 65°F (18°C) in summer or below 45°F (7°C) in winter. The prevailing winds are W or SW and most gales also come from those directions.

Entry Regulations

Ports of entry

Vlissingen (Flushing) 51°27′N 3°35′E, Breskens 51°24′N 3°34′E, Veerhaven (De Maas/Rotterdam) 51°54′N 4°29′E, Scheveningen 52°06′N 4°16′E, IJmuiden 52°27′N 4°35′E, Den Helder 52°58′N 4°47′E, Terneuzen 51°20′N 3°49′E, Terschelling 53°22′N 5°13′E, Vlieland 53°18′N 5°06′E, Lauwersoog 53°25′N 6°12′E, Delfzijl 53°20′N 6°54′E.

Some ports have customs only in the summer months, such as Roompot Sluis and Oost Vlieland.

Procedure on arrival

Although a EU country, all boats arriving from overseas must fly the Q flag and report on arrival and departure to the nearest customs office. This is strictly enforced. On arrival the customs will issue a certificate of entry, which is valid for a maximum of 12 months. During this period a yacht may leave and re-enter the Netherlands, showing the certificate on each re-entry. Foreign yachts must be registered. Any person steering a vessel capable of more than 9 knots must have a certificate of competence.
Vlissingen: The port is entered through a set of lock gates and there is a marina situated close to the lock.
Scheveningen: The marina is located in fishing harbour no. 2. The port authorities should be contacted on VHF Channel 14 for permission to enter the harbour.
IJmuiden: There can be a strong tidal stream at the entrance. The Seaport Marina IJmuiden is located at the south pier (VHF Channel 74).

Den Helder: Yachts can moor in the Royal Naval Yacht Harbour.
Delfzijl: A new yacht harbour is in operation some three miles south of the old harbour entrance.

Customs

All firearms must be licensed, and a copy of the licence carried. There are restrictions concerning signalling pistols. Very type flare pistols must be accompanied by a firearms certificate issued in the country of origin. A radio operator's licence may also be requested.

Animals must have a valid health certificate.

The yacht may not be sold, rented or borrowed while in the Netherlands, unless the appropriate taxes have been paid. Yachts from non-EU countries may stay up to 12 months, after which time they must leave the country but can re-enter after a few days, obtaining a new certificate of entry. Otherwise they become liable for VAT (Value Added Tax).

For up-to-date information, contact customs direct on *Tel.* 06 0143.

Immigration

Nationals of the European Union, United States, Canada, Israel, Japan, New Zealand, Australia, and most other European countries do not need a visa for a stay up to three months.

Navigation

Shipping traffic is very heavy along the coast. A very busy shipping route is via the Hook of Holland over the New Waterway to Rotterdam, and there is no yacht harbour in this port. In a strong westerly wind and outgoing tide from the New Waterway there can be a high tidal sea.

Inland waterways

Access to the inland waterways is from the ports of Veerhaven and the IJmuiden locks. From Den Helder there are connections via the Noord-Hollands Canal and the Zaan with Amsterdam. There is access through Vlissingen with a standing mast via the Canal through Walcheren with connections to Dordrecht and Rotterdam. There is no access from Scheveningen.

There are no speed limits on the larger rivers (except the Maas), the IJsselmeer, the open-sea channels in Zeeland, the Waddenzee and the coastal waters. However, there are speed limits in force on the canals and lakes, varying between 5 and 9 knots in different areas, which should be checked. Motorboats capable of travelling at more than 9 knots must be registered. This can be done at most larger post offices for a fee, showing proof of identity. In some areas local permission must also be obtained to travel at greater speeds.

On many of the canals and rivers yachts must keep to starboard and have their engines prepared for use. If motorsailing on the waterways, yachts are required to display forward a black cone, apex downwards.

Landing on some islands in the inland waterways is restricted. There are also restrictions concerning draft and height. However, there are certain routes that can be taken by yachts with high fixed masts without encountering any bridges. These are in the western and northern parts of Holland, such as Vlissingen to Delfzijl.

Yachts are required to have on board a copy of the Inland Waters Police Regulations, which are in force on most inland waters, the Zeeland channels (except the Western Scheldt, where its own shipping regulations apply), the IJsselmeer, and the Waddenzee. On the Dutch Rhine, the Waal and the Lek the Rhine Route Police Regulations are in force.

The Inland Waters Police Regulations are available in Part I of the *Almanak voor Watertourisme*, in Dutch only. Part 2 contains tide tables, opening times of bridges and locks, and other essential details.

It is recommended to have the latest charts on board as depths change and banks as well as shallow areas move frequently.

Fishing

There are certain regulations regarding fishing in the Netherlands and a permit must be bought. Permits can be obtained at post offices. Regulations must be respected concerning closed seasons, areas where fishing is permitted, types of rods which can be used and types of fish which can be caught.

Facilities

As can be expected in a water-based nation with a great maritime past, boating facilities are good everywhere. There are shops in all the small ports and fuel is available in most marinas and harbours on the dock. Along the coast there are marinas with repair facilities at Vlissingen and Breskens, both of which are convenient if coming from the south. There are good facilities also in Zeeland, particularly at the marinas at Zierikzee and Colijnsplaat. Good facilities are also available at Den Helder, with smaller marinas and a limited range of repair facilities at Terschelling and Vlieland. Across the Wadden Sea on the mainland, Harlingen is a picturesque port with good facilities. In the north, best facilities are at Delfzijl, which is reached by sailing up the Ems.

Further Reading

Almanak voor Watertourisme, Parts 1 and 2, from ANWB offices (Royal Netherlands Touring Club) and some bookshops.
ANWB also publishes charts of the inland waters. Small craft charts published annually by the Dutch Hydrographic Office. There is a special chart of the Province of Friesland, regularly updated.
Inland Waterways of France also has main routes in the Netherlands.
IJsselmeer Harbours
Cruising Guide to the Netherlands
Cruising Association Handbook
North Sea Passage Pilot

Further information can be obtained from:
ANWB section Watersport: *Tel.* (70) 314 7720.
KNWV: e-mail: info@KNWV.nl *Tel.* (30) 6566 550.

Website

www.visitholland.com (Netherlands Board of Tourism)

NORWAY

Norway occupies the western side of the Scandinavian peninsula, a mountainous forested land, with deep dramatic fjords cutting into the coast. The wild grandeur of the fjords gives Norway one of the most beautiful sceneries in the world. A chain of islands stretching parallel to the western coast and extending almost as far as the North Cape provide sheltered waters for cruising. The majestic fjords are less suited for cruising as the anchorages are extremely deep and the winds alternate between flat calms and violent gusts blowing almost vertically down the sides of the sheer cliffs.

Although the number of cruising boats visiting the northern part of Norway is still small, mainly because of the short sailing season and unreliable weather, there has been a marked increase in the number of yachts attracted to cold water cruising.

Practical Information

LOCAL TIME: GMT + 1. Summer time GMT + 2 from the end of March to the end of October.

BUOYAGE: IALA A

CURRENCY: Norwegian kroner (NOK) of 100 øre.

BUSINESS HOURS
Banks: Monday to Friday 0815–1500 (1530 in winter), Thursday 0815–1700.
Business: 0800–1600 Monday to Friday.
Shops: 0900–1700 Monday to Friday, 0900–1500 Saturdays.
Shopping centres: 1000–2000 Monday to Friday, 0900/1000–1600/1800 Saturdays.
Government offices: 0800–1500 Monday to Friday.

ELECTRICITY: 220 V, 50 Hz

PUBLIC HOLIDAYS
1 January: New Year's Day
Maundy Thursday, Good Friday and Easter Monday
1 May: Labour Day
17 May: Constitution Day
Ascension Day
Whit Monday
25, 26 December: Christmas

COMMUNICATIONS
International dialling access code is 00.
International calls can be made from any public phone. International operator 0115.
Page 16 of the telephone directory gives explanations in English, while various emergency numbers are given in the front.
Post office: 0800–1600/1700 Monday to Friday, Saturday 0800–1300.
The main international airport with flights worldwide is Oslo, but there are also international flights from other main cities.

MEDICAL
There is a reciprocal agreement with certain West European countries for medical treatment in the Norwegian Health Service.
Oslo Legevakt Hospital, Storgt 40.
Tel. (22) 11 70 70. Police 112, Ambulance 113.

DIPLOMATIC MISSIONS
In Oslo:
Canada: Oscar's Gate 20. Tel. (22) 466955.
Russia: Drammensun 74. Tel. (22) 55 3278.
United Kingdom: Thomas Heftyesgate 8.
Tel. (23) 13 27 00.
United States: Drammensveien 18.
Tel. (22) 448550.

A popular destination beyond continental Norway is Spitsbergen (Svalbard), which is visited by over 20 yachts each summer.

Country Profile

From the eighth to the eleventh centuries the Vikings reigned supreme in the coastal regions of north-west Europe, often terrorising the coasts of the British Isles, France and Greenland. Through their voyaging the Norsemen came in contact with the rest of the world and Norway gradually developed into a state. Christianity spread through the area in the tenth and eleventh centuries. In the thirteenth century Norway expanded westwards and established control over the Faeroes, Orkneys, Shetlands and Greenland. Norwegian vessels were roaming the North Atlantic five centuries before Columbus sailed the much more benign route to the continent which later became known as America.

The Union of Kalmar of 1397 brought Norway under Danish rule and Norway remained under Danish control for three centuries. The eighteenth century saw the Norwegian economy expand and wood, metal and fish were exported. In the 1814 Treaty of Kiel, Denmark ceded Norway to Sweden, and despite resistance the Norwegians were forced to accept it. In the nineteenth century parliamentary rule was gradually established, and after a plebiscite Norway gained independence in 1905. Social reforms were introduced, and in 1935 working-class strength brought the Labour party to power. Norway was occupied by Germany from 1940 to 1945, and after the king and government fled, Major Quisling, a Nazi supporter, ruled the country. After the war the Labour party were in power until 1965, since when there have been various governments, mainly of a moderate centre coalition. In 1972 the Norwegians voted in a referendum against Norway's proposed entry into the European Union, and again in 1994.

Agriculture is centred in the southern region and livestock raising is the most important activity. Forestry, fishing and shipping industries are important, while large North Sea gas and oil deposits have brought a considerable income in recent years.

The population is 4 million. Apart from Norwegians, Finns and Sami (Lapps) live in the northernmost region of Finnmark. Norwegian and Lappish are spoken, and the majority of the population is Lutheran. The capital is Oslo, situated at the head of a large fjord in the south of the country.

The climate is milder on the coast due to the Atlantic influences, but it is still very cold in winter. The winter coastal temperatures average 40–50°F (4–10°C), and minus 0–35°F (18°–1°C) inland. In summer the coast is around 55–60°F (13–15°C), and inland 65–70°F (18–21°C). The weather is generally rainy and changeable on the western coast, while less rainy and more predictable in the south-east. Northerly winds prevail in summer along the coast, while in winter there is a predominance of southerly winds. Winds strengthen during

The Norwegian port of Bergen.

the afternoons.

Summer weather beyond the Arctic Circle, both in continental Norway and further north, is unreliable. Visibility on most days can be poor, with low mist. Winds can be occasionally strong and the weather can change very suddenly.

Entry Regulations

Ports of entry
All ports are ports of entry except those in military areas. Frequently used ports only are listed below. Bergen 60°24′N 5°19′E, Haugesund 59°25′N 5°16′E, Stavanger 58°58′N 5°44′E, Egersund 58°27′N 6°00′E, Mandal 58°02′N 7°28′E, Kristiansand 58°09′N 8°00′E, Lillesand 58°15′N 8°23′E, Oslo 59°54′N 10°43′E, Fredrikstad 59°12′N 10°57′E, Tonsberg 59°16′N 10°25′E, Moss 59°26′N 10°40′E.

Procedure on arrival
Yachts from Nordic countries do not need to make a customs declaration provided they are not carrying an excess of dutiable stores and equipment and do not remain in Norwegian waters more than six months. Yachts from other countries should report immediately on arrival at a port of entry. Customs clearance is not strictly necessary if one has nothing to declare, but is advisable. The captain should report to customs and show the ship's documents and passports. Customs must be cleared at a quay in the main harbour before moving to a berth for yachts. Immigration must be contacted on arrival and both immigration and customs must be cleared on departure.

Customs
Firearms must be declared. All firearms must have a licence from the country of origin. Firearms must be re-exported within three months, if not an application for a permit must be made.

The requirements for the importation of animals and birds into Norway varies, depending on where the animal comes from and whether that country is rabies-free or not. Generally a health and vaccination certificate is required and the animal must be able to be identified by microchip or tattoo.

Swedish and Norwegian cats and dogs may travel without restriction between the two countries, but must have documentation if they were imported legally into either country. A comprehensive information sheet can be obtained from the Norwegian Health Authority, Central Unit, PO Box 8147 Dep., N-0033 Oslo, Norway. *Tel.* +47 22 24 19 40. Fax. + 47 22 24 19 45.

Only up to 22 lb (10 kg) of agricultural products are allowed to be imported, of which 6.6 lb (3 kg) may be meat and processed meat products from other Nordic countries. Tinned meat from all countries is allowed but fresh fruit, vegetables or dairy products are restricted imports. Eggs and potatoes may not be imported.

There are strict restrictions on the import of alcohol and a heavy tax is imposed for excess amounts. For persons over 20 the allowance is 1 litre of spirits and 1 litre wine *or* 2 litres of wine and 2 litres of beer. A deposit must be paid on excess amounts and the items placed under seal until leaving Norwegian waters. This deposit will be refunded on proof from foreign customs that the yacht has arrived in the next country.

Yachts may remain for up to one year, after which Value Added Tax must be paid. If wishing to lay up the boat, permission from customs must be obtained first and it may be necessary to have a bond from a bank. The vessel may only be used by the person to whom clearance is given and cannot be used for commercial purposes. For non-resident owners who remain more than five months in Norway, the yacht is permitted to stay for six months.

Immigration

No visas are needed for stays of up to three months by nationals of most European and Commonwealth countries, the USA, Canada, Australia, Japan, Israel and New Zealand. Extensions can be obtained from the police, but then the person will not be allowed back for a further six months.

Fishing

Anyone over 16 years old fishing for salmon, sea trout, sea char or freshwater fish in waters on common land must pay an annual fee at any post office. A local fishing licence is also compulsory and this can be obtained from sports shops, kiosks and tourist offices. The licence only covers a certain area, and can be bought for a day, week, month or whole season. Restrictions are normally stated on the licence. Live bait is forbidden.

Fishing seasons vary from district to district.

Sea fishing with rod or hand lines is open to anyone, and no fishing fee must be paid, unless fishing for salmon, sea trout or sea char. The closed season for these fish is 5 August–31 May.

Foreigners may only use hand gear such as rods or jigs. Nets and similar devices may not be used.

Restrictions

Yachts must stay in the sailing lanes marked on the charts. Sailing close to military areas is prohibited, such areas being marked on charts and usually indicated by signposts on the shore.

There are various conservation areas for sea birds along the coasts, access to which is prohibited between 15 April and 15 July, including the surrounding sea for 164 ft (50 m).

The shoreline in anchorages is normally privately owned and one should ask the owner's permission first before landing.

No fires may be lit on shore from 15 April to 15 September.

No garbage may be thrown overboard and toilets can be pumped out only well away from harbours and sailing lanes.

A warning is issued to boats cruising the fjords to pay careful attention to the height restrictions caused by overhead cables.

There are a number of special requirements for boats sailing to Spitsbergen. As a safety precaution, all cruising boats must register with the authorities in Longyearbyen, which can be done by radio. Details on the special regulations for visitors to the nature reserves can be obtained by writing to the Governor of Svalbard, 9170 Longyearbyen, Svalbard, Norway. There is also a requirement for special search and rescue insurance to be taken out by all boats going to eastern Spitsbergen.

Fees

Overtime is charged on customs clearance at weekends.

Flag etiquette

The courtesy flag must be flown from sunrise to sunset only, but not before 0800 and not after 2100. It is considered very discourteous to leave the flag flying after sunset.

Facilities

Provisioning is good everywhere, but the price of food is very high. Fuel is available in all ports. LPG containers may be refilled only in the main centres such as Oslo, Stavanger and Bergen, and it may be necessary to have the right adaptor. Sets of small craft charts are available containing details of interest to cruising yachts which are not found on ordinary charts.

The widest range of repair facilities are in the main yachting centres such as Oslo, Stavanger and Bergen, which also have the best docking facilities. Particularly recommended is Her Bern Marina situated in the old Akers shipyard right in the centre of Oslo.

Good facilities are also available at Kristiansand, where most repairs can be undertaken and there also is a chandlery and sailmaker. There are docking or mooring provisions for visiting yachts in all ports, although occasionally a dock may be privately owned and permission to use it should be obtained first.

Facilities in Longyearbyen, the administrative centre of Svalbard (Spitsbergen), are surprisingly comprehensive. Fuel and water is available on the main dock, which is reserved for commercial shipping and cruising yachts must stay at anchor. Provisioning in Longyearbyen is good as are repair facilities.

Limited supplies, fuel and water are also available at Ny Ålesund, but fuel may have to be ordered in advance. Ny Ålesund is a centre for Arctic research. There is a new dock where yachts may berth.

Further Reading

Norwegian Cruising Guide

Websites

www.tourist.no (Norwegian Tourist Board)
www.toll.no (Directorate of Customs and Excise)

POLAND

Poland lies on the southern shores of the Baltic Sea wedged between Germany and the Soviet Union, two countries whose territorial ambitions have shaped most of Poland's recent history. Poland was the first East European country to rid itself of Communist rule by democratic means and also put an end to Soviet domination. The process, which started in Poland in the early 1980s, has had reverberations, not only in Europe but all over the world.

Of all the Communist countries in Europe, Poland was the first to allow its sailors to cruise away from home. Although most limited their sailing to neighbouring Baltic countries, a few Polish yachts sailed as far as the Caribbean and some even around the world. Cruising in Poland itself is limited to the two sailing areas around the ports of Szczecin and Gdynia, the former in the estuary of the river Oder (Odra), the latter on the western shore of the Gulf of Gdansk.

Country Profile

Although Poland has been inhabited since 3000 BC, the country's history really began in the fifth century when Slavs settled between the Oder and Elbe rivers. After Christianity came to the area a duchy was established, which later divided into several duchies in the twelfth century. The Teutonic Knights took advantage of this division to conquer East Prussia and cut off Poland's access to the Baltic. The fourteenth century brought some unity to Poland under Casimir III and later Lithuania was united with Poland, and parts of White Russia and the Ukraine were absorbed. In the first half of the sixteenth century during the reigns of Sigismund I and II, Poland prospered, with economic growth and the development of a humanist culture and religious tolerance. However, after 1572 conflicts between the monarchy and the nobles embroiled the country in civil war which, coupled with wars with Russia, Turkey and Sweden, saw Poland lose territory and her great power status.

Poland's neighbours continued to intervene in her internal affairs, culminating in the partition of Poland between Russia, Prussia and Austria. In 1807–13 Napoleon formed the Grand Duchy of Warsaw, but this was abolished by the Congress of Vienna in 1815 and the land redistributed between the powers. Polish resistance and uprisings throughout the nineteenth century were repressed and many Poles emigrated. However, the independence movement remained strong, and came to the fore in the First World War.

In 1918 Poland was re-established as an independent republic, and given access to the Baltic through the Polish Corridor. Frontier disputes caused fighting with the Germans, Czechs, Russians and Ukrainians until 1921. Non-aggression pacts were signed with both the USSR and Germany in the 1930s, but the secret Molotov–Ribbentrop

Practical Information

LOCAL TIME: GMT + 1. Summer time GMT + 2 end of March to end of October.

BUOYAGE: IALA A

CURRENCY: zloty (zl).

BUSINESS HOURS
Banks: Hours very variable, 0800–1500 or 1800 Monday to Friday.
Business: 0830–1530 Monday to Friday.
Shops: Variable, 1000/1100–1800/1900 Monday to Friday, 1000–1300/1400 Saturday.
Government offices: 0800–1500 Monday to Friday.

ELECTRICITY: 220 V, 50 Hz

PUBLIC HOLIDAYS
1 January: New Year's Day
Easter Sunday, Easter Monday
1 May: Labour Day
Corpus Christi
3 May: Constitution Day
9 May: Victory Day
15 August: Assumption Day
1 November: All Saints Day
11 November: Rebirth of Polish State
25 December: Christmas Day
26 December: Boxing Day

COMMUNICATIONS
International calls can be made from telephone offices or from card phones (buy cards from post offices and kiosks).
International operator 901.
Telegrams can be sent from post offices and by telephone.
There are flights to many destinations worldwide from Warsaw. There are also international flights from Gdansk.
Good train services to Germany; ferries from Gdansk to Sweden and Finland.

MEDICAL
The medical service is good and not too expensive; however, medicines are scarce and expensive.
Gdansk Hospital, al. Zwyciestwa 46.
Tel. (058) 410000.
Emergency and police 997.

DIPLOMATIC MISSIONS
In Warsaw:
Australia: Etonska 3/5, Saska Kepa.
Tel. (02) 6176081.
Canada: Ulicia Matejki 1/5.
Tel. (02) 298051.
Germany: Dabrowiecka 30.
Tel. (02) 6173011.
Lithuania: Al. J. Ch. Szucha 5.
Tel. (02) 6253368.
United Kingdom: Aleja Roz No 1.
Tel. (02) 6281001.
United States: Aleje Ujazdowskie 29/31.
Tel. (02) 6283041.

In Gdansk:
Russia: Ulica Batorego 15.
Tel. (058) 411 088.

---

agreement provided for the division of Poland. This occurred following Germany's invasion of Poland in 1939, the immediate cause of the outbreak of the Second World War. After the war the Communists gained power and a Soviet type republic was formed. In the 1970s Western finance was sought to modernise the economy, but economic problems continued. Dissatisfaction found an outlet when in 1980 the free trade union Solidarnosc (Solidarity) was formed. A year later martial law was imposed by General Jaruzelski and Solidarity was banned, but by the end of the 1980s restrictions were eased and in 1989 a non-Communist government was elected. In 1998 Poland became a full member of NATO and is preparing to join the European Union in the year 2003.

Heavy industry remains important to the economy, mainly iron, steel, chemicals and textiles. The main agricultural products are cereals, potatoes and sugar beet, the private sector in agriculture being quite sizeable. Ten years after the end of communist rule, Poland has made the greatest economical progress of all the East European countries.

The population is 40 million, being mainly Polish with small Ukrainian and Byelorussian minorities. Polish is spoken and the majority are Roman Catholic with an Orthodox minority. Warsaw is the capital.

Winters are very cold, with snow and ice from November to March. June to August are the hottest and driest months. In summer the days are long and the Baltic coast can have pleasant variable breezes.

Entry Regulations

Ports of entry
Swinoujscie 53°55′N 14°16′E, Nowe Warpno 53°44′N 14°17′E, Trzebiez 53°40′N 14°31′E, Dziwnow 54°01′N 14°44′E, Kolobrzeg 54°11′N 15°33′E, Darlowo 54°27′N 16°23′E, Ustka 54°35′N 16°51′E, Leba 54°46′N 17°33′E, Wladyslawowo 54°48′N 18°26′E, Hel 54°36′N 18°48′E, Jastarnia 54°42′N 18°41′E, Gdynia 54°31′N 18°33′E, Gdansk 54°23′N 18°38′E, Gorki Zachodnie 54°22′N 18°47′E, Elblag 54°16′N 19°25′E, Frombork 54°22′N 19°41′E.

On inland waterways to/from Germany:
Osinow Dolny (Hohensaaten) 52°52′N 14°08′E,
Widuchowa 53°07′N 14°23′E, Gryfino 53°15′N
14°30′E.

Procedure on arrival

Foreign boats must clear in and out with customs
and immigration at all major ports. The authorities
should be contacted on VHF Channel 12 before
entering a port. English is understood, but it may
be necessary to speak slowly. The following two
ports are the only ones that can be entered under
all weather conditions.

Gdynia: The yacht basin is at the southern breakwater entrance. Yachts should moor at the harbour
master's quay on arrival for clearance then proceed
to one of the four yacht clubs. The ship's papers
may be retained until departure. One should
also clear with customs and immigration. One
must return to the harbour master's quay for
clearance on departure when the yacht may be
searched.

Swinoujscie: This commercial port close to the
Polish–German border is a convenient place to
clear into Poland for boats arriving from the west.
Boats clear in at the exposed customs quay, just
inside the harbour entrance to port, past the breakwaters but before reaching the first commercial
dock. After formalities are completed one is
allowed to move to the town quay Wladyslawa IV
near the navy basin further upriver. In the case of
unfavourable weather conditions, boats can get
permission to clear in at the town quay.

Peenestrom Channel: Yachts coming from Germany
through the Stettiner Haff (Zalew Szczecinski in
Polish) must show their papers to the Polish patrol
boat stationed at the border (marked by buoys)
before continuing to Nowe Warpno, Trzebiez or
Swinoujscie for customs and immigration clearance.
One can not continue south on the Odra River
without clearing in.

Customs

Firearms must be declared. Animals need to have a
vaccination certificate.

Immigration

Citizens of the United Kingdom do not require a
visa for up to a 180-day stay. Other countries not
requiring visas, for up to a 90-day stay, are:
Western Europe, Argentina, Bolivia, Chile, Costa
Rica, Croatia, Cuba, Cyprus, Czech Republic,
Ecuador, Honduras, Hungary, Israel, Japan,
Latvia, Lithuania, South Korea, Malta, Moldova,

Mongolia, Nicaragua, Slovak Republic, Slovenia,
Ukraine, the United States and Uruguay.
Nationals of Bulgaria, Estonia, Macedonia,
Romania and Singapore can stay up to 30 days
visa-free.

Visas, valid for 90 days, should be obtained before
arrival. Visa fees vary according to nationality.

Restrictions

There are restricted areas near Ustka and along
the Hel peninsula, where passage is occasionally
prohibited. Hel fishing harbour is now open to
foreign yachts.

Facilities

Yachting facilities have improved greatly in recent
years. Provisioning is good everywhere. Shopping
malls and smaller shops offer a wide selection of
local and imported goods. Best yachting facilities
are in the marinas at Szczecin, Trzebiez, Leba,
Gdynia, Gdansk and Gorki Zachodnie, where
there are considerable local sailing communities.
There are good marinas in Gdynia, which is municipal and has four yacht clubs, and in Gdansk on
Motlawa River in the city centre. Facilities in
Swinoujscie are very limited. Better facilities are
available at Szczecin where there are two marinas
and several yacht clubs. Marina Porta Mare on the
south shore of Dabie Lake, a few miles east of the
city, has repair facilities at the yacht clubs nearby.
This is where yachts lower their masts before continuing south on the Odra River to the German
inland waterways. Interster Marina at Goclaw is
located north of the city. Repair facilities also
exist in Kolobrzeg yacht harbour, 50 miles east
of Swinoujscie. There are many yacht clubs that
may be good sources of information if help is
needed.

Further Reading

The Baltic Sea
Polish Ports Handbook
Polish Fishing Ports
Poland – a travel survival kit

Website

www.poland.pl/tourism (National Tourism
Office)

RUSSIA

The break-up of the Soviet Union has radically altered the cruising picture in both the Baltic and Black Sea. Unfortunately, while the countries themselves have undergone a profound process of liberalisation, rules affecting the movement of foreign vessels have seen only a limited relaxation compared to the Soviet past. In this respect Russia is the worst culprit and formalities for visiting yachts are just as cumbersome as in the past. Foreign vessels, and their crews, continue to be viewed with a high degree of suspicion and the officials one has to deal with can be just as difficult and unpleasant as their Soviet predecessors. After an initial outburst of interest, the number of cruising boats visiting Russia has levelled off as sailors realise that visiting Russia on their own boat is perhaps not worth all the aggravation.

Similarly, it will be a long time before yachts are allowed to use Russia's extensive inland waterway system, which would make it possible to take a yacht from the Baltic to the Black Sea, or vice versa, through the heart of this interesting country. At the cost of thousands of lives of forced labourers, the Soviet regime created a network in Western Russia that links two lakes, six artificial inland seas, rivers and canals, which now connect the White Sea to the Baltic and the Black Sea. The Russian Inland Waterways Act, passed by Stalin in 1936, prevents all foreign vessels from using these inland waterways. Access to them will only be possible after this law is finally repealed. A few exceptions have been made and some foreign yachts somehow managed to sail from St Petersburg to the Black Sea. The Act has been amended slightly to allow foreign vessels to transit the 30 mile canal from Vyborg to the Saimaa Lake in Finland (for more details, see page 113), or to

Practical Information

LOCAL TIME: GMT + 3 (St Petersburg and Moscow), GMT + 4 end March to end September.

BUOYAGE: IALA A

CURRENCY: Rouble. Any notes printed before 1997 are no longer legal tender. A currency declaration must be completed on arrival and departure; exchange receipts should be kept to show to customs on departure. In January 1994 a decree banned all cash transactions from being in any currency but roubles. Traveller's cheques are not easily exchanged, nor are credit cards readily accepted, so one should carry sufficient cash.

BUSINESS HOURS
Banks: Variable. Most banks open at 0900/0930 and close anywhere from 1500 to 2000. Some close for lunch.
Shops: 0900–1800/1900 Monday to Saturday; most close for lunch 1300–1400.

ELECTRICITY: 220 V, 50 Hz

PUBLIC HOLIDAYS
1 January: New Year's Day
7, 8 January: Orthodox Christmas

23 February: Defence of Motherland Day
8 March: Women's Day
1–2 May: Spring and Labour Days
9 May: Victory Day
12 June: Russian Independence Day
7 November: Socialist Revolution Day
12 December: Constitution Day

COMMUNICATIONS
A train service runs all through Russia and to other CIS countries. There is an extensive internal air network and frequent flights from Moscow and St Petersburg to most European capitals. On the Black Sea coast, the only airport is at Adler, southeast of Sochi.
St Petersburg: Main post office is at Pochtamtskaya ulitsa 9, 0900–2100 Monday–Saturday, 1000–2000 Sunday. International Telephone & Telegraph Office, Bolshaya Morskaya ul. 3–5, 0900–1230, 1300-2000, Monday–Friday, 0900–1230, 1300–1700 Sunday. Also telex and fax services.
District post offices: 0900–1900, closed 1400–1500.
Green card phones can be used for local, national and international calls; buy the cards from hotels, kiosks, post offices. If possible, international calls from private phones are best; or from Intourist Hotels.

MEDICAL
Emergency treatment is free at hospitals though foreigners may have to pay for medication. Ambulance *Tel.* 03. There are private Policlinics in the main cities with imported drugs and equipment, therefore expensive.
St Petersburg: Poliklinika 2, Moskovskiy pr. 22, *Tel.* 292 62 72, 24 hour emergency service.
American Medical Center, nab. reki Fontanka 77, *Tel.* 310 96 11.

DIPLOMATIC MISSIONS
In Moscow:
Australia: Kropotkinsky Per. 13.
Tel. (095) 956 6070.
Germany: Mosfilmovskaya Ul. 56.
Tel. (095) 936 2401.
New Zealand: Povarskaya Ul. 44.
Tel. (095) 956 2642.
UK: Sofiyskaya nab. 14.
Tel. (095) 956 7200.
USA: Bolshoy Devyatinsky 8.
Tel. (095) 256 4261.
In St Petersburg:
Estonia: Bolshaya Monetnaya Ul. 14, 3rd floor. *Tel.* (812) 233 5548.
UK: Proletarskoy diktatury 5.
Tel. (812) 320 3200.
USA: Furshtadttskaya 15.
Tel. (812) 275 1701.

be able to reach some inland ports, such as Kaliningrad. Any requests, however, to take a yacht through the extensive inland waterway system are invariably turned down.

Even if not always rigidly enforced, many of the restrictions introduced during the Soviet era have remained basically unchanged, so one should not expect the same kind of freedom of movement as is enjoyed by land tourists. Although foreign yachts can now enter Russian coastal waters, obtaining visas and permission for entry remains complicated. An invitation from an authorised body, such as a yacht club, is essential. Russian consulates will issue visas for all those named in the invitation with dates of birth and passport numbers for the period and the ports stated in the invitation. A vessel which takes shelter or stops in a port not specified in the visa can expect difficulties.

The lack of adequate facilities for visiting boats, unnecessarily complicated and time consuming formalities, difficult officials and the distinct feeling that many Russians regard foreigners as nothing more than a convenient source of cash, should make anyone planning a visit to Russia consider seriously if the effort is really worth it.

Should the situation improve, from the cruising point of view, Russia has three main areas which can be visited, all very different in their own ways. The Black Sea coast is now very much diminished following the independence of Georgia and Ukraine, which also includes Crimea. The main attraction on the Baltic coast is the historic city of St Petersburg, built on the banks of the River Neva and considered the most beautiful Russian city. The sea area between St Petersburg and Kronstadt, inside a man-made seawall, is a popular cruising area for Russian sailors. A highly enjoyable detour can now be made into the Finnish Saimaa Canal, which gives access to Saimaa Lake, but whose entrance was barred in the past to foreign vessels. These restrictions have now been lifted by the Russian authorities. The Baltic enclave of Kaliningrad has been open to tourists since 1991, a small region of Russia squeezed between Lithuania and Poland and separated from the rest of Russia.

The Far East is more remote and less accessible to cruising yachts, as several sensitive areas are closed to foreign shipping. Weather considerations would probably deter most cruising yachts from sailing to the Arctic ports, which involves a long detour around the whole of Norway.

Country Profile

The largest country in the world, Russia stretches from Europe across northern Asia to the Bering Straits and the Pacific Ocean. It has coastlines on the Black Sea, Baltic Sea and Arctic Ocean as well as the Bering Sea, Sea of Okhotsk and Sea of Japan in the Pacific.

Around the fifth century the Slavs settled in the region. By the ninth century, the Russian state of Kiev developed, although the kingdom declined and Russia was conquered by the Mongols in the thirteenth century. In the fifteenth century the Muscovite principality developed into a strong state ending Mongol supremacy. The seventeenth century saw a period of political and social troubles. Russia expanded towards the Pacific, and the nobles' rights over serfs increased to the point of slavery.

Under Peter I an era of modernisation began, St Petersburg became the new capital and Russia expanded into both the Baltic and Balkan regions. Under Catherine II Russia became a leading European power, continuing an expansionist policy with the partition of Poland and acquisition of the Crimea. Unsuccessfully invaded by Napoleon in 1812, Russia took a leading role in the peace settlement of 1814–15. The 1860s saw Alexander II bring in some liberal reforms and the serfs were emancipated in 1861. Rapid industrialisation occurred at the end of the nineteenth century followed by the growth of socialist and revolutionary movements.

In 1914 Russia entered the First World War but heavy losses and defeats turned feelings against Tsar Nicolas II. Revolution broke out in February 1917, and the Tsar abdicated. The provisional government was in turn overthrown by the Bolsheviks led by Lenin. The new regime only established full control in 1921 after the Red Army defeated its opponents. In 1922 the Union of Soviet Socialist Republics was officially established. On Lenin's death in 1924 a leadership struggle ended with Joseph Stalin gaining power. In 1939 a non-aggression pact was signed with Germany and the USSR soon annexed part of Poland and the Baltic states. Germany invaded the Soviet Union in 1941, but was pushed back by a counter-offensive, the Red Army reaching Berlin in 1945. After the war relations with the West deteriorated into the Cold War and only after Stalin's death in 1953 was there some détente. Mikhail Gorbachev became head of the Communist Party in 1985, and his policies of liberalisation saw a much freer atmosphere grow in the Soviet Union, although economic problems still continued to be massive. The late 1980s saw the collapse of Communist rule throughout Eastern Europe, although when it finally happened in the Soviet Union, it took most people by surprise, especially as the transition was largely non-violent. This vast country is still struggling to shake off its totalitarian past and adapt its ailing economy to a modern world dominated by market forces. After two terms of inefficient ruling, President Yeltsin was succeeded in 2000 by Vladimir Putin under whose leadership it is hoped that the vast potential of this country will finally bring about the overdue stability and prosperity that its long-suffering people rightly deserve.

The majority of the population of 150 million is Russian now that most other national groups live in their own independent republics. In 1991, a number of former Soviet republics formed the Commonwealth of Independent States (CIS). This federation has now largely collapsed and Russia found itself involved in a prolonged conflict in Chechnya. Russian Orthodoxism is the main religion, but there are significant Islamic, Buddhist and Jewish minorities.

The climate varies greatly in this vast country, from the subtropical in the southern republics to Arctic conditions in the northern regions. Conditions along the coasts are less harsh although even in the Baltic, winters can be very cold with freezing temperatures for several months. Summer weather in the Baltic is very pleasant with white nights in June and good sailing breezes. Winters along the Black Sea coast are milder, and the summers are very hot; because the Black Sea is virtually landlocked, the winds alternate between land and sea breezes.

Entry Regulations

Foreign vessels are only allowed to visit ports which are listed on the visa or official invitation. Only the most important ports of entry are listed below, although it may be possible to obtain permission to visit other ports as well.
Baltic Sea: St Petersburg 59°53′N 30°13′E, Kaliningrad (Königsberg) 54°43′N 20°13′E, Kronstadt 59°59.6′N 29°42.5′E, Vyborg 60°42′N 28°45′E.
Black Sea: Novorossiysk 44°44′N 37°47′E, Sochi 43°35′N 39°43′E, Tuapse 44°06′N 39°05′E.
Sea of Azov: Taganrog 47°12′N 38°57′E.
Sea of Japan: Nakhodka 42°45′N 133°04′E.

Procedure on arrival

Foreign yachts must arrive with visas for each crew member obtained in advance and landfall must be made at one of the ports specified in the visa. Either a hosting club or some other institution must supply an official invitation. Yachts may be intercepted by a patrol boat on entering territorial waters. If such a vessel does not answer calls on VHF Channel 16, one should try Channel 10, which is their normal working channel.

Yachts should be attentive as to where they enter Russian territorial waters. In the Finnish Gulf it is recommended to follow the Sea Channel and cross the territorial water line between Gogland (Hochland) Island and Moshniy. At this point one should attempt to raise the authorities on VHF Channel 16. Unless instructed otherwise, one should proceed to the terminal at Kronstadt for clearance. Some yachts have been fined for entering Russian territorial waters in a non-approved place. It is forbidden to stop at any of the islands in Russian waters. Sheltering from bad weather is not considered a valid reason. The Biorkesund Passage is also closed to yachts at present. There is pressure on the authorities to open both Gogland Island and the Biorkesund Passage to yachts, which would save some sea miles.

The alternative entry point into Russia is from Finland via the Saimaa Canal (see Finland entry for further details). Here one can clear in at Vyborg or Brusnichnoye and proceed to St Petersburg via Vysozk. This route, which is used by Finnish boats, has been reported as being simpler and with less red tape.

Foreign vessels must clear in and out with both frontier guard, customs and immigration in all ports of entry. No one must leave the boat until formalities have been completed; officials will come to the boat. Foreign vessels are required to notify the authorities in the next port one intends to visit three days in advance, with a crew list, boat details and purpose of visit.

Vessels which seek shelter or stop in ports not mentioned in the visa may have difficulties. If wishing to stop at a port where there are no officials, permission to do so and clearance must be obtained from the nearest port of entry.
Kronstadt: Kronstadt base is on Kotlin Island and clearance is obtained at the terminal Fort Constantin. Official hours for customs and passport control are 0800–1800. One must wait on board for the officials – which may be some time. Boats that have cleared in in Vyborg may have to do a second clearance here as it is a different

province. After clearance one may proceed straight to one's destination at one of the yacht clubs in St Petersburg without further clearance.

St Petersburg: The 36 mile long shipping channel is through the Kronstadt Passage and Morskoy Canal. St Petersburg Radio can be contacted on 2182 kHz or Port Control on VHF Channels 16 or 26. According to regulations, when a vessel reaches buoy 19 in the approach channel, it should ask to be met by a pilot to be accompanied to the customs dock. At the moment, yachts clear at the passenger terminal, where there is a customs office. The terminal is located on the Korabelny Channel. After formalities are completed, yachts are directed to one of the yacht clubs.

Sochi: Call Port Control on Channel 16. Yachts should moor at the customs dock to starboard after entering the harbour, or, if there is space, come stern-to the short quay in front of the Port Control building in the NE corner of the harbour. All boats, even if coming from another Russian port, must clear customs, immigration and Port Control.

Procedure on departure

The authorities must be notified 24 hours in advance of departure.

Customs

Firearms must be declared and may be detained during the yacht's stay in port. There are no restrictions on animals. On arrival yachts will also be asked to declare foreign currency, narcotics, pornography, gold and silver.

Immigration

All nationalities must obtain a visa in advance. There are convenient Russian diplomatic missions in Helsinki, Nicosia (Cyprus) and Istanbul, where visas can be obtained. It is recommended to apply for a visa at the consulate where one will receive the visa, and not to try to pick it up from another consulate as the various bureaucratic formalities may differ from one place to another and often change. The consulate will advise what they require. Yachts arriving without visas for all crew members may be turned away. Difficulties will also be encountered if there are any irregularities at all with one's passport or visa – for example, if either is past its expiry date. The visa is a separate document which lists the places for which one has been given permission to visit, and the dates of one's stay. One should apply for a business or invited guest visa as this kind of visa allows for a greater flexibility in the matter of the timing of one's arrival. This type of visa is issued by the Ministry of Foreign Affairs and the consulates come under the wing of this Ministry also. Tourist visas are issued by the OVIR department in the Ministry of Home Affairs, and it is not recommended to try and obtain one of these as it takes longer. Such visas are usually very restricted in dates, as they are meant for air travellers on prearranged holidays.

To get the visa it is necessary to have an official invitation endorsed by the Ministry of Foreign Affairs and issued by one of the organisations such as yacht clubs or agencies that have an agreement with the Ministry. The first step is to fax the yacht club or agency copies of the main pages of the passports of all crew members, also giving full details of the yacht as well as the intended itinerary, mentioning each intended port of call, including ETA and ETD. The yacht club will have to pay the Ministry for authorising the invitations, so one should not waste their time and money if one is not serious about visiting Russia.

The St Petersburg Central (River) Yacht Club has an agreement with the Ministry of Foreign Affairs and is probably the best to contact. Yuri Yanin, the director, is very helpful and is keen to encourage more sailors to visit Russia. *Tel.*/Fax. (812) 235 66 36 or e-mail yanin@mail.ru.

Registration

Following the move away from tourist to business visa by sailors visiting Russia, the department of visas and registration of foreigners (OVIR) of the Ministry of Home Affairs has started insisting that all foreigners must register with them and pay a fee. The yacht clubs are trying to do this in the same way that hotels do to save visitors the nuisance of finding an OVIR office and paying this fee, but one should be prepared to add this to the list of fees to be paid.

Fees

The consular fee for the visa depends on how quickly one wants it and can vary from between US$ 80 and 150. Harbour fees and agent fees can be very high.

Facilities

Provisioning can be quite difficult as the yacht clubs are often out of town. There is usually a good selection of fresh produce which is better quality in the markets than in the large stores. Water is readily available, but the quality is sometimes questionable, so it should be treated; bottled water is often available. Fuel is difficult to obtain, so it is best to order some via a yacht club or agency.

The best facilities for foreign boats is at the St Petersburg River Yacht Club, the oldest yacht club in Russia, also called the Central Yacht Club during Soviet times. Their guest harbour is situated in the mouth of the Bolshaia Nevka river off the Peter's Passage and it is best to obtain details of how to reach them by *Tel./Fax.* (812) 235 66 36 or e-mail yanin@mail.ru. There is 24-hour security, water and electricity, showers, telephone and fax, and use of the club facilities. A chandlery is on site, there are repair facilities in a separate harbour, and a 12.5-ton crane.

Other docking possibilities are at the Naval Yacht Club, close to the marine passenger terminal and the Baltic Shipping Company Yacht Club.

The yacht harbour near Sochi's commercial harbour has basic facilities and the yacht club staff are reported as being helpful. There are mooring buoys laid down in the port but better facilities are those at the yacht club (VHF Channels 16 and 69, 0800–2000 only in summer). The yacht club can arrange fuel deliveries, or one can go directly to Pier 15 in the commercial harbour. Provisioning is very good at the open air market.

Yacht building is gathering pace as there is a great demand for cruising boats. Although not up to western standards, repair facilities are good, as local mechanics are used to improvising when spares are not available. The situation regarding marine supplies and spares is gradually improving. Ordering essential spares from abroad and clearing them through customs can take a very long time.

Further Reading

The Baltic Sea
Black Sea Cruising Guide
St Petersburg – Rough Guide

Websites

www.interknowledge.com/russia (Russian National Tourism Office)
www.yachtclub.spb.ru (St Petersburg Yacht Club)
www.bsya.iuf.net (Black Sea Yachtsmen's Association)
www.yacht-club.sochi.net (Sochi Yacht Club)

SWEDEN

Up in the north-west corner of Europe, Sweden forms half of the Scandinavian peninsula. The tongue of Sweden divides the Baltic from the North Sea and the country's two coasts offer an infinite variety of cruising. On the west coast the most attractive cruising area is from the Norwegian border to Göteborg, while on the east coast the most picturesque region is the Stockholm archipelago and the area to the south of it. To these should be added the various inland waterways, the best known being the Göta Canal, a scenic route which allows a yacht to sail from one side of Sweden to the other without the necessity to drop its mast. There are secluded anchorages and pretty villages throughout southern Sweden, making it one of the most attractive cruising destinations in Europe.

Country Profile

Inhabited from prehistoric times, the early peoples traded with the rest of Europe and from the eighth to tenth centuries the Swedish Vikings raided Russia and the surrounding region. Christianity spread only around the twelfth century, and gradually the Swedish nation developed, with Stockholm becoming the capital.

In the Union of Kalmar in 1397, Sweden came under Danish rule. Opposition to this grew and in the sixteenth century Gustave Vasa expelled the Danes and was elected king, creating a strong modern state. Sweden became a dominant European power, reaching its height under Gustave II Adolphus, when the country led the Protestant cause in the Thirty Years War. In 1660 the Danes were forced to cede the south of Sweden, leaving Sweden to dominate the Baltic region. However, the Northern War (1700–21) was costly, and Sweden lost all its German and Baltic territories except Finland. The eighteenth century saw the development of the Swedish economy and culture, until the monarchy restored its absolute rule in 1789, quashing the liberalisation in progress. Finland was ceded to Russia in 1808, while on the other hand Norway returned to Swedish rule from 1814 to 1905. The nineteenth century was a period of modernisation and liberalisation of the economy and politics, and in 1888 a free trade system was adopted.

In Gustave V's reign (1907–50) Sweden enjoyed

an unprecedented prosperous period. With the Social Democratic party dominating politics, advanced social and political legislation was implemented. Sweden remained neutral during both world wars. In 1975 a new constitution was adopted, making King Charles XVI Gustave only a figurehead monarch. In 1995 the country voted to join the European Union.

Half the land is covered in forest so the timber industry is important, as are iron ore deposits. The main industries are mechanical, electrical and engineering. Agriculture is mainly for domestic consumption, producing cereals, potatoes and raising livestock. External trade is important.

The population numbers 9.1 million. Besides Swedes there are communities of Finns, Lapps, Yugoslavs, Norwegians and Greeks. Swedish is the main language, although many speak English. The majority are Lutherans. The capital is Stockholm.

The climate is temperate due to the Gulf Stream, and the summers are pleasant. Winters are cold, the temperatures around freezing. Summer arrives only in June and the sailing season rarely lasts beyond the end of September, but has the advantage of long summer nights. The winds in summer are variable and mostly light.

Entry Regulations

Ports of entry

Customs Places P. = passport control points by which foreigners may enter and leave Sweden.

F = frontier crossing points by which foreigners may enter and leave Sweden when travelling to and from Denmark, Finland, Sweden and Norway.

North Coast: Haparanda F 65°46′N 23°54′E, Luleå P 65°35′N 22°10′E, Piteå F 65°19′N 21°30′E, Skellefteå F 64°44′N 20°57′E, Umeå P 63°50′N 20°16′E, Örnsköldsvik P 63°16′N 18°43′E, Härnösand P (no customs facilities) 62°38′N 17°56′E, Sundsvall P 62°25′N 17°20′E, Hudiksvall F 61°43′N 17°07′E, Söderhamn 61°19′N 17°06′E, Gävle P 60°40′N 17°10′E.

Stockholm Archipelago: Norrtälje F (no customs) 59°54′N 18°42′E, Kapellskär F 59°43′N 19°05′E, Stockholm P 58°19′N 18°03′E, Stockholm P 59°19′N 18°03′E, Sandhamn P (no customs) 59°17′N 18°55′E, Södertälje P 59°12′N 17°38′E, Nynäshamn P 58°54′N 17°57′E.

East Coast: Oxelösund P 58°40′N 17°07′E, Norrköping P 58°36′N 16°12′E, Söderköping P (no customs) 58°29′N 16°20′E, Västervik P 57°45′N 16°39′E, Oskarshamn F 57°16′N 16°27′E, Kalmar P 56°40′N 16°22′E.

Practical Information

LOCAL TIME: GMT + 1. Summer time GMT + 2 from the end of March to the end of October.

BUOYAGE: IALA A

CURRENCY: Swedish Krona (Skr) of 100 öre.
Besides banks, money can also be exchanged at 'Forex' exchange offices, and at post offices showing the 'PK Exchange' sign.

BUSINESS HOURS
Banks: 0930–1500 Monday to Friday (some until 1730 in larger cities).
Shops: 0900–1800 Monday to Friday, 0900–1300/1600 Saturday. Shops close earlier on days before public holidays.
Government offices: 0800–1600 Monday to Friday.

ELECTRICITY: 220 V, 50 Hz

PUBLIC HOLIDAYS
1 January: New Year's Day
6 January: Epiphany
Good Friday, Easter Monday
1 May: Labour Day
Ascension
Whit Monday
21 June: Midsummer Day
1 November: All Saints Day
25, 26 December: Christmas

COMMUNICATIONS
International dialling access code 00.
International calls can be made either from telephone offices, Tele or Telebutik, open until 2100 or dial direct from payphones with phone card (Telefonkort).
Emergency: dial 112 (free from payphones) includes police, fire, ambulance and sea rescue.
Post offices: 0900–1800 Monday to Friday, Saturday 1000–1300.
There are international flights worldwide from both Stockholm and Göteborg.

MEDICAL
Certain European countries have reciprocal agreements with Sweden for emergency treatment. The casualty department at a hospital is called Akutmottagning or Vardcentral in more remote areas. 24 hour NHS emergency number Tel. 112.

DIPLOMATIC MISSIONS
In Stockholm:
Australia: Sergels Torg 12.
Tel. (08) 613 2900.
Canada: Tegelbacken 4, 7th floor.
Tel. (08) 453 3000.
Germany: Skarpögt 9. Tel. (08) 670 1500.
New Zealand: Arsenalsgatan 8C
Tel. (08) 611 6824.
United Kingdom: Skärpögatan 6–8.
Tel. (08) 667 0140.
United States: Strandvägen 101.
Tel. (08) 783 5300.

Gotland: Slite P 57°42′N 18°49′E, Visby P 57°39′N 18°17′E.

South Coast: Karlskrona (and Dragsö) P 56°10′N 15°36′E, Ronneby P 56°10′N 15°18′E, Karlshamn P 56°10′N 14°52′E Sölvesborg F 56°03′N 14°35′E, Åhus F 55°56′N 14°19′E, Simrishamn P (report to nearest communication centre) P 55°33′N 14°22′E, Ystad P 55°26′N 13°50′E, Trelleborg P 55°22′N 13°09′E, Malmö (and Limhamn) P 55°37′N 13°00′E, Landskrona P 55°52′N 12°50′E, Helsingborg (and Råå) P 56°03′N 12°41′E, Höganäs F 56°12′N 12°33′E, Mölle P (no customs) 56°17′N 12°30′E.

West Coast: Halmstad P 56°40′N 12°51′E, Falkenberg F 56°53′N 12°30′E, Varberg F 57°06′N 12°15′E, Göteborg P 57°42′N 11°57′E, Marstrand P (no customs) 57°53′N 11°35′E, Skärhamn F (report to nearest communications centre) 57°59′N, 11°33′E, Stenungsund 58°05′N 11°49′E, Lysekil P 58°16′N 11°26′E, Uddevalla P 58°21′N 11°55′E, Kungshamn and Smögen F (report to nearest communications centre) 58°22′N 11°14′E, Strömstad P 58°56′N 11°10′E.

Communications Centres
North Coast: Haparanda *Tel.* 0922-129-49, Umeå 090-241-60, Härnösand 0611-790-82.
Stockholm Archipelago: Furusund 0176-8000-01/800-17, Stockholm 08-789-76-39/789-76-40.
East Coast: Gryt 0123-401-14/401-15.
Gotland: Visby 0498-102-45.
South Coast: Karlskrona 0455-110-63, Malmö 040-731-30/731-38/12-43-30, Heesingborg 042-17-08-02.
West Coast: Göteborg 031-63 71 50, Kungshamn 0523-307-55.

One can also contact the centres direct on VHF Channel 16 (except Haparanda).

Procedure on arrival

As Sweden is now a member of the EU, in principle yachts from other EU or Nordic countries do not have to notify customs on arrival in Sweden if there is nothing to declare, but yachts from other countries must report to customs, in a place which has a customs office, before stopping anywhere else. If visiting Göta Älv or going through the Göta Canal, one must report to the customs office before entering. Yachts may be intercepted by customs in the customs area for inspection. If arriving at a customs place outside of office hours, one must report by telephone to the nearest communication centre.

Foreign nationals may only enter and leave Sweden at passport control points, or (if travelling to or from Denmark, Finland, Iceland, Norway) via a frontier crossing point.

The customs will want a declaration of provisions and other goods on board. Also the yacht should be registered. On departure from Sweden, all yachts must make a verbal report to customs and clear passport control.

Customs offices are open 0800–1600 Monday to Friday. Outside those hours, captains must report by telephone to the nearest communications centre. The number is available from the harbour master.

Customs

Firearms must be declared on arrival and may be retained until departure.

Animals may not be brought into Sweden without special permission. Unless one has an import permit, cats and dogs will immediately be sent out of Sweden at the owner's expense. Dogs and cats may be imported from Norway and Finland with a veterinary certificate. Medicines should be declared on arrival, and be accompanied by a prescription.

Goods which may not be imported freely must normally be presented for customs clearance, put into bond or taken out of the country again. In some cases the goods may be kept on board if a cash deposit is paid for the duty owing, which will be refunded if the goods are re-exported under customs supervision within three months. This does not apply to alcohol and tobacco, only the specified amounts of which can be kept on board, which are 1 litre of spirits, 5 litres of wine, 15 litres of beer and 300 cigarettes per person. Excess of this amount will be taken ashore and returned only on departure from Sweden.

Temporary importation

Foreign flagged yachts owned by non-residents of Sweden may be temporarily imported, exempt from duty, for up to six months in any one year. Regulations are now in line with the rest of the EU, so any non-EU boats that are to spend longer than six months in Sweden must be taken out of commission and put under bond by Swedish customs.

Only vessels over 75 tons, bound for non-Nordic countries, may take on board duty-free tobacco and alcoholic products.

Immigration

No visas, but valid passports are required for stays of up to three months for nationals of most countries, including EU and most other European countries, USA, Canada, Australia and New

A peaceful anchorage on Sweden's west coast.

Zealand. Extensions can be obtained from local police stations. Persons entering Sweden from another Nordic country need only a document showing that they are a citizen of Denmark, Finland, Iceland or Norway. Identity cards only are required from citizens of Austria, Belgium, France, Germany, Italy, Luxembourg, Netherlands, Switzerland and Liechtenstein.

Restrictions

Restricted areas are clearly marked on Swedish charts, as well as by signs on the shore. In protected and controlled areas foreign yachts must remain within the channels marked on the charts. In some parts of such areas anchoring or mooring is prohibited, and in others foreign yachts may not stay longer than 24 hours. Known prohibited areas are around Göteborg, the naval base at Karlskrona and parts of the southern approaches to Stockholm. Other restricted areas are protected wildlife reserves and at certain times of the year, especially spring and early summer, access is forbidden. The restricted areas are strictly enforced,

and one may be subject to an on-the-spot fine if found to be breaking the regulations.

Laws are strict concerning the littering of the sea and shore. Garbage, oils, petrol or harmful substances must not be discharged into the water and in many places toilets must also not be pumped out.

Fishing

Scandinavians can fish for recreation on Sweden's coasts, but non-Scandinavians must have special permission from the county board or county police where they intend to fish. Fishing is not permitted in private waters, except in certain areas where a special permit is needed. There are various regulations on closed seasons and permitted fishing tackle. Spearfishing is not permitted.

Inland waterways

There are various canals linking rivers and lakes which give access to the interior of the country. The Göta Canal crosses Sweden from Göteborg to Söderköping, a distance of about 200 miles, passing through canals, the Göta River and several lakes. Fees must be paid for locks and harbour dues, and are quite high. Swedish charts are essential. As there are no fixed bridges, the canal can be navigated without dropping the mast.

There are also the canals of Falsterbo, Dalslands, Arvika and Vaddo, and the Lake Malaren near Stockholm may also be navigated. There are maximum draft as well as height restrictions on some of these canals. Maximum length: 100 ft (30 m), beam 20 ft (6 m), draft 9 ft (2.82 m), height 71 ft (22 m).

Facilities

Provisioning is easy everywhere with the exception of the remoter areas and in many places it is possible to come alongside a dock close to a grocery store. Fuel is not so widely available away from the larger centres. LPG containers can only be filled with the proper adaptor and this can only be done in some of the major towns.

There are only a few marinas, although mooring facilities are available everywhere. Most moorings belong to the Swedish Cruising Club, are painted red or blue and can also be used by foreign visitors either for short stays in daytime or for the night. Private moorings may also be used, either with permission, or if the absent owner has left a prominent green card indicating the berth is free. The biggest marinas are in Stockholm (Vasahamn) and Göteborg, and this is also where most repair facilities are located.

The standard of repair work is good throughout Sweden, but it may be difficult finding repair facilities in the more remote areas. For any major repair it is best to head for one of the larger yachting centres where almost everything is available.

The Swedish Cruising Club publishes a brochure about visitors' harbours in Sweden, called *Swedish Guest Harbours*, while plans of ports and anchorages on the east and south coasts, *Seglarhamnar pa Ostkusten*, are published by the Swedish Cruising Club. *Båtsport-kort* are Swedish charts reproduced on small scale, which are available in most Swedish bookshops.

Further Reading

The Baltic Sea
Baltic Southwest Pilot

Websites

www.tourist.se (Swedish Tourism Authority)
www.SXK.se (Swedish Cruising Club)

3 Western Europe and North Atlantic Islands

The islands of the North Atlantic have served throughout history as stepping stones for new discoveries and the routes of former explorers have been taken up by modern sailors. The southern islands – Bermuda, the Canaries, the Azores and Madeira – are visited every year by hundreds of cruising yachts on their way east or west across the Atlantic. The northern islands attract fewer cruising yachts from afar, although countries like the United Kingdom and Ireland have their own large boating communities. This is also the case with France, which has coastlines on both the Atlantic and Mediterranean, with excellent facilities on both sides.

An increasingly popular cruise undertaken by many European sailors is a circumnavigation of the North Atlantic. By taking advantage of the prevailing weather conditions, this is easily accomplished, by sailing south to Madeira and the Canaries with the Portuguese trades of summer, west with the NE trade winds of winter and back east with the westerlies, or anti-trades, of higher latitudes. These

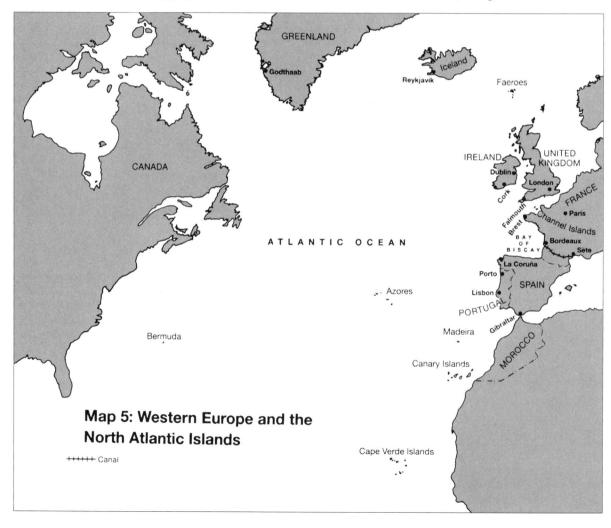

Map 5: Western Europe and the North Atlantic Islands

++++++ Canal

weather patterns are due to a permanent feature of the North Atlantic, the area of atmospheric high pressure situated near the Azores, whose name it bears. Because of its influence on sailing conditions over such a large area of the North Atlantic, the position of the Azores high must be watched carefully especially when planning an Atlantic crossing in either direction.

The sailing season in the northern islands is strictly for the summer, whereas the southern islands, being on the transatlantic circuit, have certain peak periods. Madeira and the Canaries are busiest between September and November when yachts prepare to cross to the Caribbean, while Bermuda and the Azores are busiest in May and June, when the movement is in the opposite direction. In the entire region, only Bermuda is affected by tropical storms, the hurricane season extending from July to November, with September being the most dangerous month. Although occasionally a hurricane may track eastwards, none of the other islands fall within the hurricane zone.

Horta Marina, Faial, Azores.

The best facilities are to be found in Britain and France, two of the world leaders in yachting, where there are several centres offering a full range of repair services. Facilities are also good in the most frequented islands, particularly Gran Canaria and Bermuda. Outside of these countries, repair facilities can only be described as adequate.

THE AZORES

Reputed to be the fabled Atlantis, the nine islands of the Azores lie in mid-Atlantic 900 miles off the coast of Portugal and 1800 miles from Bermuda. These volcanic islands have a scenic landscape of cones and craters, where the rich soil grows lush vegetation, both subtropical and temperate, with vividly coloured flowers growing everywhere.

Most yachts choose to stop in the Azores on their way east across the Atlantic, although some call on their way west or when sailing from the South Atlantic towards Northern Europe. Although hundreds of yachts call every year, very few of them

cruise around the islands and the majority stop only in Horta, on the island of Faial, one of the perennially favourite places of long-distance sailors. With their secluded bays, uncrowded anchorages and protected harbours, the rest of the Azores are still waiting to be discovered as a cruising destination in their own right. Besides their natural beauty, the relaxed pace of life in the islands is their main appeal. The islanders are as hospitable to visiting sailors as they were to Joshua Slocum, one of the first to call there in 1895.

Country Profile

The islands were uninhabited when, under the instigation of Prince Henry the Navigator, they were discovered by the Portuguese early in the fifteenth century, although they were known in ancient times. The Portuguese soon settled the islands and cultivated the land, and settlers came both from the Portuguese mainland and the Low Countries, the latter being Flemings fleeing religious persecution. The Azores became an important port of call for ships and Angra, with its natural harbour, became the leading town. Christopher Columbus stopped at Santa Maria on his first return voyage, and João Fernandez Labrador sailed west with Cabot's fleet and sighted the land now bearing his name.

When Spain occupied mainland Portugal in 1580, Dom Antonio, claimant to the Portuguese throne, fled to Terceira to organise his opposition. The islands fiercely resisted the Spanish invasion, but eventually Spain took control of all of them, and used them as a stopping-off point for ships returning from South America with treasure. When Portugal regained independence in 1640 the islands were each ruled by an independent governor, until in 1766 a central government was set up in Terceira. The latter supported the Liberals during Portugal's constitutional struggles in the early nineteenth century, and following the Liberal Revolution of 1832 the Azores were made a province of Portugal with three districts centred around the main ports of Horta, Angra and Ponta Delgada. Ships remained an important source of income and employment, especially the American whalers which took on many islanders as crew, due to their whaling expertise. Gradually, however, through the nineteenth century the number of ships calling declined. In 1895 the Azores were granted limited autonomy, but they remained poor and economically dependent on Portugal, although with the laying of

transatlantic cables from Faial, they became an important link in international communications. During both World Wars the islands were important bases for the Allies, and there is still a US base on Terceira. The Portuguese Constitution of 1976 made the Azores an autonomous region of Portugal with its own assembly and regional government.

The Azorean economy is mainly agricultural, the most important crops being cereals, fruit and vines, with cattle and dairy products. Fishing has recently expanded. Whaling was once an important source of income, the islanders hunting whales from small open boats, but this has recently ceased due to the whaling moratorium. There is a small tourist industry and the US air base on Terceira brings some income.

The population numbers 245,000. Many Azoreans have emigrated to North America, Brazil and Bermuda. Portuguese is the main language, although English, Spanish and French are widely understood. The majority are Roman Catholics. There is no capital of the autonomous region of the Azores, the President of the government being in Ponta Delgada and the Parliament in Horta.

The climate in the Azores is dominated by the mid-Atlantic area of high pressure which bears their name. The position of the Azores high varies with the season, being more northerly in the autumn and more southerly in the spring, usually lying to the S or SW of the islands. In winter the area can be stormy and very wet, while in the summer the Azores high can be stationary with prolonged periods of calm weather.

Entry Regulations

Ports of entry
Ponta Delgada (São Miguel) 37°44′N 25°40′W, Horta (Faial) 38°32′N, 28°38′W, Santa Cruz (Flores) 39°27′N 31°07′W, Lajes (Flores) 39°23′N 31°10′W, Angra do Heroismo (Terceira) 38°39′N 27°13′W, Praia da Vitoria (Terceira) 38°44′N 27°03′W, Vila do Porto (Santa Maria) 36°56′N 25°09′W, Vila das Velas (São Jorge) 38°40′N 28°13′W, Vila da Praia (Graciosa) 39°03′N 27°58′W.

Procedure on arrival
The Q flag should be flown at the first port of entry into the Azores. Yachts must clear in at one of the ports of entry where a transit log will be issued by the port authority to those yachts from countries *not* belonging to the European Union.

Practical Information

LOCAL TIME: GMT – 1. Summer time GMT April to October.

BUOYAGE: IALA A

CURRENCY: Portuguese escudo of 100 centavo, written 00$00. Euro from 2002. 1 euro = 200.482 PTE.

BUSINESS HOURS
Banks: 0830–1500 Monday to Friday.
Shops: 0900–1230, 1400–1800 Monday to Friday, Saturday morning.
Government offices: 0900–1200, 1400–1700.

ELECTRICITY: 220 V, 50 Hz

PUBLIC HOLIDAYS
1 January: New Year's Day
Good Friday
25 April: National Day
1 May: Labour Day
Corpus Christi
Whit Monday: Autonomy Day
10 June: Portugal Day
15 August: Assumption
5 October: Republic Day
1 November: All Saints' Day

1 December: Independence Day
8 December: Immaculate Conception
25 December: Christmas Day
There are also municipal holidays.

EVENTS
Horta: Sea Week (Semana do Mar) starting first Sunday in August, a local festival including yacht races.

COMMUNICATIONS
Area codes for Faial (Horta), Pico, Flores and Corvo 292. São Miguel (Ponta Delgada) and Santa Maria 296, Terceira, Graciosa and São Jorge 295. Area codes must be dialled for all calls, including local calls.
International dialling access code 00.
International calls can be made from post offices, hotels and some public phones, including Café Sport, Horta.
Stamps can be bought from post offices or where a 'correio' sign is shown.
There are regular flights to Lisbon from São Miguel, Faial and Terceira. There are regular flights between Ponta Delgada and Funchal (Madeira). There are charter flights from Ponta Delgada and Terceira to Boston and Toronto, and in the summer also to San Francisco. There are regular

flights between all the islands, and in summer there are ferry services, including a local ferry between Flores and Corvo.

MEDICAL
Emergency treatment is free to all. EC residents will not be charged for a hospital bed, but non-EC nationals may pay. For non-emergency consultations, a nominal fee is charged.
Emergency 112.

DIPLOMATIC MISSIONS
In Ponta Delgada:
Canada: 27-1°-Esq, Rua Dr António José de Almeida. *Tel.* 296281488.
France: 49 Rua Carvalho Araújo.
Germany: 25 Rua Dr João Francisco de Sousa. *Tel.* 296652598.
Spain: Rua Direita, Faja de Baixo. *Tel.* 296636717.
United Kingdom: 23 Rua das Almas, Pico da Pedra, Rabo de Peixe. *Tel.* 296498313.
United States: Avenida Infante Dom Henrique. *Tel.* 296282216.
In Horta:
France: 34 Rua Conde d'Avila. *Tel.* 292392780.

Clearance should also be done with customs (Alfandega) and immigration. In all ports of call in the Azores visited subsequently, the transit log must be taken along and presented to the local Guarda Fiscal office. In larger ports, the Port Authority (Capitania) should also be visited, and sometimes the Policia Maritima.

As part of Portugal, the Azores are members of the EU, with which they have a special relationship. The usual EU regulations apply, although because of their isolated position, the authorities tend to treat all arriving yachts as if coming from a non-EU country and subsequently subject them to the full range of clearance formalities.

Horta Marina: On arrival yachts should berth alongside the reception quay (minimum depth 10 ft/3 m). The marina office is open 0800–1200, 1300–2000 (seven days a week in the high season April to June). The offices of immigration, maritime police, customs (Alfandega) and Guarda Fiscal are next to the marina office in the same building. The marina staff will inform captains of the order in which these officials must be visited, both on arrival and at departure. The marina office

will assign a berth once clearance is completed. Yachts arriving after office hours should wait at the reception quay until the next morning.

On departure, one should first pay the marina fees, then take the receipt to the Guarda Fiscal and the Capitania for outward clearance.

Ponta Delgada: There is a reception dock on the port side as one enters the marina and arriving yachts are expected to stop there to be cleared in and assigned a berth. Yachts are normally met on the dock by an officer, who ensures that there is no contact with other boats before formalities are completed. This is normally done during office hours, although the Guarda Fiscal office is open 24 hours.

Angra do Heroismo: The Guarda Fiscal and Policia Maritima are by the Porto Pipas mole. With permission, yachts may come alongside there for short periods to clear if there is space.

Customs
Firearms must be declared.

There are no restrictions on animals being allowed ashore, but a rabies inoculation certificate is required.

Yachts may stay for a six-month period before becoming liable for duty.

Immigration

Visas are not required for citizens of Western European countries, Australia, Canada, New Zealand and the USA. Other nationalities may need to obtain a visa in advance. Persons travelling on a yacht in transit are normally granted a visa on arrival which is valid for a limited period: 90 days for European Union, 60 days for most other countries. Those who require a visa and arrive without one should attempt to clear in at one of the major ports of entry.

Cruising permit

A transit log (Livrete de Transito) is issued to non-EU yachts by the Capitania or Delegaoes Maritimas on arrival. All subsequent movements of the yacht are recorded in this log until departure. Yachts must clear in and out of all ports, including harbours on the same island. If arriving from Madeira, the same transit log may be used, but if arriving from mainland Portugal, a new log is usually issued.

There is a small fee to the Lighthouse Service for yachts over 79 ft (24 m).

Diving restrictions

Spearfishing within 164 ft (50 m) of a public beach, port or protected area, and spearfishing with scuba tanks anywhere, is prohibited. A permit to dive can be obtained from the Capitania.

Facilities

Yachting facilities are concentrated in the two main ports of Horta and Ponta Delgada, which cater well for day-to-day needs, but whose repair facilities are barely adequate. Limited repair facilities are available in Angra do Heroismo and Praia da Victoria on Terceira. There are also projects to build small marinas at Praia da Graciosa and Velas on São Jorge in the near future.

Provisioning in the islands is good with a better selection on the islands of São Miguel, Terceira and Faial. Limited supplies are available on the smaller islands, although local fresh produce is available everywhere. Water and fuel is also available in all ports, the latter usually having to be brought in jerrycans from filling stations.

Horta: Some 1000 yachts call every year at this well-organised and pleasant marina, where an extension is planned to be started in 2000. For hauling out, at present there is only a 25-ton travelift, although a crane can be hired in an emergency to lift a yacht on to the main wharf. A new and much larger ramp is being built in the commercial harbour. Repair facilities are constantly improving, but still only minor repairs can be undertaken locally. There is a repair yard run by the port authority and also several workshops in town which can undertake engine, electrical, radio, metalwork and sail repair. There is a small chandlery with a limited selection. Fuel and water are available in the marina and LPG bottles can also be filled. There are several supermarkets and a daily fresh produce market.

Ponta Delgada: The marina provides excellent facilities for yachts visiting the Azorean capital. The range of repair facilities is also expanding and boats can be hauled out in Ponta Delgada. Water and electricity is available on all pontoons and fuel is available at the fuelling berth. There are several supermarkets in town providing the best provisioning in the Azores and there is also a daily fresh produce market. The yacht club next to the marina is very helpful.

Terceira: The marina at Praia da Vitória has 50 berths with water and electricity with more under construction. There is a shipyard close by and a regular bus service to Angra do Heroísmo. The marina at Angra is also under construction, while the yacht club at Angra is particularly helpful to visiting yachts.

Flores: Facilities at Lajes have been improved with showers, WC, washing machines and telephone now available in the harbour area. Cruising boats anchor as there is only limited space alongside. Fuel can be delivered by tanker to the commercial wharf. A floating pontoon for dinghies and moorings buoys is planned.

Further Reading

Azores Cruising Guide
The Atlantic Islands

Websites

www.drtacores.pt (Regional Department of Tourism)
www.ciberacores.com/marinahorta (Horta Marina)
www.marina.jappdl.pt (Ponta Delgada Marina)

BERMUDA

Bermuda is an archipelago of over 150 small islands and islets, the largest linked together by causeways and bridges into a fish hook shape. The existence of coral islands so far north and only 600 miles (965 km) off the East Coast of the USA is explained by the warm waters of the Gulf Stream which bathe Bermuda and account for its mild climate.

One of the most popular landfalls in the North Atlantic, Bermuda has welcomed weary mariners for over three centuries. Although it has little to offer in the way of cruising, Bermuda attracts over 1000 yachts every year who stop here to rest and reprovision after a long passage, or simply to turn around at the finish of one of the many ocean races which run from the US East Coast. Bermuda is well geared to cope with these transient sailors, most of whom arrive from the Caribbean in April and May, some on their way to Europe, others to the USA. Later in the autumn Bermuda sees another influx as many yachts make their way south from the USA to cruise in the Caribbean.

The well sheltered St George's Harbour provides a restful anchorage from which to explore this neat and tidy little country. Such exploring is best done by land, particularly by those who are short of time and treat their stop in Bermuda as a brief but enjoyable interlude. The alternative anchorage is in Hamilton, but as all yachts have to clear in first at St George's, few bother to sail out afterwards and around the island to thread their way through the reefs to Hamilton harbour. It is easier by bus.

Country Profile

Bermuda was discovered early in the sixteenth century and named after the Spaniard Juan de Bermudez. So many ships were lost on the reefs around the islands, that they became known as 'Isles of the Devil'. Generally they were given a wide berth, and were only settled in the seventeenth century following a misadventure. In 1609 the *Sea Venture*, under the command of Sir George

Practical Information

LOCAL TIME: GMT – 4. Summer time GMT – 3 April to October.

BUOYAGE: IALA A

CURRENCY: Bermuda dollar (BD$) on a par with US$. The latter is widely accepted.

BUSINESS HOURS
Banks: 0930–1500 Monday to Friday, 1630–1730 Fridays.
Shops: 0900–1700 Monday to Saturday.
Business and government offices: 0930–1700 Monday to Friday (some close 1300–1400).

ELECTRICITY: 110V, 60 Hz

PUBLIC HOLIDAYS
1 January: New Year's Day
Good Friday
24 May: Bermuda Day
Monday nearest second Saturday in June: Queen's Birthday
Thursday and Friday before first Monday in August: Cup Match and Somers Day
1st Monday in September: Labour Day
11 November: Remembrance Day
25, 26 December: Christmas

EVENTS
International Race Week, April–May.
Newport to Bermuda Ocean Yacht Race, June of even years.
Blue Water Cruising Race, June of odd years.
Biennial Multihull Race, June of odd years.
Single-handed Race, June of odd years.
Trans-At Yacht Race, May of odd years.

COMMUNICATIONS
Area code is 441.
St George's Telecom office a few minutes' walk out of town for international calls. Open 0930–1430 Monday to Friday.
Also cardphones near the docks in St George's.
Cable & Wireless: 20 Church St, Hamilton, open 0900–1700 Monday to Saturday, International calls, telex and fax.
Main post office: Church and Parliament Streets, Hamilton.
Bermuda Harbour Radio (call sign ZBM) maintains a continuous watch on 2182 kHz, 4125 kHz, and VHF Channels 16 and 27. As well as dealing with arriving yachts, it is the Airsea Rescue Coordination Centre for the Bermuda area, and is in contact with the US and Caribbean Coast

Guards. Weather information and warnings are broadcast on Channel 27.
Weather Information for departure may also be obtained from the Yacht Reporting Centre.
Local weather: Dial 9771. Marine forecast dial 9772. Hurricane watch, dial 9773.
Bermuda Weather Service 2936659. A daily weatherfax is sent to the Yacht Reporting Centre. For Bermuda weather from overseas, dial 441 297 7977 or access www.weather.bm.
There are flights from Bermuda to London, Canada and the USA.

MEDICAL
King Edward VII Hospital in Paget East, outside Hamilton.
Tel. 236-2345.

DIPLOMATIC MISSIONS
United States: 16, Middle Road, Devonshire.
Tel. 295-1342.

Somers on an expedition to Virginia, was wrecked during a hurricane. This event lies behind the plot of Shakespeare's *The Tempest*, as the playwright was familiar with several major shareholders in the Virginia Company. After surviving on the islands for some time and building two new ships, the group continued their voyage. The Virginia Company was granted the islands by Royal Charter. In 1612 English settlers founded St George's. The settlement was never profitable, and in 1684 Bermuda was taken over by the Crown as a colony.

The inhabitants remained more interested in the sea than the land. During the American War of Independence the population stole gunpowder from St George's to send to the rebels in exchange for food and money. Bermuda was also a popular base for privateers and pirates, later becoming an important base and dockyard for the British Navy. With the advent of the steamship, tourism developed and this increased further after the First World War, especially with the establishment of airlinks. During the Second World War Bermuda was used as a US military base which ceased operation only in 1995. In 1968 a new constitution gave the country internal self-government. Bermuda is one of the oldest of Britain's self-governing dependent territories and in August 1995 a referendum voted to maintain this status.

Tourism is a prime industry, and special legislation makes Bermuda a tax haven and major international business centre. Bermudians enjoy a very high standard of living having the highest per capita income in the world. Pressure on the land is considerable, and there is little agriculture apart from that for domestic consumption.

The English-speaking population is 60,000, the majority being of African origin, with about 35 per cent of other origins, mainly European. There is a small Portuguese-speaking community. Hamilton is the capital. Anglican and Roman Catholic are the largest of 40 different religious communities.

The Gulf Stream makes the climate subtropical, with mild winters and warm humid summers. The Azores high dominates the summer months, bringing steady SW winds. June to November is the hurricane season with September the most dangerous month, although the majority of these storms pass to the west of Bermuda.

Entry Regulations

Port of entry
St George's Harbour 32°23′N, 64°40′W.

Procedure on arrival
All yachts arriving in Bermuda must clear in at the Yacht Reporting Centre at Ordnance Island, St George's Harbour, open 0800–1600 Monday to Friday. St George's is entered through the Town Cut channel. Yachts stopping elsewhere will be escorted to St George's and may be fined by Customs. After clearance yachts may then proceed to Hamilton or elsewhere in the archipelago.

The Rescue Coordination Center (RCC) Bermuda/Bermuda Harbour Radio must be contacted prior to arrival on VHF Channel 16 giving approximate time of arrival and any special requirements. The station is on call 24 hours on 2182 KHz, 4125 KHz, and VHF Channels 16 and 27. A 24-hour radar watch is also kept and unidentified vessels are called up, especially if they approach too close to the reef. The radio station will direct a yacht where to berth and how to proceed for clearance. The Q flag must be flown. The captain should have ready two crew lists and two store lists showing details of consumable stores. The customs boarding officer normally carries out immigration and health formalities as well. Customs normally monitor VHF Channel 68.

Immigration
Everyone gets granted three weeks arrival and must apply at immigration for a further three months.

Visas are required in advance for nationals of East European countries, Algeria, Cambodia, Cuba, Haiti, Iran, Iraq, Jordan, Laos, Lebanon, Libya, Morocco, Mongolia, Nigeria, North Korea, Vietnam, China, Philippines, South Africa, Sri Lanka, Syria and Tunisia and are obtainable from a British embassy or consulate. Visas are valid three months from date of issue. Visas are not required if any of the above are permanent residents of the USA or Canada.

The initial period of stay is usually 21 days. Extension applications can be made at the Immigration Department in Hamilton.

Persons who require visas to enter other countries they are sailing to after Bermuda must already have them. This applies particularly to yachts leaving Bermuda for the USA.

All visitors arriving by air are required to show a return air ticket. To avoid this for crew members arriving or leaving by air on one-way tickets, the captain or owner of a yacht must write to the Chief Immigration Officer, Department of Immigration, Ministry of Home Affairs, POB HM 1364, Hamilton HM FX (*Tel.* 295-5151) well in advance giving the name, address and nationality of any crew member, also details of the airline, flight number and date of arrival plus $15 (US or Bermuda $) for the landing permit. The latter will be sent to the captain and it permits the purchase of a one-way ticket (otherwise travel agents or airlines will not issue one). The permit must be shown on entry. If time is short, the captain can telephone with the crew details. In such cases the crew may have to buy a return ticket, but once the permit is issued, one can get a validation from the Chief Immigration Officer to allow a refund to be obtained.

Arriving by yacht and leaving by air, crew must have written proof from the owner or captain of their means of departure. The responsibility to ensure that such crew leave the island is with the captain.

Customs

All firearms and ammunition must be declared on arrival to the customs officer, who will either impound them until departure or seal them on board. Firearms include spear guns, Verey pistols and flare guns.

Animals arriving without an import permit will be restricted to remaining on board, as Bermuda has no quarantine facilities. To obtain an import permit one should apply as far in advance as possible to the Director of the Department of Agriculture & Fisheries, POB HM 834, Hamilton HM CX (*Tel.* 236-4201). Application forms are also available from any Bermuda tourist office. The animal must also have a general health certificate, and for dogs and cats, proof of a recent rabies vaccination, unless coming direct from the UK.

All medically prescribed drugs and medications must be declared on arrival. Fruit and vegetables from other countries are prohibited imports.

Yachts can stay up to six months, after which time customs will impose a duty of 33.5 per cent on the yacht's value.

Fees

An arrivals tax of $15 per person is charged, including children.

Berthing and anchorage

One may anchor in both St George's and Hamilton harbours. In St George's there are some berths available at Somers Wharf, Hunters Wharf (east), and the north side of Ordnance Island. There is limited space, but the berths are free. Contact the dockmaster on Channel 16 (callsign Dm Dm Dm) for allocation of space. Better docking facilities are available at Dockyard Marina, but this is far from most amenities. In Hamilton, yachts are restricted to the yacht club, boatyards and marinas.

Restrictions

Berthing for yachts is prohibited at all commercial docks in most cases, but contact the dockmaster for availability.

No spearfishing permitted.

Facilities

Although there is a boatyard, slipway and some repair facilities in and around St George's, the development of the Dockland Marina in the former naval dockyards has attracted some workshops to that area. Located on Ireland Island, at the opposite end of Bermuda to St George's, the new marina is adjacent to a boatyard and marine workshop with its own slipway. Although existing repair and service facilities are dispersed all over Bermuda rather than being grouped together, virtually everything one may need is available on the island even if it may take some time to find it. Marine supplies or essential parts that are unavailable can be ordered from the USA to which there are several flights every day.

Provisioning in St George's is reasonable with one supermarket within walking distance. Fuel and water are also available locally. For charts and marine supplies one has to go to the Pearman Watlington Marine Centre in Hamilton.

Further Reading

Atlantic Crossing Guide
Bermuda Yachting Guide
The Bermuda Department of Tourism publish a very useful Information Sheet for yachts, which can be obtained from: Bermuda Department of Tourism, POB HM 465, Hamilton HM BX.

Websites

www.bermudatourism.com (Bermuda Tourism Office)
www.weather.bm
www.rccbermuda.bm

THE CANARY ISLANDS

The Canary Islands consist of seven main islands and many smaller ones lying off the African coast, 300 miles south of Madeira. These high volcanic islands on the Atlantic seismic ridge lie near to

Africa, a combination of factors which explains the varied scenery, from sandy deserts to lush mountain valleys, pine forests to snow-capped Mount Teide on Tenerife, a dormant volcano rising 12,000 ft (3700 m) out of the ocean. The Canary Islands are a continent in miniature.

The seven islands of the archipelago are well spaced out so that it is only a day's sail between most of them. The logical route for most yachts arriving from the north is to visit Lanzarote and Fuerteventura first before sailing to Gran Canaria, then Tenerife, La Gomera, El Hierro and La Palma.

Traditionally the Canaries have been the logical jumping-off point for yachts crossing the Atlantic to the Caribbean, ever since Columbus started the fashion just over 500 years ago. The route pioneered by Columbus cannot be bettered and from November to January the islands are full of yachts preparing for their Atlantic crossing.

While for some it is a quick provisioning stop, other cruising yachts take advantage of what the islands have to offer and leave Europe at the end of

Orchilla lighthouse on Hierro once marked the end of the known world.

summer, so that they can spend a couple of months cruising the Canaries. The facilities for yachts have increased and improved dramatically in recent years and more cruising yachts are now spending longer in the islands and some are permanently based there. Also on the increase is the number of yachts sailing down from Europe to spend the winter months in the Canaries' pleasant climate.

Country Profile

The early population were known as Guanches, probably descended from Berbers who came over from North Africa. The islands were known to both the Greeks and the Romans and the first recorded expedition was sent by King Juba of Mauritania in 60 AD. At one time they were called the Fortunate Islands, due to the ease of life on the islands. The Roman writer Pliny, in describing the islands, called one of them Canaria from the Latin word for dog 'canis', due to the number of large wild dogs roaming the island. Originally applied to Gran Canaria, the name later came to be used for the whole archipelago.

Practical Information

LOCAL TIME: GMT. Summer time GMT + 1 March to October.

BUOYAGE: IALA A

CURRENCY: Spanish peseta (Pta) of 100 centavos. Euro from 2002. 1 euro = 166.386 ESP.

BUSINESS HOURS
Banks: 0900–1330 Monday to Saturday, some 0900–1530 Monday to Friday.
Business: 0800–1600 Monday to Friday.
Shops: 0900–1300, 1600–2000 Monday to Saturday. Some large department stores 0900–2000.
Government offices: 0800–1500 Monday to Friday, some 0700–1400 in winter.

ELECTRICITY: 220 V, 50 Hz

PUBLIC HOLIDAYS
1 January: New Year's Day
6 January: Epiphany
Maundy Thursday, Good Friday
1 May: Labour Day
30 May: Canaries Day
Corpus Christi

25 July: St James
15 August: Assumption
12 October: Columbus Day
1 November: All Saints' Day
6 December: Constitution Day
8 December: Immaculate Conception
25 December: Christmas Day

EVENTS
Carnival (Las Palmas de Gran Canaria and Santa Cruz de Tenerife).
Corpus Christi, floral carpets are laid down in many towns.
ARC Transatlantic Rally starts last Sunday in November.

COMMUNICATIONS
Area code for Gran Canaria, Fuerteventura and Lanzarote 28, for Tenerife, La Palma, Gomera and El Hierro 22. International dialling from public phones. International dialling access code 07, followed by a second dialling tone. Telefonicas: group of telephone booths with an attendant who charges you after the call is made.
Faxes can be sent and received at main post offices.

There are many flights, both regular and charter, from Tenerife, Gran Canaria and Lanzarote to all parts of Europe with links to the rest of the world. There are regular flights between the islands. Tenerife, Gran Canaria and Fuerteventura are linked by fast hydrofoil.

MEDICAL
There are medical facilities in all islands. There are also special clinics catering for foreigners in most tourist areas.

DIPLOMATIC MISSIONS
In Las Palmas de Gran Canaria:
Brazil: Nicolas EstéVanez 18. *Tel.* 277534.
Cape Verde Is: Arco 16. *Tel.* 241135.
France: Nestor de la Torre 12. *Tel.* 292371.
Germany: Franchy Roca 5. *Tel.* 275700.
Morocco: Mesa y Lopez 8. *Tel.* 262859.
Mauritania: Calle Italia 8. *Tel.* 234500.
United Kingdom: Edificio Cataluña, C/Luis Morote 6. *Tel.* 262508.
United States: Franchy Roca 5. *Tel.* 271259.

After the Roman era, the Canaries were largely forgotten until several Genoese and other European expeditions explored the islands in the thirteenth and fourteenth centuries, mainly as raiding parties for slaves with no interest in settlement. This changed when the Norman knight Juan de Bethencourt, serving Spain, subdued Lanzarote in 1402, then Fuerteventura and Hierro. The Guanches put up a fierce fight and La Gomera resisted conquest for 80 years. Gran Canaria, Tenerife and La Palma were even more difficult conquests and only in 1495 was the last Guanche resistance crushed. Three years before that Columbus sailed to the Canaries and left on his voyage to the New World from La Gomera. The new routes pioneered by Columbus opened up the Atlantic Ocean and had a big impact on the Canaries. The islands developed as a repair and provisioning centre for the increasing numbers of westbound vessels and many merchants and traders settled in the islands. Although attacked by pirates, the Dutch and the English, the islands remained under Spanish control and in 1823

the Canaries became a full Spanish province.

Thriving on trade, in the mid-nineteenth century the islands were declared a free trade area and they have remained a duty-free zone ever since. The Canary Islands now form an autonomous region of Spain with their own parliament. They are divided into two provinces, the eastern province, Las Palmas, which includes Gran Canaria, Lanzarote and Fuerteventura and the western province, Tenerife, which includes Tenerife itself, La Gomera, La Palma and El Hierro. Due to rivalry between the two main islands, the government sits alternately in the provincial capitals of Las Palmas de Gran Canaria and Santa Cruz de Tenerife.

Tourism is the main industry and has contributed to the economic boom that the islands have enjoyed. Agriculture is still important, especially market gardening, fruit, wine and some dairy products. Banana plantations are extensive in Tenerife and La Palma, while Gran Canaria specialises in tomatoes and vegetables. The revenue derived from the ports is second in importance after tourism, notably the port of La Luz y Las Palmas, which is now the most important in Western Africa. There is a large fishing industry, with fleets based on every island.

The resident population is 2 million with a tourist population of some 12 million a year. The Canary Islanders are proud of their differences from the mainland Spanish, whom they call 'peninsulares', many of whom have settled in the islands. The Spanish-speaking population is mainly Catholic.

Despite its position close to the tropics, the Canaries are not too hot in summer, 21–29°C, pleasantly warm in winter, 15–20°C, and can be regarded as an all-year cruising ground, which has earned them the title of Land of Eternal Spring. The frequency of gales is low and the islands are not affected by hurricanes. In the trade wind belt, the prevailing wind is north-easterly.

Entry Regulations

Ports of entry
Arrecife (Lanzarote) 28°57′N 13°33′W, Puerto Rosario (Fuerteventura) 28°30′N 13°51′W, Las Palmas de Gran Canaria (Gran Canaria) 28°09′N 15°25′W, Santa Cruz de Tenerife (Tenerife) 28°29′N 16°14′W, San Sebastian (Gomera) 28°05′N 17°07′W, Puerto de la Estaca (El Hierro) 24°47′N 17°54′W, Santa Cruz de la Palma (La Palma) 28°40′N 17°45′W.

Procedure on arrival
As part of Spain, the Canaries are members of the EU, with which they have a special relationship. The islands have remained outside the VAT area, although there is a low local tax on sales and services. The usual EU regulations apply, although because of their isolated position, the authorities tend to treat all arriving yachts as if coming from a non-EU country. The Schengen Agreement has complicated matters as it made provisions for only two official ports of entry, at Las Palmas de Gran Canaria and Santa Cruz de Tenerife. In practice, boats can complete formalities at the major port on any of the seven islands. On arrival the captain should report to the port authority or marina office who will advise on the correct procedure and, in the case of the marinas, will contact the relevant authorities. The Canaries are a duty-free area, so yachts are not expected to clear customs.

For the time being, most yachts arriving from overseas clear in at one of the following three ports:

Arrecife: The capital of Lanzarote has two ports used by yachts. The more northerly is the fishing harbour Puerto Naos where two pontoons have been installed for visiting yachts. In the old port of Arrecife yachts tie up to the wall inside the breakwater. In the approaches to both ports attention must be paid to the outlying reefs. Formalities are completed at the Policia Nacional, on the waterfront, almost opposite the causeway to the old fort. As docking facilities are so much better at Puerto Calero it is probably better to go directly there and return to Arrecife by taxi to complete formalities.

Las Palmas: Arriving yachts should tie up at the Texaco dock for berthing instructions. Formalities are completed in the port office.

Santa Cruz de Tenerife: Yachts berth at either Marina del Atlantico in the centre of Santa Cruz or in the fishing harbour (Darsena Pesquera) north of the city. The marina office should be contacted on arrival.

There are no restrictions on yacht movements in the Canaries, although papers may be checked at subsequent ports.

Customs
There are no restrictions on firearms or animals in the Canaries. However, customs are concerned about drug trafficking, especially from North Africa, and although they appear to be easy-going, they do keep a close eye on yacht movement.

Equipment and spare parts can be imported free of duty provided they are clearly marked as being for a yacht in transit. The use of an agent can speed up the extrication of these goods from the airport.

It is possible to lay up a boat in which case the authorities must be informed and the boat is sealed. Duty is not then liable.

Immigration
Visa exemptions and requirements are as for Spain; however, this does not appear to be applied strictly to yachts, provided the person also leaves the islands by yacht.

Passports of crew are not normally stamped on arrival, but if crew members wish to leave by air, it is essential to get their passports stamped, as otherwise they might be turned back from the airport.

Fees
There are no overtime fees as clearance is done during office hours.

Facilities

Yachting facilities in the Canaries are constantly improving and repair facilities are good, particularly on Gran Canaria. There are yacht clubs on most islands but as they are primarily social clubs, visitors are not particularly welcome.

Gran Canaria: The widest range of facilities is concentrated in the capital Las Palmas, which has a yacht harbour administered by the port authority. There are various repair workshops in the Cebadal industrial estate, close to the commercial harbour. A sailmaker operates in town. There are several chandleries, although their selection is rather limited and essential spares may have to be ordered from abroad. Charts, both Spanish and British, are available from Premanaca. There is a boatyard with a 40-ton travelift next to the yacht harbour (Muelle Deportivo) in Las Palmas.

Provisioning in Las Palmas is the best in the Canaries with several supermarkets and daily fresh produce markets. LPG bottles can be filled and fuel is available in the yacht harbour.

Gran Canaria's south coast has several good marinas at Pasito Blanco, Puerto Rico and Puerto Mogan. There are haul-out facilities at all of them as well as at the fishing harbour Arguineguin.

Tenerife: Docking facilities in the capital of Tenerife have improved dramatically with the opening of a new large marina in the very centre of the capital Santa Cruz by converting the existing container basin Los Llanos into a modern marina with the latest facilities.

Marina del Atlantico provides only docking, so for any repairs boats may still have to use the facilities of Marina Tenerife in the old fishing harbour (Darsena Pesquera) some three miles north of the city. Outside of Santa Cruz there is docking as well as some repair facilities in the marinas at Radazul, Los Gigantes and Puerto Colon. The boatyard at Los Cristianos also has haul-out and repair facilities. Provisioning is good everywhere, with well stocked supermarkets close to all marinas, all of which also have fuel, except Marina del Atlantico.

Lanzarote: Most facilities are in the capital Arrecife, around the commercial Puerto Naos. A small industrial estate in the neighbourhood provides a good range of services. Provisioning is good with supermarkets and daily market. Fuel, water and LPG are available in the commercial harbour. One of the best marinas in the Canaries is at Puerto Calero, on Lanzarote's east coast, which has a boatyard, with its own 40-ton travelift and a range

of services, including laundry and supermarket.

Fuerteventura: There is a small marina with haul-out and some repair facilities as well as fuel at El Castillo and limited repair facilities in the capital Puerto Rosario.

La Gomera: The capital San Sebastian now has its own marina, located in the northern part of the commercial harbour. The facilities of the nearby yacht club are available to marina users.

There are only basic facilities in the islands of El Hierro and La Palma, with the exception of Santa Cruz de la Palma, which has good provisioning and some repair facilities, but no docking facilities for visiting yachts.

Further Reading

Canary Islands Cruising Guide
Atlantic Islands

Websites

www.gobcan.es/turismo (Canaries Government)
www.lanzarote.net/puertocalero (Puerto Calero Marina)
marinadelatlantico@infocanarias.com (Marina del Atlantico)

CAPE VERDE ISLANDS

The Cape Verde Islands are a volcanic archipelago lying near the coast of West Africa, although the islands' culture reflects its Portuguese colonial past more than its geographical position. The islands' climate tends to be very dry, the scenery is rather bleak and they have had severe drought problems in the last 20 years. There are 10 main islands, of which São Tiago, the second largest town and the main harbour, is on São Vicente. The group divides into Barlavento (Windward group) and Sotavento (Leeward group).

The Cape Verdes are conveniently placed close to the best sailing route from the Canaries to the Caribbean and ships on transatlantic voyages have always found them a useful stopover, although now modern yachts call instead of square riggers and steamers. Most cruising yachts are on their way to the Caribbean, a few to Brazil or West Africa, particularly Senegal and Gambia. Some people have enjoyed cruising the islands more extensively,

Practical Information

LOCAL TIME: GMT − 1.

BUOYAGE: IALA A

CURRENCY: Cape Verde escudo (CVEsc) of 100 centavos. Local currency cannot be imported or exported. Foreign currency must be declared on arrival and departure.

BUSINESS HOURS
Banks: 0800–1530 Monday to Thursday.
Business: 0800–1200, 1430–1800 Monday to Friday, 0800–1200 Saturday.
Shops: 0800–1200, 1400–1800 Monday to Friday, 0900–1300 Saturday.
Government offices: 0800–1200, 1400–1800 Monday to Friday.

ELECTRICITY: 220 V, 50 Hz

PUBLIC HOLIDAYS
1 January: New Year's Day
20 January: National Heroes Day
8 March: International Women's Day
1 May: Labour Day
5 July: Independence Day
15 August: Assumption
1 November, All Saints' Day
25 December: Christmas Day

COMMUNICATIONS
International calls can be made from most post offices.
International telegrams can be sent from larger post offices.
Sal Island has the only international airport, where jets refuel on flights between Europe and South America or Africa. There are direct flights to Lisbon and a weekly service to Boston. All the other islands except Ilha Brava have domestic airports for internal flights.

MEDICAL
Hospitals: Hospital Central, Rua Martires de Pidjiguiti, Praia. *Tel.* 130.
Hospital Baptista de Sousa, Sao Vicente. *Tel.* 2030.
Treatment is very expensive although hospital emergency treatment is free on presentation of one's passport. There are limited stocks of medicines at pharmacies.

DIPLOMATIC MISSIONS
There are representatives in Praia for Brazil, France (for French Guiana and Ivory Coast visas), Germany, Portugal, Senegal, Belgium, Netherlands and Norway and the USA.
British Consulate: c/o Shell Cabo Verde, Av. Amilcar Cabral, Sao Vicente. *Tel.* 314 470.
United States: Rua Abilio Macedo 81, Praia. *Tel.* 615 616.

---

rather than just viewing them as a stop on the way to somewhere else. Facilities are basic in the Cape Verdes, but that seems to be made up for by the friendliness of their inhabitants.

Country Profile

The islands were not populated when the Portuguese discovered them in 1456. At that time they were green with vegetation, hence the name 'verde'. The Portuguese returned six years later and founded the capital of Ribeira Grande on São Tiago. Slaves were brought from West Africa to work on the plantations that were established. The islands' strategic position made them a base for the slave trade to the Americas. Some prosperity was enjoyed, but in the mid-eighteenth century a series of droughts hit the islands. These were due to an imbalance in the environment, brought about by deforestation and the introduction of goats that ate the ground vegetation. Thousands of Cape Verdeans perished in droughts in the eighteenth and nineteenth centuries and many emigrated to New England, to work in the whaling trade.

With the rise in the number of liners crossing the Atlantic the archipelago became an important coaling station for ships. The droughts continued, however, and little help was forthcoming from Portugal. After the Second World War a joint inde-

pendence movement was started by Cape Verdeans and Guinea-Bissau, another Portuguese colony. After fourteen years of guerilla warfare, independence was achieved in 1975, following the toppling in Portugal of the Salazar regime. After the 1980 coup in Guinea-Bissau, unification between the two countries was shelved, and they pursued their own path.

Since gaining independence from Portugal in 1975, the country has struggled to put its economy on a viable basis. In recent years both Portugal and the United States have given the islands aid. As the lack of rain continues to be a major problem, much of the aid goes into projects such as planting trees and building dykes and water-retaining walls. Money sent by Cape Verdeans abroad is important to the economy, for as many Cape Verdeans live overseas as on the islands. Salt mining on Sal and Maio and fish exports are other sources of income.

The islands have a total population of approximately 400,000 people of mixed African and Portuguese descent. Although the official language is Portuguese, amongst themselves Cape Verdeans usually converse in Crioulo, a local dialect closely related to Portuguese. The majority are Roman Catholics.

Rainfall is limited to a few downpours between late August and October, although there are years with little or no rain. The NE trade winds are at their strongest in the first months of the year, when they sometimes arrive laden with dust from the Sahara, which can seriously affect visibility.

Entry Regulations

Ports of entry
Mindelo 16°53′N 25°00′W, Praia 14°54′N 23°31′W, Sal 16°45′N 23°00′W.

Procedure on arrival
Visas are no longer necessary for visiting yachts arriving for short stays. Generally, formalities appear to have been simplified in an effort to attract more cruising boats to visit the archipelago. *Mindelo:* The town is in Porto Grande Bay, which is one of the best harbours in the archipelago. If there is space, one can tie up to the central dock in the inner harbour to clear in. One can come alongside or else anchor off, and immigration and port officials visit soon after arrival. One should not go ashore until cleared. Yachts must fly the courtesy flag; if a yacht does not possess one, they must buy one from the port captain. The captain must sign a form that absolves the port authority from responsibility in case of theft from the yacht. Ship's papers and passports will be held by the authorities whilst in the harbour, although a passport can be temporarily reclaimed to change travellers cheques. Yachts can clear out up to 24 hours before departure.
Praia: One should anchor in the western part of the harbour, although sometimes there is space alongside the commercial dock, where it is easier to clear in, rather than take the officials by dinghy to the boat. One should not go ashore until visited by customs and immigration.
Sal: This is the only other island where yachts can clear in. Usually customs and immigration formalities are completed at the international airport. Palmeira has a sheltered anchorage. One should fly the Q flag and the captain should check in with the police in Palmeira. The police hold passports until departure.

Customs
Firearms and animals must be declared to customs.

Immigration
Those on yachts making a short visit are issued visas on arrival. Visitors intending to spend longer in the islands need to obtain a visa in advance. In this case visas are required by all nationalities except some African countries. There are Cape Verdean diplomatic missions in many West European capitals, Boston, Washington, Dakar and Las Palmas de Gran Canaria or one can apply direct to: Ministerio de Negocios Estrangeiros, Direccão de Immigracão, Praia, writing in Portuguese. Where there is no Cape Verde mission, one should be able to obtain a visa on arrival. Visa applications need two photos.

Health
Malaria prophylaxis may be necessary in São Tiago. There is tuberculosis throughout the archipelago and cholera has been reported as a risk.

Fees
Immigration fee for visas. Clearance fee in and out.

Warning
Charts may be inaccurate, especially near Ilha da Boa Vista, which is reported to be 2 miles east of its charted position. There are several wrecks and offlying reefs not marked on the charts, especially off the east coast of the island.

Theft appears to be a problem in Mindelo and visitors are advised to employ a local watchman, usually one will be recommended by the port captain. According to the latest reports, theft appears to be a problem on all the islands. Most vulnerable are loose items left on deck, so the boat should never be left unattended for long periods, and any removable items should be secured.

Facilities

Provisioning is limited on all the islands and most food is imported and expensive. There are fresh produce markets in Mindelo and Praia, which vary in variety and quality with the seasons.
Mindelo: This is where most yachts go for a quick refuelling stop. There is a small yacht club, Clube Nautico, where visitors are welcome, and the members can help with repairs. Although not geared up to deal with yachts, the two boatyards, Internave and Onave, can handle some basic repairs and have hauling out facilities. There are no marine supplies except equipment used by fishing boats sold at hardware stores. Butane gas bottles can be refilled at ENACOL and Shell.
Praia: Water and fuel are not easily available as the suppliers prefer to sell larger quantities than those required by yachts. Fuel can be bought in jerrycans from a filling station. Water can be ordered by truck load and shared out amongst several boats. Permission is usually granted to come alongside

the commercial dock to take on larger quantities of fuel or water. Gas bottles can be filled at a filling station out of town best reached by taxi. There is a small boatyard near the harbour for local fishing boats, which can tackle simple repair jobs. There are also various workshops in town, as well as a small chandlery.

Sal: There is only a small shop and bakery in Palmeira, but Santa Maria has better supplies. Fuel and water can be bought from the fish freezing plant at Palmeira.

Further Reading

Atlantic Islands
West Africa – a travel survival kit

CHANNEL ISLANDS

'Fragments of Europe dropped by France and picked up by England' is how Victor Hugo, in exile there, described these islands lying close to Brittany but part of the United Kingdom. This cluster of five islands and many smaller islets is divided into two regions. The Bailiwick of Jersey comprises the largest island, Jersey, and its islets, while the Bailiwick of Guernsey includes Guernsey, Alderney, Herm and Sark. The Bailiwicks have their own parliaments and are proud of their autonomy, which was granted to them by King John in 1204. In many ways the culture of the islands is closer to Normandy than the United Kingdom.

The Channel Islands are a popular cruising destination both with French and British sailors, who find here some of the most hazardous sailing conditions in Europe, as well as a very special atmosphere ashore. The main hazards are strong tidal streams, concealed rocks and poor visibility. Summer weather is generally settled, but at any other time it can change very quickly. There is complete shelter in St Peter Port in Guernsey and St Helier in Jersey. There are many good anchorages in offshore winds on all the islands and the smaller ones provide an interesting alternative to the busy main ports.

Country Profile

During the period of Roman expansion into northern Europe, Gauls sought refuge on the islands.

Later Britons settled, eventually being driven out by the Norsemen, who also settled in France and gave their name to Normandy. When in 1066 the Normans led by their Duke William invaded England, the Channel Islands were already part of Normandy, but remained loyal to the English throne when in 1204 the French captured Normandy. King John, one of William's successors, in recognition for this loyalty, granted the islands their special status within the Kingdom of England. A troubled period of two hundred years followed as the French repeatedly tried to capture the islands. At the request of Edward IV, in 1483 the Pope declared the islands neutral, which brought a more peaceful era.

During the English Civil War Jersey supported the Royalist cause, and Guernsey the Parliamentarian, almost losing its privileges when the monarchy was restored. The Channel Islands became prosperous, largely due to privateering and smuggling, especially after they ceased to be neutral in 1689. Before the Royal Navy was established, the islands maintained a fleet of privateers that harassed Spanish, Dutch, French and American shipping. The French tried again unsuccessfully to gain the islands. During the French Revolutionary and the Napoleonic Wars fortifications were strengthened. However, the islands were finally invaded and occupied during the Second World War by the Germans.

After the war, the economy developed, agriculture was diversified, tourism encouraged, and the islands found a new role as a leading offshore banking and financial centre.

The population numbers 120,000. Languages spoken on the islands include English, a Norman patois, and French.

The winds during summer alternate between NW and NE. At other times, SW winds are more frequent and this is also the direction of most gales. More than strong winds, the main danger in the islands are the extremely strong tidal streams, the notorious Alderney Race reaching 8 knots on occasions.

Entry Regulations

Ports of entry
Alderney: Braye 49°43′N   2°12′W.
Guernsey: St Peter Port   49°27′N 2°32′W, Beaucette Marina 49°30′N   2°29′W.
Jersey: St Helier 49°11′N 2°07′W, Gorey 49°12′N 2°01′W.

Practical Information

LOCAL TIME: GMT. Summer time GMT + 1 from March to October.

BUOYAGE: IALA A

CURRENCY: Pound sterling (£) of 100 pence. The Channel Islands have their own money also in circulation.

BUSINESS HOURS
Banks: 0930–1530 Monday to Friday (some open Saturday mornings).
Business: 0900–1730 Monday to Friday.
Shops: 0900–1730/1800 Monday to Friday; some close Thursday afternoons.
Government offices: 0900–1730 Monday to Friday.

ELECTRICITY: 240 V, 50 Hz

PUBLIC HOLIDAYS
1 January: New Year's Day
Good Friday and Easter Monday
May Day
9 May: Liberation Day
Spring Bank Holiday
Summer Bank Holiday
25, 26 December: Christmas

COMMUNICATIONS
International dialling access code 00.
Operator 100, International operator 155.
International calls can be made from public phones in booths and post offices.

Many public phones use phone cards, which can be bought in post offices or in shops where the card sign is shown.
Emergency: dial 999.
Post offices open 0830–1700 Monday to Friday, 0830–1200 Saturday. The Channel Islands have their own stamps.
There are frequent flights to Britain and some to Europe. There is also a ferry service.

MEDICAL
Medical advice and emergency treatment can be obtained free of charge at general hospitals, but visitors must pay for consultation with a doctor and any medicines prescribed.

Procedure on arrival

Although the Channel Islands are Crown Dependencies, they are not part of the United Kingdom and customs requirements are strict. The islands are outside the VAT area of the European Union. The Q flag must be flown and it is necessary to report to customs when arriving from anywhere outside of the islands, which includes both the United Kingdom and France. It is also necessary to report to customs when moving from one administrative area to the other, such as from Guernsey to Jersey.

On arrival, normally the port control staff will give the captain customs and immigration declaration forms that must be completed as soon as possible. No one except the captain may go ashore until these have been completed.

St Peter Port: Port Control monitors VHF Channel 12. Visitors should call about one hour prior to arrival to receive berthing instructions. One of the port launches normally meets arriving yachts and directs them to a berth. A red light on the pier at the port entrance indicates large vessels are under way, and only boats of 15 m (49 ft) or less may enter or exit if keeping clear of the main fairways. Do not anchor or berth without the prior permission of the harbour master. Customs and immigration documents will be handed to you on arrival and these must be completed before anyone goes ashore. The forms should then be handed to a customs officer or deposited in one of the yellow customs boxes. All arriving vessels must clear in at the main harbour in St Peter Port before proceeding to one of the marinas.

Beaucette Marina: The harbour office monitors VHF Channels 16 and 80 seven days a week and should be contacted prior to arrival or if having difficulties in entering.

St Helier: Port Control monitors VHF Channel 14 and should be contacted before arrival. There are traffic lights controlling the entrance into the main harbour. A green light shown on Victoria pierhead means that a vessel may enter, while a red light allows vessels to leave only. Access into La Collette basin is possible at all times, although there are some draft restrictions. La Collette is used as a waiting area to proceed into St Helier Marina. St Helier Marina is closed 3 hours either side of high water and boats will be directed to a waiting pontoon. During high season it is advisable to contact the marina in advance for reservations (*Tel.* +1534 885508).

Customs

The landing of animals is strictly prohibited from vessels arriving from anywhere other than the UK, Republic of Ireland, Isle of Man or other Channel Islands. If arriving from other countries than these, animals must be securely confined below deck during the yacht's stay. Any animal found ashore or not confined will be detained and may be subject to six months' quarantine or destroyed, and the boat's captain prosecuted. Unless given express permission by a customs officer, no vessel with an animal on board may moor alongside or in the marinas.

Excess duty-free stores will be sealed. There is no sales tax in the islands.

Immigration

Requirements as for the United Kingdom. Immigration must be notified of any persons leaving or joining vessels which are arriving from or departing to places other than the UK or other Channel Islands.

Facilities

Being the favourite offshore cruising area for British yachts as well as a traditional tax-free shopping destination for the French, the Channel Islands have made an effort to improve their yachting facilities. There are now several new marinas and facilities in the old ones have also been upgraded. Repair facilities are generally good, although those in Guernsey have overtaken Jersey in the range of services offered. Provisioning is good in all centres. Both fuel and water are available in all marinas. As the Channel Islands are outside the VAT area, marinas in both Guernsey and Jersey are favourite wintering places for non-EU yachts as there are no restrictions on the length of time they are left there.

Virtually all repairs are available in St Peter Port in or around the marina. There are haul-out facilities and several chandleries offering a complete range of equipment including charts. Fuel is available on the dock. On Jersey repair facilities are centred in or around St Helier Marina, where there is a boatyard with its own chandlery, capable of any kind of repair. The Royal Channel Islands Yacht Club and the St Helier Yacht Club are particularly welcoming to visiting sailors.

Further Reading

Normandy and Channel Islands Pilot
Brittany and Channel Islands Cruising Guide
Channel Islands Pilot
Cruising Association Handbook
The Channel Islands

Websites

www.guernseymap.com (Guernsey Tourist Board)
www.jtourism.com (Jersey Tourist Board)
www.gyc.guernsey.net (Guernsey Yacht Club)
www.herm-island.com

THE FAEROES

The Faeroe Islands (Føroyar in Faeroese) are a small group of islands with a surface area of 540 square miles situated in the North Atlantic between Scotland and Iceland. They are a self-governing dependency of Denmark. The Faeroes were settled by the Vikings in the ninth century and came under Danish rule in 1380. They were granted autonomy in 1948 and have recently voted not to join the European Union, even though they are dependent on Denmark for aid. The population of 35,000 speak Faeroese, a Norse dialect akin to Icelandic, as well as Danish. English is widely understood. The majority are Lutheran.

There is a move in the Faeroes towards independence from Denmark, and the latter has made it clear that it is ready to grant the Faeroes independence if that's what the islanders want. If it does come to that, the traditional links with Denmark will undoubtedly continue under some form of partnership.

Fishing has always been the main industry, but as overfishing is depleting the traditional fishing grounds, the islands are turning to fish farming and encouraging tourism.

The capital and main port is Thorshavn on the island of Streymoy, which is the largest of the group. The smaller islands are very distinctive with precipitous cliffs and steep hills. Some of the coasts are broken by fjords providing spectacular scenery.

The weather is often unsettled and visibility is frequently poor when the land may be obscured by fog or drizzle. The incidence of summer gales is similar to other places on the West European seaboard. Sudden squalls may be experienced inside the fjords. In the summer months the long daylight hours may be enjoyed, the weather is fairly mild due to the Gulf Stream and winds are often light.

Entry Regulations

Ports of entry
Eysturoy: Fuglafjordur 62°15′N 6°49′W.
Bordoy: Klaksvik 62°14′N 6°35′W.
Streymoy (Strømø): Thorshavn (Torshavn) 62°00′N 6°45′W, Vestmanna (Vestmanhavn) 62°09′N 7°10′W.
Suduroy: Tvoroyri 61°33′N 6°48′W, Vagur 61°28′N 6°48′W.

Procedure on arrival
Normally the police board a yacht on arrival and

Practical Information

LOCAL TIME: GMT. Summer time GMT + 1 from last Sunday in March until the last Saturday in October.

CURRENCY: Faeroese krona, interchangeable with Danish krone.

BUSINESS HOURS
Banks: 0900–1600 Monday to Friday, until 1800 on Thursday. ATM machines open daily from 0600–2400.
Shops: 0900–1730 Monday to Thursday, 0900-1900 Friday, 0900–1200 Saturday.

PUBLIC HOLIDAYS
Maundy Thursday, Good Friday and Easter Monday
Fourth Friday after Easter; Prayer Day
Ascension Day
Whit Monday
Olavsoka Eve and Day
24 December afternoon
25 December: Christmas Day
Half-day holidays are taken on Workers Day, Flag Day and a Mourning Day for those lost at sea.

COMMUNICATIONS
There are air links to Copenhagen, Iceland and Scotland in the summer, and a weekly ferry to Aberdeen.
Faroese Telecom has an office at 64 Tinghusvegur in Thorshavn, open on weekdays 0800–2100 for phone calls, fax and e-mail. Emergency 112. International dialling code 009.

DIPLOMATIC MISSIONS
British Consulate, Yviri vid Strond 19, FR-110 Thorshavn. Tel. 13 510, Fax 11 318.

give customs clearance, but if not, the captain should contact customs at a port of entry.

Thorshavn Port Control monitors VHF Channel 16 permanently and the working channels are 12 and 9.

Citizens of Nordic or EU countries do not need a passport, only some form of identification. Other nationals need a valid passport. For these, visas are granted on arrival.

Suduroy: This is the most convenient landfall for boats arriving from the south. Suduroy Radio should be contacted on VHF Channel 23. The customs office overlooks the harbour at Tveraa (Tvoroyri) and formalities should be completed there.

Customs

The Faeroes are dry islands although alcoholic drinks can be purchased from a special shop at Thorshavn. There has recently been some relaxation of the licensing laws, and there are now a few licensed restaurants and pubs. Yachts are allowed small quantities on board for their own use (one bottle of spirits per person, slightly more of wine).

Navigation

The Faeroe courtesy flag should be flown, not the Danish. The flag shows a red cross with a small blue border (like the Danish white cross), on a white field.

Overhead cables cross the fjords and sounds between the islands and give a reading on radar similar to a ship.

Tidal streams run very strongly both around and between the islands, being significantly stronger at the equinox, when the tidal race may reach 11 knots in places. At the entrance to the fjords a combination of wind and tide can create a big sea, while inside the fjords if a strong tide is running one can navigate close to the steep-to sides where counter-eddies may be found. Information on dangerous overfalls and races as well as on the direction of the tides can be found in *Tidal Current around the Faeroe Islands* (*Streymkort fyri Foroyar;* ed. Fischer Heinesen) which has an English translation of essential information and is available at Jacobsen's Bokhandil, Thorshavn. *Tel.* 11 036.

Restrictions

Animals may not be landed and will be confined on board. Their presence must be declared to customs on arrival.

Facilities

There are shops in all the main ports and a supermarket in Thorshavn, so provisioning is not a problem. Fuel and water are available in Thorshavn, Tvoroyri and Klaksvik and other fishing ports. There are no special facilities for yachts and any marine supplies available are those for fishing boats. However, basic repairs can be carried out using the extensive repair and shipbuilding facilities provided for the fishing fleets.

Further Reading

Cruising Association Handbook
Faeroes, Iceland and Greenland

Websites

www.tourist.fo (Faroe Islands Tourist Board)
www.faroeislands.com (General information)
www.harbour.olivant.fo (Port of Thorshavn)

FRANCE

Blessed with both an Atlantic and a Mediterranean coastline, France has more variety to offer the cruising sailor than any other European country, from the tidal creeks and shallow estuaries of Brittany to the chic ports of the Côte d'Azur and the stark beauty of the island of Corsica. France is one of the leading sailing nations in the world and its top sailors are as well known to the general French public as its best soccer players. The booming French boatbuilding industry, which was the first to put well-designed cruising boats into mass production, has been instrumental in bringing cruising within the reach of a wider market. A sustained construction programme has resulted in a string of marinas along the entire Mediterranean coast to cater for the thriving sailing community.

For the visiting sailor, each side of France has its special attractions. The Atlantic coast calls for more attentive navigation, but brings its rewards in the many natural harbours and inlets. Although

The port of Menton on the French Riviera.

spectacular, this coast can be dangerous as there are many offlying hazards, strong tidal streams and frequent gales. This is more than made up for by such attractive ports as Morlaix, St Malo or Lézardrieux. The western coast divides into three distinct areas, the most popular and picturesque being the Brittany coast, which has many navigable rivers and the Morbihan inland sea. The central area to the Gironde has several offlying islands as well as the great rivers, the Loire and the Gironde, which lead into the inland waterways. The low-lying area stretching to the Spanish border is the least appealing as a cruising destination.

In some ways, Mediterranean France is more suited to those who prefer to find their pleasures ashore. Sailing into such glittering places as St Tropez, Cannes or Antibes is an experience that cannot be repeated and it is worth the long detour just to spend some time among the most beautiful collection of yachts in the world. For a good taste of Mediterranean France, the island of Corsica offers a wide selection of ports ideally to be visited outside of the peak summer season as it is a favourite holiday destination for French sailors.

Practical Information

LOCAL TIME: GMT + 1. Summer time GMT + 2 last Sunday in March to last Sunday in October.

BUOYAGE: IALA A

CURRENCY: French franc (FF) of 100 centimes (FF). Euro from 2002. 1 euro = 6.559 FF.

BUSINESS HOURS
Banks: 0900–1200, 1400–1600 Monday to Friday, closed either Saturday or Monday. They close early the day before a bank holiday.
Food shops: 0700–1830/1930.
Other shops: 0900–1830/1930 (many shops close all or half-day Monday; some open on Sunday mornings, especially bakers and food shops; in smaller towns shops close for lunch 1200–1400/1500 on weekdays).
Hypermarkets: 0800–2000/2100 Monday to Saturday.
Government offices: 0830–1200, 1400–1800 Monday to Friday.

ELECTRICITY: 220 V, 50 Hz

PUBLIC HOLIDAYS
1 January: New Year's Day
Easter Sunday and Monday
Ascension Day
8 May: Victory Day
Whit Monday
14 July: Bastille Day
15 August: Assumption Day
1 November: All Saints' Day
11 November: Remembrance Day
25 December: Christmas Day
Nearly all of France is on holiday in August.

COMMUNICATIONS
It is now necessary to dial the 10 digits anywhere in France, even for local calls. Local numbers are preceded by the new area codes: 01 Paris region, 02 NW France, 03 NE France, 04 SE France and Corsica, 05 SW France.
International calls can be made from public payphones, most of which take phonecards (télécarte) obtainable from post offices. In some post offices there are telephones where one can make a metered call.
Post offices open 0800–1900 Monday to Friday (0800–1200, 1400–1700 in smaller towns), 0800–1200 Saturdays.
Emergency: Fire 18, Police 17, Operator 13. There are flights worldwide from international airports at Charles de Gaulle and Orly in Paris, and Bordeaux, Lyon, Marseilles, Nice and Toulouse.

MEDICAL
Certain European countries have reciprocal arrangements with France for emergency cover.
Police 17, Fire 18, Ambulance 15.

DIPLOMATIC MISSIONS
In Paris:
Australia: 4 Rue Jean Rey, 75724. *Tel.* 01.40.59.33.00.
Canada: 35 Avenue Montaigne, 75008. *Tel.* 01.47.23.01.01.
New Zealand: 7 Rue Leonardo da Vinci, 75116. *Tel.* 01.45.00.24.11.
United Kingdom: 35 Rue du Faubourg St Honoré, 75383. *Tel.* 01.42.66.91.42.
United States: 2 Avenue Gabriel, 75382. *Tel.* 01.42.96.12.02.
In Bordeaux:
United Kingdom: 353 Blvd. Président Wilson, *Tel.* 05.56.42.34.13.
United States: 22 Cours du Marechal Foch, 33080. *Tel.* 05.56.52.65.95.
In Marseilles:
United Kingdom: 24 Avenue du Prado, 13006. *Tel.* 04.91.53.43.32.
United States: 9 Rue Armeny, 13006. *Tel.* 04.91.54.92.00.

Country Profile

Remains have been found in France of the earliest prehistoric human settlements. In historic times, the first settlers were of Ligurian and Iberian stock, followed in the sixth century BC by the Gauls, a Celtic people. Gaul was conquered by the Romans and from the resulting Gallo-Roman civilisation the French language and institutions developed. After Rome's downfall Burgundians and Visigoths settled in the south, and Franks in the north. The latter extended their rule over the whole country, and a centralised monarchy developed with the Carolingian dynasty, especially under Charlemagne. In 843 his empire was divided, and the monarchy weakened by a strong feudal nobility and numerous Viking raids on the northern coast.

From the tenth to the fourteenth centuries, royal power was gradually consolidated, while commerce, culture and Christianity thrived. External affairs were dominated by the ongoing conflict with England, who claimed much of French territory, resulting in the Hundred Years War (1328–1440). By the end of the war England retained only Calais and the French monarchy had established its authority over both the Church and the nobles. A strong modern state evolved and with the addition of Brittany in 1491, its frontiers were nearly that of present-day France.

The Protestant Reformation led to religious wars in France until the Protestant Henry IV, the first of the Bourbons, accepted Catholicism and brought religious tolerance and prosperity to the country. After his death royal absolutism reached its peak, with Louis XIV's long reign (1643–1715), which was the age of French classicism that influenced all of Europe. A series of expansionist wars weakened French finances, a problem that escalated during the eighteenth century, while the monarchy continued its absolute rule despite the growing current of ideas for reform and liberty. Then in 1789 the Revolution overthrew the old order, the king was executed and the First Republic established.

France became engaged in numerous wars in Europe, and Napoleon Bonaparte rose to power becoming Emperor and dominating Europe until his defeat in 1814–15. During the nineteenth century there was much industrialisation, and the middle and working classes sought to have a say in politics. Their aspirations led to another revolution in 1848, establishing the Second Republic. Three years later the Second Empire under Napoleon III took a more absolutist line, although some reforms were carried out in its later years. The Empire toppled following France's 1870 defeat by Prussia and the Third Republic was formed.

In the First World War France suffered heavily, both in men lost and economically, and peace was followed by an era of inflation, economic depression, and political instability. A policy of appeasement was followed towards Nazi Germany, but in 1940 France was invaded and the Third Republic fell. The Vichy government signed an armistice soon afterwards. A strong resistance movement developed, and after the war Charles de Gaulle, leader of the Free French, came to power in the Fourth Republic. In 1958 the Algerian crisis returned de Gaulle to power, and the Fifth Republic was established, giving the President greater powers. In 1995 Jacques Chirac's election as President ended socialist François Mitterand's tenure as head of state since 1981. A snap election called by President Chirac in 1997 brought to power a Socialist government led by Lionel Jospin. The next presidential election will be held in 2002.

The service industries, such as administration, commerce, banking, transport and armed forces employ around 60 per cent of the population, while agriculture only 8 per cent and industry under a third. Traditional industries have declined, whereas more modern ones such as the car manufacturing, aeronautical engineering, electrical and chemical industries are thriving. France is the leading agricultural country of the EU, producing mainly wheat, wine, meat and dairy products. Unemployment is high, while the trade balance is helped by revenues from tourism.

The population numbers 59 million, mainly French, but there are also Arab and African populations in major cities.

Paris is the capital of France. French is the main language and regional languages such as Provençal, Basque or Breton are only spoken by a few. The majority of the French are Roman Catholic.

The climate differs significantly between the Atlantic and Mediterranean coasts and so do sailing conditions. On the Atlantic side, the climate is temperate and the sailing season lasts from late spring to the autumn. The prevailing winds of summer are northerly, becoming SW when a system of low pressure comes in from the Atlantic. The strongest winds also come from the SW. Winds along the Mediterranean coast and Corsica are more variable, the strongest wind being the mistral, a northerly wind which occurs regularly and often reaches gale force.

Entry Regulations

Ports of entry

Channel/North Sea: Dunkirk 51°03'N 2°21'E, Gravelines 50°59'N 2°08'E, Calais 50°58'N 1°51'E, Boulogne 50°44'N 1°37'E, Le Touquet-Etaples 50°31'N 1°38'E, Abbeville 50°06'N 1°51'E, Dieppe 49°56'N 1°05'E, Le Havre 49°29'N 0°07'E, Caudebec-en-Caux 49°32'N 0°44'E, Le Tréport 50°04'N 1°22'E, Fécamp 49°46'N 0°22'E, Honfleur 49°25'N 0°14'E, Caen 49°11'N 0°21'W, Cherbourg 49°38'N 1°38'W, Granville 48°50'N 1°36'W, St Malo 48°39'N 2°01'W, Le Légué-St Brieuc 48°32'N 2°43'W, Paimpol 48°47'N 3°03'W, Morlaix 48°38'N 3°53'W, Roscoff 48°43'N 3°59'W.

Atlantic: Brest 48°23'N 4°29'W, Quimper 47°58'N 4°07'W, Douarnenez 48°06'N 4°20'W, Lorient 47°45'N 3°22'W, Vannes 47°39'N 2°45'W, La Trinité-sur-Mer 47°35'N 3°01'E, Concarneau 47°52'N 3°55'W, St Nazaire 47°16'N 2°12'W, Nantes 47°14'N 1°34'W, Les Sables d'Olonne 46°30'N 1°48'W, La Rochelle 46°09'N 1°09'W, Rochefort 45°56'N 0°58'W, La Tremblade 45°46'N 1°08'W, Le Château d'Oléron 45°53'N 1°12'W, Royan 45°38'N 1°02'W, Bordeaux-Bassens 44°50'N 0°34'W, Pauillac-Trompeloup 45°12'N 0°45'W, Blaye 45°07'N 0°40'W, Le Verdon 45°33'N 1°05'W, Arcachon 44°40'N 1°10'W, Bayonne 43°30'N 1°29'W, Ciboure 43°23'N 1°41'W, Hendaye-Béhobie 43°22'N 1°46'W.

Mediterranean: Port Vendres 42°31'N 3°07'E, Port la Nouvelle 43°01'N 3°04'E, Sète 43°24'N 3°42'E, Marseilles 43°20'N 5°21'E, Port St Louis du Rhône 43°23'N 4°49'E, Port de Bouc 43°24'N 4°59'E, Toulon-la Seyne 43°07'N 5°55'E, Bandol 43°08'N 5°45'E, Cassis 43°13'N 5°32'E, Hyères 43°04'N 6°22'E, La Ciotat 43°10'N 5°36'E, Le Lavandou 43°08'N 6°22'E, Sanary 43°07'N 5°48'E, St Mandrier 43°05'N 5°55'E, St Tropez 43°16'N

6°38′E, St Maxime 43°18′N 6°38′E, Fréjus-Saint Raphael 43°25′N 6°46′E, Cannes 43°33′N 7°01′E, Antibes 43°35′N 7°09′E, Nice 43°42′N 7°17′E, Menton-Garavan 43°46′N 7°30′E.

Corsica: Ajaccio 41°55′N 8°44′E, Bastia 42°42′N 9°27′E, Porto-Vecchio 41°36′N 9°17′E, Propriano 41°40′N 8°54′E, Calvi 42°35′N 8°48′E, Ile Rousse 42°39′N 8°56′E, Bonifacio 41°23′N 9°06′E.

River ports
Seine: Rouen
Moselle: Metz, Thionville
Rhine: Strasbourg, Lauterbourg, Beinheim, Gambsheim, Ottmarsheim, Huningue, Neuf-Brisach.

Procedure on arrival
As a member of the European Union, EU regulations apply. In principle therefore boats coming from another EU country do not have to clear customs, although they have to report to immigration. The situation is more relaxed when the traffic is between EU countries which have adhered to the Schengen Agreement, so boats sailing to France from Spain or Italy are not required to clear immigration. The situation is different for non-EU boats, or those with non-EU nationals on board. In such cases, on arrival in France, the captain should report to customs at a port of entry with the ship's registration papers and passports. In some places customs will visit the boat on arrival. Customs may also inspect yachts up to 12 miles off the coast. The port captain should be contacted immediately on arrival in a marina or port, and he will call customs. Alternatively, the skipper should phone customs.

Yachts must have a proper certificate of registration, the originals must always be kept on board as photocopies are not accepted. For British yachts the French authorities will accept the Small Ships Register, issued by the Royal Yachting Association, but not the International Certificate for Pleasure Navigation also issued by the RYA. They are very strict about registration certificates, and some boats have been fined for not having a satisfactory document.

Customs
Firearms must be declared.

Cats and dogs must have an anti-rabies vaccination certificate and health certificate stating if they come from a rabies-free country. Other animals must be inspected by a health official on arrival. Animals under three months old are now allowed. A maximum of three dogs and/or cats may be brought in.

EU regulations apply concerning temporary importation. Non-EU boats are now allowed to remain inside France for up to 6 months in any 12-month period. Those who wish to remain longer must deposit the ship's papers with the local customs office, who will put the vessel under bond. The clock will then be stopped until the owner returns on board. During the period the vessel is in bond, the boat must not move from its berth, and the owner or crew are not allowed to sleep on board.

Boats which are borrowed, chartered or owned by companies can be brought into France under temporary importation, but only if the same person who brought the vessel in remains in charge and takes it out of the country again. Anyone borrowing a yacht must have a letter from the owner stating that permission has been given for the yacht to be used in his or her absence. Crew changes are allowed while in France only if the same person remains in charge. The only changes of owner or captain allowed are on privately owned yachts, where the person in charge may hand over control to a member of the immediate family, namely spouse or children, who must not be resident in France. A co-owner may hand over to another co-owner, who is listed as such on the ship's papers. Delivery crews may bring in a yacht for the owner to take over, or sail a yacht out of France on behalf of an owner, as long as a proper delivery agreement is made, which the authorities may wish to see. The yacht being delivered is not allowed to stop anywhere else in France except its entry and exit points, unless forced to by weather conditions.

Yachts may not be lent, hired or sold while in French waters while under temporary importation. Those in breach of any of these conditions, will be liable for tax on the value of the yacht.

Chartering: Only bareboat charters are permitted and if the yacht is foreign owned, proper formalities must be completed. Taking on paying crew is not permitted, as this is considered to be chartering. If a yacht has paying passengers, this must be declared to customs on arrival in France, the yacht imported and TVA (Value Added Tax) must be paid.

Immigration
Nationals of Western European countries, Argentina, Australia, Brunei, Canada, Chile, Czech Republic, Hungary, Iceland, Israel, South Korea, Mexico, New Zealand, Poland, Singapore, Slovak Republic, Slovenia, Uruguay and the United States do not need visas for up to a three month stay. All other nationalities need visas which must be obtained in advance.

Inland waterways

There are various canals which cross France, still used by commercial traffic as well as yachts. The Atlantic and Mediterranean are connected by a canal route of 314 miles (503 km) with 139 locks, from Bordeaux on the River Garonne, to Castets where the Canal Latéral à la Garonne runs to Toulouse, from where the Canal du Midi leads to Sète in the Mediterranean. Other canals and river systems go into the heart of Brittany, through the centre of Paris, the eastern part of France and the Rhône river to the Mediterranean. The Northern France waterway can be entered at Dunkerque, Calais, Gravelines or St Valéry-sur-Somme, while the Brittany Canal runs from the English Channel to the Bay of Biscay through 63 locks from St Malo via Dinas, Rennes, Redan and the River Vilaine.

Normally no charge is made for the use of the waterways, with a few local exceptions. Yachts must unstep their masts, which can be done at the seaports before entry into the canals, there usually being facilities which specialise in this operation. There are certain maximum restrictions, the most important being the draft, which is normally 6 ft (1.80 m) on the main waterways from the English Channel to the Mediterranean. The Canal du Midi has a minimum depth of 5 ft 4 in (1.60 m) while the canals in Brittany have a maximum draft of 4 ft (1.20 m). A yacht drawing up to 10 ft (3 m) with a maximum height restriction of 20 ft (6 m) may be taken up the Seine as far as Paris. On all other canals and rivers, the maximum headroom is 11 ft (3.50 m) and in some places as little as 8 ft (2.50 m). There are variations and the level of water can be greatly reduced following a dry winter. The maximum speed limit is 16 mph/25 kmh on the rivers, 3.7–6.25 mph/6–10 kmh on the canals. Chemical toilets and holding tanks are compulsory.

The French Tourist Office should be contacted for a list of 'chomages' (stoppages), obtainable from the end of March onwards, which details any canals or locks closed for repairs during the year.

All vessels using the inland waterways and canals must be in possession of a valid VNF sticker (Voies Navigables de France), which can be bought for an entire year or shorter periods.

Facilities

France prides itself on having the best cuisine in the world and the quality of food is excellent everywhere. Supplies are easily available and on the outskirts of every town there are huge hyper-markets, which have an immense selection of foodstuffs and other goods. Water and fuel are available in all ports and most marinas have their own fuelling dock. LPG is widely available as it is used by many French households, but for longer stays in France it may be advisable to change over to the French system of bottles.

With the most developed yacht building industry in Europe, yachting facilities generally are of a high standard. Marinas have been built along the entire Mediterranean coast and in many places, particularly in the older ports, special docking arrangements have been made for yachts. Many ports and marinas are full to capacity and during the summer season it can be extremely difficult to find space.

Chandlery and repair facilities are widely available and small repairs can be undertaken in most ports. For more complicated or specialised jobs it is best to go to one of the major centres, where there are established boatyards and specialist companies offering a complete range of repair facilities. On the Atlantic coast, the best centres are at St Malo, Ouistreham (near Caen), Cherbourg, Brest, La Trinité, La Rochelle, Le Havre, Lorient and Bordeaux. In the Mediterranean, excellent facilities are at Antibes, in the St Tropez–Cogolin area, Toulon and Marseilles, although the latter deals mainly with commercial shipping. In Corsica, the main port of Ajaccio has the best facilities on the west coast and Bastia on the east coast.

Further Reading

North Biscay Pilot
South Biscay Pilot
North France Pilot
North Brittany Pilot
Normandy and Channel Islands Pilot
Brittany and Channel Islands Cruising Guide
Mediterranean Cruising Handbook
Cruising Association Handbook
North Sea Passage Pilot
For the French Canals:
Carte–Guide Navigation Fluviale
Cruising French Waterways
Inland Waterways of France
French Inland Waterways

Website

www.francetourism.com (Government Tourism Office)

GREENLAND

Lying close to North America, but administered by Denmark, Greenland, also known as Kalaallit Nunaat, is the world's largest island. Lying mostly within the Arctic Circle, much of the land is under ice and in places the ice cap is over 2 miles (3 km) deep. Greenland is undoubtedly the most challenging cruising destination in the North Atlantic and every year a few yachts brave the elements to explore this wild and beautiful island during the all too short summer season. The deeply indented coasts offer an infinite variety of anchorages in the steep sided fjords or among the myriad islands. By June, the west coast is clear of ice between 63°N and 69°N. It can be approached by passing well to seaward of Cape Farvel. Depending on conditions, one may have to pass as far as 100 miles offshore. July and August are the best months for cruising.

Country Profile

The native population, correctly referred to as the Inuit, probably settled in Greenland from the west. They arrived shortly before the Europeans, whose westward penetration is believed to have commenced with the arrival of some Irish monks from Iceland probably in about AD 870, who lived in isolated communities until the arrival of the Vikings a century later. The SE and SW coasts of Greenland were first explored by Eric the Red, a Viking settler from Iceland and father of Leif Ericson, towards the end of the tenth century, and Viking settlements were subsequently established there under his leadership. It is thought that Inuit of the so-called Thule culture became established on the west coast at about the same time. Although Eric the Red is presumed to have landed in AD 982, the millennium of his arrival was celebrated in the summer of 2000. There were no further known contacts with Europe until Greenland was rediscovered in the sixteenth century by the explorers Davis and Hudson. The island was colonised by the Danes from 1721 and came under their direct control in 1729. In 1953 Greenland was incorporated into Denmark, but full internal self-government was agreed in 1981. Denmark retains control of foreign affairs. In 1985 the population voted to leave the European Community, which Greenland had previously joined as part of Denmark. Because of its strategic position, Greenland is the site of several air bases.

There is a move in Greenland towards independence, and Denmark has made it clear that it is ready to grant Greenland independence if that's what the islanders want. If it does happen, the traditional links between the two countries will continue to remain strong, and there may be some form of partnership between the two.

The economy is largely dependent on fishing. The population of 56,000 is concentrated on the south-west coast, being a mix of Inuit and European, as well as a Danish minority. Danish and Greenlandic are spoken and most people are Lutheran. The capital is Godthaab, or Nuuk in Inuit.

The weather is cold all year round and the winters are particularly harsh with some ports being icebound until well into the summer. Temperatures are low even in the summer months. The prevailing winds in the southern part are S or SW, while easterly winds predominate further north. Winds are light and variable in summer. Depending on latitude, the midnight sun is visible from the end of May until the end of July.

Entry Regulations

Ports of entry

Angmagssalik 65°35′N 37°30′W (August to November navigation period), Christianshaab 68°49′N 51°11′W (May to November), Egedesminde 68°43′N 52°53′W (May to December), Faeringehavn 63°42′N 51°33′W (year round), Frederikshaab 62°00′N 49°40′W (year round), Godhavn 69°15′N 53°33′W (May to December), Godthaab 64°10′N 51°44′W (year round), Holsteinsborg 66°57′N 53°41′W (year round), Jakobshavn 69°13′N 51°06′W (May to November), Julianehaab 60°43′N 46°02′W (year round, only ice-strengthened vessels January to July), Marmorilik 71°08′N 51°17′W (May to October), Nanortalik 60°08′N 45°15′W (August to December), Narssaq 60°54′N 45°59′W (September to December), Narsarsuaq 61°09′N 45°26′W (May to October), Sukkertoppen 65°25′N 52°54′W (year round), Umanak 70°41′N 52°08′W (July to October), Upernavik 72°47′N 56°09′W (June to November).

Procedure on arrival

In spite of its association with Denmark, Greenland is not a member of the EU and therefore all arriving boats must follow the usual clearance procedure and make their first stop at a port of entry. Contact

Practical Information

LOCAL TIME: GMT – 3

BUOYAGE: IALA A

CURRENCY: Danish krone (Dkr) of 100 ore.

BUSINESS HOURS
Banks: 0930–1600 Monday to Friday, to 1800 Thursdays.
Business: 0900–1630 Monday to Friday.
Shops: Monday to Thursday 0900–1700, 0900–1900/2000 Friday, 0900–1300/1400 Saturday.
Government offices: 0900–1630 Monday to Friday.

ELECTRICITY: 220 V, 50 Hz

PUBLIC HOLIDAYS
1 January: New Year's Day
6 January: Epiphany
Maundy Thursday, Good Friday and Easter Monday
Fourth Friday after Easter: Prayer Day
1 May: Labour Day
Ascension Day
Whit Monday
5 June: Constitution Day
21 June: Midsummer
1 November: All Saints' Day
24 December afternoon: Christmas Eve
25 December: Christmas Day
31 December: New Year's Eve

COMMUNICATIONS
Post offices, offering telephone, fax and telex services, are located in all towns.

Dial 009 for international calls.
There are flights from Nuuk airport (Godthaab) to Reykjavik in Iceland, and Canada, and from Narsarsuaq and Kangerlussuaq to Copenhagen.
There are ferries and flights between the islands.

MEDICAL
There is a hospital at Godthaab and health facilities in all ports.
Emergency treatment is usually free of charge.

DIPLOMATIC MISSIONS
Canada: Nuna Air, PO Box 800, 3900 Godthaab. *Tel.* 299-25411.
British Consulate, Vestrevig 45, Nuuk. *Tel.* 299-24422, Fax 299-22409.

---

the port authorities well in advance of arrival for special permission to enter the ports, if possible 24 hours beforehand on VHF Channels 12 or 16.

Customs
The importation of firearms is forbidden.
    Animals shall be confined on board.

Immigration
The same visa requirements apply as for Denmark, which in brief means that nationals of EU and Nordic countries do not need a visa, while those of the USA, Canada, Australia and New Zealand are among those who can stay up to three months without a visa. In some ports the crew may only be allowed to land with permission from the Port Authority who will issue shore passes.

Restrictions
The military areas of Gronnedal Fladestation (naval base), Thule Air Base and Sondre Stromfjord Air Base are prohibited for yachts. All military areas must be avoided.

Ice conditions
Ice Control *Tel.* 3 52 44, 3 52 54.
    Ice Control may be contacted via coast radio stations. If the station is out of VHF range, such as when approaching Cape Farvel, contact should be made through Qaqortoq (Julianhab) Radio. Ice Control will indicate ice limits and advise on the best course to sail.

Some of the harbours are accessible all year round, but many are only accessible during the summer, and even then ice-strengthened vessels are recommended. There are ice booms placed across the harbour entrances at Jakobshavn, and one should confirm with port authorities that these booms are slackened off before entering.

Facilities

Provisions are available only in the larger settlements and the best supplies are to be found in the capital Godthaab. It is also here that the best range of repair facilities is available. Limited repair facilities are also available at Holsteinsborg and Jakobshavn, which also have slipways. Fuel and water are available in all ports.

Further Reading

Faeroes, Iceland and Greenland

Website

www.greenland-guide.gl (Greenland Tourism Office)

ICELAND

Isolated in the North Atlantic with Greenland its only neighbour, Iceland consists of one main island and numerous smaller ones. Iceland is a country of stark beauty, of mighty glaciers, hissing geysers, boiling lakes and live volcanoes. Visited by only the most intrepid yachts during its short summer, a passage to Iceland and a cruise along its rugged coasts offers an experience difficult to match anywhere else in the North Atlantic.

Country Profile

In the ninth century AD Norsemen and Irish came to settle on the island and in 930 the Althing, an assembly of free men, was formed. The Althing is considered to be the oldest democratically elected assembly in the world. In the tenth century Icelanders settled Greenland and sailed across to North America. Norway took control of Iceland in the thirteenth century, and then fell under Danish rule taking Iceland with it. Denmark established a trade monopoly for which Iceland suffered. In the eighteenth century the population was decimated by smallpox, volcanic eruptions, and a terrible famine. The nineteenth century saw a revival, as both free trade and the Althing were re-established. Autonomy was achieved in 1903, and in 1918 the independent kingdom of Iceland was formed, although still under the Danish Crown. In 1944 the Republic of Iceland was proclaimed, which made economic agreements with the Scandinavian countries. It also joined NATO and in 1958 the United States took control of Iceland's defence. In 1958–61 the 'Cod Wars' broke out with England, after Iceland extended its coastal fisheries limit to 12, then 50 in 1975, and finally to 200 nautical miles.

The fishing industry is the mainstay of the economy. The population is 276,000, half of whom live in the capital Reykjavik. The language is Icelandic and most people are Lutheran.

In spite of the closeness to the Arctic Circle, the climate is not too harsh and winters are relatively mild, mainly because of the warming waters of the Gulf Stream. The average temperatures are 10°C in summer and 1°C in winter. Prevailing winds are from the SE or E. Summer winds are often light and calms are common.

Entry Regulations

Ports of entry

Reykjavik 64°08′N 21°54′W, Akranes 64°19′N 22°05′W, Isafjördur 66°05′N 23°06′E, Saudarkrokur 65°45′N 19°36′W, Siglufjördur 66°12′N 18°52′W, Akureyri 65°41′N 18°03′W, Husavik 66°03′N 17°22′W, Seydisfjördur 65°15′N 13°55′W, Neskaupstadur 65°09′N 13°41′W, Eskifjördur 65°05′N 13°59′W, Vestmannaeyjar 63°26′N 20°16′W, Keflavik 64°00′N 22°33′W, Hafnarfjördur 64°04′N 21°55′W.

Practical Information

LOCAL TIME: GMT

BUOYAGE: IALA A

CURRENCY: Icelandic krona (ISK) of 100 aurar.

BUSINESS HOURS
Banks: 0915–1600 Monday to Friday.
Shops: 1000–1800 Monday to Friday.
Government offices: 0830–1600 Monday to Friday.

ELECTRICITY: 220 V, 50 Hz

PUBLIC HOLIDAYS
1 January: New Year's Day
Maundy Thursday, Good Friday and
Easter Monday

First day of summer (end April)
1 May: Labour Day
Ascension Day
Whit Monday
17 June: National Day
August Bank Holiday
24–26 December: Christmas
31 December: New Year's Eve

COMMUNICATIONS
There are public phone boxes only in main towns. There are payphones in post offices, shops and service stations.
Dial 00 for international access. Operator 114.
Post office 0900–1700 Monday to Friday, 0900–1200 Saturdays.
There are international flights from Reykjavik to many European cities,

Greenland, the Faeroes, the USA and Canada.
There is a weekly ferry to mainland Europe in summer.

MEDICAL
There are hospitals in all major ports and several hospitals in Reykjavik. It is advisable for EU citizens to carry Form E111 for health care.

DIPLOMATIC MISSIONS
In Reykjavik:
Canada: Sudurlandsbraut 10.
Tel. 568 0820.
United Kingdom: Laufasvegur 31.
Tel. 550 5100.
United States: Laufasvegur 21.
Tel. 562 9100.

Procedure on arrival

The captain must inform customs of the yacht's arrival. Customs will give clearance to all places within Iceland. No cruising permit is required; however, yachts must obtain from customs a permit to temporarily import the vessel for exemption from duty. *Reykjavik:* Port Control should be contacted on VHF Channel 12 for berthing instructions.

Customs

Firearms must be declared on arrival and remain under seal while in Iceland. If one does not want to have firearms under seal, one can apply for special permission to be granted by the police.

The importation of animals is prohibited. In special cases, the Minister of Agriculture will authorise an import permit on condition that strict quarantine conditions are fulfilled. Otherwise animals must remain on board.

Duty-free allowances are 1 litre spirits, 1 litre wine, and 200 cigarettes. Alternatively, the alcohol allowance can be 1 litre spirits, 6 litres beer or 1 litre wine, 6 litres beer or 2 litres of wine. The minimum age for these allowances is 20 years. The sale of alcohol in Iceland is strictly controlled.

Immigration

Most do not need visas including nationals of EU or Nordic countries, United States, Canada, Australia or Japan who can spend three months in any nine month period.

Fees

Overtime fees are charged 1700–0800 Monday to Friday, and all of Saturday and Sunday.

Facilities

Provisioning is best in Reykjavik as there is a more limited selection in the smaller places. The price of food is high everywhere. Although there are not many local yachts, repair facilities are relatively good, particularly in active fishing harbours such as Reykjavik, Isafjördur and Olafsvik. A feature along the Icelandic shores are orange huts, set up as refuges for shipwrecked sailors. Every hut has some emergency supplies and a radiotelephone.

Further Reading

Faeroes, Iceland and Greenland

Website

www.icetourist.is (Icelandic Tourist Board)

IRELAND

The North Atlantic island of Ireland is made up of two political units, the independent Republic of Ireland, also known as Eire, and the smaller region of Northern Ireland, which is part of the United Kingdom. Ireland has a coastline of nearly 3000 miles with many deep and sheltered bays.

Described by some sailing authors as one of the finest cruising grounds in the world, the only missing element to put Ireland at the top of the table is better weather. At least this is more than made up for by a profusion of perfectly sheltered anchorages.

Ireland's three coasts are very different and in their variety they cater for every requirement. The east coast is the most easily accessible for yachts coming from the United Kingdom, but Ireland's real beauty lies on its southern and western coasts. The most popular cruising area is between Cork and the Dingle Peninsula with an abundance of snug harbours and picturesque anchorages. The wilder west coast is more exposed and the distances between sheltered harbours are greater. Some 200 islands lie scattered off the west coast of Ireland and only a handful are inhabited. While the east and south-western coasts have a sizeable local boating population and also attract a number of cruising yachts, the west of Ireland is less frequented.

Country Profile

In the fourth century AD the Celts settled in Ireland and eventually the small rival kingdoms of Ulster, Connacht, Meath, Leinster and Munster developed. In the early fifth century St Patrick brought Christianity to the island, and in the sixth to seventh centuries Ireland became a flourishing cultural and religious centre. Irish monks travelled and established important monasteries on the mainland of Europe.

The seventh to eleventh centuries saw the country suffer from Viking raids and invasions. Political disunity due to rivalry between the Irish kingdoms was exploited by the Anglo-Normans, and in 1175 King Henry II imposed English rule on Ireland. In 1541 Henry VIII took the title of King of Ireland, and his religious reforms provoked revolt among the Catholic Irish. Irish land was confiscated by the English crown and given to English gentry in retaliation, while Protestant Scots settled in Ulster. In the eighteenth century some legislative autonomy was gained. The influence of the American and

Practical Information

LOCAL TIME: GMT. March to October GMT + 1.

BUOYAGE: IALA A

CURRENCY: Punt (Ir£) of 100 pence. Euro from 2002. 1 euro = 0.787564 IEP.

BUSINESS HOURS
Banks: 1000–1230, 1330–1500 Monday to Friday, most until 1700 on Thursdays.
Business: 0900–1300 Monday to Friday, 1400–1730.
Shops: 0900–1730/1800 Monday to Saturday. Late shopping 2000/2100 Thursdays and/or Fridays in many towns. Early closing days in some smaller towns. Government offices: 0900–1730 Monday to Friday.

ELECTRICITY: 220 V, 50 Hz

PUBLIC HOLIDAYS
1 January: New Year's Day
17 March: St Patrick's Day
Good Friday
Easter Monday
Whit Monday
May Day
1st Monday in June
1st Monday in August
last Monday in October
25 December: Christmas Day
26 December: St Stephen's Day

COMMUNICATIONS
Post offices open 0900–1730 Monday–Friday, 0900–1300 Saturday. Central post office, O'Connell St, Dublin, open 0800–2000 Monday to Friday, 0900–1100 Sundays and public holidays. There are frequent flights from Dublin and Cork to the UK and regular flights from Dublin and Shannon airports to European and North American destinations.

MEDICAL
EU residents are entitled to free emergency treatment, on production of the E111 form or proof of residence in the UK. There is a similar reciprocal agreement for Australian residents.

DIPLOMATIC MISSIONS
In Dublin:
Australia: Fitzwilton House, Wilton Terrace. *Tel.* (01) 676-1517.
Canada: 65 St Stephen's Green. *Tel.* (01) 478-1988.
United Kingdom: 31/33 Merrion Road. *Tel.* (01) 205-3700.
United States: 42 Elgin Road, Ballsbridge. *Tel.* (01) 668-8777.

French revolutions led to rebellion at the end of the eighteenth century, but in 1800 the Act of Union united Ireland and England. The potato famine of 1846–8 plunged the island into misery, and caused a mass emigration.

Nationalism continued to be strong, until in 1914 the Home Rule Act was passed, but its implementation was delayed until after the First World War. A nationalist rising of 1916 was repressed and guerilla warfare followed. Then in 1920 the six counties of Ulster were incorporated into the United Kingdom, and a year later the Irish Free State was formed. Civil war resulted between the provisional government and those opposing the partition of Ireland. Eventually some calm was established, and efforts made at developing the country. In 1937 a new constitution was adopted, and the name changed to Eire. The Irish Republican Army (IRA), which was formed during the First World War to fight partition, was outlawed in 1939. Neutral during the Second World War, Eire became the independent Republic of Ireland in 1948 and joined the European Community in 1972.

The six counties of Ulster, known as Northern Ireland, have remained part of the United Kingdom, although there is some internal autonomy. Following widespread civil disturbances in 1969, the British army was sent in to re-establish order. Following a ceasefire in 1994 which halted most para-military activities, there have been intensive negotiations by the Irish and British governments which culminated in the British-Irish Agreement of 1999, although its implementation has encountered many difficulties. One result of the Agreement was the establishment of six North/South Implementation Bodies, one of which, Waterways Ireland, is responsible for the management and maintenance of the inland waterways throughout the whole island.

Ireland's economy has flourished in recent years with the services industry accounting for 56 per cent of the economy, followed by industry at 39 per cent. In 1998, exports exceeded imports by nearly 15 billion and over 5 million tourists visited the country while the traditional resources of agriculture, fisheries and forestry now only account for 5 per cent of the GDP. Ireland is undoubtedly one of Europe's success stories and this is proven by its decision to join the euro ahead of the UK.

The population is 3.6 million, with immigration now exceeding emigration. Irish (Gaelic) and English are spoken.

The majority of the population are Roman Catholic, with a minority of Anglicans. In Northern Ireland the majority are Protestant, although there is a sizeable Catholic minority. The capital of Ireland is Dublin on the east coast.

Ireland has a mild humid climate influenced by the Gulf Stream. Rainfall is very heavy all year round on the western coast. Strong winds and gales are most frequently from the SW and are very common in winter. The weather is generally very changeable. The prevailing winds are westerly. Higher seas are encountered off the west coast than in any other neighbouring area.

Entry Regulations

Ports of entry
Dublin 53°21′ 6°13′W, Dun Laoghaire 53°18′N 6°08′W, Wicklow 52°59′N 6°02′W, Dundalk 54°00′N 6°23′W, Drogheda 53°43′N 6°21′W, Carlingford 54°03′N 6°11′W, Greenore 54°02′N 6°08′W, Waterford 52°07′N 6°57′W, New Ross 52°24′N 6°57′W, Dungarvan 52°05′N 7°36′W, Wexford 52°20′N 6°27′W, Cork Harbour (Crosshaven and Cobh) 51°54′N 8°28′W, Kinsale 51°42′N 8°30′W, Baltimore (summer only) 51°27′N 9°24′W, Skibbereen 51°33′N 9°16′W, Bantry 51°42′N 9°28′W, Castletown Bere 51°39′N 9°54′W, Glengariff 51°43′N, 9°33′W, Youghal 51°56′N 7°50′W, Limerick 52°40′N 8°38′W, Tralee 52°16′N 9°46′W, Galway 53°16′N 9°03′W, Westport 53°48′N 9°32′W, Sligo 54°16′N 8°28′W, Ballina 54°07′N 9°10′W, Moville 55°11′N 7°02′W, Ballyhoorisky 55°15′N 7°46′W.

Procedure on arrival
As Ireland is a member of the European Union, EU regulations apply. All boats must report to immigration. Boats from non-EU countries, or EU boats arriving from a non-EU country, must notify customs whether having dutiable stores on board or not. At night, a red light over a white light, not more than six feet apart, must be shown. On arrival the customs office should be contacted, or if no customs officer is available, the local police (Garda). The harbour master must also be notified. All dutiable, restricted and prohibited items must be declared to customs. The officer in charge of the port of departure must be notified of details of the yacht, its destination and name of the captain.

Customs
Firearms must be declared. The importation of firearms and ammunition is prohibited unless a licence is granted by the Department of Justice, Equality and Law Reform.

Importation of animals is prohibited unless accompanied by a licence from the Department of Agriculture. When animals come from the United Kingdom, unless they are domestic dogs or cats having spent at least six months in the United Kingdom, they must be cleared with the Department of Agriculture & Food.

Non-EU yachts: Yachts may be temporarily imported for private use for a maximum period of 6 months in any 12 months, whether continuous or not, without paying import charges. This also applies to the importation of spare parts and accessories to effect repairs or maintenance. This relief only applies to yachts registered outside the EU and owned by a non-EU resident. Under temporary importation a yacht may not be hired, sold or lent to a resident of the EU. Immediate relatives of the owner may use the boat if they are resident outside of the EU. The boat may be used occasionally by a EU resident, when acting on behalf of the owner and when the owner is himself/herself in the EU.

Excess dutiable stores will be placed under customs seal on arrival; these, and stores shipped from bond, must not be consumed in port without prior permission from customs and on payment of duty. They may be used while cruising Irish waters but duty must then be paid on the quantity consumed in the subsequent port. Yachts laid up or remaining longer must pay all duty owed on dutiable stores, or deposit the stores in a State Warehouse, or have them sealed on board, in which case a bond must be given by the captain or owner.

There are restrictions on the import of meat and meat products, poultry and poultry products, plants and plant products including vegetables.

Immigration
Most European countries, as well as countries such as Australia, New Zealand, Japan, South Africa, the USA, Canada and Mexico, do not require visas.

Fees
Overtime is charged on Sundays, public holidays and outside working hours 0800 to 2000 on weekdays.

Light dues must be paid by yachts over 20 tons normally kept or used outside of Ireland, the United Kingdom or Isle of Man. The annual dues for Irish and British yachts is £86. Other yachts pay £29 for each period of 30 days up to a total amount of £86.

Facilities

Provisioning in all ports on the east and south coast is good and there are several marinas scattered about. As one moves west, supplies become scarcer and the boat should be well provisioned with food, fuel and water. Repair facilities for yachts range from excellent in such major yachting centres as Cork Harbour to virtually non-existent in some of the smaller ports. The facilities at Crosshaven are possibly the best in Ireland and a whole range of repair services is available, including travelift, workshops, rigger and sailmaker. Further east, repair facilities are also available at Youghal and Waterford. There are several marinas and repair facilities in and around the capital Dublin, the best centres being at Dun Laoghaire, Howth and Malahide. The Howth Yacht Club marina has excellent docking facilities and its location is ideal for visiting Dublin. Good provisioning, fuel and LPG are available locally. The club offers temporary membership to those spending the winter here. A useful source of help are the many yacht clubs dotted about the coasts, the most famous among them being the Royal Cork Yacht Club in Crosshaven, founded in 1720 and considered the oldest yacht club in the world. Most yacht clubs have moorings for visitors who are generally made welcome everywhere.

Further Reading

South and West Coast of Ireland Sailing Directions
North and East Coast of Ireland Sailing Directions
Lundy, Fastnet and Irish Sea Pilot (Vols 2 and 3)
Cruising Association Handbook

Websites

www.ireland.travel.ie (Irish Tourist Board)
www.heritageireland.ie

MADEIRA

Madeira lies in the Atlantic some 300 miles off the African coast. Only two islands of this volcanic archipelago are inhabited, the largest, Madeira Grande, which gives its name to the whole group, and Porto Santo to the north-east. The smaller islands of the main group are Ilha Chao, Ilha Deserta Grande, and Ilheu de Bugio. The Ilhas Selvagem, north of the Canary Islands, are a wildlife refuge administered by Madeira, and yachts wishing to visit them need permission from the authorities in Madeira.

The Madeiran archipelago is one of those places whose geographical position means that it is always visited by yachts en route to somewhere else and not as a destination in its own right. Yet these islands have much to be enjoyed and many transatlantic sailors regard Madeira with special affection. The majority of yachts arrive in Madeira during October and November on their way to the Canary Islands and the Caribbean, while some leave direct from the main port Funchal to cross the Atlantic. There has also been an increase in the number of American boats cruising the Atlantic circle of Bermuda, Azores, Madeira and Canary Islands during the summer, while Madeira has also become a popular port of call in the spring, for yachts returning to Europe after wintering in the Canaries.

Country Profile

Legend says that Madeira was part of the lost kingdom of Atlantis. The islands were already known to the Phoenicians, but the Portuguese rediscovered them early in the fifteenth century. The islands were uninhabited and covered in dense forest, hence the name, which means Island of Timber. Settled by the Portuguese, prosperity soon came with the cultivation of sugar cane and wine production. Christopher Columbus lived on Porto Santo for several years after he married the daughter of the island's governor.

The islands were briefly ruled by Spain, during the period when they also occupied the mainland of Portugal. Many foreign traders settled on the island and became involved with the development of the wine trade. With the growth in the numbers of ships calling for provisions, Madeira wine rapidly became popular and sought after in many countries. It was not only for the wine, but for other fresh provisions that trading vessels and passenger ships called at Madeira, which was a very popular port of call for British ships on their voyages to all parts of the globe. It is the lush vegetation and profusion of fruit and flowers which have accounted for the island's enduring charm and Madeira has been a destination for the discerning tourist since the early twentieth century. Madeira is an autonomous region of Portugal, although in recent years there have been some calls for independence.

Agriculture is important on this fertile island, and sugar cane, bananas, sweet potatoes and fruit are grown. Orchids are one of Madeira's specialities. The tourist and fishing industries also contribute to the economy.

Practical Information

LOCAL TIME: GMT. Summer time GMT + 1 March to October

BUOYAGE: IALA A

CURRENCY: Escudo ($) of 100 centavos. Euro from 2002. 1 euro = 200.482 PTE.

BUSINESS HOURS
Banks: 0830–1145, 1300–1445 Monday to Friday.
Business: 1000–1200, 1400–1800 Monday to Friday.
Shops: 0900–1300 Monday to Saturday, 1500–1900 Monday to Friday.
Government offices: 0900–1230, 1400–1730 Monday to Friday.

ELECTRICITY: 220 V, 50 Hz

PUBLIC HOLIDAYS
1 January: New Year's Day
Good Friday
25 April: National Day

1 May
Corpus Christi
10 June: Camoes Day
Autonomy Day
15 August: Assumption
21 August: Municipal Holiday (Funchal)
5 October: Republic Day
1 November: All Saints' Day
1 December: Independence Day
8 December: Immaculate Conception
25, 26 December: Christmas

COMMUNICATIONS
International calls, fax and telex at the telephone office adjacent to the main post office, Avenida Zarco, Funchal, separate entrance, open 0830–2400 Monday to Friday, 0900–1230 Saturday.
The main post office 0830–2000 Monday to Friday, 0900–1230 Saturday. There is a special counter for post restante and the post office has its own customs department at the airport for incoming parcels.
Stamps can also be bought from

newsagents and shops where a green 'correio' sign is displayed.
There are regular international flights from Madeira and Porto Santo.

MEDICAL
EU nationals should present their E111 form at the Centro do Bom Jesus, Serviço de Migrantes, Rua das Hortas 67, Funchal. *Tel.* 22 91 61, for Portuguese medical insurance booklet. Emergency treatment is available at Hospital Cruz Carvalho, Av. Luis Camoes. *Tel.* 74 21 11, and health centres (Centro de Saude) outside of Funchal. Emergency 115, Police 22 20 22.

DIPLOMATIC MISSIONS
In Funchal:
United Kingdom: Avenida Zarco 2. *Tel.* 221221.
United States: 4 Avenida Luis Camoes, Block B, Apartment B, Edificio Infante. *Tel.* 74 34 29.

The 264,000 Madeirans were originally Portuguese, mixed with Moors, Jews, Italians and Africans. Many Madeirans have emigrated, especially to Brazil. The majority are Roman Catholics. Portuguese is the official language, although many understand Spanish, French and English. The capital Funchal is a pleasant city with attractive mosaic pavements and whitewashed buildings in the Portuguese colonial style.

The islands have a pleasant and mild climate all year round, the air temperature rarely falling below 60°F (16°C) in winter or rising above 72°F (22°C) in summer. Due to the influence of the Gulf Stream the water temperature similarly varies only between 17° and 21°C (63–70°F). The prevailing winds are north-easterly and all the ports and anchorages are sheltered from this direction. Only the more variable winds of winter and the passage of lows across the North Atlantic can cause problems, otherwise Madeira can be visited virtually all year round.

Entry Regulations

Ports of entry

Funchal (Madeira) 32°38′N 16°54′W, Porto Santo 33°03′N 16°19′W.

Procedure on arrival

Although Madeira is a member of the European Union, all boats must contact the authorities on arrival.

Funchal: The small boat harbour inside Funchal harbour is run as a marina, but virtually all spaces on the pontoons are reserved for local craft and visiting yachts are obliged to tie up alongside the harbour wall, often rafted three to four deep. Formalities are completed at the reception dock, immediately to starboard as one enters the marina. Officers from Guarda Fiscal (dealing with customs) and Policia Maritima (immigration) are here 0900–1200, 1400–1800 every day. If there is no space to come alongside, boats should anchor in the outer harbour and visit the office by dinghy. The marina monitors Channel 16 during office hours (0900–1230, 1430–1800 Monday to Friday, 0900–1200 Saturday). The Guarda Fiscal will issue a transit log to non-EU yachts arriving from outside of Madeira. Even if coming from Porto Santo, the clearance procedure must still be completed. On departure the marina office and all other officials must be visited.

Porto Santo: There are some pontoons for yachts in this large harbour. Formalities are normally completed during office hours. The captain should report to the Port Captain's office on the north side of the harbour, as well as the Guarda Fiscal and the Policia Maritima. Even if arriving from Funchal and already possessing a transit log, one still has to report to all these offices.

Customs
Firearms must be declared. Animals are not permitted to land.

Immigration
Visa exemptions and requirements as for Portugal: 90 days' stay without visa for European Union, Australia, New Zealand, up to 60 days' stay for the USA, Canada, and many others. For extensions one has to apply at the Foreigners Registration Service.

Transit log
This is issued to all yachts at either port of entry by the Guarda Fiscal, and must be presented to the authorities when visiting any other island. Even if possessing a transit log from mainland Portugal or the Azores, clearance must still be done on arrival in Madeira. A new transit log may be issued.

Fees
There are no overtime fees as clearance is done in working hours. There are harbour fees.

Restrictions
The uninhabited Ilhas Selvagem are administered from Madeira and as they are a wildlife reserve access to them is prohibited. Yachts who wish to stop must obtain special permission from the Department of Fisheries at Parque Natural da Madeira, Quinta do Bom Succeso, Caminho do Meio, Funchal. *Tel.* 22 22 66, Fax. 22 25 89.

Facilities

Funchal: Docking facilities for visitors are inadequate and during the busy months of October and November visiting yachts have no choice but to anchor in the main harbour. Shopping is good as there are several supermarkets and one in the marina itself which is open seven days a week. There is also an excellent fresh produce market. LPG bottles can be refilled locally and Camping Gaz bottles can be either exchanged or bought. For diesel fuel there is a filling station in Funchal marina located at the marina entrance, open 0900–1530. Elsewhere it must be transported by jerrycan from filling stations. There is a small chandlery opposite the marina.

There are various engineering shops in Funchal, although repair facilities are rather limited and everything revolves around the yacht club (Clube Naval do Funchal). Visiting yachtsmen are welcome at the club, which is rather far from the harbour, although the club maintains a base next to the marina. It is here that yachts can be lifted out by a 25-ton travelift operated by the yacht club. For all emergency repairs, it is advisable to contact the marina office for the names of local specialists.

Porto Santo: Water and electricity are laid on to the pontoons and there are showers at the end of the dock. The main town of Porto Santo is a long walk from the harbour, but there one can find a fresh fish and produce market, bakery and two small supermarkets. There are only basic repair facilities in Porto Santo and for any work it is best to sail over to Funchal. There are no facilities or provisioning on any of the other adjacent islands.

Further Reading

Atlantic Islands
Madeira and Porto Santo Cruising Guide

Websites

www.portugal.org/tourism (Click on Madeira map)
www.madeira-web.com (Madeira Regional Government)

PORTUGAL

Portugal occupies the western part of the Iberian peninsula with a coastline on the Atlantic Ocean. A nation of seafarers, the Portuguese started the age of discovery in the fifteenth century. Portuguese ships sailed beyond the known horizons to discover first the route around Africa to India and then around the world. Portugal's isolation in the past from Spain and the rest of Europe has produced a distinctive culture and language. Little remains of the once mighty empire except the Atlantic islands of Madeira and the Azores, which enjoy a high degree of autonomy and therefore have been dealt with separately in this book.

From the cruising point of view, mainland Portugal divides into two distinct areas, the west and the south. The ports on the west coast are situated mostly in estuaries or rivers often with bars at the entrance. Among them, the most interesting landfall is the capital Lisbon set on the River Tagus, which can be navigated right up into the centre of the city. The Algarve coast in the south has better weather and easier approaches to its small picturesque ports.

In recent years several new marinas have opened on both west and south coasts, which has greatly improved cruising the Portuguese coast.

An interesting cruising ground is the River Guadiana, which forms the border between Portugal and Spain. The river is navigable for some 20 miles as far as Pomarão, and the scenery as well as the wildlife are worth the detour. The bridge linking the two banks is reported to have an overhead clearance of at least 20 metres.

Country Profile

Portugal was originally inhabited by Iberian tribes who came into contact with Phoenicians, Greeks and Romans, the latter making the country part of their empire until the fifth century AD. The entire Iberian peninsula was overrun by Visigoths and then the Moors in the eighth century. The Portuguese kings had expelled the Moors by the eleventh century and an independent kingdom was established, its borders basically those of present-day Portugal. Portugal was unified into a state earlier than most European nations.

In the fifteenth century Prince Henry the Navigator initiated voyages of discovery into the Atlantic and along the African coast, then to the East Indies. Vasco da Gama found the sea route to India, and prosperity came with Portuguese monopoly of the spice trade. Gradually Portugal established a maritime empire. Rivalry with Spain was intense and the two countries eventually concluded a treaty, which laid out their spheres of influence. In 1580 the country was occupied by Spain and independence was only restored in 1640. By then France, England and the Netherlands were overtaking the Portuguese in maritime strength and Portugal went into decline as it failed to establish a productive economy of its own.

During the nineteenth century civil wars, economic crises, and political and constitutional conflicts kept the country weak. In 1910 the monarchy was overthrown in a revolution, but strife continued and a fascist regime was established under Antonio de Oliveira Salazar in the 1930s. After the Second World War the colonies pushed for independence and several prolonged and costly wars were fought in Africa. In 1974 the almost bloodless 'Carnation Revolution' overthrew the dictatorship and the military regime was replaced with civil government and democracy. In 1986 Portugal joined the European Union.

Portugal has predominantly an agricultural economy, but industry is developing in such fields as textiles. Tourism and fishing are important sources of revenue.

The population numbers around 10 million. Portuguese is the main language. Of Latin origin, it sounds very different from other Latin languages, although written the similarities are obvious. The majority of the population are Catholic, but there are also Protestant and Jewish minorities. The capital is Lisbon (Lisboa), 10 miles from the Atlantic on the north bank of the River Tagus, which opens into the Mar de Palha (Sea of Straw). The area has been settled since the time of the Phoenicians and the town became the capital in 1260. After an earthquake in 1755, the city was rebuilt on a grand scale.

The climate is mild and varies slightly, being cooler in the north and warmer in the south. The prevailing winds of summer are northerly. The Portuguese trades commence in about April and last until September. On the Algarve coast the northerly winds of summer are often replaced by land and sea breezes. Most gales occur in winter, when the prevailing winds are westerly. Due to their location some harbours are inaccessible in strong onshore winds.

Entry Regulations

Ports of entry
Viana do Castelo 41°41'N 8°50'W, Leixões (Porto) 41°11'N 8°42'W, Figueira da Foz 40°09'N 8°52'W, Nazaré 39°35.2'N 9°04.4'W, Peniche 39°21'N 9°22.5'W, Cascais 38°42'N 9°25'W, Sesimbra 38°26'N 9°06'W, Lisbon 38°44'N 9°07'W, Sines 37°57'N 8°52'W, Lagos 37°06'N 8°40'W, Portimão 37°08'N 8°32'W, Vilamoura 37°04'N 8°07'W, Faro 37°01'N 7°55'W.

Procedure on arrival
All boats arriving from abroad must contact either a port or marina office, which should be visited with the ship's papers (registration and ownership certificate), radio licence, insurance policy and passports or ID cards of all persons on board. A clearance form will be completed in duplicate, one

to be retained by the marina or port office, the other for police, immigration and customs. Non-EU yachts will receive a transit log (livrete de trânsito) against payment of a small fee. The log is stamped at the first port and must be stamped at the last port of departure. A receipt will be issued for the payment of the annual lights and buoys tax (taxa de farolagem). The two documents should be kept with the ship's papers while in Portuguese waters.

The marinas and yacht harbours at Viana do Castelo, Povoa do Varzim, Leixões, Nazaré, Peniche, Cascais, Lisbon (Alcantara and Marina Expo), Sesimbra, Sines, Lagos, Portimão, Vilamoura, Faro and Vila Real Santo Antonio are designated to deal with clearance formalities for cruising boats arriving from abroad.

Lisbon: The approaches to the River Tagus (Rio Tejo) are straightforward and one should keep to

the marked channel as there are a few shallows in the approaches.

Due to repair work of the Bugio lighthouse in the entrance of the River Tagus, for the time being one has to pass between a black beacon and the north coast.

Doca de Alcântara, 1.2 nm upstream of the Lisbon bridge, is the best place to come to clear in and moor (up to 24 ft (7.2 m) draft). It has been enlarged to receive more yachts. All official offices (port captain, customs & Guarda Fiscal) are located nearby. The swing bridge at the entrance to this dock opens on request (call on Channel 12).

Porto: There is a bar at the entrance to the River Douro and the entrance is dangerous in strong winds or with a heavy swell. The deep water channel is on the north side. For both mooring and clearance, it is best to use the yachting facilities in the commercial port of Leixões, which can be entered under most conditions and has a marina and three yacht clubs. It is no longer possible to dock in Porto itself, due to the destruction of the

Belem Marina in Lisbon close to the monument of Henry the Navigator.

Practical Information

LOCAL TIME: GMT. Summer time GMT + 1 from the end of March to the end of October.

BUOYAGE: IALA A

CURRENCY: Escudo ($) of 100 centavos. Euro from 2002. 1 euro = 200.482 PTE.

BUSINESS HOURS
Banks: 0830–1445 Monday to Friday.
Business: 1000–1200, 1400–1800 Monday to Friday.
Shops: 0900–1300 Monday to Saturday, 1500–1900 Monday to Friday (food shops and Lisbon supermarkets stay open later and on Sundays).
Government offices: 0900–1700 (closed for lunch 1200–1400).

ELECTRICITY: 220 V, 50 Hz

PUBLIC HOLIDAYS
1 January: New Year's Day
Shrove Tuesday
Good Friday
25 April: Freedom Day
1 May: Labour Day
Corpus Christi
10 June: Portugal Day
15 August: Assumption
5 October: Republic Day
1 November: All Saints' Day
1 December: Independence Day
8 December: Immaculate Conception
25 December: Christmas Day

COMMUNICATIONS
International calls can be made from metered booths in telephone offices in major towns or LP card phones (which also take credit cards).
Emergency: dial 112.
Post offices open 0900–1230, 1430–1800 Monday to Friday. Central post office, Praça dos Restauradores, Lisbon, open until 2200. There are regular international flights from Lisbon, Porto and Faro to most European destinations. There are also flights to America, Africa and Asia from Lisbon. There are daily flights to the Azores and Madeira.

MEDICAL
Many European nationals can get free emergency treatment if their country has reciprocal arrangements with Portugal. British Hospital, Rua Saraiva de Carvalho 49, Lisbon, Tel. 213 955 067.

DIPLOMATIC MISSIONS
In Lisbon:
Canada: Avenida da Liberdade 144. *Tel.* 21 347 4892.
Cape Verdes: Av. Restelo 33. *Tel.* 21 301 5271.
United Kingdom: Rua São Barnardo 33. *Tel.* 21 396 1191.
United States: Avenida das Forcas Armadas. *Tel.* 21 727 3300.

In Porto:
United Kingdom: Avenida da Boavista 3072. *Tel.* 22 618 4789.

floating pontoon in Gaia on the south bank of the Douro River.

Cascais: The new 600-berth marina has 100 berths intended for yachts in transit. All officials (Capitania, customs and Guarda Fiscal) are situated in the marina.

Vilamoura: Vilamoura Radio monitors VHF Channels 16 and 20 and works on Channel 62. The wide entrance leads into an outer basin used mainly by local fishing boats, from which a narrower entrance leads to the marina. For clearance, yachts must come alongside the reception dock on the port side in front of the control tower.

Procedure on departure

For EU yachts the captain should clear out at the same offices, only if leaving Portugal for a non-EU destination. For non-EU yachts departing Portugal, the transit log must be stamped by both the Capitania and the Guarda Fiscal. If arriving from or continuing on to the Azores or Madeira, customs clearance does not have to be obtained as both these island groups are administered by Portugal. However, on arrival in those places the Capitania must be contacted as normal, and a new transit log may be issued.

Customs

Firearms must be declared on arrival. All animals need an international vaccination certificate.

Duty-free goods in excess of the limits allowed are permitted as long as they remain on board.

Immigration

Visas are not required for citizens of West European countries, Canada and the USA, Australia, New Zealand, and many others. Nationals of those countries which require visas, if travelling on a yacht in transit, are normally granted a visa on arrival, which is valid for a limited period. Nationals who require a visa and arrive without one should attempt to clear in at one of the major ports. Visitors are normally allowed a 60 day stay, 90 days for EU citizens, six months for Brazilians.

Visa extensions can be obtained from the Foreigners Registration Service, Avenida Antonio Augusto de Aguiar 18, Lisbon (or regional offices).

Facilities

Provisioning is generally good and fresh produce particularly is of good quality. Fuel is available in all major ports. Repair facilities, with a few exceptions, are below the standards of neighbouring countries. The best repair facilities are concentrated in the three areas which have a local boating community: the capital Lisbon, Porto on the west coast and the large Vilamoura marina on the Algarve coast.

Lisbon: Facilities for visiting yachts are adequate and the limited number of pontoon spaces in the marinas are usually taken up by local craft. There are four different basins used by yachts, all of them situated on the north bank of the river. Coming from seaward the first is Doca de Bom Succeso, immediately past Torre de Belem. There are no special places allocated for visitors. Further upstream, past the monument to Henry the Navigator, is Doca de Belem. Visitors should tie up initially by the fuel station opposite the entrance. For a small fee visitors can use the facilities of the Associacião Naval de Lisboa (Sailing Association) which has its base there. The club secretary is also the best person to consult concerning any repair. Doca de St Amaro, just after the first suspension bridge, is often full of naval craft and harbour launches, and the best place to find space is probably Doca de Alcantara further upstream and described earlier under 'Procedure on arrival'. Expo Marina, some 6 miles upriver, was opened for Expo '98 on the site of the universal exhibition on the north bank of the Tagus. The marina has good docking facilities, but is affected by the strong current which occasionally makes manoeuvring difficult. There are various workshops in Belem and also a small chandlery, but the selection is limited. Charts are available at the Hydrographic Institute.

Porto: Repair facilities for yachts are restricted to the area around the marina in Leixoes. Either the local yacht club or the port captain's office are the best source of information on the facilities available. Most workshops are for commercial vessels, but they could work on a yacht if necessary.

Figueira da Foz: If a large sea is running at low tide this entrance can be difficult. The marina is on the north side of the entrance in the middle of the city.

Nazaré: The port and marina are south of the town.

Peniché: The marina is inside the port on the south side of the peninsula where the town of Peniché is situated.

Cascais: This new marina opened in 1999 and eventually will have a full range of services and repair facilities, including a 70-ton travelift. The marina monitors Channel 62.

Sesimbra: A small new marina has opened here inside the port.

Sines: A small well-equipped marina has opened inside the Porto Pesca (fishing harbour), which is situated within the commercial harbour. The yacht club of Sines is nearby.

Vilamoura: This large and well-run marina is very popular among North European sailors as it is a good place to leave the boat for long periods, especially if planning to set off across the Atlantic and not go into the Mediterranean. The marina offers all usual services with fuel at the reception dock. Repair facilities are the best in Portugal with a complete range of engine, sail, electrical, electronic and fibreglass repair. Carpentry and metalwork can also be done here. There is a 30-ton travelift as well as a drying out grid.

Lagos: This marina on the Algarve coast is rapidly gaining in popularity with cruising sailors. Its facilities are of the highest standard and mooring prices lower than in similar marinas elsewhere. The attractive town of Lagos is an added bonus.

Portimão: A new marina has opened on the west side of the entrance to this fishing port.

Further Reading

Atlantic Spain and Portugal
Cruising Association Handbook

Websites

www.edinfor.pt/anc (Details on marinas and ports)
www.portugal.org (Government site)
www.portugalinsite.pt (Export Promotion Corporation)

UNITED KINGDOM

The United Kingdom of Great Britain and Northern Ireland incorporates the three countries of England, Scotland and Wales, the six counties of Ulster in Northern Ireland as well as several smaller island groups such as the Scillies, Orkneys and Shetlands. The Isle of Man, situated in the Irish Sea, has a special status and enjoys a certain degree of autonomy. The Channel Islands enjoy even greater autonomy, and are therefore treated separately.

With hardly anywhere over fifty miles from the

sea, the British Isles has always been a maritime nation and produced some of the greatest sailors and navigators in history, a tradition which has continued into the modern age, when British cruising yachts were among the first to penetrate the furthest corners of the world. Sailing is a national pastime in Britain and the proportion of yachts per head of population is among the highest in the world. The most popular cruising areas are the Solent and Isle of Wight, the south west counties of Devon and Cornwall, East Anglia and the west coast of Scotland. The British Isles provide a vast cruising ground with plenty of variety, the greatest drawback being the weather, which rarely ensures enjoyable cruising conditions for more than a few days at a time. Most visiting yachts limit their cruising to the south coast, where there is an abundance of yachting facilities, but also an abundance of local craft, resulting in crowded harbours. There are many cruising attractions and more space to be found elsewhere.

Country Profile

The original inhabitants were of Iberian origin and later Celts settled the island. The Romans invaded and established the province of Britannia, the Celts fleeing west to North Wales and north to what the Romans called Caledonia, both areas resisting Roman expansion. The inhabitants of Caledonia were called Picts and this area was also settled by the Scots, a Celtic tribe originating in Ireland.

After the collapse of the Roman Empire, Germanic tribes – the Angles, Saxons and Jutes – settled, driving the remaining Celts into Wales and Cornwall. From the eighth century the Danes were constant raiders and established settlements on the east coast. Danish kings ruled in the tenth and eleventh centuries, then a Saxon dynasty was re-established, but this fell to a Norman invasion in 1066.

After several weak kings and the Hundred Years War with France, it was only in the fifteenth and sixteenth centuries under the Tudors, Henry VII, Henry VIII and Elizabeth I, that a strong modern state was forged. Wales was united with England while Scotland remained an independent kingdom until Queen Elizabeth died without an heir. Then the Stuart King James VI of Scotland became James I of England and united the two kingdoms. Scotland has still kept many of its own laws and institutions.

Under Elizabeth I there had been an era of

maritime exploration and economic expansion. Following her reign, under the Scottish Stuarts, there were conflicts between Parliament and the monarchy, civil war, and eventually parliamentary supremacy was accepted, which limited the power of the ruling monarch.

The Hannoverian dynasty came to the throne in 1714 and a period of internal stability followed, although Britain was involved in European wars and an ongoing rivalry with France. Britain's maritime power, trade, commerce and colonisation prospered. Despite the loss of the American colonies following the War of Independence, Britain gained Canada and India and continued to expand her empire. The Industrial Revolution at the end of the eighteenth century heralded an era of economic development and prosperity, which peaked in the 60 year reign of Queen Victoria in the nineteenth century.

The prosperity did not reach down to the working classes, who began to find their voice. Gradually a series of social and democratic reforms were introduced. The First World War resulted in a major loss of life and seriously weakened the economy, which took time to recover. During the Second World War, Britain again made a major war effort at great cost to the economy, although helped later by the United States. In 1945, the newly elected Labour government carried out a large-scale policy of nationalisation and social reform. In the post-war years Britain followed a policy of granting independence to the majority of its former colonies, although most remained within the British Commonwealth. The period of prosperity enjoyed in the 1950s and 60s gave way to inflation and high unemployment. After nearly two decades of Conservative rule, a Labour government led by Tony Blair came to power in 1997.

There has been a decline of traditional industries such as shipping, steel, textiles and coal, and the regions where these were concentrated suffer heavy unemployment. The chemical and electronic industries have expanded and the south-east region is more prosperous. North Sea oil and gas, and service industries offset part of the trade deficit. Agriculture is intensive and still plays an economic role.

The population is 60 million, of which the majority are English (Anglo-Saxon) with large Celtic minorities, Welsh, Scots and Irish. There are sizeable West Indian and Asian communities in larger cities, as well as of Chinese, Cypriot, Arab and African origins. Apart from English, Welsh is

Practical Information

LOCAL TIME: GMT. Summer time GMT + 1 March to October.

BUOYAGE: IALA A

CURRENCY: Pound sterling (£) of 100 pence.

BUSINESS HOURS
Banks: 0930–1530 Monday to Friday (some close 1630 weekdays, some open Saturday mornings).
Scottish Banks: 0930–1230, 1330–1530 Monday to Thursday, 0930–1530 Friday.
Business: 0900–1730 Monday to Friday.
Shops: 0900–1730/1800 Monday to Friday; some early closing Wednesdays, some close 1900/2000 Thursdays, Fridays.
Government offices: 0900–1730 Monday to Friday.

ELECTRICITY: 240 V, 50 Hz

PUBLIC HOLIDAYS
England and Wales:
1 January: New Year's Day

Good Friday and Easter Monday
May Day
Spring Bank Holiday: Last weekend in May
Summer Bank Holiday: Last weekend in August
25, 26 December: Christmas
Scotland:
2 January.
Easter Monday is not a holiday.
Northern Ireland:
17 March: St Patrick's Day
12 July: Battle of the Boyne

COMMUNICATIONS
International Tel. access code 00.
Operator 100, International operator 155.
International calls can be made from public phones.
Many use phone cards, which can be bought in post offices or in shops where the card sign is shown.
Emergency: *Tel.* 999.
Post offices open 0900–1730/1800 Monday to Friday, some 0900–1300 Saturday.
London's Heathrow and Gatwick airports are among the busiest in the world with flights to all international destinations. There are also flights to many destinations from Belfast, Birmingham, Edinburgh, Glasgow, Manchester and Newcastle.

MEDICAL
National Health Service treatment may be free for nationals of countries that have reciprocal agreements with Britain.

DIPLOMATIC MISSIONS
In London:
Australia: Australia House, The Strand WC2B 4LA. *Tel.* (020) 7379 4334.
Canada: Macdonald House, 1 Grosvenor Square, W1X 0AB.
Tel. (020) 7258 6600.
New Zealand: New Zealand House, Haymarket, SW1Y 4TQ.
Tel. (020) 7930 8422.
United States: 24/31 Grosvenor Square, W1A 1AE. *Tel.* (020) 7499 9000.

---

spoken in Wales and Gaelic in Scotland and Ireland. Church of England Protestantism is the established church, while most other denominations and religions are represented. While London is the capital of the United Kingdom, Edinburgh is the Scottish capital, Cardiff is capital of Wales and Belfast capital of Northern Ireland. A policy of devolution of central power resulted in some autonomy for Scotland, Wales and Northern Ireland in the late 1990s.

The climate is mild and temperate, being greatly influenced by the Atlantic and Gulf Stream. Rainfall is heavier on the western coasts. The spring, from March to May, can be cool and wet, while summer, from June to September, can be warm. The weather is very changeable, although occasionally there are long spells of pleasant weather when a system of high pressure remains stationary over the British Isles. Depressions tracking east across the Atlantic bring strong SW winds, usually of gale force. The prevailing winds of summer are NE, although SW winds predominate throughout the year and this is also the direction of most gales. Strong tides make navigation around the British Isles particularly difficult.

Entry Regulations

Customs Offices
England and Wales

The following offices were listed by HM Customs in 2000, and their telephone numbers were correct when going to press. However, it has been announced that there will be a reorganisation in the near future, with some of the smaller offices being grouped together, so that some phone numbers may change.

Avonmouth: Cardiff 01222 763880, also for Barnstaple, Barry, Bridgwater, Bristol, Burham-on-Sea, Clevedon, Highbridge, Lydney, Minehead, Porlock, Sharpness, Watchet, Weston-super-Mare
Swansea: 01792 652373 or Cardiff 01222 763880 – 24 hours
Berwick: 01289 307547, Hull 01482 782107 – 24 hours
Boston: Ipswich 01473 235704 – 24 hours
Cardiff: 01222 763880 – 24 hours
Colchester: Ipswich 01473 235704 – 24 hours; also for Bradwell, Brightlingsea, Burham-on-Crouch, Malson, Walton-on-the Naze, West Mersey
Brighton: 0345 231110 – 24 hours
Cowes: 0345 231110 – 24 hours; also for Yarmouth

Dover: 01304 224251 – 24 hours; also for Faversham, Folkestone, Ramsgate, Rye, Whitstable
Falmouth: 0345 231110 – 24 hours; also for Penzance
Felixstowe: Ipswich 01473 235704 – 24 hours
Fowey: 0345 231110 – 24 hours; also for Padstow, Par
Gravesend: 01474 537115 – 24 hours; also for Chatham, Faversham, London Port, Sheerness
Great Yarmouth: Ipswich 01473 235704 – 24 hours; also for Lowestoft
Hamble: 0345 231110 – 24 hours
Harwich: Ipswich 01473 235704 – 24 hours
Holyhead: 01407 762714; also for Baumaris, Caernarfon, Chester
Hull: 01482 782107 – 24 hours; also for Brough, Silloth, Workington, Whitehaven
Immingham: 01469 574748, Hull 1482 782107 – 24 hours; also for Grimsby, Scunthorpe, Trent
Ipswich: 01473 219481 – 24 hours; also for Woodbridge
King's Lynn: Ipswich 01473 235704 – 24 hours; also for Wisbech, Wells
Liverpool: 0151 922 9661, Manchester 0161 912 6977 – 24 hours; also for Birkenhead, Ellesmere Port, Heysham, Hoylake, Fleetwood, Glasson Dock, Preston, Runcorn, Southport
Lymington: 0345 231110 – 24 hours; also for Beaulieu, Christchurch
Newhaven: 0345 231110 – 24 hours
North Shields: (0191 2579441), Hull 01482 782107 – 24 hours; also for Amble, Blyth, Hartlepool, Maryport, Sunderland, Seaham Harbour
Pembroke: (01646 685807), Cardiff 01222 763880 – 24 hours; also for Aberystwyth, Fishguard, Milford Haven
Plymouth: 0345 231110 – 24 hours; also for Dartmouth, Salcombe
Poole: 0345 231110 – 24 hours
Portsmouth: 0345 231110 – 24 hours; also for Itchenor
Scarborough: (Hull 01474 537115 – 24 hours); also for Bridlington
Shoreham: 0345 231110 – 24 hours; also for Littlehampton
Southampton: 0345 231110 – 24 hours
Southend-on-Sea: Ipswich 01473 235704 – 24 hours
Teesport: Middlesbrough 01642 44011, Hull 01482 782107 – 24 hours
Teignmouth: 0345 231110 – 24 hours; also for Brixham, Exmouth, Torquay
Tilbury Dock: Gravesend 01474 537115 – 24 hours
Weymouth: 0345 231110 – 24 hours
Whitby: 01947 602074, Hull 01482 782107 – 24 hours

Scotland

If any of the following ports do not reply, call 0141 8879369, as it is manned 24 hours.
Aberdeen: 01224 212666; also for Montrose
Ayr: 01292 478548
Campbeltown: 01586 552261
Dundee: 01382 200822
Fort William: 01397 702948
Greenock: Glasgow 0141 3083618
Invergordon: 01349 852221
Inverness: 01463 222787
Islay: 01496 810337
Kirkwall: 01856 872108
Lerwick: 01595 696166
Skye: 01478 612468
Stornoway: 01851 703626
Ullapool: 01854 612852
Wick: 01955 603650

Northern Ireland

Ardglass: Belfast
Belfast: 01232 358250; also for Coleraine, Kilkeel, Larne, Londonderry, Portavogie, Warrenpoint.

Isle of Wight: Cowes and Yarmouth (see Southampton).
Isle of Man: Douglas (016246 74321).
Orkney: Kirkwall (01856 2108).
Shetlands: see Lerwick.
Isles of Scilly: St Mary's (see Plymouth).

Procedure on arrival

As a member of the European Union, EU regulations apply. Boats arriving from another EU country do not need to fly the Q flag. For boats arriving from outside the EU, the requirement to report to customs depends on the itinerary before arriving in the UK:

1 Boats arriving from another EU country only need to contact customs if there are goods to declare or non-EU nationals on board.
2 Boats arriving from a country outside the EU must telephone or contact a customs officer, who will advise on the necessary procedure.

Goods to be declared:

1 Boats arriving from another EU country:
   – any animals or birds
   – any prohibited or restricted goods
   – any duty-free stores
   – if VAT is owed on the boat.
2 Boats arriving from a country outside the EU:
   – any goods mentioned above
   – any goods in excess of the duty-free allowance.

On entering UK territorial waters (12 miles off-shore), the yellow Q flag must be flown until customs formalities have been completed. At night the flag should be illuminated. Failure to fly the flag is an offence and may lead to prosecution and a fine. Yachts are liable to be searched by customs officers at any time while cruising in UK territorial waters.

If there are animals or birds on board or any illness, health clearance must be obtained. The captain should contact the port health authority or local authority responsible for port health control by radio, 4 to 12 hours before arrival and if this is not possible immediately on arrival. Until health clearance is given no one except officials may board the vessel nor anyone leave.

On arrival in a place where there is a customs house, the captain must notify customs in person or by telephone. Notification must be made within two hours of arrival, unless arriving between 2300 and 0600, when arrival need not be notified until 0800 the following morning provided there are no birds or animals on board. Failure to notify the arrival within two hours is an offence and can lead to a fine. If notifying by telephone, in some areas a message may have to be left on a telephone-answering machine, with the yacht name, time of arrival, location of the yacht and if there are animals on board. Radio telephones can be used to notify arrival while the yacht is still at sea. All persons must await clearance on board. Goods must not be landed until customs clearance is complete.

The author's Aventura III *off London's Tower Bridge.*

Customs
Firearms and ammunition, including gas pistols and similar weapons, may not be imported.

Animals and birds must be restrained at all times, and kept confined below deck. They must not come into contact with other animals or be landed. Animals and birds may not be imported into the UK without a licence or the newly introduced animal passport. All animals will be placed in quarantine for six months at the owner's expense, immediately on arrival. The landing of a cat, dog or other rabies-susceptible animal from the Republic of Ireland, Channel Islands or the Isle of Man is not restricted provided that if the animal originated from outside of those places, it has served its full quarantine period. If on leaving the UK one intends to return with the animal, a licence must be obtained from the Ministry of Agriculture, Fisheries and Food (MAFF) before departure allowing the animal or bird to land at certain designated ports before entering quarantine.

MAFF, Government Buildings, Hook Rise South, Tolworth, Surrey KT6 7NF. *Tel.* (0208) 330 4411.

Prohibited imports include meat, poultry and many other animal products; plants and produce, including potatoes and certain other fruit and vegetables; certain articles made from endangered species including fur, ivory and reptile leather.

Radio transmitters, such as portable VHF radios, which are not approved for use in the UK, may not be operated.

Temporary importation
The following visitors to the European Union, and implicitly the UK, do not have to pay customs charges on their vessels:
- If they normally live outside the EU for at least 185 days in any 12 months
- If the vessel is exported when the owner next leaves the EU
- If the vessel is not lent, hired or sold in the EU.

Customs should be informed if the vessel may have to stay longer than the allowed period.

EU residents can have their boats based in another EU country, and leave them there without any time restrictions, without having to pay any additional duties. However, the owner may be asked to prove that duty (VAT) on the boat had been paid.

In theory all yachts are liable for VAT on importation. There are various exemptions and conditions pertaining to this and also to the exemption from VAT of yachts purchased in the UK for export. Full details can be found in a booklet published by Her Majesty's Customs & Excise, 'Pleasure craft sailing in the United Kingdom' (Notice 8 of 1996).

Departure

Customs need not be informed by boats leaving the UK for another EU country. All boats going directly to a country outside the EU *must* inform customs. Failure to do so could result in a fine.

Departing boats should complete sections 1 and 2 of Form C1331 and deliver part 1 to customs at the place of departure. It is stressed that the form must arrive at the customs office before the boat is expected to leave the UK. Part 2 should be kept on board as evidence of notification of departure. If a planned departure is delayed by more than 48 hours or abandoned, customs must be informed accordingly. Form C1331 can be obtained from customs offices or most yacht clubs and marinas.

It is no longer possible to provision the boat with duty-free goods if going to another EU country. However, both non-EU and EU boats bound for non-EU destinations should contact customs in advance to make the necessary arrangement for duty-free stores. Similarly, non-EU boats may be able to get a refund on the VAT paid on goods that are being exported outside of the EU.

Immigration

If there is anyone on board who is not an EU national, immigration must be contacted if arriving from outside the following countries or territories: UK, Isle of Man, Republic of Ireland, Channel Islands. In most yachting centres, the customs officer also acts as the immigration officer.

Nationals of EU countries do not need a visa for up to three months stay. Visas are not required for nationals of Commonwealth countries, except for Bangladesh, Fiji, Ghana, India, Burma (Myanmar), Mauritius, Tanzania, Zambia, Nigeria, Papua New Guinea, Sri Lanka, Uganda and Pakistan who require visas. Nationals of all European countries do not require visas except for Albania, Bulgaria, Bosnia-Hercegovina, the CIS, Macedonia, Yugoslavia (Serbia and Montenegro), Romania and Turkey. Nationals of all Asian, African and American countries do not require visas except for Afghanistan, Algeria, Angola, Benin, Bhutan, Burkina Faso, Burundi, Colombia, Cambodia, Cameroon, Cape Verdes, Central African Republic, Chad, China, Comoros, Congo, Croatia, Cuba, Djibouti, Dominican Republic, Egypt, Equatorial Guinea, Eritrea, Ethiopia, Gabon, Guinea, Guinea-Bissau, Haiti, Ivory Coast, Indonesia, Iran, Iraq, Jordan, North Korea, Kuwait, Laos, Lebanon, Liberia, Libya, Madagascar, Mali, Mauritania, Mongolia, Morocco, Mozambique, Nepal, Nigeria, Oman, Philippines, Peru, Qatar, Rwanda, Sao Tome e Principe, Saudi Arabia, Senegal, Sierra Leone, Slovak Republic, Somalia, Sudan, Suriname, Syria, Taiwan, Thailand, Togo, Tunisia, United Arab Emirates, Vietnam and Yemen. Visas must be obtained in advance from a British embassy or consulate. Persons requiring visas who arrive in the UK without one will be refused entry. Permission to enter is at the discretion of the immigration officer at the point of entry – he has the power to refuse entry even if one has a visa, although for those on a tourist visit with sufficient funds for their stay, entry is normally straightforward.

Facilities

Provisioning is good throughout the country. Fuel is available in most ports. LPG containers of non-UK standard are difficult to refill and for longer stays it is advisable to change over to the British (Calor gas) type bottles. Camping Gaz is widely available in camping and hardware stores. Marine supplies are also widely available with the best stocked chandleries being concentrated on the south coast and in London. Charts and marine publications are stocked by all major chandleries.

Mooring facilities vary both in quality and availability. In some of the fishing and commercial harbours these can be very basic. Not all yacht clubs have their own moorings, but when they do a place can usually be found for a visiting member of an overseas club. There are some 150 purpose-built marinas scattered about the coasts of Great Britain and Northern Ireland. All marinas operate on VHF Channel 80, which is monitored during normal working hours. Most marinas keep a number of berths for visiting yachts. Many have chandleries and also repair facilities, as well as slipways or travelifts. The most comprehensive range of repair facilities is to be found in the area between Southampton and Portsmouth where the biggest names in the British yaching industry are concentrated. It has been said that whatever cannot be fixed there probably cannot be fixed anywhere else in the world.

For those who wish to take their boat right into the heart of London, there are now three marinas to choose from, all within a relatively short distance of the centre. St Katharine's Dock, right by the Tower of London, is the best known. Only half a mile downstream are two new marinas, South Dock Marina, on the south shore of the Thames, and Limehouse Basin Marina, on the north shore. The latter is also the home of the Cruising Association, in whose new premises visiting sailors are welcome. Its excellent reference library should make it the natural choice for any cruising sailor.

The Caledonian Canal provides a convenient shortcut across Scotland. The canal is 60 miles long, has 29 locks, and 10 swing bridges. It is entered at Inverness, on the east coast, and exists at Corpach on the west coast. Boats need to purchase a permit, whose cost depends on the length of time one intends to spend in the canal, which offers attractive cruising opportunities. There are good facilities along its entire length.

Further Reading

East Coast Pilot Guide from Ramsgate to the Wash
South Coast Cruising
Shell Pilot to the English Channel
Clyde Cruising Club: Sailing directions for Scotland, Hebrides, Orkney and Shetland Islands (several volumes)
Cruising Guide to Northwest England and Wales
West Country Cruising
Channel Harbours and Anchorages
Cruising Association Handbook
North Sea Passage Pilot

Websites

www.visitbritain.com (British Tourism Authority)
www.holiday.scotland.net (Scottish Tourist Board)
www.tourism.wales.gov.uk (Welsh Tourist Board)
www.ni-tourism.com (Northern Ireland Tourist Board)

4 West Africa and South Atlantic Islands

With the exception of Senegal and the Gambia, the west coast of Africa is largely bypassed by cruising yachts and hardly any venture south of the Ivory Coast. This is the main reason why none of the countries between the Gulf of Guinea and Namibia were included in this book, but also because it was felt that for the time being most of those countries are best avoided. According to reports received from commercial ships as well as travellers in the region, the conditions that prevail in those countries, the cases of piracy, corruption, crime and diseases, as well as the total lack of facilities, should deter anyone from visiting them, particularly as by yacht one is more vulnerable than if travelling in an organised group. However, for a taste of West Africa, no place is better suited to explore by yacht than Senegal and the Gambia, whose rivers and estuaries provide an excellent cruising ground without the dangers and difficulties associated with the countries lying further south.

A completely different picture awaits the sailor at the southern tip of the continent where great changes are underway. After many years of isolation, South Africa has rejoined the international fold, while its former dependency, Namibia, has joined the ranks of independent nations. For the adventurous sailor, the islands of the South Atlantic are interesting destinations each in its own particular fashion. St Helena and Ascension have a long history of being welcome stops on the trade wind route to the equator, whereas the main attraction of Tristan da Cunha and the Falkland Islands is their very remoteness. It is indeed the even greater remoteness of Antarctica that attracts cruising boats in increasing numbers. The seventh continent is no longer the exclusive destination of scientific expeditions as sailing boats are now making their way there regularly, the majority during the short summer season, although a few have wintered there.

With the exception of South Africa, where especially in Durban and Cape Town yachting facilities are of international standards, facilities in all other places in the region are either limited or non-existent. Provisioning in some West African countries can be difficult or expensive, so the boat should be well stocked. French charts are better for Senegal and Guinea-Bissau.

ANTARCTICA

Until very recently the number of sailing boats which visited the seventh continent could be counted in single figures. The increasing popularity of Patagonia among cruising sailors has now spilled over and every year more yachts venture south of the 60th parallel. Almost without exception, their destination is the Antarctic Peninsula, which extends northwards for about 300 miles from the permanently frozen landmass. The western side of this peninsula is usually free of ice during the short summer, which makes it possible to find the occasional sheltered anchorage. In some milder years, the peninsula can be free of ice as far south as 70°S, but this is quite rare. The number of protected harbours is very small and any boat venturing that far south should be totally self-sufficient in every respect, as well as strong enough to withstand the danger of collision with floating ice, or even the possibility of being frozen in.

Almost the entire surface of the continental landmass of approximately 5 million sq miles is permanently covered by ice, the thickness of which can reach as much as 6000 ft (2000 m). In spite of the low temperatures, which never rise above freezing, Antarctic flora and fauna is very rich. To study and protect the Antarctic, and also to carry out research in various fields, the international community has agreed to administer the territory jointly. These provisions are encompassed in the Antarctic Treaty which was signed in 1959 by Argentina, Australia, Belgium, Chile, France, Japan, New Zealand, Norway, South Africa, the USSR, United Kingdom and USA, who all had maintained research stations there during the International Geophysical Year, 1957–8. The Treaty came into force in 1961; since then a total of 44 countries have acceded to it. The Treaty reserves the Antarctic area south of 60°S latitude for peaceful purposes, provides for international co-operation in scientific investigation and research, and preserves for the duration of the Treaty, the status quo as regards territorial rights and claims. In 1991 a Protocol on Environmental Protection was signed by the Treaty parties. The Protocol came into force in January 1998 following ratification by all consultative parties to the Antarctic Treaty. The Protocol consists of a framework document laying out a series of environmental principles contained in five annexes. These deal with environmental impact assessment, conservation of flora and fauna, waste disposal and management, prevention of marine pollution, and protected areas.

All expeditions to Antarctica south of 60°S must obtain permission from the national Antarctic operator or the relevant government department. The Antarctic guidelines do not apply north of 60°S.

Aventura III *in Antarctica.*

Formalities

Any vessel intending to visit Antarctica must obtain written permission from its national authority responsible for the implementation of the Antarctic Treaty and Protocol. For the time being, boats continue to arrive without such permits and this appears to be tolerated, but the situation may change. British vessels are not supposed to sail into Antarctic waters without permission from the relevant department in the Foreign and Commonwealth Office. Penalties are very severe if this ruling is not observed. The US and French authorities take a more lenient view.

Although various countries claim sovereignty over parts of the Antarctic territory, the only one relevant for cruising boats is Chile, which controls the area south of the Beagle Channel, including Cape Horn, and also claims much of the Antarctic Peninsula. As these are the areas where the majority of cruising boats would go, it is essential to complete the necessary formalities in Puerto Williams before proceeding south. This is in any case a good insurance as the most likely source of help, should

there be an emergency, is the Chilean Navy.

The Chilean authorities do not impose any restrictions on a vessel intending to visit the Antarctic Peninsula, but certain formalities must be completed in Puerto Williams, both before going and on one's return.

Once in Antarctica there are no formalities to be completed and yachts are free to cruise, subject to various restrictions. Most of these are self-imposed and self-controlled. The success of them being observed depends entirely on the captain and crew of each individual yacht, who should do everything in their power to protect the fragile environment.

Restrictions

The following rules must be observed in order to comply with the Antarctic Treaty conservation provisions. The signatories to the Antarctic Protocol take a tough view for the need to implement its various provisions. In the case of the UK, the Antarctic Act 1994 provides for any offences to be punishable by a prison sentence or fine, or both.

1 No killing or capturing of any wildlife (seals and birds) nor collection of eggs.
2 Minimal interference with plants, animals and soil. Visitors should keep their distance from wildlife, especially when breeding, and not touch or disturb them. Nothing should be removed, including plants and rocks, and historical evidence of human activity left undisturbed.
3 There are some 50 Protected Areas in Antarctica, so designated because of the need to restrict human disturbance. They can only be visited with a permit issued under the authority of an Antarctic Treaty participating government. Applications should be made to one of the Antarctic national committees or institutes. The list of areas is subject to change and an up-to-date list should be consulted prior to one's visit. There are also unofficial restricted areas near the scientific bases and on the subantarctic islands; information on these should be requested from the bases.
4 No introduction of non-indigenous flora or fauna, diseases, parasites. No pets are allowed into the Treaty area. All litter must be returned to the yacht; biodegradable waste can be disposed of at sea as far off the coast as possible – larger vessels (more than 12 crew) must go 12 miles offshore.

5 Entry into protected areas requires separate applications for permits and these would only be issued if there was an overriding benefit to scientific research.

The Chilean base Marsh, on King George Island, South Shetlands, may wish to be informed of a vessel's name and number of crew, for search and rescue information only. Marsh has a regular air link to Chile.

If wishing to visit a base, the base commander should be contacted first by VHF (Channels 12 or 16) to request permission.

Navigation

Charts may be incomplete or inaccurate; care should be taken over uncharted rocks.

Facilities

Neither provisions nor repair facilities are available and, for one's own safety, one should not expect to rely on outside help. The personnel of the research stations are usually far too busy to help out, and their resources are also limited, so help can only be expected in serious emergencies.

There are several bases along the Antarctic Peninsula and most of them are manned during the summer months, when the area is most likely to be visited by cruising boats. None of them should be visited without prior arrangement, or they should be at least contacted on VHF radio before going ashore. The nearest are the Chilean and Argentine bases in Paradise Harbour (64°53′S 62°52′W), the Ukraine base at the Argentine Islands (formerly the British Faraday base at 65°15′S 64°16′W) and the US Palmer base on Anvers Island (64°45′S 64°03′W).

The UK Antarctic Heritage Trust usually has a person on duty during the summer months at the former base, now a museum, at Port Lockroy on Wiencke Island (64°49′S 63°31′W).

BRITISH ANTARCTIC TERRITORY

The British Antarctic Territory was established in 1962 and encompasses the lands and islands within the area south of 60°S lying between 20°W and 80°W. The area of approximately 500,000 sq miles (1.3 million sq km) includes the South Orkney and

South Shetland Islands and the Antarctic Peninsula (Palmer Land and Graham Land). There is no permanent population, but there is always a number of scientists and other personnel manning the various research stations.

SUBANTARCTIC AND SOUTHERN OCEAN ISLANDS

These lie north of 60°S and the Antarctic Treaty Area, so are administered by their respective governments. Most are uninhabited and often have pristine environments unspoilt by human contact. To preserve this, visits are restricted or prohibited. Yachts should exercise strict precautions to avoid introducing non-native animals (e.g. rats) or pests, which has already occurred in some places much to the detriment of the indigenous flora and fauna. It is best to follow guidelines as those for the Antarctic.

BOUVETOYA
54°26′S 3°24′E. A Norwegian possession and protected nature reserve.

SOUTH GEORGIA AND SOUTH SANDWICH ISLANDS
South Georgia lies 800 miles ESE of the Falkland Islands, while the South Sandwich Islands are 470 miles SE of South Georgia. Argentina made claims to the islands and in 1982 invaded South Georgia, site of a British Antarctic Survey Base; three weeks later British forces recaptured it, also expelling the Argentinians who had lived on the previously uninhabited South Sandwich Islands from 1976. In 1985 all the islands ceased to be governed as dependencies of the Falklands and are now administered by the Commissioner for South Georgia and the South Sandwich Islands, based in Stanley. The British government extended its territorial jurisdiction from 12 to 200 miles offshore in 1993 to conserve fishing stocks. Argentina still maintains its claim to the islands and British naval forces patrol the islands regularly. There is a permanent military base at Grytviken, the administrative centre of South Georgia.

Port of entry
King Edward Point, South Georgia 53°56′S 34°45′W.

Procedure on arrival
Report to King Edward Point; customs and immi-

gration formalities will be carried out by the Officer in Charge or the Harbour Master. There is a harbour fee of £44.

Restrictions
Visits are only allowed with permission of the Commissioner for South Georgia and the South Sandwich Islands, Stanley, Falkland Islands.

The islands' native flora and fauna are protected under the Falkland Islands Dependencies Ordinance.

NEW ZEALAND'S SUBANTARCTIC ISLANDS
These islands lie south of New Zealand. They are administered as Nature Reserves by the Department of Conservation (DOC), PO Box 473, Invercargill, New Zealand. Tourism is allowed and various cruise ships visit the islands from New Zealand, but all visits are strictly controlled by the DOC. All indigenous flora and fauna is protected by legislation. Quarantine is strict to prevent the introduction of non-native pests; DOC officials may carry out checks at the ports of departure from New Zealand. No animals are permitted on board vessels visiting the islands.

Entry to the islands is by permit only, issued by the DOC, and a landing fee of NZ$150 is charged per person. There is an annual quota of tourists allowed to visit each site. All visitors, including those on yachts, must be accompanied by an official DOC guide.

Visits with permits are possible on the following islands, at the landing points approved by the guide: Campbell Island (52°33′S 169°09′E), Auckland Islands (50°50′S 166°00′E). The Bounty Islands (47°42′S 179°03′E) are restricted to small special interest groups. Visitors are not allowed to land on the Antipodes Islands (49°41′S 178°48′E) or Snares Islands (48°02′S 166°35′S).

AUSTRALIAN ANTARCTIC TERRITORY (AAT)
The AAT, with a total land area of 5,800,000 sq km, consists of all islands and territories south of latitude 60°S and between longitudes 45° and 160° east except for the French sector of Terre Adélie (which comprises the islands and territories south of 60°S latitude and between longitudes 136° and 142° east). The AAT is the single largest sector of the continent and covers much of east Antarctica. There are three stations (Mawson, Davis and Casey), and various summer bases and temporary field camps. There is a temporary population of scientists, ranging from about 70 in winter to 200 in summer.

AUSTRALIAN SUBANTARCTIC ISLANDS
Heard, McDonald and Macquarie Islands in the South Indian Ocean are owned by Australia. All three have uniquely unspoilt environments. Access is by permit only; applications may be made to: The Australian Antarctic Division, Kingston 7050, Tasmania, Australia.

The environment is protected by various prohibitions: the import of live organisms or dead poultry; any interference with or collecting of native life; leaving any material or waste ashore; interfering with any buildings, scientific experiments, etc.

Heard Island (53°05'S 73°30'E) and McDonald Island (53°03'S 72°36'E) have only been visited by a few scientific expeditions and remain unspoilt.

Macquarie Island (54°38'S 158°54'E) is administered by Tasmania as a Nature Reserve and limited tourism is allowed. A permit for entry can be obtained from: Tasmanian Dept. of Parks, Wildlife & Heritage, PO Box 861J, Hobart 7001, Tasmania, Australia. A landing fee is charged per person. There is a permanent research station on the island. Visits may only be made with the permission of the Australian Antarctic Division.

FRENCH SUBANTARCTIC TERRITORY (TERRITOIRE DES TERRE AUSTRALES ET ANTARCTIQUES FRANÇAISES (TAAF))
This consists of the islands of Saint-Paul, Amsterdam, Crozet and Kerguelen which are French possessions. Wildlife is protected by a National Park Act. There are several Protected Areas which may be visited by permit only. Yachts should call first at one of the TAAF research stations and contact the 'Chef de District'.

Ports of entry
Martin-de-Vives, Ile Amsterdam 37°50'S 77°35'E
Port Alfred, Ile de Possession 46°25'S 51°45'E (Iles Crozet archipelago)
Port-aux-Français, Grande Terre 48°00'S 68°45'E (Iles Kerguelen)

SOUTH AFRICAN SUBANTARCTIC ISLANDS
Marion Island 46°54'S 37°45'E
Prince Edward Island 46°38'S 37°57'E
Both these islands are nature reserves where wildlife is protected. Tourism is not encouraged. A permit to visit is necessary, obtainable from: South African Scientific Committee for Antarctic Research (SASCAR), The Foundation for Research Development, Council for Scientific & Industrial Research, PO Box 395, Pretoria 0001.

Further Reading

Antarctica: An Introductory Guide (lists addresses of national institutes)
Antarctic Treaty Handbook (gives maps and descriptions of Protected Areas)
Southern Ocean Cruising

Websites

www.quest.arc.nasa.gov/antarctica (Useful links)
www.iaato.org (International Association of Antarctic Tour Operators)
www.dotrs.gov.au/terr/aat (Australian Antarctic Territories)

ASCENSION ISLAND

A mountainous peak rising from the floor of the Atlantic Ocean, Ascension is a dormant volcanic island like Tristan da Cunha and the Azores on the mid-Atlantic volcanic ridge. Lava flows have formed a barren twisted landscape. The highest peak, Green Mountain, rises to 2817 ft (859 m). The 34 sq mile island is a communications centre for Cable & Wireless, the BBC, the RAF, the US Air Force and the European Ariane project. As a traditional port of call for ships on the Cape of Good Hope route, the few yachts that sail on this route sometimes stop at Ascension. Only short stops are normally allowed, but in genuine emergencies help is always at hand. Because of their isolation, people who work on the island are friendly and hospitable.

Country Profile

The island was discovered in 1501, and visited on and off by sailors who took turtles and eggs for food, and left goats behind. Ascension became a well-known stopping point for ships, but was only settled in 1815, when Britain feared attempts to free Napoleon from St Helena. The settlement developed and labourers came from the Gold Coast as well as freed slaves. After Napoleon's death in 1821, the island was used as a naval supply base and convalescent home for sailors. At the end of the century the Eastern Telegraph Company, now Cable & Wireless, landed a submarine cable, which marked the end of the island's isolation from the outside world. Ascension had been administered by the British Navy, but in 1922 St Helena took over this administration, while Eastern Telegraph took control on behalf of St Helena. The Americans arrived in 1942 to fortify this unprotected vital communications centre, and constructed the Wideawake Airfield, named after the thousands of wideawake terns which settle there for breeding. During the Second World War planes refuelled here on the route from Brazil to Africa. In the 1950s the United States established a missile tracking station and a NASA earth station, which tracked the Apollo missions.

Communications projects are the dominant factor in the economy. St Helenians come to Ascension to work. Income also comes from the sale of stamps. The water supply is always a concern, due to the low annual rainfall and since 1967 distilled water has been used. English is the

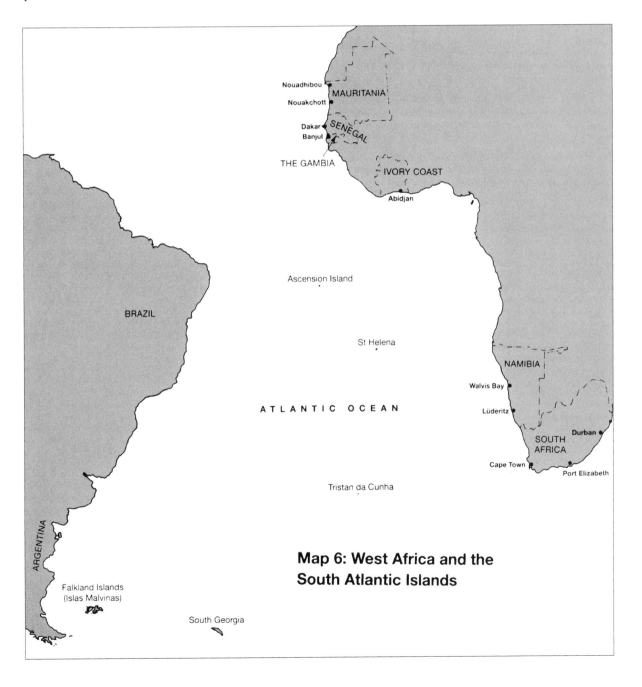

Map 6: West Africa and the South Atlantic Islands

Practical Information

LOCAL TIME: GMT

BUOYAGE: IALA A

CURRENCY: St Helenian pound (£) of 100 pence.

BUSINESS HOURS
Government offices: 0800–1630 Monday to Saturday.

ELECTRICITY: 240 V, 50 Hz

PUBLIC HOLIDAYS
1 January: New Year's Day
Good Friday and Easter Monday
Ascension Day
Queen's Birthday
Whit Monday
August Bank Holiday
25, 26 December: Christmas

COMMUNICATIONS
Cable and Wireless office for international calls.
Only military aircraft use the airport, mostly Royal Air Force. Civilian passengers are carried; contact Curnow Shipping in Britain for bookings. Fax. + 00 44 (0) 1326 212808, e-mail: reservations@curnow-shipping.co.uk.

MEDICAL
There is a hospital with limited facilities.

---

language of the island and Georgetown is the capital. The resident population is approximately 1000, comprising employees and families working for one of the organisations, being mostly St Helenians.

The climate is tropical, hot and dry. The island is under the influence of the SE trade winds for most of the year. The weather can change rapidly.

Entry Regulations

Port of entry
Clarence Bay, Georgetown 7°56′S 14°25′W.

Procedure on arrival
Yachts should anchor in the area north of the Pierhead, in a position which does not obstruct ships arriving, departing or unloading cargo. Yachts must not tie up to any buoy or mooring in Clarence Bay. Landing is permitted only at Pierhead steps. No advance notice is required of arrival, but at the earliest opportunity the captain must report to the Police Office, who also act as immigration officials, with the yacht's details, crew list and passports. This must be done within working hours, as no yachts are attended to outside of normal working hours. The crew must wait on board if a yacht arrives outside of these hours.

Crew may not leave a yacht at Ascension.

It is not allowed to clear out on the day before departure, so one should plan on leaving on a normal working day.

Customs
Firearms must remain on board. Animals must remain on board and are not allowed ashore.

Immigration
All those landing must pay an entry permit fee of £7.50 per person. Yachts may normally stay for up to three days, but the authorities are relaxed about this. The crew may go ashore between 0700 and 2300. They may only stay ashore if booked into the Georgetown Guest House. Sleeping rough is not permitted.

Health
Yellow fever vaccination certificates are required if coming from some African countries.

Fees
Light dues are payable at £1.50 per 100 tons (up to 500 tons), minimum charge £10. Medical insurance sufficient to cover a medical evacuation by air is compulsory. It is available on the island at £4 per day. Existing policies are acceptable.

Restrictions
Yachts are not allowed to anchor anywhere except Clarence Bay.

Facilities

There is no public transport or taxis, although cars may be hired. There is only a small number of bars and cafes. Fresh produce and other provisions are sometimes in short supply and may not be available for yachts even if on sale to the islanders. The Georgetown shop, although not intended for visiting yachts, has a good stock of tinned food and drinks. There is no cooking gas on the island. Water may not be freely available. Only minor repairs can be effected, although in a serious emergency one may be able to enlist the help of the AIS (Ascension Island Services) who service the island boats and lighters. The AIS should be approached if help is needed.

Further Reading

St Helena including Ascension Island and Tristan da Cunha

Website

www.ascension-island.gov.ac (Island Administrator)

FALKLAND ISLANDS

The Falkland Islands, also known as Islas Malvinas, are a British colony in the South Atlantic. The archipelago is made up of two groups of over 700 islands, East Falkland and its adjacent islands, and West Falkland. The islands lie about 480 miles north-east of Cape Horn. Port Stanley is the main town, where most people live, and the rest of the country is called the 'camp'.

The Falklands used to be an important port of call for sailing ships on the Cape Horn route and the hulks of abandoned square riggers scattered around Port Stanley harbour bear silent witness to that glorious era and its magnificent ships. The Falklands' traditional role as a convenient stop for reprovisioning has been resuscitated in the last few years by modern yachts, some sailing the classic Cape Horn route, but most being on their way to or from the Straits of Magellan, Tierra del Fuego and the Chilean canals, which are becoming an increasingly popular cruising destination. Only a few have sufficient time to stop long enough in the Falklands to cruise these wild and windswept islands. Although access is restricted in some areas, either for military reasons or because some islands are nature reserves, most of the islands can be visited and a glimpse caught of their spectacular wildlife with large colonies of penguins, sea lions and elephant seals. The weather is the greatest impediment to cruising, as it can change rapidly and without warning, but there are many protected anchorages, so that one is never too far from shelter.

Country Profile

The first recognised sighting of the islands was in 1592 by Captain John Davis in *Desire*. At the end of the seventeenth century the Englishman Strong landed, and named Falkland Sound. French seafarers christened the islands Iles Malouines after their homeport St Malo and later under Spanish influence the name became Islas Malvinas. In the eighteenth century France established a small colony at Port Louis, which two years later was ceded to Spain. The island became a penal colony and a military garrison was stationed there. At the same time Britain established an outpost on Saunders Island, West Falkland, which was expelled in 1770 by Spain, restored after the threat of war, but then later abandoned. During the South American wars of independence at the start of the nineteenth century, Spain also left the islands. Authority was re-established in 1820, when the United Provinces of the River Plate, later to become Argentina, claimed Port Louis. This settlement was destroyed by a US warship after the colonists arrested some American sealers. The Argentinian force was expelled by Britain, and the islands then became a dependency of Britain until the Argentines, still laying claim to the islands, invaded in April 1982. After a brief conflict Britain recaptured the islands. Recently relations between the two countries have been improving, although Argentina has not formally given up her claim.

In 1986 a 150 mile fisheries protection zone was declared and licence fees from Asian and European fleets have quadrupled the islands' revenue. Improvements have been made in education, infrastructure and social benefits. The islands are financially self-sufficient. British aid was granted in 1982 for redevelopment and to support economic development, but there has been no aid since then. The land is devoted to sheep grazing, the wool being exported to the UK. A British military force has been stationed on the islands since the war, or the 'conflict' as the locals refer to it.

The 2100 inhabitants are of British origin, about two-thirds being born in the Falklands. English is the only language.

The climate is temperate, although changeable. Westerlies are frequent, often strong, and their yearly average is 17 knots. Summer winds are more northerly in direction and this is also where the worst gales come from, usually with very little warning. Another local phenomenon occurring during strong westerly winds are the willywaws, violent gusts of winds which are felt in the lee of the islands and in some of the passages between them.

Practical Information

LOCAL TIME: GMT – 4. GMT – 3 second Sunday in September to third Sunday in April.

BUOYAGE: IALA A

CURRENCY: Falklands pound (£). This is not legal tender in the UK, but pounds sterling can be used in the Falklands. Money can be exchanged at the Standard Chartered Bank, Ross Road, Port Stanley. Falklands £s cannot be changed for sterling or other currencies outside of the islands. One can cash personal British cheques with a cheque guarantee card, but credit cards cannot be used.

BUSINESS HOURS
Banks: 0830–1200, 1330–1500 Monday to Friday.
Shops: 0800–1700 Monday to Friday.
Government offices: 0800–1200, 1315–1630.

ELECTRICITY: 240 V, 50 Hz

PUBLIC HOLIDAYS
1 January: New Year's Day
Good Friday
Queen's Birthday
14 June: Liberation Day
14 August: Falklands Day
October Bank Holiday
8 December: Anniversary of the Battle of the Falkland Islands
25, 26 December: Christmas

COMMUNICATIONS
Cable & Wireless for international telephone calls, telegrams and telex, open 0800–2000. Long distance calls can also be made from the Falkland Islands Company, who also allow boats to retrieve their e-mail, provided arrangements are made in advance (fic@horizon.co.fk).The Town Hall, Ross Road, houses the post office and government offices. Other government offices are in the nearby Secretariat. There are two RAF flights a week from Britain via Ascension Island and weekly flights to Punta Arenas, Chile.

MEDICAL
There is a good hospital at Port Stanley.

Entry Regulations

Ports of entry
Port Stanley 51°39′S 57°43′W.

Procedure on arrival
Port Stanley: One should report one's ETA in advance to the authorities on VHF Channel 12. All yachts must enter at Port Stanley, where clearance formalities are completed. Yachts anchor in the inner harbour, but to clear in it is usually possible to come alongside the wharf. More conveniently located is the small dock off the Falkland Islands Company office. Permission should be asked to come alongside there rather than at the commercial wharf in the eastern part of the large harbour. The boat is visited by a government official who has both customs and immigration duties. The service is prompt and efficient and there are no other clearance formalities.

Fox Bay East: This is a port of entry for vessels over 50 tons and certain restrictions apply to yachts intending to clear there. The authorities insist that anyone intending to clear at Fox Bay must give at least one week's notice. Vessels clearing in at Fox Bay must also bear the cost of return fares for customs officials to fly out from Port Stanley.

Customs
Firearms must be declared to authorities, but may be kept on board.

Animals must remain on board, unless quaran-

tined ashore with permission of the Veterinary Department. Animals must be kept below decks while the yacht is alongside a berth.

Immigration
The following nationalities do not need visas: EU countries, Australia, Canada, Cyprus, Iceland, Israel, Japan, Liechtenstein, Malta, New Zealand, Norway, Switzerland, the USA, Uruguay and dependencies of the UK. Nationals who require visas to enter the Falklands are only allowed to go ashore during daylight hours. Argentine nationals, travelling on Argentine passports, will not be permitted ashore. Exceptions are made in the case of close relatives visiting war graves. As relations with Argentina are slowly improving, current restrictions applied to Argentine yachts with Argentine crews may also be lifted.

Yachts may stay up to 30 days, unless given permission by the harbour master to stay longer.

Fees
Harbour dues are paid for an initial one-month period and are £44 for any vessel with sails as its main propulsion.

Entry fee £20, clearance fee £20.

Overtime is charged outside of working hours; customs have a minimum 2 hour charge: £19 per hour, £28.50 per hour outside office hours.

Minefields
These are left from the 1982 war, but are clearly marked and fenced off. They are mainly areas

around Port Stanley, Port Howard, Fox Bay and Fitzroy. A map of the mined areas can be obtained from the Army office in Port Stanley.

Facilities

Provisioning is good, as the local shops are well stocked and there is also some fresh produce grown locally. Large quantities of provisions can be ordered directly from the Falkland Islands Corporation. Port Stanley has become the winter base for some of the charter boats plying the South Atlantic. As a result, repair facilities have improved considerably and one should first contact the Falkland Islands Company, which has a number of skilled workers for welding, carpentry, diesel engines, electrics, freezer and fridge repairs. They can also arrange for fuel deliveries (larger quantities by tanker), laundry to be collected, the booking of flights, excursions and hire cars. Simple sail repairs are undertaken by Matthew Jackson, the local baker who is also an upholsterer. Fuel is available at the service station. LPG can only be decanted into non-standard tanks, or the tanks have to be sent by freighter to Chile for refilling, which may take up to one month. Those wishing to leave their boats for longer may store them ashore. This is done by FIPASS (Falklands Interim Port and Storage System), who operate 2 miles outside Stanley. The Falkland Islands Corporation has a 60-ton slip and can do some repairs. There is also a government slip and also a crane that can lift boats of up to 40 tons, but there are no slings available locally. Some provisions, mainly locally grown vegetables and meat, may be obtained in the other settlements. There are also some facilities in Fox Bay East, on West Falkland.

Further Reading

Falkland Island Shores
South American Handbook

Websites

www.tourism.org.fk (Falkland Islands Tourist Board)
www.fidc.org.fk (Falkland Islands Development Corporation)
www.website.lineone.net

THE GAMBIA

Surrounded on all sides by Senegal with only a narrow outlet to the Atlantic Ocean, The Gambia is a thin ribbon of land stretching along the Gambia river. The 300-mile long river is the heart of this small country, which rarely exceeds 20 miles in width. The river is navigable for 169 miles. Some 17 miles upriver lies James Island, site of an infamous slave market. Many yachts have sailed upriver recently without encountering any problems. The bird and wildlife is prolific and there are many villages along the river banks, where it is possible to stop and barter for food.

For the ordinary tourist The Gambia's prime attraction are the vast stretches of undeveloped beaches, while upriver is the much visited village of Juffure, from where the main character in the *Roots* book was abducted and taken as a slave to America. Other interesting sites are Abuko nature reserve and the Wassau burial sites, whose huge stone columns are said to be at least 1200 years old.

Country Profile

The region has been inhabited at least since AD 750. Islam was introduced during the time when it was part of the empire of Mali. The Portuguese were the first European visitors in 1455 and they introduced groundnuts and cotton. In the sixteenth and seventeenth centuries England established a garrison and slaving post at Fort James, while France had a trading post across the river. There was rivalry between them for slaves, ivory and gold and eventually The Gambia was awarded to Britain in the Treaty of Versailles at the end of the eighteenth century. Slavery was abolished in 1807, and British ships patrolled the coast trying to enforce the ban.

The Gambia was administered from Sierra Leone until 1888 when it became a British Crown Colony. Very little was done by Britain to develop the country.

Independence was gained in 1965 and The Gambia became a republic seven years later. There was a military coup in 1981, but this was ousted with the aid of Senegalese troops. A Confederation called Senegambia lasted from 1982 to 1989. The Gambia has some economic problems, but is politically stable.

The economy depends on groundnuts, which are the main crop, and efforts to diversify have not

Practical Information

LOCAL TIME: GMT

BUOYAGE: IALA A

CURRENCY: Gambian dalasi (GAD) of 100 bututs. Certain African currencies cannot be exchanged including those of Algeria, Morocco and Tunisia. CFA francs are accepted. All foreign currency must be declared on arrival.

BUSINESS HOURS
Banks: 0800–1300 Monday to Thursday, 0800–1100 Friday.
Business: 0800/0900–1500 Monday to Thursday (closed for lunch), 0800/0900–1300 Friday.
Shops: 0900–2000 Monday to Saturday, 1000–1800 Friday.
Government offices: 0800–1500 Monday to Thursday, 0800–1300 Friday, Saturday.

ELECTRICITY: 220 V, 50 Hz

PUBLIC HOLIDAYS
1 January: New Year's Day
18 February: Independence Day
Good Friday, Easter Monday
Eid el-Fitr
1 May: Labour Day
Eid el-Adha
15 August: Assumption
Mouloud
25, 26 December: Christmas

COMMUNICATIONS
Cable & Wireless: Mercury House, Telegraph Road, Banjul for telephone calls and telex. Direct international calls can also be made from one of the Gamtel offices, some open 24 hours, also offering fax services.
Post office: 0800–1300 Monday to Friday,

0800–1100 Saturday.
There are regular flights to London and African cities, plus charter flights to European destinations from November to April.

MEDICAL
The Medical Research Clinic, Fajara, is British-run. Westfield Clinic (German-run private clinic), Pipeline Road. Tel. 92213.

DIPLOMATIC MISSIONS
In Banjul:
Mauritania: 12 Clarkson Street.
Tel. 27 690.
Senegal: 10 Nelson Mandela Street.
Tel. 227 469.
United Kingdom: 48 Atlantic Road, Fajara.
Tel. 495 133.
United States: Kairaba Avenue, Fajara.
Tel. 392 858 or 392 856.

been very successful. Tourism brings some income. There is a large trade deficit.

The population is 1.2 million and the land is densely populated. The Mandinka are descendants of rulers of the old Mali empire and live mostly inland, while the Wolof live mainly in Banjul. There are also Fulani and ten other ethnic groups. Most of the population are Muslim, with some Animist and Christian minorities. English is the official language, but Mandinka, Fula, Wolof, Jola and Serahule are also spoken.

Originally called Bathurst, Banjul the capital was founded in 1816 on the tip of the peninsula at the river mouth, which is in fact an island.

The climate is tropical with two distinct seasons. The dry and more pleasant weather is from November until May, while the remainder is the wet season. The hottest months are from February to May. The winds are variable throughout the year, with the strongest winds in September and October.

Entry Regulations

Port of entry
Banjul 13°27′N 16°34′W.

Procedure on arrival
The average depth in the channel is 30 ft (9 m). Vessels should keep all buoys to starboard when

entering. Port Control keeps a continuous watch on VHF Channel 16 on weekdays and should be contacted prior to arrival.

Yachts normally proceed to the government wharf for inspection by the various officials. There may be space for a yacht to come alongside at the new commercial dock. The captain should then visit the harbour master at the Port Authority building in Wellington Street, then immigration in Anglesea Street, customs and finally health. Although the officials are very friendly, the formalities tend to be time-consuming. It has been recommended to hire a taxi and guide to do the rounds of the various offices.

The Gambia Yachting Association acts as an agent for visiting yachts and will approach yachts on arrival to offer their services with clearance formalities. The fee should be agreed in advance.

Customs
Firearms and animals must be declared.

Immigration
For a stay of up to three months no visas are required from nationals of Commonwealth countries and European Union countries with the exception of nationals of Austria, France, Spain and Portugal who do need visas. Normally seven days are granted on arrival and this can be extended to up to three months at the Immigration Office, Anglesea and Dobson Street, Banjul. Other

nationals including citizens of the United States and Japan must obtain visas in advance.

British embassies issue Gambian visas in countries with no Gambian representative. The British embassy in Dakar issues visas the same day.

Health

Proof of yellow fever vaccination is required when clearing in. Malaria prophylaxis should be started one week prior to arrival.

Cholera may be a risk. Water should be treated.

Facilities

There is good provisioning in Banjul, where there are several supermarkets. Fresh produce is also available. Fuel is available in the harbour from the Con Oil fuel barge. Some repairs can be made at the shipyard run by the port authority which also has a slipway. The Gambia Sailing Club in Banjul has some sailing enthusiasts who organise regular races and will help visitors if needed.

The Gambia Yachting Association, 45 Leman Street, Banjul. *Tel.* 229 377 can assist with provisioning, fuel, water, excursions into the interior and also guarding an unattended boat. Prices should be agreed in advance. There have been several reports of theft from yachts in the Banjul area.

Further Reading

West Africa – a travel survival kit
Cruising Guide to West Africa

Website

www.gambia.com/tourism

IVORY COAST

The Ivory Coast or La Côte d'Ivoire lies on the northern shore of the Gulf of Guinea in West Africa. Until not long ago it was regarded as the most stable regime in the region and has tried to build up its tourism as an alternative to the agriculture-dominated economy. The capital Abidjan is a pleasant modern city and most yachts who visit the Ivory Coast rarely go anywhere else, apparently content with Abidjan's transplanted French ambience.

Country Profile

As the European colonial powers extended their influence throughout Africa and especially along the coast, France became interested in establishing a trade monopoly in this region and therefore signed treaties with several local chiefs, giving France the right to trade freely in the area. Towards the end of the nineteenth century France took outright control of the region. A cash crop economy was rapidly established and the local inhabitants were used as labour on the predominantly French-owned plantations.

After the Second World War discontent grew amongst the Ivorians, who demanded a greater say in local administration, and 1948–9 saw violent demonstrations, which were repressed by the French authorities. Independence was finally achieved in 1960, under the Presidency of Felix Houphouet-Boigny, a founder member of the independence movement. France has remained quite involved with the Ivorian economy, and until the mid-1980s many French expatriates worked there, but these have been gradually replaced with Ivorians. In 1990 a serious political and social crisis led the President to end one party rule. On his death in 1993, Henri Konan Bédié became head of state.

The population is 15 million, composed of over 60 tribes, the main one being the Baoulé. There are also many expatriate workers from neighbouring African states, as well as France and Lebanon. French is the official language and also spoken are five main African languages, among them Dioula, Baoulé and Bete. Some of the population follow traditional beliefs, while 40 per cent are Muslim and 26 per cent Christian. Abidjan is still the commercial capital and main port, but the political capital since 1986 has been the former village of Yamoussoukro, the birthplace of President Houphouet-Boigny.

The climate in the south of the country is hot and humid with a high rainfall. The north is drier, November to April being the dry season and May to October the rainy season. October to May is the most pleasant time. The winds are light throughout the year, the prevailing winds being SSW Force 2 to 3. The weather has been described as perfect for all year round sailing.

Entry Regulations

Port of entry
Abidjan 5°18′N 4°00′W.

Practical Information

LOCAL TIME: GMT

BUOYAGE: IALA A

CURRENCY: West African franc (CFA Fr.). A maximum of CFA 100,000 may be exported.

BUSINESS HOURS
Banks: 0800–1130, 1430–1630 Monday to Friday.
Shops: 0800–1200, 1600–1900 Monday to Saturday.
Government offices: 0800–1200 Monday to Saturday, 1430–1700 Monday to Friday.

ELECTRICITY: 220 V, 50 Hz

PUBLIC HOLIDAYS
1 January: New Year's Day
Easter Monday, Good Friday

1 May: Labour Day
Ascension
Whit Monday
15 August: Assumption
1 November: All Saints' Day
7 December: National Day
25 December: Christmas Day
Variable religious holidays: Korite (end of Ramadan), Tabaski (Eid el Kebir).

COMMUNICATIONS
The main post office (PTT) is by the railway station in Le Plateau, Abidjan, open 0730–1200, 1430–1800 Monday to Friday; international calls can be made from here or from the Hotel Ivoire. The international airport at Abidjan has regular flights to several European and African cities.

MEDICAL
Polyclinique Internationale Sainte Anne

Marie, Deux Plateaux. *Tel.* 44 5132.

DIPLOMATIC MISSIONS
In Abidjan:
Canada: Immeuble Trade Center, 23 Avenue Nogues, Le Plateau, CP4101. *Tel.* 212009.
France: Rue Le Coeur, Le Plateau. *Tel.* 21 6749.
Mauritania: Rue Pierre et Marie Curie, Deux Plateaux. *Tel.* 35 2068.
Senegal: Residence Nabil, Rue du Commerce. *Tel.* 32 2876 (also issues visas for Gambia).
United Kingdom: 3rd floor, Immeuble Les Harmonies, Boulevard Carde and Avenue Dr Jamot, Le Plateau. *Tel.* 22 6850.
United States: 5 Rue Jesse Owens. *Tel.* 21 0979.

Procedure on arrival

Yachts should try and come to the main dock to clear customs and immigration. If there is no space, yachts normally anchor at Carena, close to the centre of town, or at the local yacht club (Centre de Voile Abidjanaise).

Customs

Firearms and animals must be declared.

Immigration

No visas are required for a stay up to three months for nationals of Andorra, Monaco, Morocco, the Seychelles, Tunisia, the USA and African ECOWAS countries. No visas are required by South Africans for stays up to 30 days. All other nationals need visas.

There are Ivorian representatives in Paris, Dakar, Rabat, Algiers and Tunis.

Health

Vaccination against yellow fever is compulsory; cholera vaccinations and malaria prophylaxis are recommended.

Facilities

Although yachting facilities are virtually non-existent, the yacht club in Abidjan welcomes visitors and may be able to help in an emergency. There are various workshops in the industrial zone south of the city. Provisioning is good and if anchored off the yacht club, it is a short walk to Gare Langunaire, from where a ferry goes to the shopping centre. Fresh produce is best at the central market in Treichville, which is the African part of Abidjan, as opposed to Le Plateau which is more French.

Apart from the anchorage off the yacht club, there is also good shelter in the lagoon, which can be navigated for a long distance but only by shallow drafted yachts, as the depths are less than 4 ft (1.20 m).

Limited facilities are available at Grand Lahou, which has a small boat club at the end of a long inlet. Provisions are available and also some repairs at a workshop, which also does welding. Minimal facilities only are available at Sassandra and Grand Bassam, the former colonial capital.

Further Reading

West Africa – a travel survival kit

Website

www.tourisme.ci

MAURITANIA

Stretching along the west coast of Africa between Morocco and Senegal, a large part of Mauritania is the Sahara Desert. The republic is based on an Islamic socialist constitution and a traditional Muslim society, and does not particularly encourage tourism. Its long coastline has very few natural harbours and the never-ending sandy beaches are its most remarkable feature. For those in search of solitude this might be sufficient attraction, but otherwise the country has very little to offer the cruising sailor.

Country Profile

Mauritania once enjoyed some prosperity, lying on the trade route between the Maghreb and West Africa. During the nineteenth century the country was added to France's large colonial possessions in West and Central Africa.

Independence from France was gained in 1960 when French West Africa was broken up. When Spain abandoned its colony in the Western Sahara, Mauritania divided the region with Morocco, but the burden of war with the Polisario guerillas seeking independence for the region led to the abandonment of Mauritania's claims to the Western Sahara.

The production of iron ore for export is the mainstay of the economy, although efforts have been made to diversify. Foreign aid remains important and much food is imported. With the exception of the iron mines, the country is very undeveloped and many people still lead an existence bordering on the primitive. Slavery was only officially abolished in 1980 and a rigid feudal system still survives in remote communities.

There are around 2 million inhabitants. The 'white' Moors, of Arab and Berber descent, make up around 90 per cent of the population. The remainder are 'black' Moors, Africans who adopted the Moorish identity, and the southern population of black Africans, related ethnically to the Senegalese. Ethnic conflict between the Moors and Africans erupted in violent riots in 1989, leading to the expulsion of thousands of black Africans, including many Senegalese living in Mauritania, over the southern border, which remains closed between the two countries. Arabic is the official language and some local languages are also spoken. Islam is the official religion. The capital is Nouakchott.

Most of the land has a harsh desert climate. The climate is better along the coast where the prevailing winds are northerly. The rainy season is from July to September, when it sometimes rains heavily. A strong swell is often felt along the coast from January to March.

Entry Regulations

Ports of entry
Nouadhibou 20°54′N 17°03′W, Nouakchott 18°02′N 16°02′W.

Procedure on arrival
Nouadhibou: This is the main commercial port. The port authority (Etablissement Maritime) should be contacted on arrival on VHF Channel 16 for instructions. There is an inner quay where a yacht can come alongside for clearance. The yacht may be searched.

Nouakchott: The port authority (Etablissement Maritime) should be contacted on VHF Channel 16. The main wharf in the port is some four miles south of the capital. This port is not protected in bad weather and if there is too much swell, a boat should put to sea.

On arrival, a currency and valuables declaration form must be completed and visitors must report to the police in the first large town.

For those travelling overland to Mali, there is a checkpoint to pass through and a number of checkpoints when travelling south to Nouadhibou.

Customs
Firearms and animals must be declared. The import of alcohol is prohibited.

Immigration
Visas are required by all visitors except the citizens of France and Italy.

There are Mauritanian representatives in Paris, Abidjan, Algiers, Dakar, Rabat and Las Palmas.

Health
Yellow fever vaccination is required. Malaria prophylaxis is recommended; cholera is a risk.

Facilities

The only repair facilities available are at Nouakchott where there is a shipyard which may take on work on a yacht in an emergency. Fuel is

Practical Information

LOCAL TIME: GMT

BUOYAGE: IALA A

CURRENCY: Ouguiya (U) of 5 khoums. The import and export of local currency is forbidden. Foreign currency must be declared on arrival. Ouguiyas cannot be exchanged outside Mauritania.

BUSINESS HOURS
Working hours: 0800–1200, 1400–1600/1800. Closed Fridays. Banks: 0730–1430 Sunday to Thursday.

ELECTRICITY: 220 V, 50 Hz

PUBLIC HOLIDAYS
1 January: New Year's Day
26 February
8 March: Women's Day
1 May: Labour Day
25 May: Africa Liberation Day
28 November: Independence Day
Also variable holidays: Mouloud, Korite (end of Ramadan), Tabaski (Eid el Kebir), First Moharem.

COMMUNICATIONS
International calls can be made in Nouakchott and Nouadhibou, through the operator. The main post office in Nouakchott, Ave. Nassar, is open daily.

There are regular flights from Nouakchott to Las Palmas de Gran Canaria, Casablanca and Paris. Flights from Nouadhibou also go to Las Palmas and Casablanca as well as to Budapest and Moscow.

MEDICAL
There is a hospital in Nouakchott.

DIPLOMATIC MISSIONS
United States: BP222, Rue Abdalaye, Nouakchott, *Tel.* 52660.
France: Rue Ahmed Ould Mohamed, Nouakchott. *Tel.* 251740.
There is a Senegalese mission in Nouakchott.

---

available in both ports and also some basic provisioning. Water should be treated.

Further Reading

West Africa – a travel survival kit

Websites

www.embassy.org/mauritania (Mauritania Embassy in Washington)
www.gksoft.com/govt/en/mr.htm (Useful links)

NAMIBIA

The latest country in Africa to gain independence, Namibia lies on the south-west coast of the continent and as a German colony used to be known as South West Africa. The easternmost area is part of the Kalahari desert, while the Namib desert stretches along the west coast. Most of the coast is inhospitable desert, but inland are many national parks and unusual dramatic scenery.

Yachts sailing this part of the Atlantic usually stop at Luderitz, an old German colonial town surrounded by the encroaching Namib desert. It is a convenient stop on the way north from Cape Town. The winds are usually favourable and so is the Benguela current, which sweeps up the western coast. The detour shortens the distance to St

Helena and, if time permits, also gives a chance to visit some of the interior of this fascinating country, which was for so long in the grip of a guerilla war.

Country Profile

The Portuguese were the first Europeans to sail along the Namibian coast in the fifteenth century on their way around the Cape of Good Hope. Other sailors to pass this way were American whalers in the late eighteenth century. Only at the end of the nineteenth century was a more permanent interest shown when Namibia became a German colony, except for the Walvis Bay enclave which was annexed by Britain. The indigenous tribes fought to preserve their independence and rebelled early in the twentieth century. Repression was fierce and nearly all the Herero tribe were annihilated. Germany relinquished her colonies at the end of the First World War and South Africa was given a League of Nations Mandate to rule South West Africa, continued after the Second World War as a United Nations Mandate.

In the 1950s nationalism and opposition to South African rule grew. SWAPO (South West Africa People's Organisation) was formed in 1960 and mounted a guerrilla war against the South Africans, which gradually escalated. In 1966 the United Nations changed the country's name to Namibia and cancelled the Mandate, but the South African government continued to administer the

Practical Information

LOCAL TIME: GMT + 1, GMT + 2 September to April.

BUOYAGE: IALA A

CURRENCY: Namibian dollar (N$). The import/export of N$ is restricted to N$500. South African rand are also accepted. Foreign currency must be declared on arrival.

BUSINESS HOURS
Banks: 0900–1530 Monday to Friday, 0830–1100 Saturday.
Shops: 0830–1700 Monday to Friday, 0830–1300 Saturday.

Supermarkets also open 1100–1300, 1600–1900 Sunday.
Business: 0730–1630/1700 Monday to Friday.

ELECTRICITY: 220/240 V, 50 Hz

PUBLIC HOLIDAYS
1 January: New Year's Day
21 March: Independence Day
Good Friday, Easter Monday
1 May: Labour Day
4 May: Casinga Day
25 May: Africa Day
26 August: Heroes Day

7 October: Day of Goodwill
10 December: Human Rights Day
25–26 December: Christmas

COMMUNICATIONS
IDD is available. International access code: 00. There are flights from Windhoek to Frankfurt and London.

DIPLOMATIC MISSIONS
In Windhoek:
United Kingdom: 116 Robert Mugabe Ave. *Tel.* 223 022.
United States: Ausspannplatz, 14 Lossen St. *Tel.* 221 601.

---

country and industry was dominated by a white minority. Finally South Africa agreed to negotiations and eventually to withdraw from Namibia. Early in 1990 the Namibians held elections, voted for a black government and independence was gained. Namibia has since been accepted into the Commonwealth.

Namibia is rich in minerals, uranium, copper, lead, zinc and diamonds, and mining is the mainstay of the economy. Agriculture and fishing are also important activities, although the former suffered from drought in the early 1990s. Foreign multinational companies still control most of business and industry, and trade is still predominantly with South Africa. Following independence, Walvis Bay and 12 offshore islands remained under South African jurisdiction, until a 1994 agreement transferred them to Namibia.

The population is 1.5 million. English is the official language and Herero, Owambo, Afrikaans, German, and some others are also spoken. The majority of the population are Christian. The capital is Windhoek.

The weather is usually hot, although it is milder on the coast. Rainfall is unreliable. Winds are mostly from the south. The cold Benguela current produces misty conditions close to the coast and up to about 5 to 10 miles offshore.

Entry Regulations

Ports of entry
Luderitz 26°38′S 15°09′E, Walvis Bay 22°57′S 14°30′E.

Procedure on arrival
Luderitz: This is a safe harbour in all weathers and the approaches are straightforward. One should contact the harbour master or Dias Point Lighthouse on VHF Channel 16 asking permission to enter the harbour. If arriving at night it is best to raft up to one of the tugs until the morning. Yachts can come alongside the commercial wharf for clearance. Customs, immigration and the harbour master's office are on the quayside.

Customs
Firearms must be declared on arrival.

Immigration
Visas are not needed by citizens of Australia, Canada, CIS, Western Europe (except Greece, which requires visas), Japan, Malaysia, New Zealand, Singapore, the USA and some African countries.

Health
Yellow fever vaccination is required if coming from an infected area. Malaria prophylaxis is recommended.

Facilities

In Luderitz the local yacht club welcomes visiting sailors and its facilities are available to visitors. Provisions are available from a selection of supermarkets and water and diesel fuel can be obtained in the harbour. There are some repair facilities here (the port is used by fishing boats working this area of the South Atlantic) and at Walvis Bay.

Further Reading

South Africa Nautical Almanac
Africa on a Shoestring
Zimbabwe, Botswana and Namibia – a travel survival kit

Website

www.iwwn.com.na/namtour (Namibia Tourism Office)

ST HELENA

The island of St Helena lies halfway between Africa and South America, with her two dependencies of Ascension over 700 miles to the north-west and Tristan da Cunha 1500 miles to the south-west. St Helena has only one harbour called The Anchorage. The rest of the coast is towering rocky cliffs backed by green slopes climbing up to the summit of Mount Acteon at 2683 ft (818 m). St Helena became known all over the world when chosen as the place of exile of Napoleon Bonaparte, and Longwood House where he lived for six years is now a museum. One of Britain's last remaining colonial possessions, an English way of life mixes with the influence of the climate and origins of the inhabitants.

St Helena's popularity as a port of call for passenger liners has now been taken over by sailing yachts, a large number of which stop there every year. A warm welcome awaits the visiting sailor ashore in Jamestown, the island's only settlement.

Country Profile

The island was discovered in 1502 by a Portuguese fleet returning from India, but was kept a secret by them, so as to keep it as a port of call for Portuguese ships on that route. In 1516 a Portuguese deserter, Fernando Lopez, stowed away on a ship, but got off at St Helena and lived there for 30 years. Then the island had lush vegetation and fruit trees, which were destroyed by wild goats left by ships. By the end of the sixteenth century a little community had established itself, and the island became known to the rest of the world. Despite Dutch efforts to claim the island, in the mid-seventeenth century the English East India Company set up base there, to protect their interests against Dutch and Spanish privateers and warships. A settlement grew in James Valley, plantations were cultivated and African slaves brought in as labour. A Dutch invasion in 1673 was foiled by Black Oliver, a slave who knew the island well and who led the English counter-attack.

In 1815 St Helena received its most famous visitor, when Napoleon Bonaparte was brought there as a prisoner, remaining with a mini-imperial French court until his death in 1821. It marked a period of prosperity for the island with the influx of naval and military personnel, but this faded after Napoleon's death. Slavery was abolished in 1832, and two years later St Helena became a Crown Colony. The British government used the island as a base for the campaign against the slave trade, and many freed slaves settled on the island. Joshua Slocum, the first single-handed circumnavigator, called there on *Spray* in 1898.

Towards the end of the nineteenth century, the opening of the Suez Canal saw the number of visiting ships fall, and many islanders left the island. The start of the twentieth century brought another brief period of activity, when 6000 prisoners from

Practical Information

LOCAL TIME: GMT

CURRENCY: St Helenian pound (£) of 100 pence, fixed at parity with £ sterling.

BUSINESS HOURS
Government offices: 0830–1600 Monday to Friday.

ELECTRICITY: 240 V, 50 Hz

PUBLIC HOLIDAYS
1 January: New Year's Day
Good Friday and Easter Monday
Queen's Birthday
St Helena's Day
Whit Monday
August Bank Holiday
December 25, 26: Christmas

COMMUNICATIONS
St Helena Radio 2182 KHz VHF Channel 16. There are regular communications with the UK and St Helena's dependencies.
Cable & Wireless: international phone calls, fax, internet bureau and telegrams.

MEDICAL
There is a small general hospital in Jamestown, also a dental surgery.

the Boer War were brought to St Helena. The development of a flax growing industry, which lasted until the 1960s, helped the shaky economy, especially during the two World Wars.

Many islanders work on Ascension, but unemployment remains a problem. Some have emigrated to Britain. There is a small fishing industry and also some revenue from the sale of stamps, the rest being made up by British aid.

The total population, most of whom live in Jamestown, Half Tree Hollow and Longwood, numbers 5000. They are a mixture of Portuguese, Dutch, English, Malay, Goanese, Madagascan, East Indian, African, Chinese, Boer, American whalers and perhaps some of Napoleon's entourage, to name only a few of the people who have contributed to the St Helenian ethnic mix. English is the main language, although there is also a local dialect. Various Christian denominations are represented.

The climate is tropical, but cooled by the SE trades, and the cold Benguela current from the Southern Ocean. The weather is warm and occasionally humid, but it varies within the island and it is sometimes foggy or misty.

Entry Regulations

Port of entry
Jamestown 15°55'S 5°43'W.

Procedure on arrival
St Helena Port Control should be called on VHF Channel 16 from 0830–1600 Monday to Friday. St Helena Radio can be contacted on Channel 16 at weekends. There are a limited number of orange mooring buoys available for yachts off West Rocks.

Formalities are simple, but should be done in working hours. No overtime is charged, but clearance on weekends is only done by arrangement. All persons must remain on board until cleared by the harbour master, customs and police.

Clearance for departure from St Helena at weekends can be given by customs on the Friday before departure.

Customs
Firearms will be placed under customs seal for the duration of the stay. Spearguns and scuba gear are not to be used during the stay unless accompanied by a member of the local diving club. There are strict laws for the protection of the underwater environment, but visitors who wish to dive can do

so with the local island club, which can be joined on a temporary basis.

Animals, plants, vegetables and fruit are prohibited without proper import documentation and must not be brought ashore.

A declaration of bonded stores is required to be handed to customs on arrival.

Immigration
A visitor will normally be issued a visitor's pass for a period of one month. No visas are required.

Health
Yellow fever vaccination is required if coming from parts of Africa where yellow fever is prevalent.

Fees
The entry fee for all persons over 12 years is £11. Harbour dues of £17.50 are payable on arrival. Payment can be made in local currency, sterling, Visa or MasterCard.

Facilities

The situation for visiting yachts has greatly improved since a number of mooring buoys were laid by the Royal Cape Yacht Club. Commuting ashore is sometimes a problem due to the surge at the landing pier. The local government has introduced a ferry service from 0400 to 2000, which although designed for the local fishermen can also be used by crews of visiting yachts. The fee is £1 per person per day. There are showers near the landing steps.

Water can be taken in jerrycans from an outlet on the main dock. Diesel fuel can be bought by jerrycan from a fuel station in town, or arrangements can be made for a 44 gallon (200 litre) drum to be delivered via the ferry service. Visiting boats are not allowed to come alongside the dock so all fuel has to be transported by launch or dinghy.

Yachting facilities are scarce, but a modest selection of fresh provisions can be obtained for the onward passage. It is advisable to arrive in St Helena with a well-stocked boat and only expect to buy a few fresh provisions locally. There is a good selection of tinned food. Larger quantities can be delivered via the ferry service. Fresh bread must be ordered in advance. Simple repairs can be carried out at the workshop dealing with the local boats.

There are no international banks, although credit cards are accepted for payment of goods in most shops. St Helena currency fixed at parity with £ sterling is used on the island. Traveller's cheques are recommended and can be cashed at the Cash Office, The Castle.

Further Reading

South Africa Nautical Almanac
St Helena including Ascension Island and Tristan da Cunha

Websites

www.sthelena.gov.sh (St Helena Government)
www.chelt.ac.uk/ess/st-helena (Useful links)

SENEGAL

The best known and most visited country by cruising sailors in West Africa, Senegal was once the centre of French West Africa and Dakar one of the most sophisticated African cities. The French influence is still noticeable and the mixture of the two cultures has produced some interesting results in music, painting and even cuisine.

The country is mostly flat except for some mountains in the far south-east and east. Several rivers, some of which are navigable for some distance inland, flow into the sea. These rivers and the offlying islands are Senegal's main cruising attraction, which brings a few cruising yachts to this part of the world every year. The most interesting area is the Casamance, a labyrinth of creeks and islets south of the river Gambia, which is populated by millions of migratory birds during the dry season.

From 1989 there has been fighting in western Casamance between government forces and separatists, and although a truce was agreed between the two sides in 1991, the latest situation should be checked before visiting this area as violence may be continuing, especially around Ziguinchor.

Country Profile

This area has been inhabited since at least 13 000 BC, one of the earliest inhabited areas of West Africa. Under successive kingdoms, it was part of the Ghana empire in the ninth to the eleventh centuries and the Mali empire in the thirteenth to fourteenth centuries. During this period Islam spread across the region. Droughts in the Sahara drove various peoples, the Wolof, Serer, Fulani and Toucouleur, south into Senegal.

In 1444 the Portuguese arrived and set up a trading post on La Gorée Island off Dakar. This became a slave trade centre and over the next 150 years intensive slave trading was carried out. The British, Dutch and French also arrived and there was rivalry between the European powers for the region. Finally the French, who had founded the town of St Louis, captured La Gorée and penetrated into the interior, becoming masters of the area. When the slave trade was banned, the French developed agriculture and followed a policy of assimilation of the local population. At the end of the nineteenth century, the Senegalese had limited French citizenship and sent deputies to the French parliament.

French West Africa covered a vast area as far as the Niger and Dakar was its capital. In the twentieth century nationalism grew and after the Second World War Léopold Senghor, a poet educated in France, led the independence movement, wanting to form a strong federal union. However, individual countries preferred to remain separate and in 1960 French West Africa dissolved into nine separate republics. Senghor became President of Senegal until he stepped down in 1980, when Abdou Niouf took over. In 1989 ethnic tensions led to serious riots in Senegal and Mauritania, and the deportation of thousands of people by both governments. The land borders remain closed between the two countries.

The economy of Senegal is mainly agricultural, groundnuts being the main crop. Some income also comes from fishing, phosphates and tourism. There is a trade deficit and much food has to be imported. There is considerable foreign aid.

The population is 8.6 million, with about one-third being Wolof, the largest ethnic group. Other peoples are Serer, Diola, Fulani, Toucouleur and Mandinka. Unlike other parts of Africa, there is a high degree of homogeneity among the ethnic groups, as language and religion are shared. Most understand Wolof and practise their own brand of the Muslim faith. French is the official language. Dakar has been the capital since 1958. South-west of the port is the city centre, where administration and businesses are based.

The climate is tropical with a rainy season between July and September. The winter months, from November to March, have more pleasant weather. The prevailing winds are northerly,

Practical Information

LOCAL TIME: GMT. Summer time GMT + 1.

BUOYAGE: IALA A

CURRENCY: West African franc (CFA Fr.). Foreign currency must be declared on arrival; exchange receipts should be kept to show customs on departure.

BUSINESS HOURS
Banks: 0800–1130, 1430–1630 Monday to Friday.
Shops: 0800–1200, 1430–1800 Monday to Saturday.
Business and government offices: 0800–1200/1430–1800 Monday to Friday, 0800–1200 Saturday (except government). During Ramadan, some open 0730–1430.

ELECTRICITY: 220 V, 50 Hz

PUBLIC HOLIDAYS
1 January: New Year's Day
1 February
4 April: Independence Day
Good Friday
Easter Monday
1 May: Labour Day
Ascension
Whit Monday
15 July: Day of Association
15 August: Assumption
1 November: All Saints' Day
25 December: Christmas Day
Variable religious holidays: Korite (end of Ramadan), Tabaski (Eid el Kebir), Mouloud (Prophet's Birthday).

COMMUNICATIONS
IDD available. International access code: 00. International calls can be made from Sonatel, 6 rue Wagare–Diouf, Dakar: 0700–2400. There are four telecentres in Dakar for phone, telex and fax services. The main post office (PTT) is Boulevard Pinet Laprade, Dakar.
There are international flights from Dakar to most African capitals and some European cities.

MEDICAL
Hôpital Principal, ave. Courbet. *Tel.* 215430. Clinique Hubert, 125 ave. Jean Jaures. *Tel.* 216848.

DIPLOMATIC MISSIONS
In Dakar:
Canada: 45 blvd. de la République. *Tel.* 823 9290.
Cape Verdes: Imm. El Fahd. *Tel.* 821 1873.
France: 1 rue Amadou Assane Ndoye. *Tel.* 823 9181.
Gambia: 11 rue de Thiong. *Tel.* 821 4476.
Spain: 45 blvd de la Republique. *Tel.* 821 1179 (visas for Canaries).
United Kingdom: 20 rue du Docteur Guillet. *Tel.* 823 7392.
United States: BP 49, ave. Jean XXIII. *Tel.* 823 4296.
All neighbouring countries are represented in Dakar, except Mauritania, and so it is possible to obtain the necessary visas.

---

although occasionally from December to May a dust laden *harmattan* blows from across the desert. Drought is sometimes a problem north of the Gambia river.

Entry Regulations

Ports of entry
Dakar 14°41′N 17°25′W, Ziguinchor 12°35′N 16°16′W, St Louis 16°02′N 16°30′W.

Procedure on arrival
Dakar: The port authority should be contacted on VHF Channel 16 for instructions. There is a fishing harbour where yachts may berth if there is space. The official requirement is to pass south and then east of Gorée Island before proceeding 2.7 miles NNE into the recommended anchorage NW of Pointe de Bel-Air. The yacht club Cercle de Voile de Dakar is nearby.

Officials may not come to the boat, so the captain should take all papers to the Port Captain's office (Commissariat Special du Port) on Boulevard de la Liberation. Immigration formalities are completed at the same place. Ship's papers are retained until departure. The office is open 0800–1230, 1400–1700 Monday to Friday.

Ziguinchor: This port lies 33 miles up the Casamance river. There is a depth of 15 ft (5 m) over the bar at the river entrance, after which the minimum depth in the navigable channel is 30 ft (9 m). The middle channel is marked by buoys, but the river should only be navigated in daylight. Yachts can come alongside a wharf in the main port, which is on the southern bank of the river.
St Louis: There is a dangerous bar at the entrance into this port, situated right on the border with Mauritania. Clearance formalities can be completed here, but the breaking bar may pose problems to a keeled yacht.

Customs
Firearms must be declared.

Animals need anti-rabies vaccinations as well as a health certificate.

Immigration
Visas are not required by nationals of the European Union (with the exception of Germany), Canada, Israel, Japan, South Africa, many African countries, Canada and the United States for up to a three months' stay. All other nationals need a visa obtained in advance. Visas are not issued on arrival.

There are Senegalese missions in Abidjan, Algiers, Banjul, Casablanca, Tunis, Praia, Rabat and Las Palmas de Gran Canaria; otherwise visas may be issued by French embassies. Entry may be denied to those whose passport shows evidence of having visited Mauritania.

Health

Vaccination against yellow fever is obligatory and against cholera recommended. Malaria prophylaxis is also recommended.

Facilities

Provisioning is good in Dakar, where there are several supermarkets. Fresh produce is available in Dakar from an open-air market near the port. The capital also has reasonable repair facilities with various workshops being located in the Medina industrial estate, north of the city. Marine equipment is non-existent, but some of the bigger engine manufacturers are represented locally and have a limited range of spares.

The Cercle de Voile de Dakar (CVD) is a yacht club with good facilities, which are available to visiting yachts. Boats can be hauled out and there is a limited range of repair services available. Water is available at the club. Duty free diesel fuel is available in the main harbour of Dakar. Camping Gaz is widely available. Non-standard LPG bottles can be filled at SENGAS, Route des Grans Moulins.

Some provisions are also available in Ziguinchor, but only the minimum can be expected in smaller places. Fuel is only available in Dakar and Ziguinchor.

Further Reading

West Africa – a travel survival kit
The Traveller's Guide to West Africa
The Rough Guide to West Africa
Cruising Guide to West Africa

Website

www.earth2000.com (Useful information and links)

SOUTH AFRICA

The Republic of South Africa lies at the southern tip of the African continent, its shores washed by the Indian and Atlantic Oceans. Much of the interior is a high semi-arid plateau, the veld, while the narrow plain along the long coast is rugged, more fertile and with a subtropical climate. An important shipping centre for more than five centuries ever since the Portuguese discovered the route to the Indies around the Cape of Good Hope, the old sailing route is now only used by cruising yachts, most of whom are on passage from the Indian Ocean to the Atlantic.

The number of cruising boats visiting South Africa has remained stable in recent years as the Red Sea route was preferred by yachts undertaking a circumnavigation. With the return of South Africa to the international fold, this has changed as more sailors are tempted to experience first hand this country's many attractions. All round the world races now include South Africa on their itinerary.

The country's convenient position and excellent yachting facilities make it a natural stopover, added to which are the many nature reserves that make South Africa an interesting place to visit. One major drawback is the weather and sailing conditions, the waters around the tip of Africa being among the most dangerous in the world.

Country Profile

The oldest inhabitants of the Cape area were the Bushmen and the Khoi-Khoi or Hottentots. By the thirteenth century several Bantu tribes had settled in the region, being forced to move gradually south and west to find new grazing lands. The Portuguese were the first Europeans to visit the Cape, when they discovered the route to India at the end of the fifteenth century. Only in the midseventeenth century were efforts made by Europeans to colonise the land, when the Dutch East India Company became interested in the area for a supply of slaves and raw materials, as well as a stopping point for ships. Dutch settlers came and gradually moved inland, forming a close-knit Boer society, with their own dialect called Afrikaans. Tension rose between the Bantu tribes and the Boer farmers, and this burst into violent conflict in the eighteenth century.

In the early nineteenth century Britain took over the colony from the bankrupt Dutch East India Company. Then British settlers started arriving, pushing the Xhosa off their land, and conflicting both with the African tribes and the Boers who resented the new regime, especially after the

Practical Information

LOCAL TIME: GMT + 2.

BUOYAGE: IALA A

CURRENCY: Rand (R) of 100 cents.
Import or export is limited to R500.

BUSINESS HOURS
Banks: 0900–1530 Monday to Friday, and
0900–1100 Saturday.
Business: 0800/0830–1630/1700 Monday
to Friday, 0830–1300 Saturday.
Shops: 0800–1700 Monday to Friday.
Government offices: 0800/0830–1630/1700
Monday to Friday.

ELECTRICITY: 220 V, 50 Hz

PUBLIC HOLIDAYS
1 January: New Year's Day
Easter Week
17 April: Family Day
27 April: Constitution Day
1 May: Workers Day
16 June: Youth Day

9 August: National Women's Day
24 September: Heritage Day
16 December: Day of Reconciliation
25–26 December: Christmas

MEDICAL
There are hospitals in all major centres
and the standards are very good.

COMMUNICATIONS
Direct dialling to Europe and North
America.
Post offices open 0800–1700 Monday to
Friday, 0830–1200 Saturday.
There are flights from Cape Town to
London and Brazil, but most of the
international flights leave from
Johannesburg.

DIPLOMATIC MISSIONS
In Pretoria:
Australia: 292 Orient St, Arcadia.
Tel. (12) 342 3740.
Canada: 5th floor, Nedbank Plaza, Church
and Beatrix Sts, Arcadia.

Tel. (12) 324 3970.
United Kingdom: (July to December)
255 Hill St, Arcadia. *Tel.* (12) 433 121.
United States: Thibault House,
877 Pretorius St. *Tel.* (12) 342 3006

In Cape Town:
United Kingdom: (January to June)
91 Parliament St. *Tel.* (21) 416 7220
(consulate: 12th floor, Southern Life
Centre, 8 Riebeeck St. *Tel.* (21) 253 670).
United States: Broadway Industries Centre,
Heerengracht, Foreshore. *Tel.* (21) 214 283.

In Durban:
United Kingdom: 10th floor, Fedlife House,
320 Smith St. *Tel.* (31) 305 3041.
United States: Durban Bay House, 29th
floor, 333 Smith St. *Tel.* (31) 304 4737.

Mozambique does not have diplomatic
relations with South Africa, but visas may
be obtained from the Mozambique Trade
Mission, 73 Market Street, Johannesburg.
Tel. (11) 234 907.

British abolished slavery in 1834. The Africans were caught between the Boers and British, being no match for superior European firepower, and already weakened by years of intertribal warfare. Tension between the Boers and the British led to the formation of the autonomous Boer republics of the Orange Free State and Transvaal.

At the turn of the century British efforts to gain control over the Boer republics led to the Boer Wars, and eventually Britain gained control over the whole country. In 1910 the Union of South Africa was established, with the white minority holding power. The first apartheid laws were passed to control black workers in the rich gold and diamond mines. After the Second World War a rise in Afrikaaner nationalism brought the National Party to power in 1948, and they reinforced the apartheid system, denying the black majority any political voice. The African National Congress was formed to campaign for the rights of black South Africans, but many of its leaders were imprisoned in the 1960s and the ANC was banned. Nelson Mandela became the best known among the imprisoned leaders and a symbol of resistance.

In 1962 the Union of South Africa became an independent republic and left the Commonwealth.

Martial law was established following riots in 1985–6 and severe repression followed, which led to several Western states imposing economic sanctions.

Frederik de Klerk, elected President in 1989, set in train a series of measures with the declared aim of putting an end to the policy of apartheid. The process accelerated after the release from prison in 1990 of Nelson Mandela, the ANC leader. International sanctions were suspended as South Africa began to dismantle the apartheid system. The general elections in April 1994, in which all citizens, regardless of race or colour, had the right to vote, brought a coalition government to power, in which the ANC had the majority and Nelson Mandela became president. Its aims to rule by consensus and reconciliation are upheld by President Mbeki who took over from President Mandela in 1999.

South Africa has the strongest economy on the African continent. The country is rich in important precious and rare mineral resources, such as gold, diamonds, chrome, titanium, uranium, coal and iron. Industry has mainly been developed for the domestic market. The Mediterranean type climate around the Cape has made agriculture important. South Africa also has the geographic advantage of controlling the route around the Cape.

The population is 45 million of which 75 per cent are Bantu, 13 per cent of European descent, mainly Afrikaaner with some British, 9 per cent mixed race and 3 per cent Indian, who were originally brought in as indentured labourers by the British in the nineteenth century. Afrikaans and English are spoken, plus several African languages, Xhosa and Zulu being the main ones. The majority are Christian. The Indians are mainly Hindu, and there are also Muslims, Jews and those who follow traditional African beliefs. Pretoria is the administrative capital, while Cape Town is the home of the legislative assembly.

The climate varies greatly between the coastal regions and inland, and also between the Atlantic and Indian Ocean coasts. Generally, it can be described as temperate in the Cape area and tropical in the rest of the country. The prevailing winds of summer are SE, replaced in winter by W or NW winds. Gales are frequent and in summer depressions come up from the Southern Ocean accompanied by cold gale force winds. Conditions are particularly bad when such gales blow against the SW flowing Agulhas current.

Entry Regulations

Ports of entry
The ports of entry are listed in the order of the route from the Indian to the Atlantic Ocean.

Richards Bay 28°48′S 32°06′E, Durban 29°52′S 31°02′E, East London 33°02′S 27°55′E, Port Elizabeth 33°58′S 25°38′E, Mossel Bay 34°11′S 22°10′E, Cape Town (Table Bay) 33°55′S 18°26′E, Saldanha Bay 33°03′S 17°56′E.

Procedure on arrival
Yachts must check in and out with customs, immigration and port captain at each port.

The captain must report to the nearest customs office within 24 hours of arrival. If a yacht arrives from abroad at a port other than a port of entry, the captain must immediately report to the port captain, and clear at an official port of entry within 24 hours. The Q flag must be flown. Formalities on arrival are complicated and time-consuming. It is necessary to obtain coastal clearance to sail between ports and the authorities must also be informed if a yacht goes out for a day sail even if returning to the same port.
Richards Bay: Yachts should moor in the small boat harbour for clearance with customs and immigration. Formalities are simpler than in other South African ports. After clearance yachts can use the facilities of the Zululand Yacht Club.
Durban: Durban Harbour Radio must be contacted to inform the Authorities in advance of one's arrival and to request permission to proceed through the entrance channel. Foreign yachts may be met by a Police Coast Patrol which will escort the yacht to a holding area, or alternatively Durban Harbour Radio may advise to proceed to the International Jetty or Small Craft Basin. Arriving yachts have to contact the following departments within 24 hours of arrival: customs, Customs & Excise Building, corner of Stanger & Victoria Embankment; Immigration, 350 Umgeni Rd, Greyville; Health, 18 Stanger St; Port Liaison Officer, Ocean Terminal building. The Point Yacht Club has a few spaces for visitors and if there is space available one may proceed there and the club will arrange all clearance formalities, both in and out.
Cape Town: The Royal Cape Yacht Club deals with all yacht movement within Table Bay Harbour, so they must be contacted first on VHF Channel 16 and not the port authority. The movement of shipping around the harbour is indicated by lights on the port captain's office, red (Ben Schoeman Dock), green (Duncan Dock) and orange (Victoria Basin). A flashing light signifies a ship is entering port and a steady light that one is leaving. Yachts should keep to starboard when entering the harbour. The yacht basin and yacht club are located at the SE end of Duncan Dock. The captain must clear with customs, situated at the main gate, and immigration (Room 535, Customs & Excise Building, outside the Adderley Street Customs Gate). On departure one must clear first with the yacht club in order to get a clearance certificate, then immigration, harbour revenue (Room 340, Customs & Excise Building) and finally customs who require the yacht club clearance certificate.
Saldanha Bay: The port captain should be contacted on VHF Channel 16 for permission to enter and leave the harbour, as well as when crossing the shipping channel between Saldanha and Langebaan. If the port captain is notified that clearance is required on arrival, the relevant officials will be informed so as to meet the yacht at the yacht club, which is located to the northwest of the bay, north of President Jetty.
Port Owen: Port Owen Marina stands by on VHF Channel 10. The marina is located up the Berg river in St Helena Bay. It is advisable to enter the river at high tide. Although not a port of entry, the marina staff can arrange transport to Saldanha for clearance.

Procedure on departure

Cape Town: Yachts departing for a foreign destination must visit the yacht club first to obtain a clearance certificate. Then the captain must proceed to the immigration office (Customs & Excise Bldg), harbour revenue office (Ben Schoeman Dock) and finally customs (Main Gate).

Customs

Firearms will be sealed by customs on board if this is possible. Otherwise firearms will be removed and bonded until departure.

Animals must obtain the necessary certificate from the State veterinary officer in the harbour area. This will permit the movement of the animal within the harbour area.

There is no limit on the length of time a foreign yacht may stay in South Africa.

Immigration

Passports must be valid at least six months beyond arrival in the country. Most nationalities do not require visas, including those of Australia, Canada, the European Union and the United States. A 90 day stay is normally granted on arrival.

For those requiring visas, they are issued free of charge. There are South African embassies in Port Louis (Mauritius) and St Denis (Réunion). It may also be possible to get a Temporary Residence Permit (TRP) as owner of a yacht by proving ownership, and as crew by possessing an air ticket home or equivalent funds.

Any crew leaving the country by other means than by yacht must inform immigration and must possess a valid air ticket to their own country or equivalent funds. Immigration must also be notified if a South African national joins the yacht for a cruise while in South African waters.

Passports are not normally stamped on arrival. If one wishes to leave a yacht and travel within South Africa, one must get the passport stamped. One is required to fill out a Temporary Residence Permit and immigration will then stamp the passport.

Health

A yellow fever vaccination certificate may be requested if arriving from some African countries. Malaria prophylaxis is recommended.

Fees

Clearance is a 24-hour service, but overtime is charged on fees after 1630 on weekdays, on all the day public holidays, and weekends.

Pilotage service is free.

Restricted areas

The diamond producing areas off Oranjemund are off limits to yachts.

Yachts can anchor in Murray's Bay in the NE of Robben Island, but must first contact Robben Island Port Control on Channel 16 for permission to enter the zone.

Anchorage is allowed at Dassen Island, but landing is forbidden.

There is a naval base in Simon's Town, False Bay, and yachts must arrange permission to enter the bay in advance with the False Bay Yacht Club, or contact the Navy on VHF Channel 16 for permission to enter.

Facilities

Yachting facilities throughout South Africa are of a high standard and as there are yacht clubs in most ports, the clubs are the best source of information on local conditions. The yacht clubs like to be contacted in advance by those wishing to use their facilities. It is not normally allowed to live aboard a yacht, but a concession is made for visiting foreign yachts as a temporary privilege. Most yacht clubs, such as those at Cape Town, Durban and Richards Bay, have their own hauling facilities or work closely with a local boatyard. For any major repair, Cape Town and Durban have a complete range of services: electronic, electrical, sailmaking, rigging, refrigeration, diesel and outboard engines, metal, fibreglass and woodwork.

Fuel and water are easily available and provisioning in all major centres is very good. LPG containers can be filled in Durban and Cape Town. Yacht clubs are also convenient places to leave the boat while visiting the interior.

The Zululand Yacht Club in Richards Bay is a good place from which to visit the Umfoloze, Hluhluwe and St Lucia reserves, while Kruger Park can be easily reached from the Point Yacht Club in Durban. For those who are concerned about the difficult passage from Durban to Cape Town, advice on the best tactics to use in these stormy waters can be obtained from the Durban Sailing Academy.

Visiting yachts can obtain a tax refund on goods bought in South Africa that are being exported. An original VAT invoice should be requested when purchasing such goods. Customs should be then contacted for the necessary formalities.

Further Reading

South Africa Nautical Almanac
East Africa Pilot
Africa on a Shoestring

Website

www.environment.gov.za (Department of Tourism)

TRISTAN DA CUNHA

The remote South Atlantic island of Tristan da Cunha came to the world's attention in 1961, when a volcanic eruption forced the entire population of 241 to be evacuated to Britain. Other islands nearby are the small, uninhabited Inaccessible, Nightingale, Gough, Middle and Stoltenhoff Islands. Since 1938 all the islands have been administered by St Helena, lying 1500 miles to the north. South Africa is the same distance to the east.

Tristan da Cunha is almost circular, the core of a volcano with steep cliffs plunging into the sea. On the north-west corner is a small habitable plateau, and the settlement of Edinburgh. The volcano's summit is bleak and often snow-covered from June to October, although the lower slopes are greener. The islanders have retained a simple way of life and little has changed over the years.

The anchorage is completely unprotected and a heavy swell is constant, worst in a north-westerly. The small boat harbour has only about 3 ft (91 cm) of water and a heavy surge from the constant swell. Yachts can rarely stay for very long, even if they want to. Yet in spite of all the difficulties, every year this remote community is visited by a few intrepid yachts.

Country Profile

In 1506 the Portuguese Admiral Tristao da Cunha reported the first sighting of the island. No landings, however, were attempted until the Dutch came the following century, and only in 1810 was a settlement established, when three Americans made their base there. A few years later England claimed the island as part of the defence of St Helena, primarily to guard against Napoleon's unlikely escape. A small garrison was established and fortifications were built. Corporal William Glass, who had been stationed there during this time, returned to settle with his wife and a few others after the garrison was abandoned, and from these beginnings the community grew. Deserters from ships, American whalers and castaways came and went. In 1876 the island was declared a British territory. The islanders grew enough to eat and to trade with passing ships. Occasional trips were made to Nightingale Island to collect guano, penguin eggs and petrel carcasses for lamp oil. The islanders still make this trip twice every year.

In the early twentieth century life was hard, and fewer ships visited, sometimes a whole year passed

Practical Information

LOCAL TIME: GMT.

CURRENCY: GBP £ Sterling. US$ and SA Rand can be exchanged; cash or travellers cheques only.

BUSINESS HOURS
Government offices: summer 0800–1230, 1330–1600 Monday to Thursday, to 1530 Friday; opens and closes half an hour later in winter.
The supermarket and post office have the same opening hours as above.
Agriculture shop: summer 0900–1230, 1330–1530; shop closes 1 hour later in winter.

PUBLIC HOLIDAYS
1 January: New Year's Day
Good Friday and Easter Monday
Queen's Birthday
Whit Monday
August Bank Holiday
25, 26 December: Christmas
Government offices close approximately 18 December to 15 January.

COMMUNICATIONS
Radio telephone calls can be booked at the post office, and telex facilities are also available.
There are regular radio communications

with St Helena and the UK.
Tristan has no airport and ships call at most three times a year on supply runs from the UK, St Helena and Cape Town. The occasional fishing boat stops at the island for provisions.

MEDICAL
There is a small hospital.

without a ship calling. Nevertheless the community survived, being 200 strong in 1939. During the Second World War a small meteorological and wireless station was built on the island and manned by the Royal Navy. The most dramatic event in Tristan da Cunha's history occurred when the volcano erupted in 1961. The evacuated islanders lived for a couple of years in England, but most of them returned as soon as the island was safe again. The lava had formed a natural breakwater and in 1967 the small boat harbour was built.

After the war a crayfish industry was developed, with a factory for canning and freezing the tails. Income is also derived from fishing royalties, the sale of stamps and aid from Britain.

The population numbers around 300, most of whom can trace their descent back to the very first settlers. Seven family names are shared among the islanders. English is the language spoken. There is both an Anglican and a Catholic church on the island.

The climate is temperate, with moderate rainfall and high humidity. The wind is strong most days, and gales are frequent all year round.

Entry Regulations

Port of entry
Edinburgh 37°03′S 12°18′W.

Procedure on arrival
No person may land at Nightingale, Alex or Stoltenhoff Islands without first clearing at Tristan and then obtaining permission from the Administrator.

One should anchor off Edinburgh settlement. Radio Tristan will contact the yacht on VHF Channel 16. Advice on anchoring can be obtained from the harbour master. The yacht will be boarded by the immigration and medical officials. The immigration official will complete formalities ashore.

The government boat carrying the officials will not take crews ashore, who must use their dinghy. In the event of a medical emergency a boat will be provided. A boat without a dinghy may apply to the Administrator for the use of a government boat, for a fee.

Yachts should maintain contact with Tristan Radio while at the anchorage, and inform them of ETD and destination.

The small boat harbour closes to visiting vessels after 1900 in the summer (October–March), and 1700 in winter (April–September), though it may close earlier on fishing days or in the event of bad weather.

Customs
Firearms and animals must be kept on board and not landed. There are restrictions on the import of alcohol.

Immigration
No visas are required.

Restrictions
Landing is prohibited on Gough and Inaccessible Islands. Landing on Nightingale, Alex or Stoltenhoff Islands is only allowed if accompanied by a local guide. The guide must be picked up from Tristan and returned the same day before nightfall. Anyone wishing to walk up the mountain on Tristan must also be accompanied by a local guide. In all cases the guide will be in charge of the party.

Fishing
Yachts wishing to fish for finfish for their own consumption must ask permission of the Administrator. Fishing for lobster is strictly prohibited.

Fees
Overtime is charged by arrangement. There is a landing fee of £5 per person.

Use of government boat for transportation ashore, £25.

Guide fees, £17 per guide.

All fees are to be paid in cash or travellers cheques at the Treasury Office in Sterling, Rand or US dollars. Yachts arriving at a weekend or public holiday should pay their fees to the Immigration Officer.

Facilities

In spite of its remoteness, yachts are usually able to obtain some basic provisions, as the islanders grow some vegetables, mainly potatoes. Yachts are recommended to obtain any supplies required immediately after immigration is cleared and fees paid, due to the unpredictable weather. The islanders are very adept at all kinds of repairs and have helped yachts in the past. The Government workshop may be able to help with repairs.

Further Reading

St Helena including Ascension Island and Tristan da Cunha

Websites

www.sthelena.se/tristan/tristan.htm (Tristan da Cunha Association)
www.website.lineone.net/~sthelena/tristaninfo.htm (Useful links)

5 Caribbean

The islands of the Caribbean are undoubtedly the most popular cruising destination in the world. This is particularly true of the Eastern Caribbean, an area which attracts a large number of cruising yachts, while the resident charter fleets seem to be forever expanding. In some parts, such as the Virgin Islands, charter yachts are already in the majority, although in the Leeward and Windward Islands the scene is still dominated by cruising boats. Another area rapidly gaining in popularity are the islands off Venezuela, both those belonging to that country and the ABC Islands, Aruba, Bonaire and Curaçao. By contrast, the Greater Antilles are mostly off the cruising track.

The popularity of the Eastern Caribbean is well deserved as the winter weather is mostly fine, the trade winds reliable and the facilities are being continually improved to cope with a constant demand. The sailing season lasts from the end of November until June, by which time the prudent sailor should be on his or her way to a hurricane-free area. The peak hurricane season is from August until October and while the majority of cruising yachts leave the area, some stay behind planning on finding shelter in a hurricane hole should a hurricane come their way.

Several years of relative peace created a false sense of security, which was shattered in the late 1980s and again in the 1990s when storms of unprecedented violence destroyed many boats.

The weather during winter, particularly from Christmas until the end of April, is very good, with steady easterly winds and not much rain. Usually winds are NE at the beginning of winter and become SE with the approach of summer. The hurricane season lasts from June through November, the most dangerous period being from the middle of August until the end of September. The whole region can be affected by hurricanes with the exception of the southern part, Trinidad and the islands off Venezuela, where tropical storms are extremely rare. As a result of a series of destructive hurricanes, most insurance companies now stipulate that boats left in the Caribbean during the hurricane season must be laid up south of 12°40'N. In practice this means Trinidad, Tobago, Grenada and Venezuela, although it is possible to obtain a dispensation and leave the boat in a well-protected marina or boatyard in St Vincent or even St Lucia.

Provisioning is better in the major centres, although most islands have shops with a reasonable selection and fresh produce is widely available. Although most islands have air links with the outside world, direct flights to Europe or North America are only available from some islands, so crew changes are best planned for such places as Barbados, St Lucia, Martinique, Guadeloupe, Antigua, Trinidad, St Martin, or Puerto Rico.

With thousands of yachts plying up and down the island chain, one is never too far away from a good supply of repair facilities. Although in many islands mooring is still on one's own anchor, the number of purpose-built marinas is growing steadily, with the highest concentration in the Virgin Islands to St Martin area. For any major repair work one should head for one of the islands having a yachting centre which can offer a complete range of services, such as the Virgin Islands, St Martin, Antigua, Guadeloupe, Martinique, St Lucia, Trinidad, or Isla de Margarita.

One local phenomenon, which anyone cruising the Eastern Caribbean will soon encounter, are the so called 'boat boys'. These are local men, not always young, offering a variety of services to visiting yachts, from supplying fresh produce to looking after the dinghy, if left unattended on the beach, or doing work on the boat itself. In some places, their insistence can be irritating, but a firm attitude usually works. It must not be forgotten, however, that unemployment in the islands is very high and most of these men are genuinely trying to earn a living in an environment in which the opportunities for paid employment are very limited. Nor should one forget that these are, after all, *their* islands and whatever the cruising sailor leaves behind is but a small price to pay for the privilege of sailing in one of the most beautiful parts of the world.

ANGUILLA

Anguilla is the most northern of the Leeward Islands in the Eastern Caribbean and one of the least developed. Long and flat, this coral island was named 'eel' in Spanish.

Anguilla's brief claim to fame occurred in 1969 when the small island was invaded by a British expeditionary force accompanied by a posse of London policemen. This is probably the only instance in which London bobbies have been used as an occupying force and their presence on the island was greeted with delight by the Anguillans. The crisis came to a head after Anguilla declared its independence from St Kitts & Nevis.

Anguilla's main attraction is her isolation and although distances to neighbouring Caribbean islands are very small, the changes that have occurred elsewhere have largely left Anguilla untouched. There are several delightful bays both on the south and north coasts of Anguilla, while those in search of blissful solitude can do no better than the Prickly Pear Cays and Dog Island, north of Anguilla.

Country Profile

Although discovered by Columbus in 1493, Anguilla was only settled in the middle of the seventeenth century by the English and remained under their influence thereafter, except for a brief period of French rule at the end of the eighteenth century. Throughout the nineteenth century Anguilla was closely associated with St Kitts, but in 1967 it refused to join with St Kitts & Nevis as an associated state. To calm the crisis British troops and police were sent in. In 1971 Britain established Anguilla as a separate administrative unit and now the island has internal self-government, while remaining a British dependency.

The lack of rainfall makes agriculture difficult, but some of the best fishing grounds in the Caribbean are found in the area. Salt-farming also contributes to the economy, both salt and fish being exported. Many of the population work abroad, although recently the tourist trade has been cautiously expanded.

The population numbers 10,000, mostly of African origin, as well as a number of European descent. The language is English. The Valley is the main centre. Of nine different religious denominations, Protestantism has the most followers. The climate is semi-tropical, dry but pleasant with an average temperature of 27°C (80°F).

Practical Information

LOCAL TIME: GMT – 4.

BUOYAGE: IALA B

CURRENCY: East Caribbean dollar (EC$).

BUSINESS HOURS
Shops: 0800–1200, 1300–1600 Monday to Friday.
Banks: 0800–1200 Monday to Friday, 1500–1700 Fridays only.
Government offices: 0800–1200, 1300–1600 Monday to Friday. Officials 0700–2400 at Blowing Point.

ELECTRICITY: 110/220 V, 60 Hz

PUBLIC HOLIDAYS
1 January: New Year's Day
Good Friday and Easter Monday
5 May: Labour Day
May Bank Holiday (variable)
30 May: Anguilla Day
Whit Monday
Second Saturday in June: Queen's Birthday
First Monday in August: Emancipation Day
First Thursday in August
First Friday in August: Constitution Day
19 September: Separation Day
25, 26 December: Christmas

EVENTS
August: Yacht race

MEDICAL
Princess Alexandra Hospital. *Tel.* 2551/2.

COMMUNICATIONS
Cable & Wireless in The Valley for international telephones, fax and telex.
The main post office is in The Valley: 0800–1530 Monday to Friday, and 0800–1200 Saturday.
International flight connections have to be made in Antigua, Sint Maarten or San Juan (Puerto Rico), to all of which there are regular flights.

Entry Regulations

Ports of entry
Road Bay 18°12′N 63°06′W, Blowing Point 18°12′N 63°06′W.

Procedure on arrival
Road Bay: Anchor in Road Bay and take dinghy to dinghy dock. Immigration and customs offices are nearby, open 0830–1200, 1300–1600. The National Park office need be visited only by those intending to dive. One should clear first with immigration, at the police station near the dinghy dock, then with customs who can be found by the big ship dock and from whom the cruising permit, if applicable, must be purchased. Because of the

serious concern over drug traffic, yachts must be sure to clear in properly. Failure to do so could result in a fine, and the boat being confiscated.

One should advise the authorities if one wishes to go anywhere outside of Road Bay as a cruising permit will be necessary. If staying less than 24 hours, one can clear customs in and out at the same time.

Map 7: The Caribbean

ATLANTIC OCEAN

British Virgin Islands

US Virgin Islands

PUERTO RICO

Anguilla

St Martin/Sint Maarten

St Eustatius   Barbuda

Saba

St Kitts

Nevis

Montserrat

Antigua

Guadeloupe

Dominica

Martinique

St Lucia

Barbados

St Vincent

The Grenadines

Grenada

Bonaire

Curaçao

Tobago

Trinidad

VENEZUELA

Blowing Point is used mainly by commercial shipping.

Customs
Firearms should be licensed and must be securely locked on board, under the captain's control only.

A valid veterinary certificate must be shown for all animals.

There is no specified time limit on how long a yacht may stay.

Immigration
US citizens need only have proof of identity.

No visas are required by nationals of EU countries, Commonwealth countries, Iceland, Japan, Liechtenstein, Norway, Switzerland, Tunisia, Turkey, Uruguay, United States and Venezuela. All other nationals require visas.

Cruising permit
Most of the anchorages around the island are marine parks and permits are needed for some of these anchorages. This formality, which in the past was applied to all visiting boats, no longer applies to privately owned cruising boats. However, all foreign boats engaged in chartering, or being chartered, are required to have a cruising permit, issued by customs. The cost of the permit depends on tonnage and the duration of a visit, for example a boat from 5 to 20 tons for a week would pay EC$125. The permit can be obtained on arrival. It also counts as a clearance certificate and with a cruising permit one need not check out with customs in order to leave Anguilla.

Fees
An overtime fee of EC$30 is charged at Blowing Point after 2400 and on public holidays, and at Road Bay outside of official hours and on Sundays and holidays. There is also a cruising permit fee. Mooring fees are charged for the use of the moorings which had been laid at various anchorages (white for the use of boats up to 55 ft (17 m); the red buoys are reserved for dive boats). Moorings can be booked when clearing in.

Restrictions
There is a prohibited area in Little Bay, following a line from a point 18°04'03.5'N and 63°04'15.7'W extending south to a point 18°13'57.6'N and 63°04'15.7'W turning east to a point 18°13'57.6'N and 63°04'12.5'W.

Anguillan waters are all protected as a national park and spearfishing and the collection of coral and shellfish are prohibited. There are also restrictions on dumping or waste disposal. Anchoring in coral is prohibited. Also prohibited are jet-skis everywhere, and water ski-ing in designated areas and anchorages.

Facilities

Repair facilities are very basic and for any major repair one has to go to neighbouring St Martin. There is a chandlery in Road Bay (Ian's Chandlery) which will also deal with some repairs. A boat builder in North Hill can handle metalwork as well as outboard engine repair. There are several supermarkets, with the Food Center in the Valley having the best selection. Fuel is available at Road Bay but must be taken in jerrycans.

Further Reading

Cruising Guide to the Leeward Islands

English Harbour, Antigua.

Websites

www.net.ai (Anguilla Tourist Board)
www.gov.ai (Official government site)

ANTIGUA AND BARBUDA

Antigua occupies a central position in the popular Caribbean cruising ground of the Lesser Antilles. Antigua administers two other islands: Barbuda, 30 miles to the north, with its only settlement at Codrington, and small uninhabited Redonda, 35 miles to the south-west.

Antigua has been blessed by nature with a beautiful coastline and by the British Admiralty with one of the most picturesque harbours in the world. English Harbour is an enclosed bay that offers protection in all kinds of weather, which is why it was used as a hurricane hole by the British West Indies fleet for nearly two centuries. English Harbour, and particularly Nelson's Dockyard, have been saved for posterity by the foresight of a British yachtsman who stopped there during a world cruise shortly after the Second World War, fell in

Practical Information

LOCAL TIME: GMT – 4.

BUOYAGE: IALA B

CURRENCY: East Caribbean dollar (EC$).

BUSINESS HOURS
Banks: 0800–1300, 1500–1700 Monday to
Thursday, 0800–1200, 1500–1700 Friday.
Bank of Antigua: 0800–1200 Saturday.
Shops: 0800–1200, 1300–1700 Monday to
Friday, 0900–1300 Saturdays.

ELECTRICITY: 110/220 V, 50 Hz

PUBLIC HOLIDAYS
1 January: New Year's Day
Good Friday, Easter Monday
First Monday in May: Labour Day
Whit Monday
Second Saturday in June: Queen's Birthday
3 July: Caricom Day
August: Carnival
1 November: Independence Day
25, 26 December: Christmas

EVENTS
Antigua Sailing Week, April/May.
Midsummer Carnival, July/August.

COMMUNICATIONS
Cable & Wireless for international
telephone calls, telex, telegrams and fax:
St Mary's Street, St John's: 0700–2200
Monday to Friday, 0700–1400 Saturday,
1600–2000 Sunday;
Dockyard Market, English Harbour:
0830–1630 Monday to Friday.
Public phones can be used for collect and
credit card calls.
Post office, High Street, St John's, open
0800–1200, 1300–1600 Monday to Friday.
VHF: Channel 68 is used as the calling
frequency by all coastal stations, including
repair companies, taxis and restaurants, so
use of this channel as a working frequency
is not permitted in Antiguan waters. It is
strongly advised that an alternative
channel is used as soon as contact is
made on Channel 68.
Mail is held at the following places:

Nicholson's Yacht Charter, English Harbour
Seagull Yachts, Falmouth Harbour
English Harbour Post Office
There are regular flights from Antigua to
other Caribbean destinations, Canada,
USA and Europe, principally London.
Emergencies: 999 or 911.
Police 462-0125.

MEDICAL
Holberton Hospital, St John's. *Tel.* 462-0251.
Adelin Medical Centre (private), St John's.
Tel. 462-0866.
Ambulance 462-0251.

DIPLOMATIC MISSIONS
In St John's:
United Kingdom: Price Waterhouse Centre,
1 Old Parham Road.
Tel. 462-0008.
United States: Queen Elizabeth Highway.
Tel. 463-6531.
Venezuela: Cross and Redcliffe Sts.
Tel. 462-1574.

love with the island and never sailed on. Due to the tireless efforts of Vernon Nicholson, the derelict port with crumbling buildings underwent a gradual metamorphosis and Nelson's Dockyard is now the undisputed centre of Caribbean yachting. The old sail lofts, powder rooms, rope walks and officers' quarters have been restored and given new roles to play, while a museum housed in the former Admiral's Residence helps bring to life this harbour's fascinating history.

Over 2000 yachts pass through English Harbour each year, many of them charter boats based in the area. Most cruising boats arrive towards the end of the winter season, in April and May, as they make their way home either to Europe or North America. They are joined by hundreds of racing enthusiasts who congregate in Antigua at the end of April for the annual Antigua Sailing Week which brings together the cream of Caribbean yachting and signals the end of the Caribbean sailing season.

Antigua's coastline is dotted with secluded coves and attractive bays and once away from the bustle of English Harbour the solitude of some anchorages is quite surprising. On the southwest coast is Jolly Harbour Marina with berthing for over 150 yachts. Further along the east coast is Mamora Bay, the secluded base of St James's Club. Visiting

sailors can anchor in the bay or ask permission to use the dock.

Those in search of absolute solitude can sail to Antigua's smaller sister, Barbuda, a coral island surrounded by a maze of reefs that over the centuries have claimed over 200 ships. Although modern charts and good sunlight reduce the hazards, the area should be treated with caution as coral growth has made even recent charts not entirely reliable.

Country Profile

In the pre-Columbian era, the Siboney inhabited Antigua, at least as far back as 2400 BC, followed by the Arawak Indians. Columbus visited the island on his second voyage in 1493, naming the island after the Church of Santa Maria de la Antigua in Seville. The English were the first to settle in 1632, and apart from a very brief French occupation, the islands remained a British possession until independence. As on many Caribbean islands, sugar cane was introduced, and slaves from Africa brought in to work the plantations. In the seventeenth and eighteenth centuries English Harbour was developed as a major naval base, and

Horatio Nelson spent much time there during his command of the Leeward Islands Squadron.

In 1967 Antigua, Barbuda and Redonda gained internal self-government, becoming first an associated state with Britain, then fully independent in 1981.

Once a major part of the economy, the sugar industry has declined, suffering especially from droughts in the arid climate. Many of the plantations have been turned to forest and pasture. There is some export of cotton and fish. However, industry is lacking, and unemployment high. Tourism plays a major role in the economy and tourist facilities are being expanded.

The population of 83,000 is mostly of African origin, with only 2 per cent of European descent. St John's on the west coast is the capital. English is spoken and the majority are Protestant with a minority of Roman Catholics. Antigua has a tropical climate, but is very dry with a rainy season from September to November. The hurricane season is from July to November.

Entry Regulations

Ports of entry

English Harbour 17°00′N 61°46′W (this includes the Dockyard and Falmouth Harbour), Jolly Harbour 17°06′N 61°53′W, St John's 17°07′N 61°52′W, Codrington (Barbuda) 17°38′N 61°49′W.

Procedure on arrival

There are certain clearance procedures common to all ports for vessels clearing into any port in Antigua:

1 The Q flag must be flown and all crew must remain on board until clearance is completed.

2 Only the captain may go ashore to clear customs and immigration with ship's papers, passports, clearance certificate from last port, as well as airline tickets for crew disembarking in Antigua.

3 If a vessel arrives after hours, the captain must ensure that no crew goes ashore until clearance has been completed at the first opportunity.

4 Crew leaving a boat must have a valid airline ticket to a country that will accept them without question. This ticket must be presented to the immigration official when being signed off the vessel.

5 Captains wishing to exchange crew members with another vessel must do so in the presence of an immigration official.

English Harbour: One should anchor in the bay (Freeman's Harbour) and hoist Q flag. The captain only should go ashore with all documents to clear. All offices are located in the old Officers' Quarters building, where customs, immigration and the Park department have to be visited, open 0800–1600 daily. After hours, the crew must remain on board until clearance can be completed. On departure from English Harbour, harbour fees must be paid at the Paymaster to collect the port clearance certificate. This should then be presented to the immigration officer, with the ship's papers and passports.

Falmouth Harbour: Yachts requiring clearance should anchor or come to the Port Authority Dock. The port office is open 0800–1600 daily.

St John's Harbour: The port facilities are at the outer end of the peninsula running west into the middle of the harbour and its use is restricted to commercial vessels. The inner harbour, between the deepwater port and town waterfront, is used by small local craft with less than 6 ft (1.8 m) draft. Yachts may come alongside either the deep water dock or, more conveniently, at the head of the Heritage Quay Dock, close to Customs House. Clearance is done at the Port Authority offices in the deepwater dock on the north side of the harbour, 0800–1200, 1300–1600 weekdays, closes 1500 Friday.

Jolly Harbour: Proceed into the marina which monitors Channel 68. Customs, immigration and port authority have an office in the marina open daily 0800–1600.

Barbuda: Customs and immigration are located in Codrington and can be reached on Channel 16. Boats coming from another country cannot clear in at Barbuda and must do so first in Antigua. Boats visiting Barbuda must have a valid cruising permit issued in Antigua.

Customs

Firearms must be registered with the police on arrival.

Animals are not allowed ashore and must remain on board at all times.

Immigration

No visas are required by nationals of EU countries, Commonwealth countries, Argentina, Brazil, Iceland, Japan, Liechtenstein, Norway, Malta, Mexico, Monaco, Peru, San Marino, Suriname, Turkey, the United States and Venezuela. All other nationals require visas in advance. Valid passports are required by all nationals except for United States citizens who may show a recognised form of identification.

On arrival, immigration will issue a visa for the duration of one's stay. It is advisable to request more than the intended time, as extensions must be obtained from the capital of St John's and can cost as much as US$100.

If crew leave the boat in Antigua, they must have a valid airline ticket out of the country; it is the captain's responsibility to provide this ticket for all persons leaving. Crew arriving to join a yacht by air must show to immigration on arrival a copy of a letter signed by the captain. Immigration must be notified of any crew departures or changes.

Fees
Port entry, depending on length, from US$2 (up to 20 feet) to $12 (120–150 feet). Also a clearance fee of approximately $3 per person.

Cruising permit from US$8 (up to 20 feet) to $20 (120–150 feet) per month. One can buy an annual cruising permit to avoid paying the charge at every entry.

Mooring fees in English Harbour and Falmouth Harbour are less for anchoring than for at the dock and are calculated per foot per day, week or month. If the fees are not paid in advance the daily rate is charged.

National Parks Authority fees are payable at Nelson's Dockyard, Antigua Slipways, Antigua Yacht Club Marina, Falmouth Harbour Marina and Catamaran Marina.

Dockyard entry is EC$5 per person, valid for duration of stay.

No overtime fees, except at St John's, where they are about EC$20.

Cruising permit
All boats in Antiguan waters must have a valid cruising permit, which should be obtained on entry and enables one to go anywhere in Antiguan waters, including Barbuda. The permit is still valid if the yacht leaves Antigua and returns within the period of the permit.

English Harbour regulations
The navigation channel from Fort Berkley to the inner harbour must be kept free. One can either anchor off the channel, or come stern to the quay. There is a dinghy speed limit of 4 knots, and all old fuel and oil must be disposed of in the special containers provided.

Procedure on departure
Port fees must be paid before collecting the port clearance certificate. This must be presented to the immigration official, together with the ship's papers and passports. Vessels must leave within 24 hours after completing clearance procedures.

Restrictions
Spearfishing is illegal in Antigua and Barbuda waters by non-Antigua nationals. The coastline between Pillars of Hercules and entrance to Mamora Bay is protected and no fishing of any type is allowed in this area.

Coast guard
The Coast guard stand by on VHF Channel 68 and 16. A boat can be searched either on entry into port from foreign waters or with a signed search warrant from a magistrates court.

Charter
If intending to charter, one must apply for an official licence from the Chief Marine Surveyor/Examiner in St John's Harbour. *Tel.* 462-1273.

Facilities

Because of Antigua's long-standing involvement with yachting, service and repair facilities are of a high standard and almost anything can be fixed on the island. Most specialised firms are concentrated within walking or rowing distance of English Harbour. Foremost among them is Antigua Slipways, which undertakes all kinds of boat repair and has a well-stocked chandlery. Electronic repair is undertaken by the Signal Locker in English Harbour and there are also two sailmakers nearby. Seagull Yacht Service in Falmouth Harbour is a marine engineering service. Jolly Harbour Marina has a full service boatyard with its own travelift. The Map Shop in St John's has a good supply of British and US charts for the North Atlantic and South Pacific.

All companies in the English Harbour area undertaking yacht or equipment repair monitor Channel 68 and this is the quickest and surest way to obtain help if anything needs to be done on the boat.

BARBUDA

All the population live in the town of Codrington. Customs and immigration are located in the boat harbour, about three miles south of Codrington, and can be called on VHF Channel 16. Outward clearance can be obtained here, but if entering, they cannot issue a cruising permit and one would have to remain in the small boat harbour. A valid cruising permit should be obtained in Antigua before going to Barbuda. Codrington village has a post office, telephone service and limited provisioning. Palaster Reef is a national park and no fishing with a speargun or rod is permitted. There are virtually no repair facilities in Barbuda and only a limited selection of supplies can be obtained there.

Charts of Barbuda have been reported as unreliable because of coral growth.

REDONDA

A 1000-ft (305-m) high rocky island with sheer cliffs, the only decent anchorage is on the southwest coast.

Further Reading

Cruising Guide to the Leeward Islands

Websites

www.antigua-barbuda.org (Department of Tourism)
www.interknowledge.com/antigua-barbuda

ARUBA

Westernmost of the ABC islands, Aruba is a convenient last stop for yachts heading for Panama. A new marina has brought a welcome change to an island which had lacked decent yachting facilities.

No longer part of the Netherlands Antilles, Aruba broke away from the other five islands in 1986 to become an autonomous member of the Kingdom of the Netherlands. The Hague is now only responsible for defence and foreign affairs, and the Queen is represented by a Governor. The island has the same status as the Netherlands Antilles.

Country Profile

Arawaks populated this island when the Spanish first landed in 1499, but it was the Dutch who established rule over the island and resisted all challenges from other European powers. Early in the nineteenth century gold was discovered, but exploitation of it had ceased by 1916. In 1929 an oil refinery was built, at that time the largest in the world, and its closure in 1985 was a shock to the Aruban economy. Tourism was rapidly developed as a cure, and recently efforts have been made to establish Aruba as an offshore business centre. Aid from the Netherlands, however, is still vital to the economy. The island has three ports, of which only the capital Oranjestad, which is sheltered behind a reef, is suitable for yachts.

Aruba is one of the few Caribbean islands where descendants of the indigenous population, the Arawaks, still live. The population of 81,000 also includes those of Spanish and Dutch origin as well as many recent immigrants. A wide range of religions are practised including Roman Catholicism, Judaism and Protestantism. Dutch is the official language, but English and Spanish are widely spoken, as well as the local language Papiamento.

Aruba lies outside the hurricane belt and has a dry climate. Temperatures are higher from August to October, although there is not a great difference to the cooler months, which are from December to February.

Entry Regulations

Port of entry
Oranjestad 12°30′N, 70°02′W.

Procedure on arrival
Oranjestad: Yachts can enter either through the northern or southern opening in the reef. Aruba Port Control should be called on VHF Channel 16, who will advise where to tie up at a dock and wait for officials. The correct courtesy flag is that of the Netherlands, but a request can be made for an Aruban flag.

Customs and immigration offices are by the harbour. On departure one must also come to the dock to obtain clearance out of Aruba.

Customs
Dogs and cats are only allowed entry with valid rabies and health certificates. Animals arriving from South and Central America are not allowed to land.

Oranjestad is a free port and therefore no customs restrictions apply.

Practical Information

LOCAL TIME: GMT – 4

BUOYAGE: IALA B

CURRENCY: Aruban florin of 100 cents. The Aruban florin cannot be exchanged outside of Aruba. The Antillian guilder is not accepted as an equivalent, and has to be exchanged in banks. US$ are widely accepted.

ELECTRICITY: 110 V, 60 Hz

BUSINESS HOURS
Banks: 0800–1200, 1330–1600 Monday to Friday, some stay open during the lunch hour.
Shops: 0800–1830 Monday to Saturday, some close for lunch. A few open on Sundays or holidays when cruise ships are in port.

PUBLIC HOLIDAYS
1 January: New Year's Day
25 January
Carnival Monday
Good Friday, Easter Monday
18 March: National Day
30 April: Queen's Day
1 May: Labour Day
Ascension Day
25, 26 December: Christmas

EVENTS
Carnival, February or March
First 2 weeks June: Aruba Hi-winds
Pro-Am International Racing
24 June: St Johns Day
6 December: St Nicolas Day

COMMUNICATIONS
International telephone calls, telegrams and telexes from the Government Telegraph and Radio Office (Setar) next to the Post Office Building, J.E. Irausquinplein, Oranjestad. Open 0730–1200, 1300–1630. There is also an ITT office at Boecoetiweg 33. Emergency: dial 115.
There are flights from Aruba to Amsterdam, Bonaire, Curaçao, Sint Maarten, Puerto Rico and several US and South American destinations.

MEDICAL
Horacio Oduber Hospital, LG Smith Blvd. *Tel.* 74300.

DIPLOMATIC MISSIONS
Colombia: Smith Blvd 52. *Tel.* 21206.
Panama: Weststraat 15. *Tel.* 22908.
Venezuela: 8 Adriane Lacle Blvd.
Tel. 21078.

Immigration

US and Canadian citizens need proof of identification only, all others need a valid passport. Proof of adequate funds may also be required to be shown.

Most nationals may enter Aruba for 14 days without a visa. For stays over 14 days, immigration must be notified on arrival, and a Temporary Certificate of Admission will be issued. Nationals of Belgium, Luxembourg and the Netherlands can remain up to three months as tourists.

Facilities

Besides the marina in Oranjestad, there are two yacht clubs where visitors may sometimes use the moorings. Down the coast from Oranjestad, near Spanish Lagoon, is the Aruba Nautical Club, which has berths, fuel, water and electricity. Members of other yacht clubs may use the facilities, but should check in advance. Between Oranjestad and Spanish Lagoon is the Bucuti Yacht Club which also has docking space and a few other facilities. Provisioning is best done in Oranjestad, where there is a good selection of fresh produce and one is moored conveniently by the town centre.

Further Reading

Yachting Guide to the ABC Islands
Cruising Guide to the Caribbean

Websites

www.arubatourism.com (Aruba Tourism Authority)
www.abc-yachting.com

BAHAMAS

Over 700 islands and 2400 uninhabited cays make up the Bahamas, its name coming from the Spanish 'baja mar', meaning shallow sea. The coral and limestone archipelago stretches south-east from Florida for nearly 500 miles (805 km).

In the world of cruising, the Bahamas stand out as a totally different experience. These low islands surrounded by clear waters of exquisite colours and unbelievable transparency have a charm all of their own. The distinctive features are the large shallow banks and coral reefs which, although a hazard to shipping, provide excellent diving and underwater scenery. The shallow depths and strong tidal currents that occur call for very attentive navigation.

To protect the fragile environment, nature reserves and underwater parks have been established in some islands, and visiting sailors are expected to do their best to cause as little damage as possible, both ashore and afloat. In particular, they should avoid anchoring in coral, which is easily destroyed by the anchor and rode. Mooring buoys have been installed at some locations, and

Practical Information

LOCAL TIME: GMT – 5. Summer time
GMT – 4 April to October.

BUOYAGE: IALA B.

CURRENCY: Bahamas dollar (B$), which
is on a par with the US dollar. US$ are
widely accepted.

BUSINESS HOURS
Banks in Nassau: 0930–1500 Monday to
Thursday, 0930–1700 Friday. Banks in
Freeport: 0900–1300 Monday to Friday,
1500–1700 Friday.
Shops: 0900–1700, or 1000–1800,
Monday to Friday. Some close Thursday or
Saturday afternoons.
Government offices: 0900–1730 Monday to
Friday.

ELECTRICITY: 110 V, 60 Hz

PUBLIC HOLIDAYS
1 January: New Year's Day
Good Friday, Easter Monday

Whit Monday
First Friday in June: Labour Day
10 July: Independence Celebrations
First Monday in August
12 October: Discovery Day
25, 26 December: Christmas

EVENTS
Early March: Cruising Regatta in George
Town, Great Exuma.
Late April: Out Island Regatta in George
Town, Great Exuma.
December 26, January 1: Junkanoo

COMMUNICATIONS
There is a public telephone, cable and
telex office open 24 hours in the
Telecommunications Building (Batelco) on
East St, Nassau. International calls can be
made from metered booths at telephone
offices on all major islands, also from
public card phones. Main post office, East
Hill Street.
There are many international flights from
Nassau and several to US and Canada

from Freeport. There are also international
flights from George Town, Exuma and
Marsh Harbour, Abaco. All inhabited islands
are linked to Nassau by internal flights.

MEDICAL
The Princess Margaret Hospital
Tel. 3222861 in Nassau is the main facility.
Doctors Hospital in Nassau, *Tel.* 322-8411,
has excellent facilities at comparable US
prices. Most inhabited islands have a clinic.
Police *Tel.* 322-4444,
Ambulance *Tel.* 322-2221.
BASRA air sea rescue monitor VHF Channel
16 or 24 hour *Tel.* 322-3877.

DIPLOMATIC MISSIONS
In Nassau:
Canada: Out Island Traders Bldg, Ernest St.
Tel. 393-2123.
Haiti: Marlborough St. *Tel.* 322-2109.
United Kingdom: Bitco Bldg, East St.
Tel. 325-7471.
United States: Mosmar Bldg, Queen St.
Tel. 322-1181.

these should be used in preference to anchors.

The proximity to the USA has profoundly affected the islands, particularly those closest to Florida, which are visited by large numbers of tourists, cruise ships and yachts. Outside of the main tourist centres, however, the Bahamas have changed little and the slow pace of life in the outer islands is their enduring charm.

Because of their convenient position, the Bahamas were used in the past as a transit point for drugs destined for the USA. A concerted effort by all countries in the region has virtually put an end to this activity. Occasionally cruising boats are stopped by the US Coast Guard while crossing to the mainland, but this is far less frequent than in the late 1980s or early 1990s.

Country Profile

On 12 October 1492, Christopher Columbus made his first landfall in the New World on the island of San Salvador. At that time the Bahamas were inhabited by the peaceful Lucayans, who were to disappear as a people within a few years, as the Spanish deported most of the population to work in the gold and silver mines in Hispaniola

and Cuba. Once plundered of their only resource, people, the Spanish left the islands alone.

From the time of the first settlement in 1629 by Protestant settlers from Bermuda escaping religious persecution, the Bahamas have remained under British rule until 1973 when they became a fully independent nation. With the development of merchant shipping between the New World and Europe, piracy became common with such renowned figures as Blackbeard finding the deserted islands and reefs perfect hiding places. At the end of the American War of Independence many loyalists fled to the Bahamas and established cotton plantations, which met with little success in the poor soil. The descendants of the slaves brought over to work on these plantations, emancipated in 1838, form the majority of the inhabitants today.

The geographical position of the Bahamas has always influenced its history, from being a refuge for gun-runners during the American Civil War to making the fortune of those running liquor to the USA during the Prohibition era. This aspect continued with the islands becoming a large transhipment area for illegal drugs on their way to the USA. The conditions which suited the seventeenth century pirate worked equally well for the twentieth century drug baron.

Over 3 million tourists visit the Bahamas every year and the majority of the population is employed in the tourist industry, which is the backbone of the economy. The absence of income tax and strict bank secrecy laws have made the Bahamas a tax haven and important financial centre. The government has made efforts to develop other areas of the economy, particularly agriculture, to help meet domestic demand.

The total population of the islands is 260,000, largely of African origin with a minority of English and American origin. Only 30 of the islands are inhabited and 75 per cent of the population lives on New Providence Island, location of the capital Nassau. The outer islands are known as the Family Islands. English is the main language. There are many religious denominations, mainly Christian, particularly Anglican and Roman Catholic.

The Bahamian climate is very pleasant, lying on the edge of the anticyclone belt. The weather is particularly pleasant in summer, between June and October, when it is cooler than on the eastern seaboard of the USA or in the Eastern Caribbean islands. Unfortunately this is also the hurricane season, which lasts from July to November. Although several years can go by without a hurricane affecting the Bahamas, occasionally they are hit by a particularly violent one, such as Hurricane Floyd in 1999, which caused extensive damage. This risk should be born in mind by those who spend the hurricane season in the Bahamas.

Entry Regulations

Ports of entry

Abaco: Walker's Cay 26°32′N 76°57′W, Green Turtle Cay 26°45′N 77°20′W, Marsh Harbour 26°40′N 75°05′W, Sandy Point 26°01′N 77°24′W.
Andros: Nicholl's Town 25°07′N 78°02′W, San Andros 24°43′N 77°47′W, Fresh Creek 24°41′N 77°50′W, Mangrove Cay 24°13′N 77°36′W, Congo Town.
Berry Islands: Great Harbour Cay 25°44′N 77°49′W, Chub Cay 25°44′N 77°49′W.
North Bimini: Alice Town 25°20′N 76°29′W.
Cat Cay: Cat Cay Club 25°33′N 79°18′W.
Eleuthera: Harbour Island 25°34′N 76°40′W, Hatchet Bay 25°20′N 76°29′W, Governor's Harbour 25°12′N 76°15′W, Rock Sound 24°53′N 76°16′W, Cape Eleuthera (sometimes) 25°12′N 76°15′W.
Exuma: George Town 23°34′N 75°49′W.
Grand Bahama: West End 26°42′N 78°59′W,

Freeport Harbour 26°31′N 78°47′W, Lucaya Marina 26°29′N 78°38′W, Xanadu Marina 26°29′N 78°42′W.
Inagua: Matthew Town 20°57′N 73°41′W.
New Providence: Any marina in Nassau 25°04′N 77°21′W.
Ragged Island: Duncan Town 22°12′N 75°44′W.
San Salvador: Cockburn Town 24°03′N 74°32′W.
Abrahams Bay on Mayaguana Island is not listed as an official port of entry, and boats trying to either clear in or out of the Bahamas there have not been able to do so. Those wishing to stop on their way out should make this clear when clearing out of the last official port of entry as one is not supposed to stop at Mayaguana without permission. Those who wish to make this their first stop in the Bahamas may only do so with permission from the local police officer, but they must complete clearance formalities at the earliest convenience at one of the listed ports of entry. Several boats have had problems at Mayaguana, which is not an official port of entry.

Procedure on arrival

Entry into the Bahamas must be made at one of the official ports of entry. The Q flag should be flown within three miles of the port and no one should go ashore until pratique has been granted. Clearance must be done on arrival and in major ports officers are on call at all hours. The Bahamas can be transited without clearing in until one arrives at a port of entry, but during transit one cannot anchor overnight or enter a port. In the out islands, the customs officer may handle all formalities, but in Nassau and other larger ports both the customs and immigration officials must be seen. Officials are supposed to come to the yacht, but in some smaller islands the captain will have to go ashore to find them. Crew must remain on board until clearance is completed. If clearing in at a marina, the marina personnel will call customs and immigration.

Duplicate copies of Maritime Declaration of Health, Inward Report for Pleasure Vessels and crew lists will have to be filled in. A cruising permit valid for one year will be granted. This document must remain on board at all times. Every crew member must complete an immigration card, so they may have to accompany the skipper to sign the individual forms. A VHF/SSB radio operator's licence may also be required.

Penalties are severe (fines, imprisonment, confiscation of the boat) for not clearing customs.

Clearance must be done on arrival, and in major

ports officers are on call at all hours; in such places one is not allowed to anchor off and wait until morning, to avoid overtime charges. The Bahamas can be transited without clearing in until one arrives at a port of entry at a convenient time, but during transit one cannot anchor overnight or enter a port. In the outer islands normally the customs officer handles all formalities, but in Nassau both the customs and immigration officials must be seen.

Movement of vessels is strictly controlled in Nassau, Freeport and George Town, where all yachts are required to clear with Nassau Harbour Control (VHF Channel 16) when entering, leaving and even changing position within these ports.

Customs

Firearms and the exact amount of ammunition must be declared and listed on the ship's declaration. Personal firearms are permitted as part of a ship's equipment on visiting yachts in Bahamian waters, but cannot be used and must remain locked on board throughout the stay. After three months, these become liable for duty and a permit must be obtained from the police. Customs inspect boats occasionally and one may also be boarded by the Royal Bahamas Defence Force, who check firearms and ammunition. Any discrepancies from the declared quantities can cause serious difficulties.

A permit costing $10 from the Ministry of Agriculture and Fisheries is required for any animals on board. Cats and dogs need a valid anti-rabies certificate, issued from ten days to nine months previously.

Vessels may remain in the Bahamas for a maximum of three years, but yearly extensions must be obtained from Bahamas Customs in Nassau. Each extension costs $500 payable by bank draft in favour of 'The Public Treasury'. Procedures for the extension should be started before the expiry of the current permit. Letters should be addressed to: Comptroller of Customs, PO Box N 155, Nassau. The number of the existing permit should be quoted and a copy enclosed for reference.

Bicycles carried on board should be registered if they are to be used ashore. Spare parts and equipment imported into the Bahamas for yachts with a valid cruising permit are free of customs duty, but may be charged 7 per cent stamp duty. Such imported parts or equipment must be accompanied by a copy of the cruising permit, which should have been sent to the shipper when ordering. Equipment sent for repair should be shown to customs when a customs form C40, showing serial

numbers, will be given to you. On reimportation of the repaired item, stamp duty may be payable on the repair charges; the serial number must match the C40.

It is illegal to sell or attempt to sell any equipment from your vessel without first declaring such items to customs and paying import duty and stamp duty, including selling to another foreign vessel on a temporary cruising permit. Bicycles carried on board should be registered at the first port of call if they are to be used ashore.

Immigration

US and Canadian citizens can enter with proof of identity only for a stay of up to three weeks. A valid passport is necessary for longer visits.

A stay of up to six months, which may be extended to eight months, is normally granted for nationals of the following countries: European Union (except Austria, Denmark, Finland, France, Germany, Ireland, Portugal, Sweden, who may stay up to three months), Iceland, Liechtenstein, Norway, San Marino, Switzerland, Turkey, and the United States. For up to a three month stay, visas are not required of: Israel, Japan, Mexico, Commonwealth countries (except Maldives, Namibia, Pakistan and Nauru, who require visas), Djibouti, Fiji and Sao Tomé. For up to two weeks, visas are not required of nationals of Latin American countries.

After the permitted time, including any extensions, has expired, one must leave the country either by boat or by air. A copy of the cruising permit, or of the extension, should be taken abroad to avoid having to show a return ticket to the airline and/or immigration when re-entering the Bahamas.

Cruising permit (transire)

All vessels receive a Temporary Cruising Permit for twelve months on payment of a flat fee of $100. The transire must be presented to officials if requested at any port visited. The permit must be retained until the cruise is finished and handed back at the port of exit. If for any reason one is not able to clear out, the transire should be posted back from the next destination. Immigration papers should also be returned.

Procedure on departure

Departure formalities are simple and boats may leave without formally clearing out although the cruising permit should be handed in to a customs officer on departure. If this is not possible, the permit should be returned by mail. However, as some countries, notably the Dominican Republic, require a clearing out document, this should be obtained on departure from the Bahamas.

Fees

Pleasure vessels clearing into the Bahamas now pay an overall fee according to a new regulation (90A), which came into force on 1 July 1999. This overall fee incorporates all previous clearance fees, as well as overtime. A flat fee is now charged whatever time of day or day of the week a vessel clears at a port of entry.

1 A fee of $100 is payable by any pleasure craft, this fee covering the compulsory fishing permit, a cruising permit and any attendance fees payable to customs, as well as any overtime and travel costs for the attendance of an immigration officer. The permit may be extended for up to two additional years for a fee of $500 per year.

2 Vessels that carry more than four passengers or crew will pay an additional fee of $15 for each person over the age of six.

Restrictions

No marine life at all may be captured in the national marine parks, Exuma Cays Land and Sea Park, Peterson Cay National Park (Grand Bahama) and Pelican Cays (Abaco). Elsewhere, fishing regulations are strict. A fishing permit, issued at the time of inbound clearance, is included in the $100. There is a minor inconsistency over fees for fishing permits, which cost $150 per annum from the Fisheries Department or $20 for a single visit (undefined as to length). There is a one mile no spearfishing zone around New Providence Island and the south coast of Grand Bahama Island, with a 200 yard zone around all other islands. On arrival a fishing permit should be requested from the customs officer; this is required by any foreign vessel fishing in Bahamian waters for non-commercial purposes. The cost of the permit at the Exuma Land and Sea Park is $50, which entitles the boat for two nights of free mooring as well as free park access for the entire year. Fishing may only be done with a hook and line, no more than six lines are allowed, and spears, fish traps, nets (other than landing nets) and spearguns (apart from the Hawaiian sling) are prohibited. Scuba gear may not be used for fishing. The maximum catch of kingfish, dolphin fish and wahoo is six in total per person and no more than 20 lb (9 kg) of scalefish, plus ten conch or six crawfish per person. The latter may only be caught in season (1 August to 31 March) and females with eggs must be left. Turtles, coral or sea mammals must not be taken,

nor any species that are undersize. It should be noted that the Royal Bahamas Defence Force regularly patrols sensitive areas and has the power to inspect any boat they suspect of flouting either these regulations or the drug laws. They monitor VHF Channel 16.

Facilities

Almost everything is available in Nassau, which has several marinas, chandleries and repair facilities. Fuel and other marine supplies are also easily available and so are provisions. There is an excellent fresh produce market at Potter's Cay. *The Yachtsman's Guide to the Bahamas* gives details of facilities available not only in Nassau, but throughout the islands.

Another popular destination with good facilities is Freeport on Grand Bahama Island. The main port is geared to dealing primarily with commercial vessels, so visiting yachts might find it more convenient to clear in at nearby Lucayan or Xanadu Marinas. Facilities at both are good and most repairs can be undertaken locally. In the outer islands George Town in Great Exuma is slowly establishing itself as a yachting centre where minor repairs can be effected. Basic supplies are available and also charts for the Bahamas. There is also a daily fresh produce market. Any parts that are not available locally can be obtained from either Nassau or Florida to which there are frequent flights.

Further Reading

Yachtsman's Guide to the Bahamas
Bahamas: Insight Guide
Cruising Guide to the Abacos and the Northern Bahamas
The Gentleman's Guide to Passages South
Bahamas Cruising Guide
On & Off the Beaten Path (Central & Southern Bahamas)
Exuma Guide
Abaco Guide (including Grand Bahama)
Near Bahamas
Exumas
Far Bahamas

Website

www.bahamas.com (Ministry of Tourism)

BARBADOS

As the most easterly of the Lesser Antilles, Barbados is a comparatively flat island and to windward of all the other islands. It is the nearest landfall for yachts crossing the Atlantic on the traditional trade wind route. The windward position of Barbados means that few yachts attempt to beat their way against the prevailing trade winds from the other islands of the Lesser Antilles to visit this island which has little to offer from the cruising point of view.

The cruising yachts that call in Barbados usually arrive after a long passage either from the Canaries or Cape Verdes across the North Atlantic or when sailing up from Brazil and the South Atlantic and make a stop before sailing on elsewhere.

Despite having a developed tourist industry which benefits from the island's good airlinks, little has been done for those arriving by sea and facilities in Carlisle Bay, the main anchorage, are very basic. The only cruising area is along the sheltered west coast, where most of the tourist development lies.

After almost 3000 miles of Atlantic Ocean, most boats make their landfall on the SE coast of Barbados, which is easily detectable at night by the strong loom of the airport lights. The east coast, exposed to the Atlantic breakers, is wild with strange rock formations along its beaches and should be given a wide berth.

Country Profile

The pre-Columbian population of Barbados were probably Arawaks, eventually driven out by the warlike Caribs. The island was named Bearded Island – Isla de los Barbados – by the Portuguese, after the bearded fig-trees found growing there. Pedros a Campos, the Portuguese explorer, landed here in 1536 on his way to Brazil, but the first settlers in the seventeenth century were English. By then the island was uninhabited, although why the Amerindians left is not known. Jamestown, near the present-day Holetown, was the first settlement, founded in 1627. A year later the rival Bridgetown, eventually to become the capital, was established. Tobacco, cotton and sugar cane crops were developed, and thousands of slaves brought over from Africa. Barbados grew into a flourishing colony and centre for maritime trade, and through the eighteenth and nineteenth centuries the influx of English settlers continued. Due to its position it

never changed hands unlike its Caribbean neighbours and remained British throughout. Barbados became independent in November 1966.

Sugar was always the cornerstone of the economy, and remains important today. Sugar, molasses, syrup and rum are exported. There is some light industry. Tourism in recent years has increased greatly, and is an important source of employment on this relatively affluent island.

The population is 280,000, mainly descendants of mixed African and European origin. There is a small white minority of English origin. English and Bajan, a dialect, are spoken. Of more than 70 religious denominations, the largest is Anglican. Barbados has a tropical climate, although as the island is further south, it rarely is hit by hurricanes. June to January is the rainy and humid season.

Entry Regulations

Port of entry
Bridgetown 13°06′N, 59°38′W.

Procedure on arrival
Clearance can only be done in the Deepwater Harbour north of Bridgetown. On approach, yachts should call the signal station on VHF Channel 12 (callsign 8PB) and will be advised where to proceed. Once permission is given, the yacht should go into the Deepwater Harbour and unless advised to the contrary come alongside the Cross Berth, in the southern corner. Because of the large fenders set up for cruise ships, this is an unsatisfactory place to tie up a sailing boat, especially if there is any surge. If so, it may be better to launch the dinghy and for the captain to visit the various offices while the rest of the crew stay with the boat. One should stay in radio contact while entering the harbour to ensure no other vessel is manoeuvring, as the harbour frequently has cruise ships berthed there. The Q flag must be flown until clearance is complete. The captain only should proceed to clear customs, health and immigration in the Customs Examination Hall behind the Cross Berth, from 0600–2200 seven days a week. Overtime rates will be charged after 1700. If arriving outside these hours, yachts may be directed by the signal station to anchor in the Quarantine anchorage in Carlisle Bay and the crew should not go ashore. The following morning the yacht must proceed into the Deepwater Harbour as outlined above.

After entry formalities are complete, a yacht may

Practical Information

LOCAL TIME: GMT – 4

BUOYAGE: IALA B

CURRENCY: Barbados dollar (BDS$).

BUSINESS HOURS
Banks: 0900–1500 Monday to Thursday,
0900–1300, 1500–1700 Friday.
Shops: 0800–1800 Monday to Saturday.
Business and government offices:
0730–1630 Monday to Friday.

ELECTRICITY: 120 V, 50 Hz

PUBLIC HOLIDAYS
1 January: New Year's Day
21 January: Errol Barrow Day
Good Friday
Easter Monday
1 May: Labour Day
Whit Monday

First Monday in August: Emancipation Day
First Monday in October: UN Day
30 November: Independence Day
25, 26 December: Christmas

EVENTS
Crop Over Festival: July, at the end of
sugar harvest.
Mount Gay Regatta: Boxing Day, three
days of yacht racing.

COMMUNICATIONS
Overseas calls, telex, telegraph and fax
from Barbados External
Telecommunications (BET) on the Wharf in
Bridgetown. Cable & Wireless, Lower
Broad Street, 0700–1900 Monday to
Friday, 0700–1300 Saturday.
Phone cards can be bought which can be
used on most English-speaking Caribbean
islands. Bridgetown main post office, open
0730–1700 Monday to Friday, others

0730–1200, 1300–1500 Monday,
0800–1200, 1300–1515 Tuesday to Friday.
There are international flights from
Grantley Adams airport to the USA,
Canada, Europe, South America and many
Caribbean destinations. There are
connecting flights from international flights
to the smaller Caribbean islands.

MEDICAL
Facilities are good. There is a reciprocal
Health Agreement with the UK.

DIPLOMATIC MISSIONS
Canada: Bishops Court Hill, Pine Rd,
Bridgetown. *Tel.* 429-3550.
United Kingdom: Lower Collymore Rock,
St Michael. *Tel.* 436-6694.
United States: Broad St, Bridgetown.
Tel. 436-4950.
Venezuela: Hastings, Christ Church.
Tel. 435-7619.

anchor in Carlisle Bay or berth in the Careenage in the centre of town. Docking space in the Careenage is limited and permission to berth there must be obtained from the harbour master at the Barbados Port Authority (*Tel.* 436-6883).

Permission has to be obtained from customs, preferably requested on arrival, if wishing to cruise or anchor along the coast away from Carlisle Bay.

On departure, the port authority's clearance must be obtained first in order to get customs clearance. Outward clearance is valid for 24 hours after it has been granted. A vessel must proceed directly to sea from the Deepwater Harbour after receiving outward clearance.

Customs

Firearms must be licensed and declared immediately to customs on arrival. They will be kept in custody until departure. Penalties for non-declaration or possessing an unlicensed firearm are severe.

Animals are not allowed to land.

Chartering is forbidden for foreign yachts.

Immigration

Passports must be valid three months beyond the length of stay.

Visas are not required for stays of up to six months for nationals of the European Union, Argentina, Colombia, Dominican Republic, Fiji, Hong Kong, Iceland, Israel, Japan, South Korea, Norway, Peru, Switzerland, Tunisia, Turkey, Venezuela, the United States, and Commonwealth countries (except South Africa, who may stay up to 30 days, and India and Pakistan, who require visas). Nationals of most East European countries, Brazil, Chile, Costa Rica and Cuba, may stay visa-free up to 28 days. All others require a visa.

Extensions are difficult to obtain, so on arrival one should state the maximum time one intends to stay. Extensions must be applied for at the immigration office in the harbour (open 0830–1630), cost BDS$12.50, and are time-consuming to obtain.

Immigration must be notified of any crew changes. Crew flying in must have a letter from the captain confirming that they will be leaving by yacht. They may still have difficulties with immigration officers at the airport if an onward air ticket cannot be shown, so it is advisable for the captain to meet crew and take the ship's papers along. If any crew are disembarking after the yacht has been cleared, they must go with the captain to inform immigration. If transferring to another vessel, both captains must go with the crew member.

Fees

Small light dues calculated by tonnage, unless under 5 tons. Stamp duty on both entry and exit amounts to BDS$50 in total.

Facilities

Most boats stay at anchor in Carlisle Bay and commute ashore by dinghy. Dinghies can be taken to the Boatyard jetty, which has some facilities for cruising boats, such as toilets, showers and laundry, as well as water. The presence of an active racing community, centred on the Barbados Yacht Club, ensures that there is a good range of repair facilities. There are two chandleries in the capital Bridgetown, which have a limited selection of marine hardware. Mannings stock charts and cruising guides for the Caribbean and are the only place to undertake rigging work, as they have both the wire and a swaging press. As Barbados is a relatively developed island, electrical, electronic, refrigeration, metal-working workshops and other facilities are found even if not catering primarily for yachts.

Most engine repair, both diesel and outboard, can be done on the island as all major manufacturers are represented locally. There is a travelift at the Shallow Draft Harbour, operated by Willie's Marine Services (*Tel.* 424 1808). Sail repair can be done via the Barbados Yacht Club, which welcomes visitors and can be of help in an emergency.

A new marine facility is being completed at Port St Charles (13°15.46′N 59°38.41′W), on the NW coast of the island. Centred around a man-made lagoon, this is a de-luxe development catering primarily for super-yachts and with prices to match. All usual facilities, as well as duty-free fuel on departure, are available. It is envisaged that when the project is finished, in 2003, it may be designated an official port of entry.

Further Reading

The Atlantic Crossing Guide

Websites

www.barbados.org (Barbados Tourism Authority)
www.portstcharles.com (Port St Charles Marina)

BONAIRE

The stunning underwater scenery is the chief attraction of this easternmost of the ABC islands and anyone with even the smallest interest in diving should use their stay to best advantage.

Bonaire is ranked as one of the top three dive spots in the world and as a result the whole island is a protected marine park.

Bonaire is less densely populated than its neighbour Curaçao and also less developed. The slow pace of life on the island and its relaxed population have an enduring charm. For visiting sailors the attraction also lies in the better than average repair and service facilities. A much needed marina was created by dredging a channel through to a salt pond close to the capital Kralendijk.

Country Profile

The island was discovered along with Aruba and Curaçao in 1499 by the Spaniard Alonso de Ojeda. At that time an Arawak tribe, the Caiquetios, lived there, and although many did not survive, they managed to retain their identity on Bonaire until the end of the nineteenth century. The Dutch took the island in 1636 and the ABC islands changed hands several times as the European powers fought for colonies in the Caribbean, although from 1816 Dutch rule was firmly established. After the Second World War demands for more autonomy grew stronger, and in 1954 the Netherlands Antilles were granted full internal autonomy.

Lacking natural resources and a good harbour, Bonaire was never as prosperous as Curaçao. The economy is fairly diversified, with salt, textiles and rice on the traditional side, and oil transhipment and radio communications more modern sources of income. Tourism is an important foreign exchange earner. The island's population numbers over 11,000 of mixed Arawak, European and African descent. They speak Dutch, the official language, and Papiamento. English and Spanish are also widely spoken. The majority are Roman Catholics, with a Protestant minority. The capital is Kralendijk.

Entry Regulations

Ports of entry
Kralendijk 12°09′N 68°17′W.

Procedure on arrival
Kralendijk: Yachts clearing in must call the harbour master on Channel 16 who will probably request that the boat comes alongside the town pier. Alternatively, customs may allow a mooring

Practical Information

LOCAL TIME: GMT – 4

BUOYAGE: IALA B

CURRENCY: Antillean guilder or florin of 100 cents.

BUSINESS HOURS
Banks: 0930–1200, 1400–1600 Monday to Friday.
Shops: 0800–1200, 1400–1800 Monday to Saturday, and for a few hours on Sundays, if there are cruise ships in port.
Business: 0800–1200, 1400–1830 Monday to Friday.

ELECTRICITY: 110/130 V, 50 Hz

PUBLIC HOLIDAYS
1 January: New Year's Day
Good Friday and Easter Monday
30 April: Queen's Birthday
1 May: Labour Day
Ascension
Whit Monday
6 September: Bonaire Day
25, 26 December: Christmas

EVENTS
Carnival in February or March

MEDICAL
St Francis Hospital. *Tel.* 8900/8445; has a decompression chamber.
Police, fire, ambulance. *Tel.* 11.
Emergency. *Tel.* 14.

COMMUNICATIONS
There is a telecommunications and post office on J.A. Abraham Blvd, Kralendijk, open 0730–1200, 1330–1700 weekdays. There are flights from Bonaire to Aruba and Curaçao, and also to New York and Miami.

DIPLOMATIC MISSIONS
Venezuela: Breedestr. Kralendijk. *Tel.* 8275.

to be picked up; these are controlled by the marina. The customs office is close by and is open 24 hours a day seven days a week and no overtime is charged. Next one must visit the immigration office located a short distance from the port above the cinema. After clearance one is free to take a mooring.

Harbour Village Marina: This is a small marina just north of Kralendijk, where clearance by customs can also be done.

Customs

All firearms are impounded until departure, including flare guns and spearguns.

To either buy or import equipment duty free one has to fill in a special form obtainable from the customs office. Customs sometimes insist on inspecting the boat before departure to see that the item is still on board.

Immigration

All require passports except nationals of Benelux countries, Germany, Canada, the United States, San Marino, Venezuela, who must show an national identity card or some other recognised form of identification.

Nationals of all countries can stay for 14 days without a visa, except for those of the Dominican Republic and some of the former Communist countries who require visas. For those intending to stay 14–28 days, a Temporary Certificate of Admission will be issued by immigration on arrival to nationals of most countries, including the Benelux countries, Germany, Spain and the UK. This can be renewed for up to three months. Nationals of most East European and still communist countries

must apply for the Certificate before arrival.

For stays exceeding 90 days all nationals require a visa.

Restrictions

Due to the marine park status of the island, spearfishing is forbidden and marine life of any description may not be removed or destroyed. Spearguns must be left with customs for the duration of one's stay as it is illegal to have a speargun in one's possession.

The authorities are making great efforts to protect the marine environment. Anchoring is prohibited everywhere except in the designated area between North Pier and Harbour Village Marina. Anchoring anywhere else, except in an emergency, is an offence. The only exception is for boats under 12 ft (4 m) who may anchor with a stone anchor. Cruising boats are now expected to have holding tanks and the discharge of any waste is prohibited. There are mooring buoys on all popular diving sites, and since 1999 a fee has been charged for using them.

The marinas collect fees on behalf of the Bonaire Underwater Park. Hurricane Lenny did considerable damage to the reefs and also to some local boats. As a result, boats may now be requested by the port captain to leave a mooring in bad weather.

Cruising boats are expected to use only VHF Channels 71, 77 and 88A, as most other channels have been allocated to local operators. Which channels to use as working channels should be ascertained when clearing in as the use of unauthorised channels can lead to fines and confiscation of equipment.

Fees
A $10 diving fee allows diving at all sites.

Facilities

There are three marinas in Bonaire: Plaza Resort, Club Nautico and Harbour Village Marina. The latter is sometimes referred to as Bonaire Marina and has the best repair facilities. Harbour Village Marina has good repair facilities. Propane bottles can be filled by leaving them at the marina office to be returned one day later. Water may be purchased at Harbour Village Marina and at Club Nautico. Fuel is available at Harbour Village Marina or from local service stations.

There are several good supermarkets in Kralendijk and although the selection might be better in Curaçao, the advantage of shopping in Bonaire is that everything is very conveniently situated. The biggest supermarket is Cultimara and there are several shops which sell case lots at a reduced price.

Further Reading

Yachting Guide to the ABC Islands
Cruising Guide to Venezuela and Bonaire

Websites

www.interknowledge.com/bonaire (Tourism Development Corporation)
www.infobonaire.com
www.abc-yachting.com

BRITISH VIRGIN ISLANDS

The Virgin Islands are an archipelago comprising hundreds of small islands and cays situated between Puerto Rico and the Leeward Islands. The western part, having some of the larger islands, is US territory, while the eastern half is a British dependency. The language and currency are shared, but the US Virgin Islands are more developed and culturally different. The largest British islands are Tortola, Virgin Gorda, Jost van Dyke and Anegada, the latter being slightly set apart, while the former are grouped together around the Sir Francis Drake channel.

There are few island groups in the world which are better suited for cruising than the Virgins. They are scenically beautiful, there are countless bays, coves and anchorages, the waters are sheltered from the strong trade winds and ocean swells and navigation is never taxing. With so many convenient hideaways and access channels it is not surprising that the islands became a favourite base for the pirates and buccaneers who in days gone by were roaming the surrounding seas in search of bounty. It is exactly these same features which attract modern-day sailors to these shores and the British Virgins are now the largest bareboat charter centre in the world. For this reason they are often less attractive to the long-distance cruising sailors, who prefer the less crowded islands of the Caribbean.

Country Profile

The original inhabitants were Arawaks and Caribs. Visited by Columbus on his second voyage, he named the islands after St Ursula and her 11,000 virgin warriors who died rather than submit to pagan assault. Soon after their discovery, the Virgin Islands' strategic position rapidly turned them into a popular stop for vessels plying between Europe and America. The Caribs, pirates and privateers all harassed the Spanish settlements and ships from the Spanish Main returning laden with gold and silver. Infamous figures such as Henry Morgan and Sir John Hawkins operated in this area and the Virgin Islands were the inspiration for R.L. Stevenson's *Treasure Island*.

As Spanish power waned, colonisation by other European nations became more serious and several countries fought over the islands. At the end of the seventeenth century England annexed Tortola, then Virgin Gorda and Anegada. Plantations were established and slaves brought in for labour. Civil government over the islands was minimal. With the slump in sugar cane and slave rebellions leading to their emancipation, economic problems occurred with a resulting labour shortage. After 1956 the British Virgin Islands became separately administered from the rest of the British West Indies, and developed more links with the US Virgin Islands. Today the British Virgin Islands have internal self-government, but remain a British overseas territory.

Much of the land is cultivated, mostly for fruit and vegetables, yet reliance on food imports means there is a high cost of living. Tourism is very

Practical Information

LOCAL TIME: GMT – 4

BUOYAGE: IALA B. The BVI changed over to the IALA B system in 1984. However, some buoys were just painted over and have been reported as revealing their original colours after a few years.

CURRENCY: US dollar (US$).

BUSINESS HOURS
Banks: 0900–1400 Monday–Friday, also 1600–1800 on Fridays.
Shops: 0900–1700 Monday–Saturday.
Supermarkets: 0700–2300 daily.
Government offices: 0830–1630 Monday–Friday.
Business: 0830–1700 Monday to Friday.

ELECTRICITY: 110 V, 60 Hz

PUBLIC HOLIDAYS
1 January: New Year's Day
Second Monday in March: Commonwealth Day
Good Friday
Easter Monday
Whit Monday
Second Monday in June: Queen's Birthday
1 July: Territory Day
Beginning of August: Summer Festival (Monday, Tuesday, Wednesday)
21 October: St Ursula's Day
14 November: Prince Charles' Birthday
25, 26 December: Christmas

EVENTS
Easter Festival, on Virgin Gorda BVI
Spring Regatta, on Tortola, March–April
BVI Festival in Road Town, early August

COMMUNICATIONS
International telephone calls, telex and fax at Cable & Wireless, offices at Wickhams Cay, Road Town, and The Valley, Virgin Gorda, open 0700–1900 Monday to Friday, 0700–1600 Saturday, 0900–1400 Sunday and public holidays.
Emergency: dial 999.
There are flights to other Caribbean destinations but no direct flights to Europe or the USA. Connections are usually made in St Thomas, USVI, Antigua or Puerto Rico.

MEDICAL
Peebles Hospital, Road Town. Tel. 494 3497.

important and is one of two pillars of a thriving economy. Tax privileges have prompted the islands' growth as an offshore business centre. English is spoken and most people are Protestant. The capital is Road Town on Tortola, the largest island in the British Virgin Islands, where about half the total population of 20,000 lives.

Entry Regulations

Ports of entry
Tortola: Road Harbour 18°25′N 64°37′W, Sopers Hole 18°23′N 64°42′W.
Jost van Dyke: Great Harbour 18°27′N 64°45′W.
Virgin Gorda: Virgin Gorda Yacht Harbour 18°27′N 64°26′W.
There are two other entry points, Port Purcell and Beef Island Airport, but yachts are not supposed to enter or clear at these.

Procedure on arrival
Ship's papers, passports and last clearance must be shown, and an inward manifest and/or outward manifest, and crew list completed. It should be noted that the British Virgin Islands and the US Virgin Islands require full customs clearance out and in when sailing between them. If, however, one's stay is short, one may be able to clear in and out at the same time.
Road Harbour: Customs and immigration are at the government dock at Road Town. One should anchor off the dock and check in with customs and immigration before proceeding elsewhere. The office is open 0830–1630 Monday to Friday, 0830–1230 Saturday.
Sopers Hole: Offices are at the ferry dock at West End. Ferries from the US Virgin Islands stop here, which can mean that clearance takes longer if a ferry arrives.
Great Harbour: Customs and immigration offices are in the same building by the dock.
Virgin Gorda: Offices are in a new government office block by the ferry jetty.

Customs
Firearms are not allowed to be kept on board and must be surrendered to Customs until departure. This law is strictly enforced. For animals, a valid health certificate issued at least two weeks prior to arrival must be shown, plus a valid anti-rabies certificate (dogs and cats) and proof that the animal is free from disease. No animals can be landed without a permit and must remain secured on board at all times. A permit may be obtained from the Department of Agriculture in Road Town by giving full details (species, sex, age, colour, country of origin, owner's name and address, means of arrival). A charge of US$5 per animal is made by customs at the time of clearance and all certificates must be presented at the same time. The penalty for breaking the law is a fine and impounding of

the animal. Yachts in transit may import spare parts free of duty. If the parts are to be fitted by a local company, 5 per cent duty on the value must be paid.

Immigration

No visas are required for nationals of Commonwealth countries, most European countries, Argentina, Brazil, Bolivia, Chile, Costa Rica, El Salvador, Ecuador, Japan, Mexico, Panama, Paraguay, Russia, Turkey, Tunisia, Uruguay, Venezuela and the United States, if the visit does not exceed six months. All other nationals require visas.

Normally a 30 day stay is given on arrival. All members of the crew must be present to clear immigration.

Charter

If a yacht is chartered complete with crew, the captain and crew are not required to pay a cruising fee, but the charter guests are. On a bareboat charter, everyone on board is required to pay the daily cruising fee.

Fees

Harbour dues and ships' dues depending on the size of the boat.

BVI registered boats pay US$2 per person per day (December 1 to April 30), and 0.75c (May 1 to November 30). Foreign registered boats pay a fee of US$4 per person per day all year round plus $10–15 per visit per boat. Visiting crewed charter boats also have to pay a departure tax of US$4 per person. These charges only apply to yachts that are chartering. Charter licence annual fee from $400 (under 40 ft/12 m) to $800 (over 50 ft/15 m).

Overtime must be paid for customs clearance outside 0830–1530 Monday to Friday, 0830–1230 Saturdays and on public holidays.

Restrictions

Non-residents must obtain a recreational fishing permit in order to fish in BVI waters. Spearfishing, lobstering and the collection of live shells is prohibited. Jet-skis are prohibited in BVI waters.

National parks

A reef protection programme is in operation in an effort to limit damage caused by visiting boats. Mooring buoys have been laid in a number of sensitive areas, which have suffered extensive damage due to increased anchoring activity. Cruising boats must obtain a National Parks moorings permit and follow these regulations:

1 The reef protection buoys are colour coded:

– Red buoys: non-diving, day use only;
– Yellow buoys: commercial dive vessels only;
– White buoys: non-commercial vessels for dive use only, on a first come first served basis and a 90 minute time limit.

2 Vessels over 55 ft (17m) LOA or 35 tons may not use the mooring system.

3 Vessels must use the existing mooring line. To avoid chafe, the line may be extended.

4 The use of the buoys are at the user's risk and neither the BVI Government, which owns the buoys, nor the BVI National Parks Trust, which manages them, will bear responsibility for any loss or injury.

Facilities

Virtually all facilities are concentrated on Tortola, particularly around Road Town, where there are several marinas and a large haulout facility at Tortola Yacht Services with full facilities and services on site. There is a large marina at Nanny Cay with a travelift, chandlery and extensive repair facilities. A smaller marina at Sopers Hole has its own slipway, whereas nearby West End Slipways offer a wider range of repair facilities including a 200-ton marine railway.

The Caribbean's first walk-in weather centre, CARIBWX, is based in Road Town. Customised weather forecasts, a daily Caribbean SSB weather net, and also daily e-mail marine forecasts are among the many services they can offer. *Tel.* 494 7559, e-mail: weather@caribwx.com, and website: www.caribwx.com.

Virgin Gorda Yacht Harbour has full marina facilities, a 60-ton lift as well as good provisioning. Only basic facilities are available on Jost van Dyke at Great Harbour. On all small islands only basic provisions can be bought, so it is best to fully provision in one of the larger centres.

Further Reading

Cruising Guide to the Virgin Islands
Yachtsman's Guide to the Virgin Islands
Cruising Guide to the Caribbean

Websites

www.britishvirginislands.com
www.bviwelcome.com

CAYMAN ISLANDS

The Cayman Islands are a British Crown Colony lying south of Cuba and west of Jamaica. Known mainly for their flag of convenience seen flying at the stern of the occasional yacht, the Caymans are very much off the cruising track.

Grand Cayman, lying some 80 miles west of its smaller sisters, has several anchorages and also a well protected marina inside a shallow lagoon. Little Cayman and Cayman Brac ('bluff' in Gaelic) are less developed and even less visited by cruising yachts than the main island. Grand Cayman's chief attraction is its underwater world, which can be described as a diver's paradise. The sea surrounding the island is a marine park and conservation area.

Country Profile

The islands were first sighted by Columbus on his last voyage to the Americas. First named Las Tortugas after the large numbers of turtles frequenting the islands, later they were called Caymanas from the Carib word for the marine crocodile found there. The turtles became a popular source of fresh meat for ships' crews sailing the Caribbean.

The first settlers were English, probably deserters from Oliver Cromwell's army, which was fighting Spain for control of nearby Jamaica. The islands were ceded to Britain in 1670 and in the following century became a popular base for pirates, Spanish privateers having driven off the early English settlers. Scottish fishermen were the next to come and settle on the islands. In 1788 ten merchant ships, a convoy from Jamaica, were wrecked off Grand Cayman and all aboard were saved by the islanders. In return King George III promised the islanders exemption from taxation. The islands were dependencies of Jamaica until the independence of the latter in 1962, when the islanders chose to remain as a direct dependency of Britain.

The original settlers were fishermen, seamen and farmers. Now the islanders enjoy a high standard of living as the Cayman Islands are a tax haven, and major offshore finance and banking centre. Tourism has also developed considerably. The English speaking population of mixed African and European descent is just under 30,000, most of whom live on Grand Cayman. The capital is George Town. Many Christian denominations are practised on the island.

The island is cooled by the prevailing north east trades, so the mean winter temperature is 75°F (24°C) and in the summer 79–84°F (26–29°C). The winter northerlies make most anchorages untenable, when shelter must be sought either off the south coast or inside North Sound. The hurricane season is June to November.

Entry Regulations

Ports of entry
Grand Cayman: George Town 19°18′N 81°23′W.
Cayman Brac: Creek 19°45′N 79°44′W.

Procedure on arrival
Port Security should be called on VHF Channel 16, which is monitored 24 hours a day. They will notify customs and immigration and keep one informed regarding boarding of the yacht. Officials are extremely strict and insist that procedures are followed to the letter; visiting boats have been fined for the smallest infringement. Boats must fly the Q flag from the moment they enter territorial waters. Boats are usually visited by the mosquito control officer who will spray the inside of the boat, for which a $25 charge is made.

Boats must clear in and out of every individual island.

George Town: Boats are normally directed by Port Security to one of the orange mooring buoys. Occasionally boats are asked to go directly to the commercial dock near customs to complete formalities. Boats must arrive with an outbound clearance from their last port of call.

Cayman Brac: Customs should be contacted on Channel 16 by boats clearing into the Caymans. Boats are expected to come alongside the customs dock on the north side of the island, but if there is too much swell one may be allowed to go to a diving buoy on the south side of the island.

Little Cayman: Although not listed as an official port of entry, the resident customs agent will deal with formalities.

Customs
Firearms are held by customs for the duration of the yacht's stay, unless a yacht is fitted with a proper safe, which can be sealed. Spearguns and their parts are prohibited, and possession of spearguns is illegal. These must be declared to customs at the first port of arrival, and will normally be taken off the boat and put under bond until departure.

There are no restrictions on animals.

Practical Information

LOCAL TIME: GMT – 5

BUOYAGE: IALA B

CURRENCY: Cayman Islands dollar (CI$)
US$ can also be used. The Cayman dollar
is tied to the US dollar at a fixed parity of
$CI1 = $US1.25 or $US1 = $CI0.80.

BUSINESS HOURS
Banks: 0900–1600 Monday to Thursday,
0900–1630 Fridays.
Government offices: 0800–1700 Monday to
Friday.
Shops: 0900–1700 Monday to Friday,
0830–1230 Saturday.
Business: 0830–1700 Monday to Friday.

ELECTRICITY: 110 V, 60 Hz

PUBLIC HOLIDAYS
1 January: New Year's Day
Ash Wednesday
Good Friday, Easter Monday
Third Monday in May: Discovery Day
Monday in June following Queen's official
birthday
First Monday in July: Constitution Day
Monday in November following
Remembrance Sunday
25, 26 December: Christmas

EVENTS
Batabano: Carnival weekend, last week of
April/beginning of May
Cayman Brac has 'Brachanal' the
following Saturday.
Million dollar month: June, sport-fishing
tournament.
Pirates Week: last week October.

COMMUNICATIONS
Post office opens 0830–1330 Monday to
Friday, 0830–1200 Saturday.
International phone booths, telex, telegram,
fax at Cable & Wireless, Anderson Square,
0815–1700.
There are flights from Grand Cayman to
Kingston (Jamaica) and several US cities.
Cayman Brac also has an international airport.

MEDICAL
Good health care is available in George
Town Government Hospital and other clinics.
Cayman Islands Divers have a
recompression chamber behind Cayman
Clinic, off Crew Road, George Town.
Tel. 555. Small hospital at Cayman Brac.

DIPLOMATIC MISSIONS
United States: Cayside Galleries,
George Town. *Tel.* 98440.

Immigration

No visas are required for a stay of up to six months by nationals of West European countries, the Commonwealth, Israel, Japan, South Africa and the United States, also Argentina, Bahrain, Brazil, Chile, Costa Rica, Ecuador, El Salvador, Guatemala, Mexico, Oman, Panama, Peru, Saudi Arabia and Venezuela. If a visa is required it can be issued on arrival.

Health

Malaria still occurs occasionally and there are lots of mosquitoes and sandflies.

Fees

Overtime fees are payable after normal working hours (0830–1630 Monday to Friday).

Marine parks regulations

The Cayman Islands have a particularly rich marine life and so strict regulations are in force to protect its beauty. Many indigenous species are protected including sea turtles, iguanas and orchids. In the Marine Parks and Environmental Zones no marine life at all may be taken, although one may fish outside protected areas. There are permanent moorings on the west coast of Grand Cayman which is a popular diving area.

Anchoring: Yachts are to use fixed moorings only. Boats of less than 60 feet (18m) may anchor in sand, as long as no grappling hook is used and no coral is touched. Anchoring is permitted in designated anchorage areas and in replenishment zones.

The main restrictions are as follows:

Damaging coral by anchor or chains is prohibited. No marine life may be taken while scuba diving. No corals or sponges may be removed.

A spear gun or seine net may not be used without a licence from the Cayman Marine Conservation Board, and then only in certain areas.

The export of live fish and other marine life is prohibited.

Fishing with gill nets or poison is prohibited.

Dumping anything at all in the sea is prohibited. All yachts need a holding tank.

Lobster: The closed season is February 1 to July 31. Only spiny lobster may be taken and six-inch tail length is the minimum size. There is a catch limit of five per person or 15 per boat per day, whichever is less.

Conch: There is a catch limit of 15 per person or 20 per boat per day, whichever is less. No one may buy or receive more than 20 conch from Cayman waters per day.

Grouper: Certain areas off the east end of each of the islands are protected for grouper spawning.

Penalties: A maximum fine of $5000 and one year in jail can be applied for contravening the regulations. Confiscation of the boat and other equipment may also be ordered. The protected areas and marine parks are clearly marked while full-time officers enforce the rules and can arrest offenders.

Facilities

There are various repair facilities in George Town including two chandleries; the one on Eastern Avenue also stocks charts. Propane bottles can be filled at a fuel station on Walker Road. A boatyard on the south side of North Sound has a travelift and some repair facilities. Fuel and water can be obtained at Governor's Marina, also in North Sound, which has the usual marina services.

There are few facilities on Little Cayman and Cayman Brac, although the latter has a commercial harbour where some provisions can be obtained and some repairs could be made in an emergency.

Further Reading

Cruising Guide to the Caribbean

Website

www.caymanislands.ky (Department of Tourism)

CUBA

Largest of the Caribbean islands, Cuba is mountainous, with rich soils, forests, mineral resources and a spectacular coastline. World-famous for its cigars and its revolution, it is another example of the wide diversity of the Caribbean nations.

The possibilities of cruising in Cuba have been fairly limited until recently, when the country began encouraging tourists to visit the island. In the past a few non-American yachts have visited the island every year, especially from those countries which always maintained diplomatic relations with Cuba. In more recent years the number of yachts has increased, although experiences seem to vary greatly, some yachts managing to cruise along the coast with little restriction, while others have had to visit the country by land, their yachts being confined to their port of entry. Fortunately the situation is changing rapidly and cruising is expected to open up in Cuba. New marinas built for sports

fishermen have made life easier, and at present any sailor following the correct procedures should expect few problems. US yachts are not forbidden from cruising in Cuba, but if they do not obtain a licence from the US Treasury Department and permission from the US Coast Guard, they may experience difficulties when returning to the USA (see under United States entry). This situation may change if relations between the two countries are normalised.

Cuba has been blessed with countless natural harbours and once the country re-opens to cruising, it will quickly become a popular destination. Because the island runs in a general SE–NW direction and the prevailing winds are easterly, ideally one should sail along Cuba's coasts in a counterclockwise direction. The US still maintains a military base at Guantanamo Bay on the SE extremity of the island. This port should only be entered in an absolute emergency.

Country Profile

When discovered by Columbus in 1492 during his first voyage, the island was populated by Arawaks. Conquered by Diego Velazquez early in the sixteenth century, African slaves were introduced by the Spanish and soon replaced the Arawaks. The following century saw a long struggle for freedom and some autonomy from Spain was gained after the 1868–78 rebellion, when slavery was abolished. The United States, seeking to expand their influence in the Americas, became involved in the rebellion of 1895–8, which led to war with Spain, in which the latter was defeated. Cuba was then ruled by the US military until independence in 1901, and even after that the US continued to play an active role in Cuban affairs. The 1920s and 30s were dominated by the dictatorship of Gerardo Machado, toppled by a military coup led by Fulgencio Batista. The latter remained in power with US protection until 1959, when after three years of guerilla warfare, Fidel Castro ended Batista's rule. Castro's socialist policies turned Cuba from the US to the Soviet sphere of influence. In 1961 the Bay of Pigs invasion attempt by anti-Castro Cubans was defeated. The Cold War reached its peak with the Missile Crisis of 1962, when the USA refused to let the Soviet Union install nuclear missiles in Cuba.

The collapse of the Soviet Union, depriving Cuba of Soviet aid and an assured market for its

Practical Information

LOCAL TIME: GMT – 5 GMT – 4 April to October

BUOYAGE: IALA B

CURRENCY: Cuban peso (Cub$) of 100 centavos. US dollars are widely accepted. Tourist tokens (Dinero Intur) can only be used in the official tourist dollar shops. Exchange receipts should be kept to be able to make purchases, and to change back Cuban pesos on departure, up to US$10. The import/export of local currency is prohibited. Tourists are only permitted to pay in US dollars or with credit cards.

BUSINESS HOURS
Banco Nacional de Cuba: 0830–1200, 1330–1500 Monday to Friday, 0830–1030 Saturday
Shops: 1230–1930 Monday to Saturday.
Government offices: 0830–1230, 1330–1730 Monday to Friday, some offices open Saturday.

ELECTRICITY: 110/120 V, 60 Hz

PUBLIC HOLIDAYS
1 January: New Year's Day
2 January: Victory of Armed Forces
1 May: Labour Day
25, 26 and 27 July: Revolution Days
10 October: War of Independence Day

EVENTS
Carnival in July

COMMUNICATIONS
International direct dialling is available at all marinas and large hotels.
The main post and telegraph office is in the Hotel Habana Libre building, Calle L y 23, Vedado, Havana. In the same building is an international telephone, telex and fax centre, open 24 hours.
Telegrams can be sent from all post offices in Havana.
Collect calls are not permitted.
The postal service is very slow.

There are flights from Havana to Canada, Jamaica, and several Central and South American and European cities.
Also international airports at Santiago de Cuba, Camagüey, Holguin and Varadero.

MEDICAL
Facilities are no longer free for foreigners in Havana and other tourist areas; foreign visitors requiring treatment will be sent to clinics where payment must be made in dollars.

DIPLOMATIC MISSIONS
Canada: 518 Calle 30, corner of Av. 7, Miramar. *Tel.* (7) 332 516.
United Kingdom: Calle 34, 708 Miramar, *Tel.* 331 771.
US interests at the Swiss embassy: Calle Calzada, between Calle L and Calle M, Vedado. *Tel.* (7) 320 551.

goods, badly affected an economy already weakened by the continuing US trade embargo. Isolation led Cuba to start improving relations with Western Europe, Latin America and the Caribbean. Some economic reforms were introduced in the 1990s, allowing Cubans to hold foreign currency and permitting some small scale private enterprise. There is the burden of a large foreign debt and the economy remains dependent on agriculture, with main exports being sugar, coffee and citrus fruit, although efforts have been made to diversify. The construction industry and tourism have expanded. However, there are still severe shortages and life for the ordinary Cuban is increasingly difficult. Large numbers have emigrated to the United States.

The process of liberalisation that occurred in other Communist countries after the collapse of the Soviet empire has been very slow to arrive in Cuba, and although there has been some relaxation, due partly to the encouragement of tourism, it is felt that there cannot be any real changes while Fidel Castro continues his firm grip on power.

The capital of Cuba is Havana, in which one fifth of the 12 million Spanish-speaking population lives. The majority are of Spanish origin, about 12 per cent are black, and a small minority Chinese.

Catholicism still is the main religion, although it is mostly of the Marxist influenced 'liberation' type. Sects such as 'santeria', a mixture of popular Catholicism and the Yoruba belief, also have a considerable following.

The climate is subtropical with November to April, the cooler dry season, being the most pleasant. The rest of the year is often humid, rainy and very hot and the hurricane season is from June to November.

Entry Regulations

Ports of entry
North Coast: Santa Lucía (Pinar del Río province) 22°41′N 83°58′W, Hemingway Marina 23°05′N 82°30′W, Acua Marina (Varadero, Lag. Paso Malo) 23°03′N 81°12′W.
South Coast: Punta Gorda (Bahia de Santiago de Cuba) 19°59′N 75°52′W, Casilda (S. Spiritus province, Trinidad) 21°45′N 79°59′W, Marina Jagua (Bahia Cienfuegas) 22°08′N 80°27′W, Marina Puerto Sol, Cayo Largo (Archipelago de los Canarreos) 21°36′N 81°34′W.
Isla de la Juventad (Isla de Pinos): Colony 21°55′N 82°46′W.

Procedure on arrival

Recommended ports of entry for yachts are the Hemingway Marina immediately to the west of Havana, as well as the other marinas and Cayo Largo. All these have tourist facilities and are used to clearing in yachts. If entering at one of the other ports, which have no tourist services on site, one should request the services of the Tourist Office (Empresas Turisticas). Formalities may take longer in these ports as they may have to refer the matter to Havana. The commercial port of Havana should not be entered as it has no provision for clearing yachts.

As soon as Cuban territorial waters are entered 12 miles off the Cuban coast a yacht must contact the port authorities or coastguard (Guarda Frontera) on VHF Channel 16 or HF 2128KHz. The various authorities operate as follows: HF(SSB) 2760KHz Red Costera Nacional (coastguard net), 2790KHz Red Turistica (tourist net); VHF Channel 68 port authorities, Channel 19 tourist services.

The following details should be communicated:

The approaches to Havana, Cuba.

name of yacht, flag, port of registry, last port of call, intended port of arrival in Cuba with approximate ETA, type of yacht and number of people on board. The captain will then be given instructions to proceed. A vessel may be sent out to escort the yacht into port. Channel 16 is also monitored by the marinas and they will also provide assistance. In no circumstances should one attempt to arrive unannounced or anchor in a bay.

Once moored in port one must wait for the officials to arrive and no one must go ashore until clearance is complete. Clearance must first be obtained from Guarda Frontera (Coast Guard), after which one will be visited by immigration, customs, agriculture department officials, ministry of transport and health officials. There is no required order for these officials. After clearance is completed, a coastwise cruising permit can be obtained. Although entry formalities are lengthy with much paperwork, the officials are usually good natured and it all adds up to the excitement of visiting this country which for so long has been off limits.

Hemingway Marina: Most visiting yachts try and enter at the large Hemingway Marina which is

receiving an increasing number of foreign yachts. There is a check-in dock in the entrance channel to the marina and clearance formalities are completed here, after which a yacht is assigned a place in the marina.

There are reefs on either side of the entrance, which is difficult to identify until fairly close in. The GPS coordinates of the sea buoy are reported as 23°05.3′N, 82°30.6′W. With an onshore wind, which is the usual direction during winter months, entering the marina is not easy and in strong winds and breaking seas, should not be attempted. The marina should be contacted on Channel 16 if help is needed. It also uses Channel 68, as a working channel, and 2790 kHz.

Santiago de Cuba: Call Morro Santiago on Channel 16. The boat will be met, boarded and possibly searched at the entrance into the harbour, and then escorted to the marina. Formalities are lengthy.

Customs

If a yacht is staying a long time in one of the marinas, firearms will be impounded by the Coast Guard (Guarda Frontera). If the yacht is cruising along the coast, firearms must be declared every time the boat checks in at a new port and may be confiscated until departure or alternatively sealed on board, placed under the responsibility of the captain. The seals and arms will be inspected when clearing out.

Animals must have health certificates and anti-rabies vaccinations. No animal may be landed without a permit from the health authority (Filosanitario) which requires a minimum two week quarantine period and costs US$25.

All plant, animal and meat products that are not canned must be declared to the health authorities on arrival. Fresh eggs and chicken may not be imported. Reasonable quantities of canned meat, dairy or vegetable produce can be imported for the crew's own consumption.

The yacht can remain as long as the length of the tourist card issued to the crew and indefinitely if based permanently in one of the marinas.

Immigration

A 30-day tourist visa is issued on arrival to all nationalities for a fee. This is renewable for a further 30 days in most major cities. This process is speeded up if some six copies of the crew list are prepared with all crew passport details.

Tourist cards are only available for one month and then renewable for one more month only. For longer stays it is advisable to arrive with a visa obtained in advance. Yachts may remain in Cuba for an unlimited period, provided this is cleared with the authorities and all docking fees are paid in advance.

Some Latin American countries will not admit someone with a passport stamped in Cuba, but if asked, Cuban officials will not stamp passports. It appears that the US government cannot stop its citizens from visiting Cuba, but for the time being it may be advisable for US citizens not to have their passport stamped in Cuba. The Cuban Interests Section and the Swiss embassy in Washington DC deal with visa applications.

Cruising permit

Once initial clearance is completed, a coastwise cruising permit (*despacho de navegación – costera*) can be obtained from the Coast Guard. This clearance permit will specify the areas the yacht wishes to visit and the length of time planned for the cruise. It is best to put all possibilities where one might want to stop on this *despacho* as it is more difficult to add new stops later on. Although the clearance permits a yacht to cruise and anchor along the coast, if any of the ports of entry mentioned above are entered, one has to go through the clearance procedure again.

When cruising along the coast, one must report to the Guarda Frontera office in every port. This is normally located at the harbour or bay entrance. All papers are usually inspected and the cruising permit is kept until departure. It is often necessary to check in with customs and immigration also, especially if moving from province to province. It should be possible for the *despacho* just to be stamped by each Guarda, but some provinces may insist on a new *despacho* being issued. Although the paperwork seems daunting, officials are usually good natured and pleasant. The authorities are making a genuine effort to attract more yachts and formalities may be eased in the future.

Fees

Entry or exit clearance fee is US$10–20 during normal working hours (0800–1700 weekdays).

Cruising permit, valid for six months, $50.

Tourist visa US$25 per person.

Restrictions

It is forbidden to land at unauthorised places along the coast and also to take any other person on board the yacht apart from those on the crew list.

Cruising boats are not allowed to fish in Cuban

waters. Scuba diving can only be done through the Tourist Office with an official instructor. Spearfishing is prohibited and no marine life, flora, fauna or any other object may be taken from the sea.

No archaeological objects should be removed, defaced or exported.

Procedure on departure

Twenty-four hours' notice of departure must be given even if sailing to another port in Cuba. Before departure one must clear out with the Guarda Frontera who will retain the *despacho* and issue a new exit *despacho* (clearance certificate). One must also clear out with customs and immigration. The boat will probably be boarded and searched before departure.

Facilities

Yachting is still in its infancy and as there are very few locally owned sailing boats, repair facilities are limited. The situation is somewhat better in the Havana area where workshops dealing with commercial craft and fishing boats may be persuaded to effect a repair on a yacht. Outside Havana, mechanical repairs are available at Cienfuego and Santiago. Except for a few makes of diesel and outboard engines, spare parts are unobtainable.

Water and electricity are laid to the berths in the new marinas. Diesel fuel is also available. At Marina Hemingway, the fuel has to be paid for in advance before the boat is taken to the fuel dock. The marina has a good range of services and Yacht Services Inc. is a useful source on local conditions. Boats can be hauled out by crane at Marina Hemingway and this is also a good place to store the boats ashore. Antifouling paint is not available anywhere. General provisioning is not easy as ration books are required to buy food in most places outside of Havana. Foreigners can only buy provisions at special shops where purchases have to be made in foreign currency. These shops are located in tourist resorts and the diplomatic area of Havana.

The Hydrographic Institute can supply nautical charts of Cuba at the port of entry if requested prior to arrival. These can be ordered from Empresa TECNOTEX, Habana. Telex 51-1039 TECTEX CU. The Institute also has other aids to navigation such as leaflets on buoyage and maritime signs of Cuba.

Further Reading

Cuba: A Cruising Guide
Cruising Guide to Cuba

Website

www.cubatravel.com (Cuba Travel Authority)

CURAÇAO

Known worldwide for the orange liqueur named after it, Curaçao is the largest of the islands in the Netherlands Antilles off the coast of Venezuela. Curaçao is very dry, with a barren landscape and an excellent natural harbour at Schottegat.

The island is a favourite stop for yachts en route to Panama. Most yachts who stop here arrive from Bonaire and the contrast between the two islands is quite striking, particularly the capital Willemstad, which is a true metropolis by Caribbean standards. In spite of the increasing number of modern buildings, the waterfront buildings have an Old World charm redolent of Amsterdam. Although it is not too comfortable to linger in Willemstad after clearing in, the big ships continually moving in and out of this busy port are a sight to behold. Many yachts choose the protected anchorage at Spanish Water while Kleín Curaçao, an uninhabited island to the south-east, is a more solitary spot.

Country Profile

The first inhabitants of the island were Arawaks, who left remains of villages and cave drawings. Although the Spanish were the first Europeans to visit Curaçao, they showed little interest in anything except the Arawaks who were transported to Hispaniola as slave labour. The Dutch were the first to develop the island, attracted by Curaçao's protected natural harbour and the island's strategic position for trade. The Dutch West India Company was established, which panned salt and traded slaves from Africa. Despite challenges from other colonial powers, the Dutch retained their rule over the island. During the eighteenth century Curaçao became a centre for pirates, American rebels, Dutch merchants, Spaniards and Creoles. After a brief English occupation during the Napoleonic Wars, the island was restored to the

Practical Information

LOCAL TIME: GMT – 4

BUOYAGE: IALA B

CURRENCY: The Antillean guilder (NAG) or florin of 100 cents. The US dollar is widely accepted. Import/export limited to NAG200.

BUSINESS HOURS
Banks: 0800/0830–1200, 1300–1600, Monday to Friday.
Shops: 0800–1200, 1400–1800/1830 Monday to Saturday. Some stay open at lunchtime.
Business: 0800–1200, 1330–1630 Monday to Friday.

ELECTRICITY: 110/220 V, 50 Hz

PUBLIC HOLIDAYS
1 January: New Year's Day
February: Lenten Carnival
Good Friday and Easter Monday
30 April: Queen's Birthday
1 May: Labour Day
Ascension
2 July: Curaçao Day
25, 26 December: Christmas

COMMUNICATIONS
All American Cables and Radio Inc. Keukenstraat, offer telecommunications services. There are flights to Aruba and Bonaire, Sint Maarten, Puerto Rico, Amsterdam, and US and South American cities.

MEDICAL
St Elisabeth Hospital, Willemstad.
Tel. 624900, Ambulance Tel. 625822; has a decompression chamber.
Police, Fire. Tel. 114.

DIPLOMATIC MISSIONS
In Willemstad:
Canada: Maduro & Curiels Bank NV, Plaza Jojo Correa 2–4. Tel. (9) 661115.
Colombia: Scharlooweg 112. Tel. (9) 614663.
Ecuador: Breedestr. 46. Tel. (9) 613222.
Panama: Mahaalweg 26. Tel. (9) 35292.
Peru: Pietermaai 20B. Tel. (9) 611212.
United Kingdom: Bombadiersweg.
Tel. (9) 369533.
US: St Anna Blvd. Tel. (9) 613066.
Venezuela: de Ruyterkade 58.
Tel. (9) 613100.

Dutch in 1816 and became a free port. Since the creation of the Netherlands Antilles in 1954, Curaçao has had full internal autonomy, and is the administrative centre for the whole group, which remains part of the Netherlands.

Following the discovery of oil in Venezuela, a refinery was established on Curaçao. Today oil is still the linchpin of the economy. Curaçao is also an important offshore financial centre and tourism a developing industry.

The population of 165,000 consists of a mixture of nearly 80 different nationalities, a result of the island's history as a thriving trading port. Curaçao is noted for its religious tolerance and a variety of religions freely celebrate their festivals there. Dutch is the official language, but English and Spanish are also widely spoken as well as the unique Papiamento.

Entry Regulations

Ports of entry
Willemstad 12°07′N 68°56′W, Spanish Water 12°04′N 68°51′W.

Procedure on arrival
The VHF working channels in Curaçao are 12 and 14.
Willemstad: At the centre of Willemstad is St Anna Bay, through which all ships pass into the large Schottegat Harbour, past the floating pedestrian bridge which opens for vessels. One should tie up at the commercial dock on the starboard side of St Anna Bay, which is near customs and immigration. The port authorities will give berthing instructions. The immigration office (Harbour Police) is located under Queen Juliana Bridge. It should not be confused with the immigration counter at the post office which is for immigrants not yacht crews. The Harbour Authority is in the same building as Harbour Police. As tying up to the dock in Willemstad for clearance is both uncomfortable and dangerous on account of the heavy wash of the constant commercial traffic, many yachts prefer to clear at Spanish Water where a customs officer will visit the boat. For immigration, one must go to the Harbour Police office in Willemstad.

Spanish Water: Boats may tie up to the reception dock at Seru Boca Marina, in the SW corner of Spanish Water, and complete customs and immigration formalities there. The marina does not usually charge if only stopping there for clearance. Alternatively, one should anchor off Sarifundy's Marina, west of the Curaçao Yacht Club. Officials will visit a yacht for clearance, if one telephones from the marina on arrival. The entrance into Spanish Water is sometimes difficult to locate and should not be attempted at night.

Procedure on departure
On departure one has to contact immigration only, not customs. After having cleared out of Curaçao

to sail to Aruba one is technically not allowed to stop anywhere en route, although the authorities do not seem to mind genuine overnight stops.

Customs

Firearms must be declared to customs, and will be removed for the duration of the stay.

Duty paid on equipment will be refunded on departure. Spares may be imported free of duty, but this must be arranged with customs at the airport and it is usually easier if the services of a local agent are employed.

Only boats flying the Netherlands Antilles flag may remain longer than six months.

Immigration

All require passports except nationals of Benelux countries, Germany, Canada, the United States, San Marino, Brazil, Mexico, Trinidad and Tobago, and Venezuela, who must show a national identity card or some other recognised form of identification.

Nationals of all countries can stay for 14 days without a visa, except for those of the Dominican Republic and some former Communist countries who require visas. For those intending to stay 14–28 days, a Temporary Certificate of Admission will be issued by immigration on arrival to nationals of most countries, including the Benelux countries, Germany, Spain and the UK. This can be renewed for up to three months. Nationals of most East European countries must apply for the Certificate before arrival.

For stays exceeding 90 days all nationals require a visa. Visas can be extended for a further three months.

Cruising permit

This is only necessary to obtain from the Harbour Authority in Willemstad by those who wish to anchor and dive along the coast. All intended anchorages must be listed on the permit.

Restrictions

The area from Jan Thiel Bay, SE of Willemstad, to East Point, is an underwater park. Permanent moorings are provided to protect the coral from damage and using one's own anchor is prohibited. No harpoons or spearguns are allowed.

Facilities

Most visiting boats anchor in Spanish Waters Bay, which is well sheltered and free of charge. There

are good docking facilities at Sarifundy's Marina and Seru Boca Marina. The latter is a new marina linked to Santa Barbara Resort, the facilities of which may be used by those in the marina. The Curaçao Yacht Club is only open to members, but visiting yachts may buy fuel at their dock. There is a wide range of haulout, repair and auxiliary services available. Antilles Slipways has a 60-ton haulout facility and full service yard.

Willemstad is more convenient than Spanish Water for provisioning and repair. There is a wide selection of goods and US-style shopping centres out of town. Fresh produce can be bought at the floating market from boats which come over from Venezuela. Free transportation is laid on several times each week from Sarifundy's Marina for those who wish to shop at two supermarkets in Willemstad. Fuel and bottled gas are reasonably priced, as Curaçao has its own oil refinery. The Curaçao Yacht Club's facilities are available to foreign visitors. Berthing space is limited, but water and fuel are available from the jetty for a small fee, and there is a slipway. Fuel is available from 1430 to 1730 on weekdays and 1000 to 1730 on weekends.

Further Reading

Cruising Guide to the Caribbean
Yachting Guide to the ABC Islands

Websites

www.curacao.com (Curaçao Tourism Development Bureau)
www.interknowledge.com/curacao
www.abc-yachting.com
www.santa-barbara-resort.com

DOMINICA

The island of Dominica, known as the Commonwealth of Dominica to distinguish it from the Dominican Republic, is one of the most mountainous of the Windward Islands. Seen from afar, this forest-clad island presents a forbidding face with its lofty peaks brushing the rain clouds that frequently shed their load to make this the lushest island in the Caribbean. Unable to compete with the beauty of her neighbours' anchorages, it

Practical Information

LOCAL TIME: GMT – 4

BUOYAGE: IALA B

CURRENCY: East Caribbean dollar (EC$).

BUSINESS HOURS
Banks: 0800–1500 Monday to Friday,
0800–1700 Friday.
Shops: 0800–1300, 1400–1600 Monday to
Friday and 0800–1300 Saturdays.
Government offices: 0800–1300,
1400–1700 Monday, closing at 1600
Tuesday to Friday.

ELECTRICITY: 220/240 V, 50 Hz

PUBLIC HOLIDAYS
1 January: New Year's Day
Carnival, Monday and Tuesday before Ash
Wednesday
Good Friday and Easter Monday
1 May: May Day
Whit Monday
First Monday in August: Emancipation Day
3 November: Independence Day
4 November: Community Day of Service
25 December: Christmas
26 December: Boxing Day

COMMUNICATIONS
For international calls, Marpin Telecoms &
Broadcasting, 11 Great Marlborough
Street. All hotels on the island offer
telephone, telex and fax services.
The post office in Roseau is on the Bay
Front.
Emergency: dial 999.
There are flights to other Caribbean
islands such as Barbados, Antigua, St
Lucia, Puerto Rica or Martinique, from
where connections have to be made for
flights to Europe and North America.

is Dominica's interior that is her main attraction.

There are various hikes for the energetic leading into the interior. One of the most interesting inland trips is to Trafalgar Falls where one can bathe in a cascade of hot sulphur water. More arduous is the hike to the Boiling Lake, which is another volcanic phenomenon. A more sedate glimpse of Dominica's varied interior can be gained by making a dinghy trip up the Indian River, which is easily reached from the anchorage in Prince Rupert Bay.

Dominica's wild interior allowed a group of the indigenous Carib population to escape extermination and the remaining Carib settlement on the east coast is open to visitors. The Caribs called Dominica 'Waitukubuli' meaning 'tall is her body', a fair description of this beautiful island which is often bypassed by cruising yachts because of the impression that they might be in danger if stopping there. Although there have been a few instances of theft from unattended yachts, Dominica is as safe as any other Caribbean island and, if basic precautions are taken, as in any other part of the world, one's stay can be both satisfying and enjoyable.

Country Profile

Dominica was sighted by Christopher Columbus on Sunday, 3 November 1493. It was inhabited by the indigenous Caribs, who fiercely resisted both French and English for possession of the island. The two powers finally came to an agreement in 1805 and France ceded Dominica to England in return for a payment. However, situated between the French islands of Martinique and Guadeloupe, French influence has persisted on the island. Dominica was neglected in the nineteenth century and only in the 1930s were efforts made to build roads and open up the interior. Further development came in the 1950s and 60s, with the expansion of agriculture and house building. In 1967 Dominica became self-governing and full independence was achieved in 1978.

Agriculture is the most important sector of the economy. Coffee was the major export in the nineteenth century until struck by disease, to be replaced by lime-growing, an important supply to the Royal Navy in the prevention of scurvy. In the 1930s bananas became the chief export, along with coconut oil, cocoa and citrus fruit. The devastation caused by hurricanes David and Allen in 1978–9 was followed by some reconstruction of roads, hotels and the airport. As for so many of its neighbours, the expansion of tourism provides some economic hope, although in Dominica there is a desire to temper tourist expansion to prevent the destruction of the 'Nature Island' of the Caribbean. Dark volcanic sand beaches are located only on the west and north coasts of the island, although the water is very calm and Dominica is rated as the fifth best dive site in the world.

Of the 72,000 inhabitants, the majority are of African descent. A small number of Caribs, the original population, live on a reservation on the east side of the island. English and Creole French are spoken, and Protestant and Roman Catholic are the main religious denominations. Roseau is the capital. Dominica is a rainy island, especially June to October, while the hurricane season from June to November should be avoided.

Entry Regulations

Ports of entry
Roseau 15°17'N 61°24'W, Portsmouth 15°32'N 61°23'W.

Procedure on arrival
Roseau: Customs and immigration are in the deep-water port. Arriving yachts should try to contact Dominica Port Authority on VHF Channel 16 for permission to anchor off the deepwater port; if there is no reply, one can wait offshore and send someone ashore with papers. Alternatively one can anchor off the Anchorage Hotel one mile south of Roseau, and make arrangements to clear from there.

Portsmouth (Prince Rupert Bay): The captain should go ashore to obtain clearance. Customs is located close by the banana warehouse. Office hours are 0800–1300, 1400–1700 on Mondays, 0800–1300, 1400–1600 Tuesday to Friday. Immigration is upstairs on the main street, Michael Douglas Blvd, opposite the dinghy dock. Customs will require three crew lists on departure.

On arrival, one should ask for a cruising permit to cover all the places one intends to visit. A cruising permit is needed to go from Roseau to Portsmouth.

Clearing out can be done the day before departure.

Customs
Firearms should be declared.

Immigration
Immigration normally grants stays of up to 21 days. Extensions are possible.

Nationals from the Commonwealth of Independent States and other East European countries may stay up to three weeks without a visa. Longer stays require a visa.

Fees
Overtime is charged outside of office hours. Also, an environmental tax of EC$4 per peson and a EC$2 levy for documentation. US$8 departure tax per boat.

Security charge US$2.

Facilities

Repair facilities are very basic, although there are a few mechanics in Roseau who can undertake repairs on diesel engines. The Anchorage Hotel provides a few facilities and repairs for visiting sailors. Water can be taken from their dock and fuel carried in jerrycans from a nearby fuel station. A similar service is offered by the Castaways Hotel further up the coast. Immediately north of Roseau, at Canefield, the owner of the Shipwreck Bar does fibreglass work and outboard engine repair. Provisioning in Roseau is reasonable, there are supermarkets and a fresh food market, while Portsmouth has a good market on Saturdays.

Further Reading

Cruising Guide to the Leeward Islands
Cruising Guide to the Caribbean

Website

www.dominica.com (Commonwealth of Dominica)

DOMINICAN REPUBLIC

One of the Greater Antilles, the island of Hispaniola, of which the Dominican Republic occupies the eastern two-thirds, is a mountainous island, cut by deep valleys and sometimes troubled by earthquakes. The other third of the island is Haiti, culturally very different to the Dominican Republic where the Hispanic culture dominates.

Described by Christopher Columbus as 'the fairest land human eyes have ever seen', until not so long ago, this beauty was denied to cruising sailors as yachting was not encouraged by the authorities in Santo Domingo. The situation is very different now; foreign yachts are welcome in most places and facilities are steadily improving, although entry formalities are still cumbersome and lengthy. Most yacht traffic takes place along the north coast as yachts make their way either east or west between the USA and the Virgin Islands or Lesser Antilles.

Because of the prevailing NE winds, the south coast offers more protected anchorages, although the more scenic bays are on the wild and rugged north coast. The capital Santo Domingo lies at the mouth of a heavily polluted river and although the city itself, the oldest in the New World, is very attractive, facilities for visiting yachts are limited. A better alternative is Boca Chica in Puerto de Andrés where one can use the facilities of the local Club Nautico.

The north coast, although scenically spectacular,

Practical Information

LOCAL TIME: GMT – 4

BUOYAGE: IALA B. Lights are reported to be unreliable in some parts of the country.

CURRENCY: Dominican Republic peso (RD$) of 100 centavos. Keep exchange receipts to change RD$ back on departure.

BUSINESS HOURS
Banks: 0800–1600 Monday to Friday.
Business: 0800–1200, 1400–1700 Monday to Friday.
Shops: 0830–1200, 1400–1800 Monday to Saturday.
Some offices and shops: 0900–1700 Monday to Friday, 0800–1300 Saturday.
Government offices: 0730–1430 Monday to Friday.

ELECTRICITY: 110 V, 60 Hz

PUBLIC HOLIDAYS
1 January: New Year's Day
6 January: Epiphany
21 January: Our Lady of Altagracia
26 January: Duarte Day

27 February: Independence Day
Good Friday
Corpus Christi
1 May: Labour Day
16 July: Foundation of Sociedad la Trinitaria
16 August: Restoration Day
24 September: Our Lady of Las Mercedes
12 October: Columbus Day
24 October: United Nations Day
1 November: All Saints' Day
25 December: Christmas Day

COMMUNICATIONS
Codetel operates local and international calls. The Codetel office in Santo Domingo is Av 30 de Marzo 12, near Parque Independencia, open 0800–2200 (there are other offices in the city), for international calls, telex and fax. Also RCA Global Communications Inc. and ITT America Cables and Radio.
Main post office (Correo Central), La Feria, Calle Rafael Damiron, Centro de los Heros, Santo Domingo, open 0700–1800 Monday to Friday, some hours on Saturday. For overseas mail, it is recommended to use

'entrega especial' (special delivery), available for a small extra charge at a separate window at post offices.
There are international flights to various Caribbean, North and South American and European destinations from both Santo Domingo and Puerto Plata international airports.

MEDICAL
Clinica Abreu, Av. Independencia y Beller, has a 24 hour emergency department, free treatment for foreigners. Padre Billini Hospital, Calle Padre Billini y Santomé, Zona Colonial, have free consultations.

DIPLOMATIC MISSIONS
In Santo Domingo:
Canada: Maximo Gomez 30. *Tel.* 685-1136.
Haiti: Juan Carlos Ramirez 33. *Tel.* 686-5778.
United Kingdom: St George School, Abraham Lincoln 552. *Tel.* 540-3132.
United States: Calle César Nicolas Penson. *Tel.* 221-2171.

only offers a handful of sheltered anchorages and as it is usually difficult to cover the distances between them in one day's sail, cruising here needs careful planning. There is no doubt that this coast is best enjoyed if heading westward, otherwise the continuous beating into the trades can mar the pleasure of discovering this unspoilt area. The best northern anchorages are to be found between Puerto Plata and Manzanillo Bay. However, the most attractive area is at Samana Bay where a large resort is to be completed shortly, although the area is still largely undeveloped and one may come across a group of humpback whales who migrate south to the bay area for the breeding season.

Country Profile

Arawaks were living on the island when Columbus visited it during his first voyage. The island was settled by the Spanish until 1697 when the French gained control of the western half. In 1804 the independent republic of Haiti was founded in the west and the Haitians plundered the eastern Spanish half of the island. Sovereignty remained in dispute until finally in 1844 the Dominican Republic was founded. After a brief return to Spanish rule in 1861–5, and then a period of instability, the Dominican Republic was annexed by the United States from 1916 to 1924. In 1930 Rafael Trujillo Molina, head of the army, took control with US support, beginning a ruthless dictatorship. He remained in power until his assassination in 1961. Economic problems are the dominant political issue, with violent demonstrations occurring in the 1980s against economic hardship.

Agriculture dominates the economy, sugar being the main crop, although efforts are being made to diversify since sugar exports declined during the 1990s. Other produce is coffee, bananas, tobacco and cocoa. There is some mining of bauxite, gold and silver, and the export of minerals, especially ferronickels, has grown. Tourism is now the most important source of foreign exchange.

The population is 8 million. The majority are a mixture of African and Spanish origins, and Spanish is spoken. Santo Domingo is the capital. Most of the population are Roman Catholics, with a Protestant minority.

The Dominican Republic lies in the outer

tropical zone, so there is little temperature variation between summer and winter. The varied relief of the large island means a diverse climate, from warm and tropical to arid and more temperate.

Entry Regulations

Ports of entry
North coast: Manzillo Bay 19°43′N 71°45′W, Puerto Plata 19°49′N 70°42′W, Puerto Duarte (Samana) 19°12′N 69°26′W, Luperon (Puerto Blanco) 19°55′N 70°56′W.
South coast: La Romana 18°25′N 68°57′W, San Pedro de Macoris 18°26′N 69°18′W, Santo Domingo 18°28′N 69°53′W, Haina 18°25′N 70°00′N.

Procedure on arrival
If possible, one should arrive during working hours, 0800–1700. Fly the Q flag and wait to be boarded, as it is illegal to land before clearance. Usually a port official will come with customs and immigration officers. The ship's papers, passports and clearance certificate from last port should be presented on arrival. Then a visitor's card for each person must be obtained.

Yachts must clear from port to port, and see customs on each arrival, but there is no charge for this. Clearance papers must be obtained from each port. Note that many ports are closed to foreign yachts, unless one has special permission. Permission should also be obtained from the Port Authority to cruise outside of the ports.

Dominican officials expect, and often request, a small present after business has been concluded. This need not necessarily be money and it is not obligatory, but it is difficult to avoid. A small gift or a small amount of money (a few dollars) will be highly appreciated.

Customs
Firearms are checked by the boarding officer. One should have certificates of ownership.

Immigration
Visas are not required for stays of up to 90 days for nationals of Argentina, Austria, Denmark, Ecuador, Finland, Greece, Iceland, Israel, Italy, Liechtenstein, Japan, Norway, South Korea, Spain, Sweden, UK and Uruguay.

Tourist cards, valid for up to 60 days from the date of entry, can be obtained on arrival for US$10, for many other nationals, including most other European countries, Australia, Canada and the United States (including Puerto Rico and USVI), French overseas departments and territories, Antigua and Barbuda, Bahrain, Barbados, Brazil, Costa Rica, Dominica, Jamaica, Mexico, Paraguay, St Lucia, St Vincent and the Grenadines, Suriname, Trinidad and Tobago, Turks and Caicos, and Venezuela. All others, including Cuba, require visas; all applications must be authorised by the authorities in the Dominican Republic.

Health
Cases of ciguatera have been reported on the north coast between Samana and Puerto Plata.

There is a risk of malaria in certain provinces.

Fees
Tourist card fee is $10 per person. Overtime fees are payable if clearing outside office hours, or if special paperwork is required.

Facilities

The best facilities are in the capital Santo Domingo which has a large number of local sailors and adequate facilities for both sail and power boats. Reasonable facilities are also available in La Romana, which is the base of a large fleet of sportsfishing boats and has two well-equipped marinas. There are adequate facilities at Puerto Plata which has seen a steady increase in yacht traffic in recent years, although a dangerous surge can affect the harbour during northerly winds. Fuel is delivered to the dock, where water is also available. There is good provisioning in town and propane bottles can be filled locally. Only basic repair facilities are available at Samaná where there is fuel and water on the dock and a good fresh produce market.

In recent years Luperon has become the favourite cruising destination, and although the marina itself is far from perfect, it is a good base from which to visit the interior including the capital Santo Domingo. Repair and other facilities are adequate and there are a number of local businesses catering primarily for the increasing number of visiting cruising boats. Foremost among these is Kiwi John's, which provides a range of services, including e-mail.

Outside of the large industrial centres, repair facilities for yachts are virtually non-existent although minor repairs can be dealt with by ordinary workshops.

Further Reading

Cruising Guide to the Caribbean
The Gentleman's Guide to Passages South

Website

www.domnicana.com.do (National Tourism Office)

GRENADA

The most southerly of the Windward Islands, Grenada or the 'Spice Island' has now fully rejoined the fold of Caribbean cruising destinations after the turmoil of a Marxist-Leninist regime and a US-led invasion. A beautiful island with lush mountains and silvery beaches, Grenada is again a sailors' favourite. Situated conveniently close to the Grenadines, with which it is linked by its smaller sisters Carriacou and Petit Martinique, Grenada is the usual turning-point north for a cruise among the Windward Islands.

Carriacou is the largest of the Grenadines and was once a great sugar-growing island. Relatively undeveloped, it is attractive with its green hills, sandy beaches, and sheltered natural harbours such as Tyrrel Bay. On Carriacou customs and beliefs of African origin have been preserved, as seen in the annual Big Drum Dances and Tombstone Feasts. A Scottish tradition has also survived in the hand-built schooners which are raced in August in the Carriacou Regatta.

Petit Martinique, island of mystery, with a reputation as a smuggling centre, is not often visited by yachts cruising the popular nearby Grenadines, which belong to St Vincent, as this means having to sail down to Carriacou to clear in and then sail back.

Country Profile

The Caribs who originally lived on Grenada called it Camerhogue. Then the Spanish first gave it the name of Concepción and later changed it to Granada after the town of Spain, becoming Grenada under French influence. Carib hostility prevented European settlement until the seventeenth century, when the French settled near present-day St George's. After a period of peaceful coexistence, the Caribs were exterminated, and those who survived threw themselves into the sea on the north coast at Morne des Sauteurs (Caribs' Leap).

Under the French a plantation economy was introduced, African slaves were brought in, and the population grew. As elsewhere, the English

Practical Information

LOCAL TIME: GMT – 4

BUOYAGE: IALA B

CURRENCY: East Caribbean dollar (EC$).

BUSINESS HOURS
Banks: 0800–1500 Monday to Thursday, to 1700 Friday.
Shops: 0800–1600 Monday to Friday, 0800–1200 Saturday.
Government offices: 0800–1145, 1300–1545 Monday to Friday.

ELECTRICITY: 220/240 V, 50 Hz

PUBLIC HOLIDAYS
1 January: New Year's Day
8 February: Independence Day
Good Friday and Easter Monday
1 May: Labour Day
Whit Monday
Corpus Christi
7, 8 August: Emancipation Day
14, 15 August: Carnival
Thanksgiving Day
25, 26 December: Christmas

EVENTS
Grenada Sailing Festival, early February
Carriacou Regatta, first week in August
Carnival, second week in August

COMMUNICATIONS
Cable & Wireless, Carenage, for long distance calls, fax and telex open 0700–1900 Monday to Friday, 0700–1000, 1600–1800 Sunday and public holidays.
Post Office, Carenage, St George's 0800–1145, 1300–1530 Monday to Thursday, to 1630 on Fridays. Saturday mornings.

There are flights to various Caribbean destinations and also to London, Puerto Rico, New York and Miami.

MEDICAL
Ambulance (St George's) Tel. 434, (St Andrews) Tel. 724, (Carriacou) Tel. 774.

DIPLOMATIC MISSIONS
In St George's:
United Kingdom: 14 Church Street, Tel. 440-3536.
United States: POB 54, Point Salines. Tel. 444-1173.
Venezuela: Upper Lucas Street. Tel. 440-1721.

St George's Harbour, Grenada.

challenged the French and Grenada was ceded to England in 1763. First tobacco and indigo were grown, then cotton, coffee and sugar, and later cocoa, nutmeg, cloves and mace were introduced, earning Grenada the name of Spice Island.

Full independence was granted in 1974, but five years later a coup overthrew the corrupt government of Eric Gairy. The New Jewel Movement established a Marxist-Leninist government led by Maurice Bishop, which moved close to Cuba and other communist countries, and thus attracted the suspicion of the USA. In 1983 Bishop and some of his followers were murdered after a power struggle and soon afterwards a joint US-Caribbean force invaded to restore order. The return to democracy has been accompanied by a marked upturn in the country's economy, which is one of the fastest growing in the region.

Agriculture is important to the economy and the main exports are nutmeg, bananas and cocoa. Recently tourism has been expanding, partly due to the new international airport.

The population is around 110,000. English is the main language and some French patois is spoken. Unlike other islands which have had a mixture of French and English rule, the French influence has not retained much strength except in the patois and place names.

The picturesque St George's, situated in a large natural harbour on the SW corner of the island, is the capital. The old town lies around the inner harbour, which is known as the Carenage. Most Grenadians are Roman Catholic or Protestant.

The climate is tropical. The hurricane season lasts from June to November, but most hurricanes pass to the north of the island.

Entry Regulations

Ports of entry
Grenada: St George's 12°03′N 61°45′W, Prickly Bay 12°00′N 61°45′W, Secret Harbour 12°00′N 61°44′W, St Davids 12°01′N 61°40′W.
Carriacou: Hillsborough 12°29′N 61°30′W.

Procedure on arrival

The Q flag should be flown. Documents to be prepared are ship's papers, four crew lists, passports, a ship's stores list, health declaration and the clearance from the previous port.

Clearance must be obtained for voyages both coastwise or foreign. If planning to cruise in Grenada one must obtain a cruising permit from customs when clearing in.

Customs and immigration work Monday to Friday 0800–1200, 1300–1600. At some locations there are officers outside these times, including weekends and public holidays, but an overtime charge will be paid.

St George's: Customs and immigration offices are located at the Blue Lagoon (ex Grenada Yacht Services) south of the Carenage. Open 0800–1600 seven days a week.

Prickly Bay: Customs and immigration are located next to the Spice Island Marine. The office is open 0800–1600, seven days a week.

Secret Harbour: Only customs located here on weekdays. For immigration at any time, as well as clearance at weekends, one needs to go to Prickly Bay. An immigration officer may be located here in the future. The entrance through the reefs, although buoyed, is difficult and should not be attemped at night.

St David's: To become a port of entry with its own officials by 2001.

Carriacou: One must stop at Hillsborough to clear in as officials do not allow boats to anchor at Tyrell Bay before clearance. This only applies to boats arriving from another country. Customs office is in the commercial harbour, immigration at the police station. In Carriacou one must also visit the Grenada port authority office, located next to customs.

Customs

Firearms must be declared to customs and will be sealed on board in a proper locker or kept ashore in custody until departure. A receipt will be issued by the police.

Animals may not be landed unless they have a health certificate and local permit from the veterinary officer. Cats and dogs need a valid anti-rabies certificate.

Medicines such as morphine in the medical stores must be declared.

Foreign flagged yachts may import parts and equipment free of duty. The parts are usually detained at customs and, to retrieve them, one needs to obtain a stamped form (C14) from the customs office where one has cleared in. An invoice or bill showing the value of the goods must be presented and customs will charge a 5 per cent fee on the declared value.

Immigration

Visas are not required by nationals of the European Union, Commonwealth (except Cyprus and Pakistan, who require visas), United States, Japan, Bulgaria, Chile, Czech Republic, Iceland, Israel, South Korea, Liechtenstein, Norway, Poland, Slovak Republic, Switzerland, Taiwan and Venezuela. All others require visas, although a visa-free stay may be granted on arrival if continuing on to another destination within 14 days.

Fees

Various fees need to be paid when clearing in: EC$45 for navigation aids, EC$12.10 per person for environmental levy. Under new legislation expected in 2000, a cruising permit will be required to cruise in Grenada, renewable monthly. The cost is expected to be around US$50 per month.

EC$40 is charged for clearing in or out outside normal working hours. This even applies if visiting the customs/immigration office during the one-hour lunch break.

Overtime fees are higher on Sundays and public holidays.

A small charge is made for the crew list form if one does not provide one's own.

Restrictions

Yachts may not anchor at Grand Anse Beach. Lobster and spear fishing is prohibited without a licence, which is issued only to Grenadians. Lobster should only be bought in season (31 October to 30 April). It is prohibited to pump bilge or waste into the water, and marine toilets may not be used within 200 metres of the beaches. There are toilets ashore at both marinas and the yacht clubs.

Facilities

Grenada's facilities are split between St George's and the south coast. In St George's, the Grenada Yacht Club operates a small marina with the usual facilities including fuel. Blue Lagoon (formerly GYS), also in St George's, has some docks but they are in a very bad state of repair. In Prickly Bay, Spice Island Marine has a small dock, chandlery, fuel and a 35-ton travelift. Secret Harbour Marina in Mount Hartman Bay is operated by The Moorings and provides a full service marina, including facilities for yachts up to 200 ft (61 m) long and 14 ft (4.2 m) draft. Grenada Marine in St David's has a 70-ton travelift, chandlery and full service yard. It is the best repair facility on the island. Henry's Safari Tours (Channel 68) offers a range of services: taxi, airport collections, laundry, provisioning, island tours and rain forest hikes.

Provisioning is good with several supermarkets and the fresh produce market in St George's is one of the best and most colourful in the Lesser Antilles. There is a supermarket with its own dinghy dock right by the lagoon as well as a hardware store with a good selection of marine equipment. There are garbage facilities ashore at both yacht marinas, the yacht club, and the main towns and villages. In Carriacou, the new Tyrrel Bay Yacht Haulout can haul out boats to 50 tons. Some docking facilities are being planned as well as a fuel dock. Next door, the Carriacou Yacht Club provides some of the other marina facilities but no docking.

Further Reading

Sailors Guide to the Windward Islands

Websites

www.grenada.org (Grenada Board of Tourism)
www.secretharbour.com
www.grenadamarine.com

GUADELOUPE

The largest of the Leeward Islands, Guadeloupe is a Département d'Outremer (Overseas Department) of France and its inhabitants are French citizens. The department includes the neighbouring islands of Les Saintes, Marie-Galante, and La Désirade as well as St Barts and St Martin. Guadeloupe is a butterfly-shaped island. Basse-Terre to the west has impressive scenery, black beaches, gorges, waterfalls and forests, and La Soufrière, a still active volcano, while to the east lies the lower Grande-Terre, more developed with its white beaches and tourist resorts. The two butterfly wings are separated by the Rivière Salée, which is navigable by

shallow draft boats. The bridge only opens at 0500 every day except Sunday and normally boats with a 6 ft (1.8 m) draft can negotiate the passage, even if occasionally they have to plough through the soft mud. The added advantage of taking this shorter route is that the sailing angle for boats continuing to Antigua is much more favourable.

The proximity between French-speaking Guadeloupe and English-speaking Antigua invariably leads to comparisons between these two rival yachting centres. While there is not much difference in the type and quality of services offered, where Guadeloupe scores is in the blend of French sophistication and Caribbean *joi de vivre* that has produced an atmosphere unmatched in any of the English-speaking Caribbean islands. The French influence has mixed with the African heritage to form a distinctive and rich culture seen in the music, cuisine and especially Carnival.

From the cruising sailor's point of view, Guadeloupe comes close to perfection. The island and her dependencies offer everything a sailor could wish for, from secluded anchorages to the latest marinas, first-class repair facilities, good provisioning as well as an excellent cuisine suited to all pockets.

Country Profile

The Caribs called the island Karukera, 'Land of beautiful waters'. Arawak archaeological finds indicate they had an advanced culture, but the Caribs who followed them were fiercer and less developed. Columbus came in 1493 and named the island Santa Maria de Guadalupe de Estremadura. Spain showed little interest in settling the island, and Carib hostility put off attempts by other countries. In 1635 a French expedition of colonisation had some success, despite conflict with the hostile Caribs. The island was briefly occupied by England, but the Treaty of Paris in 1763 returned Guadeloupe to France.

The French Revolution brought an unsettled period, Victor Hugues' rule even echoing France's bloody Terror, although slavery was briefly abolished. Emancipation of the slaves was finally achieved in 1848 largely due to Victor Schoelcher, now regarded as a national hero. In the second half of the nineteenth century indentured labourers were brought in from East India to cope with the labour shortage and social conflicts arose between various races, with resulting demands for independence. Despite equal status with Martinique, Guadeloupe is poorer and less developed and

Practical Information

LOCAL TIME: GMT – 4

BUOYAGE: IALA B

CURRENCY: French franc (Fr.) US$ sometimes accepted. Euro from 1 January 2002. 1 euro = 6.55957 FRF.

BUSINESS HOURS
Banks: 0800–1200, 1430–1630. Some banks also open on Saturday mornings. Shops: 0800–1200, 1400–1800 Monday to Friday, morning only on Saturday. Government offices: 0730–1300, 1500–1630 Monday and Friday. 0730–1300 Tuesday to Thursday. Business: 0800–1200, 1430–1700 Monday to Friday, 0800–1200 Saturday.

ELECTRICITY: 220 V, 50 Hz

PUBLIC HOLIDAYS
1 January: New Year's Day

Good Friday and Easter Monday
1 May: Labour Day
Ascension
Whit Monday
8 May: Liberation Day
14 July: Bastille Day
21 July: Schoelcher Day
15 August: Assumption
1 November: All Saints Day
11 November: Armistice Day
25 December: Christmas Day

EVENTS
Carnival starts in February with the climax on Ash Wednesday, when Vaval, the Carnival king, is symbolically burnt on the stake.

COMMUNICATIONS
Post office and telephones: Blvd Hanne, Pointe-à-Pitre and rue Dr Pitat, Basse-Terre. Phone cards can be bought for public phone booths, with direct dialling. Emergency numbers: police 82 00 89

(Pointe à Pitre), 81 11 55 (Basse-Terre). COSMA (Central Office of Maritime Security in Antilles) is based in Guadeloupe, Tel. (596) 71 92 92. Inmarsat 422 799 024. It monitors VHF Channels 16 and 11, also 2182 kHz.
There are flights from Pointe-à-Pitre to the Caribbean, and cities in South America, Canada, the USA and France.

MEDICAL
There is a good medical system. Ambulance Tel. 87 65 43. Central hospital Tel. 89 10 10.

DIPLOMATIC MISSIONS
Dominican Republic: rues St-John Perse et Frebault, Pointe-à-Pitre. Tel. 82 01 87. United Kingdom: BP 2041, Zone Industrielle de Jarry, Pointe-à-Pitre. Tel. 26 64 29. Most diplomatic representations are in Martinique.

---

politics tend to be radical. A pro-independence movement has grown in Guadeloupe, while St Barts and St Martin are more conservative. In 1983 a regional council was set up, as part of a French programme of decentralisation.

Agriculture is an important part of the economy, especially sugar and bananas, the latter being the main export. Vegetables are increasingly grown, especially for domestic consumption to combat the large amount of food imports which makes the cost of living high. There is some industry, especially around Pointe-à-Pitre. Tourism has developed, boosting the economy, yet unemployment is a problem.

The 408,000 inhabitants are a mixture of French, African and Indian descent. French is the official language, although Créole is spoken everyday. Most of the population are Roman Catholic. Situated between the sea and La Soufrière, Basse Terre is the administrative centre and capital. It is very picturesque, being one of the oldest French colonial towns in the Caribbean, founded around 1640. In Petit Cul-de-sac Marin, the bay to the south, lies Pointe-à-Pitre, the largest city and economic centre of Guadeloupe.

The climate is tropical, in the trade wind belt. The height of the land means frequent rainfall. July to September is the highest danger period for hurricanes.

Entry Regulations

Ports of entry
Pointe-à-Pitre 16°13′N 61°32′W, Marina de Rivière-Sens 15°59′N 61°44′W, Port-Louis 16°25′N 61°32′W, Deshaies 16°18′N 61°48′W, Saint François 16°15′N 61°16′W. Marie-Galante: Grand Bourg 15°52′N 61°19′W.

Procedure on arrival
Entry formalities must be completed at one of the official ports. The Q flag must be flown and only the captain may disembark to complete formalities. *Pointe-à-Pitre:* Customs and immigration are located in the harbour office. Open 0800–1700 every day.
Basse Terre: Customs is south on the main road south of the village.
Iles des Saintes: It is possible to stop at these islands by going to the local gendarmerie, although one still has to clear in again on arrival in Guadeloupe. The main anchorage is at Bourg des Saintes.
Marie-Galante: A customs office is now located in the port of Grand Bourg.

Customs
Non-French nationals on a tourist visit to Guadeloupe for less than 185 days can import two

hunting guns and 100 cartridges for each. Other firearms are not permitted. All weapons should be declared.

Animals need a health certificate, and dogs and cats need a valid anti-rabies vaccination certificate.

The yacht is considered to be temporarily imported and duty is waived for a period of six months within a 12-month period on condition that no work is done either ashore or chartering. The yacht can be left in bond with customs if one leaves the department, and this is not included in the six-month period.

Immigration

Visas are required by nationals from South Africa, Bolivia, Haiti, Honduras, El Salvador, Dominican Republic, Turkey, Australia, Dominica, St Lucia, Barbados, Jamaica, and Trinidad and Tobago. Visas can be obtained on arrival. Any non-EU citizen staying longer than three months needs an extended visa.

Charter

This is illegal in French territory, although transit with non-French passengers is allowed.

Fees

Port tax is payable depending on length of stay and size of yacht. No customs charges are made for EU countries and US yachts, although yachts from some other countries may have to pay some fees calculated by day and tonnage.

Facilities

Yachting facilities in Guadeloupe are excellent. There are several marinas (ports de plaisance) and as Guadeloupe has been chosen as the finish of several transatlantic races from France, repair and service facilities are of a high standard.

Pointe-à-Pitre has a protected harbour and an excellent marina complex (Marina Bas du Fort). All services are available in the marina complex as well as a large selection of marine supplies in several chandleries and specialised shops. There is a 27-ton travelift in the marina and two slipways at a boatyard nearby. Provisioning is of a very high standard.

Basse Terre has good repair facilities, most of them concentrated around Marina Rivière Sens. There are various repair shops and a chandlery with a reasonable selection. There is a good fresh produce market in town and a large supermarket on the outskirts.

The small fishing harbour of St François has a municipal marina offering the usual services, but only a limited range of repair facilities. Only basic facilities are available in Deshaies.

Further Reading

Cruising Guide to the Leeward Islands
Cruising Guide to the Caribbean

Websites

www.antilles-info-tourisme.com/guadeloupe (Guadeloupe Tourism Office)
www.voile-en-guadeloupe.com (Yachting information)
www.marina-pap.com/control (Marina Pointe à Pitre)

HAITI

The island of Hispaniola in the Greater Antilles is divided between Haiti and the Dominican Republic, both very different from each other. The Republic of Haiti occupies the western third of the island which is very mountainous, hence the name of Haiti, which means 'high ground'. Haitian culture is a rich mixture of African and French, and Haitians are proud of being the first black republic in the world.

Decidedly off the cruising track, the relatively few who visit Haiti by yacht find the experience either appalling or delightful. While people eventually get used to the poverty of most Haitians, it is the exasperating bureaucracy that turns most cruisers off. At least there are some compensations. One is the stunning scenery, while the other is the tasty cuisine, as despite nearly two centuries of separation, the French heritage still makes itself felt.

As in the case of Haiti's eastern neighbour, the Dominican Republic, cruising is best done from east to west as particularly during winter the strong trade winds make eastbound passages difficult.

If coming south from the Bahamas, the most convenient and interesting landfall is at Cap Haitién, as it allows a glimpse into this fascinating country's turbulent past. Above the town of Milot stands the Citadelle, a huge fortress built by self-proclaimed king Henri Christophe, at the cost of some twenty thousand lives. At the base of the trail leading to the Citadelle stand the ruins of Sans Souci, the imperial palace of one in a line of ruth-

Practical Information

LOCAL TIME: GMT – 5.
GMT – 4 April to October.

BUOYAGE: IALA B

CURRENCY: Gourde (Gde) of 100
centimes. US currency also circulates.

BUSINESS HOURS
Banks: 0900–1300 Monday to Friday.
Shops: 0800–1200, 1300–1600 Monday to
Friday, 0800–1200 Saturday. (1 hour later
October–April).
Government offices: 0700–1200,
1300–1600 (October to April 0800–1200,
1300–1800).
Business: 0700–1600 Monday to Friday.

ELECTRICITY: 110 V, 60 Hz

PUBLIC HOLIDAYS
1 January: Independence Day
2 January: Glorification of Heroes Mardi
Gras
14 April: Americas Day
Good Friday
1 May
18 May: Flag Day
22 May: Sovereignty Day
Corpus Christi
Ascension Day
15 August: Assumption
8 October: Death of Henri Christophe
17 October: Death of Dessalines
24 October: UN Day
1 November: All Saints' Day
18 November: Armed Forces Day
5 December: Discovery of Haiti
25 December: Christmas Day

EVENTS
Carnival, three days before Ash Wednesday

COMMUNICATIONS
In Port-au-Prince the Teleco office is in rue
Pavée, and the main post office is in Place
d'Italie 0800–2000 Monday to Friday,
0830–1200 Saturday.
Emergency: dial 116.
There are flights from Port-au-Prince to
several Caribbean destinations, North
America and Paris.

DIPLOMATIC MISSIONS
In Port-au-Prince:
Canada: c/o Bank of Nova Scotia, Route
de Delmas. *Tel.* 223 2358.
United Kingdom: Hotel Montana, rue
Cardozo, Pétionville. *Tel.* 257 3969.
United States: Boulevard Harry Truman.
Tel. 223 5511.

less dictators that have ruled this unfortunate country. A constrasting glimpse into Haiti's present can be gained by visiting the daily market in Cap Haitién, a colourful experience not to be missed.

The southern cruising route leads towards the capital Port-au-Prince, past several attractive harbours, none of which offer all-weather protection. Port-au-Prince lies at the head of the Gulf of Gonave and is a city of contrasts like the country itself. Beyond Cape Tiburon at Haiti's SW extremity, there are several attractive anchorages with the most scenic surroundings in the Baie des Cayes.

Country Profile

On his first voyage Columbus landed on the north coast and established the first European settlement in the New World, which was destined to be wiped out by the Tainos, who were the indigenous inhabitants of the island. Later the Tainos were eliminated by disease, war with the settlers and slavery, which led to a labour shortage. This was filled by bringing in large numbers of African slaves to work on the plantations. The Spanish neglected the western half of the island for the more profitable east and the vacuum was filled by the French, Dutch and English, while pirates had hiding places along the coasts from where they attacked the Spanish treasure fleets. In the seventeenth century France gained the upper hand and made the region

the colony of Saint Domingue and soon it was the largest sugar producer in the French West Indies.

The French Revolution sparked off discontent and a slave rebellion was led by Tourssaint L'Ouverture, the unrivalled black leader who drew up a constitution and declared himself Governor General. A year later he was captured and thrown into prison in France where he died. Napoleon wanted to reintroduce slavery, but this provoked an uprising and the French were driven out, the rebels declaring independence in 1804 under the new name of Haiti.

The following century saw further revolutions and conflicts until in 1915 the United States intervened, bringing some order to the country. Opposition to this occupation led to a revolt from 1918 to 1920 and some 2000 Haitians were killed. The USA withdrew in 1934, leaving a poor and overpopulated country. After various crises in the 1950s François Duvalier (Papa Doc), a black nationalist, was elected President. He established a repressive rule with an armed militia and thousands were killed or fled the country. In 1971 his son Jean-Claude (Baby Doc) inherited the Presidency. Discontent arose and in 1986 Baby Doc was forced to flee to France.

Establishing a democratic government after the 1990 elections proved to be almost impossible as a military coup unseated the newly elected President Jean Bertrand Aristide, who took refuge in the USA. The UN imposed sanctions and a US-led military intervention in 1994 restored President Aristide to power. Early in 1995 a UN peacekeeping force took over from the US military.

Haiti is probably the poorest country in the Western Hemisphere. It is overpopulated, lacks raw materials and the mountainous terrain is difficult to cultivate. Problems have been worsened by low agricultural productivity, low prices in world markets and hurricane damage. Coffee is the most important crop. There is a little industry and commerce, which is concentrated in the Port-au-Prince area. Tourism declined with the political troubles and the situation remains unstable, although the lifting of the trade embargo has helped the economy. There are often fuel and electricity shortages.

The population is 6.5 million, the majority being of African origin, but many are mulattos of mixed French and African descent. Conflict in the past has often been between the African and mulatto sections of the population. The languages spoken are French and Créole. Voodoo, a spirit religion with its origins in Africa, exists alongside Christianity, the population being nominally 90 per cent Catholic, 10 per cent Protestant.

The climate is tropical. It is cooler and drier from December to March, and on the coast, which is cooled by sea breezes. The hurricane season lasts from June to November.

Entry Regulations

Ports of entry
Port-au-Prince 18°33′N 72°21′W, Cap Haitién 19°46′N 72°12′W, Gonaives 19°27′N 72°42′W, Port-de-Paix 19°57′N 72°50′W, Miragoane 18°28′N 73°06′W, St Marc 19°07′N 72°42′W, Jacmel 18°13′N 72°31′W, Les Cayes 18°11′N 73°44′W, Jérémie 18°39′N 74°07′W, Petit Goave 18°26′N 72°52′W, Fort Liberté 19°41′N 71°51′W.

Procedure on arrival
Entry can only be made at an official port of entry. Clearance from the last port must be shown and five crew lists are needed. A cruising permit must be obtained from the port captain (Capitainerie).
Ibo Island: A convenient place from where to complete formalities is the small marina on Ibo Island (also referred to as Carenage Island), 9 miles north of Port-au-Prince. The marina monitors Channels 16 and 70. A bus runs from there to the capital, where entry formalities are completed in the main harbour. The immigration office is in the Port Authority building. The marina is protected on all

sides and is one of the safest hurricane holes on Haiti's north coast.
Port Morgan: Although not yet designated an official port of entry, boats that use this marina on Ile à Vache, on Haiti's south coast, can complete clearance formalities there. The marina office monitors Channels 16 and 9, and will deal with customs and immigration formalities on behalf of boats using their services. Other boats must proceed, as before, to Les Cayes and complete formalities there.

Customs
Firearms must be declared, and an authorisation for their possession must be shown to the police, plus a description of the firearms and the reasons for possessing them. Firearms must be kept on board.

Animals must be declared to customs.

Immigration
Visa are issued on arrival to all visitors from all countries with the exception of: China, Colombia, Dominican Republic and Panama.

A 90 day stay is usually given which may be extended.

Cruising permit
A 'Permis de Navigation' must be obtained from the Capitainerie at the port of entry. This permit is necessary to allow free access to all ports in Haiti.

There is no limit on the length of time a yacht may stay as long as one remains in contact with the authorities.

Health
Malaria prophylaxis is recommended. There is a red alert on AIDS.

Fees
Customs, Immigration, Health. Port charges of $50 per day may be charged if berthed alongside a quay. Light dues.

Facilities

Facilities in Haiti are generally poor, although it is possible to have some work done in the commercial harbours. The small marina Port Morgan on Ile à Vache is a useful stop when cruising along this coast. The marina has mooring alongside a quay and also on buoys. There is electricity on the dock, fuel, LPG and water (in limited quantities), also laundry and some repair facilities.

Communications at the marina are good, with international phone, fax and e-mail (portmorgan@globelsud.net). A limited range of services is available at the small marina on Ibo (Carenage) Island, 9 miles north of Port-au-Prince. Water is available on the dock, but no electricity. There is a slipway with a capacity of 25 tons. Although spare parts are almost impossible to find locally, they can be sent over by courier from Miami, from where there are frequent flights. DHL have an office at the airport.

If planning to cruise in Haiti one should carry all essential spares as practically nothing is available locally. A few ports have fuel on the dock, but in most places fuel must be either carried in jerrycans or ordered in drums and delivered by truck. Water is available everywhere, but should be treated. There is good provisioning with fresh fruit, vegetables and fish, but imported goods are scarce.

Further Reading

Cruising Guide to the Caribbean
The Gentleman's Guide to Passages South

Website

www.haititourisme.com (Haiti Tourism Office)

JAMAICA

Part of the Greater Antilles, Jamaica is one of the largest islands in the Caribbean. Lying south of Cuba, this mountainous and scenic island is known worldwide as the birthplace of reggae music.

This island of stunning beauty with its hundreds of miles of coastline and abundance of natural harbours has all the ingredients of a perfect cruising destination. Unfortunately the high level of crime, muggings and theft keeps most yachtsmen away. The often unfriendly or aggressive attitude of officials has not helped matters either, even if such attitudes can perhaps be justified by the relentless fight against drug traffic into which cruising yachts have become unwillingly entangled. While the present situation remains unchanged it is doubtful that the number of visiting yachts will increase significantly.

Country Profile

The name Jamaica comes from the Arawak word *Xaymaka*, meaning land of wood and water. Arawaks were the original inhabitants before the arrival of Christopher Columbus in 1494. Soon afterwards the first Spanish settlement was established and the Arawaks did not survive long. In 1525 Santiago de la Vega, now Spanish Town, was founded and was for a long time Jamaica's capital. The seventeenth century saw England stake its claim and capture the island from Spain. A plantation economy was developed with English and Irish settlers, based on slave labour, and Jamaica became England's main sugar-producing colony. In the early days pirates such as Henry Morgan used the island as a base.

The competition of sugar-beet meant that the cane sugar industry suffered in the nineteenth century; economic and social problems continued into this century, provoking disorders. Rival trade union movements arose, the Jamaica Labour Party and the People's National Party, whose rivalry has dominated politics since the 1944 Constitution and universal suffrage were introduced. After a brief membership of the West Indies Federation, Jamaica celebrated independence in 1962. The 1970s saw a phase of socialism and links with Cuba, followed by a more conservative period.

Once a prosperous island, Jamaica has been in recession since 1973. The bauxite mining and alumina refining industries, although still important, have declined. A large part of the land is cultivated, mostly for sugar and bananas, the main exports. Tourism, as elsewhere in the Caribbean, is the leading foreign exchange earner. However, unemployment remains very high, with its accompanying problems of poverty and crime. There has been and still is a high level of emigration away from the island, formerly to the United Kingdom and now to the USA.

Kingston is the capital. The population is 2.5 million, of which the majority are of African descent, but there are also minorities of East Indian, Chinese, Lebanese and European origins. English is spoken and also the local dialect 'Jamaica patois'. There are various religions, with a Protestant majority, some Roman Catholics as well as Jews, Muslims, Hindus and Baha'i. Rastafarianism has a significant following.

The climate is tropical and humid, and Jamaica lies in the hurricane zone. The hurricane season lasts from June to November.

Practical Information

LOCAL TIME: GMT – 5

BUOYAGE: IALA B

CURRENCY: Jamaica dollar (J$). It is advisable to shop around for better rates as those offered by banks and exchange places can vary widely.

BUSINESS HOURS
Banks: 0900–1700 Monday to Friday.
Shops: 0900/0930–1600/1730 Monday to Saturday. Shops close at 1300 on Thursday in downtown Kingston, and on Wednesday in uptown Kingston and Montego Bay.
Offices: 0830–1630 Monday to Friday.
Government offices: 0800–1700 Monday to Thursday, 0800–1600 Friday.

ELECTRICITY: 110V, 50 Hz

PUBLIC HOLIDAYS
1 January: New Year's Day
Ash Wednesday
Good Friday
Easter Monday
End of May: Labour Day
First Monday in August: Independence Day
Third Monday in October: National Heroes' Day
25, 26 December: Christmas

EVENTS
Easter Carnival
Sun Splash, annual reggae festival mid-August.
A week of celebrations around Independence Day.

COMMUNICATIONS
Jamaica Internal Telecommunications Ltd (Jamintel), open 24 hours for cables, telephone calls, fax and telex. Post offices open 0830–1630 Monday to Friday.
There are international flights from both Kingston and Montego Bay to Caribbean and North American cities and London.

DIPLOMATIC MISSIONS
In Kingston:
Canada: Mutual Security Bank Building, 30 Knutsford Blvd. *Tel.* 926-1500.
United Kingdom: 26 Trafalgar Road. *Tel.* 926-9050.
United States: Jamaica Mutual Life Center, 2 Oxford Road. *Tel.* 929-4850.

Entry Regulations

Ports of entry
Kingston 17°58′N 76°48′W, Montego Bay 18°28′N 77°56′W, Ocho Rios 18°25′N 77°07′W, Port Antonio 18°11′N 76°27′W.

Procedure on arrival
It is recommended that yachts clear in at Montego Bay or Kingston and then cruise to the other ports as officials will be easier to locate and are used to clearing cruising boats. Yachts must advise the authorities of any movements before changing ports.

The captain should provide customs with a detailed itinerary and they will then issue a cruising permit. The authorities must be notified every time one moves to another port and boats must clear in and out at every port. A yacht can only go where is stated on the permit. Yachts are monitored and if checking in late or making unauthorised stops will be fined. Yachts clearing in from foreign ports may not be allowed to dock until given permission by customs. Foreign registered boats that have already cleared into Jamaica must notify customs within 24 hours of arrival in another port. According to recent reports formalities in Jamaica are difficult and time-consuming.

Port Antonio: One can come alongside the dock at the Port Antonio Yacht Club and contact the authorities on Channel 16.

Montego Bay: Customs and immigration officials are located in the wharf area of Montego Freeport.

Proceed to the Montego Bay Yacht Club who should be contacted on Channel 16. The club is open daily from 0900 to 2400 for members, but visitors are welcomed. Officials may come to the club or the captain will be asked to go to the airport to complete formalities there. However, these policies seem to change frequently, so it may be advisable to contact the port authority or customs first and ask about the correct procedure.

Kingston: Yachts can contact Morgan's Harbour or the Royal Jamaica Yacht Club on Channel 16 and request permission to come alongside. Both these clubs are located in the Port Royal area. Arrangements can then be made to clear in at either club.

Ocho Rios: Port authority and customs have to be contacted on VHF Channel 16. One will have to anchor in this open harbour.

Customs
Firearms must be declared and will be kept in the custody of customs until departure.

Animals will be quarantined.

Yachts may stay up to six months.

Immigration
No visas are required for nationals of Commonwealth countries, Iceland, Israel, Mexico, Norway, Switzerland, Turkey for a stay of up to three months, the European Union (UK and Ireland up to six months; Denmark, Italy, Luxembourg, Netherlands, Belgium, Germany up to three months; France, Greece, Portugal and Spain up to

one month), and the United States for up to six months. Nationals of Argentina, Brazil, Chile, Costa Rica, Ecuador, Japan and Uruguay may stay up to one month without a visa; nationals of Venezuela up to 14 days. All other nationalities require visas.

Fees

Overtime is charged after 1600 Monday to Friday and at weekends for customs and immigration.

Security

Security is a problem and no yacht should be left unattended. It is advisable not to carry valuables or much money when ashore.

Facilities

Repair facilities in Jamaica can only be described as adequate and workshops willing to undertake an urgent job can only be found with local help. Duraes Boat Sales & Marina Supplies (*Tel*. 925-7633) is a good source for spares. There are two marinas in the Kingston area and both have reasonable facilities, being used mainly by locally owned boats. The Royal Jamaica Yacht Club maintains a marina-type facility about 12 miles from Kingston where cruising visitors belonging to reputable clubs are always welcome. Morgan's Harbour Club at Port Royal has similar docking facilities, as well as fuel and water available.

At Port Antonio, Port Antonio Marina has the best facilities and the staff are very helpful. Also the East Jamaica Anglers Association maintains a dock and some facilities which can be used by visitors. Similarly at Montego Bay the Montego Bay Yacht Club has good facilities, which may be used by visiting sailors. Fuel and water are available.

Provisioning with local produce is generally good, but the range of imported goods is limited, except in tourist resorts.

Further Reading

Cruising Guide to the Caribbean
Yachtsman's Guide to Jamaica
Cruising Guide to the Northwest Caribbean

Websites

www.jamaicatravel.com (Jamaica Board of Tourism)
www.jamaica-gleaner.com (Useful addresses and links)

MARTINIQUE

Martinique is the main island of the French Antilles and the most northerly of the Windward Islands. Volcanic in origin, in the north-west of the island Mount Pelée is still active. 1902 saw the last major eruption, which completely destroyed the capital St Pierre and brought Martinique to the attention of the world. The Atlantic side of this mountainous and lush island is rugged and rough, while the west coast is more sheltered, with beaches and pleasant anchorages.

Most yachting facilities are concentrated around the capital Fort-de-France which is the largest city in the Windward Islands and has a distinctly European flavour. Yachting facilities are on a par with those in Guadeloupe, with which Martinique has an ongoing rivalry.

Country Profile

The origin of the name Martinique is disputed, coming either from the Carib 'Madinina', island of flowers, or Saint Martin as named by Columbus after he saw the island in 1493. He only landed there in 1502, on his fourth voyage. Arawaks were the original inhabitants, 2000 years ago, probably exterminated by the fiercer Caribs who inhabited the island when the Europeans arrived. First to be interested in settling the island were the French and conflict with the Caribs was resolved with a treaty in 1660, but the Indians quickly died out. African slaves were then brought over to work on the sugar cane plantations.

All through the seventeenth and eighteenth centuries the French and English fought over their colonial possessions, until the 1763 Treaty of Paris established French control of Martinique and Guadeloupe in return for relinquishing claims on other territories. The French Revolution encouraged the slaves to fight for freedom, so landowners persuaded the English briefly to occupy the island to prevent this. During the Napoleonic wars the English Navy captured Diamond Rock off the coast and commissioned it as a ship, from where for 18 months it proceeded to harass the French. Slavery was abolished in 1848 and the resulting labour shortage led to indentured labourers being brought in from India and China. Martinique became a French department in 1946 and the inhabitants are full French citizens.

Agriculture has always been important to the

Practical Information

LOCAL TIME: GMT – 4.

BUOYAGE: IALA B

CURRENCY: French franc (Fr.) US$ are sometimes accepted. Euro from 1 January 2002. 1 euro = 6.55957 FRF.

BUSINESS HOURS
Banks: 0800–1200, 1430–1630. Some banks also open on Saturday mornings.
Shops: 0900–1200, 1500–1800 Monday to Saturday.
Government offices: 0800–1730 Monday to Friday, with a lunch break.

ELECTRICITY: 220 V, 50 Hz

PUBLIC HOLIDAYS
1 January: New Year's Day
Ash Wednesday
Good Friday, Easter Monday
1 May: Labour Day (Fête du travail)
Ascension
Whit Monday
8 May: Liberation Day
14 July: Bastille Day
21 July: Victor Schoelcher Day
15 August: Assumption
1 November: All Saints' Day
11 November: Armistice Day
25 December: Christmas Day

EVENTS
Sailing Week, early April
Mardi Gras Carnival

COMMUNICATIONS
Phone cards (Télécartes) for public phones can be bought from post offices, newsagents and some shops.
PTT office, rue Antoine Siger, Fort-de-France, has coin and card telephones.
Post offices are open 0700–1800 weekdays and Saturday mornings. The main post office is on Rue de la Liberté, Fort-de-France.
There are flights from Fort-de-France to Caribbean destinations, Montreal, Toronto, Miami and several cities in France.

MEDICAL
SAMU emergency services, Pierre Zobda Quitmann Hospital, Le Lamentin. *Tel.* 552000, Ambulance *Tel.* 715948.

DIPLOMATIC MISSIONS
In Fort-de-France:
United Kingdom: Route du Phare. *Tel.* 615630.
United States: 14 Rue Blenac. *Tel.* 631303.
Germany: *Tel.* 503839.
Venezuela: *Tel.* 633416.

economy, although the sugar industry has declined as elsewhere in the Caribbean. Rum exports remain important, as well as pineapples and bananas. High food imports mean the cost of living is expensive. The French government spends a lot on social services, but unemployment and a trade deficit are problems. Efforts, however, have been made to develop industry, and tourism is expanding.

The 360,000 cosmopolitan Martiniquais are a mixture of French, African and Asian origins, speaking French, as well as Créole which combines French and African languages. Most of the islanders are Roman Catholics.

The island has a high rainfall due to the mountains, June to November being the wet season. The high humidity is made tolerable by the steady trade winds. July to November is the hurricane season.

Entry Regulations

Ports of entry
Fort-de-France 14°38′N, 61°04′W, Marin 14°28′N 60°53′W, St Pierre 14°44′W 61°11′W.

Procedure on arrival
Boats must complete customs and immigration formalities at one of the official ports of entry. The original ship's registration papers must be available as copies are not accepted. Boats that may call more than once at Martinique should try to get several copies of the customs forms and maritime navigation documents as these may be filled in and deposited at a customs mailbox outside of office hours.

Fort de France: Yachts should anchor away from the ferry dock in the north-east side of the bay as the ferries are always coming and going. Customs and immigration are at the ferry terminal, open daily 0800–1100, 1500–1730. The alternative is to anchor or dock at the marina in Anse Mitan and take the ferry across the bay to visit the various offices in Fort de France.

Marin: The clearance office is in the marina, open daily 0700–1230. Both immigration and customs formalities are done at the same time. Unless intending to use the marina, arriving boats usually anchor and take their dinghy to one of the marina pontoons.

St Pierre: Customs is past the tourist office. Outside of working hours one may leave the completed forms (see note above).

For boats arriving from across the Atlantic, Cul-de-Sac Marin is perhaps a more convenient port to clear in. There is now a large charter base there.

Customs
Firearms must be declared.

Anti-rabies certificates are needed for cats and dogs.

As in any other French territory, yachts staying over six months in a consecutive 12 month period become liable for import duty, although if leaving the boat in bond and flying out of Martinique, for which special permission from customs must be obtained, this period is suspended until one's return.

Immigration

EU nationals do not need visas. US nationals may stay up to six months. Visas are required for nationals of South Africa, Bolivia, Haiti, Honduras, El Salvador, Dominican Republic, Turkey, Dominica, St Lucia, Barbados, Jamaica, and Trinidad and Tobago.

Any non-EU citizen planning a stay over three months will need a visa. In theory some non-EU citizens need a visa, but this is not applied to those arriving and leaving on the same yacht. Non-EU nationals should have a visa if planning to fly in or out of Martinique.

Procedure on departure

It is essential to clear out at one of the official ports so as to obtain the clearance certificate which is requested when clearing in at all other islands. Therefore one must try to clear out during office hours.

Fees

Most nationalities including the USA and EU countries pay nothing, but some others are charged a fee on a daily rate according to tonnage. No overtime is charged as clearance can only be arranged in office hours.

Facilities

Although the anchorage in front of Fort-de-France gets very crowded at times, at least everything is available ashore. There are good repair facilities, several well-stocked chandleries and all major engine manufacturers are represented locally. There are boatyards with slipways or travelifts. Also there are several large supermarkets as well as a good fresh produce market.

Marin is now one of the largest yachting centres in the Caribbean, with facilities to match. There are several repair shops in the marina for sail, mechanical and electronics repair, as well as a full service boatyard (Carenage) with a 60-ton travelift. There are two chandleries with a good selection of marine equipment.

Marina de Cohe is a small marina north of Fort-de-France with its own dry dock and repair facility.

Anse Mitan is the main tourist centre of Martinique and a popular spot with yachts. Marina Pointe de Bout is close by and the complex surrounding this marina offers various repair facilities, chandleries and supermarkets.

Facilities at St Pierre are very basic and the public dock was severely damaged by Hurricane Lenny. Water and fuel must be carried in jerrycans.

Further Reading

Sailors Guide to the Windward Islands

Websites

www.martinique.org (Martinique Tourism Promotion Board)
www.frenchcaribbean.com
www.caribbean-connection.com

MONTSERRAT

The island of Montserrat is a 40 square mile island in the Leewards chain and is a useful navigation mark for yachts plying between Antigua and Guadeloupe. There is no natural harbour on the island but there are a few sheltered bays on the north-west coast with Old Road Bay, Bunkum Bay, Little Bay and Rendezvous Bay being the major ones. However, winter swells can make anchorage untenable at certain times.

The dramatic eruption of the Soufriere Hills Volcano in 1995 which caused the evacuation of the population and buried the capital Plymouth in ash and rock was a severe blow for Montserrat. The entire southern two-thirds of the island is now an Exclusion Zone because of ongoing volcanic activity, and this zone includes an area one mile out to sea from Trants Bay in the east around the southern coast to Barton Bay in the west. There is no entry to shipping in this area because of the dangers of super-heated pyroclastic flows from the volcano entering the sea. Since 1995 such flows have impacted coastal waters for a distance of one mile out to sea.

The northern one-third of the island is mountainous and there are a host of walks and historical sites to see. There are also excellent vantage spots to see the effects of the volcano and the volcanic dome itself.

Visiting yachts should report to Little Bay where there are customs and immigration facilities during daylight hours. There is an emergency jetty at

Practical Information

LOCAL TIME: GMT – 4

BUOYAGE: IALA B

CURRENCY: East Caribbean dollar (EC$).

BUSINESS HOURS
Banks: 0800–1400 Monday to Friday, extended to 1500 on Fridays.
Shops: 0800–1600 Monday to Saturday.
Government offices: 0800–1600 Monday to Friday.

ELECTRICITY: 110/220 V, 60 Hz

PUBLIC HOLIDAYS
1 January: New Year's Day
17 March: St Patrick's Day
Good Friday, Easter Monday
2 May: Labour Day
June: Queen's Birthday
Whit Monday
First Monday of August: Emancipation Day
23 November: Liberation Day
25, 26 December: Christmas
31 December: Festival Day

COMMUNICATIONS
Cable & Wireless, Sweeneys, 0800–1600

Monday to Saturday for international telephones.
Post office at Government HQ at Brades, 0800–1600 Monday to Friday.
There are no flights to the island and access is by ferry from Antigua.

MEDICAL
St John's Hospital (2 km from Little Bay).
Emergency *Tel.* 999.

DIPLOMATIC MISSIONS
These are in Antigua.

Little Bay which is currently used as the island's main port of entry due to the destruction to Port Plymouth by volcanic activity.

At the time of writing the volcano is still active, so up-to-date information on the current volcanic situation should be obtained before visiting.

Country Profile

A few Caribs lived on the island when Columbus sighted it on his second voyage in 1493, naming it after the well-known abbey in Spain. In the first half of the seventeenth century, Montserrat was settled by Irish Catholics and the island became a refuge for Catholics fleeing persecution both in Ireland and Virginia.

A sugar plantation economy was developed based on slave labour. In 1768 on St Patrick's Day some slaves rebelled and all of them were executed; today the rebels are celebrated as freedom fighters. During the seventeenth and eighteenth centuries the French invaded several times, but never succeeded in permanently wresting Montserrat from British rule. In 1967 the island became self-governing as a Crown Colony of Britain and today is a United Kingdom Overseas Territory.

The population has considerably reduced because of the volcanic crisis and there are now just 4500 people living in 16 square miles in the north of the island. The major employer is in the construction field as the island rebuilds its infrastructure in the north of the island. There is some adventure tourism and a new hotel has been opened in the north.

The majority of the population is of African descent with a small number of Indian tradesmen.

English is the main language and Roman Catholic, Anglican, Methodist, Pentecostal and Seventh Day Adventists are the main religious denominations.

The climate is tropical with a low humidity. June to November is the hurricane season.

Entry Regulations

Port of entry
Little Bay 16°48′N 62°12.5′W.

Procedure on arrival
On arrival at Little Bay one should anchor in the southern part of the bay. Customs and immigration are situated inside the port authority's complex and are open during daylight hours.

Clearance from the previous port must be submitted to the port authority.

All boats must come to clear at Little Bay and permission must be obtained to anchor in other bays. Permission may depend on volcanic conditions prevailing at the time.

Customs
Firearms must be kept sealed on board.

Animals must stay on board until they have been checked by the veterinary officer.

Yachts can stay indefinitely in Montserrat without paying duty.

Immigration
Passports are required but no visas are required for nationals of the European Union, Commonwealth countries, Japan, Iceland, Liechtenstein, Norway, San Marino, Sweden, Switzerland, Tunisia, and US

citizens. All other nationals require visas although if the stay does not exceed 14 days the visa exemption may apply for most countries (except East European and communist countries). Visas can be obtained from British consulates.

Stays of up to six months are permitted for Canadian, UK and US citizens.

Cruising permit

One needs coastwise clearance to visit all other anchorages, and one must not go to any bay without a customs permit. One can apply for this permit from customs on arrival and it will be granted for a certain period. If wishing to stay longer one can return and get an extension. Clearance will depend on volcanic conditions prevailing at the time.

Procedure on departure

The captain must visit customs and, accompanied by crew, also immigration in Little Bay when clearing out. A departure tax (port dues) is to be paid at customs.

Fees

Overtime is charged after 1600 on Mondays, Tuesdays, Thursdays and Fridays, after 1130 on Wednesdays and Saturdays and all day on Sunday.

There is a port tax on departure. There are plans to charge for the cruising permit.

Facilities

There are no local facilities and no boatyards. There is neither fuel nor water at Little Bay. There is only one fuel station situated some 2 km inland from Little Bay. There are four supermarkets within a 2 km radius of Little Bay, where there is a reasonable selection, but prices tend to be expensive. There is no fresh vegetable market. There is a bar/restaurant at Little Bay and information on marine repairs can be obtained from the owner.

Further Reading

Cruising Guide to the Leeward Islands

Websites

www.geo.mtu.edu/volcanoes/west.indies/ soufriere/govt (Montserrat Volcano Observatory)

NETHERLANDS ANTILLES

The Netherlands Antilles are part of the Kingdom of the Netherlands, but have full internal autonomy. Politically one unit, the islands form two groups geographically. One group (often called the three S's), Sint Maarten, Saba and Sint Eustatius (Statia), are in the Leeward Antilles, while the second group, Bonaire and Curaçao, lie off the Venezuelan coast. The latter, with neighbouring Aruba, which is a separate political unit within the Netherlands, are also commonly called the ABC islands. To complicate matters further, the northern half of the island of Sint Maarten is Saint Martin, part of the French overseas department of Guadeloupe.

Unique to the ABC islands is the local language, called Papiamento, which is a mixture of Spanish, Portuguese, Dutch, English and some African and Indian dialects. Dating back at least to the early eighteenth century, this unusual language is in everyday use and there are both books and newspapers published in it.

The ABCs lie outside the hurricane belt and are therefore popular as a cruising ground for yachts trying to avoid the dangerous season further north. The ABC islands are also a useful stop en route to Panama.

Each Dutch island has its own distinctive character and they are so proud of their individuality, that they have been treated separately in this book:

PUERTO RICO

Puerto Rico is the most easterly island of the Greater Antilles. From the high mountain range in the interior, the land plunges down past coastal plains to the Puerto Rico Trench north of the island, which is 30,190 ft (9200 m) below sea level. Included within the US Commonwealth of Puerto Rico are the small islands of Mona to the west, and Vieques and Culebra to the east.

Frequented mainly by US cruising boats on their way to or from the Virgin Islands and Lesser Antilles, Puerto Rico has so far failed to become part of the cruising circuit, whose playground remains the islands to the east. Among the relatively few who venture west past the Virgins, even

Practical Information

LOCAL TIME: GMT – 4

BUOYAGE: IALA B

CURRENCY: United States dollar (US$). Automatic teller machines are widely available.

BUSINESS HOURS
Business and government offices: 0700–1200, 1300–1600 Monday to Friday. Banks: 0900–1430 Monday to Thursday, also 1530–1700 Friday.

ELECTRICITY: 110 V, 60 Hz

PUBLIC HOLIDAYS
1 January: New Year's Day
6 January: Three Kings Day
11 January: De Hostos birthday
Third Monday in January: Martin Luther King's Birthday
*Third Monday in February: Washington's Birthday

*22 March: Emancipation Day
Good Friday
16 April: José de Diego's Birthday.
*Last Monday in May: Memorial Day
30 June: St John the Baptist Day
4 July: Independence Day
17 July: Muñoz Rivera's Birthday
25 July: Constitution Day
27 July: Dr José Celso Barbarosa's Birthday
First Monday in September: Labour Day
*12 October: Columbus Day
*Fourth Monday in October: Veterans' Day
19 November: Discovery Day
Last Thursday in November: Thanksgiving Day
25 December: Christmas Day
*Half-holidays. Any holiday that falls on a Sunday will be observed the following Monday. US holidays are observed as well as local Puerto Rican ones.

EVENTS
The festival of St John, the island's patron saint, is the most important holiday.

COMMUNICATIONS
Private communication offices are located throughout San Juan and telephone cards are sold widely.
Blue Pages in the phone book are in English for tourists.
Post office in Hato Rey, Av Roosevelt.
There are many international flights from San Juan to Caribbean, European, North and South American destinations.
American Airlines is the main carrier.

DIPLOMATIC MISSIONS
In San Juan:
Dominican Republic: Cobian Plaza, 2nd floor. Tel. 725-9550.
Haiti: IBM Building Suite 833, Muñoz Rivera Ave, Hato Rey. Tel. 764-1392.
United Kingdom: American Airline Bldgs 1101, 1509 Lopez Landron St, Santurce. Tel. 758-9829.

---

less bother to go beyond Vieques and Culebra to visit the main island. The main reason for this reluctance is that once committed to sailing to Puerto Rico, one has either to carry on west or fight one's way back east, a prospect not enjoyed by many cruisers. The same manner of thinking also affects the local Puerto Rican sailors who seldom venture east past Culebra. As can be expected on an increasingly prosperous island like Puerto Rico, yachting is well developed, although sailing yachts are still in the minority.

For the cruising sailor who does not sail beyond the attractive outposts of Vieques and Culebra, there are a number of ports on each coast, those on Puerto Rico's south coast being both more plentiful and better protected. On the northern coast, only San Juan offers total protection from the prevailing NE winds. A busy and noisy port, the capital is a good place to reprovision and Old San Juan is an attractive well-preserved city from Puerto Rico's colonial past.

Culebra is geologically part of the Virgin Islands. The island is quietly beautiful and tourism not too developed. Dewey is the chief town, known as Culebra to the locals. Culebra was badly hit by Hurricane Hugo, when scores of boats were destroyed in the anchorage, which was previously considered to be a hurricane refuge.

Country Profile

Christopher Columbus landed on the island in 1493, accompanied by Juan Ponce de León. At that time Arawaks were the inhabitants of Borinquén, as they called it. Ponce de León, attracted by stories of gold, returned 15 years later and established the first settlement. Later the settlers moved to the site of present-day Old San Juan. Puerto Rico was one of the first parts of the Caribbean to be colonised. Columbus had named the island San Juan Bautista, after St John the Baptist whose symbol, the lamb, may still be seen on the flag. León named the new settlement's harbour 'Puerto Rico' and at some point island and port swapped names.

Puerto Rico was important to Spain as gold had been discovered on the island and the local population were used as slave labour to work in the gold mines. The island lay in a prime location between Spain and her American empire, and attacks by other maritime powers were frequent. During the seventeenth century more settlers came, and plantations were established, growing sugar, and later tobacco and coffee. At the end of the Spanish–American war in 1898, Spain ceded Puerto Rico to the United States. In 1917 the island ceased to be a colony and Puerto Ricans became US citizens, the islands becoming a US Commonwealth in the 1950s. A 1999 referendum voted by a narrow majority to remain a Commonwealth, defeating those who wished the island to become a full US state.

Federal laws apply, although not income taxes, a major incentive for US businesses to come to Puerto Rico. Since becoming a Commonwealth, industrialisation has been extensive, to replace the monoculture of sugar. Agriculture is still important as is tourism.

The population is 4 million, being mainly Roman Catholic. Spanish is the first language, although English is widely spoken. The capital is San Juan.

Rain is heavier on the northern coastal plain of Puerto Rico and the climate is more arid in the south. The hurricane season is June to November.

Entry Regulations

Ports of entry
Culebra 18°18′N 65°17′W, Ponce 17°58′N 66°39′W, San Juan 18°28′N 66°07′W, Mayaguez 18°12′N 67°07′W, Guanica 17°58′N 66°55′W, Playa de Fajardo 18°20′N 65°38′W.

Procedure on arrival
Boats arriving from outside the territory must contact customs immediately at one of the following telephone numbers: San Juan (24 hours) 729-6977, Fajardo 860-7003, Mayaguez 831-3345, Ponce 841-3133, 841-3111, Vieques 741-3232.
Culebra: Most yachts coming from the US Virgin Islands enter here. One should anchor off the main town of Dewey, which is in the narrowest part of the isthmus. The customs office is in town, halfway across the isthmus.
Ponce: A four-mile journey into town must be made to do the clearance formalities. Entry procedure is complex and takes time.
San Juan: One should notify customs and immigration on arrival, which can be done by telephone from the Club Nautico or San Juan Bay Marina. This is preferable to going to the Customs House, where the officials are busy with cruise ships and commercial vessels. They prefer to come and clear yachts at the club or the marina.
Mayaguez: This is the largest port on the west coast – it is commercial, but a convenient port of entry. One should go to the commercial dock and phone customs or clear at the customs office on the main street. Instead of entering the commercial port which is unsuitable for yachts, it is possible to

anchor at Boquerón and take a taxi into Mayaguez to clear in. Some US boats that already had $25 customs decals have managed to clear in by telephone from Boquerón.

American yachts coming from the US Virgin Islands must clear customs on arrival in Puerto Rico the same as other yachts. US boats can do this by telephone provided they have paid the annual $25 customs fee. If not, the captain will have to visit the nearest customs office to pay that fee before being considered cleared.

Immigration
All non-US residents must obtain a visa in advance. Canadians may not need a visa, but should check this before arrival. A multiple entry visa should be requested, especially if cruising from the US Virgin Islands or other US territory.

Cruising permit
This should be obtained in the US Virgin Islands, where it is issued free, otherwise a fee will be charged for it on arrival in Puerto Rico. Customs must be notified when a yacht arrives at each subsequent port or anchorage after the first port of entry even when possessing a permit.

Procedure on departure
It is normally sufficient to inform customs by telephone of one's intention to depart. Non-US nationals must return the immigration docket in their passports, issued on arrival, but this can be done by post.

Fees
Overtime is charged outside of working hours Monday to Saturday from 0900–1600. A $25 customs decal can be purchased when clearing in. This is valid for an entire calendar year throughout the USA and its territories, and exempts the boat from further customs charges.

Restrictions
Ensenada Harbour lies within a restricted area and may be closed during military activity, as there is a US Navy base at Roosevelt Roads. In the Puerto Nuevo area there are artillery and small-arms ranges extending 10 miles to seaward, although these are seldom used. The western end and parts of the south coast of Isla Vieques are also restricted naval areas. Some of these ranges are used extensively and when manoeuvres take place, the military monitors VHF Channel 16 and will advise which areas to avoid.

No garbage may be taken ashore: it must be disposed of outside of Puerto Rico. San Juan does have some garbage removal facilities, but these are not found elsewhere on the island. US marine regulations apply concerning discharge of any waste overboard. Marine Police occasionally inspect yachts and fine them for not having a holding tank with the valve in the correct position.

Health

A warning has been issued not to consume mangrove oysters or clams from street vendors because of the risk of hepatitis.

Facilities

With a large fleet of local craft, although predominantly motor yachts and sport-fishing boats, facilities are of a high standard and there are many marinas dotted around Puerto Rico's coastline. The best facilities are in and around San Juan, where there are several small shipyards, which can handle yachts and do major repair work. There are also several chandleries in San Juan and the selection of marine supplies is good. Whatever is not available can be flown within 48 hours from mainland USA.

Facilities are of a similar standard in Ponce, Puerto Rico's second city, where the Ponce Yacht and Fishing Club has a reputation of welcoming visiting sailors. The club facilities, including a travelift, may only be used by visitors if they are not being used for work on club members' craft. The usual repair facilities can be found in all commercial ports, such as Mayaguez and Fajardo, and fuel and water are normally available on the dockside. This also applies to Culebra, where repair and yachting facilities were badly affected by the devastation Hurricane Luis caused in September 1995.

A good place to haul-out is Isleta Marina to the east, where a boatyard offers repair facilities. There is a slipway and travelift, marine store and sailmaker. The adjacent marina offers the full range of services, fuel, water and electricity. There is a frequent launch service to Fajardo on the mainland, for good provisioning.

Fuel and water is available at the yacht clubs at Ponce, Boqueron and Salinas. Provisioning is good in all larger ports.

Further Reading

Cruising Guide to the Caribbean
The Gentleman's Guide to Passages South

Website

www.prtourism.com (Puerto Rico Tourism Company)

SABA

Saba is one of the northern islands in the Netherland Antilles. No other Caribbean island could better the saying that 'small is beautiful' than Saba. An extinct volcano only 2 miles (3 km) in diameter, the island rises sheer out of the sea to a lofty peak of 3084 ft (940 m). Its small size does

Practical Information

LOCAL TIME: GMT – 4

BUOYAGE: IALA B

CURRENCY: Netherlands Antilles guilders or florins. It is tied to the US dollar at a fixed rate of $US1 = NAFL 1.80.

BUSINESS HOURS
Banks: 0830–1200, 1330–1630 Monday to Friday.
Shops: 0800/0900–1200, 1400–1800.

ELECTRICITY: 110 V, 60 Hz

PUBLIC HOLIDAYS
1 January: New Year's Day
Good Friday and Easter Monday
30 April: Queen's birthday
Labour Day
Ascension Day
Whit Monday
1 November: All Saints Day
Early December: Saba Day
25, 26 December: Christmas

COMMUNICATIONS
International calls can be made from the telephone office, The Bottom.

There are flights to Statia, St Kitts and also Sint Maarten, where connections can be made to Europe, North America and Caribbean destinations.

MEDICAL
There is a medical centre on the island.
Tel. 4-63239.
Saba Marine Park Hyperbaric Facility Recompression chamber serving the entire Eastern Caribbean. Tel. 4-93295.

not offer much protection from the prevailing swell but the slight discomfort at anchor is more than made up for by the delights experienced ashore, not to speak of the wonderful underwater scenery which is reputedly the best in the entire Caribbean.

There are well-protected anchorages at Well's Bay and Ladder Bay on the west coast, while the entry formalities have to be completed at Fort Bay, which is on the SW point of the island. Fort Bay offers better protection in strong NE winds, while the previous anchorages are to be preferred in SE winds.

Until not so long ago Saba's interior was completely inaccessible and the sole way to reach the island's only villages, fittingly called Bottom, Windwardside and Hell's Gate, was to land at Ladder Bay and negotiate the 800 steps cut into the rock. Although the building of a road was deemed an impossible task by civil engineering experts, the Sabans proved them wrong by building one themselves. This amazing feat of stamina and determination was finished in 1958 and runs almost all the way around the island. With the same determination a small airport was built on the only flat area possessed by this rugged island. The villages are neat and picturesque and visitors are treated to a view of a tranquil life that has all but disappeared elsewhere. There are no beaches but the underwater scenery is remarkable. The construction of the airport, the road to the harbour in Fort Bay, and later a pier, brought in tourism on a small scale and the tourist boom of Sint Maarten is spreading over to Saba. Saba has become a duty-free area like Sint Maarten.

The population of around 1400 are mainly Roman Catholic, with some Anglican and Wesleyan. Dutch is the official language but everyone speaks English.

Entry Regulations

Port of entry
Fort Bay 17°37′N 63°15′W.

Procedure on arrival
Fort Bay: Contact the harbour master on Channels 16 or 11. In settled weather conditions one may be able to pick up a mooring off Fort Bay while clearing in ashore. Otherwise it may be necessary to carry on to the more protected anchoring area on the NW side of the island, between Ladder Bay and Well's Bay where several moorings (yellow with blue stripe) have been laid for visiting yachts. From here, Fort Bay is best reached by dinghy. One should proceed ashore and clear with the harbour master at the government building near the pier. Hours are 0800–1700 Monday to Saturday. One can check in and out at the same time, even if staying a few days. A yacht is allowed to anchor in one of the other anchorages and then visit Fort Bay by land or dinghy to clear. The alternative is to use the services of Alva Hassell, next to the Marine Park office, who will deal with all clearance formalities for a fee of $10–$30 depending on the length of the boat.

Restrictions
All the waters around Saba were made a national marine park in 1987 and anchoring is restricted to sandy areas where the coral will not be damaged. Spearfishing and the taking of coral or shells is prohibited. Marine Park officials patrol the anchorages and welcome yachts.

A fee is charged for the maintenance of the underwater park. Several mooring buoys are available for visiting boats, also some smaller buoys for the dinghy when diving in the protected area.

Fees
Moorings are free, but there is a Marine Park fee of $3 per person per week.

Facilities

Sea Saba is a diving shop based at Fort Bay. They monitor Channel 16, have a small chandlery and can order spares from Sint Maarten. Their mechanical shop can deal with emergency repairs. Fuel can be taken in jerrycans from the fuel station at the Fort Bay anchorage. Some provisioning can be done in Windwardside, which has the better shops of the two settlements.

Further Reading

Cruising Guide to the Leeward Islands

Website

www.turq.com/saba (Saba Tourist Office)

ST BARTS

In the northern group of the Leeward Islands, Saint-Barthélemy, commonly known as St Barts, is linked administratively to St Martin within the French overseas department of Guadeloupe. St Barts is an attractive island, relatively unspoiled by tourism, with white sandy beaches and volcanic hills. The picturesque harbour of Gustavia is a favourite port of call for cruising sailors who come here to provision their boats with duty-free goods. The island is surrounded by several bays and small islets, but it is in Gustavia where all the action is.

Country Profile

Christopher Columbus named the island San Bartolomé after his brother's patron saint. The French were the first to settle in the mid-seventeenth century, mostly emigrating from Normandy and Brittany. After a period of French rule, it was ceded to Sweden at the end of the eighteenth century in exchange for trading rights in the port of Göteborg. Le Carénage, present-day Gustavia, became a free port, which together with its neutrality during the great power conflicts brought prosperity and peace. The sea has always been a source of income; men-of-war, traders and pirates called and the island was used as a transhipment point for both plunder and legitimate goods. During the American War of Independence St Barts acted as a base for American privateers and American goods. Transhipment still remains an economic activity today. In the last part of the nineteenth century, after a referendum, St Barts was returned to France. The French had remained the predominant influence and today one can still see old women in the traditional white starched Breton bonnets.

St Barts relies on its free port status, its anchorages and beaches for revenue. Trade and fishing are also important. Of the 5000 inhabitants, most are of French descent and some Swedish, there being only a small percentage of people of African origin. The French that is spoken still has traces of seventeenth century dialect. Roman Catholicism and Protestantism are the main denominations. The islanders are French citizens with full rights. Gustavia is the capital, a colonial town with a French atmosphere, although named after a Swedish king.

Entry Regulations

Port of entry
Gustavia 17°55′N 62°50′W.

Procedure on arrival
Gustavia: Port captain should be contacted on Channel 16 two hours prior to arrival. Yachts anchor or moor in the pleasure port in the centre of town, separate from the commercial harbour. Proceed ashore to the port authority with papers and passports, open 0730–1230, 1430–1730

Practical Information

LOCAL TIME: GMT – 4

BUOYAGE: IALA B

CURRENCY: French franc, although US$ are widely accepted. Euro from 2002.
1 euro = 6.55957 FRF.

BUSINESS HOURS
Banks: 0800–1200, 1400–1600 (only in Gustavia).
Shops: 0800–1200, 1430–1700 Monday to Friday; morning only on Saturday.

ELECTRICITY: 220 V, 50 Hz

PUBLIC HOLIDAYS
1 January: New Year's Day
Good Friday and Easter Monday
1 May: Labour Day
8 May: Victory Day 1945
27 May: Slavery Abolition Day
Ascension
Whit Monday
14 July: Bastille Day
15 August: Assumption
1 November: All Saints' Day
2 November: All Souls Day
11 November: Armistice Day
25 December: Christmas Day

EVENTS
Carnival
24 August: St Barts Day

MEDICAL
Central Hospital. *Tel.* 27 60 35.
Emergencies. *Tel.* 27 76 03.
Gustavia Hospital. *Tel.* 27 60 35.

COMMUNICATIONS
International dialling access code 00.
Public phones use phone cards which can be bought in the post office and some shops.
There are flights to Guadeloupe, St Croix, St Martin, St Thomas and San Juan (Puerto Rico) for connections to Europe and North America.

Monday to Saturday, 0800–1200 Sunday from early December to late April. Third party insurance is occasionally requested.

Customs
Items for personal use are admitted without tax if not in excessive quantity. Otherwise, French regulations apply.

Cats and dogs over three months old are admitted if accompanied by health and anti-rabies inoculation certificates.

Immigration
Visas are required by nationals of South Africa, Bolivia, Haiti, Honduras, El Salvador, Dominican Republic, Turkey, Australia, Dominica, St Lucia, Barbados, Jamaica, and Trinidad and Tobago. Any non-EU citizen (except for Japan) staying longer than three months will need an extended visa.

Because of the duty-free status of St Barts, visa regulations are less strictly enforced than on Guadeloupe or Martinique.

Restrictions
Anchoring is not permitted in Baie St Jean. Water-skiing or jet-skiing is prohibited within 350 metres of any beach. No water sports are allowed inside Gustavia harbour. The use of barbecues is prohibited on boats docked at the quay.

Fees
Port dues are payable in the main harbour of Gustavia and they are collected by a roving harbour patrol. The daily fees depend on length and location, being lowest if anchoring in the outer harbour, higher in the inner harbour and if coming stern-to the quay. One is charged per night of stay depending on the length of boat.

Facilities

Boats either come stern-to the two quays (electricity available), on a mooring in the inner harbour or at anchor in the outer harbour. Showers are available ashore. Fresh water can be bought from the port authority. Provisioning in town is adequate and the best buy continues to be duty-free spirits, although most other goods are more expensive than in the other French-speaking islands.

Fuel can be obtained from the commercial dock at St Barth Marine open 0800–1500 Monday to Friday, 0800–1200 Saturday. Camping Gaz is available but gas bottles with US fittings cannot be filled. There are water, showers, toilets and garbage disposal at the yacht dock. Only basic repair facilities are available.

Further Reading

St Martin/Sint Maarten Area Cruising Guide
Cruising Guide to the Leeward Islands

Websites

www.st-barths.com
www.frenchcaribbean.com

ST EUSTATIUS (STATIA)

St Eustatius, affectionately known as Statia, lies north of St Kitts in the Leeward Island chain. The island's only anchorage is off the main village of Oranjestad, in Oranje Baai, which is an open roadstead where the swell usually makes itself felt. Statia is a free port, like its sister islands in the Netherlands Antilles, Saba and Sint Maarten.

Country Profile

It is difficult, if not impossible, to imagine that this tiny island was once the commercial hub of the West Indies. During the American War of Independence, when the loyal British colonies were forbidden to trade with the rebel Americans, Dutch Statia made best use of its neutrality and traded with everyone without asking questions. The small population became very rich and Statia was known as the Golden Rock. November 16, 1776, the date of the first firing in the world of an official salute to the new Stars and Stripes, is celebrated as Statia Day. Later when Britain declared war on the Netherlands, Admiral Rodney sacked Statia and confiscated its wealth. In more recent times Statia has become a forgotten corner of the Dutch Empire and most of its impoverished population have emigrated to other countries. Farming, fishing and trading have been the traditional industries and more recently oil storage and a refuelling facility have helped the economy of the poorest of the Netherlands Antilles. Tourism has come to dominate the economy, Statia being a tourist destination for discriminating travellers, who enjoy

Practical Information

LOCAL TIME: GMT – 4

BUOYAGE: IALA B

CURRENCY: Netherlands Antilles guilders or florins. It is tied to the US dollar at a fixed rate of $US1 = NAFL 1.80.

BUSINESS HOURS
Banks: 0830–1530 Monday to Thursday, 0830–1230, 1400–1630 Friday.
Shops: 0800/0900–1200, 1400–1800 Monday to Saturday.
Business: 0800–1200, 1330–1800 Monday to Friday.

Many Statians are Seventh Day Adventists and the shops they run are closed on Saturdays.

ELECTRICITY: 110 V, 60 Hz

PUBLIC HOLIDAYS
1 January: New Year's Day
Good Friday and Easter Monday
30 April: Queen's Birthday
1 May: Labour Day
Ascension Day
Whit Monday
16 November: Statia Day
25, 26 December: Christmas

COMMUNICATIONS
International calls can be made from the telephone office. Landsradio, Van Tonningenweg, 0800–1200, 1400–1700, 1800–1830 Monday to Friday.
There are flights to Saba and St Kitts and also Sint Maarten, from where connections can be made to Europe, North America and Caribbean destinations.

MEDICAL
Hospital, Prinsesweg. Ambulance.
Tel. 82371.

the tranquillity of a small place off the beaten track. The population numbers around 2100, the majority being Seventh Day Adventist, with a Roman Catholic minority. English is spoken, as well as Papiamento.

Entry Regulations

Port of entry
Oranjestad 17°29′N 62°59′W.

Procedure on arrival
Proceed ashore and check in with immigration and the harbour master at the head of the big pier, the office being normally open 0800–1700 with a lunch break.

Fees
Entry fee of $US10–15 depending on length. $10 per day mooring charge, if using one of the harbour moorings. Departure fee of $5–$10 depending on destination.

Restrictions
Diving is only allowed if you are accompanied by someone from the local dive centre.

Facilities

These are quite basic, although the situation will improve when moorings for visiting yachts are laid both in the harbour and marine park. Water can be taken on from the Golden Rock Dive Centre (Channel 11), who have their own mooring. They

can also help with engine repairs. Fuel is available by jerrycan. There are two supermarkets in Oranjestad (Duggins and Windward Islands) with a good selection of both imported and local produce. They stay open until late in the week and 0800–1330 on Sundays.

Further Reading

Cruising Guide to the Leeward Islands

Website

www.turq.com/statia (St Eustatius Tourist Office)

ST KITTS AND NEVIS

Part of the Leeward Islands in the Lesser Antilles is the Federation of St Christopher (the popular name St Kitts is more often used) and Nevis. St Kitts is a green, mountainous island with a low-lying peninsula to the south east while Nevis is smaller and circular, rising to a volcanic peak over 3000 ft (984 m) high with a dramatic crater at the top. As well as politically united, the two islands are linked by a submarine rock base, separated by the 2-mile (3-km) wide waters of the Narrows.

So near and yet so far from the English-speaking Lesser Antilles, St Kitts and Nevis are rather off the cruising track. Some people avoid them because they do not fancy a tough return beating against wind and current to more popular Antigua. Others

Practical Information

LOCAL TIME: GMT – 4

BUOYAGE: IALA B

CURRENCY: East Caribbean dollar (EC$). US$ also widely accepted.

BUSINESS HOURS
Banks: 0800–1300 Monday to Thursday also Friday 1500–1700. St Kitts and Nevis National Bank also opens Saturday 0830–1100.
Shops: 0800–1200, 1300–1600; closed Thursday afternoons.
Government offices: 0800–1200 Monday to Friday, 1300–1430 Monday and Tuesday, 1300–1400 Wednesday to Friday.

ELECTRICITY: 230 V, 60 Hz

PUBLIC HOLIDAYS
1 January: New Year's Day
Good Friday, Easter Monday
First Monday in May: Labour Day
Whit Monday
Second Saturday in June: Queen's Birthday with a parade
August Monday
September 19: Independence Day
25, 26 December: Christmas

EVENTS
Carnival, over Christmas and New Year period on St Kitts.
Culturama carnival on Nevis, July–August, ending the first Monday in August.

COMMUNICATIONS
Skantel, Cayon St, Basseterre, and Main St, Charlestown, is open 0700–1900 Monday to Friday, 0700–1400, 1900–2000 Saturday, 0800–1000, 1900–2000 Sundays and public holidays, for telephone, fax, telex and telegram.
Post offices at Bay Road, Basseterre and Main St, Charlestown, open 0800–1500 Monday to Saturday except Thursdays when they close at 1100.
There are flights from St Kitts to various Caribbean destinations as well as to Miami, New York and Toronto.

are put off by the frustrating requirement to clear in and out for every move around the islands. These factors, as well as the absence of docking facilities, have combined to make these islands some of the least frequented in the Lesser Antilles. This is surprising, because although they do not abound in scenic anchorages, the islands themselves are extremely attractive and their interesting past makes visiting ashore a worthwhile experience. As the first English settlement in the Caribbean, St Kitts is of historical interest. There are old relics, ruined forts, grand plantation houses and in Basseterre, the capital since 1727, the best preserved colonial town in the British West Indies. The main town of Nevis, Charlestown, also retains a picturesque colonial air. For the energetic there are some challenging hikes up to the top of St Kitts or the peak of the Nevis volcano. The promised development of marinas on both islands will undoubtedly change this state of affairs and place St Kitts and Nevis firmly on the Antilles cruising circuit.

Country Profile

Some archaeological remains have been found of the original inhabitants, who suffered a similar fate to those on other islands, perishing at the hands of Europeans, although not without a struggle. They called the island Liamuiga, 'fertile island'. Columbus visited the island on his second voyage and renamed it after St Christopher, the patron saint of travellers. Nevis was originally called Oualie by the Indians, meaning land of beautiful water, and the name Nieves is thought to have been given to the island by Columbus because it reminded him of the white clouds gathered around the snowy peaks of the Pyrenees, Nieves becoming corrupted over the years to Nevis.

St Kitts was the first British settlement in the West Indies, although some French also settled and for a while the island was divided between the two, still reflected in the place names. From their base in St Kitts both the English and French colonised other Caribbean islands and the relationship was often stormy.

On Nevis the natural mineral baths made the island a popular spa and Horatio Nelson, coming to water his ships, met and married Frances Nisbet, who lived on the island.

From 1816 St Kitts, Nevis, Anguilla and the British Virgin Islands were administered as a single colony until the Leeward Islands Federation was formed. St Kitts and Nevis gained independence in 1983 as a separate Federation.

On St Kitts the nationalised sugar industry dominates the mainly agricultural economy, although low sugar prices have increased reliance on foreign aid; government efforts to diversify have seen the development of electronics and data-processing industries. Nevis grows sea island cotton and coconuts. Tourism is increasingly important, helped by the good airport on St Kitts.

There are around 46,000 inhabitants, mostly of African descent, whose first language is English, although some French patois is also spoken. The majority are Protestant.

The islands are in the trade wind belt. There is plenty of rainfall on the hills, but it is less humid on the coast. The hurricane season is from June to November.

Entry Regulations

Ports of entry
Charlestown (Nevis) 17°08′N 62°38′W, Basseterre (St Kitts) 17°18′N 62°43′W.

Procedure on arrival
Charlestown: Anchor off the pier and go first to customs, which is opposite on Main Street, open 0800–1200, 1300–1600 weekdays. Then one should check in with passports at immigration in the police station, to the right down Main Street. A permit is required to visit some anchorages on Nevis, and one must return to customs for clearance to sail over to St Kitts.
Basseterre: It is possible to anchor in the deepwater port and visit the customs office ashore, open 0800–1630 Monday and Tuesday, and 0800–1600 the rest of the week, with 1200–1300 being a lunch break. At weekends or holidays the local taxi drivers can help find a customs official. Immigration is upstairs in the police station on Cayon Street, three streets inland from Bay Road.

There is no customs office at Zante Marina for the time being, but this is still the more convenient place to berth the boat and complete formalities in Basseterre which is best reached by taxi. There are plans for the clearance facilities to be reinstated at Zante Marina.

Customs
Firearms must be declared and usually are bonded on board.

Animals must be quarantined before being allowed entry. An import permit from the Ministry of Agriculture is necessary. Otherwise animals must remain on board and may only land after having been inspected by the local veterinary officer.

Immigration
No visas are required for nationals of Commonwealth countries, the European Union (except Portugal), Central America, Argentina, Bahrain, Bolivia, Chile, China, Colombia, Ecuador, Egypt, Fiji, Iceland, Israel, Japan, Jordan, South Korea, Kuwait, Liechtenstein, Monaco, Netherlands

Antilles, Norway, Oman, Paraguay, Peru, Puerto Rico, Qatar, San Marino, Saudi Arabia, South Africa, Switzerland, Taiwan, Tunisia, Turkey, Uruguay, UAE, USVI and the United States.

Visits of up to one month are normally allowed for the above, up to six months for Canadian and US citizens. All others require visas, unless the stay does not exceed 14 days, in which case visas are not required for all nationalities except those of Eastern Europe, Haiti, North Korea and Yemen.

Cruising permit
If one clears in first at Charlestown, one must clear in again at Basseterre and vice versa. On both islands, clearance is normally given only for anchoring in the port of entry, and a cruising permit must be obtained to visit any other anchorages on that island.

If wanting to visit the other island, one must return to customs and get a Boat Pass to go to the other port of entry. Here another cruising permit will have to be obtained, although one does not have to visit immigration again before clearing out.

Fees
Customs charges EC$20, which does not have to be paid again if visiting both islands. There is an overtime fee on both islands for clearance outside of working hours.

Facilities

An ambitious redevelopment project in Basseterre will radically alter the situation once it is completed as it includes a full service marina. For the time being (2000), Zante Marina offers only basic facilities, water and electricity. It is reported that protection is inadequate if the wind is south of east as a large swell enters the marina. A fuel dock is planned, but in the meantime the marina can arrange for the delivery of larger quantities by tanker. Facilities are very basic on Nevis where there are plans to build a small marina at Fort Charles, at the southern end of Charlestown. Another development on Nevis is planned at the old Newcastle harbour, on the NW side of the island near the airport. On both islands fuel must be either carried in jerrycans or ordered by tanker if the quantity warrants it. The Shell depot in St Kitts will also fill gas bottles. There is a boatbuilding firm near the deepwater harbour in Basseterre which will undertake fibreglass work and general repair. Brooks Boat Company can be contacted on VHF Channel 16, call sign BBC. There is good provisioning in Basseterre, where there are several supermarkets.

Water is also available on the dock in Charlestown, but permission to come alongside must be obtained from the harbour master. The fuel situation is similar to the one in St Kitts. The Nevis Gas Company will refill gas bottles. There is less selection in provisions than in St Kitts, but there is a good supply of fresh produce, particularly freshly caught fish.

Further Reading

Cruising Guide to the Leeward Islands

Websites

stkitts-nevis.com (St Kitts and Nevis Tourist Board)
www.port-zante.com

ST LUCIA

This volcanic island in the Windward Islands boasts some of the most spectacular scenery in the Caribbean, which has earned her the name 'Helen of the Caribbean'. The Grand and Petit Pitons peaks rise out of the sea at Soufrière Bay and there are few Caribbean anchorages to match this spot for sheer magnitude. Not far away lies Marigot Bay, a landlocked bay that reputedly hid from sight an entire British fleet during the Napoleonic wars and now shelters one of The Moorings' fleet of charter yachts. However, the main yachting centre of St Lucia is at Rodney Bay close to the northern end of the island, where an excellent marina has been set up in a dredged lagoon. To this one should add that the facilities in the well-protected port of the capital Castries make St Lucia the perfect base from which to explore the rest of the Lesser Antilles. Several marine reservations have been established in recent years, where anchoring is normally prohibited. The one at Soufrière has

Rodney Bay and Marina.

Practical Information

LOCAL TIME: GMT – 4

BUOYAGE: IALA B

CURRENCY: East Caribbean dollar (EC$). US$ also widely accepted.

BUSINESS HOURS
Banks: In Rodney Bay Marina: 0800–1500 Monday to Thursday, 0800–1700 Friday, 0800–1200 Saturdays.
Shops: 0800–1230, 1330–1600 Monday to Friday, 0800–1200 Saturday.
Government offices: 0830–1230, 1330–1630 Monday to Friday.

ELECTRICITY: 220 V, 50 Hz

PUBLIC HOLIDAYS
1 January: New Year's Day
22 February: Independence Day

Good Friday and Easter Monday
Whit Monday
Corpus Christi
Emancipation Day
Thanksgiving Day
13 December: National Day
25, 26 December: Christmas

EVENTS
Carnival: February.
Flower festivals: La Rose, August; La Marguerite, October
Jazz Festival: June
ARC Finish: December.

COMMUNICATIONS
International telephone calls with phone cards or credit cards at Rodney Bay Marina and Cable & Wireless, Bridge St, Castries, also New Dock Road, Vieux Fort.

The main post office is on Bridge Street, Castries.
There are international flights from Hewannora Airport near Vieux Fort to various European and North American cities, while inter-island flights leave from Vigie airport near Castries.

MEDICAL
Victoria Hospital, Castries. *Tel.* 4522421.
Serious emergencies are often sent to Martinique.

DIPLOMATIC MISSIONS
United Kingdom: 24 Micoud St, Castries. *Tel.* 4522484.
Venezuela: Casa Vigie, Castries. *Tel.* 4524033.
France: Vigie. *Tel.* 4522462.
The nearest US representative is in Martinique.

several mooring buoys that have been laid for the use of visiting boats.

Recently tourism has become a major revenue earner and yachting plays an important part in this development. The government has actively encouraged the establishment of yachting related businesses, aiming to make St Lucia one of the prime yachting centres in the Caribbean.

Country Profile

Arawaks were probably the first to settle on St Lucia, only to be driven out by the Caribs. The first European sighting remains a matter of controversy and it is disputed that Columbus ever came to the island in 1502 on 13 December, which is celebrated as St Lucia's Day, the national holiday. Populated by hostile Caribs, there was little interest by Europeans in settling the island until the 1600s. English efforts to settle failed, then in 1642 the French king granted it to the French West Indies Company. The Caribs continued to resist settlement, and several governors were killed. Twenty years later the English renewed their claim and a struggle for possession commenced between Caribs, French and English, the island changing hands some fourteen times before finally becoming a British Crown Colony in 1814, which it remained until independence in

1979. The majority of settlers, however, were of French origin and the French influence remained strong, still to be seen in the French patois, architecture and place names.

For many years the economy was dominated by sugar, although bananas, cocoa and coconuts have also become important exports. Tourism is now a major earner of foreign exchange.

The population is 145,000. English is the official language but many speak a French patois and most are Roman Catholic.

The island has constant trade winds with only minor differences through the year. December to June is the best time of year, when it is less humid, and there is no risk of hurricanes. The hurricane season is from June to November.

Entry Regulations

Ports of entry
Vieux Fort 13°44′N 60°57′W, Marigot Bay 13°58′N 61°58′W, Castries 14°00′N 60°59′W, Rodney Bay 14°04′N 60°58′W, Soufrière 13°50′N 61°04′W.

Procedure on arrival
On arrival the captain should go ashore to report to customs. The crew must remain on board until clearance is completed. Customs clearance from

last port is required and a local declaration form must be completed in quadruplicate (including animals, duty-free goods, firearms on board).

If staying less than three days, one can clear in and out on arrival. After clearing out, yachts have 72 hours to depart St Lucia, or 24 hours if local or charter boats.

Vieux Fort: The customs office is at the head of the large dock. Clearance may be completed 0800–1630 on weekdays only; at weekends one must clear at Hewannora Airport.

Marigot Bay: The customs office is on the right hand side by The Moorings fuel dock, open 0800–1800 every day.

Castries: Yachts clearing in must come straight to customs dock or, if there is no space, must anchor in the quarantine anchorage to the east of the customs dock. Failure to do so could result in a fine. Customs and immigration officials are available during office hours (0800–1630 weekdays).

Rodney Bay: One should tie up alongside the customs dock in the marina, which is marked by yellow posts, although this is not enforced, and boats usually dock wherever they can find a space. The captain is required to report immediately to the customs and immigration office inside the marina, open 0800–1200, 1300–1630 every day including Sunday, except Friday when it is open until 1800. The crew must not disembark until formalities have been completed. There is no docking charge if only coming to clear. The channel leading into Rodney Bay Marina has a maximum reported depth of 13 ft (4 m).

Customs

Firearms must be declared, but no action is taken if staying less than three days, after which they must be sealed on board by a customs officer. Yachts temporarily imported will have weapons held by customs in Castries or possibly by police if a longer permit is obtained.

Animals are not allowed ashore without prior inspection by the veterinary officer, who will then grant permission. Dogs will only be allowed ashore if they have been under quarantine for the last six months.

Immigration

Visas are not required for nationals of Commonwealth, Scandinavian and EU countries, Liechtenstein, Switzerland, Turkey, Tunisia, Uruguay, Venezuela and the United States.

Normally a six week stay is granted when clearing in, with a further one month extension possible. Extensions have to be obtained in Castries. A charge of 40 EC dollars is made for every three weeks extension.

Cruising permit

This is not obligatory, but permission is needed to move to any different place other than the port of entry. A cruising permit for sailing the coast or visiting other places in St Lucia is best requested when clearing in.

Procedure on departure

Yachts must clear out with customs and immigration. A new crew list must be submitted if there have been any crew changes.

If a boat is leaving with the same crew, it may do so without clearing out provided its stop is less than 72 hours, but this must be made clear when clearing in. Any boat must leave within 24 hours of having cleared out. Duty-free fuel may be purchased after clearing out. This is best done at Rodney Bay Marina where one can go directly to the fuel dock after clearing customs.

Fees

The port authority charges various fees for clearance and navigational aids, which are made up as follows:

1 Occasional licence: Boats up to 40 ft (12 m) EC$20, 41–70 ft (12.4–21 m) EC$30, over 71 ft (22 m) EC$40.
2 Pratique: boats under 100 GRT EC$10 at any time, over 100 GRT EC$20 between 0800 and 1600, EC$40 between 1600 and 0800.
3 Clearance: boats under 40 ft (12 m) EC$5, over 40 ft (12 m) EC$15.
4 Navigational aids: EC$15.
5 Charter boats must pay a licensing fee.

Overtime is payable if clearing out after hours or at weekends.

Facilities

St Lucia is constantly improving its yachting facilities and several charter companies have their base there, which means that most repair work can be undertaken locally. Good repair facilities are available at Rodney Bay Marina: a well stocked chandlery, electronics workshop, sail repair, dive shop. The boatyard has a 50-ton travelift and extensive dry storage facilities. There are two banks in the marina, as well as a small supermarket. Two large supermarkets are close by. Comprehensive repair facilities are available at Vigie near the capital Castries where the St Lucia Yacht Services offer a marina service, repair facilities, a travelift and slipway.

The Moorings charter company maintains a base of operations in Marigot Bay. The company's employees will undertake outside work if not needed to work on their own yachts. Fuel and water are available at their dock and also provisions from their supply store. The Moorings stand by on VHF Channels 16 and 85.

There are only basic services available in Vieux Fort, although some engine repair work can be undertaken at the Goodwill Fishermen's Cooperative. Some supplies as well as fresh fruit and vegetables are also available.

Further Reading

Sailors Guide to the Windward Islands
Cruising Guide to the Caribbean

Websites

www.stlucia.org (St Lucia Tourist Board)
www.st-lucia.com
www.rodneybaymarina.com

ST MARTIN

One of the northern Leeward Islands, St Martin is French while Sint Maarten, which occupies the southern half of the same island, is Dutch, part of the Netherlands Antilles. French St Martin is different from its Dutch neighbour, not only in culture, but also in terrain, as the north is hilly and forested compared to the low sandy south. Pic du Paradis is the highest point. Since 1963 St Martin has been part of the French overseas département of Guadeloupe. Both tourism and yachting have developed at a great rate during the last decade. One area where the French half of the island scores high is not surprisingly that of cuisine.

Country Profile

The Caribs were the original inhabitants of this island, which Christopher Columbus probably sighted on St Martin's Day in 1493, hence its name.

Spain showed little interest in the island and it was left to the French to settle in the north in the seventeenth century, while Dutch settled in the south. A treaty in 1648 divided the island between France and the Netherlands on the basis of peaceful coexistence, an arrangement which continues to this day.

The economy of St Martin is dominated by tourism, with the attractions of duty-free shopping, pleasant climate and good beaches. The resulting immigration has almost tripled the population, now around 35,000 on the French side. Marigot is the capital.

Entry Regulations

Ports of entry
Marigot Bay 18°04′N 63°06′W, Anse Marcel 18°07′N 63°03′W.

Procedure on arrival
One should proceed ashore and report to customs (*douane*) and police (gendarmerie). Yachts are supposed to check with immigration on arrival and departure and also when sailing between the Dutch and French sides of the island.
Marigot Bay: Clear in with immigration at the head of the dock (open daily 0700–1900).
Anse Marcel: Yachts can clear at the port office.

Customs
St Martin is a duty-free island.
Firearms must be declared.
Animals need a health certificate, and dogs and cats need a valid anti-rabies vaccination certificate.

Fees
An immigration fee of US$10 is charged for a yacht with crew, and $20 if carrying a charter party. There is an entry fee.

Immigration
A stay of up to three months is permitted. Visas are required by nationals of South Africa, Bolivia, Haiti, Honduras, El Salvador, Dominican Republic, Turkey and Australia, Dominica, St Lucia, Barbados, Jamaica, and Trinidad and Tobago. Any non-EU citizen staying longer than three months needs an extended visa.

As international flights arrive in the Dutch Sint Maarten, crew joining a boat in French St Martin have sometimes experienced difficulties with immigration officials at the airport as they did not have either an onward or return ticket. Captains of

Practical Information

LOCAL TIME: GMT – 4

BUOYAGE: IALA B

CURRENCY: French franc US$ are widely used. Euro from 2002. 1 euro = 6.55957 FRF.

BUSINESS HOURS
Banks: 0900–1200, 1400–1500 Monday to Friday.
Shops: 0900–1200/1230, 1400–1800. Monday to Saturday.

ELECTRICITY: 220 V, 50 Hz

PUBLIC HOLIDAYS
1 January: New Year's Day
Carnival, beginning of February
Good Friday and Easter Monday
Ash Wednesday
1 May: Labour Day
8 May: Victory Day 1945
Ascension
Whit Monday
14 July: Bastille Day
21 July: Schoelcher Day
15 August: Assumption
1 November: All Saints' Day
11 November: Armistice Day
25 December: Christmas Day

COMMUNICATIONS
International dialling access code 00.
If calling the Dutch side of the island, dial 3 first and then the number.
Public phones take phone cards, which may be bought from post offices and some shops.
International flights can only be made from the Dutch Sint Maarten airport. The small airport in St Martin only has flights to St Barts and Guadeloupe.

yachts expecting crew should contact immigration beforehand to avoid this problem.

Facilities

There are several established marinas and there is a possibility of more to come. Port La Royale, in the north-east corner of Simpson Bay Lagoon, offers the usual marina services, repair and engineering workshops. There are two chandleries in Marigot, a good supermarket and a fresh produce market. Port Lonvilliers marina is the best hurricane hole on the island, being completely enclosed and offering protection from every direction. Overall, repair facilities are somewhat better on the Dutch side of the island.

Further Reading

Cruising Guide to the Leeward Islands

Website

www.frenchcaribbean.com

ST VINCENT AND THE GRENADINES

Part of the Windward Islands in the Lesser Antilles, the island of St Vincent plus over 30 Grenadines

have always been a popular yachting destination. The long established cruising Mecca of the Caribbean, the Grenadines, have not lost their appeal in spite of the steady increase of sailing pilgrims who flock there. The anchorages might be better in the Virgins, the scenery more stunning in the Leewards, but the affection of discriminate cruisers for the Grenadines remains unswayed. Why this is so is difficult to say, but the fact that the Grenadines have changed so little compared to the rest of the Caribbean is probably the main reason.

Particularly encouraging is the fact that under the guidance of Prime Minister James F. Mitchell, who grew up in Bequia and is familiar with the needs of sailors, various measures have been taken to protect the fragile environment of the islands. St Vincent was also the first country in the Caribbean to ban water scooters and jet skis, abominations which have destroyed the peace and tranquillity of many resorts around the world.

Arbitrarily divided by the British Colonial Office, the Northern Grenadines are administered by St Vincent, while the smaller southern group belongs to Grenada. The island of St Vincent has been a charter base, with good facilities, for many years. A warm welcome awaits sailors in neighbouring Bequia, whose Port Elizabeth in Admiralty Bay is one of the most famous watering holes on the international cruising scene.

Bequia is a true island of sailors and boats. The seafaring tradition is very much alive among today's Bequians, most of whom are descendants of the early Scottish settlers and whaling crews. More than anywhere else in the West Indies, Bequia is the island where sailors feel truly at home.

The other Grenadines all have their special

Practical Information

LOCAL TIME: GMT – 4

BUOYAGE: IALA B

CURRENCY: East Caribbean dollar (EC$)

BUSINESS HOURS
Banks: 0800–1200/1300 Monday to Friday, plus 1400/1500–1700 Friday.
Shops: 0800–1200, 1300–1600 Monday to Friday, 0800–1200 Saturday.
Government offices: 0800–1200, 1300–1600 Monday to Friday, 0830–1200 Saturday.

ELECTRICITY: 220/240 V, 50 Hz

PUBLIC HOLIDAYS
1 January: New Year's Day
22 January: St Vincent & the Grenadines Day
Good Friday, Easter Monday

1 May: Labour Day (Fisherman's Day)
Whit Monday
First Monday and Tuesday in July: Caricom Day and Carnival Tuesday
First Monday in August
27 October: Independence Day
25, 26 December: Christmas

EVENTS
Bequia Easter Regatta
Carnival
Sport Fishing Competition

COMMUNICATIONS
Cable & Wireless, Halifax St, Kingstown for international telephone calls, fax, telex and telegraph.
Post office, Halifax St, 0830–1500 Monday to Friday, 0830–1130 Saturday.
Frangipani Yacht Services in Bequia:

International telephone calls, telex and mail service.
St Vincent, Union, Mustique and Canouan all have airports, but for international flights to North America or Europe, connections have to be made in Barbados, St Lucia or Martinique.

MEDICAL
Kingstown General Hospital. Tel. 4561185.
Emergency. Tel. 999.
Bequia Casualty Hospital, Port Elizabeth. Tel. 4583294.

DIPLOMATIC MISSIONS
In Kingstown:
France: Administrative Building, Arnos Vale Playing Field. Tel. 4562567.
United Kingdom: Granby St. Tel. 4571701.
Venezuela: Granby St. Tel. 4561374.

character, from the unspoilt Tobago Cays to exclusive Mustique, retreat of royalty and rock stars.

Country Profile

Caribs inhabited Hairoun, as they called St Vincent, when Columbus visited on his third voyage, and their hostility initially prevented European settlement. In 1675 a Dutch ship carrying settlers and slaves was wrecked on the island and only the slaves survived, mixing with the Caribs. Slaves from neighbouring islands fled to swell this population of 'Black Caribs' of whom some descendants still live on the island.

England and France disputed possession of the island and both occupied it at different times. The French encouraged the Black Caribs against the English, and a fragile peace came only at the end of the eighteenth century when a revolt was crushed, and most of the Black Caribs were deported to Roatán Island, now part of Honduras.

During the nineteenth century labour shortages brought in Portuguese and Indian immigrants. St Vincent became incorporated into the British colony of the Windward Islands. The volcano of Soufrière erupted in 1902, two days after Mount Pelée on Martinique, killing 2000 people and was a blow to an already bad economic situation. The volcano still remains active, its last eruption occurring in 1979. Full independence was gained the same year.

The soil is fertile and agriculture is important economically, bananas being the main export. Tourism also contributes considerably to the economy, but there is high unemployment.

The population of around 112,000 lives mostly on the coast and in the capital Kingstown, on St Vincent. English is the main language, but some people also speak a Créole patois. The population is predominantly Protestant and Roman Catholic.

The islands lie in the tropical trade wind zone. December to May are the best months, dry, and outside the hurricane season, which lasts from June to November.

Entry Regulations

Ports of entry
St Vincent: Kingstown 13°09′N 61°14′W, Wallilabou Bay 13°15′N 61°17′W (yachts only), Young Island Cut 13°08′N 61°12′W.
Bequia: Port Elizabeth 13°00′N 61°16′W.
Mustique: Grand Bay 12°53′N 61°11′W.
Union Island: Clifton 12°35′N 61°25′W.
Canouan: 12°42′N 61°20′W.

Procedure on arrival
Visiting yachts arriving in St Vincent territorial waters must proceed to a port of entry to clear in before stopping in any other port or anchorage.

With Q flag hoisted, one should dock or anchor in the port of entry and the captain only should go ashore. Three crew lists, clearance from previous port, passports and ship's papers will be needed. Clearance must also be done with the port authorities, customs and immigration.

Kingstown: Yachts should anchor at the new Kingstown Cruise Ship and Ferry Berth. First one should clear in with customs and then immigration, which is in town, and finally the port authority. This can take some time. Because of the lengthy formalities and difficult mooring in Kingstown, some people prefer to clear in at Bequia and visit St Vincent on the ferry, which sails there daily.

Wallilabou Bay: Wallilabou Bay is the first port of entry on the western side of St Vincent for yachts arriving into St Vincent particularly from St Lucia and Martinique. It is also the last port on that end of the island for departing yachts.

Bequia: As Bequia is more used to yachts, clearing in at Port Elizabeth can be done more quickly. In Port Elizabeth customs and immigration are in the same building as the post office, open 0900–1500.

A cruising permit will be granted by customs or Port Department on clearing in, if they are satisfied that the voyage is for cruising purposes only.

Customs

Firearms must be declared on arrival, and can be sealed on board, but if a yacht has no suitable locker, the firearms will be held in the custody of customs or police until departure.

Animals may be inspected by the veterinary officer and are not allowed ashore.

A yacht may stay up to one year subject to immigration requirements provided customs is satisfied that it is a genuine visiting yacht.

Immigration

Nationals of the UK, USA and Canada may enter for up to six months on proof of citizenship. They can get three- or six-month extensions on subsequent visits. Other nationalities will be normally granted one month on arrival for each visit, which can be extended by application to immigration, or another month gained by re-entry. No nationalities need obtain visas before arrival.

Procedure on departure

One must clear out at one of the official ports. For southbound boats, formalities are simplest at Clifton on Union Island where one can clear customs in the port, but for immigration one has to walk to the airport, which is very close.

Fees

Overtime fees for customs are payable outside of working hours, EC$38.10 Monday to Saturday, EC$55.80 Sundays and holidays. An entry tax of EC$10 per person is payable except for children under 12.

Fees are payable by yachts that are chartering as follows:

Charter licence: EC$2 per foot per month or EC$12 per foot per year. Yachts over 100 feet $2400 per year.

Day charters: A tax of EC$5 per person per day or part thereof is payable.

Cruising yachts do not pay these licence fees.

There is a EC$50 charge for a first night on a mooring at Mustique and EC$25 for subsequent nights.

Fishing

The use of spearguns or quantity fishing is not allowed unless written approval is given by the Fisheries Department. One can request this permit from customs on arrival.

Trolling and handlining a few fish for one's own consumption is allowed. There is a closed season for lobsters from 1 May to 31 August, and for turtles from 1 March to 31 July. The removal of coral is forbidden.

Restrictions

No swimsuits to be worn in towns or any business place in town or in the streets.

Facilities

The Ottley Hall Marina and Shipyard near Kingstown provides a complete range of repair and service facilities, from a 500-ton shiplift and 40-ton travelift to covered drydocks. There are also good repair facilities at Young Island and Blue Lagoon, which has been a charter base for many years. There is a small boatyard undertaking fibreglass repair and metal work, as well as various workshops specialising in electrical work, rigging and engine repair, both outboard and diesel.

Water and fuel are available at the dock in Blue Lagoon. There is also a supermarket geared specifically for charter clients, while other supermarkets can be found in Kingstown and near the airport.

The range of repair facilities on neighbouring Bequia is more limited. There are two chandleries with a good selection of spares and accessories, one also stocking charts. Water and fuel are available from the dock next to the slipway. Daffodil Marine will deliver fuel, water and ice to the boat. They also offer a laundry service. The range of provisions is less varied than in Kingstown and they tend to be more expensive. Fresh produce can be bought on the waterfront. The traditional meeting point for sailors is the Frangipani bar.

A marina development on the south-west side of Canouan offers fuel, water, Camping Gaz, basic supplies and long-distance telephones. On the other Grenadines facilities are very basic. Only essentials can be obtained in Mayereau, rather less on Petit Saint Vincent and not even that in the Tobago Cays.

Further Reading

Sailors Guide to the Windward Islands
Cruising Guide to the Caribbean

Websites

www.stvincentandgrenadines.com (Tourist Board)
www.svgtourism.com

SINT MAARTEN

Politics has little relation to geography in this small country, for Sint Maarten is part of the Netherlands Antilles, but shares the island with St Martin, which is part of the French département of Guadeloupe.

One of the most northerly of the Leeward Islands, Sint Maarten is of arid limestone, its southern part low-lying with coastal lagoons and saltpans. However, Sint Maarten is a developed island, and has some fine beaches. Tourism development has virtually exploded in recent years and the island has become one of the most popular destinations in the Caribbean.

In recent years Sint Maarten has become one of the leading yachting centres in the Caribbean, with excellent docking and a wide range of repair facilities. Its main drawback is that it lies in an area prone to be hit by hurricanes, as happened on several occasions in recent years. Boats that do not wish to use one of the marinas may anchor in Simpson Bay, although the recent construction of a large cruise ship dock has somewhat restricted the space available to yachts.

St Maarten's biggest annual event, and now one of the major regattas in the Caribbean, is the Heineken Regatta held every year during the first weekend of March.

Country Profile

The Caribs were the original inhabitants of this island, which was called St Martin by Christopher Columbus. Spain showed little interest in the island and French settled in the north, while the salt ponds attracted Dutch settlers to the southern coast. A treaty in 1648 divided the island between France and the Netherlands on the basis of peaceful coexistence, an arrangement which continues to this day. Farming, fishing, salt-extraction, and sugar were the main activities of the islanders, although with the abolition of slavery in 1863 the plantations declined. In 1954 the Dutch half, like the rest of the Netherlands Antilles, was granted full self-government while still under Dutch sovereignty.

The economy depends mainly on tourism. The island has very good airlinks, beautiful beaches, a free port status, and is prosperous. The tourist boom has seen a rapid rise in population, now over 39,000 on the Dutch side of the island. Many religious denominations are represented. Dutch is the official language, although everyone speaks English. Papiamento is spoken by immigrants from the ABC islands.

Sint Maarten has a mild tropical climate, with steady easterly trade winds. July to November is the rainy season, while December to June is dry, although conditions vary little, June to November being the hurricane season.

Entry Regulations

Port of entry
Philipsburg 18°02′N 63°03′W.

Procedure on arrival
All vessels arriving in or departing from Sint Maarten must clear immigration.
Great Bay: The immigration office is located in the harbour office and is open 0800–1200, 1300–1600 Monday to Friday, 0900–1200 Saturday and Sunday.
Simpson Bay: The immigration office is located at the police station adjacent to the channel into the lagoon. The clearance office is open 0800–1200, 1300–1630 Monday to Thursday, 0800–1200 and

Practical Information

LOCAL TIME: GMT – 4

BUOYAGE: IALA B

CURRENCY: Netherlands Antilles guilders or florins are the official currency, but US dollars are widely accepted. French francs, the currency of St Martin, are not accepted on Sint Maarten.

BUSINESS HOURS
Banks: 0830–1300 Monday to Friday, plus 1600–1700 Friday.
Shops: 0800/0900–1200, 1400–1800. Monday to Saturday.

ELECTRICITY: 110/220 V, 60 Hz

PUBLIC HOLIDAYS
1 January: New Year's Day
Good Friday and Easter Monday
First March weekend: Heineken Regatta
30 April: Queen's Birthday
1 May: Labour Day
Ascension Day
Whit Monday
All Saints' Day
11 November: St Maarten Day
25, 26 December: Christmas

EVENTS
Easter carnival mid-April
Late February/early March: Heineken Regatta

COMMUNICATIONS
Sint Maarten uses the Dutch system, which is different to the French side. If calling the French St Martin dial 06 and then the number.
There is a telecommunications office on Back Street. Landsradio, open 0700–2400; there are also offices at Simpson Bay, Cole Bay and St Peter's. The cheapest international calls can be made from Mailboxes, near Palapa Marina.
There are international flights to Europe, North America and many Caribbean destinations.

1300–1730 on Friday. During the high season it is also open 0900–1200 on Saturday and Sunday. Immigration works every day 0700–1800 and monitors Channels 12 and 16.

Clearance facilities are also available at Oyster Pond, on the east coast, which straddles the Dutch/French border.

Immigration

A valid passport is necessary for all nationals, although US citizens need only proof of citizenship. Visa regulations as for Curaçao.

Crew joining a boat have sometimes experienced difficulty with immigration officials if they are unable to show an onward ticket. Captains of yachts expecting crew are advised to contact immigration in advance.

Customs

The entire island is duty-free and therefore goods can be imported free of taxes or any formalities. Restricted goods, such as drugs, firearms and ammunition, must be declared on arrival.

Procedure on departure

Outward clearance papers are necessary if sailing to another island, even another Dutch one, though not if sailing across to French St Martin.

Fees

Departure tax, based on gross tonnage, to be paid when clearing out. There are also plans, as yet unconfirmed, to charge for the opening of the Simpson Bay Bridge and also anchoring fees in the lagoon itself.

Facilities

The Simpson Bay Bridge opens four times a day. Owners of boats passing through the bridge leading into the lagoon must sign a 'waiver of liability' before being allowed to proceed. This can be done in advance by sending the form, obtained when clearing in, by Fax. (5995-23721), to the bridge tender. The form is not necessary when leaving the lagoon, nor is it required on the French side of the bridge. The Sandy Ground Bridge, on the French side, is now also opening at certain times.

Facilities are concentrated in two main locations, on the eastern side of Philipsburg Harbour and in Simpson Bay. There are two marinas in Philipsburg, Great Bay and Bobby's, the latter offering a wide range of services as well as having a 90-ton travelift. Budget Marine is a large chandlery with an excellent selection of marine supplies. It has now moved to a new location in the most easterly corner of the lagoon. All repair work can be dealt with in the Philipsburg area and what is not available there can be found at Simpson Bay. Several charter companies maintain a base at Oyster Pond, which also has a marina. The usual repair and service facilities are available there, although not as extensive as in the other two areas of Sint Maarten. The Sint Maarten Yacht Club is located right next to the bridge of the Simpson Bay lagoon.

Water, fuel and electricity are available at all marinas. Fuel stations are open 0900 to 1600 Monday to Friday, closing at 1300 at weekends. Close to the Philipsburg marinas is a large selection of shops, several of which have dinghy docks. Better selection and prices will be found at Food Service supermarket, while the large market on the waterfront in Marigot, open Wednesday to Saturday, has the best selection of local fresh produce. The Match supermarket in Marigot is reported to have the best selection of French foods and wines. Philipsburg is a good place to buy electronic appliances, which are priced lower than in any of the neighbouring islands.

Further Reading

Cruising Guide to the Leeward Islands

Website

www.st-maarten.com (Sint Maarten Tourism Office)

TRINIDAD AND TOBAGO

The Republic of Trinidad and Tobago lies just off the Venezuelan coast, the most southerly of the Caribbean islands, and regarded by some as the most exotic. Cosmopolitan Trinidad, home of calypso and the steel drum, is famous for its Carnival called De Mas (short for masquerade). Tobago is more peaceful, and was used by Daniel Defoe as the setting for *Robinson Crusoe*, although Alexander Selkirk, on whom the story is based, was in fact wrecked on Juan Fernandez island in the South Pacific.

Until recently Trinidad and Tobago used to be less frequented by cruising boats than the islands farther north. Indeed, the islands were considered slightly out of the way, nor did they offer many cruising opportunities. The situation changed dramatically after a series of devastating hurricanes in the mid-1990s when most insurance companies started stipulating that boats must spend the hurricane season south of latitude 12°40′N, which is just north of Grenada, so it only includes that island as well as Trinidad and Tobago and Venezuela. Suddenly these places became popular destinations during the summer months, when islands farther north are indeed threatened by tropical storms. In fact, although these countries lie below the technical line, there have been hurricanes there during the last century and, especially in the case of Chaguaramas, with all its low-lying land and a

huge concentration of boats, there could be a major disaster one day. To ease matters, a small group of insurers can provide coverage during the hurricane season provided the boats are fully manned and therefore have the ability to go south quickly. Alternatively, for boats that are left in the critical area, they must be laid up in a hurricane-safe location.

Aware of Trinidad's sudden popularity, the authorities have simplified the previous cumbersome formalities, while the local businesses have made great efforts to improve yachting facilities, which now are among the best in the Eastern Caribbean. The downside of this sudden popularity (it is estimated that some 3000 cruising boats now visit Trinidad every year) has been a dramatic increase in labour charges paralleled by a drop in the quality of workmanship, so Trinidad's attraction as a destination may be short-lived.

While lacking the natural bays and anchorages of its northern neighbours, Trinidad's scenic beauty lies mostly inland. Most yachts sail to Trinidad to be there for Carnival time, when the anchorage off Port of Spain gets very crowded. This is certainly the best time to visit the island, as the Carnival is one of the most spectacular to be seen outside of Brazil.

Country Profile

The Arawaks and Caribs were the first inhabitants of the islands. On his third voyage Columbus spotted Trinidad, although no one is quite sure whether he named it after the Holy Trinity or the three distinctive peaks on the south-east of the island. Tobago's name is a corruption of tobacco, which was grown there by the Caribs.

Spain used Trinidad as a base to explore South America. Diseases and slavery soon killed off most of the native population. The late eighteenth century saw an influx of French settlers, but Spain ceded the islands to England in 1802. After the abolition of slavery in 1834, the English brought in Indian and Chinese indentured labourers to fill the labour shortage. Immigrants also came from neighbouring islands, North America, Madeira and Europe.

Tobago was first settled in 1641 when the Duke of Courland obtained a royal grant to settle on the island until it was ceded to England in the eighteenth century.

In 1888 Trinidad and Tobago were united into one Crown Colony and in August 1962 the islands

Practical Information

LOCAL TIME: GMT – 4

BUOYAGE: IALA B

CURRENCY: Trinidad and Tobago dollar
(TT$). In 2000 the rate was $US1 =
$TT6.30.

BUSINESS HOURS
Banks: 0900–1600 Monday to Friday.
Shops: 0800–1600/1630 Monday to Friday,
and 0800–1200 Saturday.
Government offices: 0800–1600 Monday to
Friday.

ELECTRICITY: 110/220 V, 60 Hz

PUBLIC HOLIDAYS
1 January: New Year's Day
Good Friday and Easter Monday
Easter Tuesday

Whit Monday
Eid el-Fitr (end of Ramadan)
Corpus Christi
19 June: Labour/Butlers Day
First Monday in August: Emancipation Day
31 August: Independence Day
24 September: Republic Day
Divali, Festival of lights
25, 26 December: Christmas

EVENTS
Carnival
Phagwah, Spring festival,
February/March
Yaum um-Nabi
Hosein festival
May: Angostura Yachting World Regatta

COMMUNICATIONS
Main Textel office, Independence Square
and 1 Edward Street, operates international

telephones, telex, fax, and is open 24
hours (there is also an office in
Scarborough).
Main post office, Wrightson Road, Port of
Spain, open 0700–1700 Monday to Friday.
There are flights from Port of Spain to
many destinations in Europe, North
America, South America and the
Caribbean. There are also flights from
Tobago to Miami, New York and Toronto
as well as Caribbean destinations.

DIPLOMATIC MISSIONS
In Port of Spain:
Canada: 3 Sweet Brick Rd, St Clair.
Tel. 622-6232.
United States: 19 Queens Park West.
Tel. 622-6371.
United Kingdom: 19 St Clair Avenue,
St Clair. Tel. 622-6371, 622-2745.
Venezuela: 16 Victoria Av. Tel. 627-9821.

became independent, the country being declared a Republic in 1976.

Coffee, sugar, cocoa and citrus fruit are cultivated in the fertile soil although agriculture has declined in importance to the economy. Trinidad is rich in mineral deposits including asphalt from the Pitch Lake on the south-west coast. Sir Walter Raleigh found the lake in 1595 and caulked his ships there. Trinidad has oil reserves, which are an important factor in the economy, although after the depression of the oil market in the 1980s, efforts were made to diversify. The discovery of natural gas reserves has boosted the petrochemicals industry, and the plastics and electronics industries are growing. Tourism is rapidly developing.

The population of Trinidad is 1.5 million, the majority being of African or Asian origin. Chinese, Portuguese, Syrian, Jewish and Latin American minorities make up Trinidad's very cosmopolitan population. Tobago has 45,000 inhabitants. English is spoken, as well as Spanish, French patois and Hindi dialects. Port of Spain is the capital of Trinidad, and Scarborough is Tobago's main town. Many different religions are practised, among them Roman Catholicism, Protestantism, Hinduism, Judaism, Islam, the syncretist creed of spiritual Baptists, and the Xango cult, which is a combination of African and Asian elements.

The islands have an equatorial climate within the trade wind belt and are almost out of the hurricane zone. June to November is the rainy season.

Entry Regulations

Ports of entry

Trinidad: Port of Spain 10°39′N 61°31′W, Chaguaramas 10°43′N 61°40′W, San Fernando 10°17′N 61°28′W, Brighton 10°15′N 61°38′W, Pointe-à-Pierre Yacht Club 10°19′N 61°28′W, Point Gourde 10°40′N 61°38′W, Point Tembladora 10°41′N 61°36′W, Point Fortin 10°11′N 61°41′W.
Tobago: Scarborough 11°11′N 60°44′W.

Procedure on arrival

Yachts entering Trinidad territorial waters are advised to call coastguard control on Channel 16 to advise of the yacht's arrival and to give an ETA.

Although Trinidad has several official ports of entry, arriving yachts should clear at either Chaguaramas in Trinidad or Scarborough in Tobago. Port of Spain is geared primarily to commercial ships, and pleasure craft may only stop there in real emergencies. Otherwise they will be sent to Chaguaramas, which has an office dedicated to clearance formalities with customs, immigration, collection of navigation dues, etc. Normal office hours are 0800–1600 Monday to Friday, although offices are open 24 hours. Regulations state that once a vessel has entered territorial waters, the captain must proceed to immigration regardless of time of day or night.

Yachts sailing to Tobago from Trinidad have to present the 'Arrival Form' to the customs officer in

Chaguaramas. He will endorse the form, which needs to be presented to customs on arrival at Scarborough. The same procedure is necessary for the reverse voyage.

Chaguaramas: Entry formalities can be completed here as there is a permanent customs office. If the dock is not occupied, yachts may come alongside the customs dock. Otherwise one should anchor nearby. A clearance-out certificate from the last port will be required.

Although boats are required to clear customs again at Scarborough if sailing from Trinidad to Tobago, with permisision from the customs officer in Trinidad one can anchor somewhere else in Tobago, such as Store Bay, and go overland to Scarborough to complete the necessary formalities.

Scarborough: One should come to the government dock to complete formalities.

Procedure on departure

Vessels must clear out of one of the two recommended ports. Yachts clear out with customs, immigration and port authority. Harbour fees are TT$50 for every 30 days in Trinidad up to a maximum TT$500 in any one year.

Customs

Firearms and ammunition must be declared on arrival and will be taken by the customs boarding officer and placed in custody at the central police station. Requests for their return prior to departure must be made to customs at least 72 hours before clearance; failure to do so may result in a delay to departure or departure without the firearms. To keep firearms in one's possession during the stay, it is necessary to apply to the Commissioner of Police for a licence.

Animals must remain on board, and may only land with the permission of the government veterinary officer and customs.

Fruits, plants and plant material must be inspected by a plant quarantine officer before being landed.

Yachts are admitted duty-free for a reasonable period of time. Boats stored for longer terms must be left in the care of an approved yard. Some formalities must be completed at customs, including a full inventory of items on board. If a yacht is left unattended, it will be necessary to complete formalities for temporary importation. This is normally carried out through Chaguaramas customs station.

Parts for yachts in transit may be imported free of duty by following the recommended procedure by customs. Only the captain of the vessel is allowed to carry duty free parts from the airport to Chaguaramas customs station, where they will be transferred on board. Parts arriving by courier will be delivered to Chaguaramas customs station. Parcels arriving via the postal service will come to the Carenage Post Office, which will notify the yacht, after which the parcel will be cleared at the Ajax Street post office in Port of Spain.

Immigration

All visitors need a valid passport. An initial visa for three months will be issued on arrival, which may be extended for another three months. One week prior to expiration a further extension may be requested upon payment of an extension fee of between $TT100 and $TT150.

Immigration will charge overtime outside of the normal working hours, which are 0800–1200, 1300–1600 Monday to Friday.

Crew departing Trinidad and Tobago by air must be signed off the vessel and signed on again when returning. The procedure requires a letter prepared by the marina or boatyard, which must be approved by the immigration officer. This approval allows for proper paperwork at the airport (or other port of exit) and an exclusion of the airport tax if executed within 24 hours of departure. This letter must be in the hands of the crew prior to departure to enable embarkation without a return ticket. This same letter will be used as authorisation for re-entry into Trinidad to rejoin the vessel. When the crew returns to Trinidad and Tobago, the master must present the crew's passport to the immigration officer at the Chaguaramas station within 24 hours to sign the crew back on the vessel.

Cruising permit

An actual cruising permit is not required; however, on arrival the captain must notify the authorities of the vessel's intended itinerary to cruise around the islands and permission must be obtained before sailing. Permission must be obtained from customs for any movement of the yacht, from one port or place to another, and to cruise the coast of either Trinidad or Tobago.

Health

A yellow fever inoculation certificate is needed if coming from an infected area in South America.

Fees

After completion of immigration formalities on arrival, the customs officer will collect $TT50 for the first 30 days of navigation dues. The balance of these dues will be collected when the boat clears out. On departure one will be charged port dues. Overtime is charged outside of working hours on weekdays and all day Saturdays, Sundays and holidays. Customs charge overtime for boarding TT$123, and clearance TT$106. Immigration overtime is TT$100.

The departure tax per person is TT$100.

Restrictions

The tanker ports at Point Fortin and Pointe-à-Pierre, and the cargo port of Point Lisas, are prohibited to yachts.

Facilities

Docking facilities have improved due to the opening of a number of new marinas. The best situated for those wishing to be close to the capital Port of Spain is the Trinidad and Tobago Yacht Club which has a limited number of berths available to visitors.

A full range of repair facilities is available at Chaguaramas, where there are several boatyards with hauling-out facilities up to 200 tons. Many boats are stored here on the hard during the hurricane season. Another area with good facilities is Carenage, where the Trinidad and Tobago Yachting Association is based. Recent reports on work carried out at most boatyards have been critical of both high costs and poor workmanship. The independent Yacht Services Association of Trinidad and Tobago is doing its best to arrest this downward trend, so it is advisable to assess the latest situation before committing to a major overhaul job.

Only basic facilities are available in Tobago. Fuel can be loaded in Scarborough by contacting National Petroleum, which will send a fuel truck to the Coast Guard dock.

Further Reading

Cruising Guide to the Caribbean
Cruising Guide to Trinidad & Tobago

Websites

www.visittnt.com (Trinidad and Tobago Tourist Board)
www.trinidadmarine.com
www.boatersenterprise.com

TURKS AND CAICOS

The British dependency of Turks and Caicos consists of about 40 low-lying cays and islands south-east of the Bahamas. Turks Island Passage separates the Turks from Caicos. The windward sides of these islands tend to be cliffs and sand dunes, while the western, leeward coasts are greener. Only a few are inhabited, most of the 14,000 inhabitants living on the principal island, Grand Turk. The group is quite a tranquil area, with stunning underwater scenery, which is strictly preserved by conservation laws.

The building of a large international airport on Providenciales capable of handling intercontinental jets has thrown this sleepy little country into the modern age. A cosmopolitan mix of expatriates has swollen the ranks of the local population to make Provo, as Providenciales is usually known, an oasis of sophistication in the midst of a watery desert.

The opening of a Club Méditerranée and other exclusive holiday resorts have produced a boom in tourism and yachting facilities are not lagging far behind. Situated conveniently halfway between Florida and the Virgins, the islands provide a useful stop in an emergency, or at least a break during a long passage. For the visiting sailor the main attractions are the clear unpolluted waters that give access to an underwater scenery of rare beauty and also the possibility of diving on some historic wrecks. The flipside of the coin is the tricky navigation among the reefs, sand banks and coral heads, with few navigation aids and those that are in place unreliable.

Country Profile

Arawaks were probably the first inhabitants, although none were left by the mid-sixteenth century. It is disputed whether Columbus sighted the islands first in 1492 or if it was Ponce de León some years later. Both Grand Turk and Caicos have been put forward as the original San Salvador where Columbus made his first landfall and this landfall controversy is still not resolved. From the sixteenth to eighteenth centuries many Spanish ships were lost on the Caicos Banks where the depth falls abruptly from about 3000 to 30 feet.

From the seventeenth century the islands were settled by the Bermudans who farmed salt there. Pirate raids were common, which probably provided the names: 'Turks' referring to the Mediterranean pirates, and 'caiques' their ships. Loyalists fleeing the American Revolution came and settled, establishing cotton and sisal planta-

Practical Information

LOCAL TIME: GMT – 5.

BUOYAGE: IALA B. Navigation aids are unreliable. In 1989 the government began changing the buoyage system to red right returning (IALA B), replacing the red left returning system.

CURRENCY: United States dollars (US$). Some Turks and Caicos coins are used.

BUSINESS HOURS
Government offices: 0800–1300 and 1400–1630 Monday to Friday, 0800–1200 Saturdays.
Banks: 0830–1430 Monday to Thursday, 0830–1230, 1430–1630 Friday.

ELECTRICITY: 110 V, 60 Hz

PUBLIC HOLIDAYS
1 January: New Year's Day
10 March: Commonwealth Day
Good Friday and Easter Monday
30 May: National Heroes Day
June: Queen's Birthday
Early August: Emancipation Day
Late September: National Youth Day
October, both variable: Columbus Day and Human Rights Day
25, 26 December: Christmas

EVENTS
Start of South Caicos regatta on Commonwealth Day
Carnival, end of August

COMMUNICATIONS
Cable & Wireless Offices on Grand Turk and Providenciales for telephone calls. Public card phones are available on all islands. These two islands, as well as South Caicos, have a modern international telephone service, although calls are quite expensive. Main post office, Grand Turk, open 0800–1600 Monday to Thursday, 0800–1530 Friday. Sub-post offices on South Caicos, Salt Cay and Providenciales. The main international airport is at Providenciales, with flights to North America. There are also flights to Nassau from other islands and to Miami from Grand Turk.

MEDICAL
There is a good hospital in Grand Turk and government clinics on the outer islands.

tions with slave labour. The islands became quite prosperous but competition from abroad meant these crops and salt panning suffered.

During the nineteenth and twentieth centuries the Turks and Caicos were ruled alternately by the British colonies of the Bahamas and Jamaica, but when the latter two became independent, nothing came of integrating the Turks and Caicos and they have remained a British Dependent Territory. Since 1976 the islands have had internal self-government. A political scandal rocked the island group, as members of government were found to be involved in the drugs trade. As a result Britain ruled directly from 1986 until 1988 when a constitutional government was restored.

Natural resources are limited, both in respect of water and fertile soil. The export of lobster and conch generates some revenue. The development of tourism and offshore financial services are now the main economic activities.

The inhabitants, numbering around 14,000, speak English and are mostly Protestant. Cockburn Town on Grand Turk is the seat of government and the largest population centre.

The islands are hot, although the trade winds make the temperature bearable. Rain is more frequent on the west coast. The hurricane season is June to November.

Entry Regulations

Ports of entry
Cockburn Town (Grand Turk) 21°28′N 71°06′W,
Providenciales 21°44′N 72°17′W, Cockburn Harbour (South Caicos) 21°30′N 71°31′W.

Procedure on arrival
Clearance formalities can be completed at the following ports and marinas:
Providenciales: South Dock (mainly for large yachts), South Side Marina, Caicos Marina and Shipyard, Sapodilla Bay, Turtle Cove Marina, Leeward Marina;
South Caicos: Government Dock, Seaview Marina;
Grand Turk: Government Freighter Wharf, Coburn Town Dock (¼ mile north of radio tower), Flamingo Cove Marina.
In all ports, customs should be contacted on Channel 16. Some of the marinas that have difficult entrances can be contacted on Channels 16 or 68, either for advice, or they may send out a pilot boat, for which a charge is usually made.
Grand Turk: If the anchorage off Cockburn Town is untenable, one should sail two miles south and anchor off the small dock. Then the harbour master should be called on Channel 16 or one can visit his office by the town dock (the northernmost dock in Cockburn Town anchorage).

A transire (cruising permit) is needed to visit the other islands. All yachts must also clear with the authorities on departure.

Customs
Firearms must be declared to customs on entry and will be taken into custody until departure. 24 hours' notice must be given to retrieve firearms on departure.

Animals must remain on board whilst in port and must be declared to customs.

Boats in transit can have parts and equipment shipped duty-free. There are two air freight flights weekly to Florida.

Immigration

A visa is not necessary with a valid passport; usually 30 days is granted on arrival, which is renewable once only for a maximum stay of six months. Visas may be required by nationals of former Eastern Bloc countries and some non-Commonwealth countries.

Fees

Overtime fees are charged outside of working hours on weekdays and all day Saturday, Sunday and on public holidays. This includes work during the lunch break. There are also customs fees and light dues.

Restrictions

Sport fishing without a permit is forbidden, as are spearguns, pole spears, Hawaiian slings and using scuba gear to take any marine life. Lobster may be taken in season (August 1 to March 31) by hand or noose.

Facilities

By far the best facilities are on Providenciales, where there are several marinas, offering the usual range of services. Access to Turtle Cove through Sellar's Cut is rather difficult, so it is advisable to contact the marina on VHF Channel 16 and ask to be guided in. Most repairs can be undertaken by the Caicos Marina & Shipyard, also located on Providenciales, which operates an 85-ton travelift and offers full repair facilities. They also have a well-stocked chandlery. The yard can be contacted on Channel 16 between 0700 and 1700. Propane bottles can be filled at the Shell station. A large marina is under construction which will become another point of entry into the country.

Facilities on the other islands, including the main island of Grand Turk, are much more limited. Fuel and some provisions can be obtained at Cockburn Harbour, on South Caicos, which is the only commercial harbour in the archipelago. In Grand Turk itself, fuel can be taken on at South Dock while water can be ordered by truck to the dock at the government pier at Governor's Beach, south of Cockburn Town. MPL Enterprises have a store in town with some marine supplies and spare parts and they also undertake engine repair. There

is a good supermarket in town. A useful pamphlet which gives details of facilities which are available and can be obtained locally is *Information for Visiting Yachtsmen*.

There is a hurricane hole in the vicinity of Cockburn Town, at North Creek or Columbus Sound.

Further Reading

Turks and Caicos Guide
Turks and Caicos Handbook

Websites

www.interknowledge.com/turks-caicos (Turks & Caicos Tourist Board)
www.turksandcaicos.tc/marinas (Details of marinas)

US VIRGIN ISLANDS

The US Virgin Islands, lying just east of Puerto Rico, have three main islands, St Thomas, St John and St Croix. Most of the other 65 islands are uninhabited. The islands have long been developed as resorts for American tourists. As a US Unincorporated Territory, the islanders are US citizens, although unable to vote in federal elections.

For most European sailors coming from the Lesser Antilles, St Thomas is their first glimpse of the USA and unfortunately the area around Charlotte Amalie does not present the best image, although scenically the US Virgin Islands are on a par with their British counterpart. The islands are a convenient landfall if coming directly from continental USA and also a good point of departure when heading for the USA, either direct or via Bermuda. As a cruising destination in itself, the US Virgin Islands have lost much of their appeal, due to the deterioration of yachting services, restrictive Coast Guard regulations and the high crime rate.

Country Profile

The Spanish were the first Europeans to settle the Virgin Islands, but as Spain's maritime power waned, other countries laid claim to the islands. St Croix was settled by the English and Dutch, these being pushed out by the Spanish and then the French. Wars, pirates and religious conflicts all made St Croix militarily and economically unprofitable for the French, and the settlers left. At the

Practical Information

LOCAL TIME: GMT – 4

BUOYAGE: IALA B

CURRENCY: United States dollars (US$).

BUSINESS HOURS
Banks: 0900–1430 Monday to Friday, plus 1530–1700 Fridays.
Government offices: 0800–1700 Monday to Thursday.
Shops: 0900–1700 Monday to Saturday.
Supermarkets: 0700–2400.

ELECTRICITY: 110/120 V, 60 Hz

PUBLIC HOLIDAYS
1 January: New Year's Day
6 January: Three Kings Day
Third Monday in January: Martin Luther King Day
Third Monday in February: President's Day

Maundy Thursday, Good Friday, Easter Monday
31 March: Transfer Day
End of May: Memorial Day
Mid-June: Organic Act Day
3 July: Emancipation Day
4 July: Independence Day
21 July: Hurricane Supplication Day
First Monday September: Labour Day
12 October: Columbus Day
Mid-October: Hurricane Thanksgiving Day
1 November: Liberty Day
Mid-November: Veterans Day
Last Thursday in November: Thanksgiving Day
25, 26 December: Christmas

EVENTS
Carnival week, end April

COMMUNICATIONS
International telephone calls can be made at various private companies.

Post offices open 0900–1700 Monday to Friday, 0900–1200 Saturday.
There are flights from St Thomas and St Croix to various US and Caribbean destinations.

MEDICAL
Medical costs are high but the standards are very good.
St Croix Hospital, 9 Diamond Bay, Christiansted. *Tel.* 778-6311.
St. Thomas Hospital, Sugar Estate, Charlotte Amalie. *Tel.* 776-8311. St John Clinic, Cruz Bay.*Tel.* 776-6400.
Police *Tel.* 915, Fire 921, ambulance 922.
Air ambulance *Tel.* 778-9177 (day), 772-1629 (night).

DIPLOMATIC MISSIONS
In Charlotte Amalie:
Dominican Republic: *Tel.* 775-2640.
United Kingdom: 1 Fortel St. *Tel.* 774-0033.

---

beginning of the eighteenth century France sold the island to Denmark. With St Thomas and St John already in Danish hands, by mid-century the Danish West Indies had become a prosperous colony. After the decline in the sugar-cane industry and the abolition of slavery, by the end of the century the economy was in bad shape. When in 1917 the USA showed an interest in acquiring the islands for a Caribbean naval base, Denmark was happy to sell them for $25 million. Nothing much changed until the 1930s, when the collapse of the sugar industry and high unemployment prompted action. Naval rule was replaced by civil government and efforts were made to improve social conditions. Only after the Second World War did the economy take off with a boom in tourism, visitors being attracted by the warm climate and unspoilt islands. This provided employment that continues today as the main source of income, bringing considerable prosperity. There is some industry, an oil refinery on St Croix and other manufacturing industries. Tax incentives have attracted some US investment.

The population is around 100,000, mainly of African origin. English is the main language, and some Spanish and Créole are also spoken. Charlotte Amalie on St Thomas is the capital, often referred to just as St Thomas. A picturesque town, with a good harbour, the influence of the Danes is still noticeable in the architecture and the traffic still drives on the left. Most religions have some follow-ing here, and one of the oldest synagogues in the Western hemisphere is in Charlotte Amalie.

The islands have a very pleasant climate, cooled by the trade winds. From November to April swells on the north coast can be a problem following heavy weather in the North Atlantic. June to November is the hurricane season.

Entry Regulations

Ports of entry
St Thomas: Charlotte Amalie 18°23′N 64°56′W, *St Croix:* Christiansted 17°46′N 64°41′W, *St John:* Cruz Bay 18°20′N 64°47′W.

Procedure on arrival
US Customs telephone numbers: St Croix 773-1011, St John 776-6741, St Thomas 774-9700. The British Virgin Islands are considered foreign locations and one must clear in with immigration every time one arrives from all other islands with the exception of Puerto Rico.
St Thomas: The captain should go ashore and obtain preliminary clearance at the offices on the western end of the waterfront next to the seaplane landing. All crew must then go with their completed papers to customs and immigration at the ferry dock. One crew member is allowed to stay on board as an anchor watch. However, if not a US national he or she will have to clear in person later at the same place.

St Croix: The yacht should berth at the wharf at Gallows Bay and the captain call customs. They will give instructions on how to proceed. Also one should call immigration, who will send an official from the airport. The customs office is above the post office on the waterfront.

St John: The captain should go to the customs office on the waterfront in Cruz Bay. All crew must also clear in with customs and immigration, with the same proviso as St Thomas.

If a yacht is going on to Puerto Rico it is advisable to obtain a cruising permit in St Thomas, issued free (otherwise on arrival in Puerto Rico a fee is charged). All yachts must clear out with customs before going to Puerto Rico.

Customs

Firearms must be declared and need a permit. For further information on firearms write to the Commissioner of Public Safety, St Thomas, USVI.

Animals should be fully documented with health and anti-rabies certificates.

Note

In their fight against drug traffic, the government of the US Virgin Islands has created a special strike force to patrol the waters of the US Virgins. Any yachts within territorial waters may be stopped, boarded and searched, and the presence of any illegal drugs on board can result in the yacht being confiscated.

Immigration

All nationalities arriving by private yacht (except for Canadians) need a valid US visa, which must be obtained in advance of arrival. Crew members must accompany the captain when clearing in as each individual must sign the entry permit.

Fees

No fees are charged Monday to Saturday 0800–1700, after which overtime rates apply. Foreign nationals arriving without a valid US visa will be fined $160.

National Park

A number of regulations have been established to protect the natural resources of the Virgin Islands National Park. The following are of direct interest to cruising sailors:

1   Do not anchor on coral and avoid damaging the reef.
2   Anchoring is prohibited in Salt Pond, Reef Bay, Great and Little Lameshur Bays. Use the white mooring buoys, with a blue band, in these locations.
3   Do not take any live or dead marine features, such as coral, shells or fans.
4   Do not tie boats to shoreline vegetation.
5   Spearfishing is prohibited throughout the park. Line fishing is permitted, but there are certain restricted areas.
6   A maximum of two male spiny lobsters (minimum size 9 in/23 cm) may be taken, and only by hand or handheld snare.

Mooring buoys have been installed for the use of cruising boats. Prohibited areas are marked by white cylinders with orange markings. For latest information it is recommended to contact the National Park administration in Cruz Bay, *Tel.* 776-6201. Occasionally they monitor Channel 16.

Facilities

Most repair facilities are concentrated around Charlotte Amalie, either in the harbour itself or the immediate vicinity. The principal marina is at Crown Bay on the western side of the bay as is the Haulover Marine Yachting Center, comprising a group of companies providing specialist services such as diesel repair, boatbuilding and sailmaking. There are several more marinas dotted around St Thomas's indented coastline, all offering the usual services.

The only other island having comparable services is St Croix, where St Croix Marine operates a full service yard and marina. They have a 300-ton slipway and 60-ton travelift, and also a well-stocked chandlery. Their marina is close to Christiansted, as is the smaller marina run by the Annapolis Sailing School. Green Cay Marina, on the NE coast, offers the best amenities but is farther out of town. Provisioning in Christiansted is very good, with several discount-type supermarkets.

Facilities on St John are much more limited, although 70 moorings were laid in Francis Bay to be used by visitors to the St John National Park. St John Island is largely unspoilt and its facilities, or lack of them, reflect this.

Further Reading

Yachtsman's Guide to the Virgin Islands
Cruising Guide to the Caribbean
Cruising Guide to the Virgin Islands

Websites

www.usvi-on-line.com
www.usvi-info.com
www.usvi.net

6 Central and North America

From the torrid jungle of Panama to the frozen wastes of Alaska, this region encompasses a vast array of cruising areas as well as some of the most famous yachting centres in the world. The coasts of Mexico and Central America are mostly visited by American yachts who have some of the best cruising spots almost on their doorstep. The United States itself has enough cruising attractions to satisfy even the most demanding sailor, which can also be said of Canada, whose western coast is of a beauty rarely matched elsewhere. While the greatest pull of the northern destinations is their scenery, a major attraction of the southern destinations, apart from their exoticism, is the opportunity to visit the remains of some of the great civilisations that once flourished in the region.

The fear of lengthy formalities and corrupt officials has dissuaded many from sailing to Spanish-speaking Mexico and Central America, but this fear is largely unfounded and in many places the officials are often more friendly than those in the USA. However, in Central American countries, some identification should always be carried when ashore. Facilities are not up to US and Canadian standards, but should anything break, help is never too far away and repair facilities are now available in most places frequented by cruising boats.

From a sailor's point of view, the main feature of Central America is the Panama Canal, a wonderful technological achievement whose operation has been largely unaffected since coming fully under Panamanian control. The transiting of yachts is now more efficient than ever before and passing through the Canal is a rewarding experience. For those whose cruising plans are blocked by continental America, there is always the possibility of crossing from one ocean to the other over land. There are several haulage companies specialising in transporting yachts across the continent at a cost comparable to the fee charged by a delivery crew.

Besides the opportunities provided by coastal cruising, much of North America is also accessible by a large network of rivers and canals. While the Intracoastal Waterway parallels almost the entire east coast of the United States, a system of canals and locks links New York to the Great Lakes, which can also be reached via the St Lawrence River. The Great Lakes are the largest inland cruising area in the world and, as their boating facilities are of the highest standard, they provide a very special cruising destination to anyone looking for something different.

BELIZE

Belize, formerly known as British Honduras, fronts the Western Caribbean Sea and borders on Mexico and Guatemala. The coastlands are low and swampy, with mangroves and lagoons, while forested mountains present a contrast in the southwest of the country. Belize's main attraction lies offshore, a 175-mile long barrier reef, second only in size to the Great Barrier Reef of Australia. Cruising inside the island-dotted reef is a unique experience and the underwater scenery is reputed to be amongst the best anywhere in the world. Between the reef and the coastal strip there are hundreds of uninhabited islands and cays, and therein lies Belize's popularity as a cruising destination. The barrier reef is not broken by many

passes and inside the reef navigation is difficult as the sea is shallow and there are not many navigational aids, but the number of secluded anchorages, unsurpassed diving and excellent fishing will ensure Belize's attraction as an alternative to the crowded Eastern Caribbean.

Country Profile

Hidden in the interior of Belize are many ruins of the ancient Mayan empire which flourished in this region from the fourth to ninth centuries, before moving to the Yucatan peninsula. In the mid-seventeenth century, the country was colonised by English settlers from Jamaica with their African slaves who came for the logwood used for textile dyes. The British government tried to secure the protection of these settlers, but did not claim sovereignty over the country. In 1821 both Guatemala and Mexico claimed Belize, claims which were rejected by Britain. In the middle of the century Guatemalan fears over an attack by the USA led to better relations with Britain, and a

Map 8: Central and North America

Practical Information

LOCAL TIME: GMT – 6

BUOYAGE: IALA B. Many of the navigation lights or marks are reported to be either out of action or missing and therefore night passages should be avoided. Even in daylight the barrier reef area should be navigated with caution.

CURRENCY: Belize dollar (BZ$). The fixed rate of exchange is BZ$2 = US$1.

BUSINESS HOURS
Banks: 0800–1300 Monday to Thursday, 0800–1200, 1500–1800 Friday.
Government offices: 0800–1200, 1300–1600 Monday to Friday.
Shops: 0800–1200, 1300–1600 Monday to Thursday, Friday 1600–2100 also, half day Wednesday and Saturday.

ELECTRICITY: 110/220 V, 60 Hz

PUBLIC HOLIDAYS
1 January: New Year's Day
9 March: Baron Bliss Day
Good Friday, Easter Saturday and Easter Monday
1 May: Labour Day
24 May: Commonwealth Day
10 September: St George's Caye Day
21 September: Independence Day
12 October: Pan American Day
19 November: Garifuna Settlement Day
25, 26 December: Christmas

COMMUNICATIONS
Belizean Telecommunications Ltd. (BTL) 1 Church Street, Belize City for telegrams, telephone calls, fax, telex, 0730–2100 Monday to Saturday, Sunday 0800–1800. Collect calls can be made to the USA, Canada, Australia and the UK.
Post office: Queen St and North Front St, Belize City, open 0800–1700 Monday to Thursday, 0800–1630 Friday.
There are international flights from Philip Goldson airport, Ladyville, 10 miles from Belize City to US and Central American cities.

MEDICAL
24 hour emergency department, St Francis Hospital, 28 Albert Street, Belize City.
Tel. (02) 77068.

DIPLOMATIC MISSIONS
In Belize City:
Canada: 29 Southern Foreshore.
Tel. (02) 31060.
Mexico: 20 North Park Street.
Tel. (02) 30193. Mexican visas can be obtained at the consulate, north of Fort George pier. It is also advisable to purchase the certified crew lists at the consulate as they may be needed when clearing into Mexico.
Panama: Cork Street. *Tel.* 44991.
United States: 20 Gabourel Lane and Hutson Street. *Tel.* (02) 77161.

In Belmopan:
Panama: 7/9 Unity Boulevard.
Tel. (08) 22714.
United Kingdom: PO Box 91, Embassy Sq.
Tel. (08) 22146.

---

convention was signed in which Guatemala recognised Belize's boundaries. Belize eventually became a British Crown Colony. Mexico later renounced its claim by treaty although Guatemala, never having ratified the original treaty, sometimes renews its claim to the territory. Independence was gained in 1981, although a British military presence is still maintained in Belize.

The economy is agricultural and the main concern is how to become self-sufficient in food production, as so much still has to be imported. Labour shortage is another problem, and the immigration of workers is encouraged. The main exports are sugar, citrus fruit and bananas, while timber and fish are also important. Tourism has developed, and there is some light industry. Oil has been found near the Mexican border.

The 200,000 inhabitants are mainly Créole and mestizo, with Indian and Garifuna minorities. The latter are descended from Black Caribs, who were deported from St Vincent in the eighteenth century. They live mostly along the southern coast and speak their own language. English is the official language, but Créole English and Spanish are also spoken as well as a Low German dialect and Mayan languages. Most Christian denominations have followers, the main ones being Roman Catholic, Anglican and Methodist. In 1970 Belmopan, some 50 miles inland, became the new capital replacing Belize City.

The tropical climate can be hot especially February to May, although the prevailing wind helps to keep the coast cooler. During winter months the anchorages are rather exposed to the northers which sweep down across the Gulf of Mexico. The hurricane season lasts from June to November.

Entry Regulations

Ports of entry
Belize City 17°30′N 88°11′W, Punta Gorda 16°06′N 88°48′W, San Pedro (Ambergris Cay) 17°56′N 87°57′W.

Procedure on arrival
All boats must clear customs, immigration and quarantine. Customs require four crew lists, four store lists and ship's papers. Yachts must clear in immediately on arrival in Belize waters, not more than 24 hours after; similarly, after clearance to

depart has been completed, yachts must leave promptly, within 24 hours. The authorities do patrol their waters to enforce this regulation.

Belize City: Clearing in formalities at Belize City, although relatively simple, are orientated towards commercial shipping and can take time as some offices are quite far away. Clearance can be accomplished more rapidly if the Belize port captain is called in advance of arrival on VHF Channel 16. Flying the Q flag, one can either anchor off or use the dock at the Holiday Inn Hotel. If anchored, a customs boat will usually come alongside and the officials will board the boat, but if not, the captain should go ashore to the customs office. In this case the captain is usually accompanied back to the boat by a customs official for the necessary paperwork. The next office to be visited is immigration, which is in town north of the police station. Because of theft from boats and lengthy formalities, cruising boats now try to avoid clearing in at Belize City.

Punta Gorda: Entry and exit formalities are much simpler here.

San Pedro (Ambergris): This is an official port of entry with customs, immigration and quarantine officers on duty. As the entrance through the reef is rather complicated, one should call San Pedro Yacht Club on Channel 16 for directions. One can go straight to the yacht club (identified by the Texaco sign) to complete formalities. San Pedro is located just south of the Mexican border and therefore convenient for yachts arriving from the north.

Cay Caulker: It is now possible to also clear in at the marina here, but one has to pay the cost of bringing out the officials from Belize City.

Procedure on departure

For clearing out at Belize City it is necessary to purchase two special clearance forms available from Angelus Press near the police station. The first office to be visited is the port authority, which is quite far and requires a taxi ride. A charge will be made depending on the tonnage of the yacht. Customs must be cleared next, and finally immigration.

Customs

Firearms and ammunition are usually removed and kept in custody by customs until clearing out.

Animals must have a health certificate and antirabies vaccination.

The importation of fruit or vegetables is prohibited and all fresh produce will be confiscated on arrival. The authorities will request a list of ship's stores (i.e. fresh produce) on arrival in port.

Yachts may remain in Belize for up to six months.

Immigration

Visas are not required for nationals of Commonwealth countries (except India), European Union, Canada, the United States. Normally on arrival a 30-day stay is given.

Other nationals require a visa to be obtained in advance. Visas can be obtained from the Belizean consulate, Chetumal, Mexico, valid for 30 days. Extensions may be obtained every 30 days for up to six months at the immigration office, Barrack Rd, Belize City. Extensions can also be arranged at the immigration offices in Ponta Gorda, Belmopan and Orange Walk. At the end of six months one must leave the country for at least 24 hours.

Health

Malaria prophylaxis is recommended.

Fees

There is a visa charge of US$25, extensions US$5. The navigation charge is calculated per ton. There is an exit fee.

Restrictions

Nature conservation is a high priority and there are many national parks, wildlife sanctuaries and nature reserves, such as Half Moon Cay Natural Monument and Hol Chan Marine Reserve, where damaging or catching any wildlife is prohibited. A permit is needed to hunt or collect any kind of wildlife and this will be granted only if it is for scientific or educational purposes.

It is prohibited to remove or export black coral, turtles or turtle products, to pick orchids in forest reserves, to spear fish in certain areas or while wearing scuba gear and to remove archaeological artefacts.

Facilities

Most of the existing facilities are in Belize City. The anchorage there is an open roadstead and often rolly. Belize City has some repair facilities, good provisioning, a limited supply of hardware but very little yachting equipment. Water and fuel are available at the dock. LPG bottles can be filled by taking a taxi to the filling station out of town.

Due to the frequency of theft from boats, few boats now go to Belize City if this can be avoided.

A convenient place to leave the boat if intending to visit the interior, which is one of the main attractions of Belize, is Mayan Marina at Moho Cay, just north of Belize City. The entrance is shallow (approximately 7 ft/2m), but the marina can be contacted on Channel 16 and will advise on the best route and also the time of high water. Some repair facilities are available, and also fuel, water and electricity. There is a frequent shuttle service to the mainland. It has been reported that Moho Cay Marina is also a good place from which to visit the Mayan sites in Guatemala, such as Tikal, and is safe to leave the boat while touring inland. Provisioning is best in Belize City and limited in other places. There is good provisioning at San Pedro, on Ambergris Cay, which also has daily flights to the mainland. The San Pedro Yacht Club has a range of facilities including fuel.

Further Reading

Cruising Guide to Belize and Mexico's Caribbean Coast
A Cruising Guide to Northwest Caribbean
Mexico & Central American Handbook

Websites

www.travelbelize.com (Belize Tourism Board)
www.belize.com (Links)

CANADA

Spanning the north of the American continent, Canada has cruising grounds on both the western Pacific coast and the eastern Atlantic coast. The majority of Canadians, however, sail inland on the Great Lakes, which can be reached either by sailing up the St Lawrence river from the Atlantic or through the Erie Canal. Some cruisers like to make the round trip by sailing to Nova Scotia, up the St Lawrence to the Lakes and then back to New York and the US east coast through the Canal.

For the decreasing number of yachts who take the northern route across the Atlantic, the island of Newfoundland, closest point to Europe, is their landfall or springboard. Cruising this northern island is strictly for summer months and even then it can be cold, wet and windy at times. The rewards are a vast choice of anchorages in small bays, har-

bours and islands and the few cruising boats sailing this far north can find complete isolation in beautiful surroundings. More often visited by foreign yachts is Nova Scotia, the first stop down-east from Maine. Halifax, the main harbour, is a large yachting centre and, like St Johns in Newfoundland, a transatlantic springboard and landfall.

On the Pacific coast British Columbia boasts one of the most beautiful and dramatic cruising grounds in the world with its snowcapped mountains, waterfalls cascading down rugged cliffs, a myriad of islands and quiet, still fjords. The 100 mile long Vancouver Island protects most of the mainland from the Pacific Ocean and so creates an inland sea. Dotted with islands and spiked with inlets, the absence of swell can provide great sailing conditions.

The most popular cruising area is the Gulf Islands in the south. There are harbours and anchorages on both sides of the Strait of Georgia, which separates Vancouver Island from the mainland. Another good cruising area is at the north of the Strait, where a cluster of islands border the magnificent Desolation Sound. North of this begins the inside passage to Alaska.

A large tidal range and strong currents make for attentive navigation, as do the hazards of floating logs and kelp. All of the area is well charted and tide rips are marked. Fog can be a hazard along this coast and radar a great boon, especially as there is a lot of other traffic – logging tugs, fishing boats, fast ferries to and from the islands and, especially near Vancouver, commercial shipping. The rewards of nature, both in scenery and wildlife, including superb fishing, more than make up for the attentive navigation needed.

Country Profile

The first inhabitants were Indian tribes who probably came over from Asia thousands of years ago. European contact commenced when John Cabot discovered Canada in 1497. Jacques Cartier explored the St Lawrence river in the sixteenth century, claiming it for France, and Quebec was founded in 1608. French settlement of New France, as the area was called, was slow at first, but increased in the seventeenth century. New France came into conflict with England, who gained Acadia (renamed Novia Scotia) and Hudson Bay, and established a naval base at Halifax. After France's defeat in the Seven Years War, in 1763 the rest of French Canada was ceded to England. New Brunswick province was

Practical Information

LOCAL TIME: GMT – 5 to – 10, add one hour for daylight saving April to October.

BUOYAGE: IALA B

CURRENCY: Canadian dollar of 100 cents (Can$).

BUSINESS HOURS
Banks: 1000–1500 Monday to Friday, occasionally Saturday.
Business: 0900–1700 Monday to Friday.
Shops: 0930–1900 Monday to Friday, some nights until 2100, 0930–1800 Saturday.
Government offices: 0900–1630 Monday to Friday.

ELECTRICITY: 110/220 V, 60 Hz

PUBLIC HOLIDAYS
1 January: New Year's Day
Good Friday, Easter Monday
Monday before 25 May: Victoria Day

1 July: Canada Day
First Monday in September: Labour Day
Second Monday in October: Thanksgiving Day
11 November: Remembrance Day
25 December: Christmas Day
26 December: Boxing Day
Also provincial holidays

COMMUNICATIONS
Overseas dialling access code 011.
Dial 0 for the operator, 411 for information.
Post offices open 0930–1700 Monday to Friday, 0900–1200 Saturday, longer in cities.
Emergency: dial 911.
Air travel within Canada is extensive, and all major cities have international flights, but particularly Montreal and Toronto. There are flights to London from both Halifax and St Johns, Newfoundland.

MEDICAL
Emergency medical treatment is available in all hospitals. Canadians have free health care, but visitors must pay, so travel health insurance is recommended.

DIPLOMATIC MISSIONS
In Ottawa:
Australia: Suite 710, 50 O'Connor St, ON K1PT. *Tel.* 236 0841.
France: 42 Sussex Drive, ON K1M. *Tel.* (613) 232-1795.
New Zealand: Suite 727, Metropolitan House, 99 Bank St, ON K1P 6G3. *Tel.* (613) 238-5991.
United Kingdom: 80 Elgin Street, ON K1P 5K7. *Tel.* (613) 237-1530.
United States: 100 Wellington Street, ON K1P 5T1. *Tel.* (613) 238-5335.

created following a large immigration of loyalists after American independence.

The provinces of Upper Canada, now Ontario, and Lower Canada, now Quebec, were created and both rebelled in 1837 in protest at England's refusal to establish a parliamentary regime. This revolt was suppressed, but three years later a united Canada was created by the English government and given internal self-government in 1848. The Dominion of Canada was established in 1867, as a Confederation of the provinces of New Brunswick, Novia Scotia, Quebec and Ontario. In the following thirty years the new country expanded its borders to include Manitoba, British Columbia, Prince Edward Island, Alberta and Saskatchewan and border disputes with the United States were resolved regarding Oregon and Alaska.

In the First World War Canada fought with the Allies and became an international power. In 1931 her independence was formally recognised. William Mackenzie King, leader of the Liberal Party, presided over Canadian politics from 1921 until 1948 almost without interruption. Fighting Germany in the Second World War, Canada's war effort pushed her to develop her industry and agriculture. In 1949 Newfoundland became a Canadian province. After the war the Liberal Party dominated politics until 1984 when the Conservative Party came to power, losing to the Liberals in 1993. In

1994 the Free Trade Agreement with the US and Mexico came into effect. Demands for greater independence by some of the population of the French-speaking Quebec province is an ongoing issue. In a referendum held in October 1995, the population of Quebec narrowly voted to remain part of Canada.

Canada has rich agricultural and mineral resources, and is a leading world producer of wheat, timber, oil and natural gas, iron, lead, zinc, copper, nickel, gold and uranium. The main industries are food processing, timber and metallurgy, while US finance has helped the development of the automobile and chemical industries. The Canadian economy is very closely tied to its neighbour and over half of external trade is with the United States.

The population numbers 31 million, mostly of British, French and other European origins, while only about 1.5 per cent are indigenous Native Canadians. Almost half are Roman Catholic, while United Church and Anglican are the next popular among the many religions practised. English and French are the official languages. Canada's capital is Ottawa, located in Ontario on the banks of the Ottawa river.

The climate varies considerably around the country. Atlantic Canada is very cold November to April (minus 10° to 4°C/15° to 50°F), while May to October is mild on the coasts. There are few

Rudyard Inlet in British Columbia.

gales in summer, but the area is affected by fog. In spring and summer up to July, icebergs can be carried into the Newfoundland area.

In Western Canada November to April is temperate on the coast, while May to October is warm and rainy. Northern Canada has subarctic conditions during the winter. The southern area, nicknamed the 'banana belt', is in the rain shadow of Vancouver Island, has milder winters and so cruising is possible all year round, while the northern sector tends to be summer cruising only. Land breezes often dictate the sailing conditions and calms are commonplace. In the summer gales are rare and west or north-westerly winds blow most afternoons.

Entry Regulations

Ports of entry
Newfoundland: St John's 47°34′N 52°41′W, Corner Brook 48°57′N 57°56′W, Fortune 46°54′N 55°38′W, Harbour Grace 47°41′N 53°13′W, Argentina 47°18′N 53°59′W.

Ontario: Portsmouth Olympia Harbour (west of Kingston) 44°12′N 76°30′W, Toronto 43°38′N 79°23′W, Brockville 44°36′N 75°38′W, Cornwall 45°01′N 74°43′W, Goderich 43°45′N 81°45′W, Welland 42°58′N 79°13′W.

Prince Edward Island: Charlottetown 46°13′N 63°07′W, Summerside 46°24′N 63°47′W.

Nova Scotia: Sherbourne 43°45′N 65°20′W, Yarmouth 43°50′N 66°07′W, Le Havre 44°17′N 64°21′W, Lunenburg 44°22′N 64°18′W, Halifax (customs *Tel.* 426-2071 0800–2200) 44°38′N 63°33′W, Parrsboro 45°23′N 64°20′W, Pictou 45°41′N 62°43′W, Port Medway 44°08′N 64°34′W, Pugwash 45°52′N 63°40′W, Sheet Harbour 44°51′N 62°27′W.

North West Territories: Frobisher 63°45′N 68°32′W.

New Brunswick: Caraquet 47°48′N 65°01′W, Chatham 47°02′N 65°28′W, Dalhousie 48°04′N 66°22′W, Newcastle 47°00′N 65°33′W, St Andrews 45°04′N 67°03′W.

Quebec: Gaspé 48°50′N 64°29′W, Port Alfred 48°20′N 70°52′W, Rimouski 48°29′N 68°31′W, Rivière du Loup 47°51′N 69°34′W.

British Columbia: Kitimat 54°00′N 128°42′W,

Nanaimo 49°10'N 123°56'W, Port Alberni 49°14'N 125°00'W, Woodfibre 49°40'N 123°15'W, Prince Rupert Harbour 54°19'N 130°22'W.

Gulf Islands: Bedwell (South Pender Island, summer only) 49°38'N 124°03'W, Sidney 48°39'N 123°24'W, Nanaimo (Vancouver Island) 49°10'N 123°56'W, North Head Harbour (Grand Manan) 49°10'N 123°56'W.

Procedure on arrival

On arrival at a port of entry, customs should be contacted on 1-888-CANPASS (the service is also available as a 1-800 number). CANPASS is a new program to streamline customs and immigration clearance. Customs will want to know the boat's name, registration number and last port of call. Customs may also request a list of ports where one intends to visit. For each person on board, provide full name, date of birth, citizenship, purpose of trip and length of stay in Canada or, in the case of returning residents, length of absence. All personal goods being imported, including firearms and weapons as well as alcohol and tobacco, must be declared. The customs officer will advise you whether you are free to leave the area and enter Canada, or if you have to wait for a customs or immigration officer to complete documents or conduct an examination. At the conclusion of the customs process, you will receive a report number for your records, as proof of reporting. This number should be displayed in a suitable place where it can be seen.

Customs

All firearms must be declared to customs on arrival. There are no permit requirements for long guns, such as rifles and shotguns, when imported temporarily for hunting, sporting or competition use while in Canada, or for in-transit movement through Canada, or for personal protection against wildlife in remote areas of Canada. Generally, restricted firearms, such as pistols or revolvers, may only be imported for gun shows and shooting competitions. If travelling through Canada between mainland USA and Alaska, restricted firearms should be shipped directly by a commercial carrier as a permit to transport is generally not issued in such cases.

Many souvenirs made of or containing animal or plant products may be controlled or, in the case of endangered species, prohibited entry into Canada. The Convention on International Trade in Endangered Species of Wild Fauna and Flora (CITES) regulates the international movement of thousands of animal and plant species and products made from them. A CITES export permit from the exporting country is required and souvenirs involving endangered species require an additional CITES import permit issued by the Canadian Wildlife Service. These CITES import permits are seldom approved for souvenirs and gifts purchased by people travelling abroad. For more information on exact permit requirements contact the CITES administrator. Telephone (819) 997-1840 or fax a request to (819) 953-6283. There is also more information on the website: www.cws-scf.ec.gc.ca/cites/index_e.html.

Some examples of the types of souvenirs that are not allowed entry into Canada under CITES include: sperm whale teeth, suntan lotion from marine turtles, large spotted cat skins and fur articles, tortoiseshell jewellery, ivory and ivory products, stuffed crocodiles and crocodile leather products, all rhinoceros products, and carapaces from marine turtles.

All alcoholic beverages and tobacco products must be declared on arrival. If you meet the age requirements set by the province or territory where you enter Canada, you can include up to 200 cigarettes, 50 cigars or cigarillos, 200 tobacco sticks, 200 grams of manufactured tobacco; also, up to 1.14 litres of liquor, or 1.5 litres of wine or 24 x 355 ml cans or bottles of beer or ale. If you bring in more than the free allowance, you will have to pay the duties that apply. If duties and taxes are payable, customs should be provided with the Visa or MasterCard number and expiry date.

Non-resident visitors may leave their boats in Canada during the off-season without payment of duties only if repair or maintenance work is to be undertaken by a bona fide marina or service outlet during that time. Before leaving a boat, the owner must advise the local customs office of the details and produce a copy of the work order, identifying the unit and showing the name and address of the owner, the type of work to be done, and the location where the work will be carried out.

Canada has complex requirements, restrictions and limits that apply to importing meat, dairy products, fruit and vegetables and other foodstuffs. Visitors can avoid problems by not bringing such goods into Canada.

Imported dogs and cats require a rabies vaccination certificate or certificate stating rabies-free status. Those from the United States require the certificate to be signed and dated by a veterinarian indicating that the animal has been vaccinated against rabies within the last three years. This certificate must provide sufficient description and detail to enable adequate identification.

Immigration

All nationalities need valid passports, except US citizens who only need valid identification. No visas are required for nationals of the USA, West European countries (except Portugal), Japan, or Commonwealth countries (except Bangladesh, Gambia, Guyana, India, Jamaica, Nigeria, Pakistan, Sri Lanka, Trinidad and Uganda). Most other nationalities require a visa to be obtained in advance. Contact should be made with a Canadian visa office abroad to determine requirements.

The length of stay, up to six months, is decided by the immigration officer at the port of entry.

Fishing licence

A fishing licence is required in British Columbia, available from most marine service outlets, fuel docks, sporting and hardware stores. The cost of an annual permit for non-residents is Can$35. There are also catch limits.

Traffic

In poor visibility, yachts can contact the local 'Traffic' (VHF Channel 13 or 14) and report their position, route and speed, and receive information on any large ships they may encounter. Fundy Traffic can be contacted on VHF Channel 11 on the way to St John and will help when visibility is bad. Halifax Traffic on VHF Channel 14 offers similar assistance to yachtsmen.

The Canadian Coast Guard monitors Channel 16.

Fees

Ports normally have 24-hour service, but some may charge overtime for clearance outside of working hours, which can vary. At St John's, overtime is charged for customs clearance between 0000–0800, approximately Can$60 if arrival is after midnight. In some ports customs may only come and clear during their working hours (0800–1700 normally).

Facilities

There are good facilities in all major yachting centres. Marine equipment and fuel is more expensive than in the USA, whereas Canadian charts are cheaper than US charts. Provisioning is very good in larger ports, but only adequate in some of the smaller places.

On the west coast, the best stocks of chandlery and general boat repair facilities are in Vancouver as well as Surrey, one of its suburbs. In Vancouver itself there are good docking facilities at the Royal Vancouver Yacht Club as well as the nearby marina and Royal Vancouver Rowing Club, all of which welcome visitors and are close to the centre. Particularly north of Vancouver, grocery stores and fuelling stations are far apart and therefore some are mentioned below.

Nanaimo, on Vancouver Island, is a good provisioning place used by the local fishing fleet, so docking space is sometimes limited. There are several marinas in Pender Harbour, with stores, post office and fuel station. Similar services are available at Sullivan Bay on North Broughton Island. Good facilities are available in Prince Rupert, although the place gets crowded when the fishing fleet is in.

On the Atlantic coast, Halifax, in Nova Scotia, has a wide range of repair facilities and services. There are three large yacht clubs in town and visitors can secure free mooring for one week at the Maritime Museum of the Atlantic in the main harbour. The Royal Nova Scotia Yacht Squadron is particularly welcoming to visiting yachts and has good facilities. Best repair facilities are at Lunenburg, an important fishing port, which has a very interesting fishing museum. Although there are barely any yachting facilities in St John's busy commercial harbour, these are concentrated in Long Pond, a narrow inlet on the west side of the Avalon peninsula. This is also the home of the Royal Newfoundland Yacht Club, which is particularly welcoming to foreign visitors. Fuel and water are available on the dock. The only marina-type facility is at Lewisport, with floating pontoons and electricity. In all other places one has to either anchor or use the government wharves. Fuel in larger quantities can be ordered to be delivered by a tanker.

Further Reading

Cruising Guide to Newfoundland
Cruising Guide to Nova Scotia Coast
Exploring the North Coast of British Columbia
Exploring the South Coast of British Columbia

Websites

www.travelcanada.ca (Canadian Tourism Commission)
www.gov.nf.ca/tourism (Newfoundland & Labrador Tourism)
www.cws-scf.ec.gc.ca/cites/index_e.html (CITES)
www.ccra-adrc.gc.ca (Canada Customs)
www.cfia-acia.agr.ca (Canadian Food Inspection Agency)
www.cic.gc.ca (Immigration Canada)

COSTA RICA

Costa Rica lies between Nicaragua and Panama, enjoys the highest standard of living in Central America and also has the reputation for being the most stable Latin American democracy. Costa Rica has coastlines on both the Caribbean Sea and the Pacific Ocean, the latter being the more attractive for cruising. Compared to its northern neighbours, Costa Rica's indented coastline presents a welcome change and a pleasant cruising ground. The hilly interior and attractive capital San José can be visited from either Puntarenas or Limón.

The most popular port of call is Golfito, rarely missed by cruising boats plying the western coast of Central America. An exciting destination lies 300 miles offshore in the Pacific, the fabled treasure island of Coco. Hundreds of expeditions have been mounted over the years to find the various treasures reputed to have been buried there, but so far nothing has been found. The island's real treasure is its unspoilt nature and Isla del Coca was declared a national park by the Costa Rican government. Even if not looking for treasure, it is worth the detour to watch the birdlife and underwater scenery teeming with fish.

Country Profile

The Caribbean coast was discovered by Columbus in 1502 during his last voyage. Costa Rica means 'rich coast', and there were rumours of vast gold treasures to be found there. Spaniards settled in the interior, where there were already thousands of farming Indians, who were decimated by European diseases. Gradually European settlement expanded, but life was hard and mostly on a subsistence level.

When in 1821 independence from Spain was declared, after a period of internal strife, Costa Rica declared itself a state in the short-lived Federal Republic of Central America; with independence, coffee became a source of prosperity and by the middle of the century exports were considerable. The government offered free land to coffee growers, thus building a prosperous land-owning peasant class. Bananas were introduced at the end of the century and these thrived and became a major crop on both the Caribbean and the Pacific coasts. President Oscar Arias Sanchez won the Nobel Peace Prize in 1987 for his Central American Peace Plan, signed by all five Central American republics but never implemented.

Costa Rica's economy has a good rate of growth, based on the export of coffee, bananas, meat, sugar and cocoa. Industry has grown, mostly in the food processing sector, but also in chemicals and plastics. However, Costa Rica still has a large foreign debt and public sector deficits as government spending on welfare is high.

The 3.5 million inhabitants are mostly white or mestizo and only about 5000 Indians are left in the whole country. Spanish is the main language. There are a number of people of African origin living along the Caribbean coast, especially in Limón, who speak Jamaican English, as their forebears came from Jamaica to work on banana plantations early in the twentieth century. Roman Catholicism is the religion of the majority. The capital is San José.

The Pacific coast of Costa Rica is drier, while the Atlantic coast has heavy rainfall. Both coasts are hot and humid. December to April are the dry months, while May to November are wet, hot and humid. The east coast is under the influence of the NE trade winds during the winter months, but the west coast has light winds and often calms. Costa Rica is rarely affected by tropical storms.

Entry Regulations

Ports of entry
Pacific: Playa del Coco 10°35′N 85°42′W, Golfito 8°38′N 83°11′W, Puntarenas 9°59′N 84°51′W, Quepos 9°24′N 84°10′W.
Atlantic: Puerto Limón 10°00′N 83°03′W.

Procedure on arrival
Formalities can be lengthy and some visiting boats have had difficulties with the officials, particularly with immigration at Golfito. Stopping along the coast before clearing into the country is not tolerated and yachts that do so will be told to proceed immediately to a port of entry. Because of problems encountered with officials in other ports, it is essential to make sure at the first port of entry that all requirements are complied with, such as the temporary importation permit. Clearance papers from the last port or country must be shown, and also that the passports have an exit stamp from immigration in the last country.

Clearance must be done with the port authority, then customs and immigration. Port officials will usually visit the yacht on entering Costa Rica. In subsequent ports of entry, the captain may go ashore to clear with the port captain and show the clearance certificate (*zarpe*). Port authority work-

Practical Information

LOCAL TIME: GMT – 6

BUOYAGE: IALA B

CURRENCY: Colon of 100 centimos.

BUSINESS HOURS
Banks: 0900–1500 Monday to Friday.
Government offices: 0800–1600 Monday to Friday.
Business: 0800–1200, 1400–1600 Monday to Friday.
Shops: 0800/0900–1200, 1300–1800/1900 Monday to Saturday.

ELECTRICITY: 110 V, 60 Hz

PUBLIC HOLIDAYS
1 January: New Year's Day
19 March: St Joseph
Easter Week, three days
April: Battle of Rivas
1 May: Labour Day
June: Corpus Christi

29 June: Saints Peter and Paul
25 June: Guanacaste Day
2 August: Virgin of Los Angeles
15 August: Mothers Day
15 September: Independence Day
12 October: Cultures Day
8 December: Immaculate Conception
25 December: Christmas Day
28–31 December, holiday in San José only

EVENTS
Holy Week: most places are shut during the week, and everything closes from Friday to Saturday.
October: Costa Rica Yacht Club Regatta in Puntarenas, visiting yachts are welcome.

COMMUNICATIONS
Internacional de Costa Rica for international phone calls. Int. operator 116. Collect calls overseas can be made from special booths in the telephone office. Instituto Costarricense de Electricidad and Compania Radiografica for cables, long-

range radio telephone and telex, San José office, Corner Calle 1 and Avenida 5, open 0700–2200.
Police Tel. 117 (127 outside cities).
There are frequent flights from San José to the USA and Latin American capitals.

MEDICAL
Facilities are generally to a good standard.
Ambulance (west coast) Tel. 221 5818.
Cruz Roja (Red Cross) Tel. 128.

DIPLOMATIC MISSIONS
In San José:
Canada: 6th floor, Edificio Cronos, Calle 3 and Ave. Central, Apartado 10303. Tel. 296 4149.
United Kingdom: Edificio Centro Colon, 11th floor, Between Calles 38 & 40, Apartado 815. Tel. 221 5566.
United States: Rohrmoser, Pavas. Tel. 220 3939.

---

ing hours 0800–1600 Monday to Friday, seven days a week in Puntarenas; overtime may be charged for clearance outside these hours.

Playa de Coco: Contact the port captain on Channel 16 for berthing instructions in the commercial port. The port captain will issue the usual *zarpe*, after which one must clear customs and immigration. Under certain conditions, and certainly in genuine emergencies, it may be possible to clear in at Flamingo Marina (10°26.5′N 85°47.50′W), but this must be arranged in advance (*Tel.* 654-4203). Transportation and agency costs will be charged to the boat.

Puntarenas: Call port captain on VHF Channel 16 for berthing instructions or anchor by the town at the end of the peninsula. All offices are close by in the port.

Golfito: On arrival call Base Naval (Naval Base) on Channel 16. The captain will be required to give his name and passport number, the vessel's name and registration number, the name of the last port, and *zarpe* number. Normally boats are directed to the quarantine area, near the commercial dock. Immigration, customs, quarantine and port officials normally visit the boat. Occasionally one may be asked to visit their offices. On completion of the formalities customs will issue a three-month cruising permit. Only after all formalities are completed

may one move to the location of one's choice, such as Banana Bay Marina, which monitors Channels 12 and 16.

Boats that have already cleared into Costa Rica at another port must visit the port captain's office to present their *zarpe*. The port captain should be contacted on Channel 16 for clearance arrangements. Customs will either board the boat on arrival or the captain has to go ashore to complete formalities. The offices of the port captain, customs and immigration are all near the big dock directly in front of the channel entrance.

Quepos: Clearance formalities are completed at the administration building. The port captain's office is on the banana pier.

Puerto Limón: Contact the port captain on Channel 16 and proceed into the commercial harbour. Visiting boats are allowed to use one of the disused commercial piers. The docks are in a bad state and tugs manoeuvring ships churn up the water, so boats should be tied up well and kept away from the dock by an anchor. Formalities are completed in the port itself.

Customs

Customs on arrival will issue a Temporary Import Certificate (Certificado de Entrada) for the yacht, valid for three months. A further extension of three months may be obtained by application to Customs in San José or Liberia.

If the captain of a yacht leaves the country by other means, responsibility for the yacht must be taken over by an authorised bonding agent until the captain's return, or until the yacht's departure from the country.

Firearms and animals must be declared. Animals must have a valid rabies vaccination certificate and a veterinarian's health certificate (certified by a Costa Rican consul). The Department of Zoology must be notified by a special Import form, obtainable from: Departamento de Zoonosis, Ministerio de Salud, 1000 San José.

Immigration

Visas are issued on arrival to nationals of most countries. There are no visa requirements for stays of up to 90 days for nationals of the European Union, Argentina, Canada, Hungary, Israel, Japan, Liechtenstein, Panama, Paraguay, Poland, Romania, South Korea, USA, and Uruguay.

No visas are required for stays of up to 30 days for nationals of Antigua, Albania, Australia, Bahamas, Bahrain, Barbados, Belize, Bolivia, Brazil, Bulgaria, Colombia, Chile, Czech Republic, Dominica, El Salvador, Grenada, Guatemala, Guyana, Honduras, Iceland, Jamaica, Kenya, Kuwait, Monaco, Mexico, New Zealand, Oman, Philippines, Qatar, Taiwan, Saudi Arabia, Slovak Republic, South Africa, St Kitts, St Lucia, San Marino, St Vincent, Singapore, Suriname, Trinidad, UAE, and Venezuela. All others require visas.

Immigration officials insist that visitors have their passports on them at all times. All crew members must be seen by the immigration official.

A passport or at least a certified copy should always be carried.

Health

Malaria prophylaxis recommended.

As dengue fever appears to be endemic in Costa Rica, the necessary precautions should be taken not to be bitten by the mosquito carrier.

Fishing licence

Any vessel with fishing equipment on board must have a licence. Application should be made to the Agriculture Department in San José: Ministerio de Agricultura, Calle 1, Avenida 1, San José.

Procedure on departure

The port captain at the port of departure will issue an international departure certificate (zarpe) speci-

fying the country of destination. Those intending to stop before leaving Costa Rican waters should make this clear when clearing out. Immigration must also be visited before departure.

Fees

Overtime is payable outside normal working hours, which are 0800–1600 Monday to Friday, except customs in Golfito which does not work on Mondays.

National Marine Parks

A permit must be obtained from the Marine Parks Division before visiting Isla del Coco or Isla del Cano. A written application should contain details of the yacht, the captain and crew, ETA and ETD: Sistem de Parques y Reservas Marinas, Servicio de Parques Nationales, Apt. 10104–1000, San José. Fax. (506) 23 69 63. There is an anchoring fee per day charged at both islands, also a landing charge per person.

Facilities

Provisioning is reasonable in Playa del Coco or at Marina Flamingo ten miles south in Bahia Potrero, where fuel and water are available on the dock. Facilities at Marina Flamingo are now the best in Costa Rica and serve a large fleet of sports fishing boats. Fuel, water and electricity are available on the docks. There is a tidal grid, a dry dock for boats up to 50 ft (15 m) (limited to 4.5 ft (1.37 m) draft), 20-ton mobile crane and a chandlery. There are also good facilities in Puntarenas where the yacht club is particularly helpful and offers a range of repair facilities including a 20-ton travelift, as well as fuel and water on the dock and 24-hour launch service. The club monitors VHF Channel 6 from 0700 to 1700 every day except Wednesday. Fuel and water are also available from Muelle Moreno. Repair and haul-out facilities at Pacific Marine, near the yacht club, and Servicio de Yates, nearer the town centre. There are also good supermarkets and an excellent fresh produce market. Coming from the south, Golfito is a good port for repairs and reprovisioning. Banana Bay Marina offers a range of facilities, such as floating docks with water and electricity, as well as duty-free fuel for boats in transit. Set up to assist cruising boats, the Jungle Club is the meeting point for visiting sailors. It offers a whole range of services, such as fuel, LPG and can arrange to have unattended boats watched. Puerto Limón, on the Caribbean side, is the main port of Costa Rica. There is good provisioning and adequate repair facilities. Trains and buses run to San José. Marina Flamingo, in Bahia Potrero, a few miles south of the border with Nicaragua, is a convenient place to obtain fuel and water. Although this is not an official port of entry, boats have been able to stop for fuel. It is reported that the chart for the area does not tally with GPS, so due care should be exercised.

Further Reading

Charlie's Charts of Costa Rica
Cruising Ports: California to Florida via Panama
Mexico & Central America Handbook
The Forgotten Middle: Pacific Coast of Central America

Website

www.tourism-costarica.com (Costa Rica Tourist Board)

EL SALVADOR

El Salvador is a small, highly populated, industrialised country on the Pacific Ocean side of Central America. The volcanic uplands in the interior provide fertile soil for coffee. Violent civil war has affected the country in recent years but the situation is steadily improving. Cruising boats are now welcome to stop in El Salvador, although the authorities still regard foreign visitors with some suspicion. Boats are likely to be intercepted, and possibly boarded, by Navy patrol boats while passing the Gulf of Fonseca before being advised to proceed to a port of entry. As in other parts of Central America, the unrest in the interior may not affect the coastal areas and therefore ports are usually safe to visit.

Country Profile

El Salvador remained largely isolated from the Spanish conquest of the continent, having no precious metals to attract the Spaniards. A small number of Spaniards settled, intermarried with the Indians and raised cattle and subsistence crops. The introduction of coffee at the end of the nine-

teenth century saw the population and prosperity grow. The prosperity was short-lived and many emigrated due to the shortage of land, and the effects of civil war.

In 1979 a military coup took place and the president was replaced by a junta. Then in 1980 the civilian José Napoleon Duarte was appointed president, and elected four years later. Political tension increased as dissatisfaction grew and efforts at land reform were unsuccessful. Eventually civil war broke out, in which thousands of people, mainly civilians, were killed, often by right-wing death squads, opposed by the left-wing guerillas, the FMLN. The peace plans of 1987 and 1989 drawn up by President Arias of Costa Rica failed to reach a solution. Finally, negotiations between the government and the guerillas led in 1992 to a peace accord ending the civil war.

Efforts to diversify away from a dependence on agriculture have resulted in El Salvador having the largest manufacturing sector in Central America, although the economy suffered some decline due to the civil war. Coffee remains the main export. Some economic reforms have been introduced to curb inflation and stimulate economic growth. Yet land ownership is concentrated in the hands of a few, and the majority of people live at subsistence level, this being a cause of instability in the past. US aid is very important to El Salvador's economy.

The 6.4 million inhabitants are mostly mestizo with a small proportion of pure Indian and European. Spanish is the main language, but English is widely understood. The majority are Roman Catholic. The capital is San Salvador, 2230 ft (680 m) above sea level in the centre of the country.

The coast is hot and humid, especially March to May, and is coolest from December to February. December and March may have spells of continuous rain for 2–3 days or even weeks. Water shortages are possible at other times of the year.

Entry Regulations

Ports of entry
Acajutla 13°36′N 89°50′W, Cutuco (La Union) 13°19′N 87°49′W.

Procedure on arrival
Contact should be maintained with the Salvadorean Navy on Channel 16, who will advise on the correct procedure.
Cutuco: The port lies 2 miles from the town of La

Practical Information

LOCAL TIME: GMT – 6

BUOYAGE: IALA B

CURRENCY: Colon (ES¢; often called peso) of 100 centavos. Guatemala and Honduras may not accept or exchange Es¢.

BUSINESS HOURS
Business: 0800–1800 Monday to Friday, 0800–1200 Saturday.
Banks: 0900–1700 Monday to Friday.
Government offices: 0800–1600 Monday to Friday.
Shops: 0900–1900 Monday to Saturday.

ELECTRICITY: 110 V, 60 Hz

PUBLIC HOLIDAYS
1 January: New Year's Day
Palm Sunday to Easter Monday for government
Maundy Thursday, Good Friday, for banks and commerce
1 May
10 May
Corpus Christi (half day)
3–5 August: August Feasts
6 August: St Saviours Day (San Salvador)
15 September: Independence Day
12 October: Discovery Day
2 November: All Souls Day
5 November (half day)
25 December: Christmas Day
Government offices are also closed 1–6 August, 24–31 December.
Banks closed: June 29, 30, December 30, 31.

COMMUNICATIONS
Antel, the state telecommunications company, for telex and telephones.
Post offices open 0900–1700 Monday to Friday.
There are some international flights from San Salvador to Miami, New York, Los Angeles, Havana, San Francisco and Central American cities.

DIPLOMATIC MISSIONS
In San Salvador:
Canada: PO Box 3078, 111 Av. Las Palmas, Colonia, San Benito. Tel. 279 4655.
United Kingdom: PO Box 1591, Paseo General Escalon 4828. Tel. 298 1763.
United States: Unit 3116 Final Blvd, Station Antiguo Cuscatlan. Tel. 278 4444.

Union. Officials may board the yacht on arrival. A departure certificate (*zarpe*) will be issued by the port captain and this must be shown at subsequent ports.

Customs
An authorisation for firearms must be obtained from the Ministry of Defence.

Animals must have a health certificate. Dogs must have a valid anti-rabies vaccination certificate.

All animal products except sealed, sterilised meat products are prohibited. Animal products from the USA, Puerto Rico, Australia, New Zealand, Japan, Jamaica and Mexico are also exempt.

Fruit is inspected and may be destroyed. Leather products may be subject to disinfection.

Immigration
All require visas, except European Union countries, Argentina, Chile, Colombia, Costa Rica, Guatemala, Honduras, Japan, Iceland, Liechtenstein, Nicaragua, Panama. Nationals of Canada, USA and Mexico require a tourist card, allowing stays of up to 90 days. Visas can be renewed for 30 days at immigration.

Health
There is a risk of malaria and dengue fever. Rabies is a serious risk, mainly transmitted by dogs and bats.

Fees
There is an entrance and exit tax of 6 colones.

Overtime is charged for clearance outside working hours (1200–1400, 1800–0800 weekdays, 1200 Saturday to 0800 Monday, and national holidays).

Restrictions
Literature that may be regarded as subversive may be confiscated or refused entry. Military style clothing is also confiscated.

Facilities

Limited supplies are available in the two main ports, which also have facilities for simple repairs. Of the two, Acajutla has the better range of workshops.

Further Reading

Cruising Ports: California to Florida via Panama
Mexico & Central America Handbook
The Forgotten Middle: Pacific Coast of Central America

Websites

www.elsalvadorturismo.gov.sv (Salvador Tourism Corporation)
www.sv/svturis.html (Links)
www.elsalvadortrade.com.sv

GUATEMALA

Among the Central American republics, Guatemala stands out as the country which has best preserved the language, customs and character of the original population. This area of Central America used to be the centre of Maya civilisation.

Much of the land is still uninhabited and most settlements are in the highlands. The Pacific coast is narrow, low and featureless, and it is the smaller Caribbean coast which attracts most cruising yachts. The Motagua and Polochic rivers drain into the Caribbean Sea, but it is the Rio Dulce which is the ultimate destination of almost every yacht cruising this part of the world. Yachts that are not hampered by too deep a draft can negotiate the bar at the entrance to the river, after which the river virtually belongs to them. Impenetrable forests come down to the water's edge where almost hidden by the thick foliage are small Indian villages. The river widens into El Golfete, a small inland lake and further on the river merges with Lake Izabal, whose entrance is guarded by the fort of San Felipe, now restored according to original plans found in the Spanish archives. There are other rivers on the Guatemalan coast, which are navigable for longer or shorter distances, giving yachts a chance to savour a different kind of cruising.

Guerilla activity in some parts of the country has resulted in Western visitors being advised by their governments to avoid travelling in Guatemala. The coastal regions do not appear to have been affected and there have been no reports of incidents from any of the popular cruising areas.

Country Profile

The Maya civilisation developed about AD 100 and after 200 years of growth entered its 'classic' period, flourishing in an area corresponding to present-day Guatemala, Belize, Honduras and parts of Mexico. Centred on the city state, the Mayans developed mathematics, agriculture, architecture and writing. This civilisation lasted until the tenth to eleventh centuries AD, when the movements of other Indians forced the Mayas to concentrate in the Yucatan peninsula. When the Spaniards arrived, there were only scattered groups of Indians living in the Guatemala area. Some Spaniards settled in the southern highlands and mixed with the people already there. Guatemala City eventually became the administrative centre for all the Central American region, which was ruled by Spain from Mexico City.

Early in the nineteenth century independence movements began to develop, precipitated by the 1820 revolution in Spain. A year later independence was declared in Guatemala City, which became the centre of a federation. For some time this was ruled by the dictator General Morazán, but revolts and warfare broke up the federation. Since then the political history of the whole region has been tempestuous. Guatemala was ruled by a succession of strong dictators, with periods of constitutional government and anarchy between. After the Second World War efforts were made to introduce social reforms. After a coup in 1954 the military took power, and the following years saw great bloodshed as the army crushed those trying to restore the reforms. The 1980s saw some moves towards democratisation, a new constitution was drafted and presidential elections held in 1985. However, the military remains strong, and although peace talks have been ongoing since 1991 between the government and guerilla forces, there continue to be outbreaks of violence.

Agricultural exports dominate the economy. Industry is growing and there are some oil reserves. The return to democracy, economic growth and improved balance of payments have seen a revival of the tourist industry.

Of the 11 million inhabitants, more than half are Indian. There are two distinct cultures, the largely self-supporting indigenous peoples of the highlands, and the Ladino commercial economy in the lowlands. 'Ladino' is a Central American term used to refer to anyone with a Latin culture, who speaks Spanish and wears western clothes, even if they are Indian.

Spanish is the official language, but there are also 20 Indian languages and some 100 dialects. The majority of the population practise a mixture of paganism and Catholicism. Guatemala City is the capital located in the centre of the country at an altitude of 5000 ft (1500 m).

The climate depends very much on the altitude and the coast is hot and humid. The Caribbean coast is occasionally affected by northers in winter. Throughout the year the local prevailing winds are easterly.

Entry Regulations

Ports of entry
Pacific: Champerico 14°18'N 91°56'W, Puerto Quetzal 13°55'N 90°47'W, San José 13°55'N 90°50'W.

Practical Information

LOCAL TIME: GMT – 6. Summer time GMT – 5 May to August.

BUOYAGE: IALA B

CURRENCY: Quetzal of 100 centavos.

BUSINESS HOURS
Banks: 0900–1500 (some have longer hours, but close for lunch).
Business: 0800–1200, 1400–1800 Monday to Friday.
Shops: 0800–1200, 1400–1800 Monday to Friday, 0800–1200 Saturday.
Government offices: 0700–1530 Monday to Friday.

ELECTRICITY: 110/220 V, 60 Hz

PUBLIC HOLIDAYS
1 January: New Year's Day

6 January: Epiphany
Wednesday of Easter week (half day)
Maundy Thursday, Good Friday, Easter Saturday
1 May
30 June: Anniversary of the Revolution
15 August (Guatemala City only)
15 September: Independence Day
20 October: Revolution Day
1 November: All Saints' Day
25 December: Christmas Day
31 December: New Year's Eve
If a holiday falls on a Saturday or Sunday, the following Monday is taken as a public holiday.

COMMUNICATIONS
Guatel for international telephones and cable open 0700–2400.
Mail is very slow, slower to the USA and

Canada than to Europe.
There are frequent international flights from Guatemala City to most American capitals, flights less frequently to Europe.

MEDICAL
Public hospitals charge a small fee for examinations.
Police *Tel.* 120, Red Cross *Tel.* 125.

DIPLOMATIC MISSIONS
In Guatemala City:
Canada: 13 Calle 8–44, Zona 10, Edificio Edyma Plaza, 8th floor. *Tel.* 336102.
United Kingdom: Edificio Centro Financiero, 7th floor, Tower Two, 7a Avenida 5–10, Zona 4. *Tel.* 321601.
United States: 7–01 Avenida de la Reforma, Zona 10. *Tel.* 311541.

Atlantic: Livingston 15°50′N 88°45′W, Puerto Barrios 15°44′N 88°36′W, Santo Tomàs de Castilla 15°42′N 88°37′W.

Procedure on arrival

On arrival yachts are normally visited by customs, immigration, police, health and port captain.
Santo Tomàs: This is Guatemala's main eastern port and headquarters of the Guatemalan Navy, and although an official port of entry, the authorities will direct yachts to clear at nearby Puerto Barrios or Livingston, on the Rio Dulce.
Livingston: Access to Rio Dulce is very difficult on account of a wide sand bar at the river entrance. Boats with a draft of over 5 ft (1.50 m) must enter at high tide and the maximum draft that can be carried through at high tide is 7½ ft (2.20 m). Advice on the state of the tide may be obtained on Channel 68. Clearance is best done here as officials are used to dealing with yachts. Fly the Q flag and the officials will come out to the yacht in office hours (closed 1300–1500), for initial clearance and inspection. Customs will take the *zarpe* from the last port and ship's papers, immigration take the passports. The captain must collect these later from the shore offices, with the necessary entry stamps as well as a new *zarpe* and cruising permit. This can all be done in one day if arriving early enough. Quetzales will be needed to pay various fees.

La Marina, the marina in Livingston, is a convenient place to stop to complete formalities and the marina can also help with formalities and visa extensions. They monitor Channel 68 and will help with negotiating the difficult entrance.
Puerto Barrios: The approaches are much easier than for Livingston, 9 miles away. Entry as well as exit formalities are dealt with quickly, as all offices are within a short walking distance. One should visit the port captain first, who will arrange for the other officials to visit the yacht.
Puerto Quetzal: This new port was built on the Pacific side to replace the old port of San José. Port Control should be contacted on VHF Channel 16 for instruction on where to berth for clearance. To ensure the safety of visiting yachts, the Navy requires that yachts come directly to the naval basin, where security is excellent. All formalities are completed from there.

Customs

Firearms and animals must be declared. Firearms will be held by police or the port captain during the stay in port. A receipt will be issued.
Animals require a veterinary health certificate and valid anti-rabies vaccination.

Immigration

Visas are not required by nationals of the European Union, Andorra, Argentina, Belize, Costa Rica,

Ecuador, El Salvador, Honduras, Israel, Japan, Liechtenstein, Nicaragua, Norway, San Marino, Switzerland and Uruguay. Tourist cards are issued on arrival, the length of the permitted stay depending on nationality, but it is usually 90 days. Nationals of Canada, Mexico and the USA do not need visas for stays of up to 90 days.

Tourist cards and boat papers can be extended by up to six months. Extensions can be obtained in Guatemala City. There is a daily fine for overstaying one's permitted time.

Passports should always be carried especially if travelling inland.

Cruising permit

Cruising yachts intending to spend longer than 30 days in Guatemala will be issued on arrival with a special permit consisting of a sticker that must be displayed prominently on the boat. The sticker will be attached by the customs officer in the first port of entry. Initially valid for 90 days, the permit can be extended in Guatemala City for a further three months.

Procedure on departure

A *zarpe* (clearance) must be obtained from immigration and the port captain must sign it. Passports must also have exit stamps from immigration.

Health

Amoebic dysentery is endemic. Malaria prophylaxis is necessary.

Fees

Immigration 10 quetzales per passport. Customs 70 quetzales.

Facilities

There is good provisioning in Puerto Barrios and a fresh produce market. Water is available from the small dock. Fuel is available from the ferry dock, but there is little depth alongside. Tecno Marine is a small boatyard offering a range of repair services as well as some marine supplies. They monitor Channel 74 and will advise on entry procedure.

At El Golfete facilities have greatly expanded in recent years, with several marinas on the river catering for visiting yachts where it is possible to leave the boat to travel inland, either to the capital or the ancient Maya sites. With the growth of a local yachting community, repair facilities have improved also. There are three fuel docks on the

Rio Dulce, all on the south side near the bridge. There is also a fuel dock at Livingston. There are now two marine stores in Rio Dulce with a reasonable selection. A wide range of repair facilities is now available and also a travelift with 63 tons capacity. All marinas standby on Channel 68.

La Marina in Livingston has a range of facilities. There are small boatyards at both Livingston and Puerto San Tomàs with haul-out facilities, but the range of repair services is limited.

Further Reading

Cruising Guide to Northwest Caribbean
Cruising Guide to Belize and Mexico's Caribbean Coast
Cruising Ports: California to Florida via Panama
Cruising Guide to the Rio Dulce
The Forgotten Middle: Pacific Coast of Central America

Websites

www.guatemala.travel.com.gt (Guatemala Tourist Commission)
www.mayaparadise.com

HONDURAS

Honduras has coastlines on both sides of Central America, while the interior is mountainous and sparsely populated. Its Pacific coast on the Gulf of Fonseca is only about 70 miles long compared to a 400-mile shoreline in the Caribbean. The country's prime sailing attraction is the Bay Islands, a perfect cruising ground whose popularity with yachts has increased steadily in recent years. Roatán, Utila and Guanaja are the main islands of this group of islands, islets and cays which spread over an area larger than the Virgin Islands, with whom their scenic beauty is on a par. For those who find the Eastern Caribbean, and the Virgin Islands in particular, too crowded for their taste, the Bay Islands provide a perfect alternative. Until recently tourism has been low key, but this will probably change following the expansion of Roatán's airport.

The rest of Honduras is less tempting to explore by sea and although the mountainous north coast is scenically attractive, the lack of harbours make

Practical Information

LOCAL TIME: GMT – 6

BUOYAGE: IALA B

CURRENCY: Lempira of 100 centavos.
US$ must be declared on arrival.

BUSINESS HOURS
Banks: 0900–1500 Monday to Friday,
0800–1200 Saturday.
Business: 0900–1200/1400–1700 Monday
to Friday, 0900–1200 Saturday, some also
open on Saturday afternoons.
Supermarkets: 0900–2200 Monday to
Saturday.
On the north coast businesses open and
close half an hour earlier than the capital.

ELECTRICITY: 110 V, 60 Hz
PUBLIC HOLIDAYS
1 January: New Year's Day
14 April: Day of the Americas
Maundy Thursday, Good Friday, Easter
Saturday
1 May
15 September: Independence Day
3 October: Francisco Morazán Day
12 October: Discovery Day
21 October: Army Day
24 December: Christmas Eve
25 December: Christmas Day
31 December: New Year's Eve

COMMUNICATIONS
Hondutel for international telephone calls,

fax and telex.
Post offices open 0800–1200, 1400–1700
Monday to Friday, 0800–1200 Saturday.
There are international flights from
Tegucigalpa, San Pedro Sula, Roatán and
La Ceiba. There is a good network of
internal flights, as well as daily flights from
the Bay Islands to the mainland.

DIPLOMATIC MISSIONS
In Tegucigalpa:
Canada: Centro Financiero Banexo, Blvd
San Juan Bosco, Payaqui. *Tel.* 3234557.
United Kingdom: Edificio Palmira, 3rd floor,
Colonia Palmira. *Tel.* 2320612.
United States: Postal 3453, Avenida La
Paz. *Tel.* 2369320.

cruising along it very difficult, while the western Pacific coast is featureless and uninteresting.

Country Profile

When the Spanish pushed east from Guatemala early in the sixteenth century, they found silver in this newly conquered land. The present-day capital Tegucigalpa, which means silver hill in the local Indian language, was founded as a mining camp in 1578. Gradually Spanish settlements spread along the north coast and this is where most of the population live today. During the nineteenth century US companies developed banana plantations in the northern lowlands and imported labour from the British West Indies and Belize.

Honduras was under Spanish colonial rule until the Central American colonies declared their independence in 1821 and formed a federation under the leadership of Guatemala City. Francisco Morazán led a Honduran army in 1828 in revolt, captured Guatemala City, and took over control of the federation. He introduced many liberal reforms, but was assassinated in 1842. The federation fell apart, and thereafter the history of Honduras as an independent republic was very troubled. Throughout the nineteenth and into the twentieth centuries the efforts of Honduras, El Salvador and Nicaragua to create a political federation came to nothing. From 1969 relations with El Salvador deteriorated, following a dispute over the illegal immigration of Salvadoreans into Honduras. Relations only returned to normal in 1980.

In 1987 the Central American Peace Plan was drawn up by the Costa Rican President, but the provisions for US military personnel and Nicaraguan contra forces to withdraw from Honduras were not carried out. Democratic elections in Nicaragua in 1990 defused the tensions between Nicaraguans and the Contra fighters operating from Honduras. The situation gradually returned to normal during the 1990s and the country embarked on an ambitious programme of economic reforms.

The Bay Islands (Islas de la Bahia) were ceded to Honduras only in 1859 by Britain, hence their less Latin atmosphere. The people of the Bay Islands are of British origin and many are still English-speaking. They are descendants of Scottish and English pirates, colonists from the Cayman Islands who arrived in the eighteenth century, and some Black Caribs, deported to Roatán from St Vincent at the end of the eighteenth century. Henry Morgan had a lair at Port Royal, Roatán, and legend says that he is buried on Utila. Also part of Honduras is Swan Island, a former US dependency, which was ceded to Honduras in 1972. The island is a navy base and should be avoided.

Honduras is a poor country, with 25 per cent unemployment, due to low investment, poor harvests and labour disputes. Agriculture is the main economic activity, coffee, bananas and timber being the main exports. Almost half the land is forested. The country has considerable mineral and oil reserves.

The population numbers 5.6 million. The main language is Spanish, but English is spoken in the north and the Bay Islands. The majority of the population are Catholic.

Rain is frequent on the Caribbean coast all year round, but heaviest from September to December. The drier months are April to May but these months are very hot. The east and north coasts have strong NE trade winds throughout the winter months. The best time to cruise the Bay Islands is at the end of winter or early spring when the northers of winter are no longer a problem.

Entry Regulations

Ports of entry
Pacific: San Lorenzo 13°25′N 87°27′W.
Atlantic: Puerto Castilla 16°01′N 86°03′W, Puerto Cortés 15°51′N 87°56′W, La Ceiba 15°47′N 86°45′W, Tela 15°47′N 87°30′W.
Bay Islands: Roatán (Coxen's Hole) 16°18′N 86°35′W, Utila 16°16′N 86°40′W, Guanaja 16°28′N 85°54′W.

Procedure on arrival
Yachts clear in with the port captain at each port, and must obtain outward clearance (*zarpe*) before proceeding to the next port.
Roatán: Known locally as Coxen's Hole, the port of Roatán is the main port of entry in the Bay Islands. The Q flag and Honduran courtesy flag should be flown to attract the attention of the officials. The boat is usually boarded by the port captain accompanied by a customs officer. A crew list must be handed in as well as the clearance papers from the last port. A 30-day cruising permit is issued which can be easily renewed. A *zarpe* will be issued by customs and filled in by the port captain. Immigration must also be visited; visas, if necessary, will be issued. Visiting yachts are sometimes asked to employ the services of a local agent to carry out the clearance formalities, although this is not compulsory as clearance formalities are fairly straightforward. Yachts heading for the Bay Islands should try and make straight for Roatán, rather than clear at one of the mainland ports as formalities are simpler and officials are used to dealing with foreign yachts.
Utila: Puerto Este is not an official port of entry but the port captain will issue a *zarpe* and give permission for a few days' stay before continuing to Coxen's Hole for full clearance.
Puerto Castilla: Anchorage off the new town is prohibited so yachts should continue another 1.5 miles east to anchor off the old town. The yacht's captain must go ashore to clear at the port captain's office by the port terminal building in the new town.
Puerto Cortés: Yachts anchor off the naval base. The captain must go into town to clear with the port captain, immigration and customs.
La Ceiba: Proceed directly into the Lagoon Marina. The office will arrange clearance with the port captain and immigration. Alternatively, one can anchor off the town and complete formalities in La Ceiba itself.
Guanaja: At Guanaja Settlement, visit the port captain, and also immigration if clearing into Honduras. Boats must not move from Guanaja until clearance formalities are complete. Boats that have gone directly to El Bight have been fined.
Swan Island: Also marked on charts as Cisne or Santanilla. Boats are expected to come to the dock on the SW side, but this should be avoided if there is any swell. In that case the boat should anchor. Documents are normally checked by the military, who will not issue a clearance certificate (*zarpe*), so papers from the previous port should not be surrendered as they may be requested at the next stop.
Amapala: A convenient and attractive place to stop on the less frequented Pacific coast, on El Tigre Island. The activities of the former commercial port were moved two decades ago to San Lorenzo on the mainland. Although not an official port of entry, boats have been able to stop here. Boats are visited on arrival by the port captain, who will request clearance certificate (*zarpe*) from the last port. Customs and immigration are visited next, their offices being on the quay. There is a small fee for all formalities, which includes the issuing of a certificate on departure.

Procedure on departure
Customs will issue a *zarpe*, to be completed by the port captain. If leaving Honduras, immigration must also be visited for an exit stamp.

Customs
Firearms and animals must be declared.

Immigration
No visas are required for nationals of the European Union, Australia, Canada, USA, Argentina, Chile, Curaçao, Costa Rica, El Salvador, Guatemala, Iceland, Japan, Liechtenstein, Malta, Monaco, New Zealand, Norway, Panama, San Marino, Switzerland and Uruguay.

A 30-day stay is granted on arrival. Extensions of

30 days, up to three months maximum, can be obtained from immigration offices.

Some identification should always be carried, as the police often do spot checks.

Health

Dysentery and stomach parasites are a problem for those travelling inland. Water must be treated everywhere. Malaria prophylaxis recommended.

Fees

Overtime charges are made for clearance outside of working hours. Agent's fees if an agent is used. There is an immigration fee per passport, and customs charge a fee for each *zarpe*.

Wildlife reserves

All of Utila Island is a sanctuary except for the settlements. Also protected in the Bay Islands are the National Marine Park of Barbareta, West End on Roatán, and most of Guanaja and its surrounding reefs. Other protected islands are: Hog Cays (Cayos Cochinos), off the Caribbean coast, Cayos Zapotillos, Swan Island (Isla del Cisne) and Miskito Cays (Cayos Misquitos) off the Mosquito coast. Boats are not allowed to anchor anywhere, but have to use one of the moorings provided to protect the reefs, for which there is no charge.

Facilities

Facilities generally have improved as more cruising boats visit Honduras. The best supermarket and local markets will be found in La Ceiba where provisioning is much cheaper than in the offshore islands. A number of mechanical workshops, chandleries and repair facilities can also be found in La Ceiba. Two new marinas, Lagoon Marina and Grand Marina, are providing 24-hour security, workshops, storage, e-mail, telephone, as well as clearance facilities. Fuel, water and electricity are available at both marinas in La Ceiba.

In the Bay of Islands, provisioning and repair facilities are good with several supermarkets on Roatán. There is less on Utila and Guanaja. For any specialised job it is better to enlist the help of one of the workshops in Roatán, which are used to dealing with yachts. There is good provisioning with many shops and a general market close to the dock in Coxen's Hole. Fuel is also available on the dock. There are also two small shipyards at French Harbour, with their own slipways, catering for the commercial shrimping fleet, so facilities are good.

One can anchor away from the commercial port of French Harbour in West Bight, where French Harbour Yacht Club has drinking water at its dock and is a good place to leave the yacht although space is limited. The yacht club can also help find the right professional for repairs. Guanaja, the easternmost island in the group, also has a reasonable range of supplies, as does Utila. All islands have regular flights to La Ceiba on the mainland.

The Honduran Navy have a haul-out facility at Puerto Cortés which yachts may be permitted to use, although it is expensive.

There is good provisioning, fuel, telephones and bank, at Amapala, on El Tigre Island, on the Pacific coast.

Further Reading

Cruising Guide to the Northwest Caribbean
Cruising Ports: California to Florida via Panama
Mexico & Central America Handbook
Honduras and Bay Islands Mariners Guide
The Forgotten Middle: Pacific Coast of Central America

Websites

www.hondurastips.honduras.com
www.hondurasinfo.hn

MEXICO

Mexico has many things of interest to offer its visitors, whether they come by air, land or sea: an ancient culture, a vibrant atmosphere unmatched anywhere else in Latin America and a landscape of varied scenery from the high mountains of the interior to the silvery beaches lapped by the Pacific Ocean and Caribbean Sea. The cruising attractions of Mexico are concentrated in two main areas, the Gulf of California (Sea of Cortez) in Baja California on the west coast, and the Yucatan Peninsula on the east coast.

While Baja California's attraction lies primarily in the incredible wildlife that inhabits the limpid waters of the Gulf of California, the Yucatan's temptations lie mostly ashore, among the awe-inspiring ruins of the mighty Mayan empire. For many years the Gulf of California has been the preferred foreign destination of Californian sailors, a

Practical Information

LOCAL TIME: GMT – 6 (east coast), GMT – 7 (Baja California Sur), GMT – 8 (Baja California Norte, summer time GMT – 7 start April to end October).

BUOYAGE: IALA B

CURRENCY: Nuevo peso (NP$) of 100 centavos.

BUSINESS HOURS
Banks: 0900–1500 Monday to Friday, open Saturday mornings in some larger towns.
Shops: 0900/1000–1300/1400 and 1500/1600–1900/2000 Monday to Saturday.
Government offices: 0800–1500 Monday to Friday.
Business: 0900–1400, 1600–1900 Monday to Friday.

ELECTRICITY: 110/120 V, 60 Hz

PUBLIC HOLIDAYS
1 January: New Year's Day
5 February: Constitution Day
24 February: Flag Day
21 March: Birthday of Benito Juarez
Good Friday (some businesses close Monday to Thursday of Holy Week)
1 May
5 May: Anniversary of Battle of Puebla
24 June: St John the Baptist
15 August: Assumption

1 September: Government Day
16 September: Independence Day
12 October: Columbus Day
2 November: All Souls Day
20 November: Anniversary of Mexican Revolution
12 December: Feast of Our Lady of Guadalupe (Mexico's patroness saint) is not an official holiday but is often observed
25 December: Christmas Day (most offices are closed from Christmas until 2 January)

EVENTS
There are lots of fiestas all year round, usually religious, with folk dances and fireworks.

COMMUNICATIONS
International calls from a long-distance concessionary (caseta de larga distancia), although these are hard to find. Ladatel public phones take cards (bought from shops and newsagents).
Dial 09 for an English-speaking international operator.
Collect calls can only be made to the USA, UK and a few European countries.
There is a service charge if the call is not accepted or the person is not reached.
International calls are heavily taxed.
Post offices (oficinas de correos) to be found in all centres although the postal system is slow. Open 0900–1300, 1500–1800 Monday to Friday, 0900–1200 Saturday.

There are many flights worldwide from Mexico City and to US cities from other places such as Acapulco.

MEDICAL
Public hospitals are cheap, but not recommended. Both the US and UK embassies in Mexico City have lists of approved doctors. Medical facilities are good in larger cities. Pharmacists are permitted to diagnose and treat minor ailments.

DIPLOMATIC MISSIONS
In Mexico City:
Australia: Plaza Polanco, Torre B, Jaime Balmes 11, Col. Los Morales. *Tel.* (5) 395-9958.
Canada: Calle Schiller 529 (Rincon del Bosque), Colonia Polanco. *Tel.* (5) 724-7900.
New Zealand: Homero 229, 11570, Col. Chapultepec Morales. Tel. (5) 250-5999.
United Kingdom: Rio Lerma 71, Col. Cuauhtémoc. *Tel.* (5) 207-2089.
United States: Paseo de la Reforma 305. Colonia Cuauhtémoc. *Tel.* (5) 211-0042.

In Acapulco:
Canada: Hotel Club Del Sol, Mezzanine floor, Costera Miguel Aleman. *Tel.* (748) 56-621.
USA: Hotel Club de Sol. *Tel.* (748) 57-207.

place so near and yet so far from their own highly developed state. Equally the Yucatan Peninsula and the offlying island of Cozumel have offered almost the same kind of contrast to yachts heading south from Florida, but rapid tourist development is already creating a skyline similar to Acapulco in the formerly deserted beaches, bays and lagoons where for centuries the tallest buildings were those of the Mayan temples.

Less than 400 miles off Mexico's western coast lies a group of islands rarely visited from the mainland except by yachts on passage to the Marquesas. Of the four Islas de Revillagigedo only two, Socorro and Clarión, are inhabited, Partida is just a rock, while San Benedicto was parched by a volcanic eruption in 1952. The lack of rainfall has resulted in an arid landscape, which is more than made up for by the spectacular underwater scenery.

Country Profile

Since 2000 BC Mexico has seen thousands of years of continuous civilisation and has over 1000 archaeological sites to show for it. Before the arrival of the Spanish conquistadors, several highly developed and complex civilisations had risen to power and fallen. Huge ceremonial cities were built, the states based on the rule of a small elite over a people tied together by strong family and community ties. By the sixteenth century the flourishing Aztec empire had succeeded the Mayas, with its capital at Tenochtitlan. An estimated 20 million people populated Mexico at this time.

Henando Cortez, leading a militarily superior force, conquered Tenochtitlan and then slowly the rest of the country, which was then called New Spain. It remained under Spanish control for 300

years. The Indians, used as slave labour, were decimated by disease, and converted by Catholic
missionaries who had followed soon after the conquistadors. Assimilation of the Indians went
smoothly in the centre of the country, but the discovery of silver in the north meant the Spaniards
pushed into a less welcoming area, where the
Indians rebelled against the invasion. The
Spaniards loaded vast amounts of silver on to their
ships to be sent back to Europe, always under the
threat of attack by pirates or privateers.

In 1810 the War of Independence began, and
although defeated, guerilla warfare continued until
independence was finally gained in 1821. Until the
middle of the century the country remained politically unstable, dominated by the struggle between
the liberals and the conservatives, while the majority of the people lived in terrible poverty.
Territory was lost to the expanding United States,
including Texas and present day California and
New Mexico. At the turn of the century President
Diaz brought some stability and prosperity, but
not to the workers or labourers. From 1911–20
revolution and civil war tore the country apart,
with Pancho Villa and Emiliano Zapata the popular heroes. Despite fierce conflict, some land
reforms were introduced, and a socialist constitution was set up, with a Federation of 31 states and
a federal district.

Since the Second World War industrialisation
has continued, helped by the oil reserves, nationalisation and moves towards democracy. However,
little progress has been made on land and agricultural reforms. Many Mexicans seek employment in
the United States. Exports to the USA are vital to
the economy. Oil has been the main source of
income since the 1970s, also minerals and plantation crops. The tourist industry is growing. Mexico
hopes to benefit from the free trade agreement with
Canada and the USA which came into effect in 1994.

The population of Mexico is 90 million.
Traditionally the gachupines, Spaniards born in
Spain, dominated the country, but were always
resented by the criollos, being those of Spanish origin but born in Mexico. The mestizos, mixed
Spanish and Indian, forming the bulk of the
population, were much poorer, but those who suffered the most were the Indians, comprising 54
different ethnic groups. The situation has not
changed a great deal to the present day.

The official language is Mexican Spanish and
there are various Indian languages. English is spoken by some, especially those involved in the
tourist industry. Roman Catholicism is the religion
of the majority. The capital is Mexico City,
although the state capitals within the federation are
also important, especially after the 1985 earthquake in Mexico City, when decentralisation was
spurred on. Mexico City is at a very high altitude,
7347 ft (2240 m) and is built on the site of the former Aztec capital Tenochtitlan.

The climate is often very hot on the coasts,
although it is more temperate at higher altitudes
and in the north. May to October is the rainy
season, and it usually rains in the late afternoon
and evening. May is the hottest month. It rarely
rains from November to April. Temperatures on
the west coast are high all year round, especially in
the Gulf of California where the wind is often light.
On both coasts the hurricane season runs from June
to October, while winter brings the occasional
norther and, on the east coast, strong trade winds.
The best time to cruise is spring and late autumn.

Entry Regulations

Ports of entry
West coast: Ensenada 31°51′N 116°38′W, Cedros
Island 28°03′N 115°11′W, Cabo San Lucas
22°50′N 109°55′W, La Paz 24°10′N 110°19′W,
Santa Rosalia 27°20′N 112°16′W, Puerto San
Carlos 24°47′N 112°07′W, Guaymas 27°54′N
110°52′W, Topolobambo 25°32′N 109°06′W,
Mazatlán 23°11′N 106°26′W, San Blas 21°32′N
105°19′W, Chacala 21°10′N 105°14′W, Puerto
Vallarta 20°37′N 105°16′W, Manzanillo 19°03′N
104°20′W, Lazaro Cardenas 17°55′N 102°11′W,
Zihuatenejo 17°37′N 101°33′W, Acapulco 16°50′N
99°55′W, Puerto Escondido 15°51′N 97°06′W,
Puerto Angel 15°39′N 96°31′W, Salina Cruz 16°10′N
95°11′W, Puerto Madero 14°42′N 92°27′W.
Islas de Revillagigedo: 18°42′N 110°58′W.
East coast: Altamira 22°25′N 97°55′W, Tampico
22°13′N 97°53′W.
Isla Mujeres 21°10′N 86°43′W, Progreso
21°17′N 89°40′W, Cancun 21°08′N 86°46′W,
Cozumel 20°30′N 86°58′W, Campeche 19°51′N
90°33′W, Veracruz 19°12′N 96°08′W, Alvarado
18°46′N 95°46′W, Ciudad del Carmen 18°39′
91°51′W, Frontera 18°37′N 92°41′W, Chetumal
18°30′N 88°17′W, Xcalak 18°16′N 87°49′W,
Coatzacoalcos 18°09′N 94°25′W.

Procedure on arrival
Formalities can be time-consuming, but in the
major ports there are maritime agents who will do
the formalities for a fee as will some of the marinas.

On arrival in Mexico, yachts must go to the nearest port of entry, with the Q and courtesy flags flying. Normally immigration must be cleared first, then customs, quarantine (not always requested) and finally the port authority (API). A fee based on tonnage is normally assessed by API at the first port of entry and must be paid at the port captain's office.

It is recommended to arrive with a Tourist Entry Form (FMT) for every crew member or visa if applicable, both obtained in advance from a Mexican consulate. If the FMT is not previously obtained one should first go to the immigration office and obtain this Tourist Entry Form. Then the captain should proceed to customs with the ship's papers, the Tourist Entry Form and clearance papers. On payment of US$10 with an international credit card (or place a bond or deposit), one will be issued with a temporary import permit. For cruising in Mexican waters a health permit will also be required. Health officials may inspect the yacht, or one may be required to visit the hospital for a health clearance. As well as the ship's papers, the captain should have six crew lists in Spanish. Crew list forms in Spanish can be obtained before arrival from a Mexican consulate for a fee, or for a similiar fee on arrival. All officials will stamp and sign all crew lists and each official will keep a copy. If entering Mexico, one should try to have as many places as one wishes to visit listed on the import permit up to the last port intended for exit from the country. This may ease the paperwork while in Mexico until the final clearance. However, officials in some ports have been reported as not recognising this import permit and insisting on issuing their own.

One must clear in and out at all subsequent ports, paying visits to the port captain and immigration if they have offices. Crew lists will have to be given to all these officials. The port captain will only sign the permit for outward clearance 24 to 48 hours before departure, and yachts should leave promptly after obtaining their departure clearance (*zarpe*). This is only given after verification that no accounts are pending at the port or marina. This departure clearance will have to be shown in the next port, along with the health permit and ship's papers. When cruising between two major Mexican ports, it is advisable to ask the official filling out the departure clearance to mention on the document any intermediate ports which one wishes to visit (puertos intermedios). The following ports also include some minor ports where normally yachts have to check in only with the port captain.

West coast

Ensenada: The port captain normally inspects boats on arrival and advises on the required procedure and the order of offices to be visited. Officials do not work at weekends. Boats are either anchored inside the breakwater or taken to Pirates Pier, a marina offering a limited range of services.

Cedros Island: Anchor off at Cedros village and report to port captain there.

Cabo San Lucas: The port captain's office is on Matamoros Street, immigration near the Pemex fuel station.

La Paz: Customs and immigration offices are in the Federal building behind the municipal quay. Port captain's office in Calle Francesco Madero north of the quay.

Mazatlán: Yachts anchor off and dinghies can be left at one of the yacht agencies on the shore. Frequent buses stop at the club gate and go into town where the offices of immigration and port captain are situated. Boats on short stays can clear in and out at the same time.

San Blas: Yachts must check in with the port captain both if moored in the small boat harbour or east of the town in the Bay of Matenchen.

Puerto Vallarta: Marina Vallarta is a convenient place to complete formalities. Port captain and customs offices are in the terminal building by the cruise ship dock. Immigration is in town. Puerto Vallarta is also reported to be the only safe harbour in the area during the hurricane season.

Manzanillo: Yachts anchor outside Las Hadas Hotel or stern-to one of the docks inside the jetty. The offices of port captain and immigration must be visited, in Manzanillo town.

Lazaro Cardenas: Call port captain on VHF Channel 16 and an official will come in a launch to check one's papers.

Zihuatenejo: The offices of port captain and immigration are behind the concrete fishing dock.

Acapulco: Yachts can either anchor outside or arrange a berth in the yacht club marina. The yacht club facilities can be used by visitors and the yacht club can arrange clearance facilities for a fee. For those who prefer to do the formalities themselves, these can be very time-consuming as the offices are spread out all over town, and the distances are great.

Puerto Escondido: The port captain's office is on the waterfront next to the naval post. If the port captain is absent, report to the senior naval officer.

Puerto Angel: Report to the port captain whose office is east of the pier, or to the senior officer at the naval post on the beach.

Salina Cruz: This commercial port is not recommended for yachts.

Puerto Madero: This is the last port on the Pacific coast for those going south. Yachts may anchor in the outer fishing harbour. The port captain and customs offices are in the inner basin, but immigration is a taxi-ride away at the airport.

Islas de Revillagigedo: One should clear with the Navy, which has a garrison there, on the main island of Socorro.

East coast

Cozumel: This island used to be a favourite place for clearing in or out of Mexico. Yachts anchor at San Miguel, on the north side of the commercial dock. The wharf is used by large ferries so one should not come alongside, unless prepared to move off at short notice. The anchorage is uncomfortable in westerlies and strong northers. The port captain's office is on the waterfront, while the customs office is at the airport. Clearing in formalities tend to be lengthy, as one has to visit several offices around town. The port captain's office has caused problems to visiting yachts in the past, which appears to have been due to a difficult official who fined several boats for arbitrary infringements of local regulations. The easier alternative is to go directly to the yacht club, which operates a marina and has an agent who deals with all necessary formalities for a fee which has been reported as being very high, another reason why many cruising boats bypass Cozumel altogether. Customs and immigration officials usually inspect boats at the yacht club and the port captain also has a representative there.

Isla Mujeres: Formalities are relatively simple as all offices are within walking distance. One has to clear in with immigration first, followed by customs, health and finally port captain. The port captain's office is on the front street opposite the ferry wharf; immigration is also on the main road and harbour master next door. A health inspection is carried out at the local hospital. Occasionally firearms are inspected, but left on board. The Navy sometimes inspects vessels in the harbour.

Xcalak: There is a port captain's office but no immigration. Check in with police also. The Navy may inspect the boat.

Procedure on departure

The port captain, customs and immigration must be visited with six more copies of the crew list, and a departure clearance form obtained from the port captain. Although this document may not be requested when clearing into the next country, one would have to show it if stopped by a Mexican Navy boat while still in Mexican waters. If wishing to stop anywhere in Mexico after clearing out, this should be put on the outward clearance by the relevant official.

The cruising permit and tourist cards must be returned.

Customs

The only firearms allowed in Mexico are sporting guns which must have a valid Mexican hunting licence, obtained in advance. Other firearms must have a permit, and be declared to the authorities on arrival, who will keep them in custody until departure. The penalties for having an unauthorised gun on board are severe and can lead to seizure of the yacht and imprisonment of the captain.

Animals require a veterinary health certificate and cats and dogs also require an anti-rabies vaccination certificate. Both certificates must be shown to a Mexican consul to obtain an import permit for the animals.

Although 'Vessels in Transit' do not have to pay import tax on boat parts, avoiding such payment is very difficult. The correct procedure is as follows: the owner of the vessel should go with the ship's papers to the port captain of the nearest marina, who will issue a letter stating that the vessel is in transit. The sender of the parts is then instructed to send the package to the port captain, marking the name of the marina and correct address, then the boat owner's name and vessel's name. 'Vessel in Transit' must appear on the package. The shipment will come directly to the port captain, thus bypassing customs and, if all runs smoothly, the goods will then be handed over to the vessel's owner without any dues to be paid. As in the case with most formalities in Mexico, things may not work out in practice, in which case the services of a customs agent will greatly simplify matters, but his fee must be weighed up against the money saved in import dues.

Immigration

Citizens of Australia, Canada, Japan, the United States, the European Union (except France), Argentina, Chile, Costa Rica, Iceland, Israel, South Korea, Liechtenstein, Monaco, New Zealand, Norway, San Marino, Singapore, Switzerland and Uruguay require a tourist card. This can be obtained from Mexican consulates, tourist offices, national airlines, or on arrival. Most other countries require a visa, to be obtained in advance.

The tourist card is valid for up to six months although often a 90 days' stay is stamped on arrival by immigration. Particularly if coming from Belize it is advisable to arrive in Mexico either with a tourist card or a visa obtained in advance. These can be obtained from the Mexican consul in Belize City. It is imperative that those who wish to stay longer ask immigration at the first port of entry to stamp the passport for the entire six-month period allowed under Mexican law.

Renewal of the tourist card beyond six months can be done in Mexico City at the Secretaria de Gobernación, Dirección General de Asuntos Jurídicos, Avenida Juarez 92, 2nd floor (postal address: CP06500), *Tel.* 535-2718. If one has proof of possessing US$500 per month of intended stay, renewal of tourist cards and visas, which can take several weeks, can be done at a local immigration office. However, in an emergency a local immigration officer can extend a card for a few days, with telephone approval from Mexico City. A tourist card is needed to leave the country, and if lost it takes about a week to replace. Passports and tourist cards must be carried at all times.

Health
Water should be treated everywhere in Mexico. Several cruising sailors have contracted parasites either from contaminated water or food which had come in contact with such water, such as salads, fruit or ice cream.

Malaria prophylaxis is recommended if visiting rural areas.

Fees
There is an immigration fee for forms and a fee for the temporary import permit from customs. Customs charge a port tax (*derechos de puerto*), the receipt for which must be shown to the port captain when clearing in. Overtime is charged for clearance outside of office hours.

Fishing licence
Each person on board must have a fishing licence, and a licence must also be purchased for the yacht. For a yacht with four crew this will amount to about US$100. Spot checks are made, and simply having fishing tackle on board is considered by the Mexican authorities sufficient reason to have a licence. The licences can be obtained in advance from the Mexican Fisheries Department, 2550 5th Street, San Diego, California 92103-6622, USA or on arrival from the local Fisheries Department.

Yacht custody
Leaving the yacht in Mexico for over six months is possible if it is left in an authorised marina, if the owner is a foreign national and not resident in Mexico. The owner or his legal representative must visit the yacht at least once a year to renew the custody.

Charter
Chartering of foreign yachts is only allowed if marketed through a marina or authorised third party if the marina or third party has entered into a rental agreement with the owner and is responsible for all fiscal obligations. A permit must be obtained from the Ministry of the Treasury and Ministry of Communications and Transport.

Restrictions
Turtles are protected and no products made from turtles are allowed to be exported.

A permit is necessary to stop at Isla Contoy, north of Isla Mujeres, which is a nature reserve. The permit can be obtained from the office of the nature reserve, located in Rueda Medina, on Isla Mujeres.

Facilities

As the number of yachts visiting Mexico is increasing, so the yachting facilities are improving. All major ports visited by cruising yachts now have a reasonable range of services and most routine repairs can be dealt with locally. In most places there is good provisioning with both supermarkets and fresh produce. Fuel is available almost everywhere, although it can be dirty. The port captain in some ports is in charge of fuelling and a permit may be needed from him or customs.

La Paz is a major gathering point for yachts wintering in Baja California and there are excellent repair facilities with three shipyards capable of handling most jobs, and a good marina with a chandlery, fuel and all the usual services.

In Manzanillo fuel and water are available on the dock, good provisioning in the neighbouring town as well as various workshops, engine repair and spares. Also Mexican charts can be bought at the Instituto Oceanigrafico in Las Brisas. At Puerto Vallarta there is a chandlery at the new marina. Opequimar offer a complete range of repair services as well as 30-ton travelift. Acapulco's yacht club offers a wide range of services to visiting yachts including fuel. There are also good facilities at La Marina in Acapulco. Other marinas on Mexico's west coast, where good facilities have been reported, can be found at Cabo San Lucas, Marina Real, near Bahia San Carlos and Marina Ixtapa. The latter is a large new marina north of Zihuatenejo. The entrance is reported to be difficult in onshore winds. Marina services in general are constantly improving and several new marinas will be opened in the near future.

In Cozumel the yacht club is run as a marina and has fuel and water, a haul-out facility and some small workshops which can undertake simple repairs.

There are daily air trips to the Maya ruins on the mainland, which can also be reached by taking the ferry to Playa del Carmen and thence by bus or taxi to the ruins. Puerto Morelos has a good boatyard and repair facilities.

Isla Mujeres is another place where yachts can be left while visiting the Mayan sites on the Yucatan peninsula at the Puerto Isla Mujeres Marina at the Club Nautico docks in protected Laguna Makax. Repair facilities here are good, with a 70-ton travelift. Fuel is also available. Puerto Aventuras Marina, a new large resort near Cancun and the international airport, is also recommended as a place to leave a yacht in safety.

Further Reading

Charlie's Charts, Western Coast of Mexico
Cruising Ports: California to Florida via Panama
Cruising Guide to Belize and Mexico's Caribbean Coast
Cruising Guide to the Northwest Caribbean
Mexico and Central America Handbook
Fodor's Mexico

Websites

www.mexico-travel.com (Ministry of Tourism)
www.mexconnect.com (Mexican Consulate visa and boating information)

NICARAGUA

Nicaragua is the largest Central American state, lying between Costa Rica and Honduras with coasts on both the Pacific Ocean and the Caribbean Sea. The capital Managua lies on the shores of Lake Managua 30 miles from the Pacific Ocean. The Miskito kingdom encompassing the Caribbean lowlands was a British protectorate until the end of the nineteenth century. Following the Sandinista revolution, the Miskito Indians fought for self-determination, and this coastal area, including the Corn Islands, has been a self-governing region since 1987. English is spoken there and the African influence is noticeable.

In recent years Nicaragua has been avoided by cruising yachts and for good reason, although with the changing political situation this is no longer the case. The shallow reef-encumbered Miskito coast has many attractive anchorages, but navigation is difficult and even in the past when the area was not off-limits, most yachts restricted their cruising to the more accessible Corn Islands. Nicaragua's decision to extend its territorial waters from the normal 12 miles to 25 miles has resulted in the seizure of some foreign flagged vessels, mainly fishing boats. In their fight against illegal fishing, the Nicaraguan authorities have confiscated boats and arrested their crews, as a result of which the USA have warned all US vessels to avoid Nicaraguan waters, both on the Pacific and Caribbean side. Cruising yachts do not appear to have been affected, but those which intend to stop in Nicaragua should proceed directly to an official port of entry.

Country Profile

Nicaragua was under Guatemalan jurisdiction until it gained independence in 1838. An American William Walker led a famous expedition to Central America in the mid-nineteenth century, setting out to conquer Mexico. Driven into Nicaragua with his bellicose followers, he captured Granada and then took control of the whole country. Walker was elected President and recognised as such by the United States. A Central American coalition fought against him, and he eventually surrendered to the US Navy. A second expedition failed, and in 1860 Walker sailed to Honduras, where he was arrested and executed.

Nicaragua was again invaded in 1912–13 when US marines were sent in to enforce a loan. The

Practical Information

LOCAL TIME: GMT – 6

BUOYAGE: IALA B

CURRENCY: Cordoba (C$) of 100 centavos.

BUSINESS HOURS
Banks: 0830–1730 Monday to Friday.
Business and government offices:
0800–1200 and 1300–1700 Monday to
Friday.
Shops: 0800–1800 Monday to Friday,
0800–1200 Saturday.

ELECTRICITY: 110 V, 60 Hz

PUBLIC HOLIDAYS
1 January: New Year's Day
Maundy Thursday, Good Friday
1 May: Labour Day
19 July: Revolution of 1979
14 September: Battle of San Jacinto
15 September: Independence Day
2 November: All Souls Day
8 December: Immaculate Conception
25 December: Christmas Day
During most of Holy Week and the
Christmas and New Year period businesses
and shops close. Holidays falling on
Sunday are taken on the following Monday.

COMMUNICATIONS
International calls can be made from public
telephones and TELCOR offices.
International access code: 164 in Managua,
02-164 elsewhere.
Post offices: 0900–1730 Monday to Saturday.
There are international flights from
Managua to other Central and North
American capitals.

DIPLOMATIC MISSIONS
In Managua:
Canada: 208 Calle del Triunfo, Frente
Plazoleta Telcor Central. *Tel.* 627 574.
United Kingdom: El Reparto 'Los Robles',
Carretera de Masaya, 4a Casa a Mano
Derecha. *Tel.* 780 014.
United States: Km 4.5 Carretera Sur.
Tel. 666 010.

---

nationalists under General Sandino fought against this occupation. The United States appointed Anastasio Somoza supreme commander of the Nicaraguan National Guard, and Sandino was killed. Following the introduction of President Roosevelt's 'Good Neighbour' policy, the United States withdrew and Somoza dominated political life until his assassination in 1956. His son, General Somoza Debayle, followed him as ruler, until he was deposed in 1979. The revolution was led by the Sandinista guerillas (FSLN), who established a government with Daniel Ortega as President. However, their socialist policies were not welcomed by their neighbours and the US-backed 'contras' mounted a counter-revolutionary war, mainly from bases in Honduras. The Sandinistas introduced reforms, but both the war and the US trade embargo damaged the economy, one of the main reasons for their defeat in the 1990 elections. President Arnoldo Aleman, who came to power in 1997, imposed a strict austerity programme which has revived the economy but has resulted in high unemployment.

The economy is based on agriculture, the main exports being coffee, cotton, sugar, meat and bananas. Industry expanded in the 1970s, but suffered due to guerilla warfare, floods and drought. Extensive political and economic reforms were introduced in the 1990s, re-privatising confiscated property, with some success in reining in the severe inflation, and the beginning of economic growth.

The 4 million inhabitants are mestizo and of Indian and African origins as well as a small number of European origin. Spanish is the main language and most are Roman Catholic.

The climate is humid and hot, December to May being the dry months, while June and October are the wettest. Violent northerly winds occasionally affect both coasts in winter, particularly the Caribbean coast. On this coast the prevailing winds are E or NE, while winds on the west coast are usually light. The coasts are sometimes affected by tropical storms, the season for which lasts from June to November. Mega-hurricane Mitch struck the country in November 1998 causing widespread devastation and thousands of deaths.

Entry Regulations

Ports of entry
Pacific: Corinto 12°28′N 87°11′W, Puerto Sandino 12°11′N 86°47′W, San Juan del Sur 11°15′N 85°53′W.
Atlantic: El Bluff 12°01′N 83°44′W.

Procedure on arrival
Corinto: This is the main port of Nicaragua. Port control keep 24-hour watch on VHF Channel 16 and should be contacted for instructions concerning clearance.
El Bluff: Yachts should dock at the customs wharf, where customs and health officials will board.

Customs
Firearms and animals must be declared. A declaration of money and valuables must be made on arrival.

Canned meats and dairy products are prohibited imports, also medication without prescriptions.

Immigration

Passports must have a validity of at least six months. For nationals of most countries a visa is not needed, only a Tourist Card purchased on arrival ($5 at airport, $7 at other borders). The Tourist Card is valid for 30 days, but extensions may be given for a nominal fee. Spanish citizens do not need a visa or a Tourist Card.

One's passport or a photocopy of one's passport should be carried at all times.

Health

Malaria prophylaxis is recommended.

Restrictions

To visit the Corn Islands, Bluefields and Puerto Cabezas, a permit must be obtained in Managua.

Facilities

Even after the cessation of hostilities, provisioning in many places is still difficult. Even essential goods are difficult to obtain in some places and this includes fuel. There are simple repair facilities in most ports.

Further Reading

Cruising Guide to the Caribbean
Mexico & Central America Handbook
The Forgotten Middle: Pacific Coast of Central America

Website

intur.gob.ni (Nicaragua Tourism Authority)

PANAMA

Panama is a country that lies at the world's cross-roads, a narrow isthmus which divides the Atlantic from the Pacific Oceans and links the two halves of the American continent. The country is dominated by the Panama Canal and the surrounding Panama Canal Area, which were incorporated fully into Panama on 31 December 1999. Balboa on the Pacific and Cristobal in the Caribbean are the two main ports and gateways to the canal. The port of Cristobal incorporates the town of Colón.

The main cruising attractions in Panama are the 365 San Blas islands off the Caribbean coast, a popular destination for yachts. The islands are the home of the Cuna Indians and their distinctive handicrafts are a popular buy. A cruising permit is required to visit these islands, but the local Panamanian officials usually treat yachts arriving from the east on their way to the mainland with a certain degree of tolerance.

On the Pacific side, the Las Perlas islands are another unspoilt cruising ground popular with boats en route to the Galapagos and South Pacific islands. Two armed robberies against cruising boats have cast a shadow over these islands and, like in other isolated parts of the world, sailors are advised to only stop in a remote anchorage in the company of another boat.

Country Profile

The name Panama means 'abundance of fish' in the local Indian dialect. The San Blas coast was discovered in 1501 by the conquistador Roderigo de Bastidas and Christopher Columbus visited the islands the following year. It was in 1513, however, that the country's fate was decided, when Vasco Nuñez de Balboa crossed the isthmus and sighted the Pacific Ocean. Panama City was founded on the Pacific side and became the starting point for Spanish conquests which fanned out north and south along the Pacific coast. All trade from the Pacific ports had to be taken overland across the isthmus, then heavily escorted ships laden with treasure left for Spain from Puerto Bello on the Caribbean side, returning later with European goods. This route was continually being attacked and in 1671 the pirate Henry Morgan looted and burnt Panama City. Finally in the mid-eighteenth century Spain abandoned the overland route for the one around Cape Horn.

During the Californian Gold Rush, the land route was again used for transport and a railway was built across the isthmus, completed in the mid-nineteenth century at great loss of life. A canal was the obvious solution and Ferdinand de Lesseps, who had successfully built the Suez Canal, started work in 1882. However, this project failed after tropical disease killed thousands of workers. In 1903 Panama declared its independence from Colombia, the fledgling state being promptly recognised by the United States who had been instrumental in its birth. Work on a canal started again under US supervision, after the surrounding

Practical Information

LOCAL TIME: GMT – 5

BUOYAGE: IALA B

CURRENCY: Balboa of 100 centesimos. Balboas are on a par with US$, which circulates as an equivalent currency.

BUSINESS HOURS
Banks: variable, usually all morning Monday to Friday.
Shops: 0700/0800–1200, 1400–1800/1900 Monday to Saturday. Many shops do not close for lunch.
Government offices: 0800–1200, 1230–1630 Monday to Friday.

ELECTRICITY: 220/110 V, 60 Hz

PUBLIC HOLIDAYS
1 January: New Year's Day
9 January: Panamanian Martyrs' Day
Shrove Tuesday: Carnival
Good Friday

1 May: Labour Day
*15 August (Panama City only)
*2 November: All Souls Day
3 November: Independence Day
*4 November: Flag Day
5 November: Independence Day (Colón only)
10 November: First Call of Independence
28 November: Emancipation Day
8 December: Mothers Day
25 December: Christmas Day
*Official holiday, banks and government offices close but not businesses.

EVENTS
Fiestas, especially Panama City Carnival, four days before Ash Wednesday.

COMMUNICATIONS
Cable & Wireless offices, in Cristobal and Balboa for international calls, open 0800–2130 daily.
International calls are also possible from the yacht clubs in both these places.

Post office in Cristobal, Cristobal Administration building, corner Av. Bolivar and Calle 9, open 0800–1600 Monday to Friday. Balboa post office, corner Avenida Roosevelt and Jamaica, open 0700–1745 Monday to Friday, 0700–1645 Saturday.
'Republic of Panama' must be written on letters or they may be returned.
There are international flights from Panama City, mainly to the USA and other Latin American capitals. Best international connections are via Miami, which acts as the regional hub.

DIPLOMATIC MISSIONS
In Panama City:
Canada: World Trade Center, Avenida 53, Marbella. *Tel.* 264 9731.
United Kingdom: Torre Banco Sur, 4th floor, Calle 53 Este. *Tel.* 269 0866.
United States: Av. Balboa and Calle 39. *Tel.* 207 7000.

---

area had been cleared of the worst diseases. The first Canal passage was finally made in 1914. The former Canal Zone was a ribbon of land under US control and included the ports of Cristobal and Balboa. In 1979 the Canal Zone was transferred to Panamanian sovereignty and the ownership of the Panama Canal itself was transferred to Panama on 31 December 1999. US involvement in Panamanian affairs came to a head in 1989, when widespread dissatisfaction led to the downfall of President Noriega, who is currently in prison in the USA.

The Panama Canal is one of the wonders of the modern world and transiting it is a unique experience. The total length of the Canal is 50 miles (80 km) and runs in a NW to SE direction, which means that the Pacific entrance lies further east than the Caribbean one. It requires about nine hours for the average ship to transit the Canal. Coming from the east a Pacific-bound vessel is raised 85 ft (26 m) in a series of three steps at Gatun Locks. Each lock chamber is 110 ft (34 m) wide and 1000 ft (305 m) long. Gatun Lake, through which ships have to travel for 23.5 miles (38 km) from Gatun Locks to the end of the Gaillard Cut, is one of the largest artificial lakes in the world. It was formed by an earth dam across the Chagres River.

Because of its historical background, no part of the Canal is more interesting than the Gaillard Cut. This portion of the Canal was cut through eight miles of rock under the command of Col. David DuBose Gaillard, whose name it now bears. It was a mammoth task requiring enormous effort and several devastating landslides occurred both during construction and after the Canal was opened. The Pacific-bound ships enter Pedro Miguel Locks at the southern end of Gaillard Cut. Ships are lowered here 31 ft (9.5 m) in one step to Miraflores Lake, a small artificial lake which separates the two sets of Pacific locks. Finally, ships are lowered the remaining two steps to sea level at Miraflores Locks, which are slightly over 1 mile (1.5 km) in length. The lock gates at Miraflores are the highest of any in the system because of the extreme tidal variations in the Pacific Ocean.

The Panamanian economy is traditionally founded on income derived from the Canal, services to incoming visitors, Canal employees, and US military personnel. It is now developing tourism, industry and copper mining, while agriculture is also important and offshore banking services.

The population numbers around 2.5 million, mostly mestizo, but also of Indian, African and Asian origin. The Cuna Indians of the San Blas Islands are descendants of the Caribs, who originally peopled much of the Caribbean islands and coasts. The Cunas are one of the few groups to survive the arrival of the Europeans. The San Blas Islands enjoy a measure of autonomy within the state of Panama. Spanish and English are the main languages of Panama and the majority of the population are Roman Catholic. Panama City, two miles from Balboa, is the capital.

The climate is hot and very humid, although cooled by the prevailing easterly winds. The dry season is January to April, and rain can be heavy in October and November. Panama is not affected by hurricanes.

Entry Regulations

Ports of entry
Cristobal 9°21′N 79°55′W, Balboa 8°57′N 79°34′W.
San Blas Islands: Porvenir 9°34′N 78°57′W, Rio Diabolo.

Round the World Rally yachts in Miraflores Lock, Panama Canal.

Procedure on arrival
Arriving yachts can clear immigration at either the Panama Canal Yacht Club in Colón if coming from the Caribbean, or at the Balboa Yacht Club if coming from the Pacific. After immigration, one must clear with customs and the port authority, both of which are within a short distance, but are best visited by taxi. The procedure for transiting the Canal is dealt with separately at the end of this section. At both Balboa and Cristobal, arriving yachts may be boarded by a Panamanian official who will complete all the initial clearance formalities. If the yacht is not boarded, the captain should go ashore, but all others must remain on board until clearance is complete.

Cristobal: Cristobal Signal Station should be contacted on VHF Channels 12 or 16 and the yacht will be directed to go to the yacht club, if there is space available, or anchor. The captain should go ashore and clear immigration first. The office is in a building to the right of the yacht club, open 0700–1500 Monday to Friday. After-hours clearance can be obtained from the immigration office in Cristobal. Next the captain should go to the

Autoridad Portuaria (port authority) to clear into Panama and obtain a cruising permit. The port captain's office is in the Panama Canal Commission building 1105, 3rd floor. If not transiting the Canal, clearance is completed at the port authority. If transiting the Canal, the captain should go to the Canal Admeasurement office. It is dangerous to walk out of the yacht club gates at any time of day or night, so a taxi should be used at all times.

Balboa: Flamenco Signal Station should be contacted on VHF Channels 12 or 16 upon arrival at the sea buoy. Yachts will be directed to pick up a mooring off the Balboa Yacht Club. Occasionally the yacht club launch will come out and the launch operator will direct the yacht to a vacant club mooring if available. On arrival, yachts are normally boarded by a Panamanian Migration and Drug Enforcement Officer. Immigration is completed ashore at the yacht club. The main yacht club building was destroyed by fire early in 1999 and both club and immigration use temporary offices.

Porvenir: One should clear with customs and immigration.

Rio Diabolo: One should check in at the police station.

Customs
Firearms must be declared on arrival and will be held in bond until departure.

Dogs need health and anti-rabies certificates and are not allowed to land. All other animals need health certificates. In practice, the procedure is quite relaxed.

Immigration
Tourist cards are required by all nationals of all countries except: Germany, Spain, UK, Austria, Chile, Costa Rica, El Salvador, Finland, Honduras, Switzerland and Uruguay. Tourist cards are free if acquired in advance, US$5 on arrival.

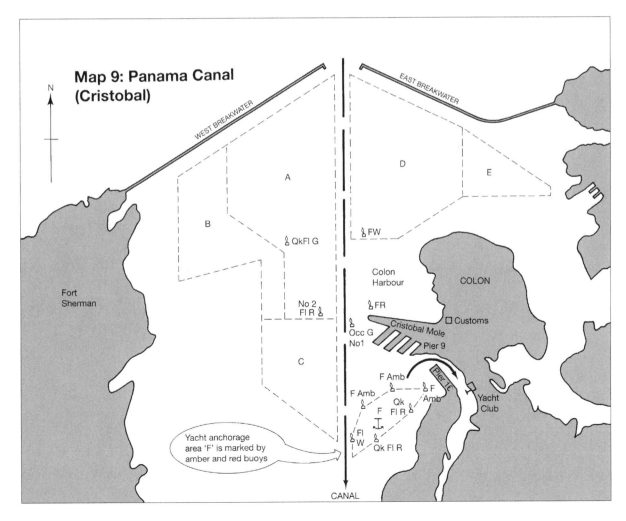

Map 9: Panama Canal (Cristobal)

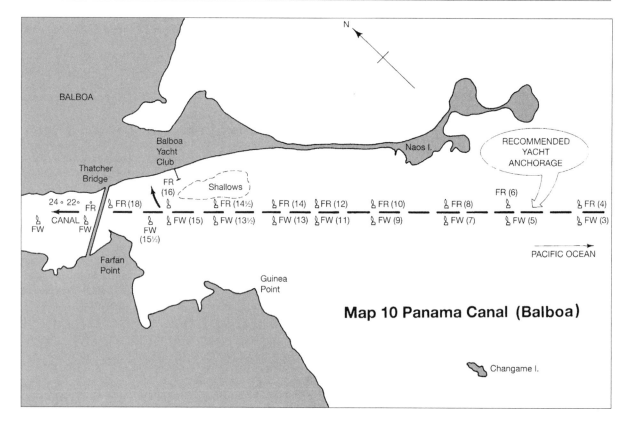

Map 10 Panama Canal (Balboa)

Visas are required but issued without charge to nationals of Colombia, Denmark, Mexico, Netherlands, Norway and the USA. Visas are valid 30 days from the date of entry, to be used within three months of issue. Extensions are possible for another 60 days. Nationals of most East European, African and Asian countries require authorisation from immigration in Panama before arrival for a visa to be issued.

In the USA, visas can be obtained from: Panamanian Consulate, 201 E Kennedy Boulevard, Suite 1400, Tampa, FL 33602, USA. *Tel.* 813-229-6860. Visitors arriving without a visa are charged US$10 per person.

Cruising permit

On arrival the port authority will issue a cruising permit which costs $20 per month for boats over 32 ft (10 m) LOA, plus $5 insurance fee. The permit is needed whether transiting the Canal or not. Yachts planning to sail to the San Blas Islands after transiting the Canal should make sure that they receive a cruising permit for these islands. Yachts clearing in Cristobal, who do not intend to stop in Balboa at all, can clear out of Panama in Cristobal, but they must do this one working day before transiting the Canal. Apparently the clearance is free in Cristobal, but costs $25 in Balboa. If intending to stop at Las Perlas, this should be mentioned on the clearance paper by the relevant officer.

Security

In Colón and Cristobal, muggings are a real threat, even in daylight. One should avoid walking anywhere outside of the port and all shopping should be done by taxi.

Health

An international yellow fever vaccination certificate is required. If just transiting the Canal, it is not necessary to take anti-malarial precautions, but is recommended outside the Canal Area.

Fees

Visa fee of US$10 if a visa is required. Clearance fee. Canal fees. Cruising permit.

Procedure for Transiting the Panama Canal

After clearing into Panama, the captain must call the Admeasures Office by calling, on the Pacific side, Flamenco Signal Station on Channel 12 or direct by telephone 272-4571, or, on the Atlantic side, Cristobal Signal Station or telephone 443-2293 to make arrangements for an inspection of the boat. In Cristobal, the office is on the second floor, Administration Building, No. 1105, and in Balboa, first floor, Building 729. An appointment will be made to visit the boat. Transit fees are based on LOA and cost $500 for boats up to 50 ft (15 m), $750 for boats between 50 and 80 ft (15–24 m), $1000 80 to 100 ft (24–30 m), and $1500 100 to 150 ft (30–46 m). A buffer deposit must also be made, which varies between $650 and $900, to cover any unforeseen costs, but is usually refunded within six weeks. Fees may now be paid only at Citibank in either Cristobal or Balboa, and no longer direct to the Panama Canal Commission. Payments can be made either in cash or by bank transfer.

The captain must then report to the Canal Operations Captain's Office (Building 910, La Boca on the Pacific side and Building 1105, third floor, Cristobal Administration Building). This officer will explain the requirements needed for the transit, which include four mooring lines not less than 120 ft (40 m) long and not less than 7⁄8″ (22 mm) diameter rope, four line-handlers (in addition to the captain), adequate fendering, and the yacht must maintain a minimum of five knots under power. If it becomes apparent at the start of the transit that the yacht is doing less than five knots, it will have to return to the starting point and will be charged for an aborted transit. Yachts with no engines can be towed through the Canal by a Commission launch, all towing charges to be paid by the yacht owner.

The captain will be given a provisional pilot time for the transit. This must be confirmed or changed by calling Marine Traffic Control *Tel.* 292-4202 or VHF Channel 12. Final arrangements must be made no later than 24 hours before the scheduled transit time. Transits can be arranged earlier and if reconfirmed or cancelled the day before the transit a delay charge will not be made. Yachts normally make the transit in two days, spending a night at Gamboa. The pilot arrives early in the morning, and leaves the yacht for the night, returning the following morning to complete the transit. The yacht will be charged a delay fee of US$400 if the transit is not cancelled before the close of working hours on the day before the scheduled transit or if the yacht is for any reason unable to commence transit. Yachts are required to maintain their transit schedule regardless of weather conditions. The cost of a Panama Canal tug is between $145 and $1650 per hour depending on circumstances.

Types of lockage

There are three different types of lockage in the Canal, and all vessels must be capable of making a centre chamber lockage. Other types are sidewall or alongside a Commission tug. Whether a yacht is assigned a sidewall or centre chamber lockage is decided by the admeasurer who will ask the preferred type of lockage, but the final decision will be made by the course adviser as this will depend on the situation at the time of lockage. This depends on hull configuration, protruding railings, awnings, high masts, and anything that could be damaged if made fast to the chamber walls.

Centre chamber lockage: The vessel is held in the centre of the chamber by two bow and two stern lines. Yachts are sometimes rafted together.

Sidewall lockage: Only two 120 ft (40 m) lines are required; lots of fenders as well as suitable spring lines will be needed as the walls are rough concrete. Care should also be taken of the rigging which may hit the walls in the turbulence.

Alongside a tug: Two 50 ft (15 m) lines will be required. This type of lockage is not safe when uplocking.

Mooring lines

Each yacht must have four line-handlers in addition to a helmsman. All lines, chocks, cleats should be inspected to ensure they are in good condition, as they will be under heavy strain during the transit. The area around the fittings must be clear of gear so that the lines can be efficiently handled.

Yacht clubs

Visiting yachts usually stay at the Panama Canal Yacht Club in Colón on the Atlantic side. Its dinghy dock can be used by yachts anchored in the harbour. Those who wish to tie up at the club pontoons can do so on payment of a daily fee. Docking facilities on the Pacific side are limited. There is a new marina in Panama City, but it is tidal and has severe draft restrictions. While the Balboa Yacht Club is being rebuilt, one may use the existing moorings and launch service, but as the charges are quite high, some may prefer to either anchor behind Naos Island, by the causeway, or out at Taboga Island. There are frequent ferries from the latter into Panama City. The Pedro Miguel Yacht Club on Miraflores Lake has some repair facilities, and is a half-hour bus ride from Panama City. Those who wish to stop at Pedro Miguel and interrupt the Canal transit must inform the port captain when making the initial arrangements for the Canal transit. The pilot will then arrange to leave or board the yacht there. Reservations at the club can be made on *Tel.* 232-4509. The

Panama Canal Commission has given notice to all three clubs located on Commission land that their current leases will not be renewed and they must therefore relocate. The situation is not at all clear, but it looks as if docking facilities at both ends of the Canal will be even worse than they are now.

Facilities

Provisioning is very good in both Colón and Panama City and there are several supermarkets with a wide selection. The best provisioning on the Pacific side is at the El Dorado shopping centre, which has excellent supermarkets. There is also a fresh produce market near the railway station in Balboa. Another good fresh produce market is held daily in Margarita, which can be reached by taxi from Colón. There is a wide range of repair facilities at both ends of the Canal with various workshops capable of dealing with diesel and outboard engines, electronic equipment and sail repair. Either yacht club will advise on the best companies to approach. The range of repair facilities is better in Panama City. There is both fuel and water at each club. Both yacht clubs have slipways and there is also a boatyard in Las Minas with haul-out facilities. Charts are available in Panama City.

Facilities in the San Blas and Las Perlas islands are very limited.

Panama Yacht Services, *Tel.*+507-229-7110, Fax. 229-3018, e-mail panamayacht@hotmail.com, provides a range of services for yachts, from provisioning to repair. It can deal with all aspects of the Canal transit, both with formalities and, if necessary, line handlers.

Further Reading

Cruising Ports: California to Florida via Panama
Captain's Guide to Transiting the Panama Canal
Cruising Guide to the Isthmus of Panama

Websites

www.panamatours.com (National Tourism Office)
www.ipat.gob.pa
www.pancanal.com (Panama Canal Commission)
This features a live video feed from Miraflores locks so that it is now possible to view a Canal transit on the internet.

ST PIERRE AND MIQUELON

St Pierre and Miquelon is a territory of France, located in the North Atlantic Ocean 15 miles off the south coast of Newfoundland. The main islands of the small archipelago are St Pierre, Miquelon (Grande Miquelon), and Langlade (Petite Miquelon), the latter two connected by a sandy isthmus.

The islands were settled by the French during the seventeenth century. They remained a French colony, except for British rule from 1713 to 1763, and again during the French revolutionary wars, being restored to France in 1814. During the Second World War, General Charles de Gaulle's Free French troops occupied the islands. The islands became an overseas department of France in 1976 and attained the status of a territorial collectivity in 1985.

Fishing and tourism are the main economic activities, and the French government provides a high subsidy. The majority of the population of around 6400 live in the capital St Pierre.

Entry Regulations

Ports of entry
St Pierre 46°47′N 56°10′W, Miquelon 47°06′N 56°23′W.

Procedure on arrival
Contact the port authority on Channel 16.

Practical Information

LOCAL TIME: GMT − 3, GMT − 2 April to October.

CURRENCY: French franc. Euro from 2002. 1 euro = 6.55957 FRF.

COMMUNICATIONS
The airport at St Pierre has flights to Paris via Montreal or Halifax. Construction of a second runway will increase links with both the American mainland and France.

MEDICAL
There is a small hospital in St Pierre.

Immigration
As for France.

Websites

www.st-pierre-et-miquelon.com (Official site)
www.miquelon.net

UNITED STATES OF AMERICA

Spanning the North American continent between the Pacific and the Atlantic Oceans, the United States is not a major cruising destination for foreign yachts and with the exception of Canadian boats, the number who visit this great country is comparatively small. Such visitors include European yachts making a detour on the way home from the Caribbean and occasionally a North European yacht which has braved the elements to cross the North Atlantic as part of a summer cruise. Being so remote from any sailing nation, except Canada, the West Coast is even less frequented.

This is rather surprising, as the USA has a lot to offer the cruising sailor, particularly the East Coast, the entire length of which can be cruised from the Florida Keys to Maine. A cruise along this coast has the added attraction of the Intracoastal Waterway, a unique system of canals, rivers and estuaries, which stretches along most of the eastern seaboard offering the chance of sailing up or down the coast in sheltered waters almost within sight of the ocean. For the foreign sailor, Florida is a perfect introduction to the United States and some of its best-known attractions are close by, such as Disneyworld or the Cape Canaveral Space Center. The waterways of the southern states wind their way through old cities, deserted estuaries and silent woods to reach the Chesapeake. This, the largest bay in the USA, has a shore line of thousands of miles and within striking distance of some of America's largest cities are secluded anchorages and snug harbours. A couple of days' sail up the coast, at the confluence of the Hudson and East rivers, lies New York, one of the few cities in the world where one can sail right through its centre. Passing almost within touching distance of Manhattan's skyscrapers and under the many bridges is an experience that cannot be repeated. New York is the gateway to the Great Lakes which can be reached by a system of canals and locks.

Alternatively, one can carry on through Long Island Sound to the heart of New England where much of modern America's history was made. Famous seafarers, whalers and explorers left from these old ports. Finally one reaches the island world of Maine where many summers could be spent exploring the countless bays, rivers and anchorages which stretch all the way to the Canadian border.

Offering less variety, the West Coast's main attractions are concentrated at its two extremes. The most popular cruising area in the Pacific Northwest are the San Juan Islands, an archipelago of some 200 islands, many of which have been declared wildlife reserves or marine parks. Beyond these islands and through Canadian waters, the Inside Passage beckons, linking Puget Sound to Alaska, America's ultimate cruising destination. An increasing number of yachts sail to Alaska for the short summer season, either by taking the inside route, or making an offshore detour by stopping first at the Hawaiian Islands. For those avoiding high latitude cruising, there is all year round sailing in the Pacific Southwest, whether in the San Francisco Bay area or the Channel Islands, off Southern California. Of the eight main islands, Santa Catalina is the best known and most popular. The other islands are less frequented and there are countless coves around their precipitous shores. Since some of the Channel Islands are either privately owned or part of the Nataional Park system, a permit to visit them must be obtained in advance by those wishing to go ashore.

Country Profile

The original inhabitants of North America probably came across the Bering Straits from Asia, and spread south through the Americas. The Red Indians, as they later became known, lived in scattered tribes. Their first contact with Europeans was not with Columbus, who only visited the offlying islands of the Caribbean, but with an expedition led by the Norseman Erik the Red, who probably touched on the eastern coast in the tenth century. European settlement began 500 years later, with the French settling in Canada, and the Spanish in Florida.

Throughout the seventeenth century English settlement took place, while the French expanded along the Mississippi, founding Louisiana. There was a large emigration from Europe to this New World. Thirteen English colonies were established and antagonism grew between the plantation South, and the bourgeois, puritan North. However, in the eighteenth century they united against both the Indians and the French, although the latter ceased to be a threat after the Treaty of Paris in 1763, when Canada was ceded to England. The French then became an ally of the American colonies in the escalating tension with England, resulting in the War of Independence in 1775–6.

The newly independent Federal Republic grew more confident in the nineteenth century and extended its territory as the western frontier was conquered and settled, Louisiana, Florida and Alaska were purchased and Texas, New Mexico and California were incorporated into the republic. The middle of the century saw antagonism growing between the agricultural southern states, which advocated free trade, and the protectionist industrialising north, the antagonism aggravated by the question of slavery. The resulting civil war led to the north's victory and the abolition of slavery. The last 30 years of the century saw the country enjoy something of a golden age, with the

At anchor off John Hopkins Glacier in Glacier Bay, Alaska.

economy growing to rival the European industrial powers.

In 1917 war was declared on Germany, but immediately after the war, the country returned to its isolationist, protectionist policy. Economic growth continued until the Wall Street Crash of 1929 set off an unprecedented social and economic crisis. Franklin D. Roosevelt introduced a New Deal Policy in an effort to combat the depression. Entering the Second World War in 1941 brought an end to isolationism, as with peace the United States' foreign policy became dominated by opposition to the expansion of the Soviet Union, and communism in general. The 1960s saw the rise of strong civil rights movements calling for an end to racial segregation, and then increasing protests against the war in Vietnam, where the USA had intervened in 1964. Under President Richard Nixon relations improved with China and the Soviet Union, and withdrawal from Vietnam occurred in 1973. The 1980s saw a return to an active foreign policy under President Ronald Reagan, and his successor, George Bush. Democrat Bill Clinton was succeeded in 2001 by George W. Bush.

Practical Information

LOCAL TIME: There are 6 time zones. GMT – 5 Eastern Standard Time, GMT – 8 Pacific ST, GMT – 10 Alaska. In most states, from the first Sunday in April to the last Sunday in October, one hour is added.

BUOYAGE: IALA B

CURRENCY: US dollar (US$)

BUSINESS HOURS
Banks: 1000–1500 Monday to Friday.
Business: 0900–1200, 1300–1700 Monday to Friday.
Shops: 0900–1800 Monday to Saturday.
Government offices: 0900–1200, 1300–1630 Monday to Friday.

ELECTRICITY: 110 V, 60 Hz

PUBLIC HOLIDAYS
1 January: New Year's Day
3rd Monday in January: Martin Luther King's Birthday
3rd Monday in February: George Washington's Birthday
Easter Weekend
1st Monday in May: Memorial Day
4 July: Independence Day
1st Monday in September: Labor Day
12 October: Columbus Day
mid November: Veterans Day
Last Thursday in November: Thanksgiving Day
25 December: Christmas Day

COMMUNICATIONS
Dial 0 for operator, 411 for information.
Emergency: dial 911 for police.
Post offices open 0900–1700 weekdays, some 24 hours in main cities.

There are flights to worldwide destinations from most major cities. Miami, New York and San Francisco particularly have many international connections.

MEDICAL
Comprehensive health insurance is essential. Only emergency cases will be treated without payment in advance.

DIPLOMATIC MISSIONS
In Washington DC:
Australia: 1061 Massachusetts Avenue NW. *Tel.* (202) 797-3000.
Canada: 501 Pennsylvania Avenue NW. *Tel.* (202) 682-1740.
New Zealand: 37 Observatory Circle NW. *Tel.* (202) 328-4800.
United Kingdom: 3100 Massachusetts Avenue NW. *Tel.* (202) 462-1340.

The United States is a vast country with many natural resources and a large agricultural production. It is also the original consumer society and imports much more than it exports, including raw materials, energy sources and finished goods. The service industries are where the majority of the population are employed. Major exports are machinery, chemicals, livestock and fertilisers, electronic equipment and computers.

The population numbers about 258 million, the majority of whom are of European origin, mainly English, German, Irish and Italian. Ten per cent of the population is of African origin and there are also large minorities of Hispanics, Chinese and Japanese. There are very few of the Indians who originally populated the continent. The main language is English, but Spanish is increasingly spoken, especially in some areas of Florida, California and New York. A predominantly Christian country, the main denominations are Protestant and Roman Catholic. Washington DC is the federal capital, while each of the 50 states have their own state capitals.

Being such a large country, the climate varies considerably, from cold and temperate in the north to tropical and desert in the south. Hurricanes occur from June to November on both the Atlantic and Pacific coasts. The Gulf of Mexico and the South Eastern seaboard are particularly at risk, although hurricanes have reached up as far as New York on occasion. On the Pacific coast, however, it is rare that a tropical cyclone reaches as far as California. The weather in the Pacific Southwest is warm throughout the year, most of the rainfall occurring during the winter months with summers being very dry. Winds are mostly westerly, except for the hot dry NE winds, the Santa Anas, that come down the mountains. The Pacific Northwest has colder and wetter weather and cruising is decidedly seasonal, from May to October, with high summer being the best time. Winds are NW or W and many days are foggy.

Entry Regulations

Complete and detailed information about arriving by yacht can be found on the following government website: www.customs.ustreas.gov/travel/vessel.htm.

Ports of entry

Yachts arriving in the USA from a foreign port must call first at a customs port or designated place where customs service is available. If in doubt it is advisable to contact the US Coast Guard on VHF Channel 16 and ask for instructions.

All yachts from a foreign port must report their arrival to US Customs immediately by telephone. Only the captain may disembark to make this report. After answering various questions about the vessel, its crew and itinerary, the captain will be told by a customs officer what to do next. US registered boats are usually told to proceed to their destination, but foreign yachts are normally inspected by customs.

South Florida (Miami Customs District)
All yachts arriving in Southern Florida in ports and marinas from Fort Pierce south and around the coast up to and including Ft Myers may call (800) 432-1216. This includes the Fort Pierce Area, Fort Lauderdale Area, West Palm Beach Area, Miami Area, Marco Island and Key West Area.

Customs telephone numbers for other states:
Alabama: Mobile (334) 441-5111, (504) 441-5895.
Alaska: Anchorage (907) 271-6309, (907) 271-6313, Juneau (907) 586-7211, Ketchikan (907) 225-2254, Sitka (907) 747-3374, Skagway (907) 983-2325, Valdez (907) 835-2355, Wrangell (907) 874-3415.
California: Los Angeles (310) 514-6013, (310) 514-6083, (310) 980-3300, San Diego (619) 557-5370, (619) 662-7209, San Francisco (415) 782-7423, (415) 782-9424/5, San Luis Obispo (805) 595-2381.
Connecticut: Bridgeport (203) 367-9487 & 9489, (800) 973-2867.
Delaware: (800) 743-7416 both places, also Dover (215) 596-1972, Wilmington (302) 573-6191.
Florida: Fernandina Beach (904) 261-6154, Ft Myers (941) 225-0041, Jacksonville (St Augustine) (904) 360-5020, Panama City (850) 785-4688, Pensacola (904) 432-6811, Pt Canaveral (407) 783-2066, Pt Manatee (941) 729-9301, St Petersburg (727) 536-7311, Tampa (813) 228-2358.
Georgia: Brunswick (912) 262-6692, Savannah (912) 232-7507, (912) 652-4400, (912) 966-0557.
Illinois: Chicago (312) 894-2900.
Louisiana: (504) 589-3771 all places, also New Orleans (504) 589-6804, Baton Rouge (504) 0261, Gramercy (504) 869-3765, Lake Charles (318) 439-5512, Morgan City (504) 384-6658.
Maine: Portland (207) 780-3228.
Maryland: Baltimore (410) 962-7986, (800) 973-2867.
Massachusetts: Boston (617) 737-2380, (800) 937-2867.
Michigan: Detroit (313) 226-3140, Grand Rapids (616) 456-2515, Port Huron (810) 985-9512, Sault Ste Marie (906) 632-2631 & 7221.
Minnesota: Baudette (218) 634-2803, Crane Lake (218) 933-2321, Duluth (218) 720-5203, Ely (218) 365-3262, Grand Marais (218) 387-1148 (May–October), Grand Portage (218) 475-2244,

International Falls (218) 283-2541, Warroad (218) 386-2796.
Mississippi: (800) 973-2867 both places, also Gulfport (601) 864-6794, Pascagoula (601) 762-7311.
New Jersey: Newark (201) 645-6561/ 2257/ 3762 & 2552, Perth Amboy (908) 442-0414 & 0416. (If one arrives in New Jersey south of the Manasquan Inlet contact Customs, Philadelphia, Pennsylvania office.)
New York: New York City: (6 World Trade Center) (212) 466-2901 (Pier 92 North River 0800–1600 only) (212) 399-2901, (Rosebank Staten Island) (718) 816-0469, Albany (518) 431-0200, (800) 827-2851, Buffalo (800) 927-5015, (716) 551-4311, Ogdensburg (800) 827-2851.
North Carolina: Morehead City (919) 726-5845/3561/2034, Wilmington (910) 343-4616.
North Dakota: Pembina (701) 825-6551.
Ohio: Cleveland (440) 267-3600, Toledo-Sandusky (888) 523-2628 (419) 259-6424, (419) 625-0022.
Oregon: Astoria (800) 562-5943, (503) 325-5541, Coos Bay (541) 267-6312, Newport (541) 265-6456, Portland no service, call Astoria.
Pennsylvania: Philadelphia (215) 597-4648, (215) 596-1971 (800) 973-2867.
Rhode Island: Newport (401) 847-2744, Providence (401) 941-6326.
South Carolina: Charleston (843) 723-1272.
Texas: (800) 973-2867 for most Texan ports, also Brownsville (956) 831-4121, (956) 548-2744, Freeport, Galvestan & Houston (713) 671-1100, (407) 975-2062, Port Arthur (409) 727-0285, Corpus Christi, Port Aransas, Port Lavaca, Port O'Connor & Rockport (512) 888-3352.
Virginia: Alexandria (703) 557-1950, Newport News (757) 245-6470, Norfolk (757) 441-6741, Richmond (804) 226-9675.
Washington: (800) 562-5943 for all Washington ports, also Aberdeen (360) 532-2030, Bellingham (360) 734-5463, Blaine (360) 332-6318, Everett (425) 259-0246, Friday/Roche Harbors (360) 378-2080, Longview (360) 425-3710, Neah Bay (206) 645-2311, Olympia (253) 593-6338, Point Roberts (360) 945-2314, Port Angeles (360) 457-4311, Port Townsend (360) 385-3777, Seattle (206) 593-6338, Tacoma (253) 593-6338, Vancouver (Canada) (604) 278-1825 & 7422.
Wisconsin: Green Bay (920) 496-0606, Milwaukee (414) 571-2875, Racine (414) 633-0286.

Procedure on arrival

The US Coast Guard have the power to board any vessel within US territorial waters and they frequently do this, particularly off Florida. They can also board any US flag vessel anywhere in the world. All vessels entering the 12 mile territorial waters must fly the Q flag.

On arrival everyone must remain on board until clearance is completed, except for the captain going ashore to report the arrival of the yacht. After doing this he or she must return on board. Failure to follow the correct procedure on arrival can lead to a substantial fine and seizure of the offending vessel.

US registered yachts: On arrival in the USA from a foreign port all US yachts must report their arrival to customs immediately, and also report any merchandise acquired abroad that is subject to duty. If an inspection is required, the customs officer will direct the yacht to an inspection area. Otherwise, US yachts are not obliged to make formal entry provided they are not engaged in trade or are violating any laws. US yachts are not forbidden from cruising in Cuba, but if they do not obtain a licence from the US Treasury Department they may experience difficulties when returning to the USA. The treasury licence allows the crew to spend money in Cuba. Lacking a licence the captain may have to prove to US officials that he or she has not spent any money in Cuba and received docking there free of charge paid for by a Cuban sponsor. Yachts returning to the USA from Cuba can expect to be boarded. The amount of difficulties reported by US yachts varies and seems to depend on individual officials. One solution to this might be to leave Cuba for another country such as the Bahamas and make one's entry into the USA from there. Cuban officials will co-operate and not stamp US passports. On leaving Florida for Cuba, it is mandatory to notify the US Coast Guard and obtain clearance for crossing the security zone into Cuban waters. Customs do not have to be notified when US boats leave for a foreign port, although as most countries require the last port clearance for their own entry procedure, it is advisable to obtain this before leaving the USA.

Foreign yachts: The captain must report the arrival of the yacht to customs immediately and make formal entry within 48 hours. Documents needed include registration papers, a declaration of both ship's stores and crew's possessions, last port clearance, and a crew list. Clearance must be completed with customs, immigration, health and agriculture. Sometimes the customs officer performs some or all of these other duties. On departure from the USA, yachts must clear out with customs.

Cruising licence

Certain countries are eligible for a cruising licence, which exempts them from having to clear in and out at any subsequent US port after entry has been made in the first port of entry. The licence is obtained from the US customs port director on arrival and is valid for up to one year. After expiry, another licence may only be issued after the vessel has left for a foreign port and returned from a foreign port at least 15 days since the previous licence expired. The countries to which this applies are Argentina, Australia, Austria, Bahamas, Belgium, Bermuda, Canada, Denmark, Germany, Finland, France, Greece, Honduras, Ireland, Italy, Jamaica, Liberia, Netherlands, New Zealand, Norway, Sweden, Switzerland, Turkey and Great Britain (including Turks and Caicos, St Vincent and the Grenadines, the Cayman Islands, British Virgin Islands, St Kitts and Nevis and Anguilla). This list is subject to change and it includes countries with which the USA has reciprocal arrangements.

Foreign yachts not eligible for a cruising licence must buy a US$25 user fee decal. These foreign yachts must also obtain a permit and clearance before proceeding to each subsequent US port.

The US authorities require that all vessels that have 406 MHz EPIRBs on board, must have these registered and be able to show proof of such registration. Those who do not comply must register their EPIRB on arrival.

Customs

Hunting and sporting firearms may be brought into the USA, provided they are taken out again on departure with any unspent ammunition. All other firearms and ammunitions are subject to restrictions and require an import permit from the Bureau of Alcohol, Tobacco and Firearms (ATF), US Treasury Dept, Washington DC 20520.

Returning US citizens do not require an import permit for firearms they have taken out of the country; however, this previous export must be proven by registering the firearms before departure with either customs or the ATF.

Cats and dogs must be free of diseases communicable to man. Vaccination against rabies is not required for cats and dogs arriving from rabies-free countries. Otherwise, dogs must have a valid rabies vaccination certificate.

Pet birds may be brought in, but will be subject to at least 30 days quarantine on arrival at the owner's expense in a Department of Agriculture facility. These facilities are only available in New York, Miami, San Ysidro, Honolulu, Hidalgo and

Los Angeles, and bird owners must enter at one of these six ports of entry. The quarantine must be arranged in advance and the quarantine fee should be paid not later than on arrival.

Further details can be obtained from the US Department of Treasury, US Customs Service, Washington DC 20229, who publish special leaflets: *Importing a Pet Bird, Pets, Wildlife.*

A foreign visitor may import a pleasure boat into the USA free of duty if it is for his or her personal use. Duty must be paid within one year of the date of importation if the boat is sold or offered for sale or charter in the USA. Boats entered for alterations or repairs, as samples for taking orders or as professional equipment and tools of the trade, may be entered without payment of duty as temporary importation under bond. The length of stay is normally one year and cannot exceed three years.

Immigration

All nationalities require a visa obtained in advance, except Canadians and Mexicans, who require only proof of their citizenship.

Fees

There are no charges for overtime inspections performed by US customs.

There are fees for formal entry, permit to proceed and clearance.

US pleasure craft and foreign yachts without a cruising licence and longer than 30 ft (9 m) LOA must pay an annual fee of US$25 for a user fee decal. In some cases purchase of the decal by boats eligible for a cruising licence may be cheaper than paying individual entry fees.

Restrictions

It is prohibited to import many food and plant products and yachts are subject to an agricultural inspection on arrival, including those arriving in the US mainland from Hawaii, Puerto Rico and the US Virgin Islands. Meat and meat products, fresh produce and plants are among the items normally confiscated. Bakery products, cured cheeses and canned meat are generally admissible.

Also restricted is the import of any wildlife and fish which are considered an endangered species by the USA, or any of their products. This includes tortoise shell jewellery, leather, whalebone and ivory, coral, skins and furs.

Foreign yachts may not charter coastwise in the United States and this includes fishing trips. Foreign vessels may carry charter guests when leaving for a foreign destination or when arriving from a foreign port.

Fishing licence

Licences are required for fishing by the states of Washington and Alaska. There are daily and annual catch limits described in the regulations for each area. Licences are available through most marine service outlets, fuel docks, sporting goods and hardware stores. The approximate cost is as follows: *Washington:* non-resident annual licence US$18. *Alaska:* non-resident annual licence US$36, non-resident 2 week licence US$20.

An Alaska Fish and Game Licence is required for fishing in National Parks such as Misty Fiords and Glacier Bay.

Pacific Northwest

The Vessel Traffic Service (VTS) on VHF Channel 14 provides a useful service in the Juan de Fuca Strait which is often fogbound and always very busy with traffic.

Visibility is often poor in the Pacific Northwest region, so radar and Loran are useful.

Facilities

Yachting facilities throughout the United States are of a high standard. There are marinas practically everywhere and the only objection visiting sailors might have are the high docking fees. Fortunately almost everywhere there is also a place to anchor at little or no cost and in some ports municipal marinas, docks or moorings are priced at a level affordable by those cruising on a restricted budget.

Provisioning everywhere in the USA is good, fuel is cheap and widely available and most ports have fuelling docks which often also have water. Marine equipment is available in most places, although the selection depends on how much local demand there is.

Repair facilities vary from place to place, being best in major yachting centres. There are too many to mention, but on the East Coast the most important centres where the whole range of repair facilities are available are the areas around the following cities: Miami, Fort Lauderdale, Beaufort/Morehead City, Baltimore, City Island (New York), Newport, Marblehead. On the West Coast: San Diego, Newport Beach, San Francisco, Seattle. In between these places there are countless smaller ports, where one can find boatyards, chandleries and all kinds of workshops.

Further Reading

The Department of the Treasury, US Customs Service, Washington DC 20229, publish leaflets on the various import restrictions, as well as details on import duty.

Charlie's Charts of The US Pacific Coast
Cruising Ports: California to Florida via Panama
The Intracoastal Waterway
A Cruising Guide to the New England Coast
A Cruising Guide to the Chesapeake
A Cruising Guide to the Florida Keys
A Cruising Guide to the Maine Coast
Embassy Guide to the Atlantic Coast

Websites

www.customs.ustreas.gov/travel/vessel.htm (US Customs)
www.state.gov/services.html (US State Department links)
www.torresen.com (List of yacht clubs)

7 South America

The South American continent provides the extremes of cruising conditions, from the trade wind-cooled Caribbean islands of Venezuela to the spectacular wilderness of Tierra del Fuego and the Chilean fjords. The most popular cruising ground for foreign yachts is the Caribbean coast, while other parts of the continent are usually visited by cruising boats as a detour on their way to somewhere else.

Many cruising yachts visit Brazil on their way to the Caribbean, either from the Canaries, Cape Verdes or West Africa, or else on their way north from South Africa. A few yachts have navigated the mighty Amazon, but north-eastern Brazil is the most popular destination, with Carnival in Bahia the main attraction, a worthy substitute for the more famous one in Rio de Janeiro, which some yachts manage to include in their itinerary. Only a few venture further south than Rio, usually on their way to Tierra del Fuego, an area which is gaining in popularity as a cruising destination in its own right. For a return to warmer climes, a sail up the west coast of South America has the advantage of favourable wind and current, although there are few cruising opportunities north of Chile. The desert-like coast of Peru is bare and unappealing, while Ecuador's only attractive area is that surrounding Guayaquil.

Sailing is not a very popular pastime in South America and the largest local boating communities are found in major centres such as Rio de Janeiro, Santos, Montevideo, Buenos Aires, Mar del Plata, Valparaiso, Callao and Guayaquil. This is also where most repair and other yachting facilities are concentrated. Unfortunately these do not coincide with the cruising areas popular with visiting yachts. For most South American destinations one should aim to carry all essential spares and be prepared to be quite self-sufficient. The one notable exception is Venezuela, whose popularity among cruising yachts sailing down from the Lesser Antilles has stimulated the development of marinas, boatyards and other facilities geared specifically for visiting yachts. Another attraction of this area is that it is very rarely affected by hurricanes, making it a good place to spend the summer season.

ARGENTINA

Argentina shares the southern tip of South America with Chile, the Andes mountains forming a natural border between the two countries. Argentine scenery varies from the high Andes and the oases in their foothills where the Spanish first settled, to the forests and plains of the north, the vast central pampas, and remote Patagonia in the south.

Not many cruising yachts brave the elements to visit Argentina, but those who do are attracted to the challenging wilderness of the Magellan Straits and Tierra del Fuego. Yachts coming from the north can get a taste of Argentina in Buenos Aires and the resorts in the Rio de la Plata estuary, where most yachting facilities are concentrated. There are only a few ports along Argentina's long coastline and there is little to see between the Rio de la Plata and the Straits of Magellan, with the notable exception of Mar del Plata, which has a thriving sailing community and facilities to match.

Country Profile

When the Incas tried to push south from the Andes, the Indians who already lived in the area prevented them expanding any further. The Indians were no more welcoming to the Spaniard Juan de Solis, who landed in present-day Argentina in 1516 and was killed by them. Magellan paid a brief visit in 1520, before his voyage to the Pacific through the straits that bear his name. Early settlement proved difficult due to Indian hostility, causing Buenos Aires, which was founded in 1535, to be abandoned for nearly fifty years. Expeditions were made into the country from Peru and Chile, and eventually towns were founded in the eastern foothills of the Andes.

From the mid-sixteenth century, Peru ruled over all Spanish possessions in South America, but Buenos Aires was not considered important and all trade went via Panama and the Caribbean. At the end of the eighteenth century the Viceroyalty of Rio de la Plata was formed and Argentine confidence

Map 11: South America

Practical Information

LOCAL TIME: GMT – 3

BUOYAGE: IALA B

CURRENCY: Nuevo peso on a par with the US dollar. Cash payments in the latter are usually accepted.

BUSINESS HOURS
Banks: 1000–1500 Monday to Friday. Government offices: central area 0700–1300 Monday to Friday; southern regions 1000–1700 Monday to Friday. Winter 1230–1930 Monday to Friday. Shops: 0900–1900 Monday to Friday, midday Saturdays. Many close for siesta and reopen around 1700. Shopping centres and supermarkets 1000–2200 Monday to Saturday.

ELECTRICITY: 220 V, 50 Hz

PUBLIC HOLIDAYS
1 January: New Year's Day
Holy Thursday, Good Friday
1 May: Labour Day
25 May: Anniversary of 1810 Revolution
10 June: Malvinas Day

20 June: Flag Day
9 July: Independence Day
17 August: Anniversary of José de San Martin's death
12 October: Columbus Day
8 December: Immaculate Conception
25 December: Christmas Day
31 December: New Year's Eve

Dates in italics will be moved to the following Monday.

EVENTS
The days before Día de la Tradición, 10 November: music and gaucho parades. 30 December: ticker tape parade in Buenos Aires.

COMMUNICATIONS
ENTEL offices: international telephone calls, cables, telex. Entel office, Av. Corrientes 705, Buenos Aires, open 24 hours. International calls also from main post office and public phones with DDI sign (DDN for national calls only). Phonecards are sold by Telefonica or Telecom.
Post office: 0800–2000 Monday to Friday, 0800–1300 Saturday. Corner of Sarmiento

and Leandro Alem, Buenos Aires. Poste Restante, State Railways Building, Av. Maipu 4, Puerto Nuevo district 0800–2000.
Emergency: Police dial 101.
There are frequent international flights from Buenos Aires. There are regular flights from Buenos Aires to all major cities in Argentina, including Ushuaia.

MEDICAL
British Hospital, Buenos Aires, Perdriel 74. *Tel.* 4309-6400.
German Hospital, Pueyrredon 1640. between Calle Berruti and Calle Juncal. *Tel.* 4827-7000.

DIPLOMATIC MISSIONS
In Buenos Aires:
Australia: Villanueva 1400. *Tel.* 4777-6580.
Canada: Tagle 2828. *Tel.* 4805-3032.
France: Cerrito 1399. *Tel.* 4819-2930.
New Zealand: Carlos Pellegrini 1427. *Tel.* 4328-0747.
United States: Avenida Colombia 4300, near Palermo Park. *Tel.* 4777-4533.
UK: Luis Agote 2412/52. *Tel.* 4576-2222.

grew after repulsing British attacks early in the nineteenth century. In 1816 independence from Spain was declared and José de San Martín led an Argentine army to free first Chile and then Peru. Despite conflict between the central government and the provinces, eventually federalism triumphed, and in the mid-nineteenth century a federal system was established, which still continues today.

The 1930s saw Argentina become one of the world's wealthiest countries, a prosperity based mainly on cattle, and trade made Buenos Aires one of the world's leading cities. It was largely an elite that enjoyed this affluence and popular discontent led to General Juan Perón becoming President in 1946, his popularity based on an alliance between the army and the working classes. During his rule, and aided by his flamboyant wife Evita, living conditions were improved for the lower classes. However, the military mounted a coup in 1955 and thereafter the country suffered political violence and economic decline. Various regimes succeeded one another, and Perón briefly returned as President. Finally, a military junta took power, establishing a repressive rule, during which thou-

sands of people disappeared. Continuing economic problems and defeat in the Falklands war in the early 1980s brought pressure for democracy. Parliamentary democracy returned to Argentina in 1983 accompanied by a gradual rapprochement with the United Kingdom as well as some modest steps towards reconciliation with the Falklands under the leadership of President Carlos Menem. He was succeeded in 1999 by Fernando de la Rua.

Argentina is a rich farming country, and 50 per cent of export earnings still come from agriculture and livestock, although the manufacturing sector is also developing. The government has implemented a privatisation programme and there has been some economic improvement after the 1980s crisis although high inflation and unemployment are still causes of popular discontent.

The population numbers 37.5 million. In the Buenos Aires province people are mostly of European origin, while in other provinces they are mestizos, a mixture of Spanish and Indian. Few pure Indians are left, most having been either absorbed or killed in wars with the early settlers. Spanish is the official language, although its pronunciation and some vocabulary are different to Castilian Spanish. English, French and Italian are also spoken. The majority are Roman Catholic. The capital is the sprawling city of Buenos Aires, lying on Rio de la Plata, into which flow the Parana and Uruguay rivers.

The Argentine climate ranges from subtropical in the north to cold temperate in Tierra del Fuego. The central zone is temperate, while Buenos Aires is hot and humid, the summer months December to February being the hottest. In Rio de la Plata the prevailing winds in summer are easterly, while SW winds are more common in winter. They are often accompanied by pamperos, violent SW squalls that affect most of Argentina's coastal waters.

Entry Regulations

Ports of entry
Buenos Aires 34°36′S 58°22′W, Mar del Plata 30°01′S 57°32′W, Puerto Madryn 42°46′S 65°03′W, Puerto Deseado 47°45′S 65°54′W, Santa Cruz 50°80′S 68°23′W, Rio Gallegos 51°36′S 68°58′W, Ushuaia 54°49′S 68°17′W.

Procedure on arrival
The ports of entry listed above are a selection only, as foreign yachts may use any Argentine port to clear in.

Yachts arriving from overseas must clear with the following authorities: naval authority (Prefectura Naval Argentina) where the ship's documents have to be presented, customs (aduanas) and immigration (migraciones).

Buenos Aires: Port control should be contacted on VHF Channel 16 for instructions on where to berth for clearance in the busy commercial harbour. After the compulsory quarantine inspection, the customs and immigration formalities are normally completed ashore. Sufficient time should be allowed for the long trip up the Plate River. A good place to stop on arrival is at the Yacht Club Argentino, reached via a buoyed channel. Formalities are completed at Prefectura Naval.

Mar del Plata: Boats should proceed to the marina, where both Yacht Club Argentino and Club Nautico are located. Either club will help with formalities. Yachts are first cleared by a health officer, followed by customs and Prefectura Naval, whose offices are in town. When clearing out, the captain must again visit the Prefectura Naval office.

Ushuaia: Visiting boats usually moor at the ASAFYN dock on the east side of the harbour. Port control should be contacted on Channel 16 as one enters the harbour. An immigration official will be sent to visit the boat. For customs it is necessary to visit the main office in the commercial harbour. Those who intend to sail north through the Beagle Channel must also clear in and out with the Chilean Navy at Puerto Williams, if continuing into Chilean waters. Those who need Chilean visas can obtain them at the Chilean consulate in Ushuaia, situated on the corner of Calle Maipu and Kuanip.

Customs
Firearms must be declared to customs.

Animals must be inspected on arrival by a veterinary health officer and must have rabies vaccination certificates.

Foreign flagged yachts are allowed to be temporarily imported for a maximum period of six months. This can be extended by leaving Argentina for a short period, such as to Uruguay or Chile.

Immigration
Citizens of neighbouring South American countries need only identity cards not passports.

No visas are required for nationals of West European countries, Canada, USA, Algeria, Barbados, Bolivia, Brazil, Chile, Colombia, Costa Rica, Dominica, Dominican Republic, Ecuador, El Salvador, Guatemala, Honduras, Hungary, Israel, Jamaica (30 days only), Japan, Mexico, Nicaragua, Paraguay, Peru, Poland, Turkey, Uruguay and Yugoslavia (Serbia and Montenegro). A three-month stay is allowed, which can be extended for another month by immigration.

Nationals of the following countries must obtain a visa before arrival: Australia, Cyprus, Guyana, Iceland, Morocco, New Zealand, Panama, South Africa, South Korea, Trinidad and Tobago, Venezuela.

One's passport should be carried at all times if travelling inland.

Health
Malaria prophylaxis is recommended, although there is no risk in some areas. Polio and measles vaccinations are recommended.

Fees
Overtime is not charged, except by immigration if called outside of office hours. There are port fees in commercial harbours.

Procedure on departure

Boats sailing from Argentina to the Falklands (Malvinas) should make this clear when completing departure formalities as, technically, as far as the Argentine authorities are concerned, they will not leave Argentina and therefore do not need to clear out. Each boat must check in regularly with the Argentine Navy on an agreed SSB frequency while sailing anywhere in Argentine waters. Sailing to the Falklands is no longer penalised, but on re-entering Argentine territorial waters the naval authorities should be informed of this at the earliest opportunity.

Restrictions

The naval bases of Mar del Plata and Puerto Belgrano (38°54′S 62°06′W) are prohibited areas.

Fishing is only permitted if in possession of a valid permit. The open season for fishing is November to February or March.

Facilities

Most yachting facilities are concentrated around Buenos Aires, where there are several resorts with yacht clubs in the Rio de la Plata estuary, such as San Isidro and Olivos. In Buenos Aires, both Yacht Club Argentino and Yacht Club Puerto Madero have marinas most conveniently located to visit the Argentinian capital. Visitors are offered one-week free docking. There are good facilities available and also a good range of marine supplies in Buenos Aires. A yacht club with good facilities is at San Fernando, 20 miles upriver from the capital, where there is a boatyard offering an excellent range of services.

Yacht Club Argentino also has a base at Mar del Plata, where it shares the inner basin of the large harbour (Puerto de Yachting) with three other clubs. Visiting sailors are very welcome here and the facilities in this large fishing port are very good, with excellent facilities and provisioning; there are good repair facilities but limited haulout facilities. This is the best place to prepare the boat for a southbound voyage and it is also a good base from which to visit inland Argentina as it has frequent flights to Buenos Aires and other destinations. Only basic facilities are available at Puerto Madryn and Puerto Deseado.

Provisioning outside of the Buenos Aires area is adequate and for yachts heading south a convenient place to reprovision is at Río Gallegos, capital of Santa Cruz province.

There is good provisioning, fuel, banks as well as LPG in Ushuaia in Tierra del Fuego, the southernmost town in Argentina. There are some repair facilities and several supermarkets. Fuel can be bought from the fuel depot on the west side of the harbour. Visiting sailors are welcome at the dock belonging to ASAFYN (Water Sports Association) whose secretary is the best source on any local information.

Further Reading

South Atlantic Coast of South America
South American Handbook
South America on a Shoestring

Websites

www.setur.gov.ar (Ministry of Tourism)
www.cibernautica.com.ar (Waypoints and charts for Uruguay and Argentina)

BRAZIL

Brazil covers nearly half the area of South America and shares borders with all of the countries except Chile and Ecuador. This vast and varied country is a land of plateaux and plains, huge rivers, rain forests and desert. Much of the interior is still unexplored, although the days of undiscovered Brazil are numbered and the rain forests of the Amazon are threatened with destruction. This unique world of incredible flora and fauna where aboriginal tribes still live a life that has not known change for thousands of years is now on the threshold of extinction.

Brazilian culture is a rich mixture of European, African and Latin American, all of which can be seen in its world-famous Carnival. It is this Carnival which brings many sailors to Brazil, those who arrive from the north sailing for Salvador in Bahia, while those coming from the south have the opportunity to see the greatest show of them all in Rio de Janeiro. In between these two cities, to the north as well as to the south, stretches a long coastline of varied scenery and just as varied climate and weather conditions. There are interesting places to explore all along the coast, but perhaps the best cruising ground is the area between São Sebastião Island and Rio de Janeiro, which has

Salvador da Bahia.

many protected anchorages and attractive scenery, slightly marred by the increasing number of oil rigs. The River Amazon also has an appeal for some cruising sailors and it can be navigated for well over one thousand miles giving the opportunity to see some of the interior of this huge country. For many sailors the first taste of Brazil lies 250 miles offshore on the island of Fernando de Noronha, while another Brazilian outpost in the Atlantic is better avoided, the St Peter and St Paul rocks near the equator, where landing is only possible in the calmest of weathers.

Country Profile

Brazil's first contact with Europe was in 1500 when the Portuguese Pedro Alvares Cabral made landfall, thinking at first it was India. He called it the island of Santa Cruz, not guessing that it was part of the same continent discovered by Columbus further north. Later the country got its present name from the hardwood 'brazil' found in its forests. Portugal developed trading posts along the coast as well as establishing sugar and spice plantations. Efforts to enslave the local inhabitants failed – they either died or fled – and West Africans were brought over to work on the plantations instead. By the seventeenth century Brazil was the largest sugar producer in the world. Then gold and diamonds were discovered, and a flood of people arrived moving inland to the mines. Gradually settlements were developed further afield and the frontiers expanded.

When Napoleon occupied Portugal, the Portuguese Royal Family fled to Brazil. After Napoleon's defeat, the King's son Dom Pedro I remained in Brazil and became Emperor on the proclamation of Brazil's independence from Portugal in 1822. Despite wars with Argentina and Uruguay, coffee and rubber exports helped prosperity slowly grow. Following an army coup in 1889, a republic was proclaimed.

Brazil's twentieth-century history has been troubled by economic crises, military coups and dictatorships. Being on the side of the Allies in the Second World War favoured the economy. Reformist governments ruled from 1956, despite

Practical Information

LOCAL TIME: GMT – 3. Summer time GMT – 2 (October to March). Fernando de Noronha GMT – 2.

BUOYAGE: IALA B

CURRENCY: Real (RI) of 100 centavos (introduced 1994).

BUSINESS HOURS
Banks: 1000–1630 Monday to Friday.
Business: 0900–1800 Monday to Friday. The lunch break is normally between 1200 and 1500.
Shops: 0900–1830/1900 Monday to Friday, 0900–1300 Saturday. Government offices: 0800–1200/1400–1800 or 0800–1700 Monday to Friday.

ELECTRICITY: 220/110 V, 60 Hz

PUBLIC HOLIDAYS
1 January: New Year's Day
6 January: Epiphany
February Carnival (Mardi Gras)
Good Friday, Easter Monday
21 April: Tiradentes Day
1 May: Labour Day
Corpus Christi
Ascension
7 September: Independence Day
12 October: Our Lady of Aparecida Day
1 November: All Saints' Day
2 November: All Souls' Day

15 November: Proclamation of the Republic
19 November: Flag Day
25 December: Christmas Day

EVENTS
Carnival starts on Friday night, four days before Ash Wednesday, and is celebrated throughout the following days and much of the nights as well. Although Rio Carnival is the most famous, it is celebrated all over Brazil.

COMMUNICATIONS
International operator 000111.
International calls can be made from state telephone company offices, hotels and post offices.
There is a 40 per cent tax on international communications.
Post office (Correios), open 0800–1800 Monday to Friday, 0800–1200 Saturday. Central PO, Rua Primeiro de Março 64, Rio. There are frequent international flights from Rio de Janeiro, São Paolo and Salvador, also a wide network of internal flights.

POLTUR
This is a special police unit set up to assist foreign visitors. In Rio de Janeiro the office is at: Avenida Afrânio de Melo Franco, Leblon. It is open 24 hours.

MEDICAL
Rio Health Collective, Ave das Americas

4430, Sala 303, Barra da Tijuca, 0900–1400, has English-speaking doctors. *Tel.* 294 0282.
The public health system is poor, although emergency treatment is free. Private treatment is expensive, so medical insurance is recommended.

DIPLOMATIC MISSIONS
Australia: Casa 1, Conjunction 16, Lago Sul SH15Q109 Brasilia. *Tel.* (61) 248-5569.
New Zealand: Rua Hungria 888–6°, São Paulo. *Tel.* (11) 212-2288.

In Rio de Janeiro:
Argentina: Praia de Botafogo 228. *Tel.* 551-5498.
Canada: 1st floor, 46 rua Dona Gerardo. *Tel.* (21) 233-9286.
France: Av. Presidente Antonio Carlos 58. *Tel.* (21) 210-1272.
Germany: Rua Pesidente Carlos de Campos 417. *Tel.* 553-6777.
United States: Av. President Wilson 147. *Tel.* (21) 292-7117.
United Kingdom: 2nd floor, Praia do Flamengo 284. *Tel.* (21) 552-1422.

In Salvador:
United Kingdom: Av. Estados Unidos, 1109. *Tel.* (71) 242-1266.
United States: Av. Presidente Vargas, 1892. *Tel.* (71) 245-6691.

pressure from the powerful multinational companies, until a military coup in 1964 established a military regime. During the 1980s Brazil moved slowly towards democracy and free elections, but her economic and financial problems remain considerable. The question of land has yet to be resolved, as most is concentrated in the hands of a few landowners and the majority of the peasants are landless. Unemployment and inflation are high. The country has extremes of poverty and riches, while a large foreign debt adds to the burden. Brazil's main exports are coffee and orange juice. Industry is slowly developing and there are rich mineral deposits of iron, bauxite and manganese. 1994 saw the signing of an agreement with Argentina, Paraguay and Uruguay to create a common market, Mercosul.

Brazil's 166 million inhabitants are mainly a mixture of Portuguese, African and native Indian, also Dutch and French in the north-east. Nineteenth-century immigration from Germany, Italy, Poland and Japan add to the mix. The indigenous Indian tribes of the interior number over 170 cultural groups and speak as many languages. Portuguese is the official language, although it is slightly different to that spoken in Portugal. Catholicism is the religion of the majority of the population, although there are also Indian and African beliefs, and the Candomblé, Macumba and Xango cults. The capital of the federal republic is Brasilia.

Brazil's climate varies greatly. Most of the northern part of the Brazilian coast is under the influence of NE winds which are strongest in the summer between December and February. The rest is in the SE trade wind belt, which predominates from March to August. During the austral winter months the SE trades have a lot of south in them, and sailing down the coast can be difficult. An eye must be kept on the weather, as the winds can change direction suddenly putting a boat on to a dangerous lee shore.

Entry Regulations

Ports of entry

Manaus (Amazonas state 3°09'S 60°01'W, Belém (Pará) 1°27'S 48°30'W, Macapá (Amapá) 1°18'S 51°01'W, São Luis (Maranhão) 2°30'S 44°18'W, Fortaleza/Mucuripe (Ceara) 3°41'S 38°29'W, Natal (Rio Grande do Norte) 5°47'S 35°11'W, Recife (Pernambuco) 8°04'S 34°52'W, Maceió (Alagoas), 9°40'S 35°44'W, Salvador (Bahia) 12°58'S 38°30'W, Ilheus/Malhado (Bahia) 14°47'S 39°02'W, Vitoria (Espirito Santo) 20°18'S 40°20'W, Rio de Janeiro 22°55'S 43°12'W, Angra dos Reis (Rio de Janeiro) 23°01'S 44°19'W, Itacuruça 22°55'S 43°50'W, Macaé 22°23'S 41°46'W, São Sebastião (São Paulo) 23°48'S 45°23'W, Santos (São Paulo) 23°56'S 46°20'W, Paranaguá (Paraná) 25°30'S 48°31'W, São Francisco do Sul (Santa Catarina) 26°14'S 48°38'W, Florianópolis Island (Santa Catarina), Rio Grande (Rio Grande do Sul) 32°10'S 52°05'W.

Procedure on arrival

Formalities can be very time-consuming everywhere, although officials are generally polite and helpful. Normally yachts are not boarded and the captain has to go into town to find the various offices. The port captain should be visited first (the Brazilian Port Authority is called PORTOBRAS, Empresas Portos do Brasil). After that, one must go to customs and the Federal Police, who deal with immigration. The order of visits is important, as certain forms have to be taken from one office to another. According to a law passed in 1999, all foreign ships are required to clear in and out with the health and quarantine office at every port. This regulation appears to be rarely imposed, nor is the quite substantial quarantine fee collected. A cruising permit (passe de saida) will be issued at the port of entry by the port captain.

Some yachts have reported having to use a special officially approved agent (despachante), whom one is introduced to on arrival. The agent takes passports and ship's papers and does the entry formalities for a fee. This usually only applies to the first entry into the country and also depends on local officials.

After having completed the initial clearance at a port of entry, one has to obtain clearance to the next port, although one is allowed to cruise and stop on the way. One should request clearance to the next port 'with stops' (con escala). At every major port en route one has to visit the port authority and Federal Police offices. This is particularly important when one enters a new state. This clearance is strictly enforced, and failure to do so can lead to on the spot fines of up to US$5000.

Recife: Proceed directly to the Cabanga Yacht Club, which will assist with clearance formalities. The club can only be reached at high water and even then there is a draft restriction of 8 ft (2.5 m).

Salvador: Boats are usually directed to Centro Nautico, which is a marina-type facility next to the ferry terminal and close to the city centre. All offices are close by and the first to be visited is the port authority located in the Navy building immediately to the east of Centro Nautico.

Rio de Janeiro: All clearance formalities must be undertaken in the commercial harbour of Rio de Janeiro, which is not recommended to be entered by yacht, as it is much more convenient to stay in one of the marinas and go to the necessary offices by public transport. Marina Gloria is the most conveniently located for a visiting yacht and the office will help with directions as the various offices are best visited by taxi.

Santos: To clear in, one has to visit various offices in the commercial harbour, but it is better to leave the boat at the Yate Clube de Santos on Ilha de Santo Amaro.

Cabedelo: There is a marina close to Joao Pessoa, capital of Paraíba state. The police visit the marina every day and one can drive with them to check in at Cabedelo where there is also a customs office. The port captain's office must then be visited in Joao Pessoa.

Fernando de Noronha: Although cruising yachts on passage to or from Brazil are now allowed to make a short stop here, this is not an official port of entry. The best place to anchor is in St Anthony Bay just off the breakwater, which provides protection from the dinghy when landing. The port captain's office is close by and he will inspect, but not stamp, passports. Occasionally he will insist on having a valid visa for Brazil, but even without one short visits will be allowed. However, one will need a visa when reaching mainland Brazil. There is a fee to be paid to the National Park based on the number of days one plans to stop. Arriving yachts must clear with the port captain's office and the Guarda Territorial.

Belém: This is the best port to enter Amazonia, but a detailed chart is essential for the Para River, which leads the 80 miles inland to Belém. Visiting boats may use a mooring at the Belém Yacht Club, which will also help with formalities.

Customs

Firearms are retained by customs, until authorisation for their possession is given by the military authorities. The firearms should then be registered with the police. In some places, such as Belém, firearms may be left on board.

Animals need a health certificate. Rabies vaccination is available upon arrival.

After six months the yacht must leave the country or it becomes liable to import tax of about 100 per cent of value.

Immigration

Passports must be valid six months from arrival date except Argentinians and Uruguayans, who only require a national identity card. A three-month permit is issued initially, renewable on request for another three months from the Federal Police on payment of a fee. Visas are not required by nationals of EU countries, Andorra, Argentina, Bahamas, Barbados, Chile, Colombia, Ecuador, Iceland, Liechtenstein, Mexico, Monaco, Morocco, Namibia, Norway, Paraguay, Peru, Philippines, San Marino, Suriname, Switzerland, Trinidad and Tobago, Venezuela and Uruguay. These regulations are meant for visitors arriving by air, and in some ports the authorities insist on everyone having a visa, even nationalities that are normally exempt. It is therefore advisable for everyone arriving by yacht to obtain a visa in advance.

All other nationalities, including Australian, New Zealand, US and Canadian citizens, need to obtain a visa before arrival.

Health

Yellow fever vaccination certificates are required by those who have been within the last three months in Africa, Bolivia, Colombia, Ecuador or Peru. The certificate must not be more than 10 years old. Those who arrive either without a certificate or who have not been vaccinated will have to be vaccinated in Brazil, which is not always done under the most hygienic conditions.

In rural areas especially, there is the risk of malaria, dengue fever, cholera, typhoid, hepatitis and yellow fever, so vaccination or prophylactic treatment is recommended.

Fees

Overtime is charged for clearance outside office hours on weekdays, and all day on weekends. There are harbour fees and light dues. A special fee is payable by those stopping at Fernando de Noronha.

Facilities

Provisioning is better in larger cities, although imported goods are both expensive and difficult to come by. There are strict price controls in an effort to curb inflation. This has led to shortages of essential goods and even rationing. Fresh produce is plentiful in most places. Fuel and water are normally available alongside at fishing docks. Diesel fuel is sometimes diluted with petrol (gasolene), but this is marked on the pump. Also petrol (gasolene) is often diluted with alcohol. Propane is available from Supergasbras depots. For cruising in local waters it is best to buy Brazilian Navy charts, which are available in Rio and Bahia. Charts for the Amazon river are available in Belém.

Yacht clubs are usually welcoming to foreign visitors, with the exception of the Rio Yacht Club, where visitors are not at all welcome. Clubs with a large fleet of yachts, often motor yachts, have good repair facilities or access to them.

There are several anchorages and marinas in Rio de Janeiro, one of the most conveniently situated being Marina Gloria close to Rio's smaller airport. The marina is very crowded with local boats, but space is usually found for visitors. There are repair facilities available as well as a chandlery. Practically everything is available in Rio, but it can take time finding it. There is a fuel dock at Marina Gloria.

Angra dos Reis, close to Rio, has a huge shipyard which also undertakes work on yachts. The repair facilities are excellent. The yard has a social club, shops and banks in the complex. There is also a good marina at Bracuhy, 23 miles from Angra.

The yacht club at Niterói welcomes visitors. There are good repair facilities, chandlery and fuel on the club dock.

Santos is close to São Paolo and has a large club, Yate Clube de Santos, on Ilha de Santo Amaro, the base of a large fleet of power boats. As a result, repair facilities are very good with all kinds of workshops and a good chandlery.

Salvador, the capital of Bahia, is a first port of call for many yachts arriving in Brazil. There is a well-stocked market and adequate repair facilities. Centro Nautico, in the centre of town, is the best place to leave the boat if planning to visit the interior, or enjoy Salvador's unique carnival. There are a number of yacht clubs in and around Salvador, and repair facilities at some of them are very good as they cater for a large local boating community. A marina is under construction in Salvador, close to Centro Nautico. Fuel is available from the yacht club dock immediately to the east. Near Cabedelo there is a boatyard with a slipway at Praia de Jacaré with moorings for yachts. Everything is available locally – fuel, gas, charts, as well as good repair and haul-out facilities. It is also reputed to be a safe place to leave the yacht while visiting the interior.

Natal is a pleasant port on the NE tip of Brazil with a good yacht club and a range of repair facilities. It is a good place to leave from for the Caribbean. At Fortaleza, the Marina Park Hotel has a boatyard with some repair facilities.

Belém is a large city 80 miles inland on the south bank of the Para river. The yacht club gives temporary membership. All services and supplies are available.

On the island of Fernando de Noronha, which is a protected National Park, only basic provisions can be obtained as well as water from the fisherman's building on the dockside. Diesel can be bought from the fuel station a short distance inland.

Further Reading

South Atlantic Coast of South America
South American Handbook
Fodor's Brazil
South America on a Shoestring

Websites

www.embratur.gov.br (Brazilian Tourism Board)
www.brazilinfo.com

CHILE

Chile is a 2600 mile long strip of land between the Andes and the Pacific Ocean, with an average width of rarely more than 100 miles. The northern area is mostly desert, and forms the frontier with Peru, while the crests of the Andes make up the eastern frontier. Around the capital Santiago is a fertile heartland, where most of the population live. To the south are lakes, rivers and forests, down to the southern tip of South America where

lies the notorious Cape Horn, the island of Tierra del Fuego, which Chile shares with Argentina, and the Magellan Straits.

An increasing number of cruising yachts are attracted to the islands and channels in the southern part of Chile, a spectacular area with magnificent fjords and imposing glaciers. The major drawback of this beautiful cruising ground, apart from its remoteness, is the weather, which is rarely pleasant. The best time for exploring this part of the world is at the height of the southern summer, from December to March, when the weather is more settled than at other times. The rest of Chile is rarely visited by foreign yachts, except those on their way to or from the southern fjordland. Chile's offshore possessions in the Pacific, Easter Island and the Juan Fernandez Islands, are dealt with separately.

Country Profile

Remains of a pre-Inca civilisation have been found in the north of Chile. When the Incas expanded their empire from their base high in the Andes, they only reached as far as the centre of present-day Chile, their advance being fiercely resisted by the Araucanian tribes. In 1520 Magellan sailed through the Straits on his voyage that was to prove to all doubters that the earth was round. Tierra del Fuego was named 'Land of Fire' by his sailors who spotted the numerous Indian cooking fires glowing on the shores. Fifteen years later a Spanish expedition from Peru searched unsuccessfully for silver and gold. Don Pedro de Valdivia led a later expedition and founded Santiago, but on pushing further south, he was killed by the Araucanians. The Indians continued to resist Spanish encroachment for three centuries.

Under the rule of the Viceroyalty of Peru, a farming colony developed, although often raided by English and French pirates. In 1810 a revolt was led against Spanish rule and an independent republic was formed in 1818. The first Chilean constitution was drafted in 1833, although internal conflict continued to trouble the newly independent state. Chile's victory in the War of the Pacific (1879–83) fought with Peru and Bolivia over the northern desert area which was rich in nitrates, brought only some Chileans considerable wealth. In the early twentieth century the decline of the nitrate trade contributed to an economic crisis, which coupled with continuing social inequalities, led in the 1920s to the rise of powerful socialist

Practical Information

LOCAL TIME: GMT – 4. Summer time GMT – 3 October to March.

BUOYAGE: IALA B

CURRENCY: Peso ($)

BUSINESS HOURS
Banks: 0900–1400 Monday to Friday.
Business: 0830–1230, 1400–1800 Monday to Friday.
Shops: 1030–1930, Monday to Friday, 0930–1330 Saturday (Santiago).
Government offices: 0800–1300, 1500–1800 Monday to Friday.

ELECTRICITY: 220 V, 50 Hz

PUBLIC HOLIDAYS
1 January: New Year's Day
Holy Week (two days)

1 May: Labour Day
21 May: Navy Day
15 August: Assumption
18–19 September: Independence Days
12 October: Discovery of America
1 November: All Saints' Day
8 December: Immaculate Conception
25 December: Christmas Day

COMMUNICATIONS
International phone calls, fax and telegraph from ENTEL.
Santiago post office open 0900–1800 Monday to Friday. 0900–1230 Saturday.
There are regular flights from Santiago international airport to European and American capitals. Lan-Chile and Ladeco Air operate domestic flights to the main cities and also to Easter Island. There are airports near the ports of Iquique, Puerto Montt and Valdivia.

DIPLOMATIC MISSIONS
In Santiago:
Australia: Gertudis Echenique 420, Las Condes. *Tel.* (2) 228-5065.
Argentina: Miraflores 285. *Tel.* 331-076.
Canada: 10th flr, Avenida Humada 11, Casilla 427. *Tel.* (2) 696-2256.
New Zealand: Avenida Isidora Goyenechea 3516, Las Condes. *Tel.* (2) 231-4204.
United Kingdom: Avenida El Bosque Norte 0125. *Tel.* 231-3737.
United States: Andres Bello 2800, Las Condos. *Tel.* 232-2600.

In Punta Arenas:
Argentina: Consulate at Avenida 21 de Mayo 1278 (open 1000–1400). It is possible to obtain a visa for Argentina here in 24 hours.

---

and communist parties. Government reforms had little success in stabilising the country, and in 1970 a Marxist coalition came to office under Salvador Allende, rapidly polarising the country between right and left. A military coup three years later saw Allende killed and a military junta led by General Pinochet take power, which at the price of severe repression brought some recovery to the economy. In more recent years gradual moves towards democracy have been made and following free elections in 1989 a civilian government was re-established.

Chile remains a leading exporter of copper, as well as other mineral resources. Forestry products are the second largest export. Agriculture, including viniculture, is important, mainly concentrated in the fertile central region.

The population of over 13 million are either of European origin or mestizo, a mixture of Spanish and Indian. In some of the rural and mountain areas, there are still a large number of Mapuche, the original inhabitants of this land. The urban areas are populated mainly by descendants of immigrants who came during the nineteenth century. Spanish is the main language and Roman Catholicism the religion of the majority.

October to April are the warmer summer months, while May to October is colder. The Chilean climate varies considerably according to latitude, being dry and hot in the north, wet and windy in the south. The coastal areas are cooled by the cold Humboldt current. In the south, the most settled weather is between December and March, which is dominated by westerly winds. In this area, northerly winds usually bring rain and poor visibility, while southerlies are accompanied by clear skies.

Entry Regulations

Ports of entry
Arica 18°29'S 70°26'W, Iquique 20°12'S 70°10'W, Mejillones 23°06'S 70°28'W, Antofagasta 23°38'S 70°26'W, Valparaiso 33°01'S 71°38'W, Valdivia 39°48'S 73°14'W, Puerto Montt 41°28'S 72°57'W, Castro 42°29'S 73°46'W, Puerto Natales 51°43'S 72°31'W, Punta Arenas 53°10'S 70°54'W, Puerto Williams 55°56'S 67°37'W.

Procedure on arrival
Foreign vessels arriving directly from a foreign port must immediately contact the port captain (Capitania del Puerto) on Channel 16. No one must disembark until this has been authorised by the maritime authority, whose representative will visit the boat accompanied by immigration (Policia de Investigaciones) and quarantine (Servicio de Salud). Once these formalities have been completed, the captain must visit customs.

Foreign vessels arriving from another Chilean port must immediately contact the port captain on Channel 16, who will inform the captain of the vessel that within two hours he needs to visit the maritime authority office to report his arrival. The Navy insists on a detailed itinerary listing every overnight anchorage. It is advisable to try to contact the naval authorities on HF radio before entering Chilean territorial waters, which both Chile and Peru consider as extending to 200 miles offshore.

Arica: Contact the port captain on Channel 16 and follow berthing instructions.

Valdivia: After entering the Rio Valdivia at Corral, the town of Valdivia, where formalities are completed, lies about 11 miles up the river. It is usually possible to also clear in at Alwoplast, which is only halfway up the river, although occasionally the Navy will insist that a boat comes upriver into Valdivia itself and moors on the dock in front of the port captain's office.

Puerto Williams: Yachts entering the Beagle Channel area should contact the Chilean Navy on VHF Channel 16. Puerto Williams is a naval base, but yachts are welcomed there. Cruising boats are usually told to proceed directly into the small western basin, close to the airport, where there is a concrete dock. Shallow-drafted boats may come on its inside, or tie up alongside the *Micalvi*, a former supply ship, now used as a yacht club by the locals. Officials will visit the boat here, after which the captain must go to the port captain's office to complete formalities. It is essential that those for whom this is the first port of entry into Chile insist on being given the compulsory customs certificate. Those who leave without it will have serious problems when clearing out of Chile.

Customs

Firearms must be declared.

There are no restrictions on animals.

Foreign yachts should obtain a customs exemption certificate on arrival. This is valid for a limited time only and must be renewed before its expiry date.

Yachts are normally allowed to stay up to six months but up to two years is possible.

Aventura III off *Romanche Glacier in southern Chile.*

Immigration

Nationals of West European countries (except France), Australia, Canada, Latin American countries, those of the former Yugoslavia, Hungary, Israel, Japan, South Africa, and the USA do not require visas for short stays. Other nationals may be required to obtain a visa in advance. Visitors are normally given a 90-day stay, which can be renewed for another 90 days. As visa requirements may be changed, it is advisable to check with a Chilean embassy or consulate before arrival.

Cruising permit

A cruising permit is issued to visiting yachts when clearing into Chile. The permit must be presented to officials at every port of call and is usually retained by the port captain until departure. A detailed itinerary must be submitted. Yachts cruising the southern archipelago have found the officials in Castro to be the most cooperative, not insisting on a precise cruising plan and issuing an open permit valid for two or three months provided a designated port was visited at the end of the proposed itinerary.

Procedure on departure

The exit permit (*zarpe*) for vessels leaving either for another Chilean port or a foreign destination must be requested by the captain, who must personally visit the port captain's office 24 hours before the intended departure time. On the day of departure, an official from the port captain's office will bring the permit to the boat. After this, the vessel must leave within one hour, otherwise the exit permit will be cancelled. In practice, the permit may be collected from the office on the day of departure.

No exit permit is necessary if leaving Puerto Williams for Antarctica as, from the Chilean authorities point of view, the vessel will not leave Chilean territorial waters. On the contrary, several boats got into trouble by not going through the correct procedure when leaving Puerto Williams for Ushuaia, in neighbouring Argentina, a routine trip which many boats do on a regular basis.

Restrictions

Access to the Chilean channels without a permit is prohibited. Both the lighthouse keepers and Navy keep an eye on yacht movement. Boats equipped with SSB must report their position to the nearest radio station at 0800 and 2000 local time daily. The frequencies to be used should be ascertained locally as it has been reported that in some areas 2182 kHz was not being monitored and 4146 kHz was being used instead. This requirement is no longer enforced so strictly, although the Navy will monitor the progress of cruising boats and insists on being kept updated on one's progress, primarily for one's own safety.

There are restricted areas in Puerto Chacabuco and Puerto Williams. The port captain must be informed if a yacht wishes to move to another anchorage within those harbours.

Some parts of the Patagonian channels are prohibited to yachts.

Facilities

There are good repair facilities and various workshops in the port area of Valparaiso, which is the port serving Santiago. There is also excellent provisioning in town.

There is a new marina at Algarrobo, near Valparaiso, run by the local yacht club. Because of the difficult entrance, the club launch will guide boats in. There are good facilities including a 25-ton travelift. Valparaiso is one hour away, for provisioning, marine equipment and charts. There are also helpful yacht clubs at Arica, Antofagasta, Caldera and Coquimbo, all of which will help with formalities, repair and leaving the boat if wishing to travel inland.

There are several good supermarkets in Valdivia, which also has the usual range of workshops. A good boatyard and sail loft operated by Alwoplast, upriver from Valdivia, provide a good range of repair services including metalwork, carpentry, fibreglass, rigging as well as haul-out. Yachts may also be left there while touring the interior, or stored, afloat or ashore, between seasons.

Fuel is available in all ports along the coast. There are two new marinas in the south. Marina del Sur in Puerto Montt has all services, including charts, as well as a 40-ton lifting platform. Also in Puerto Montt is Oxxean, a small marina with floating docks, fuel and basic facilities. A new marina has opened in Puerto Cisne (Puyuhuapi) as a supply base for the charter boats going to Laguna St Rafael. All facilities are available at Alwoplast Boatyard, which exports multihulls to the USA and Europe. In the smaller southern ports, fuel is available at Puerto Montt, Castro, Quellan, Chacabuco, Calbuco and Ralun, but as there are no pumps on the dock, it has to be carried in jerrycans. Fuel can also be obtained in Puerto Natales and, occasionally, in Puerto Eden. Those cruising the southern part of Chile must make adequate provision for this when planning their trip, whether north- or southbound. Valdivia has an excellent fuel dock upriver, in front of the bridge. In the south, propane is available in Puerto Montt, Puerto Chacabuco and Puerto Williams.

Provisioning is variable depending on the size of town, but some supplies can be bought in Puerto Montt and Castro. In smaller ports supplies are limited and expensive. There are fresh produce markets with good quality and reasonably priced produce in Valdivia, Puerto Montt and Castro. Even in remoter areas, fresh fruit and vegetables can normally be bought from local farmers, depending on the season. Fishing is excellent everywhere.

In spite of its remoteness, provisioning is surprisingly good at Puerto Williams, where there is a bank, post office, supermarket and fuel. Visitors are welcome at the local yacht club, located in a grounded ship. If cruising the southern channels, one must carry all essential supplies and spares, as these are almost impossible to obtain south of Valdivia. Those who wish to see more of inland Patagonia and do not wish to sail all the way to Punta Arenas are better off if they leave the boat in Puerto Natales. Yachting facilities in Punta Arenas are limited and this, combined with its very poor protection from wind and swell, makes it indeed a place to be visited overland, if at all.

Charts can be obtained from the Chilean Hydrographic Office, which also produces an atlas comprising all necessary charts reduced in size. Also useful for the southern area are a set of the Chilean tide and current tables.

Further Reading

Chile Cruising Guide
South American Handbook
South America on a Shoestring

Websites

www.sernatur.cl (Department of Tourism)
www.chileweb.net (Chile online)
www.telsur.cl/alwoplast (Alwoplast boatyard in Valdivia)

COLOMBIA

Colombia has a coastline on both the Pacific Ocean and the Caribbean Sea. The country is sparsely populated, the majority living on the Caribbean lowlands or in mountain valleys. The eastern part is very remote, linked only by air and river to the rest of the country. The Pacific coast from Ecuador to Buenaventura is a marshy lowland with few settlements and most of the coastal development is on the Caribbean side, which has the large towns of Cartagena, Barranquilla and Santa Marta.

The scenery along the Caribbean coast offers more contrast than any of Colombia's neighbours. From the sand dunes and desert of the Guajira peninsula to the dense forests of Darien, the coast shows an ever-changing face. Not far inland tower the majestic peaks of the Sierra Nevada de Santa Maria crowned by the snow-capped Mount Cristóbal Colón, 18,900 ft (5762 m), which can be seen from far offshore. The contrasts of nature are not the only attractions of this part of the Spanish Main as ashore one is forever reminded of the country's tumultuous past. The forts of Nueva Andalusia and the walled citadel of Cartagena bear witness to the rise and fall of the Spanish Empire.

In spite of persistent reports about the danger of cruising in Colombian waters, because of the risk of being intercepted on the high seas by a drug-running vessel, a determined campaign by the US Coast Guard, whose vessels patrol the Caribbean Sea, has made this area into one of the safest in the world, with no reports of yachts being molested on the high seas, although many have been stopped, and even boarded, by a US Coast Guard vessel. Most cruising boats visiting Colombia do so on their way from the Eastern Caribbean islands to the Panama Canal, while those heading in the opposite direction use Colombia as a convenient stepping stone in their battle with contrary winds and current. The most popular landfall is the historic city of Cartagena, whose picturesque harbour is one of the most attractive ports in the New World. While visiting Cartagena itself appears to be safe, all embassies warn against any inland travel as it is considered far too dangerous.

Also belonging to Colombia are the islands of Providencia and San Andres, visited by boats on their way north from Panama. Some of the cays and reefs further north, such as Serrana, Serranilla and Roncador also belong to Colombia, which maintains a military presence on these cays. Boats

Practical Information

LOCAL TIME: GMT – 5

BUOYAGE: IALA B

CURRENCY: Peso (Col$) of 100 centavos. A maximum of 500 pesos can be exported and not more than 60 Col$ exchanged on departure.
Travellers' cheques are difficult to change, as reportedly there are many forged American Express travellers' cheques in circulation. It is also difficult to change pounds sterling and US dollars are preferred, particularly smaller notes such as US$20 bills.

BUSINESS HOURS
Banks: 0800–1130, 1400–1600 Monday to Friday, some open until 1630 Fridays, except last Friday of the month when they shut at 1130. Some open 0800–1100 Saturday.
Shops: 0900–1230, 1430–1830 Monday to Saturday.
Business: 0800–1200, 1400–1530/1800 Monday to Friday.
Government offices: 0800–1200, 1400–1800 Monday to Friday.

ELECTRICITY: 120 V, 60 Hz

PUBLIC HOLIDAYS
1 January: New Year's Day
*6 January: Epiphany
*19 March: St Joseph
Maundy Thursday, Good Friday
1 May
*Ascension
*Corpus Christi
*Sacred Heart
*29 June: St Peter and St Paul
20 June: Independence Day
7 August: Battle of Bogotá
*15 August: Assumption
*12 October: Discovery Day
*1 November: All Saints' Day
*11 November: (week of celebration) Independence of Cartagena
8 December: Immaculate Conception
25 December: Christmas Day
*When not falling on a Monday, these are observed the following Monday.

COMMUNICATIONS
Empresa Nacional de Telecomunicaciones (ENDT): offices in all main cities for international calls, fax and other services. IDD available in main centres, but otherwise may have to go through the international operator. Phone cards are available.

Collect calls can only be made from private phones. Postal services run by two companies, Avianca and Correos de Colombia.
There are international flights from Bogotá and many internal flights between major cities.

MEDICAL
Emergency treatment in hospitals is free.

DIPLOMATIC MISSIONS
In Bogotá:
Australia: Calle 70 No. 10. *Tel.* 212-6576.
Canada: Carrera 7 No. 115-33. *Tel.* 657-9800.
New Zealand: Carrera 7 No. 73-55. *Tel.* 312-1231.
United Kingdom: Carrera 9 No. 76-49. *Tel.* 317-6690.
United States: Calle 22D-Bis No. 47-51. *Tel.* 315-0811.

In Cartagena:
Canada: Edificio Centro Ejecutivo Bocagrande, Carrera 3. *Tel.* 665-5838.

In Barranquilla:
United States: Calle 77 Carrera 68, Centro Comercial Mayorista. *Tel.* (5) 457-088.

---

that have sought shelter there have been visited by the military, but have been allowed to stay.

Country Profile

Long before Europeans arrived, Caribs lived along the northern coast, while the interior was inhabited by hunters, nomadic tribes, and the Chibchas, skilled goldsmiths who rolled their chief in gold dust every year. The other cultures of the pre-Colombian era also produced amazing goldwork. In 1500 the Spaniards sailed along the northern coast to Panama, and soon afterwards founded the settlements of Santa Marta and Cartagena. Spanish explorers pushed into the interior and Santa Fe de Bogotá was founded in 1538. The initial period of settlement saw strife between rival conquistadors, although some unity was gained in the mid-sixteenth century when the kingdom of Nueva Granada was established. In the eighteenth century this was replaced by a Viceroyalty at Bogotá, independent of the Peruvian Viceroyalty.

Influenced by the French Revolution, an independence movement developed and at the start of the nineteenth century revolts against the Spanish colonial power occurred. When the Spanish government tried to reconquer Venezuela and Nueva Granada, Simón Bolívar raised an army, crossed the Andes and occupied Bogotá. In 1819 the Republic of Gran Colombia was declared, which included today's republics of Colombia, Venezuela and Ecuador, but the latter two soon broke away leaving Nueva Granada alone, to be named Colombia later in the century.

The newly independent country was divided between Conservatives and Liberals, and civil wars and revolts continued throughout the nineteenth century. In 1885 a centralised constitution was imposed by the Conservatives, and this is still in use today. At the turn of the century there was another civil war and eventually the Liberals were defeated. Relative peace followed until 1948 when civil war broke out once again. It was ended in 1957 by a political truce, the two parties agreeing to divide power equally by means of alternative governments until 1978. In recent years, guerilla groups have been active in the country, especially after the Liberals' victory in the 1986 elections and considerable violence occurred during both 1988 and 1989. The 1991 peace talks between government and guerillas collapsed, and sporadic violence still continues in rural areas. The war against the drug barons of Medellin are another violent problem for the government, which is determined to stamp out the production of cocaine.

Agriculture is the most important sector of the economy, although the recent fall of world coffee prices has meant its replacement as the main export by sugar, bananas, cut flowers and cotton. Manufacturing is expanding, as is mining, especially oil and coal, and also precious metals, such as emeralds.

The population is over 33 million, a mixture of European, Indian and African origins. Spanish is the main language, and most are Roman Catholic. English is spoken on Isla de Providencia. Bogotá, at 8690 ft (2650 m), is the capital.

The climate varies according to altitude, the coast being tropical, hot and humid. The NE trade winds cool the coast during the winter months, while the summer has much lighter winds. Hurricanes rarely reach as far south as Colombia.

Entry Regulations

Ports of entry
San Andrés 12°33′N 81°41′W, Cartagena 10°25′N 75°32′W, Barranquilla 10°58′N 74°46′W, Buenaventura 3°54′N 77°05′W. Yachts have also been able to clear in at the following ports: Riohacha 11°33′N 72°55′W, Santa Marta 11°15′N 74°13′W.

Procedure on arrival
Yachts must clear in and out between major ports, and will be given an outward clearance (*zarpe*) for the next port. Visiting yachts must clear in with the port captain in each port. Customs and immigration formalities are completed only in the first and last ports. Yachts clearing in or out of Colombia must use an approved agent to complete the formalities for customs, immigration, port captain and health. On departure, the agent will take the papers and return them with a *zarpe*.
Barranquilla: Arriving yachts should dock wherever possible, then ask for a berthing assignment from the port captain. The yacht clubs have limited space, and anchoring is not possible in the busy river. It may be necessary to come alongside the commercial dock. The port captain's office should be visited first.
Cartagena: There is now a buoyed channel with a minimum depth of 12 ft (4 m) through Boca Grande. The local yacht club, Club Nautico, on the island of Manga, monitors Channel 16. It is possible to berth there or to anchor off. The club will contact an agent who brings the various officials. The agent's fee in 2000 was $60. The agent will also arrange the necessary extensions. Cartagena's port captain will not deal with any yacht captain direct and will insist on the use of an agent. All crew members must visit the immigration office located in the cruise ship terminal, which is best reached by taxi.
Riohacha: One should anchor off the pier and wait to be boarded. If the officers do not come out, the captain should go to customs at the far end of the dock. If there is space on the pier it may be possible to go alongside.
Santa Marta: One should come alongside the eastern dock or anchor south of the dock. Officials prefer to board at the dock.
San Andres/Providencia: Formalities are minimal at these Colombian outposts. The port captain should be contacted on Channel 16. He will recommend the use of an agent for clearance formalities, which must be completed even if coming from mainland Colombia. Visas are not required, nor issued.

Customs
Firearms must be declared.

Animals need a health certificate and an anti-rabies vaccination certificate.

Immigration
Visas are not required for visitors from most countries whose stay does not exceed 60 days; 15 day extensions may be issued by the DAS (Security Police), up to a maximum of a further three months. An exit stamp from the DAS must be obtained on departure.

Visas, if required, can be obtained on arrival, and, especially for those who have retained the services of an agent, there seems to be no difficulty in obtaining one.

Identification must always be carried; as a precaution against theft, authorised copies are acceptable, and the Security Police will witness and photocopy passports and other documents for US$20.

A Colombian cruising permit and visas can be

obtained from any Colombian embassy or consulate in one of the countries in the vicinity, such as Venezuela or Panama. There is a Colombian consulate in Colón in Panama, which is used to dealing with yachts intending to visit Colombia.

Fees

The agent's fee varies between US$60 and US$100 and is negotiable. A deal can sometimes be negotiated with the agent if more than one yacht is cleared in or out at the same time.

Security

Colombia is a major drug-smuggling area, and police and customs are especially active on the north coast, San Andrés Island and in other tourist resorts. Penalties for possession are up to 12 years' imprisonment. Searches are frequent and one should beware of anyone claiming to be a plainclothes policeman. Apparently foreign visitors have also been set up by police with planted drugs, so caution is essential. Walking alone at night is to be avoided as this is dangerous in many towns. The Tourist Office (CNT) will advise on the dangerous areas.

Health

Vaccination against yellow fever is recommended and malaria prophylaxis for the coastal and eastern jungle regions. Cholera is a risk in certain areas. Hepatitis is common.

Facilities

Provisioning is good along the Caribbean coast, particularly in larger ports, where there are both supermarkets and daily fresh produce markets. Fuel is available everywhere. There are excellent repair facilities at Cartagena, where there is a good boatyard with haul-out facilities and a complete range of services. In town, Avenida Don Pedro Heredia is the best place for non-marine hardware. Charts are available from an agent in Calle Larga near Manga. The naval base has a large sail loft and may be persuaded to do repairs. The yacht club is particularly helpful towards visitors and has marina berths.

There are also good repair facilities at Barranquilla with both haul-out and repair services, but the approaches to the port, which lies on the bank of the River Magdalena, are very difficult. Barranquilla is also considered a high security risk area. Very good facilities are also available on San Andrés Island, both in respect of provisioning and repair. Visiting yachts may anchor off and use the facilities of the San Andrés Yacht Club. Facilities are more limited in Providencia, which attracts fewer tourists than San Andrés. Both fuel and water are available on both islands, although at higher prices than on the mainland.

Further Reading

Cruising Guide to the Caribbean
South American Handbook
Fodor's South America
South America on a Shoestring

Website

www.preseidencia.gov.co (Ministry of Culture and Tourism)

ECUADOR

Straddling the equator on the west coast of South America between Peru and Colombia, Ecuador is a country of contrasts between coastal plains and rugged mountains. The lowlands of Costa is the main agricultural region of Ecuador and Guayaquil its principal city. Inland is the high Sierra and the eastern Amazon basin. In the central Sierra highlands is the capital Quito, once co-capital of the 'Tahuantinsuyo' or Inca empire; Spanish conquistadores built modern Quito on the same site.

For cruising sailors Ecuador's main attraction lies several hundred miles offshore in its Archipiélago de Colón, commonly known as the Galapagos Islands. As they form a separate entity and cruising regulations also differ from mainland Ecuador, the Galapagos are described separately in the South Pacific section.

Due to the prevailing winds and currents, the Ecuadorian coast is best cruised from south to north, which most yachts visiting Ecuador rarely do, as usually they sail from the north after having transited the Panama Canal and have to battle against wind and current. The Ecuadorean coast is arid and there are few natural harbours with the notable exception of the estuary of the River Guayas. A convenient stop can be made at Salinas, the westernmost point of Ecuador, where the boat can be left in the care of the local yacht club, while

Practical Information

LOCAL TIME: GMT − 5

BUOYAGE: IALA B

CURRENCY: Sucre of 100 centavos.
To stabilise the economy, in 2000 the currency was tied to the US dollar, now used alongside the sucre.

BUSINESS HOURS
Banks: 0900–1330 Monday to Friday, some also Saturday.
Shops: 0900–1730 Monday to Friday and 1200–1400 Saturday.
Business: 0900–1300, 1500–1900 Monday to Friday, 0830–1230 Sunday.

ELECTRICITY: 110 V, 60 Hz

PUBLIC HOLIDAYS
1 January: New Year's Day, Good Friday
1 May: Labour Day
24 May: Battle of Pichincha
25 July: Foundation of Guayaquil

10 August: Independence Day
9 October: Independence of Guayaquil
2 November: Day of the Dead
3 November: Independence of Cuenca
25 December: Christmas Day

COMMUNICATIONS
Long-distance telephone facilities are available in all main towns. IETEL telecommunications offices offer the usual services. For the international operator dial 116.
Collect calls can be made to the USA and Canada, but not Switzerland or Australia.
Central post office, Pedro Carbo y Aguirre, Guayaquil.
There are international flights from Quito to American and some West European capitals; also some from Guayaquil, which has several flights to Quito every day and one daily flight to the Galapagos Islands.

MEDICAL
Clinica Kennedy, Av. del Periodista,

Guayaquil. *Tel.* 286 963; has a good emergency department.

DIPLOMATIC MISSIONS
In Quito:
Canada: Edificio Josueth Gonzalez, Avenida 6 de Diciembre 2816 James y Orton. *Tel.* (2) 543 214.
United Kingdom: Calle Gonzales Suarez 111. *Tel.* (2) 560 669.
United States: 120 Avenida 12 Octobre y Patria. *Tel.* (2) 562 890.

In Guayaquil:
Canada: Edificio Torres de la Merced, General Cordova 800 and Victor Manuel Rendon. *Tel.* (4) 566 747.
Peru: 9 de Octubre 411, 6th floor. *Tel.* 322 738.
United Kingdom: Cordova 623 y P. Solano. *Tel.* 560 400.
United States: 9 de Octubre y Garcia Moreno. *Tel.* (4) 323 570.

visiting the interior. This is also a good place to leave for the Galapagos Islands.

Country Profile

In the mid-fifteenth century the Incas of Peru expanded into Ecuador and made it part of their empire. Later Pizarro claimed the northern kingdom of Quito, and conquered the city in 1534. Orellana, founder of Guayaquil, built ships in the Ecuadorean jungle and discovered the Amazon, which he named after the female warriors he met there; he sailed on to the Atlantic and finally Spain in the same ships.

Guayaquil gained independence from Spain in 1820, but Quito was only liberated by a force led by Bolivar's deputy Antonio José de Sucre who defeated the Spanish forces and occupied Quito. Simón Bolívar continued the war of liberation and Ecuador was drawn into a confederation with Venezuela and Colombia. Independence finally came in 1830 when the Confederation broke up.

During the nineteenth century Ecuadorean politics were dominated by the struggle between the pro-Church Conservatives and the anticlerical Liberals. From the end of the century the country experienced long periods of military rule. The 1940s and 1950s brought a period of prosperity

and constitutional rule, but then the 1960s and 1970s saw the unstable pattern of alternating civilian and military governments again. Rivalry between the Sierra and the Costa regions, as well as Peru encroaching on the eastern border, were problems that successive governments had to contend with. After the 1978 constitution ended military rule, a more stable period has ensued, although armed clashes still continue on the undemarcated border with Peru, breaking a ceasefire agreed as the result of international talks.

In the early 1970s the Ecuadorean economy was transformed from an agricultural to an oil economy. However, exports of bananas, coffee and cocoa are still important and fishing is a growing industry. Economic hardship continued into the late 1990s when there were several outbreaks of political unrest, especially among the rural population.

The 11 million inhabitants are mostly Quechua Indian or mestizo, while a small proportion of the population is of European, African and Asian origin. Spanish and Quechua are the main languages spoken and most people are Roman Catholic.

Although lying on the equator, the climate of Ecuador is very pleasant, temperatures along the coast showing little difference between seasons. The winds are mostly light southerlies. The climate in the interior is more varied and temperatures vary greatly with altitude.

Entry Regulations

Ports of entry
Manta 0°56′S 80°43′W, Esmeraldas 0°58′N, 79°41′W, Guayaquil 2°17′S 79°55′W, Salinas (La Libertad) 2°13′S 80°55′W, Puerto Bolívar 3°16′S 80°01′W.

The Galapagos Islands are dealt with separately on page 398.

Procedure on arrival
On arrival, the port captain should be contacted on VHF Channels 6 or 12, as Channel 16 is rarely used except as a general calling channel. The port captain will advise on where to berth the yacht for clearance. Yachts cruising the Ecuadorean coast must obtain a clearance (*zarpe*) before sailing to another port. The name of the next port of call is mentioned on the clearance and this must be adhered to.

The port captains require that an agent is used to complete formalities and the latter will charge large amounts ($30 to $100 reported in Esmeraldas). An agent must be used to check in and out of every port. It is advisable to enter at the ports where there are yacht clubs, such as Salinas or Guayaquil, as these ports are more used to foreign visitors and there are less problems with officials.

Guayaquil: This is the main port of Ecuador, and lies on the west bank of Guayas river, about 40 miles inland. There are two ports, the old port and the new Puerto Nuevo, on the Estero Salado, which is a saltwater estuary lying parallel to the freshwater Guayas river. Both are navigable although currents are strong. For a fee, the artificial canal, which has a depth of 9 feet at high water in parts of the entrance, can be used. The Guayaquil Yacht Club is in the old port in the centre of Guayaquil. The club can be contacted on VHF Channel 71 and it is possible to use their facilities and complete clearance formalities from there.

Esmeraldas: Yachts should anchor in the fishing boat section of the artificial harbour, opposite the port captain's office. It is more convenient to come to the Navy dock if there is space.

Salinas: Arriving yachts should report directly to the Puerto Lucia Yacht Club at Salinas on Channel 19 (from 0800 to 1800) and the yacht club will liaise with all the authorities. The approach to the yacht club marina is the waypoint buoy reported at 02°12′N 80°55′W. There are shoals close inshore to east and west of the marina entrance so the approach should be made due south from the waypoint buoy. There is a flashing white light on the tip of the breakwater and red and green channel markers. Behind the marina are two distinct tall buildings, one with a pyramid-shaped roof. The marina will assist with clearance formalities. Immigration is in the next town, Libertad, to which there is a regular bus service.

Manta: Yachts should moor in the area reserved for the local yacht club before contacting the port captain for clearance.

Customs
Firearms and animals must be declared.

Immigration
Tourist cards are granted on arrival for West European and US citizens for 15 or 30 days. Extensions of 30 days (US$10 each) are available from immigration, up to 90 days. Nationals of France, China, Cuba, North and South Korea, Taiwan and Vietnam must obtain a visa in advance. Visa requirements are not strictly enforced for those arriving by boat and short stays are granted on arrival even to nationalities that normally need visas. Passports should always be carried, especially if travelling inland.

Cruising permit
Foreign yachts cannot cruise the Ecuadorean coast without a special permit from the Ministry of Defence in Quito, which must be applied for through one's embassy. A yacht arriving without this permit is normally only given clearance for a foreign port or the Galapagos Islands (if one has a permit to go there, if not, one cannot name Galapagos as one's next destination). In practice, visiting yachts have found that it was possible to obtain permission to sail to another Ecuadorean port from the port captain at the port of entry. Sometimes this permission has to be obtained from a higher authority in Guayaquil.

Health
Amoebic dysentery is endemic in some parts of the country. Vaccination against yellow fever and malarial prophylaxis is recommended. Cholera is a risk.

Fees
A tax for light dues of US$3 per gross ton must be paid to the port captain on arrival. One should get a receipt for this payment or one will have to pay it again in the next port.

There are also immigration charges, a clearance fee and agent's fees. A charge is also made for the *zarpe*. Apparently some yachts have been overcharged and others have had to pay overtime, because they were leaving the harbour outside office hours, even when the formalities had been completed during office hours. This seems to be less of a problem in the ports of Salinas and Guayaquil, where foreign yachts are more common. Yachts should also avoid mooring in commercial harbours as yachts are charged the same rates as large ships, which are very high. There are not usually fees for anchoring in fishing harbours.

Facilities

Provisioning is adequate along the coast, but a better selection is found in larger towns. Because of a favourable exchange rate, prices are very low for both provisions and fuel. Water is sometimes scarce along the coast.

Esmeraldas is a small town with only basic necessities such as fresh produce and some hardware available. Fuel is delivered to the main dock in drums.

Good repair facilities are available in Manta, where most of the Ecuadorian fishing fleet is based. It is possible to anchor inside the harbour and take the dinghy to the yacht club dock.

The best port along the coast is Salinas, where the excellent Puerto Lucia Yacht Club welcomes visitors to their marina. Most provisioning is available locally, but for a better selection there are regular buses to Guayaquil where supplies are much better. The yacht club has docks with power and water hook-ups and Mediterranean-style moorings. Fuel is available inside the breakwater at a dock where one can come stern-to at high tide. The club has a travel-lift for 25 tons and simple repairs can be made. The yacht club is very helpful and will assist in an emergency. The marina is the most secure and best place to leave a boat while exploring the interior.

The Guayaquil Yacht Club has pontoons with electricity and water and welcomes visitors. The town is good for provisioning, although marine supplies are not available. Charts are available at the Naval Hydrographic Institute (Inocar), which has a publications store at the Governor's Palace in Guayaquil, near the Guayaquil Yacht Club. Repairs and hauling out can be done at the naval dockyard Astinave (which can be contacted on VHF Channel 21). Although it deals mainly with fishing boats, work done on yachts in the past was satisfactory. There is a branch of the Guayaquil Yacht Club at Puerto Azul, 6 miles west from Guayaquil, where there is a marina with 24-hour security guard. Smaller yachts can be hauled out and a limited range of repair is available.

Further Reading

South American Handbook
South America on a Shoestring

Websites

www.ecua.net.ec (General information and links)
www.magellanoffshore.com (Puerto Lucia Marina)

FRENCH GUIANA

French Guiana (Guyane) is an overseas department of France, sandwiched between Brazil and Suriname. The atmosphere in the country is more Caribbean, akin to Martinique and Guadeloupe than to the rest of Latin America. The low coastal regions gradually climb to the hills and forests of the interior from where twenty rivers flow down to the Atlantic Ocean. Cayenne is the capital, on the island of the same name at the mouth of the Cayenne river.

The coast itself has few ports or anchorages worth exploring, but the offlying Iles du Salut are a popular stop for sailors. These islands can only be visited after having cleared into the country. The best anchorage is on Ile St Joseph, although there are no completely protected anchorages. Also interesting to visit is the Ariane Space Centre at Kourou, west of Cayenne, although an appointment has to be made in advance. River trips, usually by canoe, are another attraction of this small country, which is only visited by a small number of cruising yachts, mainly French.

Country Profile

Columbus visited this coast in 1498, to be followed by Amerigo Vespucci, Sir Walter Raleigh and many other explorers. French settlers arrived in the sixteenth century and began extracting dye stuffs from the trees. Dutch and English attempts to gain control of the land were unsuccessful and the Peace of Breda in 1667 awarded the region to France. During the French Revolution political prisoners were deported to Guyane, a punishment which was known as the 'dry guillotine'. In 1809 an Anglo-Portuguese naval force captured the territory and handed it over to the Brazilians, until it was eventually restored to France at the end of the Napoleonic Wars.

Practical Information

LOCAL TIME: GMT – 3

BUOYAGE: IALA B

CURRENCY: French franc and euro from 2002. 1 euro = 6.55957 FRF. It is recommended to arrive with francs as it is difficult to change money.

BUSINESS HOURS
Bank de la Guyane, Place Schoelcher 0715–1130, 1445–1730, and Saturday mornings.
Business: 0800–1300, 1500–1800 Monday to Friday.

ELECTRICITY: 220 V, 50 Hz

PUBLIC HOLIDAYS
1 January: New Year's Day
Easter Monday
1 May
Ascension
Whit Monday
10 June: Slavery Day
14 July: National Day
1 November: All Saints' Day
11 November: Armistice Day
25 December: Christmas Day

COMMUNICATIONS
International telephone calls can be made from any public phone. Phone cards can be bought in tobacconists and shops.
Foreign telegrams via Paramaribo or Fort-de-France from TSF station in Cayenne.
Post office 0700–1200 Monday, Friday,

Saturday. 0700–1230 Tuesday, Wednesday, Thursday. Also 1500–1700 Monday to Friday.
There are flights from Cayenne to Paris, Miami, Caribbean and South American destinations.

MEDICAL
There are hospitals in Cayenne and Kourou.

DIPLOMATIC MISSIONS
In Cayenne:
Brazil: 12 rue L. Héder, corner Place des Palmistes. *Tel.* 30 04 67.
Suriname: 38 rue Christophe Colomb. *Tel.* 30 04 61.
United Kingdom: 16 Av. Président Monnerville. *Tel.* 31 10 34.

A penal colony was established in the mid-nineteenth century on the inaccessible Iles du Salut, which became notorious, especially Ile du Diable – Devil's Island – where political prisoners, including Alfred Dreyfus, were kept. After the Second World War the colony became part of France as the department of Guyane and the prison was finally closed, the last prisoners leaving in 1953. Yachts occasionally stop here and this seems to be tolerated by the authorities, provided one does not stay too long. There is a military post ashore and a restaurant but no other facilities. Temporary anchorage may be found in the lee of Ile Royale.

In 1983 the country was given greater internal autonomy and a regional council elected. The country's main resources are timber forests and minerals. Most food and manufactured goods are imported, mainly from France. Exports are shrimps, rum, essence of rosewood, hardwoods and gold. In recent years efforts have been made to develop local food production and to improve tourist facilities. The European Space Agency satellite launch facility at Kourou has brought some economic benefits.

The 115,000 inhabitants are of Créole, Indian, Asian and European origin (mainly French). French is the official language and most of the population are Roman Catholic.

The rainy season is from November to July, while August to December are the best months. Rainfall can be heavy in this tropical climate where temperatures average 80°F (27°C).

Entry Regulations

Ports of entry
Degrad des Cannes 4°51′N 52°16′W, Cayenne 4°56′N 52°20′W.

Procedure on arrival
Degrad des Cannes: This is the main port of French Guiana, located on the NW bank of the Mahury river. The entrance is lit and buoyed, and yachts usually anchor outside the main channel by the shore. Normally the gendarmes will come out to the yacht to check passports and ship's papers. The port captain's office should then be visited.

It has been reported that the port captain does not approve of yachts clearing in at Degrad des Cannes and insists that formalities are completed at Cayenne. The approaches to Cayenne are difficult and the buoyed channel not easy to find.
Cayenne: The capital is no longer used as a commercial port. The Cayenne Channel should only be navigated in daylight, preferably on a high tide. It is possible to come alongside the jetty two hours before and two hours after high tide. Cruising boats normally anchor at Stouppan and commute to Cayenne by road.

There are also customs offices at Kourou and Saint-Laurent-du-Maroni.

Customs
Firearms and animals must be declared.
Yachts can be temporarily imported for up to six

months without paying duty, on condition that one does not enter into commercial activity ashore. Chartering is not allowed.

It is illegal for foreign tourists or sailors to sell any of their possessions to local residents and the penalties are heavy fines. As any informers receive a large proportion of the fine, visitors have been set up by some of these local informers.

Immigration

Visas are not required for nationals of Western Europe, Canada, Argentina, Brunei, Chile, Czech Republic, Hungary, Israel, South Korea, New Zealand, Poland, Singapore, Slovak Republic, Slovenia, and the USA for one or three months, depending on nationality. If staying more than three months, one needs income tax clearance before departure. Visas are required by all other nationals and can be obtained from a French embassy or consulate.

Restrictions

A permit is necessary for visiting some Amerindian villages.

Health

Vaccination against yellow fever is obligatory except for very short stays. Malaria prophylaxis is recommended.

Facilities

Provisioning is good, but expensive. There is a fresh produce market at Cayenne, Place du Coq, on Fridays and Saturdays. Particularly good is the Match supermarket, which has an excellent selection of French goods including wine. There is only a limited range of repair facilities. Good provisioning is also available in Kourou, where emergency repairs may be possible if the help of technicians from the French space centre can be enlisted.

Further Reading

South American Handbook

Websites

www.guyanetourisme.com (Tourism Office)
www.tourisme-guyane.gf

GUYANA

Guayana means 'land of many waters' in Amerindian, which is an accurate description of this small country of many swamps and rivers on the north-east Atlantic coast of South America. Most of the population live along the narrow coastal belt, which is very low and subject to floods. A difficult coast to approach because of the shallow and muddy waters, combined with lengthy formalities, do not make Guyana a natural cruising destination. Visiting the interior is only possible with special permission. This also applies to trips up the river Berbice, which is navigable for 100 miles past the port of New Amsterdam. It is also possible to take keeled boats up the rivers Essequibo, Pomeroon, Waini and Raima, all of which are navigable for some distance inland.

The capital Georgetown has a certain charm and the few yachts which do visit Guayana rarely go anywhere else. On the right bank of the river Demerara, the town has nineteenth century houses on stilts and boulevards built along disused Dutch canals. Seawalls and dykes protect the town, which is built on an alluvial flat area below the highwater mark.

Robberies are common, both in Georgetown and inland, although rarely violent. Cruising boats are left in safety at the Coast Guard dock in Georgetown. It is recommended to visit Starbroek Market only if escorted by a local man.

Country Profile

Although the Spanish were the first to explore this coast, they were not very interested in what they found and it was the English and Dutch who were the first to settle in the seventeenth century. They disputed the ownership of the land until 1814, when the three counties of Essequibo, Berbice and Demerara were merged to form British Guiana. Initially plantations were established in the hills using African slave labour, but the poor soil forced the settlers to move down to the coast in the mid-eighteenth century. Coffee and cotton were the main crops and later sugar. In 1834 slavery was abolished and indentured Chinese and Indians plus some Portuguese from the Azores and Madeira were brought in as labour. At the end of the nineteenth century a boundary dispute with Venezuela was settled in favour of Britain, but this area is still claimed by Venezuela. In 1953 a new constitution

Practical Information

LOCAL TIME: GMT – 4

BUOYAGE: IALA B

CURRENCY: Guyana dollar (Guy$). There are strict controls on changing money, so it is better to arrive with cash than travellers' cheques. Guy$ is not convertible into foreign currency.

BUSINESS HOURS
Banks: 0800–1230 Monday to Friday, also 1500–1700 Friday.
Shops: 0830–1600 Monday to Friday, 0830–1200 Saturday, some half day Wednesday. Some shops are open Saturday afternoon.
Business: 0800–1200, 1300-1630 Monday to Friday.
Government offices: 0800–1130, 1300–1600 Monday to Friday.

ELECTRICITY: 110/220 V, 50 Hz

PUBLIC HOLIDAYS
1 January: New Year's Day
23 February: Republic Day
March: Holi Phagwa
Good Friday, Easter Monday
1 May: Labour Day
July: Caribbean Day (1st Monday in July)
1 August: Freedom Day
Divali
Youm um-Nabi
25, 26 December: Christmas
Variable: Eid el-Fitr, Eid el-Adha

COMMUNICATIONS
Guyintel, Bank of Guyana building, Georgetown for overseas telegrams, telex, fax, international calls. Collect calls cannot be made.
Main post office in North Road, Georgetown, open 0730–1600 weekdays.
Post office in Robb Street for fax.
Emergency: Police 911, Ambulance 912.
There are flights from Georgetown to Barbados, Trinidad, Brazil, Toronto and New York.

MEDICAL
Georgetown Hospital: treatment is free but doctors charge for an appointment and the hospital is poorly equipped. Also St Joseph and Davis Memorial Hospitals.

DIPLOMATIC MISSIONS
In Georgetown:
Brazil: 308 Church St, Queenstown. Tel. (2) 57970.
Canada: Young Street. Tel. (2) 72081.
France: 7 Sheriff St. Tel. (2) 65238.
Suriname: 304 Church St. Tel. (2) 56995.
Trinidad and Tobago: 91 Middle St. Tel. (2) 72061.
United Kingdom: 44 Main St. Tel. (2) 65881.
United States: 99–100 Young & Duke Streets. Tel. (2) 54900.
Venezuela: 296 Thomas St. Tel. (2) 61543.

introduced universal suffrage. Cheddi Jagan, prime minister in 1961–4, relied on the support of the Asian population, opposed by both the whites and blacks. In 1966 British Guiana was granted independence and took the new name of Guyana. Later the black leader Forbes Burnham became president to be succeeded in 1985 by Hugh Desmond Hoyte, who improved relations with the US and introduced free market policies, which were continued by Dr Jagan. In 1997 Bharrat Jagdeo became President and the next elections are due by 2001.

Guyana's main income comes from sugar and bauxite. There are sugar and rice plantations on the coast. The small country's main problem is its large foreign debt. The 1990s have seen some economic recovery, although weaknesses remain and there are frequent power cuts.

The population is about 800,000, of which half are Asian. There are also indigenous Amerindians and people of African, British, Chinese, European and American origins. English is the official language although Creole is widely spoken. The capital is Georgetown. The main religions are Christian, Hindu and Muslim.

The climate is hot and humid, especially from August to October. The wet seasons are from April to August, and November to January. Guyana lies outside of the hurricane belt.

Entry Regulations

Port of entry
Georgetown 6°49′N 58°11′W.

Procedure on arrival
One should attempt to arrive between office hours (0700 to 1500) and call the Lighthouse Service on Channel 16. Permission should be asked to dock at the customs boathouse, near the clock tower. The services of an agent must be engaged and the fee agreed in advance (approximately $100 to $150 to clear in and out). The agent will arrange for customs, quarantine and immigration officers to visit the boat. The agent should also obtain permission to leave the customs dock and go alongside the Coast Guard dock, which is reported to be the only safe place to leave a boat unattended.

Customs
Firearms and animals must be declared.

Receipts of any purchases should be kept to be shown on departure.

Immigration
All nationals require visas except those of Australia, Canada, New Zealand, the USA, Japan, South Africa, United Kingdom and other

Commonwealth countries, Belgium, Denmark, Finland, France, Germany, Greece, Ireland, Italy, Luxembourg, the Netherlands, Norway, North and South Korea, Portugal, Spain, Sweden, Switzerland and Caricom countries (who can enter without a passport if they have an ID card or driver's licence). All other countries must obtain a visa in advance. A single entry up to 30 days is normally given. Visas can be obtained in Suriname or other neighbouring countries. Visa fees vary with nationality, and visas are valid three months from the date of issue. Evidence may be required of sufficient funds. Those who arrive without a visa must give up their passport and collect it the next day before 1030 from Immigration, Camp Street, Georgetown. An extension needs the approval of the Home Department, 6 Brickdam, and takes about two weeks to process.

Restrictions

Permission is needed from the Home Affairs Ministry to visit the interior.

Health

Yellow fever vaccination certificate is required if arriving from an infected area. Malaria prophylaxis is recommended.

Fees

There is an exit tax, payable to immigration; also some high harbour dues ($89 in and $89 out reported in 1995).

Facilities

Provisions are plentiful and affordable. There is a daily fresh produce market in Georgetown. Electricity, water and fuel supplies have greatly improved and now there are rarely shortages. Permission to obtain fuel is also arranged through the agent. Only simple repairs are possible and there are no marine supplies available. The NGEC shipyard in Georgetown operates a dry dock and slipway and may do work on a yacht in an emergency. Visits to the interior can be arranged through the Tourism and Hospitality Association of Guyana at 157 Waterloo St. *Tel.* 50807, Fax. 50817.

There is a Venezuelan Embassy and obtaining the tourist cards is simpler than elsewhere. Having a visa will simplify formalities for those intending to explore the Orinoco delta.

Further Reading

South American Handbook

Website

www.interknowledge.com/guyana

PERU

With its Inca ruins, old Spanish colonial cities and the magnificent Andes dominating the centre of the country, Peru has always been one of the most fascinating countries to visit in South America. In the last few years the activity of guerilla groups, whose attacks in various parts of the country have affected foreign tourists as well as Peruvians, has made Peru much less of an attractive destination. Even before this, Peru was a difficult destination, as there are few ports along its arid coast on the Pacific. The few yachts that call normally make their base at Callao, whose welcoming yacht club used to be a good place to leave the boat while touring the interior of this intriguing country.

Country Profile

Several different cultures rose and fell in this region before the Incas came to dominate Peru and Ecuador. The Inca civilisation dates from the eleventh century AD and, expanding outwards from the Cuzco basin, by the mid-fifteenth century the Incas had conquered much of the surrounding region. A strong state was established based on a rigid ruling hierarchy, who forced the masses to build temples and cities and a priestly caste who made human sacrifices to the sun. Gold and silver were available in large amounts and the Incas were highly skilled in metalwork and architecture. But, the empire grew too unwieldy and was in the throes of civil war just before the Spanish arrived.

In 1532 a small Spanish force led by Francisco Pizarro routed the Incas and sacked Cuzco, founding Lima as the capital of the newly conquered territory. The Spanish had voyaged through all America searching for treasure, and in Peru reached the end of their quest. They looted the treasure of the Incas, and forced them to work in the silver mines. The Inca civilisation rapidly declined, its people decimated by disease, civil wars

Practical Information

LOCAL TIME: GMT – 5

BUOYAGE: IALA B

CURRENCY: Nuevo Sol (S/) of 100 centimos. Outside Lima and Cuzco, changing travellers' cheques is difficult.

BUSINESS HOURS
Banks: winter 0915–1245, summer (January to March) 0845–1130 Monday to Friday; some open in the afternoon or on Saturdays.
Shops: 0900–1230, 1600–1900 Monday to Saturday (some close Saturdays), January to March. The rest of the year 0930–1230, 1530–1900.
Government offices: January to March 0930–1130 Monday to Saturday, rest of the year 0930–1100, 1500–1700 Monday to Friday, 0930–1130 Saturday.

ELECTRICITY: 220 V, 60 Hz

PUBLIC HOLIDAYS
1 January: New Year's Day
Maundy Thursday, Good Friday
1 May: Labour Day
29 June: Saints Peter and Paul
28–29 July: Independence Day
30 August: Santa Rosa de Lima
1 November: All Saints' Day
8 December: Immaculate Conception
24, 25 December: Christmas
31 December: New Year's Eve
Most shops and businesses close during family holidays, especially July to August.

COMMUNICATIONS
ENTEL, off Plaza San Martín, Lima, for international calls, fax, telex and telegram. 24 hour offices in Lima, Av. Bolivia 347, and Jr. Cuzco 303. International calls also from CPT,

Peruvian Telephone Co., Plaza San Martin 0800–2200 daily.
Main post office, Pasaje Piura, nr Plaza de Armas, 0800–2000 Monday to Saturday, 0800–1400 Sunday.
There are regular flights from Lima to European, North and South American destinations.

DIPLOMATIC MISSIONS
In Lima or its suburbs of Miraflores and San Isidro:
Canada: Libertad 130. *Tel.* 444-4015.
Chile: Javier Prado Oeste 790, San Isidro. *Tel.* 221-2818.
United Kingdom: Natalio Sanchez 125. *Tel.* 433-4738.
United States: Av. La Encalada cuadra 17. *Tel.* 434-3000.

and slavery. From Peru, the Viceroyalty ruled over Spain's South American possessions.

The ideas of the French Revolution fired the Spanish colonies to declare independence and then fight Spain for it. In Peru independence was declared in 1821, after José de San Martín's army crossed from Chile to fight the Spanish forces. Simón Bolívar and Antonio José de Sucre, already having freed Venezuela and Colombia, completed the war of liberation and in 1826 Spain capitulated and new republics were born across the continent. Efforts by Peru and Bolivia to form a confederation in the 1830s eventually came to nothing. At the end of the century the War of the Pacific saw Peru and Bolivia defeated by Chile, and Peru lost its southernmost territory. Political instability in Peru continued into the twentieth century with strong military regimes alternating with weak civilian governments. In 1968 a reformist military junta introduced reforms to raise the living standards of the workers and rural Indians, but the country's economic problems continued. The guerilla activity of the Sendero Luminoso (Shining Path) movement has been a major problem for Peru. Although violence abated after the arrest of the guerilla leaders in 1992, there still continue to be some outbreaks.

In the economy, efforts have been made to improve agriculture, the main export crops being sugar, cotton and coffee. Mining is of some importance, while oil reserves are sufficient to provide half of the domestic consumption.

The population of over 20 million are mainly Indian and mestizo, with some of African, Chinese, European and Japanese origins. The majority are Roman Catholic. There are two official languages, Spanish and Quechua. The latter is an Inca language, spoken by millions of Indians, many of whom speak no Spanish. The Indian community is still large, most living in poverty in isolated settlements in the mountains.

The climate of coastal Peru is greatly influenced by the cold Humboldt current, which keeps temperatures cool throughout the year and often produces coastal fog. There is very little rain along the coast which is arid and desert-like. The prevailing winds are south or south-easterly and usually light.

Entry Regulations

Ports of entry
Paita 5°05′S 81°07′W, Chimbote 9°05′S 78°38′W, Callao 12°03′S 77°09′W, General San Martín 13°50′S 81°16′W, Matarani 16°59′S 72°07′W.

Procedure on arrival
The authorities expect to be advised in advance of a vessel's arrival. This is best done by calling the marine authorities (TRAMAR) on VHF or HF. They have stations at Paita, Callao and Mollendo.

Boats that have entered territorial waters (both Peru and Chile insist on 200 miles), must proceed directly to an official port of entry. It has been reported (1995) that the authorities now insist that an agent must be hired for all formalities, both on arrival and departure. This regulation is being enforced mainly in Callao.

Callao: Visiting yachts are normally directed by the yacht club launch to a club mooring. The launch attendant should be asked to inform the authorities of the yacht's arrival and request them to come to the yacht to complete clearance formalities. No one should leave the yacht until it has been boarded by the various officials, including port authority, customs, immigration and possibly security. More formalities have to be completed later at the immigration office near the commercial harbour. Shore passes will be issued, but these are not valid for travel outside Callao and Lima, so a proper visa should be requested if intending to travel inland.

Paita: On arrival contact the coastguard (costera) on VHF Channel 16.

Ancon: Cruising boats should go directly to the yacht club dock. The club will contact the authorities for clearance.

Customs

Firearms and animals must be declared. The export of objects of archaeological interest is prohibited.

Immigration

No visas are needed in advance by nationals of EU countries (except Spain), Argentina, Bolivia, Brazil, Canada, Colombia, Ecuador, Honduras, Liechtenstein, Norway, South Korea, Switzerland, Uruguay, the USA, Japan, Czech Republic, Costa Rica, El Salvador, Guatemala, Mexico, Nicaragua, Panama, Paraguay, Chile, Dominican Republic, Caribbean countries (except Cuba), and Venezuela. Tourist cards are issued on arrival by immigration, for 90 days, renewable for another 30 days. All other countries, including Australia and New Zealand, need to obtain visas in advance.

The crew of foreign yachts who wish to visit the interior should insist on being given a tourist card on arrival, particularly if intending to leave Peru for one of the neighbouring countries before returning to the yacht.

Visas or tourist cards can be renewed at Ministerio del Interior, Paseo de la Republica, Av. 28 de Julio, Lima. Some identification should always be carried, either passports or a photocopy that has been witnessed by a notary.

Health

If visiting the interior, yellow fever inoculation and malaria prophylaxis are recommended. Visitors to sites in the High Andes may be affected by altitude sickness.

Security

A high number of robberies have been reported. The use or purchase of drugs is severely punished and can lead to 15 years' imprisonment. There have been reports of the planting of drugs on foreigners by police followed by demands for high sums of money for the charges to be dropped. Guerilla activities still continue, and police and army searches are common.

United States citizens can obtain more information from the Country Officer for Peru, Office of Andean Affairs, Department of State, Washington DC.

Facilities

Callao is the port of the capital Lima, which is only a short distance inland. The Yacht Club Peruano in Callao monitors Channel 68 and has a few mooring buoys for visitors. Otherwise one should use one's own anchor. There is a 24 hour launch service. There are a number of workshops in the surrounding area and the yacht club has a travelift. Fuel and water is available from the club dock. Provisioning is good from local supermarkets and an excellent fresh produce market. Marine equipment is in very short supply. Visitors are also welcome to use the facilities of the yacht club at La Punta, close to Callao. There is a slipway for hauling out in La Punta, chandleries and other repair facilities. There is also a yacht club at Ancon, a town farther from Lima, which welcomes visitors. The new yacht club has very good facilities including a heavy-duty travelift, fuel and water on the main dock, and moorings with good security.

The port authority sells Peruvian charts, almanacs and tide tables.

Further Reading

South American Handbook
South America on a Shoestring

Website

www.mitinci.gob.pe (Ministry of Tourism)

SURINAME

Suriname before independence was known as Dutch Guiana, and lies on the north-east coast of South America between Guyana and French Guiana. There are ongoing border disputes with both neighbours. Although discovered by Spain, the Guyanas have always been considered more Caribbean than Latin American, as Spain showed little interest and the area was colonised by the other European powers active in the Caribbean area.

Suriname has a flat, marshy coast, where most of the population live, although parts of the coast remain unexplored. Uplands rise up from the coastal plain and contain mineral reserves, while the coast is indented with rivers, which makes the sea muddy and navigation more difficult. Some of the wide rivers are navigable for a considerable distance inland, but to do this requires special permission from the authorities in Paramaribo, who treat all foreigners, including those arriving on yachts, with suspicion.

In 1992 a peace agreement ended the civil war going on in the interior between government and guerillas since 1986. However, the interior remains dangerous with an increase in violent crime, and sporadic guerilla activity continuing as police authority over some areas remains lacking. In the past, some parts of the country have been closed to travellers. The latest situation should be ascertained before travelling away from the coast.

Country Profile

The coast was first sighted by Columbus in 1498. It was in the early seventeenth century that Dutch merchants began trading along what became known as the 'Wild Coast'. English settlers also came and planted tobacco. In the mid-seventeenth century the Governor of Barbados sent an expedition and an agricultural colony was founded with sugar plantations worked by African slaves. The colony grew in numbers with the immigration of Jews from the Netherlands and Italy, as well as Dutch Jews ejected from Brazil. In 1667 Suriname was conquered by the Dutch, a situation confirmed by the Peace of Breda with Britain. At the end of the eighteenth century a brief conquest was made by Britain, but Suriname was returned to the Netherlands in 1814. Soon afterwards slavery was forbidden, and instead labour was brought in from China and the East Indies.

In 1975 Suriname became an independent republic, but five years later a military coup overthrew the elected government, and a state of emergency was declared. Pressure from the Netherlands, who ceased all aid, and also from the United States, helped a gradual move back towards democracy, with a new constitution, and elections in 1988 so Dutch aid was restored. By 1987 the civil war brought the aluminium industry, responsible for 75 per cent of foreign revenue, to a standstill and destroyed much economic infrastructure. Foreign aid was suspended again during the 1990 military coup, only to be restored by the 1991 elections. The end of the civil war helped boost a modest economic recovery, but inflation is rising and wages remain low.

Agriculture is centred on the coast, the main exports being rice, sugar and citrus fruit, but food imports are high. Fishing and timber are other contributions to the national economy.

The population numbers 440,000, over half of whom are Créole. There are also Asians, Indonesians, Chinese, Amerindians, Europeans and Bush Blacks, who are descendants of slaves who escaped to the interior in the seventeenth century. Dutch is the official language, but English and a local language called Sranan Tongo, of Créole origin, are widely spoken. Some Asian languages are also spoken. The main religion is Christian, but the Hindu, Muslim and Jewish religions are also practised. Paramaribo is the capital, on the banks of the wide Suriname river eight miles from the sea.

The climate is tropical and humid, but not too hot due to the NE trade winds. Coastal temperatures are around 75–88°F (23–31°C). The rainy seasons are November to February and April to August.

Entry Regulations

Port of entry
Paramaribo 5°50′N 55°10′W.

Procedure on arrival
Paramaribo: The harbour office keeps a 24-hour watch on VHF Channels 12 and 16. A new harbour has been built one mile upstream and the old main wharf is now used by fishing vessels, so if there is space it may be possible to come alongside to complete clearance formalities. Cruising boats may also use the pilot boats dock, or anchor nearby. Formalities can be completed from here as all offices are nearby.

Practical Information

LOCAL TIME: GMT – 3

BUOYAGE: IALA B

CURRENCY: Suriname guilder (SGld) of 100 cents. It is illegal to change money except in banks. Declare foreign currency on arrival if exceeding SGld 5000 and keep exchange receipts for departure.

BUSINESS HOURS
Banks: 0700–1400 or 0800–1230 Monday to Friday, 0800–1200 Saturday.
Business: 0730–1700 Monday to Friday.
Shops: 0700–1300, 1600–1800 Monday to Thursday and Saturday (to 1900 Saturday).
Friday 0730–1300, 1700–2000.
Government offices: 0700–1500 Monday to Friday.

ELECTRICITY: 220 V, 60 Hz

PUBLIC HOLIDAYS
1 January: New Year's Day
March: Holi Phagwa
Good Friday, Easter Sunday and Monday
1 May: Labour Day
1 July: National Unity
Eid el-Fitr
25 November: Independence Day
25, 26 December: Christmas

COMMUNICATIONS
Vaillantplein: telephone and telegraph office.
Satellite calls to the USA and UK.
Open 0700–2000. Book international calls in advance. Telesur for telex and telegrams.
Post office, Kerkelein.
There are international flights from Johan Pengel International Airport, 30 miles from Paramaribo to Amsterdam, Miami, Caribbean and Latin American destinations.

MEDICAL
There are several well-equipped hospitals in Paramaribo.

DIPLOMATIC MISSIONS
In Paramaribo:
United Kingdom: POB 1300, 9–11 Van't Hogerhuysstraat. *Tel.* 472 870.
United States: POB 1821, Dr Sophie Redmondstraat 129. *Tel.* 472 900.

Customs
Firearms and animals must be declared.

The import of fruit, meat and meat products is prohibited.

Immigration
All visitors require visas obtained in advance except nationals of Denmark, UK, Antigua, Brazil, Chile, Canada, Dominica, Ecuador, Finland, Gambia, Grenada, Guyana, Israel, Japan, South Korea, Netherland Antilles, Norway, St Lucia, Sweden, Switzerland, Trinidad, who will be issued with tourist cards on arrival, for a fee of US$14. Two passport photos will have to be supplied for the registration card.

All other nationals must obtain their visa in advance. This can be obtained by writing to the Ministry of External Affairs, Department of Consular Matters, Paramaribo, enclosing a passport photo and US$50. It is cheaper and more convenient to obtain the visa at Suriname consular offices in Guyana, French Guiana or Venezuela, although this can take up to 15 days. Visas may be obtained more quickly on payment of extra fees. Suriname diplomatic missions:
Guyana: 304 Church St, Georgetown. *Tel.* 2 67844.
French Guiana: 38 rue Christophe Colomb, Cayenne. *Tel.* 30 04 61.
Venezuela: 4a Ave, entre 7 y 8a Transversal, Qta Los Milagros, Altamira. *Tel.* 2 26 12 095.
USA: 7235 NW 19 St, Suite A, Miami, FL33126. *Tel.* 305 593 2163.

Immigration formalities are time-consuming, and may be simplified in the future. Presently, the military police stamp passports on arrival for a one week stay only, so the immigration office in van't Hogerhuysstraat, Niuewe Haven, Paramaribo, must be visited, for a second stamp, and application made for a foreigner registration card, which will be valid for a stay of up to three months. This card can be collected from immigration after two weeks.

Passports must be given an exit stamp by immigration two days before departure. The military police will also give an exit stamp. An exit tax is charged.

Health
Yellow fever vaccination is recommended as is malaria prophylaxis. Cholera is a risk so all water should be boiled or purified. There is some risk of bilharzia in coastal districts.

Restrictions
Military installations must not be photographed.

Facilities

Provisioning in Paramaribo is reasonable and there is a good supply of local produce. There is a good hardware store with some boating equipment. Water is available on the dock and fuel either from the station outside the harbour gates or, in larger quantities, from the fishermen's cooperative. Only simple repairs can be effected. A shipyard operates in Paramaribo harbour and they have a dry dock and lift, where yachts can be hauled out if necessary. The tourist information office is conveniently located right by the harbour gates.

Further Reading

South American Handbook

Website

www.sr.net/srnet/InfoSurinam (Suriname online)

URUGUAY

One of the smaller South American countries, Uruguay has little coastline on the Atlantic. Lying on the northern bank of the Rio de la Plata, the name Uruguay means 'river of birds'. The Whitbread Round the World Race (now Volvo Ocean Race) put Punta del Este on the sailing map, and although it no longer calls there, the facilities remain for yachts to use. Besides Punta del Este and a few resorts in the vicinity, Uruguay holds little attraction for cruising yachts. There are more interesting things to see in the interior of this low, undulating country, which is the land of the gaucho.

Country Profile

Before the Europeans arrived, the semi-nomadic, warlike Charrúa lived here. In 1516 the Spaniard Juan Diaz de Solis landed near the site of present-day Montevideo. As there was no gold or silver to be found, the Spanish lost all interest until the end of the sixteenth century. In the following century Jesuit and Franciscan missionaries founded a settlement on Vizcairio Island. Cattle were introduced into the country and thrived so well they later became Uruguay's main commodity.

In 1680 Portugal founded a town to rival Buenos Aires on the opposite bank of the Rio de la Plata but it was Spain who founded the city of Montevideo several decades later. Montevideo changed hands several times and early in the nine-teenth century declared its independence from Buenos Aires. In 1811 José Artigas led the fight for independence against both Brazilian and Argentinian claims. Then a Brazilian force occupied Uruguay and Artigas fled to Paraguay, but in 1825 thirty-three Uruguayan exiles, the '33 Orientales', returned to lead a successful revolt against the Brazilian occupation. Uruguayan independence was declared, and eventually with British intervention peace was established and the new republic recognised by its neighbours.

Civil war followed between the Liberals and Conservatives and only in 1872 was agreement reached between the two sides, dividing the country into spheres of influence. Gradually political stability was achieved, and from the early twentieth century, a welfare state with a mixed economy was established. The 1960s saw political turmoil, and guerilla activities, which were defeated by the military in 1972. The following year a military coup occurred, but civil government was restored in 1984. In 1990 President Lacalle took office. Opposition to his social reforms and privatisation programme was widespread, and the latter was rejected by a referendum in 1992. In 1999 new elections brought Jorge Batlle to the office of President (until 2005).

Much of Uruguay's former prosperity has gone, and the model welfare state declined. Agriculture, mainly livestock, dominates the economy, Uruguay being famous for its cattle-raising cowboys called gauchos. Light industry is developing. Uruguay is a founder member of Mercosur, the Southern Common Market, set up in 1991.

The population is just under 3.1 million, the majority living in and around the only large city, Montevideo. Founded in 1726, the centre of the capital on the original site still has a colonial atmosphere. Most of the population are of Spanish or Italian origin, plus a few other European immigrants. There are no native Indians left. Spanish is the official language and Roman Catholicism the religion of the majority.

The climate is temperate but somewhat damp and windy. Winter lasts from June to September, averaging 50–60°F (10–16°C), but temperatures can drop below freezing. Summer is from December to March, when average temperatures are 70–80°F (21–27°C). The winds in the Rio de la Plata estuary are easterly in summer months. Strong SW winds called pamperos occur between June and October, occasionally reaching hurricane force.

Practical Information

LOCAL TIME: GMT – 3

BUOYAGE: IALA B

CURRENCY: Uruguayan peso of 100 centesimos.

BUSINESS HOURS
Banks: 1300–1700 Monday to Friday.
Summer 1330–1730 (Montevideo),
1600–2000 (Punta del Este).
Business: 0830–1200, 1430–1630/1900
Monday to Friday.
Shops: 0900–1200, 1400–1900 Monday to
Friday, 0900–1230 Saturday.
Government offices: mid-March to mid-
November 1200–1900 Monday to Friday.
Rest of year 0700–1230 Monday to Friday.

ELECTRICITY: 220 V, 50 Hz

PUBLIC HOLIDAYS
1 January: New Year's Day
6 January: Three Kings Day
Easter Week: Easter Monday is not a

holiday. Banks close all week, shops close
from Good Friday.
19 April: Landing of the 33 Orientales
1 May: Labour Day
18 May: Battle of Las Piedras
19 June: Artigas' Birthday
18 July: Constitution Day
25 August: Independence Day
12 October: Columbus Day
2 November: All Souls' Day
8 December: Blessing of the Waters
25 December: Christmas Day

EVENTS
Carnival: Monday and Tuesday before Ash
Wednesday
Easter Week: La Semana Criolla with rodeos
and music. Few shops and offices are open.

COMMUNICATIONS
Antel, C/Fernando Crespo 1534, open
0800–2200 daily for international calls and
telex.
Also All America Cables & Radio Inc.,
Plaza Independencia.

Post office: Calle Misiones 1328, open
0800–1845 Monday to Friday, 0800–1245
Saturday (0730 summer).
Post is unreliable and mail should be sent
registered.
Emergency: dial 999.
There are international flights from
Montevideo to Europe, North America and
all South American capitals.

MEDICAL
British hospital, Avenida Italia 2440,
Montevideo.

DIPLOMATIC MISSIONS
In Montevideo:
Argentina: Rio Branco 1281.
Tel. (2) 900 0897.
Brazil: Blvd Artigas 1257. Tel. (2) 901-2024.
Canada: Juan Carlos Gomez 1348.
Tel. (2) 915-8583.
United Kingdom: Calle Marco Bruto 1073.
Tel. (2) 622-3630.
United States: Calle Lauro Müller 1776.
Tel. (2) 203-6061.

Entry Regulations

Ports of entry
Punta del Este 34°58'S 54°57'W, Montevideo
34°54'S 56°16'W, Buceo 34°55'S 56°08'W,
Piriapolis 34°52.7'S 55°17.3'W, La Paloma
34°39'S 54°09'W, Colonia 34°06'S 57°51'W.

Procedure on arrival
Before entering any port, one must call the
Prefectura on VHF Channel 16 (try 9 or 11 if no
reply). One should call Control Montevideo (or
Punta del Este etc.), giving the ship's name.
Punta del Este: On arrival one should tie up to one of
the municipal moorings. Officials do not normally
board yachts for clearance. The marina office can
be contacted on VHF Channel 71, but the captain
has to go ashore and visit the offices. Immigration
is in town, open 1300–1900; in the summer season the officials are in the harbour office.

Customs
Firearms must be declared to customs. Animals
must be declared and may be confined on board.

Immigration
Nationals of Argentina, Bolivia, Brazil, Chile and

Paraguay need only an identity card, not a pass-
port.
Visas are not required for nationals of the
European Union (except France), Japan, Argentina,
Belize, Bolivia, Brazil, Chile, Colombia, Costa
Rica, Dominican Republic, Ecuador, Guatemala,
Honduras, Hungary, Iceland, Israel, Japan,
Liechtenstein, Malta, Mexico, Nicaragua, Norway,
Panama, Paraguay, Peru, Poland, Seychelles,
Switzerland and the USA. All are issued with a
tourist card on arrival, valid for three months,
which can be extended at Migraciones office, Calle
Misiones 1513, for a small fee.
One should carry one's passport, or a certified
photocopy, at all times.
The Ministry of Tourism sells 'Tarjeta turistica',
a card which covers medical and dental treatment,
free repatriation in case of illness and legal insurance, also car insurance for an extra fee. The cost is
not high.

Facilities

The best facilities are at Punta del Este, which has
a marina and yacht club, although the latter is not
open to visiting cruising yachts. There are plenty of

mooring buoys in the municipal marina, which can be hired for a daily fee which includes a launch service. There is good provisioning in town and fuel and water are available. There are adequate repair facilities locally and a travelift. Having had to deal with the Whitbread fleet, the local workshops have attained a certain degree of experience and most repairs can be carried out locally. However, nautical items are hard to get both in Punta del Este and Montevideo. There is a better selection in Buenos Aires, on the Argentine side of the river.

Best facilities near the capital are in the small port of Buceo, which has a yacht club with moorings available to visitors. There are good new facilities including a travelift at the protected harbour of Piriapolis. The old city of Colonia has a good marina. Available at all yacht clubs is a locally produced book with plans and photographs of all ports and anchorages along the Uruguayan coast.

Further Reading

South American Handbook
Fodor's South America
South America on a Shoestring

Websites

www.turismo.gub.uy (Ministry of Tourism)
www.cibernautica.com.ar (Waypoints and charts for both Uruguay and Argentina)

VENEZUELA

Venezuela has over 1500 miles of Caribbean coastline, off which lie 72 islands including the popular yachting destination, Isla de Margarita. Venezuela was given its name, 'little Venice', by the Spanish after seeing the Indian pile dwellings on Lake Maracaibo. A poor country throughout its history, this changed dramatically with the discovery of oil in 1914, and since then Venezuela has enjoyed a greater measure of prosperity than most Latin American countries or her Caribbean neighbours.

Lying on the direct route to Panama and also being rarely affected by hurricanes, the Venezuelan coast and particularly the offlying islands have become a very popular cruising destination in recent years. This popularity has been matched by a rapid improvement in yachting facilities and ser-

vices, with new marinas springing up all the time. The islands abound in picturesque anchorages and diving is excellent almost everywhere, particularly among the scores of islets and cays of Los Roques.

An increasingly popular destination is the Delta of the Orinoco, much of which can be explored by keeled boats. Those interested in the mountainous interior can leave their boats in the safety of one of the many marinas.

Country Profile

The Carib and Arawak tribes who lived along the coast put up little resistance to the Spanish settlers who arrived at the start of the eighteenth century. Not finding any gold, the Spanish turned to agriculture, and gradually spread through the country, mixing with the Indians and later introducing African slaves to work on the sugar plantations. After several uprisings against Spain's colonial rule in the eighteenth century, early in the nineteenth century Francisco Miranda tried twice to gain independence for the region. Simón Bolívar who followed him was more successful, crossing the Andes with his men in 1819 and capturing Bogotá. The short lived independent Gran Colombia was created, a union of present day Ecuador, Colombia, Venezuela and Panama, but in 1830 Venezuela declared itself an independent republic. A succession of dictators ruled the country into the early twentieth century. After the Second World War a more democratic regime was followed by the dictatorship of General Marco Perez Jimenez, who was eventually overthrown in 1964. Increasing instability led in 1992 to two unsuccessful military coups. In 1999 Hogo Chavez, one of the military officers who led one of the 1992 military coups, was elected President of Venezuela on a manifesto of economic and political reform.

The Venezuelan economy, dominated by petroleum, suffered during the 1980s collapse in oil prices, although stabilisation has since occurred, and efforts have been made to diversify. Venezuela has vast natural resources and is rich in energy sources. Mining and agriculture are important. Problems that remain are a large foreign debt, high food imports, as well as unemployment, illiteracy and an exodus from rural areas.

The population is over 20 million, mostly of mixed Spanish and Indian ancestry, with pure Indians living in the remoter parts, also some of African and European origins. The main language spoken is Spanish, and Roman Catholicism is the

Practical Information

LOCAL TIME: GMT – 4

BUOYAGE: IALA B

CURRENCY: Bolivar (Bs) of 100 centimos.

BUSINESS HOURS
Banks: 0830–1130, 1400–1630 Monday to Friday.
Government offices: 0830–1200, 1400–1800; these hours vary and officials have special hours for receiving the public, usually 0900–1000, 1500–1600.
Shops: 0900–1300, 1500–1900 Monday to Saturday.

ELECTRICITY: 110/240 V, 60 Hz

PUBLIC HOLIDAYS
1 January: New Year's Day
Carnival: Monday, Tuesday before Ash Wednesday
Thursday, Friday, Saturday of Holy Week
19 April: Proclamation of Independence
1 May
24 June: San Juan Bautista
5 July: Independence Day
24 July: Bolívar's Birthday
12 October: Columbus Day
25 December: Christmas Day

31 December: New Year's Eve
Extra government and bank holidays (nearest Monday to the date):
19 March: St Joseph
6 January
Ascension Day
Corpus Christi
29 June
15 August: Assumption
1 November: All Saints' Day
8 December: Immaculate Conception

COMMUNICATIONS
CANTV for international and long-distance calls, 24 hours. No collect calls can be made. Post offices are open 0800–1800. Post is slow and unreliable.
The post offices on Isla Margarita (Pampatar and Porlamar) are open 0900–1130, 1400–1630.
There are regular flights from Caracas to Europe, USA, Caribbean and South American destinations.

MEDICAL
Health care in state hospitals is free, but the standards vary and foreign visitors are advised to have medical insurance. For serious medical emergencies it may be worth contacting Hospital de Clinicas in Caracas (*Tel.* (2) 574-2011), which provides a full range of hospital and out-patients services. Many of the staff speak English. Cash payment is expected at the time of service, but fees are reported to be reasonable and the care excellent.

DIPLOMATIC MISSIONS
In Caracas:
Brazil: Piso 6 Edificio Central Gerencial Mohedano, Av. Mohedano. Visas can be granted the same day if requested at 0900, returned at 1800.
Canada: 7th floor Edificio Torre Europa, Av. Francisco de Miranda, Campo Alegre. *Tel.* (2) 951-6166.
Guyana: Edificio Los Frailes, C/ La Guanita, Chuao.
Suriname: 4a Avenida between 7a and 8a Transversal, Urb. Altmira.
United Kingdom: Torre Las Mercedes, Avenida La Estancia, Chuao. *Tel.* (2) 993-4111.
United States: Av. Francisco Miranda and Av. Principal de la Floresta. *Tel.* (2) 285-2222.

In Maracaibo:
United Kingdom: Avenida 9B, 66-146. *Tel.* (61) 73-745.
United States: Edificio Sofimara, Calle 77 and Av. 13. *Tel.* (61) 84-254.

---

leading religion. Caracas is the capital, in the central highlands, at an altitude of 3148 ft (960 m).

Venezuela has a tropical climate and there is little change between the seasons, although it is drier from December to April. The northern coast and offlying islands are under the influence of the NE trade winds, which blow strongly between December and April. Summer winds are lighter and Venezuela is very rarely affected by tropical storms.

Entry Regulations

Ports of entry
Carúpano 10°41′N 63°15′W, Puerto Sucre (Cumaná) 10°28′N 64°11′W, Puerto La Cruz 10°13′N 64°38′W, Carenero 10°32′N 66°07′W, La Guaira 10°36′N 66°56′W, Puerto Cabello 10°29′N 68°00′W, Maracaibo 10°39′N 71°36′W, Pampatar (Isla de Margarita) 11°00′N 63°47′W, Porlamar 10°56.5′N 63°49′W.

Procedure on arrival
On entry into Venezuela, one must first clear with customs, immigration and port captain, in that order. When departing for the next state one must clear out and after that in each state visited, yachts must clear in and out with customs and port captain. Immigration clearance is only required when entering and leaving the country. As clearance is done from state to state, no cruising permit is necessary. One should be aware that the rules do change often and that individual port captains often change the rules to fit their needs and interpretation of the law. There is no clearance at weekends and at the time of writing no overtime charges. It may be necessary to have an official pilot for entry into Maracaibo, La Guaira and Ciudad Bolívar. It is not recommended to clear into Maracaibo as yachts are charged the same price as large commercial vessels.
Puerto Sucre: Formalities are reasonable as the officials are used to yachts. Cumaná town is a mile away.

Carenero: One can anchor off the yacht club and there is also a marina. The port captain's office is about a mile away.

La Guaira: This is a big commercial port and yachts cannot clear in without using an agent. For a fee of up to US$100, the agent does all the paperwork and brings all the officials to the dock together. For outward clearance the agent delivers stamped passports and clearance papers to the fuel dock. Immigration is on the NW of the passenger terminal by the dock. One must clear here for Carabelleda.

Pampatar: Most yachts now bypass Pampatar as the port captain does not welcome yachts and go instead straight to Porlamar.

Porlamar: Marina Deportes Nautico (also known as Concorde Marina) monitors Channel 16 and is a good place to complete entry formalities. The services of a local agent will simplify matters and Venezuelan Marine Supply (Vemasca), which can be contacted on Channel 72, has been recommended as being prompt and reliable. They work 0830 to 1830 Monday to Saturday and answer calls for Vemasca.

Los Testigos: This is not a port of entry, so theoretically one should clear into Venezuela somewhere else before coming here. Boats are normally allowed to stop and allowed to remain 72 hours, but extensions are usually granted. Yachts are normally requested to visit the Coast Guard on Isla Iguana and also to call them again on departure. The area is occasionally patrolled by the Venezuelan Coast Guard, who will ask those who have overstayed to move on, and also insist that boats fly the Venezuelan courtesy flag.

Carúpano: Boats should anchor inside the harbour and take the dinghy to the steps. All offices are near the port and formalities are simple. Only immigration works at weekends and will clear boats on arrival. The customs and port captain offices are only open on weekdays.

Puerto La Cruz: Located on the mainland, boats should proceed to Xanadu Marina, where entry formalities can be completed.

If one wishes to stop at any of the Venezuelan islands between Isla de Margarita and Bonaire, this should be stated when clearing out of Isla de Margarita. A mention will be made on the clearance paper that permission had been granted to stop at 'puntos intermedios'. This may not always be acceptable to other officials but more and more yachts are visiting La Blanquilla without any difficulties as the local Coast Guard becomes accustomed to foreign yachts.

Los Roques: This is not an official port of entry, but boats are allowed a stay of 15 days. Most yachts prolong this by taking several days to reach Roque Grande where one has to do the clearance and also take time on departure after outward clearance. One must clear with the National Guard, Coast Guard, port captain and also the National Park service as the area is a National Park. There are fees per boat charged per length (around US$1 per foot) and about US$18 per person. One should inform the Park official where one intends to go as a special permission is needed for some areas of the Park and some areas are prohibited. There is a small fee for a diving permit if one wishes to dive.

Customs

Animals are not restricted but should have a valid health certificate and anti-rabies vaccination. There is rabies in Venezuela.

Foreign yachts may remain in Venezuela for a period of 18 months, but individuals may only stay for 90 days. This was introduced to allow people to leave their yachts in Venezuela while they returned home. Some of the agents in Puerto de la Cruz and Porlamar are able to extend this time allowance in the passport for a price. These rules may change as the marina owners put pressure on the government to realise the importance of the marine tourist industry.

Immigration

For most nationalities, it is no longer required to obtain a visa in advance and immigration procedures are dealt with on arrival. There are convenient Venezuelan consulates in Aruba, Bonaire, Martinique, Barbados, Guyana, Suriname, Trinidad and Grenada.

A passport or certified copy of the passport should be carried at all times when travelling inland, as the police and military do spot checks.

Health

Malaria prophylaxis and yellow fever vaccination are recommended. There is bilharzia in some rivers, so swimming in fresh water should be avoided.

Precautions should be taken against vampire bats on the coast from Cumaná onwards, and also the Chimaná Islands, as they may carry the rabies virus. The bats will fly on to a boat at night and bite the sleeping occupants.

Fees

There is an entry tax, a departure tax and also a cruising permit fee. These fees vary from state to state, and often also fluctuate even within the same state. There are National Park fees in Los Roques and the Moroccoy Park. There are no overtime fees. The agent fees are rising all the time, but as a good agent can save a lot of time and bother, one should try to check in advance to determine a good agent and establish their fees before using them for clearance.

Charter

Chartering is illegal in Venezuela, especially to Venezuelan citizens, and can lead to heavy fines or confiscation of the boat. An exception to this rule is when a foreign flag vessel arrives to pick up charter guests from an international flight to cruise in Venezuelan waters, these being considered as crew. This practice should be kept very low key.

Restrictions

Isla Orchilla is a military base and one should not approach as there is a restricted area.

Los Piedros (Punto Fijo) is also a military base and entry is prohibited.

Los Roques is a National Park and certain restrictions apply to fishing, lobstering or collecting shells.

Security

The number of thefts, muggings and even knife attacks reported by visiting sailors has increased in recent years. They seem to occur both on the mainland and in the islands. Margarita, Cumaná and Puerto La Cruz seem to be particularly bad areas. Outboard engines and items on deck should be secured and, if possible the dinghy should be lifted out of the water.

Facilities

Venezuela is a good place to provision, especially if continuing on to the Pacific. Prices are lower than most of the Caribbean. The selection is generally good, although shortages can occur lasting several months. Fuel is widely available and cheap. Repair facilities are generally good and the prices competitive because labour costs are low; however, a written estimate should be obtained before embarking on any major work.

The 'vessel in transit' status is not recognised in Venezuela and getting spare parts sent in can be difficult and costly. For this reason many sailors choose to get their repairs done in Trinidad or make sure they bring any necessary parts with them.

Isla de Margarita is no longer a duty-free island and now has a 8 per cent sales tax, but this is still less than the mainland where the tax is 15 per cent. Several planned marina projects have not come to fruition and there is only one marina suitable for cruising boats. A limited number of repair facilities are available. Recommended are the services of Venezuelan Marine Supply (Vemasca) in Porlamar, who can be contacted on Channel 72 between 0830 and 1830 Monday to Saturday. They run a good rigging shop, stock some spares, and will also order parts to be sent in.

There are good repair facilities and several boatyards in Cumaná, but many yachts are avoiding this area because of the rising crime rate; and several sailors have already been attacked.

The majority of cruising yachts that need work done are choosing Puerto La Cruz where there are haulout facilities and spare parts can be obtained. Puerto La Cruz has now become the boating capital of Venezuela as far as foreign vessels are concerned, due to the good shipyards and marinas that have opened in recent years. The Amerigo Vespucci marina in Puerto La Cruz operates a boatyard, where yachts can be slipped and hull repair can be undertaken. It is good for repairs and provisioning before sailing to the Pacific.

La Guaira is a large commercial port with no facilities for yachts, only worth visiting for clearance or visiting Caracas. Fuel is available on the dock and water at the military dock. It is much better to sail the six miles to Carabelleda where the marina facilities have been greatly improved recently. Various repair facilities are available and there is a boatyard. Fuel is available at the dock. Puerto Cabello is a large commercial port with good repair facilities and provisioning.

Boats heading for the Orinoco can reprovision and refuel at Guira, a large commercial port. Better facilities are available at Puerto Ordez, at the confluence of the Orinoco and Coroni rivers. There is a good yacht club, which can be used by visitors. Boats reaching the Orinoco from the south will find some supplies and fuel at Curiapo, on the Barima river.

Further Reading

Cruising Guide to Venezuela and Bonaire
Cruising Guide to the Caribbean
South American Handbook

Website

www.venezuela.gov.ve/turismo (Ministry of Tourism)

8 North Pacific Islands

No other region described in this book presents such a marked contrast as that between the highly developed and fast pace of Hawaii and the tranquil traditional lifestyle of some of the Micronesian islands. For anyone cruising the North Pacific this way of life is the most interesting feature of these widely scattered islands, some of which are hardly ever visited by yachts or any other outsiders. Most yacht movement is centred on Hawaii, which serves as a convenient turning-point for the large number of yachts sailing over from mainland North America. Hawaii is also a good platform for starting a longer cruise, whether it be to Alaska, Micronesia or the South Pacific. The latter is still the favourite and Tahiti the usual destination after Hawaii.

Most of the former UN Trust Territories of the North Pacific have chosen some degree of autonomy, although they continue to maintain strong links with the United States, who had administered them since the Second World War. The USA maintains a military presence in some places, access to which is usually prohibited to yachts. In an attempt to protect their traditional lifestyle, most Micronesian nations do not actively encourage tourism and there are certain restrictions imposed on yachts wishing to visit some of the remote islands. Many of them insist on a cruising permit to be obtained in advance, but in some places this permit is issued on arrival.

Most of the area is under the influence of the NE trade winds which are most consistent during winter, from November to March. Their strength and consistency diminishes as one moves south towards the equator. Typhoons affect the area between the Carolines and Japan, most typhoons occurring between May and December, September being the most dangerous month. Typhoons do not reach the islands east of Guam.

Facilities are situated at the two extremes, in Hawaii and Guam, with very little in between. Anyone sailing west of Hawaii must be prepared to

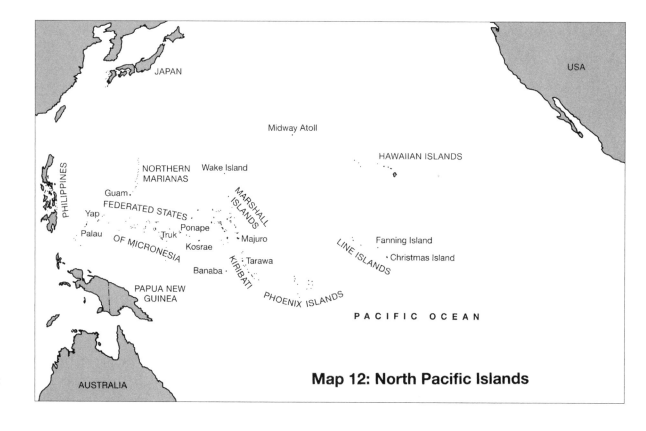

Map 12: North Pacific Islands

be able to cope with any emergency as the few facilities that are available are usually located in each territory's capital. As can be expected, facilities in Hawaii itself are of the highest order, which means that the boat can be well prepared for the projected voyage. Facilities are also good in Guam, where most of what might be needed is available.

FEDERATED STATES OF MICRONESIA

The Federated States of Micronesia (FSM) are Kosrae, Pohnpei, Chuuk and Yap, stretching over a vast expanse of Pacific Ocean just north of the equator. Geographically, these four small states are part of the Caroline Islands, consisting between them of over 600 islands, of which only 65 are inhabited.

For the cruising sailor the Federated States of Micronesia offer a chance to come in contact with a Micronesian society which has managed to preserve most of its traditions despite successive waves of foreign domination. Close links with the United States have brought a higher living standard, but also the social problems of modern life, which the islanders are making an effort to overcome. Visiting sailors, coming by sea, with which the islanders have a deep affinity, can be sure of a warm and sincere welcome.

The four individual states each have their own distinct character, which adds to the attraction of sailing there. Pohnpei, formerly known as Ponape, is a lush island with eight outlying atolls. The ruins of Nan Madol, a city of nearly one hundred man-made islets dating back to AD 1200, are worth a visit. Another attraction of Pohnpei is the excellent diving, reputedly best at Ant Atoll, 10 miles SW of Pohnpei, although the atoll is privately owned and permission must be obtained from the authorities in the capital Kolonia before a visit. An additional attraction are several waterfalls and the swimming in fresh-water pools at the base of the falls.

Kosrae is a mountainous volcanic island, with a quiet atmosphere, especially since the Congregationalist church is very strong, and on Sundays even leisure activities are disapproved of.

The State of Chuuk (formerly Truk) has 192 small islands spread over nearly 1000 square miles of ocean, many of them uninhabited. The main centre is Chuuk Lagoon, where 15 islands and 80 islets surround the huge lagoon, where an entire Japanese fleet was trapped and sunk by a surprise US air attack in 1944, and is now Chuuk's main tourist attraction. Also part of Chuuk state are the isolated Mortlocks, Hall Islands and Western Islands, where a more traditional atmosphere may be experienced.

The islands of Yap are the most isolated and traditional in their ways and the Yapese are determined to keep it that way. Yap Proper, consisting of 13 islands within a reef, is the centre of the state, while eastwards lie the 134 other islands. Yap is famous for its huge stone money, which was once transported from island to island in canoes.

Many islands, especially the more isolated ones, are attempting to return to a traditional way of life by doing without Western goods and rejecting the Western way of life. Visitors are urged to respect local customs and refrain from disturbing these people's lives. Conservative dress, especially for women, is recommended.

Country Profile

Before the arrival of Europeans all the islands had developed civilisations based on highly stratified clan societies. These social divisions remain strong today. Pohnpei was inhabited as early as AD 200, and ruled in the thirteenth century by a royal dynasty from Nan Madol city. On Kosrae by the fifteenth century a highly developed society existed with its capital on the fortressed Leluh island. Only sighted in the nineteenth century by Europeans, it was named Strong's Island and was rarely visited. On Yap remains have been found dating back to AD 200, and Yap once reigned over a considerable island empire, built on the power of sorcerers.

Out of the way of the main trade routes, little attention was paid to any of the islands until the nineteenth century, when traders, whalers and missionaries arrived. New diseases wiped out many of the islanders. The surviving inhabitants saw first the Spanish, then the Germans impose colonial rule, solely interested in exploiting the economic value of the islands' resources, and using the islanders as forced labour. The Germans fled at the start of the First World War, and the Japanese ruled the islands as League of Nation mandates. The Japanese embarked on an intensive cultivation of the islands, while the Micronesians, often outnumbered on their own islands, had little say in what went on. Then came the Second World War and the Americans gradually pushed out the Japanese, although the worst of the fighting took place elsewhere.

Practical Information

LOCAL TIME: Yap, Chuuk, GMT + 10.
Pohnpei, Kosrae, GMT + 11.

BUOYAGE: IALA A

CURRENCY: United States dollar (US$)

BUSINESS HOURS
Banks: 1000–1500 Monday to Thursday, to
1700/1800 Friday.
Shops: 0800–2100 daily.
Government offices: 0800–1700 Monday to
Friday.

ELECTRICITY: 110/120 V, 60 Hz

PUBLIC HOLIDAYS
1 January: New Year's Day
11 January: Constitution Day (Kosrae)
24 February: Sokehs Rebellion (Pohnpei)

1 March: Yap Day
31 March: Traditional Culture Day (Pohnpei)
Good Friday
10 May: Constitution Day
17 May: Kolonia Independence Day (Pohnpei)
12 July: Micronesian Day
8 September: Liberation Day (Kosrae)
11 September: Liberation Day (Pohnpei)
26 September: Charter Day (Chuuk)
24 October: United Nations Day
3 November: Self-government Day (Kosrae)
8 November: Constitution Day (Pohnpei)
1st Friday in November: Independence Day
24 December: Constitution Day (Yap)
25 December

COMMUNICATIONS
International calls via the COMSAT stations,
normally open 24 hours. Most public phones
take FSM phone cards.

The US postal system is used.
Zip codes: Pohnpei 96941; Truk 96942;
Yap 96943; Kosrae 96944;
Mail can be sent c/o General Delivery with
island zip code.
Weno, Chuuk: the post office is open
0900–1530 Monday, 0800–1530
Tuesday–Friday, 1000–1200 Saturday.
International onward connections are best
made via flights to Guam, Majuro
(Marshalls), Honolulu or Nadi (Fiji). There
are flights between the islands.

MEDICAL
Facilities are available in all the states.

DIPLOMATIC MISSIONS
Australia: Box 5, Pohnpei. *Tel.* 320 5448.
United States: Box 1286, Kolonia.
Tel. 320 2187.

After the war the United States administered the islands as part of the UN Trust Territory. In 1979 the Trust Territory voted on a common constitution, which was rejected by the Marshalls and Palau, who went their own way. The remainder formed the Federated States of Micronesia. Each state has signed a separate Compact of Free Association with the USA, which means the US retains military freedom and the islands receive aid. Each state has its own constitution, and in 1991 FSM was admitted to the United Nations.

Millions of dollars in aid come into the FSM from the USA, aimed at building the economy towards self-sufficiency. Many projects are under way, but most islanders remain subsistence farmers and fishermen. There is little paid employment except in the government sector. Fishing rights fees are an important source of income, but otherwise there are few natural resources. Kosrae is known for its citrus fruits, and Pohnpei exports black pepper.

The population is around 150,000 with the majority residing in Chuuk State. All are Micronesians, except for the Nukuro and Kapingamarangi islanders in Pohnpei state who are Polynesian. English is the language spoken by all, as well as Kosraen, Pohnpeian, Chuukese and Yapese. Some outer islands have their own languages. Most islanders are Protestants or Catholics.

Each state has its own centre, but the FSM capital is Palikir on Pohnpei. Colonia (the town is locally known as Donguch) is the capital of Yap, Tofol of Kosrae, and Weno of Chuuk.

The islands are under the influence of the NE trade winds, which blow between October and May. January to March is the dry season, while rainfall can be heavy in the summer months. The SW monsoon lasts from June to September, when there are frequent periods of calm. Strong SW gales can occur during August and September. They appear to be caused by the typhoons which are bred in this region but usually move away from the islands. Occasionally the islands are affected by typhoons. Although typhoons can occur at any time of the year, the period 1 December to 30 April may be regarded as relatively safe. In some years, the typhoon season may start early, or last longer than usual, so the weather should be watched carefully at all times. Guam has the best forecasts for the area.

Entry Regulations

Ports of entry
Pohnpei: Kolonia 6°59′N 158°13′E.
Chuuk: Weno (Chuuk Lagoon) 7°20′N 151°50′E,
Lukunor Atoll (Mortlocks) 5°30′N 153°48′E,
Satawan Atoll (Mortlocks) 5°25′N 153°35′E.
Yap: Colonia (Yap Island) 9°30′N 138°08′E,
Ulithi Atoll 9°55′N 139°30′E, Wolaei Atoll
7°21′N 143°53′E.

Kosrae: Lele/Leluh Harbour 5°20'N 163°02'E, Okat Harbour 5°21'N 162°57'E.

Procedure on arrival

All yachts, whether in possession of a permit or not, must proceed directly to a port of entry. It is forbidden to stop at any islands before clearing in. Even after having cleared into one of the four member states, one still has to complete formalities with customs and immigration on arrival in each individual state. Yachts sailing to another state may stop at outer islands on the way, even if they do not belong to the state that one has already cleared into, as long as a coastal clearance is obtained in the port of departure.

Kolonia: Kolonia port control should be contacted on Channel 16 about two hours before arrival. The operator will advise where to come alongside. For clearing in it is best to come alongside the commercial wharf as customs and immigration may wish to board the boat. Agriculture, police and health officials may also visit. If there is no space at the wharf, one can anchor and go ashore. The customs and immigration offices are housed in separate buildings in town.

Arrivals at weekends should be avoided as overtime fees will be charged. Those arriving on a Sunday may anchor at buoy number 6 and clear in on Monday morning. The ship's log may be inspected to see if the boat has made any stops before clearing in. Holding tanks may also be inspected (see Restrictions).

On departure, it is possible to clear customs in town, but immigration may insist on clearing the yacht at the commercial wharf.

Weno: The government offices are on the NW side of the island near the airport. There is a $100 clearing in fee.

Kosrae: Lele Harbour, protected by the reef and Leluh Island, is the harbour of the capital Tofol, on the eastern side of the island. Marine Resources should be contacted on Channel 16 on arrival. Customs and immigration officials will come out to the yacht at anchor in a launch. Occasionally the captain is asked to come ashore himself and meet the officials at the dinghy landing. After clearance, one should visit the Port Director at the Public Works Office in town. Clearance is also possible at Okat Harbour on the western coast.

Colonia: Tomil Harbour, the main port, is reached through a passage in the reef. If there is space yachts can come alongside a quay in the small boat harbour for clearance.

Ulithi: Clearance can be made at the government dock at Falalop.

Customs

Firearms must be declared to the police on arrival and may have to be surrendered until departure.

Animals require a veterinary certificate and must remain on board at all times. Birds such as parrots and parakeets cannot be imported without special permission from the Director of Health Services. Birds not having this permission may have to be destroyed or exported.

Immigration

Entry permits are granted on arrival for up to 30 days, with proof of adequate funds. One must clear in and out of each state, and a new entry permit of 30 days is given each time. Stays of over 30 days in one state must be applied for in advance from Chief of Immigration, PO Box PS105, Palikir, Pohnpei, Federated States of Micronesia, FSM 96941. *Tel.* 320 2606, Fax. 320 2234. Extensions of 30 days can be obtained, up to 90 days maximum, for US$10 per extension. For stays over 90 days a visa will be needed.

Cruising permit

This must be obtained in advance of arrival. One should apply in writing to the Chief of Immigration. The application should contain the following information: boat name, port and flag of registration, LOA, net and gross tonnage, crew list, detailed itinerary, intended port of entry. It takes several months to receive an answer. If the permit has not arrived by the time one is ready to leave the last port, a copy of the original application should be faxed to the above number with a request to process the application immediately. An answer is normally received within 48 hours. There is no fee for the permit. The permit is issued for one year. Any yacht arriving without the permit may be asked to leave after three days.

Health

Chuuk has been cholera free only since 1984.

Typhoid and tetanus vaccinations are recommended.

Fees

Yap: Overtime is charged after 1630 on weekdays, and at weekends: customs, immigration and health all charge $6 per hour.

Harbour fees are $0.06 times GRT divided by 24 hours.

Light dues are $0.06 times GRT. There are charges for fresh water.

Pohnpei: Overtime is charged outside of

0800–1700 Monday to Friday, and at weekends.

Harbour fee $15 entry, $5 per day for using the dock.

Truk and Kosrae: Overtime is charged outside of 0800–1700 weekdays, and all day Saturdays, Sundays and holidays.

Restrictions

When visiting outer islands of each state, not the main centres, permission must be asked for beforehand from the landowner. Even uninhabited islands and islets do have an owner. Permission is normally granted. The chief of the village should be visited first, and offered a symbolic gift. On some islands, the chiefs are now legally entitled to charge visiting yachts a landing fee.

The authorities in Chuuk no longer allow visiting sailors to dive on the many wrecks, even if accompanied by a local guide. Dives are only permitted with one of the local dive shops.

Holding tanks are becoming a requirement and officials may inspect them when clearing into Pohnpei. These restrictions were imposed because of commercial fishermen, but cruising boats were also affected. Requirements are no longer strictly enforced on yachts, but the situation may change in the future.

Facilities

Facilities vary widely across the Federation, with adequate repair facilities in the main centres and very little in the outer islands. In Sokehs Harbour in Pohnpei, Rumours Bar, Grill and Marina has some facilities for visiting yachts, including a fuel dock, dinghy dock and showers. The channel leading into the inner harbour is unmarked, so local help may be needed. There are fisheries plants in several islands and wherever there is a base for fishing boats, one can expect to find at least a modicum of repair facilities. One of the best is Yap Fisheries who maintain a 70-ton railway where boats can be hauled out and some repairs carried out.

Provisioning is good in all main centres where there is a selection of imported goods, mainly from the USA, although they tend to be on the expensive side. There are also fresh produce markets and some fresh produce can be found practically everywhere even if the selection is not always great. Water sources must be chosen carefully as often the public supply is not drinkable and should be treated. Generally, rain water is more reliable if one has access to a catchment tank, or provision should

be made to collect one's own. Water obtained locally should be treated. Rainfall is only abundant in Kosrae and Pohnpei. Fuel can be bought in all centres, usually by jerrycan, although some fisheries have pumps or can arrange to have it delivered to the dock by tanker. No fuel is available in the outer islands. Propane is usually available in Pohnpei and Chuuk, but not in Kosrae and Yap.

As in other remote cruising areas, one should carry a good supply of essential spares as the only parts that may be available locally are those used in trucks or heavy plant in use on the islands.

Further Reading

Micronesia Cruising Notes
Micronesia – a travel survival kit
Landfalls of Paradise
Micronesia Handbook

Websites

www.fsmgov.org
www.visit-fsm.org

GUAM

Guam is the largest and most populous island of Micronesia, a modern, Americanised metropolis and home to an important US military base. It is geographically the southernmost of the Mariana Islands, but forms a separate unit from the Commonwealth of the Northern Marianas. Guam is an Unincorporated Territory of the United States. Guam's close relations with the USA, and its role as a crossroads and distribution centre for the rest of Micronesia because of its air links, makes it rather different from the rest of the Pacific.

Cruising yachts will indeed find in Guam a contrasting atmosphere to the one they have experienced in other islands. The pace is faster, the buildings taller and everything can be fixed if one is prepared to pay the price. Guam is used by many American sailors as a long-term base, especially as US citizens can work in Guam without a permit.

Country Profile

The Chamorros inhabited the Marianas as early as 1500 BC, migrating east from South East Asia. A

Practical Information

LOCAL TIME: GMT + 10

BUOYAGE: IALA A

CURRENCY: United States dollar (US$)

BUSINESS HOURS
Banks: 1000–1500 Monday to Thursday,
1000–1800 Friday.
Shops: 0800–1630 weekdays.
Government offices: 0800–1700 weekdays.

ELECTRICITY: 110 V, 60 Hz

PUBLIC HOLIDAYS
US holidays:
1 January: New Year's Day
Third Monday in January: Martin Luther

King's Birthday
Third Monday in February:
President's Day
Good Friday
Last Monday in May: Memorial Day
4 July: US Independence Day
First Monday in September: Labor Day
First Monday in October: Columbus Day
24 October: United Nations Day
11 November: Veterans Day
Fourth Thursday in November:
Thanksgiving Day
25 December
Plus:
First Monday in March:
Guam Discovery Day
21 July: Liberation Day
1 November: All Souls Day
8 December: Immaculate Conception

COMMUNICATIONS
Mail can be sent to c/o General Delivery,
Agana 96910, open 0830–1700 Monday to
Friday, 1200–1600 Saturday. International
calls, IT & E Overseas Inc, Marine Drive,
Tamuning.
There are flights from Guam to the
Philippines, Japan, Indonesia, Hong Kong
and to the USA via Majuro and Honolulu.

DIPLOMATIC MISSIONS
In Hagatna:
Japan: ITC Building, Tamuning.
Tel. 646-1290.
Northern Marianas: CNMI Liaison Office,
Box 8366, Tamuning. Entry permits can be
obtained here.
Philippines: ITC Building, Tamuning.
Tel. 646-4620.

---

complex matrilineal hierarchical society developed and stone remains of this early civilisation are still visible on the island. Magellan's visit in 1521 marked the arrival of the Western world. In the sixteenth century Spain claimed the Marianas, which were valuable as a stopping point on the trade route between Mexico and the Philippines. In the next century Catholic missionaries arrived, but their efforts to suppress old traditions led to rebellions by the Chamorros. By the end of the seventeenth century there were no full-blooded Chamorro men left, either being killed in the fighting or by European diseases. Things improved as Spaniards and Filipinos settled and cultivated the island. At the end of the 1898 Spanish–American war, Guam was ceded to the United States. During the Second World War the Japanese occupied Guam, until the USA retook the island in 1944 after some fierce fighting. In 1950 a civilian government took over, Guam's population gaining US citizenship, although no vote in US elections. The close relationship between Guam and the USA is unlikely to change in view of Guam's strategic importance to the USA.

Since the 1960s Guam has seen considerable economic growth and a rise in the standard of living. The military bases are the largest employer and dominate the economy. Both the Air Force and Navy have a considerable presence here. In the 1960s travel restrictions were lifted and tourism opened up, especially from Japan. Guam is a duty-free port.

The population is 150,000. Half are Chamorro, the rest Asian and American. English is the main language and, to a lesser extent, Chamorro which has a small Spanish influence, as does the main religion, Roman Catholicism. Hagatna, previously known as Agana, has been the main centre on Guam since the Spanish period.

The climate is warm and humid. From January to April the NE trades blow, while from July to November it is rainy and stormy. Typhoons can occur between July and November.

Entry Regulations

Port of entry
Apra Harbour 13°27′N 144°40′E.

Procedure on arrival
One should contact harbour control on VHF Channels 16, 13 or 12 (call sign KUF 810) for instructions on where to berth for clearance. Yachts are directed to the commercial pier on Cabras Island near the two large cranes, or off the Marianas Yacht Club at Drydock Point. Officials will come to the yacht.

Customs
Firearms must be declared on arrival and will be sealed on board. Permits may have to be shown.

Animals must be declared and should have up-to-date health certificates. They are not allowed to land.

Immigration

US visa regulations are in force, and all nationals except US citizens are required to have a visa in advance. However, visa requirements are often waived for those arriving by yacht.

Fees

Overtime is charged for clearance outside of normal office hours.

Restrictions

The inner harbour of Apra Harbour is a US naval base and access is restricted.

Facilities

Because of the high frequency of typhoons, arrangements have been made in Apra Harbour for small boats seeking shelter during a typhoon. The refuge area is located in Piti Channel, which can be reached by boats with a maximum draft of 8 feet. The area is reputed to be well sheltered in any kind of winds.

The Marianas Yacht Club, located on Dry Dock Point south of the commercial port, can be used by visitors. Two weeks' free membership is given to members of other yacht clubs, otherwise a fee must be paid for the use of club facilities, which include showers. Some club moorings are reserved for visitors and also privately owned moorings managed by the club are occasionally made available to visitors. There are additional moorings in Piti Channel and also at Hagatna Boat Basin, a small boat harbour in East Hagatna. Repair facilities are available at Dillingham Shipyard on Cabras Island.

Fuel and water can be obtained at the fishermen's wharf in Apra Harbour or at Hagatna, which is located approximately eight miles up the coast. Advice on the difficult reef entrance to Hagatna harbour can be obtained from harbour control on VHF Channel 16.

Although an increasingly important cruising destination, yachting facilities are rather limited with only basic spares being available locally. However, as there are regular air links with mainland USA, most parts can be air freighted to Guam in a reasonable time. There are several supermarkets which have a good selection of food as well as a fresh produce market. Guam is one of the best places to reprovision in Micronesia.

Further Reading

Micronesia Cruising Notes
Micronesia Handbook
Micronesia – a travel survival kit
Landfalls of Paradise
Destiny's Landfall

Websites

www.gov.gu
www.visitguam.org (Guam Visitors Bureau)

HAWAII

Hawaii, the 50th state of the USA, is in fact an archipelago stretching across the North Pacific from the remote Kure and Midway atolls to the more developed and heavily populated islands in the east. The islands are summits of an ancient volcanic mountain range, and have stunning scenery to match. On the largest, Hawaii Island, also known as Big Island, there is Mauna Loa, over 13,000 ft (4000 m) high, an active volcano, which erupted in 1959 destroying a village and thousands of acres of crops. The other major islands are Maui, Oahu, Kauai, Molokai, Lanai, Nihau and Kahoolawe. Hawaii is very different to the rest of the Pacific, mainly due to the strong American influence, also being very developed and commercial, such as the world-famous Waikiki Beach, although the old ways do survive in some places.

The ideal landfall and start of a cruise in Hawaiian waters is the small port of Hilo on Big Island as it is upwind of the entire archipelago. Hilo is a very pleasant place to unwind after the long passage from mainland USA and also to visit the interior of the spectacular Big Island. In most places in Hawaii only part of the sightseeing can be done from the cockpit, as many of the interesting places are either inland or difficult to reach by boat. The Big Island is an excellent introduction to Hawaii with its magnificent Kilauea Volcano, orchid gardens, cane fields and scenic coastline. A definite stop on the lee side of the island is at Kealakekua Bay, where Captain Cook lost his life in 1778.

The former whaling capital of the Pacific, Lahaina on Maui island is another popular cruising stop, as is the marine park at Hulopoe Bay on Lanai with its superb underwater scenery. Busy

Entrance into Alawai Marina off Waikiki Beach, Hawaii.

Honolulu with its excellent facilities has many tempting sights which should include a visit to the Bishop Museum, especially for those planning to continue their cruise to other Pacific islands, as many of the art treasures from these islands have been collected there. A good place to take one's leave from Hawaii is the northernmost island of Kauai and its spectacular Hanalei Bay, the set for many a South Seas movie.

Country Profile

Hawaii is said to have been discovered three times, the Polynesians claiming that Hawaii Loa was the first to land there over 1000 years ago. Some say that the Spanish were the first Europeans to discover the islands, but it was more likely Captain Cook in 1778, who named them the Sandwich Islands. This great navigator lost his life in a dispute between his crew and the islanders of Kealakekua (Hawaii Island).

At the end of the eighteenth century Kamehameha the Great united all the islands under his rule, and until 1882 his family reigned, later taken over by the Kalahaua dynasty. Missionaries and traders arrived during the nineteenth century. In 1893 Queen Lili'uokalani was dethroned and a republic proclaimed. Soon afterwards the US Congress passed a resolution annexing the islands. Many attempts were made by Hawaii to be recognised as a state, a status finally achieved in 1959.

The economy mainly relies on sugar, pineapples and tourism. Handicrafts, Hawaiian-style clothes, orchids and macadamia nuts are also exported. The scarcity of land is a problem and over a million people inhabit Hawaii. Following the immigration of Chinese and Japanese in the nineteenth century, Portuguese, Spanish and Russian in the early twentieth century, Hawaii's population is very mixed. Those of Polynesian origin form only a small minority. English is the main language. All Christian denominations can be found as well as Buddhism, Shintoism and Judaism. The capital is Honolulu on Oahu Island where most of the population lives.

The climate is subtropical in the low coastal areas and temperate in the mountains. There is no rainy season but showers, sometimes downpours,

Practical Information

LOCAL TIME: GMT – 10

BUOYAGE: IALA B

CURRENCY: United States dollar (US$)

BUSINESS HOURS
Banks: 0830–1500 Monday to Thursday, 0830–1800 Friday.
Business and government offices: 0800–1630 Monday to Friday.
Shops: 0930–1730 Monday to Saturday, some stay open until 2100, some open Sundays.

ELECTRICITY: 110 V, 60 Hz

PUBLIC HOLIDAYS
1 January: New Year's Day

3rd Monday in January: Martin Luther King Day
3rd Monday in February: President's Day
26 March: Prince Kuhio Day
Good Friday
1 May: Lei Day (floral displays)
Last Monday in May: Memorial Day
11 June: Kamehameha Day
4 July: Independence Day
First Monday in September: Labor Day
September/October: Aloha Week, on Oahu
2nd Monday in October: Columbus Day
11 November: Veterans Day
Last Thursday in November: Thanksgiving Day
25 December: Christmas Day

COMMUNICATIONS
Public telephones can be credit card or coin operated.
Stamps are available at post offices, hotels

and shops.
Emergency: 911.
There are frequent flights from Honolulu to mainland USA, the Far East, Europe, Tahiti, Fiji, New Zealand and Australia.

MEDICAL
There are good medical facilities in all islands, but as the costs tend to be high, visitors are advised to have a comprehensive health insurance.

DIPLOMATIC MISSIONS
Kiribati: 850 Richards Street, Honolulu.
Northern Marianas: CNMI Liaison Office, 1221 Kapiolani Blvd, Suite 348, Honolulu, HI 96814.
Marshalls: 1441 Kapiolani Blvd, Suite 1910.

---

occur in winter. The islands are under the influence of the NE trade winds and are only rarely affected by tropical cyclones.

Entry Regulations

Hawaiian entry regulations are basically the same as the rest of the United States, but there are slight differences and regulations are usually applied in a more detailed manner. This is partly due to the fact that to arrive in Hawaii from the US mainland, yachts must leave US territorial waters.

Ports of entry
Honolulu (Oahu) 21°18′N 157°52′W, Hilo (Hawaii) 19°44′N 155°04′W, Kona (Hawaii) 19°40′N 156°02′W, Kahului (Maui) 20°54′N 156°28′W, Nawiliwili (Kauai) 21°57′N 159°21′W, Port Allen (Kauai) 21°54′N 158°36′W.

Procedure on arrival
Customs telephone numbers: Honolulu: 522-8012, 861-8462 (24 hours), Fax. 522-8018, Hilo: *Tel.* and Fax. 933-6976, Kona: 334-1850, Fax. 334-1852, Maui: 877-6013, Fax. 877-5703, Kauai: 822-5673, 822-5521 (24 hours).

Yachts must report immediately on arrival to customs and formal clearance must be made within 48 hours of arrival. Working hours are 0800–1630 Monday to Friday. Vessels that have cellphones can call customs before arriving to minimise the waiting time. After hours, one should telephone

customs. A Ships Stores Declaration and Crew's Effects Declaration must be made as well as showing the clearance from the previous port. Customs may handle immigration and health formalities in some places. One can first contact the harbour master who will inform customs. Quarantine must be notified if there are animals on board or if coming from any country outside the USA or Canada, in which case any fresh fruit, vegetables, eggs and certain food items will be confiscated and destroyed.

On arrival no one must go ashore except for the person reporting the arrival to customs, who must afterwards return to the yacht, until formalities are completed. Violations of this rule can result in heavy penalties, even forfeiture of the boat.

Yachts must enter at an official port of entry. Yachts stopping elsewhere may be liable for heavy fines. This rule also applies to US registered vessels coming from foreign ports; they must call at an official port of entry before proceeding elsewhere. American captains have been fined for making landfall at other Hawaiian ports and attempting to clear customs by telephone.

US vessels arriving from a US port on the mainland who have not stopped at a foreign port en route or have had no contact with any other vessel at sea, and who have only US citizens on board, do not need to clear customs, but must be inspected on arrival by an agricultural inspector of the State of Hawaii. They must inform the agricultural department of their arrival.

After having cleared into Hawaii, US vessels are free to go anywhere in the USA. Foreign vessels are given a cruising permit, if eligible. Foreign vessels must check in with customs at other ports of entry when they visit other islands. Precise instructions of the procedure will be given at the first port of entry.

Hilo: The harbour master will direct yachts to berth in Radio Bay.

Kahului: Yachts should berth at the commercial wharf for clearance before anchoring in the harbour.

Honolulu: Clearance is best done at Ala Wai yacht harbour.

Nawiliwili: Customs will clear yachts at the commercial wharf.

Procedure on departure

All yachts, including US registered vessels, must obtain a customs clearance for foreign destinations.

Customs

Firearms must be declared to customs. The police may issue permits.

Hawaii is rabies-free, so regulations regarding animals on board yachts are more strict than on the US mainland. Animals must be declared on arrival, and will have to be sent to the Quarantine Centre in Honolulu within 72 hours, where they must remain for 120 days or until the yacht leaves Hawaii. This includes animals arriving from the US mainland. As air transport costs from other islands are paid by the animal's owner, it is better to make Honolulu the port of entry if one has an animal on board. There is a daily fee for quarantine, which must be paid in advance; unused days will be refunded. The quarantine station should be given 24 to 48 hours' notice of departure and they will deliver the animal to the yacht. Penalties are very heavy for violation of this regulation.

Any dutiable items such as navigation equipment bought recently in the USA should be listed and certified by US customs before leaving the USA, or receipts kept showing the place of purchase, to avoid being liable for duty.

There are restrictions on importing plants and fresh produce. Fruit and vegetables may be confiscated on arrival when the yacht is inspected by the agriculture official.

Cruising permit

US regulations state that foreign yachts from certain countries can obtain a cruising licence on arrival, which exempts them from having to clear in and out in each port once the first entry clearance is completed. The countries which are eligible for this licence are Argentina, Austria, Australia, Bahamas, Belgium, Bermuda, Canada, Denmark, Finland, France, Germany, Greece, Honduras, Ireland, Italy, Jamaica, Liberia, the Netherlands, New Zealand, Norway, Sweden, Switzerland, Turkey, the United Kingdom (including Turks and Caicos, St Vincent, Cayman Islands, British Virgin Islands, St Kitts and Anguilla). This list, which includes countries that grant similar privileges to US yachts, is subject to change. The licence is issued on entry by customs. It is valid for up to one year. Successive licences are not usually granted.

Foreign yachts, whether or not holding a cruising permit, are still supposed to notify customs by telephone on arrival in major ports.

Yachts not entitled to a cruising licence must obtain a Permit to Proceed to each subsequent port and they must make entry at all major ports while cruising Hawaii.

Immigration

US citizens need proof of citizenship only.

Canadians need proof of citizenship only, unless they are arriving from outside of North America, when they must present a valid Canadian passport.

All other nationalities need a visa, which must be obtained in advance from US embassies and consulates. The passport must be valid at least six months beyond the period of stay.

Fees

Overtime is charged outside of working hours, and on Sundays and public holidays. Service will be provided at pro-rata overtime rates, not to exceed US $25 per boat.

Customs charges: A user fee of US$25 covers the annual processing. A decal will be issued for this fee and must be displayed in a prominent position.

Restrictions

A controversial regulation, which has been resisted by local sailors, is the 72 hour anchoring limit. Although brought in to deal with a large number of derelict vessels, the rule has been applied against cruising boats too. It is reported that the rule now only applies to the island of Oahu. Cruising boats are free to anchor for longer periods at all other islands, provided they are not left unattended.

Many Hawaiian bays have been designated Marine Conservation Areas, and anchoring is prohibited in some of them. The government booklet 'Marine Life Conservation Districts' gives more information on local restrictions.

Nihau Island is reserved for native Hawaiians. It can only be visited with official permission.

Military areas: Kahoolawe Island, just south of Maui, was previously used as a firing range by the US Navy. Jurisdiction has reverted to the State of Hawaii, but unexploded ordnance is still being cleared from the island. Before landing at this island, check with the customs office on Maui to get the latest information and clearance.

The Midway Islands, 28°13′N 177°24′W, at the western extremity of the Hawaiian group, are not part of the state of Hawaii, and are administered by the US Navy. Johnston Atoll 16°45′N 169°31′W is administered by the US Air Force and is to be used for dumping chemical weapons as well as other military purposes. Part of the atoll is a wildlife refuge. The waters within a three-mile radius of both Midway and Johnston are off-limits to yachts unless they have special permission. In case of a real emergency, permission to enter would probably be given. In such a case one should contact the US Coast Guard or the Rescue Coordination Centre in Honolulu.

Remote Island Wildlife Refuges: These are administered by the US Fish and Wildlife Service in Honolulu. Refuge Complex Office, PO Box 50167. Permission to land will only be given for legitimate reasons. These areas include:

The NW part of the Hawaiian archipelago, including Nihoa Island, but not Midway, from 161°W to 176°W.

Howland, Baker and Jarvis Islands, on the equator SSW of Hawaii. In 1990 they were included within Hawaii state boundaries by Congress.

Kure Island, west of Midway. Access is restricted to this island, which is administered by the state of Hawaii.

Palmyra Atoll 5°53′N 162°05′W is privately owned and permission to stop here should be obtained from the owners.

Wake Island 19°18′N 166°38′E is administered by the US Air Force but yachts can stop. The pass into the lagoon is not deep enough to enter so one has to anchor off the reef, making it only a temporary stop. Only military and contract workers live there.

Facilities

The number of marinas in Hawaii is less than one would expect in such a developed place and, on the whole, yachting facilities are below US standards. The number of cruising yachts is not very large, except in the summer months when many yachts make their way across from the mainland and facilities at marinas are stretched to the full.

With a few exceptions, all marinas are state-owned and operated. This means that they are subject to standard regulations and also that docking fees are lower than in private marinas. The basic rules are as follows: berths are assigned on a first come first served basis, but one may reserve a place either by writing a letter or telephoning in advance. The first three days are free, but those who stay longer have to pay for the entire period, including the first three days. The maximum stay in one year at any state marina or harbour is 30 days. The average cost is under $10 per day, water and electricity being included where available. Some yacht clubs also have docking facilities for visiting yachts. The Hawaii Yacht Club in Honolulu will allow visitors to use its facilities for a fee, but this is usually limited to a maximum period of two weeks.

Major repair work and services, such as hauling out and hull, engine and sail repair, are available only at Honokohau Harbour on Hawaii (Big Island), at Kewalo Basin, Keehi Lagoon and at Ala Wai Boat Harbour in Honolulu on Oahu Island. Smaller repairs can be made at Hilo, Lahaina and Nawiliwili. Fuel and water are available on the dock in most harbours, otherwise it has to be carried in jerrycans. Marine supplies in the main yachting centres are good and there are several chandleries with a wide selection, including charts. One of the best is Ala Wai Marine Stores in Honolulu. Whatever is not available locally will be ordered from the mainland and air freighted to Hawaii in 48 to 72 hours.

Provisioning is good everywhere and Hawaii is a good place to victual the boat, especially if planning to cruise the outer islands of Micronesia or the South Pacific. However, the prices are 25 per cent higher than on the mainland so all non-perishable stores should be bought before leaving the USA. LPG bottles can be filled in most places, but non-US standard bottles must be fitted with an adaptor.

Further Reading

Landfalls of Paradise
Charlie's Charts of the Hawaiian Islands
Hawaii – a travel survival kit

Website

www.visit.hawaii.org (Hawaii Visitors and Convention Bureau)

KIRIBATI

The Republic of Kiribati (pronounced 'kiribass'), formerly the Gilbert Islands, is a group of more than 30 islands situated in the centre of the Pacific Ocean around the point where the international date line and the equator cross. Besides the 16 original Gilbert Islands, Kiribati also includes Banaba (Ocean Island), the eight Phoenix Islands, and eight of the eleven Line Islands. All of the islands are low atolls enclosing lagoons, rarely more than 12 ft (4 m) above sea level. The notable exception is Banaba, which is volcanic. Little grows on these islands except coconut palms and not all of them are inhabited. Kiribati is very isolated, its small islands spread out over more than one million square miles of ocean.

Visiting this sprawling archipelago needs careful planning, a task not made easier by the insistence of the authorities that one must clear in first at the capital Tarawa before going anywhere else. While this is relatively easy if one only intends to visit the northern group of the original Gilberts, where Tarawa occupies a central position, a visit to the outer islands such as Christmas, Canton or Fanning presents almost insurmountable logistical problems because of the prevailing winds and currents. Fortunately local officials often take a rather detached view of Tarawa's instructions, as everyone on these remote islands, officials included, are usually delighted to welcome visitors to their lonely outposts. This remoteness is one of the things which makes these islands so intriguing and any amount of officialdom cannot spoil the pleasure of visiting them.

Christmas Island in particular is a convenient stopover point for boats on passage between Hawaii and French Polynesia. Site of former British nuclear tests, the island was handed over to Kiribati on that country's independence. The island is a sanctuary to millions of sea birds and access to the breeding areas is prohibited.

The main settlement, London, has yet to clean up the vast amount of rusty equipment that was dumped there, and the lasting impression of anyone visiting this side of Christmas Island is of utter desolation. In sheer contrast, Fanning Island (Tabuaerean), only 160 miles farther north, is a typical Pacific island, clean, welcoming and self-sufficient.

These Line Islands, together with Washington, belong to Kiribati and their local names have been confused, and are often wrongly depicted in nautical publications. Their correct names are: Kirimati (Christmas), Fanning (Tabuaerean) and Teraina (Washington).

Country Profile

The first inhabitants of these islands probably came from Australasia with migrations from Samoa in the thirteenth century AD. Although sighted by Spanish expeditions, the first real contact with Europeans came only in the mid-nineteenth

Practical Information

LOCAL TIME: GMT + 12, Canton Island GMT – 11, Christmas Island GMT – 10.

BUOYAGE: IALA A. Navigational aids are not very reliable and it is reported that most atolls are without lights after midnight.

CURRENCY: Australian dollar (Aus$)

BUSINESS HOURS
Banks: 0930–1500 Monday to Friday. The branch at Christmas Island closes between 1230 and 1330.
Shops: 0800–1900 Monday to Friday, half day Saturdays and Sundays.

ELECTRICITY: 240 V, 50 Hz

PUBLIC HOLIDAYS
1 and 2 January: New Year
Easter Monday
Good Friday
12, 13, 14 July: Independence Day celebrations
1st Monday in August: Youth Day
10 December: Human Rights Day
25, 26 December: Christmas

COMMUNICATIONS
Post office, Betio 0900–1200/1400–1500 Monday to Friday.
Telecom Services Kiribati (TSKL) provides excellent public phone links in all major islands, including Christmas. All the outer islands are in radio contact with Tarawa. Emergency: dial 999.

There are flights from Tarawa to Funafuti (Tuvalu), Majuro (Marshalls) and Nadi (Fiji) for international flight connections. There are internal flights to most of the other islands and Christmas Island has a weekly flight to Honolulu.

MEDICAL
Tungaru Central Hospital, Bikenibeu, South Tarawa. Tel. 28100.
Hepatitis is prevalent. Drinking water should be boiled or treated.

DIPLOMATIC MISSIONS
In Bairiki:
Australia: PO Box 77. Tel. 21184.
New Zealand: PO Box 53. Tel. 21400.
United Kingdom: PO Box 61. Tel. 21327.

century with the arrival of missionaries, whalers and blackbirders (slave traders). The islanders suffered greatly from new diseases brought by these visitors, especially measles. At the end of the century the Gilbert Islands, together with the Ellice Islands (now Tuvalu), willingly became a British Protectorate, hoping to end tribal conflicts and raiding of the population by blackbirders.

In 1890 phosphate was discovered on Ocean Island. The mining of this became an important industry and the administrative centre shifted there from Tarawa. In 1919 Christmas Island was annexed by the British, and later the other islands. During the Second World War the Gilberts were occupied by Japan and as the Americans advanced the islands were the arena for fierce fighting, especially at Betio on Tarawa. Relics of that battle still litter the shores of the lagoon today. Independence came to the Gilberts in July 1979, under their new name Kiribati.

The islanders live off fish, coconut, taro, bananas and breadfruit – everything else must be imported. The lack of resources is a problem, especially since the phosphates, once a vital source of income, have been exhausted. Some offshore mineral deposits have been found, but are not yet commercially exploited. The main exports are copra, dried seaweed and fish, and foreign currency is earned by selling fishing rights to foreign countries in the 200 nautical mile exclusive economic zone. The sale of stamps and handicrafts also contributes some income, but considerable aid comes from Australia, Japan, the EU and New Zealand. Many work on Nauru in its phosphate industry, or as merchant seamen, sending home money. Tourism is fairly important in the northern Line Islands, due to their proximity to Hawaii.

The population is over 80,000, mostly Micronesian with some Polynesian, especially in the southern islands. English is spoken as well as I-Kiribati, a Micronesian language. The capital is Bairiki, one of the islands of Tarawa, a densely populated atoll, where about one third of the population live. The main port is on the neighbouring Betio islet in the same lagoon. Protestantism and Roman Catholicism are the main religious denominations.

Most islands have an equatorial climate, while the islands to the extreme north and south of the group are tropical. November to April is the rainy season, with high humidity and stronger winds. Rainfall is not reliable and drought can be a problem for all the islands. The prevailing easterlies keep the climate pleasant, although temperatures can be high, 80–85°F (27–29°C) on average.

Entry Regulations

Ports of entry
Betio Islet on Tarawa 1°21′N, 172°55′E, Christmas (Kiritimati) Island 1°59′N 157°28′W, Fanning Island (Tabuaerean) 3°51′N 159°22′W, Ocean (Banaba) Island, 0°53′S 169°32′E.

Procedure on arrival
Tarawa: Tarawa Radio should be called on VHF Channel 16 when approaching the island and give one's ETA. The Marine Guard keeps 24-hour watch on 500, 2182 and 6215 MHz. Channel 16 is monitored only during office hours (0800–1230, 1330–1615 Monday to Friday). Having been advised beforehand, officials will be waiting in Betio when the yacht arrives. All formalities are supposed to be completed alongside in the small boat harbour in Betio, but this can only take yachts under 6 ft draft. Because of silting, the depths in the harbour are unreliable, so it may be safer for larger draft vessels to tie up to the commercial wharf on the way into Betio or anchor just outside the harbour entrance. An unmarked wreck, lying just below the surface, is close to the recommended anchorage and its position has been reported at 1°22.03′N 172°55.44′E. The customs office is at Betio and immigration officials will come over from Bairiki, where the government offices are based. The captain must show last port clearance and registry certificate.

A cruising permit should be obtained when clearing in. The authorities stipulate that in order to visit any of the other islands, one must clear in first at Tarawa and also clear out there at the end of the visit. They are strict about clearance, and Tarawa must be visited first, even if coming from the south. However, on departure it may be possible to get permission to call at an island and continue on from there out of the archipelago.

Canton: This atoll in the Phoenix Islands is a former US satellite tracking station. Only a handful of people live there and only three supply ships call a year. If one arrives with a Kiribati visa and emergency repairs have to be done, one probably can get permission to stay. The officials will request this by radio from Tarawa. The dredged ship pass should be entered near slack water and one can anchor inside the dredged turning basin. The natural pass is not recommended. The village is three miles away; officials will visit the yacht.

Tabuaerean (formerly Fanning Island): There is a wide pass on the west side but there is always a strong outflowing current. One should time one's arrival to coincide with slack water, otherwise it is possible to anchor in the lee of the island and wait for the change of tide. Once inside, the best anchorage is SE of the pass, close to the jetty. If no officials come out to inspect the yacht, the captain should disembark and visit first customs in the government offices just south of the jetty, then the chief of police who also acts as immigration officer.

Christmas Island: The pass into the lagoon is difficult to locate, so the recommended anchorage (GPS 1°59.08′N 157°28.83′W) is west of the main settlement, just off the tennis and basketball court, which is occasionally lit at night. It is relatively easy to land on the beach here and walk to the government offices to clear in. The customs, immigration and quarantine offices are all close together and each officer will come to inspect the boat. It is better to transport them in one's own dinghy as a high price will be demanded for the launch service. Firearms are taken ashore and locked up at the police station until departure.

Customs

Firearms and animals must be declared on arrival. Firearms will be taken into custody by customs until departure. Animals and agricultural produce must remain on board.

Prohibited exports are artefacts over 30 years old, traditional swords, tools and dancing ornaments.

Immigration

Most Commonwealth and EU nationals do not need a visa and will be issued one on arrival. Nationals of Australia, France, Germany, Japan and the USA must obtain a visa in advance, either from one of the Kiribati honorary consuls in Australia, New Zealand, Japan, USA, Germany and Hawaii, or from British consulates or from the Principal Immigration Office, Ministry of Home Affairs, PO Box 75, Bairiki, Tarawa. New Zealand nationals only need a visa if they plan to spend longer than 28 days, otherwise they may arrive without one.

A visitor's permit is normally issued on arrival, for one month, with extensions of one month at a time up to four months.

Fees

Visa fee is Aus$ 40. There is also a daily anchoring fee of Aus$ 0.15 per ton.

Cruising permit

In order to visit any other islands after clearing out from Tarawa one needs to obtain an official letter from customs and immigration. A letter will be issued addressed to the relevant official at each island, stating, among other things, the duration of one's allowed stop. It is therefore essential not only to obtain this letter before leaving Tarawa, but also to ensure that one's visa covers the entire proposed stay.

Facilities

Tarawa: Most facilities available in Kiribati are concentrated on this atoll which comprises several islands around a lagoon. Basic services are available at Betio, including the government shipyard which has mechanical, electrical and engineering workshops capable of small repairs. They also have a slipway which can haul yachts with a maximum draft of 7 ft. Provisions are available in Betio, but a better supermarket is located at Bairiki. Gas bottles can be filled at Betio where reasonable amounts of diesel fuel and water are also available. Drinking water should be treated, especially at Tarawa.

Christmas Island: Water is available and also diesel fuel. Provisions are limited. Telephone calls can be made from the TSKL office next to the immigration office in London.

Fanning: The few stores only stock basic supplies. Arrangements can be made to have someone bake bread. Some locally grown fruit and vegetables are usually available.

Facilities in all other islands are basic with few imported goods and a limited selection of locally produced fruit and vegetables, but there is plenty of fish everywhere. Water is often scarce and can be a problem in the southern and central parts of the group.

Further Reading

South Pacific Handbook
Micronesia Handbook
South Pacific Anchorages

Website

www.tskl.net.ki/kiribati/tourism

MARSHALL ISLANDS

In the central Pacific north of the equator, the Republic of the Marshall Islands is part of Micronesia along with Kiribati and the Mariana and Caroline archipelagos. The Marshalls comprise over a thousand small low islands, forming two chains, the eastern Ratak (towards dawn) and the western Ralik (towards sunset). Their total land surface is only 70 square miles yet they are scattered over half a million square miles of ocean. Used as a site for nuclear tests by the USA, radiation effects are still a problem in some islands.

It was the nuclear tests which put the Marshalls on the world map in the early 1950s as they were little known before and are not much better known now. The majority of yachts, which call at the Marshalls, are on their way from Hawaii to the rest of Micronesia, whose islands have escaped the nuclear pollution, which continues to blight some Marshall Islands to this day.

Country Profile

Little grows on these low coral islands, so the sea has always been the main resource for their inhabitants and the Marshallese were renowned as sailors and navigators. They navigated partly by observing the stars and patterns made by waves, but also using charts constructed of strips of wood tied together, which showed such patterns and the various islands. Visits from early European sailors were rare as the islands did not seem to have much to offer. It was an English captain, who sighted many of the islands at the end of the eighteenth century, whose name they have taken. Traders and missionaries avoided the Marshall Islands because they had acquired a reputation for violence after several traders had been attacked, some of whom had tried to abduct Marshallese women. From the mid-nineteenth century many islanders were converted by Protestant missionaries and the violence lessened.

Germany annexed the islands at the end of the century and developed the copra industry. Economic exploitation and development continued after the First World War when the islands were taken over and administered by Japan. In 1944 US forces captured the Marshalls from the Japanese after heavy fighting. Immediately after the war the Americans began nuclear testing on Bikini and Enewetok atolls, which took a terrible toll on the islanders and their way of life. Bikini, which was the site of the earliest known inhabitation in Micronesia, became uninhabitable after 23 tests. The islanders tried unsuccessfully to resettle there in the 1970s, but radiation was still too high. Enewetok, Rongelap and Utirik suffered similar fates. The USA had administered the Marshalls as part of the UN Trust Territory since 1947. The Marshalls rejected the common constitution which all members of the Trust Territory voted on in 1979, becoming a republic with its own constitution. Soon after, the Marshalls signed a Compact of Free Association with the USA. This Compact expires in 2001 and will be renegotiated. In 1991 the republic was admitted to the United Nations after the trusteeship formally ended.

People have returned to live on Bikini and Enewetok. The excellent diving at Bikini and the only diveable aircraft carrier wreck in the world, the USS *Saratoga*, attracts divers from all over the world.

Under the terms of the Compact, the USA pays over US$30 million in aid as well as providing communications, a postal service and other assistance. The military base at Kwajalein is leased by the USA for around US$12 million a year, also providing income for the Marshallese working there.

Income also comes from copra, tourism and handicrafts. The population numbers around 60,000 and are mostly Protestant. Marshallese is the official language, but English is widely spoken. Majuro Atoll is the political and economic centre. It comprises 57 islets, the larger ones joined together by a road, around an oval lagoon. The most developed of the Marshalls, the atoll's main islands Delap, Uliga and Darrit, form the DUD municipality.

The climate is tropical and temperatures show little variation throughout the year. December to April is the NE trade wind season and even in the remaining months prevailing winds tend to be easterly. Occasionally the easterly flow is interrupted by strong SW winds. Tropical storms are very rare in Majuro but not unheard of, and one at the turn of the nineteenth century killed almost everyone on Majuro. Recently, in an El Niño year, one passed close to the south of Majuro.

Entry Regulations

Ports of entry
Majuro 7°08'N 171°22'E, Ebeye Island (Kwajalein Atoll) 8°46'N 167°44'E.

Practical Information

LOCAL TIME: Majuro GMT + 12, GMT − 12 Kwajalein

BUOYAGE: IALA A

CURRENCY: United States dollar (US$)

BUSINESS HOURS
Banks: 1000–1500 Monday to Thursday, 1000–1700 Friday.
Business: 0800–1630 weekdays.
Shops: 0800–2000 Monday to Thursday, to 2200 Friday and Saturday, 0800–1800 Sunday.

ELECTRICITY: 110/120 V, 60 Hz

PUBLIC HOLIDAYS
1 January: New Year's Day

1 March: Memorial Day and Nuclear Victims Day
Good Friday
1 May: Constitution Day
1st Friday in July: Fisherman's Day
First Monday in September: Labor Day
Last Friday in September: Manit Day
21 October: Independence Day
24 October: United Nations Day
17 November: President's Day
Fourth Thursday in November: Thanksgiving Day
25 December: Christmas Day

COMMUNICATIONS
COMSAT on Delap for international calls; also at some hotels. Majuro post office, Uliga, open 1000–1530 Monday to Friday,

0800–1200 Saturday.
The Marshalls are part of the US domestic mail service so mail-order items from US mainland or Hawaii can be obtained quite quickly and cheaply.
Zip code: 96960 except Ebeye, which is 96970.
There are regular flights from Majuro to Honolulu, Guam, FSM and Fiji as well as internal flights.

MEDICAL
There are hospitals on Majuro (*Tel.* 625 3399) and Ebeye, dispensaries on the other islands.

DIPLOMATIC MISSIONS
USA: PO Box 1379, Majuro, *Tel.* 247 4011.

Procedure on arrival

Majuro: Arriving yachts should call Majuro Port Control on Channel 16 and request clearance. If no answer is received, one should anchor or pick up a mooring and proceed to the government building where customs and immigration, in adjacent offices, will effect clearance. It is not necessary to get permission to visit in advance. Occasionally, a yacht will be directed to come alongside the commercial pier in Uliga for clearance, but that is rare and customs officials rarely board yachts.

There are no charges when checking in and one does not have to visit the harbour master on arrival, although one must do so on checking out and pay a US$80 fee. If a customs official does not visit the yacht, the captain only may go ashore to clear customs and immigration at the government offices in Delap. Those arriving at weekends can wait until Monday for immigration clearance. After clearing customs and immigration, one must visit the port director's office near the head of the pier in Uliga.

When clearing out, the offices have to be visited in reverse order, first the port director, then immigration and customs.

Ebeye (Kwajalein Atoll): One should contact officials on Channel 16 for instructions where to come alongside for clearance. If there is no space, one might have to anchor. Most yachts anchor on the east side of the T-pier, between the Mobil tanks and the old dock. Formalities are similar to those in Majuro.

Customs

Firearms must be declared on arrival. Animals must also be declared on arrival.

Immigration

It is an official requirement that entry permits must be obtained in advance for stays over 30 days, but for shorter stays yachts which have arrived without a permit have been allowed to enter. One should apply for an entry permit from Chief of Immigration, Marshall Islands Government, Majuro, Marshall Islands 96960. *Tel.* 625 3181, Fax. 625 3685. There is also a consulate in Honolulu.

Cruising permit

To visit the other islands, special permission must be obtained in Majuro. A permit, one for each island, has to be applied for at the Ministry of Interior and Outer Islands Affairs, Box 18, Majuro. *Tel.* 625 3225. Each atoll is governed by a mayor and a chief from whom approval must be obtained by the Department before issuing a permit. Apparently obtaining the necessary permits is a lengthy procedure which can take several weeks in all. A fee is payable, but only if one actually visits the particular atoll or atolls for which one has permission. This fee varies for each atoll, but is usually not substantial and never exceeds $75.

Health

There may be some risk of cholera. A health certificate is required if arriving from infected areas. An AIDS test may be required for visits over 30 days.

Restrictions

Kwajalein Atoll is used by the USA as a missile testing area and the waters within a 200 mile radius may be affected. One should contact Kwajalein Atoll Control by radio beforehand if one is sailing in this area. Restricted islands are those used by the US army: Kwajalein Island is a closed military base, and the missile range includes Kwajalein and the islands up to Roi-Namur Island.

The following islands are under the Marshall Islands jurisdiction, but similar permission is needed to visit any of them: Bikini Atoll 11°30′N 165°34′E and Enewetok Atoll 11°30′N 162°24′E – these were sites of nuclear testing and are still contaminated; Rongelap Atoll 11°09′N 166°54′E is also polluted with fall-out from Bikini.

Conservative dress should be worn, especially by women, when visiting the outer islands. The drinking of alcohol is banned on many of the outer islands.

Facilities

The best facilities are in Majuro where provisioning is good with a wide selection, mostly imported from the USA, but also some local fresh fruit and vegetables. There are several supermarkets with a very good selection. Propane tanks can be refilled. Fuel is also available and is cheaper if bought in larger quantities from the commercial wharf near the container terminal. The mail service is efficient and Majuro's US postal code is 96960. As the selection is much better than in the rest of Micronesia, long-term provisioning should be done in Majuro.

Only rain water should be used in Majuro as the water on the island is contaminated. Fuel can be ordered in bulk from Mobil or in smaller quantities from filling stations. Propane is available, but it is necessary to have the right adaptors as empty containers are gravity filled. Repair facilities are limited and only minor repairs can be undertaken. Pacific International at Delap commercial harbour has a crane which can lift up to 65 tons. There are no marine supplies except for a limited selection of spares for diesel and outboard engines and a good selection of domestic hardware. Facilities in the other islands are even more limited.

Further Reading

Micronesia Handbook

Micronesia – a travel survival kit
Landfalls of Paradise
South Pacific Anchorages

Websites

www.miembassyus.org (Marshalls Embassy in Washington)
www.yokwe.net (Tourism information)

NORTHERN MARIANAS

The Commonwealth of the Northern Marianas in the Western Pacific has the special status of a US Commonwealth. The American influence is strong, although the legacy of Spanish colonial rule can also be seen. Of the 14 volcanic islands that stretch north to south in almost a straight line, the southernmost three, Saipan, Rota and Tinian, are the main islands. The Marianas may be regarded as the world's highest mountains, for their bases lie in the Mariana Trench, seven miles below the ocean surface, in the deepest part of the Pacific. Guam is geographically part of the Marianas, but politically separate.

The islands were military-dominated for many years and access was forbidden, but that is no longer the case and now the islands attract a few cruising yachts every year. Most of these come from Guam, where there is a Northern Marianas representative who can issue the necessary permit to visit the islands. The southern islands are the more developed, while some of the northern islands are wildlife reserves and cannot be visited. The entire group is subject to typhoons for most of the year, another reason why cruising boats rarely sail there.

Country Profile

The original inhabitants of the islands were Chamorros, of Indo-Filipino origin, who developed a matrilineal society of nobles and commoners. Magellan was the first European to visit the islands in 1521, but the group only got its name in the seventeenth century when a Spanish priest named them Las Marianas. They came under Spanish rule as a useful stopover for ships on the Philippines to Mexico route. At the end of the nineteenth century the Germans bought the

Practical Information

LOCAL TIME: GMT + 10

BUOYAGE: IALA A

CURRENCY: United States dollar (US$)

BUSINESS HOURS
Banks: 1000–1500 Monday to Thursday, 1000–1800 Friday.
Government offices: 0730–1130/ 1230–1630 Monday to Friday.
Shops: 0800–2100 Monday to Saturday, 0800–1800 Sunday.

ELECTRICITY: 110/120 V, 60 Hz

PUBLIC HOLIDAYS
1 January: New Year's Day
9 January: Commonwealth Day
Third Monday in January: Martin Luther King's Birthday
Third Monday in February: President's Day
24 March: Marianas Covenant Day
Good Friday
1 May: Law Day
Last Monday in May: Memorial Day
4 July: Liberation Day
12 July: Micronesia Day
First Monday in September: Labor Day
Second Monday in October: Columbus Day
24 October: United Nations Day
4 November: Citizenship Day
11 November: Veterans Day
Fourth Thursday in November: Thanksgiving Day
8 December: Constitution Day
25 December: Christmas Day

COMMUNICATIONS
ITC, Middle Road, south of Garapan centre in Saipan for international phone calls open 0800–2400 daily.

International calls can also be made from hotels and phone booths.
The islands are part of the US mailing system, so they have their own zip codes. Mail can be sent c/o General Delivery at either Saipan 96950, Rota 96951 or Tinian 96952.
Post offices, Chalan Kanoa, SW end and at Capitol Hill, Saipan. Open 0900–1600 Monday to Friday.
International flight connections are best made via Japan or Guam to both of which there are flights from Saipan.

MEDICAL
Dr Torres Hospital, Saipan. There are also hospitals on Rota and Tinian. Emergency treatment is free.

DIPLOMATIC MISSIONS
Japan: 5th floor, Yarikuchi Bldg, Garapan.
Philippines: CTC Bldg, Susupe.

Marianas and developed the copra trade, followed by Japanese rule after the First World War when Germany lost all her Pacific colonies. The Japanese introduced sugar plantations and many Japanese settled on the islands, further eroding the indigenous way of life. The Second World War saw 'Operation Forager', the costly capture of the Marianas by US forces in June and July 1944. After the war all of Micronesia was administered by the USA as a UN Trust Territory. In 1975 the Marianas voted to become a US Commonwealth, which means that although US citizens, the islanders have no vote. The Marianas are of strategic importance to the USA, from whom they receive considerable aid every year. The US controls defence and foreign policy but the Commonwealth has internal self-government. Another source of income is from tourism, most of the tourists coming from Japan.

The population is in excess of 58,000, having doubled in recent years with an influx of foreign workers, mainly Filipinos, so now Chamorros and Carolinians make up only about 48 per cent of the population. English is the main language. Also spoken are Chamorro, Carolinian, and Japanese in the tourist areas. Most islanders are Roman Catholic. Saipan is the capital, and Susupe is the government centre.

The islands lie in the typhoon zone and typhoons can occur all year round, but are more frequent between June and November. It is always warm and humid. The NE trade winds blow from January to April. As the Marianas appear to be hit by typhoons every year, extreme caution must be exercised when cruising this area. One of the safest months is February, which has the lowest incidence of typhoons. A recommended hurricane hole is in Tanapag's inner harbour, also called Smiley's lagoon, where shelter is reputed to be good from every direction.

Entry Regulations

Ports of entry

Tanapag Harbour (Saipan) 15°12′N 145°43′E. Rota 14°08′N 145°08′E and Tinian 14°58′N 145°37′E can only be used as ports of entry by yachts who have these ports specified on their cruising permit.

Procedure on arrival

The Port Superintendent must be notified of the ETA of arriving yachts.
Tanapag Harbour: The approaches to the harbour are well marked. Visiting boats may anchor in the commercial harbour or come alongside the pier by the Mobil Tanks. The port captain will give directions where to moor when contacted on VHF Channel 16. Clearance is done by quarantine, customs and immigration officials.

Customs

Firearms should have valid licences from the owner's own country. Only .22 and .410 rifles are allowed to be kept and licensed in the Northern Marianas. On entry other licensed firearms will be confiscated by customs and held until departure. All non-licensed firearms will be confiscated and destroyed.

There is a four-month quarantine for dogs and cats. The cost is approximately US$2–3 per day.

Immigration

US citizens need only proof of citizenship.

Visas are not required for stays of up to 30 days and an entry permit of up to 30 days' stay is given provided the onward passage of the yacht is assured and the crew are in possession of visas for the next destination if required. Extensions of up to 30 days can be applied for from the Immigration Office, Northern Marianas Government, Saipan.

Cruising permit

All yachts wishing to cruise in the Northern Marianas must be in possession of a permit, which must be obtained beforehand. A letter requesting the cruising permit should be written several months before the intended visit to: Chief of Immigration, Saipan, Mariana Islands, Commonwealth of the Northern Marianas 96950. A similar letter should also be sent to the Port Captain, Commonwealth Ports Authority, PO Box 1055, Saipan. Alternatively, a cruising permit can be obtained from the Northern Marianas representative in Guam or Honolulu, which will allow a yacht to call at the islands of Tinian, Rota and Saipan. Proper clearing-in procedures must be completed on arrival in these places. Yachts will be fined US$500 for cruising in CNMI waters without a permit.

Yachts wishing to visit some of the outer islands must obtain special permission from the authorities in Saipan. It is advisable also to contact the Fish and Wildlife Office in Saipan, who are extremely concerned that certain plant diseases may be introduced accidentally into the outer islands. The only inhabited islands are Alamagan, Agrihan and Pagan, the latter having been abandoned temporarily after a recent volcanic eruption. To visit Aguijan Island, south of Tinian, one must obtain a permit from Tinian's mayor.

Fees

Entry fee: US$25.
Dockage fee: under 100 feet, US$18 per day.
Immigration clearance fee: US$10.

Restrictions

Guguan, Asuncion and Maug islands are wildlife reserves and access to them is prohibited.

Facilities

Most facilities are in Saipan, which is the most developed island and attracts most tourists. Provisioning is good and there is a reasonable selection of imported goods, although they tend to be expensive. Locally grown fresh produce can be bought daily at the Farmers Market, opposite the post office, open 0800–1800 Monday to Saturday, 1000–1200 Sunday. Fuel must be bought in jerry-cans from the filling station just north of the airport. Repair facilities are modest and only simple repairs can be done locally. Outer Cove Marina, located on the east of the island in Tanapag harbour, almost due west of Monagaha Island, is a new marina with fixed concrete docks. Fuel, ice and supplies from a mobile store are available.

Tinian is less developed, but as it has a large farming community, fresh produce is easily available and of good quality. Rota is even less developed. There are a few shops in Songsong, the main settlement. Provisions in the outer islands are scarce and one should not expect to be able to buy more than the absolute minimum.

Further Reading

Landfalls of Paradise
Micronesia Handbook
Micronesia – a travel survival kit

Website

www.visit-marianas.com (Marianas Visitors Authority)

PALAU

The Republic of Palau, now known as Belau, is part of the Western Caroline Islands. The richest flora and fauna in Micronesia are found here, both on land and underwater. Closely grouped together inside a barrier reef are the high islands of Babeldaob, the main island of Koror, Peleliu, and the many Rock Islands. Just outside the reef are

Practical Information

LOCAL TIME: GMT+ 12

BUOYAGE: IALA A

CURRENCY: United States dollar (US$)

BUSINESS HOURS
Government offices: 0730–1130,
1230–1630 Monday to Friday.
Banks: 0930–1430 Monday to Thursday,
0930–1700 Friday.
Shops: 0800–2100 Monday to Saturday.

ELECTRICITY: 110/230 V, 60 Hz

PUBLIC HOLIDAYS
1 January: New Year's Day
15 March: Youth Day
5 May: Senior Citizens Day
1 June: President's Day
9 July: Constitution Day
First Monday in September: Labor Day
24 October: UN Day
4th Thursday in November: Thanksgiving
25 December: Christmas Day

COMMUNICATIONS
COMSAT station, Arakabesan Island, for
international calls, open 24 hours.

Post office, central Koror open 0800–1600
weekdays.
There are flights to Guam or Manila, from
where international connections can be made.

MEDICAL
Belau Clinic, Lebuu St, Koror has good
facilities.
There is also a government hospital at
Arakabesan.

DIPLOMATIC MISSIONS
US Liaison Office: PO Box 6028, Koror. *Tel.*
488 2920.

Anguaur and the atoll Kayangel, while to the south are a group of five small volcanic islands, stretching down towards Indonesia.

Conveniently situated on the route from the South Pacific to the Philippines, Palau lagoon and its many picturesque islands provide one of the most beautiful cruising grounds in the Pacific in one small area. This is slightly marred by the strict entry regulations, but this can be overcome by sorting out the necessary paperwork before one's arrival and, once there, by observing the rules. The effort is entirely justified as the scenery, both above and under the surface of the sea, is rarely matched elsewhere in the Pacific. The most fascinating place to visit are the Rock Islands, which are over two hundred limestone islets covered in jungle growth. Three major ocean currents meet in this area bringing food to nourish the rich marine life. The sea is teeming with turtles, manta rays, moray eels, fish of all descriptions, giant clams and even dugong. Occasionally one is brought back to earth by the sight of a wrecked ship from the bloody battles which were fought in and over these waters during the Second World War.

Strict rules apply to visits to the outer islands and because of many abuses by cruising boats in the past, the authorities treat all visitors with suspicion, and, occasionally, with a certain degree of hostility. It is even rumoured that the authorities are considering closing the Rock Islands to cruising boats altogether.

Country Profile

The Rock Islands were settled around 1000 BC and a complex matriarchal society developed. The first contact with Europeans was in the fifteenth century, when they were sighted by the Spanish, who called them the Arrecifos. At the end of the seventeenth century Spain claimed the islands, but only in the following century was real contact made when the *Antelope* was wrecked there and the islanders helped to rebuild the ship. Britain traded with the Palauans until the nineteenth century, when Spain pushed out the English. The local population was badly depleted by European-introduced diseases. After Spain's defeat in the Spanish–American War the islands were sold to Germany, which was interested in developing the islands' economy. The First World War saw the arrival of the Japanese, who had similar interests and Japanese culture and foreign immigrants overwhelmed Palauan traditional life. In the 1930s the islands were closed to the outside world while military fortifications were built. During the Second World War Palau suffered greatly from bombing and fighting.

After the war the USA administered Palau as part of the UN Trust Territory. In 1978 Palau voted against inclusion in the Federated States of Micronesia with the other states of the Caroline Islands and two years later formed a separate republic with its own constitution. However, a nuclear-free clause in the constitution was incompatible with the Compact of Free Association signed by all the former Trust Territories, which gives the USA military rights in the area in return for financial aid. An amendment was made to the constitution, but while this issue remains unresolved, the Trust Territory remains formally in existence in Palau, although not elsewhere.

Palau depends very much on US aid, although relations between the two countries remain slightly strained as the nuclear issue has not been resolved. A huge power plant built on Aimeliik has proved a drain on the economy, needing US dollars to repay large debts. Exports are mainly fish and handicrafts, plus some income from tourism. Imports of fuel and food are high.

The 18,000 inhabitants are Micronesian, speaking English and Palauan. Sonsorolese is spoken in the south-west islands. There are various Christian denominations, Catholic, Protestant and Adventist. Many of the islanders still hold traditional beliefs.

Koror is the capital.

Palau lies on the edge of the typhoon belt and is only rarely affected by tropical storms. The typhoon season is from May to November. The wet season is June to September, which is the SW monsoon. The best weather is during the NE monsoon from December to March.

Entry Regulations

Port of entry
Malakal Harbour (Koror) 7°20′N 134°29′E.

Procedure on arrival
A yacht may not stop at any other place before clearing in at Malakal, unless the Chief of Immigration grants permission, if it is in the public interest of that place or an emergency situation. A yacht in distress may anchor or land at any port in Palau but must immediately notify the nearest government official to contact the Chief of Immigration. Yachts stopping anywhere else other than Malakal will be instructed to proceed to Malakal immediately.

Malakal: The port authorities should be notified in advance of a yacht's ETA. On entry and departure, inspections will be carried out by immigration, customs, agricultural, port and quarantine officials. On departure, the inspection will be carried out by immigration.

Customs
Firearms must be declared on entry and will be removed and held by the Bureau of Public Safety until departure. Animals must be declared.

Immigration
No visas are required and visitors are granted a 30-day visa on entry. Those wishing to stay longer must apply to the immigration office in good time and not later than 7 days before the expiration of the 30-day period. No more than two extensions of 30 days each will be granted and there is a fee of $US100 for each extension.

Cruising permit
Yachts must obtain an entry permit in advance. The application should be sent well in advance to: Chief of Immigration, Division of Immigration, Bureau of Legal Affairs, PO Box 100, Koror, Republic of Palau 96940. *Tel.* 488-2496, 488-2678 or 488-2358. Fax. 488-4385.

Applications should be received at least two weeks in advance of a yacht's expected arrival to allow sufficient time for processing the application. The application must be accompanied by a fee of US$200 (as a cashier's cheque, money order or cheque drawn on local bank made payable to National Treasury of the Republic of Palau).

The application should contain the following information: boat name, port and flag of registration, LOA, net and gross tonnage, crew list, detailed itinerary, intended port of entry. It takes several months to receive an answer. If the permit has not arrived by the time one is ready to leave the last port, a copy of the original application should be faxed to the above number with a request to process the application immediately. An answer is normally received within 48 hours. If the money is not sent in advance or is not received by the time the boat gets there, a fee of US$300 must be paid on arrival.

The fee is US$300 if the permit is obtained on arrival. An extension of 30 days may be obtained at the discretion of the chief of immigration, upon payment of a fee of $US200 for each extension.

Fees
A minimum of three hours of overtime is charged per immigration officer on duty for all arrivals and departures outside of normal working hours. The amount is calculated by multiplying the average hourly overtime rate by the number of officers on duty for a vessel and the sum of the number of hours worked or multiplied by three hours, whichever is greater. There is also a $50 Malakal harbour fee, to be paid to the port captain, and a $20 Rock Islands cruising fee. Boats staying more than one month, pay additional fees of $100 per month, $50 per person and $20 Rock Islands cruising fee. All these fees have to be paid again for the third month, which is the maximum that cruising boats are allowed to stay.

Restrictions
Some parts of the Rock Islands, including the so called '70 islands', are nature reserves and access by

any boat is strictly prohibited. The port captain will show on a chart the prohibited areas.

Facilities

Most facilities are in Koror where the majority of the population live. There is a fishery cooperative in Malakal Harbour with workshops and a slipway. Nearby is a small chandlery with a limited selection. Provisioning is good with a reasonable selection of both imported goods and locally grown produce. The Royal Palau Yacht Club has a busy social programme and welcomes visiting sailors.

Its members are the best source if help is needed.

Further Reading

Micronesia Cruising Notes
Landfalls of Paradise
Micronesia – a travel survival kit
Micronesia Handbook

Website

www.visit-palau.com (Palau Visitors Authority)

9 Australia and South Pacific Islands

A voyage to the South Sea islands figures in most sailors' long-term plans, but their remoteness from the major yachting centres keeps them beyond the scope of the average cruise. This is the reason why in spite of the proliferation of yachts worldwide, the number of boats cruising the South Pacific is still relatively small and is not likely to increase much in the foreseeable future. The vastness of the Pacific Ocean and the great distances which separate most island groups make long passages a common feature of a cruise in this part of the world. The islands' isolation and general lack of facilities require the yacht to be well prepared and self-sufficient.

The region is under the influence of the SE trade winds, which are stronger and more consistent during the winter months, from May to October, with the best sailing weather between June and August. The trade winds are less reliable at other times. The western part of the ocean comes under the influence of the NW monsoon from December until March, which is also the season of tropical cyclones which affect the area south of latitude 10°S.

Most of the South Pacific is affected by tropical cyclones and the season lasts from December until the end of March. Although most cruising yachts leave the critical area by sailing either south to New Zealand or north to Papua New Guinea, some trust their luck and decide to stay in the hope of finding shelter should a cyclone come their way. The number of absolutely safe harbours is relatively small, which considerably restricts the freedom of movement during the cyclone season.

Although there are reputedly good hurricane holes at Tahiti, Vava'u, Pago Pago and Suva, the risk still exists and in some countries, such as Tahiti, Vanuatu and the Cook Islands, the authorities may insist that cruising yachts leave the country before the onset of the cyclone season.

One of the advantages of spending the summer season outside the tropics is that of being able to go to a place with good repair and service facilities. The most popular destination is New Zealand, where the Bay of Islands and Whangarei area have a complete range of facilities. Similar facilities are also available in some of the ports along Australia's east coast, although the more northern ones are themselves subject to cyclones. In the islands, the best repair centres are those which support their own boating community, such as Tahiti, Suva, Nouméa and Port Moresby. The establishment of charter operations in Raiatea and Vava'u has also brought about an improvement in the standard of facilities there. Adequate repair facilities are also available in Tongatapu and Port Vila.

AMERICAN SAMOA

The two neighbouring Samoas are very different from each other, American Samoa being a US Territory, while Western Samoa is an independent state. American Samoa comprises all the Samoan islands east of the 171° parallel, that is the main island of Tutuila, as well as Aunuu, the Manua Group, Rose Island, and Swains Island.

This US outpost in the South Seas has been best described as the place sailors love to hate. The features that attract most cruising boats to American Samoa, such as US goods, excellent provisioning and good communications, are those which have contributed to its seamier side. The Samoans have embraced the American way of life wholeheartedly, which has led to a high standard of living compared to their neighbours, but also to high criminality especially in the capital Pago Pago.

It is Pago Pago which attracts most cruising sailors, either to reprovision in its well-stocked supermarkets, or to spend the cyclone season in this scenically beautiful and well protected harbour, which unfortunately has been virtually destroyed by the local fish cannery, which fills the water with effluent and the air with revolting odours. Until there is a marked improvement in yachting facilities, Pago Pago is best regarded as a convenient reprovisioning stop and nothing more.

Outside of Pago Pago life has been affected less by this kind of progress and the other islands are not so hectic.

Country Profile

It is debated whether Manua in American Samoa or Savai'i in Western Samoa is the true ancient Samoa, cradle of Polynesia, from where intrepid navigators spread out eastwards across the South Pacific. Archaeologists have ascertained that Polynesians lived on Tutuila around 600 BC. They remained undisturbed until 1722 when the first European, a Dutchman named Jacob Roggeveen, visited the island. Few Europeans came to the islands, especially after the eleven members of a French scientific expedition led by La Pérouse were killed here in 1787. Only in 1831 did the arrival of missionary John Williams mark a more permanent European interest and the Samoans proved enthusiastic converts, going forth as missionaries themselves to convert other nations of the Pacific.

In 1900 the United States established control of Tutuila as they wanted a coaling port in the South Pacific, and later they acquired the Manua group. Tutuila was an important base for the US Navy in the Second World War and the Navy administered American Samoa until 1951, when it was taken over by the Department of the Interior. American Samoa is now an Unincorporated US External Territory, and since 1967 has had its own Constitution. The legislature consists of a Senate elected from local chiefs and a House of Representatives.

The main economic activities are tuna fishing and canning. The USA has put a lot of money into the islands. Many Samoans work temporarily overseas, especially in the United States.

The mainly Polynesian population is 60,000. Samoan and English are spoken. The main Christian denominations are Protestant, Catholic, Mormon and Methodist. Pago Pago is the capital and its harbour is the crater of an extinct volcano. It is a deep water duty-free port with three fish canneries for US, Korean and Japanese fishing fleets. Fagatogo is the business and administrative centre.

There is very heavy rainfall all year, especially from December to April, which is the cyclone season. The average temperatures are 24–31°C (75–87°F). May to November are the trade wind months and are less humid.

Entry Regulations

Port of entry
Pago Pago 14°17′S 170°41′W.

Procedure on arrival
Arriving yachts should contact Harbour Control on Channel 16 for berthing instructions, or tie up at the customs dock at Fagatogo, which is on the port side on entering the harbour. They will be boarded here by customs, immigration and agriculture officials. It is also necessary to clear in and out with the harbour master's office which will assign an

Practical Information

LOCAL TIME: GMT – 11

BUOYAGE: IALA A

CURRENCY: United States dollar (US$)

BUSINESS HOURS
Banks: 0900–1500 Monday to Friday.
Shops: 0800–1700 Monday to Friday,
0800–1300 Saturday.
Business and government offices:
0900–1700 Monday to Friday,
0800–1200 Saturday.

ELECTRICITY: 110 V, 50 Hz

PUBLIC HOLIDAYS
1 January: New Year's Day
Third Monday in January: Martin
Luther King Day
Third Monday in February:
President's Day
17 April: Flag Day
Good Friday
Last Monday in May: Memorial Day
4 July: Independence Day
First Monday in September: Labor Day
Second Sunday in October: White Sunday
Second Monday in October:
Columbus Day
11 November: Veterans Day
Last Thursday in November: Thanksgiving
25 December: Christmas Day

COMMUNICATIONS
Communications office, Fagatogo, open 24 hours, seven days a week has facilities for international direct dialling, telex, fax and telegrams.
American Samoa is tied into the US postal system. Zip code 96799.
Main post office: Lumana'i Building, Fagatogo, open 0800–1600
Monday to Friday, 0830–1200 Saturday.
Emergency: dial 911
There are flights to Honolulu, Auckland, Apia and Nadi (Fiji).

MEDICAL
LBJ Tropical Medical Center in Faga'alu Village, west of Pago Pago, has 24-hour services.

anchoring place. A yacht must not be moved without prior permission from the harbour master or one is liable to pay a large fine. When clearing out, one must come alongside the customs dock again.

If arriving at the weekend, one can anchor in the harbour and stay on board until Monday. In this case one should not anchor in the working area which leads out from the ramp, but one can anchor off the customs dock or in the north-west part of the harbour. Overtime charges may be introduced for weekend clearance.

Customs

A customs entry clearance permit is required for firearms. A Department of Agriculture entry clearance permit is needed for any animals, plants or vegetables. Animals are confined on board.

Immigration

American Samoa is considered part of the United States, and US citizens can live and work there, but they should have valid passports for entry.

On arrival other nationalities are granted a 30-

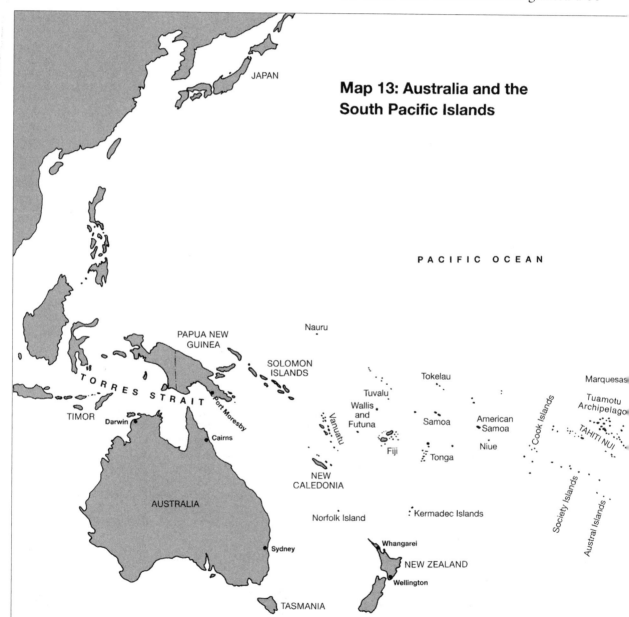

Map 13: Australia and the South Pacific Islands

day stay. Entry permits are granted to all those who can provide proof of their onward passage and have adequate funds for their stay. For extensions up to a maximum of 90 days, one should apply to the Immigration Office, Executive Office Building, Utulei, PO Box 7, Pago Pago. An exit permit is needed from immigration. It is possible that passports may be held until departure.

The Passport & Visa Office in the Administration building is open 0830–1200 Monday to Friday and can issue US visas.

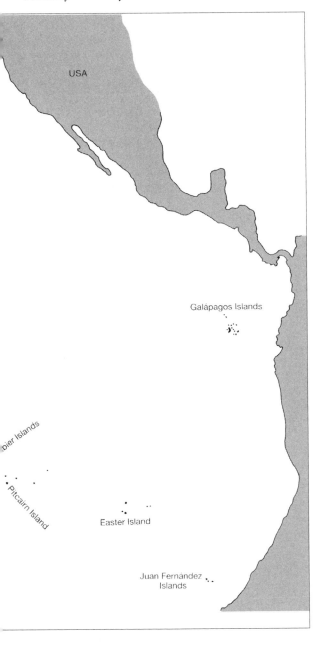

USA

Galápagos Islands

Gambier Islands

Pitcairn Island

Easter Island

Juan Fernández Islands

Fees

US$25 for clearing in and US$25 for clearing out is payable by visiting yachts as well as monthly harbour fees of approximately US$12 to US$15. These must be paid before departure as otherwise customs will not issue an outward clearance.

Restrictions

Rose Island, the easternmost island of the Samoan archipelago, is a National Wildlife Refuge administered by the US Fish and Wildlife Service in Honolulu. Permission from this service is needed to visit the island.

Facilities

Apart from the fact that most things American are available and therefore provisioning is better than in neighbouring countries, facilities for yachts in Pago Pago are quite limited. The port has put down approximately 15 moorings and these can be used by cruising boats on a first come, first served basis. The holding in the harbour is poor and it is advisable to anchor with two anchors and not leave the yacht unattended for long periods. To avoid the noise and smell of the cannery and generating plant it is best to anchor as far as possible from them.

There is no haul-out facility for yachts, although there is a marine railway for hauling out large vessels, but access to it is denied to pleasure craft even in an emergency. There is a shipyard dealing mainly with repairs on fishing boats, but it sometimes accepts work on yachts. There are some small workshops in town for engine and electrical work. Stainless steel welding and general steel work is undertaken by Mr Wu, who has a workshop in Lauli village. Best provisions can be bought at Arvenas and Tom Ho Chings, who give discounts on larger quantities, as does Burns Philp. Some of the supermarkets will deliver larger quantities to the customs dock. There is a good fresh produce market early Saturday morning at the bus station, near the port. Beer and spirits are cheaper than in countries further west, although duty-free sales are no longer available to yachts. Larger quantities of fuel can be ordered to be delivered by tanker to the customs dock. Water can be obtained from the customs dock.

Only a limited selection of marine equipment is available from one of the hardware stores (Tool Shop), but anything essential can be ordered from the USA and will arrive in approximately one week. West Marine is reported as the most reliable supplier.

Further Reading

Landfalls of Paradise
South Pacific Handbook
Samoa – a travel survival kit
South Pacific Anchorages
The Pacific Crossing Guide
Tonga Samoa Handbook

Website

www.samoanet.com/americansamoa (Office of Tourism)

AUSTRALIA

Australia is the only nation which is also a continent: a land of few rivers, a vast desert plateau in the centre, with a chain of mountains, the Great Dividing Range, to the east and narrow coastal plains to the south-east. The island of Tasmania and the Torres Strait Islands are also part of Australia and there are the overseas territories of Norfolk Island, Cocos Keeling and Christmas Island.

In spite of the large number of yachts in Australia, the number of Australian yachts cruising overseas is surprisingly small and the only explanation for this is that Australia has been blessed by nature with such beautiful and varied cruising grounds that they do not need to go and look for variety elsewhere. From the wind-swept coasts of Victoria and Tasmania to the picturesque harbours of New South Wales, the tropical islands and Great Barrier Reef of Queensland to the huge shallow bays of the Northern Territory, Australia has it all. This vast country is a world in itself and even a short cruise through some of its waters will pay unexpected rewards.

Country Profile

The Aboriginal peoples of Australia probably arrived from Asia 60,000 years ago. Isolated for so long from the rest of the world, they developed a unique culture intrinsically bound up with the land. Up to the eighteenth century, Europeans believed that a great southern continent, Terra Australis Incognita, must exist to balance the land masses of the northern hemisphere. Australia was first sighted in the sixteenth century by the Portuguese and in the early seventeenth century the Spaniard Torres sailed through the Strait that came to bear his name. Dutch sailors charted the north and west and for a while Australia was called Van Dieman's land. In 1770 Captain Cook landed on the east coast at Botany Bay. Soon afterwards Captain Phillip officially took possession of the land for Britain, on the site of present-day Sydney. Britain used it as a penal colony and many convicts were deported there, often for relatively minor crimes.

The interior of the continent was opened up only gradually, not many people settling until the discovery of gold brought a rush of fortune hunters. The Aborigines suffered from this influx – their land and often their sacred sites were taken over and many perished, hunted by the new settlers or succumbing to European-brought diseases.

Farming, particularly sheep and other livestock, was developed and railways penetrated into the interior. At the end of the nineteenth century, the six colonies which had established themselves independently formed a Federation of States within the Commonwealth. Today each state has its own capital, parliament and laws. Australia's sovereignty was formally recognised in 1931 by the British Parliament. Australian forces played an important role in both World Wars and after the Second World War, the country emerged as a modern industrial nation and power.

The rural sector produces important exports such as wool, although this has declined. Agriculture remains important, and the country being relatively free of pests and disease, Australia's quarantine laws are strict for visitors. Many unique animals can be found on this ancient continent, such as platypus, kangaroos and koalas. Australia's rich mineral resources are crucial to the economy and industry is expanding.

The population is 20 million, living mostly on the coasts and in the south-east. The majority are immigrants, mainly English, Irish, Italians, Greeks, Germans, Serbs, Croats and more recently Asians. Aborigines form only 1 per cent of the population. Also indigenous to the area are the Torres Strait islanders. English is the main language. At one time there was thought to be 500 aboriginal languages, but today there are only about four main groups still spoken. The majority of the population are Christian, mainly Protestant and Catholic. Among other religions practised include Islam, Judaism and indigenous aboriginal traditional beliefs. Canberra is the Australian Federal

Practical Information

LOCAL TIME: Western Australia GMT + 8. South Australia, Northern Territory GMT + 9½. Eastern Australia GMT + 10. Summer time + 1 from late October to late March in South Australia, NSW, Tasmania and Victoria.

BUOYAGE: IALA A

CURRENCY: Australian dollar (Aus$)

BUSINESS HOURS
Banks: 0900/1000 to 1600 Monday to Thursday, to 1700 Friday.
Shops: 0900–1730 Monday to Friday, 0900–1200 Saturday.
Thursday and Friday late night shopping until 2100.
Government offices: 0900–1700 Monday to Friday.

ELECTRICITY: 240 V, 50 Hz

PUBLIC HOLIDAYS
1 January: New Year's Day
26 January: Australia Day
Good Friday, Easter Monday
25 April: ANZAC Day
June: Queen's Birthday
First Monday in October: Labour Day

25, 26 December: Christmas
Also: State bank holidays and State Labour days

EVENTS
July: Darwin to Ambon Yacht Race
26 December: Sydney–Hobart Race

COMMUNICATIONS
Telecommunications Commission: 24-hour public telephone and telex services (Sydney, Melbourne, Brisbane, Canberra). International calls from public phones with phonecards or credit cards.
Telegrams through operator and at post offices.
Emergencies: dial 000.
There are flights worldwide from all major cities and a comprehensive internal network.

MEDICAL
Costs can be high for visitors, so medical insurance is recommended.

DIPLOMATIC MISSIONS
In Canberra:
Canada: Commonwealth Ave. *Tel.* (62) 73-3844.
Indonesia: 8 Darwin Ave, Yarralumla. *Tel.* (62) 73-3222.
New Zealand: Commonwealth Ave,

Yarralumla. *Tel.* (62) 70-4211.
Papua New Guinea: PO Box 3572, Manuka. *Tel.* (62) 73-3322.
United Kingdom: Commonwealth Ave, Yarralumla. *Tel.* (62) 70-6666.
United States: Moonah Place, Yarralumla. *Tel.* (62) 70-5000.

In Brisbane:
New Zealand: Watkins Place Bldg, 288 Edward St. *Tel.* (7) 221-9932.
Papua New Guinea: Estate Houses, 127 Creek St. *Tel.* (7) 221-7915.
United Kingdom: BP House, 193 North Quay. *Tel.* 3223-3205.
United States: 383 Wickham Terr. *Tel.* (7) 229-8955.

In Darwin:
Indonesia: Stuart Park. *Tel.* (89) 81-9352.

In Perth:
Canada: St Martin's Tower, 44 St George's Terr. *Tel.* (9) 221-1770.
New Zealand: 16 St George's Terr. *Tel.* (9) 325-7877.
United Kingdom: Prudential Bldg. 95 St George's Terr. *Tel.* (9) 322-3200.
United States: 246 St George's Terr. *Tel.* (9) 322-4466.

Capital, and each state has its own capital.

The climate varies from one end of the country to the other. It is mainly temperate except for the tropical north and central desert. The north has two seasons, wet from November to March, with the heaviest rainfall after January. The winter months of April to October are drier and more pleasant. The cyclone season is from December to March on both the Pacific and Indian Ocean coasts.

Entry Regulations

Ports of entry

Queensland: Thursday Island 10°35′S 142°13′E, Weipa 12°40′S 141°55′E, Cairns 16°56′S 145°47′E, Mourilyan Harbour 17°36′S 146°07′E, Lucinda 18°31′S, 146°20′E, Townsville 19°15′S 146°50′E, Abbot Point 19°51′S 148°04′E, Mackay 21°06′S 149°13′E, Hay Point (Dalrymple Bay) 21°16′S 149°18′E, Gladstone 23°50′S 151°15′E, Bundaberg 24°46′S 152°23′E, Brisbane 27°19′S 153°10′E, Rockhampton (Port

Alma) 23°35′S 150°52′E.
Northern Territory: Gove 12°10′S 136°40′E, Darwin 12°30′S 130°52′E, Groote Eylandt (Milner Bay) 13°52′S 136°28′E.
Victoria: Melbourne 37°50′S 145°55′E, Westernport 38°20′S 145°15′E, Geelong 38°07′S 144°23′E, Portland 38°21′S 141°37′E.
South Australia: Cape Thevenard 32°09′S 133°39′E, Port Bonython 33°01′S 137°45′E, Androssan 34°26′S 137°55′E, Port Giles 35°02′S 137°45′E, Port Lincoln 34°45′S 135°53′E, Whyalla 33°02′S 137°37′E, Port Pirie 33°11′S 138°01′E, Wallaroo 33°56′S 137°37′E, Port Adelaide 34°47′S 138°30′E, Port Stanvac 35°07′S 138°28′E.
New South Wales: Yamba (Clarence River) 29°25′S 153°23′E, Coffs Harbour 30°18′S 153°09′E, Newcastle 32°56′S 151°47′E, Sydney 33°50′S 151°15′E, Port Botany and Kurnell 34°00′S 151°14′E, Port Kembla 34°28′S 150°54′E, Eden 37°04′S 149°55′E, Lord Howe Island 30°30′S 159°50′E.
Tasmania: Port Latta 40°51′S 145°23′E, Burnie

41°03′S 145°55′E, Devonport 41°11′S 146°22′E, Launceston 41°26′S 147°08′E, Hobart 42°52′S 147°20′E.

Western Australia: Derby 17°17′S 123°37′E, Broome 18°21′S 122°15′E, Port Hedland 20°20′S 118°37′E, Port Walcott 20°40′S 117°13′E, Dampier 20°39′S 116°43′E, Exmouth 21°54′S 114°11′E, Carnarvon 24°53′S 113°40′E, Geraldton 28°47′S 114°36′E, Fremantle 32°00′S 115°45′E, Bunbury 33°19′S 115°38′E, Albany 35°02′S 117°55′E, Esperance 33°52′S 121°53′E.

Procedure on arrival

The ports of entry all have 24-hour service. There are severe penalties for stopping anywhere else before clearing in, up to an Aus$50,000 fine. One should fly the Q flag as soon as one enters Australian territorial waters.

There are particularly strict rules concerning stops in any of the islands in the Torres Strait. The area is under constant surveillance by customs planes. If an emergency stop is made at one of the islands, no one must land or have contact with any other vessel. As this is an international waterway, vessels are allowed to transit without clearing into Australia provided the above rules are observed. The nearest port of entry is at Thursday Island.

By law the captain must give a minimum of three hours' notice of arrival. One should contact any OTC (Overseas Telecommunications Commission) coastal radio station (2182 KHz or VHF Channel 16), requesting that they notify customs and quarantine of the boat name, ETA and number of people on board. If a boat has no radio, one is supposed to write to the Collector of Customs at the planned port of entry before leaving for Australia.

At the port of entry, clearance is done by customs, immigration and quarantine. They require a list of ship's stores, dutiable items, crew, and any animals on board as well as the previous port clearance. Every person on board must have a valid visa, otherwise the captain will be fined Aus$1000 for every person arriving without a visa, including the captain himself. Everyone must remain on board until clearance is completed.

Sydney: Yachts approaching Sydney should contact Sydney Maritime or Sydney Radio on Channel 16 who will direct them to the customs berth in Neutral Bay and advise the appropriate authorities.

Brisbane: Contact customs on Channel 16 and give an ETA at the customs dock. Occasionally, if the ETA falls outside working hours, customs may allow yachts to anchor at a certain point in the river and complete formalities the following morning.

Bundaberg: Boats must proceed for clearance to Bundaberg Port Marina, which is three miles upriver, as it is no longer possible to clear in at Burnett Heads Marina at the river entrance.

Cairns: On entering Cairns Shipping Channel, Cairns Harbour Control should be contacted on Channel 16 to give an ETA. Yachts arriving between 0830 and 1630 are normally told to go to Pier A at Marlin Marina. After 1630 the pier is used by excursion boats and yachts will be directed elsewhere, such as the main wharf. A more convenient place to clear in is at Halfmoon Bay Marina at Yorkey's Knob, a few miles north of Cairns, but permission to proceed directly there by yachts arriving from a foreign port must be obtained from Cairns Harbour Control.

Thursday Island: Port Control should be contacted on Channel 16, who will probably direct the yacht to the customs dock. Customs, immigration and quarantine offices are all nearby. After clearance is completed the best place to anchor is west of the second jetty.

Darwin: Yachts are normally directed to the Fishermen's Wharf for clearance. Outside working hours, the yacht may be asked to anchor in the quarantine area. Clearance is also possible at Cullen Bay Marina, but this must be agreed with Darwin Port Control before proceeding there.

Procedure on departure

Clearing out can only be done at one of the ports of entry. The documents needed to get customs clearance are passports, crew list, list of ship's stores and registration certificate. Australian yachts must be registered before leaving Australia.

After clearing out, one is not allowed to stop at any other places, but anchoring for the night or in bad weather is permitted, provided one does not go ashore.

Customs

Firearms must be declared on entry. All military-type firearms (greater than .22), machine guns, pistols, revolvers, ammunition, as well as flick knives and knuckledusters are prohibited imports, and will be sealed on board or taken into custody at the first port of entry. Arrangements can be made to transport them to the port of departure if sufficient notice is given of that port and the date of departure. Sporting rifles and shotguns may be kept on board if a permit is obtained from the police.

Foreign yachts may enter Australia for up to 12 months without paying duty or sales tax, although they may be asked to give customs a bank or cash security to the value of the duty that would be paid if the yacht were imported. If paying cash, advance notice of departure and the port of exit must be given to customs in order to get a refund.

Customs require the itinerary that the yacht proposes to follow while in Australia. Yachts are supposed to keep customs informed of their whereabouts and to notify the nearest customs office if they change their itinerary.

Prescription drugs must be declared on arrival and their consumption recorded in the log book, which customs may check on departure. The medical chest will be sealed.

Anyone over 18 years of age is entitled to bring in 1 litre of alcohol and 250 g tobacco or 250 cigarettes. All quantities in excess of this will be sealed on board.

A refund of sales tax paid on goods bought while in Australia can be obtained. On arrival one should ask customs for the special vendors form, and an Australian Tax Office refund of sales tax form. Then when buying any goods, one should ask for an itemised receipt, which shows the sales tax as a separate item. After leaving Australia, mail the tax form with the receipts for the goods bought and the sales tax will be refunded.

Cash over Aus$ 10,000 (or equivalent) must be declared on arrival and departure.

Quarantine

Yachts with animals on board may only anchor, and the animal must be kept on board and confined (in a cage or below decks) at all times. Quarantine must be notified of any intention to change mooring, as well as the proposed itinerary in Australian waters. Permission to go to a fuel dock must be obtained in advance. While at the dock, the animal must be locked below. Permission must also be obtained before sailing to another area. The boat must be locked up whenever the crew is away. There are monthly inspections at a minimum fee of Aus$65 per half hour. The authority requires a bond of Aus$500 to be placed to ensure compliance with their requirements. Failure to comply can lead to destruction of the animal, loss of the bond, and heavy fines. If embarking animals in Australia, they must have a health certificate issued by a veterinarian.

Australia is free from many human, animal and plant diseases including rabies. All foodstuffs and plants, regardless of their origin, packaging or nature, are subject to a quarantine examination on arrival. All fresh produce as well as frozen and canned meat will be removed. The quarantine laws are strict and the penalties for breaking them severe.

Immigration

All nationalities, with the sole exception of New Zealanders, must obtain a visa in advance. Until recently the captain of a yacht was exempt, but the law has been changed and he or she must also have a visa. There are Australian diplomatic missions in American Samoa, Fiji, Indonesia, Kiribati, Nauru, New Caledonia, New Zealand, Papua New Guinea, the Solomon Islands, Tonga, Vanuatu and Western Samoa, where visas can be obtained. A multiple entry visa valid for the length of the passport's validity can be obtained. A multiple visa must be obtained by those wishing to stop also at one of Australia's territories (Cocos Keeling or Christmas Island).

A single entry tourist visa is valid for up to six months within a 12 month period. Visa extensions up to one year can be applied for from the Department of Immigration, but the application itself costs Aus$200 and takes some time. When applying for an extension one will be required to show proof of funds and possibly also adequate medical insurance.

Cruising permit

This is obtained from customs on arrival, being granted when the officials are satisfied that the applicant is a genuine tourist, and has proof of sufficient funds for the maintenance of the vessel and the crew without work visas. Extensions are available from customs, upon application and assessment of the reasons. An initial six-month period is given, with provisions for extensions totalling a further six months. The permit enables foreign yachts to cruise freely between their port of entry and exit, and allows them to visit ports and places besides the official ports of entry. This permit is not for the use of anyone with the intention of using the vessel for commercial gain while in Australia.

Fees

There is a quarantine fee for the initial half-hour, followed by $60 per quarter-hour thereafter. This fee is charged even during normal working hours, when no other official fees are applicable. Quarantine also has overtime charges of $122 on weekdays and Saturdays, $150 on Sundays, and $180 on public holidays in addition to the charges noted above. Charges for yachts carrying small animals which are bonded on board are applied on top of the above fees as follows: surveillance of $120 per month, and $120 per visit or for any other requests or necessary requirements.

Overtime fees are charged by customs and immigration if formalities are completed between 1630 and 0830, at weekends or on public holidays.

There is a departure tax of Aus$10 per person over 12 years old. This is payable whether one leaves by yacht or by air.

Sales tax
A sales tax of between 4 per cent and 21 per cent is included in the price of most goods, except food, alcohol, clothing and fuel. Temporary visitors can claim exemption from this tax in two ways. One alternative is to get a good supply of 'Export Sales – Foreign Visitor Declaration' forms from the Australian Tax Office, which should be presented to the retailer at each transaction, who will then deduct the tax due and charge the net price. Many retailers are not familiar with the procedure, but on higher amounts it is worth insisting that the procedure is carried out. The second alternative is to apply for a refund to the Australian Tax Office by presenting all receipts with the tax specified on each. In the latter case, the total amount of tax must be higher than Aus$200.

Restrictions
Some restricted areas are marked on the charts.
Aboriginal Reserves and National Parks: Entry to these may be restricted and special permission is required to visit them. The Northern Territory has several of these areas on its coast. For more details, write to the Department of Aboriginal Affairs in Darwin or enquire at the port of entry.

The coast and islands west of Gove are part of the Arnhem Land Aboriginal Reserve and one needs a permit for entry, obtainable from the Lands Office in Gove.

Cotton Island is off-limits as it has sacred burial sites.

Coburg Peninsula is a National Park and permission to enter can be obtained from the Ranger Station.

Ashmore Reef is a National Park, no spearfishing is allowed.

Note: In the Northern Territory, one must remember that salt-water crocodiles can be found in the sea and estuaries. Their numbers are growing as they are a protected animal.

In New South Wales living aboard a yacht permanently is illegal, although foreign yachts that are cruising are considered more leniently. The Maritime Services Board in Pittwater are more lenient than those in Sydney Harbour.

Artefacts and protected wildlife products cannot be exported unless special permission is obtained.

Facilities

Facilities in Australia are generally good and anywhere near a yachting centre are excellent. For yachts arriving from the Pacific it is a great relief to find a country where everything is available and virtually anything can be fixed. If in need of a major overhaul or repairs, it is advisable to head for a main centre, such as Sydney, Brisbane, Cairns or Darwin, where repair facilities are of a high standard and spares readily available.

Yacht clubs everywhere are welcoming and are also a valuable source of advice concerning repairs or provisioning. Australian charts are excellent and are continually kept up to date. They are available in any port of significant size. Fuel and water are easily available and gas bottles can be filled in most places. As can be expected in such a rich and varied country, provisioning is excellent everywhere and Australia is a good place to stock up the boat for the continuation of a voyage.

Visiting yachts are welcome at the Royal Queensland Yacht Squadron base at Manly, near Brisbane, which has good facilities and is a convenient place to leave the boat to visit the interior. Cruising sailors are also welcome at the Cairns Yacht Club in central Cairns, which gives temporary membership to visitors. There are a limited number of visiting berths at Marlin Marina and most visitors have to anchor or moor across the river from the town. Half Moon Bay Marina, a few miles north of Cairns, has the best services although only basic repair facilities. Most of the companies specialising in marine repair, whether electrical, engine, electronic, fibreglass, welding or sailmaking are concentrated in the Portsmith area about two miles upstream from the city centre. The Cairns Cruising Yacht Squadron is based there, welcomes visitors and has a travelift and slipway. Larger boats can be slipped at the nearby Norship boatyard, which has a 120-tonne travelift. Fuel, water, LPG and provisions are all easily available in Cairns.

In Darwin visiting yachts used to anchor off the Darwin Sailing Club in Fannie Bay, which welcomes temporary members to use their facilities. A well stocked chandlery is on the premises. In Francis Bay there are several boatyards with haul-out facilities, both slipways and travelifts, near to the Mooring Basin, the cyclone refuge harbour where there may be some berths available when the prawnfishing boats are out. Cullen Bay Marina provides a full range of services and the best docking in the area. Due to the large fishing fleet based in Darwin, there are excellent repair facilities of all types and chandlers in the area around the Mooring Basin.

Boats bound for Darwin should join the annual 'Over the Top Cruise' organised by the Gove Yacht Club as it includes stops in several places that are normally closed to visitors.

Further Reading

Cruising Guide to the Northern Territory Coast
Cruising the Coral Coast
Australia – a travel survival kit
Australian Cruising Guide
Cruising the Coral Coast
South Pacific Anchorages
The Pacific Crossing Guide

Websites

www.tourism.gov.au (Ministry of Sports and Tourism)
www.aqis.gov.au (Quarantine Department)
www.immi.gov.au (Immigration Department)

COOK ISLANDS

The Cook Islands are made up of 15 islands, spread over an area of over half a million square miles of ocean. The Southern Group, of which Rarotonga is the main island, also comprises Aitutaki, Atiu, Mitiaro, Mauke and Mangaia. These are high and fertile and most of the 18,500 inhabitants live there. The Northern Group are the low coral atolls of Penrhyn, Manihiki, Rakahanga, Pukapuka, Nassau and Suwarrow, which is a national park. Also part of the Cooks are the atolls of Manuae, Takutea and Palmerston Island.

The affection that most cruising sailors have for the Cooks is mainly due to two legendary figures who spent a great deal of their lives on these islands. Tom Neale, a modern day Robinson Crusoe, chose to maroon himself on Suwarrow atoll, the kind of tropical retreat of which dreams are made, and welcomed any yachtsmen that called. Father George Kester also ran away to the Cooks, but not in search of solitude, for his motives were altruistic. As a missionary he dedicated his life to the spiritual well-being of the islanders as well as the material well-being of all cruising sailors who happened to call at his island, first Rarotonga and then Aitutaki.

As most yachts sail to the Cook Islands from the east, a good time to plan one's passage is after the 14 July celebrations in Tahiti are over, as the first week of August is the time when the Cooks put on their own festivities around Independence Day. Most of the action is in Rarotonga, but the other islands can be visited afterwards. Aitutaki is a popular stop and yachts are always assured of a warm welcome there. This is the case in all of the Cook Islands and as elsewhere in the Pacific, the more remote the island the more enthusiastic the welcome.

Country Profile

Folklore holds that in the early 1300s two chiefs, from Tahiti and Samoa, arrived on Rarotonga at the same time, and divided the island peacefully between them. From here it is believed that the Polynesians, forefathers of the Maori race, sailed down to New Zealand.

The first European to lay eyes on the Cooks was the Spanish explorer Mendana at the end of the sixteenth century. Others soon followed, and in the 1770s Captain Cook put many of the islands on the map. Traders and missionaries were the next to arrive, and eventually the Cooks became a British colony. The islands were handed over to New Zealand in 1901 and became independent in 1965. The Cooks today have internal self-government, with free association with New Zealand. There are very close ties to New Zealand and many Cook Islanders live there, more than on the islands.

The economy is based on tourism and agriculture. The northern islands mainly produce copra for export. Since the 1970s tourism has boomed, encouraged by the government trying to end dependence on foreign aid. However, imports are still well above exports and aid from New Zealand keeps the economy afloat.

The capital is Avarua on Rarotonga, the most developed island, which has beautiful mountainous scenery. The languages spoken are Cook Islands Maori and English. Christianity is important to the islanders and Sunday is a quiet day. The main faiths

Practical Information

LOCAL TIME: GMT – 10.

BUOYAGE: IALA A

CURRENCY: New Zealand dollar (NZ$), with local coinage.

BUSINESS HOURS
Banks: 0900–1500 Monday to Friday, 0900–1100 Saturday.
Business: 0730–1530 Monday to Friday, 0730–1130 Saturday.
Shops: 0800–1600 Monday to Friday, 0800–1200 Saturday.
Government offices: 0800–1600 Monday to Friday.

ELECTRICITY: 230 V, 50 Hz

PUBLIC HOLIDAYS
1 January: New Year's Day
25 April: ANZAC Day
Good Friday
Easter Monday
June: Queen's Birthday
4 August: Constitution Day
26 October: Gospel Day
25, 26 December: Christmas

COMMUNICATIONS
Cook Islands Telecom, Tutakimoa Road, Avarua, open 24 hours, for overseas telephone calls, telegrams and internet. Post office in Rarotonga 0800–1600 Monday to Friday for telephones, telegrams and fax.

Emergencies: police 999, fire 996, ambulance 998.
There are flights from Rarotonga to Auckland, Honolulu, Nadi and Papeete.

MEDICAL
Medical and dental facilities available 24 hours a day at Tupapa Clinic. There are modern hospitals in Rarotonga, Aitutaki and in some of the other islands.

DIPLOMATIC MISSIONS
New Zealand: Philatelic Bureau Bldg, Takuvaine Rd, Avarua, Rarotonga.
Tel. 22-201.
France: *Tel.* 22-000.
UK: Titikaveka. *Tel.* 29-311.

---

are Protestant, Catholic, Seventh Day Adventist, and Latter Day Saints.

December to March is rainy and also the cyclone season. Generally the climate is warm and sunny, but not too hot. During the winter, April to November, the islands are under the influence of the SE trade winds. However, sudden squalls can occur from other directions with little warning.

Entry Regulations

Ports of entry
Rarotonga: Avatiu 21°12′S 159°47′W.
Aitutaki: Arutanga 18°52′S 159°48′W.
Penrhyn: Omoka 9°00′S 158°04′W.
Sub-ports of entry are Pukapuka 10°53′S 165°49′W and Atiu (Avamutu) 19°59′S 158°08′W.

Procedure on arrival
For clearance, the captain must present the passports, clearance from the last port, crew list, health certificate of pratique as well as a general declaration and details of the yacht.
Rarotonga: One may clear at Avatiu, the commercial harbour. The harbour master can be contacted on VHF Channel 16 between 0800–1600 for berthing instructions. The working channel is 12. Radio Rarotonga (ZKR) monitors 2182 KHz and 4125 MHz as well as Channel 16.
Aitutaki: After entering the lagoon through the long channel one should anchor off Arutanga

village, at the entrance to the small boat harbour. Customs will come out to the boat. Boats too large should anchor outside the reef to the north of the channel and the captain should come ashore to clear. The channel has a depth of only six feet and outflowing tidal currents can reach three to four knots. There is slightly more water on the port side, which should be favoured. If in any doubt, one should ask a person to guide one in.
Penrhyn: One should anchor off Omaka village on the south side of the Taruia Pass. There is also a wharf where one can come alongside if there is no surge. After clearance one must get permission before moving elsewhere in the lagoon.

One may clear at Pukapuka and Atiu, but must pay for transporting the customs officer by air or sea.
Atiu Island: There is no harbour, so one has to anchor off the reef.

Customs
A list of firearms must be produced on arrival and these will be impounded until departure.

Animals have to be confined on board and will be checked daily by the quarantine official.

Agriculture
Animals, plants and fruit will be inspected as the Cooks are free of serious diseases and pests, and their economy depends very much on agriculture. Fruit and meat will be confiscated, so it is advisable not to arrive with a lot of fresh supplies. Fortunately good local fruit is available.

Immigration

If entering in Rarotonga a permit for up to 31 days will be given on arrival. This can be extended, on a monthly basis, up to three months maximum. Fourteen days before the permit expires one should apply for the extension. Proof of adequate funds may be requested for extensions. For longer visits a visa must be obtained from a New Zealand or British consulate before arrival in the Cooks.

In Aitutaki and other ports of entry, a 31-day permit will be given on arrival. Extensions have to be obtained in Rarotonga. If crew disembarks from the yacht, they must notify immigration and provide a baggage declaration.

Fees

Harbour fees in Rarotonga: There is a berthage charge for yachts owned by non-Cook Islands residents. Harbour fees in Rarotonga must be paid before outward clearance is given.

Avatiu Harbour: Yachts must pay a daily fee depending on length, monohulls NZ$0.55 per metre per day, multihulls NZ$ 0.70 per metre per day. There is also a small mooring fee at Aitutaki.

Visa extension fee amounts to NZ$30 per person. There is an exit fee of NZ$25 per person, NZ$10 per child (2–11 years).

Overtime is charged before 0800 and after 1600 on weekdays, and all day at weekends and public holidays.

Restrictions

Yachts may not visit any other islands in the Cooks than those mentioned as ports of entry without permission from customs and immigration. At all these islands, the captain should check in with customs and the resident administrator, if present. To visit Suwarrow atoll national park, one should obtain permission from the resident park administrator.

The authorities have placed a permanent official on Suwarrow, who lives on Anchorage Island. Although not a port of entry, boats that have cleared into the Cooks are allowed to stop there. The passports should be taken to the administrator, who will stamp them and issue a clearance certificate. A stay of four days is normally granted, which can be easily extended. Boats that have not cleared into the Cooks previously are normally allowed to remain for two or three days. Suwarrow has been declared a marine park and visitors are urged to preserve its environment. Although the lagoon provides good shelter under normal trade wind conditions, if the weather deteriorates it is advisable to put to sea immediately as the fetch in the lagoon can cause large waves, which break across the entrance making conditions hazardous.

Cruising yachts are not allowed to remain in the islands during the cyclone season, which is from December to March. Harbour masters in Rarotonga and Aitutaki may not even let transiting yachts stay overnight in port during the cyclone season.

Facilities

Avatiu harbour is the commercial port of Rarotonga. The harbour has been greatly improved but space for yachts is still limited.

There is a good selection of fruit and vegetables on this fertile island. Locally produced canned fruit juices are a good buy. Repair facilities are basic. There are no marine supplies and only one chandlery, ABC Trading Company, Rarotonga, *Tel.* 22244.

Essential spares must be ordered from New Zealand, from where there are frequent flights. Gas bottles can be filled at an office near the harbour.

There is limited provisioning and facilities in Aitutaki, although one can enter the small boat harbour to take on fuel and provisions. At Penrhyn basic provisions are available as well as some fresh fruit and vegetables. A limited amount of water can be obtained from the islanders, but as this is often in short supply it is better to try and arrive with full tanks. As the supply ship is sometimes late, the islanders prefer trading in scarce items rather than money. Items in demand are fishing gear, dry cell batteries, rope and small anchors. Boats heading west and planning to stop at Palmerston should take along a supply of fresh fruit, such as oranges, which will be greatly appreciated by the islanders.

Further Reading

Landfalls of Paradise
Charlie's Charts of Polynesia
Rarotonga and the Cook Islands – a travel survival kit
South Pacific Handbook
The Pacific Crossing Guide
South Pacific Anchorages
Tahiti Handbook

Website

www.ck (Official site)

EASTER ISLAND

Mystery surrounds this remote South Pacific island, the people who once lived here and the origins of the giant statues that are scattered all over this small island. Lying at the south-eastern point of the Polynesian triangle, yachts increasingly call at this lonely outpost of Chile to whom it belongs and from whom it is separated by over 2000 miles of ocean. Isla de Pascua, also known by its Polynesian name Rapa Nui, is totally isolated and its nearest neighbour is tiny Pitcairn, 1200 miles to the west.

In the past, yachts had to be prepared to leave the island at short notice as there was no adequate shelter and several boats had come to grief as the wind had changed direction suddenly putting them on a lee shore. There is now good protection inside the small harbour at Hanga Piko, on the west coast, but access is difficult without local knowledge and the port captain insists that a local pilot is employed, who will charge about $US100 for his services. The anchorage off the main settlement of Hanga Roa is open but sheltered from the prevailing south-easterly winds. If the wind turns, one can move to Anakena Bay, site of some of the most interesting excavations and statues on the island, or to Huituiti in the east. Swell is a problem in all these anchorages.

For those who make the long passage, there are many rewards ashore: the crater of the Rano Kau volcano and above it the sacred site of Orongo where the birdman cult was practised. At the other end of the island is the volcano Rano Raraku, where the giant statues were carved out of lava and where many still lie abandoned and unfinished.

Country Profile

Debate has raged over the history of Rapa Nui before the outside world made contact with it. Some 600 huge abandoned lava statues, up to 30 ft (9 m) high lie scattered around the island; who carved them and why remains a mystery. Easter Islanders were the only Pacific people to develop a form of writing, although no one survived who could read it.

The first European to visit the island in 1722 was a Dutchman, Jacob Roggeveen, at a time when the inhabitants had just finished a series of civil wars. The population remained stable at around 4000 until the 1850s, when Peruvian slave traders, smallpox and emigration to Tahiti saw the number of inhabitants fall considerably. At the end of the nineteenth century Chile annexed the island. Mounting an expedition to the island in 1955 the Norwegian Thor Heyerdahl tried to unravel the mystery of the statues and proposed a theory that the islanders had originated in South America. This theory is not accepted today, but nevertheless it caught the imagination of countless people around the world, making Easter Island one of the most enticing tourist destinations. Today Easter Island is a dependency of Chile, with a military governor and a local mayor. In recent years, the islanders have achieved a certain level of autonomy, but the relations with mainland Chile continue to be tense. Tourism has greatly expanded in recent years.

There are around 2500 islanders of Polynesian origin and a few hundred Chileans. Spanish is the official language, but Polynesian, closely akin to Tahitian, is spoken by the islanders. Almost all the islanders are Catholic. Hanga Roa is the only

Practical Information

LOCAL TIME: GMT – 8

BUOYAGE: IALA B

CURRENCY: Chilean peso, of 100 centesimos. US$ cash is widely accepted.

BUSINESS HOURS
Banco del Estado de Chile: 0900–1400 Monday to Friday.

ELECTRICITY: 240 V, 50 Hz; 110 V at Hotel Hanga Roa.

PUBLIC HOLIDAYS
1 January: New Year's Day
Holy Week (two days)
1 May
21 May: Navy Day
15 August: Assumption
9 September: Rapa Nui/Policarpo Day
18/19 September: Independence Days
12 October: Discovery of America
1 November: All Saints' Day
8 December: Immaculate Conception
25 December: Christmas Day

COMMUNICATIONS
International telephone calls from the telephone exchange (ENTEL).
Post office open 0900–1700 weekdays.
There is a twice-weekly flight from Santiago (Chile) that goes on to Papeete (Tahiti) and vice versa.

MEDICAL
There is a small hospital on the island.

The anchorage off Hangaroa on Easter Island.

settlement and there is a large military garrison.

From October to April the SE trades prevail. The summer, mid-November to mid-February, is when winds tend to be lighter and the seas calmer. May to September are the rainier months, when westerlies predominate. The island falls outside the cyclone belt.

Entry Regulations

Port of entry
Hanga Roa 27°09′S 109°26′W.

Procedure on arrival
On arrival the captain should contact the port captain on Channel 16. Landing the dinghy in Hanga Roa can be difficult if there is a big swell, although there is a small and shallow basin, protected by a breakwater, which is used by the fishing boats. If Hanga Roa is untenable, one can land at Hanga Piko a mile from the main settlement around Point Roa.

Entry formalities are uncomplicated and are done ashore, although sometimes officials come out to the yacht. On leaving, one must clear with customs and immigration again. Because of the difficulty in landing, it is recommended to use the services of a local fisherman, who will use his own high-powered boat to land the crew. This can be arranged via the port captain on Channel 16. Both arrival and departure formalities are normally completed at the port captain's office, at Hanga Piko.

Hanga Piko: The small harbour has been enlarged and dredged to about 8 ft (2.5 m). As the entrance is very difficult, most yachts employ a pilot, whose fee is negotiable and has been reported to vary from $100 to $150. Boats of a maximum length of 60 ft (18 m) and not much more draft than 7 ft (2 m) can find shelter inside. The final decision whether a boat will be allowed in or not depends on the port captain. The small basin is sheltered from all wind directions, but surge causes serious problems at all times, so boats must be tied fore and aft to rocks ashore. If one of the inside boats wishes to leave, all others have to move too. The harbour should be abandoned under heavy surge conditions as several yachts were damaged when this occurred.

Customs
Firearms must be declared on arrival. Animals are not allowed to land.

Immigration
Visitors are given a visa on arrival.

Restrictions
It is strictly prohibited to remove ancient artefacts.

Around one third of the island is a National Park, for which an entry fee of US$10 is charged.

Facilities

All supplies are brought in from Chile by ship or air and goods in the supermarkets are quite expensive, but the selection is very good. Some locally produced fruit and vegetables are available. There is a water tap by the dinghy landing in Hanga Roa from where water can be taken in jerrycans. Fuel is also available, but must be carried in jerrycans from the fuel station. Usually this can be arranged with the same fisherman one uses to commute ashore.

Although there are no repair facilities as such, the government has a workshop for maintenance purposes and in an emergency they would undoubtedly help.

Further Reading

Charlie's Charts of Polynesia
South Pacific Handbook
Aku-Aku
Chile and Easter Island – a travel survival kit
Landfalls of Paradise
South Pacific Anchorages
Tahiti Handbook

Website

www.netaxs.com (Easter Island home page with useful links)

FIJI ISLANDS

Fiji is an archipelago of over 300 islands, from coral atolls to large volcanic islands. About 100 are inhabited, while many of the rest are used as fishing bases and planting grounds. The International Dateline runs through Fiji, although most of the islands are just west of 180°.

For the cruising sailor, Fiji has all the ingredients of a perfect destination – beautiful islands, secluded anchorages and welcoming people. This picture of perfection is somewhat marred by a menacing array of coral reefs that almost encircle the entire archipelago. The proliferation of radar and satellite navigation has significantly reduced the danger, but many a world cruise has come to a premature end on one of Fiji's reefs.

The majority of visiting yachts arrive from the east, which is where the reefs have claimed most victims. Part of the problem is that it is forbidden to stop at any of the eastern islands before clearing in and a careful watch is kept on yacht movement by the Fijian authorities. The location of the few ports of entry complicates the task of cruise planning, especially for those hoping to visit the eastern Lau group to windward of all ports of entry. The most convenient port for those intending to cruise eastern Fiji is Levuka on the island of Ovalau.

At the crossroads of Melanesia and Polynesia, the traditional way of life is still thriving in the islands and the unthinking attitude in the past of a few visiting sailors has caused offence and animosity, which led to a strict control of cruising permits. Local etiquette should be observed and one is expected to pay a courtesy visit to the chief or headman of the island or village bearing a gift of yagona (kava). A good supply should be taken on board from Suva market. The effort that the Fijians make to preserve their traditions is exactly what makes them so interesting and visitors who observe these simple rules can be assured of a genuine welcome.

Traditions are not so strong in the western islands, some of which have been developed as tourist resorts, such as the charming Mamanuca islands, which are a short hop from Nadi airport, convenient for crew changes. Further west is the Yasawa Group, one of the most popular cruising grounds due to scenic anchorages and clear waters.

Rotuma and several smaller islands lying approximately 200 miles NNW of Fiji, form a distinctive group and although administratively linked to Fiji, ethnologically they are very different as Rotumans are Polynesians. The administrative centre is at Ahau, but as Rotuma is not an official port of entry, access to it is only allowed with prior permission from the authorities in Suva.

Country Profile

The islands were first settled by Melanesians from South East Asia around 7000–5000 BC, while the Polynesians arrived in the fifteenth century AD. European discovery spread over two to three hundred years, after being first sighted in the mid-seventeenth century by Abel Tasman. Captain Cook visited several islands in the 1770s, and Captain Bligh sailed through on his epic voyage after being cast off from the *Bounty*.

During the nineteenth century traders arrived in search of sandalwood, as well as missionaries and land speculators. The introduction of firearms saw terrible tribal wars fought by a people renowned for their savagery and cannibalism. Gradually, however, Christianity spread its influence and the chiefs requested that the islands be taken under the protection of Great Britain to put an end to their exploitation by traders and freebooters.

Labour shortages in the nineteenth and early twentieth centuries led to large numbers of Indian labourers being brought in by the British to work on the sugar plantations. Independence came to Fiji in 1970 and for some years the country enjoyed some stability and prosperity. Racial ten-

Practical Information

LOCAL TIME: GMT + 12 (the date line has been adjusted to fall east of the whole group).

BUOYAGE: IALA A

CURRENCY: Fijian dollar (FID, FI$). A maximum of FI$100 can be exported in local currency, and FI$500 in foreign currency.

BUSINESS HOURS
Banks: 0930–1500 Monday to Thursday, 0930–1600 Friday.
Shops: 0830–1700 Monday to Thursday, 0830–1300 Saturday. On Friday some stay open until 2000.
Business and government offices: 0800–1300, 1400–1630 Monday–Friday. There is strict enforcement of Sunday observance when sport and most commercial activities are banned, although essential services such as fuel stations and public transport run as normal.

ELECTRICITY: 240 V, 50 Hz

PUBLIC HOLIDAYS
1 January: New Year's Day
Good Friday, Easter Saturday and Monday
May/June: Ratu Sir Lala Sukuna Day
June: Queen's Official Birthday (second Saturday)
End July: Constitution Day
August Bank Holiday (start of the month)
October/November: Divali Day (Hindu festival of lights)
10 October: Fiji Day
25, 26 December: Christmas
Variable: Prophet Mohammed's birthday

EVENTS
July: Bula Festival in Nadi
August: Hibiscus Festival in Suva
September: Musket Cove to Vila Yacht Race
September: Sugar Festival in Lautoka

COMMUNICATIONS
Fintel (Fiji International Telecommunications Ltd) 158 Victoria Parade, Suva: international phones, telex and fax, open 24 hours, seven days a week.
Suva post office is open 0800–1630 Monday to Friday. Post offices outside Suva open 0800–1600 Monday to Friday.
Emergency: Dial 000.
Nadi in the west of Viti Levu is the main international airport with flights to many Pacific destinations as well as Australia, New Zealand, US, European and Asian destinations. There are a few international flights from Suva airport, which connects with several daily flights to Nadi.

MEDICAL
There is a minimal charge in hospitals for non-Fijians. There are also private clinics. Suva Hospital. *Tel.* 313444.

DIPLOMATIC MISSIONS
In Suva:
Australia: Dominion House, Thomson St. *Tel.* 312844.
France: 1st floor, Dominion House, Thomson St. *Tel.* 312925.
FSM: 37 Loftus St, PO Box 15493. *Tel.* 304566.
Marshalls: 41 Borron Rd, Govt Bldgs, PO Box 2038. *Tel.* 387899.
New Zealand: 10th floor, Reserve Bank Building, Pratt St. *Tel.* 311422.
Papua New Guinea: Credit Corporation Bldg, PO Box 2447. *Tel.* 304244.
Tuvalu: 8 Mitchell St. *Tel.* 300697.
United Kingdom: Victoria House, 47 Gladstone Rd. *Tel.* 311033.
United States: 31 Loftus Street. *Tel.* 314466.

sion, however, remained close to the surface, as the Indian population grew to outnumber the native Fijians. After the coalition supported by Indians and urban Fijians won the 1987 elections, Col. Sitiveni Rabuka staged a military coup to keep power with the conservative Fijians. Fiji declared itself a Republic and was expelled from the Commonwealth. A new Constitution was adopted in 1997 and came into force in 1998. It removed the racial features of the 1990 Constitution and enabled the country to resume membership in the Commonwealth in 1998 under the country's new name of Fiji Islands. The elections in May 1999 resulted in a new government with, for the first time, a Prime Minister of Indian race. A coup put down in 2000 may herald more instability.

The capital of Fiji is Suva, on the main island of Viti Levu. It is a large cosmopolitan city, with a good harbour and duty-free port. Sugar and tourism are the main Fijian industries, the latter starting to recover after the slump which affected both industries after the coup. Other industries are timber, copra and gold mining, but unemployment is high. Fiji is an important communications centre for the South Pacific, and the main campus of the University of the South Pacific is located in Suva.

The population is about 746,000, 49 per cent Fijian, 45 per cent Indian and 6 per cent of other origins. Fijian, Hindustani and English are spoken, the latter being widely used by all sections of the population. Most Fijians are Methodists, some Roman Catholic, while the Indian population are mainly Hindu with some Muslims and Sikhs.

Fiji has a mild tropical climate. From May to November the SE trades blow, making it cooler and drier, while the summer months from November to April are wet and humid. Viti Levu and Vanua Levu can have a lot of rain and Suva is renowned for sudden but short torrential downpours. Cyclones occur during the period November to April. There are very few hurricane holes in Fiji and these quickly fill up with local boats.

Entry Regulations

Ports of entry

Suva (Viti Levu island) 18°09'S 178°26'E, Levuka (Ovalau island) 17°41'S 178°51'E, Lautoka (Viti Levu island) 17°36'S 177°26'E, Savusavu (Vanua Levu) 16°47'S, 179°21'E.

On reaching Fijian waters one must first call at a port of entry to complete pratique, customs, immigration and quarantine formalities. Working hours for clearance are from Monday to Thursday 0800–1300, 1400–1630; Friday 0830–1300, 1400–1600. Overtime charges will be paid outside of these hours. Documents required prior to arrival are:

1 Clearance certificate from the previous port or country.
2 Crew lists with details of passport numbers, nationality and age.
3 Valid passports.

Vessels in excess of 100 tons must contact a yachting agent prior to arrival. There are many differences in clearance formalities for vessels over 100 tons which must be complied with.

Once cleared into Fiji, those who intend to sail to another port of entry (either directly or via the other islands) must clear out with customs from the port of entry where they cleared in first.

Procedure on arrival

Before proceeding to a port of entry, all vessels are required to communicate with Port Control on Channel 16 to request permission to enter the port, and to obtain information on vessel movements in the harbour. On entering the port, proceed directly to the designated quarantine area indicated on the chart. Fly the international Q flag and await instructions or arrival of the correct authorities. Apart from pratique, customs, immigration or quarantine officers, no one should be allowed to board the vessel, nor any person or article leave the vessel until all clearances are granted.

The Ports Authority of Fiji levies a fee applicable to all vessels entering any of the ports of Suva, Lautoka, Savusavu and Levuka. Vessels up to 100 tons pay a maximum of $F10.45.

Quarantine should be the first official to clear the vessel. The captain will be instructed to await the arrival of the health boat or to proceed directly to the wharf and await the health officer's arrival. The Department of Health levy $F33 for this clearance which must be paid at the Divisional Medical Officer's office.

Everyone needs permission from an immigration officer before they disembark. Port Control should be asked to send out an immigration officer, but if he does not meet the yacht on arrival, a message should be sent via the customs officer repeating this request. The Immigration Department may expect to be reimbursed for the taxi fare to get the officer to the wharf and back.

Suva: Contact Suva Port Control on Channel 16 at least two hours before arrival. Normally yachts are required to anchor in the quarantine area to be boarded by a quarantine official before moving to King's Wharf for the rest of formalities. It is occasionally possible to obtain radio pratique through the operator, in which case the yacht may proceed directly to King's Wharf for clearance. Immigration does not come to the boat and the captain must walk to the immigration office in town. At the same time, one can also pay the health clearance fee at the health office nearby. If King's Wharf is crowded with ships, yachts may be allowed to proceed directly to the Royal Suva Yacht Club and complete formalities there. It is advisable to arrive during normal working hours to avoid overtime charges. Clearance is normally available from 0700 to sunset Monday to Friday. Official working hours are 0800–1300, 1400–1630 Monday to Thursday, 0830–1300, 1400–1600 Friday.

Yachts arriving at the weekend at Suva have been fined for not notifying the authorities and anchoring at the yacht club until Monday.

Levuka: The authorities may not answer calls on Channel 16, so it is best to anchor near the main wharf and make one's way ashore. All offices are nearby. Occasionally officers insist on inspecting the boat, but some appear to be put off by the prospect of a wet dinghy ride. Formalities are usually simpler than Suva, so for boats coming from the east, the detour to Levuka is probably justified as on subsequently arriving in Suva one can proceed directly to the Royal Suva Yacht Club and contact the authorities from there.

Lautoka: Yachts normally proceed to Queen's Wharf and anchor in the vicinity. Arrangements are then made on Channel 16 to meet the various officials at the dock and bring them out to the boat. Normally the boat is inspected by quarantine, agriculture, customs and immigration officers.

Savusavu: Contact the marina on Channel 16 and they will call the relevant officials.

Customs

Firearms must be declared and handed over to the police to be kept in bond until departure (48 hours' notice of departure must be given). If one enters at one port and exits at another, the guns may have to be transferred to the port of departure by the police.

A bond declaration must be signed for any animals on board and they must not be allowed to land on any of the islands.

An itinerary of places and dates where one is planning to cruise until departure from Fiji is required for customs clearance.

Yachts may remain one year without paying any duty.

Any amount over 2 litres of spirits and 4 litres of wine must be sealed on board or taken ashore and bonded. Customs often check the seal before departure. Excess amounts of wine, beer or spirits, which are left unsealed for personal consumption, must be declared and import duty paid.

No fruit or plants may be landed. All such produce on board must be declared and will be inspected on arrival. Garbage should be put in sealed plastic bags and handed over to be disposed into the port incinerator.

Immigration

Passports must be valid for at least six months from the date of entry.

A visa-free stay for up to four months (provided one has enough funds or an outward ticket) is allowed for United Kingdom, United States, Canada and most European nationals. Visas are required by only a few nationalities. After four months, an extension may be obtained for up to six months.

Quarantine

On arrival in a port of entry, the captain should inform the authorities if there are any prohibited items aboard. Foreign vessels are requested to declare on arrival the following:

Foods: (tinned or packaged): meat, sausages, salami, ham, pork, poultry, eggs, fats, milk, butter, cheese.
Plants: vegetables, fruits, nuts, seeds, bulbs, mushrooms or any other articles made of plant materials.

Pets to be bonded.

Some items will not be permitted to be kept aboard the yacht for the duration of the visit in Fiji. What is allowed to stay aboard will be at the discretion of the quarantine officer at the time of inspection. Garbage should not be discharged without the permission of the quarantine officer.

Cruising permit

Vessels intending to visit any port, island or anchorage outside of Suva, Lautoka, Savusavu or Levuka need to obtain a cruising permit from customs as well as permission to cruise the islands. This permit acts as a letter of introduction to the 'Turaga ni Koro' (the village head), the 'Buli' (head of the provincial subdivision), or the 'Roko Tui' (provincial head). Cruising permits can be obtained from the Ministry of Foreign Affairs located at 61 Carnavon Street in Suva, or from the Commissioner Western's office in Lautoka, the Commissioner Eastern's office in Levuka, or the Provincial Office in Savusavu. Fijian customs and laws are strong and have to be respected. These will be explained by the Department when the permit is given.

Those who wish to visit the Lau Group must apply for a permit from the President's office. The office is located in Suva. A letter should be prepared beforehand, including the following information: detailed list of islands to be visited, itinerary and dates, reason for visit, crew list with details of ages and passport numbers, name and details of yacht.

Fees

Customs: Overtime will be charged on weekdays after 1630, FI$16.50 per hour; Saturdays, Sundays and public holidays, FI$22.50 per hour. After 2000 to 0600 weekdays, and on Saturdays, Sundays and public holidays, there is a three hour minimum charge.

Health clearance fee of $F33.

Ports Authority fee (maximum $F10.45).

Procedure on departure

Prior to departing a port of entry, whether going abroad or to another Fijian destination, one should notify Port Control of the intended destination.

Boats leaving Fiji must clear customs on departure. Clearance will not be granted unless all port and quarantine fees have been paid, so receipts for all these should be kept. Boats must leave within 24 hours of having cleared customs.

Immigration is the final authority to clear the yacht out of Fijian waters. An appointment should be made in advance of departure advising where the boat is. Immigration insist that boats depart immediately on receiving clearance. It is prohibited to stop at any island once cleared out.

Facilities

Provisioning is good in Suva with several supermarkets and an excellent fresh produce market.

Gas bottles can be filled in town and fuel is available at the yacht club. Suva is one of the few places in the Pacific where liferafts can be serviced. Suva has a reasonable range of repair facilities. The frequency of flights to Auckland means that whatever cannot be obtained or repaired in Suva can be quickly dealt with in New Zealand.

The Royal Suva Yacht Club is welcoming and has expanded its docking facilities to cater for the increasing number of visitors. An alternative anchorage with limited docking is off the nearby Tradewinds Hotel which is also used as a refuge during cyclones. Suva has the best range of repair facilities in the Central Pacific, most of which are concentrated in the vicinity of the Royal Suva Yacht Club.

Provisioning is adequate in the other islands and some fresh produce is always available. Otherwise, facilities outside of Suva are basic with some workshops in Lautoka. There is a 60-ton travelift at Neisau Marina, near Lautoka, which has also docking facilities on two floating pontoons. Two new marinas, Port Denarau and Vuda Point, have opened on Viti Levu's west coast, both being close to Nadi international airport. Across Nadi Waters on Malololailai Island, a small marina at the Musket Cove Yacht Club has a range of services, including water, fuel, supermarket and some repair facilities. Musket Cove can be contacted on VHF Channels 64 or 68 during daylight hours. The new Copra Shed Marina at Savusavu is a good base from which to explore the eastern part of the archipelago. Pickmere's Yasawa chartlets are essential for cruising the Yasawa group and are available in Lautoka.

Further Reading

Yachtsman's Fiji
Fiji Cruising Notes
Fiji Islands Handbook
Landfalls of Paradise
South Pacific Handbook
Fiji – a travel survival kit
Pacific Crossing Guide
South Pacific Anchorages

Website

www.bulafiji.com (Fiji Visitors Bureau)

GALAPAGOS ISLANDS

The Galapagos Archipelago forms a group of volcanic islands on the equator about 600 miles (965 km) west of Ecuador. There are 13 main islands and most have both English and official Spanish names. The Galapagos are known the world over for their tame and unique wildlife, sea lions, birds and iguanas, living amidst a barren volcanic scenery. Isolated from the rest of the world, evolution took a different course in these islands and the authorities want to preserve them for posterity. This is the reason for the difficulty, if not almost impossibility, for yachts to get permission to cruise these islands. In the past some yachtsmen have abused the privilege, by stealing eggs, shooting birds and causing destruction of the environment.

The Galapagos are one of the 20 provinces of Ecuador and the Ecuadorian authorities take their custody of this unique wildlife sanctuary seriously.

Recently the authorities have been more liberal in granting cruising permits to privately owned cruising boats sailing along a predetermined itinerary. There is a very high fee to be paid for this privilege ($US200 per person per day was quoted in 2000) and it is compulsory to have an official guide permanently on board. The former interdiction on stopping applied to cruising boats has now been relaxed and boats may stop at any one of the official ports. Occasionally day trips are allowed to some of the islands, when an official guide must accompany the boat, but overnight permits for private vessels are very difficult to obtain. The simplest, and cheapest, solution is to go as a passenger on a local excursion boat, or to charter such a boat and go on a chosen itinerary.

The regulations for pleasure craft are very precise:

1   According to Article 50 of the Special Law for the Conservation and Sustainable Development of the Galapagos province of 18 of March 1998, every foreign, non-commercial vessel in transit, with a maximum of 10 persons, can visit all the inhabited ports up to a maximum of 20 days. To visit the National Park areas, they can leave their ship in any selected port and utilise the services of a local tourist operator. In such a case, each person is required to pay to the Galapagos National Park Service a park entrance fee of $US100 for every person older than 12 years and US$50 for children under 12. The Park entrance fee does not include the tariffs related to anchorage fees, which must be paid to the port captain, nor any payments

Practical Information

LOCAL TIME: GMT – 6

BUOYAGE: IALA B

CURRENCY: Sucre (S) of 100 centavos. US$ are accepted.

BUSINESS HOURS
Banks: 0800–1230 Monday to Friday, at Puerto Ayora. Money changing facilities are not very good and occasionally one can get a better rate at shops or hotels than at the bank.
Shops: 0800–1200, 1400–2000 Monday to Saturday. Most food and tourist shops open Sunday morning.

ELECTRICITY: 120 V, 50 Hz

PUBLIC HOLIDAYS
Ecuadorean holidays:
1 January: New Year's Day
6 January
Monday and Tuesday before Lent (Carnival)
Holy Thursday
Good Friday, Holy Saturday
1 May
24 May: Battle of Pichincha
24 June: Birthday of Bolívar
10 August: Independence of Quito
Opening of Congress
9 October: Independence of Guayaquil
12 October: Discovery of America
1 November: All Saints' Day
2 November: All Souls' Day
3 November: Independence of Cuenca
6 December: Foundation of Quito
25 December: Christmas Day

COMMUNICATIONS
International telephone calls from IETEL, Avenida Padre Julio Herrera, Puerto Ayora 0730–1330, 1800–2100, and from the post office in Baquerizo Moreno.
Post office at Puerto Ayora on the waterfront.
There are daily flights to Guayaquil and Quito from the islands of Santa Cruz and San Cristobal.

MEDICAL
Hospital in Avenida Padre Julio Herrera, Puerto Ayora, 0800–1200, 1500–1800 Monday to Friday.

required by the immigration authorities.

Those who do not intend to visit any of the National Park areas will be considered to be a vessel in transit. This comes under the international rules that permit the entry of vessels to international ports for a maximum time of 72 hours and therefore would not require additional procedures to enter Galapagos territorial waters.

2 Should an interested person wish to visit the National Park areas with their own vessel, they are subject to other regulations as follows:
a. They must have the entry permit from the relevant naval organisation to enter territorial waters. According to the stipulations of the article 138 of the Galapagos National Park Administrative Statute, vessels with a capacity of up to 30 persons must have the authorisation of the National Park Administration Office.
b. On arrival at the islands, they must inform the port captain and pay the correspondent tariffs for lights, buoys and anchorage fee. Additionally they must complete immigration formalities.
c. The visitor entry fee must be paid at the National Park office. They will receive an itinerary to the visitors sites within the park based on the availability due to site capacity standards. The cost is US$200 per person and per day of visit.
d. Additionally, every vessel that wishes to visit National Park areas under this system must contract the services of a licensed guide authorised by the National Park Service.
e. According to article 142 of the mentioned statute, every vessel that comes to the Galapagos Islands must submit to quarantine inspections and present the fumigation certificate of the last port of call.
f. Changes in the original crew entering Galapagos is not permitted except in the case of emergencies.

Country Profile

The islands were found by accident early in the sixteenth century when a ship carrying the Bishop of Panama to Peru drifted off course. However, it is possible that South American Indians had visited the islands earlier. Named Islas Encantadas – the Enchanted Islands – for three centuries the Galapagos were used as a base by pirates, sealers and whalers. Famous sailors such as Drake, Raleigh, Cook and Hawkins stopped there for refuge and provisions. The giant tortoises, called 'galapagos' in Spanish, which could be kept alive in ships' holds for months on end, provided a source of fresh meat, and thousands were captured or killed. In 1835 the islands received their most famous visit, from HMS *Beagle* and Charles Darwin. The expedition stayed five weeks, and Darwin's observations of how the wildlife there had developed into unique species in response to their surroundings were central to his theory of evolution. Eventually the islands were settled by Ecuador and used for some time as a penal colony.

In 1959 the Galapagos were declared a national park, and organised tourism since the 1960s brings thousands to the islands every year. The islands depend very much on tourism for their income.

The population is 6000. Spanish is the main language, although English is widely spoken. The administrative centre is Puerto Baquerizo Moreno or Wreck Bay on San Cristobal Island, while Puerto Ayora in Academy Bay, on Santa Cruz Island, is the main settlement.

The climate is equatorial, cooled by the Humboldt current. December to May is the better season when the weather is pleasantly warm and the winds are light. From June to November the weather is overcast and cool. The water around the islands is surprisingly cold and the meeting of the Humboldt current and the warm air sometimes causes mist over the islands. Occasionally the Humboldt current is replaced by the warm El Niño current, a phenomenon which can affect weather conditions throughout the South Pacific.

Entry Regulations

Ports of entry
Puerto Baquerizo Moreno, Wreck Bay (San Cristobal) 0°54′S 89°37′W, Puerto Ayora, Academy Bay (Santa Cruz) 0°46′S 90°18′W, Puerto Villamil (Isabela) 0°57′S 90°58.5′W, Puerto Velasco Ibarra (Floreana) 1° 16′S 90°29′W.

Procedure on arrival
Boats must proceed directly to one of the two official ports of entry: Baquerizo Moreno or Puerto Ayora. These are the only ports where boats may clear in. Yachts should not stop anywhere but a port of entry nor must anyone go ashore without an official guide. Yachts may be boarded at any time to check if one has a guide. The penalty is a fine for stopping at outer islands without permission. All the local boats have guides on board who are in radio contact with the port authority and will immediately report any yacht breaking the regulations.

On arrival the captain must go to the port captain's office, which is close to the dock in both Puerto Ayora and Puerto Baquerizo Moreno. The port captain will grant permission for a stop, the length of which is at his discretion. It appears that the length of stay may depend on the number of yachts already anchored in the bay. As the Galapagos become an important stopover for yachts on passage, the length of stay applied to individual yachts may have to be reduced to allow for the limited anchoring space and facilities, and the ever-increasing number of yachts. A fee is payable based on tonnage. The immigration office must be visited next.

Office hours are quite flexible and permits are difficult to obtain at weekends or on public holidays, so boats arriving at such time may wait to complete formalities on the first working day.

Customs
Firearms must be declared and will be sealed on board. Animals must be confined on board.

Immigration
Visas are granted on arrival. There is no immigration fee, although occasionally visitors have been made to pay, so it is advisable to be accompanied by an interpreter to avoid any misunderstandings.

Cruising permit
Those who wish to stop longer in the archipelago, and visit the individual islands on their own boat, must obtain a cruising permit. The procedure for obtaining a cruising permit is lengthy and carries no guarantee of success. The authorities have a quota for yachts, of between four and six per month, although these quotas change from year to year. Apparently large crews of more than four or five are not desired, as they are suspected of being on an unofficial charter. Any type of chartering by foreign yachts is resisted by the local boats which have to pay a fee to charter.

Two different permits must be obtained, one from the Ministry of Agriculture for entry to the park, and one from the Navy for permission to cruise in Galapagos waters. All applications for the permit must be in Spanish. The application should be made through the Ecuadorean embassy or consulate in the country of one's origin and addressed to: Armada del Ecuador, Dirección General de Intereses Marítimos. One should also write direct to: The Director, Nacional Forestal Ministerio de Agricultura y Ganderia, Quito, Ecuador. Telex: 2291 MAG-ED.

The letters should contain details of the vessel, the names and nationalities of the captain and crew, their permanent addresses, the vessel's port of registry, the date and port of departure, the estimated duration of the journey and date of arrival in the

Galapagos and the planned itinerary. Photocopies of the first two pages of the passports of captain and crew, a photocopy of the vessel's registration certificate and a photocopy of the captain's certificate of competence should be included. Photocopies of the yacht and her crew could be a help.

The Navy should also be sent a Letter of Agreement in Spanish allowing representatives of the Navy and Board of Tourism to board the vessel if required, taking responsibility for any expenses incurred in their transport, and also undertaking to respect the plant and animal life of the park.

If a permit is granted, the Ministry of Defence will telex the approval to the port captain, who will issue a cruising permit, which also includes the official guide's name. The permit allows a yacht to visit the islands, but only with an official guide on board. All visits to the islands must be accompanied by a guide, and this includes the local charter boats. There are about 40 places around the islands where tourists with guides may go ashore.

Although more expensive, employing the services of a local agent will expedite matters and carries a better chance of obtaining a cruising permit. All fees should be agreed, in writing, in advance. Servigalapagos is one such agent who can be contacted by e-mail at pelicanb@ayora.ecua.net.ec.

Fees

Various fees need to be paid. Light and port dues are based on tonnage and the combined total in 2000 came to $4.65 per gross ton. There is also an arrival/departure fee of approximately $8 and, occasionally, an immigration fee. A fumigation fee of $50 will be charged boats that stay longer than 72 hours. Boats that take on a licensed guide will pay between $100 and $150 per day for this service. Overtime must be paid outside office hours, 0800–1700 Monday to Friday. The overtime fees are almost double the normal fee.

Everyone must pay an admission fee to the Galapagos National Park of $US100, which is valid for a year and must be paid by anyone going on one of the organised excursions. There are also municipal fees occasionally collected in the main ports and always collected from incoming passengers at one of the two airports.

Facilities

The anchorage at Baquerizo Moreno offers reasonable protection and is not as crowded as the one at Puerto Ayora. The latter is the base of a large fleet of local excursion boats and the anchorage is therefore very crowded. Supplies at both Puerto Ayora and Baquerizo Moreno are much better than in the past and the choice is surprisingly good. A lot of vegetables are now produced locally, so provisioning a boat for the onward passage is no longer a problem. There are individual farmers on both islands who will take orders for fresh produce. Fresh bread is also available.

There are very few parts available locally but essential spares can be obtained from the mainland, if one is prepared and able to wait. There are no haul-out facilities except for a drying grid in the inner harbour in Puerto Ayora. This can be used depending on the state of the tides. One must get permission from the port captain to use it.

Diesel fuel and water are occasionally difficult to obtain, so it is advisable to arrive with full tanks and not expect to find too much in the islands. Larger quantities of diesel can be obtained at the dock in Baltra (Seymor) used by the local excursion boats, but this must be arranged in advance with the Servigalapagos agency and permission to proceed there must be obtained from the port captain in Puerto Ayora. Small quantities of diesel can be bought from the fuel station in town and taken to the boat in jerrycans. At Puerto Ayora, one may get permission from the port captain to go to the military base at Baltra, where one can also get water. Water is not very good quality, but is more plentiful in the first four months of the year when enough rainwater can be collected. Larger quantities of water can be ordered from the local desalination plant in Puerto Ayora, which will deliver it by tanker to the dock, where at high tide a boat can back up close enough to reach the tanker with a long hose. Otherwise the water has to be transferred by jerrycan.

Supplies are better at Puerto Ayora. Propane bottles cannot be filled locally and have to be sent to the mainland and as this may take some time, it is better not to resort to this solution unless in dire need.

There are various guides and agents who offer to arrange supplies, fuel or transportation, afloat or ashore. They monitor Channel 11.

Because prices tend to be much higher than in mainland Ecuador, it is advisable to provision the boat for the onward passage in either Panama or at Salinas and only plan to stock up with whatever fresh produce may be available locally.

The Charles Darwin Research Station is located at Puerto Ayora. Its main focus is scientific research. Its staff of scientists work mainly on the conservation and management of the Galapagos National Park and the Galapagos Marine Resources Reserve. Visiting scientists from all over the world come to the Galapagos to perform research on a wide variety of topics, such as evolutionary biology, geology, ecotourism, climatology, and population genetics. The station is open to visitors.

The islands narrowly escaped a major ecological disaster in January 2001 when the Ecuadorian tanker *Jessica* ran aground and broke up on a reef close to San Cristobal island. Fortunately most of the 250,000 gallons of oil spilt into the sea was blown by the prevailing winds away from the neighbouring islands. An international rescue operation managed to limit the damage to the fragile environment although there are bound to be long term consequences to both fauna and flora.

The Friends of Galapagos programme tries to attract new members as many important conservation projects in the islands were funded by the generosity of existing members. FOG may be contacted by e-mail: cdrs@fcdarwin.org.ec.

Further Reading

The Pacific Crossing Guide
South Pacific Anchorages
Ecuador and the Galapagos Islands – a travel survival kit
Floreana

Websites

www.galapagos.org (Main site)
www.darwinfoundation.org (Charles Darwin Research Station)
www.parquegalapagos.org (Galapagos National Park)

JUAN FERNANDEZ ISLANDS

Some 400 miles off the coast of Chile lies a group of islands rarely visited by anyone, including yachts. The three islands, Robinson Crusoe, Alejandro Selkirk and Santa Clara, are a dependency of Chile. Discovered by Juan Fernández in 1574, one island was the home of Alexander Selkirk, a seaman who was left on the island at his own request from 1704 to 1709. It is this willingly marooned sailor whom Daniel Defoe used as the inspiration for his character Robinson Crusoe. This island now bears the fictional character's name. Alejandro Selkirk Island is 80 miles (130 km) further west. Only Robinson Crusoe Island (33°38'S, 78°50'W) is inhabited, by a population of around 500, most based in the San Juan Bautista village in Cumberland Bay. The names were given to the islands in 1935 when the group was made a national park.

The islands are visited very rarely by yachts as they are off the cruising routes. The occasional yacht that stops here is usually en route to Easter Island, Chile's other outpost in the South Pacific.

Procedure on arrival
Anchor off the village and small jetty in Cumberland Bay. The anchorage is very rolly and crowded with small fishing boats, so that swinging room is limited. It is advisable to use bow and stern anchors. The bay is unsafe in a northerly gale and one should be prepared to leave at short notice. If there is not too much swell, one can tie up alongside. Officials will come out to clear the yacht.

Facilities

Very few provisions can be obtained here, fuel could perhaps be bought from a local fisherman, and there is enough water, especially between May and November, the rainy months. The Chilean Navy have a presence here and a well equipped workshop. Visiting boats have found the Navy personnel very helpful in emergencies.

Practical Information

LOCAL TIME: GMT – 6	CURRENCY: Chilean peso. US$ cash accepted.	COMMUNICATIONS The village has a post office, wireless station, and there is an airstrip on the west end. Daily flights in summer to Santiago, subject to demand.
BUOYAGE: IALA B	ELECTRICITY: 220 V, 50 Hz	

NAURU

The Republic of Nauru is one of the smallest countries in the world, an eight square mile coral island, lying just south of the equator, west of Kiribati. A stark island with little vegetation, but very wealthy due to its phosphate resources, Nauru is hardly an enticing destination for anyone cruising the South Pacific. Nevertheless, the island can be a useful stop, especially in an emergency, for boats bound for the Solomons or Papua New Guinea. There is only an open roadstead in the lee of the island, very deep for anchoring, where some mooring buoys have been laid for ships loading phosphate. If there is not too much surge and there is space available, it may be preferable, if draft permits, to try and enter the small boat basin.

Country Profile

Before the arrival of the Europeans, this isolated island had developed its own culture, a matrilineal society which traced descent through the female line. In the late nineteenth century Nauru was proclaimed a German territory and after the First World War it was administered as a League of Nations mandate. Occupied by the Japanese during the Second World War, after the war it was administered by Australia under a UN mandate until 1968.

Phosphate was discovered in 1900, but most of the money earned from its exploitation went abroad. With Nauru's independence in 1968, the Nauruans finally gained control of the phosphate industry and a determined effort has been made to ensure the country's self-sufficiency before the phosphate is totally exhausted.

Besides its dwindling phosphate deposits, the island has no natural resources. There is a shortage of drinking water, which sometimes has to be shipped in. Phosphate is Nauru's sole asset, but this is predicted to be exhausted over the course of the next few years. As a result of the phosphate, native Nauruans are prosperous, living in a perfect welfare state. Their hope for the future lies in their extensive overseas investments, their airline Air Nauru and a role as an international tax haven.

The population is about 9500. Many are immigrant workers (I-Kiribati, Chinese, Europeans and Indians). Nauruans, who form just over 60 per cent of the population, are a mixture of Micronesian, Melanesian and Polynesian. English is spoken as well as Nauruan, which is dissimilar to other Pacific languages, being a mixture of Kiribati, Carolines, Marshalls and Solomons' influences. Yaren District is the administrative centre. Most Nauruans are Protestant.

The climate is equatorial, 81°F (27°C) being the average temperature. The island is not affected by tropical cyclones.

Entry Regulations

Port of entry
Aiwo 0°31'S 166°56'E.

Procedure on arrival
The port captain monitors VHF Channel 16 and will advise on the best procedure. If a large ship's mooring is available, he may advise a yacht to tie up to it. Entry formalities are completed ashore.

Customs
Firearms must be declared. Animals must remain on board.

Practical Information

LOCAL TIME: GMT + 12

BUOYAGE: IALA A

CURRENCY: Australian dollars (Aus$)

BUSINESS HOURS
Banks: 1000–1500 Monday to Thursday, 1000–1700 Friday.
Business: 0800–1200, 1330–1645 Monday to Friday.

ELECTRICITY: 240 V, 50 Hz

PUBLIC HOLIDAYS
1 January: New Year's Day
31 January: Independence Day
Good Friday, Easter Monday
17 May: Constitution Day
26 October: Angam Day
25, 26 December: Christmas

COMMUNICATIONS
International telephone calls at Telecom Nauru. Air Nauru has flights to various Pacific islands as well as to Australia, New Zealand and Hong Kong.

MEDICAL
There is a good hospital on the island at Denig.

DIPLOMATIC MISSIONS
Australia: Civic Centre. Tel. 5230.
British and American Embassies in Suva, Fiji, deal with enquiries relating to Nauru.

Immigration

Visitors arriving by yacht are given a 30 day visa on arrival.

Facilities

Diesel fuel is usually available, but a drum may have to be sent out by lighter. Water is difficult to obtain as there is not much to spare on the island. There is a well stocked supermarket, where fresh provisions are usually available. Emergency repairs can be carried out at one of the workshops.

Further Reading

Micronesia Handbook
Landfalls of Paradise

Website

www.airnauru.com (Practical information)

NEW CALEDONIA

In the Western Pacific, bordering on the Coral Sea, New Caledonia is the French Overseas Territory of Nouvelle Calédonie, named by Captain Cook after the Roman name for Scotland. The main island is the mountainous Grande Terre, 250 miles long and 30 miles wide. The once stunning scenery now alternates between thick forest and bare slopes mined for minerals, for the mountains of Grande Terre are almost solid mineral deposits. Grande Terre also boasts one of the largest insular coral reefs in the world, and one can sail around much of the island inside the reef. Also part of the territory are the offlying islands, the Loyalty Group to the east (Maré, Lifou and Ouvéa), the Ile des Pines, the Chesterfield Islands, and Belep Island.

New Caledonia is an interesting mixture of French and Pacific cultures. However, in recent years troubles have flared up as the indigenous Melanesians saw neighbouring countries becoming independent while they were increasingly outnumbered by immigrants, especially from France and ex-French colonies in North Africa. A separatist movement grew up demanding independence from France. Conflict was often violent, and visit-ing sailors reported that it was wise to avoid the eastern coast where most of the Melanesian popu-lation lives. More recently the situation appears to have calmed down and the violence has subsided.

Even at the height of the troubles foreign yachts were not greatly affected, as the conflict is an internal affair. New Caledonia, particularly the pic-turesque outer islands, has a lot to offer the cruising sailor. Nouméa itself is a cosmopolitan city and an excellent place to reprovision the boat, as virtually everything is available and repair facilities are very good.

Country Profile

For centuries this land was home to a Melanesian stone-age people and culture. When the first Europeans arrived towards the end of the eight-eenth century, Grande Terre had a population of 50,000, speaking 32 languages, and numerous tribes who practised ritualised cannibalism and headhunting. Captain Cook found them quite friendly when he landed on the eastern coast, but when the French explorer Entrecasteaux visited a few years later, on his search for the missing La Pérouse expedition, he found a warlike people, their character changed by famine, drought and tribal wars. Entrecasteaux also discovered the Loyalty Islands and explored the west coast of Grande Terre.

In the nineteenth century French missionaries, traders and English settlers came to the islands. The Melanesians resisted this invasion violently and there were several revolts. Britain was not par-ticularly interested in colonising the place, but the French were and in 1853 they claimed New Caledonia as a colony. They ran the island as a penal colony and brought thousands of convicts to the islands, putting them to work mining the nickel discovered on the island. Later Indonesians, Japanese and Indo-Chinese labourers were brought in to work the mines.

During the Second World War the colony declared itself on the side of de Gaulle and the Free French and it became an important American base. Today New Caledonia is part of France as an Overseas Territory. In the 1980s there were trou-bles because of the separatist movement, but the Melanesians are outnumbered by those of European and other origins, who wish to stay part of France. Violent conflict finally led to the 1988 Matignon peace accord between the French government, Kanak separatists and the pro-French settlers.

Practical Information

LOCAL TIME: GMT + 11

BUOYAGE: IALA A

CURRENCY: French Pacific franc (CFP Fr) of 100 centimes.

BUSINESS HOURS
Banks: 0730–1545 Monday to Friday.
Shops and Business:
0730–1100/1400–1800 Monday to Friday, half day Saturday. Large supermarkets 0730–1900 or 2000, Monday to Saturday, some open Sunday morning.
Tahitian, Chinese and Indonesian shops round the central square in Nouméa are open seven days a week.
Government offices:
0730–1130/1330–1730 Monday to Friday.

ELECTRICITY: 220 V, 50 Hz

PUBLIC HOLIDAYS
1 January: New Year's Day
Easter
1 May: Labour Day
8 May: 1945 Victory Day
Ascension
Whit Monday
14 July: Bastille Day
15 August: Assumption
24 September: French Treaty Day
1 November: All Saints' Day
11 November: Armistice Day
25 December: Christmas Day

COMMUNICATIONS
International dialling access code 00.
International calls can be made from PTT (general post office), rue Eugène Porcheron,
open 0715–1115/1330–1730 Monday to Friday.
Emergency: Police dial 17.
Ambulance (SAMU) 15.
From Nouméa there are flights to several Pacific destinations, Australia, New Zealand, Tokyo and Paris.

MEDICAL
CHT Hospital, rue Paul Daunier. Tel. 256666.

DIPLOMATIC MISSIONS
In Nouméa:
Australia: 19–21 Ave du Maréchal Foch. Tel. 272414.
Indonesia: 2 rue Lamartine. Tel. 282574.
New Zealand: 4 Boulevard Vauban. Tel. 272543.
United Kingdom: 14 rue du Général Sarrail, Mont Coffyn. Tel. 282153.

Mining dominates the economy, with fishing, forestry and agriculture also important. There is a wealth of minerals on Grande Terre, nickel being the most important. Tourism has also developed considerably.

The cosmopolitan population is about 164,000. Melanesians number 40–45 per cent of the population, living mainly on the east coast and the outer islands. There are more than 35 per cent Europeans, and also immigrants from Wallis, Tahiti, Indonesia, Vietnam, Vanuatu and some others. French is the official language and there are some 28 indigenous languages. Bislama is the lingua franca, a dialect akin to Pidgin English, spoken in neighbouring Vanuatu. Beliefs vary from Catholicism and Protestantism to the traditional animism of the Melanesians. Nouméa on Grande Terre is the capital.

The cyclone season is November to March, when it is more humid and warm. It is cool and dry from April to November, when the prevailing SE trades are stronger.

Entry Regulations

Port of entry
Nouméa 22°16′S 166°27′E.

Procedure on arrival
On approaching Nouméa one should call the port authority (Channel 67) or Noumea-Radio (Channel 16) or Capitainerie de Port Mosselle (Channel 69 or Tel. 277197 or 278095) requesting that the customs, immigration and quarantine services are informed of your arrival. The vessel should then proceed to the Quai des Scientifiques (visitors dock) where the officials will deal with all formalities.

Yachts must not stop anywhere else before clearing at Nouméa. Permission to visit the outer islands must be obtained in Nouméa. Yachts are no longer allowed to stop on their way out of the territory after clearance and so should return to Nouméa for final outward clearance.

Customs
Firearms are bonded by customs until departure.

Prohibited imports are birds, cats, dogs, plants and fresh fruit. Animals must stay on board. If one wishes to land an animal it must first be put in quarantine for 15 days. Boats with pets on board may face certain restrictions in cruising, unless the animal has all necessary vaccination certificates. All fruit and vegetables that do not have a treatment certificate will be confiscated and destroyed.

The maximum period a yacht may stay before becoming eligible for import duty is six months or one year in certain cases allowed by customs. A six month cruising permit is granted on arrival. This relates to the boat only and crew must conform with existing visa requirements.

Foreign vessels may now import spare parts and equipment free of duty, but the formalities must be completed at customs in advance, either by the owner or the repair yard. Similar formalities will allow the purchase of duty-free fuel on departure.

Immigration

No visa is required for up to three months for the nationals of EU countries, Andorra, Argentina, Australia, New Zealand, Iceland, Monaco, Norway, San Marino and Switzerland. Stays for French nationals are unlimited.

No visa is required for stays of up to one month by nationals of Bermuda, Brunei, Canada, Chile, Croatia, Cyprus, Czech Republic, Hungary, Japan, South Korea, Malaysia, Mexico, Malta, Poland, Slovak Republic, Slovenia, Uruguay, and the USA. Countries not mentioned above need to obtain a visa in advance. Nationals of the above countries will get one month's visa on arrival, but those who intend to spend longer in New Caledonia will find it easier if they obtain a visa in advance from a French embassy abroad.

Fees

Overtime is not usually charged.

Procedure on departure

Boats leaving for Vanuatu or Fiji can request permission for an overnight stop in the Loyalty Islands. The written application must be made at least ten days before departure and addressed to the director of customs. Before leaving Nouméa, security clearance must be also obtained from the Brigade de Surveillance in Avenue Cook.

Social customs

When sailing around the Loyalty Islands or in the north of New Caledonia, one should pay the traditional call to the chief of the tribe or village. This is an important token gesture and the usual gift is a stick of tobacco, a length of cloth or some money (500 or 1000 Pacific Francs).

Facilities

Facilities in Nouméa are extensive as there is a fairly large local yacht population. There are several chandleries, with a good supply of French charts as well as a reasonable selection of both French and New Zealand yachting equipment. There are various specialised workshops concentrated around the yacht harbour offering a wide range of services, such as engine, electrical, electronic, refrigeration, rigging and sail repair. There are two travelifts, the one at the Cercle Nautique Calédonien has a capacity of 40 tons. Although there are several marinas, the number of available berths for visitors is limited, but the new marina at Port Moselle has considerably eased the situation. There are three fuel stations in the yacht harbour. Gas bottles can be filled at all service stations. There are several large supermarkets and a fresh produce market open from 0500 to 1000.

Reasonable provisions, as well as fuel, are available in most settlements on Grande Terre. On Ile des Pins, facilities are concentrated around Kuto, where dinghies, as well as shallow-drafted boats, may come alongside the visitors dock. Good provisioning is available locally, as well as bank, telephones and fuel (by jerrycan).

Further Reading

South Pacific Handbook
Landfalls of Paradise
The Pacific Crossing Guide
South Pacific Anchorages
Cruising in New Caledonia

Websites

www.new-caledonia.com
www.new-caledonia-tourism.nc

NEW ZEALAND

The most southerly of the Pacific countries, New Zealand lies over 1200 miles east of Australia and forms the south-western point of the Polynesian triangle. It is made up of two large islands, North Island and South Island, plus a number of smaller offlying islands. New Zealand has many attractions, not least as a cruising ground outside of the cyclone zone. It is a scenic land of mountains, glaciers, bubbling hot pools, giant ferns and a unique wildlife. The North Island is rolling, green and temperate, while the South Island is more mountainous and cooler.

There are reputedly more sailing yachts per head of population in New Zealand than in any other country. The beauty and variety of the coast, as well as the challenging sailing conditions that they grow up with, is almost certainly the explanation why there are so many good sailors in New

Zealand, a country that can be best appreciated by those who visit it by boat. From the Bay of Islands in the north to wind-swept Stewart Island in the south, cruising in New Zealand can fulfil the requirements of even the most fastidious. The east coast of both islands has many harbours and anchorages, and in the summer the climate is gentle and the weather seldom threatening.

The Bay of Islands is the favourite place of entry and the cruising here is so pleasant that some visiting yachts never leave this large protected bay dotted with the many islands which gave its name. Sailing south from the Bay of Islands or Whangarei, it is worth taking an offshore tack to call at the Barrier Islands before heading for Hauraki Gulf and busy Auckland. Other highlights of a southbound trip are the capital Wellington

Kerikeri in the Bay of Islands.

and, across Cook Strait, picturesque Picton and the Marlborough Sound.

Sailing conditions around South Island are more challenging than in the benign north and those who are short of time can enjoy its majestic scenery by cruising on four wheels. This option is often taken by cruisers who leave their yachts in the protected Bay of Islands. It is particularly difficult to cruise in Fijordland with its deep windy anchorages and the awe-inspiring Milford Haven is best savoured from the deck of a locally skippered boat. Nevertheless, the east coast of South Island has several attractive harbours such as Dunedin, Timaru and Lyttleton, but not one of them matches the scenic beauty of Marlborough Sound, which also has the advantage of being more accessible.

Whether cruising New Zealand by yacht or car, one will soon understand why the locals call the islands God's Own country.

Practical Information

LOCAL TIME: GMT + 12. Summer time GMT + 13 October to early March.

BUOYAGE: IALA A

CURRENCY: New Zealand dollar (NZD/NZ$) of 100 cents. Cash over 10,000 NZ dollars or foreign equivalent must be declared to customs on arrival and departure.

BUSINESS HOURS
Banks: 0930–1600 Monday to Friday.
Business: 0900–1700 Monday to Friday.
Shops: 0900–1730 Monday to Thursday, to 2100 Friday (sometimes Thursday also).
Government offices: 0800–1600 Monday to Friday.

ELECTRICITY: 230 V, 50 Hz

PUBLIC HOLIDAYS
1 January: New Year's Day
6 February: Waitangi Day
Good Friday, Easter Monday
25 April: ANZAC Day
June: Queen's Birthday
Fourth Monday in October: Labour Day
25, 26 December: Christmas Day

EVENTS
January: Auckland Yacht Regatta
February: Waitangi Day, Bay of Islands

COMMUNICATIONS
Telecom offices for cables and telephone calls. International calls can be made from card phones.
Post office: 0900–1700 Monday to Thursday, to 2000 Friday.
Post office, Rathbone St, Whangarei, 0800–1700 Monday to Friday.
In Opua the post office is near the wharf where the yachts clear in on the corner of Williams and Marsden Rds, Paihia, open 0900–1700 Monday to Friday.
Auckland post office, Downtown Shopping Centre, Customs St, open 0900–1730 Monday to Friday.
Emergency: dial 111.
It is illegal to use marine VHF handheld radios ashore.
Auckland airport has excellent links with all parts of the world, including most Pacific nations.

MEDICAL
There are good hospitals in all towns and medical care is of a high standard.

DIPLOMATIC MISSIONS
In Wellington:
Australia: 72–78 Hobson Street, Thorndon. *Tel.* (4) 736-6411.
Canada: ICI Building, 61 Molesworth Street. *Tel.* (4) 473-9577.
Papua New Guinea: Princess Tower, 180 Molesworth St, Thorndon. *Tel.* (4) 851-247.
United Kingdom: 44 Hill Street. *Tel.* (4) 495-0889.
France: Rural Bank Building, 34–42 Manners Street. *Tel.* 384-2555.
United States: 29 Fitzherbert Terrace, Thorndon. *Tel.* (4) 722-068.

In Auckland:
Australia: Union House, 32–38 Quay Street. *Tel.* (9) 303-2429.
Canada: 48 Emily Place, City. *Tel.* 309-3690.
France: 2 Fred Thomas Drive, Takapuna. *Tel.* (9) 488-3459.
Papua New Guinea: 86 Symonds Street. *Tel.* (9) 309-8180.
United Kingdom: Faye Richwhite Bldg, 151 Queens Street. *Tel.* (9) 303-2973.
United States: Yorkshire General Bldg, Shortland and O'Connell Streets. *Tel.* (9) 303-2724.

Country Profile

The first settlers in these islands were the Maoris, a Polynesian race, who called it Aotearoa, 'Land of the long white cloud'. Probably sailing down from the Cook Islands, the first came around the tenth century AD, although the main settlement, known simply as the 'Migration', occurred in the fourteenth century AD. A warlike people, the Maoris were also fine artists, decorating their canoes and meeting houses with wooden carvings, their faces with elaborate tattoos and making jade ornaments. The first European to visit was Abel Tasman in 1642. The islands were then left alone until 1769 when Captain Cook claimed them for Britain. The first European settlers were whalers and sealers, who brought diseases and firearms, both of which caused a rapid decline in the Maori population. The arrival of missionaries in the early nineteenth century saw a decline in violence, but in stamping out cannibalism and warfare, the missionaries weakened the traditional Maori culture. The Treaty of Waitangi in 1840 between Maori chiefs and Britain made New Zealand into a British possession. Fierce conflict over the ownership of land continued between Maoris and Europeans. Gradually the situation calmed down and New Zealand became a prosperous agricultural country. Social reforms at the end of the nineteenth century introduced, among other things, pensions and the vote for women, making New Zealand one of the first countries in the world to do so.

In the early twentieth century New Zealand became a Dominion, and then slowly evolved into an independent nation. In more recent years New Zealand's non-nuclear policy has led to friction with the USA and the break up of ANZUS, the 1951 defence agreement with Australia and the United States. New Zealand's concern over French nuclear policy in the Pacific and the sinking of the Greenpeace vessel, *Rainbow Warrior*, in Auckland harbour by French saboteurs has also seen relations cool between France and New Zealand.

New Zealand is one of the world leaders in the

export of wool, lamb, beef and dairy products. A lack of mineral resources is a problem, but in general it is a prosperous country.

The population is about 3.3 million, mostly of British descent, known as Pakehas by the Maoris who number about 400,000. In Auckland there is a considerable community of other Pacific Islanders, such as Tongans, Samoans and Cook Islanders. English and Maori are the main languages and various Christian denominations are practised as well as some traditional Maori beliefs. Wellington, on the southern tip of North Island, is the capital, although Auckland is the largest city and commercial centre.

The climate is varied from the subtropical in the north to snowy mountains and glaciers in the south. The summer from November to March is the more pleasant season, while the winter is wetter and windier. South Island is generally cooler in both summer and winter. Although out of the tropical cyclone area, occasionally in February or March the tail of a cyclone reaches North Island. Lying in the westerly wind belt, the east coast is more sheltered and the main yachting centres are along that coast.

Entry Regulations

Ports of entry
North Island: Opua 35°18′S 174°08′E, Whangarei 35°44′S 174°21′E, Auckland 36°51′S 174°48′E, Tauranga 37°39′S 176°10′E, Napier 39°29′S 176°55′E, New Plymouth 39°04′S 174°05′E, Wellington 41°17′S 174°46′E, Onehunga 36°56′S 174°46′E, Gisborne 38°41′S 178°02′E, Taharoa 38°10′S 174°40′E.
South Island: Nelson 42°16′S 173°19′E, Picton 41°16′S 174° 00′E, Christchurch (Lyttelton) 43°37′S 172°43′E, Timaru 44°25′S 171°19′E, Dunedin 45°53′S 170°31′E, Invercargill (Bluff) 46°36′S 168°26′E.
Chatham Islands: Waitangi 43°57′S 176°34′E.
Arrival at any other port requires the written permission of a Collector of Customs.

Procedure on arrival
Every yacht arriving from overseas must inform customs and agricultural quarantine officers by radio or telephone of one's intended ETA. This must be done at least 12 hours before arrival. On arrival, every yacht must clear customs, immigration and undergo an inspection by an agricultural officer before clearance is complete. If a yacht is not able to contact the authorities by radio and

arrives announced, the captain must immediately contact customs or police by telephone (toll free numbers are available: Whangarei customs 0800 428 786). No one else must go ashore until clearance is complete.

Taupo Maritime Radio keeps continuous radio watch on 2182 kHz, 8291 kHz, 4125 kHz, 6215 kHz and 16420 kHz. They can also be contacted on *Tel.* +64 9 359 6655 or +64 25 961 375 (after hours). A telephone report may also be made to the Ministry of Fisheries and Agriculture in Auckland, *Tel.* +64 9 366 0345, +64 9 309 9093 or +64 25 975 171 (after hours).

On approaching the port of entry one should endeavour to confirm one's arrival. This can be done by VHF via Taupo Maritime Radio, which maintains repeaters along the coast. Alternatively, local port authority radio stations can forward an arrival confirmation. The arrival itself must be confirmed to the port on Channel 16.

Russell Radio, located in the Bay of Islands, provides weather information for the Western Pacific and runs a maritime net on 4445 kHz from 0700 to 0830, 1930 to 2030 GMT, 12353 kHz from 0400 to 0430, 2115 to 2130 GMT, 12359 kHz from 0430 to 0445, 2030 to 2100 GMT. A fee of $NZ30 is payable for this service on arrival in New Zealand. Channel 16 is monitored during daylight hours. They will inform customs and immigration of a boat's arrival if this is requested by radio.

Opua: Arriving boats are now directed into the new marina. A customs officer is stationed at Opua during the high season from November to March. At other times it may be necessary to contact Whangarei customs on 0800 428 786. In 2000 the Far North Maritime Authority have set a flat fee of $NZ100 for clearance and this includes two-night docking at the marina. An agricultural Department (MAF) inspection must be completed immediately on arrival and if additional travel expenses are incurred, or this has to be done outside of normal working hours, any costs may be charged to the yacht. It is not clear if these costs are now included in the $NZ100 flat fee. Once entry formalities are completed the crew and vessel are free to travel throughout the country and are not required to report their movements until departure.
Whangarei: Harbour control should be contacted on Channel 16 and asked to advise customs to meet the yacht on arrival. Boats should proceed to the customs and MAF wharf for clearance.
Auckland: Contact Harbour Control on Channel 16 who will direct the yacht to one of the marinas where clearance formalities can be completed.

Procedure on departure

Confirmation of departure must be given at least 24 hours prior to leaving. Once issued with a clearance certificate, yachts are required to go to sea within a reasonable time. Any delay should be reported to customs.

The same entry and departure formalities apply to New Zealand yachts as to foreign vessels.

The controversial Clause 21 of the Maritime Safety Act, requiring each pleasure craft departing New Zealand to obtain a Safety Certificate, has been repealed. On departure, boats must clear out with customs, whose officer will deal with all other formalities such as immigration.

Customs

Firearms must be declared to customs, and are normally kept in police custody until departure. If there is an onboard safe for firearms, this may be approved by the police.

Medicines should be accompanied by a prescription and be kept in their original packing.

All foreign yachts entering New Zealand on a temporary basis fill in a Temporary Import form. The duty payable is assessed, and the amount secured by declaration on entry. Departure must be within 12 months of entry. If not, this duty must be paid on the yacht and its equipment. Extensions are normally not given beyond the 12 month limit unless the yacht is unseaworthy. The duty-free allowance for each person on arrival is 1 litre spirits and 4.5 litres wine or beer. Amounts in excess of this may be liable for customs charges.

All equipment other than fixtures must be declared, although these will not be subject to duty if remaining on board and re-exported on departure. Some may have to be sealed by customs. Items to be landed must be declared to customs on arrival. Goods imported into New Zealand such as radios and navigation equipment require a Temporary Import form and a deposit to cover duty and sales tax, which will be refunded on re-export. If imported permanently, they will be subject to duty.

Purchases made in New Zealand have duty paid on them, but if they are exported a refund of duty can be obtained from customs on proof of purchase and export.

Duty-free supplies vary from port to port. Purchases may be made from a Licensed Export Warehouse before departure, to be delivered just before departure and checked by customs.

Quarantine

New Zealand has very strict regulations on the importation of animals, animal and plant products, as it is a country so dependent on agriculture and relatively free from pests and diseases. On arrival, inspection is carried out by an agriculture quarantine officer from the Ministry of Agriculture and Fisheries (MAF), who should be contacted before arrival. If that cannot be done, one should telephone MAF on arrival – they accept collect calls – or contact them through the local police. Until clearance is completed, nothing must be landed and the crew must remain on board. After clearance is completed, if it has been necessary to place any provisions under seal or if there are animals on board, regular inspections by an agriculture officer may be carried out. It may be more convenient to destroy on arrival any provisions that have to be sealed or stores that cannot be landed. Obviously it is advisable to arrive with a minimum of fresh stores.

Items that must not be landed are fruit, vegetables, plant products, foodstuffs, eggs and waste from these items, pot plants, meat and animal products. All waste must be disposed of through the proper garbage disposal system including egg containers. The agriculture quarantine officer will explain this on arrival. Until such stores are consumed or destroyed the yacht will be under surveillance and restricted to berthing at a wharf where these garbage facilities are available. Organic garbage should be disposed of before entering New Zealand territorial waters (12 mile limit). The quarantine officer may also inspect for pesticides, which must be of a formula registered in New Zealand. This can include insecticide sprays, cockroach traps and antifouling.

Bicycles, motorcycles and sporting equipment must be washed or cleaned before landing, for which a written authority is required.

Animals: New Zealand is a rabies-free country. The New Zealand authorities actively discourage animals arriving on yachts and the restrictions placed on those with animals on board are considerable. The master must place a bond of NZ$1000 for the secure custody of any pets aboard, and this will be forfeited if conditions are not met. Animals must be either placed in quarantine or securely confined and not landed. The master is required by the bond to notify the MAF 48 hours before departure from a port, indicating the next port of call in New Zealand, and notification must be given even if only moving moorings. After six months the animals must be reshipped from New

Zealand or destroyed; if not the yacht must leave the country. In the event of an animal becoming ill the MAF must be contacted immediately and private vets cannot be consulted without MAF approval. If a pet dies, its body must be given to the agriculture quarantine officer for disposal. Boats with animals on board will be inspected every 48 hours and the inspector's time is charged to the boat owner at an hourly rate. In ports where there is a MAF station, such as Whangarei, the hourly rates are NZ$57 for weekday visits and NZ$93 for weekends, with a one hour minimum charge. Boats may group together and the charges are then shared out. Charges are more expensive at outlying ports such as Opua. Any pets obtained in New Zealand must be added to the bond.

The importation of products made from endangered species is prohibited, such as: ivory, tortoise shell, whalebone, coral, crocodile, lizard or snake skins.

Immigration

Passports must be valid for at least three months beyond departure date. Australian citizens do not need visas.

A three month visitor's permit is granted on arrival to nationals of most countries. Visas can be renewed through the Ministry of Immigration. British citizens may stay for up to six months on a visitor's permit.

Anyone leaving the vessel in New Zealand may be required to show an onward ticket.

Fees

The Agricultural Department (MAF) charges time and mileage to inspect boats and this inspection must be conducted immediately on arrival. Yachts may share the cost between them. Yachts are allowed to wait until office hours to clear customs and immigration.

There are fees for visas and extensions to the visitor's permit. There are also fees for quarantine inspections.

Sales tax

A government sales tax of 12.5 per cent is charged on all goods and services. It can be avoided by yachts in possession of the 'Temporary Importation' document, provided the taxable product is affixed permanently to the yacht by the vendor. Especially those having major work done on their boats should make sure that they are not charged this tax.

Chartering

Both the yacht and the crew become liable for New Zealand tax if engaged in chartering. Normally one would have to set up a New Zealand-based company through which to charter the yacht or to use a New Zealand-based agent. These rules are under review.

Facilities

As the favourite place to spend the cyclone season in the South Pacific, New Zealand has built up a good reputation among cruising sailors as the place where everything can be fixed. The fact that hundreds of foreign yachts flock to New Zealand every year attests to this. Marine facilities are indeed of a high standard in the North Island, particularly around such yachting centres as Auckland, Whangarei and the Bay of Islands. There are haul-out and good repair facilities in all these areas. With several marinas for the considerable local yacht population in the Auckland area and also the experience of dealing with the Volvo Yacht Race every four years, and the America's Cup in 2000, facilities there are of the highest standard. In the Bay of Islands, Kerikeri Radio has come to the aid of visiting sailors by compiling a grid chart showing all anchorages as well as marine facilities available. This useful publication can be obtained from local shops and chandleries. Marine supplies are generally good and in Auckland excellent. With a very developed yachting industry of her own, New Zealand marine products are of good quality, particularly deck hardware, windlasses, paints and sails, as well as fibreglass or aluminium tenders. LPG refills are widely available, but one may need to obtain an adaptor for the local system. One must also check if the gas is compatible with the regulator if one switches from propane to butane or vice versa.

There are workshops specialising in marine services in most places and the quality of workmanship is usually high. However, one should always insist on being given a written estimate of the cost of the proposed work, as visiting sailors have encountered problems in the past when faced with bills much higher than the verbal estimate they had been first given. Facilities in South Island are less extensive, although even there one finds adequate services wherever there is a local yachting centre. Facilities are good in Marlborough Sound where there are several small boatyards.

As can be expected from a mainly agricultural

country, provisioning is very good and New Zealand is an excellent place to stock up the boat for a voyage. As many non-food items are subject to tax, temporary visitors to New Zealand can claim a refund on all the tax and duty paid on such items which are going to be taken out of the country.

Kermadec Islands

These islands may only be visited with a permit from the Department of Conservation, Private Bag 8, Newton, Auckland. The cost of a permit is NZ$26 plus tax. There is a meteorological station on Raoul Island, the most northerly group, and yachts sailing there will find they are made most welcome if they take mail for the staff. Contact Wellington *Tel.* (4) 729-379, ext. 8803.

Further Reading

Destination New Zealand
Coastal Cruising Handbook of New Zealand
Pickmere's Atlas of Northland's East Coast
New Zealand – a travel survival kit
The Pacific Crossing Guide
South Pacific Anchorages
Superyacht Guide to New Zealand

Websites

www.purenz.com (New Zealand online)
www.govt.nz (Government site)
www.nzmarine.com

NIUE

The island of Niue is one of the world's smallest states, but the largest block of coral. Niue boasts amazing caves both under the ground and the sea and the diving here is excellent. Lying on the direct route from French Polynesia to Vava'u in Tonga, Niue is a favourite stop for westbound yachts. The anchorage is off the island's west coast, close to the main settlement at Alofi. Although the anchorage offers good protection from the prevailing SE winds, in westerly winds the island is a deadly lee shore and one must always keep an eye on the weather, particularly when visiting ashore.

Country Profile

Archaeological remains show that the island was inhabited by the Polynesians at least 1800 years ago. Captain Cook charted the island in 1774, and named it the Savage Island when the islanders resisted his landing. There was little contact with the outside world until the nineteenth century when Samoan missionaries settled on the island. The London Missionary Society followed and they administered Niue until 1900 when it became a British Protectorate, later under New Zealand administration. The Niueans, not wanting total independence, chose a free association with New Zealand, which means they have New Zealand citizenship and internal self-government. Since the 1960s Niue has developed considerably in such

Practical Information

LOCAL TIME: GMT – 11

BUOYAGE: IALA A

CURRENCY: New Zealand dollar (NZ$)

BUSINESS HOURS
Banks: 0900–1400 Monday to Thursday, 0830–1400 Friday.
Shops and businesses: 0730–1530 Monday to Friday.

ELECTRICITY: 240 V, 50 Hz

PUBLIC HOLIDAYS
1 January: New Year's Day
2 January: Commission Holiday
Good Friday, Easter Monday
25 April: ANZAC Day
June: Queen's Birthday
19 October: Constitution Celebrations
Nearest Monday to 19 October: Peniamina Day
25, 26 December: Christmas

COMMUNICATIONS
Telecommunications Dept, Central Admin Bldg for overseas calls, open 24 hours.
Post office 0800–1500 Monday to Friday.

Emergency: Police 4333, Hospital 4100.
The Administration building at Alofi contains the post office, the Treasury (open 0800–1200, 1230–1430 Monday to Friday for changing money), the Telecommunications office, and the police station.
There are flights to Auckland and Fiji.

MEDICAL
Lord Liverpool Public Hospital provides medical and dental treatment. There is a 24-hour on-call emergency service.

DIPLOMATIC MISSIONS
New Zealand: Tapeu, Alofi. *Tel.* 4022.

areas as health and education. An airport was built, but tourism remains carefully controlled.

The island's economy is heavily dependent on foreign aid, and many goods have to be imported. There are some exports to New Zealand, such as passionfruit juice, lime juice, coconut products, handicrafts and honey. The sale of stamps and remittances from Niueans working overseas are important income earners.

Around 2000 people live on Niue, and many more have settled in New Zealand. Niuean, a Polynesian language, is spoken and also English. Alofi on the western coast is the main town. The islanders are mainly Protestant.

Niue has a tropical climate being in the SE trade wind belt. December to March are the wetter, more humid months, which is also the cyclone season.

Entry Regulations

Ports of entry
Alofi 19°03'S 169°55'W.

Procedure on arrival
ZKN Niue Radio keeps a 24-hour watch on both VHF and HF. On arrival contact Niue Radio on VHF Channel 16 and they will contact customs and arrange clearance. Clearance must be gained before coming ashore. It is normally possible to clear in at weekends, but it may take some time to locate the customs officer. There is an anchorage off the settlement of Alofi, but it offers no protection from westerly winds. Eighteen moorings have been put down by the Niue Yacht Club for visiting yachts. These moorings are 2–4 ton concrete blocks with large orange floats. The moorings are checked regularly and the northernmost is a double block chained together suitable for larger yachts. Contact ZKN Niue Yacht Club on Channel 10 or 16 for mooring allocation. The club also has a HF radio and they monitor 4125 or 4417 kHz around 0600 UTC from June to November.

After obtaining clearance from customs the rest of the formalities are usually completed ashore in Alofi. If there is much surge the tender can be lifted by dock crane onto the wharf and there is a trolley for moving tenders. The captain should report first to customs, at the top of the hill, then police and immigration. Passports may have to be stamped at the airport. The agriculture officer can be telephoned from the police station. Occasionally the agriculture officer may waive the inspection.

Customs
Firearms must be declared on arrival. Animals must stay on board.

Duty-free allowances are 1 litre spirits, 1 litre of wine and 200 cigarettes, but these only apply to what is actually landed.

Immigration
Australian and New Zealand citizens do not need an entry permit and all other nationalities are granted a 30-day entry permit on arrival. Extensions can be obtained from the Department of Immigration, Central Administration Building, Alofi.

Restrictions
Certain shell species are protected and the taking of shells using scuba gear is prohibited. During the year certain areas are closed to spearfishing and swimming, to protect breeding or migratory fish. The tourist office will have up-to-date information.

Social customs
Sunday observance is strict and activities such as boating and fishing are not allowed. Beachwear must not be worn in towns and villages.

Fees
The moorings cost NZ$5 per day and there is a NZ$20 departure tax per person.

Facilities

There is a reasonable selection of provisions and a weekly fresh produce market on Fridays. Water is available on the wharf. Keys for the shower and toilet block on the wharf are available at Cullings Delicatessen, Niue Tourism Office and Alofi Rentals. This block is maintained by the Niue Yacht Club, whose enthusiastic members should be consulted for any advice. Only basic repairs can be carried out on the island and there is only a limited supply of hardware. Essential spares can be ordered from New Zealand.

Further Reading

Landfalls of Paradise
South Pacific Handbook

Website

www.niueisland.com

NORFOLK ISLAND

Norfolk Island is a small volcanic island midway between Australia and New Zealand. Its fertile soil is the original home of the Norfolk pine, an excellent wood for general building. When Captain Cook discovered the island he thought it would be ideal for spars on ships but it proved to have too many knots in the timber. The island is visited mainly by Australian boats on their way to the South Pacific islands or by those sailing from New Zealand to New Caledonia and beyond. There are landing anchorages at Sydney Bay near the historic settlement of Kingston and Cascade Bay. Sheltering anchorages are at Ball Bay and Headstone where landing is very difficult. However, none can be regarded as all-weather anchorages, therefore the boat should never be left unattended and one should go ashore only in settled weather. Yachts have been lost at Norfolk Island through ignoring this warning. There are landing jetties at both Kingston and Cascade Bay, but landing the dinghy can sometimes be very difficult.

Country Profile

Norfolk is one of the oldest British settlements in the Pacific. There is some evidence of Polynesian or Melanesian habitation on the island before Captain Cook discovered and named it in 1774. A few years later an attempt was made to establish a colony, now known as the First Settlement. Timber was made from the pines and flax gathered, but life was difficult on the isolated island with no natural harbour. In the early nineteenth century Norfolk was left uninhabited for some years, then a penal colony was set up for the worst of the Australian convicts. This period of the Second Settlement was brutal and stone buildings built by the prisoners can still be seen. Finally the prison was closed in the middle of the last century.

Next to arrive were Pitcairn Islanders, brought there by Britain who decided to resettle them as their tiny island home had become overcrowded. Homesick and unhappy, some returned to Pitcairn, although many remained, forming the base of the present population. Norfolk Island is an Australian Territory, with its own assembly under the Norfolk Island Act of 1979.

Tourists from Australia and New Zealand are a major source of income. Agriculture is only for domestic consumption and food imports are high.

The population is around 2000. Most are descendants of the original Pitcairn Islanders and settlers from Australia. The Norfolk Islanders are Australian citizens. English and a Norfolkese dialect are spoken. Church of England, Catholic, Uniting Church and Seventh Day Adventist are the main religious denominations. Kingston is where the Government and Administration Buildings are located.

The climate is mild and subtropical, with a well distributed rainfall. Summer winds are S to SE and winter winds W to SW. The cyclone season is December to March.

Entry Regulations

Port of entry
Kingston 29°01'S 167°59'E.

Procedure on arrival
One can either land at Cascade Jetty, on the north side, or at Kingston Jetty, on the south side. One should notify customs and quarantine as soon as

Practical Information

LOCAL TIME: GMT + 11½

BUOYAGE: IALA A

CURRENCY: Australian dollar (Aus$)

BUSINESS HOURS
Government offices: 0845–1700
Monday to Friday.

ELECTRICITY: 240 V, 50 Hz

PUBLIC HOLIDAYS
1 January: New Year's Day
26 January: Australia Day
Good Friday, Easter Monday
6 March: Foundation Day
25 April: ANZAC Day
8 June: Bounty Anniversary Day
June: Queen's Birthday
October: Show Day
Last Wednesday, November: Thanksgiving Day
25, 26 December: Christmas

COMMUNICATIONS
International direct dialling available
for telephone calls.
There are flights to Auckland,
Brisbane, Sydney and Lord Howe
Island.

MEDICAL
Norfolk Island Hospital

possible after one's arrival if no prior contact has been made. Customs monitor VHF Channel 16 during working hours only, 0845–1700. *Tel.* 22750, Fax. 23260. There are public phones on both Cascade and Kingston jetties.

Customs

Firearms must be declared on arrival and be kept on board during the yacht's stay. Animals must be declared on arrival and remain on board.

Landing of food, including fruit and vegetables, is prohibited.

Immigration

Visa requirements are the same as for Australia. All nationals, with the exception of Australians and New Zealanders, need to obtain a tourist visa valid for a period longer than 60 days from the intended date of arrival in Norfolk Island.

This visa must be obtained prior to arrival in Norfolk Island. These can be obtained free of charge from Australian high commissions or embassies. A multiple entry visa should be requested if a yacht is en route for Australia.

Fees

Overtime is charged for clearance outside of working hours or on public holidays. Customs charge Aus$45 for under six crew and Aus$60 for six crew and over.

There is a departure tax of Aus$25 if a crew leaves the yacht and departs the island by other means.

Restrictions

Anchorage is prohibited in Anson Bay on the NW corner of the island.

Facilities

Provisioning is reasonable, but as yachts come to Norfolk from either Australia or New Zealand, one should only plan on buying the absolute minimum on the island. The main shopping centre is at Burnt Pine, in the centre of the island. There is a good selection of locally grown produce. There is no public water supply, although one may be able to load a limited amount. Repair facilities are basic and should not be relied upon. Small quantities of fuel are available, but as this is brought to the island by ship and then transferred ashore by lighter, visitors should try not to put an unnecessary strain on the island's meagre resources.

Further Reading

South Pacific Handbook
South Pacific Anchorages

Websites

www.nf (Official site)
www.norfolkisland.nf

PAPUA NEW GUINEA

Papua New Guinea consists of the eastern half of the large island of New Guinea (the western half being the Indonesian province of Irian Jaya), and hundreds of islands of all shapes and sizes, from towering active volcanoes to idyllic coral atolls.

One of the most fascinating countries in the world, Papua New Guinea is definitely best visited by cruising boat. This not only gives one the opportunity to catch a glimpse of life in a society still following ancient ways, but also avoids the lawlessness that increasingly affects the large towns of this rich, but poorly managed, country. Most cruising sailors will only come in passing contact with the less attractive features of a country that has tried to leap into the modern age from stone age in half a century. Outside of the main centres life is little changed and by using common sense one should be able to avoid the few hot spots of trouble. One such place is Bougainville Island, which was taken over by local rebels, closing the vast copper mine and forcing the Papua New Guinea security forces and police to withdraw. Peace has now been restored to the island, but the situation is still smouldering and cruising yachts are recommended to stay away. Claims to tribal lands, especially where there has been exploitation of mineral resources, could always recur. The best way to find out about changing conditions is to listen to the news, both Radio Australia and Radio New Zealand having good overseas services for the Pacific area, or by contacting one's high commission or embassy in Port Moresby, who are usually well informed. Port Moresby and Lae are particularly affected by the surge in criminality. The area around the yacht club in Port Moresby is relatively trouble-free.

There is a vast difference between these urban areas and other parts of the country, particularly the small islands. Rabaul, on New Britain Island, is a popular spot among cruising yachts, many of whom used to spend the cyclone season in its landlocked harbour, which is the crater of a volcano. The attractive town has been obliterated once by a volcanic eruption and suffered widespread destruction by an eruption in September 1994. In its aftermath, visits there were temporarily limited to three days. The latest situation should be checked beforehand. Much of the reconstruction has been completed, but it is doubtful that Rabaul will ever regain its former popularity among cruising sailors.

Madang on the northern coast of New Guinea also has a well-protected harbour in an area scattered with islands, reefs and lagoons. It has always been a popular stop, especially for those yachts taking the route north of New Guinea towards Indonesia, but it is now reported to have increasing problems similar to those afflicting Lae and Port Moresby.

The best cruising in Papua New Guinea is found among the many islands to the east of the main island, where islanders still live a peaceful life and sail large traditional canoes for fishing and trading voyages. A cruise in Papua New Guinean waters has been for many people the highlight of their world cruise, and if one chooses one's itinerary carefully it is a country well worth visiting.

Country Profile

Until the 1930s much of the highlands of Papua New Guinea and the stone age tribes who lived there were unknown to the rest of the outside world. Through the centuries, hundreds of tribes had lived apart, often two neighbouring tribes separated by a hillside of impenetrable vegetation, never knowing of each other's existence. Each had its own character and its own language, there being today several hundred different languages in PNG. It is an anthropologists' paradise. In the coastal areas and islands, however, contact with Europeans was established much earlier.

The original inhabitants probably came from South East Asia about 20,000 to 25,000 years ago. Later there were migrations from Micronesia and Polynesia, which forced the original population into the mountains or out to populate the other islands of present day Melanesia. Cultures developed with no larger a political unit than the tribe.

In the early sixteenth century the Portuguese sighted the main island, naming it 'Ilhas dos Papuas' – island of the fuzzy haired – later called 'New Guinea' by the Dutch. Traders and missionaries arrived in the nineteenth century. The Dutch claimed the western half of the main island, the

Practical Information

LOCAL TIME: GMT + 10

BUOYAGE: IALA A

CURRENCY: Kina (K/NGK) of 100 toea

BUSINESS HOURS
Banks: 0900–1400 Monday to Thursday, 0900–1700 Friday.
Business: 0800–1630 Monday to Friday.
Government offices: 0745–1200/1300–1600 Monday to Friday.
Shops: 0800–1700 Monday to Friday, half day Saturday.

ELECTRICITY: 240 V, 50 Hz

PUBLIC HOLIDAYS
1 January: New Year's Day
January/February: Chinese New Year
Easter
June: Queen's Birthday
July: Remembrance Day
16 September: Independence Day
25, 26 December: Christmas

EVENTS
May: Frangipani Festival, Rabaul
July/August: Yam festival in Trobriand Islands
June: Port Moresby Show
August: Highlands Show, Mount Hagen ⎤
September: Eastern ⎬ alternate years
Highlands Show, Goroka ⎦

COMMUNICATIONS
Telephone, telex and fax facilities are available at telephone offices, post offices and hotels.
Post offices open 0800–1600 Monday to Friday, 0900–1200 Saturday.
Papua New Guinea has a very developed internal air network. From Port Moresby there are international flights to other Pacific Islands, Australia, Singapore and Manila.

MEDICAL
Government hospitals in all major centres. Several private hospitals in the Port Moresby area. The main hospitals are Port Moresby

General, Goroka Base and Angau Memorial, and many smaller ones as well as health centres. Doctors and hospitals may ask for immediate payment for medical services, and there are sometimes shortages of medicines. Health insurance is essential.

DIPLOMATIC MISSIONS
Australia: Independence Drive, Waigani. Tel. 25 9333.
Canada: 2nd floor, The Lodge, Brampton St, Port Moresby. Tel. 21 3599.
France: 9th floor, Pacific View Apts, Pruth St, Port Moresby. Tel. 25 3740.
Indonesia: Sir John Guisa Drive, Waigani. Tel. 25 3455.
New Zealand: Waigani (PO Box 1144 Boroko). Tel. 25 9444.
United Kingdom: Kiroki St, Waigani, Boroko.
Tel. 25 1677.
United States: Armit St, Port Moresby. Tel. 21 1455.

Germans the north-east, and the British the south-east. At the start of the twentieth century the latter area was transferred to Australian control as Papua and joined with the German part after the First World War.

The Japanese occupied New Guinea in the Second World War. After the war it became the UN Territory of New Guinea and was administered by Australia. Papua remained a territory of Australia, but for administrative purposes was administered together with New Guinea. Self-government for the two entities united as Papua New Guinea was gained in 1973 and full independence two years later. The 1980s and early 1990s were marked by continuous strife on the island of Bougainville. In September 1994 a peace agreement was signed between the government and the Bougainville secessionists, providing for four neutral zones to be occupied by a Pacific peace-keeping force. The border area with Irian Jaya is also dangerous, due to the secessionist group active there. A state of emergency is sometimes declared in Port Moresby because of the violent crime there.

The economy is based on mining, timber and some food crops, particularly coffee. The country has rich deposits of minerals, gold, copper and oil. Most of the country's problems stem from the potential of this richness in an economy where the majority of the population are still subsistence farmers and much of the income has been earned by large foreign companies. There is high unemployment and a large drift to the towns by young men in search of jobs which do not exist. An economic recession caused by the Bougainville revolt has given way to recovery, with the discovery of mineral resources elsewhere and the development of light industry.

The population is around 5 million, mostly Melanesian, with some of the more eastern islands populated by Polynesians. The national languages are Motu and Pidgin (Tok Pisin), evolved to let a country of over 700 native languages understand each other. English is also widely spoken.

The main Christian denominations are Protestant and Catholic, but there are very many others, as well as local spirit and animist religions. The discovery of so many stone age tribes brought many enthusiastic missionaries and sects to the highlands, where in some towns there are more churches than any other buildings.

Port Moresby on the southern coast of Papua is the capital, with the seat of government in Waigani.

The climate is tropical. From December to March is the north-west monsoon, while the south-east monsoon is from May to December. Only the south-east of the country is affected by tropical cyclones, whose season is from December until March.

Entry Regulations

Ports of entry
Port Moresby 9°26'S 147°06'E, Vanimo 2°41'S 141°18'E, Wewak 3°35'S 143°40'E, Samarai 10°36'S 150°39'E, Oro Bay 8°50'S 148°30'E, Rabaul 4°12'S 152°11'E, Lae 6°44'S 146°59'E, Kavieng 2°34'S 150°48'E, Daru 9°04'S 143°12'E, Alotau 10°19'S 150°27'E, Kieta 6°13'S 155°38'E, Madang 5°15'S 145°50'E, Kimbe 5°32'S 150°09'E, Lorengau 2°00'S 147°15'E, Misima Island 10°40'S 152°45'E.

Procedure on arrival
The captain should proceed ashore with all papers and go to the customs and immigration offices.

In Port Moresby the customs office is in the commercial harbour south of the yacht club.

One must clear in and out of every port and failure to do so can create serious problems.

On Misima Island if requested customs may issue a clearance for Australia with permission to cruise for a reasonable period of time in the Calvados Islands en route.

Customs
Firearms, including flareguns, are either detained until departure, or sealed on board.

Animals must remain on board at all times.

Prescribed medicines containing narcotics must be declared. One must have a prescription stating that these are necessary and being used under a doctor's direction. The medicines should be kept in the original containers.

Yachts staying longer than two months are required to lodge a security on their yacht, equal to the duty on the yacht's value.

Prohibited exports are: bird of paradise plumes, artefacts dated pre-1960 and stone objects, except stone axes.

Immigration
Tourist visas for up to 60 days can be issued on arrival for nationals of Australia, Austria, Belgium, Canada, Cook Islands, Cyprus, Denmark, Fiji, France, Germany, Japan, the Netherlands, New Zealand, Norway, Portugal, Sweden, Switzerland,

Thailand, Tonga, Tuvalu, the United Kingdom and the United States. For longer visits, visas must be obtained in advance. It is recommended that visas are obtained before arriving in the country even for those nationals listed above. These can be obtained from one of the PNG embassies or high commissions. There are PNG diplomatic missions in Canberra, Brisbane, Suva, Vila, Honiara, Jakarta, Kuala Lumpur, Wellington, Manila, Washington, Tokyo, London, Paris, Berlin and Brussels. Usually visas are valid for 60 days, after which the passports have to be sent to Port Moresby for an extension. Occasionally passports have been reported lost, but they have invariably turned up later. Even if an extension has not been granted, people have been allowed to stay while the search for the missing passports is in progress. Proof of sufficient funds to support one's stay in PNG is necessary, otherwise one has to place an immigration landing bond of about US$1000, which is refundable. Passports must have a minimum one year validity from proposed date of entry.

Health

This is a high-risk malaria area, where the disease has become resistant to many of the anti-malarial drugs in use. Advice should be taken as to the most suitable anti-malarial prevention to be followed. There is also a dengue fever risk.

Cholera is a risk. Hepatitis A is endemic.

Fees

Overtime is payable for clearance after 1600 Monday to Friday, and all day Saturday, Sunday and public holidays.

Visas cost K100 per visa per person.

Facilities

There is a large number of locally owned yachts in the capital Port Moresby, where facilities are generally good. The Royal Papua Yacht Club has its own marina with 24-hour security, but most spaces are occupied by members' boats so berths are in short supply. However, visitors are welcome and every attempt is made to accommodate them or to allow the visitor to use the large work berth. Alternatively, one may anchor or moor Mediterranean-style within the marina groins. Temporary membership is granted to members of other yacht clubs. Most repair facilities are concentrated around the yacht club, whose new marina and clubhouse facility is close to the north of the previous site, the entrance at approximately 09°28'S 147°09'E. There are three chandleries close to the yacht club. What is not available can be ordered from Australia and usually obtained within 72 hours. Lohberger is a very good engineering shop nearby, which can deal with diesel and outboard engines as well as electrical repair and rigging. They also have a good supply of spares and are the agents for various electrical products. There are a number of companies providing radio and electronic repair. There are two careening facilities within the marina and mobile cranes can lift vessels up to 20 tonnes. Larger vessels can use the Steamship slipway in Port Moresby harbour. Curtain Bros Slipway at the western end of the harbour on Motukea Island can haul out large vessels and has a travelift for smaller craft. Provisioning is good with several supermarkets and fresh produce markets.

In Rabaul the local yacht club is very welcoming and helpful and will advise on where to find various repair facilities. These are satisfactory and, as in Port Moresby, what cannot be obtained locally can be ordered from Australia, although it may take a week or longer. Boats can be hauled out at Toboi Shipyard, which has a slipway. Fuel is available from the Shell dock. Provisioning is good and Rabaul has one of the best fresh produce markets in the Pacific.

Facilities in the commercial centres of Madang and Lae are adequate, while those in the smaller towns and outer islands are often basic. There are small boatyards with their own slipways dotted about the country, so one is never too far away should the need arise for some emergency repair. However, all essential spares should be carried on board and one should also provision the boat in one of the major centres before sailing to the islands, where little except a few locally grown vegetables is available.

There is a Shell fuel dock in Madang Harbour. Some facilities for boats are at the Jais Aben diving resort near Madang, where the boat can be left if touring inland.

Further Reading

Papua New Guinea – a travel survival kit
Landfalls of Paradise

Website

www.niugini.com

PITCAIRN ISLAND

Pitcairn Island is a small isolated volcanic island in the South Pacific, its closest neighbours the Gambier Islands to the west and Easter Island to the east. Only three square miles of land, with steep cliffs all around, the sole anchorage is at Bounty Bay which is tenable only in settled weather. Pitcairn is a dependency of Britain, together with the uninhabited Henderson, Ducie and Oeno islands. It is administered by the British Consulate in Auckland, New Zealand, but day-to-day affairs are run by an island council. Supply ships are supposed to call three or four times a year but there is no regular service. Other ships used to call regularly to buy fresh produce and handicrafts from the islanders, but this has declined with the cessation of passenger liners and the increase of container ships on tight schedules. Nevertheless, ships continue to call at Pitcairn, on average about one every week. Between 20 and 30 yachts stop at Pitcairn every year, where a warm welcome awaits the cruising sailor who calls at this remote community, whose entire history has been intrinsically bound up with the sea. Although the anchorage in Bounty Bay is an open roadstead, by keeping an eye on the weather, one is usually able to spend some time on the island. Everyone leaves Pitcairn with unforgettable memories of having been hosted by one of the most isolated communities in the world.

Country Profile

Pitcairn was named after the midshipman who spotted it in 1767 on board HMS *Swallow*. Some human remains have been discovered on the island, but who these original inhabitants were remains a mystery. When the island's most famous settlers, the *Bounty* mutineers, came to the island they found no one. After a long search for a hideaway, Fletcher Christian and eight of his fellow mutineers arrived here in 1790 with their Tahitian wives and six Tahitian men on board the *Bounty*. The *Bounty* was burnt and scuttled by the new settlers in the bay which bears its name in order to avoid detection. Problems arose in the small community that dared not risk contact with the outside world and there was much violence. When the community was discovered in 1808 only one mutineer had survived with 10 women and many children. In the nineteenth century efforts to resettle the Pitcairn islanders on Tahiti and Norfolk Island were not successful, although some remained on the latter.

Income is raised from the sale of stamps and handicrafts are sold to the ships that visit. Britain gives some aid. The land is fertile, and the islanders farm and fish for their own consumption. The only paid jobs are government-funded, such as for the upkeep of the generator, roads and longboats.

Around 50 people live on the island, the population having dwindled as many have left for New Zealand. All the population are descendants of the *Bounty* mutineers and their wives, infused with some other blood from sailors and missionaries who settled on the island in the nineteenth century. None of the other islands in the dependency are inhabited, although the Pitcairners sometimes visit Oeno for a holiday and to collect shells, coral and pandanus. Henderson is a bird sanctuary, where the islanders sometimes call to collect wood for their carvings. The islanders have their own dialect, a blend of Tahitian and eighteenth century sailors' English, although standard English is spoken by all. Adamstown is the only settlement.

The public square houses the courthouse, post office, Adventist church, and the *Bounty*'s anchor.

Practical Information

LOCAL TIME: GMT – 9

BUOYAGE: IALA A

CURRENCY: New Zealand dollar (NZ$). Personal cheques and travellers' cheques can be cashed at the Island Secretary's office.

ELECTRICITY: This is provided by a diesel generator for a few hours daily.

PUBLIC HOLIDAYS
1 January: New Year's Day
23 January: Bounty Day
Good Friday, Easter Monday
25, 26 December: Christmas

COMMUNICATIONS
SSB and amateur radio. There is a daily radio link with Fiji. Tel. 872 144 5372, Fax. 872 144 5373, via Inmarsat. There is a simple telephone system connecting all houses on the island, but this is not linked to the outside world. There is no airport.

MEDICAL
There is no doctor permanently on the island, but one is employed from time to time for a few months. The rest of the time there is a registered nurse at the small dispensary.

The islanders are all Seventh Day Adventists and Saturday is the day of rest.

The climate is subtropical in the SE trade wind belt, with the most pleasant weather from November to March, when the winds are also lighter and the seas smoother. Pitcairn is very rarely affected by tropical storms.

Entry Regulations

Port of entry
Bounty Bay 25°04'S 130°06'W.

Procedure on arrival
The islanders prefer to be informed by radio of a yacht's arrival. VHF Channel 16 is monitored regularly and as the transmitter is situated high on top of the island it is said to have a range in excess of 50 miles. The island is also connected to the outside world by Inmarsat. Yachts should anchor or heave-to off Bounty Bay. Anchoring in the deep bay is not advisable if the wind has any east in it. The alternative is to anchor off the west coast, which offers some shelter in the prevailing wind. The locals will advise where to find a temporary sheltered anchorage, but no one should leave the boat unattended for any length of time as weather conditions can change very quickly and at least two yachts were lost at Pitcairn when the wind turned unexpectedly. Usually the islanders send out their inflatable rescue craft to advise where to anchor and also to take the crew ashore. Landing in one's own dinghy, especially if there is a big swell, is often impossible.

Once ashore, one should pay a call to the Island Magistrate to obtain permission to land and to have one's passport stamped and signed with the impressive Pitcairn stamp. Yachts may stay as long as this permission is in force. Anyone arriving by boat must leave the island by the same means.

Customs
Firearms and animals must not be taken ashore.

Fruit, vegetable and plants may only be landed with the prior permission of the Island Council, to avoid possible infestation of indigenous crops.

Health
A declaration may be requested stating that none of the crew have been in contact with anyone suffering from a contagious disease within three weeks prior to arrival. Only visitors in good health will be permitted ashore.

Fees
The Island Magistrate will issue a landing permit, which includes various fees that are payable by each person: $NZ10 for the transfer ashore, $NZ 10 landing fee, and $NZ5 immigration fee. The boat transfer fee is only meant for a limited number of trips, so anyone staying longer should be prepared to pay more.

Restricted areas
Henderson, Ducie and Oeno: Landing on these islands is forbidden without the prior consent of the Governor, British High Commission, Wellington, New Zealand, or the permission of the Island Magistrate, in which case the landing party must be accompanied by a resident of Pitcairn.

Facilities

The cooperative store is open three times a week, but only basic foodstuffs are available depending on supplies. Fresh produce is always available and also water. If any emergency repair needs to be made, the islanders will undoubtedly help, as they have to do all the maintenance on their own boats, generator and engines, both inboard and outboard, and are practised at coping without outside help.

The islanders are extremely welcoming, but some cruising sailors have abused this generosity and overstayed their welcome. Also, one should not expect a free launch service to and from the boat, especially if, because of weather conditions, the boat is anchored off the west coast, a long distance away from the normal landing place.

Further Reading

South Pacific Handbook
Landfalls of Paradise
South Pacific Anchorages

Websites

www.lareau.org/pitcinfo.html (General information)
www.users.iconz.co.nz/pitcairn/tourist.htm

SAMOA

Samoa, formerly known as Western Samoa, comprises the two islands of Upolu and Savai'i, as well as several smaller islands. Savai'i is the largest, but Upolu is the most developed and centre of government and commerce. Robert Louis Stevenson was the first in a long line of famous travellers to be seduced by the Samoan way of life, and today's sailors can still find a Samoa whose ways have changed very little during the century since Stevenson lived here. Tusitala, meaning teller of tales, as he was affectionately called by the Samoans, is buried on top of Mount Vaea. The view from his tomb over the whole island and Apia harbour is well worth the stiff climb. Cruising along the sheltered northern coast of the two main islands, one can anchor off villages such as Asau on Savai'i, from where one can explore the interior of these verdant islands with their gushing waterfalls and lush rain forests.

Country Profile

It is said that Savai'i is the legendary Hawaiki from which the first Polynesians spread out across the Pacific. The American Samoans may dispute this, saying it was Manua, but today Western Samoa seems much more the Polynesian of the two, not having experienced the cultural invasion of America as has its neighbour. Traditions have remained strong, despite absorbing some Western influence and *fa'a Samoa*, 'the way of the ancestors', rules the lives of Samoans, centred around the extended family, with its etiquette and rituals. Foreign visitors should be aware of this and be informed of the acceptable behaviour and what actions may cause offence.

Jacob Roggeveen first sighted the Samoas in 1722, and they were named the Navigator Islands 64 years later by Bougainville. The arrival of the missionary John Williams in the 1830s marks the beginning of modern Samoan history. A German trading firm was established to trade in copra and the islands which make up present-day Western Samoa were administered by Germany from 1900 until the First World War when they were taken over by New Zealand. This was not a popular rule and in 1962 Western Samoa was the first Polynesian nation to regain its independence. In 1990 a referendum approved the adoption of universal suffrage replacing the old electorate consisting exclusively of chiefs.

The economy is mainly agricultural, producing coconuts, copra and bananas although these have all declined. Remittances from the many Western Samoans living abroad are important. The economy suffers from a large foreign debt and unemployment. Efforts have been made to diversify, and to expand both tourism and other new industries. The population is around 160,000, the great majority being pure Polynesians. Samoan and English are spoken and most islanders are practising Christians. Apia, on Upolu's north coast, is the

Practical Information

LOCAL TIME: GMT – 11

BUOYAGE: IALA A

CURRENCY: Tala (SAT/WS$) of 100 sene

BUSINESS HOURS
Banks: 0900–1500 Monday to Friday.
Shops: 0800–1200/1330–1630 Monday to Friday, 0800–1200 Saturday.
Business and government offices: 0800–1200/1300–1630 Monday to Friday.

ELECTRICITY: 240 V, 50 Hz

PUBLIC HOLIDAYS
1 and 2 January: New Year's Day
Good Friday, Easter Monday

25 April: ANZAC Day
1st Monday May: Mothers' Day
1–3 June: Independence Celebrations
2nd Monday October: White Monday
October: Arbour Day
25, 26 December: Christmas

EVENTS
1st/2nd week September: Teuila Festival
October/November: Palolo Day

COMMUNICATIONS
Telecommunications office, above main post office, open 0800–2230 daily.
Post office, Beach Rd, open 0900–1200/1300–1530 Monday to Friday.
Emergency numbers: 22222 police, ambulance 21212, fire 20404.

There are flights from Apia to Fiji, Auckland and Sydney from where further connections can be made.

MEDICAL
National Hospital in Leufisa has small charges for non-residents. *Tel.* 21212. There are also private clinics in Apia.

DIPLOMATIC MISSIONS
In Apia:
Australia: Fei Gai ma Leala Bldg, Beach Rd. *Tel.* 23411.
New Zealand: Beach Rd. *Tel.* 21404.
United Kingdom: NFP Building. *Tel.* 21895.
United States: John Williams Bldg, Beach Rd. *Tel.* 22474.

capital. It is a waterfront town, a mixture of the old and the new. Apia harbour is worth entering, for the simple reason that to get into the harbour, yachts must go around a headland called Cape Horn.

Samoa has a tropical climate with the more pleasant season being the south-east trade wind season from April to November. During the cyclone season, from December to March, the weather is hotter and wetter. As the Samoan islands are quite high, local weather conditions can be quite varied.

Entry Regulations

Port of entry
Apia (Upolu) 13°48′S 171°46′W.

Procedure on arrival
Yachts are requested to radio their ETA to the harbour master via Apia Radio 24 hours before arrival. When a yacht is within 40 miles they should confirm their arrival to Harbour Control, VHF Channel 16. Health, customs, immigration and quarantine officers will come aboard on arrival. Do not come alongside the main wharf until permission and directions are given by harbour control. The authorities insist that all clearance is done through an agent. Slade Brothers offer this service for a fee of $30 (1995).

The anchorage is south of a line extending 097°T from Cape Horn.

Customs
Firearms must be declared and will be sealed on board by customs or kept ashore until departure.

Animals are not permitted ashore.

Yachts are normally granted a 14-day permit.

Immigration
No permit or visa is necessary if staying less than 30 days.

A visa or entry permit is required if staying longer and should be obtained prior to arrival from Samoan, New Zealand or British consulates or from the immigration office in Apia.

Cruising permit
This is required if wishing to visit other harbours besides Apia. An application may be made in writing on arrival, but it is better to do so in advance. Write to the Secretary for Foreign Affairs, PO Box L 861, Apia and send a copy to the Secretary for

Transport, PO Box 1607, Apia. The letter should state the yacht's name, port of registry, the names and nationalities of the master and crew, ETA Apia, and a list of places one intends to visit, plus planned duration of stay.

On outward clearance it is possible to get permission to stop in Asau on Savai'i, before continuing on to other destinations.

Prohibited areas
It is prohibited to enter the ferry terminal ports of Mulifanua and Salelologa, except with special permission from the Ministry of Transport.

Fees
Overtime is charged outside of working hours for clearing services. There is a customs clearance fee.

Facilities

There are no facilities for visiting yachts to come alongside, only the protected anchorage off the capital Apia. Construction work is underway in the harbour and although the new breakwater will provide better protection it is doubtful that any docking arrangements will be available for visiting yachts. Provisioning in Apia is good and there are various stores to choose from. The fresh produce market is excellent. Diesel fuel is available from the fuel station north of the river. For larger quantities it is possible to order a tanker from Mobil who will send it down to the dock. There are some good hardware stores but little marine equipment.

Engine repair is undertaken by Ken-Do Engineering. Stainless steel welding and metal work can be done at Brueger Industries. There are no haul-out facilities for yachts.

All garbage must be put into sealed plastic bags and given to the quarantine office at the wharf gate for disposal. There is a charge of WS$1 per bag.

Asau on Savai'i is a well-protected anchorage, but only limited supplies are available, so it is better to provision in Apia.

Further Reading

Landfalls of Paradise
South Pacific Handbook
Samoa – a travel survival kit
The Pacific Crossing Guide
South Pacific Anchorages

Websites

www.interwebinc.com/samoa (Samoa Visitors Bureau)
www.samoa.co.nz

SOLOMON ISLANDS

The Solomon Islands are a double chain of islands in the Western Pacific stretching from Vanuatu to Bougainville. Some of the fiercest battles of the Second World War occurred here particularly on Guadalcanal. There are over 900 islands, the main ones being Guadalcanal, Choiseul, Malaita, New Georgia and Santa Isabel. The Solomons' culture, or 'custom', is rich and varied, from wood-carving to beliefs such as shark-worshipping. Many islanders still live in the traditional way.

The authorities are making a determined effort to preserve this way of life and they enjoy the full support of the customary chiefs in their endeavours. This has put some restrictions on the movement of cruising yachts but fortunately there is still a lot to see along the usual cruising route, for which special permission is not needed. Visiting yachts are welcomed in most villages, particularly by children who like to trade fruit or shells for ball-point pens, felt-tips or balloons.

One interesting island to visit is Malaita, particularly the Langa Langa lagoon, to savour village life virtually unaffected by the outside world. Another lagoon often visited by yachts for the excellent wood carvings of the villagers is Marovo lagoon in the New Georgia group.

Apart from traditional village life, when cruising through the Solomons one constantly comes across remains of the Second World War and to this day a lot of discarded military hardware is still put to good use, such as fuel tanks to catch rain-water or aircraft wings for pig enclosures. Some also find it interesting to sail through the same waters where the young Lt John F. Kennedy made his daring escape during the Second World War after his patrol boat was sunk in the Blackett Strait. Plum Pudding or Kasolo Island where he was rescued from has been aptly renamed Kennedy Island.

Country Profile

The first inhabitants probably came to these islands about four to five thousand years ago. The first European visitor was Alvaro de Mendana in 1568, who named the islands the Solomons, hoping it would hint back home of the famed King Solomon's treasure. Only at the end of the nineteenth century did Europeans such as traders and missionaries come on a more permanent basis. Many of the islanders were recruited to work on Fijian and Australian plantations and were often treated as slaves. Because of this, many Europeans were killed in retaliation and Britain made the Solomons a Protectorate in 1893 to maintain some law and order.

The Solomons' strategic position in the Pacific meant that the islands were crucial in the Pacific War. Much of the fighting was on Guadalcanal, until the Japanese were pushed out in 1943 and the island became a US base. When the war was over, many islands were left with new airstrips and roads built by both sides and the islanders were left with a new sense of national unity. The Solomon Islands became an independent nation in 1978.

The economy is basically agricultural with very little industry. Fish and timber are the main exports. Tourism is not very developed. The islands receive considerable foreign aid.

Of the 450,000 inhabitants most are Melanesian, with a few Polynesians on the south-eastern islands, plus some I-Kiribati, Chinese, and Europeans. At least 87 local dialects and languages exist and Solomon Island pidgin is used as a lingua franca. English is used in schools and businesses and is widely spoken by the younger generation especially. There are many Christian denominations. Tulagi on Florida Island was the original capital until it was flattened in the Second World War, after which Honiara, the US base on Guadalcanal, became the new capital.

The Solomons experience high temperatures and January to March are the months of heaviest rainfall. April to November is the season of the SE trades, while the rest of the year is the NW monsoon, which is also the cyclone season. Long periods of calm weather are not uncommon among the islands.

Entry Regulations

Ports of entry

Honiara (Guadalcanal) 9°25′S 159°58′E, Gizo 8°05′S 156°52′E, Noro (New Georgia) 8°13′S 157°12′E, Yandina (Russell) 9°04′N 159°13′E, Graciosa Bay (Ndende Island, Santa Cruz) 10°44′S 165°49′E.

Practical Information

LOCAL TIME: GMT + 11

BUOYAGE: IALA A

CURRENCY: Solomon Island dollar (SI$) of 100 cents.

BUSINESS HOURS
Banks: 0830–1500 Monday to Friday.
Business and government offices: 0800–1200/1300–1630 Monday to Friday.
Shops: 0800–1200/1330–1700 weekdays and half day Saturday.

ELECTRICITY: 240 V, 50 Hz

PUBLIC HOLIDAYS
1 January: New Year's Day
Good Friday, Easter Monday
Whit Monday

June: Queen's Birthday
7 July: Independence Day
25 December: Christmas Day
26 December: National Day of Thanksgiving
The provinces have their own holidays:
8 June: Temotu
29 June: Central Solomons
8 July: Isabel
1 August: Guadalcanal
3 August: Makira
15 August: Malaita
7 December: Western Solomons

COMMUNICATIONS
Solomon Telekom, next to post office: international telephone calls, fax, telex, telegrams, 0745–2200 Monday to Friday, until noon on Saturday and Sunday.
Post office, Mendana Avenue, Honiara (phones, telegrams, telex, fax)

0800–1630 Monday to Friday, 0800–1100 Saturday.
Emergency: dial 11.
There are flights from Honiara to Papua New Guinea, Fiji and Vanuatu with onward international connections.

MEDICAL
Tap water is not potable and should be boiled.
Honiara Central Hospital. *Tel.* 23600.

DIPLOMATIC MISSIONS
In Honiara:
Australia: PO Box 589. *Tel.* 21561.
New Zealand: Mendana Avenue. *Tel.* 21502.
PNG: PO Box 1109. *Tel.* 21737.
United Kingdom: Telekom House, Mendana Avenue. *Tel.* 21705.
United States: PO Box 561. *Tel.* 20725.

Procedure on arrival

One should report one's arrival to the authorities and request clearance. Stopping and going ashore at any island before clearing in is strictly prohibited and boats that do this will pay a heavy fine. This is particularly true of the eastern islands, such as Tikopia or Vanikolo, where yachts coming from Vanuatu have stopped without first clearing into the Solomons at Ndende (Nendo) Island.

Honiara: Honiara Radio can be contacted on VHF Channel 16 or on 2182 and 6213 MHz to advise authorities of a vessel's arrival. This is not compulsory but is recommended. One should anchor in the proximity of Point Cruz Yacht Club in Honiara and go ashore to contact the relevant officials. Customs is at the end of the commercial wharf area. If asked, customs will call the other officials, who may come to the yacht club to be taken out of the boat, or if not one has to go to immigration oneself.

Graciosa Bay: Yachts sailing up from Vanuatu or points east can clear into the Solomons at Ndende Island. Usually the resident customs officer will give a two-week cruising permit so the yacht can sail to Honiara and complete formalities there. Some dues have to be paid on the spot but there is now a bank at Ndende where local currency can be obtained.

Yachts cruising the islands after clearing in should check in with customs at any port where they have an office. Clearance out of the Solomons can be done from any port of entry.

Customs

Firearms must be declared, otherwise they may be forfeited. Firearms and alcohol will be sealed on board.

Animals are not to be landed. If for any reason they are landed, they will be subject to quarantine.

Exports of genuine artefacts, not replicas, require permission.

A yacht may stay in the country for a total of six months. An initial three months will be granted on arrival and this can be extended for another three months.

Immigration

Visas are not required for up to a three month stay except for nationals of Bangladesh, India, Pakistan, and Sri Lanka. All other nationals will be issued with a Visitor's Permit on arrival.

Cruising permit

Each province requires notification of yachts that wish to cruise in their areas. All the land, including uninhabited areas, is someone's property, and in order to visit any uninhabited bays or islands, one must first obtain permission from the relevant chief. It can take time to find out which chief is responsible for which place. Fishing and collecting shells are not normally allowed unless one has been given permission, nor are coconuts and produce to be taken.

The authorities in Honiara will advise where a yacht can or cannot go. There are usually no problems in calling at the main centres or at islands used to cruising yachts.

Health

Malaria is endemic in the Solomons and malarial prophylaxis is absolutely essential. Many cruising sailors have caught malaria in the Solomons recently, so the usual precautions should also be taken, such as having mosquito screens on all portholes and hatches, anchoring further offshore and possibly upwind from any village, trying to avoid going ashore in the late afternoon or early evening when mosquitoes are most active.

Fees

Attendance and overtime fees are as follows: SI$18 on weekdays, SI$22 on Saturdays, SI$24 per hour on Sundays.

One should attempt to arrive during normal working hours. In most places one can wait at anchor until the offices open, but no one should go ashore before clearance is completed.

There is a clearance fee of SI$60 per visit, and light dues of SI$100 plus 5c per ton. There are also port, immigration charges and a SI$50 quarantine fee.

Social customs

The wearing of shorts or other scanty clothing by women is not allowed.

Marovo Lagoon: Most islanders are Seventh Day Adventists so their Sabbath is from sunset on Friday to sunset on Saturday, and visitors are not supposed to go ashore here during the Sabbath.

Facilities

In Honiara there are several supermarkets with a reasonable selection and also a fresh produce market, which is best on Saturday morning. Prices are generally higher than in Vanuatu, especially for imported goods, and the selection poorer. Government charts can be bought from the Hydrographic Office, near the immigration office. These are detailed, but apparently not completely reliable, so care must be taken. Diesel can be jerrycanned from the service station on the main street near the Point Cruz Yacht Club. Larger quantities can be taken at the fuel dock in the harbour. Diesel in large quantities is only available in Honiara, Noro, on the island of New Georgia and Gizo. Dive Solomons based on Gizo is a good local contact – and not just for diving enthusiasts, for they

have extensive local knowledge, and Dirk Sieling, who runs the operation, wrote the *Solomon Islands Cruising Guide*. Propane bottles can only be refilled in Honiara.

Repair facilities in Honiara are adequate and there are a few workshops capable of tackling simple engine or electrical repair. For larger jobs there is a good shipyard, Taroaniara Shipyard, which is an Anglican Training centre, at Taroaniara on Florida Island, which is close to Honiara across Iron Bottom Sound. The yard specialises in boat building, metal and electrical work, and also has a slipway.

Repair facilities in the other islands are limited. Water should be treated everywhere including Honiara and Gizo. In many isolated villages, where money has little value, the age old barter system is still in use and one can trade with the locals to obtain fresh produce, fish, carvings and shells. One should take along a supply of useful objects such as fishhooks, fishing line, matches, sugar, rice, tobacco, clothing and shoes, coffee, soap, needles, cotton and rope.

Further Reading

Solomon Islands Cruising Guide
The Pacific Crossing Guide
South Pacific Anchorages
Landfalls of Paradise
South Pacific Handbook
Solomon Islands – a travel survival kit

Websites

www.solomons.com (Government site)
www.commerce.gov.sb (Department of Tourism)
www.tcsp.com/solomon_islands (Tourism Council of the South Pacific)
www.solomonchartes.com

TAHITI NUI

Tahiti Nui, formerly known as French Polynesia, covers an area of the South Pacific Ocean about the size of Europe. It is made up of 130 islands in five archipelagos: the Society Islands, the Marquesas, Tuamotus, Gambiers and Australs, as well as Clipperton atoll, a small French possession off Mexico. These coral and volcanic islands, some with spectacular scenery, are all very different from each other. Tahiti is the largest island and Papeete, is the capital of the Territory.

So many superlatives have been bestowed on these islands in the days since Captains Cook, Wallis and Bligh, the *Bounty* mutineers, Robert Louis Stevenson, Paul Gauguin and many others visited them, that one can only repeat some of these well-worn adjectives. As symbols of the South Seas, the islands of Tahiti Nui are indeed unbeatable and there are few sailors who do not dream of cruising one day among these enchanted isles.

From the rugged beauty of the Marquesas to the crystal clear waters of the Tuamotu atolls and the lofty peaks of the Society Islands, the variety in scenery and sailing conditions is unsurpassed anywhere in the South Pacific. Most yachts make their landfall in the Marquesas, which is a perfect introduction to this vast cruising ground. There are no man-made ports here and the swell can tuck into

the anchorages, but this is more than made up for by the beauty of these high islands.

In complete contrast are the Tuamotus, once called the Dangerous Archipelago on account of its treacherous currents and lurking reefs. Yachts used to avoid this area, but now often stop and visit the low atolls, as the hazards have diminished considerably with the advent of radar and satellite navigation. Negotiating the passes into some of the lagoons can be a difficult operation, mainly because of the strong currents, but also because few of the passes are well marked. This can be solved by careful eyeball navigation, ideally when the sun is overhead and the colour of the water gives a good indication of its depth. Generally, the weakest current occurs one hour after low water and one hour after high water.

Papeete is enjoyed by many cruisers, able to berth Mediterranean-style in the centre of the town, which is the most chic, lively and cosmopolitan in the Pacific. Development, which has not affected the outer islands, has quickened the pace in Tahiti, but in the rest of the Society Islands life is as relaxed as ever. From Moorea to Bora Bora, the Societies are still some of the most beau-

Papeete, the capital of Tahiti.

Practical Information

LOCAL TIME: GMT – 10

BUOYAGE: IALA A. The Department of Fishing has laid out buoys which are often 2–3 miles off the islands. They have radar reflectors and are lit, but have been reported as being difficult to spot.

CURRENCY: Pacific franc (PFR/CFP)

BUSINESS HOURS
Banks: 0700–1530 Monday to Friday, or 0800–1100, 1400–1700 Monday to Friday, some 0800–1100 Saturday.
Shops: 0730–1130, 1400–1730/1800 Monday to Friday, Saturday mornings. Government offices: 0730–1530 Monday to Thursday, 0730–1500 Fridays.

ELECTRICITY: 220 V, 60 Hz

PUBLIC HOLIDAYS
1 January: New Year's Day
5 March: Gospel Day
Good Friday, Easter Monday
1 May: Labour Day
8 May: Liberation Day
Ascension
Whit Monday
29 June: Heiva which starts the Tiurai Bastille Day festivities until 14 July
15 August: Assumption
1 November: All Saints' Day
11 November: Armistice Day
December: Tiare Tahiti Day
25 December: Christmas Day

EVENTS
Festival, three weeks around Bastille Day when there are song, dance and sport competitions including canoe racing.

COMMUNICATIONS
For international calls, dial 00 from post offices and public phones. Télécartes (phonecards) can be bought from post offices.
Cables through Telefrance.
Post office: Papeete Waterfront, open 0700–1200, 1500–1800 Monday to Thursday, 0700–1400 Friday, 0800–1000 Saturday.
Emergency: Police 17, Fire 18, SOS Medical 42 34 56.
There are regular flights from Tahiti to the USA, Europe, Japan, Hawaii, Chile, New Zealand and Australia. There are frequent flights to all the Society Islands, but less frequently to the other island groups.

MEDICAL
Territorial Hospital Centre at Mamao has a 24 hour casualty department. Clinique Paofai, Blvd Pomare, near yacht quay in Papeete. Cardella Clinic near the cathedral. Medical facilities are of a high standard. There are dispensaries in all populated centres.

DIPLOMATIC MISSIONS
Australia: BP 1695, c/o Qantas, Vaima Centre. Tel. 438838.
New Zealand: c/o Air New Zealand, Vaina Centre, Papeete. Tel. 430170.
UK: BP Propriété Boubiée, route Tuterai Tane, Pirae. Tel. 428457.

tiful islands in the world with the contrast of their towering volcanic peaks over lagoons set with low sandy atolls.

Entirely off the usual cruising routes are Tahiti Nui's other two groups, the Austral and Gambier islands. The latter is best visited if coming from Easter Island or Pitcairn, while the former are only a few days' sail away from Tahiti or make a convenient landfall for yachts heading towards Tahiti from New Zealand.

Even more remote and only administratively linked to Tahiti Nui is the uninhabited Clipperton atoll, some 700 miles (1125 km) off the Mexican coast. The lagoon of this atoll has no pass, but the few yachts which stop there can shelter in the lee of the reef. Landing through the surf is sometimes difficult but the diving on the surrounding reef makes up for it.

The grafting of French culture on to the Polynesian lifestyle has resulted in some strange phenomena, but on the whole the mix has worked to good effect. At no time is this more obvious than during the annual Bastille Day celebrations, the political significance of which few Polynesians care about, but every island puts on a breathtaking show of song and dance of unmatched colour and vivacity.

Country Profile

Tahiti and the surrounding islands were populated from around AD 850, but little is known of the origins of the original population. A system of chiefdoms developed, which later became a kingdom. Remains of the past are still to be found, especially the old marae temples.

Point Venus on Tahiti marks the first European visit in 1767 by Captain Wallis of the Royal Navy, searching for the great Southern Continent. He and his sailors found a welcoming people on a lush fertile island and he claimed it for Britain. Nine months later, the French explorer Bougainville claimed Tahiti for France. Next to visit was James Cook, on an expedition to observe the sun's eclipse by Venus. He made astute observations of the Tahitians and their lifestyle, including the name they gave to the island, Otaheite ('this is Tahiti'). In honour of the Royal Geographical Society, Cook named the islands Society Islands, and returned to them several times. Captain Bligh visited the islands in 1788 with the *Bounty* and the charms of Tahiti were one of the causes of the famous mutiny. The mutineers' efforts to settle on the unfriendly Australs failed. Some remained on Tahiti, while others sailed with their Tahitian wives to Pitcairn Island. The friendly islanders, who had few sexual constraints, suffered for all their contacts with European sailors, as diseases hitherto unknown to them decimated the population.

Next to arrive on the scene were missionaries, first Protestants, then Catholics. Despite requests from the Tahitians, the British refused to make the islands a Protectorate, so the islands were finally put under French protection. The Pomaré dynasty, in power since the eighteenth century, ruled until 1880, when Tahiti became a full French colony. After the Second World War the newly-named French Polynesia became a French Overseas Territory. An increase in internal autonomy was allowed in 1984, although foreign affairs, police, finance and justice are still in the hands of the French-appointed High Commissioner. The French maintain a military presence in the islands, particularly at Mururoa, an atoll in the Southern Tuamotus which is the centre of nuclear testing. The resumption of tests in 1995 not only enraged public opinion throughout the Pacific, but also resulted in violent demonstrations in Papeete by the indigenous population.

In the new Constitution French Polynesia will cease to be an overseas territory of France and will become autonomous, although the links with France will continue as before. The new status will be reflected in a new name Tahiti Nui (Greater Tahiti).

Important products are mother-of-pearl, cultured black pearls, copra, vanilla and coffee. The tourist industry also contributes to the economy. Imports, however, are high, as is the cost of living. The Society Islands are more developed than the other groups, while on the more remote islands people live more of a subsistence existence.

The population is over 220,000. Polynesians form the majority, although there are also quite a few Europeans and Chinese. There is a very mixed population in Tahiti itself, while the population of the outer islands is pure Polynesian. Tahitian and French are the main languages, although each island group has its own distinct Polynesian language. English is also quite widely spoken, especially in the tourist centres. Most are Christian of many different denominations, with a small percentage of Buddhists among the Chinese population.

The islands have a tropical climate. November to April is warm and rainy, while May to October is cooler and drier, when the islands are under the influence of the SE trade winds. The cyclone season is November to March and every year at least one cyclone affects one or more of the islands. Full cyclones rarely hit the Marquesas, but they can be affected by bad storms during the cyclone season.

Entry Regulations

Ports of entry
Society Islands: Papeete (Tahiti) 17°32′S 149°35′W, Afareaitu (Moorea) 17°32′S 149°46′W, Uturoa (Raiatea) 16°44′S 151°26′W, Fare (Huahine) 16°43′S 151°02′W, Vaitape (Bora Bora) 16°30′S 151°45′W.
Marquesas: Taiohae (Nuku Hiva) 8°56′S 140°06′W, Hakahau (Ua Pou) 9°21′S 140°03′W, Atuona (Hiva Oa) 9°51′S 139°02′W.
Austral Islands: Mataura (Tubuai) 23°22′S 149°28′W, Moerai (Rurutu) 22°27′S 151°20′W, Raima (Raivavae) 23°52′S 147°40′W.
Tuamotus: Tiputa (Rangiroa) 15°10′S 147°35′W.
Gambier Islands: Rikitea (Mangareva) 23°07′S 134°58′W.

Procedure on arrival
Papeete is the main port of entry and all yachts have to finalise their clearance here. However, because of the distances and sailing conditions, the outer islands have been made informal ports of entry, where yachts may initially clear in.

On arrival in one of the other islands, yachts should report to the local police (Gendarmerie). Failure to report may lead to a fine. The gendarme in the first port of arrival normally issues a document, which is then stamped in subsequent ports. Even on islands without a resident gendarme, the captain should take the document to the island or village chief to have it stamped. US and Canadian passport holders arriving without a visa are given a 30 day grace period and are expected to clear into Papeete (Tahiti) and complete proper formalities within that period.

Before entering or departing Papeete harbour all yachts must contact the port captain on Channel 12 or 2683 kHz. On arrival in Papeete one must report first to immigration, then to customs, then to the harbour master's office, all of which are in the Bureau des Yachts, Quai des Paquebots, close to the tourist office on the waterfront in Papeete. The offices are open 0700–1200, 1400–1700 Monday to Friday.

Yachts sailing or motoring to and from Taapuna, west channel, or Marina Taina must request permission to cross the airfield axis east or west 10 minutes before doing so by calling VIGIE on VHF Channel 12.

Aventura III at Rapa in the Austral Islands.

Permission should be obtained for any cruise which takes a yacht more than 50 miles from Tahiti. On departure yachts must clear with customs and immigration and apply for a permit to leave from the harbour master.

Hiva Oa: This is the most common port of entry for boats arriving from the east. No other islands should be visited before reporting to the officials in Atuona. The small harbour can get crowded and the swell is usually bad. Formalities are completed at the Gendarmerie in Atuona, half-a-mile (1 km) uphill. The Gendarmerie is open 0730–1200, 1400–1730 Monday to Friday. The compulsory bond can be deposited at Banque Socredo. Europeans are expected to deposit approximately $1200–1500 per person, US citizens approximately $800. Some boats have managed to pay the deposit by credit card, although they lost on the exchange rate when the deposit was cashed in. Boats intending to spend a short time (4 to 6 weeks) in Tahiti Nui are normally exempt.

Nuku Hiva: If space is available, boats may come alongside the quay in the NE corner of the harbour.

Formalities are completed at the Gendarmerie in Taiohae, open 0730–1200, 1400–1730 Monday to Friday. The bond can be deposited at the local bank if this has not been done earlier.

Mangareva: The gendarme in Rikitea will hold the passports until departure. No other formalities are needed.

Customs

Firearms and ammunition must be declared. If staying less than three days they can be kept on board, otherwise must be bonded by the authorities in each island until departure.

Animals need health certificates. They must remain on board unless permission to land is given by the veterinary service of the Ministry of Agriculture. *Tel.* 42 81 44.

Yachts may remain for up to six months in a 12-month consecutive period without paying duty. A new regulation allows a yacht, at the end of its six month stay, to be left in storage indefinitely, allowing the owner to return and cruise for six months in every year. The boatyard in Raiatea has an arrangement with customs, which allows boats left in their care to have the clock stopped while in their charge.

The import of plants and grains is forbidden.

Yachts coming from the western Pacific, such as Fiji, Tonga or the Cooks, may have to be fumigated. On arrival they should anchor off and clear formalities before tying to the quay.

Immigration

Residents of France and citizens of Francophone Africa do not need visas, only a valid passport.

All visitors need a passport valid beyond their proposed stay in Tahiti Nui.

A visa-free stay is permitted for no more than three months for nationals of the EU countries, Norway, Cyprus, Malta, Iceland, Monaco, Andorra, Switzerland and Liechtenstein. If these nationals plan to stay longer, a visa must be obtained in advance.

Citizens of the USA, Canada, New Zealand, Japan, Poland, Czech Republic, Slovakia and Hungary get 30 days' visa-free stay and must apply to immigration for a visa for a further 60 days if required. All other nationalities need a visa in advance, which can be obtained from French diplomatic missions, for example in Panama City.

Visas are normally valid for three months. Extensions of another three months are possible, but one should apply well in advance (one month) in writing to the High Commissioner in Papeete, although local immigration offices may be able to extend visas. Extensions can take up to a month to come through. Even for nationals who can get a visa on arrival, formalities are much simplified if the visa is obtained in advance. Those who need an extension over the initial 30 days must buy stamps from the post office, at a cost of approximately $30 for the additional 60 days. These are added in one's passport by the Gendarmerie. A further extension (of up to 90 days) may only be obtained by writing to the High Commissioner (Haut Commissaire, DRCL, Rue Jeanne d'Arc, Papeete) not later than 30 days before the expiration of the original visa. The alternative is to fly out to one of the neighbouring countries and restart the clock when a new visa is issued on return.

Proof may be demanded of sufficient funds for one's stay in Tahiti Nui, especially for those arriving without a visa.

Crew arriving by air to join a boat should make this clear on their visa application, also to immigration on arrival at the airport, who should give them both an entrance and an exit stamp in their passport. The exit stamp is needed to clear out by boat.

Cruising permit

A special cruising permit is necessary for yachts spending longer in Tahiti Nui. This can be obtained on arrival from customs in Papeete or the Gendarmerie in other ports. The permit is valid for six months. Extensions are only granted in Papeete, but most non-French yachts are not allowed to stay longer than six months. All yachts are required to leave Tahiti Nui before the start of the cyclone season in November, but preferably earlier.

Bond

Since the end of 1999 citizens of EU countries arriving by yacht are no longer required to post a bond (Article 3 of law no. 590 of 24 November 1999). Each person from a non-EU country on board the yacht must deposit in a Tahiti Nui bank a sum of money equivalent to a one-way air ticket back to their home country. On arrival, arrangements have to be made immediately to have money telexed or to pay money into a bank. There are banks in the Marquesas (Nuku Hiva and Hiva Oa). If arriving there as one's first landfall in Tahiti Nui, the bond must be arranged on arrival.

Because of currency fluctuation, one should insist that the money is not changed into the local currency (Pacific Franc), but kept in US dollars, so that the refund is made in the same currency as the deposit. This is possible at Banque de Polynesie. There is a handling fee of $20 and a 1 per cent charge on the total amount.

This money is normally refunded on the day before departure from Tahiti Nui. If the bond is posted in Papeete, and one leaves from Bora Bora, one must obtain a letter from the Papeete immigration officer confirming the bond. The letter and the receipt must be presented for the refund. Refunds can be in cash, or travellers' cheques, although the latter must be ordered in advance.

Yachts staying only a short period (up to one month) may be able to have the bond requirement waived. The bond can be avoided by buying tickets for flights back to one's own country. The unused tickets can be refunded, although one may have to pay a handling charge of approximately 5 per cent. If resorting to this solution, one should make sure that the tickets are refundable and also that the issuing agency will actually authorise a refund.

Fees

There is a charge for visas granted on arrival of US$30 per person. There are port charges.

Restricted areas

The approaches to the atolls of Mururoa and Fangataufa and the area around them are prohibited areas, classed as military zones.

Charter

Visiting yachts may not charter in Tahiti Nui.

People arriving by air to charter a boat need only a valid passport, return air ticket and a visa where applicable.

Restrictions

The movement of yachts is restricted in certain lagoons in the Tuamotus where there are pearl farms. Generally, one should avoid anchoring near oyster beds.

The sale of spirits is prohibited in the outer islands and visiting boats are urged not to dispense drinks freely to locals.

All fruit trees, including coconut trees, are privately owned. Fruit must not be taken without prior permission. Similarly, reefs inside lagoons are owned by families, so fishing should only be done after having asked permission to do so.

Health

Staphilococcus infections are prevalent and usually start from a small cut. The cuts should be cleaned out well, covered with an antibiotic cream and treated until healed, which can take as long as two weeks.

Filariosis (elephantiasis) is still known to exist in some islands. There is a preventative medicine, which gives protection for six months.

Facilities

The best facilities are to be found in Papeete which has several workshops in Fare Ute, on the east side of the harbour, specialising in yacht repair and maintenance. There is also a slipway and a small boatyard doing hull repairs. Nearby is a chandlery with a good selection of equipment, spares and also charts, both French and British Admiralty. There is a shipyard at Motu Uta in Papeete harbour near the main breakwater. Any spares or equipment that is not available can be ordered from France. There is no marina as such in Papeete harbour, but the waterfront has been upgraded and there is water and electricity. Yachts moor Mediterranean-style. The Tahiti Yacht Club in Arue has several docks where visitors may be able to berth if there is space available. Marina Taina with 200 berths is on the west coast and has a visitors quay for large yachts. Yachts proceeding to this marina must request permission to cross the airfield axis east or west 10 minutes before doing so by calling VIGIE on Channel 12.

The only other centre with extensive repair facilities is on Raiatea, where two charter companies have their base. Facilities are on a par with Tahiti, or even better, and have the great convenience of being grouped together. There are two boatyards in operation, with haul-out capacity to 60 tons. The yards offer a complete range of repair facilities and specialise in electrical, engine and sail repair, as well as rigging work. This is also a good place to leave the boat between seasons, either on the hard or in the small boat harbour of Apoiti.

In Bora Bora, the Club Nautique has a few moorings for yachts and provide showers, laundry, water and other services for sailors.

Provisioning is best in Tahiti and adequate in the other Society Islands. There are fresh produce markets on most islands, the most colourful being the one in Papeete. Provisions in the Marquesas are limited, although there is plenty of local fruit and vegetables. There is usually a better selection when the supply ship arrives. In the more remote areas, it is sometimes possible to barter for fresh provisions. Fuel is available in the main settlements, although it is more difficult to find in the Tuamotus. In both Atuona and Taiohae there is now fuel in the harbour – in Atuona at the dock on the east side, in Taiohae at the quay on the east side of the harbour. Propane bottles can be refilled or exchanged in Papeete, Bora Bora and Nuku Hiva.

Further Reading

Charlie's Charts of Polynesia
South Pacific Handbook
The Pacific Crossing Guide
South Pacific Anchorages
Tahiti Handbook

Websites

www.french-polynesia.com
www.tahiti.com
www.tahitiweb.com (Useful links)

TOKELAU

Tokelau lies just north of Samoa in the central South Pacific and consists of three small low coral atolls: Atafu, Nukunono, and Fakaofo. As a territory of New Zealand, the islanders are New Zealand citizens.

One of the least visited countries in the South Pacific, only a few yachts make their way to this isolated group of atolls, which lack natural harbours and for most of the year are completely cut off from the outside world. Some formalities have to be complied with before sailing for the islands, but any difficulties are justified, as they give an opportunity to visit one of the most isolated communities in the Pacific.

Country Profile

Legend says that the Maui brothers pulled the three islands out of the sea while fishing. The original population probably came from Samoa, Rarotonga and Tuvalu. Tokelau was one of the last island groups found by the Europeans, not being discovered until the nineteenth century. The islands were rarely visited until the 1840s, when missionaries, beachcombers and slavers came, the latter taking many Tokelauans to Peru. In 1889 Britain claimed jurisdiction over the islands. For some time Tokelau was administered with the Gilbert and Ellice Islands, but in 1925 administration was transferred to New Zealand, an arrangement which continues today. There is some internal autonomy, largely along traditional lines.

Copra is the only cash crop and the islanders lead a subsistence lifestyle. Some income comes from stamps, coins, handicrafts and remittances from workers overseas, mainly in New Zealand and Samoa. Licence fees are charged for foreign ships fishing in the 200 mile exclusive economic zone. New Zealand aid is the main source of income, largely for public works, government services and salaries. The islands can only support a certain number of inhabitants.

About 1600 people live in Tokelau, while there are around 4000 Tokelauans in New Zealand. The islanders are Polynesian, close to Tuvaluans. Tokelauan, akin to Samoan, and also English are spoken. Atafu is Congregationalist, Nukunono is Roman Catholic and Fakaofo has both represented. There is no administrative centre, each island having a separate local government. The Administrator resides in New Zealand but all affairs are run by the Tokelau Liaison office in Apia, Western Samoa.

From May to September the islands are under the influence of the SE trade winds. The weather is cooler than the rest of the year when it is hot, particularly from December to March, which is the cyclone season. Tokelau is on the edge of the cyclone belt, but is only rarely affected by tropical storms.

Entry Regulations

Ports of entry
Fakaofo 9°23'S 171°15'W, Nukunono 8°34'S 171°49'W, Atafu 8°34'S 172°30'W.

Procedure on arrival
Yachts have to be cleared in by the police, health and the Administration Officer. Officials normally come out to meet boats stopping at Fakaofo. In spite of the strict regulations, boats appear to be allowed to make a short stop even if they arrive without prior permission.

Practical Information

LOCAL TIME: GMT – 11

BUOYAGE: IALA A

CURRENCY: New Zealand dollar (NZ$)
One can change money at each island's administration centre.

BUSINESS HOURS
Official working hours: 0800–1630 Monday to Friday.

ELECTRICITY: There are generators on each atoll.

PUBLIC HOLIDAYS
1 January: New Year's Day
6 February: Waitangi Day
Good Friday, Easter Monday
25 April: ANZAC Day
June: Queen's Birthday
Fourth Monday in October:
Labour Day
October: Tokehehga Day
25, 26 December: Christmas

COMMUNICATIONS
There are radio stations on each of the atolls.
There are no airports on the islands.

MEDICAL
There are hospitals on all three islands.

Customs

Any firearms which are landed on any Tokelau island must be handed to the police to be kept until departure. Animals must remain on board.

Immigration

Visas are required by all nationalities before arrival. A cruising permit is required in advance but this rule does not appear to be strictly enforced for short visits.

Cruising permit

This must be authorised by the Council of Elders (taupulega) of each island that the yacht wishes to visit. In view of the difficulty of communicating with Tokelau, the Official Secretary at the Office for Tokelau Affairs in Apia, Western Samoa, can contact the Council of Elders concerned, on behalf of those seeking permits. He will radio the islands for permission. Every visitor must pass a simple physical examination to ascertain that he or she has no obvious illness.

There is no limit on how long a yacht may spend in Tokelau; however, the Council has the right to ask a yacht to leave if the island's culture, customs, rules or regulations are violated.

Office of Tokelau Affairs: PO Box 865, Apia, Western Samoa. *Tel.* 20-822. Telex: 281 SX. Telegram: TOKALANI APIA.

Fees

No fees are charged. However, a donation should be made to the village, as appreciation of the assistance given by the villagers.

Social customs

Visitors should be very conscious of the island's customs, such as paying due respect to all older persons.

Atafu is officially a dry island.

Facilities

There are no harbour facilities whatsoever, only passes for small boats through the reefs, but these are too shallow for most yachts. Normally a yacht must anchor on a shelf outside the reef, in the lee of the atoll. Fairly often conditions are not suitable for yachts to anchor.

At Fakaofo, there is an anchorage due west of Fakaofo islet, but it is exposed to the SE tradewinds. An alternative anchorage, recommended by the islanders, is NW of the island, off Fenua Fala islet. The dinghy can be landed on the nearby beach, although a strong outboard engine may be needed to get through the surfline. The island of Fakaofo is reported as being incorrectly charted.

There is one cooperative store on each island selling some staple foodstuffs, mostly imported. It is possible to buy some locally grown produce. Water is scarce everywhere.

Further Reading

Landfalls of Paradise
South Pacific Handbook
South Pacific Anchorages

Website

www.pasifika.net/pacific-action

TONGA

This Polynesian kingdom, situated in the heart of the South Pacific, consists of over 160 coral and volcanic islands, of which only 36 are inhabited. Best known among sailors is the northern group of Vava'u, whose maze of islets and reefs provides one of the best cruising grounds in the South Pacific.

The capital Nuku'alofa on the main island of Tonga-tapu is slightly more advanced than the outer islands, but even there the pace of life is unhurried and peaceful. A spacious new harbour allows visiting sailors to leave their yachts in safety while visiting this interesting island to see the mysterious trilithon at Ha'amanga, the blowholes at Houma, the flocks of flying foxes at Kolovai, the tombs of the Tu'i Tonga in the ancient capital of Mu'a or the more recently built Victorian residence of the present King.

Country Profile

Tonga was probably inhabited over 2000 years ago by migrants from Samoa. The Tu'i Tonga chiefs reigned over Tonga, and by the thirteenth century had created a Pacific empire stretching from Fiji to Niue. The first contact with Europeans was in 1616, with the Dutchmen Schouten and Lemaire. Tasman, Wallis and Cook were subsequent visitors,

Practical Information

LOCAL TIME: GMT + 13. Tonga is situated east of 180° but the International Dateline makes a detour to include Tonga west of the line. Take account of this in navigational calculations.

BUOYAGE: IALA A

CURRENCY: The Tongan dollar (T$) called Pa'anga has 100 seniti.

BUSINESS HOURS
Banks of Tonga (branches in Tongatapu, Vava'u and Ha'apai): 0930–1530 Monday to Friday and 0930–1200 Saturday. Business and government offices: 0830–1630 Monday to Friday.

ELECTRICITY: 240 V, 50 Hz

PUBLIC HOLIDAYS
1 January: New Year's Day
Good Friday, Easter Monday
25 April: ANZAC Day
4 May: HRH Crown Prince Tupouto'a's birthday.
4 June: Emancipation Day
4 July: King Taufa'ahau Tupou IV's birthday
4 November: Constitution Day
4 December: King George Tupou I Day
25, 26 December: Christmas

EVENTS
Vava'u Festival, first week in May
Ha'apai Festival, first week in June
Heilala Festival, first week in July

COMMUNICATIONS
Cable & Wireless, Queen Salote Rd, near Faua Harbour, open 24 hours, international phone calls, can send and receive faxes on 22 970, telex on 66222. Post offices at Nuku'alofa, Ha'apai, Vava'u: 0830–1600

Monday to Friday.
Emergency: dial 933.
The main gateway to international destinations is via Auckland and Fiji, and there are also flights to Honolulu via Apia, Western Samoa.

MEDICAL
Vaiola Hospital is the main medical centre for emergency treatment, Tauafa'ahau Rd. Tel. 23200. German Clinic, Wellington Rd. Tel. 22736.
Emergency – Fire 999, Police 922, Hospital 933.

DIPLOMATIC MISSIONS
In Nuku'alofa:
Australia: Queen Salote Rd. Tel. 23244.
France: PO Box 255. Tel. 23889.
New Zealand: Corner Tauafa'ahau and Salote Rds. Tel. 23122.
United Kingdom: Vuna Rd. Tel. 21020.

the latter naming them the Friendly Islands.

In the 1820s missionaries arrived and their influence helped to end the fierce tribal wars which had been raging for thirty years. In 1845 King George Tupou I founded the present royal dynasty, which can trace its origins back to the Tu'i Tonga. To avoid German colonisation Tonga put itself under British protection at the end of the nineteenth century. In 1958 full sovereignty was restored. The present king is Taufa'a-hau Tupou IV.

The economy is agricultural, based on the export of copra, bananas and coconut products. Tongan women are skilled in mat weaving, basket work and the making of tapa cloth, and there is a small handicrafts industry. There is some effort being made to start small industries relying on skilled handwork. Young Tongans are very tempted to leave for New Zealand, although strict immigration laws have made this much more difficult.

Tourism is being developed as a source of foreign revenue, but considerable aid is given to the kingdom by New Zealand, Australia and West Germany.

The Polynesian inhabitants number around 105,000. Most people speak English as well as Tongan. Christianity plays a leading role in the community. Until recently even swimming and dancing were banned on Sundays, which remains a day where all of Tonga is supposed to shut down, including the airport. The official church is Wesleyan, but there are lots of other denominations,

particularly the Church of Latter Day Saints (Mormons). Modesty in dress is essential in Tonga – in fact it is against the law to appear in public not wearing a shirt.

Nuku'alofa is the capital on the main island of Tongatapu. This is a flat coral island and heavily populated.

Tonga's climate is warm and humid, although less so than other tropical islands. December to March, which is also the hurricane season, has more rain. From April to November the SE trade winds predominate, although quick sudden squalls can occur from other directions.

Entry Regulations

Ports of entry
Nuku'alofa (Tongatapu) 21°08'S 175°12'W, Lifuka (Ha'apai) 19°48'S 174°21'W, Neiafu (Vava'u) 18°39'S 173°59'W, Niuatoputapu Island 15°58'S 173°45'W, Niuafo'ou Island 15°35'S 175°41'W.

Procedure on arrival
The Q flag must be flown. The captain should contact the harbour master or customs, who may or may not board the yacht. One must present the outward clearance from the last port.
Nuku'alofa: Nuku'alofa Harbour must be contacted on Channel 16 for clearance instructions.

Normally boats are instructed to come to Queen Salote Wharf, the large commercial wharf at the eastern end of the harbour or in the restricted anchorage area close to the wharf. If no contact is made on VHF, the boat should be taken to Queen Salote Wharf. Certain areas in the approaches to Nuku'alofa are prohibited for anchoring and these are marked on the chart. The customs offices are in a building near the cargo wharf, north of the harbour basin, open 0830–1230, 1330–1630. Boats are only cleared between 0830 and 1630 Monday to Friday and are normally boarded by immigration and agriculture officials. Fresh fruit, vegetables, some herbs and non-commercially packed eggs will be confiscated and destroyed. Yachts are not cleared in or out at weekends. If arriving outside normal hours, one should anchor with the Q flag flying close to the wharf and proceed to the wharf during appropriate times. No one should leave the vessel until properly cleared.

After clearance or if instructed by a customs official, one should then proceed to Faua, the small boat harbour or the designated yacht anchorage at Pangaimotu Island. Faua harbour just west of the Queen Salote wharf is close to Nuku'alofa town. The entrance is 8.5 ft (2.6 m) at low tide and dredged to a depth of 9–13 ft (3–4 m) inside. Yachts should moor Mediterranean-style on the north side. The area around the fish market on the south side must be kept clear for local fishing boat use.

Vava'u: On entering the harbour, one should go alongside the main wharf on the port side. Customs and immigration offices are situated by this wharf. Boats are cleared between 0900 and 1600 Monday to Friday. If arriving after hours or at weekends, boats are allowed to stay at anchor, flying the Q flag and not having any contact until clearance is completed.

Lifuka: Anchor in front of Pangai village. The customs office is by the small dock.

Niuatoputapu: This small island lying some 175 miles north of the main Tongan island group is a convenient port of entry into the Kingdom of Tonga for yachts arriving from the north. A small pass on the NW side of the island with a minimum depth of 12 ft leads through the reef. It is essential to line up the marks as the pass is very narrow. More markers lead to the anchorage area off the wharf. The plant quarantine officer will have to be taken to the boat by dinghy, but customs and immigration can be cleared ashore.

Niuafo'ou: This small island some 180 miles north of the main island group is a port of entry, although the anchorage off the main village of Angaha is not good. A better anchorage is on the northwest of the island. Clearance would have to be effected by dinghy.

Customs

Firearms must be declared on arrival and will be held in custody ashore until departure.

Dogs and parrots may be destroyed. Other pets will be confined on board. Animals, birds and plants need a quarantine certificate. Fresh produce may be confiscated. Garbage must be disposed of officially on arrival.

Yachts may remain in Tonga for longer periods, provided the necessary arrangements have been made with customs. A small daily fee is charged for boats left unattended. Equipment sent to vessels in transit may be imported free of duty.

Day sailing within the island groups is not restricted, but a Coastal Clearance Permit is required when moving between groups served by customs offices. Customs must be visited to obtain this Coastal Clearance. Harbour dues should be paid as the receipt for this will be requested in the next port. On arrival at the next island group, one must contact customs on arrival. When travelling between Nuku'alofa and Vava'u, or vice versa, one can request that the Coastal Clearance includes Ha'apai if intending to stop in that island group.

Immigration

For most nationals including Commonwealth countries, West European countries, the USA and Canada, a visa-free entry permit is issued for up to 30 days provided one has an assured onward passage and proof of sufficient funds. Some nationals, such as those from East European countries, need to notify the authorities before arrival and request permission for a visa.

Visas can be extended on a monthly basis at the immigration office in Nuku'alofa or Vava'u. One must have a valid visa at all times, so one should make sure this does not expire when moving between island groups.

Social customs

Anyone appearing in public without a shirt will be fined. Dress code is very strict as is Sunday observance, when no sporting or other strenuous activities are allowed.

Fees

Light dues: T$0.20 per GRT/month or part month.

Tonnage dues: T$4 per 15 GRT/month or part month.

Harbour fees: T$0.30 per GRT/month or part. On payment of these, a yacht will receive inward clearance for the rest of the islands, which must be shown when visiting elsewhere.

Marine reserves

There are some underwater sites of particular beauty and these have been designated as marine reserves. These reserves are for viewing only, collection of shells or marine life is prohibited and anchoring is not permitted near or in the giant clam reserves.

There are seven marine and coastal reserves around Tongatapu: Hakaumamato Reef, Pangaimotu Reef, Malinoa Island and Reef, Ha'atafu Beach, Monuafe Island and Reef, Mounu Reef Giant Clam Reserve (northwest of the yacht harbour) and Muihopohoponga Coastal Reserve on Niutoua.

Three reserves are proposed for Vava'u: the wreck of *Clan McWilliam* in Neiafu harbour, the coral gardens between Nuapapu and Vaketeitu, the Giant Clam Reserves in Hunga Lagoon, Neiafu Harbour and off Ano Beach. Giant clams are an endangered species and those tagged with a number printed on the shell or an aluminium tag should not be disturbed even outside of the reserves. Visitors are requested to show restraint in collecting other shells, by taking dead shells or buying them and limiting the number taken to one or two of each species. Over-collection of triton shells has led to an increase in crown of thorns starfish which in abundance can destroy the reef; and visitors are urged not to buy or collect tritons.

Waste disposal

Throwing any waste into the harbour or waters of Tonga is forbidden. As there are no refuse containers on the out islands, visitors are expected to carry all rubbish with them on board and dispose of it in one of the refuse containers in Faua harbour, on the wharf at Neiafu, or at the Moorings Base.

Sewage may not be pumped into the boat harbour in Nuku'alofa or Neiafu harbour. Holding tanks or toilet facilities ashore must be used. There are no pumpout facilities, so yachts are requested to discharge sewage outside of the harbour areas.

Warning

A dangerous area to avoid by boats on passage to Fiji is Metis Shoal (19°11.4'S 174°51'W), where there has been intense volcanic activity.

Facilities

In spite of Tonga's remoteness, facilities are surprisingly good and the setting up of a small industrial centre near the capital Nuku'alofa has encouraged several boating-related foreign companies to start operations in Tonga. There is now a boat builder in fibreglass, sail loft and metalwork machine shop, all of which will undertake repair work on visiting yachts. In the harbour is a small shipyard, which also undertakes metal and electrical work and there is a diesel engineer nearby. There are no chandlery or marine supplies as such, although essential spares can be ordered from New Zealand from which there are several flights a week. There are two slipways in the harbour, of up to 100 tonnes and 15 tonnes capacity. There is also a boat lift for up to 10 tonnes.

Fuel can be delivered by Shell tanker to the dockside but smaller quantities must be bought in jerrycans. Large amounts of water are delivered by tanker, although there is a water point in Faua harbour. Gas bottles can be filled at the Tonga Commodities Board. There are several supermarkets with a reasonable selection in Nuku'alofa and a good daily fresh produce market. Freshly caught fish is sold on the waterfront.

The Moorings charter operation based in Vava'u has ensured reasonably good yachting facilities in Neiafu. The Moorings maintain a workshop and can handle most repairs. They supply fuel and water. There is also a commercial slipway at Vava'u. There is a sailmaker in Neiafu. LPG bottles can be refilled locally. Paradise Hotel has dinghy docking space for visitors, water, showers and a mail service. There are two good supermarkets in Neiafu and a fresh produce market every day except Sundays. As in Nuku'alofa, gas bottles can be refilled at the Commodities Board.

Further Reading

Landfalls of Paradise
South Pacific Handbook
Cruising Guide to the Kingdom of Tonga in Vava'u
Tonga – a travel survival kit
The Pacific Crossing Guide
South Pacific Anchorages

Websites

www.vacations.tvb.gov.to (Tonga Visitors Bureau)
www.tongatapu.net.to (Informative pages specifically for yachts)

TUVALU

Formerly the Ellice Islands, the name Tuvalu means 'cluster of eight' although the group in fact consists of nine low-lying coral atolls. Only eight of them were inhabited when the name was chosen, but a small community now lives on previously uninhabited Niurakita, the southernmost island of the archipelago. The islands lie just below the equator and west of the Dateline, their nearest neighbours being Kiribati, 200 miles to the north, and Fiji, 600 miles south. With a total land area of only 11 sq miles (26 sq km), Tuvalu is one of the smallest countries in the world, spread out in half a million square miles of ocean.

The small island communities still lead a very traditional lifestyle. With the exception of the main island of Funafuti, yachts rarely visit the islands. Although some only have precarious anchorages in the lee of a fringing reef, the lagoon is accessible in at least two islands, at Nukufetau and Nanumea, and there are plans to open passes into some of the other lagoons. Particularly if sailing towards neighbouring Kiribati, one should try and obtain permission from the authorities in Funafuti to stop at some of the outer islands.

Country Profile

The first inhabitants probably arrived about 2000 years ago, mostly from Samoa, but also Tonga and Uvea (Wallis). The northern islands, especially Nui, were populated from Micronesia. A society under the leadership of chiefs developed and customs and traditions akin to Samoa remain today. The first European sighting of the islands was in 1765 and there was little other contact until the nineteenth century when traders, missionaries, and whalers came to the islands. The islands were named after the nineteenth-century politician Edward Ellice, owner of the ship *Rebecca*, which came to Funafuti in 1819. The blackbirders, who were slave traders, took hundreds of islanders to work in Peru, Fiji, Tahiti, Hawaii and Australia. The group became a British Protectorate and then part of the Gilbert and Ellice Islands colony.

During the Second World War the remoteness of the Ellice Islands spared them occupation by the Japanese. In 1943 Funafuti, the main atoll, was used by US forces as an advance base for the push to capture the Gilbert Islands. After a referendum in 1975 the Ellice Islands separated from the Gilberts and became Tuvalu, reaching full independence in 1978.

Most of the population work in subsistence agriculture. A considerable source of income is from a Trust Fund which was set up a few years ago by Australia, New Zealand and the United Kingdom. An unexpected windfall came with the offer of a US consortium to exploit the rights to Tuvalu's internet suffix .tv Apparently several US television companies are paying substantial amounts of money for the use of such an address. Other sources of revenue are the sale of postage stamps and copra, as well as the sale of fishing rights. Remittances from Tuvaluans working overseas as merchant seamen and in Nauru's phosphate industry are also important. Overseas aid remains vital to the economy.

The population is over 9000. Tuvaluans are

Practical Information

LOCAL TIME: GMT + 12

BUOYAGE: IALA A

CURRENCY: Australian dollar (Aus$) with Tuvaluan coins.

BUSINESS HOURS
Banks: National Bank of Tuvalu, 0930–1300 Monday to Thursday, 0830–1200 Friday.
Government offices: 0730–1600 Monday to Thursday, 0730–1300 Friday.
Shops: 0630–1730 Monday to Friday.

ELECTRICITY: 240 V, 50 Hz

PUBLIC HOLIDAYS
1 January: New Year's Day
7 March: Commonwealth Day
Good Friday, Easter Monday
June: Queen's Birthday
1 August: National Children's Day
1 or 2 October: Tuvalu National Day
21 October: Hurricane Day
November: Prince Charles' birthday
25, 26 December: Christmas

COMMUNICATIONS
On Funafuti the Telecommunications Centre provides long-distance telephone calls, telex and telegrams. There are satellite transceivers on each island and communications are excellent everywhere.
The airstrip on Funafuti, originally built by US forces during the war, is still in operation and there are regular flights to Fiji, Kiribati and Majuro (Marshalls). The outer islands only have links by a supply ship, which makes the rounds roughly every six weeks.

MEDICAL
There is a small hospital on Funafuti.

Polynesians and both Tuvaluan and English are spoken. All are Christian. The Church is very important in the community. Funafuti is the main island, capital and only port.

Tuvalu lies on the northern edge of the hurricane belt, and occasionally severe cyclones strike the islands, as did cyclone Ofa in February 1990. There is little seasonal change in the climate, although in October to March strong westerly winds and heavy rainfall can occur. The average temperature is 86°F (30°C).

Entry Regulations

Port of entry
Funafuti 8°31′S 179°12′E.

Procedure on arrival
Yachts should not stop at any of the other islands before clearing in at Funafuti.

Flying the Q flag, one should anchor for clearance near the wharf, where customs are located, the customs officials will come out to the yacht. The officials must be taken to the boat and back on land in the yacht's own dinghy.

Permission must be requested to visit any of the other islands. It is sometimes possible, but not guaranteed, to get outward clearance which allows stops at the northern islands if heading towards Kiribati. This concession has been abused in the past and permission to stop is no longer granted, except in very special circumstances.

Customs
Firearms must be surrendered. Animals and plants must be declared and kept on board.

Immigration
Entry visas are granted on arrival for one month, renewable for a maximum of another three months, if proof of sufficient funds can be shown.

Fees
Overtime is charged if a yacht clears in at a weekend. There is no charge during working hours.

Social customs
One should remove shoes before entering church, the maneapa (meeting house) or private homes. The drinking of alcohol in public is not permitted. Women should be covered from the neck to below the knees.

Facilities

There is a cooperative store selling mostly imported food on all the islands. Local produce is available on all islands, but the selection is limited – taro, coconuts, papaya and bananas.

Limited amounts of fuel can be obtained in Funafuti from the BP office next to the large fuel tanks north of the ship dock. LPG is available and tanks can be refilled locally. Water is scarce, as the islands rely on rainfall. In the rainy season, rain can be heavy and one can easily collect enough. There are only simple repair facilities available in Funafuti and nothing in the other islands. A laundry service is available at the Vaiaki Lagi Hotel.

Further Reading

South Pacific Handbook
Landfalls of Paradise
South Pacific Anchorages

Websites

www.members.nbci.com/tuvaluonline (Tuvalu online)
www.tcsp.com/tuvalu (South Pacific Tourism Council)

VANUATU

Vanuatu, formerly called the New Hebrides, is a group of over 80 volcanic islands in the Western Pacific. Espiritu Santo, Malekula, Efate, Erromango, Ambrym and Tanna are the main islands. Left alone by the Europeans for longer than other parts of the Pacific, Vanuatu leapt into the modern age quickly, while remaining a place where the rich Melanesian culture is kept very much alive.

It is the chance to experience a little of this fascinating culture that brings most sailors to this country which has been endowed with less cruising attractions than its neighbours. Nevertheless their beauty inspired James Michener to write his *Tales of the South Pacific* in which the island of Aoba, 25 miles west of Santo, was probably his Bali Hai. With the exception of the northern islands, the number of natural harbours is rather limited, with the notable exception of the main island Efate

Practical Information

LOCAL TIME: GMT + 11. Summer time GMT + 12 end of September to end of March.

BUOYAGE: IALA A

CURRENCY: Vatu (Vt) of 100 centimes. Aus$ are widely accepted and credit card transactions are done in Aus$.

BUSINESS HOURS
Banks: 0800–1100/1330–1500 Monday to Friday, some 0800–1100 Saturday.
Shops: 0800–1130/1400–1700 Monday to Friday, half day Saturday.
The lunch break is strictly observed.
Government offices: 0730–1130/1315–1630 Monday to Friday.
Business: 0730–1100, 1400–1700 Monday to Friday, 0730–1130 Saturday.

ELECTRICITY: 220/240 V, 50 Hz

PUBLIC HOLIDAYS
1 January: New Year's Day
Holy Thursday, Good Friday, Easter Monday
5 March: National Custom Chiefs Day
1 May: Labour Day
Ascension
30 July: Independence Day
15 August: Assumption
5 October: Constitution Day
1 November: All Saints' Day
29 November: National Unity Day
25, 26 December: Christmas

EVENTS
April/May: Land Divers of Pentecost Island
End of August: Toka Dance, Tanna Island

COMMUNICATIONS
VANITEL in Independence Park for international telephone calls, telex and fax. Open daily 0700–2200.
Post office, Kumul Highway 0730–1130/1330–1530 Monay to Friday, 0730–1100 Saturday.
Emergencies: Police Vila. *Tel.* 22222, Santo. *Tel.* 36222. Fire *Tel.* 22333, Ambulance *Tel.* 22100.

Air/Sea Rescue 22371.
There are flights from Vila to Australia, New Zealand, Nouméa, Papua New Guinea and Fiji.

MEDICAL
Central Hospital, Vila: 24 hours casualty department. *Tel.* 22100.
Medical facilities are limited outside Vila and Luganville.
Hospitals: Santo. *Tel.* 36345, Norsup. *Tel.* 48410, Lolowai. *Tel.* 38302.

DIPLOMATIC MISSIONS
In Port Vila:
Australia: Melitco House, Pasteur St. *Tel.* 22777.
France: Kumul Highway. *Tel.* 22353.
New Zealand: Prouds Bldg, Kumul Highway. *Tel.* 22933.
PNG: Room 6a, Bougainville Bldg. *Tel.* 22439.
United Kingdom: KPMG House, Pasteur St. *Tel.* 23100.

which has several attractive bays. One of the greatest attractions of the islands is a visit to the live volcano on Tanna, where one can ascend into the crater, the closest one can get to an active volcano safely anywhere in the world. Even sailing by the island one can be treated to a spectacular firework display, especially at night.

The land divers of Pentecost Island are one of the more spectacular sights in Vanuatu. Said to be the roots of the bungee jump, they are performed mostly on Thursdays and Saturdays at the southern end of the island. With some performances being more commercially orientated, one should negotiate fees for video cameras in advance and be ashore early as times and places may change quickly.

The majority of yachts usually reach Vanuatu late in the year, many of them as part of the annual Musket Cove to Vila Race in September.

Country Profile

The exact origins of the indigenous population are not known and it has been suggested that the Melanesians probably came from Africa thousands of years ago. They spread across the part of the South West Pacific which is now called Melanesia, and developed different cultures from Papua to New Caledonia. Isolation was broken when in 1606 the explorer Fernandez de Quiros, looking for land and gold for Philip III of Spain, came across Espiritu Santo, and believed it to be the mythical southern continent, which Ptolemy and Marco Polo had claimed existed. The islanders' first contact with Europeans was not propitious, as although they made efforts to be friendly, the sailors were very hostile. Quiros' findings were ignored when he returned to Spain. Over 150 years later Bougainville was the next to visit Espiritu Santo and establish that it was not a continent after all. Soon afterwards Captain Cook charted the islands, naming them the New Hebrides, although they bore little resemblance to the original Hebrides. Missionaries, whalers, sandalwood traders and blackbirders followed as they did in so many parts of the Pacific. Violence was common as the islanders tried to resist these intrusions.

By the end of the nineteenth century both French and English settlers had arrived, so the governments of both countries decided to set up a joint Naval Commission to keep law and order. German efforts to gain influence there prompted the creation of a Franco-British Condominium in 1906. It was popularly known as the Pandemonium, as it brought to the islands two sets of laws, education systems, two languages, and so on. However, it helped to keep the peace, and brought some development to the islands. Until independence, yachts could choose whether to clear in with a French gendarme or a British bobby.

During the Second World War the New Hebrides were in the forefront of the fight for the Pacific. Espiritu Santo boomed from a quiet backwater to a US base with ships, equipment and servicemen.

Independence was achieved in July 1980 and the islands became the Republic of Vanuatu. Its government is noted for the independent line they take in Pacific politics.

Vanuatu is a rural country and very fertile with crops growing all year round. Copra, cocoa, beef and, in more recent times, kava are the main produce. Tourism is Vanuatu's greatest source of revenue and is welcomed by most islanders. The capital Port Vila is a tax haven and offshore financial centre.

Port Vila, Vanuatu.

The 150,000 inhabitants are mainly Melanesians, calling themselves Ni-Vanuatu. There are also some Chinese, Vietnamese, Europeans, Australians, New Zealanders and small communities of other Pacific islanders. The national language is Bislama, which is a pidgin English. French and English are both widely spoken, and there are 115 indigenous languages. There are a large number of Christian denominations and also animist beliefs. Tanna is the centre of the Jon Frum cargo cult. Port Vila, on Efate, is the capital.

The climate is semi-tropical. There are two distinct seasons. May to October is relatively cool and dry, while November to April is hot and humid. January to March are the rainy months. The cyclone season lasts from December until the end of March.

Entry Regulations

Ports of entry
Port Vila (Efate) 17°44'S 168°18'E, Luganville (Espiritu Santo) 15°31'S 167°10'E. Tanna is scheduled to become a port of entry.

Procedure on arrival

Boats must proceed directly to one of the two ports of entry. Stopping at any of the outer islands is prohibited. Boats have been fined for stopping at Tanna before clearing in at Port Vila.

Port Vila: Entering the harbour one should fly the Q flag and call customs on Channel 16 or inform Port Vila Radio of one's arrival. Customs, immigration and quarantine will come to the boat, which should be anchored close to the yellow quarantine buoy off Hotel Rossi. Outside of office hours it may be difficult to raise authorities and one should just anchor and wait. A clearance certificate from the last port will be requested.

Espiritu Santo: On entering the harbour, one should fly the Q flag and call customs or Santo Port Control on Channel 16 or working Channel 12. They may not answer outside of office hours. If conditions are too rough to anchor by the old black quarantine buoy, one may pick up a mooring off Aore Resort on the southern side of the Segond Channel and make one's way to the customs, quarantine and immigration offices on the main wharf. It is not recommended to tie up to the quarantine buoy or the main wharf.

Tanna: Tanna was scheduled to become a port of entry in 2000 with the completion of the new airport allowing international traffic.

If visiting any other islands, one must request permission from the authorities, especially if wishing to stop at Tanna. A cruising permit is issued before leaving Port Vila and this allows the boat to stop at other places before clearing out of Vanuatu at Santo.

Occasionally, the authorities have given permission for boats to clear in and out from Banks/Torres or Tanna, even though the former are not official ports of entry. This is only possible by prior arrangement with customs and immigration and one has to pay the airfare of the officers flying in to clear the vessel plus their overtime charges. This is usually between US$300 and 400, but the cost can be shared between a group of yachts.

Yachts may be able to obtain permission to clear outwards for foreign ports via other islands within Vanuatu.

Customs

Firearms and ammunition must be declared on arrival and surrendered to customs, to be returned at departure, of which 48 hours' notice should be given. If there is a satisfactory locker on board, the arms can be sealed on board.

Private yachts are considered to be temporarily imported into Vanuatu and do not have to pay duty provided the yacht is owned by the importer and a stay of six months in a two-year period is not exceeded. Yachts must not be used commercially if temporarily imported, or they will become liable for duty.

Duty-free goods may be taken on board after clearance or when about to clear out in Port Vila, but not Luganville. One can take on duty-free in Port Vila, have it sealed until clearance outwards in Luganville. Customs may check it before clearance and the penalty for breaking the seal is a fine. One can order duty-free diesel fuel on clearing out both in Luganville and Vila.

Quarantine

Strict quarantine regulations are in force in Vanuatu and no animals, birds, reptiles, fresh meat, fruit or vegetables may be taken ashore. Also some of these goods may not be allowed to remain on board; the agricultural officer will decide this at the port of entry. If animals are landed, the owner will have to pay a substantial fine and the animal will be destroyed.

On arrival, the agriculture quarantine service's permission must be obtained to land garbage.

Immigration

On arrival immigration will issue an entry permit for one month. Extensions must be applied for to the immigration authorities, the maximum permitted stay being four months.

Anyone who leaves the yacht must obtain an air ticket out of the country immediately. The captain is responsible for notifying immigration when a crew member wishes to leave a yacht, and he will be liable for their repatriation unless released from this obligation.

No visas are required for visits of up to 30 days for nationals of Commonwealth countries, EU countries, Cameroon, People's Republic of China, Cuba, French overseas territories and departments, Fiji, Japan, South Korea, Maldives, Marshalls, FSM, Niue, Norway, Palau, Pakistan, Philippines, Singapore, Switzerland, Taiwan, Thailand and the USA. All others must obtain a visa in advance, valid up to three months, either from a British high commission or embassy, or direct from the Immigration Office in Vila, Private Bag, 014, Vila. *Tel.* 22345. The fee is VT2500 which is approximately US$25.

Health

Malaria prophylaxis is essential as malaria is endemic in Vanuatu. Conjunctivitis and the rapid infection of small cuts are a problem.

Swimming

Sharks are a serious danger in some islands, such as at Port Sandwich on Malekula, where visitors are warned not to swim. Swimming off black sand beaches should be avoided. Elsewhere it is advisable to consult the locals before swimming in the vicinity of villages. In some places, a red float close to the shore is baited with meat to catch sharks.

A taboo exists in Malekula which forbids a male to swim under a boat or canoe with women or girls on board. Those who break this strict taboo will have to pay a substantial fine to the village chief.

Fees

Overtime is charged outside of working hours on weekdays, all day Saturdays and Sundays.

Port and light dues of US$25 plus US$1 for every day spent in Vanuatu by the boat are payable to customs at the port of departure.

Vila Harbour regulations

There is an overhead power cable between the eastern side of Iririki Island and Vila, and no vessel whose height from waterline exceeds 69 ft (21 m) should try to pass under it except by passing close to the westward of the red buoy on the east (the Vila side of the cable), where the maximum clearance is 72 ft (22 m). It is an offence to contravene this rule and yachts not observing it will be fined and will also have to bear the costs of any damage. Yachts with taller masts can tie stern to the quay or anchor in the quarantine buoy area.

All vessels in Vila Harbour must show a riding light if at anchor, between the hours of sunset and sunrise.

Anchoring near Efila Island is prohibited due to a land dispute between the islanders and the authorities, so this area should be avoided.

Facilities

In Port Vila provisioning is good with some duty-free shops for visitors. There is a good market on the waterfront, opposite the Government building, Wednesday, Friday and Saturday mornings 0600–1300. Most shops are on Kumul Highway, the main street, and there are three supermarkets in town. Gas bottles can be filled opposite the Waterfront Bar at the Boreal gas shop or at the local filling station located by the large LPG tanks on the south side of the harbour.

To use the wharf outside the Waterfront Bar and Grill one should contact the local company 'Yachting World' on Channels 16 or 60. Water and fuel can be obtained at the dock, but it has been reported that the fuel contains both water and dirt and should therefore be filtered. Larger amounts of fuel can be delivered by road tanker to the commercial wharf.

Repair facilities in Port Vila are adequate and either the staff at Yachting World or one of the members of the Vanuatu Cruising Club, who share the same premises, will advise visitors on where to have things fixed locally. Repair facilities are numerous and can best be checked out by using *Yacht MIZ MAE's Guide to Vanuatu*, available locally. Radio repair can be undertaken at the Sound Centre who also stock duty-free equipment. A small company building aluminium boats undertakes metal work. Simple sail repairs can also be arranged locally.

In Santo provisioning is good from the local supermarkets and the fresh produce market. Fuel can be obtained from either Shell or Mobile and water can be obtained at Aore Resort, the main wharf, the small freighters wharf and in containers from the Beach Front Resort. There are a number of repair shops for electrical work, refrigeration repair, hardware, welding, hydraulics and engines. There are slipways for commercial vessels, but cruising yachts are recommended to use the slipway in Port Vila.

The outer islands have an increasing number of stores and shops, stocked with basic items. Especially well stocked is the one in Craig Cove (Ambrym island) and the shops in Lakatoro (Malekula). Both of these places also have banks and money changing facilities. Many small island resorts are extremely helpful to yachts and one can arrange provisions as well as guides and tours through the local village chief.

Duty-free spirits, or any other goods, should be purchased in Vila as these are not available in Luganville.

Further Reading

Landfalls of Paradise
Vanuatu – a travel survival kit
Yacht MIZ MAE's Guide to Vanuatu
The Pacific Crossing Guide
South Pacific Anchorages

Websites

www.tourismvanuatu.com (Vanuatu Visitors Bureau)
www.vanuatu.net.vu
www.tcsp.com/vanuatu (South Pacific Tourism Council)

WALLIS AND FUTUNA

Wallis and Futuna are two island groups separated by 150 miles of ocean in the central South Pacific. Since 1959 they have been joined together as a French overseas territory. Lying west of Samoa and slightly off the route to Fiji, Wallis and Futuna are not often visited by cruising yachts. The pass into the lagoon at Wallis is relatively easy to negotiate and there are several anchorages, the most popular and best protected being at Gahi Bay. There are also several small islets in the lagoon which can be used as day anchorages. Ashore one can come in contact with a relatively unspoilt Polynesian society where the rule of the traditional Polynesian chieftain, the Lavelua, still commands more respect than the French administration. The singing and dancing of the Wallisians is vigorous and one of the few places where traditional songs have not been changed by missionary influences.

A similar atmosphere survives on the smaller Futuna, which does not have a protected lagoon, but only an anchorage at Sigave Bay on the west coast.

Country Profile

The island of Uvea, as the islanders still call it, was first sighted by Captain Wallis, who renamed it after himself, while on an expedition to find the mythical southern continent. The mountainous Futuna's first contact with Europeans was with the Dutch explorer Schouten in 1616. At the end of the nineteenth century the islands became a French Protectorate. United States forces built a runway on Wallis during the Second World War, which is now the civil Hihifo airport.

Yam, taro, bananas and pineapple are the main produce of the economy. Remittances from islanders working overseas, especially in New Caledonia, and grants from France, provide important sources of income.

The Polynesian population numbers over 9000 on Wallis, and about 5000 on Futuna as well as a few hundred French nationals. About the same number of islanders live in New Caledonia and Vanuatu. Wallisian, which is similar to Tongan, and French are spoken. Most people are Roman Catholic and an interesting feature of Wallis are the massive churches built in the style of those in Normandy, rather incongruous on a tropical island. Mata Utu on Wallis is the main town.

The SE trade winds blow over the islands during the winter months from April to November. Winds are variable during summer when the weather is sometimes sultry. Westerly gales occur in summer and the islands are rarely affected by tropical storms.

Entry Regulations

Ports of entry
Mata Utu (Wallis) 13′17′S 176°08′W, Anse de Sigave (Futuna) 14°18′S 178°10′W.

Procedure on arrival
Wallis: Care should be exercised when approaching Wallis from the east as the island is reported to lie approximately two miles east of its charted

Practical Information

LOCAL TIME: GMT + 12

BUOYAGE: IALA A

CURRENCY: French Pacific franc (CFP)

BUSINESS HOURS
Government offices: 0700–1200 Monday to Friday.
Banque Indosuez, Mata Utu: weekdays except Wednesday 0900–1200, 1300–1500.
Gendarmerie: 0700–1130, 1500–1700 Monday to Friday

ELECTRICITY: 220 V, 50 Hz

PUBLIC HOLIDAYS
1 January: New Year's Day
Easter Monday
28 April: St Pierre Chanel Day
1 May
8 May: Liberation Day
Ascension
Monday after Pentecost
14 July: Bastille Day
15 August: Assumption
1 November: All Saints' Day
11 November: Armistice Day
25 December: Christmas Day

Also Wallis parishes own holidays:
14 May: Mu'a
29 June: Hihifo (Vaitapu)
15 August (Mata Utu)

COMMUNICATIONS
Long-distance calls can be made at the post office in Mata Utu.
There are twice weekly flights from Mata Utu to Nouméa (New Caledonia), Papeete (Tahiti) and Nadi (Fiji) connecting with the international network. There are also flights from Mata Utu to Futuna.

MEDICAL
Matu Utu Hospital gives free consultations.

position. Having negotiated Honikulu Pass, on the south side of Wallis lagoon, one should proceed to the main settlement at Mata Utu. One should anchor behind the small reef in front of Mata Utu. The captain should then proceed ashore and check in first with the gendarmerie, which is close to the church. The customs office is nearby and should be visited next. Both must be visited again on departure.

Futuna: One should anchor off Sigave and the captain should go ashore. One can land by dinghy at the dock and check in with customs and police in town.

Customs

Firearms must be sealed on board.

All animals must have a rabies vaccination certificate.

Yachts may stay a maximum of six months in a 12 month period without paying duty.

Immigration

Nationals of the European Union, Canada, Cyprus, Iceland, Liechtenstein, Monaco, Norway, Switzerland and the United States do not need visas. All other nationalities need visas which must be obtained in advance from a French diplomatic mission. Yachts on a short visit are usually exempt from visa requirements.

Facilities

The lagoon at Wallis is entered through the Honikulu Pass, which is easiest at slack low water. Diesel is available from the service station near the Gendarmerie. There is good provisioning in Mata Utu, where there are a few shops with a relatively good selection. The large supermarket Super-Wallis has an excellent selection, but is expensive. Fresh produce is available on both islands.

Only simple repairs can be carried out, but in an emergency one may be able to enlist the help of the military. Essential spares can be ordered from Nouméa.

Further Reading

South Pacific Handbook
Landfalls of Paradise
South Pacific Anchorages

Websites

www.wallis-islands.com
www.outre-mer.gouv.fr/domtom/wallis

10 South East Asia and Far East

Typhoons in the Far East, rumours of pirates in the Southern Philippines, restrictions on cruising in Indonesia – no other region in the world presents so many different problems to anyone planning to cruise there and all of them have combined to discourage many people from sailing to South East Asia and the Far East.

The need for a cruising permit and recurrent outbreaks of violence in Indonesia have dissuaded many sailors from visiting this part of the world. The threat of typhoons is very real in Japan and the surrounding area, although with proper planning it is possible to make the best of the safe season. The other risks are largely exaggerated and although some parts of the Philippines are considered dangerous, there have been very few reports of violent attacks on yachts in recent years although robberies are on the increase. Certain areas are best avoided and visiting sailors should also avoid the southern islands of the Philippines and the adjacent areas in Indonesia. Also to be avoided are the waters surrounding Cambodia and North Korea where the authorities do not welcome visitors of any sort. Although the People's Republic of China has now opened its frontiers to visitors, those arriving by yacht still have to go through a maze of formalities. Even Vietnam is no longer closed to foreign visitors and sailors in that part of the world have started adding Vietnam to their cruising itinerary. The same can be said of Myanmar, which also is putting an end to its long isolation. Together with Northern Malaysia and Thailand, this area has the potential to become one of the best cruising grounds in the world.

More than any other area of the world, South East Asia has long been associated with piracy. This has been on the increase in recent years and has resulted in the International Maritime Bureau (IMB) setting up a piracy centre in Kuala Lumpur. The centre monitors all reported acts of piracy and advises governments on how to combat them. Cruising boats have been affected very little, mainly because the pirates focus their attention on cargo ships. In the southern Philippines their target seems to be local fishermen. There is nonetheless some risk for yachts and therefore their owners are advised that in potentially dangerous areas, such as the Malacca Straits, the Sulu Sea, the Java Sea, off the Yemeni coast, the Somali coast and the proximity of Socotra Island, some precautions should be taken, such as sailing in company with other yachts, staying well away from the shore, ideally out of sight of land, and keeping in permanent contact by radio.

Facilities for cruising yachts vary considerably, and the countries which have their own boating communities, such as Hong Kong, Singapore and Japan, are also those where the best repair facilities are available. In all other countries facilities are very limited although in popular cruising destinations, such as the west coast of Malaysia or Phuket, facilities are rapidly improving.

BRUNEI

The full name of Brunei is Negara Brunei Darussalam. This small state, situated on the north-west side of Borneo, is made up of two separate areas divided by the Malaysian state of Sarawak. The 100 miles of coast are cultivated plain, while inland the highlands are covered by tropical rainforest. The western part is made up of Brunei-Muara, Belait and Tutong, and the eastern part is Temburong. Although small, the country is extremely rich because of its oil and gas reserves and the Sultan of Brunei is reputed to be one of the richest men in the world.

There are few anchorages on the coast and the many oil rigs make navigation difficult, especially at night. Muara at the mouth of the Brunei River has a deepwater port and from there it is 16 miles to the capital, Bandar Seri Bagawan. The offshore financial centre being developed on the island of Labuan has brought a much needed improvement in yachting facilities with the opening of a luxurious marina near the free port of Victoria.

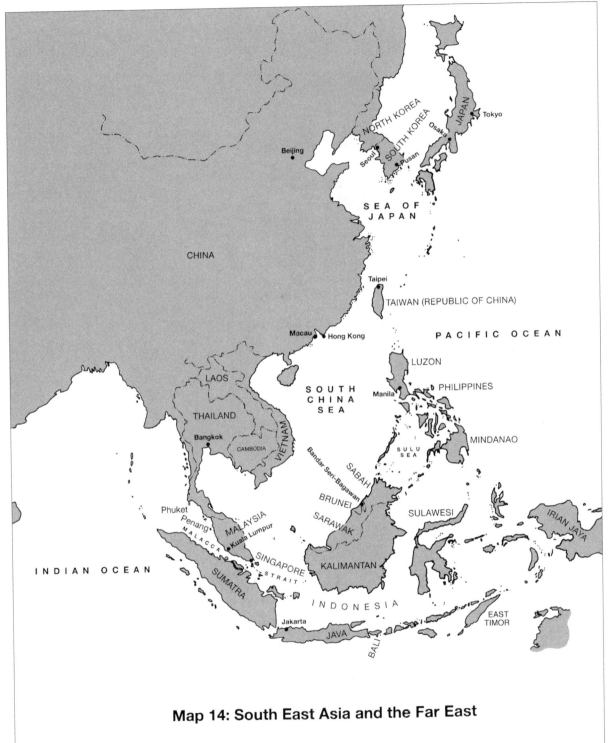

Map 14: South East Asia and the Far East

Country Profile

Negara Brunei Darussalam is Sanskrit for 'seaform'. Recent discoveries confirm that Brunei had links with countries on the Asian continent as early as the sixth to seventh centuries AD. During the fourteenth to sixteenth centuries Brunei became the centre of an empire, mainly due to the efforts of the seafaring Sultan Bolkiah, who extended his rule over much of Borneo, the Sulu Islands, and the Philippines. Islam came to Brunei in the fifteenth century. The first European to visit was Magellan in 1521, and thereafter others followed on their search for trade and territories and Brunei's empire soon disappeared.

At the end of the nineteenth century a treaty between the Sultan and Britain saw Brunei become a British Protected State. Although never a colony, Britain advised the Sultanate on all matters except those relating to custom and religion. Until the 1920s, Brunei was not seen as a very important part of the British Empire, but then oil was discovered and a new era of prosperity began. Negotiations with Britain led to a written constitution in 1959, introducing full internal self-government. Full independence was finally granted in 1984 as a monarchy.

The oil and gas industries dominate the economy, but efforts are being made to diversify, particularly to develop the agricultural sector to reduce dependence on food imports, which currently run at about 80 per cent. Because of the oil revenues, the people of Brunei enjoy very high living standards.

The population is about 300,000, mainly Malay and Chinese, some Europeans, Indians and Filipinos, also the indigenous Iban and Dusun. Malay is the official language, but English is widely spoken as well as Chinese, Iban and other native dialects. Islam is the official religion and is strictly observed by the majority. In 1991 the sale of alcohol was banned. However, other religions are freely allowed, 30 per cent being Buddhist and 5 per cent Christian. The capital is Bandar Seri Bagawan (BSB), called Brunei Town until 1970, when it was renamed after the 28th Sultan. Half the population lives in Kampong Ayer, a 400-year-old village built on stilts, which is the largest of its kind in the world.

The climate is tropical and very humid, averaging 77–95°F (25–35°C). There are heavy and sudden rains all year round, especially November to February during the NW monsoon.

Entry Regulations

Ports of entry
Muara 4°53′N 114°56′E, Kuala Belait 4°35′N 114°11′E, Bandar Seri Bagawan 4°52′N 114°55′E.

Procedure on arrival
Muara: This is the main port of this oil rich country. It is situated at the mouth of the river on which is also the capital Bandar Seri Bagawan. Port control should be contacted on VHF Channel 16. Yachts can anchor past the pier, close to the Royal Brunei Yacht Club. For clearance one must go to the ferry terminal near the cement works where customs, port authority and immigration are situated. One can go to the terminal by dinghy or by road (about 2 km from the yacht club).
Bandar Seri Bagawan: The port is up the river and is no longer used as a commercial port, but local boats use it and yachts can clear there.

Customs
Firearms should be declared to customs or police. There are no restrictions on animals.

Alcohol must be declared to customs on arrival. Non-Muslims may import up to two bottles of alcohol and 12 cans of beer.

Immigration
A visa-free stay of up to 14 days is given to nationals of most European countries, Canada, the USA, Japan, Thailand, Malaysia, Singapore, the Philippines and New Zealand. Proof of sufficient funds may be required. Nationals of these countries will require a visa if they plan to stay longer.

All other nationalities, including Australia, British overseas citizens and British dependent territories citizens, require a visa in advance, which can be obtained from Brunei or British consulates. Those requiring a visa and arriving without one may receive permission to stay 72 hours.

Fees
A visa costs B$15 if issued on arrival.

Restrictions
Muslim religious laws should be respected and no alcohol consumed in public.

Women should ensure that their heads, knees and arms are covered.

Facilities

Provisioning is good, as Brunei has a high standard

Practical Information

LOCAL TIME: GMT + 8

BUOYAGE: IALA A

CURRENCY: Brunei dollar (Br$) of 100 cents/sen. On a par with the Singapore dollar, the two currencies are interchangeable in both states. Sing$ can be imported/exported up to $1000, Br$ imported up to $1000. Indian and Indonesian banknotes are not exchangeable.

BUSINESS HOURS
Banks: 0900–1500 Monday to Thursday, 0900–1100 Saturday.
Shops: 0730–1900/2200 Monday to Thursday, Saturday.
Government offices: 0745–1215, 1330–1630 Monday to Thursday, Saturday

ELECTRICITY: 230 V, 50 Hz

PUBLIC HOLIDAYS
Muslim holidays are variable in date
1 January: New Year's Day
Chinese New Year
23 February: National Day
31 May: Anniversary of the Royal Brunei Armed Forces
15 July: Sultan's Birthday
25 December: Christmas Day
Variable: Israk Mekraj, First day of Ramadan, Anniversary of the Revelation of the Koran, Hari Raya Puasa (Idul Fitri), Hari Raya Haji (Idul Adha), Hijrah (Muslim New Year), Moulud (Prophet Mohammed's Birthday)

COMMUNICATIONS
International telephones, telex and fax available at telecommunication offices. Main post office, corner of Jln Elizabeth Dua and Jln Sultan in BSB, open 0730–1600 Monday to Thursday and Saturday.
Brunei international airport has flights to most Asian capitals, Australia, Frankfurt and London, Singapore being the most useful for connecting to European and North American destinations.

MEDICAL
The health service is good. A flying doctor service is operated. In BSB, RIPAS General Hospital, *Tel.* 42424. Ambulance 222 366, Police 222 333.

DIPLOMATIC MISSIONS
Australia: Teck Guan Plaza, 4th floor, Corner Jln Sultan and Jln MacArthur. *Tel.* (2) 229 435.
United Kingdom: Hong Kong Chambers, 3rd flr, Jln Pemancha. *Tel.* (2) 222 231.
United States: Teck Guan Plaza, 3rd floor, Jln Sultan. *Tel.* (2) 229 670.

---

of living and imported goods are widely available. The best shopping is in the capital BSB, where in the area bounded by Jln Sultan, Jln Pretty, Jln Pemancha and Jln MacArthur, one can find lots of shops. A good open-air market is held each day along the Kianggeh river, in front of a Chinese temple. Visiting yachts are welcome to use the facilities of the Royal Brunei Yacht Club in Muara and are given one month's free membership. There is a fuel barge at the river mouth.

Repair facilities for yachts are limited elsewhere and only simple repairs can be carried out.

Further Reading

Malaysia, Singapore and Brunei – a travel survival kit
Cruising Guide to Southeast Asia Volume I

Websites

www.gob.bn (Official site)
www.about_brunei/tourism
www.brunet.bn

CHINA

China is the third largest country in the world, a country of extremes from the harsh north to the tropical south. Since 1949 it had been a closed communist state, but the opening up of China in the early 1980s brought many tourists to the country. Cruising yachts have also been able to take advantage of the more tolerant attitude of the authorities, but the number of yachts that sail to China is still very small. In most places, foreign yachts are treated with suspicion and their freedom of movement is limited.

The Chinese Yachting Association is making great efforts to develop sailing as a sport and has achieved some remarkable successes in the Olympic classes. Most sailing is done on a club basis. The Yachting Association is keen to attract more foreign yachts to visit China, but is very much aware of the bureaucratic hurdles against which it is powerless.

The main fascination that China holds for visitors, including those on yachts, is the fact that most of the country has been forbidden territory for so long. Although there are countless interesting sites worth visiting in the interior, from the cruising point of view, China's coasts do not have much to offer. Most of the ports open to yachts are busy commercial harbours, facilities are virtually

Practical Information

LOCAL TIME: GMT+ 8

BUOYAGE: IALA A

CURRENCY: Renminbi (RMB) or yuan (Y) = 10 jiao. All records of exchange should be kept. One cannot import or export local currency. Foreign currency must be declared.

BUSINESS HOURS
Business and government offices: 0800–1230, 1400–1700 Monday to Friday, 0800–1200 Saturday.
Banks: 0900–1200, 1345–1630 Monday to Saturday.
Shops: 0800–1200, 1400–1800 Monday to Saturday (or 0900–2100).

ELECTRICITY: 220 V, 50 Hz

PUBLIC HOLIDAYS
1 January: New Year's Day
Chinese New Year (Spring festival), three days

8 March: International Women's Day
1 May: Labour Day
4 May: Youth Day
1 June: Children's Day
1 July: Founding of the Chinese Communist Party
1 August: Founding of the People's Liberation Army
1, 2 October: National Day

COMMUNICATIONS
International phone calls are most reasonable using card phones, which can be found in large hotels and telecommunications offices. International post and telecommunications office, corner of Sichuan Beilu and Bei Suzhou Lu, Shanghai.

MEDICAL
Hospitals are good and inexpensive in the main centres. Standards in Shanghai are among the best in the country: Shanghai No.1 People's Hospital, 190 Bei Suzhou Lu. *Tel.* (6) 324 0100.

DIPLOMATIC MISSIONS
In Beijing:
Australia: 21 Dongzhimenwai St, San Li Tun. *Tel.* (6) 532-2331.
Canada: 19 Dongzhimenwai Dajie. *Tel.* (6) 532-3536.
New Zealand: Ritan Dongerjie 1. *Tel.* (6) 532-2731.
United Kingdom: 11 Guang Hua Lu, Jian Goo Men Wai. *Tel.* (6) 532-1961.
United States: 3 Xiushui Beijie. *Tel.* (6) 6532-3831.

In Shanghai:
Australia: Suite 401, Shanghao Centre, Nanjing Xi Lu. *Tel.* (21) 6279-8098.
Canada: American International Center, West Tower, Nanjing Xi Lu. *Tel.* (21) 6279-8400.
Japan: 1517 Huaihai Zhonglu. *Tel.* (21) 6433-6639.
United Kingdom: 3/F Shanghai Centre, Nanjing Xi Lu. *Tel.* (21) 6279-7650.
United States: 1469 Huai Hai Zhonglu. *Tel.* (21) 6433-6880.

non-existent and the scenery only rarely matches that of neighbouring countries. As a cruising destination, China's attractions are rather limited.

Country Profile

An organised state existed in China in the twenty-first century BC, ruled by a succession of imperial dynasties, first based on slavery then on a feudal system. The Chinese elite were far ahead of the rest of the world in their culture and thinking, but then an isolationist attitude developed, which lasted until the nineteenth century when the European power, on the imperialist drive, sought to open China in order to exploit its vast markets. There were several wars, which resulted in Europeans securing trading concessions.

In 1912 the Imperial Regime, seen as hindering China's development into a modern state, was toppled in a republican uprising. The new republic, under Sun Yat Sen, was beset by problems and faced the opposition of the Chinese Communist Party, created in 1921, which temporarily allied with the new republican nationalist party, Kuomintang, under Chiang Kai Shek. The latter turned on the Communists and, led by Mao Tse Tung, the

Communists fled to the remote north-west. After the Second World War the civil war was renewed.

In 1949 the nationalists were defeated and fled to Taiwan, where they declared a separate state as the Republic of China. On the mainland, the People's Republic of China was proclaimed under Mao's leadership. Initially popular, the regime became too hardline for many, and the Cultural Revolution 1966–76 saw extensive purges. After Mao's death, there was a move towards flexibility, and a more pragmatic path was taken. The limits of this new spirit of reform were demonstrated by the massacre of students in Tian'anmen square in 1989. Relations with Taiwan have remained strained and the rulers in Beijing still refuse to have diplomatic relations with anyone who recognises the regime in Taipei.

China is mainly an agricultural country and there is little industry. With the lifting of economic restrictions in the early 1990s and the encouragement of foreign investment, the Chinese economy has grown rapidly although many industries remain state-owned and inefficient. Beijing (Peking) is the capital. At 1.2 billion people, China has the highest population in the world. The majority are Han, but there are also a multitude of national minorities such as Mongols, Tibetans, and

Manchus. Mandarin is the main spoken language, there being many minority languages and dialects. Written Chinese, made up of ideograms, is standard. Although officially an atheist state, many still follow traditional Chinese beliefs and Muslims, Buddhists, Lamaists and Christians also exist.

The climate along the coast is mostly temperate, although there are pronounced variations between the south and the far north. The tropical areas in the south are affected by typhoons, which are most frequent between May and October. The weather in winter is cool and the coast is under the influence of the NE monsoon. The summers are hot, humid and rainy.

Entry Regulations

Ports of entry
The following ports are those open to foreign vessels. Foreign vessels may not enter anywhere else. Basuo (Hainan Island) 19°06′N 108°37′E (also known as Dongfang), Beihai 21°27′N 109°03′E, Chiwan 22°28′N 113°53′E, Dalian 19°06′N 108°37′E, Dandong 40°08′N 124°24′E, Fuzhou 26°03′N 119°18′E, Guangzhou (Canton) 23°06′N 113°14′E, Haikou (Hainan Island) 20°01′N 110°16′E, Haimen 28°41′N 121°26′E, Huangpu 23°05′N 113°25′E, Jinshan 30°43′N 121°19′E, Jinshou 40°45′N 121°06′E, Lanshantou 35°06′N 119°22′E, Lianyungang 34°44′N 119°27′E, Longkou 37°41′N 120°18′E, Ningbo 29°52′N 121°33′E, Qingdao 36°05′N 120°18′E, Qinhuangdao 39°54′N 119°36′E, Quanzhou 24°54′N 118°35′E, Sanya (Hainan Island) 18°25′N 109°27′E, Shanghai 31°15′N 121°30′E, Shantou 23°20′N 116°45′E, Tianjin 39°06′N 117°10′E, Weihai 37°30′N 122°09′E, Wenzhou 28°02′N 120°39′E, Xiamen (Amoy) 24°27′N 118°04′E, Xingang (the foreign trade port of Beijing) 38°59′N 117°45′E, Yangpu (Hainan Island) 19°42′N 109°20′E, Yantai 37°34′N 121°26′E, Yantian 22°36′N 114°16′E, Yingkou 40°41′N 122°14′E, Zhanjiang 21°12′N 110°25′E, Zhongshan 23°03′N 113°31′E, Zhuhai 22°17′N 113°35′E (also known as Jiushou).

Yangtze River Ports: The river has a total length of nearly 4000 miles (6300 km), of which more than 1600 miles (2600 km) are navigable. During the past few years certain ports have been opened to foreign vessels but access to them is strictly controlled. There are 28 ports along the river, of which the most important are Nanjing, Nantong and Zhangjiagang.

Procedure on arrival
Intended ports must be notified one week in advance of ETA and again 24 hours before ETA.

Foreign vessels may not enter or leave ports, or shift berths within a port, without permission from the port authority and without a pilot being sent on board.

Vessels entering or leaving any port may be submitted to a quarantine examination and an inspection by the port authorities and other relevant organisations.

After having berthed in the place assigned by the port authority, the captain must present the ship's papers and crew's passports and also prepare the following documents: foreign vessel's entry report, crew list, import manifest and a customs declaration. Other documents that may be required are a valid survey certificate of vessel or builder's certificate, and the captain's certificate of competence.

Yachts intending to visit Shanghai must take onboard a pilot at the sea buoy. It has been reported that the pilot fee is extremely high, but the payment cannot be avoided as pilotage on the river is compulsory.

Before departure, the captain must submit a foreign vessel departure report, an export manifest and a list of crew replacements, if any have occurred.

In the recent past, some yachts which have visited China have not been obliged to engage the services of a pilot, although the regulations stipulate that this is compulsory. The same applies to the services of an agent, but as there is only one official organisation allowed to act as agents on behalf of foreign vessels, its services, or at least advice, should be sought by anyone planning to sail to China. China Ocean Shipping Agency (Penavico) is a state-owned company under the Ministry of Communications and is the sole organisation offering services to foreign vessels calling at Chinese ports. The company has offices located in many coastal cities.

Customs
Prohibited imports are firearms, pornographic material and any material considered politically offensive.

Valuables must be declared to customs on arrival.

Immigration
A visa is required by all visitors, obtainable in advance from Chinese embassies or consulates. The only exemptions are for citizens of Chinese

origin, as well as residents of Hong Kong holding a certificate of return issued by the China Travel Service in Hong Kong. The length of a visa varies from one to three months. Travel permits may also be required for visits to certain areas. Passports must be valid for at least two months after the date of the intended visit. After the vessel has been inspected by the authorities, in some ports crew members may have to apply to the Frontier Inspection office for landing permits.

Health

On arrival, a complete health declaration must be made. Malaria prophylaxis is recommended.

Restrictions

Vessels are prohibited from entering or passing through forbidden areas unless specially authorised by the relevant authorities. There are strict regulations concerning the access and movement of foreign vessels in Chinese territorial waters and ports. The most important regulations have been outlined, and although they may not be applied as strictly to yachts as to cargo ships or passenger vessels, anyone sailing to China should be aware of them.

No passenger or crew member of foreign vessels is allowed to photograph or make sketches of harbours.

Radios, radio telephones, radar, RDF, echo sounders, sextants, signal rockets, signal flares or signal guns shall not be used while in port. In case of an emergency or for dispatching urgent messages, one of the above may be used, but a report must be submitted immediately after usage.

Facilities

Yachting facilities and services are practically non-existent. The best repair facilities are those of the China State Shipbuilding Corporation. They control 17 yards situated in major ports along the coast. All types of repair can be carried out at these yards. Some of the ports where facilities are located are Dalian, Guangzhou (Canton), Quingdao, Shanghai and Tianjin. Although small local boatyards or workshops may be able to help in emergencies, the State Corporation should be contacted for more complex work.

Provisioning is also limited, particularly in rural areas, so one should arrive with a well-stocked boat and only rely on buying fresh produce, which is usually available. Limited facilities are available in

Xiamen (formerly Amoy), one of the few ports where sailing boats call regularly, mainly from Hong Kong. Shanghai is occasionally visited by boats from Japan, but facilities for yachts on this extremely busy river port are barely adequate. Fuel in small quantities is available in most ports; for larger amounts one may require special permission.

Further Reading

China – a travel survival kit
North East Asia
Cruising Guide to Southeast Asia Volume I

Websites

www.cnta.com (Ministry of Tourism)
www.chinats.com (China Travel Services tourist information)

EAST TIMOR

The latest country to join the community of independent nations, East Timor has only recently shaken off its colonial past. While hardly a cruising destination in its own right, once the situation reverts to normal westbound boats from Australia will be able to make at least a short stop in this small country which for the last three decades has been the focus of international news.

Country Profile

Timor is the largest and easternmost of the Lesser Sunda Islands. The island covers an area of about 11,900 sq miles (30,820 sq km). It is traversed by parallel mountain ranges of which the highest is Mount Ramelau or Tata Mailau (9,679 ft high/ 2,950 m). The economy is dominated by farming, the chief crops being maize, rice, coffee, copra and fruit. Deposits of gold and silver are found on the island, while rich oil deposits are believed to be under the surrounding ocean floor. The population of East Timor is approximately 700,000, most people being of mixed Malay, Polynesian and Papuan descent, but with a strong Portuguese influence. There is also a small ethnic Chinese community. Traditional religions predominate on Timor, and there are small Muslim and Christian communities.

The Portuguese established settlements on Timor in the early sixteenth century, and Dutch traders first landed on the island in 1613. The Portuguese and Dutch competed for influence until a series of agreements established boundaries between their territories. Dutch Timor, centred at Kupang, in the west, became part of the Republic of Indonesia in 1950. Portuguese Timor, covering the eastern half of the island, and the small area of Oe-Cusse (Ocussi Ambeno), in the northwest, was forcibly annexed by Indonesia in late 1975 just as Portugal was going to grant its colony independence. The Indonesian occupation led to a bloody conflict in which it is estimated that as many as 200,000 people have died. In May 1999, Portugal and Indonesia reached an agreement on a referendum for autonomy for East Timor, to be held in August 1999; Indonesia promised that a refusal of autonomous status would lead to full independence. Before the referendum pro-Indonesia militias in East Timor embarked on a campaign of terror and intimidation, under the passive eyes of the Indonesian army. Many people were killed and most of the island, and especially the capital Dili, were put to the torch. An international UN force, led by Australia, restored order and prepared the way to the referendum in which the majority of the East Timorese voted in favour of independence, their wish being reluctantly accepted by the authorities in Jakarta. President Abdurrahman Wahid, who came to power in 1999, has repeatedly stated his intention to normalise the situation and it is therefore expected that under his leadership the Indonesian people will accept the East Timorese decision to opt for full independence from Jakarta.

According to the Security Council resolution of 25 October 1999, until the territory obtains full independence, it will be administered under a UN mandate.

The country has yet to decide on the future form of government. Until details of the new administration become known, boats should make their way to Dili to complete clearance formalities. Up-to-date confirmation is best obtained from one of the East Timorese missions in the neighbouring countries, such as the one in Darwin.

Port of entry
Dili 8°32′S 125°32′E.

Websites

www.timor.org
www.easttimor.com (Latest news)
www.columbia.edu/icrp (Index on East Timor subjects)
www.etan.org/timor (East Timor Action Group)

HONG KONG

Hong Kong reverted to Chinese sovereignty on 30 June 1997, but its special status will continue for another 50 years.

Hong Kong is made up of the small Hong Kong Island, the commercial centre, and the Kowloon Peninsula, the main district for shopping and entertainment. Between the two lies the well-protected Victoria Harbour. Also part of Hong Kong are the New Territories, a large area on the mainland, as well as some 235 islands, many uninhabited, in the South China Sea.

Although offering limited cruising opportunities, Hong Kong is rarely bypassed by yachts cruising in the Far East, who are attracted by the excellent service and repair facilities available. There are several yacht clubs and a thriving sailing community, visiting yachts being always warmly received in this dynamic metropolis.

Country Profile

Hong Kong was ceded to Britain in 1842 after the First Opium War, when Chinese efforts to expel the European opium traders failed. When first colonised, there were few inhabitants, but archaeological discoveries have shown the area to have been populated thousands of years ago. Hong Kong became an important trade centre and gateway to China and after the Second Opium War the Kowloon peninsula was added. In 1898 a 99-year lease was granted to Britain for the New Territories. Hong Kong was occupied by the Japanese during the Second World War. In an agreement signed in 1984 China promised to respect Hong Kong's separate identity. Although there were some doubts about Beijing's long-term intentions, these were largely unfounded and Hong Kong's special status as one of Asia's economic powerhouses continues unabated.

Hong Kong is a leading producer of textiles and electrical goods as well as being a shipping, bank-

Practical Information

LOCAL TIME: GMT + 8

BUOYAGE: IALA A

CURRENCY: Hong Kong dollar (HK$) of 100 cents.

BUSINESS HOURS
Banks: 1000–1500/1600 Monday to Friday, 0930–1200 Saturday.
Offices: 0900–1300, 1400–1700 Monday to Friday, 0900–1300 Saturday.
Shops: Hong Kong Island, 1000–1800 Monday to Friday; Kowloon and Causeway Bay, 1000–2100/2130 Monday to Friday.
Government offices: 0830–1245, 1400–1700 Monday to Friday and 0900–1200 Saturdays.

ELECTRICITY: 200/220 V, 50 Hz

PUBLIC HOLIDAYS
Many holidays vary with the lunar calendar.
1 January: New Year's Day
Chinese New Year, three days
April: Ching Ming Festival
Easter
June: Queen's Birthday (two days)
June: Dragon Boat Festival
Last Saturday in August
Last Monday in August: Liberation Day
Mid-Autumn Festival
October/November: Cheung Yeung Festival
25, 26 December: Christmas

COMMUNICATIONS
Area codes: Hong Kong Is. 5, Kowloon 3, New Territories 0.
Overseas calls can be made from public phones and also from Hong Kong Telecom Offices for international phone calls, fax and telex.
Collect calls to nine countries are available on a push button basis.
Dial 013 for information.
Emergency: dial 999. Police Visitor Hotline. *Tel.* 2527 7177.
Main post offices: Connaught Pl., Hong Kong Star Ferry and 10 Middle Road, Tsim Sha Tsui, Kowloon. Open 0800–1800 Monday to Friday. 0800–1400 Saturday.
Hong Kong has excellent flight connections with all major centres of the world.

MEDICAL
Good hospitals, doctors and dentists with private and national health care.
Queen Elizabeth Hospital, 30 Gascoigne Road, Kowloon. *Tel.* (3) 2710 2111. Main emergency hospital for Kowloon and New Territories.
Queen Mary Hospital, Pokfulam Rd. *Tel.* (5) 28554111. For Hong Kong Island.
St John's Ambulance: Hong Kong (5) 2576 6555; Kowloon (3) 2713 5555.

DIPLOMATIC MISSIONS
Australia: 25 Harbour Road, Wanchai. *Tel.* 2827 8881.
Canada: One Exchange Square, 8 Connaught Place. *Tel.* 2810 4321.
New Zealand: 3414 Jardine House, Connaught Rd. *Tel.* 2877 4488.
Japan: One Exchange Square, 8 Connaught Place. *Tel.* 2522 1184.
Malaysia: 47–50 Gloucester Road. *Tel.* 2527 0921
United Kingdom: 1 Supreme Court Road. *Tel.* 2901 3000.
United States: 26 Garden Road. *Tel.* 2523 9011.

ing and insurance centre. Until recently, the New Territories were mainly agricultural, but now these are also becoming industrialised.

The population is over 6 million, mostly of Chinese origin from the southern provinces of China. There is a small European community, mostly English. Cantonese is the most widely spoken Chinese language. English is also widely spoken. Victoria on Hong Kong island is the capital. A mixture of local beliefs are practised – Confucianism, Buddhism, Taoism – and a small percentage are Christian.

The climate is subtropical. June to September is hot, humid and rainy. October to January is cooler and less humid. The typhoon season is from May to December with the highest frequency between June and September.

Entry Regulations

Port of entry
Victoria Harbour 22°18'N 114°10'E.

Procedure on arrival
The Hong Kong Port Operations Service operates on VHF Channel 12, call sign 'MARDEP' 24 hours a day. Yachts may be boarded and searched in Hong Kong territorial waters, as illegal immigration and smuggling are major problems. It is recommended to time one's arrival in daylight.

On arrival, one should proceed to the Western Quarantine & Immigration anchorage. After clearance one may go to a designated anchorage or yacht club. Within 24 hours of arrival one should report to the Port Formalities Office with the ship's papers and crew lists (Port Formalities Office, Marine Department, 3rd floor, Room 318 Harbour Building, 38 Pier Rd, Central). A General Declaration form must be completed and port and light fees paid. Any of the marinas or the Royal Hong Kong Yacht Club will advise on the correct procedure.

Procedure on departure
It is necessary to report to the Port Formalities Office again before departure with the necessary papers. A Port Clearance Permit must be obtained before departure, which is valid for 48 hours.

Customs
Firearms must be declared and handed into custody until departure.

All animals require a special permit, to be obtained in advance from the Senior Veterinary Officer, Agriculture and Fisheries Department, 393 Canton Road Government Offices, 12F Kowloon, Hong Kong.

Yachts may remain up to six months, after which a Pleasure Vessel Licence must be obtained, and the yacht must have third party insurance.

Immigration

In spite of Hong Kong's return to Chinese sovereignty, immigration regulations are different to those for travel to mainland China, where everyone must arrive with a visa obtained in advance. The situation in Hong Kong is far more relaxed and many of the previous visa requirements have remained largely unchanged. British citizens can stay for up to six months without a visa.

Nationals of many countries, including the USA, West European, South American and Asian countries, as well as Australia and New Zealand, will obtain a one-month visa on arrival, which can be

Victoria Harbour.

extended by another two months. Those allowed visa-free stays may be required to show proof of adequate funds for their stay. Other nationals require a visa to be obtained in advance from a British diplomatic mission.

Some form of photo identification such as a passport should always be carried while in Hong Kong.

Health

There may be a risk of malaria in some rural areas.

Fees

Harbour fees are HK$45/100 tons per day. Light dues are HK$37 per 100 NRT per entry. Outward port clearance is HK$50 per vessel.

Restrictions

Prohibited areas are Kai Tak Airport Area No. 1 and 100 metres from both Green Island and Stonecutters Island.

Typhoon procedures

Typhoons are most likely in September, but can

occur all year round. When a typhoon is expected, information and warnings are broadcast in 15 minute intervals day and night.

Visiting yachts may seek refuge in an approved typhoon shelter, of which there are 14 in Hong Kong for small craft, some for less than 50 m LOA, others for less than 30 m LOA. Alternatively one can secure to a government B class mooring, for which advance booking is necessary. Yachts too large for the shelters can either find a mooring or a sheltered anchorage, notifying the port authority of their position.

Facilities

There are various anchorages used by visitors, the most popular being the typhoon shelter in Causeway Bay, the small boat harbour in Aberdeen and Hebe Haven. There are several yacht clubs, which usually offer temporary membership to visitors if they are members of an overseas club or are introduced by a local member. Most clubs have some moorings and also repair facilities.

There are four major marinas, two on the east coast (Clearwater Bay Marina and Port Shelter) and two on the south side of Hong Kong Island (Aberdeen Marina and Aberdeen Boat Club). Clearwater Bay Marina has very good repair facilities, including its own travelift. Port Shelter, in Hebe Haven, offers good protection but fewer repair facilities. Aberdeen Marina is inside the typhoon shelter. Although facilities inside the marinas in Aberdeen are limited, there are many small yards in the immediate vicinity, which can undertake most repair jobs.

The Royal Hong Kong Yacht Club in Causeway Bay has the best location and is also a typhoon shelter. It has some places available for visitors on floating pontoons, but the maximum draft is approximately 10 ft (3 m). Moorings are also available, from where one commutes by sampan to the club house. Repair facilities are good and there is also a travelift. The yacht club is close to all amenities. If no space is available, it is better to try one of the marinas out of town.

Marine equipment is easily available and there is a well stocked chandlery at the Royal Hong Kong Yacht Club. Provisioning in Hong Kong is generally good and there is always a selection of fresh produce. Fuel is widely available. LPG bottles can be filled at Hong Kong Gas Co. Ltd.

Further Reading

Guide to Hong Kong Waters
Fodor's South East Asia
Hong Kong, Macau & Canton
Cruising Guide to Southeast Asia Vol. I

Websites

www.hkta.org (Hong Kong Tourism Association)
www.info.gov.hk (Government Office of Information)
www.hongkong.org (Hong Kong Trade Office)

INDONESIA

The Indonesian archipelago of 13,677 islands stretches from Australia to Asia, the largest island group in the world. The main islands are Java, Sumatra, Irian Jaya (the western part of Papua New Guinea), and Kalimantan (formerly Borneo). Indonesia is a place of tropical forests, neat terraced rice fields and active volcanoes, the most famous being Krakatoa. The culture is rich with traditions and relics from past civilisations as well as modern day arts and crafts.

For many cruising sailors Indonesia is the temptation of forbidden fruit. Access to this fascinating country is complicated by the need of a cruising and security permit (CAIT), which must be obtained in advance. Although one may be able to obtain it without the help of a local agent, the frustration and waste of time is hard to justify. The easiest way to obtain it is by joining the annual race from Darwin, which used to finish in Ambon but will now use Bali instead.

Whether taking part in this event or having obtained a permit through the approved channels, most yachts cruise the islands from east to west. Such a cruise along the island chain offers a panoramic view, each island different from its neighbour. Just as different are the myriad sailing craft one encounters along the route – single, double and treble hulled, from fragile one-man fishing boats to heavy inter-island schooners laden to the gunwhales with salt, turtles, copra or rice. Much of the inter-island traffic is done under sail and some of these craft cover thousands of miles.

On the more remote islands, rarely visited by foreign yachts, one may be greeted by a crowd of curious people. Elsewhere one can discover the

Practical Information

LOCAL TIME: GMT + 7 in the West Zone (Java, West & Central Kalimantan, Sumatra) GMT + 8 in Central Zone (South & East Kalimantan, Bali, Sulawesi); GMT + 9 in East Zone (Maluku, Irian Jaya).

CURRENCY: Indonesian rupiah (Rp) of 100 sen.

BUSINESS HOURS
Banks: 0800–1400 Monday to Friday, 0800–1300 Saturday.
Shops: 0800/0900–1700 Monday to Saturday.
Government offices: 0800–1500 Monday to Thursday, 0800–1130 Friday, 0800–1400 Saturday (this may vary between islands).
Business: 0800/0900–1600/1700 weekdays, half day Saturday.

ELECTRICITY: 220 V, 50 Hz. Some areas 110 V.

PUBLIC HOLIDAYS
Muslim, Christian, Hindu and Buddhist holidays are respected.
1 January: New Year's Day
21 April: Kartini Day
Good Friday
Ascension Day
17 August: Independence Day
25 December: Christmas Day
31 December: New Year's Eve
There are many festivals on Bali, which are public holidays, the most important being Nyepi Day in March, which is a day of curfew. Muslim & Buddhist holidays are variable:
Idul Fitri, end of Ramadan
Idul Adha, Muslim day of sacrifice
Muslim New Year
Moulud Nabi, birthday of Mohammed.

COMMUNICATIONS
International telephone calls, telex and fax from Kantor telephone offices, post offices and hotels. Central Post Office, Jln Raya Puputan Renon, Denpasar, Bali, open 0800–1400 Monday to Thursday, 0800–1100 Friday, 0800–1300 Saturday. New phones in larger cities and tourist areas take cards. International operator 102. Police 110. Ambulance 118/9.
There are international flights from Jakarta to destinations worldwide. There are also flights from Bali to Europe, Australia, the USA and Singapore. There is an extensive network of internal flights between the islands.

MEDICAL
Facilities are adequate in larger centres. Sanglah General Hospital, Denpasar. *Tel.* 27914, has a 24 hour emergency department.

DIPLOMATIC MISSIONS
In Jakarta:
Australia: Jl. M.H. Thamrin 15. *Tel.* (21) 232109.

Brunei: Wisma BCA, Jl. Jenderal Sudirman Kapling 48. *Tel.* (21) 571280.
Canada: 5th floor, Wisma Metropolitan 1, Jl. Jenderal Sudirman Kav. 29. *Tel.* (21) 510709.
France: 20 Jl. M.H. Thamrin. *Tel.* (21) 323807.
Germany: 1 Jl. M.H. Thamrin. *Tel.* (21) 323908.
Japan: 24 Jl. M.H. Thamrin. *Tel.* (21) 324308.
Malaysia: Jl. Imam Bonjol 17. *Tel.* (21) 336438.
New Zealand: 41 Jl. Diponegoro Menteng. *Tel.* (21) 330680.
Papua New Guinea: Panin Bank Centre, 1 Jl. Jenderal Sudirman. *Tel.* (21) 711225.
Singapore: Jln H R Rasuna Said, Kav. 2, Kuningan. *Tel.* (21) 5201489.
South Korea: 57 Jln Gatot Subroto. *Tel.* (21) 5201915.
Vietnam: Jln Teuku Umar 25. *Tel.* (21) 3100358.
United Kingdom: 75 Jl. M.H. Thamrin. *Tel.* (21) 330904.
USA: 5 Jl. Medan Merdeka Selatan. *Tel.* (21) 3442211.

In Bali:
Australia: Jl. Raya Sanur 146, Tanjung Bungkak, Denpasar. *Tel.* 235092.
USA: Jl. Segara Ayu 5, Sanur. *Tel.* 288478.

---

mysterious dragons of Komodo, explore the wild interior of Kalimantan, follow a funeral procession on Bali or visit the ancient ruins of Borobodur.

Benoa Harbour in Bali is the most popular port of call for cruising yachts. Bali is more on the beaten track, but the Balinese have retained a distinctive and rich culture as well as being renowned for their artistic talents.

Country Profile

Some of the Indonesian islands were populated half a million years ago, as proved by the Java man remains discovered in 1890. Gradually people migrated to Indonesia from Asia, and by the first century AD the Indian influence predominated with the growth of the Hindu and Buddhist Empires, which at the height of their power dom-inated the whole region. Empires based first in Sumatra then in Java followed, the latter surviving until the sixteenth century, marking the start of this island's dominance over the rest of the archipelago. During the fourteenth century the expansion of Islam through Arab traders marked a new era, and only on Bali does the Hindu legacy survive.

Marco Polo was the first European to arrive, landing on Sumatra in 1292, followed by the Portuguese in 1509, in search of the Spice Islands. At the end of the sixteenth century the Dutch arrived and for 300 years controlled the archipelago, which was known as the Dutch East Indies. In the early twentieth century the movement for independence gathered momentum. The Japanese occupation during the Second World War was a stimulus and in 1945 the Republic of Indonesia was declared. War with the Dutch followed until the UN intervened and in 1949 the independent state of Indonesia was recognised. Sukarno, leader of the national movement, became president, although his corrupt rule and attempts to draw closer to China were not popular. An attempted coup in 1965 by the Communist party failed. General Suharto became president in 1968, and his corrupt regime lasted until 1998, when his fall from power set in train a period of internal instability that threatens to continue for some time. East Timor's long struggle for independence came to a successful conclusion in 1999, when the disputed territory came under the occupation of a UN peacekeeping force. Ethnic and sectarian violence erupted in many parts of the country, the worst being in Ambon, which led to the suspension of the annual yacht race from Darwin. It is therefore essential that anyone planning to visit Indonesia should monitor the internal situation carefully and avoid critical areas at all costs.

Oil and rubber are important exports, also palm oil, coffee, tin and tobacco. Indonesia is rich in agricultural and mineral resources. Agriculture predominates, although efforts have been made to develop some industry. Tourism is expanding and is particularly important in Bali.

With around 195 million inhabitants, Indonesia is the fifth most populous country in the world. The Indonesians are a Malay race, but there are also Chinese and European minorities, and some aboriginal tribes in Kalimantan and Irian Jaya. Bahasa Indonesia, related to Malay, is the national language. There are 250 local languages and dialects. Often older people speak Dutch, and many speak English. Indonesians are predominantly Muslim, but Christian areas remain from colonial days, and the Balinese are Hindu. Jakarta on Java is the capital.

The climate is hot and humid. July to September is the dry season, December to January the rainiest period. Temperatures range from 75–90°F (24–33°C). The islands are under the influence of the SE monsoon from April to October and the NW monsoon from November to March, although land and sea breezes predominate close to the islands. The islands are not affected by tropical cyclones.

Entry Regulations

Ports of entry
Visa-free entry is permitted at the following ports:
Java: Tanjung Priok (Jakarta) 6°06′S 106°52′E,
Tanjung Perak (Surabaya) 7°12′S 112°44′E, Tanjung Emas (Semarang) 6°58′S 110°25′E.
Bali: Benoa 8°45′S 115°15′E, Padang Bai 8°31′S 115°35′E.
Sulawesi: Bitung 1°26′N 125°11′E, Manado 1°30′N 124°50′E.
Sumatra: Belawan (Medan) 3°48′N 98°43′E, Batu Ampar (Batam) 1°10′N 104°00′E.
South Maluku: Yos Sudarso (Ambon) 3°42′S 128°10′E.
Timor: Kupang 10°10′S, 123°34′E.

If one has a cruising permit, security clearance and also a visa obtained in advance, it is possible to enter at the first port marked on the cruising permit, even if it is not one of the above.

Although not listed as a visa-free port of entry, yachts on passage to or from Sri Lanka have been able to stop at Sabang, on Pulau Wé (5°53′N 95°19′E), a small island off the north end of Sumatra.

Procedure on arrival
Fly the Q flag, anchor and wait for officials to come to the vessel, during office hours. No one must go ashore or make contact with other vessels until clearance is complete. A small charge may be made for clearance outside of working hours. Arrival on a Friday afternoon should be avoided as many officials are Muslim and normally finish work at 1130 on Fridays.

Having waited on board for a reasonable time, if no official comes to the yacht, the captain should go ashore and contact the authorities. Usually the following offices have to be visited: quarantine, customs, immigration and port authority, in that order. Occasionally quarantine and customs may insist on inspecting the boat personally. This procedure only applies to major ports as in smaller ports, the officials may ignore the boat altogether, especially if it is anchored out of their sight.

In some ports local agents offer to deal with all formalities. Although the use of an agent is not compulsory, their fees vary between $25 and $50, which may be worth the time saved from doing the rounds of all offices oneself.

Bali: The pass through the reef leading into Benoa Harbour should not be negotiated at night. Yachts should proceed through the buoyed channel into Bali Marina, which is located in the NE part of the harbour. The marina monitors Channel 73 during office hours. The marina staff will carry out all formalities for a fee, which should be agreed in advance.

The customs, immigration and port authority offices must be visited again when clearing out of Indonesia.

Customs

Firearms may be left on board if they can be locked and sealed. If not, they will be taken ashore and bonded until the yacht leaves.

Animals must remain on board on most islands. There are severe penalties on Bali for landing animals.

In principle a yacht can stay indefinitely in Indonesia, provided the security clearance is extended.

Immigration

Passports must be valid for more than six months after date of entry.

Visas are not required for a 30 day stay for nationals of Australia, the EU, Argentina, Brazil, Brunei, Canada, Chile, Egypt, Hungary, Kuwait, Iceland, Japan, Liechtenstein, Malaysia, Malta, Mexico, Monaco, Morocco, New Zealand, Norway, Philippines, Singapore, South Korea, Switzerland, Taiwan, Thailand, Saudi Arabia, Turkey, UAE, Venezuela, Yugoslavia (Serbia and Montenegro), or the United States. All other nationalities require a visa, which must be obtained in advance. Israelis require special permission.

Those not requiring visas are given a tourist pass on arrival, which is valid for a maximum of two months, not extendable, and can only be issued at certain ports of entry (see list on previous page). If entry is made elsewhere a visa is required for all nationalities. It is, however, strongly recommended that all those arriving on yachts obtain a visitor's visa in advance from an Indonesian embassy or consulate.

Visas obtained in advance are valid for one month, extendable for up to six months. Matters are greatly simplified if one arrives with a visa, especially if planning to clear in at a smaller place. A good place to obtain them is at the Indonesian Consulate in Darwin, where one should insist on being granted a visa for three months. The extensions can cost up to US$75 and must be renewed monthly.

One should carry a large quantity of photocopies of documents, especially the cruising permit and yacht registration document, enough to be given to officials at all ports of call.

Crew wishing to join a boat or to leave Indonesia by air may find that immigration officials may want them to leave by the same means that they arrived. Their intentions should be made clear on the visa application and again on entry into the country. Crew arriving by air should have a copy of the cruising permit so as to avoid the need for a return ticket. It usually simplifies matters, if the skipper intends to temporarily leave the boat, to sign himself on as crew.

Cruising permit

Yachts without a cruising permit may stop in Indonesia, for 48 hours only, in a serious emergency and only at one of the ports of entry specified above. This may be extended in case of a genuine emergency.

Otherwise, all yachts must obtain a cruising permit and security clearance in advance. The formalities for this must be done through an approved agent. Agents should be chosen with care as yachts have sometimes not been dealt with fairly. The following details and items are required and should be sent with an application:

1. Details of the yacht (including photocopies of ship's papers).
2. The planned itinerary including last port of call before entering Indonesia, ports of call and approximate dates in Indonesia and destination after leaving Indonesia. It is wise to put down all the islands on the intended route as it is very difficult to make any changes later. Restricted areas are East Timor and Irian Jaya. Modifications may be made to the itinerary by the authorities in Jakarta.
3. Copies of the first few pages of all the crew's passports, which must be valid for six months at the time of applying for a visa.
4. A copy of a letter of acknowledgement, from the respective embassy in Jakarta or place where the cruising permit is being initiated, as an indication that they are aware that one of their citizens is sailing with his or her yacht in Indonesian waters. The wording of the letter should be approximately the following and addressed to:
   i) Department of Foreign Affairs
   ii) Department of Tourism
   iii) Department of Defence and Security
   iv) Department of Sea Communications

To Whom It May Concern

The .... Embassy, Jakarta, certifies that ....holder of...................passport number 000000 is a citizen of.......................and his/her passport is valid for travel to that country. Mr/Mrs

.... states he/she is the captain of his/her yacht .... registered number 000000 and he/she is requesting a sailing permit to enter Indonesian waters.

signed (Consul)

The cruising permit (or Clearance Approval) for Indonesian waters is valid for three months from the date of entry specified. It is important to specify this date of arrival in Indonesian waters fairly accurately on one's application, as the three months begins from this date, not the date the yacht actually arrives. If wishing to stay longer, one must have visas obtained in advance. Once in Indonesia, it may be possible to obtain a three-month extension to the original permit, by applying for a new clearance permit before arrival. The permit can easily be renewed every three months. Once all details have been sent, it is difficult to modify them, whether dates, itinerary or ports. For any substantial changes the initial fee may be charged again.

In recent years, Bali International Marina has been the most reliable source for arranging cruising permits. *Tel. +62 361 723 601, Fax. 723 604.*

Health
Malaria prophylaxis is advised. Cholera is a risk.

Restrictions
Travel to Irian Jaya requires a special permit from the State Police. Violence is possible in Northern Sumatra and South Maluku.

Fees
Overtime is charged outside of working hours. There is a harbour departure charge in Bali which is not included in the cost of the cruising permit.

Facilities

With only a handful of cruising boats calling at Indonesian ports and few locally owned yachts, it is not surprising that yachting facilities are only available in the few places where there is either a local yachting community, such as Java, or in those frequented by cruising boats, such as Bali and perhaps Ambon. The development of new marinas, such as at Carita Bay, near Java, or Nongsa, opposite Singapore, will undoubtedly bring about a long awaited change. The best situation is in Bali, still the most popular cruising destination, where there is a reasonable range of repair facilities. The opening of a marina in 1994 and the existence of a number of excursion vessels have consolidated Bali's position as a modest yachting centre. Bali International Marina offers all usual services, fuel, water and is a safe place to leave the boat if touring the interior. The marina also has a fuel dock, bar, restaurant and showers for visitors as well as being able to arrange the cruising permit. The long established Bali Yacht Services offer a range of services to visiting yachts, including entry formalities, and can be contacted on VHF Channel 11.

Spare parts and marine supplies are difficult to find and essential spares have to be ordered from Australia or Singapore. Outside of Bali, some repair facilities are available at Surabaya, on Java, where there are several boatyards, general workshops and sailmakers. Surabaya's main drawback is that it has no docking facilities for yachts and theft is a serious problem in the harbour. For any kind of repair in the outer islands, one has to rely on workshops that repair cars or trucks. The existence of a large fleet of sailing workboats means that there are small boatyards throughout the archipelago. The only spares available locally are those for some diesel engines, particularly if they are also used in trucks or heavy plant. Outboard engines are becoming more popular and some makes are now represented in the more developed centres.

Provisioning in most islands is fairly basic, although there is a good supply of locally grown fruit and vegetables everywhere. Water is available, but should be treated. Fuel is also widely available and relatively cheap as Indonesia is an oil-producing country. In some places the fuel will be delivered in drums and as it tends to be either dirty, or deliberately laced with water, filtering it properly is essential. In this respect too Bali is the best choice, with good provisioning, both imported goods and locally grown, fuel and water on the dock at Bali International Marina.

Further Reading

Cruising Guide to Southeast Asia Volume II
Indonesia – a travel survival kit
Bali & Lombok – a travel survival kit

Websites

www.tourism.indonesia.com (Ministry of Tourism)
www.balimarina.com

JAPAN

Japan is made up of four main islands that stretch about 1600 miles in a NE to SW direction off the Chinese mainland. Honshu is the largest, most heavily populated and industrialised; Hokkaido in the north is forested and mountainous; Kyushu and Shikoku to the south are smaller. There are also some 6852 smaller islands. Most of Japan is mountainous and volcanic, with frequent earthquakes. Mount Fuji, an almost perfectly symmetrical cone, is the highest point at 12,400 ft (3776 m).

Being distant from the popular cruising routes, not many cruising yachts visit Japan, but those who do find the Japanese very welcoming, often going out of their way to help visiting sailors. Until not so long ago even local yachts were a rarity as the Japanese have no tradition as a sailing nation. However, in the early 1990s the government decided to actively develop the yachting industry, more marinas were built, and various international regattas were organised. However, the one aspect that even the ingenious Japanese cannot do much about is their weather, which does not encourage cruising, for a cruise often turns into a battle against wind and current.

Fortunately this one major disadvantage is made up for by the many attractions that Japan offers the visiting sailor. One major attraction is the Inland Sea (Seto Naikai), a large body of water, connected by three passes to the surrounding ocean, which allows a yacht access into the very heart of the country. The place abounds with pretty anchorages or small fishing harbours, but there are also many marinas as well as yacht clubs, which usually offer hospitality to visitors. Those in the smaller places have only basic facilities, while in the larger towns clubs are on a par with the best yacht clubs in Europe or America. Although there is a lot of traffic in coastal waters, both commercial and fish-

Practical Information

LOCAL TIME: GMT + 9

BUOYAGE: IALA B

CURRENCY: Yen ¥ (JYE)

BUSINESS HOURS
Banks: 0900–1500 Monday to Friday.
Government offices: 0830–1700 Monday to Friday.
Business: 0900–1700 Monday to Friday, 0900–1200 Saturday.
Shops: 1000–1800 Monday to Friday, 0900–1200 Saturday.

ELECTRICITY: 100 V, 50 Hz (east), 60 Hz (west), the dividing line being approximately half way between Tokyo and Nagoya.

PUBLIC HOLIDAYS
Japan uses the western calendar, but some official publications such as tide tables use the Heisei calendar. This has the same days, but the Heisei year started in 1989 and 2000 would be 12 in the Heisei calendar.
1–3 January: New Year
2nd Monday in January: Coming of Age
11 February: National Foundation
20/21 March: Vernal Equinox

29 April: Greenery Day
3 May: Constitution Day
5 May: Children's Day
20 July: Marine Day
15 September: Respect for the Aged
23/24 September: Autumnal Equinox
2nd Monday in October: Physical Education Day
3 November: Culture Day
23/24 November: Labour Day
23 December: Emperor's birthday
When a national holiday falls on a Sunday, the following Monday is a holiday.
During Golden Week (April 29–May 5) and Obon festival (late July to the third week in August) most people are on holiday.

COMMUNICATIONS
Telephone directories in English are available in some places.
International calls can be made from hotels or post offices. Only a few public phone booths allow direct international dialling. Blue phone booths are for emergencies, operator and information.
Emergency: dial 110 police (Koban), 119 fire/ambulance (push the red button first).
Telex and telegrams can be sent from KDD (Kokusai Denshin Denwa Co. Ltd).
Post offices for stamps and telegrams: open 0900–1600 Monday to Friday.
Travel Phone: for English language

assistance and travel information: Tokyo (3) 3502-1461, Kyoto (75) 371-5649, Eastern region 0120-222800, Western region 0120-4448000.
There are international flights from all Japan's main cities, particularly Tokyo, Nagoya, Okinawa and Osaka, which have regular flights to Europe, America and Asia. There is also a good network of internal flights.

MEDICAL
Medical facilities are of a high standard and there are many English-speaking staff.

DIPLOMATIC MISSIONS
In Tokyo:
Australia: 2-1-14 Mita Minato-ku 108-0093. *Tel.* (3) 5232-4111.
Canada: 3-38 Asasaka, 7-Chome, Minato-ku, 107-0052. *Tel.* (3) 3408-2101.
New Zealand: 20-40 Kamiyama-cho, Shibuya-ku, 150-0047. *Tel.* (3) 3467-2271.
South Korea: 205 Minami-Azabu, Minato-ku 106-0047. *Tel.* (3) 3452-7611.
Taiwan: 5-20-2 Shiroganedai. *Tel.* (3) 3280-7811.
United Kingdom: 1 Ichiban-cho, Chiyoda-ku, 102-0082. *Tel.* (3) 5211-1100.
United States: 10-1 Akasaka 1-Chome, Minato-ku, 107-0052. *Tel.* (3) 3224-5151.

ing vessels, even sailing at night does not present great problems as all vessels are well lit and sailed with due considerations to other vessels. Fog may be a problem at times so having radar is essential. Although typhoons are a constant threat, weather forecasts and faxes are good and reliable, and almost every port has a typhoon shelter.

Country Profile

The earliest inhabitants of these islands probably came from Korea and China, although links with South East Asia are also a possibility. By the fourth century AD the country was already developing into a united state and a distinctive national culture emerged with Chinese, Korean and Buddhist influences. The latter mixed with Shinto became the state religion. In the eighth century in the capital Kyoto both arts and industry flourished, although the provinces remained poor and were infested with bandits, which prompted the rise of the class of 'samurai' warriors.

At the end of the twelfth century civil wars between leading clans disrupted the country and a system of military governments was created led by the 'shogun' chiefs with a puppet emperor. This form of government lasted into the nineteenth century. A period followed which rejected all foreign influences and contact with the outside world until 1853 when the American Commodore Perry's visit began the opening up of Japan. At the end of the nineteenth and in the early twentieth century, a new spirit arose, introducing industry and modernity into the country. An expansionist policy abroad led to wars with Russia and China, military rule in the 1930s and the Pacific War from 1941. Japan finally surrendered following the nuclear bombing of Hiroshima and Nagasaki in August 1945. In 1989, after the death of Hirohito, his son Akihito became Emperor.

After continuous rule by the Liberal Democratic Party since 1955, the 1990s saw corruption scandals undermine its power and coalition governments have been formed. The economy has also experienced a recession after the 1980s boom.

From the 1960s Japan became one of the world leaders in economic affairs. Expanding industries are petrochemicals, electronics, optics and motor vehicles.

The population numbers around 125 million. The Japanese are descended from a mixture of peoples from the East Asian region, although some people in the north are possibly indigenous.

Tokyo, Osaka and Yokohama are the main cities. Tokyo, the capital, is one of the world's most populous cities. Japanese is the main language and English is the second language spoken. Shintoism, which is native to Japan and a development of early shamanism and animism, is the main religion. Buddhism is also widespread and many Japanese observe the ceremonies of both religions. There is a small percentage of Christians.

The north is cold, while the south is in the monsoon belt. Most of the country is in a temperate four seasonal zone. Summer sees SE winds and a rainy season in June and July. Typhoons are most frequent mid-July to October, but can occur at any time; five to ten days' warning are usually given.

Entry Regulations

Ports of entry
Aioi 34°46′N 134°28′E, Fukuyama 34°26′N 133°27′E, Kobe 34°40′N 135°13′E, Nagasaki 32°43′N 129°50′E, Nagoya 35°03′N 136°51′E, Naha (Okinawa Island) 26°13′N 127°40′E, Osaka 34°39′N 135°24′E, Shimonoseki 33°56′N 130°56′E, Tokyo 35°41′N 139°44′E, Yokohama 35°27′N 139°40′E.

Although only the above are listed as actual official ports of entry, in practice visiting yachts could be cleared in any port, as all have the relevant offices.

Procedure on arrival
Port Control must be contacted on Channel 16 before arrival and given an ETA so that the relevant authorities can be advised. The formalities are time-consuming as there are lots of forms to fill in, but this is mostly routine and officials are always very friendly and courteous. On entry, inspections will be carried out by quarantine, customs and immigration, and maybe also the Maritime Safety Agency (coastguard). A de-ratting certificate must be shown. If one does not have a de-ratting certificate, the yacht is checked by inspectors. The customs, immigration and quarantine offices are normally in the same building in the main harbour – sometimes one can tie up to their jetty to complete the formalities. They will advise on the best berth or anchorage. Sometimes they will come to the yacht, if not the captain should go to their offices.

Clearance with customs and immigration must be carried out at every port, although this is routine and a question of filling out a lot of forms. The last port may telephone ahead to the next port to notify them of a yacht's arrival. Alternatively the number can be obtained from the last customs office and one can telephone oneself on arrival. If arriving at a weekend officials may decide only to come on Monday, but one should attempt to arrive on a weekday as immigration cannot be done on weekends. If a place does not have a customs office, one should check in and out at the local police station (Koban); in these places the Maritime Safety Agency may check the yacht themselves. The Maritime Safety Agency office can often be a useful source of local information.

Customs

Firearms and ammunition must be declared on arrival and the penalty for non-declaration is imprisonment. Arms will be sealed on board or kept in custody ashore.

If wishing to import animals, one should have all the necessary certificates and undergo quarantine inspection. Dogs require a rabies inoculation certificate and may be quarantined. Dogs may be inspected on board after 14 days. Cats do not need a certificate. Otherwise animals must be confined on board.

Immigration

In principle, all visitors must obtain visas before arriving in Japan, but for many nationalities on a visit solely for tourist purposes, the visa requirement is waived, and one is accorded the 4-1-4 status. This is a short stay status. Should one wish to enter into any other sort of activity, the regulations become very much more complicated.

No visa is required for stays of not more than six months for tourists from Austria, Germany, Ireland, Liechtenstein, Mexico, Switzerland and the United Kingdom (except for UK colonial territories).

No visa is required if staying up to three months for nationals of Argentina, Bahamas, Barbados, Belgium, Canada, Chile, Colombia, Costa Rica, Croatia, Cyprus, Dominican Republic, Denmark, El Salvador, Finland, France, Greece, Guatemala, Honduras, Iceland, Israel, Italy, Lesotho, Luxembourg, Malaysia, Malta, Mauritius, the Netherlands, New Zealand, Norway, Peru, Portugal (except for present or former Portuguese colonial territories), San Marino, Singapore, Slovenia, Spain, Suriname, Sweden, Tunisia, Turkey, Uruguay, the USA and Yugoslavia (Serbia and Montenegro).

All other nationalities must obtain a visa in advance. For citizens of a country without a visa-waiving agreement (including Australia and South Africa) on entry into Japan usually 60 days is granted, normally extendable for two further 60-

day periods, after which one must leave Japan, and re-enter having obtained another visa elsewhere.

Entry will be refused to Taiwanese and North Korean passport holders.

It is possible to obtain a multiple entry visa.

One may be able to leave the boat in Japan and re-enter for another period.

Fees

There are no charges for clearance or overtime.

Cruising permit

To cruise the Inland Sea (Seto Naikai) a cruising permit must be obtained from the Department of Transportation in Hiroshima. One must present a planned itinerary, first checking which ports are off limits.

The local tourist office can provide a map of the area which shows all the attractions.

Restrictions

A number of ports are closed to yachts, such as Urakawa (in the SE of Hokkaido), and these can only be entered in an emergency.

VHF Channel 16 is primarily a shipping communications channel and should only be used in an emergency.

Navigation

Day-sailing is recommended along the Japanese coastlines due to the very high concentration of shipping and the innumerable fishing boats, nets and aquaculture projects. Along the Hokkaido coast a hazard are the salmon nets, up to 1000 m long and lying very close to the surface.

Currents can be very strong in the Inland Sea, especially at the entrances, where they may reach 6–8 knots.

Facilities

Most things are available in Japan, but are extremely expensive in comparison to Europe or America. Chandleries are well-stocked, but expensive. Ironically, even Japanese electronic equipment costs more in Japan than abroad, particularly compared to the USA. Locally produced sails and nautical charts also cost much more than their equivalent elsewhere and the same applies to provisions, so it is best to arrive with all necessary supplies and a well-stocked boat. Local fresh produce is more reasonable. Fuel, water and LPG are available everywhere.

Repair facilities are generally good and there are

boatyards in most ports. Prices for haul-outs vary greatly, but appear to be more reasonable away from the large cities.

Marinas in the Inland Sea are generally expensive, but some of them offer free berthing to foreign visitors for a few days. There are no charges for tying up to a dock in a commercial or fishing harbour. There are many yacht clubs, most of whom give free membership to visiting foreign sailors. It is best to approach them for advice if in need of a repair job or if one cannot find something. The best marinas are in the Osaka area, where six marinas are strategically placed around the large bay. The most convenient is in the port of Osaka itself, but there may not be space available. The marina at Wakayama, on the east side of the bay, south of the new international airport at Kansai, has very good facilities and is linked by train to Osaka and beyond. There are as yet no marina facilities for visitors in the Tokyo area, while at the opposite end of the country, new marinas have now been built in Nagasaki, Sasebo and Fukuoka. Naha Harbour in Okinawa has an American Seaman's Club, near the small boat harbour, which is very helpful. They offer temporary membership and can help find workshops for repairs.

Further Reading

Japan Handbook
North East Asia
Japan – a travel survival kit
The Japan Hydrographic Department publishes harbour guide books for all of Japan, including the small harbours. Although written in Japanese, these are basically a collection of very detailed charts. They are essential for cruising in Japan, and can be ordered from the department's Service Centre, No. 3-1 5-Chome Chuo-ku, Tokyo 103-0000. *Tel.* (3) 3543-0689.

Website

www.jnto.go.jp (Japanese Tourism Office)

MACAO

On the south-eastern coast of China, Macao consists of the peninsula on which the city of Macao is built, and the islands of Taipa and Coloane in the Pearl River delta. After nearly five centuries under Portuguese administration, Macao reverted to China at the end of 1999. Similar to Hong Kong, the government in Beijing has guaranteed the unimpeded continuation of Macao's status as a centre for international commerce. The town is a fascinating mixture of old colonial styles and Chinese and as it has retained more of its old character, it is more interesting to visit than neighbouring Hong Kong.

Country Profile

Before the Portuguese arrived in the sixteenth century, there was only a Chinese village and when the Portuguese sailors asked the name, the locals replied 'A-Ma-Gao', Bay of A-Ma, who was a Chinese goddess popular with seafarers and fishermen. A-Ma-Gao became corrupted into the name Macao. Macao prospered as China and Japan began trading with the European powers. This Portuguese territory also became a base for the introduction of Christianity into China and Japan. The Dutch tried to invade Macao several times in the seventeenth century without success. This privileged trading position ended with the establishment of Hong Kong by the British in the mid-nineteenth century, only 40 miles north-east of Macao and with a better deepwater port. Macao reverted to Chinese sovereignty at midnight on 31 December 1999. An agreement with China guarantees the continuation of Macau's capitalist economy for 50 years.

The population of around 500,000 are mostly Chinese with about 3 per cent Portuguese and other Europeans. Portuguese and Cantonese are the official languages, but English is widely spoken. The main religions are Buddhism, Catholicism and Protestantism.

Temperatures average 57°F (14°C) in January and 82°F (28°C) in July and there is high humidity. The best period is the autumn, October to December. May to September is hot and humid, with occasional typhoons.

Entry Regulations

Port of entry
Macao 22°12′N 113°33′E.

Procedure on arrival
Marine Police should be contacted on Channel 16 who may allow a yacht to use their own basin in

Practical Information

LOCAL TIME: GMT + 8

BUOYAGE: IALA A

CURRENCY: Pataca of 100 avos. Hong Kong $ accepted at par value.

BUSINESS HOURS
Banks: 0900–1700 Monday to Friday, 0900–1200 Saturday.
Shops: 1000–2000 Monday to Saturday. Some close first day of each month.
Government offices: 0840–1300, 1500–1700 Monday to Friday, 0840–1300 Saturday.

ELECTRICITY: 110/220 V, 50 Hz

PUBLIC HOLIDAYS
1 January: New Year's Day
January/February: Chinese New Year
Easter
1 May: Labour Day
June: Dragon Boat Festival
September: Autumn Festival
1 October: Chinese National Day

COMMUNICATIONS
International calls can be made from the post office, Leal Senado Square open 0900–1730 Monday to Friday, 0900–1230

Saturdays. The telephone office next door is open 0800–2400 Monday to Saturday, 0900–2400 Sunday.
Emergency 999, Police 57 3333.
There are regular flights to Europe and neighbouring Asian countries. There is a hydrofoil service to Hong Kong.

MEDICAL
Government Hospital. *Tel.* 51 44 99.

the inner harbour, which has a depth of only 9 ft (2.70 m). Otherwise one should be prepared to anchor in the river, which can be quite uncomfortable and should only be used in settled weather. The outer harbour is used mainly for ferries and hydrofoils going to Hong Kong. If the yacht is not visited by officials the captain should go to the harbour master's office with the ship's papers.

On departure, the harbour master should be notified not later than six hours before departure.

Customs
Animals and firearms should be declared to customs.

Immigration
Visas for a stay of up to 20 days are granted on arrival to citizens of Australia, Austria, Belgium, Brazil, Czech Republic, Canada, Denmark, Estonia, France, Germany, Greece, India, Italy, Japan, Luxembourg, Malaysia, Mexico, New Zealand, Norway, Philippines, Poland, Portugal, Ireland, Singapore, South Africa, South Korea, Spain, Sweden, Switzerland, Thailand, United Kingdom, United States, and Uruguay. There is a fee of MOP100 for an individual visa, or MOP200 for a family visa.

Facilities

Repair facilities are available at a government workshop in the port area, which also has a slipway. However, because of the proximity of Hong Kong, it is preferable to use the better facilities available there. Provisioning is good, although the selection is not as wide as in Hong Kong.

Further Reading

Northeast Asia on a Shoestring
Hong Kong, Macau & Canton – a travel survival kit
Cruising Guide to Southeast Asia Vol. I

Websites

www.macau.gov.mo (Regional Government)
www.tourism.gov.mo (Tourism Office)

MALAYSIA

The Federation of Malaysia consists of thirteen states, eleven stretched out on the long peninsula between Thailand and Singapore plus the states of Sabah and Sarawak on the north-west coast of Kalimantan. Malaysia is a constitutional monarchy, in which the throne is occupied in rotation by the various Sultans of the principal states. It is a country of tropical rainforests and temperate highlands, which is fast modernising yet retains many traditional ways.

The west coast attracts most cruising yachts and there is plenty to see, from the attractive old city of Malacca and the fishing port of Lumut to the islands of Penang and Langkawi. The latter are close to the border with Thailand and possess the finest scenery anywhere in Malaysian waters. The east coast is less visited as it is not on a cruising route and its harbours are better protected during the SW monsoon, when few cruising yachts linger in SE Asia. The best weather is during the NE

Practical Information

LOCAL TIME: GMT + 8

BUOYAGE: IALA A

CURRENCY: Malaysian dollar or ringgit (RGT) divided into 100 cents or sen.

BUSINESS HOURS
In most places Saturday is a half day and Sunday a day of rest. In the states of Kelantan, Terengganu and Kedah, Friday is a day of rest and Thursday a half day.
Shops: 0930–1900 Monday to Friday.
Supermarkets: 1000–2200 Monday to Friday. (Some Muslim businesses close on Friday.)
Banks: 1000–1500 Monday to Friday, 0930–1130 Saturday (in some regions these close on Fridays).
Government offices: 0800–1615 on weekdays and 0800–1245 on Thursday (Kelantan, Terengganu and Kedah).

ELECTRICITY: 220 V, 50 Hz

PUBLIC HOLIDAYS
1 January: New Year's Day
1 February: Kuala Lumpur City Day
Chinese New Year

Easter Monday
1 May: Labour Day
14 May: Wesak Day
June: King's Birthday
31 August: National Day
Divali, Hindu Festival of Lights
25 December: Christmas Day
Variable: Hari Raya Puasa, end of Ramadan Moulud, Prophet Mohammed's Birthday, Hari Raya Haji, Hari Raya Qurban (Feast of the Sacrifice).
Also many local state holidays.

COMMUNICATIONS
Telephone calls from public booths and post offices. Card phones (Kadfon or Unicard) are available throughout the country.
Telegrams and telexes may be sent from main telegraph offices.
Main post office in Kuala Lumpur:
Kompleks Dayabumi.
Post offices open 0800–1700 Monday to Friday.
Directory information 104.

EMERGENCIES
Tourist police:
Malacca. *Tel.* 06-270-3238
Penang. *Tel.* 04-261-5522
Kuala Lumpur. *Tel.* 03-249-6593

Kuching. *Tel.* 082-241-133.
There are regular flights from Kuala Lumpur airport to Europe, America, Australia and the Far East, also to Sabah and Sarawak.
There are flights from Penang to Bangkok, Phuket, Singapore and Hong Kong.

MEDICAL
Government clinics will provide treatment for a cash fee. Emergency *Tel.* 999.

DIPLOMATIC MISSIONS
In Kuala Lumpur:
Australia: 6 Jalan Yap Kwan Song.
Tel. 03-248-2122.
Canada: Plaza MBF, 172 Jalan Ampagn.
Tel. 03-261-2000.
Indonesia: 233 Jln Tun Razak.
Tel. 03-984-2011.
Myanmar: 7 Jln U Thant. *Tel.* 03-242-3863.
New Zealand: 193 Jalan Tun Rasak.
Tel. 03-248-6422.
Thailand: 206 Jalan Ampang.
Tel. 03-248-8222.
United Kingdom: 186 Jln Ampang.
Tel. 03-248-2122.
United States: 376 Jalan Tun Razak.
Tel. 03-248-9011.

---

monsoon when the west coast provides an excellent lee and most yachts cruise up the coast from Singapore to Thailand.

Sabah and Sarawak along the northern coast of Kalimantan are visited by yachts en route to or from the Philippines and Hong Kong. Although slightly out of the way, a cruise to these two small states provides a unique opportunity to visit part of the interior of Kalimantan, such as a river trip into the jungle or a climb up Mount Kinabalu, which is the highest peak south of the Himalayas.

Country Profile

From ancient times the Malay peninsula has played a role in the trade routes from central Asia to the Pacific, and the influences of Indian, Chinese, Thai, Arab and European traders may be seen everywhere. The first civilisation in Malaysia was around AD 400. From the eighth to the fourteenth centuries the peninsular kingdoms were dominated by neighbouring empires. In 1511 the

Portuguese conquered Malacca, which they held until 1641 when their Dutch rivals seized it. By a treaty in 1824 the British gained possession of the city, and linking up with Penang and Singapore, gradually the entire peninsula came under British rule. The nineteenth century saw the country open up, with railways and roads built to develop the tin, rubber and timber industries. Labourers were brought in from India and China.

In the 1930s an independence movement developed, which was halted by the Japanese occupation during the Second World War, but fulfilled in 1957 when the Malay states gained independence. In 1963 Malaysia came into being as the federation of the peninsular states, Sabah, Sarawak and Singapore, the latter leaving the Federation in 1965. The end of the 1980s saw Malaysia establish relations with its Communist neighbours, including Vietnam.

Malaysia is a leading exporter of rubber, tin, timber, palm oil and pepper. Agriculture remains an important sector of the economy, as is fishing. The country has mineral reserves, oil and natural gas deposits.

The 18.6 million inhabitants are Malay, Chinese and Indian, plus the indigenous peoples of Sabah and Sarawak. Bahasa Malaysia (Malay) is the official language, but English is widely used. Also spoken are the various Chinese languages, Tamil and Arabic. Islam is the religion of the Malay majority. Buddhism, Hinduism, Christianity and Taoism are also practised. Kuala Lumpur is the capital in the west of the Malay peninsula with nearby Port Kelang on the coast serving it.

On the coast the temperatures do not rise too high in this tropical climate, averaging 70–90°F (21–32°C). November to February is the rainy season when sudden downpours are frequent, especially on the west coast. The NE monsoon is from November to March, but on the west Malaysian coast local land breezes have a major effect on sailing conditions.

Entry Regulations

Ports of entry
Malay Peninsula: Kuala Perlis 6°24′N 100°07′E, Teluk Ewa 6°26′N 99°46′E, Kuah 6°19′N 99°51′E, Kuala Kedah 6°07′N 100°17′E, Penang 5°25′N 100°20′E, Lumut 4°16′N 100°39′E, Telek Intan 4°01′N 101°01′E, Port Kelang 3°00′N 101°24′E, Port Dickson 2°31′N 101°47′E, Melaka/Malacca 2°15′N 102°35′E, Muar 2°02′N 102°34′E, Johore Bahru 1°28′N 103°50′E, Pasir Gudang/Johore Port 1°26′N 103°54′E, Pulau Langkawi 6°18′N 99°50′E, Mersing 2°26′N 103°51′E, Kuantan 3°58′N 103°26′E, Kemaman/Tanjong Berhala 4°15′N 103°28′E, Kerteh 4°28′N 103°24′E, Kuala Trenganu 5°20′N 103°09′E, Tumpat 6°13′N 102°11′E.
Sarawak: Kuching 1°34′N 110°24′E, Sibu 2°17′N 111°49′E, Bintulu 3°10′N 113°02′E, Miri 4°23′N 113°59′E.
Sabah: Labuan 5°16′N 115°09′E, Kota Kinabalu 6°00′N 116°04′E, Lahad Datu 5°02′N 118°20′E, Sandakan 5°50′N 188°08′E, Tawau 4°15′N 117°53′E.

Procedure on arrival
Yachts are only allowed to enter at one of the official ports of entry.

One must clear in with the Marine Department, also called harbour master's department (arrival report and ship's papers), immigration (crew list and passports), customs (list of ship's stores and last port clearance) and health (crew list, animals and health certificates). The health department may also require a de-ratting certificate or a de-ratting exemption certificate.

Port Klang: Proceed up the east channel to the mooring area of the Royal Selangor Yacht Club. There is a regular launch service to the club, where the office will give a map showing the location of customs, immigration and harbour master's offices, all of which are in the nearby port area.
Sarawak: Kuching is about 20 miles up the Sungai Sarawak, which is well buoyed but has strong currents and is best negotiated one hour after low tide. There is a floating pontoon in front of the town, which visiting yachts may use. All authorities must be visited, even if coming from mainland Malaysia.
Sabah: There are various marinas where one can moor the boat before proceeding into the commercial harbour to visit the various offices. Immigration must be visited first at the port authority wharf located in a small building behind the main building. Customs is next and is located on the third floor of the same building. Next to visit is the Marine Department at the Gaya Centre on the waterfront. As Sabah enjoys a certain degree of autonomy, one is supposed to clear immigration on arrival at Labuan, even if coming from Kota Kinabalu or another Malaysian state, but this is not always enforced.

Procedure on departure
Yachts must clear in and out of each port visited. When clearing out, all the above offices must be visited and a port clearance must be obtained from customs. Yachts are only allowed to leave Malaysia from official ports of entry, but if one wants to sail on to a place, which does not have facilities for clearance, permission may be obtained when the port clearance is requested.

Customs
The Malaysian authorities make it very clear that trafficking in illegal drugs carries the death penalty, and that this applies also to foreign nationals. This death penalty has been carried out.

Firearms must be declared and then sealed by the customs officer. A permit for firearms is required.

Animals will not be allowed ashore unless cleared by the health department. An import permit must be obtained from the Ministry of Agriculture, Veterinary Services Dept.

Immigration
All visitors must have a passport valid six months beyond the planned stay in Malaysia.

Visas are not required for a tourist visit (of one to three months, depending on nationality) for nationals of the following countries: the UK and the Commonwealth (except Bangladesh, India, Pakistan and Sri Lanka, who require visas), Western Europe, Algeria, Argentina, Bahrain, Czech Republic, Egypt, Hungary, Japan, Jordan, South Korea, Kuwait, Lebanon, Morocco, Oman, Qatar, Saudi Arabia, Slovak Republic, Tunisia, Turkey, UAE, Yemen and the USA.

No visa is required for a stay of less than one month for ASEAN countries; for two weeks, Afghanistan, Iran, Iraq, Libya, Syria; for one week, Albania, Baltic Republics, Bulgaria, Romania, Russia and the CIS.

All other nationalities or those planning to stay longer than the specified time must obtain visas in advance.

Citizens of Israel and Yugoslavia (Serbia and Montenegro) may not be allowed entry.

A visitor's pass is issued on arrival at the port of entry for all nationals. Its period of validity is at the discretion of the local immigration officer. Extensions are difficult to obtain. In principle, yachts may remain indefinitely, but this depends on getting extensions of the visitor's pass. All visitors, whether with or without visas, must possess adequate funds for their stay.

Langkawi: Visas for up to two years are now available to boats based at the Rebak Marina. This measure was taken by the Malaysian government in order to encourage the development of duty-free Langkawi into a major yachting centre.

Sabah and Sarawak: People who have entered at one of the ports on the Malay peninsula must obtain new visitor's passes to visit Sabah and Sarawak.

Health
Malaria prophylaxis is recommended for travels inland or to Sabah.

Fees
Overtime fees are charged for clearance after working hours, at weekends and on public holidays. Penang has a 24-hour clearance service, but overtime is payable 1800–0700. Light dues are payable at 20 cents per NRT. Harbour fees are payable according to tonnage and length.

Restrictions
The Security area Pulau Song Song and firing ranges as notified in Notices to Mariners are prohibited areas.

Facilities

The best facilities are in the Port Kelang area, where the Royal Selangor Yacht Club may be used by visiting yachts and will normally advise where to find the necessary repair facilities. The club is reached by going up the east channel at Port Klang. There are club moorings which should be used in preference to anchoring as currents are very strong in the river. There is a launch service to the club which has excellent facilities, fuel and water on the floating pontoon, a boatyard and a slipway capable of slipping boats to 55 ft (17 m) LOA. Provisioning is good and convenient, with a daily fresh produce market near the club and several supermarkets. Port Klang is also a good base for trips to the capital Kuala Lumpur, or to leave the boat for visits into the interior. There are several small boatyards, often with their own slips, on both coasts of the peninsula but as they are used to working on local craft, standards are not high. Admiral Marina at Port Dickson, 60 miles south of Port Klang, is a new well-appointed marina; there is no slipway there, but a 20-ton crane. Minor repairs can be done here, but for any major repair one has to go to Port Klang.

Haul-out facilities are now available at Pangkor, while at nearby Lumut the yacht club has a marina. The duty-free status of Langkawi makes it a good place for buying or ordering equipment, as well as beer and spirits. Facilities in Langkawi have steadily improved in recent years and the Malaysian authorities are making a determined effort to turn this area into the premier yachting centre in SE Asia. Rebak Marina has been expanded and now has a range of repair facilities as well as a drydock. It is a safe place to leave the boat while touring the interior. Because of the difficulties of importing duty-free parts and equipment into Thailand, many yachts use the services of the Sea Speed forwarding agent in Kuah, Langkawi to order essential items. There are marinas at the Langkawi Yacht Club and Rebak Marina on the small island of Rebak. Neither of these have haulout facilities. A further marina is under construction at Awana Resort. A new development is the Langasuka Boat Club, which provides a number of safe moorings and a few essential services for boats in transit to or from Thailand.

Simple repair facilities are also available at Malacca and Lumut. Engine and electrical repair can be undertaken in most centres. Marine supplies are in short supply even in Port Kelang and essential spares may have to be flown in.

A limited selection of provisions is available in all ports and fresh produce is available everywhere. Diesel fuel is widely available although it is normally delivered by drum and from barges.

As facilities in Malaysia are generally poorer than those in Singapore, yachts coming from that direction should try and have all work done beforehand.

Limited repair facilities are available in Kuching, the river capital of Sarawak, at the Industrial and Scientific Company, who also have a supply of local charts. The waterfront area has been renovated and there is a floating dock where visiting yachts can come alongside. All amenities are close by. It is also possible to anchor in the river and use the river launches to go ashore. There is a fuel barge on the outskirts of town.

In Sabah there are now a number of marinas offering a range of services. There is a new marina at the resort of Sutera Harbour, 2 miles from Kota Kinabalu, which has berths for megayachts and also a 70-ton travelift. There are good facilities at Gayana Resort and also at Tanjung Aru Marina, at Pulau Manukan, one of the islands making up a National Park close to the capital Kota Kinabalu. Some repair facilities are available and there is a fuel barge nearer town. The nearby Kota Kinabalu Yacht Club welcomes visitors, who may use its facilities. The new waterfront marina on Labuan island has very good facilities, although occasionally the swell is felt inside the marina due to a design fault.

Further Reading

Malaysia, Singapore and Brunei – a travel survival kit
Cruising Guide to Southeast Asia Volumes I and II

Website

www.visitmalaysia.com (Malaysia Tourist Board)

MYANMAR

Burma has been officially known as the Union of Myanmar since 1989. Restrictions on tourists are being eased, following the example of Vietnam and Laos, to bring in foreign currency. The gradual opening of the country to foreign visitors has also seen an increase in the number of cruising boats allowed to enter.

Myanmar is a diamond-shaped country, bounded on the north and east by Tibet, China, Laos, and Thailand, and on the west by Bangladesh and India. Its southern and western coasts front the Bay of Bengal and the Andaman Sea. Mountains surround a central fertile lowland, through which the Irrawady River runs, ending in a broad delta, on which stands the capital and main seaport Yangon (formerly Rangoon).

The southern part of the country is the most attractive cruising destination and is easily accessible from Phuket. The Thai Similan archipelago can be visited en route before making for the well sheltered Victoria Harbour, which is only 150 miles from Phuket. The Mergui archipelago, which stretches north from Victoria Harbour for some 200 miles, offers unlimited cruising possibilities among the hundreds of islands and cays.

Country Profile

From around 3000 BC successive migrations of peoples came down the Irrawady valley from Tibet and China. The first unified Myanmar state had its capital at Pagan in Upper Myanmar, founded by King Anawrahta in the 11th century and under his son Kyanzittha a civilisation flourished, mixing Buddhist and Hindu beliefs, and over 250 years building thousands of pagodas still to be seen today. The fall of Pagan to Kublai Khan in 1287 ushered in an unsettled period, until the Toungoo dynasty established a unified state during the 16th century, which lasted until the 18th century. By then the British, Dutch and French were exerting increasing pressure, having established trading posts along the coast. The Konbaung dynasty, founded in 1752, spread its rule over Burma, only to fall to the British in the 19th century. The capital was moved from Mandalay to Rangoon in 1886, which became an important port and part of the British Empire, Burma being ruled from India. Under colonial rule the country was modernised and became the world's main exporter of rice, but nationalist feelings slowly grew, causing increasing unrest in the 1920s and 1930s.

The nationalists initially supported the Japanese invasion of 1942. The war between the Allies and Japan in the Myanmar jungle was particularly bloody. In 1948 the Anti-Fascist People's Freedom League (AFPFL), whose leaders had led some anti-Japanese resistance, negotiated for independence with the British. The AFPFL under Aung San won an overwhelming majority in the

Practical Information

LOCAL TIME: GMT + 6.5

BUOYAGE: IALA A

CURRENCY: Kyat (K) of 100 pyas.
Import/export of local currency prohibited.
Foreign currency must be declared on
arrival; the amounts will be checked on
departure, as well as any exchange
receipts.

BUSINESS HOURS
Banks: 1000–1400 Monday to Friday.
Business: 0930–1630 Monday to Friday.

ELECTRICITY: 220/230 V, 50Hz

PUBLIC HOLIDAYS
4 January: Independence Day
12 February: Union Day

March: Full Moon of Tabaung
2 March: Peasants' Day
27 March: Armed Forces Day
April: Maha Thingyan (Water Festival)
17 April: Myanmar New Year
1 May: Workers Day
May: Full moon of Kason
19 July: Martyrs' Day
July/August: Full Moon of Waso
October: Full Moon of Thandingyut
November: Tazaungdaing Festival
3 December: National Day
25 December: Christmas Day
Buddhist festivals are variable, and
depend on the lunar calendar. Festivals of
the minority religions are also celebrated:
Eid al Adha, Diwali Festival, Bakri Idd,
Christmas and Easter, Karen New Year
(early January).

COMMUNICATIONS
Post and Telecommunications Corporation,
Yangon.
The international airport is a few miles
outside Yangon.

MEDICAL
National Health Service provides free care
for the population.

DIPLOMATIC MISSIONS
In Yangon:
Australia: 88 Strand Road. *Tel.* (1) 251834.
India: 545–7 Merchant St. *Tel.* (1) 282933.
UK: PO Box 638, 80 Strand Rd.
Tel. (1) 295300.
USA: 581 Merchant St. *Tel.* (1) 282055.

first elections of the newly independent Republic in 1947. Aung San and six members of his government were assassinated soon after and U Nu was made prime minister. The government faced serious rebellions by the Communists and ethnic minorities, while in foreign policy Burma took an important role in the nonaligned movement. Efforts were made to modernise the country and promote economic growth. A 1958 crisis in the AFPFL brought to power an interim military government under General Ne Win.

In 1988 anti-government riots forced Ne Win's resignation, and continuing instability caused the army to seize power. A military government was set up, ruled by the State Law and Order Restoration Council (SLORC). SLORC refused to recognise the 1990 election victory of the opposition, the National League for Democracy, led by Aung San's daughter, Daw Aung San Suu Kyi. Winner of the 1991 Nobel Peace Prize, she was held under house arrest from 1989.

Myanmar is a potentially rich country but has remained undeveloped, although recent efforts have been made to modernise. Agriculture is the mainstay of the economy, primarily livestock and fishing. Rice is the main export but has recently suffered a decline. About half the country is forested and the export of timber is important. Other exports are sugar cane, cotton, jute and rubber. There are considerable mineral and oil deposits. The government has also decided to encourage tourism, although the abuse of human rights remains something of a deterrent.

The population is around 45 million. The majority are Myanmars, related to the Tibetans and the Chinese, and there are sizeable numbers of indigenous peoples. There are also Indian and Chinese minorities. The official language is Myanmar, with its own alphabet, and some 100 other languages and dialects are spoken. Some English and Chinese are also spoken. Around 85 per cent are Buddhist, as well as Hindu, Muslim, Christian and Animist.

The NE monsoon runs from November to February. February to May is hot and dry. Most rain falls during the SW monsoon, from May to October.

Entry Regulations

Ports of entry
Yangon 16°46′N 96°10′E, Victoria Point Harbour 9°59′N 98°33′E.

Procedure on arrival
The authorities must be advised of one's ETA and the vessel must proceed without stopping to an official port of entry. Boats coming from the south should keep well away from the Burmese coast after leaving Thai territorial waters and only head inshore when ready to enter Victoria Harbour. Stopping at any islands is prohibited and should be avoided.

Victoria Point Harbour: Vessels should anchor off the Customs House Pier on the west shore of the harbour. Kawsong village, near Victoria Point, is at the frontier with Thailand. The police station stands on a hill near the point.

Customs

Inspections are thorough and firearms as well as valuables should be declared. Any currency must also be declared on arrival and may have to be accounted for on departure.

Immigration

All nationals require visas, the length of stay being granted is not more than 28 days. Visas are valid from three months from the date of issue.

Holders of North Korean passports are refused admission.

Health

Cholera is a serious risk. Malaria prophylaxis is recommended.

Facilities

Facilities for yachts are practically non-existent. Only simple repairs are available, especially where there are fishing boats. Fuel is only available in the larger ports. Fresh produce is widely available.

Further Reading

Myanmar – a travel survival kit
Thailand & Burma Handbook
Cruising Guide to Southeast Asia Volume II

Websites

www.myanmar-tourism.com
www.myanmar.com

PHILIPPINES

The Philippines are an archipelago of over 7000 islands lying between the Pacific Ocean and the South China Sea. They are divided into three regions: Luzon to the north, the Visayas in the centre, and Mindanao in the south. The islands are mountainous and volcanic with fertile plains and tropical rainforests.

The Philippines have been a popular cruising destination for many years. Day-sailing through the archipelago is undoubtedly the best way to visit this vast area and one can find a good anchorage every night. This also avoids the danger of running into one of the many unlit fishing boats, as well as their nets or traps. Cebu and the surrounding islands have some of the most attractive anchorages and places such as Romblon and Puerto Galera should not be missed.

People are extremely friendly everywhere and in spite of persistent rumours about the danger of pirates in the south of Mindanao and the Sulu Sea, no cases involving yachts have been reported for a long time, although this could well be because yachts avoid these areas. However, the uncertain political situation in some parts of the country affects security generally and yachts should try and avoid any troubled areas. Although the government is trying to stamp out corruption and also to standardise the entry and exit charges applied to yachts, the situation is confused. On the positive side, however, the Philippines have a lot to offer the cruising sailor and in spite of such inherent difficulties, it remains a country well worth visiting.

Country Profile

The islands were always a commercial centre for Chinese, Arab and Indian traders, who regularly visited them over the centuries. The indigenous population came originally from the Asian mainland and developed a distinctive culture and system of government. Ferdinand Magellan's arrival on the island of Cebu in 1521 marked the first European contact of the modern era. It was here that he lost his life at the hands of Lapulapu, a local chief. The islands were named after King Philip II of Spain, and soon afterwards the Spaniards asserted their rule, which continued until 1898. The Spanish spread Christianity in the Luzon and Visayas regions, but had less impact in Mindanao, which still shows its Islamic heritage. Manila became an important centre for the trade in silk and spices between China, the East Indies and Spanish America.

At the end of the nineteenth century, the writer Dr José Rizal came to the fore to lead a national movement. His execution by the Spanish and Spain's defeat in the war with the United States provoked a revolution, but independence was brief and the United States ruled the islands until the Second World War. Due to their strategic impor-

Practical Information

LOCAL TIME: GMT + 8

BUOYAGE: IALA B

CURRENCY: Philippine peso (PHP) of 100 centavos

BUSINESS HOURS
Banks: 0900–1600 Monday to Friday.
Government offices: 0800–1200,
1300–1700 Monday to Friday, some half days on Saturday.
Shops: 1000–2000 Monday to Friday.

ELECTRICITY: 220 V, 60 Hz, except Baguio 110 V.

PUBLIC HOLIDAYS
1 January: New Year's Day
Easter Week (Holy Thursday, Good Friday)
1 May: Labour Day
6 May: Araw ng Kagitingan (Heroes Day)

12 June: Independence Day
27 August: National Heroes Day
1 November: All Saints' Day
30 November: Bonifacio Day
25 December: Christmas Day
30 December: Dr José Rizal Day
31 December: New Year's Eve

COMMUNICATIONS
Public telephones for international calls can be found in main centres. Makati Central Post Office, corner Makati Avenue, Makati, Metro Manila.
Tourist information Hotline: 24-hour assistance for emergencies and language problems 50-16-60 or 50-17-28. Civil Defence Operation Centre: extreme emergencies such as typhoons, 77-49-71, 77-49-72.
There are flights from Manila to worldwide destinations. There is also a network of internal flights.

MEDICAL
Makati Medical Centre, 2 Amorsolo St, corner De La Rosa. *Tel.* 815 9911.

DIPLOMATIC MISSIONS
In Manila:
Australia: Bank of the Philippine Islands Building, Ayala Avenue, Corner Paseo de Roxas, Makati. *Tel.* 750-2850.
Canada: Allied Bank Centre, 6754 Ayala Avenue, Makati. *Tel.* 815-9536.
Indonesia: Salcedo St, Lagaspi Village 185/187. *Tel.* 892-5061.
New Zealand: Gammon Center, 126 Alfaro St, Salcedo Village, Makati. *Tel.* 891-5358.
Taiwan: Taipei Economic and Cultural Office, 28th floor, Pacific Star Bldg, Sen Gil J Puyat Av.
United Kingdom: Floors 15-17LV Locsin Bldg, 6752 Ayala Ave. *Tel.* 816-7116.
United States: 1201 Roxas Boulevard. *Tel.* 523-1001.

tance the islands saw heavy fighting during the Pacific War. Peace and the end of Japanese occupation led to independence in 1946. Democracy was shortlived and ended with President Marcos' imposition of martial law in 1972 and a personal dictatorship. His downfall came rapidly in the 1986 revolution, when Corazon Aquino, widow of Marcos' main opponent who had been assassinated in 1983, took over as President. A new constitution was introduced in 1987. Marcos died in exile in 1989, escaping charges of embezzlement. A period of instability followed his overthrow as the army staged several unsuccessful coups. Accusations of corruption at the highest levels of government have continued to bedevil the country into the new century.

The economy is agricultural, producing rice, maize, sugar, copra, tobacco and coffee. Fishing is also important. Rich mineral resources include gold, silver, oil and iron. Tourism is a booming industry and a major source of foreign revenue.

Most of the 64 million Filipinos are of Malay origin, with some inhabitants of Chinese, Spanish, Indian and American origins. Filipino or Tagalog is the national language. There are 111 dialects and 87 languages spoken in total. English is also widely used and some Spanish. The Philippine islands are the only Christian nation in Asia, 80 per cent of the population being Roman Catholic, a legacy from their Spanish past, while the rest are Protestant, Muslim or Buddhist. Manila is the capital on the island of Luzon and metropolitan Manila is made up of four cities.

The Philippines have a tropical climate. The rainy, SW monsoon season is from June to September, the dry season October to May. The average temperature is 81°F (27°C) and humidity is high. The Philippines have a high incidence of typhoons, which are most frequent between June and October. The best season for cruising is from early January to mid-May when the weather is pleasant and the danger of typhoons is minimal.

Entry Regulations

Ports of entry

Luzon: Manila 14°35′N 120°58′E, Aparri 18°21′N 121°38′E, San Fernando La Union 16°37′N 120°19′E, Subic Bay 14°48′N 120°16′E, Tabaco 13°22′N 123°44′E, Legaspi 13°09′N 123°45′E.
Cebu Island: Cebu City 10°18′N 123°54′E, Iloilo 10°41′N 122°35′E.
Mindanao: Davao 7°04′N 125°37′E, Zamboanga 6°54′N 122°04′E, Cagayan de Oro 8°29′N 124°39′E.

Procedure on arrival

Yachts must clear in at a designated port of entry before the crew may go ashore anywhere. Overnight stops, while proceeding to such a port, are normally tolerated but there should be no contact with anyone before proper clearance formalities have been completed. Yachts, especially those with animals on board, are expected to contact the quarantine medical officer 24 hours before arrival, but the authorities are aware of the impracticality of this requirement and may waive it, provided the yacht proceeds to an official port of entry.

Manila: The Manila Yacht Club should be contacted on arrival and they will arrange for a team of customs, immigration and quarantine officials to board the yacht. An inspection fee of varying amounts is occasionally requested by each of the officials.

Cebu City: Boats that have not cleared in elsewhere need to visit, or be visited, by customs, immigration and quarantine. Normally, if one has stopped earlier and called at a port where the passports have been stamped, the allowed length of time specified on the visa starts being counted from that moment.

Note: A bridge, which does not appear on most charts, now crosses Panaon Straits, between Leyte and Panaon. Its reported position is 10°10′N 125°08′E and its height, at mean low water, is 46 ft (14 m).

Customs

Firearms must be declared to customs on arrival. Prohibited items include pornographic material, narcotics and internationally prohibited drugs, unless accompanied by a medical prescription.

Yachts with animals on board must contact the Animal Quarantine office in Manila. *Tel.* (2) 992-836, for clearance and permit. The yacht will be inspected and a fee charged.

Immigration

Any visitor, except nationals of certain restricted countries with which the Philippines have no diplomatic relations, may enter without a visa and stay for 21 days provided their onward passage is assured.

Visas are needed by nationals of Albania, Cambodia, People's Republic of China, Cuba, Iran, North Korea, Russia, Vietnam, as well as for nationals of Brazil, Israel, Romania and Sri Lanka, if stay is longer than two months.

For stays longer than 21 days, it is necessary to get a visa in advance. The validity of the visa starts from the date one checks in at the first port of entry. It is advised that anyone planning to cruise in the Philippines should obtain a 60-day visa in advance. Extensions of this visa for a further 60 days can be obtained from immigration in either Cebu or Manila only, although some people have managed to renew their visa elsewhere. Fees vary but should be displayed in the immigration office.

A convenient place to obtain a visa in advance is the Philippine Consulate General in Brisbane, Australia. As well as passport, form and photograph signed on the reverse, one is required to submit an itinerary, date and port of entry into the Philippines and details of the vessel. The cost of the visa depends on the nationality.

Health

Malaria prophylaxis is recommended.

Procedure on departure

The amount charged for port clearance is not a set fee and a fee of up to 1000 pesos has been asked for by customs for 'special services'. This has led to some cruising boats leaving the Philippines without clearance.

Fees

Officially yachts gain free entry for one year and the only charges are for immigration visa extensions. However, in practice, many local officials charge for what they call 'special services' and may try to charge for a deratting certificate, which is not required by small pleasure craft.

Facilities

There are small boatyards in various islands and the Filipinos are skilled workers, particularly in wood. Teak is still widely available, but while its price is steadily increasing, its quality is deteriorating. General repair facilities, such as engine or electrical repair, are also available in most centres, the widest range being concentrated in and around Manila. Most marine supplies have to be imported, but local nautical charts are available both in Manila and Cebu. Manila Yacht Club offers members of other clubs the use of its services. Visiting yachts must pay a refundable deposit of US$300. Moorings are available with fees on a sliding scale increasing after four weeks and doubling again after eight weeks. There are good repair facilities around the yacht club as well as skilled workers to call on. Fuel is available in most places, provisioning is reasonable and fresh produce widely available.

Further Reading

Philippines – a travel survival kit
The Philippines – Insight Guides
Cruising Guide to Southeast Asia Volume I

Website

www.tourism.gov.ph (Department of Tourism)

SINGAPORE

Singapore is an island-state lying at the southern end of the Malay peninsula and linked to the Malaysian state of Johor by a long causeway.

This Asian metropolis used to attract visitors mainly for its duty-free shopping, but this is now a thing of the past as prices for electronics are both higher than elsewhere and often not covered by an

Raffles Marina.

international warranty. The fast moving city and overcrowded harbour has little to recommend it as a cruising destination in itself. However, as many cruising sailors arrive in Singapore after a lengthy cruise, often in undeveloped areas, this clean, well organised city has its attractions and as a convenient stop for provisioning and essential services is difficult to beat. Virtually everything is available in Singapore, although it can take time to find it. Occasionally this is frustrating, but chasing an elusive spare part in this cosmopolitan city is an experience in itself.

The opening of the luxurious Raffles Marina, in Tuas, on the west side of the island, has made Singapore much more attractive to those who prefer to dock in a marina. Those on a limited budget usually anchor as close to the Changi Sailing Club as they can, either across the river or in the next bay, as the Club rarely has any spare moorings. A recent government statement encouraging development of the leisure boating industry bodes well for the future, for once the government approves, things happen fast in Singapore. There is already more than one marina in the pipeline. The one

Practical Information

LOCAL TIME: GMT + 8

BUOYAGE: IALA A

CURRENCY: Singapore dollar of 100 cents (SIN$). Brunei notes are interchangeable, but Malaysian dollars are not.

BUSINESS HOURS
Banks: 1000–1500 Monday to Friday, 0930–1130 Saturday.
Business: 0900–1300, 1400–1700 Monday to Friday, 0900–1200 Saturday.
Shops: many open seven days a week, approximately 1000–2100.
Government offices: 0800–1300 Saturday (some offices).

ELECTRICITY: 220/240 V, 50 Hz

PUBLIC HOLIDAYS
1 January: New Year's Day
Chinese New Year
Good Friday
1 May
May: Vesak Day
9 August: National Day
October: Divali (Hindu), festival of lights
25 December: Christmas

Variable: Hari Raya Puasa, end of Ramadan, Hari Raya Haji.

EVENTS
There are many festivals of the different cultures and religions.

COMMUNICATIONS
Singapore is the telecommunications centre for South East Asia.
International direct dialling from public phones using Singapore Telecom cardphone service. Also Home Country Direct Service where calls are connected through own country operator, charged collect or against a telephone credit card.
International access code 104.
Emergency: dial 999.
GPO, Fullerton Bldg, off Collyer Quay, open 24 hours.
Singapore has frequent air links with most parts of the world and all major international airlines have flights in and out.

MEDICAL
The medical standards are high. Many doctors and dentists speak English.
Government Vaccination Centre, Institute of Health, 226 Outram Road.

Singapore General Hospital, Outram Rd. *Tel.* 222-3322.

DIPLOMATIC MISSIONS
Australia: 25 Napier Road. *Tel.* 737-9311.
Brunei: 7A Tanglin Hill. *Tel.* 474-3393.
Canada: 80 Anson Road, 14-00 & 15-01, IBM Towers. *Tel.* 225-6363.
China: 70–76 Dalvey Road. *Tel.* 734-3360.
France: 5 Gallop Road. *Tel.* 466-4866.
Indonesia: 7 Chatsworth Road.
Tel. 737-7422.
Malaysia: 301 Jervois Road.
Tel. 235-0111.
Myanmar: 15 St Marlins Drive.
Tel. 734-2637.
New Zealand: 13 Nassim Road.
Tel. 235-9966.
Philippines: 20 Nassim Road.
Tel. 737-3977.
South Korea: 101 Thomson Road, United Square, 10-02/04, 13-05. *Tel.* 256-1188.
Taiwan: Taipei Trade Representative, 460 Alexandra Road, PSA Building.
Tel. 278-6511.
Thailand: Orchard Road. *Tel.* 737-2644.
United Kingdom: Tanglin Road.
Tel. 473-9333.
United States: 30 Hill Street.
Tel. 338-0251.

---

great disadvantage of Raffles Marina is that it is far from downtown Singapore. Changi is more popular as it has a village atmosphere with a fresh produce market, good shopping and other facilities within walking distance.

Country Profile

By the seventh century AD Singapore was a trading centre of Sumatra's ancient Srivijaya empire, and by the thirteenth century had become one of its three kingdoms. Legend says that when a prince landed on the island he saw a strange animal, probably a native tiger, which he thought was a lion, hence the name 'Singa Pura' (Lion City in Sanskrit). During the fourteenth century the Javanese and Siam empires struggled with the Chinese for dominance and the city was destroyed and largely forgotten.

Only 500 years later did some Malays settle on the island and then in 1819 Sir Thomas Stamford

Raffles chose the island as a British maritime base. From where there was nothing, he planned the development of a city as a free port and international market for South East Asia. By his death in 1827 the Sultan of Johore had ceded full sovereignty of the island to Britain. Trade grew as tea, china, ivory and spices from China and Indonesia were shipped to London on the East Indiamen. Later rubber and tin contributed to the economic prosperity of Singapore. During the Second World War the Japanese occupied Singapore from 1942 to 1945. With peace came demands for self-determination and in 1959 Singapore became a self-governing state. For two years Singapore was one of the 14 States of the Malaysian Federation, but in 1965 Singapore left to become an independent republic.

As one of Asia's wealthiest nations, prosperity is very much due to its free port status. Singapore is an important transit port, the third busiest in the world, as well as a financial and industrial centre.

The population of 2.7 million are mostly

Chinese, also Malay, Indian, Eurasian (mainly of Portuguese origins), European, with small Jewish and Armenian minorities. Mandarin Chinese, English, Malay and Tamil are the four official languages spoken in this diverse cosmopolitan community. Most major religions are practised, particularly Buddhism, Taoism, Islam, Hinduism and Christianity.

The climate is hot and humid all year round with heavy rainfall especially November to January. Singapore is not affected by tropical storms and the only violent winds are the sumatras, which are strong, short-lived squalls that occur between April and November. Throughout the year the winds are light and there are frequent calms.

Entry Regulations

Port of entry
Port of Singapore 1°16′N 103°50′E.

Procedure on arrival
All approaches are well buoyed and lit, but due to the large amount of shipping, night arrivals should be avoided. Yachts arriving from the east should proceed to Changi, on the NE side of the island, and anchor in the vicinity of the Changi Sailing Club. Yachts arriving from the west should proceed to Raffles Marina in Tuas. Yachts are not boarded on arrival. In the past, immigration have sometimes insisted that yachts come to Finger Pier to clear, but as this is not only difficult but also dangerous because of the heavy traffic, one should berth somewhere else and visit the relevant offices by bus or taxi.

Within 24 hours of arrival the captain must report in person to immigration and customs. Immigration clearance must be obtained from the Seamen's Section, #03-01B World Trade Centre, 1 Maritime Square, Telok Blangah Road, Singapore 0409 *Tel.* 273-0525, 273-0053/4. From either Raffles Marina or Changi, the office can be reached by taxi or public transport. After immigration, one must report the yacht's arrival to the Port Clearance Office at the MPA One-Stop Document Centre at Tanjong Pagar Complex.

On departure the harbour fees will have to be paid at the port master's office in the MPA building.

Customs do not usually visit yachts, but random spot checks are made from time to time.

Customs
Firearms, including spear guns, need an import permit from the Marine Police. The permit must be obtained in advance – two weeks is the minimum period necessary for obtaining a permit. Firearms will then be sealed on board. Yachts arriving without a permit will, after declaring their firearms to customs, have to return to the boat with the Marine Police who will escort them to the armoury by taxi to deposit the firearms. On departure, they will be escorted back to the yacht with the firearms, for which a fee will be charged.

Animals must remain on board.

The relevant prescriptions for any prescribed medicines held on board may have to be shown to customs. The Singapore authorities have a very strict policy regarding illegal drugs and there is a death penalty for drug trafficking.

Yachts can remain indefinitely, but the captain must report to the authorities every two months.

Immigration
No visa is required for citizens of Australia, Bangladesh, Brunei, Canada, Ireland, Monaco, Malaysia, the Netherlands, New Zealand, Sri Lanka, Switzerland, the United Kingdom and the United States.

No visa is required for up to a stay of 90 days for citizens of Austria, Belgium, Denmark, Finland, France, Germany, Italy, Iceland, Luxembourg, Israel, Japan, South Korea, Norway, Pakistan, Spain and Sweden.

No visa is required for a stay of up to 14 days for citizens of Bahrain, Brazil, Burma, Egypt, Greece, Hong Kong, Indonesia, Kuwait, Mexico, the Philippines, Saudi Arabia, South Africa, Taiwan, Thailand and United Arab Emirates.

For visitors on yachts, normally immigration issues a two week pass, which must be renewed every two weeks. For stays longer than two months immigration may require proof why an extension is requested. A letter from a boatyard, saying that work is being carried out on the boat, is normally sufficient. As these restrictions apply to individuals, not to the boat itself, it is sometimes easier to take the bus to neighbouring Malaysia and obtain a new pass when returning to Singapore.

Visas are required for all other nationalities or for longer stays.

Immigration may want to see proof of sufficient funds.

Fees
The officials do not work outside working hours, so there is no overtime. Nominal harbour and light dues are calculated per GRT.

Restrictions

Some areas of the harbour, which are marked on the charts, are prohibited either for anchoring or for passing through – for example there is a height restriction of 45 ft (15 m) in the area close to the airport.

Facilities

Visiting yachts may berth at either Republic of Singapore Yacht Club, Raffles Marina, where a few pontoon spaces are available for visitors, or at Changi Sailing Club, where one can anchor across the fairway at Ubin Island, or in nearby Loyang Bay. The dinghy can be left at the club, and its facilities may be used on payment of a fee.

Two new marinas have opened in the proximity of Singapore. Sebana Cove is located on the banks of the Sebana river on the south coast of Malaysia. Nongsa Point Marina is located on the northern shore of Batam Island, in Indonesia. Arrangements are being made with the Indonesian authorities to allow yachts on short visits to come without visas and the compulsory cruising permit. Keppel Marina in Singapore should be contacted on *Tel.* 270-6665 for more information.

Repair facilities in Singapore are among the best in Asia. They are concentrated in three main areas: at Raffles Marina, Changi and Keppel Marina. Marina Yacht Services at Raffles Marina offer a complete range of repair facilities as well as a 70-ton travelift.

A boatyard operates at Changi next to the Sailing Club, which undertakes hull and general repairs, and has its own slipway. Another small boatyard with slipping facilities is Precision Craft, off Tangong Rhy Road. Hull, engine and electrical repair are also undertaken by Keppel Marina Services, who also have a travelift as well as a small chandlery. For any metal work, electrical or engine repair a highly recommended company is Juat Lip Engineering.

Although there is not one chandlery with a wide selection of goods, most items are available somewhere in Singapore and many shops dealing in marine equipment, such as outboard engines or inflatable tenders, often also stock spares. Some hardware stores and commercial ships chandlers stock stainless steel nuts, bolts and rigging. Radio equipment is also available and the prices are very competitive. For any duty-free shopping one should look out for the Good Retailer Scheme emblem (red decal with white lion).

Provisioning is excellent with many well-stocked supermarkets. Singapore is an excellent place to stock up the boat as both the selection and costs are good compared to the places one will visit next, whether west or eastbound.

Fuel is available at the fuel dock at Raffles Marina, Republic of Singapore Yacht Club and from a fuel barge opposite the Changi Sailing Club. Water, as well as LPG, is available at these locations. A complete range of charts is available from Motion Smith in downtown Singapore (*Tel.* 220-5098).

Further Reading

Malaysia, Singapore and Brunei – a travel survival kit
Cruising Guide to Southeast Asia Volumes I and II

Website

www.stb.com.sg (Singapore Tourist Board)

SOUTH KOREA

The Korean peninsula is one of rugged mountains and dramatic scenery, bordered by China to the north, with Japan to the east. The peninsula is divided at the 38th parallel into the Democratic People's Republic of Korea to the north and the Republic of Korea in the south.

Neither country is particularly welcoming to cruising yachts, but while in the North the discouragement of foreign visitors is undisguised, in the South, cumbersome and time-consuming formalities convey the same message. Although officially most of South Korea is open to cruising, the constant harassment from army, navy and police spoils the pleasure of visiting this otherwise beautiful and interesting country.

The most attractive cruising to be found is along the south coast, roughly between the ports of Kunsan and Pusan, where the coast is indented with countless coves, anchorages and hundreds of small islands. Pusan gained temporary fame as the world's sailing centre during the Seoul Olympics and the marina built for that occasion can now be used by cruising yachts. Pusan is Korea's principal port and second largest city. It is the gateway to the Hallyo Sudo Waterway, a national sea park

Practical Information

LOCAL TIME: GMT + 9

BUOYAGE: IALA B (IALA A in North Korea)

CURRENCY: Won of 100 chun. Up to US$500 can be reconverted on departure, but not outside of South Korea.

BUSINESS HOURS
Banks: 0930–1630 Monday to Friday, Saturdays 0930–1330.
Government offices: 0900–1800 Mondays to Fridays, March to October; 0900–1700 November to February; Saturdays 0900–1300.
Business: 0930–1700 Monday to Friday, 0830–1400 Saturday.
Department stores: 1030–1930 daily.
Smaller shops: 0800–2200 Monday to Friday; Saturdays half day.

ELECTRICITY: 220 V, 60 Hz. 110 V in some urban areas.

PUBLIC HOLIDAYS
1–2 January: New Year
January/February: Lunar New Year*
1 March: Samiljol/Independence Movement Day
5 April: Arbour Day
5 May: Children's Day
May: Buddha's Birthday*
6 June: Memorial Day
17 July: Constitution Day
15 August: Liberation Day
September/October: Ch'usok/Thanksgiving*
1 October: Armed Forces Day
3 October: Kaech'onjul/National Foundation Day
25 December: Christmas Day
*Variable

COMMUNICATIONS
International calls can be made from cardphones or from telephone offices near central post offices. English-speaking operator 0077. International information 0074.
Telegrams can be sent from post offices open 0900–1800 (1700 in winter), 0900–1200 Saturday or by dialling 005. Telexes 24-hour service KTI (Korean National Telegram).
Emergency: dial police 112, fire and ambulance 119.
There are regular flights from Seoul to all major destinations in America, Europe and Asia. There are international flights from Pusan and Chejud.

MEDICAL
There are good hospitals, many with English speaking doctors.

Imported medicines are expensive.

DIPLOMATIC MISSIONS
In Seoul:
Australia: Kyobo Bldg, 1-1, 1-ka, Chongno-gu. *Tel.* (2) 730-6490.
Brunei: 1-94, Tongbinggodong, Yongsan-gu. *Tel.* (2) 798-5565.
Canada: 10th floor, Kolon Bldg, 45 Mugyo-dong, Chung-gu. *Tel.* (2) 753-2605.
Indonesia: 55 Youido-dong, Yongdungp'o-gu. *Tel.* (2) 783-5372.
Japan: 18-11, Chunghak-dong, Chongno-gu. *Tel.* (2) 733-5626.
Myanmar: 723-1 Hannam-dong, Yongsan-ku. *Tel.* (2) 792-3341.
New Zealand: Kyobo Bldg, 14th flr, 1 Chongno 1-ga, Chongno-gu. *Tel.* (2) 737-9514.
Taiwan: 6th flr, Kwanghwamun Bldg, Chung-gu. *Tel.* (2) 399-2767.
United Kingdom: 4 Chong-dong, Chung-gu. *Tel.* (2) 735-7341.
United States: 82 Sejongno, Chongno-gu. *Tel.* (2) 397-4114.

In Pusan:
Japan: 1147-11 Ch'oryang-dong, Tong-gu. *Tel.* (51) 465-5101.
United States: 24 Taech'ong-dong 2-ga, Chung-gu, *Tel.* (51) 246 7791.

---

comprising hundreds of picturesque islands along the coast west of Pusan. Cheju Island, off the southern tip of the peninsula, is a useful stop for southbound yachts or those who wish to make a stop while on passage from Japan towards the Asian mainland.

Country Profile

The peninsula was settled in prehistoric times by tribes from central Asia. From the first century BC to the seventh AD three kingdoms ruled, until they were united by the strong Silla tribe. With their capital at Kyongju, the Silla era marked a flourishing of Korean culture. However, over the centuries Korea suffered repeated invasions by Mongols, Manchus and Japanese. The Yi dynasty ruled until 1910, when Japan annexed the peninsula.

The Japanese defeat in 1945 saw Korea divided between Soviet and American occupying forces. Victims of the Cold War, in 1948 two republics were proclaimed. North Korean efforts to overrun the south led to war in 1950–1 and the separation continues today. An authoritarian regime lasted until 1987 when elections and a new constitution raised hopes of more prosperity and freedom. In 1991 both North and South Korea entered the United Nations and signed an agreement of reconciliation.

The plains and mild climate has meant the pre-dominance of rice cultivation. Industry, such as textiles, shipbuilding and electrical, has grown expecially in Seoul and Pusan. Most exports go to the USA and Japan. Living standards are high, but the economy is dominated by large corporations and an extensive government bureaucracy.

The 45 million inhabitants are Koreans of Mongol origin. There is a small Chinese minority. Korean is an Ural-Altaic language akin to

Hungarian and Finnish. It is not related to Chinese, although many Chinese words have been absorbed. The han'gûl cursive alphabet is used. The main religion is Buddhism. Shamanism and Christianity are also practised. Seoul is the capital of South Korea.

The country has a temperate, seasonal climate, with rainy, hot summers and dry, cold winters. Typhoons can affect the coastal areas at any time, particularly from May to October.

Entry Regulations

Ports of entry
Cheju 33°31′N 126°33′E, Inchon 28°28′N 126°36′E, Kunsan (Gunsan) 36°00′N 126°43′E, Pusan (Busan) 35°06′N 129°04′E, Uban 35°29′N 129°24′E, Yosu 34°45′N 127°47′E.

Procedure on arrival
Pusan: It is compulsory to call port control on VHF Channel 16 or 12 and request permission to enter the harbour. If the call is not acknowledged, the vessel should be brought alongside the Navy barge moored close to the harbour entrance. The yacht may be searched here and firearms must be declared. Although foreign yachts are supposed to employ the services of a local agent to deal with all formalities, this rule is not strictly applied and one can carry out the clearing formalities oneself. This entails visits to customs, immigration and the port authority, all of which are located within the port compound. When leaving the harbour, it is necessary to stop again at the Navy barge and hand in the clearance papers. A copy will be retained, but the originals should be kept, as clearance will have to be shown at the next port of call.

Cheju: There is an Army check point just inside the harbour entrance, where one should stop for inspection. Formalities are completed inside the main harbour where yachts sometimes tie up to one of the coastguard boats. Arriving yachts are visited by quarantine, customs and immigration.

Kunsan: This is an estuarine harbour affected by strong currents. Although a port of entry, it is not recommended for yachts.

Inchon: This is the port of the capital Seoul. The port is very busy and port control should be contacted on VHF Channel 16 for instructions where to berth for clearance.

Customs
Firearms must be declared.

An up-to-date health certificate for all animals must be shown. Cats and dogs need a rabies vaccination certificate from one's country of origin and must spend 10 days in quarantine.

Everything brought into the country must be exported. Valuables should be declared on arrival. Special approval is needed from the Art & Antiques Assessment Office to export antiques and valuable cultural items.

Immigration
No visa is required for stays of less than 90 days for nationals of Austria, Bangladesh, Barbados, Bahamas, Canada, Colombia, Costa Rica, Czech Republic, Dominica, Greece, Grenada, Haiti, Hungary, Jamaica, Malta, Morocco, Poland, Liberia, Malaysia, Mexico, Pakistan, Peru, Romania, Singapore, Slovakia, Switzerland, Thailand, Belgium, Denmark, Finland, France, Germany, Iceland, Ireland, Israel, Nicaragua, New Zealand, Antigua, St Lucia, St Kitts, Trinidad, Liechtenstein, Luxembourg, the Netherlands, Norway, Spain, Suriname, Sweden, Turkey and the United Kingdom.

No visa is required for stays of less than 60 days for nationals of Italy and Portugal, and 30 days for Tunisian citizens.

All others must obtain visas.

For those whose passports contain evidence of visits to North Korea, special permission is needed to visit, and one should apply for a visa at least one month in advance.

Extensions are difficult to obtain. If longer than a 90-day stay is planned, a special long-term visa must be obtained in advance and one will have to apply for a residence certificate at the local immigration office.

Visa regulations change frequently and it is recommended that anyone planning to visit South Korea should obtain a visa in advance. There are South Korean embassies in most capitals and also consulates in neighbouring countries, such as Japan, where there are consulates in Kobe, Shimonoseki and Fukuoka, the latter being reported as the most efficient in granting a visa.

Restrictions
Entry formalities and dealings with officials are generally difficult and time-consuming, the matters being further complicated by the fact that very few officials speak English or any other foreign language. Because of the delicate nature of South

Korea's relations with North Korea, the military authorities are extremely suspicious of any foreign vessel. Also, as it is forbidden to sail in South Korean waters at night, one should time one's arrival in daylight. It is compulsory to clear in and out at every place and one is also likely to be stopped by various patrol boats belonging to the Navy, coastguard, marines or customs. One must also avoid the various firing ranges, which are not always clearly marked.

Facilities

Provisioning is good everywhere, which includes the electronic products that are manufactured in increasing quantities in South Korea. Excellent fresh produce can be bought on Cheju Island which has a large farming community. Diesel fuel can be bought in most places, sometimes being delivered by fuel barges which supply the harbour launches. LPG is widely available, as most taxis run on propane. The best repair facilities are in the Pusan area, which also has marina type docking in the Olympic Basin. Electrical, electronic and engine repair is available locally. There is also a small boatyard at Cheju where boats can be hauled out. Generally there are adequate repair facilities in all ports which have a fishing fleet.

NORTH KOREA

Communist North Korea occupies the northern half of the Korean peninsula and its capital is Pyongyang. All foreign visitors require visas, which must be applied for well in advance.

Visiting yachts are not welcome and the country is best avoided.

Further Reading

Northeast Asia on a Shoestring
Korea – a travel survival kit

Websites

www.knto.or.kr
www.visitkorea.or.kr

TAIWAN

Taiwan, officially called the Republic of China, is a large island straddling the Tropic of Cancer, about 120 miles off the Chinese mainland. Taiwan is a prosperous country, due to its exporting industry, and it is also one of unspoilt natural beauty.

Known all over the world for its yacht-building industry, Taiwan was the first Asian country to mass produce fibreglass boats and its leading position is still unassailed in the Far East. Very few of those yachts return to Taiwan, although every year a number of owners come to take possession of their craft and sail them away. Unfortunately this beautiful island is not geared up for cruising so these new owners have to savour other cruising grounds.

Country Profile

From the twelfth century AD the island was frequented by merchants and pirates. Portuguese sailors named the island Ilha Formosa, meaning 'beautiful island', at the end of the sixteenth century. The name Taiwan means terraced bay. Claimed by China, during the seventeenth century it was settled by Chinese immigrants, mainly Ming loyalists fleeing from the Manchus. Also at this time the Dutch and Spanish established themselves in the south and north respectively. At the end of the century the island was incorporated into the Chinese Empire. The Treaty of Shimonoseki in 1895, at the end of the Sino-Japanese war, saw Taiwan handed over to Japan. Japanese rule lasted until the end of the Second World War, when the island reverted to China. In 1949 Taiwan served as a refuge for Chinese nationalists led by Chiang Kai-shek, who established the Republic of China with its capital in Taipei. Until 1971 this government represented China at the United Nations. The Beijing authorities have always maintained the illegality of the Taipei government and, in recent years, have conducted a vigorous campaign for the reintegration of Taiwan. The threat of military action has been made very clear, while the offensive has also been pursued on the diplomatic front. Several countries that had relations with Taiwan were persuaded to break diplomatic contacts.

Agriculture is the main industry and the land is intensely cultivated, the main crops being sugar cane, rice, fruit and vegetables. Other industries are textiles, electrical goods and yachts, both sail

Practical Information

LOCAL TIME: GMT + 8

BUOYAGE: IALA A

CURRENCY: New Taiwan dollar (NT$) of 100 cents. All conversion receipts should be kept, so as to be able to change back any NT$ when leaving. Declare foreign currency on arrival.

BUSINESS HOURS
Banks: 0900–1530 Monday to Friday, 0900–1200 Saturday.
Shops: 0900–1200, 1330–1730 Monday to Friday.
Government offices: 0800–1200, 1300–1700 Monday to Friday.
Business: 0830–1730 Monday to Friday, 0830–1230 Saturday.

ELECTRICITY: 110 V, 60 Hz

PUBLIC HOLIDAYS
1–2 January: New Year & Founding Day
January/February: Chinese New Year
29 March: Youth Day
4 April: Women & Children's Day
5 April: Tomb Sweeping Day
1 May: Labour Day
June: Dragon Boat Festival
3 September: Armed Forces Day
September: mid-Autumn Festival
28 September: Teachers Day
10 October: Double Tenth National Day
25 October: National Day
31 October: Taiwan Restoration Day and Chiang Kai-shek's birthday
12 November: Dr Sun Yat Sen's Birthday
25 December: Constitution Day

COMMUNICATIONS
ITA main office, 28 Hangchow South Road, Section 1, Taipei, offers fax, telegram and telex services. Phonecards can be bought in shops and used at ISD phones for international calls.

General post office, Chung Hsiao Road, Taipei, open 0800–1700 Monday to Saturday.
Tourist Information Hotline:
Tel. (02) 717-3737 or Toll-free 080-211-734.
There are international flights to most Asian capitals.

DIPLOMATIC MISSIONS
In Taipei:
American Institute: Suite 7, 1 Lane 134, Hsin Yi Road, Section 3. *Tel.* (2) 709-2000 (Also 88 Wu Fu 3d Road, Kaohsiung, *Tel.* (7) 221-2444.)
Australian Commerce & Industry: Room 2605, 26th flr, International Trade Bldg, 333 Keeling Rd, Section 1. *Tel.* 720-2833.
British Trade & Cultural Office: 9th flr, 99 Jenai Rd, Section 2. *Tel.* 322-4242.
Canada Trade Office: 13th flr, 365 Fuhsing N. Rd. *Tel.* (2) 713-7268.
Japan Interchange Association: 43 Chinan Rd, Section 2. *Tel.* (2) 351-7250.

and motor. Nearly everything the economy produces is exported. By 1980 Taiwan was one of the 20 top trading nations in the world following a rapid economic growth from the 1950s, based on industrialisation and low labour costs. Moves are now being made away from manufacturing to electronics and information technology. The majority of the 20.5 million inhabitants are of Chinese origin, although some indigenous peoples live in the mountains. Mandarin Chinese is the official language, Taiwanese and Hakka are also spoken and many people speak some English. Buddhism, Taoism and Christianity are the main religions. Taipei is the capital.

The climate is subtropical with average temperatures from 70–75°F (21–24°C) and high humidity. There are mild winters from December to February. The summer from May to September is hotter and also the rainy season. Typhoons are most frequent from June to September.

Entry Regulations

Ports of entry
Koahsiung 22°37′N 120°15′E, Keelung 25°09′N 121°44′E, Taichung 24°15′N 120°30′E, Hualien 23°59′N 121°38′E, Suao 24°36′N 121°52′E.

Procedure on arrival
No other harbour apart from the above ports can be visited. At all ports of entry the port authority should be contacted on VHF Channel 16 before entering the harbour. Each vessel is obliged to contact the port authority so as to be issued with entry and exit permits, and also for the assignment of a berth. One may be required to use a shipping agent for one's application to the port authority for an entry permit.

One should call the joint inspection centre giving one's ETA and to arrange for a security inspection.

One is boarded by customs officers when clearing in.

Customs
A written declaration of firearms carried must be submitted to the customs boarding officer and firearms will be sealed on board.

Animals are not allowed ashore, unless possessing quarantine certificates from both one's home country and the Republic of China.

All electrical goods, such as stereos, televisions or video-recorders must be declared.

Immigration
Passports must be valid for more than six months.
All nationalities must obtain a visa before arrival

from a Republic of China embassy, consulate or trade mission abroad. The most convenient offices will probably be in Indonesia, Japan, Malaysia, the Philippines, Singapore or Thailand. From these offices one may obtain a visa or letter of recommendation exchangeable for a visa. The letters may be exchanged at a Republic of China diplomatic or consular office en route, or on arrival at Keelung or Kaohsuing ports, these two being the only ports where these letters may be exchanged.

A visitors' visa is valid for three months from the date of issue and is good for a single visit for a 60-day period. Provided one can give grounds, one may apply for a maximum of two extensions, each for 60 days. The Foreign Affairs Police speak English, 7 Chungsiao E Road, Section 1, Taipei. *Tel.* 381-7475. Application should be made to them for visa extensions.

Citizens of the People's Republic of China are refused entry.

Cruising permit
One must apply to the Ministry of Communications for a cruising permit if intending to visit more than one port.

Fees
Harbour fees are NT$ 207 per day. There is a health inspection fee of NT$ 600. Agent's fee is about NT$ 5000.

Facilities

Having a well developed indigenous yacht and shipbuilding industry, repair facilities are widely available in Taiwan. There are slipways in all ports and local boatyards offer a whole range of services. Provisioning is good, both for long-term stores and fresh produce.

Further Reading

Taiwan – a travel survival kit
Northeast Asia on a Shoestring

Website

www.tbroc.gov.tw (Tourism Bureau)

THAILAND

The Kingdom of Thailand, previously known as Siam, lies between Myanmar, Laos and Kampuchea on the Asian mainland jutting south into the Malay peninsula. It has two coasts, on the west bordered by the Andaman Sea and on the east around the Gulf of Thailand.

A relatively late addition to the international cruising circuit, Thailand is now visited every year by a large number of yachts and a charter fleet is also established in the area around Phuket. This large island off Thailand's west coast has jumped in less than a decade from a sleepy backwater to an international tourist resort with high-rise hotels, bars, night clubs and crowded beaches. Much of the charm of Phuket has been lost in the process and it now is an overcrowded and increasingly polluted island. Fortunately cruising yachts have the ability to seek out the less crowded places, which still abound around Phuket Island and its many offshore islets. The spectacular Ko Phi Phi is one such destination, a weathered rocky pinnacle rising like a gigantic stalagmite out of the sea.

There are also many secluded anchorages along the stretch of coast as one sails north from Malaysia. Thailand's northernmost islands have started to attract more cruising boats, some of which stop here on their way to Myanmar, which is gradually opening its gates to visiting boats.

Country Profile

Thailand is one of the few Far Eastern countries never to have been under colonial rule. Recent findings suggest it has been inhabited since the earliest Bronze Age. The Thai tribe was pushed out of southeast China and slowly populated the land in the seventh to eighth centuries AD, establishing small independent states in the north of present Thailand. After being dominated by the Khmer Empire, in the thirteenth century, the Thais fought for independence and established their own royal capital at Sukhothi, from where Thai civilisation flowered. Later the centre of power moved to Ayatthaya where Thai culture and the Buddhist religion flourished until 1767, when the city was sacked by the Burmese. Eventually Bangkok became the new capital, under King Rama I, founder of the present Chakri dynasty.

The first Europeans to visit the country made little progress against Thai hostility, although under

Practical Information

LOCAL TIME: GMT + 7

BUOYAGE: IALA A

CURRENCY: Baht (BHT) of 100 satang

BUSINESS HOURS
Banks: 0830–1530 Monday to Friday.
Shops: 0800–2000/2100 Monday to
Saturday.
Government offices: 0830–1200,
1300–1630 Monday to Friday.
Business: 0800–1700 Monday to Friday.

ELECTRICITY: 220 V, 50 Hz

PUBLIC HOLIDAYS
1 January: New Year's Day
9 February: Makha Bucha Day
January/February: Chinese New Year
6 April: Chakri Day
13 April: Songkran Festival (Thai New
Year's Day)
1 May: Labour Day
5 May: Coronation Day
May: Wisakha Bucha
July: Asalaha Bucha
July: Khow Phansa (Buddhist Lent)

August: Queen's Birthday
23 October: Chulalongkorn Memorial Day
5 December: King's Birthday
10 December: Constitution Day
25 December: Christmas Day
31 December: New Year's Eve

EVENTS
Early December, King's Cup Regatta week in
Phuket.

COMMUNICATIONS
There are public telephone offices in the
main centres for international calls.
Telecommunications Centre, 122 Phang Nga
Road, Phuket Town.
Tel. 211 199, open 0800–2400.
Tourist Police, Phuket Rd. *Tel.* (076) 212-213
(day), 212-468 (night). Main post office,
corner Suthat and Thalang Roads, Phuket
Town, open 0830–1530 Monday to Friday,
0830–1200 Saturday.
Bangkok airport is connected to all major
cities of the world. There are also
international flights out of Phuket, both
regular and charter, to Europe as well as to
Singapore and Kuala Lumpur. There is a
good network of internal flights.

MEDICAL
New Phuket International Hospital, 44
Bypass Road. *Tel.* 210-935. Emergency
999, Ambulance *Tel.* 212-297.

DIPLOMATIC MISSIONS
In Bangkok:
Australia: 37 Thanon Sathorn Tai.
Tel. (2) 287-2680.
Canada: Boonmitr Building 11-12 floors,
138 Thanon Silom. *Tel.* (2) 233-5077.
Indonesia: 600–602 Thanon Petchburi.
Tel. (2) 252-3135.
Myanmar: 132 Thanon Sathorn Nua.
Tel. (2) 234-4698.
New Zealand: 93 Thanon Witthayu.
Tel. (2) 251-8165.
Taiwan: The Far East Trade Office, Kian
Gwan Bldg, 140 Wit Thayu Road.
Tel. (2) 251-9274.
United Kingdom: Thanon Witthayu 1301.
Tel. (2) 253-0191.
United States: 125 Thanon South Sathorn.
Tel. (2) 252-5040/9.
Vietnam: 83/1 Thanon Witthayu.
Tel. (2) 251-7202.

pressure from the West in the nineteenth and early twentieth century Kings Rama IV and Rama V introduced a series of reforms. An army coup in 1932 ended the absolute power of the monarchy, and the army continues to play an important role in Thai politics.

The country is more economically stable than many of its neighbours, although sometimes there are problems on the north and east borders. Thailand has an agricultural economy, and around 80 per cent of the population are employed in agriculture, forestry and fishing. Recently efforts have been made to diversify and develop a manufacturing industry. The main exports are rice, teak, rubber and minerals, especially tin and tungsten. Thailand is probably the most popular tourist destination in South East Asia, and tourism is an important source of foreign revenue.

The population is 55 million, of whom more than 5 million live in Bangkok. As well as Thais there are also some hill tribes in the north-east and Malays in the south. Thai is the national language and has its own alphabet. Many in the north-east speak a dialect akin to Lao. English is also widely

understood. Most Thais are Buddhists, although some are Muslim, Confucian or Christian. All young men are expected to spend a minimum of three months in a Buddhist monastery. Bangkok, the capital, is a crowded metropolis, with many interesting places, from over 400 temples to floating markets and royal palaces.

The tropical climate is very humid. March to May are the hottest months and it is cooler from November to February. June to October is the rainy season and the SW monsoon, while November to May is the period of the NE monsoon. The latter is the more pleasant season on account of its weather, but also because it affords better sailing conditions along the sheltered west coast, most of whose ports are untenable during the SW monsoon.

Entry Regulations

Ports of entry
Bangkok 13°26′N 100°36′E, Phuket 7°55′N 98°24′E, Krabi 8°04′N 98°44′E, Turong.

Nai Harn Bay on Phuket Island.

Procedure on arrival

One should anchor flying the Q flag. Customs very rarely visit yachts. Within 24 hours of arrival, except at weekends, the captain must go ashore to complete entry formalities. In Phuket, the boat may be moored anywhere provided the captain then makes his way with all ship's papers and crew passports to complete formalities.

Phuket: The procedure has been simplified here as all officials are now located together at the Phuket Port Control Centre (PPCC) on the upper floor of the Fishing Lodge, next to the Lighthouse, in Chalong Bay. Customs, immigration and harbour master formalities can all be done here. Opening hours 0830–1630 Monday to Friday. Various fees must be paid in baht, depending on size of boat and length of stay. There is also a 5000 baht administration fee. A new dock was being built in 2000 in Chalong Bay and, when finished, it will have a clearance facility on its outer end. There is a general draft restriction of 10 ft (3 m) which will continue even when the new dock is built. Immigration occasionally insists that all crew members come to the office in person. Even those arriving with a visa are only given 30 days on arrival

if signed on as crew, which in 2000 was not renewable and therefore one had to sail to Langkawi to obtain another 30 days when returning.

Krabi: Formalities are apparently simpler in this mainland port. After anchoring in the harbour, the captain should go ashore to customs and immigration whose offices are in the port.

Customs

Firearms should be declared. They will be removed and held until departure, unless there is a secure locker on board, where they can be sealed under the supervision of customs officials.

There are no restrictions on animals.

Immigration

Nationals of most countries obtain 30 days on arrival except New Zealanders, who are the only ones to get 90 days. Visas for longer stays issued by Thai missions abroad are accepted if one has been signed on as a passenger, not crew. It is therefore preferable to obtain a visa abroad and arrive as a passenger. Those arriving without a visa will get 30 days on arrival.

Crew members are supposed to leave by the same means as they arrived, which can cause problems if crew members try and leave Thailand by air.

This is also solved by declaring anyone planning to leave the yacht as a passenger. If the captain wishes to leave the country, he will have to post a bond. However, if a captain knows in advance that he will be leaving the country, he should perhaps declare one of the crew members staying on the boat as captain and himself as a passenger. There must always be someone who is designated to be in charge of the boat; and it is not possible for everyone to be declared as passengers.

Fees

There are various fees, the highest being the administration fee of 5000 baht introduced late in 1999. Customs charge a departure fee.

Health

Malaria prophylaxis is recommended as there is some risk existing all year in most areas. Phuket island is reportedly free of malaria.

Facilities

Both repair and docking facilities have greatly improved in recent years. There are now marinas at the Yacht Haven, conveniently close to Phuket airport near the north of the island, and at the Boat Lagoon, close to Phuket Town. The latter has the disadvantage of having a tidally controlled access, with a maximum depth of 10 ft (3.20 m). As the entrance channel is quite complicated, assistance should be sought by calling on Channel 67. There are no draft restrictions at the Yacht Haven, which can be entered at any state of the tide. Best repair facilities are concentrated at the Boat Lagoon, which has a full service yard with two travelifts (45 and 65 tons). Ratanchai Slipways also offer a full range of services and can haul out larger boats. Rolly Tasker Sails now have a large sail loft at Chalong.

Provisioning is very good in Phuket Town, and the fresh produce market in Ranong Road is open daily. There are several supermarkets, including a Tesco Lotus hypermarket. Untreated tap water is not recommended for drinking. Fuel and water is available on the dock at the Yacht Haven and Boat Lagoon, also from a barge in Chalong Bay. Propane tanks can be refilled in Phuket Town.

Facilities in the other ports are more limited. More repair facilities are obviously available in the capital Bangkok, but it is a busy polluted city, totally unsuitable for yachts. The Royal Varuna Yacht Club has its base in Pattaya, the resort on the Gulf of Thailand which serves Bangkok. They organise the King's Cup Regatta, one of South East Asia's prime yachting events every year in Phuket.

Further Reading

Cruising Guide to Southeast Asia Volumes I and II
Southeast Asia on a Shoestring
Thailand – a travel survival kit
Thailand & Burma Handbook

Website

www.tourismthailand.org

VIETNAM

Vietnam lies between China and Laos, with its coastline on the South China Sea. After years of isolation, the late 1980s saw an opening up to independent travel. By 1995 foreign tourists were enjoying a remarkable amount of freedom to visit the interior of the country. Although there were still restrictions for cruising yachts, foreign boats could visit the main ports and there were already plans to organise a first international yacht race from Hong Kong in the spring of 1996. It is therefore likely that some restrictions will be lifted and cruising boats will be able to visit at least some parts of the country.

Ho Chi Minh City (formerly Saigon) is the largest city and main commercial centre of southern Vietnam, where evidence of the new climate of free enterprise is very much in evidence. Haiphong lies on the delta of the Red River and is the main port serving Hanoi, to which there are rail links. Nearby is the spectacular Halong Bay where some 3000 chalk islands form strange and fascinating shapes and grottoes.

Country Profile

A Bronze Age civilisation was developed around the Red River delta by the first century BC when Chinese forces invaded. Attempts to incorporate Vietnam into the Han Empire both politically and culturally met with early resistance from the Vietnamese. In AD 39 the Trung sisters led an uprising against their foreign rulers and briefly

Practical Information

LOCAL TIME: GMT + 7

BUOYAGE: IALA A

CURRENCY: New Dông. Import/export of local currency is prohibited.

BUSINESS HOURS
Shops: 0800–1900 Monday to Sunday.
Business: 0730–1200, 1300–1630 Monday to Saturday.

ELECTRICITY: 110/220 V, 50 Hz

PUBLIC HOLIDAYS
1 January: New Year's Day
January/February: Têt, Lunar New Year (three days)

7 April: Emperor-Founder Hung Vuong
30 April: Liberation of Saigon
1 May
1–2 September: National Day

COMMUNICATIONS
IDD is available only in Hanoi and Ho Chi Minh City. International calls must be made through the operator. Postal services can be slow.
There are international airports at Hanoi and Ho Chi Minh City.

DIPLOMATIC MISSIONS
In Hanoi:
Australia: Van Phuc Quarter. *Tel.* 831-7755.
China: 46 Hoang Dieu. *Tel.* 845-3736.

Indonesia: 50 Ngo Quyen Street. *Tel.* 825-7969.
Malaysia: Fortune Tower, 16B Lang Ha Street. *Tel.* 831-3400.
Philippines: 27B Trang Hung Dao Street. *Tel.* 825-7873.
United Kingdom: 31 Hal Ba Trung Street. *Tel.* 825-2510, 826-7556.
United States: 7 Lang Ha Street. *Tel.* 843-1500.

In Ho Chi Minh City:
China: 39 Nguyen Thi Minh Khai Street. *Tel.* 829-5009.
Malaysia: 53 Nguyen Dinh Chieu Street. *Tel.* 829-9023.
United Kingdom: 261 Dien Bien Phu Street. *Tel.* 829-8433.

established an independent state before Chinese reconquest in AD 43. It was a thousand years before such a feat was repeated with the founding of the Ly dynasty in the eleventh century. Under the Ly and their successors, Vietnam emerged as a strong force in South East Asia, resisting the thirteenth century invasions of Kublai Khan, and gradually expanding south as far as the Mekong delta.

The nineteenth century saw France force by military means the imperial court to accept a French protectorate. Nationalism slowly grew under colonial rule, strengthened by Japanese occupation during the Second World War, and in 1945 the Vietminh Independence League, led by communist Ho Chi Minh, declared an independent republic. France refused to give up the southern region of Cochin China, and eight years of war followed until the French suffered the defeat of their base at Dien Bien Phu. The Geneva Agreement of 1954 brought peace, along with a supposedly temporary division of Vietnam at the 17th parallel. Hostilities soon flared between the communist North and the anti-communist regime in the South, and in 1965 the US sent in troops to prevent the collapse of the latter. The resulting war caused widespread devastation and the US forces withdrew in 1973. Soon after the country was unified under the rule of the North as the new Socialist Republic of Vietnam.

The Vietnamese invasion of Cambodia worsened relations with China, while internal policies made thousands of Vietnamese flee the country. The stationing of large numbers of troops in Laos

and Cambodia was a considerable economic burden, and the collapse of the USSR meant the loss of a major ally and foreign aid donor. Relations with China improved following the withdrawal from Cambodia in 1989 and the decision of the Vietnamese government to introduce economic liberalisation and encourage foreign investment meant a rapprochement with the USA. In 1994 the US trade embargo, imposed against North Vietnam in 1964 and extended to all of Vietnam in 1975, was lifted, and eventually diplomatic relations were restored in May 1995. This was marked by an immediate improvement in Vietnam's international status. Tourism experienced a remarkable upsurge, especially once some of the restrictions imposed on foreign visitors were eased. Unfortunately this does not yet apply to visiting sailors.

Thirty years of war, high military spending, and international isolation have taken a heavy toll on the Vietnamese economy. Following world trends, in the 1990s Vietnam introduced its own form of perestroika, *doi moi*, with market reforms and privatisation, although, like the Chinese, there has as yet been little political liberalisation. Tourism is rapidly expanding. Agriculture remains dominant, employing over 70 per cent of the labour force, and rice is the main crop. Mining of coal and phosphates is important.

The population is over 70 million, the majority are Vietnamese, with about 12 per cent other nationalities. Vietnamese is the official language. Some English and French are spoken. The majority are Buddhist, as well as Taoist, Confucian, Christian and the newer sects Hoa Hao and Caodai.

The north is subtropical with dry winters and wet summers, while the south-east has a monsoon climate with the rainy season from May to October.

Entry Regulations

Ports of entry

Haiphong 20°52′N 106°40′E, Ho Chi Min City (Sai Gon) 10°47′N 106°42′E, Da Nang 16°06′N 108°18′E, Pan Thiet 10°55.4′N 108°06.3′E, Qui Nhon 13°45.7′N 109°14.8′E, Nha Trang 12°16′N 109°12′E.

Procedure on arrival

Permission to visit any port must be obtained in advance from a Vietnamese diplomatic mission abroad. This can be done at the same time as when applying for the visa, but as permission must be given by several government departments, the procedure takes time and can be very expensive.

Ho Chi Minh City: This is the main port of the country and is located approximately 40 miles up the Sai Gon river. A dredged channel leads through the shallow waters of the Mekong Delta. The Coast Guard will probably intercept the vessel when it enters territorial waters and an attempt should be made to advise them on HF radio of one's destination and ETA. The port authorities should be contacted on Channel 16 before proceeding into the port. Anchoring in the river is prohibited in the area close to the city. Port Control will give directions where to proceed. The port office and customs are located in the northern part of the commercial harbour.

Nha Trang: This east coast port is reported to be a better point of entry as the officials are more used to foreign boats as this is the finish of an annual race from Hong Kong. The area should be approached with great caution as it is encumbered by shallows. A channel leads into the port, and visiting boats are normally asked to anchor nearly one mile offshore.

Customs

Firearms and animals must be declared on arrival.

Immigration

All nationals require visas. Visas must be obtained in advance and the Vietnamese Embassy in Bangkok is reputed to be the easiest to deal with. Visas are normally valid one month. Extensions are available for one month.

The visa or entry permit must be accompanied by a photograph, and extra passport photos for each crew member may be required when clearing in.

Visas are normally issued with the point of exit from the country specified. This can be altered at an immigration office in the country.

Health

Cholera is a risk. Malaria prophylaxis is recommended.

Restrictions

Photography is not allowed in ports, airports and harbours.

Facilities

As can be expected, these are very basic. Fuel and water are available in Ho Chi Minh City and provisioning, especially with local produce, is plentiful. Repair facilities are limited although workshops dealing with local fishing boats would be able to deal with some emergencies.

Further Reading

Cruising Guide to Southeast Asia Volume I
Vietnam – a travel survival kit

Website

www.vietnamtourism.com (Vietnam National Administration of Tourism)

11 North Indian Ocean and Red Sea

Very few yachts make this area their cruising destination and usually visit when on their way from South East Asia to the Mediterranean. The only place where yachts spend longer is the Red Sea, not only those sailing north and taking their time to reach the Mediterranean, but also an increasing number who come south to spend the winter in the Red Sea and return to the Mediterranean in the spring. After many years of conflict and a bloody war, Eritrea has finally seceded from Ethiopia. Excellent cruising grounds have now become accessible south of Sudan and the Eritrean authorities positively encourage cruising yachts to visit their country. This is in marked contrast to the continuing situation on the eastern shores of the Red Sea, where Yemen and Saudi Arabia do not allow cruising in their waters.

At the southern entrance to the Red Sea, Djibouti provides a convenient stop, with a welcoming yacht club and reasonable facilities. The uncertain situation in the rest of Yemen has also affected Aden and boats should only stop there if the situation is known to be stable. At the northern end, the Suez Canal gives access to the Mediterranean and formalities for transiting the Canal are not complicated, particularly if one employs the services of an agent. Complicated and time-consuming formalities are the bane of those cruising the rest of the countries of this region and probably also the reason why more people are not tempted to visit it. Only in places used to yachts, such as Sri Lanka, the Maldives and Djibouti, are formalities easier, whereas in most other countries formalities are so complicated that they tend to spoil any pleasure of visiting them. This is particularly true of such countries as Iraq, Iran, Pakistan and Bangladesh, which are hardly ever visited by cruising yachts, the main reason why they are not featured in this book. Countries bordering on the Persian Gulf, which have started attracting cruising yachts, are now featured in more detail, not just Oman, but also the UAE and Kuwait.

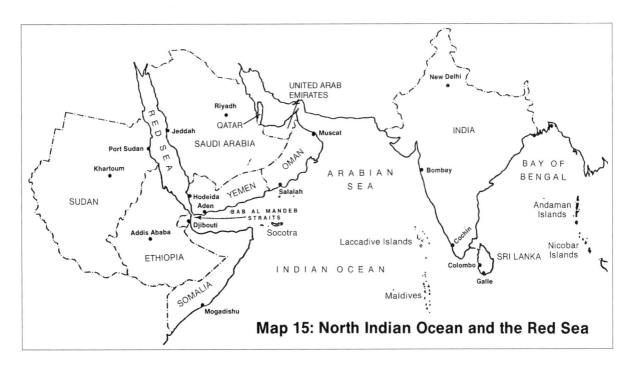

Map 15: North Indian Ocean and the Red Sea

Difficult formalities and the uncertain situation in some countries, and especially the continuing tension in the Persian Gulf, means that the number of cruising boats that stray from the traditional routes continues to be very small.

Limited or non-existent facilities are another reason why few cruising yachts are seen in the area. Having any repairs done in most places is difficult and as there are virtually no locally owned yachts, the existing workshops are not used to dealing with yachts. Marine equipment and spares are also non-existent and as even ordinary provisioning is often difficult, yachts planning to sail in this region should be as self-sufficient as possible.

Sailing in the north Indian Ocean has always been dictated by the monsoons and as Arab traders in their dhows discovered hundreds of years ago, only fools try to sail against them. The NE monsoon lasts from November to March favouring westbound passages, while the strong SW monsoon is from June to September. Tropical cyclones can occur in the Arabian Sea and Bay of Bengal particularly at the changeover of monsoons, May to June and October to November.

BAHRAIN

Bahrain is an archipelago in the southern Persian Gulf, between the Qatar Peninsula and the coast of Saudi Arabia. It is a small oil-producing country with a population of around half a million. Bahrain's strategic position has made it an important trading centre since the earliest days of civilisation. In recent history, from 1861 it was under British control, until independence in 1971. The Al-Khalifa dynasty has ruled the country since 1782. The capital is Manama. Arabic is the official language, and the majority are Sunni or Shiite Muslims.

Entry Regulations

Port of entry
Mina Sulman 26°14′N 50°35′E.

Procedure on arrival
Mina Sulman: This is the main port and is reached through a 1 mile (1.5 km) long dredged channel between Sitra and Muharraq islands. Port Control maintains permanent watch on Channel 16 and should be contacted when 3 miles offshore. Pilotage is compulsory but may be waived for small craft in daytime.

Immigration
Nationals of the UK (of UK birth) do not need a visa for a stay of up to one month. Nationals of Kuwait, Saudi Arabia, Qatar, Oman and the United Arab Emirates do not need visas. Other nationalities require a visa, valid 7 days. Visa applications require a local sponsor, which can be a hotel one is booked into, and a 'No Objection Certificate' from the Bahrain Immigration Office. Those with Israeli passports or passports containing an Israeli stamp will be denied entry.

Business hours
Generally Saturday to Thursday, although many businesses close early on Thursday. Government offices are open Saturday to Wednesday.

Diplomatic missions
United Kingdom: 21 Government Avenue, PO Box 114, Manama. *Tel.* 534 404.
United States: Bldg 979, Road No. 3119, PO Box 26431, Al-Zinj. *Tel.* 273 300.

Further Reading

Arab Gulf States – a travel survival kit

Website

www.bahrain.gov.bh (Official government site)

DJIBOUTI

The Republic of Djibouti was previously the French Territory of the Afars and Issas. It is a small country, little more than the port of Djibouti and the surrounding semi-desert hinterland, lying around the Gulf of Tadjoura in the westernmost corner of the Gulf of Aden. Djibouti's position between the Red Sea and Indian Ocean makes it a convenient port of call for both east or westbound yachts. The great majority are bound for the Mediterranean and arrive in Djibouti during the NE monsoon, mainly between January and March.

Country Profile

Before the French arrived the land was used for grazing by nomadic tribes. France occupied the area in the mid-nineteenth century to counter the British presence in Aden, making agreements with the Sultans of Obock and Tadjouran. In 1888 the construction of Djibouti was begun. At the end of the century, following a treaty with the Ethiopian Emperor, the Addis Ababa–Djibouti railway was built. As Djibouti's borders do not tally with ethnic or linguistic lines, these issues have dominated its history.

In 1949 anti-colonial demonstrations were staged by Somalis and Issas in support of Britain's attempts to unite the Italian, French and British Somalias. The French administration supported the Afars, who voted in the 1967 referendum to continue under French government. Issa opposition grew and during the 1970s the Somali Coast Liberation Front and the Ligue Populaire Africaine

Djibouti yacht club pontoons.

pour L'Independence, fought for independence. International political pressure on France and continuing internal unrest led France in 1977 to give independence to this the last French colony on the African mainland.

Revenue comes mostly from port dues and also banking, the airport and the Addis Ababa–Djibouti railway, which is Ethiopia's main outlet to the sea. French aid is important and France maintains a military presence in the country based on an agreement reached between the two countries in 1977 and renewed in 1991. The French presence has ensured a relative stability in an area renowned for its volatility. Djibouti is poor in natural resources and many still live a traditional subsistence life.

The population of over 500,000 are mainly Afars, and Issas, both being Muslim peoples. There are also minorities of French, Yemenis and refugees from neighbouring countries make up 15 per cent of the total population. Arabic and French are the official languages. Afar and Somali are also spoken. Djibouti is the capital.

It can be very hot in Djibouti, especially from

Practical Information

LOCAL TIME: GMT + 3

BUOYAGE: IALA A

CURRENCY: Djibouti franc

BUSINESS HOURS
The normal working week is Sunday to
Thursday.
Banks: 0730–1130 Sunday to Thursday.
Government offices: 0630–1300 Saturday
to Thursday. Closed on Fridays.
Shops: 0800–1200, 1600–1900 Saturday
to Thursday.

ELECTRICITY: 220 V, 50 Hz

PUBLIC HOLIDAYS
1 January: New Year's Day
1 May: Labour Day

27 June: National Day
15 August: Assumption
1 November: All Saints' Day
25 December: Christmas Day
Variable: Lailat al-Miraji, Eid al-Fitr, Eid al-
Adha, Muslim New Year, Al-Ashura,
Prophet's Birthday.

COMMUNICATIONS
International phone calls can be made with a
phone card (Télécarte) from the main post
office (PTT), Blvd de la Republique 12, open
0630–1300 Sunday to Thursday. Telephone
counter open 0630–2100 daily. International
calls with cards can also be made from the
yacht club.
There are frequent flights to Paris and some
of the neighbouring countries such as Jeddah
and Addis Ababa.

MEDICAL
Doctors and hospitals may request
immediate cash payment for treatment.

DIPLOMATIC MISSIONS
Ethiopia: BP 230. *Tel.* 35 07 18.
Egypt: *Tel.* 35 12 31.
France: 45 Blvd du Maréchal Foch, BP
2039. *Tel.* 35 09 63.
Somalia: *Tel.* 35 35 21.
Sudan: *Tel.* 35 60 94.
Yemen: BP 194. *Tel.* 35 29 75.
Oman: BP 1996. *Tel.* 35 08 52.
United Kingdom: BP 81, c/o Gellatly
Hankey et Cie. *Tel.* 35 38 44.
United States: Villa Plateau du Serpent,
Boulevard Maréchal Joffre. *Tel.* 35 39 95.

June to August, when temperatures can reach
112°F (45°C). The *khamsin* wind blows from the
desert bringing dust. October to April is a little
cooler and the winds are mostly easterly.

Entry Regulations

Port of entry
Djibouti 11°36′N 43°09′E.

Procedure on arrival
The most convenient anchorage is near the yacht
club, south of the commercial harbour. The yacht
club (Club Nautique de Djibouti) normally monitors Channel 6 during daylight hours. After
anchoring, the port captain (Capitainerie) should
be contacted on Channel 12. All formalities are
completed in the commercial harbour, which is
easily reached by dinghy.

Short term visas are issued to visiting sailors on
arrival. The ship's papers will be retained until
departure. A permit to cruise Djibouti waters is
also obtained on arrival.

Customs
Firearms are prohibited and must be declared to
customs on arrival.

There are no restrictions on animals, if their vaccination certificates are valid.

Immigration
Immigration office is open 24 hours, also located
in the port near the Capitainerie.

For stays of less than three days the visa requirements may be waived, although then immigration
will keep passports until departure.

French nationals do not need visas and can stay
up to three months. All other nationalities need to
have a visa, which should be obtained in advance,
unless planning to spend less than ten days, when
it is possible to get a transit visa on arrival. There
are few Djibouti embassies abroad, mainly in
France, the USA and Japan, but visas can be
obtained from French embassies. The usual validity is ten days.

Israelis may be prohibited entry.

Yachts may only remain in Djibouti for the duration of the owner's visa. Extensions can be applied
for at the Passport Office, police headquarters, Av
George Pompidou. Crew joining the boat by air
should obtain a visa in advance.

Health
Malaria prophylaxis is recommended. Cholera is a
risk.

Fees
Port charges are around US$80 per month. Health
dues are US$10. Light dues are US$5. There are
overtime charges outside of working hours.

Facilities

Repair facilities for yachts are rather limited, although there are a few workshops capable of carrying out simple repairs. The Djibouti Yacht Club allows visitors to use its services and will advise on the repair facilities available.

Provisioning is good, but expensive, mainly due to the presence of the French Navy. However, the French influence means food and wine are of good quality compared to Djibouti's neighbours. There is a lively market in the town centre. Although expensive, provisioning is generally better than in Aden.

Fuel and water are available in the port area. Larger quantities of fuel can be bought, by prior arrangement, from the Total fuel station at dock 14 on the north side of the main wharf. Smaller quantities can be bought in jerrycans from the fuel station behind the yacht club. Propane tanks can be filled at the Shell refinery.

Further Reading

Red Sea Pilot

Website

www.intnet.dj/public/port (Port of Djibouti)

ERITREA

With its two ports of entry, Massawa and Assab, strategically located near the extremities of the country, boats sailing in either direction can clear into Eritrea at one of the ports, daysail along the coast and then clear out at the other end. The opening of Eritrea to foreign yachts has altered the entire sailing picture in the Red Sea as it is now possible to cruise along the entire Eritrean coast in easy stages by exploring countless anchorages and offshore islands. Because of the lack of navigation aids, daysailing is strongly recommended, especially if staying close inshore. An interesting side trip for those stopping in Massawa is to the inland capital of Asmara.

The Red Sea coast stretches more than 600 miles (965 km), and it is from this body of water that the country derived its name (Erythraea, Greek for red). The coastal plain is narrow and arid, rising to highlands in the north and centre, and then falling to the broad plains of the west. In the Bay of Massawa lies the Dahlek Archipelago, a group of hundreds of islands and islets, which is a protected Marine Park. Massawa is the largest natural deepwater harbour on the Red Sea.

Country Profile

Peoples migrated to this area from the north thousands of years ago, living as nomads and traders on the Red Sea. Eritrea developed as a state in early times, under the sovereignty of the Ethiopian kingdom of Aksum which dominated the region for nearly a thousand years, until its annexation by the Ottoman Empire in the sixteenth century. From 1890 to 1941 Eritrea was under Italian colonial rule, only to be replaced by the British after Italian military defeat.

In 1952 the United Nations sanctioned the setting up of a federation with Ethiopia, within which Eritrea was to be autonomous, as a compromise between Eritrean calls for independence and Ethiopian claims upon the region. However, in 1962 Ethiopia was declared a unitary state and Eritrea was transformed into an Ethiopian province. This provoked an armed struggle for independence, led by the Eritrean Liberation Front (ELF), founded in 1958. Splits in the independence movement in the late 1970s saw the emergence of the Eritrean People's Liberation Front (EPLF). In 1974 a Marxist revolution overthrew Ethiopian Emperor Haile Selassie; the new government continued to try to defeat the EPLF, aided by Cuba and the USSR. The 1980s however saw the EPLF make major gains and in 1991 they captured Asmara, helping to precipitate an overthrow of the Ethiopian regime. The new Ethiopian government agreed to a referendum on independence, held in April 1993 with an almost unanimous vote in favour. In May 1993 Eritrea formally declared its independence.

A transitional government was set up under EPLF control (since 1994 known as the People's Front for Democracy and Justice), to prepare a constitution. Isaias Afwerki, secretary-general of the EPLF, was elected president by the National Assembly in June 1993. There followed a period of stability which was shattered early in 2000 when Ethiopia renewed hostilities, although these appeared to be short-lived as Ethiopia was herself faced with serious economic problems caused by a prolonged draught.

Thirty years of war, along with drought and

Practical Information

LOCAL TIME: GMT + 3

BUOYAGE: IALA A

CURRENCY
Nafka of 100 cents. A maximum of 1000 nafka may be imported or exported. Foreigners must use banks or authorised dealers for exchange.

BUSINESS HOURS
Banks: 0800–1130, 1300–1600 Monday to Friday, 0800–1200 Saturday.
Shops: 0800–1300, 1500–2000 Monday to Saturday (regional variations).
Offices: 0800–1200, 1400–1700 Monday to Friday, 0800–1400 Saturday (varies).

ELECTRICITY: 110 V (Asmara)

PUBLIC HOLIDAYS
1 January: New Year's Day
6 January: Epiphany
24 May: Liberation Day
20 June: Martyrs Day
1 September: Anniversary of the start of the Armed Struggle
September: Meskel
25 December: Christmas
Variable Muslim holidays: Eid al-Fitr, Eid al-Adha

COMMUNICATIONS
IDD is available in Asmara, Massawa and Assab, although it may be necessary to go through the operator.
An international airport is located in Asmara, with flights to neighbouring capitals and also to Frankfurt, Rome, and London.

MEDICAL
Yellow fever vaccinations are occasionally required on arrival and also the International Vaccination Certificate. Tetanus and hepatitis vaccinations are strongly recommended. Also, malaria prophylaxis.

DIPLOMATIC MISSIONS
In Asmara:
Canada: 4 Dejat Chebremayam Street. *Tel.* 181 940.
Djibouti: *Tel.* 114 189.
Egypt: 45 Degiat Afwerk St. *Tel.* 119 935.
Sudan: PO Box 371. *Tel.* 118 176.
United Kingdom: PO Box 5584. *Tel.* 112 0145.
United States: 34 Zera Yacob St, PO Box 211. *Tel.* 120 004.
Yemen: PO Box 5566. *Tel.* 112 396.
Also: Ethiopia, Israel and Italy.

famine, have severely damaged the economy. Agriculture is the main activity, but around 75 per cent of the population depends on food aid. There are valuable mineral resources but these have yet to be exploited. The government is trying to encourage foreign investment and private enterprise to rebuild the economy.

Eritrea's diverse population numbers 3.5 million. Tigrinya and Arabic are the official languages, and there are seven other indigenous languages. Half the population are Coptic Christians, half are Muslims. Asmara is the capital and largest city.

Temperatures remain high on the coast, in July and August even reaching 104°F (40°C). The northern coast has a rainy season from December to February but little rain falls in the south.

Entry Regulations

Ports of entry
Massawa 15°37′N 39°29′E, Assab 13°00′N 42°44′E.

Procedure on arrival
The authorities should be contacted by radio before entering any port. Yachts have reported stopping in anchorages on the way to Massawa before clearing in without experiencing problems. Sensitive areas, such as those near the border with Sudan, should be avoided. Entry formalities have to be completed again at each port of entry even if one has cleared into Eritrea already.

Massawa: The harbour master should be contacted on Channel 16 before entering the port. Yachts are normally directed to come alongside in the outer harbour. Boats are boarded on arrival and most formalities completed on board. If conditions are not favourable, one can anchor and complete formalities ashore. Port authority and immigration are in the same building and must be visited both on arrival and departure. There are no customs formalities on arrival at Massawa.

Assab: Because of the constant surge, coming alongside the dock can be dangerous, so it is advisable to anchor in the lee of the seawall. Officials rarely board yachts and formalities will be completed ashore. Assab should only be considered if the winds are unfavourable. There is little protection from strong southerlies and with these winds it is best to continue to Massawa.

Customs
Firearms must be declared. Any valuable items that are taken ashore must be declared and registered.

Immigration
Visas can be obtained on arrival. No visas are necessary for stops of less than 48 hours.

Health
Precautions should be taken against yellow fever, cholera and malaria.

Fees

Harbour fees are minimal. Visa fees of $25–$30 per person depending on nationality.

Facilities

Repair facilities are limited, although there are small boatyards and workshops that will be able to carry out simple repairs.

Provisioning, especially with locally produced goods, is good.

Fuel and water can be bought at the fishing boat dock. A local man (Mike) visits boats and offers to do laundry, help with provisioning, etc.

Further Reading

Red Sea Pilot

Website

www.netafrica.org/eritrea

INDIA

Known as Bharat in Hindi, the Republic of India covers a subcontinent bordered to the north by the Himalayas, and in the south projecting into the Indian Ocean between the Arabian Sea and the Bay of Bengal. Although a country of infinite variety, India is avoided by most yachts cruising the Indian Ocean mainly because of the complexity of entry formalities. In fact these have been simplified in recent years and officials are also reported to be more cooperative than in the past. Immigration, customs and port officials in the major ports of entry are now more familiar with visiting yachts and therefore less troublesome. Several customs and port organisations have their own sailing clubs and are therefore welcoming visiting sailors. Nevertheless, one should still comply with all official requirements. Several visiting yachts, and apparently cargo ships as well, have had items or foreign currency confiscated, because they had not been listed on the declaration filled in on arrival.

The best time to visit is between October and March. Most yachts call at Cochin, conveniently placed close to the Red Sea route. Further up the coast, the old Portuguese trading port of Goa (Mormugao) can provide an interesting and colourful interlude. However, if wishing to visit India, Bombay is the best place to head for, especially as some of the customs officials are keen and experienced sailors. The Royal Bombay Yacht Club is particularly welcoming and visiting sailors are spared some of the frustrations experienced elsewhere. Bombay is a good place from which to travel inland to experience India's rich and ancient culture.

Yachts do not normally visit the east coast, although Madras is a port of entry. India's coastal waters are teeming with small craft and especially when sailing at night one must be extremely careful, as most of them do not carry lights and collisions are a frequent occurrence.

Yachts are welcome in the Andaman Islands although few stop there. One should be in possession of a valid Indian visa. The Nicobar Islands, which lie astride the rhumb line from Phuket to Sri Lanka, are occasionally visited by yachts on passage. One needs to be in possession of an Indian visa, unless one can claim that the stop was caused by a genuine emergency. The islands have very little to offer and a stop there may have limited attraction.

Country Profile

India has been inhabited from prehistoric times, and Neolithic man originated from the Indus basin. Around 2000 BC the Aryans from Central Asia colonised north India, bringing with them the basis of Indian culture: the Sanskrit language, the religion which developed into Hinduism, and the caste system. Many empires rose and fell and in the fifteenth century contacts with Europe developed, first with the Portuguese, then the British, French and Dutch.

By the early nineteenth century Britain controlled most of India, developing the tea and cotton industries. The Indian mutiny of 1857 was only a temporary setback to British colonial power and India lay at the centre of Britain's empire. Early in the twentieth century, however, moves for independence began, and in the 1920s Mahatma Gandhi led a civil disobedience campaign. Full independence came only in 1947. The 1950 constitution created a federal state of 24 states and seven territories. India has followed a policy of non-alignment under Prime Ministers Nehru and Indira Gandhi. The latter was assassinated in 1984

Practical Information

LOCAL TIME: GMT + 5½

BUOYAGE: IALA A

CURRENCY: Rupee (RP) of 100 paise. No Indian currency may be imported or exported. So exchange receipts should be kept for reconversion on departure. Foreign currency must be declared to customs on arrival or it could be confiscated.

BUSINESS HOURS
These vary between regions.
Banks: 1000–1400 Monday to Friday, 1000–1230 Saturday.
Offices: 0930–1700 Monday to Friday, 0930–1300 Saturday (some open alternate Saturdays).
Shops: 0930–1800 Monday to Saturday.
Government offices: 0930–1730 Monday to Friday.

ELECTRICITY: 220 V, 50 Hz

PUBLIC HOLIDAYS
Public and religious holidays vary in different regions.
26 January: Republic Day
15 August: Independence Day
2 October: Mahatma Gandhi's birthday
25 December: Christmas Day

COMMUNICATIONS
Telexes and telegrams can be sent from telegraphic offices in main cities.
Post offices: 1000–1700 Monday to Saturday.
There are international flights from Goa, Cochin and Madras, both to Europe and the rest of Asia. There are also internal flights connecting the more important centres around the country.

MEDICAL
There are state operated health facilities in all towns and private consultants in urban areas. All doctors speak English.

DIPLOMATIC MISSIONS
In New Delhi:
Australia: 1/50-G Shantipath Chanakyapuri. Tel. 688-8223.
Canada: 7/8 Shantipath Chanakyapuri. Tel. 687-6500.
France: 2/50 Shantipath Chanakyapuri. Tel. 611-8790.
United Kingdom: Shantipath Chanakyapuri. Tel. 687-2161.
United States: Shantipath Chanakyapuri. Tel. 611-3033.

---

by Sikh extremists. She was succeeded by her son Ravij, himself killed by Tamil militants in 1991. Ever since the country has been ruled by the Congress or BJP parties, or by a coalition of regional parties.

India has the second highest population in the world and is a generally poor country. Agriculture employs half the population, and rice, cotton, tea and sugar are the main crops. India has substantial natural resources, both minerals and energy sources. There is some industry. The pressure of the high population sends many into the towns, even if they can find no employment.

The population, which early in 1999 passed the watershed of one billion people, thus making this the second largest nation in the world, is made up of many ethnic strains, from the Tibetan peoples of the north to the Tamils of the south. New Delhi is the capital. Hindi is the official and most widespread language and English is spoken by many. There are also 14 official regional languages and 250 dialects. India is the birthplace of both Hinduism and Buddhism, the majority of the population now being Hindu. About 10 per cent of the population are Muslim, mainly in the north, and there are also Sikhs, Jains, Pharsees, Christians and Jews.

The coastal regions can be very hot and humid and the best time to visit is during the NE monsoon from November to April, when it is dry and sunny, and if cruising the SW coast one has the benefit of more protected harbours. In the SW monsoon period the west coast is mostly unprotected, there being rain and heavy swell from June to October.

Several cities have changed their name from those used during colonialism: Mumbai (Bombay), Kochi (Cochin), Chennai (Madras).

Entry Regulations

Ports of entry
Bombay 18°54′N 72°49′E, Mormugao (Goa) 15°25′N 73°48′E, Cochin 9°58′N 76°14′E, Madras 13°05′N 80°17′E. These are the only recommended ports for visiting yachts.

Procedure on arrival
While approaching any major port, when approximately 10 miles offshore, one should call first Coast Guard on Channel 16 and then Port Control on Channels 16 or 12. Various details will be asked including an ETA. Once at the port entrance, permission to enter must be requested. Port Control will advise where to moor.
Cochin: Yachts must anchor for clearance off the steamer point on the north tip of Willingdon

Island, opposite the two jetties of the port office and the Malabar Hotel. One must not land before clearing customs, who will come out in a launch. A list must be made of *all* movable items on board, including foreign currency. This list should be specific, not general, as yachts have had items not mentioned on the list, such as binoculars, confiscated by customs. Customs will check the list, then the captain can go ashore and clear at the port office (open 1000–1700), where port dues must be paid. The customs and immigration offices must be visited next. Customs will retain the ship's papers until departure and issue a receipt. The immigration office is near the railway terminus and landing passes will be issued by them. After clearance, one may then go to the yacht anchorage south of Bolghatty Island, off the Bolghatty Hotel. Boats drawing more than 6 ft (2 m) should wait for high tide as the channel is shallow in places. Written permission from the port captain must be obtained if one moves to another area.

Mormugao: Port control should be contacted on VHF Channels 16 or 12. After anchoring in the inner harbour, the yacht is inspected by customs and possibly health. As the commercial harbour is busy with large ships, yachts are advised to clear in at the smaller port of Panaji (formerly Panjim) where customs and immigration are available. The recommended anchorage is next to the port office in Mandovi River, just short of the bridge.

Bombay: The Bombay port control operates 24 hours on VHF Channels 16 and 12, and should be contacted on arrival. Inside the harbour, one should anchor off the Royal Bombay Yacht Club by the Gateway of India. The captain should go ashore to clear customs and immigration, whose offices are in the vicinity of the anchorage.

Customs

Certain firearms and weapons are prohibited, and those permitted require a Possession Licence. All arms and ammunition will be sealed by customs and treated as bonded goods onboard the vessel.

There are no restrictions on animals.

Live plants cannot be imported. Skins of all animals, such as snakes, tigers, etc. and articles made of them, cannot be exported. There are also restrictions on the export of antiquities.

Alcohol is prohibited in some states and a Liquor Permit must be obtained from government offices.

Yachts normally can remain six months, although this can be extended.

Immigration

A tourist visa must be obtained in advance, which is valid for one or six months, so it is advisable to obtain the longer one. Entry into India must be within one month from the date of issue of the one-month visa, while the latter is valid for six months from the date of issue. Tourists must arrive within six months of the date of issue of the visa. Requests for extension for another three months by bona fide tourists are considered on merit. Applications for extensions should be addressed to Foreigners' Regional Registration Offices in New Delhi, Bombay, Calcutta, Madras or the local Superintendent of Police. Apply in advance with form and three passport size photographs.

Visas can be obtained in Colombo, Sri Lanka.

On arrival, yachtsmen are granted a landing pass which restricts them to a certain area, so permission must be obtained to travel inland. A special permit, obtainable from either Indian embassies abroad or the Ministry of Home Affairs in New Delhi, is necessary to visit certain areas, such as Sikkim, North East frontier states. The area near Tibet is out of bounds for foreign nationals.

Health

Cholera vaccination and malaria prophylaxis are recommended. Water must be treated everywhere.

Fees

Overtime fees are charged for clearance on Saturdays and Sundays.

Restrictions

There are many restricted areas in India which require special permits to visit such as the island groups of Amindivi and Laccadive (Lakshadweep) in the Arabian Sea and Nicobar and Andaman in the Bay of Bengal. When applying for the Indian visa one may also apply at the same time for the permit to visit the Andamans. Such permits are more easily obtained than in the past.

Facilities

Locally produced items and fresh produce are very cheap, as the cost and standard of living are very low. Fuel is available in Cochin, but it is preferable to use the services of an agent who will bring the fuel in 180 gallon drums alongside the yacht. The agent mark-up is typically 20 per cent. In Bombay fuel can be obtained from the Bombay ferry dock fuel station, and there is water nearby for which there is a charge. In Bombay, one must call first port control on Channel 12 for permission to change anchorage as the movement of yachts within the harbour is strictly controlled.

The Royal Bombay Yacht Club gives honorary membership to visiting sailors and allows them to use its facilities. Its members can also give advice if any repairs need to be done. In Bombay limited fibreglass repairs are possible and there is a workshop near the anchorage, where boats under 6 tons can be lifted. The yacht club anchorage is a good place to leave a yacht if wishing to travel inland. Spare parts can be air freighted from abroad without the recipient paying customs duty. Such items must arrive by air cargo and be cleared on a so-called Bill of Entry at nil rate of duty as these are spares for a foreign vessel. Customs duty exemption is not available through air courier services.

In most places along the coast there are small workshops capable of simple repairs, such as on diesel engines, electrical repair or metal work, but as spare parts are almost unobtainable, one should have all essentials on board. There are several boat-yards with slipways, but as they are not used to dealing with keeled yachts one should only use their services if absolutely necessary. As cruising along the coast offers limited attractions, those who are short of time would do better to use Cochin as a base and tour inland from there.

Further Reading

Indian Ocean Cruising Guide
India – a travel survival kit

Website

www.tourismindia.com (Ministry of Tourism)

JORDAN

Jordan's official name is the Hashemite Kingdom of Jordan. There is about 13 miles (21 km) of coastline on the Gulf of Aqaba, at the head of which is Aqaba, Jordan's only seaport. Most of Jordan is desert, with a dry raised plateau stretching down the centre of the country. The valley of the River Jordan includes the Dead Sea depression, which at 1300 ft (400 m) below sea level, is the lowest point on earth.

Cruising yachts have started visiting this inter-esting country and although the coastline itself has little to offer this is more than made up for by the attractions of the interior. Most boats that visit Jordan do so at the end of a passage up the Red Sea and the detour into the Gulf of Aqaba, before transiting the Suez Canal, is more than justified by the chance to visit not only Jordan but possibly also neighbouring Eilat in Israel. However, for the time being those who wish to call at both countries would be wiser to visit Jordan first.

Country Profile

The region which is present-day Jordan has been settled from the earliest days of history, ruled over by the empires of the Egyptians, Assyrians, Babylonians, Persians and Romans. The westward expansion of the Arabs in the seventh century ended Byzantium rule here and established Islam. From the sixteenth century Jordan formed part of the extensive Ottoman Empire, until the latter's defeat by British and Arab forces during the First World War.

Transjordan (the East Bank) and Palestine (the West Bank) were administered by Britain as a League of Nations mandate. In 1946 the mandate ended and Transjordan achieved full independence under the rule of Abdullah ibn Hussein, a member of the Hashemite dynasty which claims direct descent from the prophet Mohammed, and Emir since 1921.

In 1948 war broke out between the newly formed state of Israel and the Arab League, of which Transjordan was a member. After signing an armistice with Israel, and despite Arab opposition, King Abdullah occupied the West Bank, incorporating it into what was now the kingdom of Jordan. Following the King Abdullah's assassination in 1951 by a Palestinian extremist, his son, Hussein ibn Talal, assumed the throne. After his death in February 1999, his son Abdullah II became King.

In the 1950s tensions remained high on the border with Israel. Many Palestinians fled as refugees to Jordan and the 1960s saw an intensifying guerilla campaign by the Palestinian Liberation Organisation, making raids into Israel from Jordan. In the Six Day War of 1967 Jordan lost the West Bank to Israel. The 1978 Camp David peace agreements between Israel and Egypt saw Jordan move closer to the Palestinians, but there was worsening relations with Egypt and Syria who were closer to the Soviet camp, while the more

Practical Information

LOCAL TIME: GMT + 2, + 3 April to September.

BUOYAGE: IALA A

CURRENCY: Dinar (JD) of 1000 fils. Import/export of foreign currency is unrestricted provided it is declared. Export of JD limited to JD300. Israeli currency is prohibited.

BUSINESS HOURS
Banks: 0830–1530 Saturday to Thursday, 0830–1400 during Ramadan.
Shops: 0900–1830 Sunday to Thursday.
Government offices: 0800–1500 Sunday to Thursday.

ELECTRICITY: 220 V, 50 Hz

PUBLIC HOLIDAYS
30 January: King Abdullah II's Birthday
22 March: Arab League Day
25 May: Independence Day
9 June: King Abdullah II's Accession
10 June: Army Day
14 November: King Hussein's Birthday
Variable: Eid al-Fitr (End of Ramadan), Eid al-Adha (Feast of the Sacrifice), Islamic New Year, Mouloud (Prophet's Birthday), Leilat al-Meiraj

COMMUNICATIONS
Post offices open 0800–1800 Sunday to Thursday.
Aqaba has an international airport. There are regular flights to all neighbouring countries and also frequent flights to a number of European destinations.

DIPLOMATIC MISSIONS
In Amman:
Australia: 4th Circle, Jabal Amman.
Tel. 593 0246.
Canada: PO Box 815403, Pearl of Shmeisani Bldg, Shmeisani.
Tel. 566 6124.
Egypt: Zahran St, 3rd Circle, Jabal Amman.
Tel. 560 5175.
United Kingdom: PO Box 87, Abdoun.
Tel. 592 3100
United States: PO Box 354, Abdoun.
Tel. 592 0101.

---

conservative Jordan kept links with the West.

Following the Intifada rebellion on the West Bank, in 1988 Hussein made the surprise move of recognising the PLO as representative of the Palestinians, ending Jordan's claims to the region and breaking legal and administrative links. A policy of political liberalisation led to political parties, banned since the 1960s, being legalised in 1991. Jordanian participation in the Arab–Israeli peace talks improved relations with the USA. In 1993 the PLO and Israel's announcement of their mutual recognition and provisions for some Palestinian autonomy was officially welcomed by the Jordanian government. In October 1994 a peace agreement with Israel ended a 46-year-old state of hostilities.

The area around the River Jordan is fertile agricultural land, while the rest of the country is mainly dry plain given over to nomadic livestock. The economy has never recovered from the 1967 Israeli occupation of the West Bank which contained 80 per cent of Jordan's fruit-growing area, a principal source of exports. Foreign aid, attracted by Jordan's continuing political stability, is crucial to offset the persistent trade imbalance. The economy has suffered since the 1990 Gulf Crisis imposed world trade sanctions on Iraq as a major transhipment route. There is some light industry, phosphate mining and potash extraction from the Dead Sea area, and there has been a steady growth in tourism.

The population numbers around 4 million, almost all Arabs, with minorities of Circassians and Armenians. There are also large numbers of Palestinian refugees. Arabic is the official language. English and some French are also spoken. Over 80 per cent of the population are Sunni Muslim, with Christian and Shi'ite Muslim minorities. Amman is the capital and largest city.

Summers are usually very hot and dry, especially in the Jordan Valley. November to March is the cooler, rainy season.

Entry Regulations

Port of entry
Aqaba 29°31′N 34°59′E.

Procedure on arrival
Yachts must call the port authority on Channel 16 or 12 on arrival in Jordanian waters. Instructions will be given where to proceed. Officials will come out to the yacht in a patrol boat.

Customs
Firearms and animals must be declared.

Immigration
Shore passes will be issued on arrival. For travel inland a visa is required for all nationals except Egypt and the states of the Arabian peninsula. The validity of visas depends on the nationality, usually for three months.

Passports should be carried at all times when near the Israeli border.

Health

Cholera is a risk.

Note

Up until now yachts coming from Eilat would be refused entry into Jordan, although with the improving political climate it is possible this will change. Otherwise, it is recommended to visit Aqaba first and then Eilat, first sailing out into international waters.

Restrictions

Spearfishing and the removal of shells or coral are prohibited.

Fees

Sea tax JD6 per person.

Facilities

Water is available on the quay. Fuel must be obtained through an agent. There are small workshops where simple repairs could be undertaken.

Further Reading

Red Sea Pilot

Website

www.mota.gov.jo (Ministry of Tourism and Antiquities)

KUWAIT

Kuwait lies on the north-west coast of the Persian Gulf and has boundaries with Iraq and Saudi Arabia. The land is mainly desert, with a more fertile narrow coastal belt. About 15–20 per cent of the world's known reserves of oil lie under Kuwaiti soil.

The Iraq–Kuwait border area is dangerous and must be avoided. There are still unexploded mines along the coast and in the sea, although mine clearance is gradually making the area safe.

There are a number of locally owned yachts, mainly power, and two well endowed marinas, one near the capital, the other in the south of the country. The northern area of the Bay of Kuwait is shallow (under 16 ft / 5 m) and characterised by mud flats, whereas the southern coast of the bay and along the Arabian Gulf is deeper and has sandy beaches. Most ports are on the southern shores and there are about twenty anchorages for small boats. Although tourism is discouraged by the authorities, the few cruising boats that have visited Kuwait since the Gulf War have been allowed to stay for a limited period.

Country Profile

The island of Failaka, at the mouth of Kuwait Bay, was a trading centre from ancient times, but the mainland was only settled in the eighteenth century. Ancestors of Kuwait's present rulers, the Al-Sabah family, soon established their rule over the emirate, which became a British protectorate in 1899. In the 1930s the exploitation of oil was begun, at first by foreign-owned companies. British protection was formally ended on 19 June 1961. After the Emir had been given a share of the oil profits in 1951, the government fully nationalised the oil industry in 1975.

Iraq's invasion of Kuwait, on 2 August 1990, led eventually to the Gulf War and a liberation of Kuwait by a US-led alliance in February 1991. Pressure on the Emir to restore the 1963 constitution, suspended in 1976, led to parliamentary elections in 1992, in which opposition groups won a majority.

Since the 1970s oil production has declined so the government has diversified the economy, concentrating on light manufacturing, while overseas investments produce almost as much revenue as oil. There is also some fishing and agriculture.

The population numbers around 3 million, consisting of Kuwait Arabs, as well as large numbers of foreign workers: Arabs from other countries, Indians, Pakistanis and Iranians. The capital is Kuwait City. Islam is the official religion, most being Sunni Muslims with about one third Shiites. The official language is Arabic, but English is widely spoken.

Entry Regulations

Ports of entry

Shuwaikh 29°21′N 47°56′E, Shuaiba 29°02′N 48°10′E.

Procedure on arrival

Shuwaikh: This is the port of Kuwait City. Kuwait

Practical Information

LOCAL TIME: GMT + 3

BUOYAGE: IALA A

CURRENCY: Kuwaiti dinar (KD) of 1000 fils

BUSINESS HOURS
Banks: 0800–1200 Sunday to Thursday.
Shops: 0800/0900–1800/1900 Saturday to Wednesday.
Government offices: Saturday to Wednesday 0700–1400 summer, 0730–1430 winter, 1000–1400 Ramadan.

ELECTRICITY: 220 V, 50 Hz

PUBLIC HOLIDAYS
1 January: New Year's Day
25 February: Kuwait National Day
26 February: Kuwait Liberation Day
Also variable Muslim religious holidays: Eid al-Fitr (end of Ramadan), Eid al-Adha, Islamic New Year, The Prophet's Birthday, Leilat al-Meiraj

COMMUNICATIONS
There is an international airport near Kuwait City with frequent international and regional flights.

DIPLOMATIC MISSIONS
In Kuwait City:
Canada: PO Box 25281, Block 4, Villa 4, Al-Mutawakel, Safat. Tel. 256 3025.
United Kingdom: PO Box 2, Arabian Gulf St, Safat. Tel. 243 2046.
United States: PO Box 77, Arabian Gulf St, Safat. Tel. 242 4151.

Radio (callsign 9KK) maintains listening watch on Channel 16 between 0600 and 2400. The Harbour Master should be contacted on arrival and permission requested to enter the port. This is reached through a 4 mile (6.5 km) long dredged channel. After clearance, foreign yachts are directed to the marina run by the Kuwait Yacht Club situated 5 miles (8 km) SE of the main port. The entrance is reported to be difficult to find at night because of bright lights ashore.

For more information contact: Ports Public Authority PO Box 3874-SAFAT - 13039
Tel. +965-484-3490, 481-2623, 481-3282. Fax. 481-9714.

Customs
Firearms, alcohol, pork products and goods of Israeli origin are prohibited imports. Alcohol is prohibited in Kuwait. A permit from the Ministry of Information must be obtained to take photographs.

Immigration
All nationals require visas which must be obtained in advance, and require prior approval from the Kuwaiti authorities as well as a Kuwaiti sponsor. Tourist visas are not issued. Visas are usually valid for one month.

Israeli passport holders and those with evidence of a visit to Israel will be refused entry.

Social customs
Islamic law must be respected. Women should dress conservatively and men must not wear shorts or go shirtless in public. During the month of Ramadan, one should not eat, drink or smoke in public.

Facilities

Because of the large number of local yachts, facilities are of a high standard. There are two marinas, one near Kuwait City, referred to as the Yacht Club, the other near the Khiran tourist resort, some 60 miles (97 km) south of the capital near the Saudi border.

Facilities at the Yacht Club Marina are good, with water and electricity on the pontoons and good repair and haul-out facilities up to 40 tons. There is a fuel dock in the marina and good provisioning from a supermarket nearby. For more help contact the Kuwait Offshore Sailing Association on Tel. (965) 905 6961.

Khiran Marina has water and electricity to the berths, fuel station and other supplies. Medical services are available in the resort. The basin has a lighthouse equipped with radar and radio with a 60-mile range for guiding boats in and out of the marina, although it has been reported that the entrance is difficult and should only be attempted with local help.

Further Reading

Arab Gulf States – a travel survival kit

Websites

www.kuwait.gov.kw (Official government site)
www.kuwait-info.org (Ministry of Information)

MALDIVES

The Maldives consist of an archipelago of 1190 islands in the Indian Ocean south west of Sri Lanka, of which some 200 are inhabited. All are low-lying coral islands, grouped naturally into 26 atolls protected by surrounding reefs. The word 'atoll' is in fact derived from the Maldivian language. Administratively the Maldives are divided into 20 atoll groups. Gan Island lies south of the other islands and was a British base until 1976.

Cruising yachts are increasingly welcome in the Maldives, the government regarding yachting as a valuable contribution to their tourist industry. From the cruising sailor's point of view, the Maldives have many attractions, but one major disadvantage is the lack of all-weather anchorages. Although there are plenty of islands to visit, in most lagoons the anchorages are very deep and exposed. This is the reason for the popularity of islands such as Thulusdhoo and Himmafushi, which have shallow well-protected anchorages. Apart from this shortcoming, the Maldives are an interesting cruising ground and the diving in some atolls is excellent.

Country Profile

The origin of the Maldive islanders is not known, although it is thought that they probably came from India and Sri Lanka. Until AD 1153 the Maldivians were ruled by Buddhist kings, then an Islamic sultanate was established. The islands remained independent except for a brief rule by the Portuguese during the sixteenth century. Attacks by India in the seventeenth century were held off with the help of France. In 1887 the Maldives by agreement became a British protectorate. Since 1965 a non-aligned position has been maintained, and the Maldivians have refused to allow any foreign powers to establish military bases within the island group. The present Republic was founded by referendum in 1968. In 1988 Indian troops helped put down an attempted coup. In 1993 Maumoon Abdul Gayoom was re-elected unopposed to the Presidency for his fourth term.

The island groups are basically self-contained, relying on fishing for subsistence. Fishing has always been the major source of income, and the traditional dhoni boats can still be seen, although many are now being converted from sail to motor. Tourism has become increasingly important since its introduction in the early 1970s, helped by good airlinks via Malé International Airport. Tourist resorts have been set up on uninhabited islands, while in other islands efforts are made to preserve the purity of local culture and religion.

Malé, the capital, is the sole urban settlement, the centre of government and economic life. Of the 270,000 inhabitants, over a quarter live in Malé. The population is a mixture of Sri Lankan, Indian, Indonesian, Malay, Arab, African and European origins. Dhivehi is the main language, which is strongly influenced by Arabic, although English is widely understood. The Maldives are an Islamic country, which means certain customs must be respected. Pork and alcohol are only available on the tourist islands. A certain modesty in dress is expected.

Lying close to the equator, the monsoons are mild and calms common. The SW monsoon blows from May to October, bringing more rain and stronger winds especially in June and July. The NE monsoon lasts from November to April. Temperatures average between 77°C and 88°F (25–31°C).

Entry Regulations

Port of entry
Malé 4°10′N 73°30′E.

Procedure on arrival
Yachts can only clear in and out at Malé, although in recent years boats have been able to make unscheduled stops at Uligamu in Haa Alifu Atoll and Gan in Addu Atoll. This is only tolerated if the stops are short and no other islands are going to be visited. Those who intend to cruise other islands are asked to proceed to Malé and complete formalities there. Clearance formalities are complicated and time-consuming and visiting sailors are strongly advised to obtain the services of an agent.

Malé: On arrival the Coast Guard should be contacted on Channel 16 (24 hours), who will first ask if the vessel has an agent. If not, the vessel's particulars will be passed on to the port authority before the boat is allowed to proceed. Vessels are not allowed to enter Malé between 2300 and 0600 except with special permission from the Coast Guard. The port authority now insists that all vessels, regardless of size, need to have a pilot, although this is not strictly applied. Anchoring in Malé atoll itself is difficult because of depth. A patch with a minimum depth of 50 ft

Practical Information

LOCAL TIME: GMT + 5

BUOYAGE: IALA A

CURRENCY: Rufiya (Rf) of 100 lari. US$ accepted on the tourist islands.

BUSINESS HOURS
Friday is the day of rest.
Banks: 0900–1300 Sunday to Thursday.
Government offices: 0730–1430 Sunday to Thursday.
Shops: 0730–2200 (some do not open Friday morning).

ELECTRICITY: 220/240 V, 50 Hz

PUBLIC HOLIDAYS
7 January: National Day
2 February: Huravee Day
26 July: Independence Day
24, 25 October: National Day
3 November: Victory Day
11 November: Republic Day
10 December: Fisheries Day
Variable: Eid el-Fitr, Eid el-Adha, Islamic New Year, Mouloud, Prophet Mohammed's Birthday

COMMUNICATIONS
International calls, fax, telex and cables: Telecommunications Co. Dhiraagu, on Chandhani Magu, off Marine Drive 0700–2000 weekdays and 0800–1800 holidays.
Post office: Marine Drive east end 0730–1330, 1600–1750 Saturday to Thursday.
There are international flights from Malé to Singapore, Amsterdam and Colombo, also to Trivandrum, near Cochin.

MEDICAL
ADK Private Hospital, Sosun Magu, Henveiru, Malé. Tel. 324331.
Indira Gandhi Hospital, Maafanu, Malé. Tel. 316647.
Bandos Medical Centre (diving), Bandos Islands Resort. Tel. 440088.
There are health centres on all the inhabited atolls.

DIPLOMATIC MISSIONS
In Malé:
France: 1/27 Chandhani Magu. Tel. 323760 (for visas for Réunion, Mayotte and Comoros).
India: Tel. 323015.
Sri Lanka: Tel. 322845.
United States: Mandhu-edhuruge, Violet Magu. Tel. 322581.

(15 m) is reported at 4°10.40′N 73°29.80′E. If this place is occupied, one must be prepared to anchor nearby in depths of around 150 ft (50 m). Although one may be able to clear in oneself, the authorities usually insist on the use of an agent. Those using an agent may be able to be directed on arrival to the lagoon north of the airport, while the agent deals with formalities. As the lagoon entrance is difficult to spot, the agent will guide a boat in.

One may first be boarded by security, especially if arriving at night. Customs, immigration and health will board during office hours to carry out clearance. On departure, one should first clear immigration, then the port authority and finally customs. This can take some time.

Uligamu: Occasionally boats en route from Sri Lanka to the Red Sea stop at this northernmost island of the Maldives. Although not an official port of entry, there is now a customs official located there who will do the necessary formalities for a short emergency stop. There are strict restrictions on visiting ashore: visitors may not stay ashore after 2000, no alcohol may be taken ashore, women must be properly dressed, and no islanders may board a boat. Those who intend to visit any of the other islands must proceed to Malé and complete entry formalities there.

Gan: Short stops at this southernmost atoll are normally tolerated, but proper entry formalities must be completed at Malé.

Customs

Firearms must be declared on arrival and will be confiscated until departure. One must make sure one gets a receipt. One should have a firearms permit, otherwise on departure one has to go to the Ministry of Defence with the receipt to get approval for the return of the firearms. Customs requires nine crew lists on arrival as well as a deratting certificate.

Being a Muslim society, dogs are considered unclean and are required to be kept on board.

Prohibited imports are alcohol, pork products, and pornographic material. The export of tortoiseshell, turtleshell and whole black coral is forbidden.

As Malé is a free port, no duties are levied, but goods must be declared.

Immigration

All tourists are given a 30-day visitor's permit on arrival. For a nominal fee the permit may be extended.

Proof of sufficient funds will be required.

Cruising permit

A special permit must be obtained if wishing to sail to any other atolls besides Malé Atoll. Application should be made to the Ministry of Atolls Administration, Faashanaa Building, Marine Drive, Malé 20-05.

Health

Malaria prophylaxis is recommended.

Fees

Port charges. Agency fees. In 2000, boats up to 60 ft (18 m) were quoted an agency fee of US$150 for stays up to 15 days. This included agency fees as well as all government clearance fees. Larger boats pay proportionally more.

Anchorage fee of $5 per day for stays over 15 days.

Cruising permits for the outer islands are $10 per atoll for yachts up to 60 ft (18 m), $15–$30 for larger yachts.

Anchorage charges: the first two weeks are free, after that there is a fee according to the length of stay.

Agents

The Maldives National Shipping Company. *Tel.* + 960 323871, Fax. 324323. E-mail: mnsl@dhivehinet.mv
Hazash Enterprises. *Tel.* +960 326442, Fax. 324913. E-mail: hazash@dhivehinet.net.mv
FIFO. *Tel.* +960 317641, Fax. 317642. E-mail: fifo@dhivehinet.net.mv
When an agent has been prearranged, he should be notified 48 hours before arrival of the ETA. An ETA letter will then be sent by the agent to the Ministry of Defence and National Security, customs, port authority, immigration and quarantine. The details of the ETA letter include the following particulars:

1 Name of vessel
2 Name of master and nationality
3 Name of owner
4 Port of registration and official number
5 Gross tonnage
6 Callsign
7 HF working frequency
8 Last port of call
9 Estimated date and time of arrival
10 Number of crew

Boats needing fuel and supplies stopping in Malé for less than 72 hours can do so without an agent, but formalities will be lengthy.

Facilities

The few available facilities are all on Malé which has some small workshops capable of simple repairs. As most food has to be imported, mainly from Sri Lanka, provisions are expensive. There is a good fresh produce market on Marine Drive on the waterfront and also a fish market nearby. Fuel and even water are only available in Malé, the latter being scarce in the outer islands. In Malé, fuel and water are best obtained via one's agent, who will also arrange for garbage disposal. Fuel is also available from the State Trading Organisation, *Tel.* 323279. A few basic provisions are available at Uligamu and Gan, and if fuel is available one should be prepared to pay a high price for it. There are weekly flights to Singapore so emergency spares could be flown in. The deep water port of Gan in Addu Atoll, in the southern extremity of the archipelago, has some facilities and also an airport with regular flights to Malé. Although this is not an official port of entry, emergency stops are normally tolerated.

Further Reading

Maldives and East Indian Ocean
Indian Ocean Cruising Guide
Malways: Maldives Island Directory
Dive Maldives: A Guide to the Maldives Archipelago
Marine Life of the Maldives

Websites

www.visitmaldives.com
www.atolleditions.com.au

OMAN

Oman is a sultanate on the eastern end of the Arabian peninsula. Tourism is not encouraged and virtually all the foreigners allowed into the country come on business. Recently there has been a change of heart concerning yachts, some being allowed to stop for a few days at Mina Raysut, near the town of Salalah. However, cruising the coast is still forbidden. Boats have also been allowed to stop at Mina Qaboos (Muscat), where great changes are expected in the near future with the opening of a small marina. Practically all yachts which call in Oman are bound for the Red Sea and although a detour is necessary if coming from Sri Lanka, the route from India, particularly Bombay, passes very close to Raysut.

Country Profile

During the first centuries AD the Persians dominated the northern coastal districts. By the seventh

Practical Information

LOCAL TIME: GMT + 4

BUOYAGE: IALA A

CURRENCY: Omani rial of 1000 biaza

BUSINESS HOURS
Friday is the day of rest.
Banks: 0800–1200 Saturday to
Wednesday, 0800–1130 Thursday (opens
1 hour later during Ramadan).
Shops: 0900–1300, 1600–1930 Saturday
to Thursday.
Government offices: 0730–1430 Saturday
to Wednesday. Open and close one hour
later during Ramadan.

ELECTRICITY: 220 V, 50 Hz

PUBLIC HOLIDAYS
Muharram (Muslim New Year)
Mouloud (Prophet's Birthday)
Prophet's Ascension
Eid el-Fitr (five days)
Eid el-Adha (five days)
18 November: National Day (five days)
19 November: Sultan's Birthday

COMMUNICATIONS
There are good international telecommunications
but no central telephone exchange so
international calls are best made from hotels.
GPO, Muscat, Markaz Mutrah Al-Tijari St, open
0730–1330, 1600–1800, Saturday to
Wednesday, 0800–1100 Thursday. Fax and telex
available.
Emergency 999.
There are regular flights to Europe and South
East Asia from Seeb international airport. Salalah
airport is used only for domestic flights.

MEDICAL
Good medical care and hospitals in all
towns.

DIPLOMATIC MISSIONS
In Muscat:
Canada: PO Box 8275, Muttrah, Flat 310,
Bldg 477, Way 2907, Moosa Abdul
Rahman Hassan Bldg, Al-Noor St, Ruwi.
Tel. 791738.
New Zealand: PO Box 520. Tel. 795726.
United Arab Emirates: Diplomatic City, Al-
Khuwair, PO Box 1551. Tel. 600302.
United Kingdom: PO Box 300, Code 113.
Tel. 693077.
United States: PO Box 202, Madinat
Qaboos. Tel. 696989.

century Sohar, the Omani capital, had become one of the most important of the Indian Ocean sea ports, and gradually Omani maritime power came to dominate the Persian Gulf and Indian Ocean, controlling the main trade routes to the Far East and Africa. In the early sixteenth century the first Portuguese visited the Omani coast, establishing trading posts, and until 1650 they controlled Muscat and several other coastal settlements. From the seventeenth century the Omanis grew in power, resisting Persian invasions, and conquering Portuguese settlements in the Indian Ocean including Mogadishu, Mombasa, and the islands of Zanzibar and Mafia. The present dynasty began with Ahmad ibn Said, elected Imam in 1749. The maritime empire reached its height under Sultan Seyyid Said (1807–56) who moved the centre of his empire to Zanzibar. Omani power was eroded by European expansion and especially the growth of British influence in the Indian Ocean.

Since the decline of its trading empire Omani economy remained largely at subsistence level, based on agriculture, fishing and herding. Then in the 1960s oil was discovered, and the revenues from this soon brought the country prosperity. From 1970 Sultan Qaboos ibn Said undertook to modernise the country. In 1982 the first refinery for the domestic market was opened, and reserves of natural gas are starting to be exploited. However, a large percentage of the population remain in the agricultural sector, being nomads raising livestock. Apart from oil, the main exports are dates, limes and alfalfa.

The population of over 2.2 million consists of two main tribes, the Yemeni, and the Nizanis who came originally from north-west Arabia. In the urban areas there are minorities of Indians, Pakistanis, Baluchis and East Africans. Arabic is the official language, but there are also many dialects, and English is spoken by businessmen. The majority are Ibadi Muslim, with Sunni and Shia Muslim minorities. Non-Muslims are not permitted to enter mosques. The capital is Muscat.

April to October is very hot with high humidity along the coasts – it can reach up to 122°F (50°C) in the shade. During November to March, the period of the NE monsoon, the climate is more pleasant, with occasional rains.

Entry Regulations

Ports of entry
Mina Raysut 16°56′N 54°00′E, Mina al Fahal 23°39′N 58°32′E, Marina Bander Al Rowdha (Muscat) 23°35′N 58°37′E.

Procedure on arrival
Mina Raysut: The port should be called on Channel 16 one hour before arrival. Normally permission will be given to enter the harbour and directions should be followed as to where to go for

clearance. On arrival boats are normally boarded by quarantine, immigration, customs and harbour officials. Clearance is easier on weekdays (Saturday to Wednesday). Boats arriving outside hours on weekdays will have to wait until the following morning. Boats will not be cleared at weekends (Thursday and Friday). No one should go ashore before formalities are completed. Passport and ship's papers are retained until departure. Shore passes must be obtained to leave the port area.

Marina Bander: Contact marina on Channel 16. The marina office will contact the relevant officials for clearance.

Customs

Firearms must be declared. Dogs are not allowed to land.

Immigration

Visas are required by all nationals except those of the Gulf States. Before a visa can be obtained, everyone, except US citizens, must first obtain a No Objection Certificate (NOC). Unless one has an Omani sponsor, the NOC for tourists is usually obtained through the hotel where one is booked. The hotel should be faxed a copy of the first page of the passport and they may also require four photos. Normally one is required to stay at least three nights in the hotel that arranges the NOC. Once the NOC is issued you will have a NOC number which you give to immigration on arrival to obtain the visa.

Israeli passport holders and those with evidence of travel to Israel will be denied entry.

In practice, when you arrive by yacht a visa is not required for short visits, although the ship's papers and passports are retained until departure and a shore pass issued which allows one to travel inland.

A passport may be returned so that money can be changed, but has to be given back to the authorities afterwards.

Health

Malaria prophylaxis is recommended.

Restrictions

There is a curfew in Mina Raysut every night between 1800 and 0900, and also on Thursdays and Fridays, when yacht crews are not allowed to leave the port area.

Procedure on departure

Formalities are complicated and sufficient time should be allowed for them. All offices must be visited in turn, starting with police and finishing with the harbour master.

Warning

It has been reported that satellite fixes cannot be obtained from approximately 40 miles offshore and when approaching Mina Raysut. The authorities in Oman are aware of this phenomenon, but have not been able to offer an explanation.

Facilities

There is excellent provisioning and a fresh produce market in Salalah, which is seven miles from Mina Raysut. Some repair facilities are available in the port area. In Mina Raysut larger quantities of fuel can be ordered from the Shell depot, who will deliver it by tanker. Shell will also refill propane tanks. There is a water outlet on the main dock. Boats can be hauled out by one of the port cranes. For emergency repair, one should contact the naval base. Marina Bander al-Rowdha has water and electricity to all berths. Some mechanical and engineering repairs can be carried out here and a travelift is planned.

Further Reading

Indian Ocean Cruising Guide
Red Sea Pilot
Arab Gulf States – a travel survival kit

Websites

www.tourismoman.com
www.omanonline.com

QATAR

Qatar occupies the Qatar Peninsula, jutting north into the Persian Gulf from the Arabian Peninsula. From the early nineteenth century until the present day the Thani dynasty has ruled Qatar, although from 1916 until 1971 the country was a British protectorate. Petroleum dominates the economy, accounting for over 90 per cent of exports, and natural gas is also important.

Qatar's population numbers about 540,000, which includes a large number of foreign workers.

The official language is Arabic, although English is widely used. The majority of native Qataris belong to the Wahhabi sect of Islam. The capital is Doha.

The climate is very hot, particularly in the summer.

Entry Regulations

Port of entry
Doha 25°17′N 51°32′E.

Procedure on arrival
The Doha Port Authority maintains a continuous watch on VHF Channel 16.
Doha: The port is entered through a dredged channel. Boats drawing less than 13 ft (4 m) may proceed into the inner harbour.

Customs
The import of alcohol and pork products is prohibited.

Immigration
All nationals except those of other Gulf states and the UK require visas. UK nationals (those born and residing in the UK) may stay for 30 days visa-free. A visa application requires a local sponsor which can be a hotel. Tourist visas are issued for 14 days, renewable for another 14 days.

Israeli nationals and those whose passports contain an Israeli stamp are prohibited entry.

Practical Information
Local time GMT +3
Business Hours
Offices and shops: 0800–1200, 1600/1700–1900 Saturday to Thursday.
Government offices and embassies close Thursdays.
Public Holidays
3 September: National Day.
Variable Muslim holidays.

Diplomatic Missions
United Kingdom: PO Box 3, Doha. *Tel.* 421 991.
United States: Ahmed Bin Ali St and Al-Jazira Al-Arabiya St, PO Box 2399, Doha. *Tel.* 864 701.

Further Reading

Arab Gulf States – a travel survival kit

Website

www.qgpc.com.qa (Government of Qatar)

SAUDI ARABIA

Saudi Arabia is a vast desert country on the Arabian peninsula between the Persian Gulf and the Red Sea. Mecca, the holiest place of Islam, is sited here and Saudi Arabia is a very conservative Muslim country, difficult to visit by foreigners, except Muslims on a pilgrimage to Mecca. In order to preserve religious purity, tourism is actively discouraged. This also includes cruising yachts. A few yachts which have been forced to call at a Saudi port have been treated courteously, once the authorities have ascertained that the stop has been caused by a genuine emergency. Yachts that have either strayed into Saudi waters or have been apprehended cruising the offlying Farasan Islands without permission, have been escorted into port and detained for a few days before being allowed to go on their way. Anyone intending to sail to Saudi Arabia must approach the authorities in advance to obtain the necessary permission. Otherwise it is better to avoid its waters, unless one is forced to make an emergency stop there.

Country Profile

As the site of Mecca and Medina this area has always been of prime importance to the Islamic religion. From these holy cities the Arabs disseminated Islam to the world and spread Arab power west throughout North Africa to Spain, and east to India and Indonesia. For centuries most of the Arab peninsula was under Ottoman rule, and its peoples were largely nomadic tribes. The nineteenth century saw the rise of the fervent Wahabis, who wanted to restore Islam to its original purity, coming into conflict with the Turks. After the collapse of the Ottoman empire at the end of the First World War, Saudi Arabia came into being.

King Ibn Saud, ruling from 1932 to 1953, modernised the country and succeeding members of his family have ruled since. The stability of the country grew under King Faisal, who was assassinated in 1975, to be succeeded by his brother Khaled and then in 1982 by another brother King Fahd. The country was the base for the UN coalition forces during the 1991 war against Iraq after its invasion of Kuwait in 1990.

Most of the land is desert, and only a small area is cultivable. The vast oil reserves around the Gulf provide a huge income, which Saudi Arabia is investing in various projects in order to end its

Practical Information

LOCAL TIME: GMT + 3

BUOYAGE: IALA A

CURRENCY: Saudi riyal (SR) of 100 halalah

BUSINESS HOURS
Banks: 0830–1300 Saturday to Thursday and 1600/1700 to 1800/1900 Saturday to Wednesday.
Business: 0800–1300, 1700–2000, closing 1300 on Thursday for weekend (Thursday/Friday).
Shops: 0830–1300, 1600–1900 Saturday to Wednesday, Thursday mornings.
Government offices: 0730–1430 Saturday to Wednesday. Smoking is forbidden.

ELECTRICITY: 110/220 V, 60 Hz

PUBLIC HOLIDAYS
There are no official public holidays, but businesses close a few days before the end of Ramadan and reopen after the end of Eid el-Fitr. They close one week before 10th Dhu el-Hijja until the end of Eid el-Adhar.

COMMUNICATIONS
Jeddah GPO, Al-Bareed St, open 0700–2100 Saturday to Thursday. Telephone office, Abo Bakr Al Seddeeq St, Al-Sharafeyyah district. Emergency 999, Ambulance 997.
There are regular international flights from both Jeddah and Riyadh.

DIPLOMATIC MISSIONS
In Jeddah:
Australia: 59 Al Amir Abdullah, Al-Faisal Street, Al Hamra District 5. *Tel.* (2) 665-1303.
Canada: Headquarters Building, Zahid Corporate Group. *Tel.* (2) 667-1156.
New Zealand: c/o Associated Agencies, Sindus Bldg, Al Madian St.
Tel. (2) 651-2109.
United Kingdom: Al-Andalus St, Al-Shate'e. *Tel.* 654-2786.
United States: Palestine (Falasteen) St, Ruwais. *Tel.* (2) 667-0080.

dependence on oil revenue. A labour shortage means that a lot of Egyptian and Palestinian workers have been brought in, but also many European and American specialists. Although tourism is officially frowned upon, a considerable income is generated by the many pilgrims visiting the holy site of Mecca.

Of the more than 17 million inhabitants, many are nomadic peoples and foreign workers. Arabic is the official language, while some government officials and businessmen speak English. Riyadh is the capital.

Islam is very strictly observed in Saudi Arabia, which is the main reason why non-Islamic tourists are not welcome. Alcohol is banned and photography frowned upon. Female visitors are only allowed into the country if they are chaperoned by a male. Mecca and Medina are off limits to non-believers as are all mosques.

The climate is very hot from April to September. Winters are cooler and the weather in coastal areas is very pleasant.

Entry Regulations

Ports of entry

Yanbu' al Bahr (Yenbo or Yambo) 24°06'N 38°03'E, Mira' al Jeddah 21°28'N 39°10'E.

Procedure on arrival

Yachts are allowed to enter the above ports, which are the main ports of Saudi Arabia, only in an emergency. Port control should be contacted on VHF Channel 16 before arrival. Only the captain is allowed ashore to complete formalities. Both the yacht and crew are normally restricted to the port area, but if allowed ashore everyone must return aboard before sundown. Travel inland is not permitted, nor may anywhere else but these two ports be visited. Cruising along the coast is strictly forbidden. In an emergency, which necessitates a stop in a Saudi port, the captain should contact immediately a coastal radio station and insist on being treated according to international maritime law. While in Saudi waters, vessels must fly the Saudi courtesy flag or risk being fined.

Customs

A licence is required for firearms. Dogs are banned. Alcohol and pork products are prohibited. All alcoholic drinks and products which contain pork will be sealed on board during the duration of the stay.

Immigration

Visas are difficult to obtain as tourism is not encouraged. Anyone travelling to Saudi Arabia can only obtain a visa by either being sponsored by a local company or having a written invitation from an influential individual. Even so, visas are extremely rarely granted to sailors. In genuine emergencies, yachts have been allowed to stop for a few days in one of the major ports, but the crew's movements were restricted to the immediate port area. Entry visas are not normally issued to holders of Israeli passports, passports which have been stamped with Israeli visas, or if there is some proof that one has been or intends to go to Israel.

Restrictions

One should not take photographs of Saudi women, airports or government buildings. Fishing, swimming and the consumption of alcohol is strictly prohibited while in harbour.

Yachts are obliged to obtain a copy of *Saudi Arabian Ports Rules and Regulations* while in Saudi Arabian waters.

Facilities

Both repair facilities and provisioning are better at Jeddah, which is Saudi Arabia's main port. Fuel is easily available. There are several workshops, as well as a ship repair yard with a slipway in Jeddah, which can also undertake electrical and electronic repair. Yanbu also has some local workshops well equipped to deal with emergency repairs.

Further Reading

Red Sea Pilot
Arab Gulf States – a travel survival kit

Website

www.saudia-online.com

SOMALIA

Somalia, or the Somali Democratic Republic as it has been called since the 1969 military coup, occupies most of the NE shoulder of the African continent. With nearly 2000 miles of coast around the Horn of Africa, Somalia has the second longest coastline in the continent. The interior is mostly desert where nomadic peoples roam, with mountains to the north and plains to the south.

With the exception of a few man-made ports, there are no natural harbours and there is little to attract cruising yachts to this country. A few yachts have called in at one of the ports on the eastern coast, but most stops were dictated by emergency reasons. Some areas, especially those in the vicinity of the Horn of Africa, are considered dangerous and therefore should be avoided. Only major ports should be approached and only in serious emergencies. Sailing to Somalia is considered far too hazardous in the present circumstances and anyone

intending to sail anywhere near Somalia should obtain the latest information on the internal situation before venturing anywhere near a Somali port.

Violent crime, including looting and banditry, is common, especially in Mogadishu, while many other areas of the country are suffering from armed conflict. There is no functioning national government.

Somali pirates

Reports received in Suez from boats arriving from the Indian Ocean point to an increase in pirate activity in the vicinity of the Horn of Africa. The alleged area is centred on Ras Alula (11°59′N 50°47′E), located approximately 30 miles west of Ras Asir, on the northern Somali coast in the Gulf of Aden. Ras Alula, also marked as Ras Caluula on some charts, is the first cape west of Cape Guardafui (Ras Asir).

The waters in the vicinity of the Somali coast, both south and west of the Horn of Africa, are now considered to be dangerous for both commercial shipping and small boats. The US authorities have issued a warning advising vessels to stay at least 30 miles off the African coast. This was also confirmed by the Djibouti authorities in the wake of several attacks on cruising yachts, as well as other shipping, off the north coast of neighbouring Somalia. Some of these attacks occurred as far as 60 miles offshore. Just as dangerous are the waters off the east coast of Somalia. Because of the latest reports, boats are strongly advised to avoid passing between the island of Socotra and the African mainland, while those approaching from the east through the Gulf of Aden should stay well clear of both the Somali and Yemeni coasts, as both are considered to be dangerous. The best approach is to sail in convoy with other yachts and try to be in permanent contact with someone ashore who knows one's position at all times and could alert the authorities in an emergency.

Country Profile

The Somalis have inhabited this area for many thousands of years. Greek and Arab writers of the ancient world used to call these handsome people the 'Black Berbers'. The Egyptians, who in 1500 BC knew of the port of Mogadishu, named it the Land of Punt. Mogadishu sent frankincense and myrrh to the Arabian peninsula, and traded as far as China. The whole Somali coast was part of the Arab trading routes around the Indian Ocean, a network extending down the East African coast as far as Mozambique. This prosperity faded when

Practical Information

LOCAL TIME: GMT + 3

BUOYAGE: IALA A

CURRENCY: Somali shilling (SSh) of 100 cents. The best currency to exchange is US dollars. Saudi riyals and pounds sterling are also accepted but nothing else. Foreign currency declaration forms must be filled in on arrival and one may have to show them when changing money.

BUSINESS HOURS
Banks: 0800–1130 Saturday to Thursday. Business and shops: 0900–1300, 1600–2000 Saturday to Thursday. Government offices: 0800–1400 Saturday to Thursday.

ELECTRICITY: 220 V, 50 Hz

PUBLIC HOLIDAYS
1 January: New Year's Day
1 May: Labour Day
Eid el-Adha
26 June: Independence of Somaliland
1 July: Independence of Somali Republic
Eid el-Arifa
Hijra
Ashoura
21, 22 October: Anniversary of the 1969 Revolution
Mouloud (Prophet's Birthday)

COMMUNICATIONS
The international telephone service is relatively good.

There are international flights from Mogadishu to Rome, Frankfurt, Nairobi, Cairo and other Middle Eastern cities for onward connections.

DIPLOMATIC MISSIONS
In Mogadishu:
United Kingdom: Waddada Xasan Geedd Abtoow 7/8. *Tel.* (1) 20288. (Temporarily closed. The British embassy in Ethiopia should be contacted in emergencies: *Tel.* 00254 2 714699/719942.)
United States: Contact the US embassies in Kenya or Djibouti. *Tel.* 00254 2 334141 (Nairobi), 00253 353995 (Djibouti).
Canada: Contact the Canadian embassy in Kenya. *Tel.* 00254 2 214804.

Portugal found the sea route to India via the Cape of Good Hope. Somalia, with no resources that Europeans could exploit, was largely ignored.

In the nineteenth century Somalia was divided up between its neighbours and the colonial powers. The Sultanate of Oman controlled southern Somalia, while Britain claimed northern Somalia, and the French took Djibouti. Italy bought Mogadishu and the surrounding area from the Omanis in 1889. Ethiopia meanwhile occupied much of the Ogaden Desert, an area ethnically part of Somalia, which remains a source of bitter conflict between the two countries up to the present day.

The British and Italian Somalias both became independent in 1960, and were united soon afterwards. In 1969 a radical socialist regime came to power after a military coup and the Somali Democratic Republic was formed. The United States withdrew its aid and this was replaced by economic and military aid from the USSR, until the latter decided to also support Ethiopia and was therefore ordered out of Somalia. During the 1970s Somali guerillas, supported by the government, tried to recover Ogaden, but failed due to Russian and Cuban aid given to Ethiopia.

The prolonged civil war has left a legacy of widespread poverty and lawlessness. In 1990 rebel forces reached Mogadishu and President Barre fled. The UN intervened in 1992 to provide humanitarian aid but the murder of 24 Pakistani soldiers and escalating violence eventually forced the UN to virtually abandon Somalia to its fate, the

last of its forces withdrawing by early 1995. Although aid agencies continue to be active in the country, the country's prospects for a return to normality are grim. A loose agreement was reached in 2000 among the various political factions, but as several warlords objected to its terms it may be some time before the country has a central government.

The lack of natural resources is a major problem and the majority of the population are nomadic herdsmen. Agricultural production is mainly for domestic consumption, although some export crops are being developed. The fishing industry is expanding, but there is little else. Frequent droughts and the influx of refugees from Ogaden are both burdens on the economy.

The population of around 8 million is concentrated in the coastal towns, near the Juba and Shebelle rivers in the south, while there are scattered nomadic peoples inland. Islam is the religion of the majority, although traditional rituals may still be found. Somali is the official language, although a written form was only developed in 1972. Educated Somalis speak Arabic, some English in the north and Italian in the south. Swahili is spoken widely in southern coastal towns. The capital is Mogadishu.

The climate is dictated by the two monsoons. It is hot all year round and also humid in the rainy seasons. The temperatures are very high in summer and can reach up to 108°F (42°C) from June to September in the northern coastal towns. At the height of the SW monsoon, May to October, winds often reach gale force. The current along the Somali coast can be very strong, particularly during the SW monsoon.

Entry Regulations

Ports of entry
Mogadishu 2°01'N 4°21'E, Kismayu/Chisimaio 0°23'S 42°33'E, Berbera 10°27'N 45°01'E, Merca/Marka 1°43'N 44°46'E, Boosaaso 11°17'N 49°11'E.

Procedure on arrival
Mogadishu: Port control monitors VHF Channel 16 and should be contacted to announce the yacht's ETA and request clearance.
Berbera: Port Radio (call sign 60Y) monitors MF 500 KHz and should be contacted to advise a yacht on procedure.

Customs
Firearms will be retained. Animals should be declared.

Immigration
All nationalities must obtain visas before arrival. In the proximity of Somalia, visas can be obtained from Nairobi at International House, Marma Ngina St. A letter may be required from one's own embassy. The Italian embassy in Dar es Salaam also issues Somali visas and there is also a Somali embassy in Djibouti.

Restrictions
A permit is needed if a camera is taken ashore. Permits are issued by the National Censorship Office in Mogadishu.

Health
Yellow fever and cholera vaccination is essential. Malaria prophylaxis is also recommended. A yellow fever vaccination certificate must be shown on entry, otherwise the vaccination will be done on the spot and not under very hygienic conditions.

Fees
There are very high harbour charges.

Facilities

Provisioning is rather limited, although there is some fresh produce available depending on the season. Mogadishu is very rarely visited by yachts. The harbour is well sheltered, but the area where small boats anchor is shallow due to silting. Some repairs are possible as there are various workshops in the port in Mogadishu, but they may take time.

Further Reading

Indian Ocean Cruising Guide

Website

http://www.abyssiniacybergateway.net/somalia (Useful links)

SRI LANKA

This large island shaped like a teardrop lies to the south of the Indian subcontinent, from which it is separated by the Palk Strait. The island is one of coastal plains and central highlands covered in forests. Inland can be seen the ancient cities and palaces of one of the oldest civilisations in the world.

Sri Lanka is a popular stopping point for yachts on their way to the Red Sea. Most come from the Pacific, the Far East or South East Asia, and the traffic is mostly westbound as only a few sail to Sri Lanka from the west. Sri Lanka is also a good point of departure for cruising the Maldives, Chagos and Seychelles. As a cruising destination in itself, Sri Lanka has little attraction and the troubles that have befallen the island during the last decade, although not affecting cruising yachts greatly, have almost destroyed the tourist industry. Fighting continues between the government and Tamil Tigers and the northern and eastern parts of the country should be avoided. A state of emergency is in operation in Colombo. The rest of the island, however, remains relatively unaffected.

Virtually all yachts that call at Sri Lanka do so at the old port of Galle, conveniently located on the island's southern tip. Very few yachts cruise outside of Galle and the beautiful natural harbour of Trincomalee on the east coast is for the time being out of bounds because of recurrent political troubles, while Colombo's large commercial harbour has no attractions as there are no provisions for yachts and formalities are even more complex than in Galle.

The continuing uncertainty in the rest of the country as well as the increasingly unwelcoming attitude of the officials in Galle are strong reasons to avoid Sri Lanka for the time being and bypass it altogether. This is the only course of action while the totally unacceptable situation continues in Galle, where visiting boats are forced to anchor in the outer harbour and the clearance costs are forever rising.

Country Profile

Sri Lanka's written history begins in 544 BC with the arrival of the Indian prince Vijaya, marking the start of the Mahavansa chronicles. The Sinhalese kings ruled for 21 centuries, despite regular invasions from southern India, developing an advanced civilisation, with the Buddhist religion at its core. The third century BC was a time of painting and literature, of building monasteries and cities with elaborate irrigation schemes, and remains of all this can still be seen.

In the sixteenth century the Portuguese were the

Fishermen mending nets at Galle, Sri Lanka.

first Europeans to visit and secured a monopoly over the spice and cinnamon trades. The Sinhalese resisted annexation and continued to rule from the capital Kandy in the central highlands. The Dutch expelled the Portuguese in the mid-seventeenth century, and suffered the same fate in their turn being ousted by the British at the end of the eighteenth century. Early in the nineteenth century the island became the Crown Colony of Ceylon, and the Sinhalese King was exiled. Coffee, tea and rubber plantations were developed, and railways and roads built. Tamils were brought in from southern India as labourers.

Independence was finally regained in 1948. The name Ceylon was later changed to Sri Lanka when the country's status was changed to that of a Democratic Socialist Republic. Since 1983 tensions often followed by violent clashes have existed between the Sinhalese and Tamils. Tamils make up 18 per cent of the population and are concentrated in the north of the island. Many of them have been there for over 2000 years, but the rest are descended

Practical Information

LOCAL TIME: GMT + 5½

BUOYAGE: IALA A

CURRENCY: Sri Lanka rupee (CER or SLRe) of 100 cents. All foreign currency must be recorded on arrival on a currency declaration form, which is surrendered on departure. Unspent rupees can be reconverted.
In Galle only banknotes and travellers' cheques can be changed.
Obtaining cash on a credit card is possible only in Colombo.
Indian and Pakistani banknotes cannot be imported.

BUSINESS HOURS
Banks: 0900–1500 Tuesday to Friday, 0900–1300 Monday, Saturday.
Business and government offices: 0800/0830–1630 Monday to Friday.
Shops: 1000–1800 Monday to Friday, 1000–1400 Saturday.

ELECTRICITY: 230/240 V, 50 Hz

PUBLIC HOLIDAYS
Poya Day: the full moon day of each month is a public holiday and all offices are closed.
1 January: New Year's Day
4 February: Independence Day
13 April: Sinhalese and Tamil New Year
Good Friday, Easter Monday
1 May: Labour Day
May: full moon, Vesak Festival
22 May: National Heroes Day
June Bank Holiday
25, 26 December: Christmas
Variable: Eid al-Fitr, Eid al-Adha, Milad un-Nabi.

COMMUNICATIONS
International telephone, telex and telegraph services are available.
In Galle international telephone calls can be made via Windsor Yacht Services.
General post office, in Galle, and small one in the suburb Magalle, opening hours: 0800–1630.
There are international flights from Colombo to European and Asian destinations.

MEDICAL
Colombo General Hospital.
Karapitiya General Hospital, Galle.
Tel. 32176.
Private Hospital. *Tel.* 34060.
There are hospitals with casualty departments and private clinics in all major centres.

DIPLOMATIC MISSIONS
In Colombo:
Australia: 3 Cambridge Place.
Tel. (1) 698767.
Canada: 6 Gregory's Rd, Cinnamon Gardens. *Tel.* (1) 695841.
France: 89 Rosmead Place. *Tel.* (1) 699750.
India: 36–38 Galle Rd. *Tel.* (1) 52160.
Maldives: 25 Melbourne Av.
Tel. (1) 586762.
Myanmar: 17 Skelton Gdns.
Tel. (1) 587607.
New Zealand: c/o Aitken Spence & Co. Ltd, PO Box 5. *Tel.* (1) 27861.
Thailand: 43 Dr C W W Kannangara Mawatha. *Tel.* (1) 597406.
United Kingdom: 190 Galle Rd.
Tel. (1) 437336.
United States: 210 Galle Rd.
Tel. (1) 548007.

from more recent immigrants from neighbouring Tamil Nadu state in southern India. Tamil separatists want an independent state in the northern part of Sri Lanka. In 1987, India intervened to re-establish order, but this brought renewed fighting between Indian forces and the Tamil rebels. India finally withdrew her forces in 1990 and peace negotiations between the Tamil rebels and the government began. Peace talks broke down and the 1990s saw some of the bloodiest conflicts so far.

Sri Lanka is famous for its tea and is one of the top world suppliers. Also exported are rubber, coconut products, clothes, cinnamon, precious and semi-precious stones. Agriculture is an important part of the economy and much rice is grown for domestic needs.

The population numbers over 17 million. As well as Sinhalese and Tamils, there are also Moors, Burghers (of Portuguese and Dutch origin), Eurasians and Malays. The majority of Sinhalese are Buddhist, most Tamils are Hindu, while some Sri Lankans are Christian and Muslim. Sinhala and Tamil are the official languages and English is also widely spoken. Colombo is the capital.

The climate is tropical, with two distinct monsoon seasons. Heavy rainfall along the western coast occurs during the SW monsoon, particularly between May and September. The temperatures on the coast are usually high, while in the hills it is pleasant all year round. The island is occasionally affected by tropical cyclones, which develop in the Bay of Bengal, the worst months being November and December.

Entry Regulations

Ports of entry
Galle 6°01′N 80°13′E, Colombo 6°57′N 79°51′E, Trincomalee 8°36′N 81°15′E, Jaffna 9°40′N 79°59′E, Kankesanthurai 9°49′N 80°03′E.

Procedure on arrival
On arrival in a Sri Lankan port, the captain should inform the harbour master, or report to the nearest customs officer or police station immediately. A health officer will board the

yacht and inspect it before granting pratique. Then the yacht will be inspected by a customs officer, who will require the last port clearance. Crew lists and details of any passengers or crew who are leaving the vessel have to be given to the immigration office.

Colombo: Arriving yachts should contact the port authority on VHF Channel 16 before proceeding into the harbour. The instructions detailed above should then be followed.

Galle: Flying the Q flag, one should anchor or tie up to a mooring in the western part of the outer harbour, as visiting boats are no longer allowed to enter the inner harbour. The arrival should be timed for daylight as entering the harbour at night is prohibited. A port authority official will come out to the boat during office hours (0800–1200, 1300–1600 Monday to Friday) to fill in an arrival report (yacht details, crew list, etc.). All foreign yachts are supposed to appoint an agent and names of agents will be given by the port authority official. The agent appointed will come to the yacht after having been informed by the port authority. Usually the agent will bring the health officer for the quarantine inspection. The Don Windsor Agency can be contacted on Channel 16 one hour before arrival to arrange for the boat to be met by an agent.

The captain can come ashore in an emergency and contact customs and immigration at the gate and inform the port authority of arrival. The captain can appoint an agent whilst ashore.

Clearance must be carried out through this agent, both on arrival and departure. The agent is supposed to ensure that the captain complies with port and immigration regulations, that he has sufficient funds in foreign exchange for the fees and that all port dues and customs duties are settled before departure. The ruling concerning agents has not been confirmed officially from Colombo, although this appears to be the current procedure accepted by officials in Galle.

The port authority will indicate the area in each port where yachts may anchor. Yachts should not move from their original mooring without the harbour master's permission. Permission is also needed before hauling out a yacht. One should only land by dinghy at the appointed places in each port.

Procedure on departure

On departure a clearance certificate must be obtained from customs. If the yacht is sailing along the coast, a clearance certificate must be obtained

for calling at other ports in Sri Lanka. Access is only permitted to official ports of entry.

Customs

Firearms must be declared on arrival and held in custody by customs until departure. One must ensure that a receipt is obtained for the firearms.

Animals should not be taken ashore. Rabies is widespread and in 1989 over one hundred people died of it in Sri Lanka.

All electrical and electronic goods such as cameras or radios must be re-exported.

Customs permission has to be obtained for any item that is taken off or put on board the yacht, including ship's stores and items being repaired. In Galle the customs at the harbour gate will often check the contents of any bags carried.

Yachts may stay up to two months.

Immigration

For all nationalities arriving on a yacht, a visa is granted on arrival for one month. This visa can be extended for up to two months.

Any crew or passengers leaving the yacht in Sri Lanka must get a landing endorsement from immigration or police before leaving the harbour. It is an offence for someone who is not a crew member or no longer a crew member to move ashore without a landing endorsement. Likewise, the master may not engage any crew while in Sri Lanka without permission from immigration or police. A new crew list should be given to the police if there are any crew changes.

Health

Malaria prophylaxis is recommended.

Fees

Port dues: US$100, for one month or part thereof, which must be paid on arrival. Payment made at one port is valid for other ports. US$20 customs fee. Overtime clearance fee (approximately US$10).

Agent fee: In Galle approximately US$50 for the first 30 days or part thereof.

Customs departure tax: Rs 500

No overtime fees apply as all formalities are completed within normal working hours.

Restrictions

Anchorage in any other area in Sri Lankan territorial waters except a port of entry is forbidden to yachts, unless in distress or an emergency situation.

Facilities

Facilities are generally poor and as there are very few local yachts, the only workshops that are used to dealing with yachts are those in Galle. The fishing cooperative has a slipway, but this is temporarily out of action. There is a fuel pump on the dock, where small amounts of diesel fuel can be bought. Larger amounts can be ordered by road tanker. Water can be obtained from a tank at the fisheries dock. There are various workshops in Galle capable of electrical or engine repair. There is also a small boatyard building fibreglass boats near the old harbour, which can deal with some repairs.

A local entrepreneur, Santosh Windsor, has a yacht service company, run from his home near Galle harbour. He is the best man to contact in an emergency. His office can also be used for overseas telephone calls, mailing address and to book excursions into the interior. He can arrange most repairs including electronic, engine, and sail repair as well as metal work and welding. He can also supply courtesy flags, fill LPG bottles and arrange for essential spares to be ordered from abroad and air-freighted by courier. More complex engine or electrical repairs may have to be made in Colombo. Windsor Yacht Services also arrange visits into the interior and will also find a reliable person to watch unattended boats. Theirs is also the most reliable forwarding address for mail: 6 Closenburg Road, Magalle, Galle, Sri Lanka. *Tel.* +94 77 901046, Fax. +94 71 749803.

There are no chandleries or marine supplies either in Colombo or Galle. Marine Overseas Agency in Colombo has a stock of nautical charts and publications. There are no supermarkets in Galle and most provisioning has to be done from small grocery shops, which have a rather limited selection. There is a very good daily fresh produce market in Galle, where provisions can be bought for the onward voyage.

Further Reading

Sri Lanka – a travel survival kit
Indian Handbook
Indian Ocean Cruising Guide

Website

www.priu.gov.lk (Official government site)

SUDAN

Sudan is the largest country in Africa, but only a small part is on the Red Sea coast. The north is desert, and the south tropical and it is the country where Arab and black African cultures meet. The River Nile runs through the country from Kenya down to Egypt past Khartoum, the capital, in the centre of the country.

Most sailors only come in contact with Port Sudan, the country's main port on the Red Sea. It is a convenient stop for yachts sailing up or down the Red Sea, although its facilities are poor and nothing has been done to improve them. A dirty and crowded harbour and town, Port Sudan is a poor introduction to this vast country. Boats coming from the south might find simpler formalities in Suakin, just south of Port Sudan. The buildings of the once thriving port are now all in ruins. In the fifteenth century it was the major port of the western Red Sea. Huge camel caravans brought copper, ivory, hides and slaves from the interior, returning with cotton, spices, silks and beads. By the sixteenth century the harbour could hold 600 ships, and during the nineteenth century Suakin became even more cosmopolitan, only to prove too small for large ocean steamers. Today it is deserted, a sad ghost town of ruined buildings, where Kitchener's old headquarters can still be seen overlooking the harbour.

Port Sudan's position at the halfway point of the Red Sea also marks the point where the winds change from prevailing southerlies to northerlies. Northbound yachts, as are the majority who call here, face an uphill beat all the way to the Suez Canal, while southbound boats usually have to fight contrary winds as far as Bab el Mandeb and even beyond. If not in a great hurry, the best tactic for northbound boats is to cover as much ground as possible inside the reefs, which extend parallel to the shore along most of Sudan's coastline. This not only makes life easier but also more pleasant as the reef anchorages offer perfect shelter and the diving and fishing are superb.

Country Profile

The Ancient Egyptians called the lands to their south 'bilad al sudan', 'lands of the blacks', and they made occasional forays into it for ivory, ebony and slaves. From the fourth century Christian kingdoms ruled over the area, but from the sixth

Practical Information

LOCAL TIME: GMT + 2

BUOYAGE: IALA A

CURRENCY: Sudanese pound (£S) of 100 piastres (PT). It is illegal to export any £S on leaving. Foreign currency must be declared on arrival and departure.

BUSINESS HOURS
Banks: 0830–1230 Saturday to Thursday.
Shops: 0800–1400, 1800–2000 Saturday to Thursday.
Government offices: 0800–1430 Saturday to Thursday.

ELECTRICITY: 240 V, 50 Hz

PUBLIC HOLIDAYS
1 January: Independence Day
3 March: Unity Day
6 April: Uprising Day
Sham el Nassim (Spring Festival)
1 July: Decentralisation Day
Eid el-Fitr
Eid el-Adha
Islamic New Year
Mouloud (Prophet's Birthday)

COMMUNICATIONS
Port Sudan Post Office opens 0700–1400 Saturday to Thursday, and has a telephone counter, although it can be difficult to get international calls through.
Khartoum airport has international flights and can be reached from Port Sudan by air, train or bus. There are also flights from Port Sudan to Cairo and Jeddah, which both have good onward connections.

MEDICAL
The government hospital in Port Sudan has a 24 hour casualty department.

DIPLOMATIC MISSIONS
In Khartoum:
Egypt: Al-Gamma St. *Tel.* 72836.
United Kingdom: St 10, off Sharia Baladia. *Tel.* 777105.
United States: Sharia Ali Abdul Latif. *Tel.* 774700.
Canada: The Canadian embassy in Ethiopia deals with Sudan.
Tel. +251 1 713 022. (Addis Ababa)
There is an Egyptian consulate in Port Sudan, where it is sometimes possible to obtain an Egyptian visa.

century they were progressively taken over by the Arabs. In the north Sultans established their rule and Islam extended its influence. In 1821 the Egyptians, then under Ottoman rule, took control of north Sudan. Only the Fur Sultanate in the south-east remained independent. In 1881 Mohammed Ahmed al-Mahdi led a successful uprising against the Ottomans and a puritanical Islamic state was established. Al-Mahdi's rule was short-lived and ended in 1898, when his forces were defeated by those led by Field Marshal Kitchener from British-occupied Egypt. The southern Sultanate was also overthrown by Anglo-Egyptian forces in 1916 and as a result Sudan was made an Anglo-Egyptian condominium.

From the 1930s onwards a movement for independence grew. Civil war between the north and south began in 1955, and a year later the independent Republic of Sudan was established. The continuing war caused great economic problems for the country and civil governments alternated with military regimes. The war finally ended in 1972 and the south gained some autonomy. A civil government was established in 1986. The antagonism of the southerners was exacerbated after the declaration of Islamic Law in 1984, as there are very few Muslims in the south. Problems continue in the south with the guerilla activities of the Sudanese People's Liberation Movement. Peace talks in 1991 failed to resolve the conflict, and while it continues, travel into the interior should be avoided.

Sudan's history has been dominated by the division between north and south – the northerners have always tended to dominate the country's affairs, much to the southerners' resentment. Among the 23 million Sudanese, there are 500 ethnic groups. Northerners are generally Muslim of Arab origin and language, while the Southerners are African, animist or Christian, with no common language, and closer in lifestyle to neighbouring countries. Although Arabic is the official language, only half the population speak it. A hundred other languages are spoken, including English in the south.

Sudan is mainly an agricultural country. Cotton is the main export and the development of irrigation, especially along the Nile, is a top priority in this dry country. The foreign debt is large and in the past shortages have been a major problem.

The climate is tropical, hot and dry in the north, and rainier in the south. The Red Sea area is very hot in summer when the winds are mostly northerly. The winter months are very pleasant and the prevailing winds are from the south.

Entry Regulations

Port of entry
Port Sudan 19°37'N 37°14'E.

Procedure on arrival
Port Sudan: Call Port Control on Channel 16 or

14 before entering the port. Boats are normally directed to the anchorage in the NW part of the harbour. Everyone should remain on board until cleared by quarantine. The boat is usually visited by a local agent and all formalities are expected to be completed with his help. The services of an agent are not compulsory, but as the formalities are lengthy and complicated, it is much easier if a local agent is used, although one can do all formalities on one's own. Agency fees tend to be quite high so these must be agreed in advance. The agent will also call customs and port police. These will seal all alcoholic drinks and radio equipment on board. The agent will then arrange shore passes, for which a passport size photograph is required. The passports must then be left with immigration, which usually holds them until the following day. The ship's papers are held by the Port Office until port dues are paid, in US dollars cash, on departure.

Suakin: Boats arriving here from the south have been allowed to clear into Sudan and formalities are reported to be simpler. On arrival, call Port Control on Channel 14. The boat is usually visited by customs and quarantine. As Suakin is not an official port of entry and there is no immigration official there, only shore passes are given to the crew and these are for a short duration only. Proper formalities must be completed if continuing to Port Sudan. Formalities are simpler if one arrives with a Sudanese visa.

Yachts have been allowed to anchor along the coast before clearing in, provided no one goes ashore. Yachts stopping in Suakin can check in with the police in New Town (El Geif), which is reached over the causeway.

Procedure on departure

Port Sudan: On departure, one must clear with the port office, then pay the port dues at the Port Corporation in East Town. They insist the fee must be paid in US dollars. Next one has to clear customs, and return to the port office to get back the ship's papers.

Customs

Firearms must be declared. Animals are not allowed to land.

Immigration

Yachts in transit are normally allowed visa-free entry for a short period of stay. Visas must be obtained in advance by those who wish to spend longer in the country or who wish to visit the interior. A passport must be valid at least six months beyond the intended period of stay. Visas are valid for three months from the date of issue, for a one month stay. Extensions for two months are obtainable.

The shore pass does not allow foreigners to leave the Port Sudan area. Special travel permits must be obtained for visits inland. Those who wish to leave the country by air need a transit visa. Nationals of Israel or anyone with an Israeli stamp or visa in their passport are not allowed to visit Sudan.

Health

Cholera and yellow fever vaccinations recommended. An international certificate for yellow fever may be demanded even though it is not obligatory. Malarial prophylaxis is recommended if travelling inland, when one should also avoid swimming in fresh water, as the bilharzia parasite is endemic.

Fees

Port dues, payable in US dollars. US$10 per person for the shore pass.

Restrictions

Travel permits are necessary when travelling anywhere in Sudan. These are obtained from the Foreigners Registration Office. The country south of Kosti is closed, due to the activities of the Sudanese People's Liberation Movement. The border with Ethiopia is closed.

A photography permit is required, and can be obtained from the tourist office.

Facilities

Provisioning with fresh produce is very good in Port Sudan where there is a daily market. There are also various grocery shops, some of them selling in bulk. Fuel is available from the fuel dock in South Town. This must be arranged through the agent as foreign vessels are not allowed to buy fuel direct. Water is also available, but must be treated. There is also a good market in Port Sudakin (New Town) but one must go early in the morning. There are few other provisions and what is available is expensive. There is no bank in Suakin.

There are only limited repair facilities in Port Sudan, although there are some workshops around the harbour that can undertake simple repairs. No kind of spares are available and as flights to Khartoum are infrequent, one should not rely on being able to obtain essential spares from abroad.

Further Reading

Africa on a Shoestring
Traveller's Guide to East Africa and the Indian Ocean
Red Sea Pilot

Website

www.sudmer.com (Ministry of External Relations)

UNITED ARAB EMIRATES

The UAE is a federation of seven independent states, with coastlines on the Persian Gulf and the Gulf of Oman. Abu Dhabi is the largest state. Dubai, Ajman, Fujairah, Ras al-Khaimah, Sharjah, and Umm al-Qaiwain are known as the Northern States. The UAE interior is mainly desert; most of the 2 million inhabitants live along the coast or in inland oases.

Although cruising opportunities are very limited, a small number of foreign yachts venture into the area every year. As there is a relatively high number of locally owned yachts, mainly power, facilities are of a good standard.

Country Profile

Formerly known as the Trucial States, the Emirates were under the military protection of Britain from 1853 to 1971, when six of the states became independent as the United Arab Emirates. Ras al-Khaimah joined in 1972. The exploitation of oil and gas reserves are the main economic activity, although some effort is being made to diversify and develop other industries. The Emirates are members of the Organization of Petroleum Exporting Countries (OPEC), and formed part of the international force which defeated Iraq in the 1991 Gulf War.

Arabic is the official language and English is widely spoken. Islam is the state religion, and Islamic law should be observed by foreign visitors. Abu Dhabi is the federal capital, and the port of Dubai is the commercial centre.

June to September is the hottest, dry period of the year; October to May being more pleasant.

Entry Regulations

Ports of entry

Dubai (Port Rashid) 25°16′N 55°16′E, Jebel Ali 25°02′N 55°08′E.
Abu Dhabi: Mina Zayed 24°29′N 54°22′E.
Sharjah: Khalid 25°22′N 55°23′E.
Ras al-Khaimah: Mina Saqr 25°59′N 56°03′E.
Fujairah 25°10′N 56°22′E.
Ajman 25°25′N 55°26′E.
Umm al-Qaiwain 25°35′N 55°35′E.

Practical Information

LOCAL TIME: GMT + 4

BUOYAGE: IALA A

CURRENCY: UAE dirham (UAE Dh) of 100 fils is pegged to the US dollar. Israeli currency is prohibited.

BUSINESS HOURS
Banks: 0800–1300 Sunday to Wednesday, 0800–1200 Thursday.
Some also 1600–1930.
Business: 0800–1300, 1600–1900 Saturday to Wednesday, 0700–1200 Thursday.
Government offices: 0730–1330 Saturday to Wednesday, 0730–1200 Thursday (winter), 0700–1300 Saturday to Thursday (summer). All offices close in the afternoon during Ramadan.

ELECTRICITY: 220/240 V, 50 Hz (Abu Dhabi), 220 V, 50 Hz (Northern States)

PUBLIC HOLIDAYS
1 January: New Year's Day
6 August: Accession of HH Sheikh Zayed (Abu Dhabi only)
2 December: National Day
Variable: Start of Ramadan, Eid al-Fitr, Eid al-Adha, Muharram (Islamic New Year), Mouloud, Leilat al-Miraj

COMMUNICATIONS
IDD calls are widely available and communications generally are of very good quality.
Fax, telex and telegram services are available from ETISALAT offices.

There are international airports at Abu Dhabi, Dubai, Ras al-Khaimah, Sharjah and Fujairah, with frequent flights to destinations in Europe, the Middle East and Asia from the first two airports.

MEDICAL
Facilities are of a very high standard but are expensive.

DIPLOMATIC MISSIONS
United Kingdom: PO Box 248, Abu Dhabi. Tel. (2) 326 600, and PO Box 65, Dubai. Tel. (4) 397 1070.
United States: PO Box 4009, Al-Sudan St, Abu Dhabi. Tel. (2) 336 691.

Procedure on arrival

Dubai: Yachts should call Dubai Creek Port Control on Channel 16. The Q flag and UAE courtesy flag must be flown. The vessel will be instructed to proceed inside the creek, where clearance is made with customs and immigration. Clearance from the last port, crew lists, customs declaration and passports, with valid visas, will be requested.

Immigration

Admission is refused to nationals of Israel and holders of passports containing Israeli stamps. All nationals require visas except nationals of Bahrain, Kuwait, Oman, Qatar and Saudi Arabia, and of UK citizens for a maximum of 30 days. Visa applications must be arranged through a sponsor (UAE resident) or hotel or travel agency. A multiple entry visa should be obtained if intending to visit more than one state.

In the case of those arriving without a visa, especially if it is made clear that only a short stay is intended, immigration may retain passports and issue yacht crews with a landing pass for 48 hours.

Restrictions

All the states except Sharjah allow the consumption of alcohol by non-Muslims, but it is illegal to drink alcohol on the street or to buy it for a UAE citizen. During Ramadan it is illegal to eat, drink or smoke in public.

Facilities

As there are a number of locally owned yachts, facilities are of a good standard and there is a limited range of repair facilities available. There are two marinas in Dubai, one at the Dubai Golf and Yacht Club by the town centre, which can only be reached when the bridge over the creek opens. About 3 miles west of the town is the Dubai Offshore Sailing Club.

Further Reading

Arab Gulf States – a travel survival kit

Websites

www.uae.org.ae
www.dubaitourism.co.ae
www.emirates.org

YEMEN

Yemen lies on the south-western edge of the Arabian peninsula, with coasts on the Gulf of Aden and Red Sea. The reunification of the People's Democratic Republic (South Yemen) and the Yemen Arab Republic (North Yemen) occurred in May 1990.

Previously North Yemen had not encouraged visitors, although a few yachts had called at Hodeidah, the main port. Mainly to shelter from the weather, yachts have sometimes stopped at the Jabal Zugar and Hamish Islands. This practice seemed to be tolerated by the authorities, although one should refrain from going ashore. Also belonging to Yemen is the island of Socotra, lying off the Horn of Africa. Its inhabitants have a fierce reputation and mariners have always been advised to give the island a wide berth. It is advice still worth following as Socotra lacks good harbours and its inhabitants' reputation appears to have remained unchanged.

Yachts more often call at Aden, the former capital of South Yemen, which has been an important port since ancient times and is still a useful stop on the way to or from the Red Sea. It is a busy commercial port, which holds little attraction for cruising yachts. Formalities are complicated and the freedom of movement enjoyed by visiting sailors is full of constraints. The only other choice for a stop in this area is Djibouti, on the African coast, where facilities are better, but prices much higher, the latter being the main factor which has persuaded some cruising yachts to prefer Aden.

Country Profile

In ancient times various kingdoms ruled in Yemen, the most important being that of Saba (Sheba), the Yemenis then being known as Sabeans. The famous Queen of Sheba travelled north, with many treasures, to visit King Solomon. Myrrh and frankincense, much-prized luxuries in the ancient world, grew naturally in Yemen, and the Sabeans prospered with trade. Also they had a monopoly on the trade of goods from India and Africa, while keeping the origin of the goods a secret, so that in Mediterranean countries Saba was believed to be a very rich place. From the sixth century AD the area lost its importance, being occupied by the Ethiopians and then the Persians. The arrival of Islam in the seventh century saw Yemen become a

Practical Information

LOCAL TIME: GMT + 3

BUOYAGE: IALA A

CURRENCY: Riyal of 100 fils.

BUSINESS HOURS
Banks: 0800–1200 Saturday to Wednesday, 0800–1130 Thursday.
Business: 0800–1200, 1600–1900 Saturday to Thursday.
Government offices: 0800–1500 Saturday to Wednesday.

ELECTRICITY: 220/240 V, 50 Hz

PUBLIC HOLIDAYS
1 May
22 May: National Day
26 September: Revolution Day
14 October: National Day
30 November: Independence Day
Variable: Birthday of the Prophet, Eid El-Fitr (two days), Eid El-Adha (three days), Islamic New Year.

COMMUNICATIONS
Post office at Steamer Point in Aden 0800–1300, 1600–2000 Saturday to Thursday.
Yemen Telecommunications Co., Steamer Point, open 24 hours. Cable & Wireless, Alamnie Bldg, 26 September St, Hodeidah.

There are international flights from Sana'a to many European, Middle East and Asian destinations. Aden has flights to destinations in the Middle East and Eastern Europe, Djibouti and Cairo.

MEDICAL
Aden General Hospital.

DIPLOMATIC MISSIONS
In Aden:
United Kingdom: 28 Shara Ho Chi Minh, Khormakasar. Tel. (2) 232712.
In Sana'a:
United Kingdom: 129 Haddah Road. Tel. (1) 264081/2/3/4.
United States: PO Box 1088 Sa'awan St. Tel. (1) 238842.

---

province on the southern edge of the Islamic Empire. In the ninth century the Zaydi dynasty was established which survived until 1962.

A sultanate independent of the Zaydis established itself in the south of the country. In 1839 the British conquered Aden and established a protectorate in southern Yemen. The Turks occupied the north in 1848, and the eventual border which was settled between Britain and Turkey remained the division between the two Yemeni countries. The south stayed under British rule, but from 1959 Aden and most of the sultanates of southern Yemen increasingly pushed for independence. There was fighting against the British forces from 1963 until independence was gained in 1967. In 1970 South Yemen became the People's Democratic Republic of Yemen with a Marxist-Leninist regime.

North Yemen was occupied by the Turks from 1848 and only after they withdrew at the end of the First World War was the independence of the Zaydi kingdom finally recognised. In 1962 a *coup d'état* saw the 1100 year old Zaydi dynasty overthrown and a republic proclaimed. Until 1970 civil war continued between the royalists supported by Saudi Arabia and the republicans supported by Egypt. The Yemen Arab Republic was proclaimed in 1970.

In May 1990 the two Yemens decided to unite. The capital is Sana'a, the previous capital of North Yemen. The decision to reunite the two countries was partly to redress the arbitrary division of the country by Britain and Turkey in the last century, but mainly it was prompted by economic reasons

as oil has been discovered in the border area between them. Reunification has not brought peace and, after a bitter conflict in the early 1990s, tensions remain high.

The population of around 17 million speak Arabic and are Muslim. English is spoken by many in the town of Aden.

Yemen has a subtropical climate. May to September is the period of the SW monsoon, when it is humid and rainy. October to February is drier and cooler, with easterly winds predominating.

Entry Regulations

Ports of entry
Aden 12°48'N 44°58'E, Hodeidah 14°50'N 42°56'E, Mukalla 14°31'N 49°08'E.

Procedure on arrival
Aden: Aden Port Control should be contacted when 10 miles off to give an ETA, either on Channel 16 or 2182 kHz. They will request to be contacted again when one mile off the harbour entrance. Arriving at night should be avoided as Port Control may insist on taking on a pilot as vessels are not allowed to move within the harbour at night. The yacht anchorage is west of the customs wharf. Formalities are carried out ashore. The dinghy can be left at the ferry dock, where a customs officer will meet the captain and accompany him to the office. Immigration will be visited next, where passports are held until departure and every

crew member is issued a shore pass. The last stop is at the harbour master's office.

Hodeidah: Port Control in Hodeidah should be contacted in advance on VHF Channel 16 to advise ETA, name of vessel and other details, otherwise the yacht may not be allowed into the port. Hodeidah is approached through a 10 mile long channel. Pilotage is only compulsory for vessels over 150 GRT.

Mukalla: Boats en route to or from the Red Sea have been able to make short stops here with minimum formalities. Contact the authorities on Channel 16 who will advise where to anchor. Customs and immigration offices are in the commercial harbour near the jetty.

Customs

Firearms must be declared to customs. Animals must not be landed.

Immigration

No visas are required for sailors on a short visit who do not leave the Port of Aden area. In this case passports are held until departure and shore passes issued.

Visas are essential for all nationalities if intending to visit other parts of Yemen outside of the port of Aden. Yachts may be able to stop at Hodeidah in an emergency without the crew having visas, but the nature of this emergency should be made clear during the conversation with Hodeidah port radio.

Health

Malaria prophylaxis is recommended for travel outside of Aden, especially September to February.

Cruising permit

It may be possible to obtain a permit to cruise the South Yemen coast, obtainable from customs and the harbour master. A yacht should not stop in any coastal areas without written permission.

Procedure on departure

One must visit customs, immigration and harbour master's office for outward clearance. Departures at night are prohibited and Port Control should be contacted on Channel 16 when ready to leave.

Restrictions

Cameras are not permitted ashore and no photographs should be taken in the port area. Visiting other yachts in the harbour needs permission from customs.

It is forbidden to stop at the islands of Socotra (off Somalia), Perim and Kamaran.

The restrictions on Perim and the Hanish islands have been lifted, but it is wise to check locally on the situation between Eritrea and Yemen. The large Strait of Bab al Mandab is to be preferred to the small Strait, which has been closed to yachts in the past.

Facilities

Egyptian visas can be obtained easily at the Egyptian Consulate in Aden. Repair facilities in Aden are limited to those operated by the National Dockyard which has a slipway and undertakes general hull and engine repair, as well as electronic repairs on radios and radars. However, they are only supposed to work on commercial vessels, so one may need special approval for them to work on a yacht.

Provisioning is reasonable, with a good selection of tinned goods and staples. Prices are much lower than in neighbouring Djibouti. There is a daily fresh produce market at Steamer Point. Cheap diesel fuel can be bought at the eastern end of the customs wharf, which also has a water outlet. Propane tanks can be refilled locally. There is a Sailors Club near the anchorage which has showers and can be used by visitors on yachts.

In Hodeidah a limited amount of provisions may be obtained in the port. There is a small shipyard, with its own slipway, which repairs port craft and navy boats, so they might be able to help out in an emergency.

Further Reading

Red Sea Pilot
Yemen – a travel survival kit

Website

www.yemeninfo.gov.ye (Government Information Office)

12 South Indian Ocean

Scattered along the trade wind route from the South Pacific to the Cape of Good Hope, the islands of the South Indian Ocean are visited by a relatively small number of yachts every year. The most popular destinations are the various islands as well as the Seychelles where restrictions on cruising yachts are gradually being eased. On mainland Africa yachts are now welcome in both Tanzania and Kenya, while Mozambique also looks more positive as more yachts sail there.

The region is under the influence of the SE monsoon for most of the year, which provides good sailing conditions. The cyclone season lasts from December to the end of March, but only affects the area south of Mauritius and Madagascar, so that the more northerly islands, such as the Seychelles and Chagos, as well as most of the African coast, can be cruised safely all year round. However, to cruise the African coast, it is advisable to do it during the SE monsoon and sail from south to north so as to take advantage of favourable winds and current, by sailing first to Tanzania, stopping in Dar es Salaam, Zanzibar, Pemba and Mombasa.

Repair facilities for yachts are available in only the few places which have either a resident boating population, such as Kenya and Réunion, or a charter operation, such as the Seychelles. In all other places only basic repairs are possible. Provisioning follows the same pattern, with only basic supplies available in the smaller places and a somewhat better selection in the larger centres. Spares and marine supplies are not available throughout the region, so all essential spares should be carried on board.

CHAGOS

The Chagos archipelago is a collection of atolls, reefs and shoals in the Indian Ocean, lying between the 5th and 8th parallel south of the equator. The group has been a British Indian Ocean Territory since 1965, and the largest island, Diego Garcia, has been made available to the United States as a military base and is off limits to yachts. There are some 55 other islands, all uninhabited. The group is a British dependency and administered by the British Navy. The original Chagos inhabitants, the Illois were resettled in Mauritius. But, due to a vigorous campaign by about 2000 islanders to return to their homeland, in Nov 2000 a High Court decision in London accepted

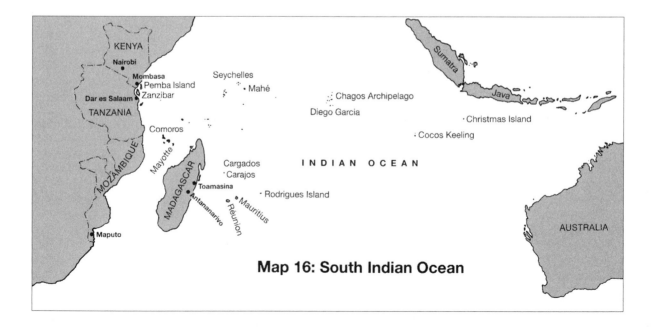

Map 16: South Indian Ocean

the validity of their claim. Arrangements are now being made for the Illois to return to Chagos but negotiations are needed with the USA who are unlikely to agree to vacate the military base on Diego Garcia which has about 3000 personnel.

Increasing numbers of cruising boats are now stopping at some of the outer islands in the group, some people even spending long periods on these uninhabited islands. This appears to be tolerated, although the islands are sometimes patrolled and one may be asked to show papers and passports. People on visiting yachts are not allowed to spend the night ashore and, at least in principle, the authorities expect yachts to spend no longer than one month in the islands. There are British police, customs and immigration officials on Diego Garcia. It is in the best interests of all sailors not to upset the present status quo by abusing this tolerance. The archipelago has the largest expanse of undisturbed coral reefs in the Indian Ocean, as well as rare and endangered species of birds and other wildlife. There are strict conservation rules, which must be observed in order to preserve this unique sanctuary in its present state.

Country Profile

From the sixteenth century the Portuguese, followed by the English and French, began sailing more directly across the central Indian Ocean to find good trade routes to the Indies, and encounters with the archipelago painted a picture of a dangerous reef-strewn area. Only from the eighteenth century however was any attempt made to accurately chart it, at first with such inaccuracy that there was confusion over whether the islands discovered were in the Chagos or the Seychelles. A French colony was established and a copra industry developed on the larger islands with slaves brought across from Africa and Madagascar. The archipelago was ceded to Britain in 1814 along with Mauritius and the Seychelles. After emancipation some former slaves remained on the islands as contract employees. The inhabitants, a mixture of African and Tamil, became known as Ilois and worked on the plantations as well a growing food for themselves. In 1965 the archipelago was detached from Mauritius and the British Indian Ocean Territory was created, which also included several of the islands of the Seychelles.

An agreement was reached by Britain and the USA in 1966 to make the Territory available for defence purposes. In 1967 the islands were pur-

chased by the Crown from the private company which ran the copra plantations, and became Crown Property. The workers and their families were resettled in Mauritius and compensation was paid to them. In 1976, the three island groups of Aldabra, Desroches and Farquhar were detached from the BIOT and became part of the newly independent Seychelles republic. The Mauritian government does not recognise the present arrangements and claims Chagos as being part of its own territory. This is not accepted by the British authorities as Chagos was only ever administered by Mauritius under the Empire.

The commanding naval officer on Diego Garcia is the British representative, and is in charge of customs and immigration.

Entry Regulations

Diego Garcia may only be entered in a serious emergency. Yachts trying to enter will be stopped outside the main pass and searched by the Navy. If an emergency stop is being made, it is best to contact the authorities on VHF Channel 16, while approaching the island, and advise them of the nature of the emergency. In the past the authorities have done their best to render assistance to yachts with genuine problems. An anchorage fee of £35 ($55) is now being charged for cruising boats.

Restrictions
The islands are a conservation area and all flora and fauna, such as turtles, coconut crabs, live coral and shells, are protected. Spearfishing is not allowed, nor should the heart of palm be taken.

Penalties for infringement of the regulations are severe.

The use of certain anchorages in the Chagos Banks, Peros Banhos and Salomon Island is prohibited. These areas are:

Great Chagos Bank: Three Brothers and Resurgent Island, Danger Island, Cow Island (Little Eagle), Nelson Island;

Peros Banhos: All the islands to the east of a line drawn between the easternmost point of land on Moresby Island and the easternmost point of land on Fouquet Island (in practice, this means that one may only anchor in the western part of the islands);

Salomon Island: One may only anchor in the designated anchorage in the landward side of the lagoon (close to Île Boddam) south of a line drawn from the southwest point of Île Diable to the southwest point of Île Poule.

Anchorages

The Egmont Islands, 70 miles north-west of Diego Garcia, have a lagoon which can be entered on its north-west side. Care should be taken when navigating in the lagoon as there are many coral heads. There is an anchorage in the SE corner by Sudest Islet, but it is not protected from the north-west.

In the NW of the archipelago, the Peros Banhos atoll consists of about 30 islets and reefs. Most anchorages offer little protection, but there is a good one in the lee of Ile du Coin in the SE of the atoll.

The Salomon Islands, south-west of Blenheim Reef, are one of the most popular anchorages with yachts. The small lagoon can be entered in the north close to Ile de la Passe and the recommended anchorage is in the south-east. The Salomon Islands offer the best all-round protection in the archipelago. Several boats were anchored there in safety when a tropical cyclone passed close by in May 1993, producing winds of up to 50 knots. Although fully fledged cyclones are not known to have passed over the archipelago directly, this incident served as a timely warning that even areas that are considered to be lying outside the known cyclone area should be treated with great caution during the cyclone season.

Further Reading

Indian Ocean Cruising Guide

Websites

www.tcol.co.uk/part_v/biot.html (British Indian Ocean Territories (BIOT))
www.nctsdg.navy.mil (US Navy)
www.msc.navy.mil/mpstwo/garcia.htm (US Military Sealift Command)

CHRISTMAS ISLAND

Christmas Island is an Australian territory lying in the Indian Ocean 260 miles south of the Sunda Strait between Sumatra and Java. The island is the tip of an extinct volcano, about 985 ft (300 m) above sea level, and the cliffs are almost continuous around its coast. The island is popular with yachts on passage to the Cocos Keeling Islands, another Australian dependency in the Indian Ocean.

Country Profile

The island was sighted early in the seventeenth century and was only later named Christmas Island on Christmas Day 1643. Inaccurate charts showed several islands during the seventeenth century, but in fact there is only one. The first recorded landing was in 1688, although not until the 1820s did anyone stop for any length of time. In the first half of the nineteenth century, the island became a regular stop for vessels supplying the Cocos Islands. Phosphate was discovered by an expedition in the 1870s, which led to Britain taking control of the island. Soon the first settlers arrived at Flying Fish Cove and phosphate mining began, Chinese labour being imported to work the mines. Mining was disrupted during the Second World War, and most of the inhabitants evacuated to Australia. Bombed by the Japanese, the island surrendered following a mutiny by the Indian troops stationed there. After the war the New Zealand and Australian governments bought the mining company, changed the name to the Christmas Island Phosphate Commission, and set up an intensive mining operation.

The mining of the phosphate reserves dominates the island's economy, although reserves of the best quality phosphate are running out. In 1987 the mine was closed by the Australian government due to industrial unrest. The mine was reopened in 1990. Tourism is being developed. Since the opening of the Christmas Island resort in 1993, the island has become a popular destination. The abundance of bird and marine life, and the fact that most of the island and surrounding reefs are now a National Park, is very popular with eco-tourists, birdwatchers and divers.

The 2300 inhabitants are Malay, Chinese and Australian. English is the main language and Islam the main religion. The best time to visit the island is during the SE trade wind season, from April to November, as the weather is more pleasant. There is no safe anchorage during the remaining months from December to March, which is the period of the NW monsoon. During this time the weather is wet, March being the wettest month.

Entry Regulations

Port of entry
Flying Fish Cove 10°25′S 105°43′E.

Procedure on arrival
The only anchorage is at Flying Fish Cove on the

Practical Information

LOCAL TIME: GMT + 7

BUOYAGE: IALA A

CURRENCY: Australian dollar (Aus$).

BUSINESS HOURS
Banks: 0930–1500 Monday to Friday.
Post office: 0800–1200, 1300–1500
Monday to Friday.
Supermarket: 1000–1700 Monday to
Friday, 0830–1130 Saturday.

PUBLIC HOLIDAYS
1 January: New Year's Day
26 January: Australia Day
Chinese New Year
Good Friday, Easter Monday
25 April: ANZAC Day
June: Queen's Birthday
Hari Raya Puasa
Territory Day
Hari Raya Haji
25, 26 December: Christmas

ELECTRICITY: 240 V, 50 Hz

COMMUNICATIONS
IDD calls can be made from the island.
Mail can be sent to Poste Restante, Post Office,
Christmas Island, Indian Ocean. It is recommended
to write 'Via Australia' on letters to ensure there is
no confusion with the Pacific Christmas Island.
There are regular air links to Perth, Jakarta and
Singapore.

MEDICAL
There is a good hospital. *Tel.* 08 9164 8333.

north-west tip of the island. Yachts should beware of the chains between the shore and the large mooring buoys. The anchorage can be badly affected by swell and yachts are sometimes advised to move either by the police or harbour master.

Arriving yachts should contact the harbour master on VHF Channel 16, who will inform customs, immigration and quarantine officers. All persons must remain on board until the yacht has been inspected and cleared. The boat is usually boarded first by a police officer, who deals with immigration and customs. Quarantine is strict, and eggs and some meat products may be confiscated, or sealed on board. Depending on the officer in charge, some fresh fruit and vegetables may be kept.

Procedure on departure
Yachts are to notify customs and immigration, located at the police station. A customs clearance form will be issued, which must be handed to customs before departure. Outward clearance is also required by the harbour master on leaving, when all bills must be settled. The immigration office is open 0800–1600 Monday to Friday.

Customs
Firearms must be declared to customs. The firearms will be kept by customs and returned when the yacht is ready to depart. Animals are not allowed to land, as there is a National Park and strict quarantine regulations are in force.

Immigration
Australian visa requirements are in force and every person must arrive with a valid Australian visa. The only exception are holders of New Zealand passports.

Fees
Aus$20 departure tax per person. Other fees may be introduced in the future. Mooring fee of Aus$50 per week.

Restrictions
Garbage must not be dumped in Flying Fish Cove, but put in receptacles near the Boat Club. Birds and turtles are protected species in the National Park.

Facilities

Because of the mining operations, facilities are relatively good. Diesel can be bought alongside the barge jetty, where it is delivered by tanker. This must be arranged with the Transport Pool. They can also arrange the filling of LPG bottles and some repairs as they have good engineering facilities. Some spare parts for engines are also available from the same source.

Provisioning is good and there is a supermarket opposite the service station, which will deliver large orders. It has been reported that the surcharge which was applied to yachts making purchases and reprovisioning in the island is no longer in force. In spite of the distance and difficulty of shipping fresh produce from Australia, the availability and prices are quite reasonable.

The Boat Club, located south of the dinghy landing, welcomes visitors. The bar operates an honour system and all outstanding bills at the Club must be settled before outward clearance is given.

Further Reading

Indian Ocean Cruising Guide

Websites

www.christmas.net.au
www.dotrs.gov.au/terr/xmas (Department of Transport and Regional Services)
www.immi.gov.au (Australian Immigration Department)

COCOS KEELING

The Cocos Keeling Islands lie about 500 miles west of Christmas Island in the South Indian Ocean. They consist of two atolls, North Keeling and South Keeling, comprising 27 low coral islands, most of them clustered around South Keeling's lagoon. Most of the smaller islands are uninhabited. Cocos Keeling is an Australian territory.

The islands are a convenient stop for westbound yachts in the South Indian Ocean. The anchorage in the lee of Direction Island has been described as being particularly beautiful. This is perhaps the reason why some yachts which call for only a few days stay longer than intended.

Country Profile

North Keeling was probably first sighted by Captain William Keeling in 1609, and gradually the rest of the group was charted. In 1826 two Englishmen settled on South Keeling. There was some disagreement and after a few years one of the men left, leaving John Clunies-Ross, who brought labourers from Malaya and established a copra plantation. In 1857 the islands were considered as belonging to Britain and were administered first from Ceylon and then Singapore. In 1886 George Clunies-Ross was granted all the land by Queen Victoria. During the First World War Direction Island was used as a cable station, and was raided by the German cruiser *Emden* in 1914. In 1955 the islands became a dependency of Australia and the Clunies-Ross family were left with only a plantation on one of the islands. A High Security Animal Quarantine Station opened on West Island in 1981. The station was closed at the end of 1999.

Meteorology and communications are important activities. The group is not self-sufficient, although some local produce is grown. Foods, fuel and all consumer items are imported from Australia. The population is about 600, being Malays and Australians. English and Malay are spoken. The best place to find out more about the fascinating history of this unique place is to visit the tourist information centre, which shares Admiralty House with the Historical Society on West Island.

The islands are under the influence of the SE trade winds for most of the year. The winds are strongest in August. During the cyclone season, from December to March, the winds are lighter. The islands are rarely affected by tropical storms.

Entry Regulations

Port of entry
Direction Island, South Keeling 12°05′S 96°53′E.

Procedure on arrival
When approaching the 12 mile limit, vessels should contact quarantine or the marine officer on Channel 20 to advise ETA. Vessels arriving at night

---

Practical Information

LOCAL TIME: GMT + 6½

BUOYAGE: IALA A

CURRENCY: Australian dollar (Aus$)

PUBLIC HOLIDAYS
1 January: New Year's Day
26 January: Australia Day
Good Friday, Easter Monday

25 April: ANZAC Day
June: Queen's Birthday
First Monday in October: Labour Day
25, 26 December: Christmas

COMMUNICATIONS
IDD calls can be made from two pay phones on West Island, which take Australian Telecom phone cards.
Mail comes weekly.

Poste Restante, Post Office, Cocos (Keeling) Islands, Indian Ocean 6799.
There is a twice weekly air service to Perth.

MEDICAL
There is a small hospital at West Island. There is a resident doctor who visits both health centres on Home Island (*Tel.* 7609) and West Island (*Tel.* 6655).

should proceed to the anchorage and advise quarantine of their arrival at 0700 the following morning. Incoming vessels must fly the Q flag and anchor approximately 250 metres offshore at Direction Island, close to the yellow quarantine buoys. No one on board should leave the vessel nor should there be any contact with anyone until clearance is completed. Neither the quarantine buoys nor any other buoys at Direction Island are suitable for yachts, which should use their own anchors.

Entrance to the lagoon of South Keeling is between Horsburgh Island and Direction Island.

Customs, immigration and quarantine are on West Island, but the officers prefer to board yachts at Direction Island. Boats are normally visited by quarantine and immigration officers at the earliest opportunity.

If arriving at the weekend, the officials should be contacted on VHF radio.

Customs

Firearms must be declared on arrival and must not leave the vessel without a permit.

Restricted goods may be bonded on board.

Quarantine

Fresh eggs, their containers and some meat products may be confiscated, or sealed on board. Depending on the officer in charge, some fresh fruit and vegetables may be kept. There are very strict quarantine regulations. If a yacht has animals on board, it must anchor outside the quarantine buoy at Direction Island. Animals must not be taken ashore. All animal and food waste must be taken to Direction Island for proper disposal where it is burnt in pits.

Immigration

The same strict immigration requirements apply as in mainland Australia and no one is allowed to arrive without a valid Australian visa, except holders of New Zealand passports. A multiple entry visa is recommended for those who intend to visit Australia and Christmas Island.

Fees

Aus$20 departure tax per person. There are high quarantine fees, similar to mainland Australia, which, with overtime, can exceed Aus$100.

Restrictions

Yachts are only allowed to anchor at Direction Island unless a special dispensation has been obtained from the marine officer.

Spearfishing or cleaning fish is not permitted on the south-east corner of Direction Island around the anchorage area, or anywhere near a beach because of the danger of attracting sharks.

Facilities

Provisions are available, but fresh food is expensive as most of it has to be flown in from Perth. A limited selection of fresh fruit and vegetables is available from Cocos Produce on West Island. Alternatively, one can order fresh vegetables, which will be brought in by plane the following week. Larger orders, when provisioning for a passage, should be placed with the main store on West Island well in advance of departure. Similarly, essential spares can also be ordered from Australia. Gas bottles can be filled on West Island, where the Australian community lives. Water is available from a tank on Direction Island and there is also a tap on Home Island jetty, but neither is drinkable. There is no duty on alcoholic drinks. Cocos Engineering on West Island (e-mail: cocos-engineering@bigpong.com, *Tel.* (08) 9162 6586, Fax. (08) 9162 6677) offers a range of mechanical and electrical repair services, as well as fuel delivery and a taxi service, by fast catamaran, from West to Direction Island.

Further Reading

Indian Ocean Cruising Guide

Websites

www.dotrs.gov.au/terr/cocos (Department of Transport and Regional Services)
www.immi.gov.au (Australian Immigration Department)

COMOROS

This small archipelago lying in the Indian Ocean between the northern tip of Madagascar and the African mainland consists of four main islands: Grande Comore (Ngazidja), Moheli (Mwali), Anjouan (Ndzuani) and Mayotte (Maore). Formerly a French colony, the islands are now independent, except for Mayotte which is an overseas territory of France and a naval base. Mayotte

Practical Information

LOCAL TIME: GMT + 3

BUOYAGE: IALA A

CURRENCY: Comoron franc (KMF). All foreign currency must be declared on arrival. French franc and US dollars accepted.

BUSINESS HOURS
Banks: 0730–1400 Monday to Thursday and 0700–1100 Friday.
Business and shops:
0800–1200/1500–1700 Monday to Thursday and Saturday, 0800–1130 Friday. Some shops open on Sundays.
Market: 0700–1800 daily.

Government offices: 0730–1430 Monday to Thursday, 0730–1100 Friday, 0730–1200 Saturday.

ELECTRICITY: 220 V, 50 Hz

PUBLIC HOLIDAYS
1 January: New Year's Day
1 May
6 July: Independence Day
The variable Muslim holidays, start of Ramadan, Eid el-Fitr, Eid el-Adha, Ashoura, Mouloud, Muharram, Leilat al-Meiraj and anniversary of death of Alkoutb Said Muhammad Sheikh Al Maarouf are also public holidays.

COMMUNICATIONS
The post offices at Moroni and Mutsamudu provide telephone, fax and telex services. Grande Comore has an international airport with flights to Paris, Africa, Germany, Mauritius and Madagascar.

MEDICAL
Only Moroni has a good hospital.

DIPLOMATIC MISSIONS
In Moroni:
France: Blvd de Strasbourg. *Tel.* 731 325.
South Africa: *Tel.* 732 812.
United States: *Tel.* 732 203.
Also – China, Mauritius and Seychelles.

---

is dealt with separately on page 535.

The islands are volcanic and Mount Kartala on Grande Comore is still active. They are mostly protected by coral reefs and the surrounding seas are rich in marine life. The coelacanth, a 350 million year old species of fish believed to be extinct, was rediscovered in Comoron waters.

Most yachts who visit the Comoros are sailing between Mauritius and East Africa, the islands being very conveniently located on that route. The underwater scenery is their prime attraction and the south side of the island of Moheli is particularly beautiful, with good snorkelling, although the anchorage at the main town Fomboni is only an open roadstead. The anchorage is not good either at Moroni, the capital, on Grande Comore. The main port of Mutsamudu has the best protection. More sheltered anchorages are to be found in neighbouring Mayotte.

Country Profile

The islands were originally settled by Malays, Africans and Arabs. Refugees from Persia, prosperous from the slave and spice trades, established a number of rival sultanates. During the seventeenth century Portuguese pirates used the islands as a base from which to attack ships returning from the East laden with goods. In the nineteenth century the Sultan of Mayotte sold his island to the French, and the rest of the islands followed suit after being subjected to French naval bombardment. France maintained strict control over the islands, and no one was allowed in or out of the islands without permission from the colonial authorities.

In 1912 Comoros was declared a colony and was under the administration of Madagascar until 1946. Some internal autonomy was granted in 1961, and after mass demonstrations in 1968, the French were forced to allow the formation of political parties. Tension grew between those for and against independence and, after a referendum, independence was unilaterally declared in 1975. Mayotte meanwhile asked France for protection and became a 'territorial community' within the French Republic. In independent Comoros, political unrest followed, radical policies were taken and relations worsened with France. The economy also deteriorated. In 1978 a coup carried out by mercenaries saw the creation of the Federal Islamic Republic of the Comoros, and a return to a more conservative line. The mercenaries remain quite powerful, and in September 1995 they staged another coup, overthrowing President Said Mohamed Djohar. French troops on nearby Mayotte intervened to restore the government.

Many Comorons work abroad in France or Africa as land shortage is a problem, most land being cultivated by foreign companies and a few Comoron families. The export of perfume from ylang-ylang, jasmine and orange trees is important. Other exports are vanilla, cloves and pepper.

The population numbers over 560,000 and are a mixture of Arab, African, Malay, Malagasy and French origins. Most of the population are Muslim. French and Arabic are the official languages, but people also speak Comoron, a mix of Swahili and Arabic. Moroni on Grande Comore is the capital.

The dry season, from May to October, is the best time to visit when the average temperature is 75°F (24°C). November to April is the rainy season, when temperatures range from 81° to 95°F (27–35°C), although the coast is cooled by sea breezes. The NW monsoon season from December to March can have high winds and cyclones.

Entry Regulations

Ports of entry
Mutsamudu (Anjouan) 12°10′S 44°24′E, Moroni (Grande Comore) 11°42′S 43°15′E.

Procedure on arrival
The port captain should be contacted on VHF Channel 16 and asked for instructions. The boat will be boarded on arrival.

Customs
Firearms must be declared to customs. Animals need a rabies vaccination and health certificate.

Immigration
Visas are required by all nationalities, but can be obtained on arrival from immigration in either Moroni (Grande Comore) or Mutsamudu (Anjouan). Two passport-size photos will be required. The visas are valid for three months.

Health
Malarial prophylaxis is essential.

Facilities

There are only limited facilities available, although at Mutsamudu, which is the main commercial port, there is a small boatyard and some workshops. Provisioning is basic, although some produce is available. Supplies are better in neighbouring Mayotte.

Further Reading

Indian Ocean Cruising Guide
Madagascar & Comoros – a travel survival kit
Traveller's Guide to East Africa and the Indian Ocean

Website

www.ksu.edu/sasw/comoros (Links)

KENYA

Kenya has 300 miles (4830 km) of coastline made up of beaches, mangrove swamps and creeks. Much of the coast is protected by coral reefs, which provide excellent diving, while the beaches are reputed to be the best in Africa. This scenic country is the most popular tourist destination in Africa with its beaches, savannah grasslands, safari parks, Lake Victoria and spectacular mountains.

Kenya is also visited by an increasing number of sailors who seek a taste of Africa, especially if they visit the interior during their stay. The coastal towns have a different character, having been subjected to the Arab influence for many centuries. Trading dhows from the Persian Gulf still ply these waters, arriving with the NW monsoon at the end of the year and leaving with the SE monsoon. They can be seen at Mombasa and also at Lamu, a small island and northernmost port of entry, whose fourteenth-century Arab town is a centre of Islamic learning. Lamu is the island of the legendary Sinbad the Sailor and the surrounding area, a small archipelago of coral-fringed islands, bears witness to the convoluted history of this part of the world. The most interesting sites are the ruined Swahili cities on Manda and Pate islands. Mombasa, also built on an island, is Kenya's chief port, its cosmopolitan atmosphere reflecting the port's history as an important Persian, Arab and Portuguese trading centre. The most popular base for visiting yachts is Kilifi, north of Mombasa, where good repair facilities are available and a yacht can be left in reliable hands, while touring the interior.

Country Profile

In Kenya remains of man have been found that are betwen 2.5 to 3 million years old. Later the country was gradually populated by migrations of Cushites, Bantu and Nilotes. Trade came to dominate eastern Africa, ivory being the main export, as Arab traders settled along the coast. The Bantus occupied the interior, and the mixture of these two peoples led to the Swahili culture and language. When the Portuguese arrived at the end of the fifteenth century Mombasa was a powerful merchant city. The Portuguese established themselves on the coast, but were later driven out by the Arabs. In 1837 the Sultanate of Oman and Zanzibar took over. The people of the interior were always suspicious of the coastal traders, and thus avoided becoming victims of the slave trade, unlike the peoples of West Africa.

Practical Information

LOCAL TIME: GMT + 3

BUOYAGE: IALA A. The lights and buoys on the coast cannot be relied upon and entry anywhere is not advisable at night.

CURRENCY: Kenyan shilling (Ksh) of 100 cents. Ksh cannot be exported and must be changed back before departure.

BUSINESS HOURS
Banks: 0900–1500 Monday to Friday. Saturday 0900–1100.
Business and shops: 0830–1230, 1400–1730 Monday to Friday, 0830–1200 Saturday.
Government offices: 0800–1200, 1400–1600 Monday to Friday.

ELECTRICITY: 220/240 V, 50 Hz

PUBLIC HOLIDAYS
1 January: New Year's Day

Good Friday, Easter Monday
1 May
1 June: Madaraka Day
10 October: Nyayo Day
20 October: Kenyatta Day
12 December: Independence Day
25, 26 December: Christmas
Also Eid el-Fitr and Eid el-Adha

COMMUNICATIONS
Kenya Post and Telecommunications Corporation provides telephones, fax, telegraph and telex. Post offices open 0800–1700 Monday to Friday, 0800–1300 Saturday. Emergency 999. Operator 0. There are frequent flights from Nairobi to Europe and other African cities. There are less frequent regular flights from Mombasa as well as many charter flights. There is also a good network of internal flights.

DIPLOMATIC MISSIONS
In Nairobi:

Australia: PO Box 30360, Development House, Moi Avenue. *Tel.* (2) 445034.
Canada: PO Box 30481, Comcroft House, Haile Selassie Ave. *Tel.* (2) 214804.
Egypt: Harambee Plaza, 7th floor. *Tel.* (2) 225991.
Mozambique: PO Box 66923. *Tel.* (2) 581857.
New Zealand: Nanak House, Kimathi St. *Tel.* (2) 331244.
Sudan: Minet ICDC House, 7th floor. *Tel.* (2) 720853.
Tanzania: PO Box 47790, Continental House. *Tel.* (2) 331056.
United Kingdom: PO Box 30465, Bruce House, Standard St, Unit 64100. *Tel.* (2) 714699.
United States: Moi/Haile Selassie Avenue, PO Box 30137. *Tel.* (2) 334141.

In Mombasa:
United States: Palli House, Nyerere Ave. *Tel.* (11) 315101.

Britain became interested in the area at the end of the nineteenth century and took over Kenya as a British protectorate. Thousands of Indian labourers were brought over by the British, some of whom settled permanently as well as the Europeans, gradually pushing out the Africans. The 1920s saw the rise of Kikuyu nationalism, the Kikuyu being the largest tribe in Kenya, culminating in the Mau Mau revolt in 1952–6. Kenya became independent in 1963. The majority of the Asians chose not to take up citizenship of the new state and were forced to leave the country. The nationalist Kenyan African National Union, led by Jomo Kenyatta, ruled the country after independence until his death in 1978. His successor Daniel arap Moi was elected to his fourth presidential term in 1992, in the first multiparty elections held in Kenya since independence.

The Kenyan economy is based on agriculture. Tea and coffee are major exports. Kenya has the largest tourist industry in Africa.

The inhabitants, over 25 million, are mainly African, with a minority of Asian, European and Arab origins. Most speak Swahili, but English is also widely spoken. Christianity is the main religion, Islam predominates on the coast, Hinduism in the Asian community and traditional beliefs are still prevalent. Nairobi in the interior is the capital.

The climate on the coast is tropical and hot. April to June is called the season of long rains, October to November the season of short rains. This monsoon weather also dictates the direction of the currents. This must be borne in mind when planning a cruise along this coast as the best period for southbound voyages is during the NW monsoon and for northbound voyages during the SE monsoon.

Entry Regulations

Ports of entry
Lamu 2°18′S 40°55′E, Mombasa 4°04′S 39°41′E, Malindi 3°13′S 40°07′E, Shimoni 4°39′S 39°23′E.

Procedure on arrival
In all ports one should report first to customs.
Lamu: Boats are boarded on arrival by quarantine and customs. All currency and valuable items must be declared, both of which will be checked against the declaration on departure.
Mombasa: One can proceed into the harbour, or call port control on VHF Channel 12 or 16 beforehand. Sometimes one is asked to wait at the first buoy for a pilot boat, although the entrance is simple and a pilot is hardly necessary.

There are two places in Mombasa where clearance is possible. Formalities appear to be simpler at the Old Port, on the northern side of Mombasa

Island, where officials are more efficient than those at Kilindini Harbour, which is the main commercial port. While clearing, one can anchor beyond the port building among the dhows. At the Old Port a launch may come out with the officials. If no one comes, the captain should go ashore and report first to customs and then immigration. Customs and immigration offices are by the jetties, which are used by small local freighters and dhows. The officials at the Old Port do not work at weekends or on holidays when it is necessary to go to Kilindini Harbour. Here it is best to proceed to the police pontoon, where one can be cleared by customs, health and immigration.

Those who need a visa will have to go to the immigration office in town, where a three-month visa is easily obtained, renewable for another three months. The visa is payable in US dollars.

Yachts can also clear at Kilifi and Shimoni, where there is customs, but immigration formalities still have to be completed in an official port of entry.

Kilifi: One can check in with customs, although immigration formalities have to be completed in Mombasa. Apparently the immigration authorities do not approve of this, although they raise no objections if a captain drives immediately from Kilifi to Mombasa with the passports in order to complete immigration formalities.

Shimoni: This port, close to the Tanzanian border, is very convenient for clearing into Kenya. There are customs and immigration offices in the port.

Customs
Firearms must be declared on arrival. These will be impounded and released only on departure.

There are no restrictions on animals, although they should have up-to-date rabies vaccinations, as rabies is endemic on the East African coast. Inoculations can be done in Mombasa if required.

There is no specified limit on the period a yacht may remain in Kenya and some have remained for several years while the owners were absent. Boats should not be left completely unattended as there have been several reports of theft.

Visiting sailors can buy or have sent out capital equipment such as engines, instruments and sails. By using a clearing agent, who will provide a bond, it is possible to avoid local importation taxes.

Immigration
Visas are not required for nationals of most Commonwealth countries (except Australia, New Zealand, Sri Lanka and British passport holders of Indian, Pakistani and Bangladeshi origin, who

require visas), Denmark, Ethiopia, Finland, Germany, Ireland, Italy, Norway, San Marino, Spain, Sweden, Turkey and Uruguay. Normally visitor's permits are issued free for three months.

All other countries require visas, but these are normally issued on arrival for three months. An extension of three months can be obtained with proof of sufficient funds. It is recommended to obtain visas in advance, as otherwise a visitor's pass will be issued on arrival only on condition that a deposit of around US$350 is made (refundable on departure).

Visas and entry permits can be extended if they are applied for in person before the date of expiry.

Health
Malaria prophylaxis is recommended, as malaria is prevalent on the coast. Do not swim in fresh water, as this may be infected with bilharzia parasites. AIDS is endemic in East Africa.

Fees
Overtime is charged on weekends and holidays.

There are light dues, government charges for which change frequently.

Foreign yachts have to pay harbour charges, which may work out cheaper if bought for one year in advance, unless one intends to spend only a short time in Kenya.

A navigation fee of approximately US$10 is payable when clearing out.

Restrictions
The authorities are trying hard to protect wildlife, and it is a serious offence to buy and attempt to export ivory, animal skins and stuffed animals.

It is forbidden to photograph ports, police, naval buildings, vessels or personnel.

Cruising permit
A transit log is necessary for any movement in Kenyan waters. The log is obtained from customs on arrival and must be presented to customs when calling at the following ports: Shimoni, Mombasa, Kilifi, Malindi and Lamu. One should inform customs of the intended itinerary, time of departure and ETA in the next port.

Facilities

Although slowly improving, yachting facilities are still limited. However, provisioning is generally good and less expensive than the Indian Ocean islands. Diesel and LPG are also reasonably priced. There is a problem of theft in some places and outboard engines, dinghies and any loose equipment should be put away or watched carefully, except in the few places where security is provided. In some places for a minimal charge one can employ a guard for the night.

The best facilities are those at Kilifi, a well protected port on a creek spanned by a bridge. The bridge has a clearance of 72 ft (22 m). One must also be careful not to touch the telephone and power lines. Swynford Boatyard, based on the southern shore beyond the bridge, operates a full service yard with hauling-out facilities for boats up to 12 tons or 40 ft (12 m) LOA, drying out grid for larger boats, mechanical, electrical and carpentry workshops as well as information on local marine services. The boatyard has moorings and fees include a night watchman for the boat if the crew make trips inland. Most visiting boats use the services of Swynford Boatyard, which is very welcoming and provides a mail service, showers, bar and water. Mail can be sent c/o Swynford Boatyard, Private Bag, Kilifi. Tel. and Fax 125 22479. Provisioning in Kilifi is good with a supermarket, fresh produce market, bank and frequent buses to Mombasa 35 miles away.

Facilities in Mombasa itself are more limited. The Mombasa Yacht Club welcomes visiting yachts and offers its facilities for a daily fee. The anchorage there is very deep, but the club has some moorings. There are several good supermarkets in Mombasa as well as a daily market. Although there are some local workshops in Mombasa, because of the proximity of Kilifi, it is better to use the boatyard there as they are used to dealing with yachts.

Limited supplies are available in Malindi, which is a tourist resort with banks and several shops. Facilities in Lamu are poor. Fuel and water have to be taken in jerrycans and there are only limited food supplies with the exception of fresh produce. The situation is similar in Shimoni, the southernmost port in Kenya.

Further Reading

Indian Ocean Cruising Guide
East Africa Pilot
Africa on a Shoestring
Traveller's Guide to East Africa and the Indian Ocean
Kenya – a travel survival kit

Websites

www.kenyatourism.org (Ministry of Tourism)
www.kenyaweb.com

MADAGASCAR

This large island off the coast of Africa is very different from its continental neighbours, since the majority of its inhabitants are descended from Malay and Asian migrants, mixed with Africans and Europeans. Centuries of relative isolation have produced an interesting culture and unique wildlife. A rugged mountain chain runs down the centre of the island, dividing the narrow tropical eastern coast from the savannah and forests of the west. The southern part is very arid.

For many years ruled by a Marxist government, the officials have not especially welcomed visiting sailors, who were invariably treated with suspicion. As a result very few yachts stopped in Madagascar. The situation is gradually changing and as the island is attracting an increasing number of tourists to its resorts, the attitude to visiting yachts has shown a marked improvement, but formalities are still quite strict. In order to get permission to sail in Madagascar, one has to write in advance to the Ports Authority at Ministère du Transport et de la Meteorologie, BP 4139, Antananarivo 101, Madagascar. *Tel.* (261) 20-22-24604, Fax. (261) 20-22-24001 with the following information:
1 date and place of departure of your yacht;
2 itinerary;
3 identity, occupation, address and passport numbers of the entire crew;
4 purpose of the trip;
5 length of stay in each port;
6 period of entry and stay in Malagasy waters.

The most attractive ports and anchorages are on the north-west coast where Antseranana, formerly known as Diego Suarez, has a beautiful natural harbour. The old town has a cosmopolitan atmosphere with its mixed population of Malagasy, Arabs, Indians, Africans and Réunionnais. Further along the coast is Madagascar's prime attraction, the picturesque island of Nossi-Be, now a thriving tourist resort. Another island worth visiting is Nossi Boraha (Ile Sainte Marie), close to Toamasina, the country's chief commercial harbour and main port of entry. The latter is a good place to stop for yachts on passage to the Cape of Good Hope. Another interesting stop for south-

Practical Information

LOCAL TIME: GMT + 3

BUOYAGE: IALA A

CURRENCY: Malagasy franc (MFr) of 100 centimes. Prices may also be quoted in piastres or ariary (1 ariary = 5MFr). Foreign currency must be declared on arrival. The immigration officer will ask for a currency declaration to be filled in on arrival, and this form has to be endorsed every time money is changed. The form, and the remaining funds, will be checked on departure.

BUSINESS HOURS
Banks: 0800–1100, 1400–1600 Monday to Friday.
Business and government offices: 0800–1130, 1400–1730 Monday to Friday, 0800–1200 Saturday.
Shops: 0800–1200, 1400–1800 Monday to Friday (some open Sunday morning).

ELECTRICITY: 220 V, 50 Hz; also 110/380 V, 50 Hz

PUBLIC HOLIDAYS
1 January: New Year's Day
29 March: Memorial Day
Good Friday, Easter Monday
1 May
Ascension
Whit Monday
26 June: Independence Day
15 August: Assumption
1 November: All Saints' Day
25 December: Christmas Day
30 December: Anniversary of the Republic

COMMUNICATIONS
There are regular flights to Europe, other Indian Ocean islands and Africa, and internal flights around the country.

MEDICAL
There are hospitals in the main centres, but the standards of medical care are fairly basic. Malaria is prevalent all year round. Water is not drinkable and should be treated.

DIPLOMATIC MISSIONS
In Antananarivo:
France: 3 rue Jean Jaures.
Tel. (2) 23700.
United Kingdom: Immeuble Ny Havana, Cite de 67 Ha.
Tel. (2) 27749.
United States: 14 Lalana Rainitovo, Antsahavola.
Tel. (2) 21257.

bound yachts is at Taolanaro, formerly Port Dauphin, the site of the first French settlement in the seventeenth century.

Country Profile

The earliest inhabitants are thought to have arrived by sea from Indonesia around 220 BC to AD 800. In this latter period the Sumatran Srivijaya empire controlled much of the Indian Ocean's maritime trade. The migrants brought crops from South East Asia, an influence which can still be seen in Malagasy agriculture. Arabs and Swahilis established towns on the coast, and from the sixteenth century the Europeans used the island as a stopping point for ships on the Cape of Good Hope route. In the eighteenth century the Merina Kingdom united the island and set about creating a modern state. France became interested in the island and invaded it in 1895, the Merina Queen was deposed and a republic declared. Madagascar became a colony and foreigners expropriated the land, developing an import–export economy with coffee as the main crop.

Having been independent for so long previously, the Malagasy grew more and more dissatisfied. In 1947–8 a violent insurrection occurred, in which several thousand Malagasy died. In 1960 independence was granted although France retained a hold on trade and military bases. Initially links were kept with France, but aspirations were not met by economic growth and in 1972 a military regime took power. The government cultivated relations with socialist countries and drew away from France. A political crisis in 1975 led to a radical socialist government coming to power. There are still disputes with France over the sovereignty of some small islands to the north, Iles Glorieuses, Juan de Nova and Europa, which are administered by France. Serious civil unrest in 1991 led to a vote for a new constitution, and the Third Republic was instituted in 1993.

The economy is predominantly agricultural, with coffee, vanilla, spices and perfume the main exports. Rice is cultivated all over the island mainly for domestic consumption. Manufacturing industry is mainly textiles and food-processing. Foreign loans and aid are important. Efforts are being made towards greater self-sufficiency. Tourism is also beginning to expand.

The 12 million inhabitants are a mixture of Malay and African. Malagasy and French are the main languages. The main religions are Christianity, Islam, and some traditional beliefs. The capital is Antananarivo in the centre of the island.

The climate is tropical. November to March is the rainy season. The SE trade wind season lasts until the end of October and the trades can be very strong at times, occasionally being accompanied by violent thunderstorms. From December to March cyclones are common on the east coast.

Entry Regulations

Ports of entry
Toamasina 18°09'S 49°25'E, Antseranana 12°16'S 49°18'E, Mahajanga 15°43'S 46°19'E, Toleara 23°22'S 43°40'E, Nossi-Be (Hell-Ville) 13°24'S 48°17'E.

Procedure on arrival
All visiting yachts are supposed to arrive with a cruising permit obtained in advance (see page 530). It is therefore advisable to have up-to-date confirmation of this requirement, either from the Ministry of Transport in Antananarivo or from a Malagasy embassy, before arriving at a Malagasy port.

Hell-Ville: Anchor off the main dock and call the port captain on Channel 16, although officials rarely visit the boat. The customs office is in the port area. Immigration formalities will be done at the police station. Malagasy currency will be needed for the visa, so some money should be changed before going to the police. The alternative is to anchor in the nearby anchorage at Crater Bay. It is possible to land there and take a taxi into Hell-Ville to complete formalities.

Customs
Firearms may be removed for the duration of the stay. Animals are not allowed to land.

Immigration
Visas are required by all nationalities. Visas are usually granted on arrival and are valid for up to three months. However, it may be advisable to obtain a visa in advance. There are very few Malagasy embassies in the world, although there are diplomatic offices in some capitals, such as London, Washington, Bonn, Paris, Rome, Brussels and Tokyo, as well as in some African capitals. For those sailing to Madagascar from neighbouring countries the most convenient places to obtain a visa from a Malagasy consulate are Mauritius, Réunion or Tanzania.

Visa extensions up to two months are available from the Ministry of Interior. A charge of 1500 MFr per month is made and one may have to submit a short letter in French explaining why the extension is wanted.

Health
If coming from continental Africa, yellow fever and cholera vaccination certificates will be required. Drinking water should be treated everywhere. Malaria prophylaxis is recommended.

Restrictions
Military and police establishments must not be photographed.

Fees
There is a small charge for visas issued on arrival. Also a reported departure fee of $40.

Facilities

There are limited facilities in Hell-Ville, but provisioning with local produce is adequate. There is fuel and minor repairs can be carried out. Elsewhere, locally grown fruit and vegetables are readily available and there are good markets in most places. The best repair facilities can be found at Mahajanga, on the west coast, which is used by many foreign shrimping boats as a base of operations. There is a ship repair yard with a slipway. They can undertake hull and engine repair. Similar facilities are also available in Toamasina, where a repair yard with a slipway and workshops is operated by the port authority.

Further Reading

Indian Ocean Cruising Guide
Traveller's Guide to East Africa and the Indian Ocean
Madagascar & Comoros – a travel survival kit

Website

www.embassy.org/madagascar (Madagascar Embassy in Washington)

MAURITIUS

Joseph Conrad called Mauritius 'sugary pearl of the Indian Ocean' to describe the sweet beauty of this island situated in the centre of that sea. A volcanic outcrop of the land bridge that once connected Africa and Asia, Mauritius lies about

500 miles east of Madagascar. Part of the Mascarene archipelago, Mauritius also includes the islands of Rodrigues, Agalega, and the Cargados Carajos archipelago.

Yachts calling in Mauritius are usually on passage westwards across the Indian Ocean and in a hurry to leave before mid-November due to the number of early cyclones that have hit the island in the past. Yet a few who have spent time cruising the Indian Ocean have dallied and enjoyed the beauty of this high island and the exotic mixture of its culture and peoples. The waterfront in Port Louis has been dramatically transformed in recent years by Caudan Development, who turned the once dirty harbour into an attractive complex, with shopping centres, restaurants, hotel and a new marina. Grand Baie on the north-west coast is the favourite anchorage with a friendly yacht club and good basic facilities.

Some cruisers also break their passage at the smaller island of Rodrigues, which is a pleasant stop due to easier formalities and friendly islanders.

The inner harbour in Mathurin Bay is very well protected and the yacht can be left there while exploring the interior, particularly the caves on the windward side of the island.

Occasionally yachts stop at the Cargados Carajos Shoals, a large reef area lying some 200 miles north-east of Mauritius. Although one is supposed to obtain prior permission to stop, this rule does not seem to be strictly enforced. However, one should ask permission from local fishermen to anchor off one of the four islands they occasionally inhabit. Over fifty islets and cays make up this small archipelago which abounds in marine life. The chart of this area is badly out of date and it is reported that the lighthouse, which is marked as being on Ile du Sud, is in fact on Ile Coco. Eyeball navigation is essential throughout this reef-infested area.

Country Profile

Mauritius was uninhabited until the end of the sixteenth century, although often visited by Arab and Malay sailors. The Portuguese were the first Europeans to visit 'Ilha do Cirne' (Isle of the Swan) at the start of the sixteenth century. That famous bird the dodo once lived here before sailors killed it off for food. In 1598 the Dutch took possession of the island, naming it after Prince Maurice of Nassau. Rivalry was considerable between the Dutch, French and English for the island, both for the valuable ebony found there and, as trade opened up with the East, for its important strategic position on the Cape of Good Hope route. In 1715 the French gained control, renaming it Ile de France, and their influence is clearly visible today. Rapid strides were made under Governor Mahé de Labourdonnais: Port Louis became the capital, the sugar industry was developed, fortifications were built and the French used their naval base for harassing ships of the East India Company.

A century later the Treaty of Paris ceded Mauritius, as well as the Seychelles and Rodrigues, to Britain, resuscitating the previous name. Emancipation of the slaves in 1833 led to labour shortages on the sugar plantations, and a large influx of labour from India occurred. With the opening of the Suez Canal, Mauritius lost some of its importance to world trade. Independence from Britain came in 1968.

The sugar industry is still the backbone of the economy, although efforts are being made to diversify away from dependence on a single crop. Tea and tobacco are now significant exports, tourism has expanded and the island is opening up to becoming an offshore financial centre.

The history of the island is reflected in its 1 million inhabitants, who are a mixture of Indian, French, English, African and Chinese origins. English is the official language, but Creole, French, Hindi and Bhojpuri are also widely spoken and Hinduism, Islam, Christianity and Buddhism make up the island's religions.

Mauritius has a subtropical climate with a high humidity and temperatures of up to 91°F (33°C). December to April has heavier rainfall, while September, October and November are the most pleasant months. The cyclone season is from mid-November to April.

Entry Regulations

Ports of entry
Port Louis 20°09'S 57°29'E, Port Mathurin 19°41'S 63°25'E.

Procedure on arrival
Port Louis: This is the main harbour and the only official port of entry and exit for Mauritius. One must clear in here before visiting any other anchorage.

One should radio one's ETA to the port authority in Port Louis, who keep 24-hour watch on

Practical Information

LOCAL TIME: GMT + 4

BUOYAGE: IALA A

CURRENCY: Mauritian rupee (MRS) of 100 cents. Only MRS 350 may be exported.

BUSINESS HOURS
Banks: 0930–1430 Monday to Friday, 0930–1130 Saturday.
Business: 0845–1630 Monday to Friday, 0900–1200 Saturday.
Shops: 1000–1800 Monday to Friday, 1000–1200 Saturday.
Government offices: 0900–1600 Monday to Friday, 0900–1200 Saturday.
Port offices: Monday to Friday 0700–1500, Saturday 0700–1300.

ELECTRICITY: 220 V, 50 Hz

PUBLIC HOLIDAYS
1, 2 January: New Year
12 March: Independence Day
1 May: Labour Day
1 November: All Saints' Day
25 December: Christmas Day
Variable religious holidays:
Yaum-un-Nabi
Thaipoosam Cavadee (Tamil)
Chinese Spring Festival
Maha Shivaratree (Hindu)
Ougadi
Eid El-Fitr
Ganesh Chaturthi
Divali, Hindu Festival of Lights

COMMUNICATIONS
International calls, telex and telegrams from Mauritius Telecom which has three offices: PLC Bldg, 43 Sir William Newoin St, open 0830–2200, Rogers House, open 0830–1700, and Cassis, open 0830–1600. Main post office, Quay Street, Port Louis,

0815–1115, 1200–1600 Monday to Friday, 0815–1145 Saturday.
There are flights to many destinations in Europe, Asia, Africa and Australia.

MEDICAL
Medical care is free in hospitals.

DIPLOMATIC MISSIONS
In Port Louis:
Australia: Rogers House. *Tel.* 208 1700.
France: 14 rue St Georges.
Tel. 208 3755.
Madagascar: rue Guiot Pasceau, Floréal.
Tel. 686 5015.
New Zealand: Anchor Bldg, Pailles.
Tel. 212 4920.
South Africa: British American Insurance Bldg. *Tel.* 212 6925.
United Kingdom: PO Box 1063.
Tel. 211 1361
United States: Rogers House.
Tel. 208 2347.

VHF Channel 16. On arrival, contact Port Louis Harbour Radio and request permission to enter. Authorities expect yachts to come alongside the customs dock, but the jetty has been damaged by larger vessels and yachts may find it difficult to lie alongside the rough dock. The radio station will usually advise arriving yachts where to dock and will also call customs and immigration. Occasionally the authorities allow a yacht to proceed directly into Caudan Marina.

Port Mathurin: Clearance can be obtained in Port Mathurin on Rodrigues island. This clearance is only valid during the stay in Rodrigues and one must clear in again on arrival in Mauritius. The port has been dredged and the buoyage no longer accords with some charts. The harbour should not be entered at night as the leading beacons can be confusing.

St Brandon (Cargados Carajos Shoals) and Agalega should not be visited without prior permission in writing from the Ministry of External Affairs & Emigration in Port Louis, except in an emergency.

Procedure on departure

Although not an official port of entry, yachts have been allowed to stay in Grand Baie and leave from there after clearing out in Port Louis. There does not seem to be a strict rule about this and a yacht wishing to clear out may be required to return to Port Louis. To clear out of Mauritius, one must buy a

customs clearance form from the chamber of commerce in Port Louis. Stamps must then be bought at the post office to be affixed on the form by customs.

Customs

Firearms must be declared on arrival.

All animals need (a) Import Permit from Ministry of Agriculture & Natural Resources & the Environment, obtained in advance; (b) health certificate from country of origin. They must be declared to customs on arrival and landing is allowed if (a) and (b) agree, otherwise animals must remain on board. Quarantine for dogs and cats is six months, for birds it is three weeks. Dogs and cats from areas where rabies has occurred in the last 12 months are prohibited.

It is prohibited to import fresh fruits from Asia east of 60°E (including India and Pakistan), plants, fresh vegetables and sugar cane.

Immigration

A three-month stay is normally granted. Visitors in transit, who arrive and depart with the same yacht, do not requie a visa. If a visa is required it may be obtained abroad from Mauritius high commissions or embassies and where these do not exist from British embassies. In Mauritius one should contact the Passport & Immigration Officer, Line Barracks, Port Louis. To extend a stay beyond three months one must apply for a visa, provided the reasons given are considered justifiable.

Health

A yellow fever inoculation is required if coming from an infected area. Malaria prophylaxis is recommended.

Restrictions

The use of harpoons for fishing is forbidden.

Facilities

The new Caudan Marina in Port Louis has greatly improved docking facilities. Electricity and water are available on the dock and there are plans to add a fuel station. Larger quantities of fuel can be delivered by truck. Provisioning is excellent. There is a dry dock in Port Louis, Taylor-Smith General Engineering, which undertakes some general repair work. Other repair facilities are available including sail repair. Fuel is available and gas bottles can be filled at the Shell depot in St Louis.

There is a good anchorage in front of the yacht club at Gran Baie, but there is an 8 ft (2.5 m) draft restriction in the channel leading into the bay.

The Grand Baie Yacht Club offers temporary membership to visiting sailors at a reasonable cost. Water and fuel can be obtained from the jetty.

In Rodrigues water and fresh provisions are available, but little in the way of repairs, although long-distance telephone communications are excellent thanks to a new satellite link. The water available in the harbour may be poor quality and should be treated. The meteorological office is extremely helpful and forecasts are made available free of charge to departing yachts.

Further Reading

Indian Ocean Cruising Guide
Traveller's Guide to East Africa and the Indian Ocean
Mauritius, Réunion & Seychelles – a travel survival kit

Websites

www.mauritius-info.com
www.mauritius.net (Mauritius Tourism Promotion Agency)

MAYOTTE

Mayotte Island is geographically part of the Comoros archipelago, a small group of islands lying between the northern tip of Madagascar and East Africa in the Indian Ocean. Politically, Mayotte is an overseas territory of France and the French Navy maintain a naval base on the island. The island is surrounded by reefs and the main harbour at Dzaoudzi is very well-protected. There are many anchorages inside the reef and diving is excellent.

The other three islands in the group, Grande Comore, Moheli and Anjouan, now form an independent republic.

Country Profile

The early history of Mayotte is described in the section dealing with the Comoros, with whom Mayotte was united until 1975, when the Comoros became independent while Mayotte chose by referendum to remain French. The economy of Mayotte is dependent on France. A deepwater port has been built, and the airport expanded, with French funding, with the hope of developing tourism.

Comoros continues to claim sovereignty over Mayotte, although Mayotte's main political party wants to remain French, and even upgrade to a Département. A referendum on Mayotte's status held in July 2000 confirmed Mayotte's continuing links with France.

The local name for Mayotte is Maore and the capital is Mamoudzou. The population of nearly 150,000 are a mixture of African, Arab, Malagasy and French origins. French and Arabic are the main languages, while the main religion is Islam.

The climate is tropical, with two seasons, the dry season lasting from May to October, with an average temperature of 75°F (24°C), and the rainy season from November to April, when both temperature and humidity are higher. The cyclone season is from December to March.

Entry Regulations

Port of entry
Dzaoudzi 12°47′S 45°15′E.

Procedure on arrival
One should contact harbour control (Commandant du Port) on VHF Channel 16, who will give direc-

Practical Information

LOCAL TIME: GMT + 3

BUOYAGE: IALA A

CURRENCY: French franc (FF), euro from 2002. 1 euro = 6.55957 FRF.

BUSINESS HOURS
Banks: 0700–1200 Monday to Thursday and 0700–1130 Friday.
Business: 0800–1200/1400–1600 Monday to Thursday, 0900–1200 Friday.

Offices and shops close 1200–1500 daily. Government offices: 0630–1400 Monday to Thursday, 0630–1200 Friday.

ELECTRICITY: 220 V, 50 Hz

PUBLIC HOLIDAYS
1 January: New Year's Day
Easter Monday
1 May
Ascension
Whit Sunday and Monday

14 July: Bastille Day
15 August: Assumption
1 November: All Saints' Day
11 November: Armistice Day
25 December: Christmas Day
Some Muslim holidays are also observed.

COMMUNICATIONS
Flights from the airport at Pamandzi to Réunion, Madagascar, Seychelles, Nairobi, Hararé and Comores. Intercontinental flights can be caught daily from Réunion.

tions about clearance procedure. A port official will board the boat on arrival and will call customs. All boats, whether French or not, must clear customs, who will issue a transit log valid for one year from the date of arrival. No other formalities are necessary until the vessel's departure.

Customs

Firearms must be declared to customs and the gendarmerie for authorisation to be held on board during stay in port.

Animals need a rabies vaccination and health certificate.

Yachts can stay up to six months in Mayotte.

Immigration

French visa regulations apply. Nationals of Western European countries, Argentina, Brunei, Canada, Chile, Czech Republic, Hungary, Israel, South Korea, New Zealand, Poland, Singapore, Slovak Republic, Slovenia and the United States do not need visas for stays not exceeding one month. All other nationalities need visas which must be obtained in advance.

Health

Malaria prophylaxis is recommended.

Fees

Overtime is charged 1700–0630 Monday to Friday and after 1200 on Saturday, also on Sundays and holidays. Customs fees are payable.

Procedure on departure

Customs must be visited for outward clearance. This must be done 18 hours before the intended departure on the following day, or before 1100 if planning to leave that same afternoon. The transit log may be reused if the vessel returns during its period of validity.

Facilities

Some repair facilities are available in Dzaoudzi. Supplies are better than in the neighbouring Comoros and most imported goods are French. There is a good market for local produce every morning.

Further Reading

Africa on a Shoestring
Indian Ocean Cruising Guide

Websites

www.maho-net.org
www.perso.wanadoo.fr/pilotage-mayotte (Harbour master official site)
www.outre-mer.gouv.fr/domtom/mayotte

MOZAMBIQUE

The People's Republic of Mozambique has some 1400 miles of coastline on the Indian Ocean. The country stretches along the eastern coast of Africa, being mostly a coastal plain rising inland to mountainous borders with Zimbabwe, Zambia and Malawi. The island area of Basaruto and the area around Maputo provide some of the best cruising. Although not particularly welcoming cruising

Practical Information

LOCAL TIME: GMT + 2

BUOYAGE: IALA A

CURRENCY: Metical (meticais) of 100 centavos. The import and export of local currency is forbidden. Foreign currency must be declared on arrival. These currency regulations are strictly enforced.

BUSINESS HOURS
Banks: 0730–1130 Monday to Friday.
Shops: 0730–1130, 1330–1730 Monday to Friday.

ELECTRICITY: 220 V, 50 Hz

PUBLIC HOLIDAYS
1 January: New Year's Day
3 February: Heroes Day
7 April: Mozambican Women's Day
1 May: Labour Day
25 June: Independence Day
7 September: Victory Day
25 September: Revolution Day
25 December: National Family Day

COMMUNICATIONS
There are flights from Maputo to Zimbabwe, South Africa, Lisbon, Madrid and Copenhagen.

DIPLOMATIC MISSIONS
In Maputo:
Canada: Av. Julius Nyerere 1128. *Tel.* 492 623.
United Kingdom: Av Vladimir Lenin 310.
Tel. 420 111.
United States: 193 Av. Kenneth Kaunda.
Tel. 492 797.

---

yachts in the past, those yachts which have stopped in one of Mozambique's ports have been treated courteously by the officials. Stopping at other places between major ports is not allowed, although in the case of those who have arrived with visas obtained beforehand, some freedom of movement was allowed. Recently the country does appear to be opening up to yachts and South African yachts have cruised there. Caution is advised if travelling inland as the presence of landmines laid during the war is a continuing hazard in spite of de-mining efforts. Crime is an ongoing problem, especially in urban areas, but also includes car jacking and highway robbery.

Country Profile

There were several independent kingdoms thriving on trade in this region before the Europeans came to Africa. Then in the late fifteenth century the Portuguese established trading posts along the coast, trading for gold, slaves and ivory from the interior. It was only at the end of the seventeenth century that colonisation began, when the Portuguese settled and established a plantation economy using slave labour, and after slavery was abolished, forced labour. Large estates were owned by these settlers and in the nineteenth century foreign companies were also given concessions. When Salazar's regime came to power in Portugal in the 1920s, protectionist measures were brought in and attempts were made to bring the colony more closely under Portuguese control. The country was not prosperous and the Africans had no say in the country's affairs.

In 1962 Frelimo was formed and mounted campaigns against the Portuguese. Frelimo gained control of several areas, where it established a socialist and more egalitarian economy. In 1975 after the revolution in Portugal, the new regime in Lisbon decided to put an end to the wasteful war and Frelimo came to power under the presidency of Samora Machel. Efforts were made to raise living standards, increase literacy, and there was extensive nationalisation. The country's resources were drained by attacks from Rhodesia, as Frelimo supported Robert Mugabe's forces. There were also attacks from the Mozambique National Resistance rebels (MNR), who were supported by South Africa. Therefore the government was forced to change its policy in order to save the economy. The Nkomati Accord was signed with South Africa and efforts made to attract foreign capital. A new constitution introduced multiparty rule, and market reforms were applied in the economy. In 1992 a peace treaty finally ended a civil war in which some 900,000 people had died. The 1994 elections were won by Frelimo President Joaquim Chissano. Since then the country has remained politically stable but the economy was badly affected by disastrous floods early in 2000.

The economy is mainly agricultural, with some limited industry. The main exports are cotton, sugar, copra, sisal and tea. Previously considerable income had come from Mozambiqueans working in the mines in South Africa, but these were expelled following the application of sanctions. Recently efforts have been made to strengthen links with the west and restrictions on tourists have been reduced. However, shortages are still a major problem and both fuel and food are rationed.

The population numbers over 15 million, made up of various tribes, the most numerous being the Makua-Lomwe. Portuguese is the official language, but many African languages are spoken. In remoter areas Portuguese is less widely spoken. Most people hold traditional animist beliefs, although there are also Christians, Muslims and Hindus. The capital is Maputo, formerly called Lourenço Marques under the Portuguese.

The climate is tropical and mostly hot and humid. The country is plagued by irregular rainfall, the rainy season being from November to March. The prevailing winds are SE to SW. Much of the coast is under the influence of sea breezes with stronger onshore winds in the afternoons. In the northern part of the coast, the SE trade winds blow during the winter months, February to June, while NE winds prevail in summer, from July to January.

Entry Regulations

Ports of entry
Maputo 25°59′S 32°36′E, Beira 19°50′S 34°50′E, Nacala 14°32′S 40°40′E.

Procedure on arrival
Maputo: The harbour is approached through two main channels, the south channel being recommended only for small vessels and those with local knowledge. Port Control maintain continuous watch on VHF Channel 16. It is possible to come alongside one of the wharfs for clearance formalities. *Beira:* The port is located in the estuary of the River Pungue and access to it is through the Maputi Channel, which is approximately 10 miles long. Small vessels can anchor inside the inner harbour. *Nacala:* Port Control maintains watch on HF 8.499 KHz.

Customs
Firearms must be declared and may be detained.

Immigration
All nationalities require visas. Those arriving without a visa may be fined US$500. Visas can be obtained in Dar es Salaam (Tanzania) and Johannesburg (South Africa). Special permission may be necessary to travel inland outside the Maputo province if the security situation is bad. A permit is needed from Ministerio de Cultura e Educacão to take anything out of the country that has been bought there, so all receipts should be kept.

Health
Malaria prophylaxis is essential, resistance to chloroquine is confirmed. Cholera is a risk.

Restrictions
It is prohibited to take photographs of public buildings, military installations or soldiers. The legacy of an authoritarian regime has left officials, and especially the military, extremely suspicious of any foreigners, so one should exercise due caution when using a camera and avoid photographing any buildings or installations that could be regarded as sensitive. There are also restrictions on diving, which is prohibited in some areas.

Facilities

Provisioning is very difficult because of frequent shortages. Fuel and food can only be bought with ration cards. It is sometimes possible to obtain some fresh produce. Repair facilities are available in Beira and Maputo, where there are dockyards dealing with repairs on fishing vessels.

Further Reading

Africa on a Shoestring
Indian Ocean Cruising Guide
East Africa Pilot

Website

www.mozambique.mz (Official government site)

REUNION ISLAND

La Réunion Island is a small French territory in the South Indian Ocean lying south-west of Mauritius. It is a useful stop for yachts sailing from the latter to South Africa. The lush interior of this volcanic island has some stunning mountain scenery, such as the Cirque de Cilaos, a crater 3935 ft (1220 m) high, once a refuge for runaway slaves, and the spa town of Cilaos with its hot springs. Piton des Neiges is the highest summit at over 9840 ft (3000 m). In the south-east of the island is Piton de la Fournaise, an active volcano, with a black lava landscape. Many people go walking through the mountains and there are lodges where overnight stops can be made. It is a last opportunity to stretch one's legs before the long and possibly rough passage to South Africa.

Juan de Nova, Europa, Bassas da India, Iles

Practical Information

LOCAL TIME: GMT + 4

BUOYAGE: IALA A

CURRENCY: French franc (FF). Euro from 2002. 1 euro = 6.55957 FRF.

BUSINESS HOURS
0800–1200, 1400–1800 Monday to Saturday.
Banks: 0800–1600 Monday to Friday.

ELECTRICITY: 220 V, 50 Hz

PUBLIC HOLIDAYS
1 January: New Year's Day
Easter Monday
1 May: Labour Day
8 May: Liberation Day
Ascension
Whit Monday
14 July: Bastille Day
14 August: National Day
15 August: Assumption
1 November: All Saints' Day
11 November: Armistice Day
20 December: Abolition of Slavery
25 December: Christmas Day

COMMUNICATIONS
International direct dialling from telephone offices. There are frequent flights to Paris, also to Mauritius and Madagascar.

MEDICAL
Two general hospitals:
Centre Hospitalier Departamental, Allée Topaze, Saint Denis. *Tel*. 02 62 90 50 50.
Centre Hospitalier Gabriel Martin, Rue Mahé de Labourdonnais, Saint Paul. *Tel*. 02 62 45 30 30.

DIPLOMATIC MISSIONS
British Consulate, 94B Avenue Leconte Delisle, Sainte Clotilde. *Tel*. 02 62 29 14 91.
Madagascar Consulate, 77 Rue Juliette Dodu, Saint Denis. *Tel*. 02 62 21 66 00.

Glorieuses and Tromelin are uninhabited islands near Madagascar. After Madagascan independence they remained French, and are administered by the Réunion Commissioner. Tromelin is claimed by both the Seychelles and Mauritius. Mauritius claims all of the islands.

Country Profile

Réunion was discovered by the Portuguese Pedro de Mascarenhas in 1513. The island was uninhabited, although visited occasionally by Malay, Arab and European sailors. In the second half of the seventeenth century French settlers and their Malagasy slaves came to the island. The island was then called Isle Bourbon, and the French East India Company administered it. Britain began to take an interest in the island, so the French government took over the administration.

In the late eighteenth century slave revolts broke out and some escaped to the interior, where they lived in communities with elected chiefs. The name of the island was changed to La Réunion after the French Revolution. Réunion was part of the French Mascarene Islands along with Mauritius and Rodrigues, and was occupied by Britain during the Napoleonic Wars. Sugar was introduced to Réunion when the French re-established their rule, and soon came to dominate the economy. With the abolition of slavery, contract labourers from India were brought in to fill the labour shortage. Later the economy suffered from competition by sugar-producing countries in other parts of the world. After the Second World War Réunion

became an overseas department of France. Although the local population would like greater autonomy in their affairs, there is little desire to make a complete break from France.

Sugar still dominates the agricultural economy. Other exports are vanilla essence and tobacco. The fishing industry is also being developed. Industry is expanding as well as banking. Trade is predominantly with France. Réunion imports almost all of its food and consumer goods from France and the cost of living is high. Unemployment is a problem and many young people have emigrated to France.

The population is around 800,000. Most Réunionais are of French, African and Indian origins. Also there are Asian and European communities and a Chinese minority. The majority are Roman Catholics, but there are also Hindus, Muslims and some Buddhists. French and Créole are the main languages. Saint Dénis on the north coast is the capital.

The average temperature on the coast is 66–88°F (18–31°C), although it is cooler in the hilly interior. The island is divided by its mountain range into the lusher, rainier windward side and the drier leeward side to the south and west. Réunion lies in the E to SE trade wind area, and the cyclone season is from December to March. The island is occasionally affected by cyclones.

Entry Regulations

Ports of entry
Pointe des Galets 20°55′S 55°18′E, Saint-Pierre 21°20′S 55°29′E.

Procedure on arrival

Pointe des Galets: One should tie up alongside the fishermen's wharf south of the entrance, or proceed farther south to the marina. Deep-drafted boats should not proceed beyond the fishermen's wharf, where the depth is 14 ft (4.5 m). Yachts should contact the Capitainerie du Port on VHF Channel 16 and they will advise on the correct procedure. Yachts which arrive outside working hours usually have to wait until offices open. Port de la Pointe des Galets is usually referred to simply as 'Le Port'.

Customs

Firearms must be declared on arrival.

Animals need rabies vaccination and health certificates.

There are restrictions on the importation of plants.

Yachts can stay up to six months in one or several visits during a 12-month period, without paying duty, as long as the crew do not enter into employment ashore or charter the vessel. If the owner wants to leave Réunion by other means, the vessel has to be put in the custody of customs until the owner's return. The ship's papers must be left with customs. This period will be deducted from the time spent in Réunion.

Immigration

French immigration regulations apply. Nationals of Western European countries, Argentina, Brunei, Canada, Chile, Czech Republic, Hungary, Israel, South Korea, New Zealand, Poland, Singapore, Slovak Republic, Slovenia, the United States and some African countries do not need visas for up to a three-month stay.

All other nationalities require visas, which should be obtained from a French embassy or consulate in advance. One should ensure that the visa given is valid for Réunion.

Facilities

Pointe des Galets is an artificial harbour about 12 miles west of the capital Saint Dénis. A new marina (port de plaisance) is now operational south of the commercial harbour. Provisioning is very expensive as the bulk of food is imported. Fuel and water can be taken on at the fisherman's wharf. There is a good morning market for local produce in the capital Saint Dénis.

Saint Pierre on the south-west coast also welcomes yachts. Saint Paul is the old capital of the French East India Company. Thanks to an active racing community, repair facilities have greatly improved. The marina has a 40-ton travelift. Essential spares can be flown in from France, but this can take at least one week.

Further Reading

Traveller's Guide to East Africa and the Indian Ocean
Mauritius, Réunion & Seychelles – a travel survival kit
Indian Ocean Cruising Guide

Website

www.la-reunion-tourisme.com

SEYCHELLES

The Seychelles lie in the south Indian Ocean and number over 100 islands, some granite, others coral atolls including one of the world's largest atolls, Aldabra. This is now a world heritage site and permission to visit it must be obtained in Mahé. Having been uninhabited by man until 200 years ago, the islands are rich in unique wildlife, such as the giant land tortoise, many species of birds, strange plants such as the giant Coco de Mer, and untouched forests. Mahé, La Digue and Praslin have all been developed for foreign visitors to enjoy these natural advantages, but the number of tourists is kept controlled.

With the reputation of being the site of the Garden of Eden, it is not surprising that the Seychelles have had such a fascination for sailors, who are forever searching for paradise on earth. The anchorages at La Digue and Prasin Islands are particularly striking and one of the chief attractions on the latter is Baie St Anne, with its thousands of Coco de Mer palms, some of them reputedly 800 years old. The gigantic nuts of these palm trees have a suggestive female shape and when they were first discovered washed up on distant shores, mystical qualities were attributed to them. As their origins remained a mystery for many hundreds of years, they were believed to grow under the sea.

The strict controls imposed on cruising yachts in the early 1990s have been gradually lifted and formalities are no longer so complicated, although

Practical Information

LOCAL TIME: GMT + 4

BUOYAGE: IALA A

CURRENCY: Seychelles rupee (SR) of 100 cents.

BUSINESS HOURS
Banks: 0830–1500 Monday to Friday.
Banque Française Commerciale:
0830–1500 Monday to Friday, 0900–1130
Saturday.
Business and government offices:
0800–1200, 1300–1600 Monday to Friday.
Shops: 0800–1200, 1330–1700 Monday to
Friday.

ELECTRICITY: 240 V, 50 Hz

PUBLIC HOLIDAYS
1, 2 January: New Year's Day
Good Friday
Easter Monday
1 May: Labour Day
5 June: Liberation Day
15 June: National Day
29 June: Independence Day
Corpus Christi
15 August: Assumption Day
1 November: All Saints' Day
8 December: Immaculate Conception
25 December: Christmas Day

COMMUNICATIONS
Cable & Wireless Ltd for telephone calls,
telex, telegraph and radio (24 hours). Also
Airtel for mobile services.
Main post office in Victoria: airmail collections
at 1500 weekdays, noon on Saturdays, open

0800–1200, 1300–1600 Monday to Friday,
0800–1200 Saturday.
Emergency: dial 999.
Seychelles International Airport on Mahé
has regular flights to Europe, Africa, Asia
and the Middle East.

MEDICAL
One can obtain emergency treatment
under the National Medical Service for a
basic fee. Main hospital, out-patients clinic;
dental clinic at Mont Fleuri.

DIPLOMATIC MISSIONS
In Victoria:
France: Arpent Vert, Mont Fleuri.
Tel. 224710.
United Kingdom: Victoria House.
Tel. 225225.
United States: Victoria House. *Tel.* 225256.

---

some restrictions remain in force. Most of these are meant to protect this truly unique environment.

Country Profile

Vasco da Gama sighted the Seychelles in the sixteenth century, but they were only occasionally visited until the French settled with their African slaves in the mid-eighteenth century. During the Napoleonic Wars the control of the islands became unsure, until they came under British control in 1814. In the nineteenth century the group was administered from Mauritius and the population expanded as slaves freed by the British Navy settled there, as well as Mauritians, Indians and Chinese. In 1903 the Seychelles were detached to form a separate Crown Colony. The Seychelles have been independent since 1976, in recent years following a moderate socialist path. The 1990s saw the end of one-party rule and the drafting of a new constitution.

Efforts are being made to raise living standards and tackle the economic problems of unemployment and a trade deficit. The traditional exports of cinnamon and copra have declined in importance in recent years. Since the opening of the international airport on Mahé in 1971, tourism has become a major factor in the economy. The fishing industry is also expanding.

The 70,000 Seychellois are a mixture of African, Asian and European origin. There are also Indians, Chinese and Europeans. The majority of the population are Roman Catholic. French and English are the official languages, but Créole is spoken by most people. Victoria, on Mahé, is the capital. Mahé is the economic and political centre of the Seychelles, and most of the population live there.

The climate is tropical, but outside of the cyclone belt. Temperatures average 75–86°F (24–30°C). The NW monsoon lasts from November to April, while from March it is hotter and the winds are lighter until the SE monsoon sets in from May to October.

Entry Regulations

Port of entry
Port Victoria (Mahé) 4°37′S 55°27′E.

Procedure on arrival
All vessels visiting the Seychelles are reminded that Port Victoria is the only port of entry and exit, and that both on arrival and departure for a foreign port vessels must call at Port Victoria to complete clearance formalities.

The port control keeps a 24-hour watch on VHF Channel 16. On arrival, one should fly the Q flag and anchor about 3.3 cables north of the Victoria Lighthouse, bearing 274°T. Do not go directly to the yacht club. The health, customs, immigration and security officials usually board the yacht for clearance. The Entomological Department requires yachts to be sprayed on arrival.

Once cleared, yachts may proceed into the inner harbour to anchor as directed by the port authority. Within 24 hours, weekends and public holidays excluded, the captain must report to the Port Office, Mahé Quay, through the Port Security Gate on Latanier Road. An arrival form must be completed and the boarding fee paid. Three crew lists and the ship's papers should be taken, and the latter will be held until departure. The captain must report to Immigration, Independence House, Victoria, with crew lists and passports.

The authorities recommend having at least ten copies of crew lists, as other departments will also ask for them.

Procedure on departure
On departure from the Seychelles, one must first visit the immigration office two working days prior to departure with all passports and permits. One day before departure, one must obtain port and customs clearance, the latter from the customs office, Latanier Road.

Port clearance is needed to visit any of the other islands. Clearance must be made within working hours (0800–1200, 1300–1600 Monday to Friday). Before leaving Victoria to visit other islands, port control must be advised on VHF Channel 16. Usually one is asked to come to the commercial wharf for a security check before being allowed to leave. The same operation must be followed on one's return, when a yacht is subjected to an incoming security check before being allowed to anchor.

On the other islands, one must check in with local police or the Island Manager, who will sign the clearance form which must be returned to the port office within 24 hours of one's return to Victoria. At weekends and public holidays the form can be left at Mahé Quay police station.

Customs
All arms and ammunition, including spearguns, must be handed to the police or customs on arrival and a receipt obtained. The bonded firearms will be returned on departure.

The Seychelles are rabies-free so regulations regarding animals are strict. Yachts with animals on board will only be allowed to visit other islands if pets are not let ashore. They must always be kept confined on board in port. Only with special written permission from the Veterinary Section may animals be taken ashore. Illegal landing of animals can lead to a heavy fine, imprisonment and confiscation of the animal, which may be destroyed.

Stores under bond will be sealed and are not to be used while in the Seychelles without payment of duty. Customs officers may ask for a declaration of all food and provisions on board, but dutiable goods will not be charged duty, if they are declared properly and are for personal consumption.

Immigration
Normally a visitor's permit for two weeks is given on arrival. This is extendable up to three months. One should apply for the renewal at least one week before expiry of the existing permit. Crew leaving the yacht in the Seychelles must first obtain an authority from immigration. If crew are arriving by air to join a yacht, the captain must give immigration written confirmation prior to their arrival.

Health
Cholera and yellow fever vaccination certificates are required if coming from a known infected area.

Fees
Harbour dues are charged on a daily basis and vary in accordance with the length of stay. For vessels less than 20 GRT, the fees vary between 50 and 75 Seychelles Rupees (5SR = US$1). Vessels between 20 and 100 GRT pay between 75 and 100 SR. Port dues must be settled on a weekly basis. There is a fee of SR100 for Pratique. There is a charge of SR200 for fumigation of the yacht on arrival.

Landing fees are applicable on most islands.

Port fees must be settled before an extension to the visitors passes can be granted.

Restrictions
Anchoring in North West Bay, Mahé (Beau Vallon Bay) is strictly prohibited outside the marked and buoyed areas for which mooring buoys are provided.

It is forbidden to spend the night in any anchorage except for the following designated anchorages:
Schedule A (islands within 60 miles of Mahé): Yacht Basin, Port Victoria; Baie-Ste-Anne, Praslin; La Passe (within one mile offshore), La Digue; Bird Island/Ile aux Vaches, Denis and Fregate, all within three miles from the shore.
Schedule B (islands 60 to 240 miles from Mahé): within three miles from the shore. No anchorage or landing is allowed around African Banks Island, Remire Island and Ile aux Cocos.
Schedule C (over 240 miles from Mahé): within three miles from the shore.

The authorities should be consulted concerning islands in schedules B and C.
National Park: Shell or coral collecting and spearfishing in protected areas is forbidden. The

environment should not be disturbed in these areas. Penalties can be a large fine and imprisonment. The protected areas, including the sea up to 400 m offshore, are as follows:

1. Mahé from Rat Island south to Pointe au Sel, also from North East Point north to the Carana Beach Hotel.
2. The Sainte Anne Marine National Park (the islands of Ste Anne, Cerf, Long, Moyenne, Round).
3. The islands of Cousin, Curieuse and Cachée.
4. Praslin from Anse Boudin east to Pointe Zanguilles.
5. La Digue: La Passe lighthouse north to Gross Roche.

Chartering is not allowed unless a licence has been obtained. Spearfishing is prohibited.

Facilities

With the increase in the number of cruising yachts visiting the Seychelles and also because some charter boats are based there, facilities are steadily improving. All repair services are concentrated in Victoria, where there are several boatyards with slipways. The largest is Naval Services, which undertakes electrical, engine and transmission repair as well as metal work. There are other companies dealing with electronics, sails, rigging, fibreglass and refrigeration work. Only a limited amount of marine supplies is available locally. Fuel can be taken on at the commercial wharf in Port Victoria, but the cost is very high. LPG bottles can also be filled and there are several supermarkets with a good selection as well as a daily fresh produce market. There is no marina at the moment, although there are plans to build one in the future. For the time being yachts use the facilities of the Seychelles Yacht Club in Port Victoria's inner harbour, where visitors are welcome. The anchorage in front of the club is well protected and visitors are given one month's complimentary membership. The club has a bar, restaurant and laundry; there is also fuel on an adjacent dock.

Further Reading

Indian Ocean Cruising Guide
Seychelles Nautical Pilot
Mauritius, Réunion & Seychelles – a travel survival kit

Websites

www.seychelles-online.com (Official government site)
www.webltd.com/tourism

TANZANIA

The United Republic of Tanzania came into existence as the result of political union between mainland Tanganyika and the offshore islands of Zanzibar and Pemba. The largest country in East Africa, the mainland boasts some fine scenery, the volcanic Rift Valley with its many lakes, the high steppes and savannahs rising from the coast up to Mount Kilimanjaro, which at 19,335 ft (5895 m) is Africa's highest mountain. A concerted effort is being made to protect the environment, and a large part of the country has been declared national parks and reserves.

In line with a general opening up of the country to tourism, cruising yachts are now welcome to all parts of the country and even areas which were closed in the past, such as Pemba Island, are now accessible by sea. The underwater scenery and marine life are of comparable beauty to the spectacular interior of the country. The main attractions inland are the game parks, such as the Serengeti or Ngorongoro, which can be visited by leaving the yacht in the care of one of the yacht clubs. The spice island of Zanzibar is worth a visit to see the relics of its colourful trading history.

Country Profile

In the Rift Valley ancient remains of Stone Age man have been discovered. Around 100 BC Bantu-speaking peoples came from the west and mixed with the original inhabitants and other peoples from the north. Along the coast, Arabic and Bantu merged into the Swahili language, named Swahili from the Arabic word for coast. Towns were established, which thrived on trade from the interior, especially slaves, gold and ivory. In the tenth century Persians came, bringing Islam to the region. From the fifteenth century the Portuguese became rivals in trade, but Arab and Swahili traders still dominated the area. The interior remained less developed and the Europeans did not explore there until the eighteenth century, when famous explorers as Livingstone and Stanley went deep inland.

Practical Information

LOCAL TIME: GMT + 3

BUOYAGE: IALA A

CURRENCY: Tanzanian shilling (TSh) of 100 senti. Some services, such as entry to the national parks, must be paid in convertible foreign currency.

BUSINESS HOURS
Banks: 0830–1230 Monday to Friday, 0830–1130 Saturday, 0900–1130 Sunday.
Business: 0730–1430 Monday to Friday.
Shops: 0800–1200, 1400–1715 Monday to Saturday.
Government offices: 0730–1530 Monday to Friday.

ELECTRICITY: 230 V, 50 Hz

PUBLIC HOLIDAYS
1 January: New Year's Day
12 January: Zanzibar Revolution Day
Good Friday, Easter Monday
26 April: Union Day
1 May: Labour Day
8 August: Saba Saba (Peasants Day)
9 December: Independence Day
25, 26 December: Christmas
Variable: Eid el-Fitr, Eid el-Hadj, Moulud

COMMUNICATIONS
Tanzania is fully integrated in the global communication systems. International calls can be made from most places, and internet services are available in almost all major towns.
Air Tanzania operates internal flights to all major towns. There are international flights from Dar es Salaam, Kilimanjaro, and Zanzibar. Foreigners must pay for international air tickets in convertible foreign currency.

DIPLOMATIC MISSIONS
In Dar es Salaam:
Canada: 38 Mirambo St.
France: Ali Hassan Mwinyi Road, PO Box 2349 (visas for Francophone countries can be obtained here). Tel. (51) 34961.
Kenya: NIC Investment House, Samora Machel Avenue, PO Box 5231, Junction with Mirambo Street. Tel. (51) 31502.
Madagascar: Magoret Street, PO Box 5254. Tel. (51) 41761.
Mozambique: 25 Garden Avenue. Tel. (51) 33062.
Sudan: 64 Upanga Road, PO Box 2266. Tel. (51) 32022.
United Kingdom: Hifadhi House, Samora Machel Avenue, PO Box 9200. Tel. (51) 29601.
United States: 140 Msese Road, Kinondoni, PO Box 9123. Tel. (51) 66010.

The island of Zanzibar was ruled by Oman and became so prosperous from trade in slaves and spices, especially cloves, that in 1840 the Sultan Seyyid Said moved his capital there from Muscat. Zanzibar became a British protectorate in 1890.

In 1885 the German East Africa Company took over the mainland, which was administered by Germany until the First World War. After the war, Britain took over Tanganyika under a League of Nations mandate to be followed by a United Nations mandate.

In 1954 the Tanganyika Africa National Union (TANU), led by Julius Nyerere, began its campaign for independence, and this was achieved in 1961. Two years later Zanzibar followed suit, and in 1964 a violent revolution ousted the Sultan. The same year Zanzibar united with Tanganyika to form the new nation of Tanzania, although Zanzibar retains some autonomy.

After independence, efforts were made to establish a socialist state based on collective agriculture, the village economy and traditional way of life. Tanzania's support for refugees from Uganda led to an invasion by Idi Amin's forces in 1978. Tanzania responded and waged war not only to defend itself, but also to liberate the people of Uganda and topple the expansionist dictator Idi Amin.

The economy was weakened by the break-up in 1977 of the East African Economic Union (Tanzania, Kenya and Uganda), which had been in place since independence. In 1985 Nyerere, president since independence, resigned and was succeeded by Ali Hassan Mwinyi, although Nyerere remained chairman of the ruling party until 1990. The 1990s have seen moves towards a multiparty system.

The economy is mainly agricultural depending on coffee, cotton, sisal, tea and cloves. A large trade deficit, population growth, foreign debt, poverty and droughts have put a considerable burden on the economy. The aim of achieving self-reliance and a radical socialist state has not worked and recently the government has opened up the economy to foreign capital. Tourism has been encouraged, although it suffered from the closure of the border with Kenya after the Economic Union broke up. This border has recently been reopened.

The population is about 27 million, made up of over 100 tribal groups, mainly Bantu-speaking. The people of Zanzibar and Pemba are a mixture of African, Arab, Comoron and Shirazi (Persian) origins. Ki-Swahili is the official language, although English is widely spoken. There are also many African languages, including Sandawe the 'click' language. In Zanzibar most of the population is Muslim. On the mainland, Christianity, traditional beliefs and Islam all have their followers. Dar es Salaam has been the capital since 1891.

The climate depends on the altitude, being temperate in the mountains and tropical along the coast. The rainy months are April, May, November and December. The coast is very hot and humid especially during the NW monsoon which lasts from December to April. The SE monsoon is from May to October.

Entry Regulations

Ports of entry
Dar es Salaam 6°49'S 39°19'E, Tanga 5°04'S 39°06'E, Mtwara 10°15'S 40°12'E, Zanzibar 6°10'S 39°11'E.

Procedure on arrival
Tanga: This is usually the first port of entry into Tanzania if coming from the north, and a popular place to obtain clearance. Smaller than Dar es Salaam, the offices are closer together and the officials less busy. Tanga Signal Station maintains 24-hour watch on VHF Channel 12. Captain C.J.E. Pearson, Harbour Master, Harbour Pilot and Commodore of Tanga Yacht Club will advise yachts on procedure during office hours. Customs formalities are completed at the office on Dhow Wharf, beyond the commercial wharf, then immigration clearance is obtained from the town office, close to the post office.

Dar es Salaam: Yachts should anchor in the inner harbour flying the Q flag and await customs, immigration and port health officials. Port officials usually work 0700–1700.

Officials rarely come to a boat for clearance, so it is probably better to anchor off the Dar es Salaam Yacht Club, take the dinghy to the Msasani slipway and then take a taxi to the immigration and customs offices in town. Landing at the yacht club is prohibited before clearance is completed.

Customs
Firearms must be declared to customs who will seal them on board in a secure locker.

There are no restrictions on animals as long as they have a health certificate, although they should have had a rabies vaccination for their own protection.

Immigration
Many European, African and British Commonwealth nationals do not require visas.

A full list of immigration requirements can be found under the heading of Consular Affairs on the website http://www.tanzania-online.gov.uk. Nationalities who do require a visa may obtain it on arrival.

Cruising permit
There are no restrictions for yachts on coastal cruising, although a transit log must be obtained from customs on arrival for cruising inside Tanzania. The transit log may be inspected if stopping at Pemba Island.

Health
Yellow fever vaccination certificate is required. Malaria prophylaxis is recommended. One should not swim in fresh water, because of the danger of the bilharzia parasite. AIDS is endemic in East Africa.

Restrictions
Photographs must not be taken of police stations, prisons, party offices, military areas, bridges or dams.

As a Muslim island, it is advised that visitors to Zanzibar wear clothes that cover the body from the chest down to the knees, especially during visits to public places such as markets, bus stations or hospitals.

Facilities

Provisions are sometimes in short supply. Occasionally there are temporary water shortages due to power failures and all water should be treated and possibly filtered as well. Both the Dar es Salaam and Tanga Yacht Clubs are particularly welcoming to visiting yachts. Most visitors try and leave their yachts in the care of a yacht club to travel inland. Theft is a problem and a yacht should be properly watched at all times. In Dar es Salaam this applies during the day as well as at night and it is not recommended to stay in the inner harbour longer than it takes to complete clearance. Some simple repairs are possible in the bigger ports, but any spares must be flown in from abroad.

Further Reading

Indian Ocean Cruising Guide
East Africa Pilot
Traveller's Guide to East Africa and the Indian Ocean
Africa on a Shoestring

Website

www.tanzania-online.gov.uk (Tanzania Embassy in London)

SECTION III

1 IALA Maritime Buoyage System

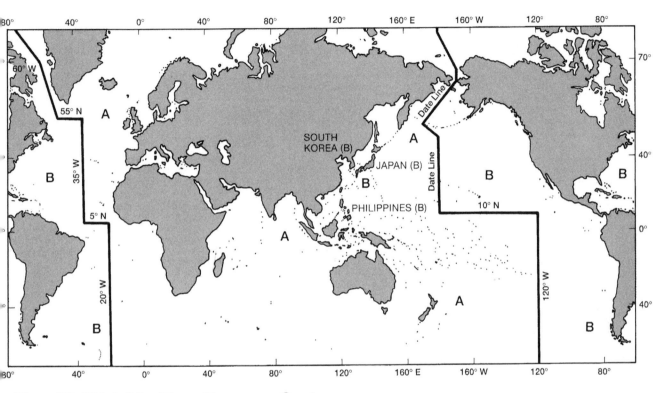

Map 17: IALA Maritime Buoyage System

BUOYAGE REGIONS A AND B

2 International Direct Dialling Codes

Region 1   Mediterranean and Black Sea

Albania	355	Greece	30	Romania	40
Algeria	213	Israel	972	Slovenia	386
Bulgaria	359	Italy	39	Spain	34
Croatia	385	Lebanon	961	Syria	963
Cyprus	357	Libya	218	Tunisia	216
Egypt	20	Malta	356	Turkey	90
Georgia	995	Monaco	33	Ukraine	380
Gibraltar	350	Morocco	212	Yugoslavia	381

Region 2   Northern Europe

Belgium	32	Germany	49	Norway	47
Denmark	45	Latvia	371	Poland	48
Estonia	372	Lithuania	370	Russia	7
Finland	358	Netherlands	31	Sweden	46

Region 3   Western Europe and North Atlantic Islands

Azores	351	Faeroes	298	Ireland	353
Bermuda	1 441	France	33	Madeira	351 91
Canary Islands	34	Greenland	299	Portugal	351
Cape Verde Islands	238	Iceland	354	United Kingdom	44
Channel Islands	44				

Region 4   West Africa and South Atlantic Islands

Ascension Island	247	Mauritania	222	Senegal	221
Falkland Islands	500	Namibia	264	South Africa	27
Gambia	220	St Helena	290	Tristan da Cunha	n/a
Ivory Coast	225				

Region 5   Caribbean

Anguilla	1 264	Jamaica	1 876
Antigua and Barbuda	1 268	Martinique	596
Aruba	297	Montserrat	1 664
Bahamas	1 242	Puerto Rico	1 787
Barbados	1 246	Saba	599 4
Bonaire	599 7	St Barts	590
British Virgin Islands	1 284	St Eustatius	599 3
Cayman Islands	1 345	St Kitts and Nevis	1 869
Cuba	53	St Lucia	1 758
Curaçao	599 9	St Martin	590
Dominica	1 767	St Vincent and Grenadines	1 784
Dominican Republic	1 809	Sint Maarten	599 5
Grenada	1 473	Trinidad and Tobago	1 868
Guadeloupe	590	Turks and Caicos	1 649
Haiti	509	US Virgin Islands	1 340

Region 6   Central and North America

Belize	501	Guatemala	502	Panama	507
Canada	1	Honduras	504	St Pierre et Miquelon	508
Costa Rica	506	Mexico	52	USA	1
El Salvador	503	Nicaragua	505		

Region 7   South America

Argentina	54	Ecuador	593	Suriname	597
Brazil	55	French Guiana	594	Uruguay	598
Chile	56	Guyana	592	Venezuela	58
Colombia	57	Peru	51		

Region 8   North Pacific Islands

Federated States of Micronesia	691	Marshall Islands	692
Guam	1 671	Northern Marianas	1 670
Hawaii	1 808	Palau	680 9
Kiribati	686		

Region 9 Australia and South Pacific Islands

American Samoa	684	New Caledonia	687	Solomon Islands	677
Australia	61	New Zealand	64	Tahiti Nui	689
Cook Islands	682	Niue	683	Tokelau	690
Easter Island	56	Norfolk Island	672 3	Tonga	676
Fiji	679	Papua New Guinea	675	Tuvalu	688
Galapagos Islands	593	Pitcairn	n/a	Vanuatu	678
Juan Fernandez Islands	n/a	Samoa	685	Wallis and Futuna	681
Nauru	674				

Region 10 South East Asia and Far East

Brunei	673	Myanmar	95
China	86	Philippines	63
Hong Kong	852	Singapore	65
Indonesia	62	South Korea	82
Japan	81	Taiwan	886
Macao	853	Thailand	66
Malaysia	60	Vietnam	84

Region 11 North Indian Ocean and Red Sea

Bahrain	973	Kuwait	965	Somalia	252
Djibouti	253	Maldives	960	Sri Lanka	94
Eritrea	291	Oman	968	Sudan	249
India	91	Qatar	974	UAE	971
Jordan	962	Saudi Arabia	966	Yemen	967

Region 12 South Indian Ocean

Chagos	n/a	Kenya	254	Mozambique	258
Christmas Island	672 4	Madagascar	261	Réunion	262
Cocos Keeling	672 2	Mauritius	230	Seychelles	248
Comoros	269	Mayotte	269	Tanzania	255

3 Chart Agents and National Hydrographic Offices

British Admiralty Chart Agents

ANTIGUA
The Map Shop
St Mary's Street, ST JOHN'S
Tel. 809 462 3993

ARGENTINA
N H Neilson & Co Ltd
Australia 1770, 1296 BUENOS AIRES
Tel. 210501

AUSTRALIA
Boat Books
109 Albert Street
BRISBANE QLD 4000
Tel. 3229 6427

The Chart and Map Shop
14 Collie Street
FREMANTLE WA 6160
Tel. 9335 8665

Ivimey & Associates Pty Ltd (Boat Books)
31 Albany Street, Crows Nest, SYDNEY,
NSW 2065
Tel. 029 4391133

BELGIUM
Martin & Co
37 Oude Leeuwenrui, ANTWERPEN B 2000
Tel. 03 232 8532

BERMUDA
Pearman, Watlington & Co Ltd
Front Street, HAMILTON
Tel. 809 29 1233

BULGARIA
Navigation Maritime
1 Blvd Primorski
9000 VARNA
Tel. 2122 580

CANADA
Maritime Services Ltd
3440 Bridgeway Street, VANCOUVER BC
V5K 1B6
Tel. 604 294 4444

CHILE
Ian Taylor y Cia Ltda
Prat 827 Oficina 301, Casilla 752
VALPARAISO
Tel. 259096

CYPRUS
Theseas Savva
118 Franklin Roosevelt Ave
LIMASSOL
Tel. 05 355899

DENMARK
Iver Weilbach & Co A/S
Toldbodgade 35, KOBENHAVN DK 1253
Tel. 01 13 5927

EGYPT
Marinkart
29 Ramses Street, BOR SAÎD FREEZONE
Tel. 320148

Marinkart
14 Gohar Alkaid Street, Port Tewfik, SUEZ
Tel. 332 355

FIJI
Carpenter's Shipping
Tofua Street, Walu Bay, SUVA
Tel. 312 244

FINLAND
Oy Maritim AB
Wavulinsvagen 4, 00210 HELSINGFORS
Tel. 40 502 6400

FRANCE
Nautic Service
ZAC de Rogerville/ Oudalle
76700 HARFLEUR (Le HAVRE)
Tel. 02 3551 7530

Riviera Charts
Galerie du Port
26-30 rue Lacan
06600 ANTIBES
Tel. 04 9334 4566

Librairie Maritime Outremer
17 rue Jacob
75006 PARIS
Tel. 01 4633 4748

GERMANY
Seekarte (Kapt A. Dammeyer)
Korffsdeich 3, Vd Europahafen
2800 BREMEN 1

Nautischer Dienst (Kapt Stegmann & Co)
Maklerstrasse 8, 2300 KIEL 17
Tel. 0431 33 1772

GIBRALTAR
Gibraltar Chart Agency Ltd
4 Bayside, GIBRALTAR
Tel. 76293

GREECE
John S. Lazopoulos & Co
85 Akti Miaouli, GR-185 38 PIRAIEVS
Tel. 41 31 902

GRENADINES
Bo'sun's Locker, Port Elizabeth
BEQUIA, St Vincent
Tel. +1 78 44 58 36 34

HONG KONG
Geo Falconer (Nautical) Ltd
Room 806-7 The Hong Kong Chinese Bank Building,
61–65 Des Voeux Road, Central
Tel. 2854 2882

ICELAND
Attavitathjonustan EHF
Eyjarslod 9
127 REYKJAVIK
Tel. 551 5475

INDIA
C & C Marine Combine
25 Bank Street
MUMBAI 400 001
Tel. 2660 525

IRELAND
Windmill Leisure & Marine Ltd
3 Windmill Lane, Sir John Rogerson's Quay,
DUBLIN 2
Tel. 6 772008

ITALY
Cooperative per Azioni Armamento
Imprese Marittime ARL
Via XX Settembre 17-19
16121 GENOVA
Tel. 010 542 304

JAPAN
Cornes & Co Ltd
Towa Bldg, 2-3 Kaigan Dori, Chuo-Ku KOBE
Tel. 078 332 3361

Cornes & Co Ltd
Yokohama Daiei Building 6th floor,
2-10 Hon Cho, Naka-Ku, YOKOHAMA 231
Tel. 045 664 6512

KOREA
Korea Ocean Development Co Ltd
1 GA71-1 Nampo-Dong, Jung-ku, BUSAN
Tel. 466 0760

MALAYSIA
Motion Smith
Lot 20 Jalan 225
46100 Petaling Jaya 03
SELANGOR
Tel. 03 7874 3422

The Industrial & Scientific Co Ltd
53 Lee Chong Lin Industrial Estate,
KUCHING, Sarawak

MALTA
Thos C Smith & Co Ltd
12 St Christopher Street, VALLETTA
Tel. 245071

NETHERLANDS
Datema-Delfzijl BV
Hogelandsterweg 8
9936 BH Farmsum
DELFZIJL
Tel. 0596 635 252

Kelvin Hughes Observator
Niuewe Langeweg 41
3194 DC HOOGVLIET/ ROTTERDAM
Tel. 010 4167 622

NEW ZEALAND
Trans Pacific Marine Ltd
30 Quay Street, AUCKLAND 1
Tel. 303 1459

RNZN Chart Agency
Burns Avenue, Takapuna, AUCKLAND 9
Tel. 486 5350

NORWAY
Nautisk Forlag AS
Drammensveien 130
Skoyen
0213 OSLO
Tel. 2254 7650

PANAMA
Islamorada International SA
BALBOA-ANCON
Tel. 228 6069

PORTUGAL
J Garraio & Ca Lda
Avenida 24 de Julho 2-10 D, 1200 LISBOA
Tel. 347 3081

SINGAPORE
Motion Smith
1st Floor Marina House, 78 Shenton Way,
Mistri Road, SINGAPORE 0207
Tel. 2205098

SOUTH AFRICA
The Tyneside Shop No. 5, John Ross House,
Victoria Embankment, DURBAN 4001
Tel. 0313 377005

SPAIN
Suisca SL
Avda de Los Consignatorios 7
35008 LAS PALMAS de GRAN CANARIA
Tel. 928 220000

SRI LANKA
Marine Overseas Agency
Paul VI Centre, 3rd floor, Room 8,
24 Malwatta Road, COLOMBO 11
Tel. 3 26262

SWEDEN
Aktiebolaget Nautic
Skeppsbroplatsen 1, S411 21 GÖTEBORG
Tel. 031 100885

Nautiska Forlaget A/B
Slussplan 5
104 65 STOCKHOLM
Tel. 08 677 0000

TRINIDAD
Marine Consultants (Trinidad) Ltd
43 Charles Street, PORT OF SPAIN
Tel. 625 1309

TURKEY
Deniz Malzeme Ltd
Sirketi Tophane, Iskele Cad No. 17,
ISTANBUL
Tel. 2434334

UNITED STATES OF AMERICA

Tradewind Instruments Ltd
2540 Blanding Avenue, ALAMEDA
Nr San Francisco, California 94501
Tel. 415 523 5726

Boxell's Chandlery
68 Long Wharf, BOSTON,
Massachusetts 02110
Tel. 617 523 5678

Bahia Mar Marine Store
801 Seabreeze Boulevard,
FORT LAUDERDALE, Florida 33316
Tel. 305 764 8831

Pacific Map Centre
647 Auahi Street, HONOLULU,
Hawaii 96813
Tel. 808 531 3800

Safe Navigation Inc
107 East 8th Street,
LONG BEACH, California 90813
Tel. 213 590 8744

New York Nautical Instrument and Service
Corporation
140 West Broadway, NEW YORK 10013
Tel. 212 962 4523

Captain's Nautical Supplies
138 NW 10th Street, PORTLAND,
Oregon 97209
Tel. 503 227 1648

Captain's Nautical Supplies
1914 4th Avenue, SEATTLE,
Washington 98101
Tel. 206 448 2278

Bluewater Books & Charts
Southport Center,
1481 SE 17th Street Causeway,
FORT LAUDERDALE, Florida 33316
Tel. 305 763 6533   *Fax.* 305 522 2278

California Nautical Chart Center Inc
344 East 4th Street, LONG BEACH,
California 90802
Tel. 310 432 7292   *Fax.* 310 432 3363

The Armchair Sailor
543 Thames Street, NEWPORT,
Rhode Island 02840
Tel. 401 847 4252   *Fax.* 401 847 1219

URUGUAY
Marine Technical Services
Florida 1562, MONTEVIDEO
Tel. 985161

UNITED KINGDOM, CHANNEL ISLANDS

Aberdeen
Thomas Gunn Navigational Services
62 Marischal Street, Aberdeen AB1 2AL
Tel. 01224 595045

W.F. Price & Co. Ltd
Wapping Wharf
BRISTOL BS1 6UD
Tel. 0117 929 2229

Falmouth
Marine Instruments of The Bo'sun's Locker
Upton Slip, Church Street, Falmouth,
Cornwall TR11 3PS
Tel. 01326 312414

Glasgow
Kelvin Hughes
375 West George Street, Glasgow G2 4LR
Tel. 0141 221 5452

London
Kelvin Hughes
145 The Minories, London EC3N 1NH
Tel. 020 7709 9076

Plymouth
The Sea Chest Nautical Bookshop
Queen Anne's Battery Marina
PLYMOUTH PL4 0LP
Tel. 01752 222 012

St Peter Port (Guernsey)
Boatworks Plus Ltd
Castle Emplacement, St Peter Port,
Guernsey, Channel Islands
Tel. 01481 26071

Southampton
Kelvin Hughes
19–23 Canute Road, Eastern Docks,
Southampton SO1 1FJ
Tel. 023 80634911

US Defence Mapping Agency Agents

ARGENTINA
Securnavi SA
Av Luis M Campos 653,
BUENOS AIRES 1426

AUSTRALIA
Victoria
Boat Books & charts
214 St Kilda Road
ST KILDA 3182

New South Wales
Ivimey and Associates Pty Ltd
31 Albany St,
Crows Nest, SYDNEY 2065

Queensland
Boat Books
109 Albert St, BRISBANE 4000

The Navigation Center,
9C Palmer St,
SOUTH TOWNSVILLE 4810

BELGIUM
Bogerd NAVTEC NV
Oude Leeuwenrui 37
2000 ANTWERPEN
ANTWERP B-2000

BERMUDA
Dockyard Marina
SANDYS MA 1

CANADA
British Columbia
Alexander Marine Ltd
570 Davie St, VANCOUVER V6B 2G4

Alexander Marine
570 Davie St
VANCOUVER

Bosun's Locker
580 Johnson St
VICTORIA V8W 1MA

Maritime Services Ltd,
Division of Triton Holdings Inc,
3440 Bridgeway St, VANCOUVER V5K 1B6

Newfoundland
Campbell's Ships Supplies
PO Box 274, 689 Water St, West,
ST JOHN'S A1C 5J2

Nova Scotia
Gabriel Aero-Marine Instruments Ltd
1576 Hollis St, HALIFAX B3J 1V4

Quebec
Marine Press
295 Mountain St
MONTREAL

McGill Maritime Services Inc
369 Place D'Youville, MONTREAL H2Y 2G2

DENMARK
Iver C. Weilbach & Co A/S
35 Toldbodgade, COPENHAGEN DK-1253

ENGLAND
Kelvin Hughes
145 The Minories, LONDON EC3N 1NH

FRANCE
Librairie Maritime
55 Avenue de la Grande Armée
PARIS

Outremer Librarie Maritime
17 Rue Jacob, PARIS 75006

GERMANY
Bade & Hornig
Stubbenhuk 10, D-2000
HAMBURG 11

Eckardt & Messtorff
Rodingsmarkt 16,
D-2000 HAMBURG 11

GREECE
J & D Athanassiadis S/A
Kastoros St,
No 78/A PIRAEUS

HONG KONG
Geo Falconer (Nautical) Ltd
806-7 Hong Kong Chinese Bank Bldg,
61–65 Des Vouex Rd, Central District

Hong Kong Ship Supplies Co
Room 1614, Melbourne Plaza, 33 Queen's Rd,
Central District

ITALY
Cooperative Armamento Imprese Marittime
Piazza S, Sabina N 2, GENOA 16124

Societa Italiana Radio Marittima
Via San Benedetto 14, GENOA 16126

JAPAN
Japan Hydrographic Charts & Publications Co Ltd
Kobe Branch, Shosen-Mitsui Bldg No 5,
Kaigan-Dori, Chuo-Ku, KOBE

Japan Hydrographic Charts & Publications Co Ltd
Konwa Bldg, No 12-22, 1-Chome, Tsukiji,
Chuo-Ku, TOKYO

Nippon Oceanic Survey Co Ltd
Matsui Bldg, 1st Floor, 17–22 Shinkawa,
1-Chome, Chuo-Ku, TOKYO 104

MEXICO
Convoy S.A.
Avenida Miguel Aleman 906-A
Col. Lazaro Cardenas
MAZATLAN

NETHERLANDS
L J Harri BV
'Schreerstoren', Prins Hendrikkade, 94–95,
AMSTERDAM 1012 AE

Datema Delftzijl
Veerhaven 10
ROTTERDAM

NETHERLANDS ANTILLES
Tropical Sails
Great Bay Marina
Philipsburg, SINT MAARTEN

NEW ZEALAND
Trans Pacific Marine Ltd
29 Jellicoe St
Downtown
AUCKLAND 1

NORWAY
Navicharts A/S
Masteveien 3
HAGAN

PANAMA
Islamorada International SA
Building 808
Balboa Road
BALBOA

PERU
Direccion de Hidrografia y Navegacion de la Marina
Avda Gammara No 500, Chucuito,
CALLAO 1

SCOTLAND
Kelvin Hughes
Pegasus House, 375 W George St,
GLASGOW G2 4LR

Thomas Gunn Naval Services
62 Marischal St
ABERDEEN

SINGAPORE
Motion Smith
70 Shenton Way, 02-03 Marina House,
SINGAPORE 0207

E.W. Liner Charts & Pubs
54b Jalan Mariam
SINGAPORE 1750

SOUTH AFRICA
Time & Tide
31 Parry Rd, DURBAN 4001

SPAIN
Deposito Hidrografico SA
Avda Marques de L'Agentera,
BARCELONA 5

Fernando Blanco Montejo
28009 Lope de Rueda 27, MADRID 9

Blanco Montejo
C-Aleman 44
35006 LAS PALMAS de GRAN CANARIA
Canary Islands

SWEDEN
Aktiebolaget Nautic
Skeppsbroplatsen 1,
GÖTEBORG S-411 18

Kartbutiken
Kungsgatan 74
111 22 STOCKHOLM

Agents in United States Possessions

GUAM
Coral Reef Marine Center
PO Box 2792, Marine Drive Asan,
AGANA 96910

PUERTO RICO
Miramar Marine
749 Las Palmas St
Marginal Sur Exp Munez Rivera
SAN JUAN 00903

VIRGIN ISLANDS
Lighthouse Marine
Viraco Park
ST THOMAS

Marine Warehouse East
Red Hook
ST THOMAS

Agents in the United States

HAWAII
Ala Wai Marine Ltd
1651 Ala Moana Blvd, HONOLULU 96815

Pacific Map Center
560 N Nimitz Hwy
Suite 206a
HONOLULU

National Hydrographic Offices

ARGENTINA
Servicio de Hidrografia Naval
Avenida Montes de Oca 2124, 1271
BUENOS AIRES

AUSTRALIA
Royal Australian Navy Hydrographic Service
PO Box 1332, NORTH SYDNEY, NSW 2059

BELGIUM
Dienst der Kust Hydrografie Administratief Centrum
Vrijhavenstraat 3, B-8400 OOSTENDE

BRAZIL
Directoria de Hidrografia e Navegação
Rua Barão de Jaceguay S/No
Ponta da Armação, 24000 NITEROI-RJ

CANADA
Canadian Hydrographic Service
615 Booth St, OTTAWA Ontario K1A 0E6

CHILE
Instituto Hidrografico de la Armada
Casilla 324, VALPARAISO

CUBA
Instituto Cubano de Hidrografia
Av. 47 # 2829 e/ 28 y 38
Rpto Kohly, CIUDAD DE LA HABANA

DENMARK
Kort-og Matrikelstyrelsen
Rentemestervej 8
2400 KØBENHAVN NV

ECUADOR
Instituto Oceanográfico de la Armada
Avenida 25 de Julio
Base Naval Sur
Casilla de Correos 5940, GUAYAQUIL

EGYPT
Idaret Al Misaha Al Baharia
Ras el Tin, EL ISKANDARIYA

FIJI
Fiji Hydrographic Service
Marine Department, SUVA

FINLAND
Merenkulkuhallitus
Karratt-Ja Väyläosasto
00 181 HELSINKI

FRANCE
Etablissement Principal de Service
Hydrographique
et Océanographique de la Marine
13 rue du Chatellier BP 426, 29275 BREST CEDEX

GERMANY
Deutsches Hydrographisches Institut
Bernhard-Nocht-Strasse 78, Postfach 200
D-2000 HAMBURG 4

GREECE
Hellenic Navy Hydrographic Service
TGN 1040 ATHÍNAI

ICELAND
Sjómaelingar Islands
Seljavegur 32, REYKJAVIK

INDONESIA
Dinas Hidro-Oseanografi
Jalan Pantai Kuta V No. 1, Ancol Timur,
JAKARTA

ITALY
Istituto Idrografico della Marina
Passo Osservatorio 4, 16134 GENOVA

JAPAN
Kaijohoan-Cho Suiro-Bu (Hydrographic
Department of Maritime Safety Agency)
No. 3-1 Tsukiji 5 Chome, Chuo-Ku,
TOKYO 104

MALAYSIA
Hydrographic Department, Department of Navy
Ministry of Defence, Jalan Padang Tembal,
KUALA LUMPUR 50634

MEXICO
Direccion General de Oceanografia Naval
Eje 2 Oriente
Tramo H. Escuela Naval Militar No. 861
Edificio B, Col. Los Cipreses
Delegacion Coyoacan, MEXICO DF

NETHERLANDS
Dienst der Hydrografie van de Koninklijke Marine
171, Badhuisweg, 2597 JN's, GRAVENHAGE

NEW ZEALAND
Hydrographic Office, Lambton House
160 Lambton Quay, WELLINGTON

NORWAY
Norges Sjøkartverk
Lervigsveien 36, PO Box 60, 4001
STAVANGER

PERU
Direccion de Hidrografia y Navegacion de la Marina
Avda Gamarra No. 500, Chucuito, CALLAO 1

PHILIPPINES
The Surveys Department, National Mapping &
Resource Information Authority (NAMRIA)
421 Barraca St, San Nicolas, MANILA

POLAND
Biuro Hydrograficzne Marynarki Wojennej
PRL 81-912 GDYNIA 12

PORTUGAL
Instituto Hidrograficio
Rua das Trinas 49, LISBOA

RUSSIA
Glavnoe Oupravlenie Navigatsii I
Okeanografii
Ministetstva Oborony
8 11 liniya B-34, ST PETERSBURG

SINGAPORE
Hydrographic Department
Port of Singapore Authority
78 Keppel Rd, No. 2-28 Tanjong Pagar Complex,
SINGAPORE 089 55

SOLOMON ISLANDS
Solomon Islands Hydrographic Unit
Survey & Cartographic Division
PO Box G13, HONIARA

SOUTH AFRICA
The Hydrographer SA Navy
Hydrographic Office
Private Bag XI, Tokai 7966, CAPE TOWN

SPAIN
Instituto Hidrográfico de la Marina
Tolosa Latour No. 1 CADIZ

SWEDEN
Sjökarteavdelningen
S-601 78, NORRKÖPING

THAILAND
Hydrographic Department, Royal Thai Navy
Krom Utoksastr, Royal Thai Navy
Aroon-amarin Road
BANGKOK 10600

TRINIDAD AND TOBAGO
Hydrographic Unit
2B Richmond Street, PORT OF SPAIN

TURKEY
Seyir Hidrografi ve Osinografi Dairesi
Baskanligi
Çubuklu 81647, ISTANBUL

USA
National Oceanic & Atmospheric Administration
(NOAA) National Ocean Service
SSMC Building 3
1315 East West Highway
SILVER SPRING
Maryland 20910-3282
(Waters of USA, Great Lakes, Hawaii, Puerto Rico)

Defence Mapping Agency Hydrographic
Topographic Centre (DMAHTC)
6500 Brookes Lane, WASHINGTON D.C. 20315
(Worldwide except tidal waters of USA and its
possessions)

URUGUAY
Servicio de Oceanografia Hidrografia y
Meteorologia de la Armada
Capurro 980, Casilla de Correo 1381
MONTEVIDEO

VENEZUELA
Comandancia General de la Marina
Direccion de Hidrografia y Navegación
Apartado Postal No. 6745, Carmelitas,
CARACAS

Websites

There are several stores selling charts, marine publications and cruising guides. The latter may also be ordered directly from the publishers, who have their own websites:

www.adlardcoles.co.uk (Adlard Coles Nautical)
www.pbg.mcgraw-hill.com/im/im-home.html
   (International Marine Publishers, USA)
http://www.motorbuch.de (Pietsch Verlage,
   Germany)
www.loisirsnautiques.com (Loisirs Nautiques,
   France)

www.imray.com (Imray, Laurie, Norie & Wilson,
   UK)
www.cruisingguides.com (Caribbean Cruising
   Guides)
www.bookharbour.com (Kelvin Hughes, UK)
http://www.bluewaterweb.net/ (Bluewater
   Books and Charts, Fort Lauderdale)
http://www.seabooks.com/ (Armchair Sailor,
   Newport)
http://www.armchairsailorseattle.com (Armchair
   Sailor, Seattle)

4 Glossary of Useful Terms in French, Spanish and Portuguese

Clearance Formalities

English	Français	Español	Português
yacht harbour	port de plaisance	dársena de yates	doca de recreio
harbour master's office	capitainerie du port	comandancia de marina	capitania
customs office	bureau de douane	aduana	alfandega
pilot station	station de pilotage	caseta de prácticos	estaçao de pilôtos
prohibited area	zone interdite	zona prohibida	zona proibida
dock	bassin, dock	dique	doca
breakwater	brise-lames	rompeolas	quebra-mar
mole	môle	muelle	molhe
slipway	cale de halage	varadero	rampa
landing steps	escalier de débarquement	escala de desemarque	secada de desembarque
mooring	amarrage	amarradero	cabeço
dolphin	duc d'Albe	noray	duque de alba
skipper	capitaine	patrón	patrao
crew	équipage	tripulación	tripulaçao
Certificate of Registry	Certificat de Francisation	Patente de Navegación	Certificado de Registro
Ship's Articles	Rôle d'equipage	Rol	Rol de Equipagem
Ship's Log	Livre de bord	Bitácora	Diário de Bordo
Bill of Health	Patente de santé	Patente de Sanidad	Certificado de Saúde
pratique	libre-pratique	plática	livre prática
insurance certificate	certificat d'assurance	poliza de seguro	cetificado de seguro
charter party	charter-partie	contrato de flete	fretador
customs clearance	libre-sortie, congé de douane	despacho de aduana	despacho
bonded stores	sous douanes, en franchise	viveres precintados	mantimentos desalfandegados
passport	passeport	pasaporte	passaporte

Charts and Publications

English	Français	Español	Português
Pilot, Sailing Directions	Instructions Nautiques	Derrotero	Pilôto, Roteiro da costa
Nautical Almanac	Almanach Nautiques	Almanaque Náutico	Almanaque Náutico
Tide Tables	Annuaire des Marées	Tabla de Mareas	Tabela Marés
List of Lights	Livre des Phares	Cuaderno de Faros	Lista de Faróis
Notices to Mariners	Avis aux Navigateurs	Aviso a los Navegantes	Avisos aos Navegantes
North, South	Nord, Sud	Norte, Sur	Norte, Sul
East, West	Est, Ouest	Este, Oeste	Este, Oeste
scale	échelle	escala	escala
lighthouse	phare	faro	farol
fixed light (F)	feu fixe (F.f)	luz fija (f)	luz fixa (F)
flashing light (Fl)	feu à éclats (F.é)	luz de destellos (dest)	relampagos (Rl)
quick flashing light	feu scintillant	luz centelleante	relampagos rápidos
occulting light (Oc)	à occultations (F.o)	luz de ocultaciones	ocultaçoes (Oc.)
group occulting light (OC)	à occultations groupées (F.2.o)	luz de grupos ocultaciones	grupo n. ocultaçoes
alternating light	à changement de coloration	luz alternativa	alternada
intermittent	feu intermittent	luz intermitente	intermitente
interrupted	feu interrompu	luz de grupos de centelleos	interompida
quick flashing (IQ)			
fixed and flashing (F FL)	fixe blanc varié par un éclat (F.b.é.)	luz fija y destellos (f.dest.)	fixa e com relampagos (F.RI)

	Français	*Español*	*Português*
light buoy	bouée lumineuse	boya luminosa	bóia luminosa
whistle buoy	bouée sonore à sifflet	boya de silbato	bóia de apito
bell buoy	bouée sonore à cloche	boya de campana	bóia de sino
can buoy	bouée plate, cylindrique	boya cilindrica	bóia cilindrica
conical buoy	bouée conique	boya cónica	bóia cónica
spar buoy	bouée à espar	boya de espeque	bóia de mastro
pillar buoy	bouée à fuseau	boya de huso	bóia de pilar
barrel buoy	bouée tonne	barril	bóia de barril
topmark	voyant	marca de tope	alvo
fixed beacon	balise fixe	baliza fija	baliza fixa
floating beacon	balise flottante	baliza flotante	baliza flutuante
chequered	à damiers (dam)	damero, a cuadros	aos quadrados (x)
horizontal stripes	à bandes horizontales	franjas horizontales	faixas horizontais
vertical stripes	à bandes verticales	franjas verticales	faixas verticais
black (B. blk.)	noir (n)	negro (n)	preto (pr)
red (R)	rouge (r)	rojo (r)	vermelho (vm)
green (G)	vert (v)	verde (v)	verde (vd)
blue (bl)	bleu (bl)	azul (az)	azul
yellow (Y)	jaune (j)	amarillo (am)	amarelo (am)
white (W)	blanc (b)	blanco (b)	branco (b)
orange (Or)	orange (org)	naranjo	côr de laranja
violet (Vi)	violet (vio)	violeta	violeta
brown	brun	marrón	castanhao
grey	gris	gris	cinzento
high water	pleine mer	pleamar	preia-mar
low water	basse mer	bajamar	baixa-mar
flood	marée montante	entrante	enchente
ebb	marée descendante	vaciante	vasante
spring tide	eau vive	marea viva	águas-vivas
neap tide	eau morte	aguas muertas	águas-mortas
one	un	uno	um
two	deux	dos	dois
three	trois	tres	três
four	quatre	cuatro	quatro
five	cinq	cinco	cinco
six	six	seis	seis
seven	sept	siete	sete
eight	huit	ocho	oito
nine	neuf	nueve	nove
ten	dix	diez	dez
eleven	onze	once	onze
twelve	douze	doce	doze
thirteen	treize	trece	treze
fourteen	quatorze	catorce	catorce
fifteen	quinze	quince	quinze
sixteen	seize	diecisés	dezaseis
seventeen	dix-sept	diecisiete	dezasete
eighteen	dix-huit	dieciocho	dezoito
nineteen	dix-neuf	diecinueve	dezanove
twenty	vingt	veinte	vinte
thirty	trente	treinta	trinta
forty	quarante	cuarenta	quaranta
fifty	cinquante	cincuenta	cinquenta
sixty	soixante	sesenta	sessenta
seventy	soixante-dix	setenta	setenta
eighty	quatre-vingt	ochenta	oitenta
ninety	quatre-vingt-dix	noventa	noventa
one hundred	cent	cien	cem
thousand	mille	mil	mil

5 Bibliography

Abaco Cruising Guide, Stephen Pavlidis, Seaworthy Publications.

Adriatic Pilot, T. & D Thompson, Imray, Huntingdon.

Aku-Aku, Thor Heyerdahl, Unwin Hyman, London.

Atlantic Spain and Portugal, Imray, Huntingdon.

Atlantic Crossing Guide, ed. Anne Hammick, Adlard Coles Nautical, London.

Atlantic Islands, Imray, Huntingdon.

Atlantic Pilot Atlas, Adlard Coles Nautical, London.

Australian Cruising Guide, Alan Lucas, Imray, Huntingdon.

Azores Cruising Guide, World Cruising Publications.

Bahamas Cruising Guide, Matthew Wilson, International Marine.

The Baltic Sea, Barry Sheffield, Imray, Huntingdon.

Baltic Southwest Pilot, Mark Brackenbury, Adlard Coles Nautical, London.

Bermuda Yachting Guide, Bermuda Maritime Museum.

Biscay Spain, Robin Brandon, Imray, Huntingdon.

Black Sea Cruising Guide, Rick and Sheila Nelson, Imray, Huntingdon.

Blue Guide Greece, A & C Black, London.

Blue Guide Israel, A & C Black, London.

Boating Guide to Mexico, West Coast Edition, John Rains, Point Loma Publishing, San Diego.

Brittany and Channel Islands Cruising Guide, David Jefferson, Adlard Coles Nautical, London.

Canary Islands Cruising Guide, World Cruising Publications.

Captain's Guide to Transiting Panama Canal, David Wilson, Compass Publishing.

Carte-Guide Navigation Fluviale, Editure Cartographique Maritime.

Channel Harbours and Anchorages, Adlard Coles Nautical, London.

Channel Islands Pilot, Malcolm Robson, Adlard Coles Nautical, London.

The Channel Islands, Nick Heath, Imray, Huntingdon.

Charlie's Charts North to Alaska, Charles Wood, Surrey, British Columbia.

Charlie's Charts of Costa Rica, Margo Wood, Surrey, British Columbia.

Charlie's Charts of Hawaii, Charles Wood, Surrey, British Columbia.

Charlie's Charts of Polynesia, Charles Wood, Surrey, British Columbia.

Charlie's Charts of the US East Coast, Charles Wood, Surrey, British Columbia.

Charlie's Charts of the US Pacific Coast, Charles Wood, Surrey, British Columbia.

Charlie's Charts, Western Coast of Mexico, Charles Wood, Surrey, British Columbia.

Chile, Ian and Maggy Staples, Tony and Coryn Gooch, Imray, Huntingdon.

Clyde Cruising Club: Sailing Directories for Scotland, Hebrides, Orkney and Shetland Islands (several volumes).

Coastal Cruising Handbook of New Zealand, Royal Akarana Yacht Club, New Zealand.

Cruising Association Handbook, Cruising Association, London.

Cruising French Waterways, Hugh McKnight, Adlard Coles Nautical, London.

Cruising Guide to Abaco, Steve Dodge, Cruising Guide Publications.

Cruising Guide to Belize and Mexico's Caribbean Coast, Freya Rauscher, Westcott Cove Publishing.

Cruising Guide to Cuba, Simon Charles, Cruising Guide Publications.

Cruising Guide to Germany and Denmark, Brian Navin, Imray, Huntingdon.

Cruising Guide to Labrador, ed. Sandy Weld, Puffin Press, Weston, MA, USA.

Cruising Guide to Maine, 2 vols, Don Johnson, Westcott Cove Publishing.

Cruising to New South Wales, Alan Lucas, Horwitz Grahame, Cammeray, Australia.

Cruising Guide to Newfoundland, ed. Sandy Weld, Puffin Press, Weston, MA, USA.

Cruising Guide to Northwest England and Wales, George Griffiths, Imray, Huntingdon.

Cruising Guide to Panama including San Blas, Lars Akerholm.

Cruising Guide to Puget Sound, Migeal Scherer, International Marine.

Cruising Guide to Southeast Asia, Stephen Davies and Elaine Morgan, Imray, Huntingdon.
Volume I: The South China Sea, Philippines, Gulf of Thailand to Singapore.
Volume II: Papua New Guinea, Indonesia, Singapore, Malacca Strait to Phuket.

Cruising Guide to Trinidad and Tobago, Chris Doyle, Cruising Guide Publications.

Cruising Guide to the Abacos and Northern Bahamas, D Wyatt, Westcott Cove Publishing Co., Stamford, Connecticut.

Cruising Guide to the Caribbean, Michael Marshall, Adlard Coles Nautical, London.

Cruising Guide to the Caribbean, William T. Stone and Ann M. Hays.

Cruising Guide to the Chesapeake, Blanchard & Hays Stone, Putnam's, New York.

Cruising Guide to the Florida Keys, Frank Papy, Ridgeland, South Carolina.

Cruising Guide to the Isthmus of Panama, Tom and Nancy Zydler, Seaworthy Publications.

Cruising Guide to the Kingdom of Tonga in Vava'u, The Moorings, Cruising Guide Publications, Florida.

Cruising Guide to the Leeward Islands, Chris Doyle, Cruising Guide Publications, Florida.

Cruising Guide to the Maine Coast, Hank & Jan Taft, International Marine.

Cruising Guide to the Netherlands, Brian Navin, Imray, Huntingdon.

Cruising Guide to the New England Coast, Duncan & Ware, W.W. Norton, New York.

Cruising Guide to the Northern Gulf Coast, Claiborne Young, Pelican, USA.

Cruising Guide to the Northern Territory Coast, J. Knight.

Cruising Guide to the Northwest Caribbean, Nigel Calder, International Marine.

Cruising Guide to the Nova Scotia Coast, John McKelvy, Pilot Press.

Cruising Guide to the Rio Dulce, Frank Schooley.

Cruising Guide to the Sea of Cortez, ed. Nancy Scott, Cruising Guide Publications.

Cruising Guide to the Virgin Islands, Nancy and Simon Scott, Cruising Guide Publications.

Cruising Guide to Venezuela & Bonaire, Chris Doyle and Jeff Fisher, Cruising Guide Publications.

Cruising Guide to West Africa, Steven Jones, Imray, Huntingdon.

Cruising in New Caledonia, Marc Rambeau.

Cruising Ports, California to Florida via Panama, John Rains, Point Loma Publishing, San Diego.

Cruising the Coral Coast, Alan Lucas, Horwitz Grahame, Cammeray, Australia.

Cruising the San Juan Islands, Bruce Calhouan, Norton, New York.

Cuba: A Cruising Guide, Nigel Calder, Imray.

The Danube, A River Guide, Rod Heikell, Imray, Huntingdon.

Destination New Zealand, Graham Brice and Christopher Carey.

Dive Maldives: A Guide to the Maldives Archipelago, Tim Godfrey, Atoll Editions.

East Africa Pilot, Delwyn McPhun, Imray.

East and North Coasts of Ireland Sailing Directions, Irish Cruising Club, Imray.

East Coast Pilot Guide from the Wash to Ramsgate, Derek Bowskill, Imray, Huntingdon.

East Spain Pilot, Robin Brandon, Imray, Huntingdon.

Embassy Complete Boating Guide to Florida's East Coast, Embassy Marine Publishing, USA.

Embassy Guide to the Atlantic Coast, Embassy Guides.

Embassy Guide to the Bahamas, Embassy Guides.

Embassy Guide to Maine, Embassy Guides.

The Exuma Guide, Stephen Pavlidis, Seaworthy Publications.

Exploring North British Columbia, D. Douglass

Exploring South British Columbia, D. Douglass

Exploring the Inside Passage to Alaska, D. Douglass, Find Edge Productions.

Faeroes, Iceland and Greenland, Imray, Huntingdon.

Falkland Island Shores, Ewen Southby-Tailyour, Adlard Coles Nautical, London.

Fiji Cruising Notes, Phil Cregeen, Migrant.

Fiji Islands Handbook, David Stanley, Moon Publications.

Firth of Clyde, Clyde Cruising Club.

Floreana, Margret Wittmer, Anthony Nelson, Shropshire.

Fodor's Brazil, Fodor Publications Ltd.

Fodor's South America, Fodor Publications Ltd.

Foreign Port Forms, Imray, Huntingdon.

The Forgotten Middle: Pacific Coast of Central America, Roy and Carol Roberts.

French Inland Waterways, Cruising Association, London.

The Gentleman's Guide to Passages South, Bruce Van Sant, Cruising Guide Publications, Clearwater, Florida.

The Greek Islands, Ernle Bradford, Collins, London.

Greek Waters Pilot, Rod Heikell, Imray, Huntingdon.

Grid Chart of the Bay of Islands, Kerikeri Radio, PO Box 131 Kerikeri, New Zealand.

Guida Mar da Costa Brasileira, Aloysio Gomez Cameiro.

Honduras & Bay Islands Mariners Guide, Rick Rhodes.

IJsselmeer Harbours, Hilary Keatinge, Barnacle Marine.

Imray Mediterranean Almanac, ed. Rod Heikell, Imray, Huntingdon.

Indian Ocean Cruising Guide, Rod Heikell, Imray, Huntingdon.

Indonesia Handbook, Moon Publications.

Inland Waterways of France, Imray, Huntingdon.

The Intracoastal Waterway, Jan & Bill Moeller, International Marine.

Intracoastal Waterway Facilities Guide, Robert & Barbara Smith, Paradox Publishing, USA.

Ionian, Rod Heikell, Tetra Sailing Guides.

An Island to Oneself, Tom Neale, Collins, London.

Islas Baleares, Anne Hammick, Imray, Huntingdon.

Isles of Scilly, John and Fay Garey, Imray, Huntingdon.

Italian Waters Pilot, Rod Heikell, Imray, Huntingdon.

Japan Handbook, Moon Publications.

Landfalls of Paradise, Earl Hinz, Marine Enterprises, Marina del Rey, California.

Lundy & Irish Sea Pilot, David Taylor, Imray, Huntingdon.

Madeira & Porto Santo Cruising Guide, World Cruising Publications.

Marine Atlas of the Hawaiian Islands, A. P. Balder, Uni. Hawaii Press.

Malways: Maldives Island Directory, Tim Godfrey, Atoll Editions.

Marine Life of the Maldives, Tim Godfrey, Atoll Editions.

Mediterranean Almanac, ed. Rod Heikell, Imray.

Mediterranean Cruising Handbook, Rod Heikell, Imray, Huntingdon.

Mediterranean France & Corsica, Rod Heikell, Imray, Huntingdon.

Mediterranean Spain, Costas del Sol and Blanca, Robin Brandon, Imray, Huntingdon.

Mediterranean Spain, Costas del Azahar, Dorada and Brava, Robin Brandon, Imray, Huntingdon.

Micronesia Cruising Notes, Phil Cregeen, Migrant.

Mull of Kintyre to Arnamurchan, Clyde Cruising Club.

Nicaraguan Handbook, David Stanley.

Normandy and Channel Islands Pilot, Mark Brackenbury, Adlard Coles Nautical, London.

North Africa, Hans van Rijn, Imray, Huntingdon.

North and East Coast of Ireland Sailing Directions, Irish Cruising Club, Imray, Huntingdon.

North and East Coast of Scotland, Clyde Cruising Club.

North Biscay Pilot, Adlard Coles Nautical, London.

North Biscay Cruising Guide, Nick Heath, Imray, Huntingdon.

North Brittany Pilot, Adlard Coles, revised by Nicholas Heath, Adlard Coles Nautical, London.

North France Pilot, T. & D Thompson, Imray, Huntingdon.

North Sea Passage Pilot, Brian Navin, Imray, Huntingdon.

Northern Territory Coast, A Cruising Guide, John Knight, 81 Alawa Crescent, Casuarina, NT 5792 Australia.

Norwegian Cruising Guide, John Armitage and Mark Brackenbury, Adlard Coles Nautical, London.

100 miles of the Great Barrier Reef, David Colfelt.

On and Off the Beaten Path, Stephen Pavlidis, Seaworthy Publications.

Orkney Islands, Clyde Cruising Club.

Outer Hebrides, Clyde Cruising Club.

Pacific Crossing Guide, Michael Pocock, Adlard Coles Nautical, London.

Pickmere's Atlas of Northland's East Coast, Transpacific Marine, Auckland.

Red Sea Pilot, Elaine Morgan and Stephen Davies, Imray, Huntingdon.

Reed's Caribbean Almanac, ed. Catherine Degnon, Thomas Reed.

Rough Guide to West Africa, Jim Hudgens.

Sail Thailand, Collin Piprell.

Sailors Guide to the Windward Islands, Chris Doyle, Cruising Guide Publications, Florida.

St Helena including Ascension Island and Tristan da Cunha, Tony Cross, David & Charles, Newton Abbot.

Seychelles Nautical Pilot, Alain Rondeau, Imray, Huntingdon.

The Shell Channel Pilot, John Cuncliffe, Imray, Huntingdon.

Shetland Islands, Clyde Cruising Club.

Solomon Islands Cruising Guide, Dirk Sieling, Island Cruising Co.

South Africa Nautical Almanac, Tom Morgan.

South and West Coast of Ireland Sailing Directions, Irish Cruising Club, Imray, Huntingdon.

South Atlantic Coasts of South America, Pete and Annie Hill, Imray, Huntingdon.

South Biscay Pilot, Robin Brandon, Adlard Coles Nautical, London.

South Coast Cruising, Mark Fishwick, Yachting Monthly, London.

South Pacific Anchorages, Warwick Clay, Imray, Huntingdon.

Straits Sailing Handbook, Colin Thompson, Sheppards & Co, Gibraltar.

Superyacht Guide to New Zealand, Jill Malcolm

Traveller's Guide to East Africa and the Indian Ocean, IC Publications Ltd, London.

Traveller's Guide to North Africa, IC Publications Ltd, London.

Traveller's Guide to West Africa, IC Publications Ltd, London.

Turkey and the Dodecanese Cruising Pilot, Robin Petherbridge, Adlard Coles Nautical, London.

Turkish Waters and Cyprus Pilot, Rod Heikell, Imray, Huntingdon.

Turks & Caicos Guide, Stephen Pavlidis, Seaworthy Publications.

Turks & Caicos Handbook and Yachtsman's Guide, J. Blake.

Vetus Marina Guides: Havengids Nederland, and *Marina Guide Méditerranée,* Vetus den Ouden, Netherlands.

Virgin Anchorages, Nancy and Simon Scott, Cruising Guide Publications.

Votre Livre de Bord (Mediterranée).

Votre Livre de Bord (Mer du Nord – Manche – Atlantique).

World Cruising Routes, Jimmy Cornell, Adlard Coles Nautical, London.

West Country Cruising, Mark Fishwick, Yachting Monthly, London.

Yachting Guide to the South Shore of Nova Scotia, Arthur Dechman, USA.

A Yachtsman's Fiji, Michael Calder, The Cruising Classroom, Forestville, Australia.

Yachtsman's Guide to the Bahamas, Tropic Isle Publishers Inc, Florida.

Yacht Miz Mae's Guide to Vanuatu, Nicola Rhind and Thomas Mueller.

Yachting Guide to the ABC-Islands, Gerard van Erp, Yachting Guides.

Yachtsman's Directory to Spain and Portugal, Richard Ashton, Publi-Nautic.

The Yachtsman's Guide to Jamaica, John Lethbridge, Imray, Huntingdon.

Yachtsman's Guide to the Virgin Islands, Tropic Isle Publishers Inc, Florida.

Yachtsman's Pilot to the West Coast of Scotland (several volumes), Martin Lawrence, Imray, Huntingdon.

Tourist Guides

Lonely Planet Publications:
These small paperback guides, which are aimed at the independent traveller who wants to visit out of the way places, and has a limited budget, are eminently suitable for cruising sailors. They cover many places off the mass tourism track. *Shoestring* guides cover a large region, or even an entire continent. The *Travel Survival Kits* concentrate on one country in more detail. See the Further Reading sections of individual countries.

Travel & Trade Publications:
These series of handbooks cover large regions in considerable detail.
Caribbean Islands Handbook, Central American and Mexico Handbook, South American Handbook
South East Asia Handbook, Indonesia Handbook, India Handbook, Thailand & Burma Handbook, Indonesia, Malaysia & Singapore Handbook
North Africa Handbook, East Africa Handbook

Moon Publications:
Publish a series of useful guides to the Pacific, by David Stanley: *Micronesia Handbook, South Pacific Handbook, Tahiti-French Polynesia Handbook, Tonga-Samoa Handbook.* Highly recommended.

Index of Countries